Southeast Asia

The Holy See of Cao Daism in Tay Ninh, Vietnam. Unique to Vietnam, Cao Dai draws its beliefs from a variety of world religions. Onlookers can watch the noon processional service from a balcony overhead. See chapter 6. © John Elk III Photography.

A Barong dancer in Bali—an example of the integration of religion, mythology, music, dance, and art in everyday Balinese life. See chapter 10. © Cliff Hollenbeck Photography.

Pura Ulu Danau Temple, Lake Bratan, Bali—one of the most photographed temples on the island. See chapter 10. © John Elk III Photography.

Southeast
Asia

2nd Edition

by Jennifer Eveland, Lynn A. Levine
and Beth Reiber

Hungry Minds™

Best-Selling Books • Digital Downloads • e-Books
Answer Networks • e-Newsletters • Branded Web Sites • e-Learning
New York, NY • Cleveland, OH • Indianapolis, IN

Published by:

Hungry Minds, Inc.

909 Third Ave.
New York, NY 10022

www.frommers.com

ISBN 0-7645-6312-2
ISSN 1098-9455

Editor: Amy Lyons
Production Editors: Stephanie Lucas, M. Faunette Johnston
Photo Editor: Richard Fox
Design by Michele Laseau
Cartographer: Roberta Stockwell
Production by Hungry Minds Indianapolis Production Services
Front cover photo: Rice Terraces in Bali, Indonesia. Torleif Svensson/The Stock Market
Back cover photo: In Chiang Mai, Thailand, a man gives two elephants a bath.
    Neil Emmerson/The Image Bank

SPECIAL SALES

For general information on Hungry Minds' products and services, please contact our Customer Care department; within the U.S. at 800-762-2974, outside the U.S. at 317-572-3993, or fax 317-572-4002. For sales inquiries and reseller information, including discounts, bulk sales, customized editions, and premium sales, please contact our Customer Care department at 800-434-3422.

Manufactured in the United States of America

5   4   3   2   1

Contents

List of Maps

ABOUT THE AUTHORS

Jennifer Eveland (Thailand, Malaysia, Singapore, Vietnam, Laos, Cambodia, and Myanmar) was a child when she and her family first moved to Singapore, and after returning to the United States, she was drawn again and again to the magic of Singapore, East Asia, and Southeast Asia. She is the author of *Frommer's Singapore & Malaysia* and *Frommer's Thailand*, and currently lives in Singapore.

Jennifer would like to acknowledge a few special friends who have contributed laughs and fun to her life in Asia and her travels for this book—Noke Methinee Prathoomsuvarn You Corn Dog Queen; Andrew Chan with the most comfortable sofa in Bangkok; that funky guy Duc who pops up every time she goes to Vietnam; The Buddha Snake; Les Drolets Alain and Mical Mercier Oulevey; Michele "The Hudak" Brace; and most especially Ben and Groovy at Bojangles in Singapore.

Lynn A. Levine (Bali & Lombok and The Philippines) is the author of *Frommer's Turkey* and co-author of *Frommer's Italy from $70 a Day*. The spirit of adventure has inspired her to repeatedly quit 9 to 5 jobs, and an uncontrollable urge to tell people where to go has helped her thrive under Frommer's assigments. Lynn splits her time among Manhattan, Florence, Italy and the Jersey suburbs and is frequently accompanied on her travels by her faithful Jack Russell Terrier, Buster.

Lynn would like to thank Stan Maringka of IDCI Inc. for the "straight up" on Indonesia, Ketut and Putu for providing an insider's view of Lombok, Martin and Julie O'Neill for their tireless advice on Bali, Steve and Heather Sargison for help and comic relief in Cebu, Nadine for the best cappuccino in the Philippines, and Philippine Airlines Corporation. Special thanks also to Kelly Regan for that first shot, and to my mom, without whom none of this would be possible.

Beth Reiber (Hong Kong) worked for several years in Germany as a freelance travel writer for major U.S. newspapers and in Tokyo as the editor of *Far East Traveler*. Now a freelancer again and residing in Lawrence, Kansas, with her husband and two young children, she is the author of several Frommer's guides including *Frommer's Hong Kong, Frommer's Portable Hong Kong, Frommer's Japan*, and *Frommer's Tokyo*, and is a contributor to *Frommer's Europe from $70 a Day*.

Beth would like to thank some very special people who graciously extended their help in the preparation of this book: Peter Randall, Diana Budiman, and Mandy Lo of the Hong Kong Tourist Association; and Teresa Costa Gomes of the Macau Government Tourist Office.

AN INVITATION TO THE READER

In researching this book, we discovered many wonderful places—hotels, inns, restaurants, shops, and more. We're sure you'll find others. Please tell us about them, so we can share the information with your fellow travelers in upcoming editions. If you were disappointed with a recommendation, we'd love to know that, too. Please write to:

Frommer's Southeast Asia, 2nd Edition
Hungry Minds, Inc.
909 Third Avenue
New York, NY 10022

AN ADDITIONAL NOTE

Please be advised that travel information is subject to change at any time—and this is especially true of prices. We therefore suggest that you write or call ahead for confirmation when making your travel plans. The authors, editors, and publisher cannot be held responsible for the experiences of readers while traveling. Your safety is important to us, however, so we encourage you to stay alert and be aware of your surroundings. Keep a close eye on cameras, purses, and wallets, all favorite targets of thieves and pickpockets.

WHAT THE SYMBOLS MEAN

✪ Frommer's Favorites

Our favorite places and experiences—outstanding for quality, value, or both.

The following abbreviations are used for credit cards:

AE	American Express	EC	Eurocard
CB	Carte Blanche	JCB	Japan Credit Bank
DC	Diners Club	MC	MasterCard
DISC	Discover	V	Visa
ER	EnRoute		

FIND FROMMER'S ONLINE

www.frommers.com offers up-to-the-minute listings on almost 200 cities around the globe—including the latest bargains and candid, personal articles updated daily by Arthur Frommer himself. No other Web site offers such comprehensive and timely coverage of the world of travel.

The Best of Southeast Asia

by Jennifer Eveland, Lynn A. Levine, and Beth Reiber

To the Western visitor, Southeast Asia is an assault on the senses, an immersion into a way of life utterly unlike that to which we're accustomed. From bustling cities like Hong Kong, Singapore, and Kuala Lumpur to tiny fishing villages in Vietnam and the Philippines, from the jungles of Malaysian Borneo to the deluxe resorts of Bali, from the temples of Luang Prabang in Laos to the bacchanal of Patpong in Thailand, Southeast Asia offers a glimpse of the extraordinary, an explosion of colors, sounds, smells, textures, and *life* that will send you home with a wider vision of the human experience. In this chapter, we'll share our picks of the region's unrivaled highlights.

1 The Most Unforgettable Travel Experiences

- **Riding the Star Ferry (Hong Kong).** To reacquaint myself with the city, one of the first things I do on each return trip is hop aboard the Star Ferry for one of the most dramatic—and cheapest—5-minute boat rides in the world. Hong Kong's harbor is one of the world's busiest, and beyond it rises one of earth's most breathtaking skylines. See chapter 4.

- **Gazing upon Hong Kong from Victoria Peak (Hong Kong).** You don't know Hong Kong until you've seen it from here. Take the tram to Victoria Peak, famous for its views of Central, the harbor, and Kowloon beyond, followed by a 1-hour circular hike and a meal with a view. Don't miss the nighttime view, one of the most spectacular and romantic in the world. See chapter 4.

- **Making merit (Thailand).** In Thailand, Buddhist monks do not earn income, but survive on gifts of food and necessary items given by devoted Buddhists in the community. The monk in his gold-colored robes who walks from house to house each morning is not begging for food, but is offering an opportunity for the giver to receive merit. In contributing to the monk's survival, the giver of food and gifts is supporting the *sangha*, the monkhood, and therefore becomes closer to Buddhist ideals. I once had the opportunity to make merit at a small temple. The captain of the boat I was aboard escorted me to the abbot, to whom I presented a bucket filled with all-purpose items, following the customs the captain taught me. In return I was blessed with a prayer, and a deeper view of the ways in which the Thai people respect their

Southeast Asia

CHINA

Red River

MYANMAR
(BURMA)
See Chapter 12

Luang
Prabang

Hanoi
Haiphong

Macao
Hong Kong
See Chapter 4

Haikou
Hainan

*Gulf of
Tonkin*

Chiang
Mai

LAOS
See Chapter 7

Yangon

Vientiane

THAILAND
See Chapter 5

Hue
Da Nang
Hoi An

Bangkok

VIETNAM
See Chapter 6

*Andaman
Sea*

Ko Samet
Pattaya

CAMBODIA
See Chapter 12

Phnom
Penh

*South
China
Sea*

Nha Trang

*Gulf of
Thailand
(Gulf of Siam)*

Ko Samui

Ho Chi Minh City
(Saigon)

Palawan

Phuket

*Langkawi
Island*

*Penang
Island*

Kota
Bharu

Peninsular
Malaysia

Kuala Terengganu

Kuala
Lumpur

Kuantan

Tioman Island

Kota
Kinabalu

Bandar Seri
Begawan

BRUNEI

Sabah

MALAYSIA
See Chapter 9

Malacca

Johor Bharu

SINGAPORE
See Chapter 8

Kuching

Sarawak

Strait of Malacca

Sumatra

*Kalimantan
(Borneo)*

Java Sea

INDONESIA

Flores

Jakarta

Java

Bali
See Chapter 10

Lombok
See Chapter 10

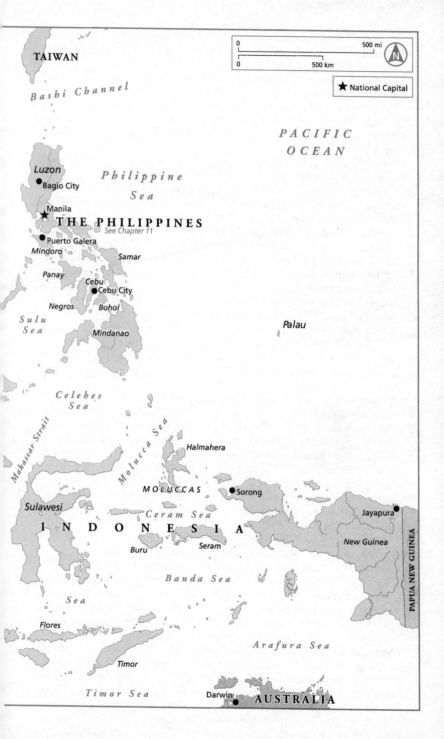

religion. If you are interested in making merit this way, talk to your hotel's concierge. You may be able to join kitchen staff as they head to a nearby monastery in the early morning. See chapter 5.

- **Staying in a village stilt house (Vietnam).** It's as much due to a lack of tourist facilities as to personal choice, but traveling to the northern hills and far south of Vietnam, you may find yourself bunked in a local house, many traditionally built on stilts that sit out over water or mountain. This will be a supremely unique experience; staying in stilts provides the best chance of really seeing how the villagers live. See chapter 6.

- **Participating in a Baci ceremony (Laos).** The Baci is a touching Lao ceremony used to say welcome or farewell and to honor achievements. Participants sit in a circle and receive group blessings, after which there is traditional dancing and *lao lao*, rice wine. It's a chance for the ultra-friendly Lao people to express their hospitality to you, their honored guest. See chapter 7.

- **Sipping a Singapore Sling in the Long Bar (Raffles Hotel, Singapore).** Ahhhh, the Long Bar. Home of the Singapore Sling. I like to come in the afternoons, before the tourist rush. Sheltered by long timber shutters that close out the tropical sun, the air cooled by lazy punkahs (small fans that wave gently back and forth above), you can sit back in old rattan chairs and have your saronged waitress serve you sticky alcoholic creations while you toss back a few dainty crab cakes. Life can be so decadent. OK, so the punkahs are electric, and, come to think of it, the place is air-conditioned (not to mention that it costs a small fortune), but it's fun to image the days when Somerset Maugham, Rudyard Kipling, or Charlie Chaplin would be sitting at the bar sipping Slings and spinning exotic tales of their world travels. Drink up, my friend; it's a lovely high. See chapter 8.

- **Walking the streets of Georgetown (Penang, Malaysia).** Evidence of former British colonization and early Chinese, Indian, and Arab immigration is apparent in many major cities in Malaysia, but Penang has a special charm. In some ways the city still operates the way it did half a century ago. The shophouses are filled with small businesses—bicycle repair shops, hardware stores, Chinese medicine halls, coffee shops. From upstairs windows you can still see laundry hanging on bamboo poles. Life hums in these streets, and for anyone who has witnessed the homogenization of Singapore, or the modernization of Kuala Lumpur, Penang is a charming reminder of what life may have been like in these old outposts. See chapter 9.

- **Observing open-air public cremations (Bali).** As Hindus believe that cremation is the only way a soul can be freed of its earthly body and travel to its next incarnation (or to enlightenment), cremations are joyous occasions, full of floats and fanfare that can resemble a Mardi Gras parade. Complicated towers hold the body, carried aloft by cheering men. At the burning ground, the body is placed in a receptacle resembling a winged lion, a bull, or some other fabulous creature, and set on fire. It's beautiful and awesome, a marvelous show of pageantry and faith, and yet a natural part of everyday life. See chapter 10.

- **Sharing an Ifugao tradition (Batad, Philippines).** Make the strenuous hike to the village of Batad, where you can watch the Ifugao people cultivating and maintaining their magnificent rice terraces. You will walk along the terraces and down many (I mean many) stairs and finally be among the villagers. Most likely you'll be invited inside a traditional nipa hut. Ask to taste the rice wine and you will not only get a glass and a course on how they make it, but you will be shown many hunting treasures like boar and monkey skulls as well as a most touching heirloom: grandpa's bones in a bag. It's a traditional practice among the Ifugao people to keep the bones of their ancestors. See chapter 11.

- **Sunset at El Nido (Palawan, Philippines).** "Have you ever seen heaven?" a local boy asked me while I was lounging on the beach. Before I could reply, he simply pointed to the horizon and left. Filipinos pride themselves on having beautiful, heavenly sunsets and no matter how many times they see it, they always stop to admire it. I was looking out over the calm South China Sea. Falling coconuts and the distinctive drawling croak of the monitor lizard were the only sounds I heard. The breeze was a whisper and everything else natural seemed to settle back in awe of the sky's portrait. See chapter 11.

2 The Best Small Towns & Villages

- **Chiang Saen (Thailand).** Crumbling 11th-century temples and a splendid museum take you back to the birthplace of the Lanna Kingdom, one of Thailand's wealthiest and most influential. The neighboring Golden Triangle, notorious trade point for the international opium industry, snaps you back to modern realities. See chapter 5.
- **Hoi An (Vietnam).** The small size of Hoi An belies its importance to Vietnam; it was once a major trading port, with canals leading right up to merchants' quarters for easy delivery of goods. The canals are now peaceful streets, but not much else has changed. Almost every building in central Hoi An is a historic Vietnamese-, Japanese-, and Chinese-influenced residence or meeting hall. See chapter 6.
- **Kuala Terengganu (Malaysia).** The capital of Malaysian handicrafts has yet to be plotted on any standard tourist itinerary. Explore the city's cottage industries and experience a more orthodox side of Malaysian Islam in this quiet cultural gem. See chapter 9.
- **Luang Prabang (Laos).** This town, sanctioned a World Heritage site by UNESCO for its dozens of glorious Buddhist temples, also happens to be a charming retreat. Shady lanes are lined with French-style country homes that have been restored and converted to house cafes, galleries, shops, and some quaint guesthouses. The sunset over the lazy Mekong is the perfect end to a day spent in Luang Prabang. See chapter 7.
- **Ubud (Bali).** This is the teeming center of Bali, bursting with art and greenery and some of the best food on the island. Even though it's dependent on tourism and far from a typical Bali village, you still get a sense of a real town, with real life going on around you. Ubud is the richest region in Bali for art production and, as it's centrally located, is the perfect base for exploring the rest of the island. See chapter 10.
- **Sagada (Northern Luzon, Philippines).** Green hills, cliff-side hiking trails, Saturday markets, and life untouched by the hand of tourism mark this intriguing, small, quaint, and beautiful village in Mountain Province, home to the colorful Ifugao people. See chapter 11.

3 The Best Beaches

- **Chaweng Beach (Ko Samui, Thailand).** Chaweng is total fun in the sun. The beach itself is gorgeous, with bungalows nestled in the trees just beyond the sand. Behind the beach lies a small town full of life, from wonderful Thai and seafood eateries to shopping to wild nightlife options. See chapter 5.

- **Phan Thiet (Vietnam).** Phan Thiet is the latest paradise to be discovered in Vietnam. Right now it's developed enough to be comfortable without being overrun. Imagine a white sand beach near a small fishing village, only 3 miles from Saigon, with a lovely resort that costs only a little more than US$60 a night. Put a new golf course designed by Nick Faldo nearby and you've got Phan Thiet. See chapter 6.
- **Nha Trang (Vietnam).** What makes Nha Trang so much fun is the very Vietnamese resort flavor that surrounds it, including masseuses and manicurists wandering along the sands peddling their services, and inexpensive, delicious, and abundant seafood. The coast also faces gorgeous outlying islands, to which there are all manner of available boat trips: snorkeling, diving, and just plain drinking. See chapter 6.
- **Tanjong Rhu (Langkawi, Malaysia).** This huge secluded cove has one of the longest stretches of private beach I've ever seen. Wide with soft sand, the beach has cooling shady spots provided by palm trees overhead and beautiful deep blue waters for good swimming. Best of all, there's only one resort here (and they keep the beach picture perfect), so you won't have to elbow for space or suffer jet skis. See chapter 9.
- **Juara Bay (Tioman Island, Malaysia).** This beach is what they meant when they coined the word "isolated." Be prepared to live like Robinson Crusoe—in tiny huts with cold-water showers, many with no electricity at all. But, oh, the beach! A wide crescent of palm-lined sand hugging the clearest blue water, and with very few other people in sight. See chapter 9.
- **Lombok (Indonesia).** The pure white sand beaches of Lombok, with clear aqua-blue water lapping against them, are sometimes so private you can have one all to yourself. And it's just a short hop from neighboring Bali. See chapter 10.
- **Boracay (Philippines).** Despite the criticism that it's become overrun with tourism, Boracay's talcum-white sand beaches still remain enchanting and postcard perfect. The calm, clear waters are just right for snorkeling, diving, or just relaxing. Life couldn't get much better than simultaneously getting a 1-hour back massage for US$3 and a manicure for US$1. Her name was Sinead and her red vest said "Massage 63." These numbered back healers comb the white beaches until shortly after dark, so don't worry, they'll find you. After rubbing coconut oil all over you, their magic hands will have you feeling better than the tin man after a lube job. See chapter 11.

4 The Best Outdoor Adventures

- **Phang-nga Bay (Thailand).** From the island of Phuket, sea canoe operators guide visitors through the caves hidden deep inside the craggy island-rocks of Phang-nga Bay. Outside, the islands thrust up to the sky, their jagged edges laced with scattered trees. Lie flat in your canoe to slip through the small cave openings, inside which you'll find magnificent chambers believed to have once hidden pirate operations. See chapter 5.
- **Sea kayaking in Halong Bay (Vietnam).** The more than 3,000 arresting limestone karst formations rising out of Halong Bay's peaceful blue-green waters provide a natural obstacle course for paddling. Moving among them, you'll pass in and among intriguing grottos and caverns. Nights are spent camping out in natural parks or on the deck of a mother ship. See chapter 6.
- **Caving in Vang Vien (Laos).** There are countless caves and caverns hidden in the magnificent mountains surrounding Vang Vieng, a small village along the Nam Song River. Some of them are well known and some are barely on the map.

Either way, exploring them and the small town below is truly an adventure. See chapter 7.

- **Tioman Island or Redang Marine Park (Malaysia).** If you scuba dive or would like to learn how, the waters here are packed with exciting corals and creatures accessible through experienced dive operators. Snorkeling trips are also common, and reveal the magic of the sea to those who wish to stay closer to the surface. See chapter 9.

- **Jungle Trekking in Taman Negara (Malaysia).** With suitable options for all budgets and levels of comfort and desired adventure, Malaysia's largest national park opens the wonders of primary rain forest and the creatures who dwell in it to everyone. From the canopy, walk high atop the forest to night watches for nocturnal life. This adventure is as stunning as it is informative. See chapter 9.

- **Hiking Gunung Agung (Bali).** Bali's highest mountain/volcano, Gunung Agung (9,888 ft. or 3,014m high), is utterly sacred to the Balinese, who believe it to be the center of the world. Climbing it is a serious trek that absolutely calls for a guide and proper supplies. Most hotels can arrange for it, but you will have to start out in the middle of the night or very early in the morning to make the top by sunrise. See chapter 10.

- **Riding an elephant at the Elephant Safari Park (Pesanggaran, Bali).** Take a jostling, swaying trip through the jungle, then be sure to do the optional elephant bath. This entails mounting an elephant bareback, arms about a guide's waist, and riding along as the animal slowly walks into a deep pool of (clean) river water. At the handler's command the elephant rears up and plunges in to its knees, submerging you up to your chin. Maybe the most fun I had in Bali. See chapter 10.

- **Experiencing underwater Philippines (Palawan, Philippines).** In El Nido, all I could hear was the rhythmic hissing of packaged air being sucked into my lungs and bubbles being exhaled. I felt no weight, only freedom and extreme curiosity. For the nondiver, the experience of the first introductory dive is amazing. And for seasoned scuba divers, you already understand the privilege and beauty of visiting the foreign living room of the coral reefs. Bat fish, puffer fish, angel fish, lion fish, moray eels, turtles, and, yes, sharks—all are represented here in the Philippines, considered one of the best diving destinations in the world. See chapter 11.

- **Swimming with whale sharks (Luzon, Philippines).** In Donsol Lake, near the town of Legazpi in Southern Luzon, await the world's largest fish. You have an unforgettable opportunity to get up close and personal with these gentle giants as you snorkel above them and beside them. Be careful not to get too close to their huge mouths! See chapter 11.

- **Trekking Mount Pinatubo (Philippines).** The lunar-looking Lahar, the gritty sand and ash that Pinatubo spewed into the atmosphere when it erupted in 1991, makes you feel like you are on the moon or in some sci-fi flick. The 5-hour hike through the lahar fields and hot sulfuric ravines is well worth the wet shoes and intense heat. Below the crater rim is a hot but gorgeous aquamarine lake. Take a swim in its buoyant waters and watch the smoke escaping from the earth's crevices. Beware of quicksand. See chapter 11.

5 The Most Intriguing Temples, Shrines, Palaces & Archaeological Sites

- **The Giant Buddha (Hong Kong).** Laze on the open aft-deck during the hour-long ferry ride to Lantau island (and enjoy great views of the harbor and skyline along the way), followed by a ride over lush hills to see the world's largest, seated, outdoor bronze Buddha, located at the Po Lin Monastery. Complete your pilgrimage with a vegetarian meal at the monastery. See chapter 4.

- **The Grand Palace & Wat Phra Kaeo (Bangkok, Thailand).** These two places are number-one on every travel itinerary to Bangkok, and rightly so. The palace is indeed grand, with mixtures of traditional Thai and European Victorian architecture. Wat Phra Kaeo, the royal temple that houses Thailand's revered and mysterious Emerald Buddha, is a small city in itself, with a dozen or more picturesque outer buildings and monuments that devour rolls of film. See chapter 5.

- **Ayutthaya (Thailand).** Before Bangkok, there was Ayutthaya. This was the thriving capital of Siam that the first Europeans saw when they visited Amazing Thailand. A rich and powerful kingdom of over a million inhabitants, the monarchy supported the arts, especially literature, and as the city grew, international trade was encouraged. All that remains are brick remnants of a grand palace and many temples that were sacked during the Burmese invasion. It's best to hire a guide who can walk you through and point out the significance of each site. See chapter 5.

- **Emperor Jade Pagoda (Saigon, Vietnam).** The Emperor Jade, a classical Chinese temple, looks like the movie set of what an exotic pagoda should look like. Filled with smoky incense and bowing worshippers, it's chockablock with fantastic carved figurines depicting heaven, hell, and everything in between. See chapter 6.

- **Tomb of Khai Dinh (Hue, Vietnam).** Khai Dinh was an egotistic, eccentric emperor, which was bad for the people of Vietnam but great for the tomb he left behind. A gaudy mix of gothic, baroque, and classical Chinese architecture, the exterior is remarkable, and the stunning interior is completely covered with intricate glass and ceramic mosaic work. See chapter 6.

- **Wat Xieng Thong (Luang Prabang, Laos).** The glittering Xieng Thong, built in 1560, sits grandly on a peninsula jutting out into the Mekong River. The facades of two of its buildings are covered by glittering glass mosaics; another building contains an ornate chariot with the heads of seven dragons and the remains of a king. There are also about a dozen English-speaking monks roaming the premises, all excellent conversationalists. See chapter 7.

- **Plain of Jars (Xieng Khouang, Laos).** How did hundreds of huge stone urns, one almost 10 feet tall, come to be placed on a few meadows in northern Laos? No one really knows. The most prevalent explanation is that the urns were made by prehistoric folk in the area about 2,000 years ago, to be used as sarcophagi. See chapter 7.

- **Thian Hock Keng (Singapore).** One of Singapore's oldest Chinese temples, it is a fascinating testimony to Chinese Buddhism combined with traditional Confucian beliefs and natural Taoist principles. Equally fascinating is the modern world that carries on just outside the old temple's doors. See chapter 8.

- **Jame Mosque (Kuala Lumpur, Malaysia).** Built at the central point of the city, this is one of the oldest mosques in Kuala Lumpur. It is the heart of Malay Islam, as evidenced by the Muslim shops, eateries, and daily activities carrying on in the streets surrounding it. See chapter 9.

- **Jalan Tokong (Malacca, Malaysia).** This street, in the historical heart of the city, has a Malay mosque, a Chinese temple, and a Hindu temple living peacefully side-by-side—the perfect example of how the many foreign religions that came to Southeast Asia shaped its communities and learned to coexist in harmony. See chapter 9.

- **Gunung Kawi (Bali).** Gunung Kawi is a shrine consisting of monolithic fauxtombs, the origin and purpose of which remain unknown—a fact that only adds to their power and mystery. An outstanding, awe-inducing sight. See chapter 10.

6 The Best Museums

- **National Museum (Bangkok, Thailand).** From pre-history to recent events, this museum—the former palace of the brother of King Rama I—answers many questions about Thai history and culture through the ages. Inside buildings that are themselves works of fine Thai design, you'll find Buddha images, ancient arts, royal paraphernalia, and fine arts. Rama's sister also lived here, and her house is decorated in the same style as it was in the late 1700s. See chapter 5.
- **Vietnam History Museum (Saigon, Vietnam).** This museum does an all-round good job of presenting Vietnam's (particularly South Vietnam's) culture and history. From prehistoric objects to imperial housewares and exhibits on ethnic minorities, you'll be able to easily take in the show thanks to the extensive English explanations. See chapter 6.
- **The Cham Museum (Danang, Vietnam).** This open-air colonial structure houses the largest collection of Cham sculpture in the world. Not only are relics of this ancient Hindu-inspired culture rare, but the religious artwork itself—more than 300 pieces of sandstone—is voluptuous, captivating, and intense. See chapter 6.
- **Images of Singapore (Sentosa Island, Singapore).** No one has done a better job than this museum in chronicling for the public the horrors of the Pacific Theatre and Japanese Occupation in Southeast Asia. Video and audio displays take you on a chronological journey through Singapore's World War II experience. The grand finale is the Surrender Chambers, life-sized wax dioramas of the fateful events. Oh yeah, and there's also dioramas depicting historical figures throughout Singapore's early development, as well as depictions of traditional cultural festivals. See chapter 8.

7 The Best Festivals & Celebrations

- **Chinese New Year (Hong Kong and Singapore).** If you're in Southeast Asia around the end of January, beginning of February, hop up to Hong Kong or down to Singapore for the festivities. It's a 3-day party, with parades (complete with dragons and stilt-walkers) and fireworks. See chapters 4 and 8.
- **Songkran (Thailand).** Every year from the 13th to the 15th of April, Thais welcome the New Year (according to their calendar), and since Songkran falls in the middle of the hottest season in an already hot country, how do you think people celebrate? Every Thai heads out into the streets with water guns and buckets of ice water (sometimes laced with talcum powder, just to add to the mess), and spends the next 3 days soaking each other, and *you.* Foreigners are especially favorite targets. Don't get mad, arm thyself: Water bazookas are on sale everywhere. Have a ball! See chapter 5.
- **Mid-Autumn Festival (Vietnam).** This lunar celebration, usually taking place in late September or early October, has the stuff of all great holidays: color, pageantry, and adorable children, who dance and parade through towns carrying paper lanterns they've made themselves. See chapter 6.
- **That Luang Festival (Vientiane, Laos).** Thousands of Buddhist followers from all over the country, and even a few neighboring countries, converge on the spectacular That Luang temple in Vientiane. There are alms-giving ceremonies and flower processions, and then the whole affair dissolves into a carnival that stretches over several days. See chapter 7.
- **Thaipusam (Singapore and Malaysia).** Around the end of January, beginning of February, Hindus celebrate Thaipusam. Men give thanks for prayers answered

by carrying kavadis, huge steel racks attached to their bodies with skewers piercing the skin. Cheeks are pierced and fruits are hung from the skin using sharp hooks. A parade of devotees carry these things in a deep trance—and the next day they wake up virtually unharmed. See chapters 8 and 9.

- **Masskara Festival (Bacolod City, Philippines).** Bring your beads, masks, and pig-catching and pole-climbing skills for this event, held every October 6 to 19 in Bacolod City, Negros Island. You'll be dancing in the streets all in the name of lifting the spirits. Locals and tourists come from all over for this festival. It's the Filipino version of Mardi Gras or Carnival. See chapter 11.

8 The Biggest Cultural No-Nos

- **Photographing a villager without permission in Vietnam.** There's nothing a visitor wants more than to take away indelible images of the colorful, rustic lifestyles of the Vietnamese ethnic minorities. However, many rural people are superstitious about photographs or may resent the intrusion of privacy. Ask first. See chapter 6, plus "Etiquette Tips," in chapter 2.
- **Losing your temper in Laos or Thailand.** The Lao and Thai people enjoy a Buddhist sensibility in their daily life, approaching even unfortunate events with calm cheerfulness. They would be shocked and dismayed at anger or ill temper, and raising your voice won't achieve any purpose whatsoever. No matter how frustrated you become, keep it under wraps, or the people around you will see to it you never get where you need to go. See chapters 7 and 5, plus "Etiquette Tips," in chapter 2.
- **Looking (or being) poor in Singapore.** You probably won't run into too many cultural faux pas in cosmopolitan Singapore, but in Singapore, poverty is the pits. Bring your smartest clothes if you want to impress people here. See chapter 8, plus "Etiquette Tips," in chapter 2.
- **Using offensive body language in Bali, Malaysia, Thailand, or Laos.** Muslims, Hindus, and Buddhists all reserve the left hand for "unclean" toilet duties, never for pointing at anyone or thing, handing objects to others, eating, or touching other people. Similarly, in Buddhist and Hindu cultures the head is revered as the most sacred part of the body, while the feet are the lowest. Never touch another person's head or shoulders, not even a child's. Never point or gesture with your feet, or use your feet to perform any tasks other than walking. See "Etiquette Tips," in chapter 2.
- **Hanging clothes to dry in Bali.** Or otherwise out in public (off hotel balconies and chairs and the like). See chapter 10, plus "Etiquette Tips," in chapter 2.
- **Showing too much skin (regional).** Except perhaps in Hong Kong and Singapore and in heavily touristed areas, modest Southeast Asians accept beachwear at the beach, revealing vacation clothing at resorts, and sexy attire at discos. Everywhere else, dress with respect for the locals and their traditions. See "Etiquette Tips," in chapter 2.
- **Wearing shorts or short skirts to a temple or mosque (regional).** It'll get you tossed out. See "Etiquette Tips," in chapter 2.

9 The Best Resorts & Luxury Hotels

- **The Peninsula Hotel (Hong Kong).** Hong Kong's most famous hotel exudes elegance, from its Rolls-Royce fleet to the white-gloved doormen who stand at attention outside the palatial, gilded lobby. Rooms in the 32-story tower sport unparalleled views of Victoria Harbour, and even jaded travelers are likely to be impressed with the sheer breadth of amenities offered here. See chapter 4.

- **Island Shangri-La Hong Kong (Hong Kong).** Viennese chandeliers, Oriental carpets, and more than 500 paintings and artwork adorn this, the tallest hotel on Hong Kong Island. The 17-story atrium features a marvelous 16-story-high Chinese painting, believed to be the largest landscape painting in the world. Spacious, impeccable rooms face either the Peak or Victoria Harbour—both stunning views. See chapter 4.
- **The Oriental Hotel (Bangkok, Thailand).** The original address in Thailand, The Oriental has seen modernization detract from its charms of yesterday, but there's still ambience all around. See chapter 5.
- **The Amanpuri (Phuket, Thailand).** A seductive bungalow resort in exquisite Thai style that will thrill even the most discerning guests. See chapter 5.
- **The Regent (Chiang Mai, Thailand).** Luxurious Thai-style suites, excellent restaurants, a multitude of activities, and the most amazing swimming pool you've ever seen await you. Don't forget to meet their resident water buffalo family—they work the resort's private rice paddies. See chapter 5.
- **Ana Mandara (Nha Trang, Vietnam).** The details are perfect in this small-scale resort, from the incense burning in the open longhouse-style lobby to the small signs identifying tropical fish in the lobby's pond. Each stylish room has the air of a secluded hut with its own verandah, many overlooking the palm-lined coast. Both the food and the staff's smiles are perfect. See chapter 6.
- **Raffles Hotel (Singapore).** For Old World opulence, Raffles is second to none. A pure fantasy of the days when tigers still lurked around the perimeters. See chapter 8.
- **Four Seasons Hotel (Singapore).** Elegance and warmth combine to make this place a good bet. Consider a regular room here before you book a suite elsewhere. See chapter 8.
- **The Regent (Kuala Lumpur, Malaysia).** For my money, the Regent offers the smartest decor, best service, and best selection of facilities in the whole city. See chapter 9.
- **The Aryani Resort (Kuala Terengganu, Malaysia).** An exotic retreat, Aryani combines local Terengganu flavors with all the pampering you'd want from a getaway resort. See chapter 9.
- **Shangri-La's Rasa Sayang Resort (Penang, Malaysia).** The oldest resort on the beach has claimed the best stretch of sand and snuggled the most imaginatively modern yet traditionally designed resort in gardens just beyond. See chapter 9.
- **Four Seasons (Jimbaran, Bali).** With its individual bungalows and plunge pools overlooking the blue blue sea and its famous Four Seasons pampering, Four Seasons Jimbaran is one of the great hotels in the world. See chapter 10.
- **Amandari (Ubud, Bali).** Its individual bungalows overlooking a deep green gorge, the Amandari offers another sybaritic Bali experience. If you can afford it (or the Four Seasons Jimbaran), do. Even if you can't, do. See chapter 10.
- **Amanpulo (North of Palawan, Philippines).** There is none finer in all of the Philippines than this exclusive resort, situated on its own private island north of Palawan. A peaceful oasis for rich, famous, and powerful people who want to be pampered with private Jacuzzis, private beaches, personal service, and your very own personal motorized cart to tote you around the beautiful surroundings. See chapter 11.

10 The Best Hotel Bargains

- **Bossotel Inn (Bangkok, Thailand).** Located in a prime spot, close to the Chao Phraya River, the Bossotel is the perfect budget answer to the Shangri-La and Orientals that dominate accommodations along the river. See chapter 5.
- **River Ping Palace (Chiang Mai, Thailand).** If you're going to travel on a budget, do it with style—and style is what River Ping Palace has wrapped up in its old Thai-style teak mansion buildings. See chapter 5.
- **Caravelle Hotel (Saigon, Vietnam).** The Caravelle is exemplary of the many bargains to be had in Saigon. Just renovated, it features plush, comfortable rooms in a huge downtown hotel with all the amenities, including a deluxe gym and spa and the hippest bar in Saigon. All this for US$89 per double room and US$160 a suite, including breakfast. See chapter 6.
- **Anou Hotel (Vientiane, Laos).** The Anou is clean, bright, and friendly, and in a fantastic downtown location. The big rooms, going for US$25 to US$35, feature real wood floors and comfortable beds, and the suites are huge. This is the kind of hotel that makes Southeast Asia such a marvelous budget destination. See chapter 7.
- **RELC International Hotel (Singapore).** For a safe and simple place to call home in Singapore, RELC can't be beat. One wonders how they keep costs so low when their location is so good. See chapter 8.
- **Traders Hotel (Singapore).** Value-for-money is the name of the game, with all sorts of promotional packages, self-service launderettes, vending machines, and a checkout lounge just a few of the offerings that make this the most convenient hotel in the city. See chapter 8.
- **Swiss-Inn (Kuala Lumpur, Malaysia).** Tucked behind the market tents in Chinatown, this bargain find has the look of a higher quality hotel, but in mini-size. If you plan on spending your time out exploring the city, why pay more for empty space? See chapter 9.
- **Heeren House (Malacca, Malaysia).** Bargain or no bargain, this boutique hotel in the heart of the old city is *the* place to stay in Malacca if you want to really get a feel of the local atmosphere. See chapter 9.
- **Telang Usan Hotel (Kuching, Malaysia).** An informal place, Telang Usan is homey and quaint, and within walking distance of many major attractions in Kuching. See chapter 9.
- **The homestay/losmen of Bali.** These small-time accommodations will give you a large, comfortable (though no-frills) room or bungalow with a big, often fancy breakfast for about US$5 a night for two. See chapter 10.
- **Dolarog Resort (El Nido, Palawan, Philippines).** The peaceful huts are situated on their own private island and will give you that same "away from it all feel" that the exclusive resorts guarantee—but for only around US$30 a night! See chapter 11.

11 The Best Local Dining Experiences

- **Dining on dim sum (Hong Kong).** Nothing conveys a sense of Chinese life more vividly than a visit to a crowded, lively Cantonese restaurant where trolleys of dim sum in bamboo steamers are wheeled from customer to customer during breakfast and lunch. Simply peer into the passing bamboo baskets and choose what appears the most tempting. A great way to start the day. See chapter 4.

- **Taking high tea at the Peninsula (Hong Kong).** The British rulers may be gone, but their legacy lives on in the afternoon tea, complete with finger sandwiches and scones. Virtually all upper-class hotels offer afternoon tea, but none can compare with the experience offered in the lobby of Hong Kong's most venerable hotel, long a favored people-watching spot. Come for afternoon tea, listen to classical music, and gaze away. See chapter 4.
- **Street food (Bangkok, Thailand).** On every street, down every alley, you'll find someone setting up a cart with an umbrella. Noodles, salads, and satay are favorites, and some hawkers set up tables and stools on the sidewalk for you to take a load off. Thai cafe life! See chapter 5.
- **Pho (Vietnam).** Don't leave the country without sampling one if not many bowls of this delicate noodle soup, made with vermicelli-thin rice noodles, chicken (*ga*) or beef (*bo*), and several fresh accompaniments, according to the chef's whim: basil, mint, chile peppers, bean sprouts. There are regional variations to boot. See chapter 6.
- **Kua Lao (Vientiane, Laos).** Kua Lao is traditional Lao cuisine in a like setting, including music. Situated in a restored colonial, with a series of dining rooms, it is the premier Lao restaurant in the country. The extensive menu goes on for pages. There is an entire page of vegetarian entrees, and another entire page of something you don't see often: traditional Lao desserts. See chapter 7.
- **Hawker centers (Singapore).** Think of them as shopping malls for food—great food! For local cuisine, who needs a menu with pictures when you can walk around and select anything you want as it's prepared before your eyes. See chapter 8.
- **Gurney Drive (Penang, Malaysia).** Penang is King for offering a variety of Asian cuisine, from Chinese to Malay to Indian and everything else in between. Visiting this large hawker center by the sea is like taking "Intro to Penang 101." See chapter 9.
- **Satri's Warung (Bali).** With 24 hours' advance notice, Satri's will cook you a smoked duck or—our favorite (we dream of it all the time)—banana chicken feast, a whole bird, plus three plates of salad or fabulous vegetables, rice, and fruit for dessert, for about US$7 for two. See chapter 10.
- **What's inside pot no. 1? (Philippines).** In many of the Philippines' towns on almost all its islands, the best food can be found not at the five-star resorts but on the counter in front of a family's home. As you stroll along the street you'll notice four or five silver pots lined up in a row. Feel free to have a peek and ask the cook what's inside—maybe pork adobo, chicken curry, pig knuckles. Pull up a chair, choose your pot, and experience true Filipino cuisine. See chapter 11.

12 The Best Markets

- **Stanley (Hong Kong).** Stall after stall of casualwear, silk clothing, bathing suits, tennis shoes, accessories, and souvenirs and crafts imported from China make this a shopper's paradise. After a day of bargaining, I like to recuperate in one of Stanley's trendy yet casual restaurants. See chapter 4.
- **Temple Street Night Market (Hong Kong).** Highlights include shopping for casual clothing, music, toys, and accessories; enjoying a meal at a *dai pai dong* (roadside food stall); watching amateur street musicians; and having your fortune told. See chapter 4.
- **Chatuchak Weekend Market (Bangkok, Thailand).** Words cannot describe it. It's so big, I'm thinking of selling homing devices to people who are afraid they'll get lost inside. Don't buy a thing until you spend at least a half day wandering

down the endless aisles eyeballing the multitude of merchandise available. See chapter 5.

- **Night Bazaar (Chiang Mai, Thailand).** Most of those gorgeous handicrafts you find all over Thailand are made in the north, and at Chiang Mai's sprawling Night Bazaar you'll find the widest selection, best quality, and best prices. See chapter 5.
- **Hoi An Central Market (Hoi An, Vietnam).** On the banks of the busy Perfume River lies this entire city block of narrow, roofed aisles. Produce of every description is for sale inside—handicrafts, household items, and services such as facials and massages—and on the outskirts, an entire warehouse is devoted to silk and silk tailoring. See chapter 6.
- **Morning Market (Vientiane, Laos).** Laos's famous market is three huge buildings with traditional tiered roofs. Silver handicrafts, fabrics, jewelry, electronics, books, and much, much more occupy each building's several floors. The aisles are wide and made for wandering and poking through the wares, and the proprietors are friendly, gentle bargainers. See chapter 7.
- **Arab Street (Singapore).** Sure, Singapore is a shopper's paradise, but it needs more places like Arab Street, where small shops lining the street sell everything from textiles to handicrafts. Bargaining is welcome. See chapter 8.
- **Central Market (Kuala Lumpur, Malaysia).** One-stop shopping for all the rich arts and handicrafts Malaysia produces—and it's air-conditioned, too. See chapter 9.

13 The Best Shopping Bargains

- **Custom-tailored clothes (Hong Kong).** Nothing beats the thrill of having something custom-made to fit you perfectly. If this is your dream, make a trek to a tailor one of your first priorities, so that you'll have time for several fittings. See chapter 4.
- **Hill tribe handicrafts (Night Bazaar, Chiang Mai, Thailand).** From unusual silver designs to colorful embroidery, you'll fill your birthday and holiday shopping list in about an hour, and it'll cost you a fraction of your budget. See chapter 5.
- **Antiques (Thailand).** Before you head out on vacation, visit some Asian galleries in your home country and take a look at the prices of the items you like. Once you're here you'll be amazed at how little these things really cost. Most places will be glad to pack and ship purchases for you, and you'll still come out ahead. See chapter 5.
- **Tailored silk suits (Thailand and Hanoi, Hoi An, and Saigon, Vietnam).** For a fraction of what you'd pay at home, you can have a lined silk (or wool) suit tailored in a day or less, including a fitting or two. Bring pictures of your favorite designer outfits for a clever copy, and an empty suitcase or two for the trip home. See chapters 5 and 6.
- **Silver or lacquer handicrafts (Vietnam).** You'll find amazingly good workmanship and prices throughout the country, particularly for lacquerware. You can bargain like a demon, but be careful to ensure that the silver is genuine. See chapter 6.
- **Handwoven textiles (Laos).** The Laos handweave textured fabrics, piece by piece, on primitive wooden looms. Such painstaking work costs more than a few dollars, but ranging from sophisticated silk to gaily colored ethnic prints, the designs are pure art and uniquely Laotian. See chapter 7.

- **Silver filigree jewelry (Malaysia).** This fine silver is worked into detailed filigree jewelry designs to make brooches, necklaces, bracelets, and other fine jewelry. See chapter 9.
- **Pewter (Malaysia).** Malaysia is the home of Selangor Pewter, one of the largest pewter manufacturers in the world. Their many showrooms have all sorts of items to choose from. See chapter 9.
- **Fabric and wood carvings (Bali).** Even though as a tourist you may spend more than a local, just about anything you buy in Bali (but especially fabric and wood carvings, particularly those you commission) is dirt cheap, particularly when you see how much the same item goes for back home. See chapter 10.

14 The Hottest Nightlife Spots

- **Patpong (Bangkok, Thailand).** Yes, *that* Patpong. If go-go bars and sex shows aren't your style, you'll still find plenty to do. After you're finished shopping in the huge night market, there are plenty of restaurants, pubs, and discos that cater to folks who prefer more traditional nightlife. See chapter 5.
- **Saigon (Vietnam).** From the tawdry Apocalypse Now bar to rooftop garden scenes like Saigon-Saigon and cool jazz spots like Q-Bar, Saigon is famous for its rollicking nightlife. Most evenings begin with an elegant French or Vietnamese dinner at amazingly reasonable prices and then move on to incessant bar-hopping in the city's compact downtown, mingling with trendy locals and fun-loving expats. See chapter 6.
- **Singapore (The Whole City).** Nightlife is becoming increasingly sophisticated in Singapore, where locals have more money for recreation and fun. Take the time to choose the place that suits your personality. Jazz club? Techno disco? Cocktail lounge? Wine bar? Good old pub? They have it all. See chapter 8.
- **Bangsar (near Kuala Lumpur, Malaysia).** Folks in Kuala Lumpur know to go to Bangsar for nighttime excitement. A couple blocks of concentrated restaurants, cafes, discos, pubs, and wine bars will tickle any fancy. Good people-watching, too. See chapter 9.
- **Kuta Beach (Bali).** The Tijuana or Tangiers of Bali, Kuta is one big nightlife spot. Drink till you drop. See chapter 10.
- **Makati (Manila, Philippines).** Bring your trendiest outfit and shoes for some of the most jet-setting watering holes in Southeast Asia. The Giraffe, Venezia, Zu, and Euphoria are a few names to throw around. For a more bohemian experience, check out the spots in Malate like Verve Room or Hobbit House. See chapter 11.

2

Introducing Southeast Asia

by Jennifer Eveland

While the rest of the world's continents fit into nice tidy compartments—North America, South America, Europe, the Middle East, Africa—Southeast Asia seems more like a hodgepodge of islands than anything surely defined. Take a closer look at this region and you'll see that the nations that make up Southeast Asia—Cambodia, Indonesia, Laos, Malaysia, Myanmar, Singapore, Thailand, and Vietnam—many times have more differences than similarities. Differences in geographical features, history, religious and cultural heritage, and political and economic viewpoints make this an incredibly diverse part of the world.

1 The Region Today

The region's many differences also mean many choices for vacationers. Some travel as far as halfway around the world to visit—but with so much diversity, how can you decide which is the perfect beach or the most intriguing cultural adventure? In this chapter I provide an overall view of the region and explain some of the special features and unique attractions of each destination to help you decide. I also point out some important issues to help you steer clear of trouble spots—there are a few. And in the chapters that follow, we'll help you plan your trip from soup to nuts.

Geographically speaking, Southeast Asia does not lack in gorgeous scenery. The lush tropical rain forests of peninsular Malaysia and Borneo are some of the oldest in the world, and Singapore is one of only two cities that can boast tropical rain forest within the city's limits. The islands and beaches of the region support famous resort areas in Phuket (Thailand) and Bali (Indonesia), plus countless other gorgeous islands and beaches that are relatively under-exploited. Divers and snorkelers flock from around the world for stunning coral reefs bursting with colorful life in Thailand, Malaysia, Philippines, and Indonesia. Every country offers terrific natural diversity, opening up all kinds of choices for postcard-perfect experiences and exciting outdoor adventure.

Southeast Asia's cultural diversity is also complex. Consider the Sri Lankans who transplanted Theravada Buddhism, with its serene and orthodox ways, throughout Myanmar, Thailand, and Laos. Or the Indian traders who brought ancient Hinduism to Cambodia, influencing the architecture of the magical city of Angkor, in contrast to the Hindus who settled on Bali, mixing their dogma with local animism to create a completely unique sect. Meanwhile, seafaring Arab merchants imported Islam to coastal areas of Malaysia and Indonesia, adding a further element to the "oriental mystique" of these countries. Then there's Vietnam, the only Southeast Asian nation to fall directly under the control of past Chinese empires, whose cultural influences are still strong to this day. As if that weren't enough, Europeans from the late 1400s onward brought colonial elegance to cities like Hong Kong, Singapore, Penang, and Malacca, to name just a few. Basically, to cross an international border in Southeast Asia is to enter a completely different world from the one you just left.

Economic and political development have influenced tourism greatly. While cosmopolitan Hong Kong and Singapore guarantee the best luxury hotels, finest dining, and most refined cultural attractions, up and coming cities such as Manila, Kuala Lumpur, Bangkok, and Ho Chi Minh City promise cultural curiosities around every street corner as they struggle to justify traditional customs with modern development. And as Thailand's almost 3 decades of tourism development have created excellent facilities for travelers, those looking for a more down-and-dirty experience can head off to Myanmar or Laos, almost completely new to the industry, and off the beaten path of most tourism agendas. Basically, for every luxurious Bali there's a laid-back Tioman Island (Malaysia). For every crazy Hong Kong there's a charming Penang.

While we're on the subject, it's important to talk about those Southeast Asian nations that present trouble spots for travelers, in terms of politics and economics. The sections that follow will discuss political turmoil in more detail, but basically you'll want to become aware of possible violence in Laos and Cambodia, as well as certain areas of Indonesia, Malaysia, and the Philippines. To make sure you're up-to-the-minute regarding political turbulence, check with the U.S. Department of State's Web site posting current travel warnings (http://travel.state.gov/travel_warnings.html).

HONG KONG

OK, OK, you got us. Hong Kong is not *officially* part of Southeast Asia; however, we know many of you will be stopping over in this happening hub and figure we'll save you some trouble by including the information you need in this guidebook. Even if it isn't a stop on the way, the incredible skyline alone is worth the trip. At night, the way the neon lights color Victoria Harbor—it has to be the world's most awesome cityscape next to New York.

The first reason people come to Hong Kong is for the **shopping**—the entire city is a Chinese emporium of cheap goods, exotic finds, and luxury bargains galore. The second is for the **dining**—everything from a 10-course Chinese banquet fit for royalty to mouthwatering prawn wonton soup in a dingy shop front. Despite the city's **museums and exhibits,** many of which are excellent, and its well-maintained Chinese Taoist **temples,** the best sights to see are the streets themselves. Spend an afternoon getting lost in the backstreets of **Yau Ma Tei** or **Mong Kok** and discover scenes of daily life and old traditions like street markets and incense-saturated family altars. If you have the time, **Macau,** the charming Portugal-meets-China settlement, is only an hour away.

THAILAND

Thailand sees more international travelers each year than any of its neighbors, enticing everyone from luxury vacationers to young shoestring backpackers, Japanese junkets and European group tours. You'll find professionals spinning their wheels for business ventures, tourists prowling for that "One Night in Bangkok" and soul-searchers hanging around for the Buddhist dharma and Asian hospitality. Most travelers to Southeast Asia either start here or end up here.

Most people fly into **Bangkok,** staying for a few days to take in the city's bizarre mix of old and new: royal palaces and skyscrapers, pious monks amid rush-hour commuters, sidewalk noodle vendors serving bankers in suits, not to mention the city's nightlife—with that seedy element that has made it infamous. Heading south, you'll find the legendary beaches and resorts of **Phuket** island, while **Ko Samui,** in the Gulf of Thailand, provides a lesser-developed "alternative" to Phuket. Another attraction to Thailand, the northern hills around **Chiang Mai,** present a world of adventure trekking and tribal culture that has been well-developed for visitors. Throughout the country are opportunities for **outdoor adventure** and **extreme sports,** organized by very professional firms that you can count on for safety and reliability.

And at the end of the day, there's that unbeatable taste of the **Thai cuisine**—tangy soups, hearty coconut curries, and the freshest seafood.

VIETNAM

If the thought of Vietnam stirs flashbacks of televised war coverage or scenes from dark movies, guess again. One of the fastest growing destinations in the region also happens to be one of the most beautiful, most friendly, and most convenient places to travel.

What's my favorite feature of Vietnam? All its major destinations fall in a line—go from north to south, starting in Hanoi and ending in Ho Chi Minh City, or vice versa. Tourist bus routes let you pay one price, but plan your own itinerary so that you can make stops along the way for as long as you wish. You just can't get more convenient than that.

Ho Chi Minh City, or Saigon, is the gateway to the beautiful **Mekong Delta** region. Heading north you'll pass through **Dalat,** a hill station in the cool mountains, then down to **Nha Trang,** an emerging seaside town. Further north, **Hoi An** is one of the region's most charming villages, and chock full of shopping galore. Still further north, the former capital city at **Hue** is filled with many architectural gems of Chinese and European influence. But the merging of cultures is never more evident than in **Hanoi,** where the best elements of Vietnamese, French, and Chinese cultures collide. From here, head east off to see the gorgeous **Halong Bay,** with hundreds of craggy rock formations plunging straight up from the sea, or travel north to visit Vietnam's hill tribe people in the mountains that divide northern Vietnam from China.

LAOS

Travelers who complain that Thailand's become too touristy, look to Laos. Here is a country where foreigners are still greeted as gracious guests rather than cash cows. Rarely will you find a tour bus or tacky souvenir stall, just quiet towns with laid-back markets, townsfolk carrying on their crafts in pretty street scenes, and farmers tending their chores in the beautiful countryside—the pace of life set by peaceful Buddhist values.

Some people fear that Laos will break into the "Tour Coach" market at any moment, and the country's gorgeous historic temples will turn into *DisneyLaos.* The good news? It's not going to happen soon. The bad news? That's because since March of 2000 many small bombs have exploded in the capital city and other tourist areas, including places like Wattay Airport near Vientiane, a restaurant frequented by tourists, the capital city's morning market and central bus terminal, and a hotel in the southern city of Pakse. Combined with the country's poor travel infrastructure and the tons of unexploded ordnance in the countryside, Laos is starting to look like another Holiday in Cambodia.

How heartbreaking. A trip to Laos can be such a rewarding experience. For a capital city, Vientiane is startlingly parochial. With every other building dedicated to an international development agency, it's an eye-opening reminder that Laos is one of the top 10 poorest countries in the world. Next stop, **Luang Prabang,** UNESCO World Heritage site—a paradise of gorgeous Buddhist temples—dozens of them amid shady streets that lead to the Mekong River. If you have time, **Xieng Khouang,** in the east of Vientiane, is the home of Southeast Asia's Stonehenge, **The Plain of Jars,** huge mysterious stone monoliths that have somehow survived bombs and guerilla insurgents.

SINGAPORE

All of Southeast Asia's cultures seem to converge on Singapore, making it perhaps one of the best places to begin your exploration of the region. Excellent **museums** explore Asian civilizations, Southeast Asian art, even World War II history. The city's hundreds of restaurants provide a wealth of choices in terms of **cuisine,** for a glimpse of regional specialties in one stop. And some of the best regional **fine arts, crafts and antiques** end up in Singapore showrooms.

I'll be honest with you, Singapore gets trashed regularly by complaints of it being too Western, too modern, too sanitary—too Disneyland. Walk the streets of **Chinatown, Little India,** and the Malay Muslim area at **Kampong Glam** and you can see where the buildings have been renovated and many former inhabitants have retired from traditional crafts. But some of these places have a few secrets left that are very rewarding if you are observant. For the past 200 years Singapore has invented itself from many contributing cultures. If you consider the country today, it is still keeping up that tradition.

MALAYSIA

Possibly one of the most overlooked countries in Southeast Asia, Malaysia is one of my favorites for one very special reason. It's not Thailand! After so much time spent traveling around Thailand listening to every hawker yell "Hello! Special for you!" and every backpacker bragging about 5-dollar roach-infested guesthouses, I look forward to Malaysia just to escape the tourism industry. Beaches on the islands of **Langkawi** and **Sabah** are just as beautiful as Thailand's and resorts here are equally as fine. The quaint British colonial influences at **Penang, Malacca,** and **Kuching** (Sarawak) add to the beauty, as does the mysterious Arab-Islamic influences all over the country. Not to mention an endless number of outdoor adventures from mountain climbing to jungle trekking to scuba diving—in fact the rain forest here is far superior.

Why is Malaysia so underestimated? To be honest, after experiencing the relative "freedom" and tolerance of Thai culture, many travelers find Malaysian culture too strict and prohibitive. Personally, I think it's a fair trade—in Thailand when I talk to Thai people, I'm often treated like a tourist with a fat wallet. In Malaysia, when I meet local people I end up having interesting conversations and cherished personal experiences. And I don't have to suffer through blatant prostitution and drug abuse—the sad, sleazy side of the Thai tourism industry.

One word of caution regarding travel in Malaysia: On April 23, 2000, a group of tourists were kidnapped from the diving resort at Sipadan Island, off the east coast of Sabah (Malaysian Borneo). Abu Sayyaf, the Filipino Muslim separatists who were responsible for the incident, still remain at large in the southern islands of the Philippines close to Borneo. Exercise caution when traveling to this area.

BALI (INDONESIA)

No doubt the whole world is familiar with the trouble facing Indonesia. Since the economic crisis in 1997, the country's been plagued with civil unrest: first the struggle for East Timor independence, followed by rioting in the capital, Jakarta. Today, unrest continues, including frightening cannibalistic ethnic clashes in Kalimantan on Borneo and fighting between Muslims and Christians on most major islands. Additionally, a rise in anti-American sentiment has incited violence outside the U.S. Embassy in Jakarta, and witch-hunts for American tourists in Solo, near the ancient temple at Borobudur on Java. Meanwhile, despite injections of IMF funds and major changes in leadership, the economy continues to stall, spin, crash, and burn.

Unbelievably, amid all the political, social, and economic troubles, Bali has gone unscathed. After a brief dip in tourism arrivals in 1997, the island and its resorts resumed business as usual to top leisure markets. There's virtually no sign of violence, unrest, or economic crisis to speak of.

The beaches remain the stuff of legend—supporting dreamy resorts dripping with tropical ambience, world renowned among romantic honeymooners and well-heeled paradise seekers. Sports enthusiasts flock here for surfing, snorkeling, scuba diving, swimming, windsurfing, as well as a number of on-land challenges. People who can pull themselves away from the seaside will venture into villages lively with friendly local smiles and markets packed with eye-boggling local handicrafts and treasures to bargain for. The artistic and intriguing community in Ubud is just as fascinating as the gorgeous scenery around the town, full of sacred Hindu temples, mysterious royal tombs, rice paddies, gorges, and rivers. It's a small wonder why so many other tropical destinations seek to imitate Bali's unique architectural and creative style, but really you have to experience the real thing to believe it.

THE PHILIPPINES

With countless offerings for the adventure traveler and nature lover, Philippines remains a top destination for climbing, trekking, animal watching, scuba diving, windsurfing, beach bumming—you name it. With 7,107 islands in total, you can't throw a stone without hitting a beach; however, tourism development has come quietly for Philippines, as it's had to compete with Thailand and Indonesia.

From the cosmopolitan (and crazy) capital, Manila, you can kick off an extensive exploration of the country's Spanish colonial heritage and local traditions. Nearby mountains open up a world of underground caverns and above-ground hiking paths, as well as dangerous volcanoes. If you're only in it for the resorts, head straight for **Boracay** or **Mactan** island, the most well-developed resort destinations. For scuba and snorkeling head for **Bohol** and **Mindoro,** both very relaxed and laid-back resort areas. But to really get away from civilization, check out **Palawan,** a pristine wonderland with some of the most secluded resorts and amazing nature adventures.

While the security situation has improved in most areas of the country, making travel the safest it's been in years, there are still some areas to avoid. While rebel activity is primarily restricted to the southwestern islands, especially Mindanao, some areas, such as the Cordillera and Bicol regions of Luzon, see rebel activity. Since April 2000 the Abu Sayyaf terrorist group have kidnapped many locals and tourists, including a group from the nearby Malaysian dive resort at Sipadan in eastern Sabah.

CAMBODIA & MYANMAR

Both Cambodia and Myanmar (Burma) are endowed with magnificent scenic beauty and unique cultures, and offer fascinating and profound travel experiences to visitors. Cambodia's Angkor Wat and Myanmar's countless temples at Bagan are two of Southeast Asia's—and the world's—most amazing sights. Unfortunately, the progressive approach to world relations and tourism shown by neighboring Vietnam has not yet been emulated by these countries' governments, whose policies still reflect disarray, repression, and an inability to deal constructively with internal and external problems.

After being closed to tourism for years due to a series of wars and the actions of repressive governments, these countries are showing some signs of encouraging more visitors by upgrading the quality of their infrastructure.

For a decade now **Ang San Suu Kyi,** Myanmar's leading voice of democracy, has spoken out against any activity that might put money into the hands of the oppressive military regime that imprisons her. However, human rights groups are only beginning to debate the merits of tourism in Myanmar. Perhaps tourism will attract global exposure that could prove helpful in the long run?

Meanwhile, although much of Cambodia remains a dangerous prospect for leisure travel, the recent addition of direct flights to Siem Reap, gateway to the ancient city at Angkor, have simplified the experience altogether.

Still, as general difficulties, both in terms of political consequences and safety concerns, still exist, we've chosen to present these destinations with caution. In chapter 12, we've provided the most sensible travel options.

2 A Southeast Asian Cultural Primer

A vast diversity of ethnic groups people Southeast Asia. Whether living in modern cities or remote hills, each group has its own special cultural practices, which are often influenced by religion. With so much mingling and mixing of peoples occurring throughout Southeast Asian history, it should come as no surprise that the region's cornucopia of cultures have intertwined and adopted various elements, beliefs, and practices from each other.

THE CULTURAL MAKEUP OF SOUTHEAST ASIA
HONG KONG

Although Western culture has had a strong impact on Hong Kong (fact: 5 of the world's 10 busiest McDonalds are located here), it still preserves its connection to many aspects of Chinese culture passed down from ancestors. Fortune-telling, astrology, superstition, and ancestor worship still play a role in the daily life of a people whose religions may include elements of Buddhist, Taoist, and Christian beliefs. In the morning, you may see men and women practicing the ancient art of tai chi in the shadow of a skyscraper, while in the evening, outside a temple, you might encounter a fortune-teller interpreting someone's future.

Whether it's entertainment, cuisine, or the arts, the Chinese influence in Hong Kong is unmistakable. Among the most popular cultural pursuits are **puppet plays,** which tell the story of Chinese dynasties, and **Chinese Opera** (wayung), which is performed in the more modern Cantonese style as well as the classic Beijing style.

While the majority of Hong Kong's 30,000 restaurants serve Cantonese-style Chinese food, there is also a good selection of establishments serving Shanghai, Beijing, Hangzhou, Szechuan, and many other varieties of Chinese cooking.

English is spoken widely in Hong Kong, as the island's two official languages are Chinese (Cantonese) and English.

THAILAND

Over centuries, migrating cultures have blended to create what is known as "Thai" today. From early waves of Southern Chinese migrants, combine Mon peoples from Burma, Khmers from Cambodia, Malays and Lao people—it is said that Thailand's King Rama I could trace ancestry to all these, plus European, Indian, Han Chinese, and Arab families. Of the 75% of the population that call themselves Thai, a great number of people in northeastern Isaan are of Lao ancestry. In the past century, Thailand has also become home to many migrating hill tribes in the north—tribes who've

Buddha & Buddhism

Buddhism is the primary religion of Thailand, Laos, Vietnam, Burma, and Cambodia, and is practiced to a lesser extent in the other Southeast Asian nations. It is a religion without a God, mystical in the sense that it strives for the intuitive realization of the oneness of the universe. It requires that individuals work out their own salvation as commanded by the Buddha himself, to "look within, thou art the Buddha," and in his final words, to "work out your own salvation with diligence." Buddhism has one aim only: to abolish suffering. It proposes to do this one step at a time, by each person ridding him- or herself of the causes of suffering, which are desire, malice, and delusion.

Other aspects of the philosophy include the law of **karma,** whereby every action has effects and the energy of past action, good or evil, continues forever and is "reborn." Merit can be gained by entering the monkhood (and most males do so for a few days or months), helping in the construction of a monastery or a stupa, contributing to education, giving alms, or performing any act of kindness, no matter how small. When the monks go daily with their bowls from house to house, they are not begging, but are offering people an opportunity to make merit by supporting them; similarly, people at temples selling caged birds, which devotees purchase and set free, are allowing people to gain merit through this act.

Buddha himself was a great Indian sage, born **Siddhartha Gautama** in the sixth century B.C. A prince, he spent his boyhood carefully sheltered from the outside world, and when he finally left the palace walls he encountered an old man, a sick man, and a corpse. He concluded that all is suffering and, resolving to search for relief from that suffering, he went into the forest and lived there for many years as a solitary ascetic, ultimately achieving enlightenment and nirvana (escape from the cycle of reincarnation) while sitting under a sacred fig tree.

Upon his death, two schools arose. The oldest and probably closest to the original practice is **Theravada** (Doctrine of the Elders), sometimes referred to less correctly as **Hinayana** (the Small Vehicle), which prevails in Sri Lanka, Burma, Laos, Thailand, and Cambodia. The other school is **Mahayana** (the Large Vehicle), which is practiced in China, Korea, Vietnam, and Japan.

Buddha images are honored and revered in the Eastern tradition; they are not idols of worship but images that in their physical form radiate spirituality and convey the essence of Buddhist teachings—serenity, enlightenment, purity of mind, purity of tongue, and purity of action. Similar energy is believed to inhabit the miniature Buddha amulets that are worn as talismans to protect against evil spirits.

come from Vietnam, Laos, Myanmar, and Southern China, many as refugees. As you travel south toward the Malaysian border, you find Thai people who share cultural and religious affinity with their southern Malay neighbors. Also in the past 50 years, Thailand has seen a boom in Chinese immigrants. They're difficult to pinpoint because immigration laws have required they change their name to a Thai equivalent.

The Thais are a warm and peaceable people, with a culture that looks heavily to Indian and Sri Lankan influences. Early Thais adopted many Brahman practices that today are evident in royal ceremony and social hierarchy—Thailand is a very class-oriented culture. Even their cherished national story, the *Ramakien,* subject of almost all Thai classical dances and temple murals, finds its origin in the Indian Hindu epic, the *Ramayana.* Thai Buddhism follows the Theravada sect, imported from Sri Lanka, along with the classic bell-shaped stupa seen in many temple grounds.

Perhaps the two main influences in Thai life today are spirituality and the royal family. In every household throughout the country you'll find a spirit house to appease the property's former inhabitants, a portrait of the king in a prominent spot and perhaps pictures of a few previous kings, a dais for Buddha images and religious objects, and portraits of each son as he enters the monkhood (as almost all sons do). And in Thailand, unlike the Western world, even the younger generations are as spiritually active as their older kin.

VIETNAM, LAOS, CAMBODIA & BURMA

Together the countries of Vietnam, Cambodia, Laos, and Burma make up one of the most ethnically diverse regions of Southeast Asia. Outside of the cities, little English is spoken in any of these countries except by tour guides and others who have frequent contact with Western visitors. Much of the architecture and art in Cambodia, Laos, and Burma is influenced by Buddhism and includes some of the world's most renowned temples along with exquisitely sculpted Buddha images. The temple complexes of Angkor Wat in Cambodia and Bagan in Burma are among the architectural wonders of the ancient world, while the finest temples in Laos are found in the ancient capital of Luang Prabang.

One important point to note: the ethnic minorities, or hill tribes, of northern Vietnam, Laos, Thailand, and Myanmar (Burma) all share a common heritage with each other, originating either from Himalayan tribes or southern Chinese clans. You'll find startling similarities in the customs and languages of all these people.

VIETNAM   In Vietnam, the ethnic Vietnamese are a fusion of Viet, Tai (a southern Chinese group), Indonesian, and Chinese who first settled here between 200 B.C. and A.D. 200. While Vietnam has no official religion, several religions have significantly impacted Vietnamese culture, including **Buddhism, Confucianism, Taoism, and Animism.** Animism, which is the oldest religious practice in Vietnam and many other Southeast Asian countries, is centered around belief in a spirit world. Ancient cultural traditions lean toward borrowings from the mandarins of old Chinese dynasties that claimed sovereignty over Vietnam. In the 1900s, the French added a smattering of their own culture. Today, the modern culture can best be described as "capitalism." Be prepared—everybody here has something to sell you.

LAOS   In Laos, approximately half the population is ethnic Lao descended from centuries of migration, mostly from southern China. A landlocked country with little natural resources, Laos has had little luck entering the global trade scene and remains dependent on the international donor community. If you think the Thais are laidback, then you'll have to check the Laos for a pulse. In fact, their culture is most often compared with the Thais because quite a great deal of Thai culture finds its roots in Laos, although the Thais will never admit it, as they often look down upon their northern neighbors.

CAMBODIA   The population of Cambodia is made up primarily of ethnic Khmers who have lived here since around the second century A.D. and whose religion and culture have been influenced by interaction with Indians, Javanese, Thais, Vietnamese, and Chinese. It's been a long time since the achievements of the Khmer Empire, and it seems this country's only other claim to fame are its killing fields during the reign of terror under communist dictator Pol Pot that claimed millions of Khmer lives. These days there's still a whiff of danger in the air, thanks to heavy crime in the capital, landmines from decades of nonstop fighting, and gangster-style elements in the countryside. Realizing the value of tourist dollars to the ancient city of Angkor, the authorities have struggled to maintain order near the site.

MYANMAR (BURMA)   The majority of Myanmese people come from the Burmans. Today these are the people who hold positions of power in the government, occupying most of the territory of central and south Myanmar. A small group of Mons, descended from an ancient civilization that once ruled, still exists in the east and southeast of the country. The northern hills are occupied by scores of hill tribes, the most vocal of which is the **Shan.** While the international community is aware that many tribes are fighting for "independence," it is interesting to note that for many of these people, they already have their own state, but feel they are fighting Myanmese who are trying to occupy it.

SINGAPORE

Seventy-eight percent of Singaporeans trace their heritage to migrating waves from China's southern provinces, particularly from the Hokkien, Teowchew, Hakka, Cantonese, and Hainanese dialect groups. Back then the Chinese community was driven by rags to riches stories—the poor worker hawking vegetables who opened a grocery store, then started a chain of stores and now drives a Mercedes Benz. This story still motivates them today.

But it's not just Chinese who have dominated the scene. The island started off with a handful of Malay inhabitants, then came the British colonials with Indian administrators, followed by Muslim Indian moneylenders, Chinese merchants, Chinese coolie laborers, and Indian convict labor, plus European settlers and immigrants from all over Southeast Asia. Over 2 centuries of modern history, each group made its contribution to "Singaporean culture."

Today, as your average Singaporean struggles to balance traditional values with modern demands of globalization, his country is raked over the coals for being sterile and overly-Westernized. Older folks are becoming frustrated by younger generations who discard traditions in their pursuit of "The 5 Cs"—career, condo, car, credit card, and cash. Temples and ethnic neighborhoods are finding more revenue from tourists rather than the communities they once served. While many lament the loss of the good old days, most are willing to sacrifice a little tradition to be Southeast Asia's most stable and wealthy country.

MALAYSIA

Malaysia's population consists primarily of ethnic **Malays,** labeled **Bumiputeras,** a political classification that also encompasses tribal people who live in peninsular Malaysia and Borneo. Almost all Malays are Muslim, with corresponding conservative values running throughout the land. While the ruling government party supports an Islam that is open and tolerant to other cultures, a growing minority favors strict Islamic law and government, further marginalizing the country's large Chinese and Indian population. These foreign cultures migrated to Malaysia during the British colonial period as trading merchants, laborers, and administrators. Today, Malaysia recognizes ethnic **Chinese** and **Indian** citizens as equals under national law. However, government development and education policies always seem to favor Bumiputeras.

Among the favorite Malaysian recreational pastimes are **kite flying,** using ornately decorated paper kites, and top spinning. Some still practice **silat,** a Malaysian form of martial arts.

BALI

No country in Southeast Asia has a more ethnically diverse population than Indonesia, with more than 350 ethnic groups with their own languages and cultures scattered among the 6,000 inhabited islands of this vast archipelago of more than 14,000 islands.

Of all the islands, Bali stands out for its especially rich cultural life, which is inextricably linked with its Hindu beliefs. In Bali life doesn't imitate art, life is art, as virtually everyone is involved in some sort of daily artistic endeavor, whether it's painting, dancing, or playing a musical instrument. Flower offerings to the gods are a common sight and the Balinese are forever paying homage to Hindu deities at more than 20,000 temples and during the 60 annual festivals on the island.

The majority of the island's population is native Balinese; there are quite a few people from other parts of Indonesia, and they are there for work opportunities. English is widely spoken in the tourist parts of Bali, which means just about everywhere you go someone will speak enough English to help you out.

THE PHILIPPINES

The Philippines, where **English** is one of three official languages along with Spanish and the Filipino dialect Tagalog, stands out from the rest of Southeast Asia as the only predominantly Christian country in the region. Islam is also practiced, with the Muslim population concentrated on the Philippines' second largest island, Mindanao.

Filipinos are primarily of **Malay** ancestry, with mixtures of **Spanish, Chinese,** and other groups. Altogether, several hundred languages and dialects are spoken in the islands.

ETIQUETTE TIPS

"Different countries, different customs," as Sean Connery said to Michael Caine in *The Man Who Would Be King*. And while each country covered in this book will prove that rule by having their own twists on etiquette, some general pointers will allow you to go though your days of traveling without inadvertently offending your hosts. (For etiquette tips on individual countries, see the country chapters.)

GREETINGS, GESTURES & SOCIAL INTERACTION

In these modern times, the **common Western handshake** has become extremely prevalent throughout Southeast Asia, but it is by no means universal. There are a plethora of traditional greetings, so when greeting someone—especially an older man and even more especially a woman, of any age—it's safest to wait for a gesture, or observe those around you, then follow suit. In Muslim culture, for instance, it is not acceptable for men and women not related by blood or marriage to touch.

In interpersonal relations in strongly Buddhist areas (Laos, Vietnam, and Thailand) it helps to **take a gentle approach to human relationships.** A person showing anger or ill temper would be regarded with surprise and disapproval. A gentle approach will take you farther.

A delicate matter that's best to get out of the way immediately: In countries with significant Muslim and Hindu cultures (Malaysia, Singapore, Indonesia, Bali) **only use your right hand in social interaction.** Traditionally, the left hand is used only for personal hygiene. Not only should you eat with your right hand and give and receive all gifts with your right hand, but you should make sure all gestures, especially **pointing** (and even more especially, pointing in temples and mosques), are made with your right hand. In all the countries discussed in this book, it's also considered more polite to point with your knuckle (with your hand facing palm down) than with your finger.

In all the countries covered in this guide, ladies seated on the floor should never sit with their legs crossed in front of them—instead, always tuck your legs to the side. Men may sit with legs crossed. Both men and women should also be careful **not to show the bottoms of their feet,** which are considered the lowliest, most unclean part of the body. If you cross your legs while on the floor or in a chair, don't point your soles toward other people. Also be careful not to use your foot to point or gesture. **Shoes should be removed** when entering a temple or private home. And don't ever step over someone's body or legs.

On a similar note, in Buddhist and Hindu cultures the head is considered the most sacred part of the body; therefore, **do not casually touch another person's head**— and this includes patting children on the head.

DRESSING FOR CULTURAL SUCCESS

The basic rule is **dress modestly.** Except perhaps on the grounds of resorts and in heavily tourist areas such as Bali's Kuta and Thailand's beaches, foreigners displaying navels, chests, or shoulders or wearing short shorts or short skirts will attract stares. While shorts and bathing suits are accepted on the beach, you should avoid parading around in them elsewhere, no matter how hot it is.

Understanding Feng Shui

Have you ever noticed how some homes seem to give off terrific vibes the moment you enter the front door while others leave you feeling disturbed and wanting to get out fast? The Chinese believe feng shui (pronounced fung shway and meaning "wind and water") has a lot to do with these positive and negative feelings.

The earliest known record of feng shui dates from the Han dynasty (202 B.C.–A.D. 220) and the practice is still widely and highly regarded in Asia today. In essence, the idea of feng shui revolves around the way physical surroundings relate to the invisible flow of chi (natural energy), which must move smoothly throughout the home or business in order for life to play itself out beneficially. Walls, doors, windows, or furnishings can throw off this flow through their color, balance, placement, or proportion—even by their points on the compass. Your bed, for example, placed on the wrong wall or facing the wrong way, could encourage chi to rush into a room and out again, taking wealth and health with it. If your bed is situated directly under an exposed beam, you might as well make a standing appointment with the chiropractor, 'cause that's some baaad feng shui.

In Singapore and Hong Kong, particularly (as both have large Chinese populations), company presidents regularly call upon feng shui masters to rearrange their office furniture, and the master is usually the first person called in on new construction jobs to assess the building plans for their adherence to good feng shui practices. It's not uncommon to hear stories about buildings being partially torn down late in the construction process, simply because a master hadn't examined the plans earlier and, when finally consulted, had deemed that the structure did not promote good feng shui. The extra cost is considered a valid investment— after all, what's a few dollars saved now if bad feng shui will later cause the business to fail? For the average homeowner who doesn't want to consult a feng shui master (or can't afford to), a plethora of books is available to advise on creating successful living spaces.

For every life situation there's a feng shui solution. And don't worry what people will think when they see those four purple candles in the corner of your living room or the pair of wooden flutes dangling from an exposed beam. Let 'em laugh—you'll be grinning all the way to the bank.

Getting in Touch with Your Inner Haggler

In the smaller shops and at street vendors throughout Southeast Asia, you'll find that prices are never marked, and it will be expected that you bargain. The most important thing to remember when bargaining is to keep a friendly, good-natured banter between you and the seller. It's all in a day's work for him. Before you start out, it's always good to have at least some idea how much your purchase is worth, to give you a base point for negotiation. Shop around, ask questions. A simple "How much?" is the place to start, to which they'll reply with their top price. Never accept the first price! Try a smile and ask, "Is that your best price?" Sometimes they'll ask what your paying price is. Knock the price down about 50%—they'll look shocked, but it's a starting point for bidding. Just remember to smile and be friendly, and you should be able to negotiate something you both can agree on. Caveat: If it's a larger, more expensive item, don't get into major bargaining unless you're serious about buying. If the shopkeeper agrees on what you say you're willing to pay, it's generally considered rude to not make the purchase. If no agreement is made, however, you can always say thank you and walk away. See individual country chapters for more on shopping.

TEMPLE & MOSQUE ETIQUETTE

Many of Southeast Asia's greatest and most remarkable sights are its places of worship, usually Buddhist wats, Hindu temples, and Islamic mosques (masjids). When visiting these places, more so than at any other time, it's important to observe certain rules of decorum.

When visiting the **mosques,** be sure to dress appropriately. Neither men nor women will be admitted wearing shorts. For the ladies, please do not wear short skirts or sleeveless, backless, or low-cut tops. Both men and women are required to leave their shoes outside. Also remember: Never enter the mosque's main prayer hall. This area is reserved for Muslims only. No cameras or video cameras are allowed, and remember to turn off cellular phones and pagers. Friday is the Sabbath day, and you should not plan on going to the mosques between 11am and 2pm on this day.

Visitors are welcome to walk around and explore most **temples** and **wats.** As in the mosques, remember to dress appropriately—some temples may refuse to admit you if you're showing too much skin—and to leave your shoes outside. Photography is permitted in most temples, though some, such as Wat Phra Kaeo in Thailand, prohibit it. Never climb on a Buddha image, and if you sit down, never point your feet in the direction of the Buddha. Do not cross in front of a person who is in prayer. Also, women should never touch a monk, try to shake his hand, or even give something to one directly (the monk will provide a cloth for you to lay the item upon, and he will collect it). Monks are not permitted to touch women, or even to speak directly to them anywhere but inside a temple or wat.

3

Planning a Trip to Southeast Asia

by Jennifer Eveland

The country chapters in this guide provide specific information on traveling to and getting around in all of Southeast Asia's individual countries, but in this chapter, we'll give you some region-wide tips and info that will help you plan your trip.

1 Passport & Visa Requirements at a Glance

Most countries covered in this guide require that citizens of the U.S., U.K., Canada, Australia, and New Zealand have only a **passport** for entry; Vietnam, Laos, Cambodia, and Myanmar (Burma) require citizens of these countries to have **visas.** Most countries expect travelers to enter via international airports. If you plan to enter Vietnam, Laos, Cambodia, and Myanmar either overland or by boat, you'll have to obtain **special permission** from the consulate when you obtain your visa. See individual country chapters for more specific information.

BALI   Visitors from the U.S., Australia, most of Europe, New Zealand, and Canada do not need visas. They will be given a stamp that allows them to stay for 60 days, provided they are entering the country through an officially designated gateway: Ngurah Rai Airport or the seaports of Padang Bai and Benoa. If you want to stay longer than 60 days, you must get a tourist or business visa before coming to Indonesia. Tourist visas are valid only for 4 weeks and can not be extended, while business visas can be extended for 6 months at Indonesian immigration offices.

MYANMAR (BURMA)   Myanmar consulates issue visas for tourist visits of up to 4 weeks. Be warned: They may refuse your application if they suspect you represent a media firm or a pro-democracy or human rights organization. Look like a tourist.

CAMBODIA   All visitors are required to carry a passport and visa. A 1-month visa can be obtained upon entry at the Phnom Penh or Siem Reap international airports for US$20. Bring two passport photos for your application.

HONG KONG   A valid passport is the only document most tourists, including Americans, need to enter Hong Kong. Americans can stay up to 1 month without a visa. Australians, New Zealanders, Canadians, and other British Commonwealth citizens can stay

3 months without a visa, while citizens of the United Kingdom can stay for 6 months without a visa.

LAOS   Residents of every Western country need a passport and visa to visit Laos. Although the official time limit is 15 days, most people get 30 days for just asking. If you haven't organized your visa in your home country, travel agents in Thailand and Vietnam can arrange them for you with little hassle. Contrary to rumor, you do not need to book an organized tour to obtain a visa, so don't believe any travel agents who tell you so. Further, some provinces require you check in with local police as you travel through.

MALAYSIA   To enter Malaysia you must have a valid passport. Citizens of the United States do not need visas for tourism and business visits. Citizens of Canada, Australia, New Zealand, and the U.K. do not require a visa for tourism or business visits not exceeding 1 month.

THE PHILIPPINES   For stays of up to 21 days, only a passport and a return or continuing ticket are required. If you wish to stay longer than 21 days, you can obtain a 59-day visa from a Philippine embassy or consulate in your country.

SINGAPORE   To enter Singapore you'll need a valid passport. Visas are not necessary for citizens of the United States, Canada, the United Kingdom, Australia, and New Zealand. Upon entry, visitors from these countries will be issued a 30-day pass for a social visit only, except for Americans, who'll get a 90-day pass.

THAILAND   All visitors to Thailand must carry a valid passport with proof of onward passage (either a return or through ticket). Visas are not required for stays of up to 30 days for citizens of the U.S., Australia, Canada, Ireland, New Zealand, or the U.K.

VIETNAM   Residents of the U.S., Canada, Australia, New Zealand, and the United Kingdom need both a passport and a valid visa to enter Vietnam. A tourist visa usually lasts for 30 days and costs US$50, although some people are inexplicably able to get longer visas upon request. Multiple-entry business visas are available that are valid for up to 3 months, but you must have a sponsoring agency in Vietnam and it can take much longer to process. For short business trips, it's less complicated simply to enter as a tourist.

PASSPORT INFORMATION FOR FIRST-TIMERS & RENEWERS

Important tip: prior to your departure make two photocopies of your passport and all relevant visa stamps inside. Leave set one with family back home and bring the other with you. This way you can lock up your (priceless) document in the hotel safe, but still carry a copy with you for identification. Also, you'll be glad to have copies if your passport is lost or stolen. They certainly simplify matters for the authorities. If you've never had a passport before, see the information below for application procedures. You can download passport applications from the Internet sites listed below.

UNITED STATES   If you're applying for a first-time passport, you need to do it in person at one of 13 passport offices throughout the U.S.; a federal, state, or probate court; or a major post office (though not all post offices accept applications; call the number below to find the ones that do). You need to present a certified birth certificate as proof of citizenship, and it's wise to bring along your driver's license, state or military ID, and social security card as well. You also need two identical passport-sized photos (2 in. by 2 in.), taken at any corner photo shop (not one of the strip photos, however, from a photo-vending machine).

For people over 16, a passport is valid for 10 years and costs US$60 (US$45 plus a US$15 handling fee); for those under 16, it's valid for 5 years and costs US$40. If you're over 16 and have a valid passport that was issued within the past 12 years, you can renew it by mail and bypass the US$15 handling fee. Allow plenty of time before your trip to apply; processing normally takes 3 weeks but can take longer during busy periods (especially spring). To find your regional passport office, call the **National Passport Information Center** (☎ 900/225-5674 [this is not a toll-free call]; http://travel.state.gov/passport_services.html).

CANADA   You can pick up a passport application at one of 31 regional passport offices or most travel agencies. The passport is valid for 5 years and costs US$60. Children under 16 may be included on a parent's passport but need their own to travel unaccompanied by the parent. Applications, which must be accompanied by two identical passport-sized photographs and proof of Canadian citizenship, are available at travel agencies throughout Canada or from the central **Passport Office, Department of Foreign Affairs and International Trade,** Ottawa, Ont. K1A 0G3 (☎ 800/567-6868; www.dfait-maeci.gc.ca/passport). Processing takes 5 to 10 days if you apply in person, or about 3 weeks by mail.

THE UNITED KINGDOM   To pick up an application for a standard 10-year passport, visit your nearest passport office, major post office, or travel agency. You can also contact the **London Passport Office** at ☎ 020/7271-3000 (www.open.gov.uk/ukpass.ukpass.htm). Passports are £28 for adults and £14.80 for children under 16.

IRELAND   You can apply for a 10-year passport, costing IR£45, at the **Passport Offices** at Setanta Centre, Molesworth Street, Dublin 2 (☎ 01/671-1633; www.irlgov.ie/iveagh). Those under age 18 and over 65 must apply for a IR£10 3-year passport. You can also apply at 1A South Mall, Cork (☎ 021/272-525) or over the counter at most main post offices.

AUSTRALIA   Apply at your local post office or passport office or search the government Web site at **www.dfat.gov.au/passports/.** Passports for adults are A$126 and for those under 18 A$63.

NEW ZEALAND   You can pick up a passport application at any travel agency or Link Centre. For more info, contact the **Passport Office,** P.O. Box 805, Wellington (☎ 0800/225-050). Passports for adults are NZ$80 and for those under 16 NZ$40.

2 Money

At the risk of making light of international economic turmoil, there's one fact that's hard to ignore: The East Asian financial crisis created some good travel bargains in these parts. Now that a few years have passed many countries are on the road to recovery. Prices are no longer rock bottom; however, travel savings are still to be had, especially after you consider that foreign exchange values are in your favor. A few exceptions should be noted. Singapore and Hong Kong's travel industries remain strong, catering heavily to the business travel market, so you'll find it tougher to negotiate sweet deals. Also, the luxury resorts on Phuket and Bali are still going strong—Bali, unlike many other parts of Indonesia, has experienced very little of the social turmoil plaguing the rest of the country. Alternately, moneywise now is a great time to plan vacations in Malaysia, Vietnam, and the Philippines.

In this section we'll introduce you to the region's post-crisis economic outlook and its currencies, and discuss taxes and exchange.

IN THE WAKE OF THE SOUTHEAST ASIAN FINANCIAL CRISIS

After 3 decades of stellar economic growth, the East Asian Economic Miracle took a nose dive in mid-1997. On July 2 of that year, Thailand became the first to raise the alarm when it floated its currency, a move that caused the baht to devalue 20% in the week to follow. On its tail, the Malaysian ringgit, Indonesian rupiah, and Philippine peso suffered similar fates.

The world watched as the economic scene unfolded, revealing a Southeast Asian legacy of suspicious government ties to industry, massive overseas borrowing, overbuilt property markets, and lax bank lending practices. The booming economies had been susceptible to the seduction of cheap and plentiful foreign money and the whim of currency speculation. Borrowers that once carried too much debt became hopeless in the face of plummeting local currency values. Loans defaulted, businesses closed, unemployment rose. Nations that once took pride in over 8% annual GDP growth rates stared down the barrel of growth rates below 1%. While leaders paddled to stay afloat, economists had a field day.

Now, a few years after the turmoil, it's evident which countries fared better than others. **Indonesia** was the hardest hit by the crisis and still continues to suffer despite a change in political leadership and truckloads of IMF money and advice. Its currency, the rupiah, experiences tremendous fluctuations to this day. Even more unfortunate, many parts of the country have fallen into states of social unrest and violence. Bali seems to be the only area unaffected.

Malaysia turned down IMF advice and proceeded with its own reforms. The value of the Malaysian ringgit has been pegged at 3.80 to the dollar, and so far the country appears to be managing through the storm, with much debate, however. In early 2001, **Thailand** voted in a new prime minister to try, once again, to combat its financial troubles. So far it is too soon to tell how successful any new measures will be.

Many foreign investors have pulled out of **Vietnam,** putting a damper on the country's big plans to shift to a free-market economy. The opening of the Vietnamese market was met with much excitement and international buzz, and now the country scrambles to keep business hotels filled.

On the other hand, consider **Laos,** which was dependent on foreign aid to hold its economy together even before the crisis. Crisis, what crisis?

EFFECTS OF THE CRISIS ON TOURISM

A couple of years ago we reported on great bargains to be had in Southeast Asia. Now many hotels, airlines, and travel organizers have returned to pre-crisis rates, and have curbed special packages and promotions. Still, if you consider exchange rates, you're still getting a good deal. The pre-crisis Thai baht, for example, was worth 25B to the U.S. dollar. The best rate to be had was in January 1998, when the baht dropped in value to 55B to the dollar. Today it fluctuates between about 40B to 43B to a dollar. And you'll find similar stories with other countries here.

You will find the least savings if you book a tour through an agent in your home country. They'll realize the benefit of being paid in a strong currency. You'll get much better prices booking through agents in-country.

International luxury hotels have adopted several strategies for weathering the crisis—among them quoting rates in U.S. dollars as opposed to local currency, a policy that prevents them from losing their shirts amid unpredictable currency values. In some instances, however, room rates are still lowered. Four-star and three-star hotels, as well as guesthouses, have discounted standard room rates. A word of advice: Never accept the first offer. Competition is fierce, so always ask for a discount rate, package deal, long-term stay rate, off-peak rate—anything you can think of. Then ask them to throw in free breakfast.

Retail sales have become a big problem for Southeast Asian economies. The locals have really tightened their belts, causing shop owners to panic. Singapore, that infamous shop-a-holic fantasy, has seen many businesses close from the strain. As a result, you'll see all kinds of sales, enticing offers, and great deals. People want to make a sale. The downside of this is that many shops have closed. For that matter, so have many restaurants and nightspots.

The bottom line is travel bargains to Southeast Asia are not the same as they once were, but while nations still struggle to put themselves back together you'll be able to save money while currencies are in your favor.

CARRYING MONEY & GETTING THE BEST EXCHANGE RATES

There was a time when travelers depended heavily on traveler's checks when making a trip, but that was before the days of credit cards and easy cash access through ATMs. We learned a couple years ago that an ATM had been installed in Antarctica, and if that doesn't say something about how easy it is to get access to your money in the world today, I don't know what does.

That said, Southeast Asia still has many areas where you will not find ATMs and where, except in large hotels, you'll even have a hard time using credit cards. For this reason, I recommend using a combination of traveler's checks, credit cards, and cash when traveling to this part of the world.

TRAVELER'S CHECKS   Traveler's checks have long been the most popular way to carry money since they are replaceable if lost or stolen and are also widely accepted at exchange bureaus in major airports as well as at most banks and hotels (unlike other parts of the world, Southeast Asia has almost no restaurants or shopping establishments that accept these notes as payment). I recommend exchanging them at banks and currency exchange booths controlled by banks rather than at hotels, which typically charge the highest commissions.

While a number of companies offer traveler's checks, the most widely recognized are **American Express** traveler's checks. They come in denominations of US$20, US$50, US$100, US$500, and US$1,000. You'll pay a service charge ranging from 1 to 4%. Card members can also get American Express traveler's checks over the phone by calling ☎ **800/721-9768,** or online at www.americanexpress.com. AAA members can obtain checks without a fee at most AAA offices.

Second to AmEx, **Thomas Cook** (☎ **800/223-7373** in the U.S. and Canada; www.thomascook.com) also offer traveler's checks. Call for a location near you.

If you opt to carry traveler's checks, be sure to keep a record of their serial numbers, separately from the checks of course, so you're ensured a refund in an emergency.

AUTOMATED TELLER MACHINES (ATMs)   ATMs, which are commonplace in Hong Kong, Singapore, Malaysia, Philippines, and Thailand, are another means of obtaining local currency. Be sure to check that your card uses either the widely accepted MasterCard/Cirrus or Visa/PLUS networks. Use of an ATM gives you the best bank rate of the day and exceeds the rates offered by change bureaus and hotels. You'll be surprised how every provincial capital seems to have at least one ATM machine. However, if your itinerary includes Vietnam (where ATM access is limited to the two major cities), or Laos, Cambodia, or Myanmar, do not rely on this method to fund your trip. Carry traveler's checks. See individual country chapters for more information on ATM availability.

CREDIT CARDS   Credit cards are invaluable when traveling. They are a safe way to carry money and provide a convenient record of all your expenses. Major credit cards, including American Express, Visa, and MasterCard, are widely accepted in Southeast Asia's larger hotels, some restaurants, and some shops. Some banks may also be willing to give you a cash advance against your card, but prepare for hefty interest rates.

Bear in mind that a lot of businesses will try to weasel some sort of "credit card processing surcharge" out of you, perhaps up to 4%. Your credit card company will tell you that the practice is not acceptable and should be reported to the issuing bank immediately. But let's be honest here—no self-respecting souvenir vendor in Phuket's going to give two shakes about that threat! But I have had some vendors back down if I insist I won't pay the fee. Usually I try not to shop with my credit cards anyway—cash will always demand a better price.

You'll also want to keep them close. Thailand is one of the world's hot spots for credit card fraud. When handing your card over, watch them run one copy of the receipt only. Keep all charge slips and when you get back home, check them against your billing statement. I once found a mysterious charge for US$400 worth of gems from a Bangkok shop. Yikes!

Every credit card company has an emergency assistance number that you can call to report lost or stolen cards. They may be able to wire you a cash advance off your credit card immediately, and in many places, they can deliver an emergency credit card in a day or two. For each country, we've listed emergency numbers to call if your card is lost or stolen.

EXCHANGING CURRENCY   When arriving at an airport, it's a good idea to change only a small amount into local currency (enough to get from the airport to the hotel) since you will get a better exchange rate at a money changer or ATM. If you're carrying most of your money as traveler's checks, change only as many checks into the local currency as you will need so that you don't end up with an excessive amount when departing the country.

The **best exchange rates** often are available through local money changers that, depending on the country, may or may not have government approval. For example, in Singapore and Malaysia money changers operating out of booths in shopping centers and small shops offer the best rates.

THE PREVALENCE OF THE U.S. DOLLAR

Because of the devaluation of many of Southeast Asia's currencies during the financial crisis, we're faced with a situation where many businesses—particularly hotels—prefer doing business in U.S. dollars to dealing in local currency, a practice that helps them stay afloat amid fluctuating currency values. In places like Vietnam and Laos, everybody down to the smallest shop vendor quotes prices in U.S. dollars. Consider Laos, where the *largest* paper note available does not equal one U.S. dollar—the Lao government simply does not have the resources to print larger bills. It's just easier to settle big ticket items with a few U.S. notes than with stacks of local money.

While dealing in U.S. dollars can make things less complicated, always keep in mind local currency values so you know if you're being charged the correct amount. I usually carry local currency in an envelope—outside I convert dollars to local money to make a "cheat sheet" so I don't have to fuss with divisions in my head, which can get confusing if you're going to two or three countries one after the other.

In this book, we've listed **hotel, restaurant, and attraction rates** in whatever form the establishments quoted them—in U.S. dollars (designated as US$) where those were quoted, and in local currencies (with U.S. dollar equivalents) where those were used.

Note that with the exception of the Singapore dollar, Malaysian ringgit, and Hong Kong dollar (which have remained stable), all other Southeast Asian national currencies are still in a state of flux, so before you budget your trip based on rates we give in this book, be sure to check the currency's current status. CNN's Web site has a convenient **currency converter** at **http://cnnfn.cnn.com/markets/currencies/**.

WORKING WITH THE LOCAL CURRENCY

You will have to rely primarily on local currency when traveling in the countryside and/or visiting towns and villages situated off the main tourist routes where neither traveler's checks or credit cards are accepted. No matter where you travel, its always a good idea to have some U.S. dollars handy, preferably in small bills, which may help ease you through any unforeseen emergencies. The U.S. dollar has long been the most readily accepted foreign currency throughout Southeast Asia.

Below we've listed the currencies of all countries in this guide, with their denominations.

MYANMAR (BURMA)   The main unit of currency is the kyat (pronounced chat) which is made up of 100 pyas. Kyats come in notes with denominations of 1, 5, and 10. There are also 1 kyat coins and coins of 1, 5, 10, 25, and 50 pyas. The exchange rate is stable at approximately **6.50 kyat to US$1.** It is illegal to carry Myanmese currency out of the country, so be sure to exchange whatever you have remaining when you leave the country.

CAMBODIA   The monetary unit is the riel, which is available in 50, 100, 200, 500, 1,000, 5,000, 10,000, 20,000, and 50,000 riel notes. Cambodia's volatile exchange rate typically fluctuates from **2,500 to 3,750 riels to US$1.** It's a good idea to bring a supply of U.S. dollars since the dollar is considered Cambodia's second currency and is accepted by many hotels, guesthouses, and restaurants (in fact, some establishments prefer dollars to local currency—see discussion above).

HONG KONG   The basic unit of currency is the **Hong Kong dollar,** which is divided into 100 **cents.** Three banks, the Hongkong and Shanghai Banking Corporation, the Bank of China, and, to a lesser degree, the Standard Chartered Bank, all issue their own colorful notes, in denominations of HK$10 (which is being phased out), HK$20, HK$50, HK$100, HK$500, and HK$1,000. Coins are minted in bronze for 10¢, 20¢, and 50¢ pieces, in silver for HK$1, HK$2, and HK$5, and in nickel and bronze for HK$10. The exchange rate is **HK$7.80 to US$1.**

Throughout Hong Kong you'll see the dollar sign ("$"), which of course refers to Hong Kong dollars, not U.S. dollars. To avoid confusion, this guide identifies Hong Kong dollars with the symbol "HK$" (followed in parentheses by the U.S. dollar conversion).

INDONESIA (BALI)   The rupiah (Rp) is the main currency, with bills of Rp100, 500, 1,000, 5,000, 10,000, 20,000, and 50,000, and coins in denominations of 25, 50, 100, and 500. Indonesia's currency was hit hard in 1998 and 1999, leading to exchange rates that fluctuated wildly—from a pre-crisis rate of approximately Rp2,300 to US$1, the rupiah plunged to Rp14,700 to US$1 in July 1998 and at press time was hovering around **Rp9,000 to US$1.**

It is hard to say at press time precisely what things should cost—even the prices listed could be entirely different by the time you arrive.

LAOS   The primary unit of currency is the kip (pronounced "keep"), which comes in denominations of 5,000, 2,000, 1,000, 500, 100, 50, 20, 10, and 5. The exchange rate is approximately **7,600 kip to US$1.** As in Cambodia, many tourist establishments prefer payment in U.S. dollars. In many areas of Laos, both U.S. dollars and Thai baht are preferred over the local currency

MALAYSIA   The ringgit, which is also referred to as the Malaysian dollar, is the unit of currency and prices are marked RM. One ringgit equals 100 sen, and notes come in RM1, RM2, RM5, RM10, RM20, RM50, RM100, RM500 and RM1,000. Coins come in denominations of 1, 2, 5, 10, and 50 sen, and one ringgit coins. Since the economic crisis, the value of the ringgit has been set at **RM3.80 to US$1.**

PHILIPPINES   The Philippines peso, which is divided into 100 centavos, is available in 2, 5, 10, 20, 50, and 100 peso bills, as well as 1, 5, 10, 25 and 50 centavo and 1 and 5 peso coins. The exchange rate is approximately **50 pesos to US$1.**

SINGAPORE   The Singapore dollar (commonly referred to as the "Sing" dollar) is the unit of currency, with notes issued in denominations of S$2, S$5, S$10, S$20, S$50, S$100, S$500, and S$1,000; coins come in denominations of 1, 5, 10, 20 and 50 cents and the gold-colored S$1. The exchange rate is approximately **S$1.67 to US$1.**

THAILAND   The Thai baht, (noted as "B") which is made up of 100 satang, comes in colored notes of 10 baht (brown), 20 baht (green), 100 baht (red), and 500 baht (purple). Coins come in denominations of 1 baht, 5 baht, and 10 baht; also 25 and 50 satang. The exchange rate is approximately **41B to US$1.**

VIETNAM   The main unit of Vietnamese currency is the dong, which comes in denominations of 200, 500, 1,000, 2,000, 5,000, 10,000, 20,000, and 50,000 notes. There are no coins. While it is officially against the law to accept U.S. currency, many tourism facilities in the cities take dollars. However, in the countryside and well away from major cities only dong are accepted. The exchange rate is approximately **14,500 VND to US$1.**

TIPPING & TAXES

While tipping is always a matter of individual discretion, it is not expected by most hotels and restaurants throughout Southeast Asia, which add a 10 to 15% service charge to the bill. The only places where tipping is expected are major upscale hotels, restaurants, and bars that cater to Western tourists. You should also tip personal guides a small amount of currency.

Airport departure taxes, which vary in amounts from country to country (see the individual country chapters for rates), are commonplace and must be paid in local currency (though some countries accept U.S. dollars) prior to leaving on an international flight.

3 When to Go

With a few exceptions, whenever and wherever you travel in Southeast Asia, you are likely to encounter hot and humid weather. All of Southeast Asia lies within the tropics, and the countries closest to the equator—Singapore, Malaysia, Indonesia, the Philippines, and southern Thailand—have the hottest annual temperatures. Vietnam, Laos, Cambodia, Burma, and the rest of Thailand located 10 to 20 degrees above the equator also have high humidity but slightly "cooler" temperatures. The mountainous northern regions of Myanmar, Thailand, Laos, and Vietnam get pretty chilly during the winter months between November and March, so bring a pullover.

Monsoon winds make weather patterns confusing to keep track of. The basic rule of thumb is this: Between the months of October through February, winds from the northeast create heavy rainfall and rough seas along the eastern coasts of Vietnam, Cambodia, Thailand (including Ko Samui), Malaysia, and Singapore; however, western coasts along Thailand (including Phuket) and Malaysia are peaceful and calm. In May the winds shift, bringing rains and swelling seas from the northwest down upon the western coasts of Myanmar, Thailand, and Malaysia until October. Most everyplace feels a dry and hot spell in March and April—Bangkok swelters! The cooler months of October through March are also the most pleasant times to visit Hong Kong, while the most rain usually falls between July and September, during typhoon season.

Singapore, Malaysia, and the Philippines are hot and humid year-round, with annual average maximum and minimum daily temperatures of 90° and 72° and year-round humidity above 90%. Most major cities are located at or near sea level, where average daytime temperatures are in the 80° to 90° range year-round. The best way to escape the heat and humidity is to head for the hills and mountains in the higher altitude regions of Thailand, Malaysia, Vietnam, Burma, Laos, and the Philippines.

HOLIDAYS, CELEBRATIONS & FESTIVALS

Some of the holidays celebrated in Southeast Asia may affect your vacation plans, either positively (because you'll get to see the destination at its most festive, as for instance during Chinese New Year) or adversely (because some businesses and attractions may be closed on national holidays). See the individual country chapters for listings of the major holidays celebrated in each country.

PACKING TIPS

Depending on where you travel in Southeast Asia, you'll experience a range of temperatures, though mostly what you'll feel is year-round tropical heat. Some northern hill areas of Laos, Thailand, and Vietnam can dip into the 40s (°F) during the cool season (November through February), though even during this period temperatures in the southern parts of the countries will remain in the 70s and 80s.

Lightweight clothing in natural fibers (or breathable travel gear) is essential in the tropical heat, as are a hat and a pair of sunglasses. For sightseeing, the most practical clothing will be lightweight cotton long pants or a long skirt (below the knee) and a cotton T-shirt. Especially if your sightseeing takes you to royal palaces or religious buildings where local customs favor conservative attire—no shorts or miniskirts, and please cover your shoulders (no tank tops). In Malaysia, when visiting mosques, women will need a scarf to cover the head, and a long blouse and long skirt to cover the body.

For everyday wear, except at resorts and the beach, **avoid wearing shorts in Vietnam, Laos, and more conservative areas of Malaysia.** I highly recommend a light sweater for airports, bus trips, or theaters where air-conditioning always seems to be set at deep-freeze.

A pair of rugged open **sport sandals** is also a must, and a pair of **rubber flip-flops** come in handy in hotel rooms with tile or wood floors, and for use in public showers. If you're going in and out of temples (as is always the case for sightseeing) you'll be happy to have shoes that slip off and on easily. Also, bring shoes that fit loosely. If you come from colder climates, your feet will swell from the heat, as well as from being on them all day while you're taking in the sights. Don't even trust your favorite pair: If they're a snug fit, they'll turn into your worst enemies before long. Pack **wool socks** if you plan to hike. They're breathable, repel moisture, and are better at preventing blisters than cotton socks.

Film is easy to get in all of these countries, and is usually much cheaper than in the West (the exceptions being Singapore and Hong Kong, where it costs about the same). If you're thinking of **renting a bike** along the way, bringing your own helmet isn't a bad idea. Most toiletries, even Western brands, are easily available at pharmacies and stories in the big cities. A pair of **your own plastic chopsticks or a small cutlery set** may also come in handy.

Here's a checklist of items you don't want to be without:

- Antacid tablets
- Anti-diarrhea medicine
- Anti-bacterial cream

- Anti-itch cream
- Bandages
- Acetaminophen, aspirin or ibuprofen for fever or pain
- Batteries (it's also a good idea to bring an extra camera battery)
- Bug repellent
- Contact lenses
- Cotton swabs
- Dramamine
- Film
- Hydration powder packets
- Mild laxative tablets
- Moist towelette packets
- Full supply of any medications you need to take
- Nylon or fast-drying shorts
- Padlock and wire cable (comes in handy to lock your bag up and attach it to anything)
- Plastic bags for everything and anything (wet clothes, shells, sand, etc.)
- Rain poncho/small umbrella
- Sunscreen
- Tampons (Note that maxi pads are available everywhere.)
- Tissues (lots of them; in some countries you'll rarely find a square of toilet paper around)
- Trash bags (to line your luggage or for protection on ferry crossings)
- Water purifying tablets
- Waterproof sandals

4 Getting There

If you're flying to Southeast Asia, you will more than likely arrive via one of the region's three main hubs: Hong Kong, Bangkok, or Singapore, from where you can pick up flights to any other destination in Southeast Asia. Your home country's national carriers will almost certainly connect with all three of these airports. Check also with Southeast Asian-based airlines for fare deals: Cathay Pacific, Thai Airways International, Malaysian Airlines, Philippine Airlines, and Singapore Airlines. Finally, many times booking agents can dig up some unconventional flights for better savings. For example, the cheapest flights between Bangkok and Singapore are via Royal Nepal Airlines or Biman Bangladesh Airlines (with considerable savings). Travel agents in Vietnam recommend, from North America, either Cathay Pacific via Hong Kong, or Eva Air via Taipei (Taiwan) for the best rates and routes. The point being, unless you are taking advantage of a frequent flyer scheme, be creative when selecting your routes. See the appendix for airline phone and Web site information, and see the individual country chapters for more specific and detailed travel information.

If you have to overnight in Hong Kong, Bangkok, or Singapore, hotel accommodations are available plus dining options and some shopping without your having to clear immigration, but you may want to consider overnighting in town for a better meal and maybe a nightlife option or two. If you're stopping over in Singapore for only a few hours you can swim at the airport pool (no kidding), have a massage, or take a special coach tour of the city for free. All three airports have duty free shops (Singapore's is cheapest) and some business center have facilities such as Internet access and overseas calling and faxing.

TO HONG KONG

The following carriers fly to Hong Kong's Chek Lap Kok Airport.

FROM THE UNITED STATES   United Airlines, Northwest Airlines, Cathay Pacific Airways, China Airlines, Singapore Airlines, Thai Airways International, and Hong Kong's Dragonair.

FROM CANADA   Cathay Pacific Airways, Canadian Airlines International, Air Canada, Singapore Airlines, and China Airlines.

FROM THE UNITED KINGDOM   Cathay Pacific Airways, British Airways, Virgin Atlantic Airways, Singapore Airlines, China Airlines, and Dragonair.

FROM AUSTRALIA   Cathay Pacific Airways, Qantas Airways, Ansett Australian Airlines, Singapore Airlines, and Dragonair.

FROM NEW ZEALAND   Air New Zealand and Cathay Pacific Airways.

TO SINGAPORE

The following carriers fly to Singapore's Changi Airport.

FROM THE UNITED STATES   Singapore Airlines has the most weekly flights from the U.S. to Changi International Airport. United Airlines and Northwest Airlines are the only U.S. airlines offering flights to Singapore.

FROM CANADA   Singapore Airlines provides service from Canada, along with Canadian Airlines International.

FROM THE UNITED KINGDOM   You can fly to Singapore via Singapore Airlines, British Airways, and Qantas Airways.

FROM AUSTRALIA   Singapore Airlines, Qantas Airways, Ansett Australian Airlines, British Airways, and KLM Royal Dutch Airlines all provide service to Singapore.

FROM NEW ZEALAND   Singapore Airlines and Air New Zealand offer New Zealand-Singapore flights.

TO BANGKOK

The following international airlines provide service to Bangkok's Don Muang International Airport.

FROM THE UNITED STATES   Service is provided by the national carrier, Thai Airways International, as well as United Airlines, Northwest Airlines, Cathay Pacific Airways, All Nippon Airways, Asiana Airlines, Japan Air Lines, China Airlines, Eva Airways, Korean Air, Malaysia Airlines, and Singapore Airlines.

FROM THE UNITED KINGDOM   Airlines with flights from the U.K. to Bangkok include Thai Airways International, British Airways, and Singapore Airlines.

FROM CANADA   Canadian Airlines International flies to Bangkok from Vancouver via Hong Kong 4 days a week.

FROM AUSTRALIA   Service is provided by Qantas Airways, Thai Airways International, Singapore Airlines, and British Airways.

FLYING FOR LESS: TIPS FOR GETTING THE BEST AIRFARES

Passengers within the same airplane cabin are rarely paying the same fare for their seats. Business travelers who need to purchase tickets at the last minute, change their itinerary at a moment's notice, or get home before the weekend pay the premium rate, known as the full fare. Passengers who can book their ticket long in advance, who don't mind staying over Saturday night, or who are willing to travel on a Tuesday,

Wednesday, or Thursday after 7pm, will pay a fraction of the full fare. Here are a few other easy ways to save.

1. **Keep tabs on airline discounts.** Periodically, airlines lower prices on their most popular routes. Check your newspaper for advertised discounts or call the airlines directly and ask if any **promotional rates** or special fares are available. You'll almost never see a sale during the peak summer vacation months of July and August, or during the Thanksgiving or Christmas seasons; but in periods of low-volume travel, you should pay no more than US$400 for a cross-country flight. If your schedule is flexible, ask if you can secure a cheaper fare by staying an extra day or by flying midweek. (Many airlines won't volunteer this information.) If you already hold a ticket when a sale breaks, it may even pay to exchange your ticket, which usually incurs a US$50 to US$75 charge.

   Note, however, that the lowest-priced fares are often nonrefundable, require advance purchase of 1 to 3 weeks and a certain length of stay, and carry penalties for changing dates of travel.

2. **Consolidators, also known as bucket shops, are a good place to find low fares.** Consolidators buy seats in bulk from the airlines and then sell them back to the public at prices below even the airlines' discounted rates. Their small boxed ads usually run in the Sunday travel section of your newspaper, at the bottom of the page. Before you pay, however, ask for a confirmation number from the consolidator and then call the airline itself to confirm your seat. Be prepared to book your ticket with a different consolidator—there are many to choose from—if the airline can't confirm your reservation. Also be aware that bucket shop tickets are usually nonrefundable or rigged with stiff cancellation penalties, often as high as 50% to 75% of the ticket price.

   Council Travel (☎ **800/226-8624;** www.counciltravel.com) and **STA Travel** (☎ **800/781-4040;** www.sta.travel.com) cater especially to young travelers, but their bargain basement prices are available to people of all ages. **Travel Bargains** (☎ **800/AIR-FARE;** www.1800airfare.com) was formerly owned by TWA but now offers the deepest discounts on many other airlines, with a 4-day advance purchase. Other reliable consolidators include **1-800-FLY-CHEAP** (www.1800flycheap.com); TFI Tours International (☎ **800-745-8000** or 212/736-1140), which serves as a clearinghouse for unused seats; or "rebaters" such as Travel Avenue (☎ **800/333-3335** or 312/876-1116) and the Smart Traveller (☎ **800/448-3338** in the U.S. or 305/448-3338), which rebate part of their commissions to you.

3. **Search the Internet for cheap fares.** See the "Cyber Deals for Net Surfers" section below for tips.

4. **Book a seat on a charter flight.** Discounted fares have pared the number available, but they can still be found. Most charter operators advertise and sell their seats through travel agents, thus making these local professionals your best source of information for available flights. Before deciding to take a charter flight, however, check the restrictions on the ticket: You may be asked to purchase a tour package, to pay in advance, to be amenable if the day of departure is changed, to pay a service charge, to fly on an airline you're not familiar with (this usually is not the case), and to pay harsh penalties if you cancel—but to be understanding if the charter doesn't fill up and is canceled up to 10 days before departure. Summer charters fill up more quickly than others and are almost sure to fly, but if you decide on a charter flight, seriously consider cancellation and baggage insurance.

5. **Look into courier flights.** Companies that hire couriers use your luggage allowance for their business baggage; in return, you get a deeply discounted

ticket. Flights are often offered at the last minute, and you may have to arrange a pretrip interview to make sure you're right for the job. **Now Voyager,** open Monday to Friday from 10am to 5:30pm and Saturday from noon to 4:30pm (☎ 212/431-1616), flies from New York. Now Voyager also offers noncourier discounted fares, so call the company even if you don't want to fly as a courier.

6. **Join a travel club** such as **Moment's Notice** (☎ 718/234-6295) or **Sears Discount Travel Club** (☎ 800/433-9383, or 800/255-1487 to join), which supply unsold tickets at discounted prices. You pay an annual membership fee to get the club's hot line number. Of course, you're limited to what's available, so you have to be flexible.

CYBER DEALS FOR NET SURFERS

It's possible to get some great deals on airfare, hotels, and car rentals via the Internet. Grab your mouse and surf before you take off—you could save a bundle on your trip. The Web sites highlighted below are worth checking out, especially since all services are free. Always check the lowest published fare, however, before you shop for flights online.

Arthur Frommer's Budget Travel (www.frommers.com)   This site offers detailed information on 200 cities and islands around the world, and up-to-the-minute ways to save dramatically on flights, hotels, car reservations, and cruises. Book an entire vacation online and research your destination before you leave. Consult the message board to set up "hospitality exchanges" in other countries, to talk with other travelers who have visited a hotel you're considering, or to direct travel questions to Arthur Frommer himself. The newsletter is updated daily to keep you abreast of the latest breaking ways to save, to publicize new hot spots and best buys, and to present veteran readers with fresh, ever-changing approaches to travel.

Microsoft Expedia (www.expedia.com)   The best part of this multi-purpose travel site is the "Fare Tracker": You fill out a form on the screen indicating that you're interested in cheap flights from your nearest airport to up to three destinations, and, once a week, they'll e-mail you the best airfare deals. The site's "Travel Agent" will steer you to bargains on hotels and car rentals, and with the help of hotel and airline seat pinpointers, you can book everything right on-line. This site is even useful once you're booked. Before you depart, log on to Expedia for maps and up-to-date travel information, including weather reports and foreign exchange rates.

Travelocity (www.travelocity.com)   This is one of the best travel sites out there, especially for finding cheap airfare. In addition to its "Personal Fare Watcher," which notifies you via e-mail of the lowest airfares for up to five different destinations, Travelocity will track the three lowest fares for any routes on any dates in minutes. You can book a flight right then and there, and if you need a rental car or hotel, Travelocity will find you the best deal via the SABRE computer reservations system (a huge travel agent database). Click on "Last Minute Deals" for the latest travel bargains, including a link to "H.O.T. Coupons" (www.hotcoupons.com), where you can print out electronic coupons for travel in the U.S. and Canada.

The Trip (www.thetrip.com)   This site is really geared toward the business traveler, but vacationers-to-be can also use The Trip's exceptionally powerful fare-finding engine, which will e-mail you every week with the best city-to-city airfare deals for as many as 10 routes. The Trip uses the Internet Travel Network, another reputable travel agent database, to book hotels and restaurants.

E-Savers Programs   Several major airlines offer a free e-mail service known as E-Savers, via which they'll send you their best bargain airfares on a regular basis. Here's how it works: Once a week (usually Wednesday), or whenever a sale fare comes up, subscribers receive a list of discounted flights to and from various destinations, both international and domestic. Here's the catch: These fares are usually only available if you leave the very next Saturday (or sometimes Friday night) and return on the following Monday or Tuesday. It's really a service for the spontaneously inclined and travelers looking for a quick getaway. But the fares are cheap, so it's worth taking a look. If you have a preference for certain airlines (in other words, the ones you fly most frequently), sign up with them first. See the appendix for a listing of airline Web sites.

One caveat: You'll get frequent-flier miles if you purchase one of these fares, but you can't use miles to buy the ticket.

Smarter Living (www.smarterliving.com)   If the thought of all that surfing and comparison shopping gives you a headache, then head right for Smarter Living. Sign up for their newsletter service, and every week you'll get a customized e-mail summarizing the discount fares available from your departure city. Smarter Living tracks more than 15 different airlines, so it's a worthwhile time-saver.

5 Getting Around Between Countries

Basically, flying in Southeast Asia is the best way to go between and within countries, in terms of time conservation and convenience. It is also the most expensive, but if your time is short, it is definitely worth the cost. That said, sometimes half the fun of traveling is getting there—like that nightmare 10-hour bus journey I suffered, bumping and bouncing from Savannakhet to Pakse in southern Laos, where the only fellow passenger who spoke English could only repeat "I love you!" the whole trip. All 10 hours of them. But do you think I'll forget that guy? Or how about the marathon train trip I took from Chiang Mai in northern Thailand to Singapore. The train broke down in Surat Thani, then we were all kicked off at the Malaysian border where we hopped a bus for Butterworth. Then my outstation taxi broke down 40 kilometers outside of Kuala Lumpur before I finally got on the last leg of the trip. It was almost 3 days of frustration made joyous by some of the most fascinating characters along the way. This is the stuff travel is made of; those stories that begin, "I'll never do it again, but what a trip!"

BY PLANE

Depending on your specific itinerary, you may fly on international carriers including Silk Air (the regional arm of Singapore Airlines), Malaysia Airlines, Thai Airways International, Cathay Pacific Airways, Vietnam Airlines, Myanmar Airways International, or Garuda Indonesia, as well as various domestic carriers including Pelangi Air and Berjaya Air in Malaysia; Air Mandalay in Burma; Lao Aviation in Laos; Royal Air Cambodge and Kampuchea Airlines in Cambodia; or Bangkok Airways, P.B. Air, or Angel Airlines in Thailand. Competing airlines can often offer more interesting routes for you to select from.

Also bear in mind that international airports are not restricted to capital cities. In addition to Bangkok, Thailand has international access via Chiang Mai and Chiang Rai (to China, Burma, and Laos); U-Tapao and Phuket (to Cambodia); Phuket and Ko Samui (to Singapore and Kuala Lumpur). You can fly into Malaysia to Penang, Langkawi, and Tioman Island and to Borneo destinations direct from Singapore. Burma has international access to Mandalay; Laos has international access at both Luang Prabang and Pakse in addition to the capital Vientiane. Vietnam has international flights to either Ho Chi Minh City or Hanoi. The best new development is the opening of international access at Siem Reap, the access city to Angkor Wat in

Cambodia—now you can fly directly to the site from Bangkok, U-Tapao (near Pattaya), Phuket, Singapore, and other cities.

Basically, be sure to research all flight options for the most direct routes and best fares. Each chapter gives specific details for booking these flights.

BY TRAIN

With a few exceptions, trains that operate throughout Southeast Asia are poorly maintained, overcrowded, and slow. The most popular rail route—and the only one with interconnecting service between countries in all of Southeast Asia—runs from Singapore to Bangkok (and vice versa) through the heart of the Malaysian peninsula, with stops along the way at the cities of Johor Bahru, Malacca, Kuala Lumpur, and Butterworth (for Penang). It takes 6 hours from Singapore to Kuala Lumpur and another 35 hours from KL to Bangkok. You can board the train at the Singapore Rail Station in Tanjong Pagar, at the Kuala Lumpur Central Railway Station on Jalan Hishamuddin, and in Bangkok at the Hua Lamphong Railway Station on Rama IV Road.

Upscale travelers with unlimited budgets can book passage on one of the world's foremost luxury trains, the Eastern & Oriental express, which covers the distance between Singapore and Bangkok in 42 hours. Find more details in either the Singapore or Thailand chapters.

BY BUS

While not the most comfortable option, buses save money and provide access to some places not available via commercial flights. Popular overland routes include Vietnam to Laos (between Hue/Danang and Savannakhet), Vietnam to Cambodia (between Ho Chi Minh City and Phnom Penh), Thailand to Cambodia (between Bangkok and Phnom Penh) and extensive routes from southern Thailand, throughout Malaysia, and down to Singapore. If you decide to travel this way, be sure to get express permission to enter Laos, Vietnam, and Cambodia via an overland checkpoint.

BY BOAT

More and more people adventure down the Mekong, starting at Chiang Khong in Northern Thailand and ending in Luang Prabang in Laos. Get your visas from travel agents in Chiang Mai, and you'll have no problems. Thailand and Laos have a few border crossings over the Mekong, the most popular of which is the Friendship Bridge connecting Nong Khai (the last stop on Thailand's northeastern rail route) to Vientiane, Laos's capital. And during my research for Vietnam I heard that very soon travel companies will provide Mekong River tours from Ho Chi Minh City to Phnom Penh.

6 Package Tours & Escorted Tours

Before you start your search for the lowest airfare, you may want to consider booking your flight as part of a travel package such as an escorted tour or a package tour. What you lose in adventure, you'll gain in time and money saved when you book accommodations, and maybe even food and entertainment, along with your flight.

ESCORTED TOURS

Packaged travel may not be the option for you if you like to navigate strange places at whim. If you like to plan your coordinates in advance, however, many package options will enable you to do just that—and save you money in the process.

Some people love escorted tours. They let you relax and take in the sights while a driver fights traffic for you; they spell out your costs up front; and they take you to the maximum number of sights in the minimum amount of time with the least amount of hassle. If you do choose an escorted tour, you should ask a few simple questions before you buy:

What is the cancellation policy? Do they require a deposit? Can they cancel the trip if they don't get enough people? Do you get a refund if they cancel? If you cancel? How late can you cancel if you are unable to go? When do you pay in full?

How busy is the schedule? How much sightseeing do they plan each day? Do they allow ample time for relaxing by the pool, shopping, or wandering?

What is the size of the group? The smaller the group, the more flexible the itinerary, and the less time you'll spend waiting for the rest of your group. Tour operators may be evasive about this, because they may not know the exact size of the group until everybody has made their reservations; but they should be able to give you a rough estimate. Some tours have a minimum group size and may cancel the tour if they don't book enough people.

What is included in the price? Don't assume anything. You may have to pay for transportation to and from the airport. A box lunch may be included in an excursion, but drinks might cost extra. Beer might be included, but wine might not. Can you opt out of certain activities, or does the group leave at a certain time every day, with no exceptions? Are all your meals planned in advance? Can you choose your entree at dinner, or does everybody get the same chicken cutlet?

PACKAGE TOURS

Package tours are not the same thing as escorted tours. They are simply a way to buy airfare and accommodations at the same time. For popular destinations like Bali and Thailand, they are a smart way to go, because they save you a lot of money. In many cases, a package that includes airfare, hotel, and transportation to and from the airport will cost you less than just the hotel alone would have, had you booked it yourself. That's because packages are sold in bulk to tour operators, who then resell them to the public at a cost that drastically undercuts standard rates.

Packages, however, vary widely. Some offer a better class of hotels than others. Some offer the same hotels for lower prices. Some offer flights on scheduled airlines, while others book charters. In some packages, your choice of accommodations and travel days may be limited. Some packages let you choose between escorted vacations and independent vacations; others will allow you to add on just a few excursions or escorted day trips (also at lower prices than you could locate on your own) without booking an entirely escorted tour. Each destination usually has one or two packagers that are usually cheaper than the rest because they buy in even greater bulk. If you spend the time to shop around, you will save in the long run.

FINDING A PACKAGE DEAL

The best place to start your search is the travel section of your local Sunday newspaper. Also check the ads in the back of national travel magazines like *Travel & Leisure, National Geographic Traveler,* and *Condé Nast Traveller.* One of the biggest packagers in the Northeast, Liberty Travel, usually boasts a full-page ad in Sunday papers. You won't get much in the way of service, but you will get a good deal. Check your local directory for one of its many local branches nationwide, or visit the Liberty Web site at www.libertytravel.com. **American Express Vacations** (☎ 800/241-1700; www. leisureweb.com) is another option. Check out its **Last Minute Travel Bargains** site, offered in conjunction with Continental Airlines (www6.americanexpress.com/ travel/lastminutetravel/default.asp), with deeply discounted vacation packages and reduced airline fares that differ from the E-Savers bargains that Continental e-mails weekly to subscribers. Northwest Airlines offers a similar service. Posted on North-west's Web site every Wednesday, its Cyber Saver Bargain Alerts offer special hotel rates, package deals, and discounted airline fares.

Another good resource is the airlines themselves, which often package their flights together with accommodations. Fly-by-night packagers are uncommon, but they do exist; when you buy your package through the airline, however, you can be pretty sure that the company will still be in business when your departure date arrives.

The biggest hotel chains and resorts also offer package deals. If you already know where you want to stay, call the resort itself and ask if they can offer land/air packages.

TOUR OPERATORS SPECIALIZING IN SOUTHEAST ASIA

Whether you want to ride an elephant through the jungle, trek among indigenous people, shake hands with an orangutan, swim beneath a waterfall, snorkel in a clear blue lagoon, lounge on a white sand beach, or wander through exotic markets, there's a Southeast Asia tour packager for you, offering a wide range of travel options using the finest and most reliable travel services available in the region.

Among the most experienced and knowledgeable tour operators specializing in Southeast Asia are **Absolute Asia** and **East Quest.** Both companies offer a diverse blend of cultural and adventure travel programs and will customize tours and design itineraries to suit each individual's particular interest. Anyone traveling with Absolute Asia has three options: follow the itinerary as is, combine it with another itinerary, or design your own trip.

All tour operators offer escorted package tours for groups and can also customize packages for independent travelers. See individual country chapters for in-country tour operators specializing in each country.

Abercrombie & Kent. 1520 Kensington Rd., Suite 212, Oakbrook, IL 60523-2141. ☎ **800/323-7308.** Fax 630/954-3324. www.aandktours.com.

Well-known luxury tour operator Abercrombie & Kent's Southeast Asia programs are highlighted by two comprehensive itineraries. Tours include Myanmar, Thailand (including spa tours in Thailand), Cambodia, Hong Kong, and other destinations. These tours also include stays at the finest hotels in Southeast Asia, such as the Oriental in Bangkok and the Mandarin Oriental in Hong Kong.

Absolute Asia. 180 Varick St., 16th fl., New York, NY 10014. ☎ **800/736-8187.** Fax 212/627-4090. www.absoluteasia.com. E-mail: Info@absoluteasia.com.

Absolute Asia, experienced since 1989, began by planning private tours in Thailand and Indochina and expanded to include all of Southeast Asia and beyond. Today they offer an array of innovative itineraries, specializing in individual or small group tours customized to your interests, with experienced local guides and excellent accommodations. Talk to them about tours that feature art, cuisine, religion, antiques, photography, wildlife study, archaeology, soft adventure—they can plan a specialized trip to see just about anything you can dream up—for any length of time. They can also book you on excellent coach programs in Indochina.

Asia Transpacific Journeys. 2995 Center Green Court, Boulder, CO 80301. ☎ **800/642-2742** or 303/443-6789. Fax 303/443-7078. www.southeastasia.com. E-mail: travel@southeastasia.com.

Coordinating tours of every corner of Southeast Asia and the South Pacific, Asia Transpacific Journeys deals with small groups and custom programs that include luxury hotel accommodations. Their new 22-day Passage to Indochina tour takes you through Laos, Vietnam, and Cambodia's major attractions with a well-planned itinerary. A highly recommended choice.

Backroads. 801 Cedar St., Berkeley, CA 94710-1800. ☎ **800/462-2848** or 510/527-1555. Fax 510/527-1444. www.backroads.com.

For those who want to explore Southeast Asia by bicycle, cycling and hiking specialist Backroads has a 12-day Vietnam tour and an 8-day Thailand Golden Triangle tour. They also have a 9-day bike, walk, and snorkel tour in Bali.

Imaginative Traveller. 1 Betts Ave., Martlesham Heath, Suffolk IP5 3RH. ☎ **0208/ 742-8612.** Fax 0280/742-3045. www.imaginative-traveller.com.

This UK-based firm gets rave reviews every time, organizing all sorts of cycling, trekking, and motorcycling adventures throughout Southeast Asia, particularly Indochina.

Latitudes Expeditions East. 1363 McAllister St., San Francisco, CA 94115. ☎ **800/ 580-4883** or 415/440-6472. www.weblatitudes.com. E-mail: info@weblatitudes.com.

Another excellent choice for travel in Southeast Asia, Latitudes not only specializes in the countries of this region, but has, in addition to cultural, nature, and luxury tours, adventure and outdoor sporting tours like cycling and rafting, plus spa and health packages.

7 Health & Insurance

GENERAL AVAILABILITY OF HEALTH CARE FACILITIES

The best hospitals and health care facilities are located in the large cities and major tourist centers of countries which have the greatest number of Western tourists—i.e., Singapore, Hong Kong, Malaysia (Kuala Lumpur), Thailand (Bangkok), and the Philippines (Manila). In rural areas of these countries and throughout the lesser developed countries of Vietnam, Cambodia, Laos, and Burma, there are limited health-care facilities, as hospitals are few and far between, and generally of poor quality. Even in heavily touristed Bali, you're better off evacuating to one of the more developed countries if faced with a serious medical situation.

COMMON DISEASES

Among Southeast Asia's tropical diseases carried by mosquitoes are **malaria, dengue fever,** and **Japanese encephalitis.** Reports about malaria prophylactics differ depending on who you talk to. While most local health agencies tell you not to waste your time with anti-malaria drugs, the CDC still advises people to take these tablets, most of which cause uncomfortable side effects. In truth, your only sure way to avoid mosquito-borne diseases is to not get bit. Repellents that contain **DEET** are the most effective, but can cause adverse reactions to the skin. I've never trusted herbal "all-natural" lotions, that for me always seem to attract mosquitoes. However, I found a great product: Johnson's Baby Clear Lotion Anti-mosquito (in the baby-care section of your pharmacy) provides terrific DEET-free mosquito protection. It works, it's gentle enough for babies and it's available throughout Southeast Asia (BYO to Myanmar, Cambodia, and Laos). Also be aware that malaria mosquitoes bite in the evening. Dengue fever mosquitoes bite during the day.

Hepatitis A may be contracted from water or food, while cholera epidemics sometimes occur in remote areas. Bilharzia, schistosomiasis, and giardia are parasitic diseases that can be contracted from swimming or drinking from stagnant or untreated water in lakes or streams.

Anyone contemplating sexual activity should be aware that HIV is rampant in many Southeast Asian countries, along with other STDs such as gonorrhea, syphilis, herpes, and hepatitis B.

The **International Association for Medical Assistance to Travelers (IAMAT)** (☎ **716/754-4883** or 416/652-0137; www.sentex.net/~iamat) offers tips on travel and health concerns in the countries you'll be visiting, and lists local English-speaking doctors. The **United States Centers for Disease Control and Prevention** (☎ **404/ 332-4559;** www.cdc.gov) provides up-to-date information on necessary vaccines and health hazards by region or country (by mail, their booklet is US$20; on the Internet, it's free). The **U.S. State Department's 24-hour travel advisory** (☎ **202/647-5225;** http://travel.state.gov/travel_warnings.html) also lists the latest information on diseases affecting a particular country.

DEALING WITH THE HEAT & HUMIDITY

Limit your exposure to the sun, especially during the first few days of your trip and, thereafter, from 11am to 2pm. Use a sunscreen with a high protection factor and apply it liberally. Also, Asians are still big fans of parasols. Don't be shy about using an umbrella to shade yourself.

Remember that children need more protection than adults do. Always make sure to drink plenty of bottled water, which is the best defense against heat exhaustion and the more serious, life-threatening heatstroke. Also, remember that coffee, tea, soft drinks, and alcoholic beverages should not be substituted for water, as they are diuretics that dehydrate the body. In extremely hot and humid weather, try to stay out of the midday heat and confine most of your daytime traveling to early morning and late afternoon. If you ever feel weak, fatigued, dizzy, or disoriented, get out of the sun immediately and go to a shady, cool place. To prevent sunburn, always wear a hat and apply sunscreen to all exposed areas of skin.

DIETARY PRECAUTIONS

Unless you intend to confine your travels to the big cities and dine only at restaurants that serve Western-style food, you will likely be eating many foods that you don't normally consume. This may lead initially to upset stomachs and/or diarrhea, which usually lasts just a few days as your body adapts to the change in cuisine. Except for Singapore, where tap water is safe to drink, **always drink bottled water (never use tap water for drinking or even brushing teeth).** It's also recommended to peel all fruits and vegetables and avoid raw shellfish and seafood. Also, beware of ice unless it is made from purified water. (Any suspicious water can be purified by boiling for 10 minutes or treating with purifying tablets.) If you're a vegetarian, you will find that Southeast Asia is a great place to travel, as vegetarian dishes abound throughout the region. In terms of hygiene, restaurants are generally preferred to street stalls. Be sure to carry diarrhea medication as well as any prescription medications you may need. It's also a good idea to carry your own set of plastic chopsticks or a small cutlery set, just in case you suspect the cleanliness of those that are presented to you at a restaurant.

So, how can you tell if something will upset your stomach before you eat it? Trust your basic instincts. I've been plenty sick my share of times, and have found that each time I get into trouble I've usually felt dread from the start. If your gut tells you not to eat that fried chicken knee, don't eat it. If your hosts insist, but you are still afraid, explain about your "foreigner tummy" with a regretful smile and accept a cup of tea instead.

WHAT TO DO IF YOU GET SICK AWAY FROM HOME

It can be hard to find a doctor you can trust when you're in an unfamiliar place, and in some countries covered in this guide, medical care is simply not up to Western standards. Try to take proper precautions the week before you depart, to avoid falling ill while you're away from home. Amid the last-minute frenzy that often precedes a vacation break, make an extra effort to eat and sleep well—especially if you feel an illness coming on.

If you worry about getting sick away from home, you may want to consider **medical travel insurance** (see the section on insurance, below). In most cases, however, your existing health plan will provide all the coverage you need. Hospitals and doctors here will not accept your policy, but many insurance companies will allow you to submit receipts for reimbursement.

If you suffer from a chronic illness, consult your doctor before your departure. For conditions like epilepsy, diabetes, or heart problems, wear a **Medic Alert Identification Tag** (☎ 800/825-3785; www.commedicalert.org), which will immediately alert doctors to your condition and give them access to your records through Medic Alert's 24-hour hot line. Membership is US$35, plus a US$15 annual fee.

Pack prescription medications in your carry-on luggage. Carry written prescriptions in generic, not brand-name form, and dispense all prescription medications from their original labeled vials. Also bring along copies of your prescriptions in case you lose your pills or run out.

If you wear contact lenses, pack an extra pair in case you lose one.

The International Association for Medical Assistance to Travelers (IAMAT) and the U.S. Centers for Disease Control and Prevention (see above for contact info) list English-speaking doctors in the countries you'll be visiting. Also note that when you're abroad, any local consulate can provide a list of area doctors who speak English. If you do get sick, you may want to ask the concierge at your hotel to recommend a local doctor—even his or her own.

INSURANCE

There are three kinds of travel insurance: trip cancellation, medical, and lost luggage coverage. **Trip cancellation insurance** is a good idea if you have paid a large portion of your vacation expenses up front. The other two types of insurance, however, don't make sense for most travelers. Rule number one: Check your existing policies before you buy any additional coverage.

Your existing health insurance should cover you if you get sick while on vacation (though if you belong to an HMO, you should check to see whether you are fully covered when away from home). If you need hospital treatment, most health insurance plans and HMOs will cover out-of-country hospital visits and procedures, at least to some extent. However, most make you pay the bills up front at the time of care, and you'll get a refund after you've returned and filed all the paperwork. Members of **Blue Cross/Blue Shield** can now use their cards at select hospitals in most major cities worldwide (☎ 800/810-BLUE or www.bluecares.com/blue/bluecard/wwn for a list of hospitals). For independent travel health-insurance providers, see below. Your homeowner's insurance should cover stolen luggage. The airlines are responsible for US$1,250 on domestic flights if they lose your luggage; if you plan to carry anything more valuable than that, keep it in your carry-on bag.

The differences between travel assistance and insurance are often blurred, but in general the former offers on-the-spot assistance and 24-hour hot lines (mostly oriented toward medical problems), while the latter reimburses you for travel problems (medical, travel, or otherwise) after you have filed the paperwork. The coverage you should consider will depend on how much protection is already contained in your existing health insurance or other policies. Some credit- and charge-card companies may insure you against travel accidents if you buy plane, train, or bus tickets with their cards. Before purchasing additional insurance, read your policies and agreements over carefully. Make sure your policy covers **emergency evacuation,** since medical care in some Southeast Asian countries (Vietnam and Laos, for instance), is still substandard. Also check that your insurance covers motorbike riding if there's any chance you'll choose that method of getting around. Call your insurers or credit/charge-card companies if you have any questions.

Some credit cards (American Express and certain gold and platinum Visas and MasterCards, for example) offer automatic flight insurance against death or dismemberment in case of an airplane crash.

If you do require additional insurance, try one of the companies listed below. But don't pay for more than you need. For example, if you need only trip cancellation insurance, don't purchase coverage for lost or stolen property. Trip cancellation insurance costs approximately 6 to 8% of the total value of your vacation.

Among the reputable issuers of travel insurance are:

- **Access America,** 6600 W. Broad St., Richmond, VA 23230 (☎ **800/ 284-8300**)
- **Travel Guard International,** 1145 Clark St., Stevens Point, WI 54481 (☎ **800/826-1300**)
- **Travel Insured International, Inc.,** P.O. Box 280568, East Hartford, CT 06128 (☎ **800/243-3174**)
- **Columbus Travel Insurance,** 279 High St., Croydon CR0 1QH (☎ **020/ 375-0011** in London; www2.columbusdirect.com/columbusdirect)
- **International SOS Assistance,** P.O. Box 11568, Philadelphia, PA 11916 (☎ **800/523-8930** or 215/244-1500), strictly an assistance company
- **Travelex Insurance Services,** P.O. Box 9408, Garden City, NY 11530-9408 (☎ **800/228-9792**).

Companies specializing in accident and medical care include:

- **MEDEX International,** P.O. Box 5375, Timonium, MD 21094-5375 (☎ **888/MEDEX-00** or 410/453-6300; fax 410/453-6301; www. medexassist.com)
- **Travel Assistance International** (Worldwide Assistance Services, Inc.), 1133 15th St. NW, Suite 400, Washington, D.C. 20005 (☎ **800/821-2828** or 202/ 828-5894; fax 202/828-5896)
- **The Divers Alert Network (DAN)** (☎ **800/446-2671** or 919/684-2948) insures scuba divers.

8 Tips for Travelers with Special Needs
FOR TRAVELERS WITH DISABILITIES
Except for the modern, upscale international hotels, most buildings in Southeast Asia are not wheelchair-accessible or user-friendly when it comes to handling the special needs of disabled travelers. That said, a disability shouldn't stop anyone from traveling. There are more resources out there than ever before that can help you get around the obstacles. *A World of Options,* a 658-page book of resources for disabled travelers, covers everything from biking trips to scuba outfitters. It costs US$35 (US$30 for members) and is available from **Mobility International USA,** P.O. Box 10767, Eugene, OR 97440 (☎ **541/343-1284,** voice and TDD; www.miusa.org). Annual membership for Mobility International is US$35, which includes their quarterly newsletter, "Over the Rainbow." In addition, **Twin Peaks Press,** P.O. Box 129, Vancouver, WA 98666 (☎ **360/694-2462**), publishes travel-related books for people with disabilities.

The **Moss Rehab Hospital** (☎ 215/456-9600) has been providing friendly and helpful phone advice and referrals to disabled travelers for years through its **Travel Information Service** (☎ 215/456-9603; www.mossresourcenet.org).

You can join **The Society for the Advancement of Travel for the Handicapped (SATH),** 347 Fifth Ave., Suite 610, New York, NY 10016 (☎ 212/447-7284; fax 212/725-8253; www.sath.org) for US$45 annually, US$30 for seniors and students, to gain access to their vast network of connections in the travel industry. They provide information sheets on travel destinations, and referrals to tour operators that specialize in traveling with disabilities. Their quarterly magazine, *Open World for Disability and Mature Travel,* is full of good information and resources. A year's subscription is US$13 (US$21 outside the U.S.).

Travelers with disabilities may also want to consider joining a tour that caters specifically to them. One of the best operators is **Flying Wheels Travel,** 143 West Bridge (P.O. Box 382), Owatonna, MN 55060 (☎ 800/535-6790). They offer various escorted tours and cruises, with an emphasis on sports, as well as private tours in minivans with lifts. Other reputable specialized tour operators include **Access Adventures** (☎ 716/889-9096), which offers sports-related vacations; **Accessible Journeys** (☎ 800/TINGLES or 610/521-0339), for slow walkers and wheelchair travelers; **The Guided Tour, Inc.** (☎ 215/782-1370); **Wilderness Inquiry** (☎ 800/728-0719 or 612/379-3858); and **Directions Unlimited** (☎ 800/533-5343).

You can obtain a copy of **Air Transportation of Handicapped Persons** by writing to Free Advisory Circular No. AC12032, Distribution Unit, U.S. Department of Transportation, Publications Division, M-4332, Washington, D.C. 20590.

Vision-impaired travelers should contact the **American Foundation for the Blind,** 11 Penn Plaza, Suite 300, New York, NY 10001 (☎ 800/232-5463), for information on traveling with Seeing Eye dogs.

FOR GAY & LESBIAN TRAVELERS

If you have Internet access, check out **www.utopia-asia.com**, an excellent resource for homosexual travelers in Asia, including tips for even Vietnam, Burma—you name it. From there you can also find links to local bulletin boards and chats where you can learn about issues specific to each country. As far as the actual traveling is concerned, most Southeast Asian countries don't deal with public displays of affection between straight couples, much less gay or lesbian couples. To avoid offending local sensibilities, discretion is always advised.

The **International Gay & Lesbian Travel Association (IGLTA)** (☎ 800/448-8550 or 954/776-2626; fax 954/776-3303; www.iglta.org), links travelers with the appropriate gay-friendly service organization or tour specialist. With around 1,200 members, it offers quarterly newsletters, marketing mailings, and a membership directory that's updated quarterly. Membership often includes gay or lesbian businesses but is open to individuals for US$150 yearly, plus a US$100 administration fee for new members. Members are kept informed of gay and gay-friendly hoteliers, tour operators, and airline and cruise-line representatives. Contact the IGLTA for a list of its member agencies, who will be tied into IGLTA's information resources.

General gay and lesbian travel agencies include **Family Abroad** (☎ 800/999-5500 or 212/459-1800; gay and lesbian); **Above and Beyond Tours** (☎ 800/397-2681; mainly gay men); and **Yellowbrick Road** (☎ 800/642-2488; gay and lesbian).

There are also two good, biannual English-language gay guidebooks, both focused on gay men but including information for lesbians as well. You can get the *Spartacus International Gay Guide* or *Odysseus* from most gay and lesbian book stores, or order them from **Giovanni's Room** (☎ 215/923-2960), or **A Different Light Bookstore**

(☎ **800/343-4002** or 212/989-4850). Both lesbians and gays might want to pick up a copy of *Gay Travel A to Z* (US$16). The *Ferrari Guides* (www.q-net.com) is yet another very good series of gay and lesbian guidebooks.

Out and About, 8 W. 19th St. no. 401, New York, NY 10011 (☎ **800/929-2268** or 212/645-6922), offers guidebooks and a monthly newsletter packed with good information on the global gay and lesbian scene. A year's subscription to the newsletter costs US$49. *Our World,* 1104 North Nova Rd., Suite 251, Daytona Beach, FL 32117 (☎ **904/441-5367**), is a slicker monthly magazine promoting and highlighting travel bargains and opportunities. Annual subscription rates are US$35 in the U.S., US$45 outside the U.S.

FOR SENIORS

The most common complaint I hear from seniors here concerns the heat! Take extra precautions to avoid overheating your system—bring plenty of sunscreen and a good hat. Asians are very fond of parasols to shield the sun, so feel free to join them. Also, be firm with your tour operator to make sure you've enough time to rest. Some of these people will have you running day and night with not enough time to sit and breathe in between.

As for senior citizen discounts, Singapore and Hong Kong offer discounted entrance to museums and attractions, but I'm warning you—in Singapore the qualifying age is 55 years so don't pitch a fit if they offer you the discount without your asking! As for other countries, I'm sad to say, they'll think you're crazy just for asking. Restaurants never offer discounted meals, and at hotels, you'll find discounts at international chains, but locally run establishments will have no special plans for seniors. **Members of the American Association of Retired Persons (AARP),** 601 E St. NW, Washington, D.C. 20049 (☎ **800/424-3410** or 202/434-2277), get discounts not only on hotels but on airfares and car rentals, too. AARP offers members a wide range of special benefits, including *Modern Maturity* magazine and a monthly newsletter.

The **National Council of Senior Citizens,** 8403 Colesville Rd., Suite 1200, Silver Spring, MD 20910 (☎ **301/578-8800**), a nonprofit organization, offers a newsletter six times a year (partly devoted to travel tips) and discounts on hotels and auto rentals; annual dues are US$13 per person or couple.

Mature Outlook, P.O. Box 9390, Des Moines, IA 50306 (☎ **800/336-6330**), began as a travel organization for people over 50, though it now caters to people of all ages. Members receive discounts on hotels and receive a bimonthly magazine. Annual membership is US$19.95, which entitles members to discounts and, often, free coupons for discounted merchandise from Sears.

Golden Companions, P.O. Box 5249, Reno, NV 89513 (☎ **702/324-2227**), helps travelers 45-plus find compatible companions through a personal voice-mail service. Contact them for more information.

The Mature Traveler, a monthly 12-page newsletter on senior citizen travel, is a valuable resource. It is available by subscription (US$30 a year) from GEM Publishing Group, Box 50400, Reno, NV 89513-0400. Another helpful publication is *101 Tips for the Mature Traveler,* available from Grand Circle Travel, 347 Congress St., Suite 3A, Boston, MA 02210 (☎ **800/221-2610** or 617/350-7500; fax 617/346-6700).

Grand Circle Travel, 347 Congress St., Suite 3A, Boston, MA 02210 (☎ **800/221-2610** or 617/350-7500), is one of the hundreds of travel agencies specializing in vacations for seniors. Many of these packages, however, are of the tour-bus variety, with free trips thrown in for those who organize groups of 10 or more. Seniors seeking more independent travel should probably consult a regular travel agent. **SAGA**

International Holidays, 222 Berkeley St., Boston, MA 02116 (☎ **800/343-0273**), offers inclusive tours and cruises for those 50 and older. SAGA also sponsors the more substantial **"Road Scholar Tours"** (☎ **800/621-2151**), which are fun-loving but with an educational bent.

If you want something more than the average vacation or guided tour, try **Elderhostel** (☎ **877/426-8056;** www.elderhostel.org) or the University of New Hampshire's **Interhostel** (☎ **800/733-9753**), both variations on the same theme: educational travel for senior citizens. On these escorted tours, the days are packed with seminars, lectures, and field trips, and the sightseeing is all led by academic experts. **Elderhostel,** 75 Federal St., Boston, MA 02110-1941 (☎ **877/426-8056;** www. elderhostel.org), arranges study programs for those aged 55 and over (and a spouse or companion of any age) in 78 countries around the world, including Asia. Most courses last about 3 weeks and many include airfare, accommodations in student dormitories or modest inns, meals, and tuition. Write or call for a free catalog, which lists upcoming courses and destinations. Interhostel takes travelers 50 and over (with companions over 40), and offers 2- and 3-week trips. The courses in both these programs are ungraded, involve no homework, and often focus on the liberal arts. They're not luxury vacations, but they're fun and fulfilling.

FOR FAMILIES WITH CHILDREN

I don't see a lot of parents traveling with small children in Southeast Asia, and I'm not sure why. Bring your child to some of these countries and he'll be smothered with attention. The Thais are especially fond of mischievous children—you'll make a million friends. However, there are a few concerns that should be mentioned. Women who are breastfeeding need to keep feedings limited to private places, especially in Muslim countries here. And children's tummies will definitely be more susceptible to wee beasties in water and food that can cause diarrhea and more serious problems, so look out for everything they put in their mouths. Another safety concern, hotel pools and public beaches *do not* have lifeguards. As for baby-sitting, all hotels can arrange a baby-sitter (with advance notice) to come stay with your children for the evening, so there's no problem there.

Several books on the market offer tips to help you travel with kids. Most concentrate on the U.S., but two, *Family Travel* (Lanier Publishing International) and *How to Take Great Trips with Your Kids* (The Harvard Common Press), are full of good general advice that can apply to travel anywhere. Another reliable tome, with a worldwide focus, is *Adventuring with Children* (Foghorn Press).

Family Travel Times is published six times a year by TWYCH (Travel with Your Children; ☎ **888/822-4388** or 212/477-5524), and includes a weekly call-in service for subscribers. Subscriptions are US$40 a year for quarterly editions. A free publication list and a sample issue are available by calling or sending a request to the above address.

FOR WOMEN TRAVELERS

Women traveling together or alone will find touring this region particularly pleasant and easy (as evidenced by the fact that this book was written by women). The Buddhist and Islamic codes of conduct and ethics followed by many mean that you will be treated with respect and courtesy. However, I've heard some Western women complain about being eyeballed in Muslim Malaysia—only to discover later that they were walking around in miniskirts and bikini tops through town. I've also noticed an alarming number of women sunbathing topless, especially in Thailand. It appears tolerated, but that's only because your hosts wish to avoid confrontation. Deep inside it is very embarrassing.

While you will almost never find local women dining or touring alone, as a visitor, your behavior will be accepted. You will rarely, if ever, be approached or hassled by strangers. At the same time, you can feel free to start a conversation with a stranger without fear of misinterpretation. Note that if you are traveling with a man, public displays of affection are not welcome, and it's you, the female, who will be scorned. Also, you will have to take even more care than your male counterpart to dress modestly, meaning no cleavage- or midriff-baring tops, miniskirts, or short shorts. Otherwise, you risk offending people on the grounds of either religious or local moral standards.

All this said, it's still not advisable to take risks that you wouldn't normally take at home. Don't hitchhike, accept rides, or walk around late at night, particularly in dimly lit areas or in unfamiliar places. Be acutely aware of purse or jewelry snatchers in large cities. When meeting strangers in nightclubs, for example, buy your own drinks and keep an eye on them.

FOR SINGLE TRAVELERS

Many people prefer traveling alone. When you book hotels, specify a single room, which is almost always discounted form the standard double rate. **Travel Companion** (☎ 516/454-0880) is one of the oldest roommate finders for single travelers. Register with them and find a trustworthy travel mate who will split the cost of the room with you.

Several tour organizers cater to solo travelers as well. **Experience Plus** (☎ 800/ 685-4565; fax 907/484-8489) offers an interesting selection of single-only trips. **Travel Buddies** (☎ 800/998-9099 or 604/533-2483) runs single-friendly tours with no singles supplement. **The Single Gourmet Club** (133 E. 58th St., New York, NY 10022; ☎ 212/980-8788; fax 212/980-3138) is an international social, dining, and travel club for singles, with offices in 21 cities in the USA and Canada, and one in London.

You may also want to research the **Outdoor Singles Network** (P.O. Box 781, Haines, AK 99827). An established quarterly newsletter (since 1989) for outdoor-loving singles, ages 19 to 90, the network will help you find a travel companion, pen-pal, or soul mate within its pages. A 1-year subscription costs US$45, and your own personal ad is printed free in the next issue. Current issues are US$15. Write for free information or check out the group's Web site at www.kcd.com/bearstar/osn.html.

Hong Kong 4

by Beth Reiber

Viewed from Victoria Peak, Hong Kong surely rates as one of the most stunning cities in Southeast Asia, if not the world. In the foreground rise the skyscrapers of Hong Kong Island, numerous, dense, and astonishingly tall. Beyond that is Victoria Harbour, with its incredibly busy traffic of everything from the historic Star Ferry to cruise liners, cargo ships, and wooden fishing vessels. On the other side is Kowloon Peninsula, growing larger seemingly by the minute with ambitious land reclamation projects, housing estates, and ever-higher buildings, all against a dramatic backdrop of gently rounded mountains.

If this is your first stop in Asia, Hong Kong will seem excitingly exotic, with its profusion of neon Chinese signs, roasted ducks hanging in the windows of restaurants, colorful street markets, herb medicinal shops, fortune-tellers, and crush of people, 98% of whom are Chinese.

If you're arriving from elsewhere in Asia, however, Hong Kong may seem welcomingly familiar, with its first-class hotels, restaurants serving everything from California-style pizzas to French haute cuisine, easy-to-navigate transportation system, English language street signs, and gigantic shopping malls.

Hong Kong's unique blend of exotic and familiar, East and West, is due of course to its 156 years as a British colony—from 1842, when Britain acquired Hong Kong Island as a spoil of the first Opium War, to its 1997 handover to the Chinese. As a Special Administrative Region (SAR), Hong Kong has been guaranteed its capitalist lifestyle and social system for 50 years, and for the casual observer, little seems changed. English is still an official language, the Hong Kong dollar remains legal tender, and entry formalities are largely the same. Although Hong Kong is pricier than most other Asian destinations, the Asian financial crisis has made it more affordable than ever, with reduced hotel rates and competitive restaurant prices.

Shopping remains Hong Kong's chief draw, whether it's bargain hunting at one of its many street-side markets or browsing upscale boutiques at air-conditioned malls. Dearer to my heart is the justifiably celebrated dining: Hong Kong boasts what is arguably the greatest concentration of Chinese restaurants in the world, along with top-notch restaurants serving cuisines from around the globe. The city has also revved up its sightseeing attractions, offering museums, parks, temples, and other amusements. If all you want to do is lie on a beach

Hong Kong Region

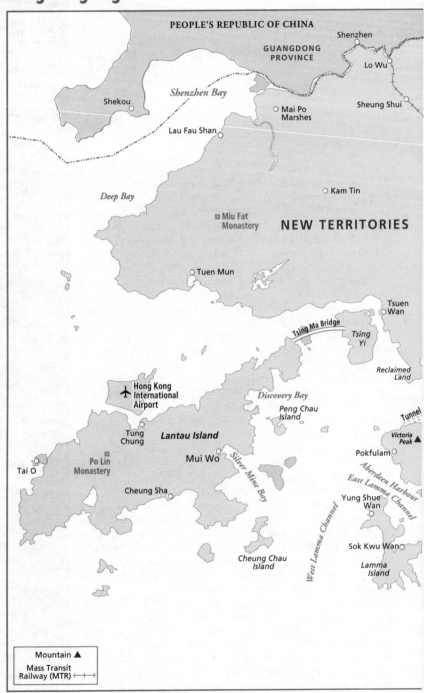

PEOPLE'S REPUBLIC OF CHINA

GUANGDONG
PROVINCE

Shenzhen

Lo Wu

Shenzhen Bay

Shekou

Mai Po
Marshes

Sheung Shui

Lau Fau Shan

Deep Bay

Kam Tin

Miu Fat
Monastery

NEW TERRITORIES

Tuen Mun

Tsuen
Wan

Tsing Ma Bridge

*Tsing
Yi*

*Reclaimed
Land*

Hong Kong
International
Airport

Discovery Bay

*Peng Chau
Island*

Tunnel

Tung
Chung

Lantau Island

*Victoria
Peak* ▲

Pokfulam

Tai O

Po Lin
Monastery

Mui Wo

Silver Mine Bay

Aberdeen Harbour

East Lamma Channel

Cheung Sha

Yung Shue
Wan

Sok Kwu Wan

West Lamma Channel

*Cheung Chau
Island*

*Lamma
Island*

Mountain ▲

Mass Transit
Railway (MTR) ┼─┼─┼

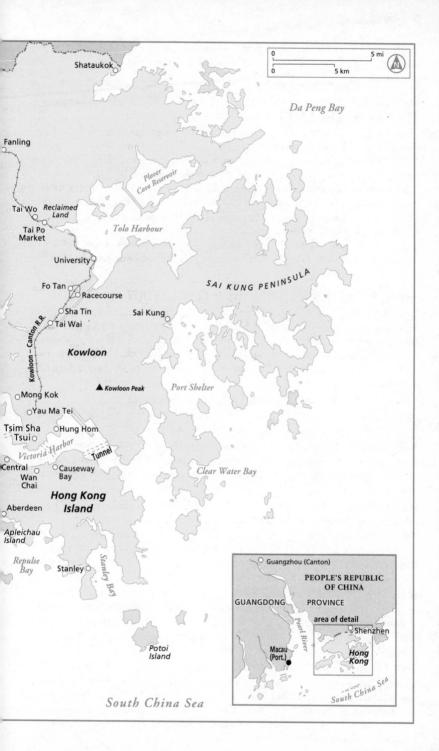

Shataukok

Da Peng Bay

Fanling

Plover Cove Reservoir

Tai Wo   Reclaimed Land

Tai Po Market

Tolo Harbour

University

SAI KUNG PENINSULA

Fo Tan

Racecourse

Sha Tin   Sai Kung

Kowloon–Canton R.R.

Tai Wai

Kowloon

Port Shelter

▲ *Kowloon Peak*

Mong Kok

Yau Ma Tei

Tsim Sha Tsui

Hung Hom

Victoria Harbor

Tunnel

Central   Causeway Bay

Wan Chai

Clear Water Bay

Hong Kong Island

Aberdeen

Apleichau Island

Repulse Bay   Stanley

Stanley Bay

Potoi Island

South China Sea

0   5 mi
0   5 km

Guangzhou (Canton)

PEOPLE'S REPUBLIC OF CHINA

GUANGDONG   PROVINCE

area of detail

Shenzhen

Hong Kong

Macau (Port.)

Pearl River

South China Sea

55

or get away from it all, you can do that, too. And Macau, with its fascinating blend of Portuguese and Chinese cultures, is just an hour's boat ride away.

1 Getting to Know Hong Kong

THE LAY OF THE LAND

Hong Kong, covering 652 square kilometers (404 sq. miles), can be divided into four distinct parts: **Hong Kong Island** with the Central District, the Western District, Wan Chai, and Causeway Bay, and with such major attractions as Hong Kong Park, Victoria Peak, Stanley Market, Ocean Park, and the Zoological and Botanical Gardens; **Kowloon Peninsula** with Tsim Sha Tsui and its many hotels, restaurants, museums, and shops at its tip, as well as the Yau Ma Tei and Mong Kong districts and the KCR Kowloon-Canton Railway Station in Hung Hom with service to mainland China; the vast **New Territories,** which stretch north from Kowloon all the way to the Chinese border and now house approximately half of Hong Kong's people, primarily in huge public-housing estates in satellite towns; and **260 outlying islands,** most of them barren and uninhabited.

HONG KONG NEIGHBORHOODS & CITY LAYOUT

CENTRAL DISTRICT This is where the story of Hong Kong all began, when a small port and community were established on the north end of the island by the British in the 1840s. Today, Central serves as Hong Kong's nerve center for banking, business, and administration, and boasts some of Hong Kong's most innovative architecture, a handful of exclusive hotels, high-end shopping centers, and bars and restaurants catering mostly to Hong Kong's white-collar workers.

LAN KWAI FONG Named after an L-shaped street in Central, this is Hong Kong's most well-known nightlife and entertainment district, occupying not only Lan Kwai Fong but overflowing onto neighboring streets like D'Aguilar and Wyndham.

MID-LEVELS Located halfway up Victoria Peak, the Mid-Levels is a popular residential area with its swank apartments, views of Central, lush vegetation, and slightly cooler temperatures. Serving white-collar workers who commute down to Central every day is the Hillside Escalator Link, the world's longest people-mover.

SOHO This new dining and nightlife district, flanking the Hillside Escalator Link that connects Central with the Mid-Levels, is popular with Mid-Levels residents and those seeking a quieter, saner alternative to the crowds of Lan Kwai Fong. Dubbed SoHo for the region "south of Hollywood Road," it has since blossomed into an ever-growing neighborhood of cafe-bars and small, intimate restaurants specializing in ethnic and innovative cuisine.

WESTERN DISTRICT West of the Central District, the Western District is one of the oldest, most traditional areas on Hong Kong Island, a fascinating neighborhood of shops selling herbs, ginseng, dried seafood, and other Chinese products. It's also famous for Hollywood Road, long popular for its many antiques and curio shops, and Man Mo Temple, one of Hong Kong's oldest temples.

WAN CHAI Few places in Hong Kong have changed as dramatically or noticeably as Wan Chai, located east of the Central district. Once notorious for its sleazy bars, easy women, tattoo parlors, and sailors on leave, Wan Chai has become respectable (and nearly unrecognizable) with new, mostly business-style hotels, more high-rises, the Hong Kong Arts Centre, the Hong Kong Convention and Exhibition Centre, and a small but revitalized nightlife scene.

CAUSEWAY BAY   Just east of Wan Chai, Causeway Bay is a popular shopping destination, with its Japanese department stores and clothing, shoe, and accessory boutiques. On its eastern perimeter is Victoria Park.

ABERDEEN   On the south side of Hong Kong Island, Aberdeen was once a fishing village but is now studded with high-rises and housing projects. However, it is still known for its hundreds of sampans, junks, boat people, and a couple of huge floating restaurants.

STANLEY   Located on the quiet south side of Hong Kong Island, this former fishing village is home to Hong Kong's most famous market, selling everything from silk suits to name-brand shoes, casual wear, and souvenirs.

KOWLOON   North of Hong Kong Island, across Victoria Harbour, is Kowloon, 7.74 square kilometers (4.8 sq. miles) that were ceded to Britain "in perpetuity" in 1860. Kowloon includes the districts Tsim Sha Tsui, Tsim Sha Tsui East, Yau Ma Tei, Hung Hom, and Mong Kok. Boundary Street in the north separates it from the New Territories.

TSIM SHA TSUI   At the southern tip of Kowloon Peninsula, Tsim Sha Tsui (also spelled "Tsimshatsui") is where most tourists stay and spend their money, since it has the greatest concentration of hotels, restaurants, and shops (some of my friends call it the "tourist ghetto"). Tsim Sha Tsui boasts an excellent art museum, a cultural center for the performing arts, Kowloon Park, one of the world's largest shopping malls, a broad selection of international restaurants, a jumping nightlife, and Nathan Road, appropriately nicknamed the "golden mile of shopping."

TSIM SHA TSUI EAST   East of Tsim Sha Tsui, Tsim Sha Tsui East was built entirely on reclaimed land and is home to several expensive hotels, entertainment centers, shopping and restaurant complexes, science and history museums, and, on its eastern edge, the KCR Kowloon-Canton Railway Station, with train service to the New Territories and China.

YAU MA TEI   Just north of Tsim Sha Tsui on Kowloon Peninsula is the Yau Ma Tei district (also spelled "Yaumatei"). Like the Western District, Yau Ma Tei is also very Chinese, with an interesting produce market, a jade market, and the fascinating Temple Street Night Market.

MONG KOK   On Kowloon Peninsula north of Yau Ma Tei, Mong Kok is a residential and industrial area, home of the Bird Market, the Ladies' Market on Tung Choi Street, and countless shops catering to Chinese.

A LOOK AT THE PAST

Although Hong Kong has been inhabited for at least 6,000 years and became part of the Chinese Han dynasty approximately 2,200 years ago, its modern history begins a mere 160 years ago, under conditions that were less than honorable. During the 1800s, tea was being imported to England in huge quantities from China, the only place it was grown. In exchange for the tea, the Chinese would accept only silver bullion, and furthermore, they forbade the British to enter their kingdom, with the exception of a small trading depot in Canton.

However, the British hit upon a trading commodity that proved irresistible to many Chinese: **opium.** Produced in India and exported by the East India Company, this powerful drug enslaved everyone from poor peasants to the nobility, and before long China was being drained of silver that was traded to support a drug habit. The Chinese emperor, fearful of the damage being wreaked on society and alarmed by his country's loss of silver, declared a ban on opium imports in the 1830s. The British

Recommended Books

Even though it is now dated, one of my favorite books about Hong Kong is Jan Morris's *Hong Kong* (Random House, 1988), which traces the evolution of the British colony from its birth during the Opium Wars to the late 1980s and makes for fascinating armchair reading. A good follow-up is Christopher Patten's *East and West: China, Power, and the Future of Asia* (Times Books, 1998), reflections from Hong Kong's last governor of the years leading up to the handover, negotiations with the Chinese, and what the future might bring. Other intimate views of the city are *Hong Kong: Borrowed Place, Borrowed Time* (Praeger, 1968) by Richard Hughes, a foreign correspondent who lived in Hong Kong for several decades and was said to have been the inspiration for several characters in John Le Carré's novels; and *Hong Kong: Somewhere Between Heaven and Earth* (Oxford University Press, 1996), edited by Barbara-Sue White and a collection of poems, short stories, excerpts from novels, diaries, and other reflections on Hong Kong by Chinese and Europeans from all walks of life in Hong Kong, including historical accounts.

Fictional works that bring Hong Kong to life are Richard Mason's *The World of Suzie Wong* (World Pub., 1957) and Han Suyin's *A Many-Splendored Thing* (Little Brown, 1952), an autobiographical account of life in Hong Kong shortly after the Chinese revolution in the late 1940s and early 1950s. James Clavell's *Tai-Pan* (Atheneum, 1966) is a novel about Hong Kong's beginnings; *Noble House* (Delacorte Press, 1981) is its sequel. John Le Carré's *The Honourable Schoolboy* (G.K. Hall, 1977) details the activities of George Smiley, acting head of the British Secret Service in Hong Kong. A more recent publication is Paul Theroux's *Kowloon Tong* (Houghton Mifflin, 1997), the story of a British expatriate born and raised in Hong Kong but who lives as an outsider, never having learned Chinese and failing to grasp what's at stake when shortly before the British handover he's offered a large sum of money for his family's business by a Chinese mainlander.

simply ignored the ban, smuggling the illegal cargo up the Pearl River. In 1839, with opium now India's largest export, the Chinese confiscated and destroyed the British opium stockpiles in Canton. The British declared war, and eventually won the struggle. As a result of this first **Opium War,** waged until 1842, China was forced to open new ports for trade, to agree to an exorbitant cash indemnity for the loss of the destroyed opium, and to cede Hong Kong Island in perpetuity to the British in a treaty that China would never recognize. Not only was this **Treaty of Nanking** demoralizing to the Chinese, it also ensured that their country would remain open to the curse of opium. After the second Opium War (1856—1858), Kowloon Peninsula was added to the colony, followed in 1898 (within the 99-year-lease dictated by Britain) by the New Territories and over 200 outlying islands.

But back in 1842 when the British took control of Hong Kong Island, where some 7,000 Chinese lived in its farming and fishing communities, Britain's prospects for developing a thriving port did not look rosy. Although it had a deep and protected harbor, no one, including the Chinese, was much interested in the island itself, and many in the British government considered its acquisition an embarrassing mistake. What's more, no sooner had the island been settled than a typhoon tore through the settlement. Repairs were demolished only 5 days later by another tropical storm. Fever and fire followed, and the weather grew so oppressive and humid that the colony seemed to be enveloped in a giant steam bath.

Yet as the number of headstones in the hillside cemetery multiplied, so did the number of the living. By 1846, the population had reached an astonishing 24,000. By the turn of the century the number had swelled to 300,000. British families lived along the waterfront and called it **Victoria** (now the Central District), slowly moving up toward the cooler temperatures of Victoria Peak. The Chinese, barred from living in the Peak and other European neighborhoods, stayed in a shantytown farther west, now known as the **Western District.** A typical Hong Kong dwelling consisted of four Chinese families and their animals in one room. Conditions were so appalling that when the bubonic plague struck in 1894 it raged for almost 30 years, claiming more than 20,000 lives.

Most of the newcomers to Hong Kong were mainland Chinese, who arrived with the shirts on their backs and nothing to lose. Every turmoil that sent a shudder through China—famine, flood, or civil war—flung a new wave of farmers, merchants, peasants, coolies, and entrepreneurs into Hong Kong. Everyone's dream was to make a fortune; it was just a matter of timing and good *joss* (luck). The Chinese philosophy of hard work and good fortune found fertile ground in the laissez-faire atmosphere of the colony.

Hong Kong's growth in the 20th century was no less astonishing in terms of both trade and population. In 1911 the overthrow of the Manchu dynasty in China sent a flood of refugees into Hong Kong, followed in 1938 by an additional 500,000 immigrants. Another mass influx of Chinese refugees arrived after the fall of Shanghai to the Communists in 1950. From this last wave of immigrants, including many Shanghai industrialists, emerged the beginnings of Hong Kong's now-famous textile industry.

As a British colony, Hong Kong was administered by a governor appointed by the queen. There were no free elections, and the Legislative Council, Hong Kong's main governing body, was also appointed. As 1997 drew nearer, marking the end of the 99-year lease on the New Territories, it soon became clear that China had no intention of renewing the lease or renegotiating a treaty it had never recognized in the first place. Finally, after more than 20 rounds of talks and meetings, Britain's Prime Minister Margaret Thatcher signed the Sino-British Joint Declaration of 1984, agreeing to transfer all of Hong Kong to Chinese Communist rule on June 30, 1997. For its part, China declared Hong Kong a **"Special Administrative Region,"** granting it special privileges under a "one country, two systems" policy that guaranteed Hong Kong's capitalist lifestyle and social system for at least 50 years after 1997. As such, Hong Kong would remain largely self-governing, and its people would retain rights to their property, freedom of speech, and ability to travel freely in and out of Hong Kong. Throughout the negotiations, residents of Hong Kong were never consulted about their future.

Then came the events of June 1989 in Beijing's **Tiananmen Square,** in which hundreds of students and demonstrators were ordered shot by Chinese authorities in a brutal move to quash the pro-democracy movement. China's response to the rebellion sent shock waves through Hong Kong and led to rounds of angry protest. Those who could, emigrated, primarily to Australia, Canada, and the United States; at its height, more than 1,000 people were emigrating each week. The vast majority of Hong Kong Chinese remained, however, confident or at least hopeful that China realized it had more to gain by keeping Hong Kong as it was.

On June 30, 1997, the last British governor sailed out of Hong Kong, and Tung Chee-hwa, appointed by Beijing, became the new chief executive of the Special Administrative Region (SAR). Mainland China celebrated the event as the end of more than 100 years of shame.

Today, the question foremost in every visitor's mind is, "How much has Hong Kong changed since the handover?" The answer: not much. Entry formalities for Americans and most other nationalities remain unchanged. English remains an official language, and the English names of buildings, streets, and attractions remain the same. The Hong Kong dollar, pegged to the U.S. dollar, remains legal tender, and in most hotels, restaurants, and shops that cater to tourists, it's business as usual.

The most visible differences are the replacement of the Union Jack and colonial flag with China's starred flag and a new Hong Kong flag emblazoned with the bauhinia flower, as well as new coins and stamps. But these are really subtle changes. The British population dropped more than 10 percent in the first 6 months after the handover, forcing some bars, restaurants and other establishments that had long catered to the expat community to close down. Tourism fell as well, forcing hotels and restaurants to downsize and cut their prices. Meanwhile, the **Asian economic crisis** has brought an influx of new expatriates looking for work, most notably Filipinos. And although border regulations between Hong Kong and China have remained unchanged, the SAR has been deluged with a new flood of mainlanders—an estimated 50,000 a year. All this despite the exodus of manufacturers to Shenzhen across the Chinese border, where the cost of production and labor is cheaper. Hong Kong is also wrestling with unprecedented levels of pollution.

But Hong Kong has always been a city in transformation, with changes occurring at a dizzying pace: relatively new buildings are torn down to make way for even newer, shinier skyscrapers; whole neighborhoods are obliterated in the name of progress; reclaimed land is taken from an ever-shrinking harbor; and traditional villages are replaced with satellite towns. Hong Kong's city skyline has surged upward and outward so dramatically since my first visit in 1983, it sometimes seems like decades rather than a year or two must have elapsed each time I see it anew. Change is commonplace, and yet it's hard not to lament the loss of familiar things that have suddenly vanished; it's harder still not to brood over what's likely to come. But Hong Kong, founded by the narcotics trade and created to make money, has always been an ever-changing place. There are strikingly few monuments or statues to the city's past. Even the city's original settlement long ago lost most of its colonial-age buildings.

But don't worry. If this is your first trip to Hong Kong, you're much more likely to notice its Chinese aspects than its Western elements. Live fish awaiting their end at open-air seafood restaurants, bamboo scaffolding, herb medicinal shops, street-side markets, Chinese characters on huge neon signs, wooden fishing boats, shrines to the kitchen god, fortune-tellers, temples, laundry fluttering from bamboo poles, dim sum trolleys, and the clicking of mahjongg tiles all conspire to create an atmosphere overwhelmingly Chinese.

HONG KONG'S PEOPLE & CULTURE

With a population of approximately 6.8 million, Hong Kong is mostly Chinese—some 98% of its residents are Chinese, more than half of them born in Hong Kong. But the Chinese themselves are a diverse people and they hail from different parts of the country. Most are **Cantonese,** from southern China, the area just beyond Hong Kong's border—hence, Cantonese is one of the official languages of the city. Other Chinese include the **Hakka,** traditionally farmers, whose women are easily recognizable by their hats with a black fringe, and the **Tanka,** the majority of Hong Kong's boat population. Hong Kong's many Chinese restaurants specializing in Cantonese, Szechuan, Chiu Chow, Pekingese, Shanghainese, and other regional foods are testaments to the city's diversity.

Hong Kong is one of the most densely populated areas in the world, at about half the size of Rhode Island, with a total land area of slightly more than 645 square kilometers (400 sq. miles). The best place to appreciate this is atop Victoria Peak, where you can feast your eyes on Hong Kong's famous harbor and, as far as the eye can see, mile upon mile of high-rise apartments. If Hong Kong were a vast plain, it would be as ugly as Tokyo. But it's saved by undulating mountain peaks, which cover virtually all of Hong Kong and provide a dramatic background to its cityscape and coastal areas.

Most public housing is in the New Territories, in a forest of high-rises that leaves foreign visitors aghast. Each apartment building is approximately 30 stories tall, containing about 1,000 apartments and 3,000 to 4,000 residents. Seven or eight apartment buildings comprise an estate, which is like a small town with its own name, shopping center, recreational and sports facilities, playgrounds, schools, and social services. Each apartment is indescribably small by Western standards—approximately 76 square meters (250 sq. ft.), with a single window. It consists of a combination living room/bedroom, a kitchen nook, and bathroom, and is typically shared by a couple with one or two children. According to government figures, every household in Hong Kong has at least one television; many have one for each member of the household, even if the house consists of only one or two rooms. But as cramped, unimaginative, and sterile as these housing projects may seem, they're a vast improvement over the way much of the population used to live. They also account for most of Hong Kong's construction growth in the past 2 decades, especially in the New Territories.

CULTURAL LIFE

Much of Hong Kong's drama is played in its streets, whether it's amateur Chinese opera singers at the famous Temple Street Night Market, a festival featuring parades or dances, a fortune-teller in front of a Taoist temple, or a morning practitioner of *tai chi* (Chinese shadowboxing) going through the slow, dance-like motions of this ancient form of exercise in a public park. Virtually everything the Chinese consider vital still thrives in Hong Kong, including ancient religious beliefs, superstitions, traditional Chinese medicine, wedding customs, and festivals based on the Chinese lunar calendar.

Of the various Chinese performing arts, **Chinese opera** is the most popular and widely loved. Dating back to the Mongol period, it has always appealed to both the ruling class and the masses. Virtue, corruption, violence, and lust are common themes, and performances feature elaborate costumes and makeup, haunting atonal orchestrations, and crashing cymbals. The actor-singers train for years to achieve the high-pitched and shrill falsettos that characterize Chinese opera. The costumes signify specific stage personalities: Yellow is reserved for emperors, while purple is the color worn by barbarians. Unlike Western performances, Chinese operas are noisy affairs, with families coming and going during the long performances, chatting with friends, and eating.

2 Planning a Trip to Hong Kong

VISITOR INFORMATION

Though the information supplied by the Hong Kong Tourist Association offices abroad are sometimes not as up-to-date or as thorough as those available in Hong Kong itself or through the Internet (**www.hkta.org**), before you leave home, it's worth contacting a local HKTA office for general information and a map.

IN THE UNITED STATES

- **New York:** 115 E. 54th St., 2nd floor, New York, NY 10022-4512 (☎ **212/ 421-3382;** fax 212/421-4285; e-mail: hktanyc@hkta.org). **Chicago:** 401 N.

Michigan Ave., Suite 1640, Chicago, IL 60611 (☎ **312/329-1828;** fax 312/329-1858; e-mail: hktachi@hkta.org). **Los Angeles:** 10940 Wilshire Blvd., Suite 2050, Los Angeles, CA 90024-3915 (☎ **310/208-4582;** fax 310/208-1869; e-mail: hktalax@hkta.org).

In Canada

- **Toronto:** Hong Kong Trade Center, 3rd floor, 9 Temperance St., Toronto, ON M5H 1Y6 (☎ **416/366-2389;** fax 416/366-1098; e-mail: hktayyz@hkta.org).

In the United Kingdom

- **London:** 6 Grafton St., London W1X 3LB, England (☎ **0171/533-7100;** fax 0171/533-7111; e-mail: hktalon@hkta.org).

In Australia & New Zealand

- **Sydney:** Hong Kong House, Level 4, 80 Druitt St., Sydney, NSW 2000, Australia (☎ **02/9283 3083;** fax 02/9283-3383; e-mail: hktasyd@hkta.org).
- **Auckland:** P.O. Box 2120, Auckland, New Zealand (☎ **09/307-2580;** fax 09/307-2581; e-mail: hktaauk@hkta.org).

In Hong Kong

The **HKTA** has an office at the **Hong Kong International Airport** located in the arrivals hall, just past Customs. It's open during peak hours, generally from 7am to 11pm daily. In town, there are two HKTA offices on both sides of the harbor. In Kowloon, there's a convenient office in Tsim Sha Tsui in the Star Ferry concourse, open daily 8am to 6pm. On Hong Kong Island, a larger, main HKTA office is located in the Central District at 99 Queen's Rd. Central, also open daily 8am to 6pm. It's rather inconvenient, however, about a 10-minute walk west of the Star Ferry pier and Central MTR station.

Otherwise, if you have a question about Hong Kong, you can also call the **HKTA Visitor Hotline** (☎ 852/2508 1234), available daily from 8am to 6pm. After hours, a telephone-answering device will take your call, and a member of HKTA will contact you.

The HKTA publishes a large assortment of free, excellent literature about Hong Kong. "The Official Hong Kong Guide," published monthly, is a booklet available at HKTA offices and in the guest rooms of most upper- and medium-range hotels. It contains a lot of practical information, including a short description of Chinese foods, shopping tips, a rundown of organized sightseeing tours, an overview of Hong Kong's major attractions, and a listing of festivals, events, and exhibits being held that month.

"Traveller's Guide" is a booklet that also gives general information on sightseeing, shopping, dining, and organized tours. Another useful booklet is "The Official Dining, Entertainment & Shopping Directory," which lists addresses and telephone numbers for hundreds of restaurants, nightlife venues, and shops. "Museums & Heritage" describes Hong Kong's most important historical monuments, architectural treasures, and museums dedicated to Hong Kong's past.

You can also get a free map of Hong Kong from HKTA, providing close-ups of Tsim Sha Tsui, the Central District, Wan Chai, and Causeway Bay. There are also brochures outlining each of HKTA's organized tours. In addition, invaluable leaflets are available showing the major bus routes throughout Hong Kong, as well as ferry schedules to outlying islands.

To find out what's going on during your stay in Hong Kong, pick up "Hong Kong Diary," a HKTA leaflet published weekly which tells what's happening in theater, music, and the arts, including concerts and special exhibitions in museums. Be on the lookout, too, for free city magazines distributed to venues throughout town with information on concerts, exhibitions, the cinema, and special events, including *HK Magazine, Where Hong Kong,* and *bc.* In addition, "Hong Kong Life," published as a supplement by the *Hong Kong Standard* newspaper on Sunday, describes what's going on in Hong Kong during the next week; the *South China Morning Post* carries an entertainment section on Friday.

ENTRY REQUIREMENTS

A valid passport is the only document most tourists, including Americans, need to enter Hong Kong. Americans can stay up to 1 month without a visa. Australians, New Zealanders, Canadians, and other British Commonwealth citizens can stay 3 months without a visa, while citizens of the United Kingdom can stay for 6 months without a visa.

CUSTOMS REGULATIONS

Visitors are allowed to bring in, duty free, 1 liter of alcohol and 200 cigarettes (or 50 cigars or 250 grams of tobacco). There are no restrictions on currencies brought into or taken out of Hong Kong.

MONEY

The basic unit of currency is the **Hong Kong dollar,** which is divided into 100 **cents.** Three banks, the Hongkong and Shanghai Banking Corporation, the Bank of China, and, to a lesser degree, the Standard Chartered Bank, all issue their own colorful notes, in denominations of HK$10 (which is being phased out), HK$20, HK$50, HK$100, HK$500, and HK$1,000. Coins are minted in bronze for 10¢, 20¢, and 50¢ pieces, in silver for HK$1, HK$2, and HK$5, and in nickel and bronze for HK$10.

Throughout Hong Kong you'll see the dollar sign ("$"), which of course refers to Hong Kong dollars, not U.S. dollars. To avoid confusion, this guide identifies Hong Kong dollars with the symbol "HK$" (followed in parentheses by the U.S. dollar conversion).

CURRENCY EXCHANGE & RATES   Since 1983, the Hong Kong dollar has been pegged to the U.S. dollar at a rate of approximately HK$7.80 to each US$1. However, when exchanging money at banks, hotels, and currency exchange offices, you'll receive less than the official conversion rate, generally from 7.77 (at a bank) to 7.25 (at a hotel). For the sake of convenience, all conversions in this chapter are based on HK$7.70 to US$1 (or HK$1 = US13¢), then rounded off. For British readers, the exchange rate is approximately HK$12.25 to £1 (or HK$1 = 6 pence).

ATM machines are found throughout Hong Kong, including the airport, Star Ferry concourses in Kowloon and Central, all major MTR subway stations, and major banks like the Hongkong and Shanghai Banking Corporation. Although the exchange rate is probably the best you'll find, commission fees eat up the advantage unless you exchange amounts high enough to warrant the fee. Credit cards are accepted at most hotels and major restaurants and shops; note, however, that when bargaining at shops, you'll do better if you pay in cash.

Otherwise, banks offer the best exchange rate, though rates can vary. Some offer a good rate but charge a commission; others may not charge commission but have lower rates. Most charge a commission on **traveler's checks** (unless, of course, you're cashing American Express checks at an American Express office), but the exchange rate is better for traveler's checks than cash. **Banking hours** are generally Monday through Friday from 9am to 4:30pm and Saturday from 9am to 12:30pm, though some banks stop their transactions an hour before closing time.

Most plane tickets now include departure tax in their price, but if yours doesn't, you'll be required to pay HK$50 (US$6.50) for both adults and children.

Hotels give a slightly less favorable exchange rate but are open nights and weekends. Money changers are found in tourist areas, especially along Nathan Road in Tsim Sha Tsui. Avoid them if you can, since they often charge a commission or a "changing fee," or give a much lower rate.

WHEN TO GO

Hong Kong's peak tourist season used to be in the spring and fall, but now tourists are flocking to the territory year-round. No matter when you go, therefore, make hotel reservations in advance, particularly if you're arriving during the Chinese New Year or one of the festivals described below. Major conventions and trade fairs can also tie up the city's hotel rooms.

CLIMATE   Because of its subtropical location, Hong Kong's weather is generally mild in winter and uncomfortably hot and humid in summer, with an average annual rainfall of 89 inches. The most pleasant time of year is late September to early December, when skies are clear and sunny, temperatures are in the 70s, and the humidity drops to 70%. January and February are the coldest months, with temperatures often in the 50s. In spring (March to May), the temperature can range between 60°F and 80°F and the humidity rises to about 84%, with fog and rain fairly common. That means there may not be much of a view from the cloud-enveloped Victoria Peak.

By summer, temperatures are often in the 90s, humidity can be 90% or more, and there's little or no relief even at night. This is when Hong Kong receives the most rain; it's also typhoon season. However, Hong Kong has a very good warning system, so there's no need to worry about the physical dangers of a tropical storm. The worst that can happen is that you may have to stay in your hotel room for a day or more, or that your plane may be delayed or diverted.

PUBLIC HOLIDAYS   Hong Kong has 17 public holidays a year, including some of the festivals described below. The majority are Chinese and therefore are celebrated according to the changing lunar calendar. Since most shops, restaurants, and attractions remain open except during the Chinese New Year, the holidays should not cause any inconvenience to visitors. Banks, however, do close.

Public holidays are: New Year's Day (January 1), Chinese Lunar New Year (2 days falling between the end of January through mid-February), Easter (Good Friday, Saturday, Easter Sunday, and Easter Monday), Ching Ming Festival (early April), Labor Day (May 1), Buddha's Birthday (end of April or May), Tuen Ng Festival (Dragon Boat Festival, June), Establishment Day of the Special Administrative Region (Hong Kong's return to China; June), day following the Mid-Autumn Festival (September), National Day (October 1), Chung Yeung Festival (October), Christmas Day (December 25), and the first weekday after Christmas.

HEALTH CONCERNS

No shots or inoculations are required for entry to Hong Kong from the United States, but you will need proof of a vaccination against cholera if you have been in an infected area during the 14 days preceding your arrival. Check with your travel agent or call the Hong Kong Tourist Authority if you are traveling elsewhere in Asia before reaching Hong Kong.

If you need a prescription from a Hong Kong doctor filled, there are plenty of drugstores in the territory. They will not, however, fill prescriptions from elsewhere.

Generally, you're safe eating anywhere in Hong Kong, even at roadside food stalls. Stay clear of local oysters and shellfish, however, and remember that many restaurants outside the major hotels and tourist areas include MSG in their dishes as a matter of course.

GETTING THERE
BY PLANE

Hong Kong's outdated Kai Tak airport was retired in 1998, replaced with the much larger **Hong Kong International Airport** (☎ 852/2181 0000), situated about 15 miles from Hong Kong's central business district at Chek Lap Kok. In the arrivals hall, just past Customs, visitors can pick up English-language maps and sightseeing brochures and get directions to their hotel at the **Hong Kong Tourist Association (HKTA),** open daily during peak hours from 7am to 11pm. Also in the arrivals hall are the **Hong Kong Hotel Association,** open daily from 6am to midnight, where you can book a room in one of some 60 member hotels free of charge, and the **Macau Government Tourist Office,** open daily from 9am to 1pm, 1:30 to 6pm, and 6:30 to 10:30pm.

FROM THE UNITED STATES & CANADA   Airlines that fly nonstop between North America and Hong Kong include Canadian Airlines International (☎ 800/426-7000; www.cdnair.ca), with daily flights from Vancouver; Cathay Pacific Airways (☎ 800/233-2742; www.cathay-usa.com), with daily service from Los Angeles, Vancouver, and Toronto; Singapore Airlines (☎ 800/742-3333; www.singaporeair.com), with daily service from San Francisco; and United Airlines (☎ 800/241-6522; www.united.com), with daily service from San Francisco, Los Angeles, and Chicago. Northwest Airlines (☎ 800/225-2525; www.nwa.com), Japan Airlines (☎ 800/525-3663; www.japanair.com), Korean Air (☎ 800/438-5000; www.koreanair.com), and Philippines Airlines (☎ 800/435-9725; www.philippineair.com) also fly to Hong Kong from the U.S., but make stops en route.

FROM THE UNITED KINGDOM   Cathay Pacific (☎ 171/747 8888; www.cathaypacific.com), British Airways (☎ 0845 77 33377; www.britishairways.com), and Virgin Atlantic Airways (☎ 01293 747 747; www.virgin.com) offer daily nonstop service from London to Hong Kong.

FROM AUSTRALIA   Both Cathay Pacific (☎ 131747) and Qantas (☎ 131313; www.qantas.com) offer daily nonstop service from Sydney and Melbourne. From New Zealand, Cathay Pacific (☎ 0508 800454) offers daily nonstop service from Auckland.

Getting Into the City from the Airport

The quickest, most efficient way to get to downtown Hong Kong is via the sleek **Airport Express Line** (☎ 852/2881 8888), located straight ahead after entering the arrivals hall. Trains run every 10 minutes between 6am and 1am and take 20 minutes to reach Kowloon Station (off Jordan Street at the old Jordan Ferry Pier and near hotels in Tsim Sha Tsui and Yau Ma Tei) and 24 minutes to reach Hong Kong Station (on Hong Kong Island, just west of the Star Ferry terminus). Fares are HK$60 (US$7.80) to Kowloon and HK$70 (US$9.10) to Central. Both Kowloon and Hong Kong stations are served by the Mass Transit Railway (MTR) subway system and by taxi service. In addition, free shuttle bus service from both stations deposits passengers at major hotels, departing every 20 minutes between 6am and 11pm.

There is also bus service from the airport. **Airport Shuttle** (☎ 852/2377 0733) provides door-to-door service to major hotels for HK$120 (US$15.60). Slower, with more stops, are **Cityflyer Airbuses** (☎ 852/2873 0818) serving major downtown areas. Most important for tourists are Airbus A21, which travels through Mong Kok, Yau Ma Tei, Jordan, and Tsim Sha Tsui; and Airbuses A11 and A12, which travel to Hong Kong Island. Buses depart every 10 to 15 minutes, with fares costing HK$33 (US$4.30) to Kowloon and HK$40 (US$5.20) to Central and Causeway Bay.

The easiest way to travel from the international airport, of course, is to simply jump in a taxi, which is quite cheap in Hong Kong but expensive for the long haul from the airport. Depending on traffic and your final destination, a taxi to Tsim Sha Tsui costs approximately HK$300 (US$38.95), while a taxi to the Central District will cost about HK$350 (US$44.45). There's also an extra luggage charge of HK$5 (US$0.65) per piece of baggage.

GETTING AROUND

Each mode of public transportation—bus, ferry, tram, and train/subway—has its own fare system and requires a new ticket each time you transfer from one mode of transportation to the other. However, if you're going to be in Hong Kong more than a couple days and will be traveling extensively on the subway or train (including the Airport Express Line), consider purchasing the **Octopus,** which allows users to hop on and off trains, subways, and most (but not all) buses and ferries without having to purchase tickets each time or fumble for exact change. Sold at all MTR subway stations and some ferry piers, this electronic smart card costs HK$150 (US$19.50), including a HK$50 (US$6.50) refundable deposit.

Otherwise, transportation on buses and trams requires the exact fare, making it imperative to have a lot of loose change with you wherever you go.

BY SUBWAY   Hong Kong's **Mass Transit Railway (MTR)** is modern, easy to use, and much faster than the older modes of transportation. Built to transport commuters from the New Territories and linking Kowloon with Hong Kong Island, the MTR consists of four color-coded lines. Single-ticket, one-way fares range from HK$4 to HK$26 (US$0.50 to US$3.40), depending on the distance. Plastic credit-card size tickets are inserted into slots at entry turnstiles. *Be sure to save your ticket until the end of your journey,* when you will again insert it into the turnstile (only this time you won't get it back). The MTR operates daily from 6am to 1am. Note that there are no public restrooms at MTR stations. For general inquiries, call the MTR Hotline at ☎ 852/2881 8888.

BY TRAIN   The **Kowloon-Canton Railway (KCR) East Rail** is useful for traveling north from Kowloon to the New Territories. You can board the train at the KCR Kowloon-Canton Railway Station in Hung Hom (near Tsim Sha Tsui East) or at Kowloon Tong station, also a subway stop. The KCR offers express through-trains to Guangzhou, Shanghai, and Beijing, as well as local commuter service for towns in the New Territories. Sheung Shui is the last stop if you don't have a visa for China. Departing every 3 to 10 minutes daily from approximately 5:35am to midnight, the commuter train from Kowloon to Sheung Shui takes only a half hour and costs HK$9 (US$1.15) for ordinary (second) class and HK$18 (US$2.35) for first class one-way. If you're curious about the New Territories, its scenery, and satellite towns, this is a fast, cheap, and painless way to see it.

BY BUS   Hong Kong buses are a delight—especially the British-style double-deckers—and are good for traveling to places where subways don't go, such as to the southern part of Hong Kong Island and throughout the New Territories. The HKTA has individual leaflets for Hong Kong Island, Kowloon, and the New Territories that show bus routes to most of the major tourist spots, indicating where you can catch the bus, its frequency, and where to get off.

Major bus terminals include Exchange Square in the Central District, Admiralty Station, and the Outlying Islands Ferry Piers, all on Hong Kong Island, and in Tsim Sha Tsui in front of the Star Ferry concourse. Depending on the route, buses run from about 6am to midnight, with fares ranging from HK$1.20 to HK$45 (US$0.15 to US$5.85). Unless you have an Octopus card, good on most buses (see above), *you must have the exact fare,* which you deposit into a box as you get on. Drivers often don't speak English, so you may want to have someone at your hotel write down your destination in Chinese.

BY TRAM Tramlines, found only along the north end of Hong Kong Island, are a great, nostalgic way to travel through the Western District, Central, Wan Chai, and Causeway Bay. Established in 1904, these old, narrow, double-decker affairs clank their way from Kennedy Town in the west to Shau Kei Wan in the east, with one branch making a detour to Happy Valley. Enter the trams from the back and try to get a front-row seat on the top deck. Regardless of how far you go, you pay the exact fare of HK$2 (US$0.25) into a little tin box next to the bus driver as you exit. Trams run daily from 6am to 1am.

BY STAR FERRY A 5-minute trip across Victoria Harbour on one of the white-and-green ferries of the Star Ferry Company, in operation since 1898, is one of the most celebrated rides in the world and one of Hong Kong's top attractions. It costs only HK$1.70 (US$0.22) for ordinary (second) class; if you really want to splurge, it's HK$2.20 (US$0.28) for first class on the upper deck. Ferries ply the waters between Central and Tsim Sha Tsui daily from 6:30am to 11:30pm, with departures every 3 to 5 minutes, except for early in the morning or late at night, when they leave every 10 minutes. Don't miss it.

BY OTHER FERRIES Besides the Star Ferry, there are other ferries crossing the harbor between Kowloon and Hong Kong Island, including ferries between Central and Hung Hom, hoverferries between Central and Tsim Sha Tsui East, and ferries between Tsim Sha Tsui and Wan Chai.

There's also a large fleet serving the outlying islands, with most ferries departing Hong Kong Island from the Outlying Islands Ferry Piers located just west of the Star Ferry terminus in Central. The latest schedules and fares are available from the Hong Kong Tourist Association (HKTA) or by calling the Hong Kong Ferry Company Ltd. (HKF) (☎ **852/2542 3081** or 852/2542 3082).

BY TAXI As a rule, taxi drivers in Hong Kong are strictly controlled and fairly honest. Taxis free to pick up passengers display a red "for hire" flag in the windshield during the day and a lighted taxi sign on the roof at night. Fares start at HK$15 (US$1.95) for the first 2 kilometers (1.24 miles), then are HK$1.40 (US$0.18) for each 200 meters (275 yd.). Luggage costs an extra HK$5 (US$0.65) per piece, and taxis ordered by phone add a HK$5 (US$0.65) surcharge. Trips through tunnels cost extra: HK$20 (US$2.60) for the Cross-Harbour Tunnel, HK$30 (US$3.90) for the Eastern Harbour Crossing, HK$45 (US$5.85) for the Western Harbour Tunnel, and HK$5 (US$0.65) for the Aberdeen Tunnel.

BY MAXICABS & MINIBUSES These small buses are the poor person's taxis; although they are quite useful for the locals, they're a bit confusing for tourists. There are two types of vehicles: the green-and-yellow ones, called **maxicabs,** which follow fixed routes, charge fixed rates ranging from HK$2 to HK$22.50 (US$0.25 to US$2.90) depending on the distance, and require the exact fare as you enter; and the red-and-yellow **minibuses,** which have no fixed route and will stop when you hail them. Fares for these range from HK$2 to HK$20 (US$0.25 to US$2.60), depending on the distance, but are often higher on rainy days, race days, or cross-harbor trips. You pay as you exit; just yell when you want to get off.

BY CAR   Rental cars are not advisable in Hong Kong and hardly anyone uses them, even businesspeople. Nothing is so far away that you can't get there easily, quickly, and cheaply by taxi or public transport, and parking is at a premium. If you're unconvinced, Avis, Budget, and Hertz have branches here, along with a couple of dozen local firms. A valid driver's license is required, and remember, traffic flows on the left-hand side of the street.

BY RICKSHAW   Rickshaws hit the streets of Hong Kong in the 1870s and were once the most common form of transport in the colony. Now they're almost a thing of the past—no new licenses have been issued for years. A few ancient-looking men hang around the Star Ferry terminal in the Central District, but I've never once seen them hauling a customer. Instead, they make money by charging HK$50 (US$6.50) for tourists who want to take their picture. If you do want to take a ride, they'll charge up to HK$100 (US$13) to take you around the block, by far the most expensive form of transportation in Hong Kong. Be sure to negotiate the price first.

Fast Facts: Hong Kong

American Express   American Express offices are located up on the first floor of the Henley Building, 5 Queen's Rd. Central, in the Central District (☎ **852/ 2110 2008**), and at 48 Cameron Rd. (☎ **852/2311 3399**) in Tsim Sha Tsui. Both offices are open Monday through Friday from 9am to 5pm and on Saturday from 9am to 12:30pm.

Business Hours   Although opening hours can vary among banks, banking hours are generally Monday through Friday from 9am to 4:30pm and Saturday from 9am to 12:30pm. Keep in mind, however, that some banks stop their transactions an hour before closing time.

Most business offices are open Monday through Friday from 9am to 5pm, with lunch hour from 1 to 2pm; Saturday business hours are generally 9am to 1pm.

Most shops are open 7 days a week. Shops in the Central District are generally open from 10am to 6pm; in Causeway Bay and Wan Chai, from 10am to 9:30pm; in Tsim Sha Tsui, from 10am to 9 or 10pm (and some even later than that); and in Tsim Sha Tsui East, from 10am to 7:30pm. As for bars, most stay open until at least 2am; some stay open until the crack of dawn.

Doctors & Dentists   Most first-class hotels have medical clinics with registered nurses, as well as doctors on duty at specified hours or on call 24 hours. Otherwise, the concierge can refer you to a doctor or dentist. See below for hotels with in-house physicians. The U.S. consulate can also provide information on English-speaking doctors. If it's an emergency, dial 999 or contact one of the recommendations under "Hospitals," below.

Drug Laws   Penalties for possession, use, and trafficking in illegal drugs are strict, and convicted offenders can expect lengthy jail sentences and fines. Just say no.

Electricity   The electricity used in Hong Kong is 220 volts, alternating current (AC), 50 cycles (in the U.S. it's 110 volts and 60 cycles). Most hotels have adapters to fit shavers of different plugs and voltages, but for other gadgets you'll need transformers and plug adapters (Hong Kong outlets take plugs with three rectangular prongs).

Embassies & Consulates   Since visa, passport, and other departments may have limited open hours, you should telephone for exact opening hours. **United States:** 26 Garden Rd., Central District (☎ **852/2523 9011**). **Canada:** 12th Floor of Tower One, Exchange Square, 8 Connaught Place, Central District (☎ **852/2810 4321**). **U.K.:** 1 Supreme Court Rd., Central District (☎ **852/ 2901 3000**). **Australia:** 23rd and 24th floors, Harbour Centre, 25 Harbour Rd., Wan Chai, on Hong Kong Island (☎ **852/2827 8881**). **New Zealand:** 65th floor of Harbour Centre, 25 Harbour Rd., Wan Chai, on Hong Kong Island (☎ **852/2525 5044**).

Emergencies   All emergency calls are free—just dial **999** for police, fire, or ambulance.

Hospitals   The following hospitals can help you around the clock: Queen Mary Hospital, 102 Pokfulam Rd., Hong Kong Island (☎ **852/2855 4111**); Hong Kong Adventist Hospital, 40 Stubbs Rd., Hong Kong Island (☎ **852/2574 6211**); and Queen Elizabeth Hospital, 30 Gascoigne Rd., Kowloon (☎ **852/ 2958 8888**).

Internet/E-mail   All upper-range and most medium-priced hotels in Hong Kong are equipped with data ports that allow guests to use laptop computers. Internet access is generally available upon purchase of an Internet access card for HK$100 (US$13), valid for unlimited use for 5 days. Otherwise, many hotels offer business centers as well, most equipped with computers and Internet access (fees may be charged).

Outside hotels, **Pacific Coffee** is a chain of coffee shops, several with a couple of computers customers can access for free, including shop 1002 in the International Finance Center (IFC), above Hong Kong Station in Central (☎ **852/ 2868 5100**), open Monday to Saturday from 7am to 10pm and Sunday 8:30am

---

Telephone Dialing Info at a Glance

- **To place a call from your home country to Hong Kong:** Dial the international access code (011 in the U.S., 0011 in Australia, 0170 in New Zealand, 00 in the U.K.), plus the country code (**852**), plus the phone number (for example, 011-852-0000 00000).

- **To place a call within Hong Kong:** Simply dial the local number.

- **To place a direct international call from Hong Kong:** Dial the international access code (**001**) plus the country code, the area or city code, and the number (for example, 001-01-212/000-0000).

- For local directory assistance: Dial 1081.

- To reach the international operator: Dial 10013.

- **To call AT&T direct:** Call ☎ 800/96 1111; for MCI call ☎ 800/961121; and for Sprint call ☎ 800/96-1877.

- **International country codes** are as follows: Australia 61, Burma 95, Cambodia 855, Canada 1, Indonesia 62, Laos 856, Malaysia 60, New Zealand 64, the Philippines 63, Singapore 65, Thailand 66, U.K. 44, U.S. 1, Vietnam 84.

to 9pm; and in the Peak Tower on Victoria Peak (☎ **852/2849 6608**), open Monday to Thursday 8am to 10:30pm and Friday to Sunday 8am to 11pm.

Languages   English and Cantonese are the two official languages. Most residents of Hong Kong speak Cantonese, and English is generally only understood in hotels and tourist shops.

Liquor Laws   The drinking age in Hong Kong is 18. The hours for bars vary according to the district, though those around Lan Kwai Fong and Tsim Sha Tsui stay open the longest, often till dawn.

Police   You can reach the police for an emergency by dialing ☎ **999,** the same number as for a fire or an ambulance. There's a crime hot line (☎ **852/2527 7177**), a 24-hour service that also handles complaints against taxis.

Post Offices/Mail   Most hotels have stamps and can mail your letters for you. Otherwise, most post offices are open Monday through Friday from 9:30am to 5pm and Saturday from 9:30am to 1pm. The main post office is on Hong Kong Island at 2 Connaught Place, in the Central District near the Star Ferry concourse; it has longer hours, Monday to Saturday 8am to 6pm and Sunday 8am to 2pm. On the Kowloon side, post offices are located at 405 Nathan Rd., between the Jordan and Yau Ma Tei MTR subway stations; and at 10 Middle Rd., 1 block north of Salisbury Road in Tsim Sha Tsui. Airmail letters up to 20 grams and postcards cost HK$3.10 (US$0.40) to the United States or Europe. Mailboxes are a bright orange-red. For general inquiries, call ☎ **852/ 2921 2222.**

If you don't know where you'll be staying in Hong Kong, you can still receive mail via the post office. Have it sent to you "Post Restante" at the General Post Office, 2 Connaught Place, Central District, Hong Kong Island, which is located near the Star Ferry terminus. It will hold mail for 2 months; when you come to collect it, be sure to bring along your passport for identification.

Safety   Hong Kong is relatively safe for the visitor, especially if you use common sense and stick to such well-traveled nighttime areas as Tsim Sha Tsui, Lan Kwai Fong, or Causeway Bay. The main thing you must guard against is pickpockets, who often work in groups to pick men's pockets or slit open a woman's purse, quickly taking the valuables and then relaying them on to accomplices who disappear in the crowd. You should also be on guard on crowded public conveyances such as the MTR. To be on the safe side, keep your valuables in your hotel's safety-deposit box and carry your passport or large amounts of money in a money belt.

Taxes   Hotels will add a 10% service charge and a 3% government tax to your bill. Restaurants and bars will automatically add a 10% service charge, but there is no tax. There's an airport departure tax of HK$50 (US$6.50) for adults and children older than 12, but this is usually—but not always—included in your ticket price. If you're taking the boat to Macau, you must pay a Hong Kong departure tax of HK$19 (US$2.45), which is already included in the price of your boat ticket.

Telephone & Fax   Local calls made from homes, offices, shops, and restaurants are free, so don't feel shy about asking to use the phone. From public phone booths, a local call costs HK$1 (US$0.13) for each 5 minutes; from hotel rooms, about HK$4 to HK$5 (US$0.50 to US$0.65). For directory assistance, dial ☎ 1081 for local numbers, 10013 for international inquiries.

Most hotels will handle faxes and overseas calls and offer direct dialing. Otherwise, long-distance calls can be made from specially marked International Dialing Direct (IDD) public phones. The cheapest and most convenient method for making international calls is with a PhoneCard, which comes in denominations ranging from HK$50 to HK$300 (US$6.50 to US$39) and is available at Star Ferry piers, HKTA information offices, and machines located beside telephones. You can also charge your telephone call to a major credit card by using one of about 100 credit-card phones in major shopping locations.

As this book goes to press, the cost of a direct-dial call to the United States, made by dialing 001-1-area code-telephone number, is HK$6.80 (US$0.90) per minute. Otherwise, you can make a collect call from any public or private phone by dialing 10010. You can also make cashless international calls from any telephone in Hong Kong by using Home Direct, which gives you immediate and direct access to an operator in the country you're calling. For information on dial access numbers for Home Direct, phone locations, places where phone cards can be purchased and operated, time zones, or other matters pertaining to international calls, call 10013.

Time Zone   Hong Kong is 13 hours ahead of New York, 14 hours ahead of Chicago, and 16 hours ahead of Los Angeles. Hong Kong does not observe daylight saving time, so subtract 1 hour from the above times in summer.

Tipping   Even though restaurants and bars will automatically add a 10% service charge to your bill, you're still expected to leave small change for the waiter. A general rule of thumb is to leave 5%, but in most Chinese restaurants where meals are usually inexpensive it's acceptable to leave change up to HK$5 (US$0.65). In the finest restaurants you should leave 10%.

You're also expected to tip taxi drivers, bellhops, barbers, and beauticians. For taxi drivers, simply round up your bill to the nearest HK$1 or add a HK$1 (US$0.15) tip. Tip people who cut your hair 5% or 10%, and give bellhops HK$10 to HK$20 (US$1.30 to US$2.60), depending on the number of your bags. If you use a public restroom with an attendant, you may be expected to leave a small gratuity—HK$2 (US$0.25) should be enough. In addition, chambermaids and room attendants are usually given about 2% of the room charge.

Toilets   The best places to track down public facilities in Hong Kong are in its many hotels. Fast food restaurants and shopping malls are another good bet. There may be an attendant on hand who will expect a small tip of about HK$2 (US$0.25). Note that there are no public facilities at any of the MTR subway stations.

Water   It's perfectly safe to drink Hong Kong's water, but visitors prone to upset stomachs should stick to bottled water, which is widely available. In summer, it's wise to carry bottled water with you.

3 Accommodations

The good news is that many hotels, in the wake of the Asian financial crisis and a decrease in tourism since the 1997 handover, have been offering promotional packages or reduced rates. The bad news is that rates are still high compared to those of most Southeast Asian destinations, and inexpensive hotels are few and far between. The rates listed below are the hotels' official, or "rack" rates, but you should be able to do better by calling the hotel directly and asking whether any promotional fares are available. Remember too that rates can vary significantly within a hotel, depending on views and height: rooms on the highest floors facing famous Victoria Harbour are understandably the most expensive. At any rate, because of trade fairs held at Hong Kong's expanded convention center, you'd be wise to make room reservations several months in advance.

Although the greatest concentration of hotels is on the Kowloon side, Hong Kong is so compact and easily traversed by public transportation that location is not the issue it is in larger, sprawling metropolises. Hong Kong's top hotels are among the best in the world, many with sweeping views of Victoria Harbour and offering superb service and amenities, including so-called "executive floors" catering mostly to business travelers with such added luxuries as express check-in, private lounge, complimentary breakfast and cocktails, and often in-room fax machines and other perks. Moderate hotels comprise the majority of hotels in Hong Kong. They have rather small rooms compared to their American counterparts, cater largely to tour groups, and usually offer such in-room amenities as hair dryers, room safes, cable or satellite TV with in-house pay movies, and tea- and coffee-making facilities, as well as a tour desk and no-smoking rooms. Inexpensive hotels are in short supply and offer just the basics of bathroom, air-conditioning, televisions, and telephones.

TAXES & SERVICE CHARGES   Keep in mind that prices given in this book are for room rates only—a 10% service charge and 3% government tax will be added to your bill.

KOWLOON
VERY EXPENSIVE

○ **The Peninsula Hotel.** Salisbury Rd., Tsim Sha Tsui, Kowloon, Hong Kong. ☎ **852/ 2920 2888** or 800/262-9467 in the U.S. Fax 852/2722 4170. www.peninsula.com. E-mail: pen@peninsula.com. 300 units. A/C MINIBAR TV TEL. HK$2,900–HK$4,600 (US$377– US$598) single or double; from HK$5,200 (US$656) suite. AE, CB, DC, MC, V. MTR: Tsim Sha Tsui.

This is Hong Kong's most famous hotel, the place to stay if you are an incurable romantic, have a penchant for the historical, and can afford its high prices. Built in 1928, it exudes elegance from its white-gloved doormen to one of the largest fleets of Rolls-Royces in the world. Priding itself on service, it maintains one of the highest staff-to-guest ratios in Hong Kong. Its lobby, reminiscent of a Parisian palace with high gilded ceilings, pillars, and palms, has long been Hong Kong's foremost spot for people-watching. In 1993, a magnificent 32-story tower was constructed behind the older hotel, providing breathtaking views of Victoria Harbour from guest rooms fitted with amenities almost beyond belief. Even jaded travelers are likely to be impressed. Spacious rooms are all equipped with a silent fax machine with your own personalized phone number (written messages are sent via fax; telephone messages by voice mail); computer hookups; TV with laser-disc/CD player (free CDs and movies available); three telephones with two lines in the bedroom and a hands-free phone in the bathroom (local calls are free); room safe; and a box in the closet where attendants can place your morning newspaper or take your dirty shoes for complimentary cleaning. Huge bathrooms are equipped with their own TV, mood lighting, separate bath and shower stall, and two sinks, each with a magnifying mirror. It may be worth the extra money to spring for a harbor view, since inland views are a disappointment and those in the older part of the hotel are slightly claustrophobic.

Every restaurant in the Peninsula comes highly recommended. For decades, the hotel's premier restaurant has been Gaddi's, offering traditional French cuisine as well as live music and dancing in the evening. Equally popular is the tower's top-floor

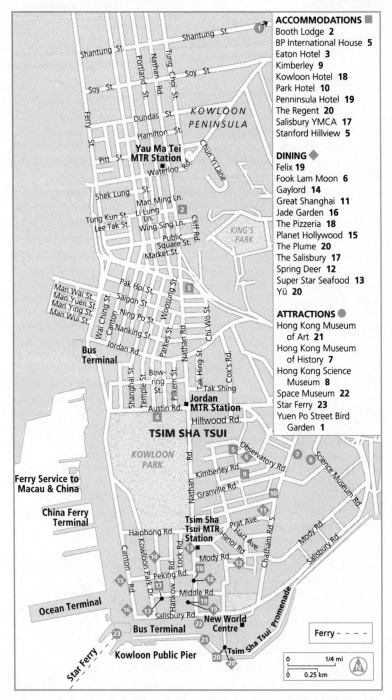

ACCOMMODATIONS ■
Booth Lodge **2**
BP International House **5**
Eaton Hotel **3**
Kimberley **9**
Kowloon Hotel **18**
Park Hotel **10**
Penninsula Hotel **19**
The Regent **20**
Salisbury YMCA **17**
Stanford Hillview **5**

DINING ◆
Felix **19**
Fook Lam Moon **6**
Gaylord **14**
Great Shanghai **11**
Jade Garden **16**
The Pizzeria **18**
Planet Hollywood **15**
The Plume **20**
The Salisbury **17**
Spring Deer **12**
Super Star Seafood **13**
Yü **20**

ATTRACTIONS ●
Hong Kong Museum of Art **21**
Hong Kong Museum of History **7**
Hong Kong Science Museum **8**
Space Museum **22**
Star Ferry **23**
Yuen Po Street Bird Garden **1**

KOWLOON PENINSULA

Yau Ma Tei MTR Station

KING'S PARK

Bus Terminal

Jordan MTR Station

TSIM SHA TSUI

KOWLOON PARK

Ferry Service to Macau & China

China Ferry Terminal

Tsim Sha Tsui MTR Station

Ocean Terminal

New World Centre

Bus Terminal

Kowloon Public Pier

Star Ferry

Tsim Sha Tsui Promenade

Ferry - - - -

| 0 | | 1/4 mi |
| 0 | 0.25 km | |

restaurant, Felix, which features an avant-garde interior designed by Philippe Starck, innovative Pacific Rim crossover cuisine, dramatic views of Hong Kong, and a bar and disco. Other good choices include The Verandah for Continental cuisine, Chesa for Swiss food, Spring Moon for Cantonese specialties, and Imasa for traditional Japanese food. The Lobby is Hong Kong's best spot for people-watching and afternoon tea.

Hotel amenities include an indoor swimming pool with sun terrace, health club with exercise equipment, Jacuzzis, saunas, steam rooms, solariums, rooftop helipad, soundproofed music room with grand piano where guests can practice, designer-brand shopping arcade, business center, beauty salon, barber, tour desk, concierge, 24-hour room service, Rolls-Royce limousine service, free newspaper, free shoeshine, nightly turndown, baby-sitting, same-day laundry service, in-house nurse, and complimentary welcoming tea.

The Regent Hong Kong. 18 Salisbury Rd., Tsim Sha Tsui, Kowloon, Hong Kong. [[☎ **852/ 2721 1211** or 800/545-4000 in the U.S. and Canada. Fax 852/2739 4546. www.rih.com. E-mail: reservations.rhk@fourseasons.com. 602 units. A/C MINIBAR TV TEL. HK$2,950–HK$4,250 (US$383–US$552) single or double; from HK$5,000 (US$649) junior suite. Children under 19 stay free in parents' room. AE, CB, DC, MC, V. MTR: Tsim Sha Tsui.

The Peninsula's biggest rival, The Regent Hong Kong boasts what may well be the best views of Victoria Harbour from Tsim Sha Tsui. In fact, you can't get much closer to the water than this—the hotel is located on a projection of reclaimed land and sits on more than 120 pylons sunk into the harbor. Built in 1981 of polished rose granite and rising 17 stories high, it has a bare lobby of polished granite and marble, with the magnificent view of the harbor and Hong Kong Island serving as the lobby's focal point. The Regent (a Four Seasons hotel) also has some of Hong Kong's best restaurants, all with great views, an exclusive shopping mall, and the world's largest fleet of Daimler limousines outside the U.K. The outdoor pool's sun terrace and whirlpools overlook the harbor, as do two-thirds of the rooms, with floor-to-ceiling and wall-to-wall windows. The remaining (less expensive) rooms face the outdoor swimming pool and landscaped sun terrace; some of these are actually larger than the harbor-view rooms. All rooms feature such updated facilities as a room safe and a cordless keyboard and TV that provide Internet and e-mail access (fee: HK$158/US$20.50 per 24 hours), as well as a dedicated data port for quick computer link-up. Fax machines are available free of charge. Worth noting are the Regent's spacious bathrooms, each fitted in Italian marble with a sunken bathtub and separate shower unit, and an air purification system in all guest rooms. But unlike most deluxe hotels, there are no designated executive floors, the underlying concept being that all rooms should offer the same degree of efficient and personalized service.

Other facilities include a business center, exercise studio (open 24 hours), health spa, upscale shopping arcade, beauty salon, concierge, 24-hour room service, house doctor, baby-sitting, free newspaper, free bottled water, nightly turndown, limousine service, same-day laundry service, and complimentary welcoming tea.

The **Plume** is one of Hong Kong's finest French restaurants, while **Yü** is the city's trendiest seafood restaurant. **Lai Ching Heen** is an elegant Cantonese restaurant, while the **Harbour Side** offers a harbor view along with its inexpensive snacks and meals throughout the day. **Club Shanghai,** decorated like a 1930s Shanghai nightclub, offers live music and dancing.

MODERATE

BP International House. 8 Austin Rd., Tsim Sha Tsui, Kowloon, Hong Kong. ☎ **852/2376 1111** or 800/223-5652 in the U.S. and Canada. Fax 852/2376 1333. www.megahotels. com.hk. E-mail: bpi.reservations@megahotels.com.hk. 535 units. A/C TV TEL. HK$990–HK$1,450 (US$129–US$188) single; HK$1,100–HK$1,500 (US$143–US$195) double;

HK$1,600–HK$1,800 (US$208–US$234) Corporate double; from HK$3,100 (US$403) suite. Children under 13 stay free in parents' room. AE, DC, MC, V. MTR: Jordan.

This is one of the newer moderately priced lodgings in Tsim Sha Tsui, built in 1993 and rising 25 stories above the north end of Kowloon Park. The word "House" in its name is misleading, since it is actually a rather large hotel, modern with a spacious but utilitarian lobby and catering mainly to tour groups, school excursions, and budget-conscious business travelers. In addition to a Chinese restaurant and coffee shop, there are vending machines that dispense beverages on each floor and a token-operated laundry (though laundry and dry-cleaning services are available). Within the same building is a full-line health club (for an extra fee), and the indoor and outdoor public swimming pools in Kowloon Park are just a stone's throw away. The guest rooms, located on the 14th through 25th floors, are clean, pleasant, and modern, with satellite TV and voice mail. Although the hotel is located inland, the best and priciest rooms offer great views of the harbor (with height limitations in Kowloon now removed due to the relocation of the airport, however, you can expect taller buildings to eclipse those views). Business travelers usually opt for one of the Corporate Rooms on the top three floors, which provide such extras as minibars, room safes, hair dryers, and radios.

Kimberley Hotel. 28 Kimberley Rd., Tsim Sha Tsui, Kowloon, Hong Kong. ☎ **852/2723 3888** or 800/223-5652 in the U.S. and Canada. Fax 852/2723 1318. www.kimberley.com.hk. E-mail: kh-rsvn@kimberley.com.hk. 546 units. A/C MINIBAR TV TEL. HK$1,100–HK$1,750 (US$143–US$227) single; HK$1,200–HK$1,850 (US$156–US$240) double; from HK$2,150 (US$279) suite. AE, DC, MC, V. MTR: Tsim Sha Tsui.

Opened in 1991, the 20-story Kimberley is on the northern edge of Tsim Sha Tsui, about a 15-minute walk from the Star Ferry. It caters to both the tourist and business trade, including many Japanese. Guest rooms, constructed with V-shaped windows that let in more sunlight and allow for more panoramic—though unscenic—views, are equipped with hair dryers, very firm beds, phone in the bathroom, and tea- and coffee-making facilities. The most expensive rooms are on higher floors and are larger, but even these are rather small. Facilities include two restaurants serving Japanese and Chinese food, coffee shop offering lunch and dinner buffets, cocktail lounge, shopping arcade, business center, sauna (extra fee charged), fitness room, putting green, and golf cage. Services include free newspaper, room service (6am to midnight), same-day laundry service, house doctor, and baby-sitting.

✪ Kowloon Hotel. 19–21 Nathan Rd., Tsim Sha Tsui, Kowloon, Hong Kong. ☎ **852/2929 2888** or 800/262-9467 in the U.S. Fax 852/2739 9811. www.peninsula.com. E-mail: khh@peninsula.com. 736 units. A/C MINIBAR TV TEL. HK$1,300–HK$2,000 (US$169–US$260) single; HK$1,400–HK$2,100 (US$182–US$273) double; from HK$3,500 (US$454) suite. AE, CB, DC, MC, V. MTR: Tsim Sha Tsui.

If you like high-tech, this is the place for you. The Kowloon is a modern glass-walled structure right behind The Peninsula (both hotels are under the same management). The Star Ferry is just a few minutes' walk away. Although rooms are minuscule, with no views from their V-shaped bay windows, the hotel offers the most technically advanced rooms in its price category. Every room boasts an interactive telecenter (a multi-system TV offering satellite programming and linked to a central computer), which doubles as a word-processor, interfaces with an in-room fax machine (each with its own private number and serving also as a printer), gives free access to the Internet (guests receive personal e-mail addresses), and provides such information as up-to-the-minute flight details, incoming messages, hotel bills, and video games. Guests can also retrieve voice mail messages electronically from outside the hotel. Other room features include tea- and coffee-making facilities, room safe, and hair dryer. Facilities include a business center, a shopping arcade, and four restaurants, including a very good pizzeria and a restaurant specializing in international buffets. Services include free newspaper, limousine service, baby-sitting, same-day laundry service, and room service (from 6:30am to 2am).

Park Hotel. 61–65 Chatham Rd. S., Tsim Sha Tsui, Kowloon, Hong Kong. ☎ **852/2366 1371.** Fax 852/2739 7259. www.parkhotel.com.hk. E-mail: hotel@parkhotel.com.hk. 423 units. A/C MINIBAR TV TEL. HK$900–HK$1,300 (US$117–US$169) single; HK$1,000–HK$1,400 (US$130–US$182) double; from HK$2,000 (US$260) suite. 1 child under 12 can stay free in parents' room. AE, DC, MC, V. MTR: Tsim Sha Tsui.

Built in 1961 and kept up-to-date with renovations, the clean and comfortable Park has long been one of the best-known medium-priced hotels in Kowloon. You can't go wrong staying here. Especially popular with Australians and Asians, this hotel probably has the largest rooms in its price range, a plus if you're tired of cramped quarters, and rooms come with hair dryers, room safes, and tea- and coffee-making facilities. The best rooms are those on the upper floors of the 16-floor property; the lower floors can be noisy, especially rooms facing the street. Facilities include Western and Cantonese restaurants, coffee shop, bar, shopping arcade, and beauty salon. Services include room service (6:30am to 12:50am), medical service, baby-sitting, same-day laundry service, and limousine service. Its location on the border between Tsim Sha Tsui and Tsim Sha Tsui East, across from the Science Museum and Museum of History, is not as convenient as that of many other hotels in this category, though it is within walking distance of the MTR (about 6 minutes) and hoverferry service to Central (about 8 minutes).

✪ **Stanford Hillview Hotel.** 13–17 Observatory Rd., Tsim Sha Tsui, Kowloon, Hong Kong. ☎ **852/2722 7822** or 800/858-8471 in the U.S. Fax 852/2723 3718. www.stanfordhillview.com. E-mail: sfhvhkg@netvigator.com. 163 units. A/C MINIBAR TV TEL. HK$1,080–HK$1,480 (US$140–US$192) single or double. Long-term rates available. AE, DC, MC, V. MTR: Tsim Sha Tsui.

This small, intimate hotel, built in 1991, is near the heart of Tsim Sha Tsui and yet it's a world away from it too, located on top of a hill in the shade of some huge banyan trees next to the Royal Observatory with its colonial building and greenery. Knutsford Terrace, an alley with trendy bars and restaurants, is just a couple minutes' walk away. Its lobby is quiet and subdued (quite a contrast to most Hong Kong hotels) and its staff is friendly and accommodating. The hotel has a business center, a fitness room, and outdoor golf-driving nets, as well as a restaurant offering international buffets and à la carte menus of Western and Asian dishes. All rooms have data ports and tea- and coffee-making facilities. The most expensive are on higher floors; ask for one that faces the Observatory. Room service is available from 7am to 11pm, and there's also same-day laundry service and baby-sitting. All in all, a very civilized place, but it is a hike uphill to the hotel.

INEXPENSIVE
✪ **Booth Lodge.** 11 Wing Sing Lane, Yau Ma Tei, Kowloon, Hong Kong. ☎ **852/2771 9266.** Fax 852/2385 1140. 53 units. A/C MINIBAR TV TEL. HK$620–HK$1,200 (US$81–US$156) single or double. Rates include breakfast. AE, MC, V. MTR: Yau Ma Tei.

About a 30-minute walk to the Star Ferry but close to the Jade Market, Temple Street Night Market, Ladies' Market, and MTR station, Booth Lodge is just off Nathan Road on the seventh floor of the Salvation Army building. It has a comfortable lobby and an adjacent coffee shop offering à la carte dining and very reasonably priced lunch and dinner buffets with Chinese, Japanese, and Western selections. Best is the restaurant's outdoor brick terrace overlooking a wooded hillside, where buffet barbecues are held Friday and Saturday evenings. Rooms, all twins or doubles and either standard rooms or larger deluxe rooms, are clean and most have hair dryers. Some that face Nathan Road have views of a harbor in the distance, though those facing the wooded hillside are quieter. There's laundry service, as well as a tour desk.

✪ **Eaton Hotel.** 380 Nathan Rd., Yau Ma Tei, Kowloon, Hong Kong. ☎ **852/2782 1818.** Fax 852/2782 5563. www.eaton-hotel.com. E-mail: inquiry@eaton-hotel.com. 464 units. A/C MINIBAR TV TEL. HK$750–HK$2,600 (US$97–US$338) single or double. AE, DC, MC, V. MTR: Jordan.

This accommodation has more class and more facilities than most others in its price range, making it one of my top picks. A handsome, 21-story hotel located above a shopping complex not far from the night market on Temple Street, it features one of the longest hotel escalators I've ever seen, which takes guests straight up to the fourth-floor lobby. The lobby lounge is bright and cheerful, with a four-story glass-enclosed atrium that overlooks a garden terrace with a water cascade, where you can sit outside with drinks in nice weather. The guest rooms are small but come with such comforts as feather duvet, tea- and coffee-making facilities, hair dryer, pay movies, safe, voice mail, and data ports. Rooms on the top floors and in a new addition are more expensive, with fax machines and fancier decor, including some innovatively designed rooms with views of a distant harbor. Otherwise, the best views are of Nathan Road. Facilities include a very good Cantonese restaurant, coffee shop, cozy bar with a "colonial" atmosphere and terrace seating, nice but small rooftop pool with sunning terrace, fitness room, and business center. Services include complimentary newspaper, room service (7am to 2am), baby-sitting, and same-day laundry service.

✪ **The Salisbury YMCA.** Salisbury Rd., Tsim Sha Tsui, Kowloon, Hong Kong. ☎ **852/ 2369 2211.** Fax 852/2739 9315. www.ymcahk.org.hk. E-mail: room@ymcahk.org.hk. 365 units. A/C. HK$660 (US$86) single; HK$705–HK$865 (US$92–US$112) double; from HK$1,200 (US$156) suite. Dormitory bed HK$190 (US$25). AE, DC, MC, V. MTR: Tsim Sha Tsui.

For decades the overwhelming number-one choice among inexpensive accommodations in Hong Kong has been the YMCA on Salisbury Road, which has the good fortune of being right next to The Peninsula Hotel on the waterfront, just a 2-minute walk from both the Star Ferry and subway station. Although the Salisbury may seem expensive for a YMCA, the location and facilities are worth the price; here you have Tsim Sha Tsui's cheapest rooms with harbor views. Modern and spacious, the Salisbury YMCA welcomes families as well as individual men and women, with 19 single rooms (none with harbor view) and more than 280 double rooms (the most expensive of which have great harbor views), as well as suites (with and without harbor views). Although simple in decor, rooms are on a par with those at more expensive hotels, with such in-room amenities as telephones with voice mail, satellite TVs with complimentary in-house movies, data ports, stocked refrigerators, tea- and coffee-making facilities, safes, and hair dryers. For budget travelers, there are 14 dormitory-style rooms, available only to visitors staying in Hong Kong fewer than 10 days (write or fax for reservations; walk-ins are also accepted). There are three food and beverage outlets, including the **Salisbury Restaurant,** which serves buffet meals. A sports facility boasts two indoor swimming pools (one a lap pool, the other a children's pool, both free for all hotel guests except those in the dormitory) and a fitness gym, two squash courts, and indoor climbing wall (fee charged). There's a fourth-floor terrace with play equipment for children. Laundry service, baby-sitting, and room service (7am to 11pm) are available.

CENTRAL DISTRICT
VERY EXPENSIVE

✪ **Island Shangri-La Hong Kong.** Pacific Place, Supreme Court Rd., Central, Hong Kong. ☎ **852/2877 3838** or 800/942-5050 in the U.S. and Canada, or 852/2877 3838. Fax 852/2521 8742. www.shangri-la.com. E-mail: isl@shangri-la.com. 565 units. A/C MINIBAR TV TEL. HK$2,300–HK$3,450 (US$299–US$448) single; HK$2,500–HK$3,650 (US$325–US$474) double; from HK$5,600 (US$727) suite. Children under 18 stay free in parents' room. AE, DC, MC, V. MTR: Admiralty.

Hong Kong Island's tallest hotel (measured from sea level) offers the ultimate in extravagance and luxury, rivaling the grand hotels in Paris or London. More than 700 Viennese chandeliers, lush Tai Ping carpets, artistic flower arrangements, and more than 500 paintings and artwork adorn the hotel. The 17-story atrium, which stretches from the 39th to the 56th floor, features a marvelous 16-story-high Chinese painting, believed to be the largest landscape painting in the world. The hotel is enhanced by the connecting Pacific Place shopping center, with its many options in dining; Hong Kong Park is across the street. Rooms, among the largest in Hong Kong and the largest on Hong Kong Island, face either the Peak or Victoria Harbour and feature marble-topped desks, data ports and dual phone lines to accommodate personal computers, a hands-free phone, Chinese lacquerware TV cabinets and movies on demand, silk bedspreads, a safe, free bottled water, and oversize bathrooms equipped with two sinks, separate tub and shower areas (in the harbor-view rooms only), bidet, bath scales, and even jewelry boxes. Fresh flowers and teddy bears placed on pillows during nightly turndown are nice touches. Guests paying rack rates receive such additional services as free transportation from and to the airport, free laundry and dry cleaning throughout their stay, complimentary breakfast, free local telephone calls, and a late 6pm check out.

Petrus is the hotel's signature restaurant, occupying a prime spot on the top floor and serving continental cuisine with a view. Next door is **Cyrano,** a lounge offering jazz entertainment every night and stunning views of the harbor. The **Lobster Bar** is *the* place to go for meals featuring the sea's best crustacean, but for casual dining with a breezy Californian atmosphere, highly recommended is the **Island Café,** specializing in buffets. Other restaurants serve Cantonese and Japanese fare.

Facilities and services include outdoor heated swimming pool (big enough for swimming laps), Jacuzzi, sauna, steam bath, health club, 24-hour business center, drugstore, barbershop, beauty salon, shopping arcade, concierge, free newspaper, 24-hour room service, same-day laundry service, welcoming tea, nightly turndown, limousine service, baby-sitting, medical clinic, and free shuttle service to Queen's Pier in Central and the Convention Centre.

✪ **Mandarin Oriental.** 5 Connaught Rd., Central, Hong Kong. ☎ **852/2522 0111** or 800/526-6566 in the U.S. and Canada. Fax 852/2810 6190. www.mandarin-oriental.com. E-mail: reserve-mohkg@mohg.com. 542 units. A/C MINIBAR TV TEL. HK$2,800–HK$4,500 (US$364–US$584) single; HK$3,050–HK$4,750 (US$396–US$617) double; from HK$5,500 (US$714) suite. AE, CB, DC, MC, V. MTR: Central.

With so many newer hotels on Hong Kong Island, the Mandarin, a 25-story landmark built in 1963, seems like a familiar old-timer. Famed for its service and consistently rated one of the top hotels in the world, it has a great location in the heart of Hong Kong's business district (not far from Star Ferry) and attracts mostly a business clientele. Its restaurants are among the best in Hong Kong, but its indoor pool is disappointingly small. Spacious rooms face either the harbor or inland (those facing the harbor even come with binoculars), most with balconies, which is rare for Hong Kong but admittedly noisy. Rooms feature all the amenities and facilities you could possibly want, including two phone lines and data ports, and purified tap water for drinking, but if you are still in need of something, the staff will make every effort to fulfill your wishes.

Several of the restaurants have a well-deserved reputation for excellent cuisine, including the **Mandarin Grill** for seafood, the **Man Wah** for Cantonese food, and the very trendy **Vong** with its Asian-influenced French food and spectacular views. **The Captain's Bar,** just off the hotel lobby, is an intimate, cozy bar popular with Central's executive and professional crowd, while the **Chinnery,** with more than 100 single malt whiskies, remained off-limits to women until, incredibly enough, 1990.

Other facilities and services include a fitness center, sauna, whirlpool, business center, art gallery, shopping arcade, Cuban-style cigar divan, beauty salon, barbershop, tour desk, concierge, secretarial services, complimentary fruit basket, free newspaper, 24-hour room service, nightly turndown, same-day laundry service, house doctor, limousine service, and baby-sitting.

CAUSEWAY BAY/WAN CHAI
VERY EXPENSIVE

Grand Hyatt Hong Kong. 1 Harbour Rd., Wan Chai, Hong Kong. ☎ **852/2588 1234,** or 800/233-1234 in the U.S. and Canada. Fax 852/2802 0677. www.hongkong.hyatt.com. E-mail: info@grandhyatt.com.hk. 570 units. A/C MINIBAR TV TEL. HK$3,200–HK$3,500 (US$416–US$454) single; HK$3,450–HK$3,750 (US$448.50–US$487) double; HK$3,950–HK$4,250 (US$513.50–US$552.50) Regency Club executive floor double; from HK$5,500 (US$715) suite. Children under 12 stay free in parents' room (maximum: 3 persons per room). AE, DC, MC, V. MTR: Wan Chai.

In a city with so many first-class hotels and such stiff competition, sooner or later a hotel had to exceed all the others in opulence and grandeur. Seemingly no expense was spared in creating Hyatt International's Asian flagship hotel. Its lobby, decorated to resemble the salon of a 1930s art deco luxury ocean liner, flaunts space, with huge

Tips for the Business Traveler in Hong Kong

- **Bring plenty of business cards.** They are exchanged constantly, and you'll be highly suspect without them (if you run out, hotel business centers can usually arrange to have new ones printed within 24 hours). When presenting your card, hold it out with both hands, turned so that the receiver can read it. Chinese names are written with the family name first, followed by the given name and then the middle name.
- **Use formal names for addressing business associates,** unless told to do otherwise. You'll find that many Hong Kong Chinese used to dealing with foreigners have adopted a Western first name.
- **Shaking hands is appropriate** for greetings and introductions.
- **Business attire**—a suit and tie for men—is worn throughout the year, even in summer.
- **Entertainment** is an integral part of conducting business in Hong Kong, whether it's a meal in which the host orders the food and serves his or her guests, an evening at the race tracks, or a round of golf.
- **If an invitation is extended, it is understood that the host will treat.** Do not insist on paying; this will only embarrass your host. Accept graciously, and promise to pick up the tab next time around.

Central District

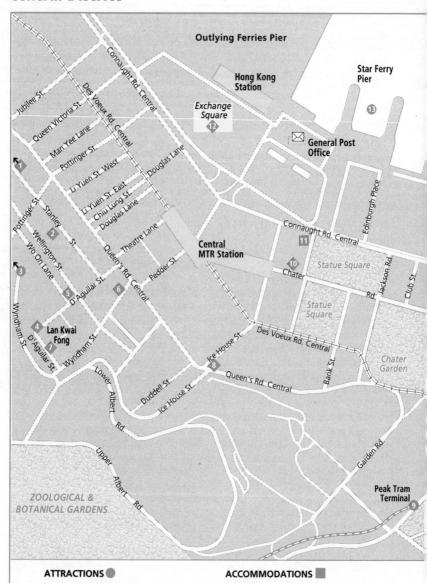

ATTRACTIONS ●
Hong Kong Museum of
    Medical Science **3**
Man Mo Temple **3**
Peak Tram Terminal **9**
Star Ferry **13**

ACCOMMODATIONS ■
Empire Hotel **18**
Grand Hyatt **20**
Harbour View International **20**
Island Shangri-La **16**
Madarin Oriental **20**
The Park Lane **11**

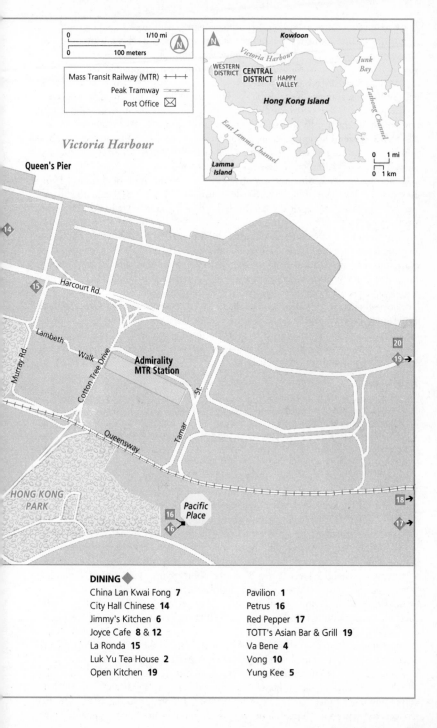

Victoria Harbour

Queen's Pier

0   1/10 mi
0   100 meters

Mass Transit Railway (MTR) ┼┼┼┼
Peak Tramway ═════
Post Office ⊠

Kowloon

Victoria Harbour

WESTERN
DISTRICT   CENTRAL
           DISTRICT   HAPPY
                      VALLEY

Junk
Bay

Hong Kong Island

East Lamma Channel

Tathong Channel

Lamma
Island

0   1 mi
0   1 km

Harcourt Rd.

Lambeth

Walk

Murray Rd

Cotton Tree Drive

Admirality
MTR Station

Tamar St.

Queensway

HONG KONG
PARK

Pacific
Place

DINING ◆

China Lan Kwai Fong **7**
City Hall Chinese **14**
Jimmy's Kitchen **6**
Joyce Cafe **8** & **12**
La Ronda **15**
Luk Yu Tea House **2**
Open Kitchen **19**

Pavilion **1**
Petrus **16**
Red Pepper **17**
TOTT's Asian Bar & Grill **19**
Va Bene **4**
Vong **10**
Yung Kee **5**

black granite columns, massive flower arrangements, palm trees, bubbling fountains, and furniture and statuettes reminiscent of that era. Located on the waterfront near the Convention Centre and only a 5-minute walk from the Wan Chai Star Ferry pier that delivers passengers to Tsim Sha Tsui, it offers smart-looking, contemporary rooms. Pluses are the specially made beds with Egyptian cotton sheets, sliding clothes rack in the closet, and coffee table books. Rooms also have fax machines with personalized numbers, data ports, cordless keyboards to access the Internet and e-mail through an interactive TV at speeds 50 times faster than a conventional modem (fee: HK$85/$11 per 24 hours), voice mail, on-command movies, free bottled water, safes, and marble bathrooms complete with 18-karat-gold fixtures, separate bathtub and shower areas, and bathroom scales and magnifying mirrors. Some 70% of the rooms provide a harbor view, while the rest offer a view of the free-form pool (one of Hong Kong's largest, with views of the harbor and surrounded by lush landscaping) and garden with partial glimpses of the harbor. Extra pampering is offered by the Regency Club's eight floors.

Other facilities and services include a children's pool, two rooftop tennis courts, golf driving range, jogging track, Jacuzzi, fitness club, business center, beauty salon, concierge, free newspaper, 24-hour room service, limousine service, baby-sitting, nightly turndown, complimentary shuttle to Central and Admiralty MTR station, and same-day laundry service.

The bright and airy **Grissini** serves authentic Milanese cuisine, while **One Harbour Road** is a split-level upscale Cantonese restaurant. **JJ's** is one of Hong Kong's hottest and largest nightspots, featuring live music, a disco, separate bar areas, and even a pizza parlor. More intimate is the **Champagne Bar,** with Hong Kong's most extensive list of the bubbly stuff and live entertainment.

EXPENSIVE

The Park Lane. 310 Gloucester Rd., Causeway Bay, Hong Kong. ☎ **852/2293 8888** or 800/223-5652 in the U.S. and Canada. Fax 852/2576 7853. www.parklane.com.hk. E-mail: info@parklane.com.hk. 792 units. A/C MINIBAR TV TEL. HK$1,700–HK$2,800 (US$220–US$364) single or double; HK$3,000–HK$3,500 (US$390–US$454) Premier Club executive rooms; from HK$4,500 (US$584) suite. Children under 12 stay free in parents' room (maximum: 3 persons per room). AE, DC, MC, V. MTR: Causeway Bay.

Although it's inland, I've always liked the location of this hotel—across from huge Victoria Park (good for joggers) and close to many area restaurants, shops, and department stores. First opened in 1974 and extensively renovated in 1994, it attracts primarily business travelers with rooms that vary in price according to floor level and view—the best are those facing Victoria Park with the harbor beyond. All rooms come with king-size bed or two double beds, voice mail, and safes. Hotel facilities and services include a fitness center, business center, shopping arcade, 24-hour room service, same-day laundry service, free newspaper, house clinic, baby-sitting, limousine service, same-day film processing, and nightly turndown. Extra perks available to guests who stay on Premier Club executive floors include complimentary breakfast, cocktails, shoe polishing, clothes pressing, fruit basket, fax machines, free local calls, and drinks.

Located on the top floor with views of Victoria Park and the harbor, **27 Restaurant & Bar** serves international cuisine with an Asian twist. **Stix** is a combination bar/American restaurant/dance club. Hotel facilities and services include a fitness center with exercise room, sauna, massage, steam bath, and Jacuzzi; business center; hair salon; shopping arcade; tour desk; concierge; 24-hour room service; same-day laundry service; free newspaper; house clinic; baby-sitting; limousine service; same-day film processing; and nightly turndown.

MODERATE

⭘ **Empire Hotel.** 33 Hennessy Rd., Wan Chai, Hong Kong. ☎ **852/2866 9111,** or 800/830-6144 in the U.S. and Canada. Fax 852/2861 3121. www.asiastandard.com. E-mail: ehhresa@asiastandard.com. 345 units. A/C MINIBAR TV TEL. HK$1,400–HK$1,800 (US$182–US$234) single or double; HK$2,000 (US$260) Empire Plus room; from HK$2,200 (US$264) suite. AE, DC, MC, V. MTR: Wan Chai.

Nicely situated in Wan Chai and popular with mid-level business travelers for its convenience to Central, this hotel offers good value, with many of the same amenities, services, and facilities found in larger, higher-priced hotels, including a rooftop outdoor heated swimming pool (large enough for swimming laps); fitness room; sauna; business center; concierge; tour desk; Western, Shanghainese, and Cantonese restaurants; and wine bar.

Rooms, with rates based on the size of the room (none provide a view of the harbor), are comfortable and pleasant, equipped with a safe, tea- and coffee-making facilities, hair dryer, fax machine, and the Data View Information System, which allows guests to receive messages on their television sets, check flight schedules, check information (on stocks, finance, or shopping), play video games, and view the hotel services directory. There are also in-house pay movies and satellite programs. Services include a free newspaper, room service (6:30am to midnight), same-day laundry service, free shuttle service to Hong Kong Station in Central, limousine service, medical and dental services, and baby-sitting.

⭘ **Harbour View International House.** 4 Harbour Rd., Wan Chai, Hong Kong. ☎ **852/ 2802 0111.** Fax 852/2802 9063. www.harbour.ymca.org.hk. E-mail: hvihymca@netvigator. com. 320 units. A/C MINIBAR TV TEL. HK$1,150–HK$1,650 (US$149–US$214.) single or double. Children under 12 stay free in parents' room. AE, DC, MC, V. MTR: Wan Chai.

Opened in 1986, this YMCA occupies a prime spot on the Wan Chai waterfront, next to the Hong Kong Arts Centre and not far from the Convention Centre. Rooms, all twins or doubles, are simple but functional. Facilities and services include a coffee shop, one restaurant with a view of the harbor serving Chinese and Western food, room service (7:15am to 11:30pm), baby-sitting, and laundry service. Best of all, more than half the rooms have V-shaped windows that face the harbor—one of the least expensive views in Hong Kong. Rooms that face inland are even cheaper.

4 Dining

Dining is one of *the* things to do in Hong Kong. Not only is the food excellent, but the range of culinary possibilities is staggering, with an estimated 8,700 restaurants to choose from. Most are Chinese, offering what may well be the greatest concentration of Chinese restaurants in the world and specializing in regional cuisines ranging from Cantonese and Pekingese to Shanghainese and Szechuan.

Other national cuisines are also popular, including French, Italian, American, Thai, Indian, and Japanese. Although Hong Kong's most well-known, exclusive restaurants have long been located in first-class hotels accustomed to catering to well-heeled visitors, neighborhood establishments offering health-conscious menus, Pacific Rim crossover cuisine, or innovative dishes created by talented, ambitious chefs have exploded onto the culinary scene in recent years. I'm convinced you can eat as well in Hong Kong as in any other city in the world.

Another welcome trend is the fact that dining prices in Hong Kong have actually fallen since the handover, especially for fixed-price meals. Especially good bargains are the buffets (available at many hotel restaurants), particularly those offering international cuisines, and fixed-price lunches. Avoid dining from 1 to 2pm on weekdays, the traditional lunch hour for office workers, and keep in mind that closing hours are strictly observed, with the last orders usually taken at least 30 minutes beforehand.

You can expect to spend more than HK$300 (US$39) for dinner per person, excluding drinks, for **expensive** restaurants, HK$150 to HK$300 (US$19.50 to US$39) for **moderate** restaurants, and less than HK$150 (US$19.50) for **inexpensive** restaurants. In addition, a 10% service charge will be added to your bill.

CANTONESE CUISINE   The majority of Chinese restaurants in Hong Kong are Cantonese; this is not surprising since most Hong Kong Chinese are originally from Canton Province (now called Guangdong). It's also the most common style of Chinese cooking around the world and probably the one with which you're most familiar. Among Chinese, Cantonese cuisine is considered the finest, and many Chinese emperors employed Cantonese chefs in their kitchens.

Since the Cantonese eat so much seafood, your best choice in a Cantonese restaurant is fish. Among the recommended choices are garoupa (a local fish), pomfret, red mullet, sole, abalone, and sea cucumber. Shark's-fin soup is an expensive delicacy. Other Cantonese specialties include roast goose, duck, and pigeon; panfried lemon chicken; and stir-fried minced quail and bamboo shoots rolled in lettuce and eaten with the fingers.

Another popular Cantonese dish is dim sum, eaten for breakfast and lunch and with afternoon tea; in Hong Kong it is especially popular for Sunday family outings. It consists primarily of finely chopped meat, seafood, and vegetables wrapped in thin dough and then either steamed, fried, boiled, or braised. Dim sum can range from steamed dumplings to meatballs, fried spring rolls, and spareribs.

Many Cantonese restaurants offer dim sum from about 7:30am until 4pm, traditionally served from trolleys wheeled between the tables, but nowadays available from a written menu. The trolleys are piled high with steaming bamboo baskets, so ask the server to let you peek inside. If you like what you see, simply nod your head. A serving of dim sum usually consists of two to four pieces on a plate and averages about HK$20 to HK$30 (US$2.60 to US$3.90) per plate. Your bill is calculated at the end of the meal by the number of plates on your table or by a card stamped each time you order a dish. But it's more than just the price that draws me to traditional dim sum restaurants—they are noisy, chaotic, and the perfect place to read a newspaper or gossip. No one should go to Hong Kong without visiting a dim sum restaurant at least once, as much for the atmosphere as for the food.

For a light snack or late-night meal, try *congee,* which is a rice porridge popular for breakfast and usually topped with a meat, fish, or vegetable. Many of Hong Kong's countless, cheapest restaurants specialize in congee, as well as noodles in soup, the most famous of which is probably *wun tun meen,* noodle soup with shrimp dumplings.

PEKINGESE CUISINE   Many Pekingese dishes originated in the imperial courts of the emperors and empresses and were served at elaborate banquets. This theatrical flamboyance is still evident today in the making of Pekingese noodles and the smashing of the clay around "beggar's chicken." Because of its northern source, the food of Peking (or Beijing) tends to be rather hearty, and richer than Cantonese food. Liberal amounts of peppers, garlic, ginger, leeks, and coriander are used. Noodles and dumplings are more common than rice, and roasting is the preferred method of cooking.

Most famous among Peking-style dishes is Peking (or Beijing) duck, but unfortunately a minimum of six persons is usually required for this elaborate dish. The most prized part is the crisp skin, which comes from air-drying the bird and then coating it with a mixture of syrup and soy sauce before roasting. It's served by wrapping the crisp skin and meat in thin pancakes together with spring onion, radish, and sweet plum sauce.

Another popular dish prepared with fanfare is beggar's chicken: a whole chicken is stuffed with mushrooms, pickled Chinese cabbage, herbs, and onions, wrapped in lotus leaves, sealed in clay, and then baked all day. The guest of honor usually breaks open the hard clay with a mallet, revealing a tender feast more fit for a king than a beggar.

For do-it-yourself dining, try the Mongolian hot pot, where diners gather around a common pot in a scene reminiscent of campfires on the Mongolian steppes. One version calls for wafer-thin slices of meat, usually mutton, to be dipped in a clear stock and then eaten with a spicy sauce. Another variety calls for a sizzling griddle, over which thin-sliced meat, cabbage, bean sprouts, onions, and other vegetables are barbecued in a matter of seconds.

SHANGHAINESE CUISINE   A big, bustling city, Shanghai does not technically have a cuisine of its own. Rather, it incorporates the food of several surrounding regions and cities, making it the most diverse cuisine in China. Because of the cold winters in Shanghai, its food is heavier, richer, sweeter, and oilier than Cantonese or Pekingese food. Because the hot summers can spoil food quickly, specialties include pickled or preserved vegetables, fish, shrimp, and mushrooms. Some dishes are heavy on the garlic, and portions tend to be enormous. The dishes are often stewed, braised, or fried.

The most popular Shanghainese delicacy in Hong Kong is freshwater hairy crab (flown in from Shanghai in autumn) steamed, and eaten with the hands. Other Shanghainese dishes include "yellow fish" (braised eel with huge chunks of garlic) and "drunken chicken" (chicken marinated in Chinese wine). As for the famous hundred-year-old egg, it's actually only several months old, with a limey, pickled-ginger taste. Breads, noodles, and dumplings are favored instead of rice.

SZECHUAN CUISINE   This is my favorite Chinese cuisine—the spiciest, hottest, and with the most fiery style of cooking. The culprit is the Szechuan chile, fried to increase its potency. Seasoning also includes chile-bean paste, peppercorns, garlic, ginger, coriander, and other spices. Foods are simmered and smoked rather than stir-fried. The most famous Szechuan dish is smoked duck; it's seasoned with peppercorns, ginger, cinnamon, orange peel, and coriander; marinated in rice wine; then steamed; and then smoked over a charcoal fire of camphor wood and tea leaves.

Other specialties include panfried prawns in spicy sauce, sour-and-peppery soup, sautéed diced chicken in chile-bean sauce, and dry-fried spicy string beans. Most Szechuan menus indicate which dishes are hot.

KOWLOON
EXPENSIVE

✪ **Felix.** In the Peninsula Hotel, Salisbury Rd., Tsim Sha Tsui. ☎ **852/2920 2888**, ext. 3188. Reservations required. Main courses HK$190–HK$280 (US$24.70–US$36.35). AE, CB, DC, MC, V. Daily 6pm–2am (last order 10:30pm). MTR: Tsim Sha Tsui. PACIFIC RIM/ EAST-MEETS-WEST.

Located on the top floor of the Peninsula's new tower, this strikingly avant-garde restaurant comes as something of a shock in the otherwise staid and traditionally conservative hotel. But what else can you expect from a restaurant designed by Philippe Starck, who was given free rein to create one of Hong Kong's most unusual settings? Your first hint that Felix is not your ordinary dining experience begins with the elevator's wavy walls, which suggest a voyage to the world beyond. The wave pattern continues inside the restaurant—a huge aluminum wavy wall and two glass facades curve seductively to reveal stunning views of the city. Off to the sides of the high-ceilinged dining area, done mostly in mahogany, are two eye-catching zinc cylinders, which vaguely resemble gigantic snails and contain cocoon-cozy bars and what may be one of the world's tiniest discos, complete with a heat-sensitive floor that illuminates dancers' movements. Be sure to check out the rest room for the thrill of its slightly exhibitionist setting. The dining area itself is rather—what can I say—stark, with various styles of tables in marble, glass, and wood, all devoid of such "superfluous" decorations as table linen or flowers. The chair backs, also designed by Starck, are embellished with portraits of himself and his friends, but such details may be overlooked when the restaurant is full. Indeed, even the view tends to take second place in this self-conscious, people-watching setting. The food, featuring Pacific Rim ingredients brought together in East-meets-West combinations, is quite good but also secondary to the setting. Dishes have ranged from a ginger-marinated sea bass on wasabi potatoes with Asian mustard to a hibachi filet of steak with a spicy crab glaze and a smoked chile-tomato sauce.

✪ **Fook Lam Moon.** 53–59 Kimberley Rd., Tsim Sha Tsui. ☎ **852/2366 0286.** Main courses HK$90–HK$190 (US$11.70–US$24.70); dim sum HK$24–HK$50 (US$3.10–US$6.50). AE, DC, MC, V. Daily 11:30am–2:30pm and 6–11:30pm. MTR: Tsim Sha Tsui. CANTONESE.

Upon entering this restaurant (look for the shrine to the kitchen god at the entrance), you immediately feel as if you've stepped back a couple of decades to a Hong Kong that has all but vanished. Considered by some Hong Kong old-timers to be the best Cantonese restaurant in the world, Fook Lam Moon specializes in exotic dishes, including shark's fin, bird's nest, and abalone, served in a variety of ways, as well as more down-to-earth dishes such as fried crispy chicken and panfried lobster bars. Shark's fin, however, is the obvious number-one choice, with 19 different renditions listed on the menu. If you feel like splurging, prices for half a bowl of shark's fin begin at HK$250 (US$32.50). If you aren't careful, you could end up spending a small fortune, but whatever you order it's apt to be memorable. You can also come for dim sum, served daily until 2:30pm.

There's another branch in Wan Chai at 35–45 Johnston Rd. (☎ 852/2866 0663; MTR: Wan Chai), with the same hours.

✪ **The Plume.** In the Regent Hotel, Salisbury Rd., Tsim Sha Tsui. ☎ **852/2721 1211,** ext. 2256. Reservations required (request a window seat). Main courses HK$270–HK$380 (US$35.10–US$49.40); fixed-price dinner HK$480–HK$720 (US$62.40–US$93.60). AE, DC, MC, V. Mon–Sat 7–11pm. MTR: Tsim Sha Tsui. CONTINENTAL/EAST-MEETS-WEST.

Some people consider The Plume the best European restaurant in Hong Kong. Certainly it feels like a great restaurant, sitting right over the water with a grand view of Hong Kong Island and offering very interesting nouvelle cuisine served by an excellently trained staff. Dinner begins with a complimentary serving of Indian bread and goose-liver pâté. The menu, which features only original creations that mix the best of the East and the West, changes every day but always includes the house specialty: a delicate cream of artichoke soup with beluga caviar. Other items have included caramelized bay scallops with lime oil and herb salad, and encrusted bresse pigeon and goose liver with Shanghai baby pak choi in perigord butter. Fixed-price meals include a vegetarian menu. In any case, the food is so imaginative and full of surprises that epicures will want to set up camp.

Yù. In The Regent Hotel, Salisbury Rd., Tsim Sha Tsui. ☎ **852/2721 1211,** ext. 2340. Reservations required (request a window seat). Main courses HK$210–HK$330 (US$27.25–US$42.85). AE, DC, MC, V. Daily 6–11pm. MTR: Tsim Sha Tsui. SEAFOOD.

There's no mistaking what this restaurant serves—it's all right there in front of you, swimming blissfully in a 40-foot "bubble wall," unaware that its days are numbered.

On the other side of the restaurant spreads a stunning view of Victoria Harbour. Located in the swank Regent Hotel but trendily low-key, Yü offers a nice concept—fresh seafood for cautious diners reluctant to tempt fate by ordering locally caught fish in the cheaper, noisier, and more colorful seaside restaurants favored by Hong Kong Chinese. Of course, you pay a mountain more to eat here, but from the looks of things there are plenty of takers. All the seafood, including a variety of garoupa, trout, and other fish, lobsters, crabs, prawns, abalone, mussels, and oysters, are kept alive in tanks until the moment they're ordered. Colorful cards show the day's catch, which can be prepared according to the diner's wishes. However, many diners stick to the imported oysters or begin their meal with the seafood platter—fresh seafood laid on a mountain of ice, including oysters, shrimp, prawns, mussels, and lobster, served with different sauces. Another good choice is the lobster bisque or seafood basket, a variety of bamboo-steamed seafood. Sautéed lobster with black beans and fine noodles is the restaurant's signature dish. There's also a sushi bar, and, surprisingly, vegetarian choices.

MODERATE

✪ **Gaylord.** 23–25 Ashley Rd., Tsim Sha Tsui. ☎ **852/2376 1001.** Main courses HK$62–HK$198 (US$8.05–US$25.70); lunch buffet HK$95 (US$12.35). AE, DC, MC, V. Daily noon–2:30pm and 6–11pm. MTR: Tsim Sha Tsui. INDIAN.

This long-established, first-floor restaurant in the heart of Tsim Sha Tsui is classy and comfortable, with private booths and overstuffed sofas. Singers perform in the evenings. It's popular for its authentic North Indian classics, including tandoori, lamb curry cooked in North Indian spices and herbs, chicken cooked in hot fiery vindaloo curry, prawns cooked with green pepper and spices, and fish with potatoes and tomatoes. There are a dozen vegetarian dishes, and the lunchtime buffet, served every day except Sundays and public holidays until 2:30pm, is a winner.

✪ **Great Shanghai.** 26 Prat Ave., Tsim Sha Tsui. ☎ **852/2366 8158.** Main courses HK$75–HK$210 (US$9.75–US$27.25). AE, DC, MC, V. Daily 11am–2:30pm and 6:30–11pm. MTR: Tsim Sha Tsui. SHANGHAINESE.

Established in 1958, this well-known spot in Tsim Sha Tsui is a big old-fashioned dining hall. It's about as close as you can get to food the way Mom used to cook, assuming, of course, you're from Shanghai. In addition to its bright lights, white tablecloths, and army of waiters in green shirts, Great Shanghai has a gigantic menu with more than 300 items, most in the HK$85 to HK$140 (US$11.05 to US$18.20) range. Since the area of Shanghai has no cuisine of its own, it has borrowed heavily from neighboring provinces, including Szechuan. Try the Shanghainese dumplings, prawns in chile sauce, vegetarian imitation goose, diced chicken with cashews, cold chicken in wine sauce, Szechuan soup, or Peking duck (sliced meat and crispy skin rolled in thin pancakes). The house specialty is beggar's chicken for HK$260 (US$33.80), which is a whole chicken stuffed with herbs, mushrooms, and other ingredients, wrapped in lotus leaves, sealed in clay, and baked all day. It's available only at night (call in your order by mid-afternoon). My own particular favorite is braised shredded eel, but all eel dishes here are good. I've also left the ordering entirely up to the waiter and ended up with a good, well-rounded sampling of Shanghainese food.

Jade Garden Restaurant. Star House (4th floor), 3 Salisbury Rd., Tsim Sha Tsui. ☎ **852/2730 6888.** Main courses HK$58–HK$138 (US$7.55–US$17.90); dim sum HK$16–HK$38 (US$2.10–US$4.95). AE, DC, MC, V. Mon–Sat 10am–3pm and 5:30–11:30pm; Sun and holidays 8am–11:30pm. MTR: Tsim Sha Tsui. CANTONESE.

Jade Garden is part of a wildly successful chain of restaurants owned by the Maxim's Group (other establishments in the group include Sichuan Garden, Shanghai Garden,

Peking Garden, and Chiu Chow Garden, the latter two with branches in Star House). Popular with large Chinese families, Jade Garden is also easy for the Chinese-food novice. Thus, if you don't know much about Chinese food, feel that you should try it, but still aren't very keen on the idea, Jade Garden may be for you. A plus is the view of the harbor afforded by some of the window-side tables. As in most Cantonese restaurants, lunch is dim sum served from trolleys pushed through the aisles. If you'd rather order from the menu or come for dinner, you might consider drunken shrimp in soup, pan-fried stuffed bean curd, fried prawns with lemon peel and orange, or, if you feel like splurging, barbecued Peking duck, which costs HK$290 (US$37.70).

In Tsim Sha Tsui, Jade Garden has another branch at 25–31 Carnarvon Rd. (☎ 852/2369 8311), open daily from 7:30am to midnight. On the Hong Kong side, there's a Jade Garden in the Jardine House at 1 Connaught Place in Central (☎ 852/2524 5098; MTR: Central), open daily from 11am to 3pm and 5:30 to 11:30pm.

✪ The Pizzeria. In the Kowloon Hotel, 19–21 Nathan Rd., Tsim Sha Tsui. ☎ **852/2929 2888**, ext. 3322. Pasta and pizza HK$115–HK$140 (US$14.95–US$18.20); main courses HK$150–HK$195 (US$19.50–US$25.30); lunch buffet HK$140 (US$18.20); fixed-price dinner HK$318–HK$348 (US$41.30–US$45.20). AE, CB, DC, MC, V. Daily noon–3pm, and 6–11pm. MTR: Tsim Sha Tsui. ITALIAN.

Located on the second floor of the Kowloon Hotel (just behind The Peninsula), this casual and bustling dining hall with large windows is one of my favorite places in Tsim Sha Tsui for a relaxed meal at reasonable prices, especially when I want great pizza or pasta and don't feel like dressing up. Despite its name, the restaurant specializes in pasta, with an à la carte menu that changes often but has included such mouthwatering choices as lobster lasagne enriched with fresh spinach and mushrooms, tortellini with mushrooms and truffles in an herb-cream sauce, and ink noodles in a lobster tarragon sauce. There are eight different kinds of pizza, and main courses have included grilled prawns with thyme olive oil in a bed of spinach and saffron risotto, and roasted spring chicken with pancetta, rosemary gravy and pesto polenta. Save room for dessert—they're all delicious.

Planet Hollywood. 3 Canton Rd., Tsim Sha Tsui. ☎ **852/2377 7888.** Main courses HK$78–HK$198 (US$10.15–US$25.75). AE, DC, MC, V. Daily 11:30am–midnight. MTR: Tsim Sha Tsui. AMERICAN.

The escalator ride up to this establishment and the music that accompanies it is like the entrance to a theme park, and that theme is Hollywood. If you're star crazy, this is where you can gawk at such movie memorabilia as the doll Chuckie from *Child's Play,* the car used by Bruce Lee in the *Green Hornet* TV series, and Sharon Stone's ice pick from *Basic Instinct.* When I ate lunch there, Jackie Chan was holding a press conference about his latest film. Large screens show Hollywood hits. The menu includes everything from blackened shrimp and buffalo wings to sandwiches, burgers, pastas, pizzas, fajitas, steak, ribs, and fish and chips, as well as some local dishes such as Hainanese chicken rice and wok-fried beef in oyster sauce. On weekdays, a fixed-price lunch is available until 2pm for HK$50 (US$6.50) which includes a trip through the salad bar and one of a dozen main dishes.

✪ Spring Deer Restaurant. 42 Mody Rd., Tsim Sha Tsui. ☎ **852/2366 4012.** Small dishes HK$50–HK$90 (US$6.50–US$11.70). AE, MC, V. Daily noon–2:30pm and 6–11pm. MTR: Tsim Sha Tsui. PEKINGESE.

An old favorite in Hong Kong, this long-established restaurant offers excellent Pekingese food at reasonable prices. It's cheerful and very accessible to foreigners, but don't expect anything fancy. In fact, your tablecloth may have holes in it, but it will be clean—and the place is usually packed with groups of loyal fans. This is one of the best places to come if you want to try its specialty—honey-glazed Peking duck, which costs HK$280 (US$36.40). Since you'll probably have to wait 40 minutes for the duck if you order it during peak time (7:30 to 9:30pm), it's best to arrive either before or after the rush. Chicken dishes are also well liked, including the deep-fried chicken in soy sauce, and the handmade noodles are excellent. Most dishes come in small, medium, and large sizes; small is suitable for two people. Remember, you'll want to order one dish each, plus a third to share. Unfortunately, since Spring Deer is crowded with groups, the lone diner is apt to be neglected in the shuffle; it's best to come here only if there are at least two of you.

INEXPENSIVE

The Salisbury. In the Salisbury YMCA, 41 Salisbury Rd., Tsim Sha Tsui. ☎ **852/2369 2211,** ext. 1026. Lunch buffet HK$98 (US$12.75); dinner buffet HK$218 (US$28.35). AE, DC, MC, V. Mon–Sat noon–2:30pm, daily 6:30–9:30pm. MTR: Tsim Sha Tsui. INTERNATIONAL.

One of the cheapest places for a filling meal in Tsim Sha Tsui is the YMCA's main restaurant, a bright and cheerful dining hall located on the fourth floor of the south tower. Best are the buffets: the lunch buffet includes a roast beef wagon, as well as other meat dishes, soups, salads, and desserts, while the dinner buffet includes many more entrees plus unlimited soda or beer.

Super Star Seafood Restaurant. 91–93 Nathan Rd., Tsim Sha Tsui. ☎ **852/2366 0878.** Main dishes HK$65–HK$120 (US$8.45–US$15.60); fixed-price menu HK$260–HK$300 (US$33.80–US$39); dim sum HK$19–HK$23 (US$2.45–US$3). AE, DC, MC, V. Daily 8am–midnight. MTR: Tsim Sha Tsui. CANTONESE SEAFOOD.

Walk past the tanks filled with fish, lobsters, and crabs, up to this lively Cantonese restaurant on the first floor, very popular with local Chinese. As its name implies, the restaurant specializes in seafood; recommended are the deep-fried stuffed crab claws, sliced sole with spice and chile, baked lobster with minced spinach, and fish in season. I like it most, however, for the dim sum, served until 5pm daily in a typical Chinese setting. There's no English menu, so you'll just have to choose from the offerings of the various trolleys as they're wheeled past your table.

CENTRAL DISTRICT
EXPENSIVE

China Lan Kwai Fong. 17–22 Lan Kwai Fong, Central. ☎ **852/2536 0968.** Reservations recommended. Main dishes HK$105–HK$245 (US$13.65–US$31.80); fixed-price lunch HK$128–HK$138 (US$16.60). AE, DC, MC, V. Mon–Fri noon–3pm, Sat–Sun 11:30am–3pm; Sun–Thurs 6:30–11pm, Fri–Sat 6:30pm–midnight. MTR: Central. CANTONESE.

This retro-styled restaurant in trendy Lan Kwai Fong is one of Hong Kong's hottest and classiest Chinese restaurants, decorated with antiques, hanging lanterns, ceiling fans, and even birds giving song from inside wooden cages. While the emphasis is on Cantonese food, it offers specialties from other regions as well, including Shanghai, Beijing, and Szechuan. Prawns, for example, are available in six variations, from stir-fried with chiles (Szechuan) to sautéed with black bean and green pepper (Cantonese). Garoupa comes fresh from the restaurant's own tanks. Peking duck (costing HK$380/US$49.35) and beggar's chicken (order in advance for HK$480/US$62.35) are also available. An all-you-can-eat dim sum brunch is available weekends and holidays for HK$128 (US$16.60).

La Ronda. In the Furama Kempinski Hotel (30th floor), 1 Connaught Rd., Central. ☎ **852/ 2848 7422.** Reservations required at dinner. Lunch buffet HK$240 (US$31.20); dinner buffet HK$380 (US$49.40). AE, DC, MC, V. Daily noon–2:30pm and 6:30–10:30pm. MTR: Tsim Sha Tsui. INTERNATIONAL.

A revolving, 30th-floor restaurant with stunning views! The buffets are quite a spread too, offering salads, appetizers, desserts, and international cuisine ranging from sushi and roast beef to curries and Chinese and Western dishes. The food, while mediocre, is more than compensated for by the view, and there's live entertainment nightly.

✪ **Petrus.** In the Island Shangri-La (56th floor), Pacific Place, Supreme Court Rd., Central. ☎ **852/2820 8590.** Reservations recommended. Jacket required. Main courses HK$320–HK$520 (US$41.55–US$67.55); fixed-price lunch HK$278–HK$328 (US$36.10–US$42.60); fixed-price dinner HK$700–HK$850 (US$90.90–US$110.40). AE, DC, MC, V. Mon–Sat noon–3pm, daily 6:30–10:30pm. MTR: Admiralty. FRENCH.

Simply put, the views from this 56th-floor restaurant are breathtaking, probably the best of any hotel restaurant on the Hong Kong side. The only place with a better view is atop Victoria Peak. If you can bear to take your eyes off the windows, you'll find the restaurant decorated like a French castle, with the obligatory crystal chandeliers, black marble and gilded columns, statues, thick draperies, impressionist paintings, murals gracing dome-shaped ceilings, and classical music playing softly in the background. The cuisine emphasizes contemporary Alsatian creations, including light, healthy fare made with olive oil rather than the heavier cream and butter. The menu changes often but has included such intriguing combinations as green asparagus fricassée with roasted prawn and deep-fried egg, and Guinea fowl pie filled with mushroom and chestnut served with duck liver sauce and truffles. As expected, the wine list—particularly the bordeaux—is among the best in Hong Kong. In any case, with the impressive blend of great views, refined ambience, and excellent cuisine, this restaurant is a top choice for a splurge, romantic dinner, or special celebration.

✪ **Va Bene.** 58–62 D'Aguilar St., Central. ☎ **852/2845 5577.** Reservations required. Pasta HK$178–HK$188 (US$23.15–US$24.45); main courses HK$188–HK$258 (US$24.45–US$33.55); fixed-price lunch HK$138 (US$17.90). AE, DC, MC, V. Mon–Fri noon–3pm and daily 7pm–midnight (last order 10:30pm). MTR: Central. ITALIAN.

This upscale restaurant, in the middle of Central's Lan Kwai Fong nightlife district, strives for the simplicity of a rustic Italian villa with its sponged, mustard-hued walls, sky-blue ceiling, and rows of terra-cotta pots serving as the main decorations. With consistently excellent food and under the exuberant and watchful eye of maitre'd and co-owner Pino Piano, Va Bene is extremely popular with Hong Kong's well-heeled expat community, making it a lively and boisterous—though cramped—spot for a meal. Perhaps you'll want to start with carpaccio (wafer-thin beef tenderloin served with white mushrooms and shavings of Parmesan), artichokes cooked in olive oil and garlic, or ravioli with spinach and ricotta cheese. As a main course, you can choose from a number of veal, beef, and seafood offerings, including veal scaloppini; braised sea bass with white wine, rosemary, garlic, and chickpeas; or pan-roasted sirloin steak served with artichokes and red wine sauce. Good Italian wines, great desserts, and attentive service round out the evening.

Vong. In the Mandarin Oriental Hotel (25th floor), 5 Connaught Rd., Central. ☎ **852/2825 4028.** Reservations required. Main courses HK$188–HK$308 (US$24.40–US$40); fixed-price lunch HK$228 (US$29.60). AE, DC, MC, V. Daily noon–3pm and 6pm–midnight. MTR: Central. FRANCO-ASIAN.

Chef Jean-Georges Vongerichten, who made a name for himself with several well-known New York restaurants, set Hong Kong abuzz when he opened much-talked-about Vong on the 25th floor of the Mandarin Oriental Hotel. Matching Petrus for its spectacular views of the harbor, this chic, black-and-gold-decorated venue serves what may well be the best interpretation of East-meets-West Franco-Asian cuisine in the eastern hemisphere, with exquisite combinations that set taste buds buzzing with excitement. Appetizers range from shrimp satay dipped in a fresh oyster sauce to sautéed foie gras with ginger and mango. Main courses are all tempting—perhaps you'll choose the spiny lobster with Thai herbs, the steamed sea bass in cardamon sauce with Savoy cabbage and watercress, or the chicken marinated in lemongrass with sweet rice steamed in banana leaf. If choosing only one dish causes anguish, order the Tasting Menu for HK$488 (US$63.45) per person (as long as the whole table is willing to go along). The only complaint is that Vong is so popular and busy, its noise level and activity approaches that of an outdoor market, making it a good place for people-watching but not for a romantic tête-à-tête.

MODERATE

Jimmy's Kitchen. 1 Wyndham St., Central. ☎ **852/2526 5293.** Main courses HK$116–HK$191 (US$15.05–US$24.80). AE, DC, MC, V. Daily 11:30am–3pm and 6–11pm. MTR: Central. CONTINENTAL.

This restaurant opened in 1928, a replica of a similar, American-owned restaurant in Shanghai. Now one of Hong Kong's oldest Western restaurants, Jimmy's Kitchen had several homes before moving in the 1960s to its present site. Some of its waiters are descendants from the original staff. The atmosphere reminds me of an American steakhouse, with white tablecloths, dark-wood paneling, and elevator music, but it's a favorite with older foreigners living in Hong Kong and serves dependably good, unpretentious European food. The daily specials are written on a blackboard, and an extensive à la carte menu offers seafood, steaks, salads, soups, chicken, Indian curries, and hearty German fare. A good old standby.

There's a branch at 29 Ashley Rd. in Tsim Sha Tsui (☎ **852/2376 0327**), open daily from noon to 11pm (MTR: Tsim Sha Tsui).

Joyce Café. The Atrium, One Exchange Square, Central. ☎ **852/2810 0807.** Reservations required. Main courses HK$98–HK$168 (US$12.75–US$21.80). AE, DC, MC, V. Mon–Sat noon–2:30pm, tea time 3–5pm, happy hour 5–8pm. MTR: Central. EAST-MEETS-WEST CROSSOVER.

Located in an office building next to Hong Kong Station, this is *the* restaurant for beautiful professionals, who stay that way apparently by dining on the light and healthy food for which this sophisticated establishment is famous. Pastas, salads, and sandwiches are its mainstay, though by no means are they ordinary. Pastas, for example, prepared Western or Asian style, range from fusilli with asparagus, mozzarella, sun-dried tomatoes, pine nuts, and chile al pesto to Shanghai vegetable wontons, made with eight different kinds of vegetables. Crab claws deep fried with prawns and spinach make a great beginning, followed, perhaps, by a Japanese obento lunch box, available vegetarian or with fish. There are enough fruit and vegetable juices to make you sprout leaves. Who knows, after a few meals here, we might be able to actually fit into some of the designer clothing sold in neighboring Central.

✪ **Luk Yu Tea House.** 24–26 Stanley St., Central. ☎ **852/2523 5464.** Main courses HK$100–HK$220 (US$13–US$28.60); dim sum HK$25–HK$55 (US$3.25–US$7.15). MC, V. Daily 7am–10pm. MTR: Central. CANTONESE.

Luk Yu, first opened in 1933, is the most famous teahouse remaining in Hong Kong. In fact, unless you have a time machine, you won't get any closer to old Hong Kong than at this wonderful Cantonese restaurant, with its ceiling fans, spittoons, individual wooden booths for couples, marble tabletops, wood paneling, stained-glass windows, and abacus-wielding cashier. It's one of the best places to try a selection of Chinese teas, including bo lai, jasmine, lung ching (a green tea), and sui sin (narcissus or daffodil). But Luk Yu is most famous for its dim sum, served daily from 7am to

5:30pm. The problem for foreigners is that the place is always packed with regulars with their own reserved seats, and the staff is sometimes surly to newcomers. And if you come after 11am, dim sum is no longer served by trolley but from an English menu with pictures but no prices, which could end up being quite expensive unless you ask before ordering. If you want to come during the day (certainly when Luk Yu is most colorful), try to bring along a Chinese friend. Otherwise, consider coming for dinner when it's not nearly so hectic and there's an English menu listing more than 200 items, including all the Cantonese favorites.

Pavilion. 3 Tun Wo Lane, Central. ☎ **852/2869 7768** or 2973 0642. Main courses HK$180–HK$190 (US$23.40–US$24.65). AE, DC, MC, V. Mon–Sat noon–2:30pm and 7–10pm (last order). Closed holidays for lunch. MTR: Central. CONTINENTAL.

Although not south of Hollywood Road (from which SoHo derives its name), Pavilion is very much a part of the new SoHo dining and nightlife scene and may well qualify as the best restaurant in the area. You'll find it off Cochrane, at the end of a short alley on the other side of a plastic (!) hedge. The restaurant, which adjoins the Petticoat Lane bar and a tapas bar under the same ownership, is not much larger than a walk-in closet; on the wall is a quote by M.F.K. Fisher that proclaims provocatively "Almost everyone has something secret he likes to eat." If you're claustrophobic, try to get a seat alfresco in the romantic courtyard. The changing menu is limited to about three pastas and seven entrees, but they're always right on. Examples of past dishes include egg tagliatelle pasta topped with fresh crab meat, chive cream sauce, and caviar; lightly grilled salmon on chile and coriander mashed potato, topped with grilled prawn and pink peppercorn sauce; and beef medallions wrapped in bacon and served on new potatoes, with a warm salad of green beans, bell peppers, grilled shiitake mushrooms and veal stock reduction.

✪ Yung Kee. 32–40 Wellington St., Central. ☎ **852/2522 1624.** Main courses HK$65–HK$150 (US$8.45–US$19.50); dim sum HK$12–HK$24 (US$1.55–US$3.10). AE, DC, MC, V. Daily 11am–11:30pm. MTR: Central. CANTONESE.

Yung Kee started out in 1941 as a small shop selling roast goose, which it did so well that it soon expanded into a very successful Cantonese enterprise. Through the years it has won numerous food awards and is the only restaurant in Hong Kong ever to be included in *Fortune* magazine's top 15 restaurants of the world. Its specialty is still roast goose with plum sauce, cooked to perfection with tender meat on the inside and crispy skin on the outside and available only for dinner for HK$380 (US$49.40). Other specialties include roasted suckling pig or duck, cold steamed chicken, barbecued pork, bean curd with prawns, any of the fresh seafood, and hundred-year-old eggs (which are included with each meal). Dim sum, available from an English menu, is served daily until 5pm.

INEXPENSIVE

City Hall Chinese Restaurant. City Hall (2nd floor), Low Block (the one closest to the harbor), Central. ☎ **852/2521 1303.** Reservations recommended, especially at lunch. Main courses HK$70–HK$160 (US$9.10–US$20.80); dim sum HK$17–HK$38 (US$2.20–US$4.95). AE, V. Mon–Fri 10am–3pm and 5:30–11:30pm, Sat 10am–11:30pm, Sun and holidays 8am–11:30pm. MTR: Central. CANTONESE.

Decorated in Chinese red, this large restaurant on the second floor of city hall offers a view of the harbor and is so popular at lunchtime that you'll probably have to wait if you haven't made a reservation. The clientele is almost exclusively Chinese, and the food includes the usual shark's-fin, bird's-nest, abalone, pigeon, duck, vegetable, beef, and seafood dishes. The food is fast but average; better, in my opinion, is the dim sum, served from trolleys until 3pm (ask for the dim sum menu in English). Lunchtime fare also includes various noodle and rice dishes, all priced less than HK$100 (US$13).

CAUSEWAY BAY/WAN CHAI
EXPENSIVE

TOTT'S Asian Grill & Bar. In the Excelsior Hotel, 281 Gloucester Rd., Causeway Bay. ☎ 852/2837 6786. Reservations recommended for dinner (request a window seat). Main courses HK$108–HK$288 (US$14.05–US$37.44); fixed-price lunch buffet HK$198 (US$25.70). AE, DC, MC, V. Mon–Sat noon–2:30pm; daily 6:30–11pm. MTR: Causeway Bay. ASIAN/EAST-MEETS-WEST.

This flashy restaurant seems to suffer from an identity crisis: gigantic Chinese paint brushes at the entrance; a blood-red interior with zebra-striped chairs. I don't know whether I'm in Africa or China until I look at the fabulous view from the restaurant's 34th-floor perch. This is Hong Kong at its most eclectic and funky, and though the setting seems contrived, the restaurant itself is relaxed, fun, and highly recommended for its innovative and varied fusion cuisine. Come early for a drink at the bar (happy hour is 5 to 8pm); or retire there after dinner for live music and dancing nightly except Sunday. A glass-enclosed kitchen reveals food being prepared in woks, over charcoal grills, and in tandoori and wood-burning pizza ovens. The menu is surprisingly diverse in cuisine and prices, allowing diners to eat modestly priced dishes like smoked salmon pizza with roasted onions, capers, tomato, zucchini, and herbs, or go all out on tandoori roasted salmon filet on basil whipped potatoes and crisp vegetable chips. It's also a good choice for those who want dining and entertainment all at the same place.

MODERATE

⭕ **Red Pepper.** 7 Lan Fong Rd., Causeway Bay. ☎ 852/2577 3811. Reservations recommended, especially at dinner. Small dishes HK$80–HK$125 (US$10.40–US$16.25). AE, DC, MC, V. Daily 11:30am–11:15pm (last order). MTR: Causeway Bay. SZECHUAN.

Open since 1970, the Red Pepper has a large following among the colony's expatriates, many of whom seem to come so often that they know everyone in the place. It's a very relaxing, small restaurant, with a rather quaint decor of Chinese lanterns and carved dragons in the ceiling. Specialties include fried prawns with chile sauce on a sizzling platter, sour-pepper soup, smoked duck marinated with oranges, and shredded chicken with hot garlic sauce and dry-fried string beans. Most dishes are available in two sizes, with the small dishes suitable for two people.

INEXPENSIVE

⭕ **Open Kitchen.** Hong Kong Arts Centre (6th floor), 2 Harbour Rd., Wan Chai. ☎ 852/2827 2923. Main courses HK$68–HK$88 (US$8.85–US$11.45). AE, MC, V. Daily 11am–11pm. MTR: Wan Chai. INTERNATIONAL.

This self-serve cafeteria, bright with natural lighting, gets my vote as the best place in Wan Chai for an inexpensive and quick meal. Not only does it offer a good selection of food at very reasonable prices, but it also boasts a view of the harbor and even has a tiny outdoor terrace. True to its name, chefs working in an open kitchen prepare everything from lamb chops, grilled steak, and tandoori chicken to grilled Cajun salmon and spring chicken. There are four or five kinds of pasta, along with choices of sauce. Lighter fare includes a salad bar, soups, sandwiches, sushi, quiche, and desserts.

AROUND HONG KONG ISLAND
VICTORIA PEAK

Cafe Deco. Peak Galleria, Victoria Peak. ☎ 852/2849 5111. Reservations required (request window seat with view). Pizzas and pastas HK$94–HK$133 (US$12.20–US$17.25); main courses HK$94–HK$227 (US$12.20–US$29.50); fixed-price lunch, Mon–Fri only, HK$168 (US$21.80). AE, DC, MC, V. Daily 10am–11pm (last order). Peak tram. INTERNATIONAL.

No expense was spared, it seems, in designing this chic, airy restaurant with its wood inlaid floor, authentic art deco trimmings (many imported from the United States and Europe), and open kitchen serving cuisines of China, Japan, Thailand, India, Italy, and Mexico. Ever since it opened in 1994, a nattily dressed crowd has been clamoring to get in. In the evening (except Sunday), diners are treated to live jazz. All this is secondary, however, to the restaurant's real attraction—the best view of Hong Kong in town. The view alone is reason enough to dine here, though some of it has been stolen with the completion of the Peak Tower's viewing platform. To assure a ringside window seat, be sure to make reservations for the second floor at least 2 weeks in advance, emphasizing that you don't want your view obstructed by the Peak Tower. The food, designed to appeal to visitors from around the world, is as trendy as the restaurant, with an eclectic mix of international dishes and ingredients, including tandoori kabobs and dishes, Asian noodles, grilled steaks and chops, oysters, pizzas, create-your-own pastas, soups, sandwiches, salads, and desserts. Some of the entrees fall short of expectations; the pizzas, however, are great and may be the best items on the menu. The salads are generous enough for two to share.

Marché Mövenpick. Peak Tower (levels 6 & 7), 128 Peak Rd., Victoria Peak. ☎ **852/2849 2000.** Main courses HK$62–HK$75 (US$8.05–US$9.75); fixed-price lunch Mon–Fri HK$78 (US$10.15); dinner buffet Mon–Thurs HK$278 (US$36.10), Fri–Sun HK$298 (US$38.70). AE, DC, MC, V. Daily 11am–11pm. Peak tram. INTERNATIONAL.

This Swiss chain has been very successful in Europe with its "marketplace" concept in self-service dining, and with the international crowds that visit the Peak, my guess is that it will do quite well here, too. For one thing, its location in the Peak Tower affords great views over Hong Kong. The food is reasonably priced and varied enough to please even fickle palates, the staff is efficient and friendly, and there's even a children's corner, with a small slide, toys, crayons, and other diversions, making it a good place for families. Upon entering, you'll be given a card, which is stamped each time you add a dish to your tray. There are various counters offering different foods, including salads, pizza, pasta, vegetables, sushi, Chinese dishes, and entrees ranging from grilled pork chops and roasted spring chicken to king prawns and sole. You can take as much or as little as you wish—if you're coming for drinks, try to hit the daily 4–7pm happy hour.

STANLEY

✪ **Stanley's French Restaurant.** Oriental Building (1st & 2nd floor), 90B Stanley Main St., Stanley. ☎ **852/2813 8873.** Reservations required. Main courses HK$165–HK$235 (US$22.45–US$30.50); fixed-price lunch HK$85–HK$155 (US$11.05–US$20.15). AE, DC, MC, V. Daily noon–3pm and 6:30–10:30pm. Bus: no. 6, 6A, 6X, or 260. FRENCH.

Whatever you save by bargain-shopping at Stanley Market may well go toward a meal at Stanley's Restaurant, and I can't think of a better place to spend it. This is an absolutely charming spot, refined, cozy, and romantic. There are two floors of dining, both with ceiling fans, wooden floors, and open windows facing the sea, making for dreamy, relaxed dining. Although the menu changes often, for starters you might try Caesar salad, considered a house specialty, or the lobster and spinach bisque with sherry. Examples of what's been offered in the past include soya-flavored filet of black cod, roast quail with goose liver and chestnut filling, and prime beef sirloin with Cajun spices on gratinéed spinach and crisp potatoes. There are also daily specials, written on a blackboard that will be brought to your table.

ABERDEEN

Jumbo Floating Restaurant. Aberdeen Harbour, Hong Kong Island. ☎ **852/2553 9111.** Main courses HK$80–HK$400 (US$10.40–US$52); dim sum HK$20–HK$30 (US$2.60–US$3.90). Table charge HK$8 (US$1.05) per person. AE, DC, MC, V. Mon–Sat 11am–11pm; Sun 8am–11pm. Bus: no. 7 or 70 from Central to Aberdeen, then the restaurant's private boat. CANTONESE.

No doubt you've heard about Hong Kong's floating restaurants. Although often included in organized nighttime tours, they're no longer touted by the tourist office as a must-see—there are simply too many other restaurants that are more authentic, are more affordable, and have better food. If you're set on the idea, the Jumbo Floating Restaurant, which claims to be the largest floating restaurant in the world, is your best bet. Simply take the bus to Aberdeen and then board one of the restaurant's free shuttle boats, with departures every few minutes. In the evenings, the restaurant even offers free 20-minute free sampan rides through the Aberdeen typhoon shelter on a first-come, first-serve basis. As for the restaurant, it has more reds, golds, and dragon motifs than you've ever seen in one place. Dishes include everything from noodles and rice combinations to fresh lobster, scallops, grouper balls, and fresh seafood (prawns are a particular favorite). Dim sum is served from trolleys until 4pm—certainly the least expensive way to enjoy the floating restaurant experience.

5 Attractions

Every visitor to Hong Kong should eat dim sum in a typical Cantonese restaurant, ride the Star Ferry across Victoria Harbour, and, if the weather is clear, take the Peak Tram for the glorious views from Victoria Peak. If you have more time, I also recommend the Hong Kong Museum of Art for its collection of Chinese antiquities, Stanley Market for its inexpensive fashions and souvenirs, an excursion via ferry to one of the outlying islands, joining a special-interest organized tour, and a stroll through the Temple Street Night Market.

✪ VICTORIA PEAK

At 399 meters (1,308 ft.), Victoria Peak is Hong Kong Island's tallest mountain and offers spectacular views; if possible, go on a clear day. Since the peak is typically cooler than the sweltering city below, it has always been one of Hong Kong's most exclusive places to live. More than a century ago, the rich reached the peak via a grueling 3-hour trip in sedan chairs, transported to the top by coolies. In 1888 the **peak tram** began operating, cutting the journey to a mere 8 minutes.

The easiest way to reach the Peak Tram Station, located in Central on Garden Road, is to take the No. 15C open-top shuttle bus that operates between the tram terminal and the Star Ferry in Central (turn left from the ferry pier). Otherwise, the tram terminal is about a 10-minute walk from the Star Ferry. Trams depart from Peak Tram Station every 10 to 15 minutes between 7am and midnight. Round-trip tickets cost HK$30 (US$3.90) for adults, HK$14 (US$1.80) for senior citizens, and HK$9 (US$1.15) for children.

Upon reaching the Peak, you'll find yourself at the very modern **Peak Tower,** designed by British architect Terry Farrell and looking for all the world like a Chinese cooking wok. Head straight for the viewing terrace on Level 5, where you have one of the world's most breathtaking views, with the skyscrapers of Central, the boats plying Victoria Harbour, Kowloon, and the many hills of the New Territories undulating in the background.

Of the two attractions located in Peak Tower, most well known is **Ripley's Believe It or Not! Odditorium,** Level 3 (☎ **852/2849 0698**). It contains oddities (and replicas of oddities) collected by Robert L. Ripley on visits to 198 countries over 55 years, including a shrunken head from Ecuador, torture devices from around the world, a two-headed calf, and models of the world's tallest and fattest men. Be forewarned that some of the items are purely grotesque, or, at best, out of date in a more politically correct world. It's open daily from 9am to 10pm and costs HK$65 (US$8.45) for adults and HK$46 (US$5.95) for senior citizens and children. **Peak Explorer,** Level 6 (☎ **852/2849 0866**), is a 36-seat motion-simulator theater that features changing, 8-minute fast-paced films and seats that move, jerk, roll, and rock in accordance to the action on the screen. It's open daily from 9am to 10pm and costs HK$45 (US$5.85) for adults and HK$32 (US$4.15) for children.

But the best thing to do atop Victoria Peak, in my opinion, is to take an hour-long circular hike on Lugard Road and Harlech Road, located just a stone's throw from the Peak Tower. Mainly a footpath overhung with banyan trees and passing lush vegetation alternating with secluded mansions, the road snakes along the side of the cliff, offering great views of Central District below, the harbor, Kowloon, and then Aberdeen and the outlying islands on the other side. This is one of the best walks in Hong Kong; at night, the lit path offers one of world's most romantic views. Don't miss it.

MUSEUMS

Keep in mind that municipal museums are closed December 25 and 26, January 1, and the first three days of the Chinese New Year (traditionally around the end of January/beginning of February). Private museums are usually closed additionally on bank holidays.

✪ **Hong Kong Museum of Art.** Hong Kong Cultural Centre Complex, 10 Salisbury Rd., Tsim Sha Tsui. ☎ **852/2734 2167.** Admission HK$10 (US$1.30) adults; HK$5 (US$0.65) children, students, and senior citizens. Free admission Wed. Fri–Wed 10am–6pm. MTR: Tsim Sha Tsui.

If you visit only one museum in Hong Kong, this should be it. Located on the Tsim Sha Tsui waterfront just a 2-minute walk from the Star Ferry terminus, this museum has a vast collection of Chinese antiquities and fine art, including ceramics, bronzes, jade, cloisonné, lacquerware, bamboo carvings, women's costumes (look for the fist-sized shoes for bound feet), and textiles, as well as paintings, wall hangings, scrolls, and calligraphy dating from the 16th century to the present. The Historical Pictures Gallery is especially insightful, with 1,000 works in oils, watercolors, pencil drawings, and prints that provide a visual account of life in Hong Kong, Macau, and Guangzhou (Canton) in the late 18th and 19th centuries. Another gallery displays contemporary Hong Kong works by local artists. A bonus is the beautiful backdrop of Victoria Harbor.

Hong Kong Museum of History. 100 Chatham Rd. South, Tsim Sha Tsui. ☎ **852/2724 9042.** Admission HK$10 adults (US$1.30), HK$5 (US$0.65) children and senior citizens. Free admission Wed. Tues–Sat 10am–6pm, Sun and holidays 1–6pm. MTR: Tsim Sha Tsui (a 20-min. walk from exit B2). Bus: 5 from the Star Ferry bus terminal.

Moving from cramped quarters in Kowloon Park to this new facility in the summer of 2001, this museum outlines 6,000 years of Hong Kong history, from its beginnings as a Middle Neolithic settlement to its development as a fishing village and then to a modern metropolis. Through displays that include replicas of fishing boats, furniture, clothing, and items from daily life, the museum introduces Hong Kong's ethnic groups and their traditional means of livelihood, customs, and beliefs. These include the Tanka, who lived their entire lives on boats, the Five Great Clans who settled in what is now the New Territories and built walled communities, and the Hakka, primarily rice farmers. My favorite part of the museum is a re-created street of old Hong Kong, complete with a Chinese herbal medicine shop originally located in Central until 1980 and reconstructed here. There are also 19th- and early-20th-century photographs, poignantly showing how much Hong Kong has changed through the decades.

Hong Kong Museum of Medical Sciences. 2 Caine Lane, Mid-Levels, Hong Kong Island. ☎ **852/2549 5123.** Admission HK$10 (US$1.30) adults, HK$5 (US$0.65) children and senior citizens. Tues–Sat 10am–5pm, Sun and holidays 1–5pm. MTR: Central; then bus no. 26 from Des Voeux Rd. in front of Hongkong Bank headquarters to Man Mo Temple; walk up Ladder St. to Caine Lane.

This unique museum, located in the Edwardian-style former Pathological Institute founded 100 years ago to combat the colony's most horrific outbreak of bubonic plague, charts the historical development of medical science in Hong Kong. Several rooms remain almost exactly as they were, including an autopsy room and a laboratory filled with old equipment, while others serve as exhibition rooms devoted to such areas as the development of dentistry and radiology (note the X-ray of the bound foot). But what makes the museum particularly fascinating is its comparison of traditional Chinese and Western medicines—it's the only medical museum in the world to do so—and its funding of research into Chinese medicine. Included are displays on acupuncture and Chinese herbs.

Hong Kong Science Museum. 2 Science Museum Rd., Tsim Sha Tsui East. ☎ **852/2732 3232.** Admission HK$25 (US$3.25) adults, HK$12.50 (US$1.60) children, students, and senior citizens. Free admission Wed. Tues–Fri 1–9pm, Sat–Sun and holidays 10am–9pm. MTR: Tsim Sha Tsui.

The mysteries of science and technology come to life with plenty of hands-on exhibits sure to appeal to children and adults alike. More than 500 exhibits are devoted to the life sciences; light, sound and motion; virtual reality; meteorology and geography; electricity and magnetism; computers and robotics; construction; transportation and communication; occupational safety and health; energy efficiency; and food science and home technology. One area is specially designed for children between the ages of 3 and 7.

Hong Kong Space Museum. Hong Kong Cultural Centre Complex, 10 Salisbury Rd., Tsim Sha Tsui. ☎ **852/2734 2722.** Admission to Exhibition Halls HK$10 (US$1.30) adults; HK$5 (US$0.65) children, students, and senior citizens; free admission on Wed. Space Theatre HK$24–HK$56 (US$3.10–US$7.25)) adults; HK$12–HK$28 (US$1.55–US$3.65) children, students, and senior citizens. Mon, Wed–Fri 1–9pm, Sat–Sun and holidays 10am–9pm. MTR: Tsim Sha Tsui.

Located opposite The Peninsula Hotel on the Tsim Sha Tsui waterfront, the Space Museum is easy to spot with its white-domed planetarium. It consists of two parts: exhibition halls and the Space Theatre. The Hall of Space Science explores humankind's journey to space, with exhibits on ancient astronomical history, manned space flights, and future space programs. There are also several interactive rides and exhibits, including a ride on a virtual paraglider (a harness that holds occupants aloft with the same approximate gravity they'd experience walking on the moon) and a multi-axis chair developed for astronaut training to give the sensation of tumbling through space. The Hall of Astronomy presents information on the solar system and solar science. Space Theatre, with a 75-foot domed roof, presents both Omnimax screenings and Sky shows with a Zeiss star projector that can project up to about

9,000 stars. Forty-minute to hour-long shows range from celestial phenomena like the Milky Way to such wonders of the world as the Great Barrier Reef. Call for show schedules.

✪ **Sam Tung Uk Museum.** Kwu Uk Lane, Tsuen Wan. ☎ **852/2411 2001.** Free admission. Wed–Mon 9am–5pm. MTR: Tsuen Wan.

Although located in the New Territories but easily accessible from either Central or Tsim Sha Tsui in about 25 minutes via MTR, this excellent museum is actually a restored Hakka walled village, built in the 18th century by members of the farming Chan clan. Consisting of tiny lanes lined with tiny homes, it encompasses four houses that have been restored to their original condition, an ancestral hall, two rows of side houses, an exhibition hall, and an adjacent landscaped garden. The four houses, without windows, are furnished much as they would have been when occupied, with traditional Chinese furniture (including elegant blackwood furniture), farm implements, kitchens, and lavatories. Although as many as 300 clan members once lived here, the village was abandoned in 1980; today the museum is a tiny oasis of tiled-roofed houses in the midst of modern high-rise housing projects.

TEMPLES

For information on Po Lin Monastery and its adjacent Giant Tian Tan Buddha, refer to the section on "Outlying Islands," below.

Man Mo Temple. Hollywood Rd. and Ladder St., Western District, Hong Kong Island. ☎ **852/2803 2916.** Free admission. Daily 8am–6pm. Bus: no. 26 from Des Voeux Rd. Central (in front of the Hongkong Bank headquarters) to the second stop on Hollywood Rd., across from the temple.

Hong Kong Island's oldest and most important temple was built in the 1840s and is named after its two principal deities: Man, the god of literature, who is dressed in red and holds a calligraphy brush; and Mo, the god of war, wearing a green robe and holding a sword. Ironically, Mo finds patronage from both the police force (shrines in his honor can be found in all Hong Kong police stations) and triad secret societies. Two ornately carved sedan chairs in the temple were once used during festivals to carry the statues of the gods around the neighborhood. But what makes the temple particularly memorable are the giant incense coils hanging from the ceiling, imparting a fragrant, smoky haze. They are purchased by patrons seeking fulfillment of their wishes, such as good health or a successful business deal, and burn for as long as 3 weeks.

Wong Tai Sin. Wong Tai Sin Estate, Kowloon. Temple daily 7am–5:30pm; gardens Tues–Sun 9am–4pm. Free admission to temple, though donations of about HK$1 (US$0.13) are expected at the temple's entrance and for Nine Dragon Wall Garden; admission to Good Wish Garden HK$2 (US$0.26) extra. MTR: Wong Tai Sin and then a 3-min. walk (follow the signs).

Located six subway stops northeast of Yau Ma Tei in the far north end of Kowloon Peninsula, Wong Tai Sin is Hong Kong's most popular Taoist temple. Although the temple itself dates only from 1973, it adheres to traditional Chinese architectural principles with its red pillars, two-tiered golden roof, blue friezes, yellow latticework, and multicolored carvings. What makes the temple popular, however, is that everyone who comes here is seeking information about his or her fortune—from advice about business or horse racing to determining which day is most auspicious for a wedding. Most worshippers make use of a bamboo container holding numbered sticks. After lighting a joss stick and kneeling before the main altar, the worshipper gently shakes the container until one of the sticks falls out. The number corresponds to a certain fortune, which is then interpreted by a soothsayer at the temple. You can wander around the temple grounds, on which can be found halls dedicated to the Buddhist Goddess of

Mercy and Confucius; the Nine Dragon Garden, a Chinese garden with a pond, waterfall, and a replica of the famous Nine Dragons mural (the original is in Beijing's Imperial Palace); the Good Wish Garden, a replica of the Yi He Garden in Beijing with circular, square, octagonal, and fan-shaped pavilions, ponds, an artificial waterfall, and rocks and concrete fashioned to resemble animals; and a clinic with both Western medical services and traditional Chinese herbal treatments.

PARKS & GARDENS

HONG KONG PARK—Opened in 1991, Hong Kong Park, Supreme Court Road and Cotton Tree Drive, Central, features a dancing fountain at its entrance; Southeast Asia's largest greenhouse, with more than 2,000 rare plant species; an aviary housing 800 exotic birds in a tropical rain-forest setting with an elevated walkway; various gardens; a children's playground; and a viewing platform. The most famous building on the park grounds is the **Flagstaff House Museum of Tea Ware** (☎ 852/2869 0690), the oldest colonial building in Hong Kong. Completed in 1846 in Greek Revival style for the commander of the British forces, it now displays some 500 pieces of tea ware ranging from earthenware to porcelain, primarily of Chinese origin and dating from the seventh century to the present day. (Don't miss the museum shop, which sells beautifully crafted teapots and tea.) Hong Kong Park is also host to free, 1-hour *tai chi* (shadow boxing) lessons in English sponsored by the Hong Kong Tourist Association every Tuesday, Friday, and Sunday at 8:15am. An ancient Chinese regimen designed to balance body and soul through slow, ballet-like movements, tai chi takes place at the Garden Plaza on a first-come, first-serve basis; contact **HKTA** (☎ 852/2508 1234) for more information. Finally, since the marriage registry is located at the edge of the park, the gardens are also a favorite place for wedding photographs, especially on weekends and auspicious days of the Chinese calendar. The park is open daily from 6:30am to 11pm, the greenhouse and aviary are open daily from 9am to 5pm, and the Flagstaff House Museum of Tea Ware is open Thursday through Tuesday from 10am to 5pm. Admission is free to everything. To reach the park, take the MTR to Admiralty Station, then follow the signs through Pacific Place.

KOWLOON PARK—Occupying the site of an old military encampment first established in the 1860s, Kowloon Park, Nathan Road, is Tsim Sha Tsui's largest recreational and sports facility, boasting an indoor heated Olympic-size swimming pool, three outdoor leisure pools linked by a series of waterfalls, an open-air sculpture garden featuring works by local and overseas sculptors, a Chinese garden, a fitness trail, an aviary, a maze formed by hedges, a children's playground, and a bird lake with flamingos and other waterfowl. Not far from the Tsim Sha Tsui MTR station (take exit A1), the park is open daily from 6am to midnight, with free admission.

KOWLOON WALLED CITY PARK—Although it doesn't boast the varied attractions of Hong Kong's other parks, the Kowloon Walled City Park, Tung Tau Tsuen Road, is perhaps the city's finest and a must for garden enthusiasts. The largest re-creation of a classical Southern China garden outside mainland China, its beautifully landscaped grounds include man-made hills, ponds, streams, pines, boulders, bonsai, bamboo, flowers, and pavilions. Also fascinating is the history of the site, formerly a Chinese fort and later becoming the infamous Kowloon Walled City, ignored by British authorities and a haven for squatters, refugees, criminals, prostitutes, and drug addicts until 1994, when it was demolished. To reach the park, take the MTR to Lok Fu station and then walk 15 minutes on Junction Road to Tung Tau Tsuen Road; or take bus no. 1 from the Star Ferry in Tsim Sha Tsui to the stop opposite the park. It's open daily from 6:30am to 11:30pm and admission is free.

YUEN PO STREET BIRD GARDEN—Songbirds are favorite pets in Chinese households; perhaps you've noticed wooden bird cages hanging outside shops or from apartment balconies, or perhaps you've even seen someone taking his bird for an outing in its cage. To see more of these prized birds, which are valued not for their plumage but for their singing talents, visit the fascinating Yuen Po Bird Garden, Prince Edward Road West, Mong Kok, which consists of a series of Chinese-style gateways and courtyards lined with stalls selling songbirds, beautifully crafted wood and bamboo cages, live crickets and mealy worms, and tiny porcelain food bowls. Nothing, it seems, is too expensive for these tiny creatures. This garden is very Chinese and a lot of fun to visit; young children love it. Take the MTR to Prince Edward Road station and walk 10 minutes west on Prince Edward Road West, turning left at the railway overhead onto Yuen Po Street. Admission is free and it's open daily from 7am to 8pm.

ZOOLOGICAL AND BOTANICAL GARDENS—Established in 1864, the Zoological and Botanical Gardens, Upper Albert Road, Central, are spread on the slope of Victoria Peak, making it a popular respite for Hong Kong residents; if you're tired of Central and its traffic, this is a pleasant place to regain your perspective. Arrive early, around 7am, to see Chinese residents going through the slow motions of *tai chi* (shadowboxing), a disciplined physical routine of more than 200 individual movements, designed to exercise every muscle of the body and bring a sense of peace and balance to its practitioners. In the gardens themselves, which retain some of their Victorian charm, flowers are almost always in bloom, from azaleas in the spring to wisteria and bauhinea in the summer and fall. More than 1,000 species of plants, most indigenous to tropical and sub-tropical regions, include Burmese rosewood trees, varieties of bamboo, Indian rubber trees, camphor trees, and the Hong Kong orchid. The small zoo houses 600 birds, 90 mammals, and 20 reptiles, including jaguars, monkeys, Palawan peacocks, a Burmese python, and kangaroos. The eastern part of the park, containing most of the botanical gardens and the aviaries, is open daily from 6am to 10pm, while the western half with its reptiles and mammals is open daily from 6am to 7pm. Admission is free. Take the MTR to Central and then walk 15 minutes up Garden Road; or take bus nos. 3B or 12 from the Jardine House on Connaught Road Central.

HORSE RACING

If you're here anytime from September through mid-June, join the rest of Hong Kong at the horse races. Introduced by the British more than 150 years ago, horse racing is by far the most popular sporting event in Hong Kong, due largely to the fact that, aside from the local lottery, racing is the only legal form of gambling in Hong Kong. Winnings are tax free.

There are two tracks—**Happy Valley** on Hong Kong Island, which you can reach by taking the tram to Happy Valley or the MTR to Causeway Bay; and **Sha Tin** in the New Territories, reached by taking the KCR railway to Racecourse Station. Races are held Wednesday evenings and some Saturday and Sunday afternoons. The lowest admission price is HK$10 (US$1.30), which is for the general public and is standing room only. If you want to watch from the more exclusive club members' enclosure, are at least 18 years old, and have been in Hong Kong fewer than 21 days, you can purchase a temporary member's badge for HK$50 (US$6.50), available on a first-come, first-served basis by showing your passport at either the Badge Enquiry Office at the main entrance to the members' private enclosure (at either track) or at the off-course betting center near the Star Ferry concourse in Central.

You can also see the races by joining one of two "Come Horse Racing" tours, sponsored by the Hong Kong Tourist Association and limited to individuals 18 years of age and older who have been in Hong Kong fewer than 21 days. The Classic Tour, costing

HK$490 (US$63.65), includes a pre-race Western-style buffet, entry badge to the luxurious Visitors' Box in the Hong Kong Jockey Club's Members' Enclosure, transportation, guide services, and even hints to help you place your bets. The EZ Race Tour, costing HK$120 (US$15.60), includes transportation and admission to the Betting Lounge within the Members' Enclosure. For bookings, call the Come Horseracing Tour Reservations Hotline at ☎ **852/2366 3995.**

OUTLYING ISLANDS

An excursion to an outlying island provides not only an opportunity to experience rural Hong Kong, but also the chance to view Hong Kong's skyline and harbor by ferry, and very cheaply at that. I recommend either Lantau, famous for its giant outdoor Buddha and monastery serving vegetarian meals, or Cheung Chau, popular with families for its unhurried, small-village atmosphere and beach. Both islands are reached in less than an hour via ferries that depart approximately every hour or so from the Outlying Ferries Pier, located less than a 5-minute walk west of the Star Ferry in the Central District. (For information on ferry schedules and prices, drop by the HKTA for a free timetable.) On weekdays and before noon on Saturday, tickets cost HK$10 (US$1.30) for ordinary class and HK$16.80 (US$2.20) for deluxe. Ferries cost slightly more on Saturday afternoons, Sundays, and holidays, and are also more crowded. I highly recommend deluxe class, since this upper-deck ticket entitles you to sit on an open deck out back, a great place to sip coffee or beer when the weather is nice and watch the harbor float past. In addition, deluxe cabins are the only ones that are air-conditioned.

In addition to the ferries above, there is also a faster hoverferry service used mostly by commuters, as well as infrequent ferry service from Tsim Sha Tsui's Star Ferry concourse on Saturday afternoon and Sunday. You can also reach Lantau via the Tung Chung MTR Line.

LANTAU

Hong Kong's largest island and twice the size of Hong Kong Island, Lantau has a population of only 45,000. As home of Hong Kong's new international airport, however, that is expected to grow to more than 200,000 by the year 2111, with most new residents concentrated in a new satellite town called Tung Chung.

Luckily, more than half of the mountainous and lush island remains preserved in county parks. After taking the ferry from Central to Silvermine Bay (called *Mui Wo* in Chinese) or the MTR to Tung Chung, you'll see some of this wonderful countryside on the 45-minute bus ride to the **Giant Tian Tan Buddha,** the largest seated outdoor bronze Buddha in the world, and the nearby **Po Lin Monastery.** Both are situated on the plateau of Ngong Ping at an elevation of 750 meters (2,460 ft.). The Giant Buddha, more than 30 meters (100 ft.) tall and weighing 250 tons, is reached via 268 steps and offers great views of the surrounding countryside. Admission to the viewing platform is free and is open daily from 10am to 6pm.

Before ascending the stairs to the Buddha, however, stop by the ticket counter at the bottom of the steps to purchase a meal ticket for Po Lin Monastery, famous for its vegetarian meals (☎ **852/2985 5248**). Your ticket will be for a specific time, at an assigned table. Two different meals of soup, vegetarian dishes, and rice are available: the ordinary, HK$60 (US$7.80) meal is served in an unadorned dining hall, and the procedure is rather unceremonious, with huge dishes of vegetables, rice, and soup brought to communal tables covered with plastic tablecloths. Grab a Styrofoam bowl and chopsticks and help yourself. Packed with families, the dining hall here is certainly colorful. The HK$100 (US$13) "Deluxe" meal is served in an adjacent "VIP Room" and is popular mostly with foreigners. Meals here are served on china plates, and the food is a notch above the cheaper meal. Both, however, are good and are available daily from noon to 4pm. No credit cards are accepted.

Be sure to explore the grounds of the colorful monastery, established near the turn of the century by reclusive Buddhist monks. Its ornate main temple houses three magnificent bronze statues of Buddha, representing the past, present, and future, and boasts a brightly painted vermilion interior with dragons and other Chinese mythical figures on the ceiling.

CHEUNG CHAU

If you have only a few hours to spare and don't want to worry about catching buses and finding your way around, Cheung Chau is your best bet. It's a tiny island (only 1 square mile) with more than 25,000 people living in a thriving fishing village. There are no cars on the island, making it a delightful place for walking around and exploring. The island is especially popular with Chinese families for its rental bicycles and beach, but my favorite thing to do here is to walk the tiny, narrow lanes of Cheung Chau village.

Inhabited for at least 2,500 years by fisherfolk, Cheung Chau still supports a sizable population of fishing families, and fishing remains the island's main industry. Inhabited junks are moored in the harbor, and the waterfront where the ferry lands, known as the **Praya,** buzzes with activity as vendors sell fish, lobster, and vegetables. The village itself is a fascinating warren of narrow alleyways, food stalls, open markets, and shops selling everything from medicinal herbs to toys.

The best thing to do is simply explore. About a 3-minute walk from the ferry pier is **Pak Tai Temple,** near a playground on Pak She Fourth Street. Built in 1783, it's dedicated to the "Supreme Emperor of the Dark Heaven," long worshipped as a Taoist god of the sea. As you roam the village, you'll pass open-fronted shops selling incense, paper funeral objects such as cars (cremated with the deceased to accompany him or her to the next life), medicinal herbs, jade, rattan, vegetables, rice, and—a reflection of the island's increasing tourist trade—sun hats, sunglasses, and beach toys. You'll also pass people's homes; their living rooms hold the family altar and open onto the street. This is the traditional Chinese home, with the family business and communal rooms on the ground floor and the bedrooms up above. On the other side of the island (directly opposite from the ferry pier and less than a 10-minute walk away), is **Tung Wan Beach,** the most popular beach on the island.

ORGANIZED TOURS

For information and pamphlets on the following tours, stop by HKTA office; many hotels also have tour desks.

BOAT TOURS   One of the most popular cruises is a 1-hour trip aboard a **Star Ferry,** with boats departing from the Star Ferry piers in both Central and Tsim Sha Tsui three to four times daily between 12:30pm and 7pm. Tickets, which include complimentary drinks, cost HK$150 (US$19.50) for adults and HK$100 (US$13) for children and can be booked at the Star Ferry terminals. Otherwise, **Watertours** (☎ 852/2926 3868), Hong Kong's largest tour operator of boat and junk cruises, offers everything from 2-hour cruises to more than a half dozen longer boat trips, including Chinese junk cruises to Aberdeen and sunset and evening cruises.

SPECIAL-INTEREST TOURS   Offered by the Hong Kong Tourist Association (☎ 852/2508 1234) are the **"Land Between" Tour,** which takes visitors through the vast New Territories with stops at a Buddhist monastery, a traditional rural market, a bird sanctuary, and a fishing village; and the **Heritage Tour,** which covers historic Chinese architecture in the New Territories, including the Sam Tung Uk walled village (now a museum) and an ornate mansion. **Gray Line's** (☎ **852/2368 7111**) special-interest tours include the **Feng Shui Tour,** which explores the Chinese principles of establishing harmony with nature in the construction of new buildings, and the **Hong Kong Lifestyles Tour,** which explores life in Hong Kong with a session of tai chi, a dim sum breakfast, and visits to a market and temple.

6 Shopping

Shopping has always been one of the main reasons people come to Hong Kong, and at first glance the city does seem to be one huge department store. Good buys include products from the People's Republic of China (porcelain, jade, cloisonné, silk handicrafts and clothing, hand-embroidery, jewelry, and artwork), Chinese antiques, clothing, shoes, jewelry, furniture, carpets, leather goods, luggage, handbags, briefcases, Chinese herbs, watches, toys, and eyeglasses. As for electronic goods and cameras, they are not the bargains they once were, though good deals can be found in recently discontinued models, such as last year's Sony Discman. Hong Kong is a duty-free port, so there is no sales tax.

Tsim Sha Tsui boasts the greatest concentration of shops in Hong Kong, particularly along Nathan Road. Be sure to explore its side streets, especially Mody Road for shops specializing in washable silk and casual clothing and Granville Road for luggage shops and export overruns. One of the largest malls in the world stretches along Canton Road.

For upscale shopping, Central is where you'll find international designer labels, in boutiques located in the Landmark and Prince's Building. Causeway Bay caters more to the local market, with lower prices, small shops selling everything from shoes and clothing to Chinese herbs, several Japanese department stores, and a large shopping complex called Times Square.

Antiques and curio lovers usually head for Hollywood Road and Cat Street on Hong Kong Island, where everything from snuff bottles to jade carvings is for sale. Finally, one of my favorite places to shop is Stanley Market on the southern end of Hong Kong Island, where vendors sell silk clothing and business and casual wear, as well as Chinese crafts and products. Another good place to shop for Chinese imports and souvenirs is at one of several Chinese craft emporiums.

Because shopping is such big business in Hong Kong, most stores are open 7 days a week, closing only for 2 or 3 days during the Chinese New Year. Most stores open at 10am, and remain open until 6pm in Central, 9pm in Tsim Sha Tsui, and 9:30pm in Causeway Bay. Street markets are open every day.

WARNING   Hong Kong is a buyer-beware market. To be on the safe side, try to make major purchases at HKTA member stores, which display the HKTA logo (a round circle with a red Chinese junk in the middle) on their storefronts. About 750 member stores are listed in *The Official Dining, Entertainment & Shopping Directory,* available free at HKTA offices. Still, it's always a good idea to obtain a receipt from the shopkeeper with a description of your purchase, including the brand name, model number, serial number, and price for electronic and photographic equipment; for jewelry and gold watches, there should be a description of the precious stones and the metal content. If you're making a purchase using a credit card, you should also ask for the customer's copy of the credit-card slip, making sure "HK$" appears before the monetary total.

SHOPPING A TO Z
ANTIQUES

Several of the Chinese-product stores, listed below under "Chinese-product Empori-ums," stock antiques, especially porcelain. You can also find antiques and collectibles in Harbour City, a megamall in Tsim Sha Tsui, particularly along the so-called "Silk Road" arcade on level 3 of Zone D (the Hongkong Hotel Arcade). Many hotel shop-ping arcades have at least a few shops specializing in antiques. Otherwise, the most famous area for antiques and chinoiserie is around **Hollywood Road** and **Cat Street,** both above the Central District on Hong Kong Island. Hollywood Road twists along for a little more than half a mile, with shops selling Qing and Ming dynasty furniture, original prints, scrolls, porcelain, clay figurines, silver, and rosewood and blackwood furniture, as well as fakes and curios. Near the western end is Upper Lascar Row, pop-ularly known as Cat Street, where sidewalk vendors sell snuff bottles, curios, and odds and ends.

Cat Street Galleries. 38 Lok Ku Rd., Central. ☎ **852/2543 1609.** MTR: Central. Bus: no. 26 (from Des Voeux Rd. Central in front of the Hongkong Bank) to the second stop on Holly-wood Rd.

Cat Street Galleries, on Cat Street, houses several individually owned booths of arts and crafts and expensive antiques from the various dynasties. It's open Monday through Friday from 11am to 6pm and Saturday 10am to 6pm.

Charlotte Horstmann and Gerald Godfrey. Shop 100D, Ocean Terminal, Harbour City, 3 Canton Rd., Tsim Sha Tsui. ☎ **852/2735 7167.** MTR: Tsim Sha Tsui.

A favorite for more than 40 years, this small shop, located in Zone C (Ocean Termi-nal) of the Harbour City shopping mall on Canton Road, is an emporium of expen-sive, top-quality Asian antiques. Since the shop itself is rather small, be sure to make an appointment to see the adjoining 10,000-square-foot warehouse. Its stock varies, but Chinese art and jade are well represented; antiques from Indonesia, Thailand, Cambodia, India, and Korea are usually also available. It's open Monday through Sat-urday from 9:30am to 6pm.

China Art. 15 Hollywood Rd., Central. ☎ **852/2542 0982** or 852/2840 0816. MTR: Cen-tral. Bus: no. 26 (from Des Voeux Rd. Central in front of the Hongkong Bank) to Hollywood Rd.

This family-owned shop is one of Hong Kong's best for antique Chinese furniture, including chairs, tables, and wardrobes, mostly from the Ming dynasty (1368–1644). It's open Monday through Saturday from 10:30am to 7pm and Sunday from 11am to 7pm.

Dragon Culture. 231 Hollywood Rd., Sheung Wan. ☎ **852/2545 8098.** MTR: Central. Bus: 26 (from Des Voeux Rd. Central in front of the Hongkong Bank) to the second stop on Hollywood Rd.

One of the largest purveyors of antiques in Hong Kong, Victor Choi began collecting Chinese antiques in the 1970s, traveling throughout China from province to province and to all the major cities. With a second gallery nearby at 184 Hollywood Rd. (☎ 852/2815 5227) and another one in New York, he carries Neolithic pottery, three-color glazed pottery horses from the Tang Dynasty, Ming porcelains, bronzes, jade, wood carvings, snuff bottles, calligraphy, paintings, brush pots, stone carvings, and more, and also provides authenticity. The main shop is open Monday through Saturday from 10am to 6pm.

True Arts & Curios. 89 Hollywood Rd., Central. ☎ **852/2559 1485.** MTR: Central.

This tiny shop is so packed with antiques and curios that there's barely room for customers. You'll find snuff bottles, porcelain, antique silver, earrings, hair pins, and children's shoes (impractical but darling, with curled toes). But the true finds here are some 2,000 intricate wood carvings, pried from the doors and windows of dismantled temples and homes. You'll find them hanging from the ceiling and in bins, many of them dusty and grimy from years of neglect. The best ones are carved from a single piece of wood, masterpieces in workmanship and available at modest prices. It's open Monday through Saturday from 10:30am to 6:30pm and Sunday from 2:30 to 6:30pm.

CHINESE CRAFT EMPORIUMS

In addition to the shops listed here which specialize in traditional and contemporary arts, crafts, souvenirs, and gift items from China, there are several souvenir shops at Stanley Market that carry lacquered boxes, china, embroidered tablecloths, figurines, and other Chinese imports.

✪ **Chinese Arts and Crafts Ltd.** Shop 230, Pacific Place, 88 Queensway, Central. ☎ **852/2523 3933.** MTR: Admiralty.

In business for more than 30 years, this is the best upscale shop for Chinese arts and crafts and is one of the safest places to purchase jade. You can also buy silk dresses and blouses, arts and crafts, antiques, jewelry, watches, carpets, cloisonné, furs, Chinese herbs and medicine, rosewood furniture, chinaware, Chinese teas, and embroidered tablecloths or pillowcases—in short, virtually all the upmarket items China produces. It's a great place for gifts in all price ranges. This shop, located at Pacific Place, is open daily from 10:30am to 7pm.

Other branches include: Star House, 3 Salisbury Rd., Tsim Sha Tsui (☎ **852/2735 4061;** MTR: Tsim Sha Tsui), open daily from 10am to 9:30pm; and in the China Resources Building, 26 Harbour Rd., Wan Chai (☎ **852/2827 6667;** MTR: Wan Chai), open daily 10:30am to 7:30pm.

✪ **Shanghai Tang.** Pedder Building, 12 Pedder St., Central. ☎ **852/2525 7333.** MTR: Central.

Step back into Shanghai of the 1930s at this upscale, two-level store with its gleaming wooden and tiled floors, raised cashier cubicles, ceiling fans, and helpful clerks wearing classical Chinese jackets. This is Chinese chic at its best, with neatly stacked rows of traditional Chinese clothing ranging from cheongsams and silk pajamas to padded jackets, caps, and shoes—all in bright, contemporary colors and styles. If you're looking for a lime-green or shocking pink Mao jacket, this is the place for you. You'll also find funky accessories and home furnishings, from Mao-emblazoned watches to '30s-style alarm clock remakes, beaded picture frames, silver chopsticks, and fuchsia-colored serving trays. It's open Monday through Saturday from 10am to 8pm and Sunday from 11am to 7pm.

DEPARTMENT STORES

Lane Crawford Ltd. Lane Crawford House, 70 Queen's Rd. Central, Central. ☎ **852/2118 3388.** MTR: Central.

This locally owned upscale department store, with large clothing departments for the whole family, has branches on both sides of the harbor and is similar to established chain stores in England and the United States. The main store is open daily from 10am to 7:30pm. Other branches can be found at: Pacific Place, 88 Queensway, Central (☎ **852/2118 3668;** MTR: Admiralty); Times Square, 1 Matheson St., Causeway Bay (☎ **852/2118 3638;** MTR: Causeway Bay); and Shop 100, Ocean Terminal, Harbour City, 3 Canton Rd., Tsim Sha Tsui (☎ **852/2118 3428;** MTR: Tsim Sha Tsui).

Mitsukoshi. 500 Hennessy Rd., Causeway Bay. ☎ **852/2576 5222.** MTR: Causeway Bay.

Mitsukoshi first opened as a kimono shop in Japan in the 1600s and is still one of Japan's most exclusive stores. Today it houses the boutiques of well-known designers of shoes, accessories, and clothing—with high prices to match. It also carries lingerie, cosmetics, and household goods. It's open daily from 10:30am to 10pm.

Seibu. Pacific Place, 88 Queensway, Central. ☎ **852/2868 0111.** MTR: Admiralty.

One of the largest department store chains in Japan (its Tokyo store is the third-largest department store in the world), this was Seibu's first store to open outside Japan. An upscale, sophisticated department store targeting Hong Kong's affluent yuppie population, it is the epitome of chic, from its art deco Italian furnishings to fashions from the world's top design houses. More than 65% of its merchandise is European, and 25% is from Japan. The Loft department carries well-designed housewares and gifts, while Seed is the place to go for the latest fashions. The food department is especially good, stocking many imported items that are not available elsewhere in Hong Kong. Open Sunday through Wednesday from 10:30am to 8pm and Thursday through Saturday from 10:30am to 9pm.

FASHION

Hong Kong has been a center for the fashion industry ever since the influx of Shanghainese tailors fleeing the 1949 communist revolution in China. If you're looking for international designer brands and if money is no object, the **Landmark,** located on Des Voeux Road Central, Central, is an ultrachic shopping complex, with boutiques for Gucci, Tiffany, Polo/Ralph Lauren, Missoni, Helmut Lang, Versace, Sonia Rykiel, Louis Vuitton, Lanvin, and Christian Dior. **The Peninsula Hotel** and **The Regent Hotel,** both in Tsim Sha Tsui, have shopping arcades filled with designer names.

For trendier designs catering to an upwardly-mobile younger crowd, check out the **Joyce Boutique** chain, the first international fashion house in Hong Kong, established in the 1970s by Joyce Ma to satisfy Hong Kong women's cravings for European designs. Today her stores carry clothing by Issey Miyake, Jean-Paul Gaultier, Yohji Yamamoto, Rei Kawakubo (Comme des Garcons), and others on the cutting edge of fashion. You'll find Joyce shops at 16 Queen's Rd. Central, Central District (☎ **852/2810 1120;** MTR: Central); and 23 Nathan Rd. in Tsim Sha Tsui (☎ **2367 8128;** MTR: Tsim Sha Tsui).

For a wider range in prices, the department stores listed above are best for one-stop shopping for the entire family, as are Hong Kong's many malls and shopping centers. Otherwise, small, family-owned shops abound in both Tsim Sha Tsui and Stanley Market, offering casual wear, washable silk outfits, and other clothing at very affordable prices. Cheaper still are factory outlets and street markets (see below).

FACTORY OUTLETS   Savvy shoppers head for Hong Kong's factory outlets to take advantage of excess stock, overruns, and quality-control rejects. Because these items have been made for the export market, the sizes are Western. Bargains include clothes made of silk, cashmere, cotton, linen, knitwear, and wool. Most outlets are located on Kowloon Peninsula in an area known as **Hung Hom,** clustered in a large group of warehouse buildings called **Kaiser Estates** on Man Yue Street. Another good place for outlets is the **Pedder Building,** 12 Pedder St., Central. For a list of factory outlets along with their addresses, telephone numbers, and types of clothing, pick up the free pamphlet, *Factory Outlets for Locally Made Fashion and Jewellery,* available at HKTA offices. Most outlets are open from 9 or 10am to 6pm Monday through Friday, with shorter hours on Saturday; some are open Sunday as well.

MARKETS

STANLEY   Stanley Market is probably the most popular and best-known market in Hong Kong. Located on the southern coast of Hong Kong Island, it's a great place to buy inexpensive clothing, especially sportswear, cashmere sweaters, casual clothing, silk blouses and dresses, and linen blazers and suits. Men's, women's, and children's clothing is available. Although prices are not the bargain they once were, I buy more of my clothes here than anywhere else in Hong Kong, especially when it comes to cheap, fun fashions. The inventory changes continuously—one year it seems everyone's selling washable silk; the next year it's linen suits or Chinese traditional jackets. In recent years, souvenir shops selling crafts and products from China have also gained popularity.

To reach Stanley, take bus nos. 6, 6A, 6X or 260 from Central's Exchange Square bus terminal near the Star Ferry. The bus ride to Stanley takes approximately 30 minutes. From Kowloon, take bus no. 973 from Mody Road in Tsim Sha Tsui East or from Canton Road in Tsim Sha Tsui. Shops are open daily from 9 or 9:30am to 6pm (to 7pm on Saturday and Sunday).

LI YUEN STREET EAST & WEST   These two streets are parallel pedestrian lanes in the heart of the Central District, very narrow and often congested with human traffic. Their stalls are packed with handbags, clothes, scarves, sweaters, toys, baby clothes, watches, makeup, umbrellas, knickknacks, and even brassieres. Don't neglect the open-fronted shops behind the stalls. These two streets are located just a couple of minutes' walk from the Central MTR station or the Star Ferry, between Des Voeux Road Central and Queen's Road Central. Vendors are open daily from 10am to 6pm.

JADE MARKET   Jade, believed by the Chinese to hold mystical powers and to protect its wearer, is available in all sizes, colors, and prices at the Jade Market, located on Kansu Street in two temporary structures in the Yau Ma Tei District of Kowloon. Unless you know your jade, you won't want to make any expensive purchases here, but it's great for bangles, pendants, earrings, and inexpensive gifts, as well as inexpensive freshwater pearls from China. It's open daily from 10am to about 3pm and is located near the Jordan MTR station.

LADIES' MARKET   Stretching along Tung Choi Street (between Argyle and Dundas streets) in Mong Kok, Kowloon, Ladies' Market specializes in inexpensive women's and children's fashions, shoes, socks, hosiery, jewelry, sunglasses, watches, handbags, and other accessories. Some men's clothing is also sold. Although many of the products are geared toward local tastes and sizes, an increase in tourism has brought more fashionable clothing and T-shirts, and you may find a few bargains here. In any case, the atmosphere is fun and festive, especially at night. The nearest MTR station is Mong Kok. Vendors are open daily from about noon to 10:30pm.

TEMPLE STREET NIGHT MARKET   Temple Street in the Yau Ma Tei District of Kowloon is a night market that comes to life when the sun goes down. It offers T-shirts, jeans, menswear, watches, lighters, pens, sunglasses, jewelry, CDs, mobile phones, electronic gadgets, alarm clocks, luggage, and imitation designer watches. Bargain aggressively, and check the products carefully to make sure they're not faulty or poorly made. The night market is great entertainment, a must during your visit to Hong Kong. Although vendors begin setting up shop around 3pm, it's at its liveliest daily from about 7 to 10pm. It's located near the Jordan MTR station.

MEGAMALLS & SHOPPING CENTERS

Harbour City. Canton Rd., Tsim Sha Tsui. MTR: Tsim Sha Tsui.

This is the largest of the megamalls in Hong Kong, and probably the largest in Asia. Conveniently located right next to the dock that disgorges passengers from cruise liners and just to the east of the Star Ferry, it encompasses several zoned areas, all inter-connected by air-conditioned walkways and stretching more than a half mile along Canton Road. Altogether there are more than 700 outlets selling clothing, accessories, jewelry, cosmetics, antiques, electronic goods, furniture, housewares, toys, Asian arts and crafts, and much more. There's enough to keep you occupied for the rest of your life, but this is an especially good place on a rainy or humid day when you'd rather be inside than out. Outlets include Lane Crawford, Marks & Spencer, Burberry, DKNY, Front First (concession for local fashion designer Walter Ma), Jean-Paul Gaultier, Plantation, Salvatore Ferragamo, Vivienne Tam (another Hong Kong designer), Bally, Luis Vuitton, Gold Pfeil, and Toys "Я" Us. Some shops are closed on Sunday but otherwise the hours are from about 10 or 11am to 8pm.

Pacific Place. 88 Queensway, Central. MTR: Admiralty.

Anchored by three first-rate hotels, Pacific Place has a mall with 200 retail outlets and restaurants and three major department stores (Marks & Spencer, Lane Crawford, and Seibu). Shops include the Body Shop, Cartier, Cerruti 1881, Hermès, Hugo Boss, Kenneth Cole, Vivienne Tam, Plantation, Prada, Shu Uemura, Tiffany & Co., and Chinese Arts and Crafts Ltd.. Most are open daily from about 10:30am to 8pm.

7 Hong Kong After Dark

Hong Kong's nightlife is concentrated in Tsim Sha Tsui, in Central's entertainment areas of Lan Kwai Fong and SoHo, and in Wan Chai. If you're watching your Hong Kong dollars, take advantage of "happy hour," when many bars offer two drinks for the price of one or drinks at reduced prices. Furthermore, many pubs, bars, and lounges offer free live entertainment, from jazz to Filipino combos, which you can enjoy simply for the price of a beer. Remember, however, that a 10% service charge will be added to your bill.

To find out what's going on, pick up "Hong Kong Diary," a free HKTA leaflet published weekly. *HK Magazine,* a weekly distributed free at restaurants, bars, and other outlets, is aimed at a young readership with its revues of plays, concerts, and events in Hong Kong's alternative scene. Finally, the *Hong Kong Standard* publishes its entertainment section of Sunday, while the *South China Morning Post* carries an entertainment section on Friday.

THE BAR SCENE
KOWLOON

Blue Note. In the Kowloon Shangri-La Hotel, 64 Mody Rd., Tsim Sha Tsui East. ☎ **852/ 2721 2111**, ext. 8916. MTR: Tsim Sha Tsui.

Offering free live jazz performed by international (mostly American) musicians, this intimate, dimly lit bar is a great place to relax, listen to music, and enjoy good harbor views. Live music is featured Monday through Saturday from 8:30pm to 12:30pm, but you might wish to come early for happy hour, available from 5 to 8:30pm.

Chasers. 2–3 Knutsford Terrace, Tsim Sha Tsui. ☎ **852/2367 9487**. MTR: Tsim Sha Tsui.

One of several bars lining the narrow, alleylike Knutsford Terrace, which parallels Kimberley Road to the north, this is among the most popular, filled with a mixed clientele that includes both the young and the not-so-young, foreign and Chinese. It features a house Filipino band nightly from 11pm, playing rock, jazz, rhythm-and-blues, and everything in between, free of charge. Open Monday through Friday from 3pm to 6am and Saturday and Sunday from noon to 6am.

Delaney's. 71–77 Peking Rd., Tsim Sha Tsui. ☎ **852/2301 3980.** MTR: Tsim Sha Tsui.

This upmarket Irish pub is decorated in Old-World style with old posters and photographs. Its convivial atmosphere gets an extra boost from live Irish bands playing 2 nights a week (at last check, Friday and Saturday), free of charge. Big soccer and rugby events are shown on a big screen. A menu lists Irish stew, beef and Guinness pie, corned beef and cabbage, and other national favorites. Hours are daily from 10:30am to 2:30am. There's another Delaney's in Wan Chai at 18 Luard Rd. (☎ **852/2804 2880**).

Ned Kelly's Last Stand. 11A Ashley Rd., Tsim Sha Tsui. ☎ **852/2376 0562.** MTR: Tsim Sha Tsui.

This is a lively Aussie saloon, attracting a largely middle-aged crowd with free live Dixieland jazz or swing Monday through Saturday from 9pm to 2am. It serves Australian chow and pub grub, and happy hour is from 11:30am to 9pm. Open daily from 11:30am to 2am.

CENTRAL DISTRICT

Bull and Bear. Hutchinson House, 10 Harcourt Rd., Central. ☎ **852/2525 7436.** MTR: Central.

The huge, sprawling Bull and Bear was at the forefront of Hong Kong's English-pub craze, opening back in 1974. Notorious from the beginning, it can get pretty rowdy on weekend nights; one British expatriate described it as a "meat market." For lunch, it attracts mainly business types with its steak-and-kidney pie, salads, sandwiches, and daily specials. Happy hour is from 5 to 9pm; it's open Monday through Saturday from 8am to midnight.

California. 24–26 Lan Kwai Fong St., Central. ☎ **852/2521 1345.** MTR: Central.

Located in Central's nightlife district, this chic bar was once the place to see and be seen—the haunt of the young nouveaux riche. Newer establishments have since encroached upon California's exalted position, but it remains a respected and sophisticated restaurant/bar. You might consider starting your night on the town here with dinner and drinks—the restaurant features a changing menu from an innovative American chef, though hamburgers (the house specialty) are hugely popular. Happy hour is 5 to 9pm. On Friday and Saturday nights from 11pm to 4am, it becomes a happening disco, with DJs playing the latest hits. It's open Monday through Thursday from noon to midnight, Friday and Saturday from noon to 4am, and Sunday from 6pm to midnight.

Dublin Jack. 37 Cochrane St., Central. ☎ **852/2543 0081.** MTR: Central.

With its bright red exterior, it's easy to spot this Irish pub next to the Hillside Escalator Link in Central's SoHo entertainment district. But often packed with expats on their way home to the Mid-Levels after a day's work in Central, it can be hard to elbow your way in through the door. Happy hour is from noon to 8pm on weekdays, from 3 to 8pm on weekends. Open daily from noon to 2am.

MadDogs. 1 D'Aguilar St., Central. ☎ **852/2810 1000.** MTR: Central.

Catering to a mellow crowd of professional people during early evening hours and a wilder bunch at night, this is one of Hong Kong's longer-standing, most popular English pubs, with a traditional decor reminiscent of Britain during its imperial heyday. Happy hour is Monday through Friday from 11am to 10pm and Saturday and Sunday from 4 to 10pm. There's a DJ every night except Sunday. It's open Monday through Thursday from 11am to 2am, Friday from 10am to 3am, Saturday from 11am to 3am, and Sunday from 10am to 2am.

CAUSEWAY BAY/WAN CHAI

Joe Bananas. 23 Luard Rd., Wan Chai. ☎ **852/2529 1811.** Cover Thurs HK$50 (US$6.50), including 1 drink, after 10pm; cover Fri–Sat HK$100 (US$13), including 2 drinks, after 10pm. MTR: Wan Chai.

Under the same management as MadDogs, this combination bar/restaurant/disco has long been one of the most popular and hippest hangouts in Wan Chai. Called "JB's" by the locals, and decorated like an American diner with its jukebox, posters, and music memorabilia, it offers dancing every evening after 10pm, but a cover is charged only Thursday through Saturday (though women get in free until 1am). Open Monday through Saturday from 11am to 6am and Sunday from 5pm to 5am.

DANCE CLUBS/DISCOS

Club 97. 9 Lan Kwai Fong, Central. ☎ **852/2810 9333.** No cover Sun–Wed, HK$97 (US$12.60) Thurs–Sat. MTR: Central.

This small, cavelike disco, decorated in funky "Moroccan" style with black-and-white tiles, mirrors, and tiny lights reminiscent of stars, is fun and usually crowded to capacity. In fact, it's so small that it sometimes feels like a private party—even more so because it's officially a members-only disco. However, nonmembers are allowed in if the place isn't too crowded; plan for a weeknight. It's easy to strike up a conversation with your neighbors here, since they are generally a mixture of expatriates and Chinese. A gay happy hour takes place every Friday from 6 to 10pm. All in all, a very retro-hip joint. Hours are Monday to Thursday 9pm to 4am, Friday 6pm to 10pm and again from 11pm to 6am, Saturday 10pm to 6am, and Sunday 10pm to 2am.

Club Shanghai. In the Regent Hotel, Salisbury Rd., Tsim Sha Tsui. ☎ **852/2721 1211,** ext. 2242. No cover. MTR: Tsim Sha Tsui.

Nostalgia for 1930s Shanghai and its real or perceived decadence have captured the collective imagination of Hong Kong's clubgoers (all too young to have actually experienced the 1930s), but few venues pull it off as successfully as this classy lounge in the Regent Hotel. Bathed in dim, red lights, it features waitresses in high-collared slit dresses gliding past stuffed armchairs draped with lace antimacassars, potted palms, fringed lampshades, and decorative opium pipes. Although the focus is on live music and dancing, you can also come just for the harbor views. It's open Monday to Thursday 8pm to 1:30am and Friday and Saturday from 8pm to 2am.

JJ's. In the Grand Hyatt Hotel, 1 Harbour Rd., Wan Chai. ☎ **852/2588 1234,** ext. 7323. Cover HK$100 (US$13) Mon–Thurs (including 1 drink), HK$200 (US$26) Fri–Sat (including 2 drinks). No cover before 8:30pm. MTR: Wan Chai.

This upscale, glitzy entertainment complex was the first in Hong Kong to offer several diversions under one roof, making it a good choice for those who like to move from one scene to the next without actually having to go anywhere. Decorated in a style that is part Victorian and part whimsical, giving it an eccentric and playful ambience, it consists of a main bar, a disco with house tracks and laser lights, a restaurant serving pizza and sandwiches, and a room with live music featuring jazz or rhythm-and-blues. JJ's is open Monday through Thursday from 5:30pm to 2am, Friday from 5:30pm to 3am, and Saturday from 6pm to 4am. Happy hour is Monday through Friday from 5:30 to 8:30pm.

Propaganda. 1 Hollywood Rd., Central. ☎ **852/2868 1316.** Cover (including 1 drink) Thurs HK$80 (US$10.40), Fri HK$120 (US$15.60), Sat HK$200 (US$25.95). No cover Mon–Wed, before 10:30pm Thurs, or after 3:30am Fri; reduced cover before 10:30pm Thurs–Sat. MTR: Central.

Hong Kong's most popular gay disco, Propaganda is located in the SoHo nightlife district, with a discreet entrance in a back alley. The crowd is 95% gay, but everyone is welcome. Come late if you want to see this alternative hot spot at its most crowded. It's open Monday through Wednesday from 9pm to 3:30am, Thursday from 9pm to 4am, Friday from 9am to 5pm, and Saturday from 9pm to 6am.

PERFORMING ARTS

To obtain tickets for the Hong Kong Philharmonic Orchestra, Hong Kong Chinese Orchestra, Chinese opera, and other performances and events, call the **Urban Council Ticketing Office (URBTIX)** at ☎ **852/2734 9009,** or drop by outlets located at the Hong Kong Cultural Centre, 10 Salisbury Rd. in Tsim Sha Tsui, or at City Hall, Low Block, 7 Edinburgh Place in Central, both open daily from 10am to 9:30pm.

Chinese Opera.

Chinese opera predates the first Western opera by about 600 years, though it wasn't until the 13th and 14th centuries that performances began to develop a structured operatic form, along with distinct regional styles. Most popular in Hong Kong are Peking-style opera, with its spectacular costumes, elaborate makeup, and feats of acrobatics and swordsmanship; and the less flamboyant but more readily understood Cantonese-style opera. Plots usually dramatize legends and historical events and extol such virtues as loyalty, filial piety, and righteousness. Accompanied by seven or eight musicians, the performers sing in shrill, high-pitched falsetto, a sound Westerners may not initially appreciate.

For visitors, the easiest way to see a Chinese opera is during a festival, such as the Hong Kong Arts Festival, held from about mid-February through early March each year. Otherwise, Cantonese opera is performed fairly regularly at Town Halls in the New Territories, as well as in City Hall in Central, but tickets, generally ranging from HK$100 to HK$230 (US$13 to US$29.85), usually sell out well in advance. Contact HKTA for an updated schedule.

Hong Kong Chinese Orchestra.

Established in 1977, the Hong Kong Chinese Orchestra is the world's largest professional Chinese-instrument orchestra, with 85 musicians performing both new and traditional works using traditional and modern Chinese instruments and combining them with Western and Chinese orchestrations. Performances are held at the Hong Kong Cultural Centre, 10 Salisbury Rd., Tsim Sha Tsui (☎ **852/2734 2009**), and at City Hall, Edinburgh Place, Central District (☎ **852/2921 2840**), with tickets ranging from HK$60 to HK$120 (US$7.80 to US$15.60).

Hong Kong Philharmonic Orchestra.

The Hong Kong Cultural Centre, 10 Salisbury Rd. in Tsim Sha Tsui (☎ **852/2734 2009**) and City Hall in Central (☎ **852/2921 2840**), are home of the Hong Kong Philharmonic, founded in 1975 and performing regularly from September to June and at other scheduled events throughout the year. Its conductor is David Atherton; guest conductors and soloists appear during the concert season. In addition to Western classical pieces, its repertoire is enriched by works commissioned from Chinese composers. Tickets range from HK$60 to HK$270 (US$7.80 to US$35.10).

8 A Side Trip to Macau

Macau was established as a Portuguese colony in 1557, centuries before the British acquired Hong Kong. Just 65 kilometers (40 miles) west of Hong Kong, across the

Pearl River Estuary, Macau is a small and unpretentious provincial town, only 24.7 square kilometers (9.5 sq. miles) in area and reminding old-timers of what Hong Kong used to look like decades ago. But with its unique mixture of Portuguese and Chinese cultures, Macau feels different from Hong Kong, different from China, different from anywhere else. Maybe it's the jumble of Chinese signs and stores mixed in with pastel-colored colonial-style buildings, the temples alongside Catholic churches, the flair of Portugal blended with the practicality of the Chinese. There are beaches, churches, fortresses, temples, gardens, museums, and fascinating neighborhoods to explore, as well as casinos and restaurants serving wonderful Macanese cuisine.

On December 20, 1999, Portugal's 400 years of rule came to an end when Macau was handed back to China. Like Hong Kong, Macau is a Special Administrative Region of China, permitted its own internal government and economic system for another 50 years after the Chinese assumed control.

ENTRY REQUIREMENTS

Americans, Canadians, Australians, Irish, British, and New Zealanders need only **passports**—no visas—for stays up to 20 days. Macau's official currency is the **pataca** (ptc), pegged to the Hong Kong dollar at a rate of $103.20 patacas to HK$100 (or 8 patacas for each US$1). However, because Hong Kong dollars are readily accepted everywhere in Macau at a rate of HK$1 to 1 ptc, even on buses and for taxis (though you are likely to receive change in patacas), it's not worth the hassle to exchange money for short stays. Hotel rates are generally quoted only in Hong Kong dollars, and unused patacas *cannot* be used in Hong Kong. Like the Hong Kong dollar, the pataca is identified by the "$" sign, sometimes also written "M$" or "MOP$." To avoid confusion, I have identified patacas by the shortened "ptcs."

ARRIVING

BY BOAT   Macau is easily accessible from Hong Kong by high-speed jetfoil, with most departures from the **Macau Ferry Terminal,** located just west of the Central District in the Shun Tak Centre, 200 Connaught Rd., on Hong Kong Island. Situated above Sheung Wan MTR station, the terminal houses jetfoil ticket offices, as well as the Macau Government Tourist Office (Room 336, on the same floor as boats departing for Macau). Limited service is also available from Kowloon, from the newer China Hong Kong Terminal on Canton Road, Tsim Sha Tsui.

The fastest, most convenient way to travel to Macau is via a 55-minute ride on a **jetfoil,** operated by TurboJET (☎ **852/2859 3333**), with departures from the Macau Ferry Terminal every 15 minutes from 7am to 5:30pm and every 30 to 60 minutes throughout the night. One-way fares Monday through Friday are HK$232 (US$30.15) for super class and HK$130 (US$16.90) for economy class; fares on Saturday, Sunday, and holidays are HK$247 (US$32.10) in super class and HK$141 (US$18.35) in economy. Fares for night service (from 5:45pm to 6am) are HK$260 (US$33.75) in super class and HK$161 (US$20.95) in economy class. Senior citizens older than 60 and children younger than 12 receive a HK$15 (US$1.95) discount. Departure taxes are included in the fares.

Tickets can be purchased at the Macau Ferry Terminal or at any MTR Travel Service Centre found at several MTR stations, including Tsim Sha Tsui, Hong Kong, Admiralty, and Causeway Bay. You can also book by credit card by calling ☎ **852/ 2921 6688.** Note that passengers are allowed only one hand-carried bag, not to exceed 22 pounds, with one additional piece checked in 20 minutes prior to departure for a fee ranging from HK$20 to HK$60 (US$2.60 to US$7.80), depending on weight.

Macau

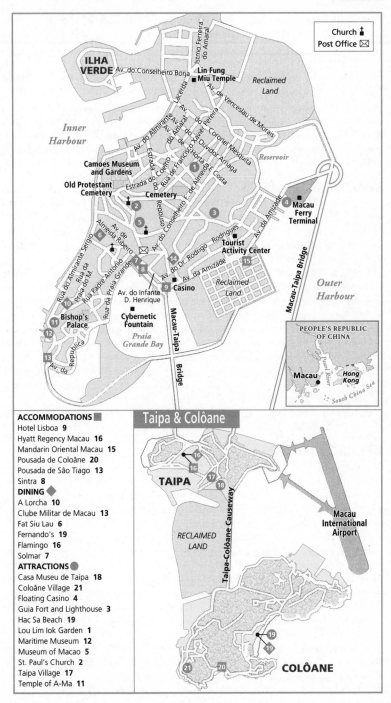

Church ✝
Post Office ✉

ILHA VERDE

Av. do Conselheiro Borja

Istmo Ferreira do Amaral

Lin Fung Miu Temple

Reclaimed Land

Av. de Venceslau de Morais

Inner Harbour

Av. do Almirante
Av. do Amaral
Av. do Coronel Mesquita
Av. do Ouvidor Arriaga
Rua de Francisco Xavier Pereira
Horta e Costa
Rua do Campo

Estrada do Cemitério

Camões Museum and Gardens

Old Protestant Cemetery

Cemetery

Estrada do Repouso

Av. de Almeida Ribeiro

Reservoir

①

②

③

④ **Macau Ferry Terminal**

⑤

⑥

Av. do Dr. Rodrigo Rodrigues

Tourist Activity Center

Av. da Amizade

Macau-Taipa Bridge

Outer Harbour

⑦
⑧

⑭ **⑮**

Av. do Dr. Rodrigo Rodrigues

Av. da Amizade

⑨ **Casino**

Rua do Almirante Sérgio
Rua da Praia do M.
Rua Padre António
Rua da Praia Grande

Av. do Infante D. Henrique

Reclaimed Land

⑩

Bishop's Palace

Cybernetic Fountain

⑪

⑫

Av. da República

⑬

Praia Grande Bay

Macau-Taipa Bridge

PEOPLE'S REPUBLIC OF CHINA

Pearl River

Macau ●

Hong Kong

South China Sea

Taipa & Colôane

TAIPA

⑯
⑯
⑰
⑱

Taipa-Colôane Causeway

RECLAIMED LAND

Macau International Airport

⑲
⑲

⑳
㉑

COLÔANE

113

In Macau, you'll arrive at the new **Macau Ferry Terminal,** located on the main peninsula. After going through Customs, be sure to stop by the Macau Government Tourist Office for a map and brochures. In the arrivals hall is also a counter for hotels operating free shuttle buses. Otherwise, city buses 3, 3A, and 10 travel from the terminal to Avenida Almeida Ribeiro, the main downtown street. The fare is $2.50 ptcs (US$0.30).

BY PLANE   Macau's International Airport, located on Taipa Island and connected to the mainland by bridge, serves flights mainly from China and a few other Asian cities. Several first-class hotels offer complimentary transfer on request. Otherwise, airport bus AP1 travels from the airport to the ferry terminal and Hotel Lisboa; the fare is $6 ptcs (US$0.80). A taxi to the Lisboa costs approximately $40 ptcs (US$5.20).

VISITOR INFORMATION

There are two **Macau Government Tourist Offices** (MGTO) in Hong Kong—in the arrivals lobby of the International Airport, open daily from 9am to 10:30pm (closed for lunch from 1 to 1:30pm and dinner from 6 to 6:30pm), and in room 336 on the third floor of the Macau Ferry Terminal, Shun Tak Centre, in Central (☎ **852/2857 2287**), open daily from 9am to 5:30pm.

In Macau, you'll find a MGTO at the Macau Ferry Terminal, located just outside Customs and open daily from 9am to 10pm; there is also a MGTO at Macau International Airport, open for all incoming flights. For complete information, stop by the main Macau Government Tourist Office, Largo do Senado, 9 (☎ **853/315 566**), located in the center of town on the main plaza just off Avenida Almeida Ribeiro and open daily from 9am to 6pm. Other tourist information offices are located at St. Paul's Church and the Macau Cultural Center, both open daily from 9am to 6pm; and at **Guia Fort and Lighthouse,** open daily from 9am to 5:30pm. Be sure to pick up a free map of the city, brochures on everything from churches to fortresses, and the tourist tabloid *Macau Travel Talk.*

Finally, you can also obtain information on Macau by visiting its Web site at **www.macautourism.gov.mo;** its e-mail address is mgto@macautourism.gov.mo.

GETTING AROUND

Macau comprises a small peninsula and two small islands—Taipa and Colôane, linked to the mainland by bridges and a causeway. The peninsula—referred to simply as Macau and surrounded by an Inner and an Outer Harbour—is where you'll find the city of Macau, as well as the ferry terminal and most of its hotels, shops, and attractions. Macau's main road is Avenida Almeida Ribeiro; about halfway down its length is the attractive Largo do Senado, or Senate Square, Macau's main plaza.

Because the peninsula is only 2½ miles in length and a mile at its greatest width, you can walk most everywhere. If you get tired, jump into one of the licensed metered **taxis,** all painted black and beige and quite inexpensive. The charge is $10 ptcs (US$1.30) at flagfall for the first 1.5 kilometers (0.9 miles), then $1 ptc (US$0.13) for each subsequent 250 meters (825 ft.). There's a surcharge of $5 ptcs (US$0.65) if you go all the way to Colôane. There is no surcharge, however, for the return journey to Macau.

Public buses run daily from 7am to midnight, with fares costing $2.50 ptcs (US$0.30) for travel within the Macau Peninsula, $3.30 ptcs (US$0.45) for travel to Taipa, and $4 ptcs to $5 ptcs (US$0.60 to US$0.65) for travel to Colôane. Buses heading for Taipa and Colôane Islands make a stop in front of the Hotel Lisboa, located on the peninsula near the Macau-Taipa Bridge. The MGTO has a free map with bus routes.

There are also **pedicabs,** tricycles with seating for two passengers. Once the most common form of transportation in Macau, increased traffic and rising affluence have rendered them almost obsolete. Today pedicab drivers vie mostly for the tourist dollar, charging about $150 ptcs (US$19.50) for an hour of sightseeing. Be sure to settle on the fare, the route, and the length of the journey before climbing in.

Finally, if you want to drive around on your own, you can see Macau by **Moke,** a small, Jeep-like vehicle. However, because traffic on the peninsula is so congested, I recommend hiring a Moke only for exploring the islands. Mokes rent for $480 ptcs (US$62.40) per 24 hours Monday through Friday and $500 ptcs (US$65) per 24 hours on Saturday, Sunday, and holidays, and are available from **Happy Mokes,** with a location at the Macau Ferry Terminal, level 1, counter 1025 (☎ **853/726868**). Drivers must be at least 21 years old and must have held a driver's license for at least 2 years. Contact the Macau tourist office for more information. *Note: Driving in Macau is on the left.*

ACCOMMODATIONS

In addition to the rack rates given below (quoted in Hong Kong dollars), there is a 10% hotel service charge and a 5% government tax. If you plan on visiting Macau in late November, when the Grand Prix is held, you should book well in advance.

EXPENSIVE

✪ **Hyatt Regency Macau.** 2 Estrada Almirante Marquês Esparteiro, Taipa Island, Macau. ☎ **853/831234,** or 800/233-1234 in the U.S. and Canada, or 852/2956 1234 for reservations in Hong Kong. Fax 853/830195. www.macauhyatt.com. E-mail: hyatt@macau.ctm.net. 326 units. A/C MINIBAR TV TEL. HK$1,600–HK$1,750 (US$208–US$227) single or double; HK$1,900 (US$247) Regency Club; from HK$2,400 (US$312) suite. Children under 12 stay free in parents' room (maximum 3 persons per room). AE, DC, MC, V. Free shuttle bus from ferry terminal and airport, or bus no. 28A from the ferry terminal.

If you're looking for a resort getaway with a tropical, Mediterranean atmosphere, extensive recreational facilities for the entire family, great restaurants, and comfortable rooms, the Hyatt is a good choice. Located on Taipa Island and offering free shuttle service to the mainland, the hotel boasts a sprawling, 3-acre spa and sport complex set amidst lush greenery with an outdoor heated pool open year-round, four flood-lit tennis courts, two squash courts, fitness rooms, and more. It's also a good choice for families with its wading pool, playground, games room, and wonderful child-care center for children ages 2 to 8 (open Sunday through Friday from 10:30am to 7:30pm, and Saturday and holidays from 9:30am to 9pm). For children ages 5 to 12, there's Camp Hyatt, with fun activities offered weekends and school and public holidays. The guest rooms, with rattan furnishings and Asian artwork, offer all the usual amenities, including satellite TV with pay in-house movies, room safe, data ports, and a voice-mail system. The least expensive rooms face inland toward new apartment construction, while the best rooms offer views of the Outer Harbour and Macau's rapidly changing skyline.

Other facilities and services include a multi-purpose court for volleyball, basketball, and badminton; aerobics class; rental bicycles; male and female spas with sauna, steam room, Jacuzzi, massage and solarium; hair salon; games room with table tennis and pool tables; business center; free shuttle to the ferry, airport, and Hotel Lisboa; same-day laundry service; 24-hour room service; free newspaper; in-house nurse and doctor on call 24 hours; and baby-sitting. In short, you could easily unwind here for days.

The Chinese is a hip Cantonese restaurant specializing in country-style cooking, while the **Flamingo** is a Macanese restaurant with a tropical hot-pink setting, terrace seating, and views of a small lake. There's a swim-up bar in the swimming pool, a restaurant with themed lunch and dinner buffets and international à-la-carte menu, a cocktail lounge with live entertainment, and a 24-hour casino. If you like exploring or dining on local cuisine, the quaint Taipa Village is only a 15-minute walk away.

○ **Mandarin Oriental Macau.** 956–1110 Avenida da Amizade, Macau. ☎ **853/567888,** or 800/526-6566 in the U.S. and Canada, or 852/2881 1288 for reservations in Hong Kong. Fax 853/594589. www.mandarinoriental.com. E-mail: mandarin@macau.ctm.net. 435 units. A/C MINIBAR TV TEL. HK$1,600–HK$1,900 (US$208–US$247) single or double; HK$2,000– HK$2,200 (US$260–US$286) Mandarin floors; from HK$4,600 (US$597) suite. AE, DC, MC, V. Free shuttle bus from ferry terminal and airport.

A companion hotel of the Mandarin Oriental in Hong Kong and the Oriental in Bangkok, this exclusive property is conveniently located about a 7-minute walk from the ferry terminal in the direction of downtown. Although a huge land-reclamation project has robbed the hotel of much of its harbor views, the hotel claimed a small portion of reclaimed land for its new, state-of-the-art resort facility, which includes an outdoor, beautifully landscaped swimming pool (heated in winter and chilled in summer); a water slide, pool, playground, and day-care center for the kids; a fitness room and aerobics studio; a spa offering five types of massage, body scrubs, wraps, and facials; and the Outdoor Adventure Learning Centre, which offers a rock climbing tower and a flying trapeze.

Although the hotel's exterior is rather nondescript, the interior is beautifully designed and elegantly decorated throughout with imports from Portugal, including blue-and-white tiles, chandeliers, tapestries, and artwork. The marble lobby features a carved teak staircase leading up to the second floor, where you'll find the hotel's small but sophisticated casino, with a separate room for slot machines. The guest rooms, equipped with safes, a voice-mail system, data ports, tea- and coffee-making facilities, and satellite TVs with in-house movies, are decorated in soft pink or green with Portuguese fabrics and natural teak, and the bathrooms are marbled and spacious. The least expensive rooms face inland, while the best rooms (on the top four Mandarin executive floors) face the sea and feature large balconies.

Italian cuisine is offered at **Mezzaluna,** the hotel's premier restaurant. At the **Dynasty** you can eat dim sum and other Cantonese food, while the **Cafe Girassol** is open 24 hours a day except on Thursday and specializes in Macanese/Portuguese and Asian cuisine, with great breakfast, lunch, and dinner buffets. **Fresco MediterAsian Grill** offers alfresco dining with a view of the pool and low-fat cuisine that blends Thai, Greek, Italian, Chinese, and Portuguese ingredients. The **Embassy Bar** features a live band every night except Monday from 10pm to 1am, while the casino is open 24 hours.

Other facilities and amenities include sauna; steam room; Jacuzzi; 2 hard-court and 2 artificial-turf floodlit tennis courts; 2 indoor squash courts; a multi-purpose court for basketball, badminton, and volleyball; business center; shopping arcade; book kiosk; beauty salon; 24-hour room service; car rental; doctor on call 24 hours; babysitting; parcel and packing service; same-day laundry and dry cleaning; free shuttle bus to the ferry and airport.

○ **Pousada de São Tiago.** Avenida da República, Fortaleza de São Tiago da Barra, Macau. ☎ **853/378111,** or 852/2739 1216 for reservations in Hong Kong. Fax 853/552170. www. saotiago.com.mo. E-mail: saotiago@macau.ctm.net. 24 units. A/C MINIBAR TV TEL. HK$1,540–HK$1,880 (US$200–US$244) single or double; from HK$2,100 (US$273) suite. AE, DC, MC, V. Free shuttle bus (on request) or bus no. 28B from ferry terminal.

Built around the ruins of the Portuguese Fortress da Barra, which dates from 1629, this delightful small inn on the tip of the peninsula is guaranteed to charm even the most jaded of travelers. The entrance is dramatic—a flight of stone stairs leading

Jugglers, dancers and an assortment of acrobats fill the street.

She shoots you a wide-eyed look as a seven-foot cartoon character approaches.

What brought you here was wanting the kids

to see something magical while they still believed in magic.

America Online Keyword: Travel

With 700 airlines, 50,000 hotels and over 5,000 cruise and vaca-

tion getaways, you can now go places you've always dreamed of.

Travelocity.com
A Sabre Company
Go Virtually Anywhere.

"WORLD'S LEADING TRAVEL WEB SITE, 5 YEARS IN A ROW" WORLD TRAVEL AWARDS

I HAVE TO CALL THE TRAVEL AGENCY AGAIN. DARN, OUT TO LUNCH. NOW I HAVE TO CALL THE AIRLINE. I HATE CALLING THE AIRLINES. I GOT PUT ON HOLD AGAIN. "INSTRUMENTAL TOP-40" ... LOVELY. I HATE GETTING PUT ON HOLD. TICKET PRICES ARE ALL OVER THE MAP. HOW DO I DIAL INTERNA-TIONALLY? OH SHOOT, FORGOT THE RENTAL CAR. I'M STILL ON HOLD. THIS MUSIC IS GIVING ME A HEADACHE. I WONDER IF SOMEONE ELSE HAS CHEAPER FLIGHTS. FORGET IT, CAN'T TAKE IT ANYMORE ... I'M HANGING UP.

YAHOO! TRAVEL
100% MUZAK-FREE

Booking your trip online at Yahoo! Travel is simple. You compare the best prices. You click. You go have fun. Tickets, hotels, rental cars, cruises & more. Sorry, no muzak.

YAHOO!®
Travel
travel.yahoo.com

through a cavelike tunnel that was once part of the fort, with water trickling in small rivulets on one side of the stairs. Once inside, guests are treated to the hospitality of a Portuguese inn, with bedroom furniture imported from Portugal and the use of stone, brick, and Portuguese blue tile throughout. The outdoor swimming pool is a great place to while away an afternoon, and most of the rooms, all of which face the sea, have balconies. Although lacking the recreational resort facilities of other hotels in this category, this place is a true find, perfect for a romantic getaway. The Maritime Museum and A-Ma Temple are within easy walking distance; you can also walk to the city center in about a half hour.

Amenities include baby-sitting, same-day laundry and dry-cleaning service, medical and dental service, free newspaper, room service (7am to 11:30pm), and complimentary shuttle to and from the ferry pier on request. Cafe Da Barra, with an elegant, drawing-room ambience, is open for dinner with a mix of classic Portuguese and Continental cuisine. Os Gatos, which offers dining on either a banyan-shaded outdoor patio with glimpses of the sea or in a glass-enclosed air-conditioned room, serves specialties from Macau, Portugal, and the Mediterranean region.

MODERATE

Hotel Lisboa. Avenida da Amizade, Macau. ☎ **853/577666,** or 800/44-UTELL in the U.S. and Canada, or 852/2546 6944 for reservations in Hong Kong. Fax 853/567193. www. macau.ctm.net/~lisboa. E-mail: lisboa@macau.ctm.net. 928 units. A/C MINIBAR TV TEL. HK$1,350–HK$2,350 (US$175–US$305) single or double; from HK$3,800 (US$493.50) suite. Children under 13 stay free in parents' room. AE, DC, MC, V. Free shuttle bus or bus nos. 3, 3A, 28A, 28B, or 28C from the ferry terminal.

The Lisboa is in a class by itself. Built in 1969, it's a Chinese version of Las Vegas— huge, flashy, and with a bewildering array of facilities that make it almost a city within a city. I always get lost in this hotel. Located near one of the bridges to Taipa island, it also has great feng shui, which may explain why its casino is one of the most popular in Macau. You certainly can't get much closer to the action than the Lisboa; it is very popular among the Hong Kong Chinese and tour groups from China and Taiwan, making its lobby rather noisy and crowded. Its casino, one of the largest, never closes, and there are countless restaurants, shops, and nighttime diversions, including the Crazy Paris Show, a revue of scantily clad European women. Other facilities include an outdoor heated swimming pool, fitness center, sauna, large shopping arcade, electronic games room, beauty salon, and barber shop. One advantage to staying here is that buses to the outlying islands and other parts of Macau stop at the front door. As for the rooms, they're located in an older wing, a newer wing, and a tower completed in 1993 which offers the best—and most expensive—harbor views, including rooms with traditional Chinese architecture and furniture. Otherwise, rooms seem rather old-fashioned in color schemes of green, pink, or orange, but they do boast satellite TV with 18 channels and pay movies, room safe, and hair dryer. In short, this is the place to be if you want to be in the thick of it. I suspect some guests check in and never leave the premises, though downtown Macau is only a 5-minute walk away. Guests enjoy 24-hour room service, same-day laundry service, house doctor, money-exchange banks, complimentary shuttle service, free newspaper on request, and baby-sitting.

Pousada de Colôane. Praia de Cheoc Van, Colôane Island, Macau. ☎ **853/882143.** Fax 853/882251. 22 units. A/C MINIBAR TV TEL. HK$680–HK$750 (US$88–US$97.50) single or double. AE, MC, V. Bus: nos. 21A, 25, or 26 from Lisboa Hotel (tell the bus driver you want to get off at the hotel).

This small, family-owned property, perched on a hill above Cheoc Van Beach with views of the sea, is a good place for couples and families in search of a reasonably priced isolated retreat. More than 30 years old but recently removed, it's a relaxing, rather rustic place, with modestly furnished rooms, all of which have large balconies and face the sea and beach. There is an outdoor swimming pool, a smaller children's pool, a playground, an outdoor terrace where you can have drinks, and a Portuguese restaurant. *Note:* The hotel was closed for renovation at press time; call to make sure it has reopened.

Sintra. Avenida de D. João IV, Macau. ☎ **853/710111,** 800/44-UTELL in the U.S. and Canada, or 852/2546 6944 for reservations in Hong Kong. Fax 853/567769. www.macau. ctm.net/~sintra. E-mail: bcsintra@macau.ctm.net. 240 units. A/C TV TEL. HK$680–HK$960 (US$88–US$125) single or double; HK$880–HK$1,080 (US$114–US$140) executive floor; from HK$1,480 (US$192) suite. Children under 13 stay free in parents' room. AE, DC, MC, V. Free shuttle bus or bus nos. 3A or 10 from the ferry terminal.

This moderately priced hotel (under the same management as Hotel Lisboa) enjoys a prime location in the heart of Macau, within easy walking distance of Avenida de Almeida Ribeiro (Macau's main street). Originally built in 1975 but completely over-hauled in the mid-1990s, it offers large rooms with satellite TVs and pay movies. The higher-priced rooms are even larger and occupy higher floors; individual bookings (not through a travel agency) are often upgraded to one of these rooms if space permits. Executive rooms occupy the top floor feature such extras as complimentary buffet breakfast, newspaper, fruit basket, shoe shine, and a welcome drink. The hotel's one restaurant (open 24 hours) serves Western and Chinese food, including dim sum breakfasts and buffet lunches, and there's a business center, a shopping center, a sauna (for men only), 24-hour room service, and same-day laundry service.

DINING

As a former trading center for spices and a melting pot for Portuguese and Chinese cultures, it's little wonder that Macau developed its own very fine Macanese cuisine. One of the most popular dishes is African chicken, grilled or baked with chiles and piri-piri peppers. Other favorites include Portuguese chicken (baked with potatoes, tomatoes, olive oil, curry, coconut, saffron, and black olives), bacalhau (codfish), Macau sole, caldeirada (seafood stew), spicy giant shrimp, baked quail and pigeon, curried crab, Portuguese sausage, and feijoada (a Brazilian stew of pork, black beans, cabbage, and spicy sausage). And don't forget Portuguese wine, inexpensive and a great bargain.

Note: Restaurants will add a 10% service charge to your bill.

EXPENSIVE

Clube Militar de Macau. Avenida da Praia Grande, 795. ☎ **853/714009.** Reservations recommended for lunch. Main courses HK$90–HK$120 (US$11.70–US$15.60); fixed-price lunch or dinner HK$90 (US$11.70); lunch buffet HK$130 (US$16.90). AE, MC, V. Daily noon–3pm and 7–11pm. Bus: nos. 3, 3A, 10, 10A, or 10. MACANESE/PORTUGUESE.

This is certainly one of Macau's most atmospheric dining halls, located in the century-old Military Club and opened to non-members in 1995. Painted a bright pink, this striking colonial building boasts an old-fashioned dining hall with tall ceilings, whirring ceiling fans, arched windows, wooden floor, and displays of Chinese dish-ware. If you order from the menu, it's best to stick to the classics, such as codfish, seafood stew in a white wine sauce, sirloin steak Portuguese style, stewed lamb leg in red wine, or African chicken. Most popular, however, is the lunch buffet. The restaurant's list of Portuguese wines is among the best in town.

✪ Flamingo. In the Hyatt Regency Hotel, Taipa Island. ☎ **853/831234.** Reservations recommended Sat–Sun. Main courses HK$68–HK$130 (US$8.85–US$16.90); fixed-price lunch HK$78 (US$10.15). AE, DC, MC, V. Daily noon–3pm and 7–11pm. Bus: nos. 11, 21, 21A, 28A, or 33. MACANESE/PORTUGUESE.

If I had time for only one memorable meal in Macau, this would be a serious contender. Decorated in hot pink, this restaurant has a great Mediterranean ambience, with ceiling fans, swaying palms, and a terrace overlooking lush landscaping and a duck pond. An air-conditioned enclosure was recently added for lightweights unaccustomed to alfresco dining, but for me the real pleasure of dining here is the terrace. The bread is homemade, and the specialties are a unique blend of Portuguese, Chinese, African, Indian, and Malay spices, resulting in delicious Macanese fare as well as traditional Portuguese dishes. Try the spicy king prawns with chile sauce, curried crab, African chicken with chile-coconut sauce, grilled sardines, codfish, or Macanese fried rice with chorizo, shrimp, chicken, and vegetables. A strolling three-man band sets the mood.

MODERATE

A Lorcha. Rua do Almirante Sergio, 289. ☎ **853/313193.** Reservations recommended for lunch. Main courses HK$50–HK$82 (US$6.45–US$10.65). AE, MC, V. Wed–Mon 12:30–3:30pm and 7–11pm. Bus: nos. 1, 1A, 2, 5, 6, 7, 8, 9, 10, 10A, 11, 18, 21, 21A, or 28B. PORTUGUESE.

Just a stone's throw from the Maritime Museum and A-Ma Temple, this is your best bet if you find yourself hungering for Portuguese food in the area. Look for its white-washed walls, an architectural feature repeated inside the tiny restaurant with its low, arched ceiling. Casual yet often filled with businesspeople, it offers stewed broad beans Portuguese-style, codfish in a cream sauce, fried shrimp, clams prepared in garlic and olive oil, and other traditional, consistently good dishes.

Fat Siu Lau. Rua da Felicidade, 64. ☎ **853/573585.** Main courses HK$45–HK$135 (US$5.85–US$17.55). No credit cards. Daily 11:30am–11:30pm. Bus: nos. 3, 3A, 5, 6, 7, 8, 10, 11, 18, 19, 21, or 21A. MACANESE.

This is Macau's oldest restaurant (dating from 1903), and though trendier restaurants have stolen the spotlight, it remains a good standby. The three floors of dining have been renovated in upbeat modern art deco, but the exterior matches all the other storefronts on the handsome renovated street—whitewashed walls and red shutters and doors. Macanese specialties include roast pigeon marinated according to a 90-year-old secret recipe; spicy African chicken; curried crab; garoupa stewed with tomatoes, bell pepper, onion, and potatoes; and grilled king prawns.

Fernando's. Praia de Hac Sa, 9, Colôane. ☎ **853/882264** or 853/882531. Main courses HK$60–HK$148 (US$7.80–US$19.20). No credit cards. Daily noon–9:30pm. Bus: nos. 21A, 25, or 26A. PORTUGUESE.

For years Fernando's was just another shack on Hac Sa Beach, hardly distinguishable from the others (it's the one closest to the beach, below the vines). But then a brick pavilion was added out back, complete with ceiling fans and an adjacent open-air bar (a good place to wait for a table; reservations are not accepted), and now everyone knows the place. The strictly Portuguese menu includes a wide range of seafood, feijoada, veal, chicken, pork ribs, suckling pig, and salads. The bread comes from the restaurant's own bakery, and the vegetables are grown on the restaurant's own garden plot across the border in China. Only Portuguese wine is served. Very informal, and not for those who demand pristine conditions—there is no air-conditioning, not even in the kitchen.

✪ **Galo.** Rua dos Clérigos, 45, Taipa Village, Taipa Island. ☎ **853/827423** or 853/827318. Main courses HK$40–HK$140 (US$5.20–US$18.20). No credit cards. Daily 11:30am–3pm and 5:30–10:30pm. Bus: nos. 11, 22, 28A, 33, or 34. PORTUGUESE/MACANESE.

A delightful, two-story house in Taipa Village has been converted into this informal and festively decorated restaurant specializing in local cuisines and unique creations of the talented owner/chef. "Galo" means rooster in Portuguese; look for the picture of the rooster outside the restaurant. Its menu, which includes photographs of each dish, offers such house specialties as Macau crabs, prepared with a mixture of Shanghainese and Macanese ingredients rather than curry. You might also want to try giant prawns, mussels, African chicken, Portuguese broad beans, or the mixed grill. In any case, be sure to start out with the *sopa da casa* (house soup), made from potatoes, red beans, onions, and vegetables simmered in broth from boiled beef and sausages. Delicious!

ATTRACTIONS

✪ St. Paul's Church. Rua de São Paulo. ☎ **853/358444.** Free admission. Grounds open daily 24 hrs.; museum Wed–Mon 9am–6pm. Bus: nos. 3, 3A, or 10 to Largo do Senado square (off Avenida Almeida Ribeiro), then follow the wavy, tiled sidewalk leading uphill to the northeast for about 10 mins.

The most famous structure in Macau is the ruin of St. Paul's Church. Crowning the top of a hill in the center of the city and approached by a grand sweep of stairs, only its ornate facade and some excavated sites remain. It was designed by an Italian Jesuit and built in the early 1600s with the help of Japanese Christians who had fled persecution in Nagasaki. In 1835 the church caught fire during a typhoon and burned to the ground, leaving only its now-famous facade. The facade is adorned with carvings and statues depicting Christianity in Asia, resulting in a rather intriguing mix of images that includes a Virgin Mary flanked by a peony (representing China) and a chrysanthemum (representing Japan), and a Chinese dragon, Portuguese ship, and demon. Beyond the facade is the excavated crypt, where glass-fronted cases hold the bones of 17th-century Christian martyrs from Japan and Vietnam. Here, too, is the tomb of Father Allesandro Valignano, who founded the church and helped introduce Christianity in Japan. Next to the crypt is the underground Museum of Sacred Art, which contains religious works of art produced in Macau from the 17th to the 20th centuries, including 17th-century oil paintings by exiled Japanese Christian artists, crucifixes of filigree silver, and carved wooden saints.

✪ Museum of Macau. Citadel of São Paulo do Monte (St. Paul Monte Fortress). ☎ **853/357911.** Admission $15 ptcs (US$1.95) adults, $8 ptcs (US$1.05) senior citizens and children. Tues–Sun 10am–6pm. Located next to St. Paul's Church.

A must-see, this very ambitious project provides an excellent overview of Macau's history, local traditions, and arts and crafts. It's located beside St. Paul's Church in the bowels of ancient Monte Fortress (which was destroyed by the same fire that gutted St. Paul's). Displays, arranged chronologically, commence with the beginnings of Macau and the arrival of Portuguese traders and Jesuit missionaries. Particularly interesting is the room comparing Chinese and European civilizations at the time of their encounter in the 16th century, including descriptions of their different writing systems, philosophies, and religions. Other displays deal with the daily life and traditions of old Macau, including festivals, wedding ceremonies, and industries ranging from fishing to fireworks factories. Displays include paintings and photographs of Macau through the centuries, traditional games and toys, an explanation of Macanese cuisine and architecture, and a re-created Macau street.

✪ Maritime Museum. Largo do Pagode da Barra, 1. ☎ **853/595481.** Admission HK$10 (US$1.30) adults, HK$5 (US$0.65) children, free for senior citizens and children under 10. Sun and holidays, half price. Wed–Mon 10am–5:30pm. Bus: nos. 1, 1A, 2, 5, 6, 7, 8, 9, 10, 10A, 11, 18, 21, 21A, or 28B.

Macau's oldest museum, ideally situated on the waterfront of the Inner Harbour where visitors can observe barges and other boats passing by, does an excellent job tracing the history of Macau's lifelong relationship with the sea. It's located at the tip of the peninsula, across from the Temple of A-Ma, in approximately the same spot where the Portuguese first landed. The museum begins with dioramas depicting the legend of A-Ma, protectress of seafarers and Macau's namesake, and continues with models of various boats, including trawlers, Chinese junks, Portuguese sailing boats, and even modern jetfoils. There are also life-size original boats on display, ranging from the sampan to an ornate festival boat. Various fishing methods are detailed, from trawling and gill netting to purse seining, as well as various voyages of discovery around the world. There is also a small aquarium, but best of all are the museum's 30-minute boat tours aboard a restored fishing junk, with sailings at 10:30am, 11:30am, 3:30pm, and 4pm daily except Tuesday and the first Sunday of the month. Cost of the trip is $10 ptcs (US$1.30) for adults and $5 ptcs (US$0.65) for children. Senior citizens and children younger than 10 sail free.

Temple of A-Ma. Rua de S. Tiago da Barra. Free admission. Daily 8am–5pm. Bus: nos. 1, 1A, 2, 5, 6, 7, 8, 9, 10, 10A, 11, 18, 21, 21A, or 28B.

Macau's oldest temple is situated at the bottom of Barra Hill at the entrance to the Inner Harbour, across from the Maritime Museum. With parts of it dating back more than 600 years, it is dedicated to A-Ma, goddess of seafarers. According to legend, a poor village girl seeking free passage was finally taken aboard a small fishing boat, the only boat to survive a subsequent typhoon. When the craft landed, the young girl revealed herself to be A-Ma, and the fishermen repaid their gratitude by building this temple on the spot where they came ashore. At any rate, the temple was already here when the Portuguese arrived, and they named their city A-Ma-Gao (Bay of A-Ma) after it. The temple contains images of A-Ma and stone carvings of the Chinese fishing boat that carried her to Macau. The temple has good feng shui, spreading along the steep slope of Barra Hill with views of the Inner Harbour, with several shrines set in the rocky hillside and linked by winding paths through moon gates.

Lou Lim Iok Garden. Estrada de Adolfo Loureiro. Admission $1 ptc (US$0.13). Daily from dawn to dusk. Bus: nos. 5, 9, 12, 22, or 28C.

Macau's most flamboyant Chinese garden was built in the 19th century by a wealthy Chinese merchant and modeled after the famous gardens in Soochow. Tiny, with narrow winding paths, bamboo groves, a nine-turn zigzag bridge (believed to deter evil spirits), and ponds filled with carp, it's a nice escape from the city. If possible, come in the morning, when the garden is filled with Chinese doing tai chi exercises, musicians practicing traditional Chinese music, and bird lovers strolling their birds in ornate wooden cages.

TAIPA & COLÔANE ISLANDS

Closest to the mainland, **Taipa** has exploded with new construction in recent years, but it's still worth seeing **Taipa Village,** a small, traditional community with narrow lanes, two-story colonial buildings painted in yellows, blues, and greens, and hanging baskets of flowers. Village life remains in full view here, with children playing, women sorting the day's vegetables on towels in the street, and workers carrying produce and goods in baskets balanced from poles on their shoulders. There are a number of fine, inexpensive restaurants here, making dining reason enough to come. For sightseeing, don't miss the **Casa Museu da Taipa (Taipa House Museum),** on Avenida da Praia (☎ 853/827088). It's one of five colonial-style homes lining the banyan-shaded street that once belonged to Macanese families in the early 1900s. Combining both European and Chinese designs and furnishings as a reflection of the families' Eurasian heritage, the Casa Museu displays a dining and living room, kitchen, and upstairs bedrooms filled with period furniture. A couple of the other former homes contain displays relating to the history of Taipa and traditional regional costumes of Portugal. Open hours are daily from 10am to 8pm, and admission is free. Bus nos. 11, 22, 28A, 33, and 34 all go to Taipa Village.

Farther away and connected to Taipa via causeway and a huge strip of reclaimed land, **Colôane** is less developed than Taipa. It's known for its **beaches,** particularly Cheoc Van and Hac Sa, both with lifeguards. To reach them, take bus nos. 21A, 25 or 26A. Farther along the coast is the laid-back, quaint community of **Colôane Village,** with its sweet **Chapel of St. Francis Xavier,** built in 1928 and dedicated to Asia's most important and well-known Catholic missionary.

For more information on Taipa and Colôane, pick up a free pamphlet from the Macau tourist office called *Macau, Outlying Islands.*

SHOPPING

A duty-free port, Macau has long been famous for its jewelry stores, especially those offering gold jewelry along Avenida do Infante D. Henrique and Avenida de Almeida Ribeiro. Portuguese wines are another good bargain, as are Chinese antiques and leather garments. In recent years, a number of fashionable clothing boutiques have also opened in the center of town, but more colorful are the clothing stalls near Largo do Senado square, many of which sell overruns and seconds from Macau's garment factories.

GAMBLING

The most sophisticated of Macau's 11 casinos are located in hotels—the **Mandarin Oriental, Hyatt Regency, Kingsway Hotel, Holiday Inn,** and **Hotel Lisboa,** all open 24 hours. Among those catering primarily to Chinese, none is more interesting than the ornately decorated **Floating Macau Palace Casino,** moored in the Outer Harbour not far from the Mandarin Oriental Hotel. Open 24 hours, it's worth strolling through for a look at Chinese gambling.

NIGHTLIFE

One of the few benefits to have arisen from the otherwise hideously sterile reclaimed-land development on the Outer Harbour is the Docks, an unofficial name given to a string of sidewalk cafes and bars lining Avenida Dr. Sun Yat-Sen near the Kun Iam Statue. They're great places for a drink and watching the parade of people file past. True to Macau's Mediterranean roots, the action doesn't start until after 10pm and is at its most frenetic after 1am.

Thailand 5

by Jennifer Eveland

In the end of the last century the Tourism Authority of Thailand kicked off a new tourism campaign called "Amazing Thailand." They could not have chosen a better adjective. Amazing are the clear blue waters that lap at sandy palm-lined shores on Thailand's coasts and islands. Amazing are the country's thousands of ornate and historic temples that house serene Buddha images amidst the sweet smell of jasmine. Amazing are the Thai people, their warm smiles welcoming visitors to enjoy their world. Every experience is a thrill, from a sampling of the renowned spicy Thai cuisine to shopping adventures in sprawling bazaars to the sexy shows that entice guests to experience "sanuk," fun Thai-style, for there is no better place in Southeast Asia to experience both the exotic and the pleasurable. Thailand invites the world to experience the allure of the Orient, while providing endless opportunities for the relaxation and good times that holiday travelers seek. Thailand is truly amazing.

The world has caught on to Thailand's magic. The country for years has enjoyed some of the highest tourism rates in the region, and even amidst the economic crisis that had almost every Southeast Asian nation scurrying for tourism dollars, Thailand managed to increase its tourism traffic. Indeed, the collapse of the Thai baht in July 1997 accounts for much of this increase, as the currency stretches a long way to make a fantastic vacation even more enjoyable. At the time of writing, the baht still was a bargain at about 43 baht per dollar, as opposed to the pre-crisis 25 baht per dollar.

One benefit of the developed tourism industry is the accessibility of the country to outsiders. While venturing into the unknown, you will rarely feel uneasy. Regional and local transportation, Western-style accommodations, and locals well-versed in rudimentary English allow foreigners to roam with relative ease and comfort. And despite often incomprehensible cultural differences, widespread travel has increased the ease with which the Thai people greet outsiders and allow for foreign tastes and manners.

1 Getting to Know Thailand

THE LAY OF THE LAND

In the center of Southeast Asia, Thailand is located roughly equidistant from China and India, sharing cultural affinities with both. It borders Burma (Myanmar) to the north and west, Laos to the northeast, Cambodia (Kampuchea) to the east, and Malaysia to the south. Thailand's southwestern coast stretches along the Andaman Sea, and its southern and southeastern coastlines border the Gulf of Thailand (still often called the Gulf of Siam).

Thailand covers approximately 289,668 square kilometers (180,000 sq. miles)—about the size of France. The country, which the Thais often compare in shape to the profile of an elephant's head, facing right, is divided into six major geographic zones, within which there are 73 provinces.

THE REGIONS IN BRIEF

NORTHERN THAILAND   Northern Thailand (the forehead of the elephant) is a relatively cool mountainous region at the foothills of the Himalayas. Like most of Thailand, the cool hills in the north are well suited for farming, particularly for strawberries, asparagus, peaches, litchis, and other fruits. At higher elevations many hill-tribe farmers cultivate opium poppies, a crop that is rarely profitable (and ruinous to farmers who become addicted) though the agricultural program advanced by the king is introducing more productive crops. The cities in the north covered in this chapter are Chiang Mai and Chiang Rai.

THE CENTRAL PLAIN   The Central Plain is an extremely fertile region, providing the country and the world with much of its abundant rice crop. The main city of the area is Phitsanulok, northeast of which are the impressive remains of Sukhothai, Thailand's first capital. To the south is Lopburi, an ancient Mon-Khmer settlement.

THE SOUTHEAST COAST   The southeast coast is lined with seaside resorts, such as Pattaya and the islands Ko Samet and Ko Chang. Farther east, in the mountains, is Thailand's greatest concentration of sapphire and ruby mines.

WESTERN THAILAND   On the opposite side of the country, west of Bangkok, are mountains and valleys carved by the Kwai River, made infamous during World War II by the "Death Railway," built by Allied prisoners of war who worked and lived under horrifying conditions, and a bridge (made famous by the film *Bridge on the River Kwai*) over the river near Kanchanaburi. Just to the north of Bangkok (which is in every way the center of the country, along the Chao Phraya River banks) is Ayutthaya, Thailand's second capital after Sukhothai.

THE SOUTHERN PENINSULA   The long, narrow Southern Peninsula (the elephant's trunk), extends south to the Malaysian border, with the Andaman Sea on the west and the Gulf of Thailand on the east. The eastern coastline along the gulf extends more than 1,802 kilometers (1,125 miles); the western shoreline runs 716 kilometers (445 miles) along the Andaman Sea. This region is the most tropical in the country, with heavy rainfall during monsoon seasons. The northeast monsoon, roughly from November to April, brings clear weather and calm seas to the west coast; the southwest monsoon, March to October, brings similar conditions to the east coast. There are glamorous beach resorts here (people visit them even during the rainy season; it doesn't rain all day), such as the western islands of Phuket and nearby Ko Phi Phi. Ko Samui, off the east coast, is a bit more relaxed and not yet as expensive as the former two.

ISAAN   Finally, Isaan, the broad and relatively infertile northeast plateau (the ear of the elephant), is the least developed region in Thailand, bordered by the Mekong River *(Mae Nam Khong* in Thai). Isaan is dusty in the cool winter and muddy during the summer monsoon. Fewer tourists make their way to Isaan than any other part of the country, so we've opted not to cover it in this chapter.

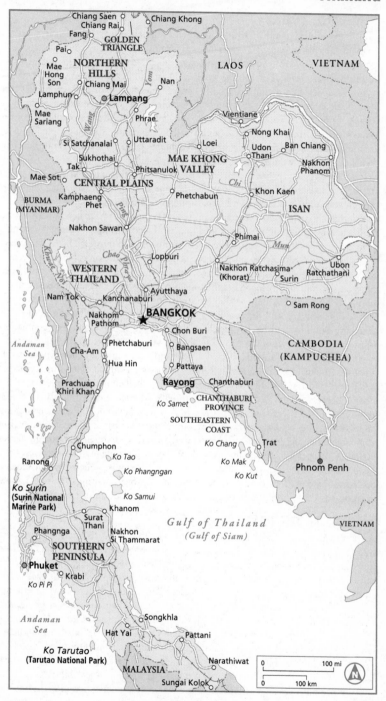

THAILAND TODAY

Today, under a pyramid of king, nation, and religion, Thais enjoy greater freedom than any people in Asia and continue to tenaciously hold their nation together. The government is a constitutional monarchy (though the constitution is still biased toward military rule). The country's political structure remains relatively flexible, yet many Thais feel that despite constant changes in leadership as political parties form new alliances and old political figures are recycled, the government remains more or less the same mixture in a different cup. King Bhumibol Adulyadej holds a position outside of government, but is recognized as the defender of all Thai people. On a few occasions he's put his foot down when government monkey business is not beneficial to his people. His word is always heeded.

The nation's most pressing concern at the time of writing, and most likely for years to come, is recovery from the **economic crisis** and the politicians who stall the legislative process to protect their own business interests. Reform proposals for debt restructuring that are desperately needed to jump start the economy have been stonewalled in parliament by politicians who are linked to many failed businesses. Media reporting of political activities is wide open, especially in comparison to most of Thailand's ASEAN (Association of Southeast Asian Nations) neighbors, and the press here can't seem to resist any story involving accusations of corruption in politics. In international relations, at the time of writing, Thailand's main concerns involved its immediate neighbors Cambodia and Myanmar. Refugees crossing over both borders have squeezed Thailand's resources, and pressure from the West to stop drug trafficking from Myanmar have put Thailand in the middle of some heated regional and global situations (though none of these should affect law-abiding visitors to the country in any way).

In January 2001, Thailand elected a new and very unusual Prime Minister. Mr. Thaksin Shinawatra, a telecommunications industry fat cat, was voted into office on a populist platform. His first task has been to put Thailand back on the road to economic recovery. So far Mr. Taksin seems to have adopted a policy similar to that of neighboring Malaysia's controversial Dr. Mohamad Mahathir. Rather than promote increased market transparency and accountability, he has chosen a nationalistic approach, scrapping International Monetary Fund advice to open and expand market liberalization for an increasingly "closed door" policy blocking out foreign investment. Economists fear the worst, however Mahathir's protectionist policies, which shocked the world, haven't been entirely unsuccessful. At the time of writing, Thaksin's administration has yet to prove itself, but should certainly provide an interesting battle.

A LOOK AT THE PAST

Archaeologists believe that Thailand was a major thoroughfare for *Homo erectus* en route from Africa to China and other parts of Asia. Modern civilization did not arrive in Thailand until about a thousand years ago when waves of people migrated from central and southern China, settling primarily in what is now Vietnam, Laos, Thailand, and Burma. These people, who are called *Tai,* became dispersed over a vast area of space, sharing a cultural and linguistic commonality. Their descendents are the core bloodline of the Thai people of today, plus some tribal peoples of Burma, Laos, southern China, Vietnam, and others in northeastern India. The **early Tais** lived in nuclear families with a dozen or two households forming an independently ruled *muang,* or village, eventually establishing loosely structured feudal states where both lord and villager benefitted—the lord from manpower and the villager from stability.

From the sixth century, Southeast Asia underwent a gradual period of **Indianization.** Merchants and missionaries from India introduced Brahmanism and Buddhism to the region, as well as Indian political and social values, and art and architectural preferences. Around the sixth century A.D., the **Mon,** migrants from Burma, were responsible for establishing Sri Lankan Buddhism in central Thailand. The Mons supported extensive religious establishments, usually Buddhist, and their religious life was reinforced by regular contact with India, visiting monks, imported sacred scriptures, and works of art.

By the early ninth century A.D., the **Khmer** Empire had risen to power in Cambodia, spreading into surrounding areas. Magnificent Khmer temples, originally built for the worship of Hindu deities, were constructed in outposts further and further from the Cambodian center of the empire. Brahmanism, having been introduced by traders from southern India, influenced not only Khmer religion and temple design (with the distinct corncob shaped *prang*, or tower), but government administration and social order as well. Angkor Wat, Cambodia's great ancient temple city, was built during the reign of **Suryavarman II** (1113–115?). The last great Khmer ruler, **Jayavarman VII** (1181–1219), extended the empire to its furthest limits—north to Vientiane, west to Burma, and down the Malay peninsula. It was he who shifted Khmer ideology toward Buddhism, building temples in Khmer-style, but with a Buddhist purpose. Many historians believe the decline of the Khmers was due to this over-extension of their territories.

In 1259 several powerful centers of Tai power in northern Thailand, southern China, and Laos were united by **King Mengrai,** who established the first capital of the **Lanna Kingdom** at Chiang Rai in 1263, and later at Chiang Mai in 1296. The Lanna Kingdom saw the rise of a scholarly Buddhism, with strict adherence to orthodox ways. Citizens enjoyed the benefits of infrastructure projects for transportation and irrigation; developed medicine and law; and created artistic expression through religious sculpture, sacred texts, and poetry. But the Mongols, under the fierce expansionist leadership of **Kublai Khan,** forced their way into the region. Mengrai, forming strategic alliances with neighboring kingdoms succeeded in keeping the Mongols at bay.

In the vacuum left by the departing Khmers, a tiny kingdom based in **Sukhothai** rose to fame after its crown prince Rama single-handedly defeated an invasion from neighboring Mae Sot at the Burmese border. Upon his coronation in 1279, **Ramkhamhaeng,** or "Rama the Bold," set the scene for what is recognized as the first truly Siamese civilization, mixing all the people of the central plains—Tai, Mon, Khmer, and indigenous populations, with threads of India and China interwoven in their cultural tapestry. In response to the Khmer's hierarchical rule, Ramkhamhaeng established himself as an accessible king. He was a devout Buddhist, adopting the orthodox and scholarly Theravada Buddhism. A patron of the arts, the king commissioned many great Buddha images, initiated splendid architectural achievements, and developed the modern Thai written language. After his death in 1298, his successors failed to rule wisely and Sukhothai's brilliant spark faded almost as quickly at it had ignited.

Next came the kingdom of **Ayutthaya,** which swallowed what was left of Khmer outposts and the Sukhothai kingdom. Incorporating the strengths of its population— Tai military manpower and labor, Khmer bureaucratic sensibilities, and Chinese commercial talents, the empire grew wealthy and strong. Following Khmer models, the king rose above his subjects atop a huge pyramid-shaped administration. A huge fortified city was built—with temples that glittered as any in Sukhothai. This was the Kingdom of Siam that the first Europeans, the Portuguese, encountered in 1511.

Burmese invasion forces took Chiang Mai's Lanna Kingdom in 1558 and finally Ayutthaya in 1569. However, during the occupation, **Prince Naresuan,** descended from Sukhothai kings, in an historic battle scene atop an elephant, challenged the

Burmese crown prince and defeated him with a single blow. Ayutthaya continued through the following 2 centuries in grand style, and while its Southeast Asian neighbors were falling under colonial rule, the court of Siam retained its own sovereignty. It has the distinction of being the only Southeast Asian nation never to have been colonized, a point of great pride for Thais today. Unfortunately the final demise of Ayutthaya would be two more Burmese invasions in the 1760s.

The Siamese did not hesitate to build another kingdom. **Taksin,** a provincial governor, rose to power on military excellence, charisma, and a firm belief that he was divinely appointed to lead the land. Rebuilding the capital at Thonburi, on the western bank of the Chao Phraya River (opposite present-day Bangkok), within 3 years he'd reunited the lands under the previous kingdom. But Taksin suffered from paranoia—he had monks killed, and eventually his own wife and children. Regional powers were quick to get rid of him—he was swiftly kidnapped, covered in a velvet sack, and beaten to death with a sandalwood club.

These same regional powers turned to **Chaophraya Chakri** in 1782 to lead the land. Crowned **King Ramathibodi,** he was the first king of Thailand's present dynasty—the **Chakri Dynasty.** He moved the capital across the river to Bangkok, where he built the **Grand Palace** and great temples. The city grew around a network of canals, with the river as the central channel for trade and commerce. Rama I reinstated Theravada Buddhist doctrine, re-established the state ceremonies of Ayutthaya, and revised all laws. He also wrote the *Ramakien,* based upon the Indian *Ramayana,* a legend that has become the subject for many Thai classical arts.

King Mongkut (1851–1868) with his son, **King Chulalongkorn** (1868–1910), lead Siam into the 20th century as an independent nation, establishing an effective civil service, formalizing global relations, and introducing industrialization-based economics.

It was King Mongkut who hired Anna Leonowens (of *The King and I*) as an English tutor for his children. Thai people want everyone to know that Mongkut was not the overbearing, pushover fop described in her account. Historians side with the Thais, for she is barely mentioned in court accounts—the story had its origins more in her imagination than in reality.

During the reign of **King Prajadhipok,** Rama VII (1925–1935), the growing urban middle class became increasingly discontent. Economic failings and bureaucratic bickering weakened the position of the monarchy, which was delivered its final blow by the Great Depression. In 1932 a group of mid-level officials staged a coup d'etat and Prajadhipok abdicated in 1935.

Democracy had a shaky hold on Siam. Over the following decades, government leadership changed hands fast and frequently, many times the result of hostile takeover with the military at the helm. In 1939, the nation adopted the name "Thailand"—land of the free.

During **World War II** democracy was stalled in the face of the Japanese invasion in 1941. Thailand chose to side with the Japanese, but at the war's end, no punitive measures were taken against Thailand; the Thai ambassador in Washington failed to deliver his country's declaration of war against the allies.

Thailand managed to stay out of direct involvement in the **Vietnam War;** however, it continues to suffer repercussions from the burden of refugees. The U.S. pumped billions into the Thai economy, bringing riches to some and relative affluence to many but further impoverishing the poor. Communism became an increasingly attractive political philosophy, and a full-scale insurrection seemed imminent. In June 1973 thousands of Thai students demonstrated in the streets, demanding a new constitution and the return to democratic principals. Tensions grew until October when

Wats 101

The wat, or Buddhist temple/monastery, is the defining architectural structure in Thailand. Bangkok alone has over 400, with thousands more spread out across the land.

With their Chinese wooden building techniques, polychromatic schemes, and Japanese-influenced carved flowing lines, the **Sukhothai-era Thai wats** (13th and 14th centuries) represented the first "pure" Thai Buddhist style, and it was during this time that the mainstays of Thai wat architecture were created. They include (in order of artistic importance): the *phra chedi* (stupa), *bot, wihaan, phra prang, mondop,* and *prasat.*

The dome-shaped **phra chedi**—usually called simply *chedi* and better known in the West as stupa—is the most venerated structure and an elaboration of the basic mound. Originally it enshrined relics of the Buddha—later of holy men and kings. A stupa consists of a dome (tumulus), constructed atop a round base (drum) and surmounted by a cubical chair representing the seated Buddha, over which is the *chatra* (umbrella) in one or several (usually nine) tiers.

The **bot** (*ubosoth* or *uposatha*) is where the *bhikku* (monks) meditate and all ceremonies are performed. It consists of either one large nave or one nave with lateral aisles built on a rectangular plan where the Buddha image is enshrined. At the end of each ridge of the roof are graceful finials, called *chofa* (meaning "sky tassel"), which are reminiscent of animal horns but are thought to represent celestial geese or the Garuda (a mythological monster ridden by the god Shiva). The triangular gables are adorned with gilded wooden ornamentation and glass mosaics.

The **wihaan** (*vihara* or *viharn*) is a replica of the bot that is used to keep Buddha images.

The **phra prang,** which originated with the corner tower of the Khmer temple, is a new form of Thai stupa, elliptical in shape and also housing images of the Buddha.

The **mondop** may be made of wood or brick. On a square-pillared base the pyramidal roof is formed by a series of receding stories, enriched with the same decoration tapering off in a pinnacle. It may serve to enshrine some holy object or it may serve as a kind of library and storeroom for religious ceremonial objects, as it does at Wat Phra Kaeo in Bangkok.

The **prasat** ("castle") is a direct descendant of the Khmer temple, with its round-topped spire and Greek-cross layout. At the center is a square sanctuary with a domed *sikhara* and four porchlike antechambers that project from the main building, giving the whole a steplike contour. The *prasat* serves either as the royal throne hall or as a shrine for some venerated objects, such as the *prasat* of Wat Phra Kaeo in Bangkok, which enshrines the statues of the kings of the present dynasty.

armed forces attacked a demonstration at Thammasat University in Bangkok, killing 69 students and wounding 800, paralyzing the capital with terror and revulsion.

The constitution was restored, a new government was elected, and democracy once again wobbled on. Many students, however, were not yet satisfied and continued to complain that the financial elite were still in control and still resisting change. In 1976 student protests again broke out, and there was a replay of the grisly scene of 3 years before at Thammasat University. The army seized control to impose and maintain order, conveniently spiriting away some bodies and prisoners, and another brief experiment with democracy was at an end. Thanin Kraivichien was installed as prime minister of a new right-wing government, which suspended freedom of speech and the press, further polarizing Thai society.

In 1980 Prem Tinsulanonda was named prime minister, and during the following 8 years he managed to bring remarkable political and economic stability to Thailand. The Thai economy continued to grow steadily through the 1980s, fueled by Japanese investment and Chinese capital in flight from Hong Kong. Leadership since then has seen quite a few changes, including a military coup in 1991, and another student crackdown in 1992. It was under General Chavalit Yongjaiyudh's administration that the economic crisis hit Thailand in July 1997. While his government sat on their hands in indecision over how to proceed, connections between public officials and bad financial institutions became more apparent and international investors lost confidence in Thailand. While in August 1997, Thailand accepted $17 billion in bailouts from the International Monetary Fund, political in-fighting stalled the government's action until November of the same year, when Chuan Leekpai, a previous PM, was elected into office again, to try to straighten things out.

THAILAND'S PEOPLE & CULTURE

The Thais are a true melting pot of many people and cultures. They descended from ancient and more recent immigrants from southern China who for centuries absorbed Mon, Khmer, Laotian, Persian, Indian, and Malay people and influences. Today, the people of modern Thailand cannot credit their ethnic identity as anything other than Thai. The hill tribe peoples of the north are descended from Tibeto-Burman people who migrated down the Himalayas to the hills of northern Indochina.

RELIGION

Thai culture cannot be fully appreciated without some understanding of **Buddhism,** which is followed by 90% of the population. Although Buddhism first came to Thailand in the third century B.C., when missionaries were sent from India, it was not until the 14th century that the *sangha* (monastic order) was established. The king entered the order, thus beginning the close connection between the royal house and the *sangha* that continues to this day. (For more information, see the section on Buddha and Buddhism in chapter 2.)

Other religions and philosophies are also followed in Thailand, including Islam, Christianity, Hinduism, and Sikhism. Sunni Islam is followed by more than two million Thais, mostly in the south. Even after centuries of evangelism, there are only a quarter of a million Christians living in the country.

ETIQUETTE

Disrespect for the royal family and religious figures, sites, and objects will cause great offense. While photography is permitted in temples (except for Wat Phra Kaeo), never climb on a Buddha image, and if you sit down, never point your feet in the direction of the Buddha image. Women should never touch a monk or give something to one directly. A monk will provide a cloth for you to lay the item upon, and he will collect it.

Thais consider the feet the lowest part of the body, so pointing your feet at someone is considered offensive. Shoes should be removed when entering a temple or private home. And don't ever step over someone's body or legs. Alternately, the head, as the highest part of the body, should never be touched, not even in jest.

Perhaps the most important advice I can give is this: In public never show anger, temper, or frustration. The Thai people consider such public displays a sign of a less developed, primitive being. While banging your fist on the counter may get you better service back home, in Thailand you'll be promptly ignored. You'll catch more bees with honey.

A lovely Thai greeting is the *wai:* Place your palms together, raise the tips of your fingers to your chin, and make a subtle bow from the waist while bending your knees slightly. The person of lower social status initiates a wai. In general, you should not wai to children and to someone providing a service to you. Also, don't expect a monk to return a wai; they're exempt due to their unique social status.

Address a Thai person by his or her first name preceded by "Khun." For example, Methinee Pratoomsuvarn should be properly addressed as Khun Methinee. Don't be surprised if you are solely addressed by your first name—such as Mr. John or Ms. Mary. Closer Thai friends will use nicknames, which are usually much easier to remember.

Even though this is a tropical country and you've probably come in search of the ultimate beach experience, it is offensive to the Thais to see tourists bare themselves in public, wear bathing suits around town, or go topless on the beach. It is particularly inappropriate for men or women to wear shorts, halter tops, or miniskirts in temples. Cover thyself in the presence of the Buddha.

THAI CUISINE: TIGER PRAWNS TO PAD THAI

Enjoying exquisite food is one of the true joys of traveling in Thailand. If you aren't familiar with Thai cooking, imagine the best of Chinese food ingredients and preparation combined with the sophistication of Indian spicing and topped off with red and green chiles. The styles of cooking available in Bangkok run the gamut from mild northern khan toke to extremely spicy southern curries. Basic ingredients include a cornucopia of shellfish, fresh fruits, and vegetables—asparagus, tamarind, bean sprouts, carrots, mushrooms of all kinds, various kinds of spinach, and bamboo shoots, combined with pungent spices such as basil, lemongrass, mint, chile, garlic, and coriander. Thai cooking also uses coconut milk, curry paste, peanuts, and a large variety of noodles and rice.

Among the dishes you'll find throughout the country are: *tom yum goong,* a Thai hot-and-sour shrimp soup; satay, charcoal-broiled chicken, beef, or pork strips skewered on a bamboo stick and dipped in a peanut-coconut curry sauce; spring rolls, similar to egg rolls but with a thinner crust and usually containing only vegetables; *larb,* a spicy chicken or ground-beef concoction with mint-and-lime flavoring; salads, most with a dressing of onion, chile pepper, lime juice, and fish sauce; *pad thai* ("Thai noodles"), rice noodles usually served with large shrimp, eggs, peanuts, fresh bean sprouts, lime, and a delicious sauce; *khao soi,* a northern curried soup served at small food stalls; a wide range of curries, flavored with coriander, chile, garlic, and fish sauce or coconut milk; spicy *tod man pla,* one of many fish dishes; sticky rice, served in the north and made from glutinous rice, prepared with vegetables and wrapped in a banana leaf; and Thai fried rice, a simple rice dish made with whatever the kitchen has on hand. "American fried rice" usually means fried rice topped by an easy-over egg and sometimes accompanied by fried chicken.

A word of caution: Thai palates relish incredibly spicy food, normally much more fiery than is tolerated in even the most piquant Western cuisines. Protect your own palate by saying *"Mai phet, farang,"* meaning "Not spicy, foreigner."

Traditionally, Thai menus don't offer fancy desserts, but the local fruit is luscious enough. Familiar fruits are pineapple (served with salt to heighten its flavor), mangoes, bananas, guava, papaya, coconut, and watermelon, as well as the latest rage, apples grown in the royal orchards. Less familiar possibilities are durian, in season during June and July, which is a Thai favorite, but an acquired taste, as it smells like rotten onions; mangosteen, a purplish, hard-skinned fruit with delicate, whitish-pink segments that melt in the mouth, available April to September; jackfruit, which is large and yellow-brown with a thick, thorned skin that envelops tangy-flavored flesh, available year-round; longan, a small, brown-skinned fruit with very sweet white flesh available July to October; tamarind, a spicy little fruit in a pod that you can eat fresh or candied; rambutan, which is small, red, and hairy, with transparent sweet flesh clustered round a woody seed, available May to July; and pomelo, similar to a grapefruit, but less juicy, available October to December. Some of these fruits are served as salads—the raw green papaya, for example, can be quite good.

LANGUAGE

Thai is derived principally from Mon, Khmer, Chinese, Pali, Sanskrit, and, increasingly, English. It is a tonal language, with distinctions based on inflection—low, mid, high, rising, or falling tone—rather than stress, and can elude most speakers of Western languages. One interesting aspect of the language that can be confusing to first-time visitors is that the polite words roughly corresponding to our sir and ma'am are not determined by the gender of the person addressed but by the gender of the speaker; females say *ka*, and males say *krap*.

English is spoken in the major cities at most hotels, restaurants, and shops, and is the second language of the professional class, as well as the international business language.

Unfortunately there is no universal transliteration system, so you will see the usual **Thai greeting** written in Roman letters as *sawatdee, sawaddi, sawasdee, sawusdi,* and so forth. Some consistency has been imposed in transliterating place names. For example, you will still see the Laotian capital written Wiang Chan as well as Vientienne or Viantiane, and the word *Ratcha* ("Royal"), as in Ratchadamnoen, can be rendered *Raja, Radja,* and *Raj.* Sometimes you'll see Ko Samet as Koh Samed, or the ancient city of Ayutthaya spelled Ayudhya, but for most destinations, the spelling has been more or less standardized as presented in this chapter.

Central Thai is the official written and spoken language of the country, and most Thais understand it, but there are three other major dialects: **Northeastern-Thai,** spoken in Isaan, and closely related to Lao; **Northern Thai,** spoken in the northwest, from Tak Province to the Burmese border; and **Southern Thai,** spoken from Chumphon Province south to the Malaysian border. The hill tribes in the North have their own distinct languages, most related to Burmese or Tibetan.

USEFUL THAI PHRASES

Hello   **sa-wa-dee-krup (males); sa-wa-dee-ka (females)**
How are you?   **sa-bai-dee-rue**
I am fine   **sa-bai-dee**
Excuse me   **kor-tod-krup (males); kor-tod-ka (females)**
I understand   **kao-jai**
I don't understand   **mai-kao-jai**
Do you speak English?   **khun-pood-pa-sa-ang-rid-dai-mai**
Not spicy please   **kor-mai-ped**
Thank you   **kop-koon-krup (male); kop-koon-ka (female)**
How much?   **tao-rai**

That's expensive   **paeng**
Discount   **lod-ra-ka**
Where is the toilet?   **hong-nam-yoo-hee-nai**
Stop here   **yood-tee-nee**

2 Planning a Trip to Thailand

VISITOR INFORMATION

The **Tourism Authority of Thailand (TAT)** recently published a new collection of up-to-date pamphlets and maps on a ton of destinations throughout the country, even places that aren't on the usual travel agenda, and will post them upon request. Current schedules for festivals and holidays come in especially handy when planning your trip. Once in country, you'll also find good, privately produced maps and tourist publications—many free—available at most hotels and many businesses.

On the Internet, visit **Sawadee Thailand** at **www.cs.ait.ac.th/tat/index.html**, the TAT's virtual travel information center; or **Welcome to Thailand** at **www.mahidol. ac.th/Thailand/Thailand-main.html** for cultural, geographic, historical, and economic information.

IN THE UNITED STATES & CANADA

- **Los Angeles:** 3440 Wilshire Blvd., Suite 1100, Los Angeles, CA 90010 (☎ **213/ 382-2353;** fax 213/389-7544).
- **Chicago:** 303 East Wacker Dr., Suite 400, Chicago, IL 60601 (☎ **312/ 819-3990;** fax 312/565-0359).
- **New York:** 5 World Trade Center, Suite 3443, New York, NY 10048 (☎ **212/ 432-0433;** fax 212/912-0920).
- **Canada:** While there is no TAT office in Canada, the Chicago office represents this region.

IN AUSTRALIA & NEW ZEALAND

- **Sydney:** Level 2, National Australia Bank House, 255 George St., Sydney 2000, N.S.W. (☎ **02/9247-7549;** fax 02/9251-2465).
- **New Zealand:** Like Canada, New Zealand has no TAT representative of its own, but the office in Sydney can forward information upon request.

IN THE UNITED KINGDOM

- **London:** 49 Albemarle St., London WIX 3FE (☎ **071/499-7679;** fax 071/ 629-5519).

ENTRY REQUIREMENTS

All visitors to Thailand must carry a valid **passport** with **proof of onward passage** (either a return or through ticket). Visa applications are not required if you are staying up to 30 days and are a national of 41 designated countries, including Australia, Canada, Ireland, New Zealand, the U.K., and the U.S. New Zealanders may stay up to 3 months. Visa extensions may be obtained at the nearest immigration office and cost 500 baht. Visitors who overstay their visa will be fined 200 baht (US$4.65) for each extra day, payable in cash upon exiting the country.

CUSTOMS REGULATIONS

Tourists are allowed to enter the country with 1 liter of alcohol and 200 cigarettes (or 250 grams of cigars or smoking tobacco) per adult, duty free. There are no restrictions on the import of foreign currencies or traveler's checks, but you cannot export foreign currency in excess of 10,000 baht (US$232.56) unless declared to Customs upon arrival.

MONEY

The Thai unit of currency, the **baht,** is written on price tags and elsewhere as the letter B crossed with a vertical slash. In this chapter I've written it as B, as in "100B". One baht is divided into 100 **satang,** though you'll rarely see a satang coin. Yellow-colored coins represent 25 and 50 satang; silver-colored coins are 1B, 5B, and 10B. Bank notes come in denominations of 10B (brown), 20B (green), 50B (blue), 100B (red), 500B (purple), and 1,000B (khaki). While the rate is still experiencing some flux following the 1997 Asian economic crisis, it's still relatively stable, hovering around 40B per U.S. dollar. For this book I used an exchange rate of 43 baht per U.S. dollar. Obtain the latest money conversions before you plan your trip. For up-to-date conversions, visit the currency chart at www.xe.net/ict.

Most major banks in Bangkok now have **automated teller machines,** and ATMs are increasingly common in major tourist spots. The largest banks in Thailand all perform account debit and cash advance services through the Cirrus/MasterCard or PLUS/Visa networks (try **Bangkok Bank, Thai Farmers Bank,** and **Bank of Ayudhya**). Things to keep in mind: The fee for a withdrawal is US$1.25 per transaction, and time changes between here and home may affect your ability to withdraw cash on 2 consecutive business days.

Traveler's checks are negotiable in most banks, hotels, restaurants, and tourist-oriented shops, but you'll receive a better rate by cashing them at commercial banks.

Nearly all international hotels and larger businesses accept **major credit cards,** but few accept personal checks. Despite protests from credit-card companies, many establishments add a 3% to 5% surcharge for payment. Use discretion in using your card—all major credit card companies list Thailand as a high-risk area for fraud. Don't let your card out of your sight, even for a moment, and be sure to keep all receipts. I generally don't like to use credit cards outside hotels anyway, as many retailers will give better discounts for cash payments.

In small towns and remote places, cash is the name of the game.

LOST/STOLEN CREDIT CARDS & TRAVELER'S CHECKS   To report a lost or stolen credit card, you can call these service lines: American Express ☎ 02/273-0022; Diners Club ☎ 02/238-3660; JCB (Japanese Credit Bank) ☎ 02/631-1938; MasterCard ☎ 02/232-2039; and Visa ☎ 02/256-7324.

WIRING EMERGENCY FUNDS

Western Union now has branches throughout Bangkok and many provincial capitals—thanks to partnerships with Central Department Store and Bangkok Metropolitan Bank. The service allows you to either send or receive cash worldwide immediately at local branches connected with Western Union offices worldwide. One word of warning—cash sent in foreign currencies will be exchanged to Thai baht using a seriously awful exchange rate. Use this service only in emergency, and in the smallest necessary amounts. Call the Western Union Customer Service Center in Bangkok at 02/254-7000. Their head office is at Central Department Store, Chidlom Branch (3rd floor, 1027 Ploenchit Rd.; ☎ **02/655-7777,** ext. 3357).

WHEN TO GO

CLIMATE   Thailand has two distinct climate zones; tropical in the south, and tropical savanna in the north. The northern and central areas of the country (including Bangkok) experience three distinct seasons. The hot season lasts from March to May,

The Thai Sex Industry & AIDS

Every day you're in Thailand, in any part of the country, you will see foreigners enjoying the company of Thai women and men. Although prostitution is illegal, it's as much a part of the tourism industry as superb hotels and stunning beaches.

With a legacy of royal patronage and social acceptance, the oldest profession has been part of Thailand's economy for centuries, although in the 19th century most brothels were operated by the Chinese and the majority of commercial sex workers (CSWs) were foreign until the 1930s. Today this burgeoning industry is still publicly ignored, and since the subject is controversial, the number fluctuates depending on whom you talk to. Some groups will say only 80,000 while others will put the number as high as 800,000.

Thailand has aggressively developed research and education programs on the subject of AIDS. The largest nongovernmental organization in Thailand, the PCDA, led by the courageous and innovative public health crusader Meechai Viravaidya, has enlarged the scope of its rural development programs from family planning and cottage-industry schemes, to distributing condoms and running seminars for CSWs. Even the royal family is in on it: Her Royal Highness, Princess Chulaporn Walailuke, founder of the Chulaporn Research Institute and an internationally known activist, sponsored the 1990 International Global AIDS Conference in Bangkok, and continues to be active.

These recent efforts must be working somewhat, as an increasing number of women and men refuse clients who won't wear a condom. According to the Thai government's Department of Communicable Diseases, AIDS Divisions, in 1999 it was estimated as many as 119,259 carry the AIDS virus, but the Population & Community Development Association claims that over 1 million is a more accurate account. In 1998 32,935 Thais died of AIDS-related illnesses, and that number is expected to double in the next decade.

If you patronize commercial sex workers, take proper precautions; wear a latex condom.

---

with temperatures averaging in the upper 90s Fahrenheit (mid-30s Celsius); with April the hottest month. This period sees very little rain, if any at all. The rainy season begins in June and lasts until October; the average temperature is 84° F (29°C) with 90% humidity. While the rainy season brings frequent showers, it's rare for them to last for a whole day or for days on end. Daily showers will come in torrents, usually in the late afternoon or evening for maybe 3 or 4 hours—many times bringing floods. If you plan on trekking in the north, I don't recommend going during this time, when you'll be slogging through mucky trails. The cool season, from November through February, has temperatures from the high 70s to low 80s Fahrenheit (26°C), with moderate and infrequent rain showers. In the north during the cool season (which is also the peak season for tourism), day temperatures can be as low as 60°F (16°C) in Chiang Mai and 41°F (5°C) in the hills.

The southern Malay Peninsula has intermittent showers year-round, and daily ones during the rainy season (temperatures average in the low 80s [30°C]). If you're traveling to Phuket or Ko Samui, it will be helpful to note that the two islands alternate peak seasons somewhat. Optimal weather on Phuket occurs between November and April, when the island welcomes the highest numbers of travelers and the most expensive resort rates. Alternately, Ko Samui's great weather lasts from about February to October. Refer to each destination's section for more information about peak seasons and weather patterns.

PUBLIC HOLIDAYS   Many holidays are based on the Thai lunar calendar; check with TAT for the current year's schedule and for holidays and festivals specific to certain regions.

The national holidays as well as New Year's Eve (December 31) and New Year's Day (January 1) are: Makha Puja (February full moon), Chakri Day (April 6), Songkran (Thai New Year, April 12–14); Coronation Day (May 5), Visakha Puja (May full moon), Asalha Puja (July full moon), Her Majesty the Queen's Birthday (August 12), Chulalongkorn Day (October 23), His Majesty the King's Birthday (December 5), and Constitution Day (December 10).

GETTING THERE
By Plane

Bangkok International Airport (a.k.a. Don Muang Airport) links all Southeast Asian nations with every other corner of the world. Since Bangkok is a regional hub, you might find yourself stopping through en route to other destinations, even if you don't plan to visit Thailand. Refer to chapter 3, "Planning a Trip to Southeast Asia," for information about reaching Thailand from outside Southeast Asia.

Thai Airways International (head office: 485 Silom Rd., Bangkok; ☎ 02/ 280-0060; www.thaiair.com) covers virtually all Southeast Asian nations in its routing.

The best way to insure the most economical airfare on direct flights to Thailand is to call a registered travel agent for your reservations and booking. Some of the best fares on direct flights can come from unexpected airlines. From Cambodia you can take Bangkok Airways, Kampuchea Airlines or Royal Air Camboge. From Hong Kong: Cathay Pacific, China Airlines, Emirates, Gulf Air, Japan Airlines, or Sri Lankan Airlines. Indonesian routes are serviced by Garuda Indonesia; and from Laos there's Lao Aviation. From Myanmar you can fly Biman Bangladesh Airlines or Myanmar Airways International, and from Malaysia you can fly Malaysian Airlines. From the Philippines you can take Egypt Air, Lufthansa German Airlines, or Philippine Airlines. From Singapore try Biman Bangladesh Airlines (one of the least expensive flights), Cathay Pacific, Finnair, Pakistan International Airlines, Royal Nepal Airlines (another good fare), Singapore Airlines, Swissair, or Turkish Airlines. Vietnam Airlines provides service from Vietnam.

Another important consideration is your desired point of entry. The above flights are to Bangkok, but there are additional direct flights into Chiang Mai from Kuala Lumpur, Singapore, and Vientiane and Luang Prabang in Laos; flights to Phuket from Hong Kong, Kuala Lumpur, Singapore, and Phnom Penh and Siem Reap in Cambodia; flights to Ko Samui from Singapore, and to U Tapao (Pattaya) from Phnom Penh.

Don't forget that if you leave Thailand by air, you'll be required to pay 500B (US$11.63) **international departure tax.**

By Train

Thailand is accessible via train from Singapore and peninsular Malaysia. Malaysia's Keretapi Tanah Melayu Berhad (KTM) begins in Singapore (☎ 65/222-5165), stopping in Kuala Lumpur (☎ 603/273-8000) and Butterworth (Penang) (☎ 604/ 323-7962) before heading for Thailand, where it joins service with the **State Railway of Thailand.** Bangkok's Hua Lamphong Railway Station is centrally located on Krung Kassem Road (☎ 02/223-7010 or 02/223-7020). Taxis, tuk-tuks, and public buses are just outside the station.

The *Eastern & Oriental Express* (www.orient-expresstrains.com), sister to the Venice Simplon-Orient-Express, runs once a week between Singapore and Bangkok in exquisite luxury, with occasional departures between Bangkok and Chiang Mai. For international reservations, from the U.S. and Canada call ☎ **800/524-2420,** from Australia ☎ 3/9699-9766, from New Zealand ☎ 9/379-3708, and from the U.K. ☎ 020 7805 5100. From Singapore, Malaysia, and Thailand contact E&O in Singapore at (☎ 65/392-3500).

BY BUS

From every major city in peninsular Malaysia (and even Singapore), you can pick up a bus to Thailand—at least to Hat Yai in southern Thailand, from where you can transfer to another bus to your destination. Stop by the bus terminal in any city to find out about time schedules. VIP buses cost more but have fewer seats, which means more leg room. Traveling up the peninsula by bus is arduous, at best. If you can take the train, you'll be far more comfortable with a sleeping berth and a little walking space.

GETTING AROUND

Transportation within Thailand is accessible, efficient, and inexpensive. If your time is short, fly. But if you have the time to take in the countryside and care to see a bit of provincial living, travel by bus, train, or private car.

BY PLANE

Domestic routes provided by Thai Airways, Bangkok Airways, and Angel Air make flying not only some of the most convenient traveling in the Kingdom, but some of the cheapest as well. Time was Bangkok served as the hub for almost all connections between domestic flights, but these days you can find flights between provincial cities without stopping in Bangkok; for example, flights between Pattaya, Ko Samui, and Phuket.

Bangkok International Airport (Don Muang) can be reached at ☎ **02/535-2081** for domestic flights only. Most domestic flights are on **Thai Airways,** part of Thai Airways International, 6 Lam Luang Rd., Bangkok (☎ **02/535-2084**), with Bangkok as its hub. Flights connect Bangkok and 25 domestic cities, including Chiang Mai, Chiang Rai, and Phuket. There are also connecting flights between many cities.

Bangkok Airways (Head office: 60 Queen Sirikit National Convention Center, New Ratchadaphisek Road; ☎ **02/229-3456**) covers routes between Bangkok, Ranong, Sukhothai, Chiang Mai, Ko Samui, Phuket, Krabi, and Pattaya (U-Tapao). The new **Angel Airlines** (3rd floor, Tower B, Benjajinda Bldg., 499 Vibhavadi Randsit Rd.; ☎ **02/953-2260**) serves Bangkok and Singapore, and domestically Bangkok, Chiang Mai, and Phuket.

BY TRAIN

From Bangkok, the **State Railway of Thailand** provides regular service to destinations north as far as Chiang Mai, northeast to Udon Thani, east to Pattaya, and south to Thailand's southern border, where it connects with Malaysia's Keretapi Tanah Melayu Berhad (KTM) with service to Penang (Butterworth), Kuala Lumpur, and Singapore. Complete schedules and fare information can be obtained at any railway station, or by calling **Hua Lampong Railway Station** directly at ☎ **02/223-7010** or 02/223-7020. Advance bookings can be made by calling ☎ 02/223-3762 or 02/224-7788.

Fares are a bit tricky to figure out at first because they use a double charge system. The first charge depends on the distance you travel between stations; for example, a trip from Bangkok to Hua Hin (229km) is 202B (US$4.70) for first class travel, 102B (US$2.37) for second class, and 44B (US$1.02) for third. From Bangkok to Chiang Mai (751km) the rates are something more like 593B (US$13.79) for first class, 281B (US$6.53) for second, and 121B (US$2.81) for third.

The second, or "supplementary charge," is relative to the speed at which you travel and the comfort level you desire. There are more than a few different trains, each running at a different speed. The fastest is the Special Express, which is used primarily for long-distance hauls. These trains cut travel time by as much as 60%, and have sleeper cars, which are a must for the really long trips. Supplementary charges range from 40B (US$0.93) for Rapid Train to 120B (US$2.79) for Special Express with catering service. Sleeping berth supplementary charges are from 100B (US$2.33) for a second class upper berth on a Rapid Train to 520B (US$12.09) per person for a double first class cabin.

Warning: On trains, pay close attention to your possessions. Thievery is common on overnight trips.

By Bus

Thailand has a very efficient and inexpensive bus system, highly recommended for budget travelers and short-haul trips. Options abound, but the major choices are public or private, air-conditioned or non-air-conditioned. Most travelers use the private, air-conditioned buses. Ideally, buses are best for short excursions; expect to pay a minimum of 50B for a one-way ticket. Longer-haul buses are an excellent value, but their slowness and lack of comfort can be a real liability.

There are three main bus terminals in Bangkok, each servicing a different part of the country. Buses to and from the southern peninsula originate at the **Southern Bus Terminal** (☎ **02/435-1199**) on Charan Sanitwong Road, across the river at the Bangkok Noi Station. Buses to the east coast arrive and depart from the **Eastern Bus Terminal** (☎ **02/390-1230**) on Sukhumvit Road opposite Soi 63 (Ekamai Road). Buses to all the northern areas are at the **Northern Bus Terminal** (☎ **02/272-5761**) on Phahonythin Road near the Chatuchak Weekend Market.

Warning: When traveling by long-distance bus, pay close attention to your possessions. Thievery is common, particularly on overnight buses when valuables are left in overhead racks.

By Car

Renting a car is almost too easy in Thailand. I don't recommend driving yourself in Bangkok because the traffic patterns are very confusing and jams are entirely frustrating. Outside the city, it's a good option, though Thai drivers are quite reckless. One caution: In many places, should you have an accident you will most likely be held responsible, regardless of actual fault. Many times the person believed most able to pay is the person who ultimately foots the bill.

Among the many car-rental agencies, the company that offers the best cars and insurance policies at the most competitive rates is **Budget Car and Truck Rental.** They have offices in Bangkok (☎ **02/203-0250;** fax 02/203-0249; www.budget.co.th; e-mail: rez@budget.co.th) as well as Chiang Mai, Chiang Rai, Hua Hin, Krabi, Phuket, Pattaya, and Ko Samui. A Suzuki Caribian Mini 4WD soft top costs 1,375B (US$31.98) per day, while the top-end Honda Accord full-sized sedan goes for 2,700B (US$62.79) per day. Discounts apply for weekly rentals. I've checked out Hertz and Avis, who also have offices around the country, and Budget seems to be the best deal.

Thailand drives on the left side of the road at a maximum speed limit of 60kmph inside a city and 80kmph outside.

TIPS ON ACCOMMODATIONS

Thailand has all kinds of accommodations, from world-renowned luxury hotels and resorts to great backpacker hotels and bungalows. Some pricier places have recently taken to quoting rates in U.S. dollars as opposed to Thai baht as a buffer against fluctuating currency values. In places like Phuket and Ko Samui, you have a rainy season which brings with it special rates that can be between 30 and 50% off the rack rates. Other places, such as Hua Hin and Cha-Am, impose peak-season surcharges. The prices listed in this book are rack rates quoted at the time of publishing, and are subject to change. However, be prepared to negotiate with reservations agents—these places almost always have special discounts, packages, or free service add-ons for extra value.

TIPS ON DINING

While Bangkok and the major tourist areas have a wide variety of quality international restaurants, of course you have a wide range of Thai food options as well, from fine dining to local coffee shop fare to street food. As for street food, be cautious: Check out the stall to see that it's clean and ingredients are fresh. If it passes your muster, the food's probably OK to eat. In smaller towns, your only options will be Thai food, with some Chinese and Western selections on the menu. Most places expect to use less spice for foreigners, but you can always remind the waiter. (Conversely, make sure you ask for spicy if you want the chiles, since some places will automatically turn down the heat when they see you coming.)

TIPS ON SHOPPING

In shopping malls and boutiques, where prices are almost always marked, you will be expected to pay full rate for any item. However, in markets and smaller shops, bargaining is the name of the game. Keep it nice and sporting and you should be fine. If you spend a long time negotiating or suggest a price that is accepted, then you may be considered rude if you walk away without finishing the sale. In rural areas such as the north, where some local people derive a large percentage of their income from handicrafts sales, I refrain from ferocious bargaining—the kind lady selling the silver bangle can probably do more with the extra 10 baht than I can. Keep in mind, however, that in high-traffic tourist areas, prices are always inflated. A major annoyance is the horrible 3% charge shops try to tack onto credit card purchases. There have been times when I've talked the shop owner into not charging me, but then there have been times when I've walked out of the store without making the purchase. They're not supposed to charge you extra, but of course nobody is really enforcing it.

Fast Facts: Thailand

American Express   The American Express agent in Thailand is Sea Tours Company, with offices in Bangkok, Phuket, and Chiang Mai. In Bangkok the Sea Tours office is at 88–92 Phayathai Plaza Building, 8th floor, 128 Phayathai Rd.; ☎ 02/216-5783; fax 02/216-5757.

Business Hours   Government offices (including branch post offices) are open Monday to Friday 8:30am to 4:30pm, with a lunch break between noon and 1pm. Businesses are generally open 8am to 5pm. Shops often stay open from 8am until 7pm or later, 7 days a week. Department stores are generally open 10am to 7pm.

Doctors   In Bangkok and major tourist destinations you'll find hospitals and clinics with English-speaking staff, all of whom are well trained. Often these clinics are stocked with better equipment than places back home, and care is of high standard quality. Consultation is usually as low as 300B (US$6.98) per visit.

Drug Laws   While illegal narcotics are more readily available in Thailand, and drug laws don't include the death penalty like neighboring Malaysia and Singapore, many tourists make the mistake of misreading Thailand's drug policy. Consumption or possession of marijuana, hallucinogenic mushrooms, LSD, opium, or opiate relatives are very much illegal, and carry penalties of 1 to 10 years of jail time plus 10,000B to 500,000B (US$232 to US$11,628) in fines, and you can expect to receive persona non grata status after you've served your time. Each year about 1,000 tourists are prosecuted for drug crimes.

Electricity   All outlets—except in some luxury hotels—are 220 volts, 50 cycles, AC. Outlets are two-pronged, flat or round.

Embassies   In Bangkok: United States, 120 Wireless Rd. (☎ **02/205-4000**); Australia, 37 South Sathorn (☎ **02/287-2680**); U.K., 1031 Witthayu (Wireless) Rd. (☎ **02/253-0191**); Canada, 15th floor, Abdulrahim Place, 990 Rama 4 Rd. (☎ **02/636-0540**); New Zealand, 93 Wireless Rd. (☎ **02/254-3865**).

Emergencies   Anywhere in the country, if you run into any emergency situation—police, medical, or fire, call the Tourist Police at ☎ 1699. Ignore all other emergency numbers—the person at the other end of the line is unlikely to understand English.

Hospitals   In Bangkok, the private Bumrungrad Hospital, 33 Sukhumvit 3 Rd., Nana Nua (☎ **02/667-1000**), and Bangkok Nursing Home, 9/1 Convent Rd. between Silom and Sathorn roads (☎ **2/632-0550**), deliver quality care with an English-speaking staff. Don't let the name fool you. Bangkok Nursing Home is actually an excellent full-service facility. Consultation visits cost about 300B (US$6.98). For major emergencies, you'll need your passport and a deposit of no more than 20,000B (US$465.12) before you're admitted. Credit cards are accepted.

In Pattaya, the Pattaya International Hospital is on Pattaya Soi 4, Pattaya 2nd Rd. (☎ **038/428-374**). The Phuket International Hospital is at 44 Chalermprakiat Ror 9 Rd. in Phuket town (☎ **076/249-400**). In Chiang Mai, McCormick Hospital, Kaew Narawat Road (☎ **053/241-107**), is your better bet for English-speaking staff.

Internet/E-mail   Service is available almost everywhere in the country, with Internet cafes popping up even on sleepy islands. Usage rates vary from about 2B (US$0.05) per minute to 300B (US$6.98) per hour.

Language   Central Thai is the official written and spoken language of the country, and most Thais understand it, even if their main language is one of the three other major dialects: Northeastern Thai, Northern Thai, and Southern Thai. English is spoken in the major cities at most hotels, restaurants, and shops, and is the second language of the professional class, as well as the language used for international business.

Liquor Laws   Thailand does have liquor laws, but you'll be hard pressed to see them enforced. The law that prohibits sale of alcoholic beverages to children under 18 years of age is never enforced. It seems public drunken behavior is almost compulsory in the tourist party zones in Bangkok, Pattaya, Ko Samui, Phuket, Chiang

Mai, and anywhere else you see a bar. Like everywhere else in the world, fines are imposed for those found driving while under the influence of alcohol.

Newspapers & Magazines   There are two main domestic English-language dailies, the *Bangkok Post* and the *Nation*.

Police   In Bangkok and all over the country, the extremely helpful Tourist Police can be reached at 1699. You do not need to dial an area code before the number.

Post Offices/Mail   You can use "poste restante" as an address anywhere in the country; this way, you can have mail sent to you addressed care of "Poste Restante, GPO, [Name of City]." You'll have to pay a minimal fee (a few baht) when you pick up your mail. Airmail postcards to the U.S., Australia, Canada, the U.K., and New Zealand cost 12B (US$0.28) for a small sized card; first-class letters cost 19B (US$0.44) per 5 grams.

Safety   For the average tourist, your only danger may be from pickpockets or those who would take your things on overnight train or bus trips. Keep your belongings close at hand. Almost all hotels have safes, whether in guest rooms or at the lobby.

If anything bad or suspicious happens to you, make sure you talk to the Tourist Police immediately. These guys have the power to be very helpful, and take complaints seriously: they've been known to lock everyone inside a bar until a "lost" wallet is recovered.

Tales of visitors being drugged by commercial sex workers are not urban myths. People have woken up the next morning to find not only their suitcase and money belt gone, but their hotel room stripped to the studs as well. To be safe, limit such relations to locals who work in clubs. If anything is amiss, you know where to find them the next day.

Last word: Don't gamble. Thai card games are set up to take your money.

Telephone & Fax   Major hotels in Bangkok, Pattaya, Phuket, Chiang Mai, and the provincial capitals have international direct dial (IDD) and long-distance service, and in-house fax transmission. Hotels levy a surcharge on local and long-distance calls, which can add up to 50% in some cases. Credit card or collect calls are a much better value, but most hotels also add a hefty service charge for them to your bill.

Most major post offices, usually open 7am to 11pm, have special booths for overseas calls, as well as fax and telex services. There are Overseas Telegraph and Telephone offices (also called OCO or Overseas Call Office) open 7 days a week and 24 hours a day throughout the country for long-distance international calls and telex and fax services. Local calls can be made from any red public pay telephone. Calls cost 3B (US$0.07) for the first minute, with additional 1B coins needed after hearing multiple beeps on the line. Blue public phones are for long-distance calls within Thailand, and use coins. Card phones can be found in most airports, many public buildings, convenience stores, and larger shopping centers. Cards can be purchased in several denominations at the Telephone Organization of Thailand offices or at some convenience stores.

Time Zone   Bangkok and all of Thailand are 7 hours later than GMT (Greenwich Mean Time). During winter months, this means that Bangkok is exactly 7 hours ahead of London, 12 hours ahead of New York, 15 hours ahead of Los Angeles, and 2 hours behind Sydney. Daylight saving time will add 1 hour to these figures.

Telephone Dialing Info at a Glance

- **To place a call from your home country to Thailand,** dial the international access code (011 in the U.S., 0011 in Australia, 0170 in New Zealand, 00 in the U.K.), plus the country code (**66**), plus the Thailand area code (Bangkok 2, Pattaya 38, Hua Hin 32, Surat Thani and Ko Samui 77, Phuket 76, Chiang Mai and Chiang Rai 53), followed by the six- or seven-digit phone number (for example, from the U.S. to Bangkok, you'd dial 011+66+2+000-0000).

- **To place a call within Thailand,** you must use area codes if calling between states. Note that for calls within the country, area codes are all preceded by a zero (i.e., Bangkok 02, Pattaya 038. Hua Hin 032, Surat Thani and Ko Samui 077, Phuket 076, Chiang Mai and Chiang Rai 053).

- **To place a direct international call from Thailand,** dial the international access code (001), plus the country code of the place you are dialing, plus the area code, plus the residential number of the other party.

- To reach the international operator, dial 100.

- **International country codes** are as follows: Australia 61, Burma 95, Cambodia 855, Canada 1, Hong Kong 852, Indonesia 62, Laos 856, Malaysia 60, New Zealand 64, the Philippines 63, Singapore 65, U.K. 44, U.S. 1, Vietnam 84.

Tipping   If a service charge is not added to your restaurant check, a 10% to 15% tip is appropriate. In small noodle shops, a 10B (US$0.23) tip may be given if the service is particularly good. Give hotel porters 20B (US$0.47) per bag (in very expensive hotels, I'll double it to 40B/US$0.93 per bag). Tipping taxi drivers is not expected, but carry small bills, as many cab drivers either don't have (or won't admit having) small change.

Toilets   By and large, rest rooms are readily available in the major areas of the country at hotels and restaurants, but expect to pay around 5B (US$0.12) for usage in public areas like bus and train stations. You also may encounter "squatters," ceramic bowls mounted at floor level. Keep your balance and bring your own toilet paper.

Touts   People will offer to take you to shops (usually jewelry shops) with "special bargains." Tuk-tuk drivers and "helpful folks" who chat you up on the street are particularly suspect. These guys are all seeking commissions from the shop owners, you'll never get the bargains promised, and the jewelry is always fake.

Water   Don't drink the tap water, even in major hotels. Most hotels provide bottled water in or near the minibar or in the bathroom; use it for brushing your teeth as well as for drinking. Bottled water in convenience shops costs under 10B (US$0.23). Most restaurants serve bottled or boiled water and ice made from boiled water. If a local place looks dodgy, don't trust the ice, or the water for that matter.

3 Bangkok

From the moment you arrive, Bangkok will grip your senses. Streets throb with traffic. The world's most opulent hotels cohabitate with squat buildings gray from smog. On every corner, street vendors fill the air with savory smells, and stalls packed with souvenirs, handicrafts, and cheap buys seem to clog every sidewalk. In the mornings, business people rush to work with cellular phones pressed to their ears while monks draped in saffron robes glide peacefully through the crowds. In the evenings, if the fiery and delicious Thai cuisine isn't racy enough, there's a nightlife unrivaled by any other city on the planet. Bangkok will suck you in with promises of a most exotic vacation, and will never fail to deliver.

Vintage 19th-century photographs of Bangkok show vivid images of life on the Chao Phraya River, bustling with vessels ranging from the humblest rowboat to elaborate royal barges. Built along the banks of the broad, S-shaped river, the city spread inland through a network of klongs (canals) that rivaled the intricacy—though never the elegance—of Venice.

As Bangkok became more densely populated and developed, more and more of the klongs were filled in to create broad thoroughfares. Cars, buses, motorcycles, and tuk-tuks (motorized three-wheeler rickshaws) followed, and today, the resultant rush-hour traffic jams are so horrendous (commuters spend, on average, 40 working days per year waiting in traffic!) that, once again, one of the best ways to travel around the city is via the river.

"Old Bangkok," or the **Historic District** nestled next to the Chao Phraya River, contains most of the city's historical sights such as the Grand Palace and most of the city's original wats (temples with resident monks). Following the river south, you'll run into the narrow lanes of Bangkok's **Chinatown.** Further down, a few of Bangkok's best hotels, including the famous Oriental Hotel, have made their mark on the city. Inland from the river, Bangkok's **central business district** is situated on Sathorn, Silom, and Surawongse roads, beginning at Charoen Krung Road (sometimes still referred to by its old name, New Road) leading all the way to Rama IV Road. Connecting from here is **Wireless Road,** where many of the larger foreign embassies have built huge compounds. Bangkok's **main shopping thoroughfare,** on Rama I Road, between Payathai and Ratchadamri roads, sports huge modern shopping complexes like the World Trade Center and Siam Square. Follow Rama I east and you'll run into Sukhumvit Road. While Sukhumvit isn't in the hub of the tourist area, it has a large concentration of expatriate residences, which makes for all sorts of good international restaurants, inexpensive shopping, and nightlife.

Get to know the Thai word *soi,* meaning lane. Main thoroughfares in the city have individual names, with many of the smaller side streets numbered in sequence for identification purposes. For example, Sukhumvit Soi 5 is the home of the Amari Boulevard Hotel, while Sukhumvit Soi 8, a few minutes' walk east and across the street, is where you'll find Le Banyan restaurant. Once upon a time each little soi had an individual name—yikes! Some are still known today, such as Nana Tua, Sukhumvit Soi 4, and its sister Nana Nua, Sukhumvit Soi 3.

VISITOR INFORMATION

The **TAT's** main office is at Le Concorde Office Building, 202 Ratchadaphisek Rd. (☎ 02/694-1222), but the more convenient location is at 4 Ratchadamnoen Nok Ave., a short walk from the Khao San Road area (☎ 02/282-9773). Call the **Tourist Service Line** at ☎ 1155 for all sorts of general inquiries.

GETTING THERE

Because most people enter Thailand via Bangkok, specific information on travel to Bangkok is covered in the country's "Getting There" section earlier in this chapter.

BY AIR   Most travelers arrive at Bangkok International Airport (Don Muang), which has domestic (☎ 02/535-2081) and international (☎ 02/535-1111) terminals. The airport has conveniences such as currency exchange offices, restaurants, post offices, hotel reservations counters, duty free shopping, and emergency medical service. **To get to central Bangkok,** limousines can be booked at the Arrival Hall starting from 650B (US$15.12). Just outside of the Arrivals Hall you'll be able to catch a cab for less: the metered fare plus 50B (US$1.16) airport pickup surcharge—about 250B to 300B (US$5.81 to US$6.98). For the best deal, check the Airport Shuttle Bus on the ground level of the Arrivals hall to see if your hotel is along one of the four routes. It'll only set you back 100B (US$2.33).

BY TRAIN   Passengers arriving by train will alight at the Hua Lamphong Railway Station (☎ **02/223-7010** or 02/223-7020) on Krung Kassem Road in central Bangkok. There never fails to be a line of taxis and tuk-tuks waiting outside.

BY BUS   If you're arriving from the southern parts of Thailand, or from Malaysia, you'll come into the Southern Bus Terminal (☎ **02/435-1199**) on Charan Sanitwong Road, across the river near the Bangkok Noi Station. From east coast destinations, you'll arrive at the Eastern Bus Terminal (☎ **02/390-1230**) on Sukhumvit Road opposite Soi 63—Ekamai Road. From northern areas of the country you'll be dropped at **Northern Bus Terminal** (☎ **02/272-5761**) on Phahonyothin Road near the Chatuchak Weekend Market. Metered taxis are either waiting at these terminals, or are easy enough to flag down.

Getting Around

Prepare yourself for traffic jams and pollution. Bangkok's notorious motor vehicle problem still remains a major issue, despite all sorts of ideas to lessen the load. The best one is the brand new BTS Skytrain, which rockets you over the bottle-necks below. While taxis are your next best bet, try to get around by boat to some of the sights, such as the Grand Palace, Wat Po, and the National Museum, for peace of mind as well as the fascinating river scenery.

BY SKYTRAIN   The **Bangkok Mass Transit System (BTS),** known as the "sky-train" is just about the hottest thing going in Bangkok. The elevated railways system brilliantly whisks you above the maddening traffic. While coverage isn't too extensive, there is access to Bangkok's central areas. The Silom Line takes runs from the Chao Phraya River at the King Taksin Bridge (next to the Shangri-La Hotel), along Sathorn and Silom roads, past Sala Daeng (at Patpong), and up Ratchadamri Road to the Siam Square shopping area. Here you can change to the Sukhumvit Line to head north to the Chatuchak Weekend Market near the airport, or go east down Ploenchit and Sukhumvit roads. Purchase single-journey tickets or stored-value tickets at each station for fares between 10B and 40B (US$0.23 and US$0.93).

BY TAXI   Unless you venture to the outer residential neighborhoods, you're never at a loss for a taxi in Bangkok. Metered taxis can be flagged down from sidewalks, and will swing by hotels and shopping malls looking for fares. The meter starts at 35B (US$0.81) for the first 2 kilometers, and increases by about 5B (US$0.12) per kilometer thereafter (increases will also depend on how fast traffic is moving). Basically, for most trips around town you won't spend more than 100B (US$2.33). Tipping is not expected, but many will fumble for change in search of one. If you encounter a cabbie who tries to negotiate a fare up front, insist he use the meter. A useful tip: many drivers come from Isaan in the northeast of the country, and have terrible English. It's always a good idea to have the concierge or desk clerk at your hotel write your destination for you in Thai before you venture out.

BY TUK-TUK   These are some crazy little vehicles: three-wheeled scooters with an open cart, complete with flashing lights, metallic ornamentation, bright colors, and

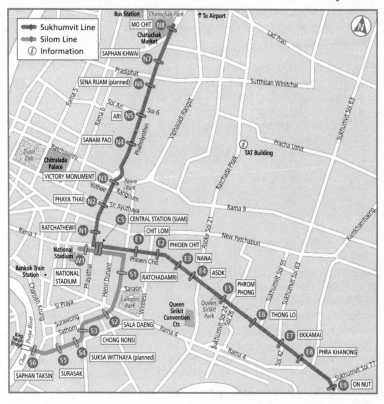

rumbling motors. Drivers will negotiate the fare before you set out; make sure you bargain. The fun part is that these guys are kamikazes, zipping through traffic as you grip the bars for support. The not so fun part is when you're stuck in traffic with exhaust fumes smoking all around you. Use them for short trips, and never during rush hour.

Be wary of tuk-tuk drivers touting shopping trips. A lot of these drivers lurk in tourist areas, trying to chat folks up to come and see his friend's gem shop or his brother's tailor, but they're just trying to get commission, and you'll be ripped off. Make sure your driver takes you where you want to go, and *only* where you want to go.

BY CAR & DRIVER   A great option for sightseeing in comfort is to hire a car and driver for a day or half-day. The larger hotels can arrange these for you, but a cheaper alternative is to contact a local travel agent or car rental company. **World Travel Service Ltd.,** 1053 Charoen Krung Rd., 10500 Bangkok (☎ **02/233-5900**), can also provide an English-speaking tour guide and can help arrange a suitable itinerary.

BY BOAT   Once upon a time Bangkok was a city of waterways, not unlike Venice. While today most *klongs,* or canals, have been paved over for motor vehicle traffic, some remain, and the mighty Chao Phraya River is still considered the lifeline of the city. Today, the most common form of transportation around the city is by taxi, but if you can take a trip somewhere via the river or a klong, you'll experience a wonderful side to the city; a tranquil ride through neighborhoods, past temples and the Grand Palace. It is highly recommended.

The **Chao Phraya Express Company** (☎ 02/222-5330) will shuttle you between the many piers on either side of the river (almost all maps indicate the location of the piers), the most common ones being the piers at the Oriental Hotel, the River City Complex (Wat Muang Khae Ferry Pier), and the Grand Palace (Tha Chang Ferry Pier).

The cost depends on how far you go. It is usually between 5B and 10B (US$0.12 and US$0.23). Look for the Chao Phraya Express logo on the side of the boat, and be prepared to jump quick as they briefly pull up to the pier.

At the ferry piers you can also charter a private long-tail boat to take you through the klongs in Bangkok and on the Thonburi side of the river. For only 300B (US$6.98) an hour, the trip is incredibly fun, passing riverside houses and shops and seeing how the locals live. Go to the pier at the River City Complex next to the Sheraton Hotel.

BY MOTORCYCLE TAXI   If tuk-tuk drivers aren't kamikaze enough, you always have motorcycle taxis. Distinguished by their colored vests, these guys are great for getting you where you want to go in a jiffy, even if traffic is bumper to bumper. Just hop on the back. They'll weave you through, so be careful not to knock your knees on the sides of buses. At about 5B to 40B (US$0.12 to US$0.93) for a short trip, they're a bargain.

BY BUS   Bangkok has an extensive and dependable system of city buses. Maps are available at bookstores and magazine stands marked with the more popular routes. A trip on an air-conditioned bus will set you back only 6B (US$0.14). Beware of pickpockets and purse slashers, a serious problem on crowded rush hour buses.

ON FOOT   Bangkok's heat, humidity, and air pollution prohibit walking long distances. Besides, half the sidewalks seem to be in a state of perpetual ruin. If you're walking around a limited area, you'll be fine. Walking around Old Bangkok, the area near the Grand Palace, and many of the city's wats is not too difficult, as long as you start in the morning while it's still cool.

Fast Facts: Bangkok

Banks/Currency Exchange   Banks with money changers and ATMs are easy to find in the areas around hotels and shopping malls. Bangkok Bank, Thai Farmers Bank, and Bank of Ayudhya are Thailand's three biggest banks, and they will accept debit and cash advance cards on the MasterCard/Cirrus and Visa/PLUS networks.

Internet/E-mail   You've got a million options here. If you're staying near Khao San Road in Banglamphu, you can't throw a stone without hitting an Internet cafe. You can also look around the Patpong area, on Silom and Suriwongse roads—check in the shopping malls. You'll also find them around the Siam Square shopping area. Down Sukhumvit Road, a few of the sois are packed with them. Access rates will vary between 2B (US$0.05) per minute and 300B (US$6.98) per hour. There are so many to choose from I recommend asking your hotel concierge for the nearest one. Don't be tempted to use the Internet in your hotel's business center. The expense is alarming.

Police   The Tourist Police can be reached at ☎1699.

Post Office/Mail   The General Post Office (☎ 02/233-1050) is on Charoen Krung Road between the Oriental Hotel and the Sheraton Royal Orchid Hotel.

Telephone   Bangkok's city code is 2.

ACCOMMODATIONS

Because of the currency fluctuation of recent years, many luxury hotels have chosen to quote room rates in U.S. dollars. All prices listed are the official published tariff. Be sure to ask for discount offers, and any extra add-on incentives (free breakfast or airport transfer, etc.) when you book. Also, expect these prices to jump during the holiday peak season between December 20 and January 10. Except for those quoted for budget accommodations, all prices do not include additional 7% service charge and 7% Value Added Tax (VAT).

ALONG THE RIVER

Very Expensive

✪ **The Oriental.** 48 Oriental Ave., Bangkok 10500. ☎ **800/526-6566** in the U.S. and Canada; 800/2828-3838 in Australia, New Zealand, and the U.K.; 02/236-0400. Fax 02/236-1937. www.mandarin-oriental.com. 396 units. A/C MINIBAR TV TEL. 10,750B–13,330B (US$250–US$310) double; 18060B–38,700B (US$420–US$900) suite. AE, DC, EC, MC, V. On the riverfront off Charoen Krung Rd. (New Rd.); 5-min. walk from Saphan Taksin station.

The Oriental has long been in the pantheon of the world's best hotels. Its history goes back to the 1860s when the original hotel, no longer standing, was established by two Danish sea captains soon after King Mongkut (Rama IV) reopened Siam to world trade. The hotel has withstood occupation by Japanese and American troops and played host to a long roster of Thai and international dignitaries and celebrities, most famously writers such as Joseph Conrad, Somerset Maugham, Noel Coward, Graham Greene, John Le Carré, and James Michener. Jim Thompson, of Thai silk trade fame, even served briefly as the hotel's proprietor. New buildings have been added—the first in 1876, the larger and more modern pair in 1958 and 1976—so that today it's more modern than colonial, though it retains considerable charm.

Shangri-La Hotel. 89 Soi Wat Suan Plu, Charoen Krung Rd. (New Rd.), Bangkok 10500. ☎ **800/942-5050** in the U.S. and Canada; 800/222-448 in Australia; 800/442-179 in New Zealand; 181/747-8485 in the U.K.; 02/236-7777. Fax 02/236-8579. www.shangri-la.com. 850 units. A/C MINIBAR TV TEL. 9,030B–19,350B (US$210–US$450) double; from 16,770B (US$390) suite. AE, DC, MC, V. Adjacent to Sathorn Bridge, with access off Chaoren Krung Rd. (New Rd.) at south end of Silom Rd. Saphan Taksin station.

The opulent but thoroughly modern Shangri-La, on the banks of the Chao Phraya, boasts acres of polished marble, a jungle of tropical plants and flowers, and two towers with breathtaking views of the river. The higher priced guest rooms have a view of the river, but all rooms are decorated with lush carpeting and teak furniture, and have marble baths. The views are terrific from the higher floor deluxe rooms, and most have either a balcony or a small sitting room, making them closer to junior suites and a particularly good value for on-the-river upscale accommodations. For such an enormous place, the level of service and facilities is surprisingly good. The super-luxurious Krung Thep Wing adds another 17-story, river-view tower to the grounds, as well as a riverside swimming pool and a restaurant and breakfast lounge. Guests register in their spacious rooms, surrounded by colorful Thai paintings and glistening Thai silk.

Extravagance at Shangri-La means nine separate dining choices, including the riverside Coffee Garden and Menam Terrace (which offers a huge international buffet dinner); popular Shang Palace for Chinese food; and one of Bangkok's prettiest settings for Thai cuisine, Sala Thip (see "Dining," below). Angelini and Edogin round out international restaurants with Italian and Japanese cuisine, respectively. The hotel's river cruiser, the *Ayutthaya Princess,* motors up the Chao Phraya to Ayutthaya daily and makes a 3-hour dinner cruise.

Bangkok Accommodations & Dining

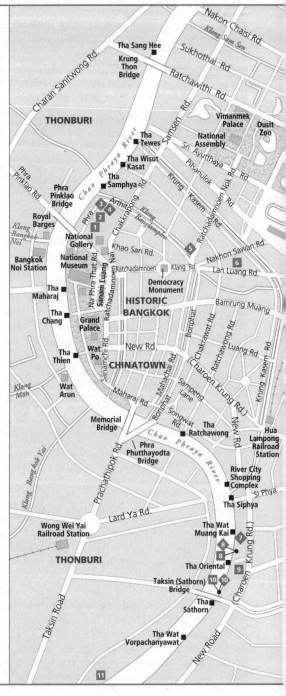

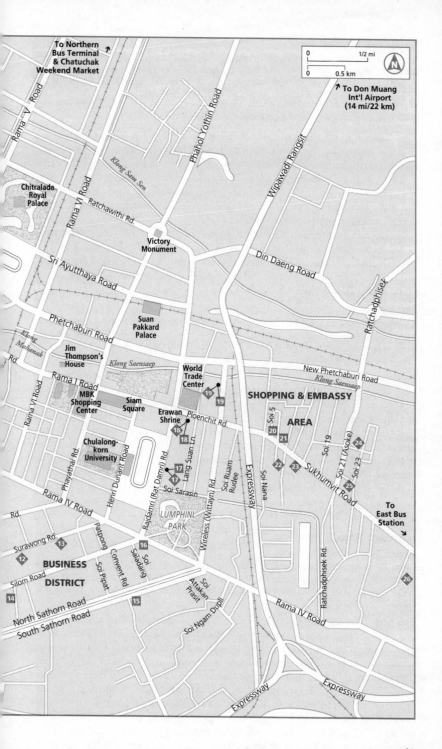

To Northern
Bus Terminal
& Chatuchak
Weekend Market

0   1/2 mi
0   0.5 km

To Don Muang
Int'l Airport
(14 mi/22 km)

Rama V Road

Rama VI Road

Phahol Yothin Road

Wipatwadi Rangsit

Klong Sam Sen

Chitralada
Royal
Palace

Ratchawithi Rd.

Victory
Monument

Din Daeng Road

Ratchadphisek

Sri Ayutthaya Road

Phetchaburi Road

Klong Mahanak

Suan
Pakkard
Palace

Jim
Thompson's
House

Rd.

Klong Saensaep

World
Trade
Center

New Phetchaburi Road

Klong Saensaep

Rama I Road

MBK
Shopping
Center

Siam
Square

Erawan
Shrine

Ploenchit Rd.

SHOPPING & EMBASSY

Soi 5

AREA

Soi 19

Soi 21 (Asoke)

Soi 23

Rama VI Road

19

19

18

18

Chulalong-
korn
University

Phayathai Rd.

Henri Dunant Road

Lang Suan Ln.

Rajdamri (Rat Damri) Rd.

17

17

Soi Sarasin

Soi Ruam
Rudee

Sukhumvit Road

20

21

22

23

24

25

To
East Bus
Station

Rama IV Road

Wireless (Wittayu) Rd.

Soi Nana

Expressway

LUMPHINI
PARK

Rd.

Surawong Rd.

13

Patpong

Soi
Saladang

16

12

BUSINESS

Soi Phat

Convent Rd.

Soi
Attakan
Prasit

Ratchadphisek Rd.

Silom Road

DISTRICT

14

15

North Sathorn Road

South Sathorn Road

Soi Ngam Dupli

Rama IV Road

26

Expressway

Expressway

149

Expensive

Marriott Royal Garden Riverside Hotel. 257/1–3 Charoen Nakhorn Rd., Thonburi, Bangkok 10600. ☎ **800/344-1212** in the U.S. and Canada; 0800/951-000 in the U.K.; 02/ 476-0021. Fax 02/476-1120. 420 units. A/C MINIBAR TV TEL. 5,590B–6,450B (US$130– US$150) double; 6,665B–451,500B (US$155–US$10,500) suite. AE, DC, MC, V. On the Thonburi (east) side of the Chao Phraya River, north of the Krung Thep Bridge, 15 min. by boat from River City. 10-min. walk from Saphan Taksin station.

This luxuriously sprawling complex on the banks of the Chao Phraya is across the river and a few miles downstream from the heart of Bangkok. As you board the hotel's long-tail boat and make the short trip down river, you will feel the crazy city release you from its grip. Once at the hotel, you'll think you're at a resort, with the three wings of the hotel surrounding a large landscaped pool area with lily ponds and fountains, and a wonderful spa for a uniquely calming Bangkok experience. Boats go to and from River City shopping mall every half-hour.

Dining options here lean toward the big international names—Trader Vic's Polynesian Restaurant and Benihana Japanese-American Steak House—as well as their own Garden Café (Thai and international cuisine), the Rice Mill Chinese Restaurant, and the Riverside Terrace for beef and seafood. They also operate an evening dinner cruise aboard the *Manhora,* a beautifully restored rice-barge.

Moderate

✪ Bossotel Inn. 55/12–14 Soi Charoen Krung 42/1 (off Charoen Krung Rd., on Soi 42, toward the Shangri-La Hotel), Bangrak, Bangkok 10500. ☎ **02/630-6120.** Fax 02/ 237-3225. 46 units. A/C MINIBAR TV TEL. 800B (US$18.60) double. AE, MC, V. 5-min. walk from Saphan Taksin station.

It's not on the water and there isn't a view to speak of, but the spiffy, renovated new wing of the Bossotel, in particular, warrants consideration.

Many of the guests are either long-term visitors or repeat offenders, because, quite frankly, Bossotel delivers large, clean rooms in a fantastic location without draining your wallet. While rooms are very basic, the furniture and decor don't clash (believe me, that's impressive for a budget hotel in these parts). While the lobby coffee shop stops room delivery service at around 10:30pm, the continental and local food has improved greatly over the past year, as has the service. They also have HBO and CNN in the guest rooms, as well as laundry service and a small business center. Check out the traditional Thai massage on the second floor—hotel guests can get a very good 2-hour massage for only 240B (US$5.58). Unbelievable.

HISTORIC BANGKOK
Expensive

Royal Princess. 269 Larn Luang Rd., Pomprab, Bangkok 10100. ☎ **02/281-3088.** Fax 02/280-1314. www.royalprincess.com. 170 units. A/C MINIBAR TV TEL. 3,600B–4,300B (US$83.72–US$100) double; from 6,500B (US$151.16) suite. AE, DC, MC, V. East of Wat Saket.

This first-class hotel near the Grand Palace in the Ratanakosin Island area more than lives up to the high standards of the Thai-owned Dusit Thani Hotels and Resorts family. Completed in 1989, its proximity to government offices brings a steady flow of official visitors, but it's also great for travelers interested in the sights of old Bangkok.

Public spaces are wall-to-wall marble, and bustle with activity, yet the scale is intimate. Guest rooms are very tastefully furnished and bright. While higher-priced deluxe rooms have balconies overlooking the tropically landscaped pool, the superior rooms of the same style look out over the neighborhood. It's a 10-minute taxi ride to either the Grand Palace or Vimanmek Palace, and though the area lacks a diversity of dining, the authentic flavor of this old neighborhood more than compensates.

Inexpensive

Bangkok has a small area that is well-known and well-used by budget travelers and backpackers. **Khao San Road,** a 10- to 15-minute walk from the National Museum, is lined on both sides with guest houses, cafes, Internet cafes, and souvenir stands. The place crawls with travelers, so you'll probably find a more authentic Bangkok experience elsewhere. Still, it's cheap and convenient. Reservations are rarely taken seriously. Just show up and shop around—front office folks are glad to show you a room or two. Also, don't expect any budget places to accept credit cards.

One of my favorites, the **New Merry V. Guesthouse** (18–20 Phra Athit Rd., Banglamphu, Bangkok 10200; ☎ **02/280-3315**), charges 250B (US$5.81) for a double with fan and 380B (US$8.84) for double air-conditioned, all with attached bath. There's a laundry facility, storage lockers, bulletin board, and Internet cafe, and it's conveniently located across from the Phra Athit boat pier.

Peachy Guesthouse (10 Phra Athit Rd., Banglamphu, Bangkok 10200; ☎ **02/281-6471**) charges 200B (US$4.65) for a large, bright room—Spartan but clean, with a ceiling fan. Communal toilets and cold-water showers on each floor are kept very clean.

THE BUSINESS DISTRICT
Very Expensive

The Dusit Thani. Rama IV Rd., Bangkok 10500. ☎ **02/236-0450**; 212/697-8600 in the U.S. and Canada; 02/9416-5523 in Australia; 181/307-7693 in the U.K. Fax 02/236-6400. www.dusit.com. 530 units. A/C MINIBAR TV TEL. 8,170B (US$190) double; from 11,180B (US$260) suite. AE, DC, JCB, MC, V. At corner of Silom and Rama IV rds. opposite Lumpini Park. Sala Daeng station.

"The Dusit" continues to be a favorite meeting place for locals, the expatriate community, and visiting celebrities, as after 28 years of operation, it retains its reputation as one of Bangkok's premier hotels. The lobby, while grand, is not the same marble and mirror disaster as some of the newer hotels in Asia. Splashing lobby fountains, exotic flower displays, and a poolside waterfall cascading through dense foliage make it a welcome retreat at the end of a day's sightseeing. Unfortunately, the old gal could stand some renovations; some of the guest rooms look a little too well worn. Superior rooms in the Executive Wing are newly redone (1996), and far fresher.

Of the hotel's eight restaurants, the Mayflower (Chinese) and the Benjarong (Thai) are ranked among the finest in Bangkok. The top-floor California/Asian fusion cuisine Tiara Restaurant has a sensational view over the city. The popular Pavilion Coffeeshop (open 24 hours), and Chinatown Restaurant are relatively less expensive choices. There are also a steakhouse and an excellent Vietnamese restaurant, as well as Japanese eateries, the latter two especially popular with businesspeople.

✪ **The Sukhothai.** 13/3 S. Sathorn Rd., Bangkok 10120. ☎ **800/223-6800** in the U.S. and Canada; 800/222-033 in Australia (Sydney 02/9377-8444); 800/441-016 in New Zealand; 800/181-123 in the U.K.; 02/287-0222. Fax 02/287-4980. www.sukhothai.com. E-mail: beaufort@ksc11.th.com. 224 units. A/C MINIBAR TV TEL. 10,320B–12,040B (US$240–US$280) double; from 14,190B (US$330) suite. AE, DC, JCB, MC, V. South of Lumphini Park, near intersection of Rama IV and Wireless rds., next to the YWCA.

Inside The Sukhothai, visitors find a welcome, if studied, serenity. Avoiding the hype of high-rise, the hotel's maze of low pavilions combines crisp, contemporary lines with earthy textures and tones. Broad, colonnaded public spaces surround peaceful lotus pools. Symmetry and simplicity form the backdrop for brick chedis, terra-cotta friezes, and celadon ceramics evoking the ancient kingdom of Sukhothai.

Large guest rooms carry the same signature style in fine Thai silk, mellow teak, and celadon tile. Gigantic luxurious bathrooms feature oversized bathtubs, separate shower and toilet stalls, plus two full-size wardrobes. Technologically up-to-date, these smart rooms also have personal fax machines and Internet connections. The Sukhothai is second to none in excellent service and assured sense of privacy.

The Colonnade restaurant hops at Sunday brunch, when live jazz accompanies a gorgeous champagne international buffet—reservations a must. Celadon, their excellent Thai restaurant, was recently expanded to meet demand.

Expensive

Holiday Inn Crowne Plaza. 981 Silom Rd., Bangkok 10500. ☎ **800/465-4329** in the U.S. and Canada; 800/553-888 in Australia; 0800/442-888 in New Zealand; 0800/897121 in the U.K.; 02/238-4300. Fax 02/238-5289. 726 units. A/C MINIBAR TV TEL. 7,267B–8,557B (US$169–US$199) double; from 11,137B (US$259) suite. AE, DC, MC, V. On Silom Rd. 1 block above (east of) Charoen Krung Rd.

Crowne Plaza, Holiday Inn's upmarket chain of hotels, provides high quality service and a level of luxury unexpected by those familiar with standard Holiday Inn accommodations in the U.S. This is the top choice for families traveling to Bangkok; while there is an 500B charge for an extra bed, there's no charge for children under 19 years of age accompanying parents. Their very comfortable guest rooms are lovely, with masculine striped fabrics offsetting floral prints for a soft and homelike appeal. Rooms in the Plaza Tower are an especially good value, though smaller than those in the Crowne Tower, with high ceilings that give a spacious feel, and oversized porthole windows, framed by heavy drapery, overlooking the city. The location is very convenient, near the expressway, a short walk from the river (and the Shangri-La and Oriental), in the middle of the gem-trade district. The huge lobby seating areas are always humming with travelers who are either resting from a day's adventure, or waiting to begin a new one.

The Window on Silom Restaurant serves one of Bangkok's better breakfast buffets. In the afternoon, the hotel serves a fine high tea in the Orchid Lounge. The Thai Pavilion and the Mogul-cuisine Tandoor serve lunch and dinner.

THE SHOPPING/EMBASSY AREA

Very Expensive

Grand Hyatt Erawan Bangkok. 494 Ratchadamri Rd., Bangkok 10330. ☎ **800/ 233-1234** in the U.S. and Canada; 02/254-1234. Fax 02/254-6308. www.hyatt.com. E-mail: reservation@erawan.co.th. 400 units. A/C MINIBAR TV TEL. 11,180B–12,255B (US$260–US$285) double; from 15,480B (US$360) suite. AE, DC, JCB, MC, V. Corner of Ratchadamri and Rama I Rds. 5-min. walk from Chidlom station.

When the Thai government attempted to build this hotel 50 years ago, so many spooky occurrences happened on the site that a special spirit house, or shrine, was erected on the property to appease the spirits before the building could be completed. Honoring the four-faced Brahma god Than Tao Mahaprom, the Erawan Shrine gets its common name from the three-headed Erawan elephant, the Brahma god's steed. To this day the shrine is never neglected, for throngs of wish-seekers come daily to offer joss, fruits, flowers, and teak elephant statues.

Step from Bangkok's busy shopping district into this hotel's majestic lobby—with old columns and balustrades reminiscent of colonial architectural styles and indoor landscaping—a perfect setting for afternoon tea. The works of dozens of contemporary Thai artists grace hallways and spacious rooms, where earth-toned silks, celadon accessories, antique-finish furnishings, parquet floors, Oriental rugs, large bathrooms, and city views abound. In addition to the facilities one expects from a five-star hotel, there is a delightful fifth-floor pool terrace, where a waterfall tumbles down a rocky wall into a full-size hot tub. Of the half-dozen or so in-house restaurants, the ones that stand out are The Chinese Restaurant, for its excellent Cantonese cuisine and sleek design, and Spasso, for its innovative Italian fare and trend-setting restaurant-cum-nightclub concept.

✪ **The Regent.** 155 Ratchadamri Rd., Bangkok 10330. ☎ **800/545-4000** in the U.S. and Canada; 800/022-800 in Australia; 800/440-800 in New Zealand; 0800/917-8795 in the U.K.; 02/251-6127. Fax 02/253-9195. www.regenthotels.com. 356 units. A/C MINIBAR TV TEL. 9,890B–10,750B (US$230–US$250) double; 16,340B (US$380) cabana room; from 1,290B (US$330) suite. AE, DC, MC, V. South of Rama I Rd. Ratchadamri station.

Think of The Regent as a modern palace. From your first entrance into the massive lobby you'll be captivated by the grand staircase, huge and gorgeous Thai murals and gold sun bursts on the vaulted ceiling. The impeccable service begins at the front desk, where guests are greeted, then escorted to their room to complete their check-in and enjoy the waiting fruit basket and box of chocolates. An air of luxury pervades each room, put forth by the traditional style Thai murals, handsome color schemes, and a plush carpeted dressing area off the tiled bath. The more expensive rooms have a view of the Royal Bangkok Sport Club and race track. Cabana rooms and suites face the large pool and terrace area, which is filled with palms and lotus pools.

Dining options at the hotel include the informal Spice Market, one of the finest Thai restaurants in the city (see "Dining," below). At Shintaro you can enjoy Japanese cuisine in a contemporary setting, while their new Italian-American restaurant serves up some hearty pastas, and has caught on as a hot spot for power lunches.

Expensive

Amari Boulevard Hotel. 2 Soi 5, Sukhumvit Rd., Bangkok 10110. ☎ **02/255-2930.** Fax 02/255-2950. www.amari.com. 315 units. A/C MINIBAR TV TEL. US$128–US$163 double; from US$240 suite. AE, DC, MC, V. North of Sukhumvit Rd., on Soi 5. 5-min. walk from Nana station.

The Sukhumvit Road area doesn't provide the best street access to the sights in old Bangkok, but who needs street access when there's a perfectly good klong nearby? All you need do is hop a water taxi and take a fascinating trip through Bangkok's old "back alleys" to the Chao Phraya. Besides, many people choose to stay in the Sukhumvit Road area to be close to major shopping malls and plentiful food and entertainment options. Amari Boulevard offers two kinds of rooms. The newer Krung Thep Wing has spacious rooms with terrific city views, while the original wing has attractive balconied rooms that are a better value. When rooms are discounted 40% to 60% in the low season, this hotel is a very good value.

Hilton International Bangkok at Nai Lert Park. 2 Wireless Rd., Bangkok 10330. ☎ **800/HILTONS** in the U.S; 800/222-255 in Australia; 0800/448-002 in New Zealand; 02/253-0123. Fax 02/253-6509. www.hilton.com. 338 units. A/C MINIBAR TV TEL. 5,590B–9,030B (US$130–US$210) double; from 13,115B (US$305) suite. AE, DC, JCB, MC, V. Between Ploenchit Rd. and New Phetchaburi Rd.

Set in lushly landscaped Nai Lert Park, near the British and American embassies, this tropical paradise is something of a mixed blessing—you will sleep far from the madding crowds, but you may find the taxi ride to the river or tourist sights a minor nuisance (though the adventurous will ride the convenient klong boat to the Grand Palace Area). However, after a long day of business or sightseeing, returning to the peaceful tranquility of the Hilton has the very comfortable feeling of returning home. The airy atrium lobby, with its classic teak pavilion and open garden views, ranks as one of the great public spaces in Bangkok. And the gorgeous free form pool in landscaped gardens is a total resort experience. The spacious guest rooms all have bougainvillea-draped balconies; the most preferred (and expensive) rooms overlook the pool.

Food service is outstanding and very good value here. The "coffee shop," Suan Saranrom, is a grand dining area overlooking the garden; it has, for many years, been voted the best Thai restaurant in a Bangkok hotel. The elegant Ma Maison offers excellent French cuisine. Genji, the Japanese restaurant; a cozy lobby bar; and an evening poolside grill are other possibilities.

Moderate

✪ **City Lodge.** 137/1–3 Sukhumvit Soi 9, Bangkok 10110. ☎ **02/253-7705.** Fax 02/255-4667. 28 units. A/C MINIBAR TV TEL. 910B (US$21.16) double. MC, V. Corner of Sukhumvit and Soi 9. Nana station.

Budget watchers will appreciate the two small, spiffy City Lodges. Both the newer lodge on Soi 9, and its nearby cousin, the older, 35-room City Lodge on Soi 19 (☎ 02/254-4783; fax 02/255-7340), provide clean, compact rooms with simple, modern decor. Each has a pleasant coffee shop (facing the bustle on Sukhumvit Road at Soi 9; serving Italian fare on Soi 19), a small but friendly staff, and privileges at the rooftop swimming pool at the more deluxe Amari Boulevard Hotel on Soi 5. All three belong to the Amari Hotels and Resorts Group. No frills here, but still a lot of comfort for your money.

DINING

Chances are your hotel will have at least one or two options for in-house dining—some hotels boasting four or more different options. In fact, some of Bangkok's best dining is in its hotels, and I've included some of the better choices in this chapter. Usually the more authentic dining experience is out around town—from noodle hawkers on the sidewalks to traditional Thai dishes served in beautiful local settings. Bangkok also has some fine international dining establishments with guest chefs from Europe and America.

ALONG THE RIVER

Very Expensive

Normandie Grill. In the Oriental Hotel, 48 Oriental Ave. ☎ **02/236-0400.** Reservations required. Main courses 600B–1,600B (US$13.95–US$37.21); set dinner 3,500B (US$81.40). AE, DC, MC, V. Mon–Sat noon–2:30pm and 7–10:30pm; Sun 7–10:30pm. Off Charoen Krung (New Rd.), overlooking the river. FRENCH.

The ultra-elegant Normandie, atop the renowned Oriental Hotel, is the apex in formal dining in Thailand, both in price and quality. Surprisingly, the staff is made up of some of the most friendly and relaxed folks you'll ever meet. The room glistens in gold and silver, from place settings to chandeliers, and the warm tones of golden silks. Some of the highest rated master chefs from France have made guest appearances at Normandie. They add their own unique touches to a menu which features mouthwatering grilled meats and rich classic French cuisine. Reservations are a must, as the dining room is relatively small, and a jacket and tie are required.

Expensive

✪ **Sala Thip.** The Shangri-La Hotel, 89 Soi Wat Suan Plu. ☎ **02/236-7777.** Reservations recommended. Main courses 200B–450B (US$4.65–US$10.47). AE, DC, MC, V. Daily 6:30–11pm. Overlooking Chao Phraya River, near Sathorn Bridge–Saphan Taksin BTS station. THAI.

Sala Thip, on the river terrace of the Shangri-La Hotel, is arguably Bangkok's most romantic Thai restaurant. Classical music and traditional cuisine are superbly presented under one of two aged, carved teak pavilions perched over a lotus pond or at outdoor tables overlooking the river. (For those who crave a less humid environment, grab a table in one of the air-conditioned dining rooms.) Although the food may not inspire aficionados, it is skillfully prepared and nicely served. Set menus help the uninitiated with ordering: the many courses include Thai spring rolls, pomelo salad with chicken, a spicy seafood soup, snapper with chile sauce, and your choice of Thai curries. Keep your eyes peeled for masked dancers performing between the tables at various intervals. They're real fun.

Moderate

Harmonique. 22 Chaoren Krung (New Rd.) Soi 34. ☎ **02/237-8175.** Reservations not accepted. Main courses 70B–200B (US$1.63–US$4.65). No credit cards. Mon–Sat 10am–10pm. THAI.

A nice little restaurant find, Harmonique's special character oozes from the courtyard walls of this old mansion. Small dining rooms set with cozy antiques and marble-top tables are inviting and friendly. While the cuisine here is Thai, it's not exactly authentic—much of it is leans toward Western tastes, and there's a big Chinese influence here. But it's all still very good—the sizzling grilled seafood platter is nice and garlicky (chiles on the side), and they also feature nice Thai salads. Avoid this place on a weekend at dinnertime—I could have been invisible for all the service I got. Other times of the week, the staff is far better.

HISTORIC DISTRICT
Moderate

✪ **Bangkok Bar and Restaurant.** 591 Phra Sumen Rd. (north of Democracy Monument). ☎ **02/281-6237.** Reservations recommended on weekends. Main courses 70B–150B (US$1.63–US$3.49). No credit cards. Daily–2am. THAI.

A recent entry on the capital's dining scene, Bangkok is fresh and bold—a great alternative to places with more hype than taste. In a renovated 150-year-old mansion alongside Klong Banglamphu, all your senses are visited with local contemporary art on the walls (don't forget to walk upstairs for more exhibit space), deep jazz and funk rhythms wafting through the air, and good Thai food—be warned it's spicy. After scraping half the green chiles off my sea bass—steamed with lemon, garlic, and chile—it was pretty swell (I swear, it was atomic!). But there are plenty of dishes that are not so spicy—the chicken wrapped in pandan leaves is crispy and savory, and the coconut milk soup has a great creamy and sweet flavor. With a full bar and interesting cocktails, this place will be a success for years to come.

Ton Pho Restaurant. 43 Phra-Athit Rd., Banglamphu (1 block north of Phra-Athit ferry pier). ☎ **02/280-0452.** Reservations recommended on weekends. Main courses 50B–260B (US$1.16–US$6). JCB, MC, V. Daily 11am–10pm. THAI.

Another great choice for dining along the Chao Phraya River, Ton Pho is closer and easier to find, plus you still have a lovely riverside venue. I was lucky one day to have my lunch while watching the Royal Barges, the delicate gilt boats that parade the royal family through the city on special occasions, practice on the river. Their menu has a large selection of seafood specials, plus chicken and beef dishes (although the beef here was a bit too tough for my tastes)—and their soups are lovely. Call the TAT to find out about Royal Barges practice, then make your reservations for some great lunch entertainment.

Inexpensive

Commé. Phra-Athit Rd. ☎ **02/280-0647.** Reservations not accepted. Main courses 50B–120B (US$1.16–US$2.79). No credit cards. Tues–Sun 6pm–2am. Opposite Ton Pho, 1 block north of Phra-Athit ferry pier. THAI.

Phra-Athit Road has enjoyed a recent spark of trendy new restaurants and cafes in the past few years. Quite the place to hang out, it has the double happiness of being hip and affordable at the same time. Of all the places here, I like Commé. Small and brightly lit, the staff is laid back and good humored, the art will always give you something to talk about, and the menu (although somewhat limited) is quite good—and surprisingly inexpensive for the quality and quantity. They serve beer; otherwise, BYO.

BUSINESS DISTRICT
Expensive

✪ **Spice Market.** The Regent, 155 Ratchadamri Rd. (south of Rama I Rd.). ☎ **02/251-6127.** Reservations recommended. Main courses 150B–400B (US$3.49–US$9.30). AE, DC, MC, V. Daily 11:30am–2:30pm and 6:30–11pm. Ratchadamri BTS station. THAI.

Many contend that the Spice Market is the city's finest pure Thai restaurant. The theatrical decor reflects the name: burlap spice sacks, ceramic pots, and glass jars set in dark-wood cabinets around the dining area playfully re-create the mercantile feel of a traditional Thai shop house. The food is artfully presented, authentically spiced, and extraordinarily delicious. House specialties include *nam prik ong,* crispy rice cakes with minced pork dip; *nua phad bai kapraow,* fried beef with chile and fresh basil; and *siew ngap,* red curry with roasted duck in coconut milk. The menu's "chile rating" guarantees that spices are tempered to your palate.

Moderate

✪ **Somboon Seafood.** 169/7–11 Surawong Rd. ☎ **02/233-3104.** Seafood at market prices (about 800B/US$18.60 for 2). No credit cards. Daily 4–11pm. Just across from the Peugeot building. SEAFOOD.

OK, this one's definitely for those who would sacrifice atmosphere for excellent food. Packed nightly, you'll still be able to find a table (the place is huge). The staff is extremely friendly—between them and the picture menu you'll be able to order the best dishes and have the finest recommendations. Peruse the large aquariums outside to check out all the live seafood options like prawn, fishes, lobsters, crabs—guaranteed freshness. The chile crab is especially excellent (the house specialty), as is the tom yang goong (they'll be glad to tone down the spice for any dishes here).

Inexpensive

The Mango Tree. 37 Soi Anumarn Ratchathon. ☎ **02/236-2820.** Reservations recommended. Main courses 90B–350B (US$2.09–US$8.14). AE, DC, MC, V. Daily 10am–2pm and 6–10pm. Off west end of Surawong Rd., across from Tawana Ramada Hotel. THAI.

Reader John D. Connelly of Chicago brought this excellent classical Thai restaurant to Frommer's attention. A lovely 80-year-old Siamese restaurant house with its own tropical garden, it offers a quiet retreat from the hectic business district. Live traditional music and classical Thai decorative touches fill the house with charm, and the attentive staff serve well-prepared dishes from all regions of the country. Their green chicken curry, which is mild, and their crispy spring rolls are both excellent—but the menu is extensive, so feel free to experiment. Only trouble is, the food isn't exactly authentic. It's toned down for foreign palates, but it's still quite decent.

THE SHOPPING/EMBASSY AREA
Expensive

The Chinese Restaurant. Grand Hyatt Erawan, 494 Ratchadamri Rd. ☎ **02/254-1234.** Reservations recommended. Main courses 250B–900B (US$5.81–US$20.93). AE, DC, MC, V. Daily 12:30pm–2:30am and 6:30–10pm. Corner of Ploenchit Rd, Chidlom BTS station. CHINESE.

Style and substance are harmoniously blended in this ultra-elegant gourmet Cantonese restaurant. Crackled glass partitions section off dining areas while allowing light to sparkle through—tres atmospheric. Recommended is their exceptionally light dim sum, including some imaginative vegetable and seafood combinations wrapped in seaweed, instead of the typical rice flour pastry. Their shark's fin, the highlight of any respectable Chinese restaurant, is very good. A delightful gastronomic experience with great service.

Genji Restaurant. Hilton International Bangkok at Nai Lert Park, 2 Wireless Rd. ☎ **02/253-0123.** Reservations recommended; required for a tatami room. Main courses 100B–1,200B (US$2.30–US$28); set dinners 850B–2,000B (US$19.77–US$46.51). AE, DC, MC, V. Daily noon–2:30pm and 6:30–10:30pm. In Nai Lert Park, north of Ploenchit Rd. JAPANESE.

One of the best Japanese restaurants in Bangkok is located in a great hotel that caters to a large Japanese clientele. If you go to Genji for lunch you'll likely discover a room full of Japanese businesspeople, a good sign for sushi eaters. Lunch served from the set menu is not only delicious but also an excellent value. At dinner there are both set menus and an enormous selection of à la carte dishes such as excellent sushi, sashimi (1,800B/US$41.86 for sushi imported from Japan and 350B/US$8.14 for the local fish), and *makizushi*, a rich hot-pot concoction, plus a variety of fish and seafood, as well as Kobe beef.

✪ **Le Banyan.** 59 Sukhumvit Soi 8. ☎ **02/253-5556.** Reservations recommended. Main courses 350B–1,500B (US$8.14–US$34.88). AE, DC, MC, V. Mon–Sat 6–10pm. 1 block south of Sukhumvit Rd., Nana BTS station. FRENCH.

In a league with the top hotel French restaurants, this local favorite serves fine classic French cuisine that impresses even the most discriminating. Located on a quiet Sukhumvit soi, the restaurant's name is inspired by a spreading banyan tree on the edge of its garden compound. Dining rooms are warmly furnished, with sisal matting and white clapboard walls adorned with Thai carvings, old photos, and prints of early Bangkok.

The most popular house special is pressed duck for two: Baked duck is carved and pressed to yield juices that are combined with goose liver, shallots, wine, and Armagnac or calvados to make the sauce. The sliced meat is lightly sautéed, and when bathed in the sauce, creates a sensational dish. Other fine choices include a rack of lamb à la Provençale and salmon with lemongrass. All are served with seasonal vegetables and can be enjoyed with one of their reasonably priced wines. A friendly and capable staff help make this a memorable dining experience.

Moderate

Lemongrass. 5/1 Sukhumvit Soi 24. ☎ **02/258-8637.** Reservations highly recommended. Main courses 120B–550B (US$2.79–US$12.79). AE, DC, MC, V. Daily 11am–2pm and 6–11pm. South of Sukhumvit Rd. on Soi 24. Near Phrom Phong BTS Station. THAI.

This place hops with happy patrons, many of whom are repeat offenders—locals and expatriates alike. The old Thai mansion is handsomely converted and furnished with antiques. Despite occasional complaints about small portions and slow service, the waiters will help you with the menu, which contains a full spectrum of Thai cuisine, including fiery southern dishes. Try house favorites pomelo salad or chicken satay. Also excellent is the *tom yang kung* (a spicy sweet-and-sour prawn soup with ginger shoots), and the tender and juicy lemongrass chicken.

Seafood Market & Restaurant. 89 Sukhumvit Soi 24 (Soi Kasame). ☎ **02/261-2071.** Reservations recommended on weekends. Seafood at market prices; fish 1,950B–625B (US$45.35–US$14.53) per kilo, Alaskan king crab at high of 1,800B (US$41.86) per kilo, cuttlefish 245B (US$5.70) per kilo. Daily 11:30am– midnight. AE, DC, JCB, MC, V. SEAFOOD

Chances are you've never had a dining experience like this, and if you're a seafood fan, you'll love it. After you've been seated, look over the list of preparation styles, then walk to the back and take a shopping cart. Peruse the no fewer than 40 different creatures of the sea, either live or on ice, all priced by the kilo. Pay for it all at the cashier, then cart it back to the table. Waiters are skilled at making perfect suggestions for your catch, and what comes out of the kitchen is divine. I had the most tender squid broiled in butter and the meatiest grouper I've ever imagined, deep-fried with chiles. Cooking charges and corkage are paid separately at the end of the meal. Cooking charges range from 60B to 120B (US$1.40 to US$2.79).

Inexpensive

Cabbages & Condoms. 10 Sukhumvit Soi 12. ☎ **02/229-4610.** Reservations recommended. Main courses 70B–200B (US$1.63–US$4.65). Daily 11am–10pm. AE, DC, MC, V. THAI.

Here's a theme restaurant with a purpose. Opened by local hero Meechai Viravaidya, founder of the Population & Community Development Association, the restaurant helps fund population control, AIDS awareness, and a host of rural development programs. Set in a large compound, the two-story restaurant has air-conditioned indoor dining, but if you sit on the garden terrace, you're in a fairyland of twinkling lights in romantic greenery. The house recommends the *sam lee dad deao,* which is a huge deep-fried cotton fish with chile and mango on the side. Another great dish is the *kai hor bai teoy,* fried boneless chicken wrapped in pandan leaves with a dark sweet soy sauce for dipping. There's also a large selection of vegetable and bean curd entrees.

Before you leave, be sure to check out the gift shop's whimsical condom-related merchandise. The restaurant apologizes for not providing after-dinner mints, but feel free to help yourself to a free condom instead.

✪ **Le Dalat.** 47/1 Sukhumvit Soi 23. ☎ **02/258-4192.** Reservations recommended at dinner. Main courses 130B–180B (US$3.02–US$4.19). AE, DC, MC, V. Daily 11:30am–2pm and 5–10pm. Just north of Sukhumvit Rd. VIETNAMESE/FRENCH.

Le Dalat's fine food and lovely garden setting make for a charming evening. The restaurant is casual, understatedly elegant, on two floors of an old Thai house done up in Vietnamese and Chinese antiques. Vietnamese-trained Thai chefs prepare excellent and authentic cuisine. Go for the *bi guon* (spring rolls with herbs and pork), *chao tom* (pounded shrimp laced on ground sugarcane in a basket of fresh noodles), and *cha ra* (fresh filet of grilled fish). In nice weather, you'll enjoy dining in the gracefully landscaped outdoor garden. A very highly recommended restaurant.

ATTRACTIONS

When Rama I established Bangkok as the new capital city in the 1780s, he built a new palace and royal temple on the banks of the Chao Phraya River. The city sprang up around the palace and spread outward from this point as population and wealth grew. Today this area contains most of Bangkok's major historical sites, including a great number of **wats,** or Buddhist temples, that were built during the last 200 years. The city's attractions may seem like wat after wat, but they are each very unique in character, employing different architectural elements, cultural influences, and histories of their own. If you're short on time, the most interesting and easily accessible wats to catch are Wat Phra Kaeo, the royal wat that houses the Emerald Buddha at the Grand Palace, and Wat Po, home of the reclining Buddha.

BANGKOK'S WATERWAYS

The history of Bangkok was written on its waterways, which until recent years were the essential focus of the city's life. As Ayutthaya was before it, Bangkok came to be known as the "Venice of the East," but sadly, many of these klongs have been paved over for avenues. The magnificent Chao Phraya River ("the River of Kings"), however, continues to cut through the heart of the city, separating the early capital of Thonburi from today's Bangkok. On the Thonburi side, the klongs still branch off into a network of arteries that are relatively unchanged as the centers of neighborhood life. For an intimate glimpse of traditional Thai life, schedule in a few hours to explore the waterways. You'll see people using the river to bathe, wash their clothes, and even brush their teeth at water's edge (a practice not recommended to tourists). Floating kitchens in sampans serve rice and noodles to customers in other boats.

There are several approaches to touring the klongs. Both **Sea Tours** (Suite nos. 88–92, 8th floor, Payathai Plaza Rajthavee; ☎ **02/216-5783**) and **World Travel** (1053 Charoen Krung (New Road); ☎ **02/5900**) offer standard group tours: The basic canal tour is organized around a so-called "Floating Market" in Thonburi, but it's become very touristy and crowded (morning trip 8:30am to noon, price about 800B/US$18.60 per person). Better yet, charter a long-tail *hang yao* for about 300B (US$6.98) an hour—expect to negotiate the price, and agree on the charge *before* you get in the boat. You'll find boats for hire at the Tha Chang ferry pier near Wat Phra Kaeo or the pier at River City Shopping Complex. Beware of independent boat operators that offer to take you to the nearby Thonburi Floating Market or to souvenir or gem shops. Take your time and explore Klong Bangkok Noi and Klong Bangkok Yai, with a stop at the Royal Barges Museum on the way back.

BANGKOK'S HISTORICAL TREASURES

The Grand Palace. Near the river on Na Phra Lan Rd. near Sanam Luang. ☎ **02/222-0094**. Admission 125B (US$2.91). Price includes Wat Phra Kaeo and the Coin Pavilion inside the Grand Palace grounds, as well as admission to the Vimanmek Palace (near the National Assembly). Daily 8:30am–3:30pm; most individual buildings are closed to the public except on special days proclaimed by the king. Take the Chao Phraya Express Boat to the Tha Chang Pier, then walk first east, then south.

The Grand Palace is almost always the first stop on any sightseeing agenda. Rama I built the oldest buildings in the square-mile complex when he moved the capital from Thonburi to Bangkok in the 1780s. It was the official residence and offices of the kings until 1946, when the royal family moved to Chitralada Palace. These days, the palace is used only for royal ceremonies and as the royal guesthouse for visiting dignitaries. The focal point of the compound is the Chakri Maha Prasad, an intriguing mixture of Victorian architecture topped with a Thai temple-style roof that today houses the ashes of royal family members. To the left, the Amarinda Vinichai Hall is the venue for the highest royal ceremonies, including coronations. To the right of Chakri Maha Prasad stands the Dusit Hall, a perfect example of Thai architecture in the highest order. The Grand Palace compound also has a Royal Decorations and Coin Pavilion—its main draw is air-conditioning.

Wat Phra Kaeo. In the Grand Palace complex. ☎ **02/222-0094**. Admission included in the Grand Palace fee of 125B (US$2.91). Daily 8:30am–3:30pm.

When Rama I built the Grand Palace, he included this temple, the royal temple most revered by the Thai people. The famed "emerald" Buddha, a 2-foot tall northern Thai style image made from green jasper, sits atop a towering gold altar. The statue dons a different costume for each of the three seasons in Thailand, changed by the king himself, who climbs up to the image as it can be lowered for no one.

Historians believe that artists created the statue in the 14th century. The emerald Buddha hid inside a plaster Buddha image until 1434, when movers accidentally dropped it, setting it free. The king at Chiang Mai demanded it be brought to his city, but three attempts failed. Each time the elephant transporting the image stopped at

Bangkok Attractions

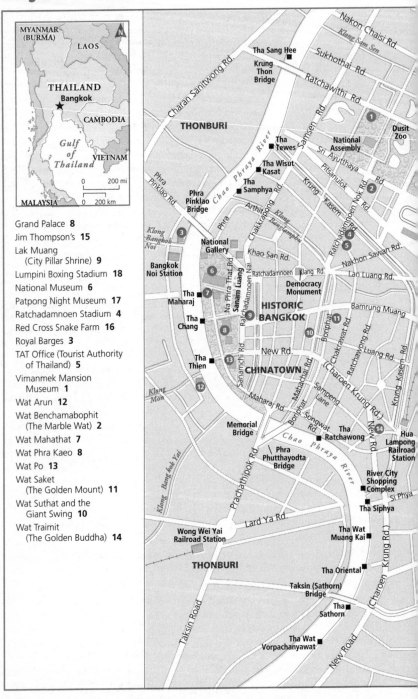

Grand Palace **8**

Jim Thompson's **15**

Lak Muang
(City Pillar Shrine) **9**

Lumpini Boxing Stadium **18**

National Museum **6**

Patpong Night Museum **17**

Ratchadamnoen Stadium **4**

Red Cross Snake Farm **16**

Royal Barges **3**

TAT Office (Tourist Authority
of Thailand) **5**

Vimanmek Mansion
Museum **1**

Wat Arun **12**

Wat Benchamabophit
(The Marble Wat) **2**

Wat Mahathat **7**

Wat Phra Kaeo **8**

Wat Po **13**

Wat Saket
(The Golden Mount) **11**

Wat Suthat and the
Giant Swing **10**

Wat Traimit
(The Golden Buddha) **14**

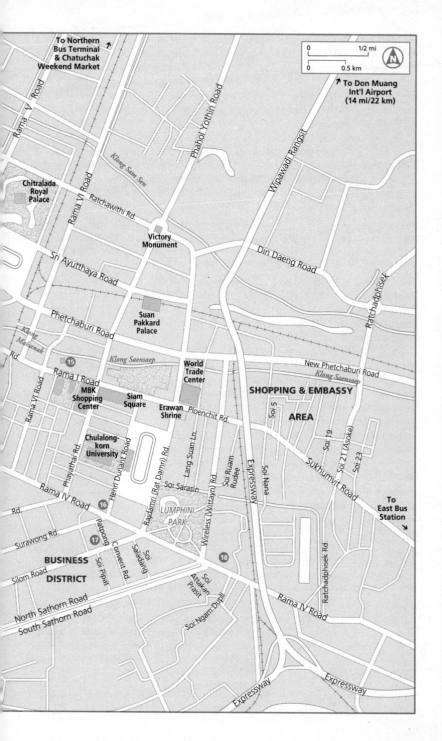

the same spot in Lampang, so the king gave in to the will of the spirits and built a *chedi* (a sacred monument) for it there. 32 years later, King Tiloka of Chiang Mai brought the image to Chiang Mai. The emerald Buddha stayed in the Wat Chedi Luang until 1552, when a later king from Luang Prabang carted it off to Laos. When the king moved the capital of Laos to Vientiane, the image followed him. Rama I finally recaptured the statue in a successful invasion of Laos, and placed it in Wat Phra Kaeo, where it remains today.

The wat compound is a small city in itself, including a library with stunning Ayutthaya style mother-of-pearl inlay doors, a reliquary like a golden bell-shaped Sri Lankan style chedi, a *wihaan* (hall) bejeweled with chipped porcelain mosaics, and a miniature model of Angkor Wat, the sprawling temple complex at the ancient Khmer capital, with its corn-shaped chedis. Murals on the surrounding walls tell the story of the *Ramayana*.

✪ **The National Museum.** Na Phra That Rd. ☎ **02/224-1333.** Admission 40B (US$0.93). Wed–Sun 9am–4pm. Free English-language tours: Buddhism Culture, Wed at 9:30am; art, culture, religion, Thurs 9:30am; call the museum or check a newspaper for more details and current schedule. About a half mile north of Grand Palace.

The National Museum, a short (15-min.) walk north of the Grand Palace and the Temple of the Emerald Buddha, is the country's central treasury of art and archaeology. It was originally the palace that the brother of Rama I built as part of the Grand Palace complex in 1782. Rama V converted the palace into a museum in 1884. Today it is the largest museum in Southeast Asia.

To see the entire collection, plan on at least 3 hours. If you're rushed, go straight to the Red House, a traditional 18th-century Thai building that was originally the living quarters of Princess Sri Sudarak, sister of King Rama I. It's furnished in period style, with many pieces originally owned by the princess.

Another essential stop is the Phuttaisawan (Buddhaisawan) Chapel, built in 1787 to house the Phra Phut Sihing, one of Thailand's most revered Buddha images, brought here from its original home in Chiang Mai. The main building of the royal palace contains gold jewelry, some from the royal collections, and Thai ceramics, including many pieces in the five-color bencharong style. The Old Transportation Room contains ivory carvings, elephant chairs, and royal palanquins. There are also rooms of royal emblems and insignia, stone carvings, wood carvings, costumes, textiles, musical instruments, and Buddhist religious artifacts. Fine art and sculpture are found in the newer galleries at the rear of the museum compound.

The Royal Barges National Museum. On Klong Bangkok Noi, north of the Phra Pinklao Bridge, Thonburi. ☎ **02/424-0004.** Admission 30B (US$0.70). Daily 9am–5pm. Take a taxi over the Phra Pinklao Bridge or take a ferry to Tha Rot Fai ("Railway Landing"), walk west along the street parallel to and between the tracks and the klong until you come to a bridge over the klong, cross the bridge and follow the wooden walkway.

If you've hired a long-tail boat on the Chao Phraya, stop by this unique museum housing the royal barges. These elaborately decorated sailing vessels, the largest over 50 yards long and rowed by up to 60 men, are used by the royal family on state occasions or for high religious ceremonies. The king's barge, the *Suphanahong,* is decorated with red-and-gold carvings of fearsome mythological beasts, like the Garuda or the dragon on the bow and stern.

Vimanmek Mansion Museum. 193/2 Ratchavitee Rd., Dusit Palace grounds. ☎ **02/281-1569.** Admission 50B (US$1.16); free if you already have a 125B (US$2.91) ticket from the Grand Palace and Wat Phra Kaeo. Daily 9am–4pm. North of the National Assembly Building.

Built in 1901 by King Chulalongkorn the Great (Rama V) as the Celestial Residence, this large, beautiful, golden teakwood mansion was restored in 1982 for Bangkok's bicentennial and reopened by Queen Sirikit as a private museum with a collection of the royal family's memorabilia. An intriguing and informative hour-long tour takes you through a series of apartments and rooms (81 in all) in what is said to be the largest teak building in the world. The original Abhisek Dusit Throne Hall houses a display of Thai handicrafts, and nine other buildings north of the mansion display photographs, clocks, fabrics, royal carriages, and other regalia. Classical Thai and folk dance and martial art demonstrations are given daily at 10:30am and 2pm.

Jim Thompson's House. Soi Kasemsan 2. ☎ **02/216-7368.** Admission 100B (US$2.33). Daily 9am–4:30pm. On a small soi off Rama I Rd., opposite the National Stadium.

Jim Thompson was a New York architect who served in the OSS (Office of Strategic Services, now the CIA) in Thailand during World War II and afterward settled in Bangkok. Almost single-handedly he revived Thailand's silk industry, employing Thai Muslims as skilled silk weavers and building up a thriving industry. After expanding his sales to international markets, Mr. Thompson mysteriously disappeared in 1967 while vacationing in the Cameron Highlands in Malaysia. Despite extensive investigation, his disappearance has never been resolved.

His Thai house is composed of six linked teak and theng (harder than teak) wood houses from central Thailand that were rebuilt according to Thai architectural principles, but with Western additions (such as a staircase and window screens). In some rooms the floor is made of Italian marble, but the wall panels are pegged teak. Volunteers guide you through rooms filled with Thompson's splendid collection of Khmer sculpture, Chinese porcelain, Burmese carving (especially a 17th-century teak Buddha), and antique Thai scroll paintings.

THE WATS

Wat Po. Maharat Rd., near the river. ☎ **02/222-0933.** Admission 20B (US$0.47). Daily 9am–5pm; massages offered until 6pm. About a half mile south of the Grand Palace.

Wat Po (Wat Phra Chetuphon), the Temple of the Reclining Buddha, was built by Rama I in the 16th century and is the oldest and largest Buddhist temple in Bangkok. Considered Thailand's first public university, the temple's many monuments and artworks explain principles of religion, science, and literature.

Most people go straight to the enormous Reclining Buddha in the northern section. It's more than 46 meters (140 feet) long and 16 meters (50 feet) high, and was built during the mid-19th-century reign of Rama III. The statue is brick, covered with layers of plaster and always-flaking gold leaf; the feet are inlaid with mother-of-pearl illustrations of 108 auspicious *laksanas* ("characteristics") of the Buddha. Behind the Buddha, a line of 108 bronze bowls, each also representing one of the laksanas, awaits visitors to drop coins (acquired nearby for a 20B (US$0.47) donation for luck).

Outside, the grounds contain 91 *chedis* (stupas or sacred mounds), four *wihaans* (halls), and a *bot* (the central shrine in a Buddhist temple). The Traditional Medical Practitioners Association Center teaches traditional Thai massage and medicine. Stop in for a massage (250B per hour), or ask about their 7- to 10-day massage courses.

Wat Mahathat (Temple of the Great Relic). Na Phra That Rd. ☎ **02/222-6011.** Optional donation 20B (US$0.47). Daily 9am–5pm. Na Prathat Rd., near Sanam Luang Park, between the Grand Palace and the National Museum.

Built to house a relic of the Buddha, Wat Mahathat is one of Bangkok's oldest shrines and the headquarters for Thailand's largest monastic order. Also the home of the

Mahachulalongkorn Buddhist University, the most important center for the study of Buddhism and meditation, Wat Mahathat offers some programs in English.

Adjacent to it, between Maharat Road and the river, is the city's biggest amulet market, where a fantastic array of religious amulets, charms, talismans, and traditional medicine is sold. Each Sunday hundreds of worshippers squat on the ground studying tiny images of the Buddha with magnifying glasses, hoping to find one that will bring good fortune or ward off evil.

Wat Arun (Temple of Dawn). West bank of the Chao Phraya, opposite Tha Thien Pier. ☎ **02/465-5640.** Optional donation 20B (US$0.47). Daily 9am–5pm. Take a water taxi from Tha Tien Pier (near Wat Po) or cross the Phra Pinklao Bridge and follow the river south on Arun Amarin Rd.

The 86-meter-high (260-foot-high) Khmer-inspired tower rises majestically from the banks of the Chao Phraya, across from Wat Po. This religious complex served as the royal chapel during King Taksin's reign (1809–24), when Thonburi was the capital of Thailand.

The original tower was only 16 meters (50 feet) high, but was expanded during the rule of Rama III (1824–51) to its current height. The exterior is decorated with flower and decorative motifs made of colorful ceramic shards donated to the monastery by local people, at the request of Rama III. At the base of the complex are Chinese stone statues, once used as ballast in trading ships, gifts from Chinese merchants. Wat Arun is a sight to behold shimmering in the sunrise, but truly the best time to visit is in late afternoon for the sunset.

Wat Benchamabophit (the Marble Wat). Si Ayutthaya Rd. ☎ **02/281-2501.** Optional donation 20B (US$0.47). Daily 9am–5pm. South of the Assembly Building near Chitralada Palace.

Wat Benchamabophit, which tourists call the Marble Wat because of the white Carrara marble of which it's constructed, is an early 20th-century temple designed by Prince Narai, the half brother of Rama V. It's the most modern and one of the most beautiful of Bangkok's royal wats. Many smaller buildings nearby reflect a melding of European materials and designs with traditional Thai religious architecture. Walk inside the compound, beyond the main bot, to view the many Buddhas that represent various regional styles. During the early mornings, monks chant in the main chapel, sometimes humming so intensely that it seems as if the temple is going to lift off.

Wat Saket (The Golden Mount). Ratchadamnoen Klang and Boripihat rds. Free admission to wat; admission to the chedi 5B (US$0.12). Chedi daily 9am–5pm.

Wat Saket is easily recognized by its golden chedi atop a fortresslike hill near the pier for Bangkok's east-west klong ferry. The wat was restored by King Rama I, and 30,000 bodies were brought here during a plague in the reign of Rama II. Rama V built the golden chedi to house a relic of Buddha, said to be from India or Nepal, given to him by the British. The concrete walls were added during World War II to keep the structure from collapsing.

The Golden Mount, a short but breathtaking climb that's best made in the morning, is most interesting for its vista of old Rattanakosin and the rooftops of Bangkok. Every late October to mid-November (for 9 days around the full moon), Wat Sakhet hosts Bangkok's most important temple fair, when the Golden Mount is wrapped with red cloth and a carnival erupts around it, with food and trinket stalls, theatrical performances, freak shows, animal circuses, and other monkey business.

Wat Suthat and The Giant Swing. Sao Chingcha Sq. ☎ **02/222-0280.** Optional donation 20B (US$0.47). Daily 9am–5pm. Near the intersection of Bamrung Muang Rd. and Ti Thong Rd.

The temple is among the oldest and largest in Bangkok, and Somerset Maugham declared its roofline the most beautiful. It was begun by Rama I and finished by Rama III; Rama II carved the panels for the wihaan's doors. It houses a beautiful 14th-century Phra Buddha Shakyamuni that was brought from Sukhothai, and the ashes of King Rama VIII, Ananda Mahidol, brother of the current king, are contained in its base. The wall paintings for which it is known were done during Rama III's reign.

The huge teak arch—also carved by Rama II—in front is all that remains of an original giant swing, which was used until 1932 to celebrate and thank Shiva for a bountiful rice harvest and to ask for the god's blessing on the next. The minister of rice, accompanied by hundreds of Brahman court astrologers, would lead a parade around the city walls to the temple precinct. Teams of men would ride the swing on arcs as high as 82 feet in the air, trying to grab a bag of silver coins with their teeth. Due to injuries and deaths, the dangerous swing ceremony has been discontinued.

Wat Traimit (The Golden Buddha). Traimit Rd. Optional donation 20B (US$0.47). Daily 9am–5pm. West of Hua Lampong Station, just west of the intersection of Krung Kasem and Rama IV rds.; walk southwest on Traimit Rd. and look for a school on the right with a playground. The wat is up a flight of stairs overlooking the school.

Wat Traimit, which is thought to date from the 13th century, would hardly rate a second glance if not for its astonishing Buddha, which is nearly 10 feet high, weighs over 5 tons, and is believed to be cast of solid gold during the Sukhothai period. It was discovered by accident in 1957 when an old stucco Buddha was being moved from a storeroom by a crane, which dropped it and shattered the plaster shell, revealing the shining gold beneath. This powerful image has such a bright, reflective surface that its edges seem to disappear, and it is truly dazzling.

CULTURAL PURSUITS

Anyone can tell you that cultural curiosities don't merely exist in the structures of buildings or cloistered in special collections. Begin your travel plans with an inquiry at the Tourism Authority about upcoming **traditional festivals** and ceremonies. The TAT (Ratchadamnoen Nok Avenue; ☎ 02/282-9773) has up-to-date information about celebration dates and locations, and encourages all visitors to attend even the smallest events.

Muay thai, or **Thai boxing,** stretches beyond the boundaries of spectator sport in its presentation of Thai mores evident in pre-bout rituals, live musical performances, and the wild gambling antics of the audience. In Bangkok, the Ratchadamnoen Stadium (Ratchadamnoen Nok Avenue; ☎ 02/281-4205) hosts bouts every Monday, Wednesday, Thursday, and Sunday while the Lumphini Stadium (Rama IV Road; ☎ 02/251-4303) has bouts on Tuesdays, Fridays, and Saturdays. Tickets are 1,000B (US$23.26) for ringside seats, 440B (US$10.23) standing room only, and 220B (US$5.12) if you don't mind crowding in the cage at the back. Shows start between 5pm and 7:30pm, depending on the stadium.

OK, so it's not exactly culture, but you'll have a hard time getting out of Thailand without encountering some kind of snake show. Bangkok's biggest venue is at the **Red Cross Snake Farm** (1871 Rama IV Rd.; ☎ 02/252-0161). There are slide shows and snake-handling and venom milking demonstrations weekdays at 11am and 2pm; on weekends and holidays at 11am only. The farm is open daily Monday to Friday 8:30am to 4pm; Saturday and Sunday 8:30am to noon; admission is 70B (US$1.63). It's located at the corner of Rama IV Road and Henri Dunant.

I can't begin to tell you what a joy a good **traditional Thai massage** can be. In the city there are countless massage places everywhere, and the quality of your massage can range from poor to stellar, regardless of price. Be aware that many "massage parlors" cater to gentlemen, with services beyond standard massage expectations. The best Thai massage I've ever had (consistently) is a short walk from the BTS Phrom Pong station (Po Massage, 14/5 Sukhumvit Soi 33; ☎ **02/261-0055; 250B/US$5.81** for 2 hours!!). Also good to try: **Po Thong Thai Massage** (Basement, Fortuna Hotel, Sukhumvit Soi 5; ☎ **255-1045;** 300B/US$6.98 per hour), or **Arima Onsen** (37/10-11 Soi Surawong Plaza, Surawong Road; ☎ 02/235-2142). The home of Thai massage, **Wat Po,** school to almost every masseuse in Bangkok, has good cheap massages in an open air pavilion within the temple complex—a very interesting experience (Chetuphon Road, ☎ **221-2974; 250B/US$5.81** per hour).

Thai cooking classes teach you all you need to know about Thai ingredients, Thai regional cuisine, cooking techniques, and menu planning. Oriental Hotel's program offer four half-day programs at US$120 per person, but you can join in for 1 or 2 days only, if you'd like. Call them at ☎ **02/437-6211** for booking and information.

For Thais, **cockfighting** is a tradition as old as the hills. Country farmers raise cocks to be fighters, for the hope of bringing in a good one and making a small fortune. In markets, fighting cocks are kept under dome basket cages—in the animal section of Chatuchak Weekend Market (see below) you can see the birds up close. At the north end of the market you might catch a demonstration or an actual fight.

Wat Mahathat serves as one of Thailand's two Buddhist universities. As such, it has become a popular center for **meditation lessons** and practice, with English-speaking monks overseeing the technique—Vipassana, also called Insight Meditation. Call the temple in the mornings at ☎ **02/623-6337** or in the afternoons at ☎ **02/623-6326, ext. 132.** Classes are held daily from 7 to 10am, 1 to 4pm, and again from 6 to 8pm. The length of time needed for practice and the results obtained will vary from individual to individual.

Thai **modern arts** let you peer into the world of Thai values and viewpoints through a range of talents and techniques. The good people at About Café and Studio (402–8 Maitreejit Rd. near the railway station; ☎ 02/623-1742) are on the cutting edge of arts exhibition. You can also check out exhibits at the Chulalongkorn Art Gallery (7th Floor, Center of Academic Resources, Chulalongkorn University, Phayathai Road; ☎ **02/218-2961**) and The National Gallery (4 Chao Fa Rd.; ☎ 02/ 282-2639).

SHOPPING

Don't even think about leaving Bangkok with money left over. With a huge assortment of **Thai silks,** tailors on every block, classical artwork and antiques, hill-tribe handicrafts, fine silver, beautiful gemstones, porcelain, and reptile skin products, shopping is your destiny in Thailand. I haven't even started describing all the **street bazaars** where you can find cheap batik clothing, knockoff watches, jeans and designer shirts, and all sorts of souvenirs. A friend of mine likes to pack a "goodie bag" when she comes to Thailand, an empty bag that she fills throughout her stay. Inevitably it's overflowing by day three. Whatever your travel budget, set aside a large chunk of it for the many items you just won't resist.

The main shopping mall drag is Rama I Road between Ratchadamri and Phyathai roads, where you'll find the **World Trade Center,** with department stores Isetan and Zen Central; **Gaysorn Plaza** for haute couture; **Siam Center** for trendy styles; and **Mah Boon Krong,** a huge local mall filled with bargains. **Siam Square,** also on Rama I Road just across from Siam Center, sprawls through alleys filled with food, small vendors with bargains, hip boutiques, and Bangkok's Hard Rock Cafe. Just north of here on Phetburi Road is **Phanthip Plaza,** Bangkok's computer mall. For antiques go to **River City,** off Charoen Krung Road overlooking the Chao Phraya River, which is just packed with reputable dealers selling everything Thai, Khmer, Chinese, and otherwise.

When you're ready for the real Bangkok shopping experience, head on down to **Chinatown. Thieves' Market,** at Chakkarat and Charoen Krung roads, is a maze of new, and some old, finds. Off Pahurat Road is the **Pahurat Cloth Market,** with fabrics from all over the region. **The Old Siam** shopping mall on Triphet Road has some great handicraft places. For a longer shopping trip, there's **Sampeng Lane,** stretching for blocks and blocks; this narrow alley is lined with wholesalers with everything from paper supplies and beads and lace to batik sarongs and religious supplies.

Everyone will tell you the ultimate shopping experience is at the **Chatuchak Weekend Market**—and they are so right! Chatuchak is crazy shopping. Located about 30 minutes north of central Bangkok near the airport, it's block after block of small stalls packed with clothing, leather goods, accessories, cheap jewelry, textiles, handicrafts, souvenirs, antiques, household items, tools and mechanical wares, pottery, live pets (from fish to fighting cocks), plants, fresh and dried foods, and other sundries. Start early, at around 9am, and give yourself at least the whole morning. Food vendors and drink stands will help you rest and cool off.

Night markets are also a thrill in Bangkok. The most famous one is at **Patpong,** which goes up at around 6 or 7pm nightly and carries on till around 3am or so. It promises all sorts of souvenirs, crafts, and knockoff deals, but make sure you bargain well. Also, if you're in the **Sukhumvit** area, there's an afternoon and evening bazaar every day beginning at Sukhumvit Soi 1 and running down farther than you can walk.

Special areas with high concentrations of shops are along **Silom Road,** where you'll find many **tailors** and **gem dealers;** and along Charoen Krung Road between the Shangri-La and Royal Orchid Sheraton Hotels for **antiques and art dealers.**

BANGKOK AFTER DARK

Bangkok is probably the only city in the world that gets hotter after the sun goes down. You can cool off with a drink at a beer pub or cocktail lounge, or heat things up with a night at the discos. You needn't be too worried about your safety in most of the city, as Bangkok is fairly safe for tourists, save for the occasional pickpocket. Taxis and tuk-tuks are on hand through the night and early morning.

For the best local theater, nothing beats **Thai boxing.** For further information, see above.

THE BAR & CLUB SCENE

If a nice cocktail is in order, the **Shangri-La Hotel Lobby Lounge** (89 Soi Wat Suan Phlu, New Road; ☎ 02/236-7777) has live performances Monday through Saturday of light pop and soft sounds. In the Sukhumvit Road area, **The Landmark** Hotel Piano Bar (138 Sukhumvit Rd.; ☎ 02/254-0404) has live piano favorites daily except Sundays. Another swell lobby bar is at **The Dusit Thani** (Rama VI Road; ☎ 02/236-0450) for live jazz and light pop nightly, including Sundays.

There are quite a few bars around town that cater to a wide array of tastes. The quintessential Irish pub in town is **Delaney's** (Convent Road, Silom; ☎ 02/266-7160), famous for Irish eats, televised sports, and Guinness draught. **The Barbican** (9/4–5 Soi Thaniya, Silom Road; ☎ 02/234-3590), attracts a cool crowd with happy hour specials, great food and snacks, and my favorite jukebox in Bangkok. For micro-brewery fans, **Brauhaus Bangkok** (Sukhumvit Soi 24; ☎ 02/261-0238), Bangkok's original, brews its own light and dark libations.

For a little music with your fun, the **Hard Rock Cafe** (424/3–6 Siam Square Soi 11; ☎ 02/254-0830) has live rock and pop (and great burgers). **Riva's** (Sheraton Grande Sukhumvit Hotel, 250 Sukhumvit Rd.; ☎ 02/653-0333) has excellent live performances of funky beats that'll make your feet move. Those who prefer something

Travel Tip: Where to Find Nightlife Listings

Keep your eyes peeled for the hip Bangkok *METRO Magazine* and *Time Out Bangkok,* which carry great listings on restaurants, pubs, and local happenings around town.

a little jazzier might want to check out the Oriental Hotel's **Bamboo Bar** (Oriental Lane off Charoen Krung Road; ☎ **02/236-0040**).

If music makes you move, the best discos are **Concept CM2** (Novotel Siam, Siam Square Soi 6; ☎ **02/255-6888**), **Narcissus** (112 Sukhumvit Soi 23; ☎ **02/258-2549**), and **Taurus** (Sukhumvit Soi 26 beside Four Wings Hotel; ☎ **02/261-3991**). All are trendy, happening places with hip music and even hipper clientele. Dress to impress.

Cabaret shows are quite a hit with tourists in Thailand, and you'll find shows in almost all the major tourist areas. Choreographed lip-sync numbers are oftentimes hilarious, and the costumes and sets would turn RuPaul's pancake green. In Bangkok, the two biggest are **Calypso** (Basement, Asia Hotel, 296 Phayathai Rd.; ☎ **02/ 261-6355**) and **Mambo** (Washington Square Theater, Sukhumvit Soi 22; ☎ **02/ 259-5128**). Tickets run between 600B and 800B.

THE SEX SHOWS

Last but not least, the nightlife Bangkok is most famous for: the racy go-go bars and sex shows. They are centered around three areas in the city, Patpong, Nana Complex, and Soi Cowboy. The largest and most famous of the three, **Patpong** (located between Silom and Surawong roads), boasts four streets of clubs with discos and bars, eateries, go-go clubs, gay bars, karaoke clubs, massage parlors, seedy hotels, and the famous sex shows, which to be honest are more bizarre than sexy. There's also a huge outdoor night bazaar. Patpong is full of touts trying to lure you inside to see their sex show, but be careful. Some places charge steep covers and all sorts of additional unexplained charges may appear on your check, and you may not be allowed to leave without paying. Remember the **Tourist Police** (☎ **1699**), who have a police box on Surawong Road, if you have problems. To prevent being ripped off, go to either **Fire Cat** (for shows) or **King's Castle** (fun for guessing which ladies are in fact girls, or *katoey* boygirls). While seedy, both are reputable. **Nana Complex** (Sukhumvit Soi 21 and Soi 23) is a virtual mini-mall-a-go-go, with three stories of go-go bars to choose from. Finally, **Soi Cowboy** (running parallel to Sukhumvit Soi, between Soi 21 and Soi 23), originally made famous during the Vietnam War, has fallen into sleepier times since Nana and Patpong took over. Clubs here are small and a little more laid-back these days.

All of the clubs will allow patrons to bring a dancer out of the club after paying a bar penalty. While prostitution in Thailand is technically illegal, the law is almost never enforced. Furthermore, it is *recommended* for safety reasons that gentlemen who are going to seek paid female companionship request the company of bar dancers. For special safety precautions regarding the sex industry in Bangkok, see "The Thai Sex Industry & AIDS" box.

4 The Eastern Seaboard

Thailand's beaches along the Gulf of Thailand (also known as the Gulf of Siam) are world-renowned for their clean white sand, palm groves, and warm water. Today, most areas are served by a sophisticated tourism infrastructure and indulgent accommodations. Although no sandy crescent is protected from the hotel developer's hand, there are still areas that are relatively quiet.

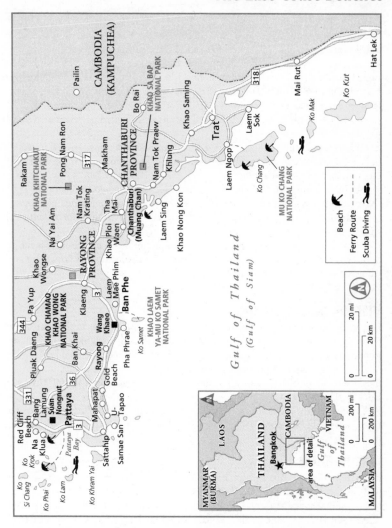

Pattaya, the oldest and most decadent of Thailand's resorts, lures people seeking a break from the big city because of its proximity to Bangkok (2½ hours by bus). But don't come for the beach. Pattaya is better known as the sex playground of Southeast Asia while its beaches rot from tourist pollution. The local government has been cleaning up Pattaya Bay and enacting strict new waste management guidelines, but there's still far more work to be done. **Ko Samet** is the star of Rayong Province: a small island (somewhat protected as a national park) whose primitive bungalows create a very different feel from Pattaya's swinging hotels. Picture postcard bays and soft white sands make this the tropical island many come to Thailand to experience. It's easily reached by a 45-minute ferry ride from the tiny port of Ban Phe (3½ hours from Bangkok by bus); though isolated, it gets crowded on weekends due to its popularity with foreign low-budget tourists and Thais, especially during holidays.

5 Pattaya

You'll hear Pattaya, 147 kilometers (91 miles) east of Bangkok, called anything from "Asia's premier resort" to "one big open-air brothel"—its legacy as Thailand's R&R capital for Vietnam-weary American troops. It does indeed have several hundred beer bars, discos with scantily-clad Thai teens, massage parlors, and transvestite clubs all jammed together along a beachfront strip. But it has another more elegant and sophisticated side in its big international resorts, retreats set in sprawling, manicured seaside gardens.

OK, let me be honest here. If you want fun and relaxation on idyllic tropical beaches, don't come to Pattaya. The bay is a toilet—I wouldn't go near the water without a prescription for an antibiotic.

If you want to see crazy scenes from a wild nightlife—go-go bars, loose bar girls, cheap booze, and plenty of trouble to be had, then Pattaya's your kinda place. Come to think of it, I wouldn't go near the bars without a prescription for an antibiotic either.

Pattaya has struggled to present a family resort atmosphere, and it surprises me just how many families come here to vacation. Really, if you're looking for something more wholesome, bypass Pattaya for tranquil Ko Samet or check out Hua Hin on the other side of the Gulf.

VISITOR INFORMATION

Last year I was disappointed to learn that the previously conveniently located **TAT office** (once in the center of Beach Road) has lost the battle with increasing rents and moved to a location south of Pattaya City, up the mountain on the road between Pattaya and neighboring resort Jomtien. You can hop any Jomtien-bound songtao and they'll drop you off at the office for 20B (US$0.47). The address is 609 Thappraya Rd. (☎ 038/429-113).

A couple of free publications, *What's On Pattaya* and *Explore Pattaya and the East Coast,* are widely distributed to hotels and guesthouses. They each contain pretty good maps.

GETTING THERE

BY AIR Bangkok Airways (in Bangkok ☎ 02/229-3456; in Pattaya ☎ 038/412-382; in Koh Samui ☎ 077/422-234) has direct flights to U-Tapao, 30 kilometers (19 miles) south of Pattaya, from both Koh Samui and Phnom Penh in Cambodia. To call U-Tapao Airport dial ☎ 038/245-595. Taxis are not on standby at the airport, but many of the larger hotels can arrange pickup if you book in advance.

BY TRAIN From Bangkok's Hua Lumphong Railway Station (☎ 02/223-7010 or 02/223-7020), the State Railway of Thailand operates a daily train to the Pattaya Railway Station off Siam Country Club Road (☎ 038/429-285). Trip time is 3 hours 45 minutes; cost is 31B (US$0.72). For speed and convenience almost everybody takes the bus.

BY BUS The most common and practical form of transportation to Pattaya is the bus. Buses depart from Bangkok's Eastern Bus Terminal (on Sukhumvit Road opposite Soi 63—Ekamai Road; ☎ 02/390-1230) every half-hour beginning from 5am until 10pm daily. For air-conditioned coach, the fare is 77B (US$1.79). The bus station in Pattaya for air-conditioned buses to and from Bangkok is on North Pattaya Road (☎ 038/429-877). From there, catch a songtao to your destination (see "Getting Around," below).

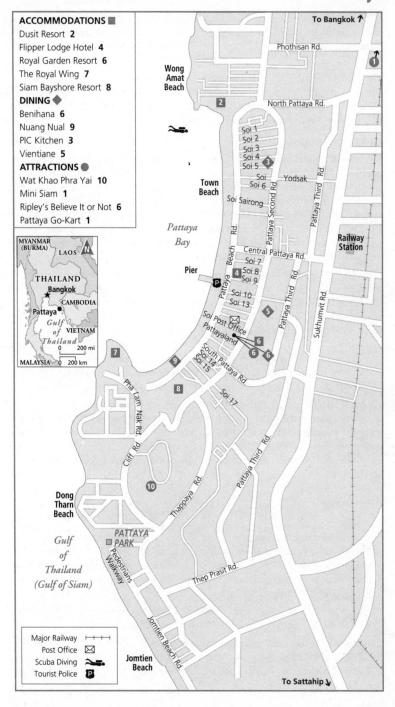

Pattaya

To Bangkok ↑

ACCOMMODATIONS ■
Dusit Resort **2**
Flipper Lodge Hotel **4**
Royal Garden Resort **6**
The Royal Wing **7**
Siam Bayshore Resort **8**
DINING ◆
Benihana **6**
Nuang Nual **9**
PIC Kitchen **3**
Vientiane **5**
ATTRACTIONS ●
Wat Khao Phra Yai **10**
Mini Siam **1**
Ripley's Believe It or Not **6**
Pattaya Go-Kart **1**

MYANMAR (BURMA)
LAOS
N
THAILAND
Bangkok ★
CAMBODIA
Pattaya ●
Gulf of Thailand
VIETNAM
0   200 mi
MALAYSIA 0   200 km

Phothisan Rd.

Wong Amat Beach

North Pattaya Rd.

Soi 1
Soi 2
Soi 3
Soi 4
Soi 5
Soi
Soi 6
Yodsak

Town Beach

Soi Sairong

Pattaya Bay

Central Pattaya Rd.

Railway Station

Pattaya Beach Rd.
Pattaya Second Rd.
Pattaya Third Rd.

Pier
P

Soi 7
Soi 8
Soi 9
Soi 10
Soi 13

Soi Post Office
Pattayaland

South Pattaya Rd.
Soi 14
Soi 15

Soi 17

Sukhumvit Rd.

Pha Lam Nak Rd.

Cliff Rd.

Thappaya Rd.

Dong Tharn Beach

Gulf of Thailand (Gulf of Siam)

PATTAYA PARK

Pedestrians Walkway

Thep Prasit Rd.

Jomtien Beach Rd.

Jomtien Beach

Major Railway ├─┼─┤
Post Office ✉
Scuba Diving 🤿
Tourist Police P

To Sattahip ↓

Thai Airways operates the **Thai Limousine Service** with departures from Bangkok International Airport (Don Muang). Coaches leave three times daily and cost 200B (US$4.65) per person. For information call ☎ **02/533-6208.** In Pattaya call ☎ **038/ 429-347.**

BY PRIVATE CAR   Taxis to Pattaya can be arranged at the taxi counters of Bangkok International Airport for 1,250B (US$29.07), or from Bangkok can be booked through **World Travel Service Ltd.,** 1053 Charoen Krung Rd., 10500 Bangkok (☎ **02/233-5900**) for about the same price.

GETTING AROUND

BY MINIBUS OR SONGTAO   *Songtao* (also called minibuses or baht buses), covered pickups with two wooden benches in the bed, cruise the major streets for passengers and are the best and cheapest form of transport. Flat fares within Pattaya should be 10B for short trips in the main area. If you're going to North Pattaya, pay around 20B (US$0.47), and for Jomtien pay 30B (US$0.70). Rates are fixed by the local governments, and some drivers will try to overcharge you. Negotiate firmly, or walk away and find someone honest. Some hotels operate their own minibuses, but they charge much more for the same bumpy ride.

BY CAR   There are plenty of car rental agencies, and you can negotiate the price with most, especially outside the high season. Call **Budget** (☎ **038/720-613;** advertised specials as low as 990B/US$23.02 per day for a Suzuki Caribian) for a better-priced vehicle with good maintenance and a sound insurance policy. All along Pattaya Beach Road, local car rental agencies offer Caribians and huge souped-up Jeeps for between 700B and 1,500B per day (US$16.28 to US$34.88). Car quality and rental agreements can vary, so I recommend shopping around to check out the vehicles each has available. You can try **VIA Car Rent** (215/15–18 Pattaya 2nd Rd. opposite Royal Garden Plaza (☎ **038/426-242**). They have a good local reputation (with TAT as well).

BY MOTORCYCLE   For those who dare brave the often drunk and reckless foreign drivers in downtown Pattaya, 150cc motorcycles rent for about 200B (US$4.65) a day without insurance. (Ask for a helmet!) Big choppers and Japanese speed bikes (500cc) will go for about 500B to 800B (US$11.63 to US$18.6) per day. Like the independent car-rental agencies, motorcycle rentals also differ in bike quality and insurance agreements.

Fast Facts: Pattaya

Banks/Currency Exchange   There are many independent money-changing booths; many bank exchanges (with better rates) stay open 24 hours. They're all easily located on any of the Pattaya maps available, with ATMs as well. Believe me, you don't have to look far when people want you to spend!

Internet/E-mail   There are little Internet centers everywhere; the average charge seems to be 2B/minute (US$0.05). I like the classy Pattaya K@fe Net at 219/59–60 Soi Yamato Beach Rd. (☎ **038/421-050**).

Hospital   If you need an ambulance, call either Pattaya Memorial Hospital at ☎ **038/429-422** or Bangkok Pattaya Hospital at ☎ **038/427-751.** Bangkok Pattaya Hospital can handle standard outpatient services as well, with English-speaking staff.

Police   In Pattaya, the number for the Tourist Police is ☎ **1699** or ☎ **038/ 429-371**.

Post Office/Mail   The post office is suitably located on Soi Post Office, the street just before the Royal Garden Plaza (☎ **038/429-341**).

ACCOMMODATIONS

Dusit Resort. 240/2 Pattaya Beach Rd., Pattaya City 20150, Chonburi. ☎ **038/425-611.** Fax 038/428-239. www.dusit.com. 474 units. A/C MINIBAR TV TEL. 5,415B (US$ 125.93) garden view double, 6,121B (US$ 142.35) seaview double; from 10,711B (US$ 249.09) suite. AE, DC, MC, V. North end of Pattaya Beach.

This beautifully landscaped resort offers water sports, a good health club, and some nightlife (far from the seedy side of Pattaya). Straddling a bluff on the north end of the main beach, the Dusit has two pools and sun decks, access to two small but well-kept sandy beach coves, several dining outlets, and a small shopping arcade. Most of the balconied rooms overlook Pattaya Bay, but the best values are the garden view rooms in Wing B, which face manicured lawns, hibiscus beds, and a side view of the sea. Tastefully modern rooms trimmed with stained wood offer all-marble bathrooms, hair dryers, and bathrobes. Landmark deluxe rooms have large bathrooms with separate bath tubs and shower stalls, plus outdoor showers on their large balconies, as well as comfortable and luxurious sitting areas.

The Dusit has several dining options, including the Empress for panoramic views and gourmet Chinese food. There's an okay coffee shop and a delightful lobby lounge that serves evening drinks with live musical accompaniment.

Flipper Lodge Hotel. 520/1 Soi 8, Pattaya Beach Rd., Pattaya City 20260, Chonburi. ☎ **038/426-401.** Fax 038/426-403. 126 units. A/C MINIBAR TV TEL. 720B–855B (US$16.74–US$19.88) double. AE, MC, V. Midbeach strip, off Soi 8.

A life-size statue of Flipper The Dolphin dominates the lobby of this fave budget choice in the middle of the beach strip. The decor is basic, but the older rooms are clean and the new ones are quite attractive; their sea-view rooms can't be beat for the price. The pool is a bit on the short side, but the attractive open-air coffee shop serves some pretty good Thai and continental fare. A budget choice you can trust amid a sea of dubious contenders.

✪ **Royal Garden Resort.** 218 Beach Rd., Pattaya City. ☎ **800/344-1212** in the U.S. and Canada; 0800/951-000 in the U.K.; 038/412-120. Fax 038/429-926. 300 units. 4708B–5885B (US$109.49–US$136.86) double; from 9416B (US$218.98) suite. AE, DC, JCB, MC, V.

Smack in the center of Pattaya Beach (you really can't get a better location), Royal Garden surprises guests with its large courtyard garden and landscaped pool area. You'd hardly know Pattaya City was just beyond the walls. With their helpful staff and handsome accommodations, this resort makes for a great retreat. Spacious balconied rooms have views of the gardens or the sea, and many creature comforts not found in other hotels, including an in-house video-on-demand service. The adjoining Royal Garden Plaza makes your dining and entertainment options even more attractive. Their pool is the largest in Pattaya, while their fitness center is modern and well-equipped. There's also tennis, and the resort can arrange any water-sports activity you so desire.

My favorite here is the Benihana Japanese-American Steakhouse (which I've reviewed separately in this chapter) for fun and great food. The Garden Café Restaurant, for à la carte and buffets, organizes regular food festivals. At night you can relax in the Elephant Lounge, or enjoy beer and pub food at Delaney's Irish Pub.

Magazines for Visitor Info

People keep publishing more and more freebie magazines on this place. There's *Explore Pattaya & The East Coast, What's On Pattaya, Accommodation Pattaya, Pattaya Pocket Guide,* plus maps pulished by all sorts and available everywhere. The information appears to be similar in each, and you can count on it being pretty accurate—it just looks like a lot of ad space to me.

The Royal Wing. Royal Cliff Beach Resort. 353 Phra Tamnuk Rd., Moo 12, Pattaya City 20260, Chonburi. ☎ **038/250-421.** Fax 038/250-486. www.royalcliff.co.th. 86 units. A/C MINIBAR TV TEL. 12,359B double (US$ 287.42). AE, DC, MC, V. On cliff, south of Pattaya Beach.

The dazzling Royal Wing is treated both by guests and its capable Swiss management as a separate entity within the impressive Royal Cliff resort (call the resort at the above number for information on its other resort accommodation options). The level of service here is more personal (butlers on call 24 hours), and the rooms are more regally furnished than anywhere else in town.

Each guest is catered to personally, with butlers unpacking your luggage on arrival and beach chaise lounges reserved with your brass nameplate. The large, bright, quietly tasteful rooms—decorated throughout with teak and fine pastel Thai cottons—are spaced around the cliff. For maximum privacy, each has two balconies, draped in fuchsia or orange bougainvillea, overlooking Pattaya Bay. The free-form swimming pool has small bow bridges and waterfalls that add an extra exotic touch. The beach is small but uncrowded and well-maintained.

The hotel offers daytime or romantic evening poolside dining at La Ronde, an elegant lobby bar, and the Palm Terrace for breakfast or lighter fare. The Benjarong Restaurant serves French and continental fare with a hint of Thai. Guests can try the Thai Market or Seafood Market open-air pavilion (see "Dining," below), as well as the facilities at the nearby Royal Cliff or Royal Cliff Grand.

Siam Bayshore Resort. 559 Beach Rd., Pattaya City 20260, Chonburi. ☎ **038/428-678.** Fax 038/428-730. 272 units. A/C MINIBAR TV TEL. 1,600B (US$ 37.21) double. AE, MC, V. Far south end of beach, across from city park.

For comfort, quiet, seclusion, and value in Pattaya, you'll have a hard time beating this excellent hotel. Rooms are large and attractively furnished with most of the amenities of the more luxurious hotels, including individually controlled air-conditioning, free in-house movies, 24-hour room service, laundry, and baby-sitting. The hotel grounds are attractively landscaped and well maintained, and facilities include two pools, a private beach club, four lighted tennis courts, volleyball and table tennis, nearby watersport facilities, and an exercise room.

DINING

Benihana. 2nd Level, Royal Garden Plaza. ☎ 038/425-029. AE, DC, JCB, MC, V. Call for lunch and dinner hours. JAPANESE/AMERICAN.

Most American readers are thinking, "Benihana? In Thailand?" Well, for those of you who've sampled tom yam gung and pad thai until it's coming out your ears, you'll be happy to visit this place. It has all the fun of Benihana's original restaurants—fantastic teppanyaki grill displays performed by chefs who have as much humor as skill, and the food is just great. The beef is like butter. Come here for a good time and a lot of laughs. You won't be disappointed.

Nuang Nual. South Pattaya Rd. ☎ **038/428-708.** Reservations required for large groups. 70B–350B (US$1.63–US$8.14); seafood at market prices. AE, MC, V. Daily 10am–11pm. SEAFOOD.

At night, when South Pattaya Road becomes a pedestrian mall, take a walk past the noisy open-air watering holes and colorful souvenir shops to Nuang Nual. The entrance is as brightly lit as a supermarket, and looks like one too, with rows upon rows of all sorts of creatures of the sea in tanks or on ice in coolers. The maitre d' will escort you to your table on the huge outdoor patio overlooking the bay, and hand you a menu which is more or less a book. Choose your creature, and they'll prepare it to your specifications: Thai style, Chinese, or Western. On my last visit, the squid dish I had was incredibly tender. They also have meats and vegetable dishes, as well as soups and fried rice and noodles. Get there early so you can get a table with a good view.

✪ **PIC Kitchen.** Soi 5 Pattaya 2nd Rd. ☎ **038/428-374.** 75B–320B (US$1.74–US$7.44). AE, DC, MC, V. Daily 8am–noon. THAI.

Named for the Pattaya International Clinic PIC Hospital next door (don't worry, they're unrelated) PIC Kitchen is highly recommended for its wonderful atmosphere. Small Thai teak pavilions, both air-conditioned and open-air, have seating areas on the floor, Thai style, or at romantic tables. Delicious and affordable Thai cuisine is served à la carte or in lunch and dinner sets. The spring rolls and deep-fried crab claws are mouthwatering. Other dishes come panfried, steamed, or charcoal grilled, with spice added to taste. At night, groove to a live jazz band from 7pm to 1am.

Vientiane. 485/18 Pattaya Second Rd., ☎ **038/411-298.** Main courses 60B–200B (US$1.40–US$4.65). AE, DC, MC, V. Daily 11am–midnight. On east side of 2nd Rd., between Soi 14 and Soi Post Office. LAO/THAI.

The large menu of this busy place includes Lao, Vietnamese, Chinese, and Isaan (northeastern Thai) specialties, plus the chef's suggested "not-too-hot dishes." The distinctively flavored roast chicken is particularly delicious and the seafood fresh, not overcooked, and in generous portions. Excellent sea crab costs 60B (US$1.40) per 100gm portions. The only drawback is its location on a noisy street, so head for the air-conditioned (smoking section) dining room or as far back as possible.

ATTRACTIONS
PATTAYA BEACH

This 4-kilometer (2½-mile) strip may seem harmless to the naked eye, but be warned, the rumors you've heard are true. It's very, very polluted. Rapid growth of the tourism sector was not accompanied by growth of pubic facilities works, and for years waste has been disposed of improperly, ironically destroying the very attraction that drew travelers here in the first place. As if raw sewage isn't enough, the waste attracts many varieties of poisonous sea snakes.

Water activities still reign in the area, but for swimming you should either stick to the very north of Pattaya Beach near the Dusit Resort, or head a little south to Jomtien Beach (which isn't the most attractive beach, in my opinion). The best option is to take a day trip to one of the islands in the Gulf of Thailand.

On Pattaya Beach there's windsurfing (150B/US$3.49 per hour), parasailing (250B/US$5.81 for 5 minutes), canoeing (100B/US$2.33 per hour), and catamaran sailing (400B–600B or US$9.30–US$13.95 per hour). You can wander along the beach to find guys who arrange these activities.

On Jomtien you can find even more activities than on Pattaya Beach. To get to Jomtien Beach, grab a songtao on Beach Road or Pattaya 2nd Road for around 30B (US$0.70). Swimming is centered around the northern section of Jomtien Beach, while the southern parts are for other water sports such as catamarans, parasailing, waterskiing, and windsurfing.

Day trips to Ko Lan (Coral Island) or nearby Ko Pai are best if you want cleaner and less crowded beaches. Ko Lan, 7.7 kilometers (4.8 miles) west of Pattaya, has beaches with eateries, overnight accommodations, water sports, and other facilities. On weekends it gets very crowded, so you may want to try Ko Pai, which is beautiful, but has no facilities at all. The local ferryboat to Ko Lan costs 20B (US$0.47) per person and takes 45 minutes. The last ferry back is at 5pm. For a speedboat hire expect to pay 800B to 2,000B (US$18.60 to US$46.51) per day. Once at the island, you can take a motorcycle taxi to the various beaches for between 20B and 50B (US$0.47 to US$1.16). The easiest way to arrange the boat trip is through the **TAT office** (☎ **038/429-113**). You will also need to see them for arrangements to Ko Pai.

Snorkeling and **scuba diving** are popular because of Pattaya Bay's clear waters (20m to 25m average visibility), colorful coral reefs (including mushroom, lettuce, brain, and staghorn corals), and tropical fish (white- and black-tip sharks, stingrays, angelfish, and many others). Nearby Ko Larn, Ko Sak, and Ko Kroh can be reached within 45 minutes by boat. There are a number of good dive shops with PADI and NAUI certified instructors in the area. I liked the people at **Dolphin Diving Center** (183/31 Moo 10, Soi Post Office; ☎ **038/427-185**), who take small groups out for two daily dives—total cost including equipment, two tanks, transport, a hot meal, and a divemaster guide is about 2,800B (US$65.12). Overnight dives can also be arranged.

For sports enthusiasts, **golf** is second only to water activities, and for reputation the area around the resort is known as the "Golf Paradise of the East," with international-class courses within a 40-kilometer (25-mile) radius of the city. If you're willing to travel a little, the finest course is at Bangphra International Golf Club (45 Moo 6, Tambon Bang Phra, Sri Racha; ☎ **038/341-149;** fax 02/341-151). This par 72 championship course was designed in 1958 by a Japanese team, and redone in 1987. It's considered the prettiest course in the area. Also try The Laem Chabang International Country Club (106/8 Moo 4 Tambon Bung, Sri Ratcha; ☎ **038/338-351;** fax 038/372-273), a nine-hole course designed by Jack Nicklaus; or the Siam Country Club (50 Tambol Poeng, Banglamung; ☎ **038/249-381;** fax 038/249-387), believed to be one of the country's most challenging courses.

When your skin is charred, your head is waterlogged, and you want a change of pace from all that beach living, Pattaya has a few worthwhile activities, both fun and cultural. On the culture side of life, there's **Wat Khao Phra Yai** on Big Buddha Hill (Pratumnak Road between South Pattaya and Jomtien). This 10.8-meter (32.5-ft.) gold colored stucco Buddha, believed to be the protector of the city, peers out into the sea. The view of the bay is quite nice from the wat as well. Pattaya also has a **Mini Siam** theme park (387 Sukhumvit Rd. near North Pattaya Road; ☎ **038/421-628**), with replicas of major Thai attractions like the Temple of the Emerald Buddha and the Bridge over the River Kwai and, strangely, some European monuments as well. They're open daily from 9am to 9pm, and charge 200B (US$4.65) for adults and 100B (US$2.33) for children.

There's a huge and highly entertaining elephant park only 18 kilometers (11 miles) from the city. **Nong Nooch** stages performances three times daily—with elephants performing alongside some 100 dancers, musicians, and performers for spectator crowds of up to 1,000. Cultural performances, music, Thai boxing, audience participation, and dozens of funny photo ops make this really touristy activity a load of laughs. Make your booking from Nong Nooch direct at ☎ **038/429-321.** They arrange shuttles from Pattaya at either 8:30am or 1:15pm with return. The half-day trip costs 350B (US$8.14) per person.

For something completely unusual, the **Ripley's Believe It or Not** showcase (3rd Floor, Royal Garden Plaza, 218 Beach Rd.; ☎ **038/710-294;** open 10am to midnight daily; admission 150B/US$3.49) is hilarious, with unusual exhibits and odd facts from around the globe. Just next door is the Ripley's Motion Master simulator ride. Both are highly recommended if you're traveling with your children.

The **Pattaya Elephant Village** (see the Elephant Desk at the Tropicana Hotel, Beach Road; ☎ **038/423-031**) stages elephant shows daily at 2:30pm. You can also arrange for a little jungle trekking on elephant back. If that's not quite your speed, check out **Pattaya Go-Kart** (Sukhumvit Road next to Mini Siam; ☎ **038/422-044**) with a 400-meter track that is also suitable for children. Rates run between 100B and 200B (US$2.33 to US$4.65) per 10 minutes, depending on the power of your kart.

PATTAYA AFTER DARK

At first sight, Pattaya is an assault on the senses. Electricity bills must be staggering from the neon signs, light up billboards and colored bulbs down every soi. Take a stroll down the South Pattaya pedestrian area ("Pattayaland") where every alley is lined with open air watering holes with bar girls hanging around hoping for a lucky catch. Go-go bars are everywhere, with sex shows the sort you'd find in Bangkok's Patpong. Pattaya Land 1 and Pattaya Land 2, near South Pattaya, are "Boyz Town," with rows of gay go-go clubs. This spectacle is the nightlife most come to Pattaya to experience. (Pattayaland is actually pretty cruel in the light of day, when lonely old guys blink bleary-eyed atop barstool perches listening to "Hotel California" for the umpteenth time.)

For cleaner fun, there are some lively bars and discos in the city. **Hopf Brew House** (219 Beach Rd.; ☎ **038/710-650**) brews its own beer served by the glass, goblet, or ampolla, to the beat of a live band. For discos, the largest is **Palladium** (Pattaya 2nd Rd.; ☎ **038/424-933**), a gigantic club with the largest dance floor you've ever seen pulsating with pop and dance beats and a great light show. The smaller **Disco Duck** (Little Duck Pattaya Resort Hotel, Central Pattaya Road; ☎ **038/428-065**) has a fun atmosphere, catering to middle-class Thai folks from Bangkok, with live bands, videos, and light shows.

Pattaya's most beautiful *katoeys* (transsexuals) don sequinned gowns and feather boas to strut their stuff for packed houses nightly. At **Alcazar** (78/14 Pattaya 2nd Rd., opposite Soi 5; ☎ **038-410-505**) the shows are at times hilarious. If you've seen a cabaret show elsewhere in Thailand, you may be disappointed to see familiar acts, which are standard in almost every show.

6 Ko Samet

Beautiful **Ko Samet** first became popular with Thais from the poetry of Sunthon Phu, a venerated 19th-century author and Rayong native who set his best-known epic on this "tropical island paradise." In the 21st-century Samet remains a slice of heaven. From a lazy beach chair under a shady coconut palm, you can dig your toes into soft white powder sand while you contemplate whether you want to jump into the glittering green sea or order another fruit punch and have a massage. At night the beach turns into a fairy land of glittering lights and barbecue pits—sumptuous seafood feasts under the stars.

Ko Samet Survival Gear

Some tips: Arm yourself with **mosquito repellent,** and if you plan to stay in a smaller bungalow, hang a mosquito net over your bed. A **flashlight** is also a good idea for finding your way after dark and in the smaller bungalows that turn off electricity in the late evening. You might want to bring along a **towel.** The bigger resorts have towels, but the cheap bunglaow places don't. **A good sarong** is the ultimate—beach blanket, towel, wrap, bed sheet, sun shield. I never leave home without at least two.

Lucky for us a shortage of potable water kept rampant commerce and tourism at bay for many years. In 1981, Samet became part of the six-island **Khao Laem Ya— Samet National Park,** a designation meant to preserve its relatively undeveloped status. However, since then, small-scale construction has boomed, and there are now more than 50 licensed bungalow hotels with nearly 2,500 rooms on the 6-kilometer-long (3.6-mile-long) island. In 1990, a TAT-sponsored effort to close the national park to overnight visitors met with such fierce resistance that 4 days later Samet was reopened for business as usual. Until inadequate water supplies, waste treatment, and garbage disposal are dealt with, the TAT encourages visitors to go to the still lovely Samet for day trips only, but that rarely happens.

These days Samui welcomes a diverse crowd, from Thai and expatriate weekenders unwinding from the stress of the big city to international travelers who seek an idyllic beach life that over-exploited Pattaya can not provide. For this reason, weekends and public holidays get pretty crowded, rooms become scarce, and resorts tack on up to 20% rate surcharges. Book early, or better yet, come during the week. Monday through Friday this place is quiet and lovely. Another planning consideration—Samet follows the same weather patterns as Bangkok. Basically, from December through April you can expect less rain, but more people. May through August is hit or miss as far as rain goes, but I've always had good luck. September through November the weather gets iffy, rainwise.

The small island's northern half is triangular, with a long tail leading to the south that looks somewhat like a kite. Most of the beaches are on the east coast of the tail; although Ko Samet is only about 1 kilometer (six-tenths of a mile) wide, it has a rocky spine and there are few paths that connect the two coasts. Passengers alight from the ferry at **Na Dan,** the island's main port. It's a 10-minute walk south past the **health center** and school to **Hat Sai Kaeo** (Diamond Beach, on the northeast cape), the island's most developed and crowded beach, which is linked by a dirt path to 10 other small beach developments. Most day-trippers take the regular ferry and then catch one of the songtaos that meet the boats and travel inland as far as Vong Deuan beach. You can also catch a ride with one of the individual resort ferries or hike the shoreline path between beaches.

The beaches at Hat Sai Kaeo, Ao Pai, and Vong Deuan have the best facilities but are also the most expensive, basically because everything, including water, must be imported from the mainland. Keep in mind, on Samet, even the finest resorts are simple no-frills operations. Air-conditioning is extra; a hot water shower is nonexistent.

GETTING THERE

BY BUS Buses leave Bangkok every hour between 7am and 10pm for the 3½-hour journey, departing from the Eastern Bus Terminal (☎ **02/390-1230**) on Sukhumvit Road opposite Soi 63 (Ekamai Road). The one-way trip to Ban Phe, the town where

you catch the ferry to Ko Samet, costs 108B (US$2.51). The bus terminal in Ban Phe is just across the street from the ferry pier. To get from Pattaya, you'd have to transfer buses in Rayong. Best to take a minivan, directions to follow.

BY MINIVAN from Bangkok, a few travel agencies operate their own minibuses to Ban Phe. **S. T. Travel** has a minibus leaving from its office at 102 Rambutri Rd. (at Khao San Road), Banglamphu, daily at 8am. Trip time is 3½ hours; cost is 480B (US$11.16) round-trip. Call them in Bangkok (☎ **02/281-3662**) or in Ban Phe (☎ **038/651-461**) for schedule information and reservations. They're convenient if you're staying in the Historic District or near Khao San Road; otherwise, take the bus. It's cheaper, it's just as comfortable, and the schedule is far more flexible.

Minivans leave from Pattaya to Ban Phe at 8am, noon, and 3:30 daily (trip time: 1 hour; 300B/US$6.98 round-trip). This one is more convenient, since public buses don't connect these two cities directly. Contact **Samet Island Tour** (109/22 Moo 10 Pratumnuk Rd., Pattaya, ☎ **038/710-76;** or on Ko Samet at the Malibu Garden Resort, 77 Vong Deuan Beach mobile, ☎ **01/218-5345**).

BY TAXI Samet Island Tour in Pattaya can arrange a private car to take you to Ban Phe for 800B (US$18.60) one-way. Call them at the number above for details and booking. From the pier in Ban Phe you can hire a taxi back for the same price.

FERRIES TO KO SAMET   During the high season, from November to April, ferries leave Ban Phe pier for the main port, Na Dan, every half hour. Trip time is 40 minutes, cost 80B (US$1.86) round-trip. The first boat departs at 9:30am and the last at 5pm (call Nuanthip Pier at ☎ 038/651-508). Several other agents in Ban Phe sell passage on their own boats to Vang Deuan beach; departures are at least a few times daily. One-way fare is 100B (US$2.33) round-trip (call Samet Island Tour in Ban Phe, ☎ 038/651-057).

From the ferry landing on Samet, you must either catch a water taxi to the other beaches (20B to 60B/US$0.46 to US$1.40 per person, depending on your destination) or take a songtao to other beaches (10B to 50B/US$0.23 to US$1.16 per person). There is one road on Samet connecting the main town, Na Dan, halfway down the eastern shore of the island to Vong Deuan. Beyond that you're stuck traversing footpaths.

One note about water taxis and songtao. They don't like to make the trip for only one or two passengers, and prefer to either wait until more people show up, or will charge you a premium. A water taxi could soak you for up to 300B (US$6.98), and a songtao could run you into the ground for 400B (US$9.30), especially if it's getting dark and they know you have no other choice but to use their service. It's a tough situation, especially since Thai etiquette asks you to refrain from blowing your top. If you do lose your temper, don't be surprised if you're refused a ride altogether.

The Thai government charges a parks admission fee of 20B per entry to the island. A ranger is usually on hand to greet each ferry-load to collect payment.

Fast Facts: Ko Samet

Banks/Currency Exchange   Ko Samet is pretty much a cash-only operation, except for Vong Deuan Resort and Malibu Garden Resort, where you can use Visa and MasterCard to settle your tab. While there are no ATMs on the island, many resorts will change money.

Post Office/Mail   Talk to your resort front desk for postal services or directions to nearby services.

Provisions   In Na Dan, Hat Sai Kaew, and Vong Deuan, you'll find small provision shops for basic goods.

Telephone   International and domestic phone access is available through the major resorts on all beaches.

ACCOMMODATIONS

The two best beaches on Ko Samet are Ao Pai, for its peace and quiet, and Vong Deuan beach, for its conveniences. Ao Pai is smaller, with bungalows set in the jungle, just a hop from the beach, the best of which are the **Ao Pai Huts** (☎ 01/ **353-2644**), along the main dirt road about 10 minutes' ride (20B/US$0.47) from the main jetty. These simple bungalows are tidy and well constructed, with clean bathrooms and space to put your baggage. During the busy season rates are 500B (US$11.63) with air-conditioning, and 300B (US$6.98) with fan. During off-peak season rates run 300B and 150B (US$6.98 and US$3.49), respectively. Rates apply for both single and double occupancy.

Vong Deuan beach offers the best variety of accommodations, but it gets a greater volume of traffic. Still, the sandy cove is quite large, and the mood here tends to be more active and fun. **Vong Deuan Resort** (☎ **01/446-1944;** Bangkok contact **02/392-4390**) has bungalows that are more modern and come with a few amenities— like towels. Bungalows with air-conditioning run from 1,100B to 1,200B (US$25.58 to US$27.91), with fan from 800B to 900B (US$18.60 to US$20.93). On Vong Deuan Beach, you can also try **Malibu Garden Resort** (Ban Phe ☎ **038/651-057** or Pattaya **038/710-676**), where the more expensive rooms have hot water, television, even a refrigerator—luxury items on Samui. Air-conditioned bungalows cost between 1,500B and 2,200B (US$34.88 to US$51.16). Bungalows with fans only are from 800B to 1,600B (US$18.60 to US$37.21).

DINING

You will just have to forage for nuts and berries.

Just kidding! All of the bungalows offer some sort of eating experience, mostly bland local food and sticky tropical cocktails, all with daily Western breakfast offerings. On Vong Deuan and Hat Sai Kaew you'll find nightly seafood barbecues with a good selection of fresh sea creatures, and the prices are very fair. A few bars open up to serve drinks until late. If you're staying in Ao Pai, a few neighboring places entice dinner guests with video screenings of recently released movies, which are always popular. In Ao Pai, Naga Bar on the main road is quiet, with a fairly decent menu, a beer selection, and a bakery that has surprisingly wonderful fresh goods in the mornings.

SPORTS & OUTDOOR ACTIVITIES

Windsurfing is particularly popular with weekenders from Bangkok. The island's best is said to be north of Hat Sai Kaeo (Diamond Beach), around the cape that bulges out of Samet's east side. The rocky north coast is even more challenging, with strong currents and sometimes erratic winds caused by the deep channel between the island and the mainland. Windsurfers are available at most guesthouses for 100B to 175B (US$2.33 to US$4.07) per hour, without instruction. Hat Sai Kaeo also has jet skis for rent at about 1,200B per hour (US$27.91).

You can book any of the speedboats at the beaches for round-island tours at about 1,500B (US$34.88) for the boat, and for snorkeling on the rocky uninhabited western side of the island, which is said to be the best for underwater life. They'll be happy to do a morning drop and afternoon fetch.

7 The Southern Peninsula

From Bangkok, follow Thailand's narrow Malay Peninsula south through tropical terrain, past coconut plantations worked by clever monkeys and coastal villages that experience "rush hour" at dawn with the return of colorful fishing boats. To the Thai people, the south represents a robust side of life. The weather here gets a bit more hot and steamy, Thai dialects turn coarse and tough (and according to the rest of the country, so do the people), and the local food sets mouths on fire with fresh chiles. Visitors know this part of the country best for the gorgeous tropical islands off the peninsula's long coastlines.

In the Andaman Sea, world-famous Phuket draws countless visitors each year on its reputation for idyllic beaches and stellar resorts. To counter the glamour and hype of **Phuket, Ko Samui** in the Gulf of Thailand developed its own image of scaled-down, home-grown tropical paradise. While these two islands get the lion's share of visitors, seaside **Hua Hin and Cha-Am,** Thailand's oldest beach resort destination, entertain mostly locals and expatriates popping down from hectic Bangkok.

Southern Peninsula: East Coast

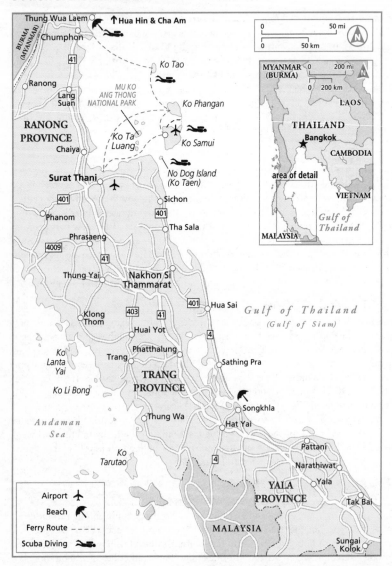

8 Hua Hin & Cha-Am

Hua Hin and Cha-Am, neighboring villages on the Gulf of Thailand, form the country's oldest resort area. Developed in the 1920s as a relaxing getaway for Bangkok's elite, Thailand's "Riviera" was a mere 3 or 4 hours' journey from the capital by train, thanks to the southern railway's completion in 1916. At the same time, Thailand opened its first golf course here, the Royal Hua Hin Golf Course, sealing this area's fate as a perfect golfing vacation destination.

When Pattaya, on Thailand's eastern coast, hit the scene in the 1960s, it lured vacationers away from Hua Hin and Cha-Am. If you ask me, it only makes this the perfect place to get away from the usual tourist din. The clean sea and wide beaches support excellent and unique resorts, plus there's the added thrill of nearby historic Phetchaburi, Khao Sam Roi Yod National Park, and islands for snorkeling trips.

Hua Hin and Cha-Am share similar weather with Bangkok. Visit from November through April for the most sunshine. The rest of the year you'll have frequent showers and some overcast days, but it is improbable it will rain all the time. The mid-December to mid-January holiday peak season demands advance bookings and hotel surcharges ranging from 500B to 1,500B per night.

VISITOR INFORMATION

Find the **Hua Hin Tourist Information Service Center** (☎ **032/511-047**) in the center of town tucked behind the city shrine at the corner of Damnoenkasem and Petchkasem Roads (open daily 8:30am to 4:30pm). In Cha-Am the TAT office (☎ **032/471-005**) is inconveniently located on the corner of Petchkasem Road and Narathip Road about 1 kilometer from the main beach area (the main Beach Road is about 1 kilometer away).

A decent source of information, *The Observer* packs a lot of advertisers and tidbits from the local expatriate community into a small, regularly updated magazine. There are a few free map handouts floating around at hotels.

GETTING THERE

BY AIR   While there is a domestic airport in Hua Hin, no airlines have serviced it for years.

BY TRAIN   Reach both Hua Hin and Cha-Am via the train station in Hua Hin. From Bangkok's Hua Lampong Railway Station (☎ **02/223-7010** or 02/223-7020) catch one of six daily express diesel railcars (trip time: 4 hours; first class 262B/US$6.09, second class 162B/US$3.77), or one of four daily rapid trains (second class 142B/US$3.30, third class 84B/US$1.95). The Hua Hin Railway Station (☎ **032/511-073**) is at the tip of Damnoenkasem Road, which slices through the center of town straight to the beach. Pickup truck taxis (*songtao*) and *tuk-tuks* wait outside to take you to your hotel starting at 50B (US$1.16).

BY BUS   Most agree that the bus is the better choice for travel from Bangkok to Hua Hin and Cha-Am because it takes less time. Air-con "blue buses" depart from Bangkok's Southern Bus Terminal (☎ **02/435-1199**) every 40 minutes from 3am to 9pm (trip time: 3 hours; 110B/US$2.56).

Buses from Bangkok arrive in Hua Hin at the Air-conditioned Bus Station on Sra-song Road, 1 block north of Damnoenkasem Road (☎ **032/511-654**). From here it's easy to find a songtao or tuk-tuk to take you to your destination. If you travel from Bangkok to Cha-Am, you'll be dropped at the small kiosk on the main beach road, from where you can catch a taxi.

GETTING AROUND

Despite decades of tourist traffic, Hua Hin remains a small town that is simple to navigate. The main artery, Petchkasem Road, runs parallel to the waterfront about 4 blocks inland. The wide Damnoenkasem Road cuts through Petchkasem and runs straight to the beach. Cha-Am, a 25-minute drive north on Petchkasem Road, is much smaller than Hua Hin, with a far different feel. Most of the life centers on Ruamchit Road, which is also known as Beach Road—hugging the beach on one side, and rows of shops, restaurants, hotels, and motels on the other. Cha-Am's resorts line the 8-kilometer (5-mile) stretch of beach that runs south from the village all the way to

Hua Hin. If you're staying in one of these resorts, you'll either spend a lot of time in residence, or pay the hotel taxis to take you to either town.

Pickup truck taxis (songtao) and tuk-tuks make their way along the main streets of Hua Hin and Cha-Am, passing the railway station and bus terminals at regular intervals. Fares begin at 50B (US$1.16) within town, while stops at outlying resorts will run up to 200B (US$4.65). Trips between Hua Hin and Cha-Am cost 200B to 300B (US$4.65 to US$6.98). In both towns motorcycle taxi fares begin at 20B (US$0.47) and to resort areas 100B (US$2.33). Trishaws, or samlors, can be found around the center of Hua Hin and can be hired for short distances as low as 20B (US$0.47).

For car rental, **Budget** (☎ 032/514-220) has the best rate at 1,375B per day (US$31.98) for a Suzuki Caribian. Cheaper alternatives can be rented from stands near the beach on Damnoenkasem Road, where a Caribian goes for around 800B (US$18.60) per day. These places and others around town will also rent 100cc motorcycles for under 200B (US$4.65) per day.

Fast Facts: Hua Hin & Cha-Am

Banks/Currency Exchange   In Hua Hin, your major **banks** are along Petchkasem Road to the north of Damnoenkasem, and **money changers** are peppered throughout the town. In Cha-Am there are a few exchange booths and ATMs along the beach road.

Internet/E-mail   Both Hua Hin and Cha-Am have Internet cafes along the well-traveled roads. For the best price (1B/US$0.02 per minute) and atmosphere check out Cups & Comp at 104/1 Naeb-Khehars Rd. (☎ 032/511-369). It's open daily from 9am to midnight.

Hospital   The **Hua Hin Hospital** (☎ 032/520-391) is located in the north of town along Petchkasem Road. The Thonburi Cha-Am Hospital (☎ 032/433-903) is off Narathip Road close to the Petchkasem intersection.

Police   Tourist police can be reached at ☎ 1655 nationwide.

Post Office/Mail   The main post office in Hua Hin (☎ 032/511-063) is on Damnoenkasem Road near where it intersects with Petchkasem.

ACCOMMODATIONS IN HUA HIN & CHA-AM

Hua Hin's resorts are relatively close to the town, with guesthouses clustered in the town itself. Cha-Am offers a host of inexpensive and casual guesthouses along the main beach road for as low as 300B to 500B (US$6.98 to US$11.63) per night. Hop from house to house and look at rooms till you find something you like (trust me, trying to make advance reservations by phone is just begging for frustration). For the best resorts in the area, the 8-kilometer (5-mile) strip of prime beach between the two villages hosts a variety of high-rise condo-hotels, luxury resorts, casual bungalow spots, and dingy budget motels. I've selected the best options below.

The Cha-Am Methavalai Hotel. 220 Ruamchit Rd., Cha-Am 76120. ☎ **032/471-028.** Fax 032/471-590. 118 units. A/C MINIBAR TV TEL. 3,276B (US$76.19) double; 6,751B (US$157) suite (rates include tax). AE, DC, JCB, MC, V.

Compared to the other choices for accommodations in Cha-Am village, the Methavalai is certainly the better bet. This large hotel is modern and well suited for the demands of international travelers. Located on the main Beach Road in Cha-Am, it's convenient to the restaurants, shopping, and small nightlife scene in town. Large guest rooms in soft palettes are peaceful, and all have balconies with a sundeck. The only downfall is you have to share the beach here with residents of the many motels along the strip. Instead, you can always opt for their large outdoor lagoon shaped pool. The Komain Coffee Shop serves room service around the clock, and the Chevalier Supper Club has live music performances nightly. I've reviewed the Sontalay Terrace beachside restaurant in the dining section of this chapter. When you call for reservations ask for room rate discounts of up to 50%.

Chiva-Som International Health Resort. 73/4 Petchkasem Rd., Hua Hin, 77110. ☎ **032/536-536.** Fax 032/511-615. www.chivasom.net. 57 units. A/C MINIBAR TEL. All double rates are quoted per person. 18,060B (US$420) ocean view double; 21,672B (US$504) Thai Pavilion; 27,520B–43,000B (US$640–US$1,000) ocean view suite. Nightly rate includes 3 spa cuisine meals per day, health and beauty consultations, daily massage, and participation in fitness and leisure activities. AE, DC, V, MC. 5-min. drive south of Hua Hin.

Chiva-Som will strip away any wear and tear the modern world can dish out, both mentally and physically. Choose a guest room in the main building for the fabulous morning sunrise over the water, or a bungalow with either ocean or garden view for extra privacy. Each are decorated in cooling natural tones and warm wood with traditional Thai touches throughout.

The centerpiece is the spa. Carefully planned to ensure privacy and relaxation, the menu for treatments is phenomenal, with health and beauty consultation, numerous facial and body treatments, medical treatments, diet programs, and fitness activities including personal training, swimming, yoga, tai chi, and Thai boxing. All facilities provide top-of-the-line equipment and first-rate tutelage. The outdoor pool sits beside the beach, while the bathing pavilion has an ozonated indoor swimming pool, steam room, cold plunge pool, and large Jacuzzi. There's also a library, full beauty salon facility, and first class fitness center and gymnasium. Make sure you ask about their special packages.

Dusit Resort and Polo Club. 1349 Petchkasem Rd., Cha-Am 76120. ☎ **032/520-009.** Fax 032/520-296. www.dusit.com. 305 units. A/C MINIBAR TV TEL. 5,885B–6,473B (US$136.86–US$150.53) double; 12,947B (US$301.09) Landmark suite (includes tax). AE, DC, MC, V.

Built for the country's elite and the well-heeled foreign tourist, the Dusit combines the amenities and facilities of the best international deluxe resorts with an English country and polo club theme. The grandly elegant marble lobby features bronze horses, plush carpets, and seating areas, with hunting-and-riding oil paintings hung throughout. Hall doors have polo mallet handles; each public area follows suit with "horsey" artwork and decor.

Guest rooms are spacious, with English country touches and oversized marble bathrooms. Room rates vary with the view, although every room's balcony faces out over the lushly landscaped pool. Patios for the ground floor Lanai Rooms are landscaped for privacy, but you can still run straight out to the pool and beach.

For all its air of formality, the resort is great for those who prefer swimsuits and T-shirts to riding jodhpurs. In fact, there's no polo field around at all, but if you'd like to go riding, the resort does care for its own stables. The beach is meticulous and calm, and all sorts of water sports with instruction are available. Other facilities include tennis courts, squash courts, and a fitness center.

✪ **Hotel Sofitel Central.** 1 Damnoenkasem Rd., Hua Hin 77110. ☎ **800/221-4542** in the U.S. and Canada; 800/642-244 in Australia; 0800/444-422 in New Zealand; 032/512-021. Fax 032/511-014. www.sofitel.com. 214 units. A/C MINIBAR TV TEL. 6,591B–7,533B (US$153.28–US$175.19) double; 10,358B–16,949B (US$240.88–US$394.16) suite (rates include tax). DC, JCB, MC, V. In the center of town by the beach.

The Hua Hin Railway Hotel opened in 1922 in response to the demand for luxury accommodations in the newly emerging resort town. Adapted from European styles, the brick and wood design incorporated long shady verandahs with whitewashed wood detail under a sloped red tile roof. Sofitel treasures the heritage of this old beauty, creating a hotel museum and preserving the hotel's original 14 bedrooms.

Subsequent additions and renovations have expanded the hotel into a large and modern full-facility hotel without sacrificing a bit of its former charm. While the original rooms have their unique appeal, the newer rooms are larger, brighter, and more comfortable. With furnishings that reflect the hotel's old beach resort feel, they are still modern and cozy. Great location in the center of Hua Hin.

Of the resort's seven food and beverage outlets, the Palm Seafood Pavilion is the finest, and is reviewed in the "Dining" section. Other options include Thai cuisine at Salathai Restaurant, continental cuisine at the Railway Restaurant, high tea served in the hotel's original lobby, and cocktails at the nostalgic Elephant Bar.

Sofitel's three magnificent outdoor pools are landscaped for sundecks with shady spots. The new Spa Health Club, in its own beachside bungalow, provides full service health and beauty treatments, and the new fitness center sports fine equipment with recent additions. Nature walks through the grounds, tennis, squash, badminton, putting (on two greens), croquet, golf trips, tours, and water sports will keep you plenty busy.

Jed Pee Nong Hotel. 17 Damneonkasem Rd., Hua Hin 77110. ☎ **032/512-381.** Fax 032/ 532-2036. 25 units. MINIBAR. 500B (US$11.63) single or double with fan; 700B (US$16.28) double with A/C. No credit cards. On the main street near the town beach.

This recently built hotel with a Chinese flair is located less than 100 meters from the Sofitel Central's elegant driveway. It's so clean and well kept that it's a good choice. A bevy of family or local workers maintain the tiny garden filled with songbirds and fountains, a small pool, and the simple balconied rooms. Many rooms are carpeted and have air-conditioning. The higher-priced rooms have better decor and hug the pool, cabana style. There's also a Thai seafood restaurant off the lobby and laundry service.

✪ Royal Garden Village. 43/1 Petchkasem Beach Rd., Hua Hin 77110. ☎ **800/344-1212** in the U.S. and Canada; 0800/951-000 in the U.K.; 032/520-250. Fax 032/520-259. 162 units. A/C MINIBAR TV TEL. 4,270B (US$99.3) double; 5,320B (US$123.72) beach terrace; 8,600B–9,100B (US$200–US$211.63) suite. AE, DC, JCB, MC, V.

A series of elegantly designed Thai-style pavilions, this resort feels like a "village" away from the town center, off the main road. The open-air sala-style lobby is tastefully decorated with ornately carved teak wooden lanterns, warm wood floors, and furniture with rose-colored cushions. A series of teak pavilions each houses 12 guest rooms. Consistent with the lobby, rooms are furnished in Thai style with teak-and-rattan furniture. Superior rooms have a garden view and deluxe rooms overlook the sand and sea. For a few dollars more, the beach terrace rooms have large patios, perfect for requesting a fun (or romantic) barbecue set up by the staff.

Regent Chalet. 849/21 Petchkasem Rd., Cha-Am 76120. ☎ **032/451-240.** Fax 032/ 451-277. www.regent-chaam.com. 660 units. A/C MINIBAR TV TEL. 4,120B (US$95.81) double; 5,885 (US$136.86) family suite; 14,124B (US$328.47) bungalow suite. AE, MC, V.

I'm sure Regent Chalet gets a lot of business because of name association, but the resort is not related to the famous Regent chain with hotels in Bangkok, Chiang Mai, and other Asian cities. Still, Regent Chalet is a popular choice in Cha-Am. The entire resort is a huge complex with 660 rooms and suites, three outdoor pools, Jacuzzi, fitness center, massage, four tennis courts, two squash courts, land and water sports, and choice of restaurants. Sounds overwhelming? Well, in a quiet little section to the side of the resort grounds is the Regent Chalet, the resort's separate bungalow facility. The best part is you enjoy a more relaxed and rustic experience, but still have access to all the offerings of the larger resort—the best of both worlds. Bungalows are either on or close to the beach, with rattan and bamboo furniture in true beach home style. The last time I visited, a resident baby elephant made an appearance for an afternoon bath and snacks. Very, very cute.

DINING

If you wake up at about 7am and walk to the piers in either Hua-Hin or Cha-Am, you can watch the fishing boats return with their loads. Workers sort all varieties of creatures, packing them on ice for distribution around the country. Still, much of the catch remains behind to be consumed locally. In Cha-Am, look for the docks at the very north end of the beach and stroll past to the open-air restaurants looking out over the water. Come here for lunch and enjoy enormous fish for 150B (US$3.49), huge juicy tiger prawns for 500B (US$11.63) per kilo (compare that to 1,850B/US$43.02 per kilo in Bangkok's Seafood Market)—there's scallops, squid, clams, cockles, mussels, a few varieties of prawn, snails, crabs, lobsters, all kinds of fish—all of it fresh like you've never seen before. Four of us gorged ourselves on a Mount Olympus-style seafood feast and spent under 600B (US$13.95). Truly unbelievable.

Itsara. 7 Napkehard St., Hua Hin. ☎ **032/530-574.** Reservations recommended Sat dinner. Main courses 60B–290B (US$1.40–US$6.74). MC, V. Mon–Fri 10am–12pm; Sat–Sun 2pm–12am. Seaside, a 40B–70B (US$0.93–US$1.63) samlor ride north from the town center. THAI.

Formerly called Ban Tuppee Kaow, Itsara resides in a two-story greenhouse built in the 1920s—not especially well maintained, though it is atmospheric. By the sea, the terrace seating is the best in the house, with views of the beach. During weekend lunches it's quiet and peaceful. Specialties include a sizzling hot plate of glass noodles with prawn, squid, pork, and vegetables. A large variety of fresh seafood and meats are prepared steamed or deep fried, and can be served with either salt, chile, or red curry paste. Beer, Mekhong whiskey, and soft drinks are available.

Meekaruna Seafood. 26/1 Naratdamri Rd., Hua Hin. ☎ **032/511-932.** Main courses 120B–500B (US$2.79–US$11.63). AE, DC, MC, V. Daily 10am–10pm. Near the fishing pier. SEAFOOD.

This small family-run restaurant serves fresh fish prepared in many Thai and Chinese styles on a wooden deck overlooking the main fishing pier in Hua Hin. The menu is in English (with photographs), and you'll find the lack of hype—compared to the other fish places with their flashy entrances and hustling touts—refreshing. Naturally, a place like this has great tom yam goong—also try fried crab cakes, fish served in any number of styles, and my favorite—baby clams fried in chile sauce. Wear bug repellent!

Palm Seafood Pavilion. Hotel Sofitel Central, 1 Damnoenkasem Rd., Hua Hin. ☎ **032/ 512021.** Reservations recommended. Main courses 540B–800B (US$12.56–US$18.60); seafood buffet 650B (US$15.12) per person. AE, DC, MC, V. Daily noon–2:30pm and 6–10:30pm. On the waterfront end of Main St. CONTINENTAL.

Hotel Sofitel Central's crystal pavilion close to the beach offers a very romantic dining experience. Attentive but discreet service, beautiful table settings and linen, soothing mood music, and excellent, elegantly prepared food all contribute in pleasing harmony. The menu changes quite often, but always highlights fresh seafood, which is prepared in continental style with Asian touches. For something different I tried the simmered pomfret with Chinese plums, bacon, and mushrooms smothered in sautéed vegetables, which was light, healthy, and full of flavor. They also do a mean salmon poached with white wine in lobster sauce with sliced lobster and mushrooms. With a fine selection of wines and a dessert menu that is an eyeful of sweet goodies, this is the best choice for fine dining in Hua Hin. Be sure to call ahead, as they frequently book private barbecues and parties.

Sontalay Terrace. The Cha-Am Methavalai Hotel, 220 Ruamchit Rd. (Beach Rd.), Cha-Am. ☎ **032/433-250.** Main courses 80B–250B (US$1.86–US$5.81). AE, DC, JCB, MC, V. THAI/WESTERN SEAFOOD.

Operated by the Methavalai Hotel, but located across the street on a beach terrace under the trees, this seafood joint is perhaps the classiest offering in town. In the afternoons, lunch and snacks are served from their menu, which includes sandwiches and burgers, while at dinner, tables are romantically lit by candles and overhead torches hung from the trees. I was going to try their lobster thermidor so I could report it to you people, but got sidetracked by a savory baked rice with seafood flavored with ginger and soya and the fried herb chicken wrapped in pandan leaves (with tangy sweet chile sauce on the side). If the lobster is as good as these other dishes, I'm sure you'll love it.

THINGS TO SEE & DO IN HUA HIN & CHA-AM

While most of the larger resorts will plan **water sports** activities for you upon request, you can still arrange your own from operators on the beach. Jet skis (which most of the resorts have given up due to accidents and pollution) can still be rented from these guys for 500B (US$11.63) per hour, in addition to windsurfing gear (300B/US$6.98 per hour) and Hobie Cats (600B/US$13.95 per hour). Call **Western Tours** (11 Damnoenkasem Rd., Hua Hin; ☎ **032/512-560;** fax 032/512-560; 1,500B/US$34.88 per person) for **snorkeling trips** to outer islands. **Lucky Sea Tours** (cellular ☎ **01/ 824-9419;** 750B/US$17.44 per person) will take you **fishing** on a Thai fishing boat which heads out for nearby Ko Singtao (Lion Island), when they get enough takers. Scuba diving trips are coordinated by **Coral Divers** (7 Naresdamri Rd., Hua Hin; cellular ☎ **01/432-8180;** 1,500B–2,000B/US$34.88–US$46.51 per person), in addition to fishing, snorkeling, and island-hopping trips at Ko Singtao. Scuba trips are only as deep as 5 meters around the small island.

Meanwhile, back on terra firma, the other favorite activity in Hua Hin and Cha-Am is **golf,** and some really fine courses may lure you out despite the heat. The best places to try are the centrally located Royal Hua Hin Golf Course and the Springfield Royal Country Club, which is also home to the Springfield Golf Academy staffed with PGA pros. Reservations are suggested and necessary most weekends. **Royal Hua Hin Golf Course** (Damnoenkasem Road near the Hua Hin Railway Station; ☎ **032/ 512-475,** or 02/241-1360 in Bangkok), Thailand's first championship golf course, opened in 1924 and was recently upgraded. It features topiary figures along its fairways and is open daily 6am to 6pm. **Springfield Royal Country Club** (193 Huay-Sai Nua, Petchkasem Road, Cha-Am; ☎ **032/471-303;** fax 032/471-324), was designed by Jack Nicklaus in 1993, this course is clever in design in a beautiful valley setting.

Outside the resort areas, there are a few wonderful natural and cultural attractions. Set aside a day for a trip to **Phetchaburi** (see section following Hua Hin and Cha-Am). Just outside Hua Hin visit the **Mareukatayawan Palace,** also known as the Teakwood Mansion (open 8:30am to 4pm daily, free admission). Built and designed in 1924 by King Rama VI, it served for many years as the royal summer residence, but is now open to the public.

If You Get Stuck in Surat Thani

Surat Thani, 644 kilometers (400 miles) south of Bangkok, is believed to have been an important center of the Sumatra-based Srivijaya Empire in the 9th and 10th centuries. In recent history, the small town served as the jumping-off point to the resort island of Ko Samui. But with the opening of the airport on Samui, numerous flights connect the island with Bangkok, Phuket, and other domestic and international departure points. Still, if you're traveling overland via train or bus, you'll have to spend at least a few hours in this little town. There's not a lot to keep you hanging around, except for juicy fresh oysters harvested nearby. For travel information, see the Ko Samui section below.

If you find yourself in Surat Thani for an overnight, the best place to stay is the **Wang Tai Hotel** (1 Talad Mai Rd., Surat Thani 84000; ☎ **077/283-020; fax 077/281-007**). Double room rates range from 850B to 1,000B (US$19.77 to US$23.26) and they accept American Express, MasterCard, and Visa. A 25B (US$0.58) tuk-tuk ride from the center of town, it does have the advantage of being next to the TAT office and it's the only place that is somewhat modern. Otherwise, there are a few good budget guesthouses in town operated by travel companies.

For information about Surat Thani, Ko Samui, or Ko Phangan, contact the **TAT office** in Surat (5 Talad Mai Rd.; ☎ **077/288-818**). Major banks along Talad Mai Road have ATMs and will perform currency exchanges. The **Post Office** and **Overseas Call Office** (☎ **077/272-013**) are together on Na Muang and Chonkasean roads near the center of town. The **Taksin Hospital** (☎ **077/273-239**) is at the north end of Talad Mai Road. The **Tourist Police** (☎ **077/281-300**) are with the TAT on Talad Mai Road.

For a little nature, **Khao Sam Roi Yot National Park** is a great day trip. The "Mountain of Three Hundred Peaks" is comparatively small in relation to the nation's other parks, but has nice short hikes to see panoramic views of the sea and surrounds, plus a look at wildlife. Of the park's two caves, Kaew Cave is the most interesting, housing a sala pavilion that was built in 1890 for King Chulalongkorn. Call **Western Tours** (☎ **032/512-560**; 700B/US$16.28 per person). A half-day trip to the **Pala-U waterfall** close to the Burmese border (63km/39 miles west of Hua Hin) is another nature trekking option. Nature trails take you through hills and valleys until you end up at the falls. The driver can stop at the Dole Thailand pineapple factory for a tour and tasting (☎ **032/571-177**; open daily 9am to 4pm; 200B/US$4.65 admission), and at the Kaew Cave.

Shopping action is had throughout the small streets in the center of Hua Hin, where you can find tailors and souvenir shops. The day market along Damnoenkasem Road just at the beach displays local crafts made from seashells, batik clothing, and many other handicraft finds. At night the 2-block long night market on Dechanuchit Road west of Phetchkasem Road packs in hawkers with sweet foods, cheap clothes, and all sorts of fun trinkets.

If you're looking for **nightlife** in the area, your best bet is Hua Hin. While Cha-Am has a couple notable spots, the wild west saloon style Jeep Pub (☎ **032/472-311**) and the Tiki style Bamboo Bar (☎ **032/433-292**), both on Soi Cattriya off Ruamchit (Beach) Road, Hua Hin, have a greater variety of life. A 15-minute stroll through the sois between Damnoenkasem, Poolsuk, and Dechanuchit Roads near the beach reveals all sorts of small places to stop for a cool cocktail and some fun. Hua Hin's main disco, Doodles (☎ **032/512-888**), is at the Melia Hotel on Naresdamri Road. For a little nighttime Thai culture the small shack of a **boxing** stadium on Poolsuk Road has occasional Friday night bouts (9pm; admission 250B or US$5.81). Announcements are tacked up around the village.

A SIDE TRIP TO PHETCHABURI

Phetchaburi's palace and historically significant temples highlight a fabulous day trip. There are many tour operators who coordinate day trips to Phetchaburi from Hua Hin; it's a mere 50-minute drive away. Western Tours (11 Damnoenkasem Rd.; ☎ **032/512-560**) organizes day excursions for 700B per person. While the Phra Nakorn Khiri and Khao Luang Cave are the two main stops on every tour itinerary, the city has a few other gems that are never included in the standard package. To see these I recommend hiring a car through the Hua Hin Tourist Information Service Center (☎ 032/511-047) for 1,200B (US$27.91).

The main attraction is **Phra Nakhorn Khiri** (☎ **032/428-539**), a summer palace atop the hills overlooking the city. Built in 1858 by King Mongkut (Rama IV), it was intended as not only a summer retreat for the royal family, but for foreign dignitaries as well. Combining Thai, European, and Chinese architectural styles, the palace buildings include guesthouses and a royal Khmer-style *chedi,* or temple. Once accessible via a 4-kilometer hike uphill, you'll be happy to hear there's a funicular railway to bring you to the top. The ride is 30B (US$0.70) adult, 10B (US$0.23) child; hours are Monday to Friday 8:15am to 5pm, Saturday to Sunday from 8:15am to 5:50pm. The museum is 40B (US$0.93) admission, and opens daily from 9am to 4pm.

Another fascinating sight at Phetchaburi, the **Khao Luang Cave,** houses over 170 Buddha images underground. Find a guide outside for 40B (US$0.93). If you're not with a group, it's a good idea—their English isn't too hot, but they do point out many cave features that might otherwise be missed. A 20B (US$0.47) donation is optional once inside.

Standard tours rarely include **Wat Yai Suwannaram.** One of very few remaining royal temples built during the Ayutthaya period, the teak ordination hall was moved from Ayutthaya after the second Burmese invasion on the city. The proof is in the axe chop battle scar on the building's carved wood doors. Inside, murals represent religious scenes filed with Brahmans, hermits, giants, and deities. The young monk apprentices will seek out a key and take you inside.

The other wat with impressive paintings, **Wat Ko Keo Suttharam,** also dates back to the 17th century, but with murals from the 1730s. These are far more representational and, of some interest to Westerners; there are several panels depicting the arrival in the Ayutthaya court of European courtesans and diplomats (including a Jesuit dressed in Buddhist garb).

Another amazing wat, the Khmer **Wat Kamphaeng Laeng,** shows just how far the Khmer empire extended. Originally constructed during the reign of Jayavaraman VII (1157–1207) as a Hindu shrine, it was once covered in decorative stucco, some of which remains. During the Ayutthaya period, it was converted to a Buddhist temple.

As for spending the night in Phetchaburi, I don't really recommend it, as there are no comfortable accommodations around. For a lunch break, **Num Tien** (539 Moo 1, Phetchakasaemkao Rd.; ☎ **032/425-121**) still reigns as the best lunch eatery in town. An open air cafe cooled under a columned verandah, this well established restaurant serves a combination of Thai and Chinese specialties at cheap prices.

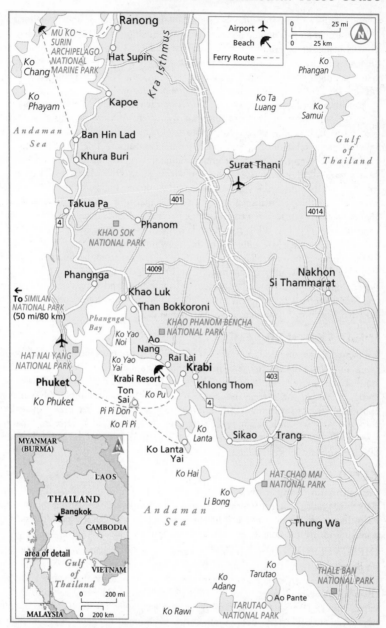

Airport ✈
Beach 🏖
Ferry Route - - - -

0   25 mi
0   25 km

Ranong

MU KO
SURIN
ARCHIPELAGO
NATIONAL
MARINE PARK

Hat Supin

Ko
Chang

Ko
Phayam

*Andaman
Sea*

Kapoe

Kra Isthmus

Ban Hin Lad

Khura Buri

Takua Pa

4

KHAO SOK
NATIONAL PARK

Phanom

401

4009

Phangnga

← To SIMILAN
NATIONAL PARK
(50 mi/80 km)

Khao Luk
Than Bokkoroni

*Phangnga
Bay*

Ko Yao
Noi

HAT NAI YANG
NATIONAL PARK

Ko Yao
Yai

Ao
Nang

Rai Lai

KHAO PHANOM BENCHA
NATIONAL PARK

Krabi

Phuket

Krabi Resort

Ton
Sai

Ko Pu

Khlong Thom

403

Ko Phuket

Pi Pi Don

4

Ko Pi Pi

Ko
Lanta

Sikao

Trang

Ko Lanta
Yai

Ko Hai

Ko
Li Bong

HAT CHAO MAI
NATIONAL PARK

*Andaman
Sea*

Thung Wa

Ko Ta
Luang

Ko
Samui

Ko
Phangan

*Gulf
of
Thailand*

Surat Thani

4014

Nakhon
Si Thammarat

Ko
Tarutao

Ko
Adang

Ao Pante

THALE BAN
NATIONAL PARK

Ko Rawi

TARUTAO
NATIONAL PARK

MYANMAR
(BURMA)

LAOS

THAILAND

Bangkok

CAMBODIA

area of detail

*Gulf
of
Thailand*

VIETNAM

0   200 mi
0   200 km

MALAYSIA

9   Ko Samui

The island of Ko Samui lies 84 kilometers (52 miles) off Thailand's east coast in the Gulf of Thailand, near the mainland commercial town of Surat Thani. Since the 1850s, Ko Samui has been visited by Chinese merchants sailing from Hainan Island in the South China Sea to trade coconuts and cotton, the island's two most profitable products.

Ko Samui's coconuts are among Southeast Asia's most coveted, principally for their flavor. More than two million coconuts a month are shipped to Bangkok. Much of the fruit is made into coconut oil, a process that involves scraping the meat out of the shell, drying it, and pressing it to produce a sweet oil. To assist farmers with Ko Samui's indigenous breed of tall palm trees, monkeys are trained to climb them, shake off the ripe coconuts, and gather them for the boss man.

You'll hear Ko Samui compared to Phuket all the time. While Phuket enjoys international fame (or notoriety, depending on your point of view) as a gorgeous beach resort heaven, Ko Samui attracts those who want to avoid the hype and settle for more down-to-earth relaxation. Once upon a time Ko Samui's fine beaches were less crowded, and simple bungalow accommodations and eateries made for a more off-the-beaten-path island experience. As Ko Samui's reputation as the "alternative Thai island" grew, so did the number of visitors landing on its shores. Increasing demand inspired the opening of an international airport in 1988, that now has over 20 packed daily flights. In recent years big resorts are getting in on the action, opening up huge accommodations à la Phuket. While they provide more comforts and facilities, in some ways they lack the carefree Ko Samui charm that drew travelers here in the first place.

The high season on Ko Samui is from mid-December to mid-January. January to April has the best weather, before its gets hot. October through mid-December are the wettest months, with November bringing extreme rains and fierce winds that make the east side of the island rough for swimming. Some years, the island's west side is buffeted by summer monsoons from the mainland.

WHAT'S ON IN KO SAMUI

Ko Samui has an enormous amount of independently produced literature for visitors. Good magazines to keep your eyes peeled for are *Accommodation Samui,* with detailed hotel, restaurant, and other listings; *What's on Samui,* for adverts and articles about things to do on the island; and *Samui Guide,* with practical tour and transport specifics. There are at least a half-dozen map guides. I like the free map provided by Bangkok Airways, with major beaches highlighted. The small Tourist Information Center (☎ 077/420-504) in Nathon, on the waterfront street to the left of the piers, also has some useful information.

GETTING THERE

Getting to Ko Samui is more simple than it at first appears. Direct flights from Bangkok, Phuket, Pattaya (U-Tapao), and even Singapore make visiting the island a snap. In addition there are several bus and train options to Surat Thani (the nearest mainland town) that connect to ferry and speedboat services.

DIRECT FLIGHTS TO KO SAMUI   Seventeen flights depart daily from Bangkok on Bangkok Airways (in Bangkok ☎ 02/229-3456), pretty much one every 40 minutes or so between the hours of 8am and 5pm. Two daily flights from Phuket (Bangkok Airways **Phuket** office ☎ 076/225-033), and another daily from the U-Tapao airport near Pattaya (Bangkok Airways Pattaya office ☎ 038/412-382), connect these major beach destinations, with additional Bangkok Airways flights connecting the northern cities through Bangkok. From Singapore, Bangkok Airways flies direct each day (Singapore office ☎ 65/545-8481). In addition, you can also fly directly between Samui and Phnom Penh four times a week (Phnom Penh office ☎ 855-23/300-409). Their offices in Samui are at 54/4 Moo 3, Tambon Bo Phud, Chaweng (☎ 077/422-512) and at the airport (☎ 077/425-601).

Ko Samui

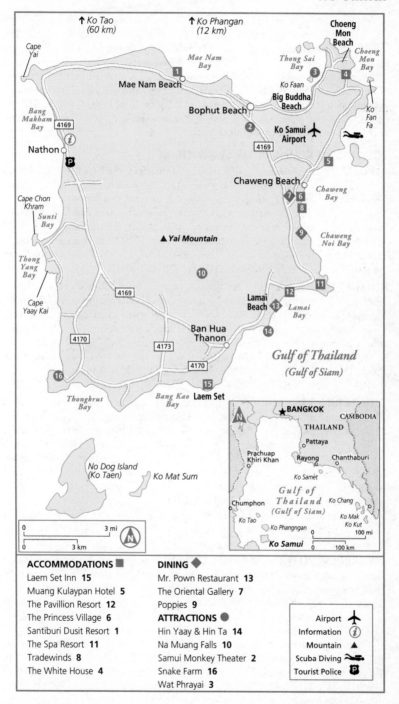

ACCOMMODATIONS ■
Laem Set Inn **15**
Muang Kulaypan Hotel **5**
The Pavillion Resort **12**
The Princess Village **6**
Santiburi Dusit Resort **1**
The Spa Resort **11**
Tradewinds **8**
The White House **4**

DINING ◆
Mr. Pown Restaurant **13**
The Oriental Gallery **7**
Poppies **9**
ATTRACTIONS ●
Hin Yaay & Hin Ta **14**
Na Muang Falls **10**
Samui Monkey Theater **2**
Snake Farm **16**
Wat Phrayai **3**

Airport ✈
Information ⓘ
Mountain ▲
Scuba Diving
Tourist Police 🅿

Ko Samui Airport is a great little airport—open air pavilions with thatch roofs surrounded by gardens and palms. You'll really feel like you've landed in paradise. If you're staying at a larger resort, airport minivan shuttles can be arranged when you book your room. If not, just out at the main road you'll find songtao, pickup truck taxis, that can take you to the beach you're staying at. If there are many of you, trips can be as low as 30B (US$0.70), depending on how far you're going. For one or two people going a longer distance, they may try to up the price to over 100B (US$2.33). If you depart Ko Samui via the airport, there's an additional 150B (US$3.49) airport tax that's usually added to your ticket charge.

GETTING TO KO SAMUI VIA SURAT THANI

AIR/FERRY PACKAGE Thai Airways (☎ 02/535-2084 in Bangkok or 077/272-610 in Surat Thani) has two daily flights from Bangkok to Surat Thani (trip time: 70 minutes). While Thai Airlines offers a shuttle to Surat Thani town, if you're heading direct to Ko Samui, you'll want to pre-arrange a combination shuttle bus and ferry trip through Songserm Travel. Songserm's main office is in Bangkok (33/11–12 Changwattana Rd., Pakkret; ☎ 02/984-5600; fax 02/984-5641), with branches in Surat Thani (30/2 Moo 3; ☎ 077/285-124; fax 077/285-127) and on Ko Samui (64/1–2 Nathon Pier; ☎ 077/421-316; fax 077/420-167).

TRAIN/FERRY PACKAGE Ten trains leave daily from Bangkok's Hua Lampong station to Surat Thani (trip time: 13 hours; second-class sleeper 468B/US$10.88, second-class seat 288B/US$6.70). Minitrucks meet trains to transport passengers to Surat Thani town, but Songserm Travel can arrange a train station pickup to take you direct to the ferry to Ko Samui. Songserm's main office is in Bangkok at 33/11–12 Changwattana Rd., Pakkret (☎ 02/984-5600; fax 02/984-5641), with branches in Surat Thani (30/2 Moo 3; ☎ 077/285-124; fax 077/285-127) and on Ko Samui (64/1–2 Nathon Pier; ☎ 077/421-316; fax 077/420-167).

BUS/FERRY PACKAGE Songserm has daily bus and ferry packages from Bangkok, and other cities in the peninsula. Buses depart from Bangkok's Khao San Road (172 Khao San Rd., Banglamphu; ☎ 02/281-1463) and their main office (33/11–12 Changwattana Rd., Pakkret; ☎ 02/984-5600; fax 02/984-5641); and from Phuket (51–53 Satun Rd.; ☎ 076/222-570). Prices vary; from Bangkok an air-con bus/ferry package is 230B (US$5.35), while if you want VIP travel (with larger reclining seats) you'll pay 500B (US$11.63) for the combination ticket. From Phuket, the air-con package trip costs 350B (US$8.14).

Songserm has offices in Surat Thani (30/2 Moo 3; ☎ 077/285-124; fax 077/285-127) and on Ko Samui (64/1–2 Nathon Pier; ☎ 077/421-316; fax 077/420-167).

BY EXPRESS BOAT FROM SURAT THANI Early morning boats connecting Ko Samui to the mainland run a circuit from Surat Thani to Ko Samui, Ko Phangan, Ko Tao, and on to Chumphon north of Surat Thani and back again. The total trip is about 4 hours, while the Surat–Samui leg is 2½ hours. Rates are as follows: Surat–Samui 150B (US$3.49); Samui–Phangan 95B (US$2.21); Phangan–Tao 250B (US$5.81); Tao–Chumphon 400B (US$9.30).

Contact **Songserm:** in Surat Thani (30/2 Moo 3; ☎ 077/285-124; fax 077/285-127); in Ko Samui (64/1–2 Nathon Pier; ☎ 077/421-316; fax 077/420-167); in Ko Phangan (44/43 Moo 1, Thong Sala Pier; ☎ 077/377-046); in Ko Tao (Mae Had Beach; cellular ☎ 01/229-5630); and in Chumphon (66/1 Thatapao Rd.; ☎ 077/502-023). In most cases, they can arrange your transportation to the ferry pier.

If you miss the morning boat from Surat Thani, **Phantip** (☎ 077/421-221) has an afternoon bus and ferry package for comparable prices.

You probably won't have to worry about transportation once you reach Nathon, Ko Samui's ferry pier. Touts on the ferry offer very cheap rides, some as low as 20B (US$0.47) if they can get a packed truckload from the boat (and be warned, they'll tie people to the roof if they can get an additional 20B for it). If you have no accommodations booking, many will even make a few stops along the way so you can check a few places out before deciding. If you wait until you reach the pier, there are many more songtao waiting to take people to their destinations.

GETTING AROUND

BY SONGTAO   Songtao, pickup truck taxis, are the easiest and most efficient way to get around the island. They advertise their destinations to such beaches as Lamai, Chaweng, and Mai Nam with colorfully painted signs. From Nathon most go north and clockwise as far as Chaweng; some head south as far as Lamai; an interchange is necessary at a pavilion near Chaweng Noi for those wishing to proceed further in either direction. You can hail one anywhere along the round-island road. To visit a site off the beaten track (or one other than that painted on a truck's sign), ask the driver to make a detour. Check when your songtao stops running. It's usually around sundown, but some will hang around outside the discos in Chaweng to take night owls home to other beaches. The cost is 20B to 40B (US$0.47 to US$0.93) one-way, with steeper fares after hours.

BY MOTORCYCLE OR JEEP   Ko Samui's roads are narrow, winding, poorly maintained, and not lighted at night. In the island's first decade of tourism, more than 350 foreigners died in vehicle accidents. Still, renting a bike or jeep is the easiest way around if you want to get out to see all of the different beaches. Use extreme caution, and wear a helmet when on a moped or motorcycle. Your defensive driving skills will be required to navigate around slow motorcycles and the occasional wandering dog.

For good car rentals at an affordable price, **Budget** (☎ 077/427-188) will pick you up with your car at the airport or jetty, or deliver to your resort. They charge 1,375B (US$31.98) for a Suzuki Caribian. At the beach towns every one of the many tour operators will rent you a Caribian for 700B to 900B (US$16.28 to US$20.93) a day. These guys are real lax about the whole business of international driver licenses. You don't even necessarily have to prove you can drive, just show your passport and pay the man. Sound scary? You should see their insurance policies.

Many other places along the beaches will rent you a motorcycle—anything from a scooter for 150B (US$3.49) a day to a chopper for 700B to 900B (US$16.28 to US$20.93) a day. Insist they provide a helmet.

Fast Facts: Ko Samui

Banks/Currency Exchange   Find major banks in Nathon, along Taweratphakdee Road, running parallel to the waterfront road. Money-changing facilities are available at each beach.

Internet/E-mail   For Internet service on Chaweng head for the Go Internet Café opposite the Central Samui Beach Resort (☎ 077/230-535). The best Internet and business services overall are at Sawadee Internet Service (131 Moo 4, T. Maret Lamai, Lamai Beach; ☎ 077/231-176).

Police   For Tourist Police emergencies dial ☎ 1699.

Post Office/Mail   The main post office (☎ 077/421-013) is near the Tourist Information Center by the waterfront, but you probably won't want to hike all the way back to the main pier to post a letter. Any hotel or bungalow will handle it for you.

Telephone   There are pay telephones, both coin and card, and in the main villages at Chaweng and Lamai beaches you can find overseas calling offices to call home and send or receive faxes. The area code is 077.

RESORTS & BUNGALOWS ON KO SAMUI

Every habitable cove on Ko Samui has at least one bungalow complex and snack cafe, but each community has a different personality. Chaweng is the most popular beach, with plentiful accommodations, restaurants, nightlife, shopping, and conveniences. The next popular beach is Lamai. It's a little shorter than Chaweng, but has some good and less expensive options for bungalows and restaurants. I've concentrated on these two areas, as they have the most activity, but I've also included a few quiet and atmospheric resorts on other parts of the island. You'll want to look into these places if you value the quiet relaxing life.

FYI, Chaweng is the longest beach with the most sea sports activities, but has the most shallow water. The deepest bay, for good swimming, is at Mae Nam (where you'll find the Dusit Santiburi resort). For the best snorkeling and skin diving, check out the rocky area between Chaweng and Lamai beaches. This information may impact where you decide to stay.

When planning your trip keep in mind the highest peak season rates are between December 20 and January 10, when rooms are up to double the usual price. After January 10, rooms get cheaper, but still reflect "peak season" increases. Prices again jump up during the summer peak season from mid-July to mid-September. Which means for the best accommodations bargains, try to come between either May and mid-July or between mid-September and mid-December. In the reviews that follow I've included current peak and off-peak prices as a guideline.

CHAWENG & CHAWENG NOI BAYS

The two Chaweng beaches (the main "**Chaweng**" and south "**Chaweng Noi**") are undoubtedly the most popular destinations on Ko Samui—for better or worse. The benefits of Chaweng are the many conveniences provided by consumer demand—you have more money changing, Internet, laundry, travel and rental agencies, medical facilities, shopping, restaurants, and nightlife, not to mention more choices for accommodations. Chaweng can be a blast if you don't mind a little hustle and bustle. If you bore easily from hours on the beach or get waterlogged from the surf, there are plenty of activity options just near the beach.

The drawback of Chaweng is the crowds. Travelers draw businesses, which in turn draw more travelers. It seems the latest sport is Chaweng Bashing—putting the place down for being grotesquely touristy and overdeveloped. In defense of Chaweng, most of the people I hear putting the place down usually end up spending time here for one reason or another!

The main island circle road (Highway 4169) is ³⁄₁₀ to 1.8 miles inland from the beach, but there's a one-lane road closer to the water. The beach here is the longest on the island, and despite the crowds remains surprisingly clean, with soft white sand edged with coconut palms. Resorts snuggle between the beach and the main road like little villages.

ACCOMMODATIONS
IN CHAWENG

✪ **Muang Kulaypan Hotel.** 100 Moo 2, Chaweng Beach Rd., Koh Samui 84320, Surat Thani. ☎ **077/230-850,** or 02/713-0668 for Bangkok reservations. Fax 077/230-031 or 02/713-0667. E-mail: Kulaypan@sawadee.com. 40 units. A/C MINIBAR TV TEL. Peak season 2,800B–4,600B (US$65.12–US$106.98) double; 5,100B (US$118.60) suite. Off-peak 1,900B–3,100B (US$44.19–US$72.09) double; 3,500B (US$81.40) suite. AE, MC, V Northern tip of Chaweng Beach.

I've never seen a resort like this in Thailand. Within this newer two-story building, designers have combined warm natural woods and rich local textiles with clean contemporary lines and stylistic minimalism. While rooms are sparse, it's all part of the design concept—think of it as a sort of minimalist approach to resort decor. Grace in simplicity, with some tasteful Thai touches. The four poster platform bed is the centerpiece, and all rooms have either balconies or private gardens. Overall the effect is very cooling. Budsaba Restaurant serves all kinds of cuisine—including many vegetarian selections. The pool is just lovely, with gardens and a great view. This resort is perhaps one of the most attractive you will find in Chaweng, especially for the price tag.

✪ **The Princess Village.** 101/1 Moo 3, Chaweng Beach, Ko Samui 84320, Surat Thani. ☎ **077/422-216.** Fax 077/422-382. 12 units. A/C MINIBAR. Peak season 3,400B–4,600B (US$79.07–US$106.98) double; 4,800B–5,200B (US$111.63–US$120.93) suite. Off-peak 2,050B–3,250B (US$47.67–US$75.58) double; 3,400B–3,850B (US$79.07–US$89.53) suite. AE, MC, V. Middle of Chaweng Beach.

If you've wondered what sleeping in Jim Thompson's House or the Suan Pakkard Palace—both in Bangkok—might be like, try the regal Princess Village. Traditional teak houses from Ayutthaya have been restored and placed around a lushly planted garden. Several have sea views and each is on stilts above its own lotus pond; use-worn stairs lead up to a large verandah with roll-down bamboo screens.

Inside, you'll find a grand teak bed covered in embroidered silk or cotton and antique furniture and artwork worthy of the Ramas. Small, carved dressing tables and spacious bathrooms contain painted ceramics, silverware, a porcelain dish, a large khlong jar for water storage, or other Thai details amid the modern conveniences. Traditional shuttered windows on all sides have no screens, but lacy mosquito netting and a ceiling fan, combined with sea breezes, create Thai-style ventilation. The view from the terrace cafe on the beach creates a wonderful setting for an afternoon beer.

Tradewinds. 17/14 Moo 3, Chaweng Beach, Ko Samui 84320, Surat Thani. ☎ **077/230-602.** Fax 077/231-247. 20 units. A/C MINIBAR. Peak season 2,500B–3,000B (US$58.14–US$69.77) double bungalow; off-peak 1,500B–2,000B (US$34.88–US$46.51) double bungalow. AE, DC, MC, V.

In the center of Chaweng, Tradewinds has one of the best locations of the beach's accommodations. Step out the front door and you're in the center of the fun: restaurants, clubs, shopping. Meanwhile, the other side of the resort opens out to Chaweng's long, lovely beach. From the higher-priced bungalows you can step right off your front porch into the sand. The other bungalows are placed in shady secluded gardens, not far from the beach. All are modern and fully furnished with large beds and rattan furnishings. Spotless and bright, they're perfect for travelers who want the intimate feeling of a bungalow village but don't want to sacrifice modern conveniences. If you don't want to go out for a meal, the superb Thai restaurant (with Western selections as well) is romantically situated on the beach.

Tradewinds is home to Samui's catamaran sailing center, and also arranges daily snorkeling, trekking, and kayaking trips.

DINING
IN CHAWENG

⊙ **The Oriental Gallery.** 39/1 Moo 3, Chaweng Beach. ☎ **077/422-200.** Reservations recommended during peak season. Main courses 60B–200B (US$1.40–US$4.65). AE, MC, V. Daily 2–11:30pm. THAI.

Opened in 1991, the Oriental Gallery combines a fine arts and antiques gallery with a swanky little cafe. Gorgeous treasures fill the dining area, both indoors and in the small outdoor patio garden. You'll almost be too busy admiring the pieces to look at the menu, which features some appetizing Thai soups, noodle dishes, and more. The selections are prepared and presented with similar good taste, and are not too spicy for tender foreign tongues. The friendly and knowledgeable gallery owners are around to chat about Thai antiques and art, and to explain any pieces that catch your eye.

Poppies. South Chaweng Beach. ☎ **077/422-419.** Reservations recommended during peak season. Main courses 80B–240B (US$1.86–US$5.58). AE, MC, V. Daily 7am–10pm. THAI/INTERNATIONAL.

Famous for its Bali-style seaside feel, Poppies is equally famous for fresh seafood by the beach. The romantic atmosphere under the large thatch pavilion is enhanced by soft lighting and live international jazz music. Guest chefs from around the world mean the menu is ever changing, but you can be sure their seafood selections are some of the best catches around. A good place, especially if you're romancing someone special.

LAMAI BAY

The long sand beach on Lamai Bay is comparable to Chaweng's (see "Chaweng & Chaweng Noi Bays," above), but the clientele is decidedly rowdier and more colorful, if not always younger. Though there are many bungalows, few are above the most primitive of standards, and they tend to attract backpackers. I've only listed one resort here, because it's the only place that's comfortable enough for me to recommend. However, there's lots of new construction, most of it in the budget category, and a range of cafes, bars, discos, tourist services, and bungalows make Lamai the cheapest resort on the island.

The north end of the beach strip is known as Coral Cove, a rocky area where bungalows are built up on the hillside. South of it, along the inland lagoon where fishermen moor their boats, there's a paved service road and beach access lane, both between the shoreline and the main island circle road. Public minitrucks cruise the inner service road and will deliver you to the "back door" of most of the beachfront bungalows. Lamai Noi is the quieter south end of the beach, somewhat removed from the fray by its autonomous network of inland service roads.

ACCOMMODATIONS
In Lamai

The Pavillion Resort. Lamai Beach, Ko Samui 84140, Surat Thani. ☎ **077/424030.** Fax 077/424420. 50 units. A/C MINIBAR. Peak season 3,440B–4,257B (US$80–US$99) double in hotel wing; 4,041B–4,859B (US$94–US$113) cottage. Off-peak 2,623–3,440B (US$61–US$80) double in hotel wing; 2,838B–3,440B (US$66–US$80) cottage. AE, DC, MC, V. North end of Lamai Beach.

One of Lamai's newer facilities, this resort has attached rooms in a hotel block and Polynesian-style octagonal bungalows, all scattered throughout the beachfront grounds (there are limited sea views). It is possibly the most deluxe accommodation you'll find on Lamai. Hotel rooms are nicely appointed, each with its own safe, and have good-sized patios for sunbathing. The larger bungalows have a campy primitive feel, as well as the comfort of a private bath and hot water. The pool and dining pavilion are right on the surf—combined with ground-floor hotel rooms, it makes for comfortable, easy access resort for the disabled. The proximity to Lamai's nightlife is a plus for most guests, while the beachside swimming pool and Jacuzzi, with cafe dining and bar, provide a very quiet escape from the goings-on in the rest of Lamai.

The Spa Resort. 171–2 Moo 4, Lamai Beach, Koh Samui 84320, Surat Thani. ☎ **077/ 230-855.** Fax 077/424-126. www.spasamui.com. 18 units. 250B–1,800B (US$5.81–US$41.86) year-round. MC, V. North of Lamai Beach.

Book your reservations well in advance! For long-term stays or just a daytime spa visit, The Spa Resort Health Center has a fantastic reputation on the island (and beyond). From chi kung, yoga, Thai massage, fasting, herbal cleansing, plus health and beauty face and body treatments—they'll plan everything, and at an affordable price. Their latest promotion was for Thai massage, herbal steam, cleansing facial, and body wrap for only 700B (US$16.28)! Accommodations are the simplest of the simple—no air-conditioning, TV or telephones; your only luxuries are fans and private bathrooms. Higher priced bungalows are those situated closer to the beach. Their vegetarian restaurant serves dishes with particular care to cleansing bodies. At these prices anyone can enjoy the benefits of spa life.

Outside Chaweng & Lamai

✪ **Laem Set Inn.** 110 Moo 2, Hua Thanon, Laem Set, Ko Samui 84310, Surat Thani. ☎ **077/424-393.** Fax 077/424-394. www.laemset.com. 15 units. Peak season 3,225B (US$75) bungalow with fan, 5,160B (US$120) air-conditioned bungalow, 8,600B (US$200) suite. Off-peak: 2,580B (US$60) bungalow with fan, 4,300B (US$100) air-conditioned bungalow, 8,600B (US$200) suite. AE, MC, V. Arrange hotel transfers when you book your room.

This is lauded in fashion magazines, newspaper travel sections, and guidebooks as one of the most delightful small resorts blending a cozy hideaway into the handsome hillside. Kayaks, mountain bikes, and snorkel gear are available to explore this location's stunning scenery. The elevated pool seamlessly blends with the gulf, reflecting sea and sky. The pavilion restaurant serves gourmet fare and delicious Thai seafood.

The most exclusive accommodation is the private two-bedroom house, transplanted from a nearby island and converted to a suite, decorated with hand-hewn furniture and native grace. The Ma-rat suites are two connected bedrooms and an open, eight-bed sleeping loft draped with mosquito netting that's perfect for a bevy of children. Large porches bookend the bedrooms and provide a perch for drinking in views beyond the pounding surf of No Dog Island. The basic screened-window, fan-cooled rooms are comfortable, but less charming than the thatched bungalows, which have beds canopied with mosquito netting and a large loft above. This boutique inn (it was built as a private club) has a handcrafted feel, far from the crowds, rustic and intimate. It's unique—an ideal getaway.

Santiburi Dusit Resort. 12/12 Moo 1, Tambol Mae Nam, Ko Samui, Surat Thani 84330. ☎ **077/425-031.** Fax 077/425-040. www.dusit.com. 73 units. A/C MINIBAR TV TEL. Peak season 20,382B–28,896B (US$474–US$672) Equatorial rooms and suites; 22,274B–26,058B (US$518–US$606) villa; 46,870B (US$1,090) 2-bedroom beach suite. Off-peak 13,072B–14,749B (US$304–US$343) Equatorial rooms and suites; 13,244B–20,640B (US$308–US$480) villa; 25,542B (US$594) 2-bedroom beach suite. AE, DC, JCB, MC, V.

A quiet getaway, this tranquil resort—the name means peaceful town—is a village of palatial pavilions informally arrayed around the largest swimming pool on the island (an oval more than 150 feet, or 50 meters, long). A small river winds through its lush tropical gardens to the long, clean beach. Modeled after a mountain retreat built by

King Rama IV more than a century ago and strongly influenced by Western neoclassical architecture, yet distinctly Thai, it evokes that earlier era without neglecting modern comfort and convenience. Guests are welcomed by the sounds of splashing water and a relaxed but attentive staff in a cool, intimate lobby that opens onto the spacious 23-acre compound. Rooms are large, lush, and inviting, with the special warmth of natural teak, traditionally styled furniture, handwoven fabrics, and other distinctive Asian touches; the bathrooms are especially large. Three dining establishments, one Thai, one East-meets-West, and a poolside cafe, mean you don't have to trek to the nearest beach for variety. Dusit will arrange any water sports you'd like. There are also tennis courts, a squash court, and a fitness center.

The White House. 59/3 Moo 5, Choeng Mon Beach, Ko Samui 84320, Surat Thani. ☎ **077/245-315.** Fax 077/245-318. 40 units. A/C MINIBAR TV TEL. Peak season 4,600B–5,100B (US$107–US$118) double; from 5,600B (US$130) suite. Off-peak 2,600B–3,100B (US$60 –US$72) double; from 3,600B (US$84) suite. AE, MC, V. On Choeng Mon Beach.

This new resort in the graceful Ayutthaya style, built around a central garden with a lotus pond and swimming pool, is dripping with atmosphere. The lobby—almost a museum—is impeccably decorated with original Thai artwork and images. Spacious and elegant rooms with tea and coffee service flank a central walkway that's lined with orchids and other attractive plants in large pots. Down by the beach there's a pool with a bar and an especially graceful teak sala. The resort's quality Swiss management team, with proven success on Ko Samui, assures a pleasant stay. White House, in the northeastern part of the island, is far from the action of Chaweng and Lamai, but there are jeep and motorbike rentals available.

Dining In Lamai

Mr. Pown Restaurant. 124/137 Moo 3, Lamai Beach. ☎ **01/970-7758.** Seafood at market prices. Daily 10am–10pm. MC, V. SEAFOOD.

Of all the seafood places along the main drag in Lamai, Mr. Pown is the nicest. Fresh seafood is carefully laid on ice in front of the entrance, so you can choose your own toothy fish or local lobster. A patio of a restaurant, tables near the front railing are great fun for people watching. The menu is an extensive list of seafood of all kinds prepared in many Chinese, Thai, and Western styles. There's also an assortment of accompanying Chinese and Thai soups, and vegetable and meat dishes. Be warned, the lobster is delicious, but expensive.

Exploring the Island

Local aquanauts agree that the best **scuba diving** is off Ko Tao, a small island north of Ko Phangan and Ko Samui. Since conditions vary with the seasons, the cluster of tiny islands south of Samui, Mu Ko Angthong National Park, are often more reliable destinations. Follow the advice of a local dive shop on where to go. Easy Divers, in operation for over 10 years, has locations in Chaweng (on the beach road next to Silver Sand Resort; ☎ 077/230-548) and Lamai (main road between Sand Sea Resort and Lamai Resort; ☎ 077/231-190). They offer all sorts of PADI courses, daily dive tours to 13 different sites, international safety standard boats, good equipment, and complete insurance packages.

Some of the finest **snorkeling** off Ko Samui is found along the rocky coast between Chaweng Noi and Lamai bays. Several shops along Chaweng Beach rent snorkeling gear for about 100B per day. For **catamaran sailing,** check out Tradewinds Resort in Chaweng (☎ 077/230-602). Run by John Stall, one of the pioneer bungalow operators here, he is familiar with local sailing conditions and great routes.

Ko Samui's famed **Wonderful Rocks**—the most important of which are the sex-organ shaped **Hin Yaay & Hin Ta** (Grandmother and Grandfather Stones)—are located at the far southern end of Lamai Beach. To get to them, walk about an hour south of Chaweng Beach, or take any minitruck to Lamai Beach and get off at Paradise Bungalows.

The gold-tiled **Wat Phrayai** (Big Buddha), more than 24 meters (80 ft.) tall, sits atop Ko Faan (Barking Deer Island), a small islet connected to the shore by a dirt causeway almost 305 meters (1,000 ft.) long. Though of little historic value, it's an imposing presence on the northeast coast and is one of Samui's primary landmarks. It's open all day; 20B (US$0.47) contribution recommended. It's easy to reach, just hop on any songtao going to Big Buddha Beach. You can't miss it.

The main island road forks at Ban Hua Thanon in the southeast corner. Past the village of Ban Thurian, the road climbs north past **Na Muang Falls,** a pleasant waterfall once visited by many kings of the Chakri dynasty. After the rainy season ends in December, it reaches a height of almost 30 meters (100 ft.) and a width of about 20 meters (66 ft.). Na Muang is a steamy 5-kilometer (3-mile) walk from the coast road and makes for a nice bathing and picnic stop. Feel free to trek to the falls on the back of an **elephant**. Na Muang Trekking (cellular ☎ 01/397-5430) will take you for a half-hour trip or longer.

Along Samui's main roads, you'll find little hand-painted signs along the lines of "Monkey Work Coconut." These home-grown tourist spots show off monkey skills involved in the local coconut industry—very interesting how they're trained to climb the trees, identify ripe coconuts, twist them from the tree and collect them from the bottom when they're finished. Trainers really utilize the beasts' natural smarts and talents—monkeys who might otherwise end up picking through resort garbage cans to eke an existence from tourism encroachment. The proper **Samui Monkey Theater** (☎ 077/245-140) is just south of Bophut village on 4169 Road. Shows are a little more vaudeville than the "working" demonstrations—with costumes and goofy tricks—a lot more fun for kids than for adults, who are more likely to just feel sorry for the poor little guys.

I defy you to find a Thai tourist spot without the requisite **snake farm,** complete with young men who taunt audiences with scary serpents, catching them with their bare hands (and sometimes their teeth). It's a lot of laughs to see the audience squirming all over each other in semi-amused horror. Samui's snake farm is at the far southwest corner of the island on 4170 Road (☎ 077/423-247), with daily shows at 11am and 2pm.

The spa scene on Ko Samui has really skyrocketed in recent years. Resorts like **The Spa Resort** (between Chaweng and Lamai Beaches; ☎ 077/230-855); **Health Oasis Resort** (Bang Po Beach near Mae Nam, ☎ 077/420-124); and **Axolotl Village** (Bang Po Beach near Mae Nam, ☎ 077/420-017), offer full-service health and beauty treatments, including yoga, meditation, chi kung, international styles of massage, herbal steam treatments, facials, and body wraps, plus lectures on health. All feature health cuisine in their restaurants and long- and short-term health programs for guests. I also recommend these places for people who just want to pop in for a day of relaxation. If it happens to be bad weather—can you think of a better way to get out of the rain and still enjoy Samui? I've recommended The Spa Resort in the "Accommodations in Lamai" section above, mainly because its location is secluded yet near the conveniences of Chaweng and Lamai beaches. Understand, however, the health resorts on Ko Samui are not Chiva Som or Banyan Tree—they're more new age than Guerlian (no doubt the effect of Ko Samui's development as an alternative vacation island).

If you're tempted to shop here, a good bit of advice is—don't! There's very little in terms of local crafts production on the island—most everything is imported from the mainland. That, and the high tourist traffic, naturally ups prices. But there's plenty of shopping around, especially in Chaweng (tailors, souvenirs, handicrafts, jewelers), but do yourself a favor by saving your money for Bangkok (or Chiang Mai), where you'll find a better selection of the same items for a better price.

KO SAMUI AFTER DARK

Some of the nights that you're on Samui your dinner will be interrupted by a roaming pickup truck with a crackling PA system blaring out incomprehensible Thai. These guys advertise local Thai boxing bouts. Grab one of their flyers for times and locations, which vary. It's iffy whether or not the TAT office can tell you about upcoming bouts, but you can try.

Some resort restaurants stage dinner theatre with Thai performances, but the schedules change regularly. Check with the **Santiburi Dusit Resort** (☎ **077/425-031**). They do wonderful poolside theme nights, and the food is always excellent. Ask about their Floating Market parties, where people float various Thai foods around on wooden canoes in the pool, right up to your table! Another venue known for throwing fine dinner performances is the **Imperial Samui Hotel** (☎ **077/422-020**).

For bars and discos, Chaweng has the action. The main fun seems to always be happening at **The Reggae Pub** (indicated on just about every island map—back from the main road around the central beach area). A huge thatch mansion, the stage thumps with some funky international acts, the dance floor jumps (even during low season they do a booming business) and the upstairs pool tables are good for sporting around. Just outside is a collection of open air bars, also found along Chaweng's beach road.

If you ask me, the best thing to do is buy a bottle of wine from a grocer or your hotel, walk to the beach, spread out a sarong and gaze at the stars. But, if it happens to be Sunday afternoon, truck on over to **The Secret Garden Pub** on Big Buddha Beach (☎ **077/245-253**) for live music and a barbecue on the beach. Many a famous performer has jumped up on the stage here, including a *certain* guitarist for the Grateful Dead. Call ahead of time and they can book you on one of their free shuttles (one at 3pm and another at 4pm). I'm telling the truth when I say there have been times where the pub has hosted thousands. Not exactly "secret," but highly recommended.

10 Phuket

No other Thai destination has changed so rapidly as Phuket, yet it remains Thailand's finest resort destination. At its best, this island is almost idyllic. It has long sandy beaches and picturesque coves, warm tropical waters of the Andaman Sea, excellent snorkeling and scuba diving, ideal windsurfing conditions, inland rain forest and mountains, and the best seafood in all of Thailand. Over the past 20 years, Phuket's resort community has developed excellent properties—both exotic and luxurious—that can compete with the best of Bali. Today, as groups pour in from Singapore, Hong Kong, Germany, and Italy, low-key travelers head for nearby Ko Pi Pi, or Ko Samui on the Gulf.

Some of the resorts are disarmingly attractive and elegant. The "Miami Beach" strip of concrete and steel is rarely seen on Phuket, with the exception of Patong beach, which will alarm you with its gaudy tourism and sleaze. Mostly you'll find serene bays framed by tastefully designed retreats that are modeled after hillside villas or luxury bungalows. It's nearly impossible to find a totally secluded beach, but there are a number of very attractive and comfortable facilities with a high level of service—not a bad

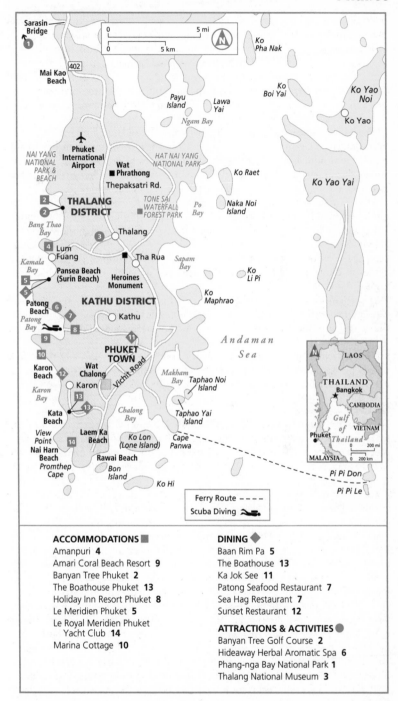

ACCOMMODATIONS ■
Amanpuri **4**
Amari Coral Beach Resort **9**
Banyan Tree Phuket **2**
The Boathouse Phuket **13**
Holiday Inn Resort Phuket **8**
Le Meridien Phuket **5**
Le Royal Meridien Phuket
    Yacht Club **14**
Marina Cottage **10**

DINING ◆
Baan Rim Pa **5**
The Boathouse **13**
Ka Jok See **11**
Patong Seafood Restaurant **7**
Sea Hag Restaurant **7**
Sunset Restaurant **12**

ATTRACTIONS & ACTIVITIES ●
Banyan Tree Golf Course **2**
Hideaway Herbal Aromatic Spa **6**
Phang-nga Bay National Park **1**
Thalang National Museum **3**

trade-off for those in search of all the luxuries. If you're traveling with a family, want to be pampered, or are looking for action, Phuket might be the place for you.

The peak season on Phuket extends from November to April, with the late-December/early-January holiday season demanding the highest rates. The monsoon winds arrive in May and last through October. During the monsoon season rains come often (with sunny patches in between storms) and the seas swell and become too rough for sea activities. Fewer people come to Phuket during this time, so resorts offer discounts of up to 50% of the peak period rate.

The name "Phuket" is derived from the Malay "Bukit," meaning mountain, and hills dominate much of the island, spilling their craggy rocks on the gentle beach coves below. From most high points you can see a number of nearby islands and islets, among them hourglass-shaped Ko Pi Pi, off the southern shore. In parts of the interior, open-pit mining for tin and other metals has scarred the land.

Phuket's most attractive beaches are on the west coast, extending from Nai Harn, on the southern tip, to Bang Tao, about 30 kilometers (19 miles) north. Most bungalows and new resorts are in between, along the Kata, Kata Noi, Karon, Karon Noi, Patong, and Surin corridor. A coastal road linking most of these beaches has been completed. For now, travel between some of the beaches north of Patong requires a detour to the interior, although some stretches are navigable with four-wheel-drive vehicles.

In the northern and inland sections of the island, peasants still use basic tools and water buffalo to work the fields. In contrast, road crews tear up agricultural lanes along the perimeter of these centuries-old farms to create wide, modern thoroughfares for the tourist trade.

This section is largely dedicated to activities on the western coast of the island, mainly the Karon and Patong beaches where most people spend their time. However, many fine resorts are outside of these areas, so they're included as well.

GETTING THERE

BY PLANE **Thai Airways** (☎ 02/535-2084 in Bangkok) flies over 10 times daily from Bangkok from 8am to 9pm (trip time: 1 hour and 20 minutes). Thai Airways' office in Phuket is at 78 Ranong Rd. (☎ 076/211-195). **Bangkok Airways** (☎ 02/229-3456 in Bangkok or 077/422-234 in Ko Samui) connects Phuket with Ko Samui twice daily. Bangkok Airways' office in Phuket is at 158/2–3 Yaowarat Rd., Phuket Town (☎ 076/225-033). Also keep in mind that you can get here directly from Singapore (Silk Air), Malaysia (Malaysia Airlines), and Siem Reap, Cambodia (Bangkok Airways).

The attractive, modern Phuket International Airport is located on the north end of the island. There are banks, money-changing facilities, car rental agents, and a post office. The Phuket Tourist Business Association booth can help you make hotel arrangements if you haven't booked a room already. Many resorts will fetch you from the airport upon request for a fee, usually steep. The airport limousine counter, operated by Tour Royale (☎ 076/341-214), offers many options for getting to your hotel from the airport. The most economical way is via minibus, which operates every hour on the hour from 9am to 11pm daily. Stopping between Patong, Kata, Karon, and Phuket town, prices run from 80B to 180B (US$1.86 to US$4.19), depending on how far you're going. Taxi service from the airport, also arranged at the limousine counter, will cost around 360B (US$8.37) to Phuket town or 540B (US$12.56) to Kata beach. The VIP Volvo transfer will set you back between 480B and 750B (US$11.16 and US$17.44).

BY BUS Two air-conditioned VIP buses leave daily from Bangkok's Southern Bus Terminal (☎ 02/435-1199), on Charan Sanitwong Road (trip time 13 hours; 690B/US$16.05), as well as an additional government air-conditioned bus at 457B (US$10.63).

The **intercity** bus terminal is at the city Park Complex on Phangnga Road (☎ 076/211-480), east of Phuket town just opposite the Royal Phuket City Hotel. For information on how to get from here to the beaches, see "Getting Around," below.

BY MINIVAN Minivans from Surat Thani leave on a regular schedule throughout the day. Call ☎ 077/286-131 for booking and hotel pickup (160B/US$3.72).

WHAT'S ON IN PHUKET

Some great local publications to pick up include the free *Phuket Food-Shopping-Entertainment,* packed with hotel and restaurant write-ups and ads for many of the island's activities. The monthly ultra-glossy *Greater Phuket Magazine* provides in-depth articles and photo essays about the island and its people. The Tourism Authority of Thailand is on the ball in Phuket, though you have to travel all the way into Phuket town to see them at 73–75 Phuket Rd. (☎ 076/211-036). The people behind the counter know everything there is to know about travel in the area.

GETTING AROUND

BY SONGTAO Not to confuse you, but in most other parts of Thailand a songtao is a pickup truck taxi, while on Phuket a songtao refers to the giant colored buses. The terminal is in front of the Central Market on Ranong Road in Phuket town. Fares to the most popular beaches range from 15B to 25B (US$0.35 to US$0.58). Songtao are typically scheduled to operate every 30 minutes from 7am to 5pm, but usually run whenever there is a full load of passengers or produce. Unfortunately, you can only take these buses from town to beach or back again. They do not operate routes between beaches.

BY TUK-TUK Not to confuse you even further, while in most other parts of Thailand a tuk-tuk is a motorized three-wheeled vehicle, on Phuket they call minitruck taxis tuk-tuk (what otherwise would be called songtao). Within Phuket they cost about 10B or 20B (US$0.23 to US$0.47) for local trips, more or less, depending on your destination. They also wander up and down the beach areas for short trips along the strip.

Tuk-tuks are the only way to travel between beaches, and these guys will try to eke every baht out of you. Here's your rule of thumb: 300B (US$6.98) from town to the airport, 150B (US$3.49) from town to Patong Beach, 150B (US$3.49) from Patong Beach to Karon Beach.

BY MOTORCYCLE TAXI Drivers in colored vests will try to talk you into a ride as you pass by, both in Phuket town and Patong beach. As in other towns, drivers here are identified by their colored vests. For a quick jot within town or Patong beach, they're recommended, but don't let these guys talk you into a trip between beaches. I really doubt it's safe enough.

BY CAR When you self-drive on Phuket, you have to be extra special careful. Coastal and inland roads have serious hills and curves that appear out of nowhere. Motorcycles swarm like bees, and Thai drivers will pass anything on a blind curve without so much as a care. Your defensive driving skills will come in real handy.

Budget has the best price and service, good cars, and comprehensive insurance policies—their lowest priced offering, the Suzuki Caribian sport vehicle, goes for 1,375B (US$31.98) per day. They'll meet you at the airport or deliver to your resort. Call the airport desk at ☎ 076/205-396, or the Patong beach office at ☎ 076/296-592.

Inexpensive Suzuki Caribians can be rented from almost all travel agents and hotels at the beach areas for prices between 700B and 900B (US$16.28 and US$20.93) per day. World Rent a Car (opposite the airport; ☎ **076/205-359**) goes as low as 700B (US$16.28) per day, and can greet you at the airport with a car or deliver one to your resort. Lining the beach at Patong, there are a ton of independent agents who hang around under umbrellas.

BY MOTORCYCLE   Also along the Patong strip, the same car rental guys will provide you with a bike for cheap. A 100cc Honda scooter goes for 200B (US$4.65) per day, while a 400cc Honda CBR rice burner or a 600cc Honda Shadow chopper will set you back 500B (US$11.63) per day. If you plan to rent for longer, make sure to negotiate for a discount rate. Wear your helmet, keep to the left, and let cars pass. For God's sake, wear clean underpants! I shudder to think of all the horror stories I've heard about vacation motorcycle accidents.

Fast Facts: Phuket

American Express   The **American Express** agent in Phuket is Sea Tours (☎ **076/218-417**), 95/4 Phuket Rd., Phuket town, 1 block south of the TAT.

Banks   Banks are located in Phuket town, with many larger branches on Ranong and Rasada roads. There are bank offices at the airport, as well as branches of major Thai banks at Kata, Karon and Patong beaches. **Money changers** are also around, at banks and in major shopping areas on each beach.

Hospitals   The Bangkok Phuket Hospital at 2/1 Hongyok-Uthit Rd. (off Yaowarat Road in Phuket town (☎ **076/254-421**) has English speaking staff and high quality facilities.

Internet   **Internet service** is fairly easy to find on the island. In Phuket town, head for Internet KSC at the ECC Building, 73/1–2 Rasada Rd., across from **Thavorn Hotel,** ☎ **076/214-496;** rates are 3B (US$0.07) per minute.

Police   The emergency number for the **Tourist Police** is **1699.** For **Marine Police** call ☎ **076/342-518.**

Post Office   The General Post Office in Phuket town (☎ **076/211020**) is at the corner of Thalang Road and Montri Road. You'll probably find it more convenient just to post from your hotel reception.

ACCOMMODATIONS
KATA & KARON BEACH

These are among the island's most attractive beaches, about 20 kilometers (12 miles) southwest of Phuket town and several miles north of Nai Harn. By day, the beaches are beginning to resemble Saint-Tropez, with rows of rented beach chairs and umbrellas lining the fine white sand, at times packed and even hectic in the high season.

The two beaches are separated by a rocky promontory but are quite similar, in both ambience and development. A few primitive bungalows and an occasional hotel behemoth interrupt the long coastline.

The Boathouse Phuket. 2/2 Patak Rd., Kata Beach, Phuket 83100. ☎ **076/330-557.** Fax 076/330-561. E-mail: boathouse@phuket.sawadee.com. 36 units. A/C MINIBAR TV TEL. Peak season 7,400B (US$172) double, 15,000B (US$349) suite, with considerable discounts for off-peak season. AE, DC, MC, V.

With its own beach at the quieter south end of Kata Beach, this small inn is a favorite. All the comfortable, attractive rooms face the sea, each with a terrace overlooking the huge Jacuzzi pool in the courtyard. The beach-side pool is small, with nearby massage and therapy facilities. Nothing about the hotel calls attention to itself; it's the well-trained, friendly, attentive staff that makes it special. The Boathouse high-style Thai and Continental restaurant serves some of the best food on the island and boasts one of the best wine "cellars" in Thailand. They also offer discount theme packages: Health Holidays, inclusive of massage and herbal steam treatments, and a Thai Cooking Class weekend getaway.

Marina Cottage. 120 Patak Rd., Kata Karon Beach, Phuket 83000. ☎ **076/330-625.** Fax 076/330-999. 104 units. A/C MINIBAR TV TEL. Low season 3,440B (US$80) garden double; 4,816B (US$112) pool view double; 5,504B (US$128) ocean view double. Peak season 4,300B (US$100) garden double; 6,020B (US$140) pool view double; 6,880B (US$160) ocean view double. MC, V. On bluff at south end of Karon Beach road.

These simple Thai cottages, tucked in the woods above the cusp of Kata and Karon beaches, are connected with a network of passageways and sky bridges through palm trees and forest. They are better equipped and more accommodating than most bungalows along these beaches, and each has its own balcony. All are a hike down to the rocky shore; rates vary according to the view. Some rooms have air-conditioning. A pleasant restaurant cottage serves good, inexpensive Thai food, and has a nice view of the sunset. During low season they also offer a "Buy 4 nights and get the 5th night free" promotion.

The Marina Cottage is home to **Marina Divers** (☎ **076/381-625**), a PADI International Diving School, which conducts classes, rents equipment, and leads expeditions around the island reefs.

PATONG BEACH

Patong has a proliferation of hotels and guesthouses, and yes, the night life scene includes go-go girls and massage parlors. Unfortunately, Patong has now strayed far into the realm of the tacky and become a kind of soul brother to Pattaya (or Tijuana, Mexico, for that matter). Despite pollution controls and water treatment, the beach is not terribly clean, and there's often a funky smell. Even with this warning, many people love it and flock to the place for its nightlife. Patong is hardly a virgin island paradise (as many people probably think based on glitzy hotel brochures), but it can be fun for those seeking a heady dose of after-dark activities.

Amari Coral Beach Resort. 2 Meun-Ngern Rd., Patong Beach, Phuket 83150. ☎ **076/ 340-106.** Fax 076/340-115. 200 units. A/C MINIBAR TV TEL. Peak season 6,880B–7,998B (US$160–US$186) double; from 11,094B (US$258) suite. Off-peak 5,418B–6,536B (US$126–US$152) double; from 8,987B (US$209) suite. Additional peak season surcharges apply Nov–Jan. AE, DC, MC, V. Far south end of Patong Beach.

The Coral Beach stands on the rocks high above Patong, at the southern tip well away from the din of Patong's congested strip, but close enough to enjoy the mayhem. While the beachfront is lacking—the rocks prevent swimming and water sports other than snorkeling—the two swimming pools overlook the huge bay, as does the terrace lobby, resort restaurants, and guest rooms. With seafoam tones, balconies, and full amenities, you'll not miss any of the comforts of home. Although there are several dining alternatives, the best is La Gritta, an Italian seafood terrace restaurant that overlooks the broad bay. Great for a sunset drink; open 6 to 11pm. Tennis courts, badminton courts, squash, windsurfing, a scuba diving center, and a long-tail boat jetty round out the list of facilities.

Holiday Inn Resort Phuket. 52 Thaweewong Rd., Patong Beach, Phuket 83150. ☎ **800/ HOLIDAY** in the U.S. and Canada; 800/553-888 in Australia; 0800/442-888 in New Zealand; 0800/897-121 in the U.K; 076/340-608. Fax 076/340-435. 272 units. A/C MINIBAR TV TEL. Peak season 6,450B (US$150) double; 8,084B (US$188) suite. Off-peak 5,246B (US$122) double; 2,580B (US$160) suite. AE, DC, EC, MC, V. Patong Beach strip.

The buildings at this Holiday Inn are modern, concrete blocks; guest rooms are furnished with rattan furniture and have balconies. The resort fronts the beach and offers water sports, including diving. This property has become especially popular with European groups, as is reflected in its restaurant offerings. Although there is little to distinguish it, the Holiday Inn is one of Patong's better accommodations. Restaurants like Seabreeze Café, Sam's Steakhouse, Suan Nok Thai Restaurant, and The Pizzeria Restaurant give you quite a bit of dining options. Nonsmoking floors, outdoor swimming pool, tennis courts, fitness club, water sports, self-service launderette, game room, Kids Club, sauna, and massage give you quite a bit of activity options.

OUTSIDE KATA, KARON & PATONG

✪ **Amanpuri.** Pansea Beach, Phuket 83110. ☎ **076/324-333.** Fax 076/324100. 43 units. A/C MINIBAR TEL. Peak season 22,575B–27,520B (US$525–US$640) garden view pavilion; 32,250B–54,180B (US$750–US$1,260) ocean view. Off-peak 18,060B–21,930B (US$420–US$510) garden view pavilion; 25,585B–40,635B (US$595–US$945) ocean view pavilion. AE, DC, MC, V. North end of cove.

The discreet and sublime Amanpuri is the Phuket address for visiting celebrities, from Hollywood and elsewhere. Small wonder, as it's the most elegant and secluded resort in Thailand and quite possibly all of Southeast Asia, for that matter. The lobby is an open-air pavilion with a standing Buddha, a lovely swimming pool, and stairs leading to the beach. Superior Pavilion Suites are freestanding houses creeping up the dense coconut palm grounds from the main building. Each is masterfully designed in a traditional Thai style, with teak and tile floors, sliding teak doors, exquisite built-ins, and well-chosen accents, including antiques. Private salas (covered patios) are perfect for romantic dining or secluded sunbathing. For special mood setting, check under the bathroom sinks for heavenly incense and burners. Less expensive suites are available inland from the resort, across the road. Two restaurants, the Restaurant Amanpuri and the Terrace, serve Western cuisine (including imported rarities that are hard to find in Thailand) and great Thai dishes. For excitement, they have their own yacht fleet, water-sports equipment and instruction, swimming pool, tennis and squash courts, fitness center, sauna, and private beach. For quiet times, there's a library with books, videos, and CDs (stereo systems are standard in each room).

✪ **Banyan Tree Phuket.** 33 Moo 4, Srisoonthorn Rd., Cherngtalay District, Amphur Talang, Phuket 83110. ☎ **800/525-4800** in the U.S. and Canada; 800/251-958 in Australia; 0800/ 964-470 in the U.K.; 076/324-374. Fax 076/324-375. 86 units. A/C MINIBAR TV TEL. Peak season 20,640B (US$480) garden villa; 26,660B (US$620) jacuzzi villa; 36,206B–40,764B (US$842–US$948) pool villa. Off-peak 17,630B (US$410) garden villa; 22,790B (US$530) jacuzzi villa; 30,960B–55,900B (US$720–US$1,300) pool villa; 64,070B (US$1,490) 2-bedroom villa. AE, DC, MC, V. North end of beach.

Banyan Tree is part of Laguna Phuket, a sprawling resort consortium that includes four other resorts and an 18-hole golf course, all connected by ferries. Far from the crowds of rowdy Patong and Karon beaches, Banyan Tree is a famous hideaway for honeymooners and people who just want to relax. Private villas with walled courtyards (many with private pool or Jacuzzi) are spacious and grand, lushly styled in teakwood with an outdoor bath and a platform bed under large Thai murals depicting the *Ramakien,* the story of the *Ramayana.* The resort can arrange private barbecues at your villa, and massage under each villa's sala, an outdoor Thai-style pavilion. The reception area is a large open sala with lovely lotus pools. Within the main building are the resort's five main restaurants for a choice of Thai, Mediterranean, Southeast Asian, and other international cuisine.

The Banyan Tree Spa wins awards every year. A small village in itself, the spa provides a wide range of beauty and health treatments in relaxing rooms, plus Jacuzzi, sauna, steam, hair styling, fitness pavilion (with daily meditation lessons), separate spa pool, and cafe serving delicious light and healthy dishes.

Banyan Tree's main pool is one of the most amazing I've ever seen: a free-form lagoon, landscaped with greenery and rock formations, with a water canal whose currents gently pull you through the passage. In addition to the Banyan Tree Phuket Golf Club, there are three outdoor tennis courts, sailing, windsurfing, and canoeing. The resort can arrange pretty much any activity, both inside and outside the resort. For added options, Banyan Tree guests have signing privileges at the sister resorts of the Laguna consortium.

Le Meridien Phuket. 8/5 Tambol, Karon Noi, P.O. Box 277, Relax Bay, Phuket 83000. ☎ **800/225-5843** in the U.S. and Canada; 800/622-240 in Australia; 0800/454040 in New Zealand; 0800/404040 in the U.K.; 076/340-480. Fax 076/340-479. 470 units. A/C MINBAR TV TEL. Peak season 8,385B–13,760B (US$195–US$320) double. Off-peak 6,708B–13,760B (US$156–US$320) double. Additional peak season surcharges apply Nov–Jan. AE, DC, EC, MC, V. Relax Bay airport shuttle bus.

Le Meridien Phuket is tucked away on secluded Relax Bay, with a lovely 600-yard beach and 40 acres of tropical greenery. This is one of the largest (verging on huge) resorts on the island, and during the high season it's almost always packed with European vacationers. The advantages of a larger resort are its numerous facilities—two swimming pools huge enough to windsurf in, beach water sports, four tennis courts, putting green and practice range, and one of the best fitness centers I've ever seen. My favorite thing, though is the brilliant Penguin Club, a professionally staffed and highly creative day-care center that kids just seem to love. The large building complex combines Western and traditional Thai architecture, and one of the advantages to its U-shape layout is that it ensures that 80% of the rooms face the ocean. The modern furnishings in each cheerful room are of rattan and teak, with a hi-fi and balcony with wooden sundeck chairs. No fewer than 10 restaurants give you all kinds of choice: Asian, beachside barbecue, Italian, Japanese, seafood, royal Thai, plus pubs with games and live shows.

✪ **Le Royal Meridien Phuket Yacht Club.** 23/3 Viset Rd., Nai Harn Beach, Phuket 83130. ☎ **800/225-5843** in the U.S. and Canada; 800/622-240 in Australia; 0800/454040 in New Zealand; 0800/404040 in the U.K.; 076/381-156. Fax 076/381-164. 110 units. A/C MINBAR TV TEL. Peak season 12,857B (US$299) double. Off-peak 10,063B (US$234) double. Additional peak season surcharges apply Nov–Jan. AE, DC, JCB, MC, V. Above Nai Harn Beach, 18km (11 miles) south of Phuket.

Le Meridien recently took over the Phuket Yacht Club, one of the earliest luxury accommodations in Phuket, and has taken the resort to new heights in quality. Perched above the northern edge of Nai Harn, looking down at the public beach and yachts beyond, the Yacht Club rivals nearly anything on the island for setting—from its pagoda-style entryway to the terraced gardens overflowing with pink and white bougainvillea. All rooms view the beach, the Andaman Sea, and Promthep Cape from their landscaped, red-tiled balconies. Newly redecorated guest rooms are spacious and decorated with cheerful fabrics and wicker furniture; most bathrooms have sunken tubs and are fully stocked with high-quality amenities. The Phuket Yacht Club has a pool, a newly renovated fitness center, and three dining venues—beachside Mediterranean fare, Italian in the elegant dining room, or Asian and International cuisine on the patio.

DINING
IN PHUKET TOWN

✪ **Ka Jok See.** 26 Takuapa Rd., Phuket town. ☎ **076/217-903.** Reservations recommended for weekends. Main courses 150B–380B (US$3.50–US$9). Tues–Sun 6pm–midnight (kitchen closes around 11pm). No credit cards. A short walk from Rasada Rd. THAI.

This is one of my favorite restaurants in Thailand. I love the ambience—a small shophouse in town with tiled floor and wood beamed ceiling, antiques and old memorabilia by candlelight, and cool old jazz wafting throughout. Ka Jok See is smart and chic; cozy and intimate. They prepare fabulous dishes like goong-saroong, the house specialty, shrimps wrapped in vermicelli then fried lightly. The dipping sauce is a unique creamy mustard concoction. I also had an excellent smoky grilled eggplant and shrimp salad and the stir-fried beef curry, which were both out of this world. This place is worth a venture from the beach for an evening. Look for the shophouse hidden behind all the plants—they have no sign.

IN PATONG

Baan Rim Pa. Kalim Beach Rd., north end of Patong Beach. ☎ **076/340-789.** Reservations required. Main courses 250B–1,200B (US$6–US$28). Daily noon–2:30pm and 6–10pm. AE, DC, MC, V. THAI.

In a beautiful Thai-style teak house, Baan Rim Pa has dining in the romantic indoor setting or with a gorgeous view of the bay from outdoor terraces. This restaurant is one of the most popular restaurants on the island, for locals who wish to entertain as well as for visitors, so be sure to reserve your table early. Thai cuisine features seafood, with a variety of other meat and vegetable dishes, including a rich duck curry and a sweet honey chicken dish. The seafood basket is a fantastic assortment of prawns, mussels, squid, and crab.

Patong Seafood Restaurant. Patong Beach Rd., Patong Beach. ☎ **076/340-247.** Reservations not accepted. Main courses 80B–250B (US$2–US$6.80); seafood at market price. Daily 7am–11pm. AE, DC, MC, V. SEAFOOD.

Take an evening stroll on the lively Patong beach strip and you'll find quite a few open-air seafood restaurants displaying their catches of the day on chipped ice at their entrances. The best choice of them all is the casual Patong Seafood, for the freshest and the best selection of seafood, including several types of local fish, lobster, squid (very tender), prawn, and crab. The menu has a fantastic assortment of preparation styles—with photos of popular Thai noodles and Chinese stir-fry dishes. Service is quick and efficient. The place fills up quick, so it's best to arrive here early.

✪ **Sea Hag Restaurant.** 78/5 Soi Permong III, Patong Beach. ☎ **076/341-111.** Reservations recommended for weekend dinner. Main courses 80B–200B (US$1.90–US$4.65). Daily 11am–2pm, 5pm–midnight. No credit cards. THAI.

The name is far from appealing, but everything else about the place is, making it one of Patong's favorite joints for local residents and travelers. The food is superb (the baked seafood in curry is absolutely amazing), and the casual dining atmosphere captures a local style of grace with an easy charm.

IN KARON

Sunset Restaurant. 102/6 Patak Rd., Karon Beach. ☎ **076/396-465.** Main courses 80B–180B (US$1.86–US$4.19), seafood at market price. Daily 8am–11pm. AE, DC, MC, V. SEAFOOD

While Patak Road, running perpendicular to the main beach road, doesn't really have a view of the sunset, this restaurant is notable for its fine seafood, prepared in both local and Western styles. Their lobster thermidor and Western-style steamed fish are fresh and scrumptious, as well as their mixed seafood platters. Thai dishes are either spicy or tempered upon request, depending on your preference. Simple tables have neat batik cloths, which is about the only nice touch in the decor. Nevertheless, it's a favorite spot for foreigners living in Phuket, and one of the best places in this part of the island.

IN KATA

✪ **The Boathouse.** The Boathouse Inn, 114 Patak Rd. ☎ **076/330-557.** Reservations accepted. Main courses from 200B (US$4.65); seafood sold at market price. Daily 7:30am–11pm. AE, DC, MC, V. THAI/INTERNATIONAL.

So legendary is the Thai and Western cuisine at the Boathouse, that the inn where it resides offers popular holiday packages for visitors who wish to come and take cooking lessons from its chef. Inside the restaurant, a large bar and separate dining area have nautical touches, while outside huge picture windows, the sun sets on a deep blue sea. Cuisine is nouvelle, combining the best of east and west and the best ingredients in satisfying portions. If you're in the mood for the works, the Phuket lobster is one of the most expensive dishes on the menu, but is worth every baht. The Boathouse also has an excellent selection of international wines. Bon appetit.

SPORTS, OUTDOOR ACTIVITIES & ATTRACTIONS

Most of your **water sports** activities are almost exclusively on Patong Beach—centralized for convenience, but restricted to one beach, so swimmers can enjoy other beaches without the buzz of a jet ski or power boat. There are no specific offices to organize such activities; just walk to the beach and chat up the guys under the umbrellas who'll set up activities from impromptu operations. **Jet skis** can be rented out for 30 minutes at 700B (US$16.28), and a 10-minute **parasailing** ride is 600B (US$13.95). You'll also find **Hobie Cats** for around 600B (US$13.95) per hour, as well as **windsurf** boards for 200B (US$4.65) per hour. Hobie Cat sailing and windsurfing is popular at other bays as well, and are usually rented through the major resorts, that also provide sailing instruction for an extra charge.

For yachting, Phuket can't be rivaled in Southeast Asia. Facilities for recreational boating are better than anywhere else, while Phuket is a **sailing** dream come true, with the crystal blue waters of the Andaman Sea and gorgeous island scenery. A great guide, *Sail Thailand,* accurately documents everything sailors need to know. It's distributed in the U.S., U.K., and Australia, or you can contact Artasia Press (☎ **02/861-3360;** fax 02/861-3363).

Every December Phuket hosts the increasingly popular King's Cup Regatta, in which almost 100 international racing yachts competed. For more information check out the Web site at www.kingscup.com.

In the smaller bays around the island, such as Nai Harn Beach or Relax Bay, you'll come across some lovely **snorkeling** just close to the shore. For the best coral just off the shoreline, trek up to Had Nai Yang National Park for the long reef in clear shallow waters. Most skin divers prefer day trips to outer islands such as the Similan Islands, Ko Phi Phi, or the newest favorite, Raya Island (pronounced by the Thais as "Laya" Island). The best times to snorkel are from November to April before the monsoon comes and makes the water too choppy. Almost every tour operator arranges group day-long boating trips with hotel transfers, lunch, and gear.

The island's over 45 **scuba** operators are testimony to the beautiful attractions that lie deep in the Andaman Sea. Sites at nearby coral walls, caves, and wrecks can be explored in full day, overnight, or long term excursions. All operators advertise full

PADI courses, Divemaster courses, and 1-day introductory lessons. Let me rave for a moment about **Dive Master's** EcoDive 2000, planned under the supervision of marine biologists and environmentalists, this unique program takes small groups beyond the standard dive routes to pristine areas, educating divers about sea creatures and eco-diving. Contact Dive Master in Phuket at 75/20 Moo 10, Patak Road, Chalong (☎ **076/280-330**); or plan your trip in advance through their Bangkok office (☎ **02/259-3195;** fax 259-3196). **Fantasea Divers** is the oldest and most reputable firm on Phuket. Their main office is at Patong Beach at 219 Ratchautit Rd. (☎ **076/340-088;** fax 076/340-309), but they have other branches along Thaveewongse Road (the main beach road) in Patong.

For an unforgettable adventure, try a **sea kayak** trip to **Phang-nga Bay National Park**, an hour and a half drive north of Phuket (3 hours by boat) off Thailand's mainland. Between 5 and 10 million years ago, limestone thrust above the water's surface, creating over 120 small islands. These craggy rock formations (the famous scenery for the James Bond classic, *The Man With the Golden Gun*) look like they were taken straight from a Chinese scroll painting. Sea kayaks are perfect for inching your way into the many breathtaking caves and chambers that hide beneath the jagged cliffs. The company to pioneer the cave trips, Sea Canoe (in Phuket town, 367/4 Yaowarat Rd.; ☎ **076/212-252**) is a very eco-friendly group, and the most professional around. The full-day trip is about 3,000B (US$69.77) per person.

Meanwhile, back on terra firma, it wouldn't be an Asian resort without **golf.** The best course on Phuket is the **Banyan Tree** Club & Laguna (34 Moo 4, Srisoonthorn Road, at the Laguna Resort Complex on Bang Tao Bay; ☎ **076/324-350;** fax 076/324-251), a par 71 championship course with many water features. The **Blue Canyon Country Club** (165 Moo 1, Thepkasattri Road, near the airport; ☎ **076/327-440;** fax 076/327-449), is a par 72 championship course with natural hazards, trees, and guarded greens. An older course, the **Phuket Country Club** (80/1 Vichitsongkram Rd., west of Phuket town; ☎ **076/321-038;** fax 076/321-721), has beautiful greens and fairways, plus a giant lake.

When you're ready to take in a little culture, the first place to stop is the **Thalang National Museum** toward the eastern side of the island on Sri Soonthorn in Thalang District off Highway 402 just past the Heroine's Monument (☎ **076/311-426;** open daily from 9am to 4pm; admission 30B/US$0.70). There are extensive displays about Phuket's indigenous cultures, the history of the Thais on Phuket, and crafts from the southern Thai regions. There's also a fascinating image of the Hindu god Vishnu that dates from the ninth century A.D., evidence of the presence of Indian merchants long ago, and their influence on the Thai people.

Phuket may not be the center of traditional Thai culture like its northern cousins, Bangkok or Chiang Mai, but there are a few **Buddhist temples** on the island that are quite notable. I highly recommend this little window to Thai culture, especially if Phuket is your only stop in Thailand. The most unique temple is **Wat Pra Tong,** located along Highway 402 in Thalang just south of the airport. Years ago, a boy fell ill and dropped dead after tying his buffalo to a post sticking out of the ground. It was later discovered that the post was actually the top of a huge Buddha image that was buried under the earth. Numerous attempts to dig out the statue failed—during one attempt in 1785, workers were chased off by hornets. Everyone took all this failure to mean that the Buddha image wanted to just stay put, so they covered the "post" with a plaster image of The Buddha's head and shoulders and built a temple around it. Near Wat Pra Tong, **Wat Pra Nahng Sahng** (also on Highway 402, at the traffic light in Thalang) houses three very interesting Buddha images. Made from tin, a local natural resource once considered semi-precious, each image has a smaller Buddha in its belly.

The most famous temple among the Thais is **Wat Chalong.** Chalong was the first resort on Phuket, back when the Thais first started coming to the island for vacations. Nowadays, the discovery of better beaches on the west side of the island has driven most tourists away from this area, but the temple still remains the center of Buddhist worship.

Playful monkeys add a fun dimension to bars, restaurants, and guesthouses around Thailand, where the adorable creatures are kept as pets. Many times, however, these gibbons are mistreated. Raised in captivity on unhealthy food in restricted living conditions, and subjected to human companionship exclusively, many develop psychological problems. Depression and despondency becomes common for maladjusted monkeys, with violent outbursts occurring sometimes. Bar monkeys end up drinking alcohol, and are force-fed uppers to keep them awake and lively—to the delight of tourists who aren't aware of the inevitable destruction it causes. The Gibbon Rehabilitation Project, off Highway 4027 at the Bang Pae waterfall in the northeastern corner of the island (☎ **076/260-492**), cares for wayward gibbons, offering them safe haven and teaching them how to relate with other gibbons in natural surroundings. Volunteer staff guide visitors to see gibbons that are still "humanized," some of which are hard-luck cases. The rest are strictly secluded to ensure their rehabilitation. The project is open daily from 10am to 4:30pm. Admission is free, but a donation is desperately needed; 1,000B (US$23.26) takes care of one gibbon for a year.

If you've come to Phuket to decompress from daily life, slow down, and cool out, I can't think of a better way to accomplish this than a visit to one of Phuket's **spas.** The most famous and exclusive facility here is The Spa at the Banyan Tree Phuket (33 Moo 4, Srisoonthorn Road, Cherngtalay). Operated by the Banyan Tree Resort, this spa has won Conde Nast reader's choice awards for best spa in the world. In pavilions secluded by garden settings, choose from many types of massage, plus body and facial treatments for health and beauty. To make reservations call ☎ **076/324-374.** Expect to pay for the luxury—figure an average of 1,500B (US$34.88) per treatment.

If the expense of a spa visit makes you even more stressed out, then **The Hideaway Herbal Aromatic Spa** (47/4 Soi Nanai, Patong, ☎ **076/340-591;** and a new location at 116/9 Moo 6, Patak Road, Kata, ☎ **076/330-914**) is the place for you. A tiny compound of open-air thatch salas are tucked into a hillside, where the relaxed and informal staff prepare baths, and perform traditional Thai massage and aromatic herbal face, foot, and hair treatments using age-old Thai beauty treatments. Their signature skin care products will make your body feel like silk. For those used to the usual generic spa routine, this homegrown place is a welcome retreat, and surprisingly affordable, too. At around 400B (US$9.30) for a single treatment, you can have the works for what it costs for a single treatment at a resort spa.

There's a small point at the southern tip of the island that everybody will tell you has the best view of the **sunset**. And they're right. From the cliffs atop Promthep Cape, the view of the sky as it changes colors from deep reds to almost neon yellows can't compete with the best fireworks. The sun usually sets between 6:15 and 6:45. Get there early on weekends. The place isn't exactly a secret.

SHOPPING

Although Patong beach is a virtual bazaar by night, shopping is not a recommended activity in Phuket. Thailand's best shopping for quality antiques and handicrafts is found in Chiang Mai and Bangkok. Most of what you're going to find here are seashell souvenirs and batik beach wear (imported from India, no less). All of the handicrafts you do find have been shipped in from up north. If you're heading that way, shop at the source for better selection and value, for prices in Phuket are grossly inflated. A shop owner tried to sell me a batik wrap skirt for 380B (US$8.84)—exactly like the one I bought in Pattaya for 120B (US$2.79)!

The exception is the gift shop at the Phuket Shell Museum. Their huge shop has high quality shell products for the home, novelty items, and fun shell souvenirs. They also have all varieties of gorgeous perfect seashells for sale, some of them massive. You could only pray to find one of these on the beach. Friends and family love them. Open daily from 8am to 7pm, the museum is at 12/2 Moo 2, Viset Road, Rawai Beach (just south of Chalong Bay); ☎ **076/381-266.** Admission is 100B for adults; children free.

PHUKET AFTER HOURS

From the huge billboards and glossy brochures, **Phuket FantaSea,** the newest theme attraction, seems like it could be touristy and tacky. But, to be perfectly honest with you, I had a fabulous time. A giant theme park, Phuket FantaSea is as slick as Universal Studios. The festival village entrance, lined with more shopping than you can imagine plus games, entertainment, and snacks, keeps you busy until they serve the forgettable buffet dinner. Afterwards, proceed to the Palace of the Elephants for the show—which is incredibly entertaining, very professional, and oftentimes amazing. Don't fear the hype. Phuket FantaSea is at Kamala Beach, north of Patong, on the coastal road. Call ☎ **076/271-222** for reservations. The park opens at 5:30pm; the buffet begins at 6:30pm and the show at 9pm. Tickets for the show are 1,000B (US$23.26) for adults and 700B (US$16.28) for children, while optional dinner and hotel transfer is extra.

Phuket also has a resident cabaret troupe at Simon Cabaret (100/6-8 Moo 4, Patong Karon Road; ☎ **076/342-011;** shows at 7:30pm and 9pm nightly; 750B/US$17.44) between Patong and Karon beaches. It's a featured spot on every planned tour agenda, so be prepared for busloads. However, I still think the cabaret is a fun and interesting thing to see—many of the tourists who attend are Asians, and the show mainly caters to them, with lip-sync performances that in turn make all the Koreans laugh, the Japanese laugh, the Chinese laugh. It can be a lot of fun. In between the comedy are dance numbers with pretty impressive sets, costumes, and naturally, transsexuals.

Every night you can catch **Thai boxing** at Vegas Thai Boxing in Patong at the Patong Simon Shopping Arcade on Soi Bangla. Bouts start every night from 7pm and last until 3am. Best of all, admission is free.

Patong nightlife is a wild time. Lit up like Las Vegas, the beach town hops like Saturday every night of the week. Shops and restaurants stay open late, and there's a never ending choice of bars (both straight and gay), nightclubs, karaoke lounges, snooker halls, massage parlors, go-go bars, and sex shows (à la Patpong). Needless to say, Patong has a draw for those interested in sex tourism—most of the bars have hostesses who are not shy.

Patong has a couple fun discos. The centrally located Banana Club (94 Thaweewong Rd.; ☎ **076/340-301**) has a fun mix of foreigners and locals, and a good DJ spinning dance music and chart hits; it's almost always packed to the gills. My other favorite choice is Safari (28 Sririrat Rd., Patong Hill; ☎ **076/340-310**), just south of Patong beach. This giant Polynesian tiki-hut throbs with dance music, provided either by resident DJs or, in peak season, live international bands.

SIDE TRIPS FROM PHUKET

Ko Phi Phi, actually a pair of islands—Phi Phi Don and Phi Phi Le, were once the darlings of the backpacker set. Phi Phi Don, the larger of the two, was loved for its fabulous beaches, great snorkeling, and remote location. As dozens of bungalow complexes sprouted along the beaches, development went unchecked, pollution got out of hand, and corals started to fall to pieces. You'll be happy to know that Ko Phi Phi has started cleaning up its act as Thailand has become more aware of its environmental problems. The winter of 1998/99 saw this small pair of islands making international headlines when Hollywood came to town to shoot *The Beach* based upon the Thailand-based novel by Alex Garland. The film's star, Leonardo DiCaprio, drew all kinds of rubbernecks to these parts, as well as environmental protection groups who, ironically, howled loudly about the negative effects the production might have on the environment here.

Boats to Phi Phi generally leave at 8:30am and take an hour and a half to complete the journey. Companies will arrange for your transfer to the jetty for an extra cost (from 50B to 200B/US$1.16 to US$4.65, depending on your hotel's location). During the high season—from November to April—these companies will sometimes run an afternoon boat at 2:30pm if there's demand. **Songserm** (☎ **076/222-570**) has both ferries (250B to 350B/US$5.81 to US$8.14 per person) and a speedboat (350B/US$8.14). Round-trip, with returns in the afternoon, costs between 450B and 650B (US$10.47 and US$15.12). While the boats depart for Phi Phi year-round, you may want to be careful from May through October, when monsoon winds cause them to rock heavily—I've seen more than a few people lose their lunch over the side of the boat. Not a pretty sight.

Pi Pi Le proves the most popular day trip from Pi Pi Don, and it's a fun excursion. Boats depart from Ton Sai town and take you on a tour that includes stops at the Viking Cave, known for its swallow nests (which fetch up to US$2,000 per kilo and are the key ingredient of bird's nest soup), cave paintings with vessels that look like Viking ships (thus the name of the cavern), inland bays with dramatic rock formations, and small beaches for swimming and snorkeling. Songserm (☎ **01-229-2480**), along the main street in town, will take you on a day trip there, plus include lunch and snorkel gear, for 350B (US$8.14) per person. Note: Some of the Phuket-based day trips include stops at Pi Pi Le.

If you stay overnight on Phi Phi Don, the nicest place is **P.P. Princess Resort** (103 Moo 7, Tambon Ao Nang, Amphur Muang, Krabi 81000; ☎ **075/612-188;** fax 075/620-615). There's an office on Phuket 2/39 Montri Rd., in Phuket town; ☎ **076/210-928;** fax 076/217-106. High season (November to April) rates are 2,000B to 3,000B (US$46.51 to US$69.77) garden bungalow; 3,250B (US$75.58) beachfront bungalow; 4,500B (US$104.65) suite bungalow. Low season (May to October) rates are 1,500 to 2,000B (US$34.88 to US$46.51) garden bungalow, 2,250B (US$52.33) beachfront bungalow; 3,250B (US$75.58) suite bungalow. These beach bungalows are different from any others I've seen, especially within this moderate price category. While the bungalows and private decks are not huge, smooth stained woods and huge glass windows bring the outside indoors. You can't help but feel surrounded by nature. The garden and beachside bungalows are identical, only the location changes with the price. Just next door is Sea Fun, where you can arrange all your water activities.

The nine islands that form the Similan archipelago are so pristine that they have been cited by diving authorities as among the best in the world for undersea exploration. The beaches that encircle all nine islands are fine, white sand bordered by lush forests that lead to rocky interiors. Snorkeling is superb. The only development is on Ko Muang (also known as Ko 4), which has a park's office and a few very basic bungalows.

The Similan archipelago is 80 kilometers (50 miles) northwest of Phuket. Excursion boats take both day-trippers (it's a long way but worth it) and campers to Similan daily for about 1,700B (US$39.53) including food and snorkel equipment. **Seatran Travel** (☎ **076/211-809**) has a boat that departs every morning at 8am, and can provide hotel transfers. Note that this trip is very much affected by weather conditions (both for travel and diving), so plan to visit from November to May (February and March are the best months) when the western monsoons are at their quietest. Under no circumstances should you fail to bring sunscreen with the highest possible rating; it's likely that the sun will be as hot and bright as you've ever encountered, and you can burn in as little as 10 minutes on the beach!

11 An Introduction to Northern Thailand

The southern regions of Thailand may be a vacation paradise of beaches and blue waters, but when many Thais nationals think of a holiday, they head for the northern hills, where the air is cooler and the atmosphere more culturally stimulating. The historic cities of **Chiang Mai**, **Chiang Rai**, and the small but interesting **Golden Triangle** (Chiang Saen), a former cowboy town for the opium trade, are a welcome change for visitors who want to experience Thailand's beauty beyond the beaches.

Northern Thailand is comprised of 15 provinces, many of them sharing borders with Burma (Myanmar) to the north and west and Laos to the northeast. This verdant, mountainous terrain, which includes Thailand's largest mountain, Doi Inthanon, at 8,408 feet (2,563m), supports nomadic farming and teak logging at high altitudes and systematic agriculture in the valleys. Traditionally, opium poppies were the main cash crop for the people here, but government efforts have largely replaced their cultivation with rice, tobacco, soybeans, corn, and sugarcane.

A SHORT REGIONAL HISTORY

The tribal people living in the northern hills are actually recent immigrants in the grand scheme of the history of these parts, migrating only within the past 100 years or so from neighboring Burma, Tibet, Laos and Southern China to escape political strife and fighting.

The majority of northern Thais trace their heritage to the Tai people who migrated from Southern China in waves between the first and eighth centuries A.D. King Mengrai, a brilliant leader who united the Tai tribes, established the first capital of the Lanna Kingdom at Chiang Rai in 1262 A.D. It was about this time that Kublai Khan invaded Burma. For added protection, King Mengrai forged ties with the Sukhothai Kingdom to the south, and in 1296 moved his capital to Chiang Mai. For the next century, the Lanna Kingdom absorbed most of the northern provinces, and in alliance with the Sukhothai, held off invasion from the Mons and Khmers. Ayutthaya, after taking control of Sukhothai, tried to conquer Chiang Mai and failed each time. The Lanna Kingdom enjoyed wealth and power until 1556, when the Burmese captured the capital. It remained in their hands until 1775, when King Taskin (of Ayutthaya) took it for Siam.

A LOOK AT THE HILL TRIBES

Since the 1970s, foreigners have caught on to the beauty of the north and to the cultures of the unique **hill tribe people** who live here. Northern Thailand is home to the majority of Thailand's half-million plus tribal peoples, who live in villages that are a trek away from civilization and who often come to the larger cities to sell their excellent handicrafts and share their culture with visitors.

While many Thais in the central and southern regions of the country acknowledge the original Chinese Thais as their ancestral lineage, the people of the hill tribes retain a separate identity. They are divided into six primary tribes: the Karen, Akha (also known as the Kaw), Lahu (Mussur), Lisu (Lisaw), Hmong (Meo), and Mien (Yao),

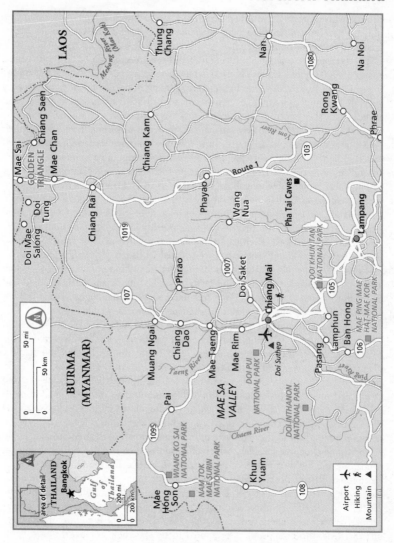

each with subgroups that are linked by history, lineage, language, costume, social organization, and religion. With close ethnic, cultural, and linguistic ties to the cultures of their Laotian, Southwestern Chinese, Burmese, and Tibetan ancestors and neighbors, the hill tribes remain to this day different from the Thais of central and southern Thailand, retaining their own traditional costumes, religion, art, and way of life.

Numbering over a quarter-million—almost half of the entire tribal population—the **Karen** are the largest tribal group in Thailand and are among the most assimilated of the hill tribes, making it difficult to identify them by any outward appearance; however, the most traditional tribespeople wear silver armbands and don a beaded sash and headband, and the single women wear all white. In nearby Burma (Myanmar), it's estimated that there are more than four million people of Karen descent (and of Buddhist belief), many of whom have settled along the Thai-Burmese border. For years, Burma's military government has been battling Karen rebels seeking an autonomous home-land, and many Burmese Karen have sought refuge in Thailand.

The **Hmong** are a nomadic tribe scattered throughout Southeast Asia and China. About 65,000 Hmong live in Thailand, while there are approximately four million liv-ing in China. In Thailand, the Hmong generally dwell in the highlands, where they cultivate opium poppies more extensively than any other tribal group; corn, rice, and soybeans are also grown as subsistence crops. As with most of the other tribes, the Hmong are pantheistic and rely on shamans to perform spiritual rites, though their elite is staunchly Catholic. Like the Chinese, with whom they resided for so many cen-turies, Hmong are skilled entrepreneurs, and many are beginning to move down from the hills to pursue a less rigorous and more profitable life in other occupations.

The **Lahu** people, of whom about 40,000 abide in Thailand, are a fractured group with a great many subdivisions, and if any tribe reflects the difficulties of maintaining a singular cultural identity in the tumult of migration, it's the Lahu. Consider Lahu religion: Originally animist, they adopted the worship of a deity called G'ui sha (pos-sibly Tibetan in origin), borrowed the practice of merit-making from Buddhism (Indian or Chinese), and ultimately incorporated Christian (British/Burmese) theol-ogy into their belief system. In addition, they practice a kind of Lahu voodoo as well as follow a messianic tradition. The Lahu are skilled musicians, their bamboo and gourd flutes being the most common instruments sold in the Night Market in Chi-ang Mai. They welcome strangers more than any other tribe in Thailand.

There are now estimated to be 33,000 **Mien** living in Thailand, concentrated in Chiang Rai, Phayao, Lampang, and Nan provinces. Even more than the Hmong, the Mien are closely connected to their origins in southern China. They incorporated the Han (Chinese) spoken and written language into their own, and many Mien legends, history books, and religious tracts are recorded in Chinese. The Mien people also assimilated ancestor worship and a form of Taoism into their theology, in addition to celebrating their New Year on the same date (relying on the same calendar system) as the Chinese. Mien farmers practice slash-and-burn agriculture but do not rely on opium poppies; instead they cultivate dry rice and corn. The women produce rather elaborate and elegant embroidery, which often adorns their clothing. Their silver work is intricate and highly prized even by other tribes, particularly the Hmong.

The **Lisu** are one of the smaller ethnic minorities in northern Thailand, represent-ing less than 5% of all hill-tribe people. They arrived in Chiang Rai Province in the 1920s, migrating from nearby Burma, occupying high ground and growing opium poppies as well as other subsistence crops. Like their Chinese cousins (many have intermarried), the Lisu people are reputed to be extremely competitive and hard-working. Even their clothing is brash, with brightly colored tunics embellished with hundreds of silver beads and trinkets. The Lisu are achievers who live well-structured lives. Their rituals rely on complicated procedures that demand much from the par-ticipants. Everything from birth to courtship to marriage to death is ruled by an ortho-dox tradition, much borrowed from the Chinese.

Of all the tradition-bound tribes, the **Akha**, accounting for only 3% of all minori-ties living in Thailand, have probably maintained the most profound connection with their past. At great events in one's life, the full name (often more than 50 generations of titles) of an Akha is proclaimed, with each name symbolic of a lineage dating back more than a thousand years. All aspects of life are governed by the Akha Way, an all-encompassing system of myth, ritual, plant cultivation, courtship and marriage, birth, death, dress, and healing. They are widely spread throughout southern China, Laos, Vietnam, and Burma (Myanmar), the first Akha migrating from Burma to Thailand in the beginning of the 20th century. They are "shifting" cultivators, depending on subsistence crops, planted in rotation, and raising domestic animals for their livelihood. The clothing of the Akha is among the most attractive of all the hill tribes: Simple black jackets with skillful embroidery are the everyday attire for both men and women.

WEATHER

There are three distinct seasons in the North. The **hot season** (March through May) is dry with temperatures up to 86°F (30°C); the **rainy season** (June through October) is a bit cooler, with the heaviest daily rainfall in September; and the **cool season** (November through February) is brisk, with daytime temperatures as low as 59°F (21°C) in Chiang Mai town and 41°F (5°C) in the hills. November to May is the best time for trekking, with February, March, and April (when southern Thailand gets extremely hot) usually being the least crowded months. Trekkers beware during the rainy season when paths become mud-slides due to frequent showers.

12 Chiang Mai

The largest and most well known city in the north, Chiang Mai is the primary gateway to the hills and people who live there. The city itself is a treasure trove of small but magnificent temples and, without argument, the epitome of shopping for Thai and hill tribe arts and handicrafts. If you can be seduced away from the city limits, you'll find cottage industries, hill tribe villages, and natural wonders.

Chiang Mai begins at the **"Old City,"** a square fortress surrounded by a moat, and some remains of its original massive walls. Several of the original gates have been restored and serve as useful reference points. Within the Old City are three of the area's most important wats (temples): Wat Chedi Luang, Wat Phra Singh, and Wat Chiang Man.

Most of the major streets radiate from the Old City and fan out in all directions. The **main business and shopping area** is the half-mile stretch between the east side of the Old City and the Ping River. Here you'll find **Chiang Mai's Night Market,** many shops, hotels, and restaurants.

GETTING THERE

BY AIR   **Thai Airways** (☎ **02/280-0070**), **Bangkok Airways** (☎ **02/229-3456**), and **Angel Airlines** (☎ **02/953-2260**) all service Chiang Mai, running 15 flights daily from Bangkok between them. They each have ticketing offices in Chiang Mai. Thai Airways is at 240 Prapokklao Rd. (☎ 053/210-042, or ☎ 053/211-044 at the airport); Bangkok Airways (☎ 053/281-519) and Angel Airlines (☎ 053/270-222, extension 2281) are at the Chiang Mai Airport. For general airport information, dial ☎ 053/270-222.

The Chiang Mai Airport is also connected to many international cities in Southeast Asia. There are daily flights to and from Yangon and Mandalay in Myanmar provided by **Air Mandalay** (☎ **053/818-049** in Chiang Mai). A daily flight from Vientiane, Laos, via **Lao Aviation** (☎ **021/212-051** in Vientiane or **053/418-258** in Chiang Mai), and three flights per week from Singapore aboard **Silk Air** (☎ **65/221-2221** in Singapore or **053/276-459** in Chiang Mai) attest to the easy access of this northern destination.

Taxis wait outside the airport, and can be booked at the ground transportation counter for about 120B (US$2.79). Thai Airways also offers a shuttle, which is less direct but costs about half the price.

BY TRAIN   Of the seven daily trains from Bangkok to Chiang Mai, the 8:10am Express Diesel Railcar (11 hours; 681B/US$15.84 second-class sleeper berth). The other trains take between 13 and 15 hours for the trip, but second-class sleeper berths are comparable in price (but some trains don't have sleeper cars at all). Private sleeper cabins (1,193B/US$27.74), available on certain express and rapid trains, should be reserved as early as possible. Purchase tickets at Bangkok's **Hua Lampong Railway Station** (☎ 02/223-7010) up to 90 days in advance. For local train information in Chiang Mai call ☎ 053/245-363, for advance booking call ☎ 053/242-094. Tuk-tuks hang around for travelers as they arrive. The short trip to town is only around 40B or 50B (US$0.93 or US$1.16).

BY BUS   There are several buses to chose from, depending on your budget and the level of comfort you desire—either one you choose the trip is still 11 hours. From **Bangkok's Northern Bus Terminal** (☎ 02/272-5761) on Phahonyothin Road near the Chatuchak Weekend Market, 5 daily VIP buses provide the most comfort, with larger seats that recline (570B/US$13.26), government air-conditioned buses cost 369B (US$8.58). The **Arcade Bus Station in Chiang Mai** is on Kaew Nawaratt Road (☎ 053/242-664), to the northeast of the Old City. There are minibus services to take you the short trip from the station to town.

GETTING AROUND

BY TAXI   Good luck finding one, as they don't cruise the streets, sticking to regular fares from the airport. Major hotels and travel agencies can provide car and limo services, but at a premium. A good bit of advice if you arrive by plane: Check out your taxi driver. Many of these guys speak English well enough and are familiar with the city and its attractions. I even met one who had a neatly bound portfolio of letters written by travelers who recommended his excellent services. These guys can be hired by the hour or day and will take you anywhere you want to go. Negotiate like a crazy person.

BY TUK-TUK   This can be a convenient way to get around if you're a firm negotiator. They can be flagged down pretty much everywhere. By the way, the guys who hang around outside major hotels will always quote you top dollar. Walk up the street a bit and flag down another one and you'll get a far better deal. And be careful of the tuk-tuk drivers who try to take you shopping or to places you don't want to go. They'll hustle you if they can. Most trips around town should be no more than 40B to 100B (US$0.93 to US$2.33).

BY SEELOR (SONGTAO)   Most of the locals get around by these pickup truck mini-buses, and they are the most recommended form of transportation for trips around the city. These red trucks can be flagged down if they're going in your general direction. Tell the driver where you're going (you may want to get someone at your hotel to write it in Thai for you), and if he can fit it in with the rest of the passengers' routes, you're on. Pay him when you reach your destination—anywhere from 10B to 20B (US$0.23 to US$0.47), a real bargain.

BY PRIVATE CAR   For the best value car rentals call **Budget Rent-a-Car** (189/17–19 Wualai Rd., ☎ 053/202-871). Suzuki Caribians start at 1,375B (US$31.98) per day, with Toyotas, Volvos, and Mercedes climbing up the price scale to about 3,500B (US$81.4) per day. Weekly discounts are available, as are chauffeured cars. Drivers will require an international driver license, and good insurance coverage will be provided.

Chiang Mai

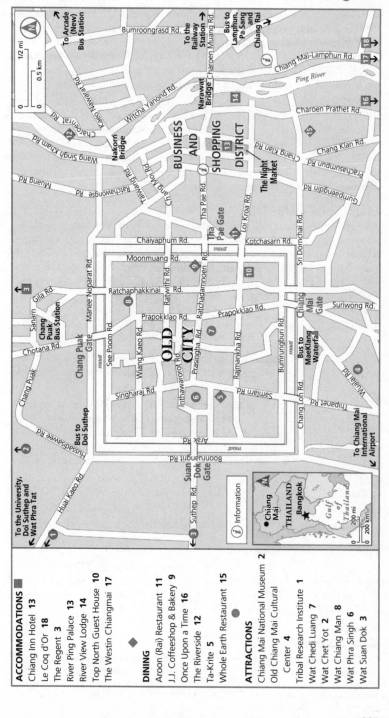

ACCOMMODATIONS ■
Chiang Inn Hotel **13**
Le Coq d'Or **18**
The Regent **3**
River Ping Palace **13**
River View Lodge **14**
Top North Guest House **10**
The Westin Chiangmai **17**

DINING ◆
Aroon (Rai) Restaurant **11**
J.J. Coffeeshop & Bakery **9**
Once Upon a Time **16**
The Riverside **12**
Ta-Krite **5**
Whole Earth Restaurant **15**

ATTRACTIONS ●
Chiang Mai National Museum **2**
Old Chiang Mai Cultural
    Center **4**
Tribal Research Institute **1**
Wat Chedi Luang **7**
Wat Chet Yot **2**
Wat Chiang Man **8**
Wat Phra Singh **6**
Wat Suan Dok **3**

For the cheapest alternative I've used **North Wheels** (127/2 Moonmuang Road; ☎ **053/216-189**) with great success. They'll greet you at the airport, and drop you there when you leave, or make deliveries to your hotel, no problem. They even took me back to the lot to let me inspect and select the car I wanted—a Suzuki Caribian for 750B (US$17.44) a day—not bad. Don't even bother reading the insurance policy, it looks like a joke but there's no punch line. Trust me.

BY MOTORCYCLE Many guest houses along the Ping River and shops around Chaiyapoom Road (north of Tha Pae Road in the Old City) rent 100cc motorcycles for about 200B per day (US$4.65). 250cc Honda, are commonly available and a good choice because of their added power and large fuel tanks; they rent for about 550B (US$12.79). Wear a helmet, and expect to leave your passport as security (don't leave any credit cards). Traffic congestion makes driving within the city dangerous, so employ all your defensive driving techniques.

VISITOR INFORMATION

The **TAT** office is at 105/1 Chiang Mai-Lamphun Road, 400 meters south of the Nawarat Bridge on the east side of the Ping River (☎ **053/248-604**). There are a couple free magazines circulating—*Guidelines Chiang Mai* and *Welcome to Chiang Mai and Chiangrai*—available at hotels and businesses, which contain detailed maps, as well as useful and interesting information. I personally think the latter is better for maps and useful information.

Fast Facts: Chiang Mai

Banks/Currency Exchange You'll find branches for every major bank (with ATMs and money-changing services) on Changklan Road in the area around the Night Market.

Internet/E-mail Look in or around guesthouses in the Old City. Assign Internet has two branches, the most convenient across from MacDonald's in Chiang Mai Pavilion at the Night Market on 145/23 Chang Klan Road, ☎ 053/818-911, with another branch outside the northwest corner of the Old City at 12 Huay Kaew Shopping Center, Huay Kaew Road across from Central Department Store ☎ 053/404-550.

Post Office The main Post Office is at 402 Charoenmuang Rd. (☎ 053/241-070).

Tourist Police Tourist Police in Chiang Mai can be reached at ☎ 1155.

ACCOMMODATIONS

The largest number of hotels is concentrated in the business and shopping district to the east of the Old City, and staying in these hotels is very convenient for reaching most attractions, restaurants, and night spots. In addition, some smaller and very charming hotels sit on the banks of the Ping River. These tend to reflect more local character, and can be very relaxing.

VERY EXPENSIVE

✪ **The Regent.** Mae Rim–Samoeng Old Rd., Mae Rim, Chiang Mai 50180. ☎ **800/545-4000** in the U.S. and Canada, 800/022-800 in Australia, 0800/440-800 in New Zealand, 0800/282-245 in the UK, or 053/298181. Fax 053/298190. 67 suites. A/C MINIBAR TV TEL. US$320–US$410 pavilion suite; US$900–US$2,000 residence suite. AE, DC, MC, V. 20 min. north of city off Chiangmai–Maerim Rd.

Northern Thailand's finest resort is well isolated from the bustle of the city on 20 acres of landscaped grounds in the Mae Rim Valley. The beautiful central garden includes two small lakes, lily ponds, and terraced rice paddies (which are maintained by the resort); and two-story Lanna-style pavilions are clustered informally around it. Spacious suites are understatedly elegant with polished teak floors and vaulted ceilings, decorated with traditional Thai fabrics and art, each with an adjoining private sala (open-air pavilion). Bathrooms are particularly large and luxurious, with two vanities and a big sunken tub and separate shower, overlooking a secluded garden.

The pool is a spectacle. As you stand at the head, the false edge at the opposite end seems to drop off into the paddy fields below and rise into the mountains beyond. At night, torches are lit in the fields, providing a mysterious aura to the views from the resort's restaurants. This luxury retreat spares no detail for your vacation enjoyment, with a modern fitness studio, luxurious spa with massage and sauna, two lighted tennis courts with full-time pro, and mountain bikes with maps of the surrounding countryside. On a whimsical note, Regent is the only resort in the world to boast its own resident family of water buffalo, and they are the most pampered and prissy beasts you've ever seen. If you're worried about being far from Chiang Mai, the resort provides regular shuttles to and from the main business and shopping district.

The Westin Chiangmai. 318/1 Chiangmai-Lamphun Rd., Chiang Mai 50007. ☎ **053/ 275-300.** Fax 053/275-299. 528 units. A/C MINIBAR TV TEL. 5,800B–8,600B (US$134.88–US$200) double; from 12,500B (US$290.7) suite. AE, DC, JCB, MC, V. South of city center, across Mengrai Bridge on east bank of river.

Chiang Mai's newest and best high-rise hotel is isolated across the river just south of town. The attractive lobby is both spacious and welcoming, and the staff is friendly and well-trained (making this place particularly well-suited for business travelers). The rooms are large and plush, with subdued colors and attractive teak furnishings, each with a view. Amenities include a swimming pool, fitness center, beauty salon, 24-hour room service, tour desk, complimentary shuttle to and from airport, voice mail.

EXPENSIVE

Chiang Inn Hotel. 100 Chang Klan Rd., Chiang Mai 50100. ☎ **053/270-070.** Fax 053/ 274-299. 190 units. A/C MINIBAR TV TEL. 1,300B (US$30.23) double; from 7,000B (US$162.79) suite. AE, DC, MC, V. 2 blocks south of Tha Pae Rd., 2 blocks west of river, just north of Night Market.

The renovated Chiang Inn is right across the street from the Chiang Inn Plaza, an arcade of Western chain eateries like MacDonald's and Dunkin Donuts, but it's set back from the lively street and quieter at night than you'd expect. The compact, teak-paneled lobby has a homey yet elegant feel and is almost always crowded with Europeans. Spacious rooms are clean but are decorated in a bland fashion that's not much in keeping with the price of the facility. Still, for location, the Chiang Inn is tops. Be warned, though, the Chiang Inn is a favorite hangout for tuk-tuk drivers who try to charge visitors an arm and a leg and take them to places they don't wish to visit.

✪ **River View Lodge.** 25 Charoen Prathet Rd., Soi 2, Chiang Mai 50100. ☎ **053/ 271109.** Fax 053/279019. 36 units. A/C TEL. 1,450B–2,200B (US$33.72–US$51.16) single or double. MC, V. On river 2 blocks south of Thae Pae Rd.

Veteran shopper and mapmaker Nancy Chandler stays here when in Chiang Mai, and for good reason. First of all, River View's location on the river makes for a peaceful retreat, and yet it's only a short walk to the city's main business and shopping district. Second, the atmosphere is fabulous, from the antiques (all for sale) scattered throughout the hotel's public spaces to the quaint, shady garden that separates the small swimming pool from the open-sided cafe restaurant. Large guest rooms have fresh terra-cotta tile floors with sparse but well-maintained furnishings and no-fuss decor. Bathrooms have shower stalls only, and some of the rooms have wall-to-wall carpeting that doesn't feel as cooling as the tiled rooms. Rates vary depending on the view, and many rooms have balconies.

MODERATE

River Ping Palace. 385/2 Charoen Prathet Rd., Chiang Mai 50100. ☎ **053/274-932.** Fax 053/273-675. 11 units. A/C MINIBAR. 600B–900B (US$13.95–US$20.93) double; 1,400B suite (US$32.56). AE, MC, V. On the river, a 20-minute walk south of the Night Market, between Monfort College and the Mengrai Bridge.

If you really want a taste of old Thailand, check into the River Ping Palace for a night. This old, lovingly restored compound of once-private teak houses has been converted into a guesthouse, dressed in four-poster beds with romantic mosquito netting, antique cabinets, rattan armchairs, Victorian brass wall sconces, framed historical photos, and unique accessories. The upstairs lanai overlooking the river is especially wonderful for enjoying lazy afternoon cocktails. The only complaint is that the facility is not exactly modern—it's difficult fitting so many functioning bathrooms into the old dame, so you must sacrifice a little convenience, especially during rainstorms when the roof gets leaky in spots. The management fights a never-ending battle to keep up with maintenance. At time of writing, the suite room, located in its own teak house, was under renovation. Still, in all, it's ambiance and authenticity in one wild package. Its restaurant, Once Upon a Time, serves excellent northern cuisine, and is reviewed later in this section.

INEXPENSIVE

○ Top North Guest House. 15 Moon Muang Rd., Soi 2, Chiang Mai 50100. ☎ **053/298-900.** Fax 053/278-485. 90 units. A/C. 500B (US$11.63) air-conditioned double; 300B (US$6.98) fan double. MC, V.

This is not your average guesthouse. Tucked away on one of the old city's narrow lanes, the quiet Top North is like a mini hotel. Quiet and comfortable, guests are invited to relax by the pool, which is large for the price, or sit for a spell in the cool Thai/Western coffee shop. Rooms are big, with clean tiled floors, large bathrooms (with bathtubs!) and the most unique blue and white stencil painting on the walls. Top North also has a good tour operation that organizes treks and an Internet café on premises.

DINING
EXPENSIVE

Le Coq d'Or. 68/1 Koh Klang Rd. ☎ **053/282-024.** Reservations recommended for weekend dinner. Main courses 320B–850B (US$7.44–US$19.77). AE, DC, MC, V. Daily 11am–2:30pm and 7pm–[11pm. Five-minute drive from the Westin. FRENCH.

In a romantic English country house setting, Coq d'Or is second to none in Chiang Mai for excellent atmosphere, food, presentation and service. Well-trained waiters serve a small, but mouthwatering assortment of imported beef, lamb and fish in French and continental styles on white linen and china. My chateaubriand came perfectly rare, with a delicate gravy and bernaise on the side. For starters, the salmon tartar wrapped in smoked salmon is served with toast, a sour cream and horseradish sauce and capers. They have a nice wine list to compliment your meal. Don't wait for a special occasion.

MODERATE

Once Upon a Time. 385/2 Charoen Prathet Rd. ☎ **053/274-932.** Reservations recommended. Main courses 80B–200B (US$1.86–US$4.65). AE, MC, V. Daily 4:30pm–midnight. Lunch is served during festivals or by request. West side of river, just north on Mengrai Bridge. THAI.

If you want the best Thai food, in the most beautiful compound of restored teak houses, there's no better choice. The two-story teak dining pavilion shares a tranquil garden with the charming River Ping Palace guesthouse. Downstairs serves specialties such as *hohmok,* an array of seafood soufflés made with prawn, mussels, or fish and coconut milk; mildly spiced grilled duck in a coconut-milk curry; *pla chon,* fresh river fish served with dipping sauces; and delicious and distinctive *gai yang,* barbecue chicken. Upstairs, under the peaked roof, diners can sit on cushions in the khan toke-style and sample the same specials or an array of northern Thai dishes, including pork curry and piquant chili pastes.

✪ **The Riverside.** 9–11 Charoenrat Rd. ☎ **053/243-239.** Reservations recommended for weekend dinner. Main courses 65B–200B (US$1.51–US$4.65). AE, MC, V. Daily 10am–1am. East side of river, north of Narawatt Bridge. THAI/INTERNATIONAL

Casual and cool is what Riverside is all about. A tavern with riverside terrace views—make sure you get there before the dinner rush so you get your pick of tables. There's live music, from blues to soft rock, great Thai and western food (including burgers), and a full bar. Even if you just stop by for a beer, it's a convivial place that always has a jolly crowd. Full of conversation and laughter, small wonder it's such a favorite with travelers, locals and expatriates. Riverside also operates a night cruise at 8pm for 50B per person.

Whole Earth Restaurant. 88 Sri Dornchai Rd. ☎ **053/282-463.** Reservations recommended. Main courses 60B–250B (US$1.40–US$5.81). No credit cards. Daily 11am–10pm. 2 blocks west of river, off Chang Klan Rd. VEGETARIAN/ASIAN.

If you're looking for Asian food in the typically California/health food/Western vein, head for this New Age place in a traditional Lanna Thai pavilion. The extensive menu is prepared by a gifted Pakistani chef and is part vegetarian, Thai, and Indian. The old pavilion has an indoor air-conditioned non-smoking section, and a long open-air verandah set for dining with a view of the gardens (they'll bring a fan to your table upon request). In a good location, near to the main shopping and business areas, Whole Earth gets busy at lunch and dinner, so try to call ahead if you can.

INEXPENSIVE

✪ **Aroon (Rai) Restaurant.** 45 Kotchasarn Rd. ☎ **053/276-947.** Main courses 20B–60B (US$0.47–US$1.40). No credit cards. Daily 9am–2:30pm and 5:30–1pm. 2 blocks south of Tha Pae Gate outside Old City. NORTHERN THAI.

For authentic northern food, adventurous eaters should try this nondescript garden restaurant. Their *khao soi,* filled with egg noodles and crisp-fried chicken bits and sprinkled with dried, fried noodles, is spicy and coconut-sweet at the same time. Chiang Mai sausages are served sliced over steamed rice; puffed-up fried pork rinds are the traditional (if not cholesterol-free) accompaniment. Dishes are all made to order in an open kitchen, so you can point to things that interest you, including the myriad fried insects, beetles, and frogs for which this place is famous. They've added a new attraction—prepackaged spices and recipes for make it yourself back at home.

JJ Coffee Shop and Bakery. Corner of Moonmuang and Ratchadamnoen Rds. ☎ **053/211-070.** Main courses 40B–220B (US$0.93–US$5.12). V. Daily 7am–10pm. In Old City across from Tha Pae Gate. INTERNATIONAL.

Probably the closest thing I've seen to a diner in Thailand, JJ's has spotless booths and tables lining the long windowfront, rock and roll music and a wait staff with more personality than most places. The extensive menu includes excellent sandwiches and burgers, with good fries. They also have Thai dishes, but the western food is particularly recommended. Breakfasts are tops, and reasonably priced. Excellent bakery goods are sold next door, in the lobby of the Montri Hotel. There's a second branch at the Chiang Inn Plaza, 100/1 Chang Klan Road, with the same hours.

✪ **Ta-Krite.** 7 Samlarn Rd., Soi 1. ☎ **053/278-298.** Main courses 50B–120B (US$1.16–US$2.79). No credit cards. Daily 10am–11pm. Walk south from Wat Phra Sing and turn right on Soi 1. THAI.

This small restaurant packs a lot of charm, with lots of green plants, lovely locally-made blue and white pottery, and old finds here and there. Serving Thai cuisine more common to the central parts of the country, the house specialty is the duck curry in a coconut gravy hot with chilies and sweetened with fruits. It's also nice to know that their produce comes from the Royal Project. A great place to stop for a sight-seeing lunch-break, their Quick Lunch specials are numerous and only cost between 25B and 30B (US$0.58 and US$0.70)!

DINING WITH A CULTURAL SHOW

Old Chiang Mai Cultural Center. 185/3 Wualai Rd. ☎ **053/274-093.** Reservations required. Set dinner and show 270B (US$6.28). Nightly show at 7pm. Efficient hotel pickup and return can be arranged by the center when you call for reservations. THAI.

I don't know about you, but I like to avoid the really touristy activities—and usually the planned "dinner and traditional show" is one of the most dreaded things on my itinerary. But, to be honest, the Cultural Center does an honorable job. Yes, you must face the busloads of tourists, but the show is fun, with traditional Thai dancing (including male sword dances, which are kinda cool) that are entertaining. Despite their busy workload, waiters and waitresses still stop to check on you from time to time, and while the food, northern style dishes served in traditional khan-toke style (small portions of assorted dishes in bowls served on a tray), is only palatable, they never let your bowls become empty. Afterwards, a display of tribal costumes and dances is presented in an outdoor pavilion. Overall not bad, but if you skip it I won't be offended.

ATTRACTIONS

After Bangkok, Chiang Mai has the greatest concentration of exquisitely crafted wats (temples) in the country—more than 700 of them. Assuming you aren't planning a wat-by-wat tour, you can see all the principal sights in one day if you start early in the morning, particularly if you travel by tuk-tuk.

Wat Chedi Luang. Prapokklao Rd., south of Ratchadamnoen Rd. Suggested contribution 20B (US$0.47). Daily 6am–5pm.

Because it's near the Tha Par Gate, most visitors begin their sightseeing at Wat Chedi Luang, where there are two wats of interest. This complex, which briefly housed the Emerald Buddha (now at Bangkok's Wat Phra Kaeo), dates from 1411, when the original chedi was built by King Saen Muang Ma. The already massive edifice was expanded to 280 feet (85m) in height by the mid-1400s, only to be ruined by a severe earthquake in 1545, just 11 years before Chiang Mai fell to the Burmese. A Buddha still graces its exterior.

The remarkable nagas (serpents) guarding the stairway entrance to the typical northern viharn (the large hall where Buddha images are housed) are exceptionally ornate and ferocious. Next to the tall gum tree on the left is a shrine honoring Sao Inthakhin, also referred to as the City Pillar. It is believed that the upkeep of this wat is directly related to the well-being of Chiang Mai.

Wat Phan Tao, also on the grounds, has a wooden viharn and bot (the temple where the main Buddha is enshrined), a reclining Buddha, and fine carving on the eaves and door.

Wat Phra Singh. Samlarn Rd. and Ratchadamnoen Rd. Suggested contribution 20B (US$0.47). Daily 6am–5pm.

This compound was built during the zenith of Chiang Mai's power (its chedi was built in 1345) and is one of the more venerated shrines in the city. The beautiful 14th-century library to the right of the compound contains delicate manuscripts on mulberry bark, while the vihaarn, the building that contains Buddha images, houses a northern-style Buddha that is renowned throughout the region for its beauty. The building's walls are covered in elaborate murals that tell stories from Buddhist tradition and illustrate scenes from daily life in Chiang Mai's past glory.

Wat Chiang Man. Wiang Kaeo and Ratchaphakkinai rds., in the Old City near the northern Chang Puak Gate. Suggested contribution 20B (US$0.47). Daily 6am–5pm.

Thought to be Chiang Mai's oldest wat, this was built during the 14th century by King Mengrai, the founder of Chiang Mai, on the spot where he first camped. It's believed to have been a royal temple. Like many of the wats in Chiang Mai, this complex reflects many architectural styles. Some of the structures are pure Lanna, with black wood carvings reflecting the northern style and the skills of northern craftsmen. Others show influences from as far away as Sri Lanka; notice the typical row of elephant supports. Wat Chiang Man is most famous for its two Buddhas: Phra Sritang Khamani (a miniature crystal image also known as the White Emerald Buddha) and the marble Phra Sri-la Buddha. Unfortunately, the wihaan that safeguards these religious sculptures is almost always closed.

Wat Suan Dok. Suthep Rd. From the Old City, take the Suan Dok Gate and continue 1 mile west. Suggested contribution 20B (US$0.47). Daily 6am–5pm.

I like this complex less for its architecture (the buildings, though monumental, are undistinguished) than for its contemplative spirit and pleasant surroundings. The temple was built amid the pleasure gardens of the 14th-century Lanna Thai monarch King Ku Na. Unlike most of Chiang Mai's other wats (more tourist sights than working temples and schools), Wat Suan Dok houses quite a few monks who seem to have isolated themselves from the distractions of the outside world. Among the main attractions in the complex are the bot, with a very impressive Chiang Saen Buddha (one of the largest bronzes in the north) dating from 1504 and some garish murals; the chedi, built to hold a relic of the Buddha; and a royal cemetery with some splendid shrines.

Wat Chet Yot. Superhighway near the Chiang Mai National Museum, north of the intersection of Nimanhemin and Huai Kaeo roads about half a mile, on the left. Suggested contribution 20B (US$0.47). Daily 6am–5pm.

Wat Chet Yot (also called Wat Maha Photharam) is one of the central city's most elegant sites. The chedi was built during the reign of King Tilokkarat in the late 15th century (his remains are in one of the smaller chedis), and in 1477 the World Sangkayana convened here to revise the doctrines of the Buddha. The unusual design of the main seven-peaked rectangular chedi was copied from the Maha Bodhi Temple in Bodh Gaya, India, where the Buddha first achieved enlightenment. The temple also has architectural elements of Burmese, Chinese Yuan, and Ming influence. The extraordinary proportions; the angelic, levitating devata figures carved into the base of the chedi; and the juxtaposition of the other buildings make Wat Chet Yot (Seven Spires) a masterpiece. The Lanna-style Buddha hidden in the center was sculpted in the mid–15th century; a door inside the niche containing the Buddha leads to the roof, on which rests the Phra Kaen Chan (Sandalwood Buddha). There is a nice vista from up top, but only men are allowed to ascend the stairs.

Chiang Mai National Museum. Superhighway, just north of the seven-spired Wat Chet Yot. ☎ **053/221-308.** Admission 80B (US$1.86). Wed–Sun 8:30am–4pm. Closed holidays.

This modern complex houses the province's fine collection of Lanna Thai art. Woodwork, stonework, and the many religious images garnered from local wats, all well labeled, help to chronicle the distinct achievements of the Lanna Kingdom from the 14th to 18th centuries. These works reveal how Burmese religious art grew more influential over the years of occupation. Knowledge of both cultures will serve you well while touring the north. Note the display of weapons that were used to combat the Burmese.

Tribal Research Institute. Chiang Mai University, 4km (2.4 miles) west of the Old City, off Huai Kaeo Rd. ☎ **053/210-872.** Free admission. Daily 9am–4pm.

If you plan to go trekking or have any interest in the hill-tribe people, visit this facility. The institute conducts research, publishes excellent books and brochures, coordinates trekking groups, and runs a small, informative museum devoted to the ethnographic legacy of the northern tribal groups. There's an informative library next door.

OUTSIDE THE CITY

Wat Phra That. Suggested contribution 20B (US$0.47). Daily 7am–5pm; come early or late to avoid the crowds.

The jewel of Chiang Mai, Wat Phra That glistens in the sun on the slopes of Doi Suthep mountain. One of four royal wats in the north, at 3,250 feet (1,000m), it occupies an extraordinary site with a cool refreshing climate, expansive views over the city, the mountain's idyllic forests, waterfalls, and flowers.

In the 14th century, during the installation of a relic of the Buddha in Wat Suan Dok (in the Old City), the holy object split in two, with one part equaling the original's size. A new wat was needed to honor the miracle. King Ku Na placed the new relic on a sacred white elephant and let it wander freely through the hills. The elephant climbed to the top of Doi Suthep, trumpeted three times, made three counterclockwise circles, and knelt down, choosing the site for Wat Phra That.

The original chedi was built to a height of 26½ feet. Other structures were raised to bring greater honor to the Buddha and various patrons. The most remarkable is the steep 290-step naga staircase, added in 1557, leading up to the wat—one of the most dramatic approaches to a temple in all of Thailand. To shorten the 5-hour climb, the winding road was constructed in 1935 by thousands of volunteers under the direction of a local monk.

Doi Inthanon National Park. Admission 10B (US$0.23). Daily sunrise–sunset. Camping is allowed in the park, but you must check with the TAT or the national park office to obtain permits, schedule information, and regulations.

Thailand's tallest mountain (at 8,408 feet/2,563m), Doi Inthanon is 29 miles (47km) south of Chiang Mai. It crowns a 360-square-mile (581 sq km) national park filled with impressive waterfalls and wild orchids. Doi Inthanon Road climbs 30 miles (48km) to the summit. Along the way is the 100-foot-high Mae Klang Falls, a popular picnic spot with food stands. Nearby Pakan Na Falls is less crowded because it requires a bit of climbing along a path to reach. At the top of the mountain, there's a fine view and two more falls, Wachirathan and Siriphum, both worth exploring.

TREKKING FROM CHIANG MAI

Tourism in the north developed slowly during the 1970's, but really took off in the early 80s, when backpackers and other assorted intrepids made their way north to see this unique region and the colorful people who inhabit it. Today, travelers are still drawn to the hilltribe villages in search of a special experience—to come in contact with cultures that are unspoiled by modern development—to witness life here as it has been for past centuries. With this ideal in mind, all trekking companies advertise their offerings as "non-tourist," "authentic," "alternative," or "remote" to set their tours and treks apart from tacky tourist operations or staged cultural experiences. The truth is, despite what these touts promise, not one village exists that has not experienced the modern world in some way.

The encroachment of civilization is inevitable, and tourists aren't the only ones to blame. The Thai government has made efforts to incorporate the tribes into the national political culture, environmentalists have worked to spare precious forests that are destroyed by their slash-and-burn agricultural techniques and the royal family has taken huge strides to introduce crops to replace their staple opium production. Despite the overall positive effects of these efforts, the tribal peoples now must struggle to maintain their cultural identities, livelihoods and centuries-old ways of life. But don't let this discourage you from joining a trek or tour. If you seek a truly *authentic* experience, come not to see primitive people, as the tour promoters suggest. Rather, come to learn how these cultures on the margin of society grapple with complex pressures from the national and international scene to maintain their unique identities. Within this frame of reference you will find your authentic experience.

There are two kinds of hilltribe operators in northern Thailand, those that offer **tribal village tours,** and others that coordinate jungle treks. The former puts together large and small groups to visit villages that are close to major cities and towns. If you join one of these groups, you'll travel by van or coach to up to half-dozen villages, each inhabited by a different tribe, and you'll spend about an hour in each one. These villages have had decades of exposure to foreigners, and because they are connected by roads, have some modern conveniences. This type of trip is carried out professionally by **Gem Travel,** 29 Charoen Prathet Road ☎ 053/272-855, fax 053/271-255. They'll provide transportation, a guide and lunch—for two, the cost is 1,500B (US$34.88) per person, but this figure decreases if you can join a group.

The second kind of trip is the **jungle trek,** which is longer, with smaller groups (about 4 to 10 people) and closer contact with tribal people. These will last anywhere from three days and two nights to two weeks if enough people are interested to make the longer trip worthwhile. Your journey will combine trekking both by jeep and on foot, accompanied by a local guide, with some bamboo rafting and elephant trekking thrown in for variety. Don't be intimidated by the trekking aspect, the guides keep a controlled pace, and even if you're not perfectly fit, you shouldn't have a problem keeping up. For **short-term jungle trekking,** The **Wild Planet** is a highly reputable outfit. Treks from Chiang Mai stop at Lisu, Lahu, and Karen villages. A 2-day/1-night trip is 3,200B (US$74.42) per person if you join their regular tour; the 3-day/2-night tour is 4,200B (US$97.67). Their head office in Bangkok is at No. 9 Thonglor Soi 25, Sukhumvit 55, Prakanong. ☎ 02/233-0997, fax 02/712-8748 www.wild-planet. co.th. In Chiang Mai, Charoen Prathet Road between Diamond Hotel and SK Money Changer ☎ 053/277-178.

BIKE TOURING

Chiang Mai Green Tour (29–31 Chiangmai-Lamphun Rd.; ☎ and fax 053/247-374) organizes **half-day or full-day mountain bike** trips to Chiang Mai's city attractions, Lamphun, the Elephant Conservation Center, or to nearby farming villages. The full day trip runs at 1,400B (US$32.56) per person.

SHOPPING

While traveling through the many regions of Thailand you're sure to find Thai arts and handicrafts in abundance in shops and at souvenir stalls. Most of the truly creative and unique items are made in the north part of the country, and if Chiang Mai is on your itinerary, your best bet is to delay any purchases until you've arrived here. Not only will you find the best selection of jewelry, embroidery, silks, pottery, carved wood, and religious artifacts, but you'll probably buy them at a much more reasonable price as well.

The centerpiece of Chiang Mai shopping is the famous **Night Bazaar.** In the late afternoon merchants set their tents on the sidewalks along Chang Klan Road beginning at the intersection of Loi Kroa Road. Until about 11pm nightly the street and the alleys beyond become a maze of good excuses to blow your vacation cash.

The **Anusarn Market,** located just southwest of the Night Bazaar, closes an hour earlier, but has less tourist traffic and more bargains.

Dedicated shoppers will have to devote at least half a day to shopping along the Chiang Mai–Sankamphaeng Road (Route 1006). It runs due east out of Chiang Mai, and after several kilometers becomes lined with shops, showrooms, and factories extending another 5.4 miles (9km). Here you'll find places like **Chiang Mai Silverware** (62/10–11 Sankamphaeng Rd.; ☎ 246-037) for bronze and silver; **Shinawatra Thai Silk** (145/1–2 Sankamphaeng Rd.; ☎ 053/338-053) for high quality silk; **Iyara Art** (35/4 Moo 3, Sankamphaeng Rd.; ☎ 053/339-450) with all sorts of curio items and antiques, plus Buddha and other religious images.; and **Baan Celadon** (7 Moo 3, Chiang Mai–Sankamphaeng Rd.; ☎ 053/338-288), for ceramics, to name just a few temptations. Most are open daily from 8am to 6pm. If you plan on doing a lot of shopping, joining a "shopping tour" group is the best idea. These half-day or full-day excursions are planned by just about every tour operator. If you hire a private car, you can take your time, stopping at each place to peruse.

CHIANG MAI AFTER DARK

Most folks will spend at least one night at the Night Bazaar for an evening full of shopping adventure, and if you get tired and hungry along the way, stop at **Galare Food & Shopping Center** (89/2 Chang Klan Road, on the corner of Soi 6, behind the bazaar; ☎ 053/820-320). Free nightly traditional Thai folk dance and musical performances grace an informal beer garden where shoppers stop for a drink or pick up inexpensive Chinese, Thai and Indian food from stalls around. Just behind, local singer-guitarists play more modern selections. For an impromptu bar scene, duck into one of the back alleys behind the Night Bazaar mall that are lined with tiny bars.

Most discos and lounges, located in major hotels, feature live music, whether it's a quiet piano bar or a rock pub featuring a Filippino band. The lobby bar at the **Empress Hotel** (Chang Klan Road; ☎ 053/270-240) features live R&B and pop songs in a relaxed lounge setting, and well as **The Royal Princess Hotel's Casablanca Room** (112 Chang Klan Rd.; ☎ 053/281-033). The casual tavern atmosphere and live pop and rock nightly at **The Riverside Restaurant & Bar** (9–11 Charoenrat Rd.; ☎ 053/243-239) gets my business every time. The **Bubble Disco in Pornping Tower** (46 Charoen Prathit Rd.; ☎ 053/270-099) and **Crystal Cave Disco** at Empress Hotel (Chang Klan Road; ☎ 053/270-240) are two of the most popular discos in the city. Pick up a copy of *Welcome to Chiang Mai & Chiang Rai* magazine at your hotel for listings of events that are happening while you're in town.

13 Chiang Rai

Chiang Rai (485 miles/780km NE of Bangkok; 112 miles/180km NE of Chiang Mai) is Thailand's northernmost province; the mighty Mae Kok River (known to most readers as the Mekong of Vietnam fame) shares borders with Laos to the east and Burma to the west. The scenic Mae Kok River, which supports many hill-tribe villages along its banks, flows right through the provincial capital of Chiang Rai.

Chiang Rai is 1,885 feet (575m) above sea level in a fertile valley, and its cool refreshing climate, tree-lined riverbank, small Night Market, and easy-to-get-around layout lures travelers weary of traffic congestion and pollution in Chiang Mai.

It's a small city, with most services grouped around the main north-south street, Phahonyothin Road, until it turns right (east) at the **Clock Tower,** after which it's called Ratanaket. There are three noteworthy landmarks: the small clock tower in the city's center; the **statue of King Mengrai** (the city's founder) at the northeast corner of the city, on the superhighway to Mae Chan; and the **Mae Kok River** at the north edge of town. Singhakai Road is the main artery on the north side of town, parallel to the river. The bus station is on Prasopsuk Road, one block east of Phahonyothin Road, near the Wiang Inn Hotel. The Night Market is on Phahonyothin Road near the bus station.

GETTING THERE

BY PLANE   Thai Airways has three direct 85-minute flights daily from Bangkok to Chiang Rai (☎ 02/535-2048 in Bangkok); and two 40-minute flights daily from Chiang Mai (☎ 053/210-042 in Chiang Mai). **Angel Air** (☎ 02/953-2260 in Bangkok or ☎ 053/922-295 in Chiang Rai) connects Bangkok and Chiang Rai with direct flights daily.

The new **Chiang Rai International Airport** (call Thai Airways for airport and flight information; ☎ 053/793-048) is about 10km (6.2 miles) north of town. Taxis hover outside and charge from 60B (US$1.40) for a lift to town.

BY BUS   **The 4-hour bus journey can be made from Chiang Mai's Arcade Bus Station (☎ 053/242-664), with 12 departures throughout the day. Tickets are 102B (US$2.37). Make sure you take the 4-hour bus—there's an older route that still operates and takes about 6 hours. Chiang Rai's **Khon Song Bus Terminal (☎ 053/711-369) couldn't be more conveniently located—on Phrasopsook Road off Phaholyothin Road near the night market just in the center of town. Tuk-tuks and samlors are easy to catch here, for trips around town for 30B to 60B (US$0.70 to US$1.40).

**BY CAR   **The fast and not particularly scenic route from Bangkok is Highway 1 North, direct to Chiang Rai. A slow, scenic approach on blacktop mountain roads is Route 107 north from Chiang Mai to Fang, then Route 109 east to Highway 1.

VISITOR INFORMATION

The **TAT** (☎ 053/744-674) is located at 448/16 Singhakai Rd., near Wat Phra Singh on the north side of town, and the Tourist Police are next door. The monthly *Welcome to Chiang Mai and Chiang Rai* is distributed free by most hotels, and had a good, reliable map of the town.

GETTING AROUND

**BY TRISHAW OR TUK-TUK   **You'll probably find walking the best method of transport. However, there are *samlors,* bicycle trishaws, parked outside the Night

Market and on the banks of the Mae Kok River; they charge 10B to 30B (US$0.23 to US$0.70) for in-town trips. During the day there are tuk-tuks, which charge 30B to 60B (US$0.70 to US$1.40) for in-town trips.

BY BUS   Frequent local buses are the easiest and cheapest way to get to nearby cities. All leave from the bus station (☎ **053/711-369**) on Prasopsuk Road near the Wiang Inn Hotel.

BY MOTORCYCLE   Two local companies are recommended: **Soon Motorcycle,** 197/2 Trirath Rd. (☎ **053/714-068**), and **Lek House,** 95 Thanalai Rd. (☎ **053/713-337**). Daily rates run about 550B (US$12.79) for a 250cc motorcycle, 180B (US$4.19) for a 100cc moped, and 15B (US$0.35) for a helmet.

BY CAR   For a quality vehicle with good insurance coverage at a fair price, call **Budget** in Chiang Rai at ☎ **053/740-442.** They'll greet you at the airport or deliver the car anywhere. At **P.D. Tour & Car Rental Services,** Phahonyothin Road opposite the Wangcome Hotel (☎ **053/712-829;** fax 053/719-041), a Jeep goes for about 800B (US$18.6) per day and a sedan for 1,200B (US$27.91), not including gas.

Fast Facts: Chiang Rai

Banks/Currency Exchange   Several bank exchanges are located on Paholyothin Road in the center of town.

Internet/E-mail   There are plenty of Internet cafes, especially on the soi that leads off Paholyothin Road to Wiangcome Hotel, but the best one is Chiang Rai Cyber Net (☎ 053/752-513) just opposite form the hotel. Rates are 30B (US$0.70) per hour.

Post Office/Mail   The post office is on Utrakit Road 2 blocks north of the clock tower, also near the TAT.

Tourist Police   The **Tourist Police** (☎ 053/717-796) are next to the Tat on Singhakai Road.

ACCOMMODATIONS
VERY EXPENSIVE

✪ **Dusit Island Resort Hotel.** 1129 Kraisorasit Rd., Amphur Muang 57000, Chiang Rai. ☎ **053/715-777.** Fax 053/715-801. www.dusit.com. 271 units. A/C MINIBAR TV TEL. US$60–80 double; from US$100 suite. AE, DC, MC, V. Over bridge at northwest corner of town.

Chiang Rai's best resort hotel occupies a large delta island in the Mae Kok River. It's sure to please those looking for international luxury and resort comforts, though at the expense of local flavor and homeyness. The dramatic lobby is a soaring space of teak, marble, and glass, as grand as any in Thailand, with panoramic views of the Mae Kok. Rooms are luxuriously appointed in pastel cottons and teak trim, but have thin walls that let in noise form adjacent rooms. The Dusit Island's manicured grounds, outdoor pool, tennis courts, fitness center, and billiards room create a resort ambience, but that shouldn't dissuade you from exploring the town.

EXPENSIVE

Wiang Inn. 893 Paholyothin Rd., Amphur Muang 57000, Chiang Rai. ☎ **053/711-533.** Fax 053/711-877. 256 units. A/C MINIBAR TV TEL. 1,883B–2,354B (US$43.79–US$54.74) double; from 4,700B (US$109.30) suite. AE, DC, MC, V. Center of town, south of bus station.

Wiang Inn offers full amenities, a helpful staff, several dining venues, a large pool, a reputable tour desk, and a convenient location, around the corner from the bus station and opposite the Night Market. Large rooms are trimmed in dark teak, with pale teak furniture and Thai artwork, including Lanna murals over the beds and ceramic vase table lamps. It's very well maintained, despite the steady stream of tour groups—which make an early booking advisable. Facilities are limited to a small pool and a massage center, but it is the best choice for a centrally located place to stay.

MODERATE

✪ **The Golden Triangle Inn.** 590 Paholyothin Rd., Amphur Muang 57000, Chiang Rai. ☎ **053/711-339.** Fax 053/713-963. 39 units. AC. 600B–900B (US$13.95–US$20.93) double. MC, V. Two blocks north of bus station.

A charming little hotel that offers comfort and lots of style and character, Golden Triangle is set in lush gardens—once inside you'd never believe bustling Chiang Rai is just beyond the front entrance. Large rooms have terra cotta tiled floors, traditional-style furniture, and reproductions of Lanna artifacts and paintings. The owners and management are very down-to-earth and extremely helpful, and their operations are very well-organized and professional. Their restaurant is excellent, and is reviewed separately in this chapter, as is their travel agency. My favorite pick for Chiang Rai.

DINING

Cabbages & Condoms. 620/25 Thanalai Rd. ☎ **053/719-167.** Main courses 70B–200B (US$1.63–US$4.65). MC, V. Daily 10am–11pm. THAI.

Sister restaurant to Cabbages & Condoms in Bangkok the Population & Community Development Association has opened this northern branch to help support population control, AIDS awareness and a host of rural development programs in the north. An extensive Thai menu, with local catfish specialties, is excellent. It's popular for tour groups, who also come for the exhibit upstairs (see Things to See & Do later in this section), but don't let that keep you away—it's good food for a good cause.

✪ **Golden Triangle International Cafe.** Golden Triangle Inn, 590 Phaholyothin Rd. ☎ **053/711-339.** Main courses 80B–250B (US$1.86–US$5.81). MC, V. Daily 8am–10:30pm. THAI.

The decor, antique artefacts and photos, is an ode to old Chiang Rai, as the owner grew up in the town, and loves it well. The best reason to eat here is for the menu, which is almost like a short book explaining Thai dinner menus, the various dishes that make up a meal, and describing the ingredients and preparation of each. Choosing your own noodle dishes gives you the chance to experiment with various tastes, and they are prepared in quick and tasty fashion. Go for the regional treats—especially the curry sweetened with local litchies.

ATTRACTIONS
EXPLORING CHIANG RAI'S WATS

Wat Phra Kaeo. On Trairat Rd. on the northwest side of town, just north of Ruang Nakhon Rd.

Phra Kaeo is the best known of the northern wats because it once housed the Emerald Buddha now at Bangkok's royal Wat Phra Kaeo. Near its Lanna-style chapel is the chedi, which (according to legend) was struck by lightning in 1436 to reveal the precious green jasper Buddha. There is now a green jade replica of the image on display.

Wat Phra Singh. 2 blocks east of Wat Phra Kaeo.

The restored wat is thought to date from the 15th century. Inside is a replica of the Phra Singh Buddha, a highly revered Theravada Buddhist image; the original was removed to Chiang Mai's Wat Phra Singh.

Wat Doi Tong (Phra That Chomtong). Atop a hill above the northwest side of town, up a steep staircase off Kaisornrasit Rd.

This Burmese-style wat offers an overview of the town and a panorama of the Mae Kok valley. It's said that King Mengrai himself chose the site for his new Lan Na capital from this very hill. The circle of columns at the top of the hill surrounds the new lak muang (city pillar), built to commemorate the 725th anniversary of the city and King Bhumibol's 60th birthday. It is often criticized for its failure to represent local style. (You can see the old wooden lak muang in the wihaan of the wat.)

VISITING THE HILL TRIBES

Most of the hill-tribe villages within close range of Chiang Rai have become somewhat assimilated by the routine visits of group tours. If your time is too limited for a trek, several in-town travel agencies offer day trips to the countryside. Prices are based on a two-person minimum and decline as more people sign up; rates include transportation and a guide.

The best operation in Chiang Rai is **Golden Triangle Tours** (590 Phaholyothin Rd.; ☎ **053/711-339**; fax 053/713-963; e-mail: gotour@loxinfo.co.th). With about 20 different day and overnight trips, their experience has created offerings that are well in tune with what travelers seek in this area. For hill tribe treks, they have day trips, and longer trips from 2 days and 1 night to 6 days and 5 nights. **Day trips** to surrounding villages include light trekking (1,300B/US$30.23 per person for 2 to 3 people). If you include elephant trekking it's 1,700B (US$39.53) per person for 2 to 3 people. Longer treks with overnights in villages are available. You'll encounter numerous Akha, Hmong, Yao, Karen or Lahu tribes, depending on the length of your trip.

Before your trek it's a good idea to stop by the **Hill Tribe Museum** (620/25 Thanalai Rd., east of Wisetwang Rd.; ☎ **053/719-167**; open daily 8:30am to 5pm; admission is a suggested contribution of 50B/US$1.16). With the help of international volunteers, The **Population and Community Development Association** created a good 20-minute slide show to help visitors understand the different cultures of the nine major hill tribes. Its informative narration and the museum's well-labeled displays will teach you more, in less than an hour, than a day trip through the countryside.

LONG-TAIL BOAT TRIPS ON THE MAE KOK RIVER

The **Mae Kok River** is a fascinating attraction here for its beautiful scenery on both the Thai and the Lao banks. You can hire a long tail boat to zip you up and down the river, stopping at sites along the way. Charter boats begin at 7am, and can be booked at any time until 11pm. A full-day trip to Thathon and back costs 2,100B (US$48.84) for boat hire. You'll have the option to stop at the Buddha cave, a temple within a cavern; an elephant camp, for trekking; a hot spring; and a riverside Lahu village. If you have limited time, you can hire a boat to only on or two attractions from 300B to 700B (US$6.98 to US$16.28), depending on the stops you make. The ferry pier is beyond the bridge across from the Dusit Island Resort. Call **C.R. Harbour** ☎ **053/750-009** for information and taxi pick-up.

Maesalong Tours (882-4 Phaholyothin Rd.; ☎ **053/712-515**; fax 053/711-011) conducts half-day river cruises north of Chiang Saen, with a stop on the Lao side at the small riverside town of Muang Mom (US$40 per person). A full-day cruise includes additional stops at Stone Forest, with its picturesque natural rock formations, plus sand beaches and additional Lao villages (US$60 per person).

SHOPPING

The recent influx of tourists has made Chiang Rai a magnet for hill-tribe clothing and handicraft products. You'll find many boutiques in the Night Market (see "Chiang Rai After Dark," below), as well as some fine shops scattered around the city. Most are open daily from 8:30am to 10pm and accept credit cards. There's much less available than in Chiang Mai, but prices are reasonable.

Chiang Rai Handicrafts Center, 273 Moo 5, Phahonyothin Rd. (☎ 053/713-355), is the largest of the hill-tribe shops, with a huge selection of well-finished merchandise, an adjoining factory, and a good reputation for air-mail shipping.

CHIANG RAI AFTER DARK

Most visitors stroll through the Night Market and shop for souvenirs. It's really a miniversion of the more famous market in Chiang Mai. Shops clustered along Phahonyothin Road near the Wiang Inn, and around the two lanes leading off it to the Wangcome Hotel, stay open till 10pm.

There's a small and rather tawdry nightlife district west and south of the Clock Tower along Punyodyana Road, a private lane with clubs named Lobo, La Cantina, My Way, Mars Bar, and Butterfly. You can also hit the disco or karaoke bar at the **Inn Come,** across from Little Duck on the superhighway, or have a draught beer and toss a few darts at the **Cellar Pub,** at the Dusit Island Resort.

14 Chiang Saen & the Golden Triangle

The small village of Chiang Saen (581 miles/935km NE of Bangkok; 148 miles/239km NE of Chiang Mai) has the sleepy, rural charm of Burma's ancient capital of Pagan. The single lane road from Chiang Rai (37 miles/59km) follows the small Mae Nam Chan River past coconut groves and rice paddies guarded by water buffalo. Little Chiang Saen, the birthplace of expansionary King Mengrai, was abandoned for the new Lanna Thai capitals of Chiang Rai, then Chiang Mai, in the 13th century. With the Mae Khong River and the Laos border hemming in its growth, modern developers went elsewhere. Today, the slow rural pace, decaying regal wats, crumbling fort walls, and overgrown moat contribute greatly to its appeal. After visiting the excellent museum and local sites, most travelers head west along the Mae Khong to the Golden Triangle, the north's prime attraction.

GETTING THERE

BY BUS   Buses from Chiang Rai's Kohn Song Bus Terminal (☎ 053/711-369) leave every 15 minutes from 6am to 6pm (trip time: 1½ hours; 20B/US$0.47). The bus drops you on Chiang Saen's main street. The museum and temples are walking distance, for convenient day trips, and songtao are across the street for trips to Golden Triangle (about 10B/US$0.23). (I'll bet you a dollar the drivers are still under that little sala hut playing checkers.)

BY CAR   Take the superhighway Route 110 north from Chiang Rai to Mae Chan, then Route 1016 northeast to Chiang Saen.

VISITOR INFORMATION

There is no TAT, so make sure you talk to TAT in Chiang Rai before your trip. The staff at the few guest houses speak some English and try to be helpful.

GETTING AROUND

Route 1016 is the village's main street, which intersects after 550 yards (500m) with the Mae Khong River. Along the river road, there are a few guest houses to the west, and an active produce, souvenir, and clothing market to the east. There's so little traffic it's a pleasure to walk; all of the in-town sights are within 15 minutes' walk of each other and are impossible to miss.

BY BICYCLE OR MOTORCYCLE   It's a great bike ride (45 minutes) from Chiang Saen to the prime nearby attraction, the Golden Triangle. The roads are well paved and pretty flat. **Chiang Saen House Rent Motor,** on the river road just east of the main street intersection, has good one-speed bicycles for 30B (US$0.70) per day and 100cc motorcycles (no insurance, no helmets) for 180B (US$4.19) per day.

BY SAMLOR   Motorized Pedicabs hover by the bus stop in town to take you to the Golden Triangle for 60B (US$1.40) one-way. Round-trip fares with waiting time are negotiable to about 250B for about two hours.

BY SONGTAO   *Songtao* (truck taxis) can be found on the main street across from the market; rides cost only 10B (US$0.23) to Golden Triangle, or to nearby guesthouses.

BY LONGTAIL BOAT   Long-tail boat captains down by the river offer Golden Triangle tours for about 350B (US$8.14) per boat (seating eight) per half-hour. Many people enjoy the half-hour cruise, take a walk around the village of Sob Ruak after they've seen the Golden Triangle, and then continue on by bus.

FAST FACTS: CHIANG SAEN & THE GOLDEN TRIANGLE

Everything You Need   Siam Commercial Bank, the bus stop, post office, and police station, and the Chiang Saen National Museum are all on main street. There is a currency exchange booth at the Golden Triangle.

ACCOMMODATIONS & DINING

✪ **Le Meridien Baan Boran Hotel.** Golden Triangle, Chiang Saen 57150, Chiang Rai. ☎ **800/225-5843** in the US and Canada; 1800/622-240 in Australia; 0800/454-040 in New Zealand; 0800/404-040 in the UK; 053/716-678. Fax 053/716-702. 110 units. A/C MINIBAR TV TEL. US$76–US$107 double. AE, DC, MC, V. Above river, 12km (7.5 miles) northwest of Chiang Saen.

In stunning contrast to most new hotels, this one is a triumph of ethnic design. You'll never question whether you're in the scenic hill-tribe region because the Le Meridien Baan Boran's elegance and style depend on locally produced geometric and figurative weavings, carved teak panels, and pervasive views of the juncture of the Ruak and Mae Khong rivers. On a hilltop just 1.2 miles (2km) west of the infamous Golden Triangle, the balconied rooms have splendid views. This oasis of comfort has attached rooms that are so spacious and private you'll feel like you're in your own bungalow. Tiled foyers lead to large bathrooms and bedrooms furnished in teak and traditionally patterned fabrics. The Yuan Lue Lau is a lovely, casual dining pavilion with river views. Thai and continental set menus or main courses, snacks, and breakfast are served. Frequent barbecues and buffets are held on a lower, river-view terrace.

ATTRACTIONS

Allow at least half a day to see all of Chiang Saen's historical sights before exploring the Golden Triangle. To help with orientation, make the museum your first stop.

Chiang Saen National Museum. 702 Paholyothin Rd., ☎ **053/777-102.** Admission 30B (US$0.70). Wed–Sun 9am–4pm. Closed holidays.

The museum houses a small but very fine collection of the region's historic and ethnographic products, including large bronze and stone Buddhas dating from the 15th to 17th centuries, pottery from Sukhothai-era kiln sites, and handicrafts and cultural items of local hill tribes.

Wat Pa Sak. about 220 yards west of the Chiang Saen Gate (at the entrance to the village). Admission 25B (US$0.58). Daily 8am–5pm.

The best preserved of the town's wats, Pa Sak is set in a landscaped historical park that contains a large, square-based stupa and six smaller chedis and temples. The park preserves what's left of the compound's 1,000 teak trees. The wat is said to have been constructed in 1295 by King Saen Phu to house relics of the Buddha, though some historians believe its ornate combination of Sukhothai and Pagan styles dates it later. The area's oldest wat is still an active Buddhist monastery.

Wat Phra Chedi Luang. Daily 8am–5pm.

Rising from a cluster of wooden dorms, Wat Phra Chedi Luang (or Jadeeloung) has a huge brick chedi that dominates the main street. The wat complex was established in 1331 under the reign of King Saen Phu and was rebuilt in 1515 by King Muang Kaeo. The old brick foundations, now supporting a very large seated plaster Buddha flanked by smaller ones, are all that remain.

Wat Mung Muang.

Mung Muang is the 15th-century square-based stupa seen next to the post office. Above the bell-shaped chedi are four small stupas. Across the street, you can see the bell-shaped chedi from **Wat Phra Bouj,** which is rumored to have been built by the prince of Chiang Saen in 1346, though historians believe it's of the same period as Mung Muang.

THE GOLDEN TRIANGLE

The infamous Golden Triangle (12km/7.5 miles northwest of Chiang Saen) is the point where Thailand, Burma and Laos meet at the confluence of the broad, slow, and silted Mae Khong and Mae Ruak rivers. They create Thailand's north border, separating it from overgrown jungle patches of Burma to the east and forested, hilly Laos to the west. The area's appeal as a vantage point over forbidden territories is quickly diminishing as there is now a legal crossing into Laos from nearby Chiang Khong.

Nonetheless, a "look" at the home of ethnic hill tribes and their legendary opium trade is still fascinating. Despite years of DEA-financed campaigns, the annual yield is still nearly 4,000 tons—about half of the heroin sold in the United States. The "surrender" of the notorious drug lord, Khun Sa, and his Muang Tai Army to the military dictators of Burma (Myanmar) effected little change—there were plenty of others waiting to take his place.

The appeal of this geopolitical phenomenon has created an entire village—Sob Ruak—of thatch souvenir stalls, cheap river-view soda and noodle shops, and very primitive guesthouses. The **House of Opium** (212 Moo 1; ☎ 053/784-062) is tiny and packed with visitors (if you see a lot of tour buses outside, go across the street and have a drink until they leave). Displays walk you through the opium process, from poppy cultivation, opium harvesting, drug production, and opium consumption. It makes a killing on camp appeal, but I really found it pretty neat.

Golden Triangle doesn't take too long to see, so I recommend a relaxing afternoon beer at **Jang's Place,** a small local establishment just across from the sandbar. Be warned: You may get so comfortable you'll never leave. Don't worry, though, they'll send out for food.

6 Vietnam

by Jennifer Eveland

Per square inch, Vietnam has as much to offer a traveler as any country in the world, packing at least seven distinct national identities into a relatively small total area. The country has over 2,000 years of its own history to boast, and while occupation by the Chinese, French, and Americans has left its brutal imprints on the Vietnamese story, it has also left a rich cultural smorgasbord. Chinese and French food, language, and architecture have been assimilated smoothly into Vietnamese culture and exist as attractive embellishments to an already fascinating nation.

An ancient Confucian university, a Zen monastery, a Buddhist temple built in the Hindu style, a Vietnamese puppet show, French country chalets and gourmet restaurants—you'll find them all in Vietnam. The Kingdom of Cham, an Indian- and Khmer-influenced nation, also made what is present-day Vietnam its home from the 2nd through 18th centuries, leaving a stunning legacy of art in its temples and sculpture.

Ethnic Vietnam can be seen by visiting some of the country's more than 54 minority groups, usually living in rural, mountainous areas. Their distinct clothing, language, and customs present another side of the country entirely.

Then there is the land of natural beauty. From tall mountains and craggy limestone formations to dense jungles, river deltas, and pristine beaches, Vietnam's ecological treasures alone are worth a trip. Adventure and outdoor travel outfitters have discovered the country of late, and many travelers come to trek, bicycle, and paddle their way through the country. On the other side of the spectrum, luxurious Vietnam is available in the form of five-star hotels and idyllic seaside resorts.

Wartime Vietnam is here, too. In fact, if you want to see the country's past in terms of its wars, you can easily do so. American veterans and history buffs of all nationalities visit former bases and battle sites. The Vietnamese, though, would rather put their turbulent history behind them. This sentiment is almost a public policy. You'll hear people repeating it like a mantra, and you'll find few even willing to talk about the wars on a casual basis.

Rather, the Vietnamese are going forward to establish their country as a unified whole, a unique entity in the world, a strong nation at peace at last. From the smallest northern village to frantic Saigon in the south, all seem to be rushing to develop infrastructure as quickly as possible, to make money and embrace foreign investment and tourism. Thanks in part to this policy, the country truly has developed in leaps and bounds. If you've never been to Vietnam before, you'll be amazed at how easy it is to navigate. Everybody seems to speak English and to be somehow connected with the tourism industry. Everybody wants to sell you something, too, but that can work to your advantage: You'll have your pick of tour guides, ticket agents, and chauffeurs. That may not be necessary, though; Vietnam's relatively good roadways and newly efficient air system make much of this small country within very easy reach of the casual traveler.

A *final word:* Go now. The region's financial crises led many of Vietnam's expatriate community and much of its business travel clients to flee the scene. Hotel and restaurant prices are as low as they'll ever be, and many tour operators are still giving big discounts.

1 Getting to Know Vietnam

THE LAY OF THE LAND

Vietnam is an S-shaped peninsula that borders China to the north, Laos to the west, and Cambodia to the southwest. Covering about 128,000 square miles, it is roughly the size of Italy. It has a varied and lush topography with two deltas, tropical forests, craggy mountains and rock formations, and a coastline that stretches for 2,025 miles, much of it white sand beaches. Vietnam can also claim thousands of islands off its coast.

THE REGIONS IN BRIEF

THE NORTH   The northern highlands, occupying the entire northwest tip of Vietnam, are known for their scenic beauty, with craggy mountains hovering over sweeping green valleys. The inhabitants of the region are ethnic minorities and hill tribes, scratching out a living from subsistence farming and still somewhat isolated from civilization. Popular tourism destinations are **Sapa, Lao Cai, Son La,** and **Dien Bien Phu,** the former French military garrison. Vietnam's tallest mountain, Fansipan, 3,143 meters (10,312 ft.), hovers over Sapa near the border with China in the northwest, part of the mountain range the French dubbed "The Tonkinese Alps." The **Red River** Delta lies to the east of the highlands. It is a triangular shape off the **Gulf of Tonkin,** an extension of the South China Sea. In the Gulf is spectacular **Halong Bay,** 3,000 limestone formations jutting up from still blue waters. South of the highlands but still in the northern region is **Hanoi,** Vietnam's capital city.

THE CENTRAL COAST   To the east is the central coastline, location of major cities **Hue, Hoi An,** and **Danang.** Hue is Vietnam's former capital and imperial city from 1802 to 1945. Hoi An, a major trading port in the mid–16th century, still shows the architectural influences of the Chinese and Japanese traders who passed through and settled here, leaving buildings that are still perfectly preserved. Danang, Vietnam's fourth-largest city, is a port town whose major attractions include the museum of Cham antiquities and nearby China Beach. Major flooding in the year 2000 caused immeasurable damage to the lowlands here, which will be apparent if you try to navigate Highway 1, which, at the printing of this book had yet to be repaired.

THE SOUTH CENTRAL COAST & HIGHLANDS   The central highlands area is a temperate, hilly region occupied by many of Vietnam's ethnic minorities. Travelers are most likely to visit historical **Dalat,** a resort town nestled in the Lang Bien Plateau, established by the French at the turn of the century as a recreation and convalescence center. On the coast is **Nha Trang,** Vietnam's pre-eminent sea resort.

THE MEKONG DELTA   Farthest south, the Mekong Delta is a flat land formed by soil deposits from the Mekong River. Its climate is tropical, characterized by heat, high rainfall, and humidity. The delta's sinuous waterways drift past fertile land used for cultivating rice, fruit trees, and sugar cane. The lower delta is untamed swampland. The region shows the influences of ancient Funan and Khmer cultures, and the scars as well from war misery, particularly in battles with neighboring Cambodia. **Saigon (Ho Chi Minh City)**, Vietnam's largest cosmopolitan area, lies just past its northern peripheries.

VIETNAM TODAY

As a destination, Vietnam is impressive for the sheer variety of what it can offer. A history of more than 1,000 years has developed a rich and varied culture, heavily spiced with remnants of other occupants like the Chinese, French, and Cham, a Hindu culture that has largely disappeared. Vietnam's 54 ethnic groups, many of them hill tribes living in remote villages, also make it ethnically one of the most diverse in Southeast Asia. The land's topography, with grandiose mountains, lush tropical forests, and beaches of plush sand, is perfect for trekking, paddling, biking, and every water sport you can name. Its major cities, Hanoi and Saigon, are exciting and cosmopolitan, and have countless cultural and historical attractions, as well as accommodations from budget to ultra-deluxe. As a rapidly developing nation, Vietnam is inexpensive and yet comfortable enough to appeal to travelers of all tastes.

A LOOK AT THE PAST

Vietnam began in the Red River Valley, around the time of the third century B.C., as a small kingdom of Viet tribes called Au Lac. The tiny kingdom was quickly absorbed into the Chinese Qin dynasty in 221 B.C., but as that dynasty crumpled it became part of a new land called Nam Viet, ruled by a Chinese commander. In 111 B.C., it was back to China again, this time as part of the Han empire. It was to remain part of greater China for the next thousand years or so. The Chinese form of writing was adopted (to be replaced by a Roman alphabet in the 17th century), Confucianism was installed as the leading ideology, and Chinese statesmen became the local rulers. Few effectively challenged Chinese rule, with the exception of two nobleman's daughters, the Trung sisters, who led a successful but short-lived revolt in A.D. 39.

In 939, the Chinese were finally thrown off and the Vietnamese were left to determine their own destiny under a succession of dynasties. The kingdom flourished and strengthened, enough for the Vietnamese to repel the intrusion of Mongol invaders under Kublai Khan from the north in the mid–13th century, and armies from the kingdom of Champa from Danang and the east. Gathering strength, Vietnam gradually absorbed the Cham empire and continued to move south, encroaching upon Khmer land, taking the Mekong Delta and almost extinguishing the Khmer as well. There followed a brief period of Chinese dominance in the early 1400s, but the biggest risk to the country's stability was to come from the inside.

Torn between rival factions in court, the country split along north-south lines in 1545; the north following the Le dynasty, the south, the Nguyen. The country was reunited under emperor Gia Long in 1802, but by the 1850s the French, already settled and on the prowl in Indochina, launched an offensive that resulted in the Vietnamese accepting protectorate status 3 decades later.

Although the French contributed greatly to Vietnamese infrastructure, the proud people bridled under colonial rule. In 1930, revolutionary Ho Chi Minh found fertile ground to establish a nationalist movement. As in China, World War II and occupation by the Japanese in 1940 helped fuel the movement by creating chaos and nationalist fervor, and upon the retreat of the Japanese, Ho Chi Minh declared Vietnam an independent nation in August 1945.

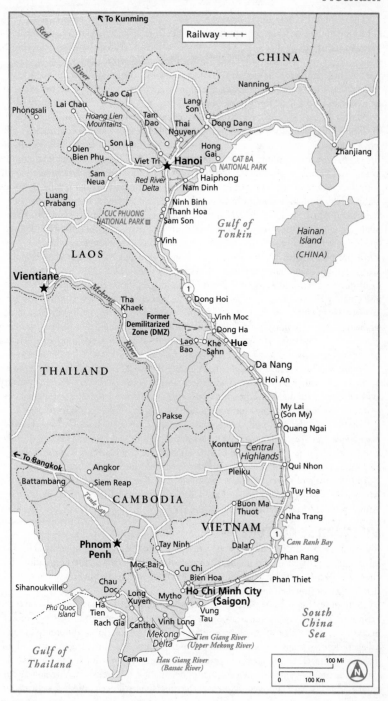

Vietnam

To Kunming

Railway ┼┼┼

CHINA

Red River

Nanning

Lao Cai

Lai Chau

Phongsali

Lang Son

Hoang Lien Mountains

Tam Dao

Thai Nguyen

Dong Dang

Son La

Dien Bien Phu

Viet Tri

Hong Gai

★ **Hanoi**

Zhanjiang

CAT BA NATIONAL PARK

Sam Neua

Haiphong

Red River Delta

Nam Dinh

Luang Prabang

Ninh Binh

Thanh Hoa

Sam Son

CUC PHUONG NATIONAL PARK

Vinh

Gulf of Tonkin

Hainan Island (CHINA)

LAOS

★ **Vientiane**

Mekong

Tha Khaek

Dong Hoi

Vinh Moc

Former Demilitarized Zone (DMZ)

Dong Ha

Lao Bao

Khe Sahn

Hue

THAILAND

River

Da Nang

Hoi An

Pakse

My Lai (Son My)

Quang Ngai

Kontum

Central Highlands

To Bangkok

Angkor

Pleiku

Qui Nhon

Battambang

Siem Reap

Tuy Hoa

Tonle Sap

CAMBODIA

Buon Ma Thuot

Nha Trang

VIETNAM

Cam Ranh Bay

★ **Phnom Penh**

Tay Ninh

Dalat

Moc Bai

Phan Rang

Cu Chi

Bien Hoa

Phan Thiet

Sihanoukville

Chau Doc

Long Xuyen

Mytho

Ho Chi Minh City (Saigon)

South China Sea

Ha Tien

Phú Quoc Island

Vung Tau

Rach Gia

Cantho

Vinh Long

Mekong Delta

Tien Giang River (Upper Mekong River)

Gulf of Thailand

Camau

Hau Giang River (Bassac River)

0 — 100 Mi

0 — 100 Km

241

The French did not agree, however, and the two sides fought bitterly until 1954. The French, having lost a decisive battle at Dien Bien Phu, agreed to a cease-fire at the Geneva Convention that year. The two sides determined that the country would be split along north and south at the Seventeenth Parallel, with the Viet Minh (League for the Independence of Vietnam) having control of the north and the French supporters having control of the south. Elections were to be held in 2 years to determine who would lead a new, unified Vietnam.

Mainly because of resistance from an American-supported regime in the south, led by Ngo Dinh Diem, the elections were never held. The communists continued to gain power and Diem was assassinated, putting the southern regime in peril. Finally, in 1965, American president Lyndon Johnson dispatched the first American combat troops to Danang to prop up the south. The Soviet Union and China weighed in with assistance to the north. The rest is history. After a decade of heavy fighting that took 58,000 American and as many as four million Vietnamese lives, the communists took Saigon on April 30, 1975. In 1976, north and south were officially reunited. Rather than enjoying the newfound peace, Vietnam invaded Cambodia after border skirmishes in 1978. China, friend of Cambodia, then invaded Vietnam in 1979.

In the mid 1980s, Vietnam began moving toward doi moi, a free-market policy, to save itself from bankruptcy. To further ingratiate itself with the international community, it withdrew its army from Cambodia in 1989, and as the 1990s began, the country began opening to the world. It further reorganized its economy toward a market-oriented model, sought diplomatic relations, and in 1991 signed a peace agreement with Cambodia. In 1994, America capitulated and lifted its long-standing trade embargo against Vietnam, and the two countries established diplomatic relations in 1995. Vietnam also joined ASEAN (Association of Southeast Asian Nations).

Today, Vietnam is flourishing. It has become the world's third largest rice exporter. Its per capita income increases steadily each year, though pockets of extreme poverty still remain in rural areas. Foreign investment, at least until the recent regional economic crises, was booming. And tourists are increasingly discovering its pleasures.

For historical background during the French occupation, read Graham Greene's *The Quiet American;* for history on the American War, Neil Sheehan's *A Bright Shining Lie* is considered the standard bearer; Michael Herr's *Dispatches* is another view. A few movies to whet your appetite: *Indochine,* a 1992 film with Catherine Deneuve set during the time of the communist revolution; *The Scent of Green Papaya,* 1994, story of an elite Vietnamese family and their servant girl; and *Cyclo,* 1995, about youth gangs in present-day Vietnam.

VIETNAMESE CULTURE

Vietnam has a cultural landscape as varied and colorful as its topography. The Viet ethnic group is well in the majority, comprising about 88% of the population, but there are 53 other minority ethnic groups, many of whom are hill tribes living in villages largely untouched by modern civilization.

Though Vietnam has rushed into modernization over the past several years, the economy is still largely agrarian, with farmers, fishermen, and forestry workers accounting for 73% of the workforce and most of the population still residing in small villages. The Vietnamese have a strong sense of family and of community, and are accustomed to close human contact and far-reaching interrelationships. This may be one of the reasons why, despite centuries of occupation by foreigners, Vietnamese cultural traditions have survived. Moreover, outsiders are still welcomed. Americans, in fact, will get a wide smile and thumbs-up, although the reception is notably better in the south than in the north. As a Saigon taxi driver put it, "America number one!

America and Vietnam, we just had a little problem." A classic understatement. One final note on the subject: Most westerners don't know that since the end of **"The Vietnam War"** this country has engaged in two other wars—one with Cambodia and another with China. To many Vietnamese, the war with the United States is considered ancient history.

CUISINE

Each region has its specialties, but the hallmarks of Vietnamese food are light, fresh ingredients, heavy on the rice, pork, and fish, with fresh garnishes such as mint, coriander, fish sauce, and chile pepper. Two of the local dishes you're most likely to encounter are *pho,* a noodle soup in a clear broth, and *bun cha,* fresh rice noodles with barbecued pork in sauce. Chinese-influenced dishes can be found, including hot pot, a cook-your-own group activity where fresh vegetables and chunks of meat and fowl are dipped into boiling broth and then consumed. The French have left their mark as well. Along with excellent restaurants, you'll find espresso and crusty French bread on every street corner.

THE ARTS

Ancient, distinctive Vietnamese art forms remain today, like **water puppetry,** where wooden hand puppets actually dance across water, and **cheo,** traditional **folk opera.** There is an emerging interest in fine arts, with countless galleries in almost every major Vietnamese city, and an emphasis on traditional techniques such as lacquer and silk painting and wood blocking. **Vietnamese music,** using string and woodwind instruments, bamboo xylophones, and metal gongs, is delicate, distinctive, and appealing. **Literature** has existed since the forming of the nation in folklore, proverbs, and idioms singular to each village and ethnic group and passed down from century to century. Many of the old tales have been translated and printed in books that you can easily find in a foreign-language bookstore.

RELIGION

About 70% of all Vietnamese are **Buddhists,** mainly Mahayana, 10% are **Catholics,** and the rest **Confucianists, animists** (believing in gods of nature), or followers of the unique Vietnamese religion **Cao Daism,** an interesting combination of the major world faiths. **Islam** and **Protestantism** also have small pockets of believers. While we're on the topic of -isms, it's hard for the casual observer to see any observance of communism at all, other than the prevalence of state-owned entities.

ETIQUETTE

Although the Vietnamese are generally tolerant of foreign ways, they dress very modestly. Foreigners displaying navels, chests, or shoulders or wearing hot pants will attract stares. Butt thongs and nude beach bathing are out of the question. Some temples flat-out refuse to admit persons in shorts, and some smaller towns like Hoi An post signs asking tourists to dress "appropriately," which means you may have a run-in with the police if you don't.

Unfortunately, one by-product of the relative newness of tourism in Vietnam is an eagerness to separate you from your money. This so-called communist state is in fact relentlessly capitalist. The child hawkers, "tour guides," and cyclo drivers can be extraordinarily persistent, following you for blocks, grabbing your arm, and hounding you at temples and open-air restaurants. Even if you don't want to be rude, avoiding eye contact and saying nothing is the best way to extricate yourself. It can be wearying, and hopefully the whole scene will calm down soon.

LANGUAGE

The ancient Vietnamese language, though not complex structurally, is tonal and therefore difficult for many Westerners to master. In its earliest written form, nom, it was based on the Chinese pictographic writing forms, but in the 17th century a French scholar developed a Roman alphabet for it. Today, most city dwellers seem to speak at least a little English or French. They will be eager to practice with you, especially if you are alone, although few people speak well enough for you to get close with them.

USEFUL VIETNAMESE PHRASES

English	Vietnamese	Pronounced
Hello	*xin chao*	seen chow
Good bye	*tam biet*	tam bee-et
Yes	*vang*	vahng
No	*khong*	kawng
Thank you	*cam on*	cahm un
You are welcome	*khong co gi*	kawng koe gee
Excuse me	*xin loi*	seen loy
Where is	*o dau*	er dow
Turn right	*re phai*	ray fie
Turn left	*re trai*	ray chrai
Toilet	*nha ve sinh*	nya vay shin
Hotel	*khach san*	kak san
Restaurant	*nha hang*	nya hahng
Potable water	*nuoc khoang*	nook kwang
I don't understand	*toi khong hieu*	toy kawng hew
How much?	*bao nhieu*	baugh nyew
When?	*luc nao*	look now
I need a doctor	*toi can bac si*	toy cahn back see
Hospital	*benh vien*	ben vee-in
Antibiotic	*thuoc khang sinh*	dook kahng shin

2 Planning a Trip to Vietnam

VISITOR INFORMATION

Vietnam's national tourism administration is a government agency rather than a font of information, although it does have a fairly good Web site at www.vietnamtourism. com. It operates mainly through its state-run tourism agencies, **Saigontourist** (www. saigon-tourist.com) and **Vietnamtourism** (www.gotovietnam.com), with offices all over Vietnam. They provide comprehensive services including tours and bookings. The following Web sites are also very helpful: www.vietnamembassy-usa.org (the Vietnam Embassy in the U.S.) and www.thingsasian.com/destination/vietnam (a colorful online magazine with excellent travel articles on dining and destinations).

ENTRY REQUIREMENTS

Residents of the U.S., Canada, Australia, New Zealand, and the United Kingdom need both passports and a valid visa to enter Vietnam. A tourist visa usually lasts for 30 days and costs US$50, although some people are inexplicably able to get longer visas upon request. It will take a week to 10 days to process, and must be submitted with your passport, the application, and two passport photos. You will receive a copy of the application, which must be submitted to the immigration officials checking

Tours for Vietnam Veterans

Travelers who come to Vietnam these days comprise those from all walks of life, but a goodly percent of them are, surprisingly, American Vietnam veterans. It's not unusual to run across groups or individuals as you make your way across the country, some simply seeing how the story ended or others on more somber missions, such as staging memorial services.

There are even tour operators specializing in veteran return visits. One such group is the Global Spectrum in Washington, D.C. Richard Schonberger, himself a veteran of the 101st Airborne Division, arranges group and private tours for about 250 veterans a year for Global. He says veterans account for about 15% of the company's annual Vietnam business.

Itineraries are often tailored to a division's history, though there are few remaining bunkers or barbed wire to see. Most groups visit general operating areas. An itinerary might include starting out in Saigon with an excursion to the Cu Chi tunnels, going down to the Mekong Delta, then heading up to Qui Nhon and to the Central Highlands and Pleiku, then on to Danang, China Beach, Hue, and of course, the De-militarized Zone (DMZ), also known as the 17th Parallel.

But why would a veteran want to return to Vietnam, scene of terror and destruction?

"One of the things we found is that most vets didn't get a taste of real Vietnamese culture, and most want to experience that the second time around," Schonberger says. Further, "Probably the most uniform reaction of veterans is a feeling of closure and healing," he says. "When you can cross the Ben Hai River at the DMZ and actually walk from north to south, that's when you really know the war is over."

For more information, contact **The Global Spectrum,** 5683 Columbia Pike, Suite no. 101, Falls Church, VA 22041 (☎ **800/419-4446** or 703/671-9619; fax 703/671-5747; www.vietnamadventuretours.com; e-mail: info@vietnamspecialists.com); or **Nine Dragons Tours,** P.O. Box 24105, Indianapolis, IN 46224-0105 (☎ **800/909-9050** or 317/329-0350; fax 317/329-0117; www.nine-dragons.com; e-mail: tours@nine-dragons.com).

your passport when you leave the country. Once inside Vietnam, you can extend your visa twice, each time for 30 days, according to Saigontourist, which, along with many travel agencies and state-owned hotels, is empowered to extend your visa. If someone gives you trouble about extending your visa, stick to your guns and ask around. Multiple-entry business visas are available that are valid for up to 3 months, but you must have a sponsoring agency in Vietnam and it can take much longer to process. For short business trips, it's less complicated simply to enter as a tourist.

If you are flying in, you will automatically be assigned either Hanoi or Saigon as entry points. If you plan to enter the country overland, you must specify your points of entry and departure and stick to them. Check your visa to make sure it's correct when you get it. If you change your plans once you're in the country, you can change the points of exit through a travel agency. Otherwise, you can face fines of up to US$40 when you try to leave.

VIETNAMESE EMBASSY LOCATIONS
IN THE UNITED STATES
- **Vietnam Embassy:** 1233 20th St. NW, Suite 400, Washington, DC 20036 (☎ **202/861-0737;** fax 202/861-0917)
- **Consulate General of Vietnam:** 1700 California St., Suite 430, San Francisco, CA 94109 (☎ **415/922-1577;** fax 415/922-1848)
- **Permanent Mission of Vietnam to the United Nations:** 866 UN Plaza, Suite 435, New York, NY 10017 (☎ **212/644-0594;** fax 212/644-5732)

IN CANADA
- **Vietnam Embassy:** 470 Wilbrod St., Ottawa, Ontario, Canada K1N 6M8 (☎ **613/236-0772;** fax 613/236-2704)

IN THE UNITED KINGDOM
- **Vietnam Embassy:** 12–14 Victoria Rd., London W8-5RD, U.K. (☎ **0171/ 937-1912;** fax 0171/937-6108)

IN AUSTRALIA
- **Vietnam Embassy:** 6 Timbarra Crescent, Malley, Canberra, ACT 2606 (☎ **2/ 6286-6059;** fax 2/6286-4534)
- **Consulate General of Vietnam:** 489 New South Head Rd., Double Bay, Sydney, NSW 2028 (☎ **02/9327-2539;** fax 02/9328-1653)

CUSTOMS REGULATIONS
The first and most important thing to remember is not to lose your entry/exit slip, the colored piece of paper that will be clipped to your passport upon arrival. If you do, you may be fined. If you are entering the country as a tourist, you do not need to declare electronic goods and jewelry if these things are for personal consumption. Declaration forms are only to make sure you're not importing goods without paying a tariff. You must declare cash in excess of US$3,000 or the equivalent. You can also import 200 cigarettes, 2 liters of alcohol, and perfume and jewelry for personal use. Antiques cannot be exported, although the laws are vague and irregularly enforced. If you're buying a reproduction, have the shop state as much on your receipt, just in case.

MONEY
The official currency of Vietnam is the **dong (VND),** which comes in notes of 100,000, 50,000, 10,000, 5,000, 1,000, 500, and 200.

CURRENCY EXCHANGE & RATES   At the time I did my research, the exchange rate was 14,595 Vietnamese VND to 1 U.S. dollar. The U.S. dollar is used as an informal second currency, and most things more than a few dollars are quoted as such. I've listed prices in this guide as they are quoted, and conversions were calculated at a rate of 14,607 VND per US$1. Every hotel, no matter how small, will gladly change money for you. Most times my U.S. dollars were bought at a rate of 14,400 VND for every 1 U.S. dollar, which is not bad. You may squeeze an extra 100 VND or so to the dollar from the black market. Changers usually loiter outside banks or post offices. Count the money you're given carefully, and be alert to counterfeits. The bigger the bill you change, the better your rate. Don't accept torn or very grubby bills, as you may have a problem reusing them. It may make more sense to pay in U.S. dollars whenever possible, unless you get a very good exchange rate on the black market.

Banks in any city I've mentioned can cash traveler's checks for you, in U.S., Canadian, and Australian dollars or pounds sterling, although U.S. dollars get the best rate.

Travel Tip

Film is cheap in Vietnam at about US$2.50 per roll, and the quality of developing services is good. If your camera breaks down, though, have it fixed at home. Disposables are available.

A service charge of anywhere between US$1 to US$4 will be levied. Vendors usually don't like to accept traveler's checks, however. Hanoi and Saigon each have a few Automated Teller Machines (ATMs) that dispense cash in dong and dollars.

As a general rule, credit cards are accepted only at major hotels, restaurants, tour guide operators, and some shops in Hanoi and Saigon, though they're increasingly accepted outside these two major cities. Any Vietcombank branch, as well as big foreign banks, will handle credit card cash withdrawals.

LOST/STOLEN CREDIT CARDS & TRAVELER'S CHECKS To report lost or stolen cards or traveler's checks, call the nearest branch of Vietcombank. Otherwise, you can go to a post office to place a collect call to the card's international toll-free collect number for cash and card replacement. The international numbers are operational 24-7, and are as follows: **Visa** Global Customer Assistance Service ☎ **410/581-3836** and **MasterCard** Global Services ☎ **314/542-7111.** Note that foreigners aren't permitted to make collect calls, so you'll have to get a Vietnamese to assist you. Or you can use AT&T, whose access number in Vietnam is ☎ **12010288.** For American Express, visit or call the nearest representative office, listed below in "Fast Facts."

WHEN TO GO

PEAK SEASON For some reason most people end up coming to Vietnam from September through April, the official "peak season" which doesn't necessarily present them with the best weather. See "Climate," below.

CLIMATE Vietnam's climate varies greatly from north to south. The north has four distinct seasons, with a chilly but not freezing winter from November to April. Summers are warm and wet. Dalat, in the central highlands, has a temperate climate year-round. The south (which means Nha Trang on down) has hot, humid weather throughout the year, with temperatures peaking March through May into the 90s. In addition, the south has a monsoon season from April to mid-November, followed by a "dry" season.

If, like many people, you're planning to do a south-north or north-south sweep, you may want to avoid both the monsoons and heat in the south by going sometime between November and February. If you're planning a beach vacation, however, keep in mind that the surf on the south central coast (China Beach, Nha Trang) is too rough for water sports from October through March.

PUBLIC HOLIDAYS Public holidays are New Year's Day (January 1), Tet/Lunar New Year (early to mid-February; state holiday lasts 4 days), Saigon Liberation Day (April 30), International Labour Day (May 1), National Day (September 2). Government offices and tourist attractions will be closed.

While **Tet** (the lunar new year, in late January/early February) is Vietnam's biggest holiday, it's a very family-oriented time. Much of the country will close down, including stores, restaurants, and museums, and accommodations may be difficult to find.

HEALTH CONCERNS

Health considerations should comprise a goodly part of your Vietnam trip planning, even if you're only going for a few weeks. You'll need to cover all the bases to protect yourself from tropical weather and illnesses, and will need to get special vaccinations if rural areas are on your itinerary. You should begin your vaccinations as necessary at least weeks prior to your trip, to give them time to take effect. If you follow the guidelines here and those of your doctor, however, there's no reason you can't have a safe and healthy trip.

DIETARY PRECAUTIONS

First, you'll want to avoid contaminated food and water, which can bring on a host of ills: bacillary and amoebic dysentery, giardia (another nasty intestinal disease), typhoid, and cholera, to name a few. **Take note: There is no public potable water in Vietnam. Drink only bottled or boiled water, without ice** except in very upscale places that assure you that they make their own ice from clean water. **Wash your hands often** with soap, particularly before eating, and eat fruit only if you have peeled it yourself. **Try to avoid uncooked food.** This is difficult with Vietnamese cuisine, which uses fresh condiments; and of course you'll want to try the fresh fruit milk shakes, ice cream, and so forth. So use your best judgment. Find the cleanest small restaurants (tip: look at the floors) and carry your own pair of plastic or disposable chopsticks or eating utensils for the inevitable moment a restaurant gives you a pair of used wooden ones.

If despite all your precautions you still fall ill with diarrhea or stomach problems, stick to easily digested foods until it clears up. Any Vietnamese will tell you to eat rice porridge and bananas and drink lots of weak green tea, which is sound advice. Yogurt (packaged only—avoid the fresh on-the-street stuff) can also help replenish necessary bacteria you may lose. You should also dose yourself with a rehydration solution to replace lost salt in the body. Bring some with you. In a pinch, you can purchase it at pharmacies in Vietnam. Once you feel like branching out, try a bowl of *pho ga*, noodle soup with shredded chicken. Should your symptoms persist for more than a few weeks, seek medical attention, and if you become ill after returning home, tell your doctor about your travels.

VACCINATIONS

The following vaccinations are important for Vietnam: Hepatitis A or immune globulin (IG), Hepatitis B, typhoid, and Japanese encephalitis if you plan to visit rural areas during the rainy season or stay longer than 4 weeks, and rabies if you're planning to go to rural areas where you might be exposed to wild animals. You should also consider booster doses for tetanus-diphtheria, measles, and polio.

Malaria is not a problem in the cities, but if you're going rural you should take an oral prophylaxis. Most Vietnamese mosquitoes are chloroquine-resistant, so mefloquine, also known as Larium, is commonly prescribed. It can have side effects, including dizziness and nausea. Before taking Larium, tell your doctor if you are pregnant or planning on becoming pregnant. The best prevention is to wear clothing that fully covers your limbs, and to use an insect repellant that contains DEET (diethylmethyltoluamide). Some people have allergic reactions to DEET, so test it at home before you leave.

GETTING THERE
BY PLANE

There is a myriad of air routes into Vietnam. You can fly almost any carrier that goes into Bangkok, Hong Kong, Taipei, or Tokyo and get a regional carrier from there. If

Travel Tip

Dress codes in Vietnam are casual except for the most normal of big city restaurants, so pack with this in mind. Keep it light, too, as you end up carrying your own goods more than once or twice along the way.

you're not picky about your choice of carrier or connection destination, there are great bargains to be had on the heels of the region's economic crises. One travel agent tipped me on great flight deals from North America aboard both Cathay Pacific (via Hong Kong) and EVA Air (via Taipei). See the section "Getting There," in chapter 3 for more international flight tips.

Pretty much every country in Southeast Asia is connected to both Hanoi and Ho Chi Minh City. Malaysia Airlines, Singapore Airlines, Thai Airways International, and Royal Camboge Airlines each flies regular routes from its home base, but prices may be expensive compared with those for flights on Vietnam Airlines. Vietnam Airlines has the benefit of being price-regulated by the government. It connects Vietnam (Ho Chi Minh City) with Vientiane, Phnom Penh, Siem Reap, Bangkok, Kuala Lumpur, Singapore, and Manila. Just about the only Southeast Asian country without a direct connection is Myanmar.

Reconfirmation of your ticket out of Vietnam is a must. Call your airline's in-country office at least 72 hours before your departure. Be prepared for a 25,124 VND (US$1.72) airport departure tax for each domestic flight, and a US$12 departure tax for your international flight out.

BY BUS

From Laos it is possible to enter Vietnam overland via a bus ride from Savannakhet in the south. It's 520 kilometers (323 miles) to Danang (105,043 Lao kip/US$13.82) or 405 kilometers (252 miles) to Hue (83,000 Lao kip/US$10.92). Buses leave at midnight. For more information contact the Lao National Tourism Authority in Savannahket at ☎ 041/212-755. You will need permission from the Vietnam Embassy to enter the country via this route when you obtain your visa.

GETTING AROUND

It is almost ridiculously easy to get around Vietnam. First, it seems like everybody is in the tourist business. A passerby on the street could probably book you a tour, if you asked. Along with established government-run and private tour agencies, hotels and cafes provide booking services. They all feed into a few big contractors, like tributaries into a river, so prices for the same services can vary. There hasn't been much of a problem with fraud yet, but do stick with the well-established agencies, tourist cafes, or hotels.

BY PLANE   Vietnam Airlines is the only domestic airline carrier in the country, but prices are reasonable and the service good. Seats are usually easy to come by. Purchasing tickets is again very easy; many major hotels have V.A. agents in the lobby.

BY TRAIN   Vietnam's major rail network runs from Hanoi to Saigon and back, with stops along the way including coastal towns like Hue, Danang, and Nha Trang. The Reunification Express is ironically the non-express train; there is an express route as well. To give you an idea of timing, from Hanoi all the way to Saigon is 34 hours on the express train; from Hanoi to Hue about 14 on an overnight express. It's an interesting way to get around, although not much cheaper than flying. Make sure you get

Vietnamese do like to smoke. Only top-end restaurants serving Western cuisine are likely to have a **nonsmoking section.** Some major hotels do; inquire when making a booking.

"soft sleeper" seats. Air-conditioning will cost you an additional price per ticket but may be most welcome, depending on when you're there. Hotels and tour agencies will gladly arrange tickets for you, to simplify the process.

BY BUS/MINIVAN   Public buses are not an option. Most times the bus driver will just shoo you off like a pest. Then again, why would you want to use one? The last time I went from Nha Trang to Hoi An I counted 18 public bus breakdowns. The passengers seemed to have fun, though, all huddled on the side of the road chatting and playing cards. Most tour agencies run **open-ticket tours** that connect all the major points: Saigon, Dalat, Nha Trang, Hoi An, Danang (optional), and Hue. You can travel either direction north to south or vice versa for about US$20. The bus (or sometimes minivan) leaves every morning; you just decide the day before if you want to be on it. It gives you tremendous freedom to plan your own itinerary. Both the **Kim Café** and **Sinh Café,** with branches in Hanoi and Saigon and all stops between, operate the open tickets, and also provide bus service between Hanoi and Hue. In the past year, Sinh Café has really beat out Kim Café in terms of convenience and service.

BY CAR   For all practical purposes, it is possible to rent a car in Vietnam only if it comes with a driver. However, it is a good way to see things outside of a city, or to take a 1-day city tour of major sights. Any major hotel or tour agency can assist you. For distances of longer than a few hours' drive, stick to minivans for safety, unless you have a very trustworthy driver and a heavy-duty vehicle.

TIPS ON ACCOMMODATIONS

A recent building boom followed by the regional currency crisis has brought hotel prices crashing down here. Always ask for seasonal reductions or promotional rates; discounts can be as high as 50% of the rack rate. While this means that deluxe hotels now have mid-range prices, the level of cleanliness and amenities is so high that you can stay in lower range hotels, pay very little, and still come away smiling. A 20% Value Added Tax (VAT) was instituted in January 1999, but expect differences in how hotels follow the policy. Inquire carefully. You need only book far ahead for the most popular hotels; see individual cities and towns for details.

TIPS ON DINING

Many of the world's finest culinary traditions are represented in Vietnam, including French, Chinese, Japanese, and, of course, Vietnamese. Explore all of your options, particularly in the French arena, as you won't find lower prices anywhere. This should not, however, preclude you from dipping into street stalls. They offer fantastic local delicacies like *bun bo* (cold rice noodles with fried beef), *banh khoi* (crispy thin rice-based crepes filled with chopped meat and shrimp), and *chao* (rice porridge with garnishes of meat, egg, or chiles). Note that many upscale places levy a 10% government tax plus a 5% service charge, or may be adding the new 20% VAT.

TIPS ON SHOPPING

Bring an empty suitcase. Vietnam offers fabulous bargains on silk, both as fabric and made-to-order clothing, as well as lacquerware, silver, and fine art. Hanoi is probably best for most buys, particularly paintings; save the lacquerware and home furnishings for Saigon. Further, the goods are meant to be bargained for, except for those in the most upscale shops.

Fast Facts: Vietnam

American Express   Amex is represented by agencies in both Hanoi and Ho Chi Minh City. Be warned, they do not provide complete travel services, but can direct you if you lose your card. Exotissimo Travel, 24–26 Tran Nhat Duat, Hanoi, ☎ **04/828-2150;** Exotissimo Travel, Saigon Trade Center, 37 Ton Duc Thang St., HCMC, ☎ **08/825-1723.** Hours are Monday to Friday 8am to 5pm.

Business Hours   Vendors and restaurants tend to be all-day operations, opening at about 8am and closing at 9 or 10pm. Government offices, including banks, travel agencies, and museums, are usually open from 8 to 11:30am and 2 to 4pm.

Crime   Violent crime isn't common in Vietnam, but petty thievery, especially against tourists, is a risk. Pickpocketing is rampant, and Ho Chi Minh City (HCMC) has a special brand of drive-by purse-snatching via motorbike. Don't wear flashy jewelry or leave valuables in your hotel room, especially in smaller hotels. There are small-time rackets perpetrated against tourists by taxi and cyclo drivers, usually in the form of a dispute on the agreed-upon price after you arrive at your destination. Or the driver doesn't seem to have change. Simply agree on a price by writing it down first.

Doctors & Dentists   Vietnamese health care is not yet up to Western standards. However, there are competent medical clinics in Hanoi and Saigon (see "Fast Facts," in individual sections) with international, English-speaking doctors. The same clinics have dentists. If your problem is serious, it is best to get to either one of these cities as quickly as possible. The clinics can arrange emergency evacuation. If the problem is minor, ask your hotel to help you contact a Vietnamese doctor. He or she will probably speak some English, and pharmacies throughout the country are surprisingly well stocked. Check the products carefully for authenticity and expiration dates. The Vietnamese are big believers in prescription drugs, although there are still some folk remedies around.

Drug Laws   Possessing drugs can mean a jail sentence, and selling them or possessing quantities in excess of 300 grams means a death sentence. Don't take chances.

Electricity   Vietnam's electricity carries 220 volts, so if you're coming from the U.S., bring a converter and adapter for electronics. Plugs are either the two-round-prong or two-flat-prong variety. If you're toting a laptop, bring a surge protector. Big hotels will have all these implements.

Embassies   Embassies are located in Hanoi at the following addresses: **United States,** 7 Lang Ha St., Ba Dinh District (☎ **04/843-1500**); **Canada,** 31 Hung Vuong St., Ba Dinh District (☎ **04/823-5500**); **Australia,** 8 Dao Tan, Van Phuc Compound, Ba Dinh District (☎ **04/831-7755**); **New Zealand,** 32 Hang Bai St., Hoan Kiem District (☎ **04/824-1481**); **United Kingdom,** 31 Hai Ba Trung St., 4th Floor, Hoan Kiem District (☎ **04/825-2510**).

Emergencies   Nationwide emergency numbers are as follows: For police, dial 113; fire, 114; and ambulance, 115. Operators speak only Vietnamese.

Hospitals In Hanoi, **International SOS** medical services can be found at 31 Hai Ba Trung St.; call their 24-hour service center for emergencies at ☎ **04/ 934-0056.** They have both Vietnamese and foreign doctors. In Ho Chi Minh City, International SOS is at 65 Nguyen Du St., District 1, 24-hour hot line ☎ **8/829-8424.**

Internet/E-mail There are gobs of Internet cafes in cities throughout Vietnam, many of them in popular guesthouse and hotel areas. At cafes rates are dirt cheap—400 VND (about US$0.02 per minute) is considered expensive. Most of the larger hotels also offer access, even for nonguests.

Language Vietnamese is the official language of Vietnam. Older residents speak and understand French. While English is widely spoken among those in the service industry in Hanoi and Saigon, it is harder to find in other tourist destinations. Off the beaten track, arm yourself with as many Vietnamese words you can muster (see "Useful Vietnamese Words & Phrases," earlier in this chapter) and a dictionary.

Liquor Laws There are virtually no liquor laws in Vietnam as far as age limits and when or where you can buy the stuff. You should avoid drunk motorbike driving, though, just as you would at home.

Police You won't find a helpful cop on every street corner—just the opposite. Count on them only in cases of dire emergency, and learn a few words of Vietnamese to help you along. Moreover, police here can sometimes be part of the problem. Especially in the south, you and your car/motorbike driver might, for instance, be stopped for a minor traffic infraction and "fined." If the amount isn't too large, cooperate.

Post Offices/Mail A regular airmail letter will take about 10 days to reach North America, 7 to reach Europe, and 4 to reach Australia or New Zealand. Mailing things from Vietnam is expensive. A letter up to 10 grams costs 13,000 VND (US$0.09) to North America, 11,000 VND (US$0.76) to Europe, and 9,000 VND (US$0.62) to Australia/New Zealand; and postcards, respectively, 8,000 VND (US$0.55), 7,000 VND (US$0.48), and 6,000 VND (US$0.41). Express mail services such as FedEx and DHL are easily available and are usually located in or around every city's main post office.

Safety Vietnam is considered a safe place to visit, but take heed of the following: First, the chaotic bike, motorbike, and car traffic can literally be deadly, so be cautious when crossing the street; maintaining a steady pace helps. In a taxi, belt up if possible, and lock your door. Second, women should play it safe and avoid going out alone late at night. Third, and most important: Beware of unexploded mines when hiking or exploring, especially through old war zones such as the DMZ or My Son. Don't stray off an established path, and don't touch anything.

Taxes A 20% V.A.T. tax was instituted for hotels and restaurants in January of 1999, but expect variation in how it's followed. Upscale establishments may add the full 20%, and some may even tack on an additional 5% service charge. Others may absorb the tax in their prices, and still others will ignore it entirely. Inquire before booking or eating.

Telephone & Fax Most hotels offer International Direct Dialing, but with exorbitant surcharges of 10 to 25%. It is far cheaper to place a call from a post office. There are plenty of phone booths. They accept phone cards (local and international) that can be purchased at any post office or phone company

Telephone Dialing Info at a Glance

- **To place a call from your home country to Vietnam:** Dial the international code (011 in the U.S., 0011 in Australia, 0170 in New Zealand, or 00 in the U.K.), plus the country code (84), the city code (4 for Hanoi, 8 for Ho Chi Minh City, 54 for Hue, 511 for Danang, 510 for Hoi An, 63 for Dalat, 58 for Nha Trang), and the phone number (for example, 011 + 84 + 4 + 000-0000).
- **To place a call within Vietnam:** First dial "0" before the city code. Note that not all phone numbers have 7 digits, and establishments may have several different numbers, one for each line.
- **To place a direct international call from Vietnam:** Most hotels offer International Direct Dialing, but with exorbitant surcharges of 10 to 25%. Faxes often have high minimum charges. To place a call, dial the international access code (00) plus the country code, the area or city code, and the number (for example, to call the U.S., you'd dial 00 + 01 + 000/000-0000).
- **International country codes are as follows:** Australia 61, Myanmar 95, Cambodia 855, Canada 1, Hong Kong 852, Indonesia 62, Laos 856, Malaysia 60, New Zealand 64, the Philippines 63, Singapore 65, Thailand 66, U.K. 44, U.S. 1.
- Post offices in Vietnam also provide international calling services. If you must call home, this is your best cost-saving option.

branch. A local call costs 1,000 VND per minute (US$0.07). See the "Telephone Dialing Info at a Glance" box in this section for more specific information.

Time Zone   Vietnam is 7 hours ahead of Greenwich Mean Time, in the same zone as Bangkok. It is 12 hours ahead of the U.S. and 3 hours behind Sydney.

Tipping   Tipping is common in Hanoi and in Saigon. In a top-end hotel, feel free to tip bellhops anywhere from 10,000 VND to US$1. Most upscale restaurants throughout the country now add a service surcharge of 5 to 10%. If they don't, and/or if the service is good, you may want to leave another 5%. Taxi drivers will be pleased if you round up the bill (again, mainly in the big cities). Use your discretion for tour guides and others who have been particularly helpful. Contrary to rumor, boxes of cigarettes as tips don't go over well. The recipient will say regretfully, "I don't smoke," when what he really means is "Show me the money." Exceptions to this are chauffeurs or minibus drivers.

Toilets   Public toilets (*cau tieu*) are nonexistent in Vietnam outside of tourist attractions, but you'll be welcome in hotels and restaurants. Except for newer hotels and restaurants, squat-style toilets prevail. You'll often see a tub of water with a bowl next to the toilet. Throw some water in the bowl to flush. Finally, bring your own paper and antiseptic hand wipes—just in case.

Water   Water is not potable in Vietnam. Outside of top-end hotels and restaurants, drink only beverages without ice, unless the establishment promises that it manufactures its own ice from clean water. Bottled mineral water, particularly the reputable "La Vie" and "A&B" brands, is everywhere. Counterfeits are a problem, so make sure you're buying the real thing, with an unbroken seal. A sure sign is typos. "La Vile" water speaks for itself.

3 Hanoi

Vietnam's capital, Hanoi ranks among the world's most attractive and interesting cities. It was first the capital of Vietnam in A.D. 1010, and though the nation's capital moved to Hue under the Nguyen dynasty in 1802, the city continued to flourish after the French took control in 1888. In 1954, after the French departed, Hanoi was declared Vietnam's capital once again. The remnants of over 1,000 years of history are still visible here, with that of the past few hundred years marvelously preserved.

Hanoi has a reputation, doubtless accrued from the American war years, as a dour northern political outpost. While the city is certainly smaller, slower, and far less developed than chaotic Saigon, its placid air gives it a gracious, almost regal flavor. It is set amidst dozens of lakes of various sizes, around which you can usually find a cafe, a pagoda or two, and absorbing vignettes of street life.

Among Hanoi's sightseeing highlights are the **Ho Chi Minh mausoleum and museum,** the **National Art museum,** the grisly **Hoa Lo prison** (also known to Americans as the infamous Hanoi Hilton), and the **Old Quarter,** whose ancient winding streets are named after the individual trades practiced there. Hanoi is also Vietnam's cultural center. The galleries, puppetry, music, and dance performances are worth staying at least a few days to take in. You may also want to use the city as a base for excursions to Halong Bay and Cat Ba island, to Cuc Phuong nature reserve, or north to Sapa.

GETTING THERE

BY PLANE   Hanoi is one of Vietnam's major international gateways, the other being Saigon. For details, see the country's "Getting There" section, earlier in this chapter.

The airport is located about 45 minutes' drive outside the city. If you haven't booked a hotel transfer through your hotel, an airport taxi costs US$12. To save a few dollars, you can take the Vietnam Airlines minivan into town. It costs US$2 for a drop-off at the Vietnam Airlines office, but sometimes for an extra buck you can get the driver to drop you at your hotel.

GETTING AROUND

Hanoi is divided into districts. You will most likely spend most of your time in the Hoan Kiem (downtown) and Ba Dinh (west of town) districts, with perhaps a few forays into Dong Da (southwest) and Hai Ba Trung (south). Most addresses include a district name. If they don't, ask. You'll want to plan your travels accordingly, as getting from district to district can be time-consuming and expensive.

BY BUS   Hanoi has only **buses** in the way of public transport, and they are extremely crowded and using them can be difficult if you don't speak Vietnamese.

BY TAXI   Taxis can be hailed off the street, at hotels, and at major attractions. The meter should read 14,000 VND (US$0.97) to start, and 4,000 to 5,000 VND (about US$0.30) for every kilometer thereafter. You can also call for a cab. There are a few companies, including **Vina Taxi** (☎ **04/811-1111**) and **52 Taxi** (☎ **04/852-5252**). Make sure the cabbie turns on the meter, and that you're given the right change. If the driver doesn't seem to have change, tell him or her you'll wait until it's obtained.

BY CAR   Renting a car is convenient. You can book one with driver for about US$33 a day (or US$5 per hour, minimum 3 hours.). If an upscale hotel quotes you more, call a **tourist cafe** (combination eateries and travel agents) or the dependable **Galaxy Hotel.**

BY MOTORBIKE   If you're feeling especially brave, you can rent your own motorbike. Most tourist cafes and mid- to low-range hotels offer them, as do the numerous street corner entrepreneurs. The price should be about US$6 or US$7 per day. Ask for a helmet. You'll be offered rides constantly as well. Be my guest! It always seems to cost US$1.

BY CYCLO   Cyclos are two-seated carts powered by a man on a foot-pedal bike riding behind you. You can flag them down anywhere, particularly near hotels and tourist attractions. Being trundled along among whizzing motorcycles isn't always very comfortable, and is definitely unsafe at night. It's nice for touring the Old Quarter, however, with its narrow streets. Bargain with the driver before setting out. You can pay as low as 10,000 VND (US$0.69) for a short haul, 15,000 VND (US$1.03) for a longer haul. You can also hire by the hour for about US$2.

BY BICYCLE   Another option is to rent a bicycle for the day for about US$1 from a hotel or tourist cafe. Again, it's an easily available method but one best used during the day. Bring your own helmet from home.

VISITOR INFORMATION & TOURS

Most tour companies are based in Saigon; however, many have branches in Hanoi. Operators can usually assist with local tours as well as country-wide services.

- **Ann's Tours.** 26 Yet Kieu, Hoan Kiem District (☎ 04/822-0018; fax 04/ 832-3866; e-mail: anntours@yahoo.com). Ask for the manager, Mr. Hoan. They offer private deluxe tours to Halong Bay and elsewhere. We've had feedback from Frommer's readers who tell us what great experiences they've had with this operation.
- **Buffalo Tours.** 11 Hang Muoi (☎ 04/828-0702; e-mail: buffalo@netnam.org. vn). This reputable outfit offers a range of standard tours, and some adventure options.
- **Handspan.** The main address is 80 Ma May St. (☎ 04/962-0501; www. handspan.com; e-mail: handspan@hn.vnn.vn). An excellent option for organized trips around Hanoi, in the northern hills and Halong Bay, plus some adventure options.

TOURIST CAFES

A good option for tours and transport for 1- or 2-day excursions to sites like Halong Bay is to visit one of Hanoi's "tourist cafes," which are small eateries/Internet cafes and travel agents all rolled into one. Mini-trip prices to Halong Bay and Cat Ba Island range from US$16 to US$28, but the lodging provided is quite basic. You'll see them everywhere, but a good bet is the **A-Z Queen Café,** 50 Hang Be St., Hoan Kiem District (☎ 04/934-37280860). Or try **Sinh Café,** 24a and 52 Hang Bac St., Hoan Kiem District (☎ 04/824-3842).

Fast Facts: Hanoi

Banks/Currency Exchange   Major banks in Hanoi include: Australia New Zealand Bank (ANZ), 14 Le Thai To St., ☎ 04/825-8190. Citibank, 17 Ngo Quyen St., ☎ 04/825-1950. Vietcombank, 198 Tran Quan Khai, ☎ 04/ 826-8045. ATMs are located at ANZ Bank and Citibank.

Internet/E-mail   The **Emotion CyberNet Café** at 60 Tho Nhuom and 52 Ly Thuong Kiet (☎ 04/934-1066; e-mail: emotioncafe@hn.fpt.vn), across from the Hanoi Hilton, sells snacks and Internet access.

Hanoi Accommodations & Dining

Church ✝
Parking 🅿
Post Office ✉

West Lake

Lake Truc Bach

Thuy Khue

Quan Thanh ④

Phan Dinh Phung

BA DINH DISTRICT

③①

③②

Duong Hung Vuong

Hoang Dieu

Nguyen Tri Phuong

②⑨

Doi Can

③⓪

Ong Ich Khiem

Le Hong Phong

Dien Bien Phu

②⑥

←① Kim Ma ✉

Duong Tran Phu

②⑦

②⑤

Nguyen Thai Hoc

②⑧

②④

Trinh Hoai Duc

Nguyen Khuyen

🅿

Quoc Tu Giam

Ngo Hao Nam

N Thinh Hao

Ton Duc Thang

Lake Van Chuong

Duong Le Duan

Quan Tho

Kham Thien

Nguyen Luong Bang

De La Thanh

Ngo Cho Kham Thien

DONG DA DISTRICT

Lake Xa Dan

Lake Ba Mau

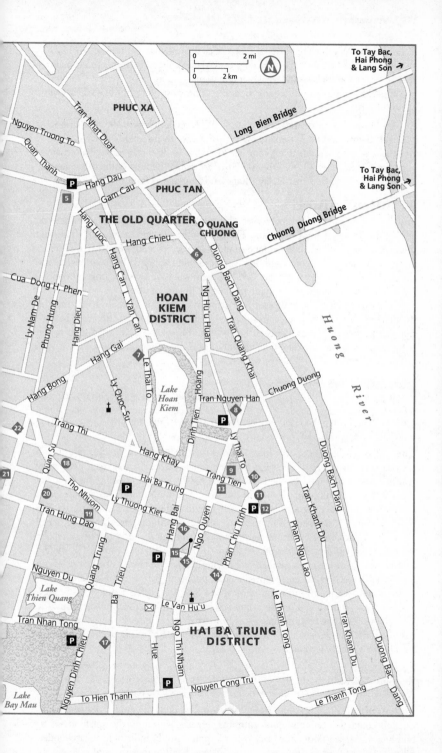

Post Office/Mail   The General Post Office is located at 6 Dinh Le St., Hoan Kiem District (☎ **04/825-7036**). It's open daily 6:30am to 10pm. You can also send faxes or telexes, and make international phone calls. FedEx (☎ **04/826-4925**) is located in the same building as the post office but have their own storefronts.

Telephone   The city code for Hanoi is 04. Most hotels provide international direct dialing, although none allow you to access an international operator or AT&T, whose Vietnam access code is 12010288. To do that, you will have to go to the General Post Office (above). There are public phone booths throughout the city for local calls that accept phone cards purchased from the post office.

ACCOMMODATIONS

From historic charm to ultra-efficient business hotel to budget hole-in-the-wall, you'll find what you want in Hanoi. The top-end hotels tend to be a bit sterile and business-oriented—I felt like the lone sundress in a sea of suits—but they offer every facility a holiday-maker could wish for. Amenities and cleanliness levels are high across the board: Virtually every hotel over US$10 a night will have a phone, air-conditioning, in-room safes, and hair dryers. Children under 12 usually stay free.

Ask for discounts! The Southeast Asia economic crisis hit Vietnam hard, and still maintains an impact here. Occupancy has declined precipitously, and every reservations desk offers rate cuts, many of up to 50%. Shown here are listed high-season (Oct–Feb) rates. Use them as guidelines only. Prices do not include a government VAT (Value Added Tax) of 20% except where noted.

VERY EXPENSIVE

Hanoi Daewoo Hotel. 360 Kim Ma St., Ba Dinh District. ☎ **04/831-5000.** Fax 04/831-5010. www.hanoi-daewoohotel.com. E-mail: info@hanoi-daewoohotel.com. 411 units. A/C MINIBAR TV TEL. US$199 double; US$269–US$359 executive floor room; US$319–US$1,500 suite. AE, DC, JCB, MC, V.

This 5-year-old high-rise is the kind of hotel that makes you open your mouth and say "aaaaah." Marble, marble everywhere, sumptuous fabrics, palm trees. Everything is done large—the hotel lobby, the bars, the rooms with king beds, the 80-meter (262-ft.) long, curving pool. It's almost too large. The plush rooms are decorated with an Asian flavor, and the halls are graced with over 1,000 interesting modern paintings by Vietnamese artists. Thick, soft linens are blissful. Bathrooms are surprisingly small in the lower-end rooms but quite well appointed, with hair dryers *et al.* There's a lobby lounge and a pool bar. The nightclub (Club Q) has five karaoke rooms. For dining, Edo (Japanese) and La Paix (Italian) are among the best restaurants in Hanoi—both are formal, expensive, excellent power lunch spots with private rooms; Café Promenade features Asian and European buffets; and Silk Road offers Chinese (Cantonese and Szechuan) food. There are three non-smoking floors, and a very efficient Business Center—perhaps the best in Hanoi—with Internet access. Elsewhere, the young staff has a slightly stunned air, as if they simply woke up one morning to find themselves working in a big, fancy hotel.

Hilton Hanoi Opera. Hilton Hanoi Opera, 1 Le Thanh Tong St., Hoan Kiem, Hanoi. ☎ **800/774-1500** or 04/933-0500. Fax 04/933-0530. www.hilton.com. 269 units. A/C MINIBAR TV TEL US$210–US$230 double; US$250 executive room.

This brand new hotel opened just before the millennium in grand style—the reproduction colonial exterior is quite stunning, especially next to the splendid Opera building. On seven floors, the place is just as grand inside and still has that wonderful new feeling. Standard rooms are spacious and handsome with comfortable beds, closet space, and good desk space. Television with satellite service, daily newspaper delivery, voice-mail telephone system, and in-room Internet access keep business travelers up to speed. Plus the hotel has plenty of features for vacation travelers as well. The staff is professional and well trained.

✪ Sofitel Metropole Hanoi. 15 Ngo Quyen St., Hanoi. ☎ **800/221-4542** or 04/826-6919. Fax 04/826-6920. E-mail: Sofmet@netnam.org.vn. 244 units. A/C MINIBAR TV TEL. US$230–US$280 double; from US$290 suite. AE, DC, JCB, MC, V.

The Metropole is one of the world's treasures: truly elegant and with a long past and a list of past guests that reads like a Who's Who of the 20th century. In fact, there's a history book being written solely about this place. Built in 1900, the hotel had a major renovation in 1992 and added a second building in 1994. Medium-sized rooms in the original building have wooden floors, cane furniture, and high ceilings, historic yet not really luxe. Sizable modern bathrooms, but little touches like wood-frame mirrors, fresh flowers, and toiletries in hand-painted ceramics are just right. The staff couldn't be nicer or more efficient. The pool is small but the Bamboo lounge alongside is roomy and comfortable. The health club with sauna and massage is superb and actually has a great street view. There are two restaurants. Le Beaulieu is the best in Hanoi for classic French fare. It is relatively formal but offers fantastic value dinner buffets on occasion. Among the three bars, the Met Pub is one of Hanoi's places to be seen, have a beer, and listen to live music. The downtown location can't be beat, and there's a nice mix of tourists and businesspeople here. Push for a room in the Old Wing; the newer is already showing signs of wear and is far less fetching, with more modern, less historic decor, although the rooms are slightly larger. If you must stay there, ask for a room with a pool view.

EXPENSIVE

Galaxy Hotel. 1 Phan Dinh Phung St., Hanoi. ☎ **04/828-2888.** Fax 04/828-2466. 60 units. A/C MINIBAR TV TEL. US$99 double; US$125 suite. AE, DC, JCB, MC, V.

The Galaxy is king of the tour group hotels, but don't let that stop you. If you elect to stay here, it will quickly become a home away from home. A recently renovated, but colorless, 1918 building, it's located right on the edge of the Old Quarter. Good-sized rooms are spotless and very comfortable, although the fuzzy TV reception drove me nuts and the pillows were merely little wads of cotton in a case. There is an Asian restaurant on the premises and a nice little bar with current Western magazines. The breakfast (included in the price) is good, and even has pancakes and sausage.

Beware: Travelers have reported cut-off phone service and closed front desks in the middle of the night. Yet the incredibly nice staff tries very, very hard and always remembers your name.

Guoman Hotel. 83A Ly Thuong Kiet St., Hanoi. ☎ **04/822-2800.** Fax 04/822-2822. 149 units. A/C MINIBAR TV TEL. US$75–US$80 double; US$120–US$180 suite. AE, JCB, MC, V.

This is your Basic Good Hotel, and with the price I have to say that it's a bit of a steal if you're looking for comfort and service. Only a year and a half old, right now the Guoman caters to the business crowd, but with its central location and nice amenities, it's a great choice for all. Its size and attitude, in fact, say "chain" more than "business." Rooms are big, carpeted, and very nicely if blandly furnished, and they still have that brand-new feeling. They are very well-equipped, with coffeemakers, safes, and even a power outlet and phone jack for laptops—truly a rarity in Vietnam. Other highlights: comfy just-right firm beds, fat pillows, and big spic-and-span marble and tile bathrooms. There are three non-smoking floors—another rarity in Vietnam.

Meritus Westlake Hanoi. 1 Thanh Nien Rd., Ba Dinh District. ☎ **04/823-8888.** Fax 04/ 829-3888. www.meritus-hotels.com. E-mail: sales-mktg.mwh@meritus-hotels.com. 322 units. A/C MINIBAR TV TEL. US$105–US$200 double; from US$210 suite. AE, JCB, MC, V.

This hotel was launched in September of 1998. It's an extremely nice business hotel. Ask for a room with a view of West Lake. You'll find standard upscale pastel and crème hotel decor, with slightly cramped nonsuite rooms, although all have every gizmo you could wish for, including coffeemakers. The beds have very firm mattresses, and the bathrooms have a separate shower.

MODERATE

Dan Chu Hotel. 29 Trang Tien St., Hanoi. ☎ **04/825-4344.** Fax 04/826-6786. 41 units. A/C MINIBAR TV TEL. US$35–US$75 double. AE, DC, JCB, MC, V.

This is an old hotel with a funky but pleasant feeling, right in the heart of the downtown district. Big, atmospheric, high-ceiling rooms are spotless and have carved wood furniture, the all-too-common ugly polyester bedspreads, and clean but spare bathrooms with hair dryers. There are laundry services, car rental, massage and sauna, and a restaurant and very good gift shop on the premises. Satellite TV and in-room safes, too. The deluxe rooms have historic wood shutters and a single long balcony that overlooks the active street scene below. It's an interesting view with very noisy side-effects.

Eden Hotel. 78 Tho Nhuom St., Hanoi. ☎ **04/942-3273.** Fax 04/824-5619. 22 units. US$50 double; US$99 suite. AE, DC, JCB, MC, V.

The floors of the Eden Hotel wind in varied levels around its outdoor garden atrium. The somewhat dark, attractive rooms are carpeted, and feature traditional Asian carved-wood furniture and fresh flowers—a nice touch. The standard and deluxe rooms are small, and I mean small, although the suite does have two rooms and a big bathroom. It must be mentioned here that the mattresses are foam, but they are extremely sturdy and comfortable. Bathrooms are basic and spotless, without bathtubs except in the suites. On the premises are The Pear Tree, a popular bar with billiards, and a small continental restaurant. It's a very casual but nice place. A friendly staff, even if they are all teenagers. The Eden is often full with budget travelers, so book early.

Hoa Binh Hotel. 27 Ly Thuong Kiet St., Hoan Kiem District, Hanoi. ☎ **04/825-3315** or 04/825-3692. Fax 04/826-9818. E-mail: kshoabinh@hn.vnn.vn. 100 units. A/C MINIBAR TV TEL. US$50–US$60 double. AE, DC, JCB, MC, V.

The Hoa Binh is a good, atmospheric choice. Comfort and history meet at just the right level for Vietnam, and you are reminded every minute that you are in Hanoi. Built in 1926, the attractive colonial has a colonnaded lobby with winding wooden stairs and sizable rooms with original light fixtures, molded ceilings, and gloss-wood furniture. Only the hideous polyester bedspreads and drapes and spongy mattresses ruin the effect. The bathrooms are very plain and small but spotless. Hand-held showers, though. The hotel is in a prime downtown location, and the bar has a view of the city. On the ground floor (but not hotel-owned) is the excellent restaurant Le Splendide—see "Dining." Hoa Binh has good facilities: two restaurants, a sauna, massage, laundry, a tailor, a barber, and karaoke.

Thang Loi Hotel. Yen Phu St., Hanoi. ☎ **04/829-4211.** Fax 04/829-3800. E-mail: thangloihtl@hn.vnn.vn. 80 units. US$80 double. AE, JCB, MC, V.

It's anything but fancy—it's a low-slung group of concrete buildings—but for a truly unique hotel experience, try Thang Loi. It resembles a summer camp lodge. The hotel was a gift from Cuba, which explains the rather dour, Cold War–era exterior, but it actually protrudes on pontoons over West Lake. Most of the immaculate but plain rooms have a balcony overlooking fisher women standing in the lake, working with baskets. The spongy mattresses are a little off-putting, as is the garish decor in the suites and the puckered carpets, but rooms have hair dryers, safes, and even scales. There's an outdoor pool, tennis courts, a barbershop, and a small sauna/massage center. The staff speaks little English but they're so nice you don't care. An odd but likeable spot.

INEXPENSIVE

Hoang Cuong Hotel. 15 Nguyen Thai Hoc St., Hoan Kiem District, Hanoi. ☎ **04/822-0060.** Fax 04/822-0195. 10 units. A/C MINIBAR TV TEL. US$15–US$30 double. AE, DC, JCB, MC, V.

This attractive little gem is one of the best among Hanoi's budget choices, and located on the same street as many of them, near the Old Quarter. Family-run, the rooms are large and carpeted, with attractive inlaid Asian furniture and very firm foam mattress beds. There are some nice details, like hair dryers, hot water thermoses, and fans in the room. The tile bathrooms are functional and spotless. There is no elevator, and room prices are based on how far you'll have to hike up the six or so flights of stairs. But you'll soon become firm friends with the very nice staff.

DINING

It's hard to have a bad meal in Hanoi. The French influence is here in both classical and in Vietnam-influenced versions, neither to be missed, especially at these prices. Almost every ethnic food variation is well represented in the city, in fact, and you'll be hard pressed to choose among them.

Hanoi has savory specialties that must be sampled. For that, hit the streets and dine in local, small eateries. *Pho,* by far the most popular local dish, is noodles with slices of beef (*bo*) or chicken (*ga*), fresh bean sprouts, and condiments. Pho Bo, at 49 Bat Dan, is one of the city's best. *Bun cha,* a snack of rice noodles and spring rolls with fresh condiments, has made Dac Kim restaurant (at No. 1 Hang Manh, in the Old Quarter) city-renowned. *Banh cuon* is meat and mushroom wrapped in a fresh rice crepe. Fantastic at Banh Cuon Nong, 17 Cha Ca in the Old Quarter.

EXPENSIVE

Il Grillo. 116 Ba Trieu (in the north of Hai Ba Trung District). ☎ **04/822-7720.** Reservations recommended on weekends. Main courses 110,000–336,000 VND (US$7.50–US$23). AE, JCB, MC, V. Daily 11am–11pm. CLASSIC ITALIAN.

Il Grillo is a family-run classic Italian restaurant with a very casual, intimate atmosphere, print tablecloths, hand-painted pottery, and chalkboard specials. You won't find any Vietnamese here, but it's a favorite with the expat crowd and by virtue of its size seems to ward off big tour groups. Portions are huge and good, and the service is friendly and attentive, including personal attention from the Italian owners. The ribeye steak is a house specialty and the pasta with clams and shredded carrots unique and delicious, as is the pasta with truffles. Most spectacular, however, were the fresh, bursting-with-flavor starters: bruschetta, prosciutto, salad with anchovies. Simple yet gorgeous. There's also a nice Italian wine list.

Le Splendide. 44 Ngo Quyen St. (Hoa Binh Hotel, Hoan Kiem District). ☎ **04/826-6087.** Reservations recommended. Main courses 102,000–278,000 VND (US$7–US$19). AE, MC, V. Daily 11am–midnight. TOULOUSIAN FRENCH.

A huge stained-glass window, chandeliers, and a long blonde-wood bar contribute to the utter charm of this place, as does the helpful manager, Antoine. The atmosphere is elegant but youthful, even though it's a favorite with lunching business folk and

Restaurant Tip

Note that many upscale restaurants in Hanoi levy a 5% service charge on top of the 10% government tax.

___

embassy staff. The menu (in English as well as French and Vietnamese) features house specialties of cassoulet, confit de canard pollè, and baked tournedos topped with foie gras. Everything is impeccably prepared and presented. Classic French deserts such as crème brûlée and fondue au chocolat are a triumph, and there's a relatively long wine list. Le Splendide is a lovely, quiet place to linger over a memorable meal, or over the live jazz on Friday nights.

The Press Club. 59A Ly Thai To St., Hoan Kiem District. ☎ **04/934-0888.** Reservations recommended. Main courses 117,000–255,000 VND (US$8–US$17.50); prix fixe menu 291,000 VND (US$19.95). AE, JCB, MC, V. Daily noon–2pm and 5[nd10:30pm. Weekend brunch 11am–3pm. CONTINENTAL.

Subdued and elegant, this place states firmly, in hushed tones, "power lunch." The indoor restaurant is sizable yet private, done in dark tones of maroon and forest green with solid-looking wood furniture and detailing. There is outdoor seating on the terrace, next to a pseudo-jazz band, which imparts a more casual atmosphere. The service is impeccable. The menu is full of safe Continental standards: antipasto starters, goat cheese salad, tuna steak, smoked trout, red snapper with capers. It is cooked to perfection, however, and the deserts are outstanding. Try the banana créme brûlée, or iced coffee and praline parfait with Amaretto cream.

For a more casual, inexpensive alternative or for lunch, try the downscaled **Deli** on the first floor—an expat standby, famous for its sandwiches and gourmet pizzas.

MODERATE

Al Fresco's. 23L Hai Ba Trung St., Hoan Kiem District. ☎ **04/826-7782.** Main courses 80,000–161,000 VND (US$5.50–US$11). No credit cards. Daily 9:30am–10:30pm. TEX-MEX.

Run by Australian expats, which practically guarantees a good time, Fresco's is two floors of a friendly, casual little open-air place. It has checkered tablecloths, good oldies music, and a great view on the second floor to the street below. The place serves very good Tex-Mex, pizza, chicken wings, and the like. The ribs are the house specialty, but the fajitas are simply out of this world, too. Desserts are good old standbys like brownies à la mode. There is a healthy wine list featuring name-brand Australian wines and some inexpensive Bulgarian and Chilean reds.

✪ **Brother's Café.** 26 Nguyen Thai Hoc. ☎ **04/733-3866.** Buffets 73,000 VND and 146,000 VND (US$5 and US$10). AE, DC, MC, V. Daily 11am–2pm and 6–10pm. VIETNAMESE.

Brother's is one of the best places to eat these days. The buffet features dishes such as salted chicken, sweet and sour bean sprouts, shrimp, noodles, and spring rolls; a full dessert table of sweet tofu, sweet baby rice, dragon fruit, and other exotic offerings; and fresh lemon or melon juice. Dinner features grilled items—shrimp, fish, lamb, pork—and a glass of wine. Part of the restaurant is in an exquisitely decorated colonial; the other part of it in a dreamy garden out back. From the pressed linen napkins to tiny fresh flowers, Brother's gets every detail just right.

Indochine. 16 Nam Ngu St., Hoan Kiem District. ☎ **04/942-4097.** Main courses 29,000–161,000 VND (US$2–US$11); set lunch 73,000 VND (US$5). MC, V. Daily 11:30am–10pm. VIETNAMESE.

This place has long been a favorite with the expat and tourist crowd, and is said to be "the" place to eat in Hanoi. Yet while the food was beautifully presented and very good, I found it a bit lackluster, and the staff just didn't seem to have a clue. Perhaps it was an off night, as everyone else seems to rave about the place. There certainly are some fine things on the menu, such as the crab spring rolls, flavorful chicken and banana flower salad, and grilled prawns in banana leaves. It is well worth a visit for the beautiful colonial setting, with both indoor and outdoor patio seating, amazingly good prices, and live Vietnamese classical music nightly.

Khazana. 41B Ly Thai To St., Hoan Kiem District. ☎ **04/824-1166.** Reservations recommended on weekends and for groups of 4 or more. Main courses 73,000–146,000 VND (US$5–US$10). MC, V. Sun 6:30–10pm; Mon–Sat 11:30am–2pm and 6:30–10pm. NORTHERN INDIAN.

This is surprisingly good North Indian food, far beyond my expectations for Hanoi, and judging from other local reviews, others seem to agree. The surroundings are elegant but not very ethnic: small round tables with Western settings, a marble floor, Indian art, impeccable service. It's a favorite of the business lunch crowd. Manager Shankar Dutta explains with loving care the ingredients of each dish, if you ask, and is justly proud of Goan fish curry, *tandoori gulistan* (batter-fried cottage cheese), and *taar korma* (spiced mutton). The dishes were fresh and bursting with flavor. Even the samosas were special.

✪ **Seasons of Hanoi.** 95B Quan Thanh. ☎ **04/843-5444.** Reservations recommended, especially for groups. Main courses 40,000–60,000 VND (US$2.76–US$4.14). MC, V. Daily 11:30am–2pm and 6–11pm. VIETNAMESE.

The atmosphere is picture-perfect at Seasons: intimate, candlelit, romantic, earth-colored surroundings in a casual yet beautifully restored colonial with authentic native furniture. There are two floors. Try to sit on the first, to avoid tourists traveling in packs. The spring rolls are heaven, as are the tempura soft-shell crabs. Fish is everywhere on the menu—fried, boiled, on kabobs, and in hot pots. If you fancy it, try the sautéed eel with chile and lemongrass. That is, unless you don't decide on the fried chicken in panda leaves first. Everything comes beautifully presented, and main courses rest on flaming warming plates. A nice wine list accompanies.

INEXPENSIVE

Le Café des Arts de Hanoi. 11b Ngo Bao Khanh, Hoan Kiem District (in the Old Quarter). ☎ **04/828-7207.** Main courses 29,000–219,000 VND (US$2–US$15). No credit cards. Daily 9am–11pm (bar open until midnight). BISTRO FRENCH/CONTINENTAL.

After strolling round Hoan Kiem Lake, stop off its northwest end for a drink or a bite at this friendly bistro-style eatery, run by French expats and open all day. Spacious, with tiled floors and shuttered windows looking into the narrow Old Quarter street below, the cafe features casual rattan furniture and a long, inviting bar. It also doubles as an art gallery, which explains the interesting paintings hanging throughout. The Vietnamese art crowd also provides some attractive local color. Most inviting, however, is the excellent food. Ask for the special of the day, and stick to bistro standbys like the omelets or a *croque madame*—toasted bread and cheese sautéed in egg—and house specialty *salade bressare* (very fresh chicken and vegetables in a light mayonnaise sauce). There is also good house wine by the glass.

Mother's Pride. 6C Phan Chu Trinh. ☎ **04/826-2168.** Main courses 24,000–28,000 VND (US$1.66–US$1.93). No credit cards. Daily 10am–10:30pm. WESTERN/HOME STYLE MALAYSIAN.

Cheap and good, Mother's is a great local favorite. The main attraction is simple Malay dishes served over rice. Try the chicken curry or sweet and sour prawns. The house soup is tangy with crispy fresh basil and bean sprouts. The fresh fruit juices—smoothies really—are fantastic, the apple particularly. Mother's also serves pizza, onion rings, chicken wings, and other snacks. Unfortunately, there is no atmosphere to speak of.

✪ **Tamarind Café.** 80 Ma May St. ☎ **04/926-0580.** Main courses 25,000–40,000 VND (US$1.72–US$2.76). MC, V. Daily 9am–11pm. VEGETARIAN.

Tamarind has the nicest wait staff I've yet to encounter. Even if you're not a vegetarian, this welcoming cafe's inventive menu will tickle your fancy. Soups, such as carrot and ginger or vegetarian wonton, take the chill off Hanoi winter nights. Other inventive options here include Malay quesadillas, tofu stuffed with soy sauce vermicelli and vegetables, and an all-day breakfast served with delicious homemade fruit condiments. Fruit shakes and excellent teas round out the meal.

Snacks & Cafes

One of the main attractions around Hoan Kiem Lake is **Fanny's Ice Cream,** 16 Hang Bong, which serves exquisite French-style ice cream and sorbets from 8am to 11pm. For great coffee and desserts try ✪ **Moca Café,** at 14–16 Nha Tho (☎ **04/ 825-6334**).

ATTRACTIONS

While sightseeing, remember that state-owned attractions will usually close for lunch from 11:30am to 1:30pm (or thereabouts). Also, foreigners will be charged approximately twice what the Vietnamese are charged, so you'll pay 10,000 VND (US$0.69) for most public attractions. Don't bother arguing.

Ba Dinh District

West Lake. Bordered by Thuy Khue and Thanh Nien sts.

In Hanoi, West Lake is second only to Hoan Kiem as a nerve center for the city, steeped in legend and sporting several significant pagodas. Vietnam's oldest pagoda, Tran Quoc, was built in the sixth century and is located on Cayang Island in the middle of the lake, a beautiful setting. It has a visitors' hall, two corridors, and a bell tower, and its monument was constructed by an early Zen sect. Quan Thanh Temple, by the northern gate, was built during the reign of Le Thai To King (1010–1028). It is dedicated to Huyen Thien Tran Vo, the god who reigned over Vietnam's northern regions. Renovated in the 19th century, the impressive temple has a triple gate and courtyard, and features a 12-foot bronze statue of the god. West Lake is also a hub of local activity, particularly on weekends when families go paddle-boating on it.

Ho Chi Minh's Mausoleum. On Ba Dinh Square, Ba Dinh District. Tues–Thurs and Sat 8am–11am.

In an imposing, somber granite and concrete structure modeled on Lenin's tomb, Ho lies in state, embalmed and dressed in his favored khaki suit. He asked to be cremated, but his wish was not heeded. A respectful demeanor is required, and a dress code may be imposed, with no shorts or sleeveless shirts allowed. Note that the mausoleum is usually closed through October and November, when Ho goes to Russia for body maintenance of an undisclosed nature. The museum may be closed during this period as well.

Ho Chi Minh's Museum. 3 Ngo Ha. Left of One Pillar Pagoda, near Ba Dinh Square. Ba Dinh District. ☎ **04/845-5455.** Admission 10,000 VND (US$0.69). Tues–Sun 8–11:30am and 1:30–4pm.

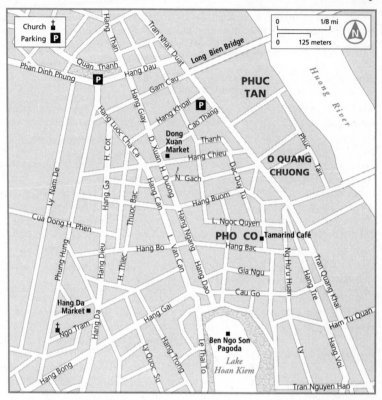

English-language explanations help to piece together the fragments of Ho's life and cause on display here. There are personal items on display and photos and documents detailing the rise of the nation's communist revolution. Completely unique to Vietnam are the conceptual displays symbolizing freedom, reunification, and social progress through flowers, fruit, and mirrors. Have a look.

Ho Chi Minh's Residence. Behind the Presidential Palace. Admission 10,000 VND (US$0.69). Tues–Sun 8–11am and 1:30–4:30pm.

Ho's residence, the well-known house on stilts, is behind the Presidential Palace, a gorgeous French colonial building built in 1901 for the resident French governor. Shunning the glorious structure nearby, Ho instead chose to live here from 1958 to 1969. The simple stilt house does have its charms, facing an exquisite landscaped lake. The basement was a meeting place for the politburo; upstairs are the bedroom and a study. Behind the house is a garden of fruit trees, many of them exotics imported from other lands, including miniature rose bushes and areca trees from the Caribbean.

One-Pillar Pagoda. Right of Ho Chi Minh Museum, near Ba Dinh Square. Ba Dinh District.

To the right of the Ho Chi Minh Museum is the unique One Pillar Pagoda, a wooden structure built in 1049 that sits on stilts over a lake. A king of the Ly dynasty, Ly Thai Thong King, had it built after having a dream in which Bodhisattva Avalokitesvara, the Goddess of Mercy, presented him with a lotus flower. The existing pagoda is a miniature reproduction of the original, which was said to represent a lotus emerging from the water. It is certainly interesting, and a visit to pray for fertility or good health reportedly has miraculous results. However, you will not be admitted if you're wearing shorts.

Army Museum. 28A Dien Bien Phu St. ☎ **04/823-4264.** Admission 10,000 VND (US$0.69). Tues–Sun 8–11:30am and 1:30–4:30pm.

This building opened in 1959, and presents the Vietnamese side of the country's struggle against colonial powers. There are three buildings of odds and ends from both the French and American wars here, including evocative photos. Most interesting, though, is the actual war equipment on display, including aircraft, tanks, bombs, and big guns, some with signs indicating just how many of which enemy the piece took out. There is a tank belonging to the troop that crashed through the Presidential Palace gates on April 30, 1975, Vietnamese Liberation Day. Outside there is also a spectacular, room-sized bouquet of downed French and U.S. aircraft wreckage. Also on the grounds is Hanoi's ancient flag tower (Cot Co), constructed from 1805 to 1812. The exhibits have English translations, which makes this an easy and worthwhile visit.

✪ Vietnam Fine Arts Museum. 66 Nguyen Thai Hoc. ☎ **04/846-5801.** Admission 10,000 VND (US$0.69). Tues–Sun 9:15–11am and 1–5pm.

The very worthwhile arts museum features Vietnamese art of the 20th century, up to the 1970s or so. While the presentations are a bit crowded and rustic, there are explanations in English, and much of the art is outstanding, though you won't really see any works of an innovative or controversial nature. Entire rooms are devoted to the Vietnamese style of lacquer and silk painting, woodblock and folk art. Techniques are explained—a nice touch. Interesting also are the modern works of wood statuary interspersed among the exhibits. Some are patriotic in nature, but many are humorous social commentaries. The top floors are devoted to prehistoric artifacts and Buddhist sculptures, some of which are huge and impressive. Don't miss the famous 11th-century Goddess of Mercy (Kouan Yin) with her thousand arms and eyes in the far left-hand room, second floor. Best of all, the museum itself is in an old colonial and, unless there's a tour group milling around, you can stroll around in relative serenity and rest on one of the many benches provided. The gift shop has some nice modern works from known artists for sale.

Dong Da District

Temple of Literature and National University (Van Mieu–Quoc Tu Giam). Quoc Tu Giam St. ☎ **04/845-2917.** Admission 10,000 VND (US$0.69). Daily 8am–5pm.

If Vietnam has a seat of learning, this is it. There are two entities here: Van Mieu, a temple built to worship Chinese philosopher Confucius in 1070; and Quoc tu Giam, literally "Temple of the King who Distinguished Literature," an elite institute established in 1076 to teach the doctrines of Confucius and his disciples. It existed for over 700 years as a center for Confucian learning. Moreover, it is a powerful symbol for the Vietnamese, having been established after the country emerged from a period of Chinese colonialism that lasted from 179 B.C. to A.D. 938. As such, it stands for independence and a solidifying of national culture and values.

What exists today is a series of four courtyards that served as an entrance to the university. Architecturally, it is a fine example of classic Chinese with Vietnamese influences. Still present are 82 stone stelae—stone diplomas really—erected between 1484 and 1780, bearing the names and birthplaces of 1,306 doctor laureates who managed to pass the university's rigorous examinations. Beyond the final building, known as the sanctuary, the real university began. Damaged in the French war, it is currently being restored.

HOAN KIEM DISTRICT

✪ **Hoa Lo Prison (Hanoi Hilton).** 1 Hoa Lo St., off Quan Su St. ☎ **04/824-6358.** Admission 10,000 VND (US$0.69). Tues–Sun 8am–4:30pm.

For sheer gruesome atmosphere alone, this ranks near the top of the must-see list. Constructed by the French in 1896, mainly to house political prisoners, the Vietnamese took it over in 1954. It was subsequently used to house prisoners of war. From 1964 to 1973, it was a major POW detention facility. United States senator John McCain was a particularly famous inmate, as was ambassador to Vietnam Pete Peterson and Lieutenant Everett Alvarez, officially the first American pilot to be shot down over Vietnam.

Only part of the original complex is left. The rest of the original site was razed and is ironically occupied by a tall, gleaming office complex. To the west is the guillotine room, still with its original equipment, and the female and Vietnamese political prisoners' quarters. The courtyard linking the two has parts of original tunnels once used by a hundred intrepid Vietnamese revolutionaries to escape in 1945. There are no English explanations, so try to see the prison with a guide or ask some of the folks working there for help, as a few speak English.

Quan Su Pagoda. 73 Quan Su St., as it intersects Tran Hung Da, Hoan Kiem District. Daily 8–11am and 1–4pm.

Quan Su is one of the most important temples in the country. Constructed in the 15th century along with a small house for visiting Buddhist ambassadors, in 1934 it became the headquarters of the Tonkin Buddhist Association and today it is headquarters for the Vietnam Central Buddhist Congregation. It's an active pagoda and usually thronged with worshippers; the interior is dim and smoky with incense. To the rear is a school of Buddhist doctrine.

✪ **Old Quarter & Hoan Kiem Lake.** Bordered by Tran Nhat Duat and Phung Hung sts.

The Old Quarter evolved from workshop villages clustered by trades, or guilds, in the early 13th century. It's now an area of narrow, ancient, winding streets, each named for the trade it formerly featured. Even today, streets tend to be either for silk, silver, or antiques. It's a fascinating slice of centuries-old life in Hanoi, including markets that are so pleasantly crowded the street itself narrows to a few feet. Hoan Kiem is considered the center of the city. It is also known as the Lake of the Recovered Sword. In the mid–15th century, the gods gave emperor Le Thai To a magical sword to defeat Chinese invaders. While the emperor was boating on the lake one day, a giant tortoise reared up and snatched the sword, returning it to its rightful owners. Stroll around the lake in the early morning or evening to savor local life among the willow trees, particularly elders playing chess or doing tai chi. In the center of the lake is the Tortoise Pagoda; on the northern part is Ngoc Son pagoda, reachable only by the Bridge of the Rising Sun and open daily from 8am to 5pm.

Hanoi Opera House. 1 Trang Tien St.. ☎ **04/933-0113.** Intersection of Le Thanh Tong and Trang Tien sts., District 1.

This gorgeous, historic art nouveau building was built near the turn of the century. Unfortunately, to get inside you'll have to attend a performance, but that should be enjoyable as well (see "Hanoi After Dark").

SIGHTS OUTSIDE THE CITY CENTER

Vietnam Ethnology Museum. Nguyen Van Huyen, 6km (3.75 miles) west of town. ☎ **04/756-2193.** Admission 10,000 VND (US$0.69). Tues–Sun 8:30–11:30am and 1:30–4:30pm.

If you're interested in learning more about the 53 ethnic minorities populating Vietnam's hinterlands, stop in at this new museum. The different groups, with their history and customs, are explained via photos, videos, and displays of clothing and household and work implements. You'll need to take a taxi to get here, though.

ACTIVITIES

Bicycles are easily rented from almost every hotel for about US$1 a day. **Handspan,** 116 Hang Bac (☎ **04/828-1996**), offers a 1-day bike tour of the city and lunch—a great introduction. There is also quite a jogging scene in Hanoi around the Botanical Gardens, Lenin Park, and Hoan Kiem Lake. Get your run in before about 6:30am, though, before traffic starts to snarl. The **Clark Hatch Fitness Center** at the Metropole Hotel (☎ **04/826-6919**) has top-end equipment, sauna, and Jacuzzi with day rates for nonguests.

SHOPPING

Hanoi is a fine place to shop, and features Vietnamese specialties such as silk, silver, lacquerware, embroidered goods, and ethnic minority crafts. Silk is good quality and an easy buy. Shops will tailor a suit in as little 24 hours, but allow yourself extra time for alterations. Many of the shops are clustered along Hang Gai, a.k.a. "Silk Street" on the northeast side of the Old Quarter. **Daily hours are generally from 8am to 9pm.** A silk suit will run from about US$25 to US$65, depending on the silk, and a blouse or shirt US$15 to US$20. Virtually every shop takes credit cards (MC, V). Bargain hard for all but the silk; offer 50% of the asking price and end up paying 70% or so.

Khai Silk, with branches at 96 Hang Gai (☎ **04/825-4237**) and 121 Nguyen Thai Hoc St. (☎ **04/823-3508**), is justly famous for its selection, silk quality, and relatively pleasant store layout. Also try **Thanh Ha Silk** (114 Hang Gai; ☎ **04/ 928-5348**) and **Oriental House** (28 Nha Chung; ☎ **04/828-5542**). **Tan My** at 109 Hang Gai (☎ **04/826-7081**) has exquisite embroidery work, especially for children's clothing and bedding.

For silver, antique oddities and traditional crafts, try **Hong Hoa** on 18 Ngo Quyen St., near the Metropole Hotel (☎ **04/826-8341**), which has a good selection. **Giai Dieu,** on 82 Hang Gai (☎ **04/826-0222**), has interesting lacquer paintings and decorative items, so stop in, as you'll probably be in the neighborhood at some point. There is also a branch at 93 Ba Trieu St. Silver jewelry, handbags, and other ornaments are sold at 80 Hang Gai St. For fine ceramics, look to **Quang's Ceramics,** at 22 Hang Luoc St. (☎ **04/828-3440**) in the Old Quarter. Unique lacquerware, including business card holders and tissue boxes, can be had at **DeltaDeco,** 12 Nha Tho St. Wood, stone, and brass lacquer reproduction sculptures of religious icons are at **KAF Traditional Sculptures and Art Accessories,** 31B Ba Trieu St. (☎ **04/822-0022**).

ART GALLERIES

Vietnam has a flourishing art scene, and Hanoi has many galleries of oil, silk, water, and lacquer paintings (see above). Don't forget to bargain here, too. One of the best is **Nam Son,** at 41 Trang Tien ☎ **04/826-2993.** Others: **Thanh Mai,** 64 Hang Gai St. (☎ **04/825-1618**); **Apricot Gallery,** 40B Hang Bong St. (☎ **04/828-8965**); and **Thang Long,** 15 Hang Gai (☎ **04/825-0740**) in the Old Quarter.

HANOI AFTER DARK

When it comes to nightlife, Hanoi is no Saigon, but there are a variety of pleasant watering holes about town and a few rowdy dance spots. Hanoi is also the best city in which to see **traditional Vietnamese arts** such as opera, theater, and water puppet shows. Invented during the **Ly dynasty** (1009–1225), the art of water puppetry is unique to Vietnam. The puppets are made of wood and really do dance on water. The shows feature traditional Vietnamese music and depict folklore and myth. Book for the popular puppets at least 5 hours ahead.

THEATER & PERFORMANCE

Thang Long Water Puppet Theater, 57B Dinh Thien Hoang St., Hoan Kiem District (☎ **04/824-5117** or 824-9494), hosts a nightly show at 8 pm. Admission is US$4.

The **Hanoi Opera House** (Hanoi Municipal Theatre), 1 Trang Tien St., Hoan Kiem District (☎ **04/933-0113**), hosts performances by local and international artists. The **Hanoi Traditional Opera,** 15 Nguyen Dinh Chieu, Ba Dinh District (☎ **04/826-7361**), has shows on Monday, Wednesday, and Friday at 8pm.

Central Circus, in Lenin Park, Hai Ba Trung District (☎ **04/822-0277**), has shows at 7:45pm daily except Mondays. It's a real circus, done on a small scale, so only see it if you're desperate to entertain the kids.

Finally, **The Daewoo Hotel,** 360 Kim Ma St., Ba Dinh District (☎ **04/831-5000**), often hosts visiting jazz bands.

BARS, PUBS & DISCOS

The old standard in town is **Apocalypse Now,** 5C Hoa Ma (☎ **04/971-2783**). A down and dirty joint with black walls, a thatched-roof bar, and lights with "blood" streaks on them. Everybody comes—backpackers, locals, expats—and it's all somehow great fun. Plus it's open later than practically any bar in Hanoi, until 4am or so—this is definitely an "end of the night" place. While they don't serve food, they do serve up great music and beer for US$1. There's a pool table and a small dance floor as well.

If you want to be at the coolest place in town go to **B @ 1 Bar,** 19 Chan Cam, off Phu Doan in the Old Quarter (☎ **04/825-1368**). The DJs spin the latest dance tunes and the place has a real laid-back attitude.

For a more upscale experience, you'll want to call the **Daewoo Hotel** to find out if they're featuring **live jazz** performances on the dates you're in town. It's at 360 Kim Ma St. (☎ **04/831-5000**).

For another good bar experience try a cocktail at the famous **Press Club,** 59A Ly Thai To (☎ **04/934-0888**).

EXCURSIONS FROM HANOI

HALONG BAY

Halong Bay, a natural wonder, is 3,000 islands of varying sizes in the Gulf of Tonkin, many housing spectacular limestone grottos. It has been declared a UNESCO World Heritage Site. The bay itself is a 4-hour drive from Hanoi among often almost unbearably bad roads, and usually includes at least one overnight stay. Given the logistics, the trip is best done via an agent or with a group. When you book a tour with an overnight stay, you'll probably cruise on a junk for 4 to 6 hours along the bay, stopping to explore two grottos. You may pause for a swim as well. If you're really pressed for time, the tourist cafes do a daily trip for US$24 per person, departing Hanoi at 7am and getting you back by midnight. But that's really pushing it. Overnight trips can cost anywhere from US$16 to upwards of US$150 for one overnight. It depends on whether you hire a bus or a private driver, where you stay, and what you eat. Sinh Café does a fine job on the low end, and Ann's Tourist on the higher (see "Visitor Information & Tours," earlier in this chapter).

To really get off the tourist track, also consider one of the 2- or 3-day **sea kayaking** adventures offered by Buffalo Tours or Handspan Adventure Travel. These trips cost around US$180 for 3- or 4-day trips.

Cuc Phuong National Park

Cuc Phuong, established in 1962 as Vietnam's first national park, is a lush mountain rain forest with more than 250 bird and 60 mammal species, including tigers, leopards, and the unique red-bellied squirrel. The park's many visitors—and poachers—may keep you from the kind of wildlife experience you might hope for in the brush, however. It's still the perfect setting for a good hike, and features goodies like a 1,000-year-old tree, a waterfall, and Con Moong Cave, where prehistoric human remains have been discovered. Cuc Phuong is a good day trip from Hanoi, and some tourist cafes offer programs for as little as US$20 (if you have 4 people in your group). It is also possible to overnight there in the park headquarters.

Hoa Lu

From A.D. 968 to 1010, Hoa Lu was the capital of Vietnam under the Dinh and first part of the Le dynasties. It is located in a valley surrounded by awesome limestone formations, and is known as the inland Halong Bay. It is a similarly picturesque sight, and much easier to reach. Most of what remains of the kingdom are ruins, but there are still temples in the valley, renovated in the 17th century. The first honors Dinh Tien Hoang and has statues of the king. The second is dedicated to Le Dai Hanh, one of Dinh's generals and the first king of the Le Dynasty, who grabbed power in 980 after Dinh was mysteriously assassinated. Hoa Lu can easily be seen on a day trip from Hanoi. Seat-in-coach tours from a tourist cafe run about US$13 per person.

The Far North

The north and northwest highland regions are becoming increasingly popular destinations for hardy travelers. As well as breathtaking landscapes amidst the **Tonkinese Alps,** one of the main attractions of going farther afield is the **villages of the ethnic minority hill tribes,** among them the Muong, Hmong, Tai, Tay, and Dao. The villagers truly haven't seen many outsiders, and visits from foreigners usually involve a lot of staring and some friendly touching on both sides. If you can make it this far, it will be a rewarding experience.

By far the easiest travel destination in the north is **Sapa,** a small market town and gathering spot for many local tribes. You can trek out to nearby villages, or simply wait for members of the various hill tribes to come to sell their wares. Their costumes alone are an eyeful: colorful embroidered tunics embellished with heavy silver ornaments. Saturday nights, there once was a **"love market"**—young people would get together to search for prospective mates, but these days the tradition has died down a bit. Fansipan, Vietnam's highest peak, stands majestic and misty nearby at 3,143 meters (10,312 ft.).

Another relatively easy destination is **Mai Chau,** a gorgeous valley about 4 hours from Hanoi. It is the homeland of the ethnic Tai people. The road is somewhat better than the one to Sapa, and the destination not yet as developed. **Dien Bien Phu** to the far northwest is a former French commercial and military outpost, and the site of one of Vietnam's biggest military victories over the French. You can fly directly to Dien Bien Phu from Hanoi.

This region is definitely one in which independent travel could prove to be extremely challenging if not well nigh impossible. The best way to take in the splendor of the natural surroundings is to do perhaps a 4- or 5-day tour, with a jeep and driver. You could tackle only one or two of the destinations in a 2-day trip. **Ann's Tours,** 26 Yet Kieu, Hoan Kiem District (☎ **04/822-0018;** e-mail: anntours@yahoo.com), offers custom-tailored, reasonable packages. Every tourist cafe offers a Sapa package, but keep in mind that low-end travel to this area will be particularly rugged (packages run between US$25 and US$30 per person for 4 days and 3 nights). Other groups offer adventure travel in the region, including camping and hiking. **Handspan Adventure Travel** organizes both light, intermediary, and tough treks with homestays for between US$75 and US$102 per person (minimum two people); plus jeep tours (US$160 to US$180). **Buffalo Tours** also has an excellent reputation, offering similar tours. Some do involve arduous climbing and overnights in hill tribe villages without electricity and running water.

4 An Introduction to the Central Coast

Many of Vietnam's most significant historical sites, and some of its best beaches, are clustered along its central coast. Here you'll find Hue, the former Vietnamese capital, with its Imperial City and emperors' tombs. Here also is Hoi An, a historic tiny trading town that had its heyday in the 17th century, with more than 800 perfectly preserved classic Chinese and Vietnamese houses and temples. Formerly the seat of the Cham kingdom from the 2nd through 14th centuries, the central coast also has the greatest concentration of Cham relics and art, the highlight of which is the Cham Museum at Danang. And you can sample the Vietnamese beach scene in its youthful stages at China Beach and Cua Dai. The proximity and convenient transportation between towns means you'll be able to cover ground efficiently. Danang and Hoi An are so close, about half an hour by car, that you can easily stay in one and make day trips to the other.

GETTING THERE
BY PLANE   You can fly into both Hue and Danang from Saigon or Hanoi.

BY TRAIN   Both Hue and Danang are stops on the north-south rail line.

BY CAR/BUS/MINIVAN   A tourist cafe bus or minivan trip from Hanoi to Hue will take about 17 grueling hours and cost US$9. Driving with a rented vehicle and driver is possible, but will probably cost several hundred dollars and isn't the safest way to travel, as road quality will be uneven.

GETTING AROUND
BY CAR/BUS/MINIVAN   The three main coastal towns in the central part of the country are linked by roads that have been hit hard by major flooding in 2000. Potholes are an understatement, and in the dust that gets kicked up dries out your throat pretty quickly. You can easily rent a car or get a seat on a bus or minivan in any of the towns, in a hotel or booking agency—if you take a bus be prepared for the trip taking a bit longer than they advertise, due to the poor condition of the roads. From Hue to Danang is about 3½ hours; from Danang to Hoi An about 90 minutes. See individual city listings for suggested prices.

5 Hue

Hue (pronounced "hway") was once Vietnam's imperial city, the capital of the country from 1802 to 1945 under the Nguyen dynasty. Culturally and historically, it may perhaps be the most important city in the entire country. While much of it (tragically including most of Vietnam's walled citadel and imperial city) was decimated during the French and American wars, there is still much to see. One of the most interesting sights is simply daily life on the **Perfume River,** a mélange of dragon and houseboats and long-tail vessels dredging for sand. You'll visit many of the attractions, including the tombs of **Nguyen dynasty emperors,** by boat. The enjoyable town has a seaside-resort sort of air, with a laid-back attitude, low-slung, colorful colonial-style buildings, and strings of lights at outdoor cafes at night. There are many local cuisine specialties to sample as well.

You may want to plan for a full-day **American war memorial excursion** to the nearby demilitarized zone (DMZ), the beginning of the Ho Chi Minh trail, and underground tunnels at Vinh Moc.

GETTING THERE

BY PLANE   Hue connects from both Hanoi and Saigon. A taxi from the airport costs 73,000 VND (US$5). There's also an airport bus that will pick you up at your hotel and take you on the half-hour trip to the airport for 25,000 VND (US$1.72). Book through your hotel's front desk or any tour operator in town.

BY TRAIN   Trains depart daily from both Hanoi and Saigon to Hue. A trip from Hanoi to Hue takes 14 hours on an express, soft-berth compartments with A/C are available.

BY CAR   If you're coming from the south, Vietnamtourism Danang can arrange a car from Danang to Hue for 584,000 VND (US$40). The trip takes about 3½ hours.

BY BUS   While public buses are definitely not recommended, many travelers choose to take an overnight private bus or minivan from Hanoi to Hue. Tickets are 131,000 VND (US$9) through one of Hanoi's tourist cafes (see "Visitor Information & Tours," earlier in this chapter), and the trip takes an excruciating 17 hours, with several rest stops.

Hue is also the last (or first) stop on the Open Tour ticket, unless you're booked through to Hanoi.

GETTING AROUND

Taxis are much cheaper here than in Hanoi: 6,000 VND (US$0.41) starting out and 6,000 VND for each kilometer after. Call **Gili** at ☎ **054/828-282.** As Hue is relatively small, renting a cyclo by the hour for 20,000 VND (US$1.38) works well. Even the tiniest hotel provides motorbike rentals at 70,000 to 80,000 VND (US$4.83 to US$5.52) per day and bicycles for 10,000 VND (US$1).

VISITOR INFORMATION

There are a number of tour companies in Hue through which you can book boat trips and visits to the DMZ. Every hotel will also be able to assist you, although the tour companies will be cheaper, especially for car services.

The **Huong Giang Company,** at 17 Le Loi St. (☎ **054/832-220** or 054/832-221; fax 054/821-426; e-mail: hgtravel@dng.vnn.vn), organizes the usual tours to the tombs and the DMZ, although they are more flexible than most in terms of hours and

Hue

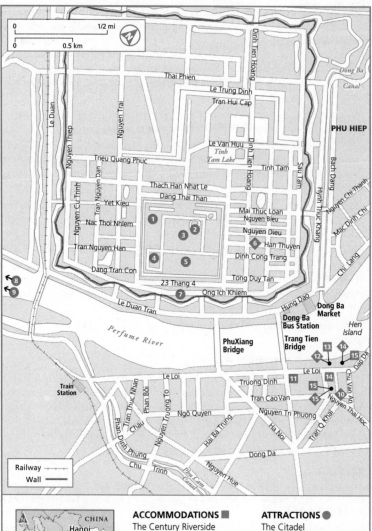

ACCOMMODATIONS ■
The Century Riverside
  Hotel 12
Dong Loi Hotel 15
Hoa Hong Hotel II 14
Hotel Saigon Marin 11
Huong Giang Hotel 13

DINING ◆
Club Garden 10
Hoa Mia Restaurant 13
La Carambole 15
Lac Thanh Restaurant 6
Riverside Restaurant 12

ATTRACTIONS ●
The Citadel
  & Imperial City 1
The Flag Tower 7
Forbidden Purple City 2
The Imperial Tombs 9
Nine Dynastic Urns 4
Thai Binh Reading
  Pavilion 3
Thai Hoa Palace 5
Thien Mu Pagoda 8

transport. They are Hue's most upscale and efficient group, and also the most expensive. An all-day tour by car and boat, with guide, to the Citadel and tombs, with lunch, is US$25. If you want a private boat to take you up the Perfume River, they can organize one for you for US$20. And to the DMZ, they'll take you for US$13.

On the other hand, **Sinh Café V,** 7 Nguyen Tri Phuong. (☎ **054/848-262**), does a DMZ seat-in-coach tour for US$11 per person, and can book a group boat up the river for US$2 per person.

Fast Facts: Hue

Banks/Currency Exchange Most hotels change currency in Hue, but note that the rate isn't as good as in the two main cities. Vietcombank is at 46 Hung Vuong St. (☎ 054/846-058).

Internet/E-mail At 8 Hung Vuong, you can't miss ISC Internet next to the giant green signs of the Fujifilm developing center. If you're by the Century Hotel, down the street just across from the hotel at 6A Pham Ngu Lao you'll also find service. Rates are 300 to 400 VND (about US$0.02 to US$0.03) per minute.

Post Office/Mail There are mini–post offices in the Century and Huong Giang hotels. The main post office is at 8 Hoang Hoa Tham St., and is open from 7am to 9pm. You can also place international calls there.

Telephone The city code for Hue is 54. You can place IDD calls at the post office (above).

ACCOMMODATIONS

There are three upscale hotels in Hue; the rest are budget places of varying quality, and there are some duds. Always ask to see the rooms first if it's not a hotel I recommend. Don't expect the service you might get in Saigon, except that all provide tour services and almost all include breakfast in their prices. Even though hotels insist that they accept American Express, they may refuse it when it's time to pay. As always in Vietnam, the prices are eminently flexible, so press for a discount.

EXPENSIVE

The Century Riverside Hotel. 49 Le Loi St., Hue. ☎ **800/536-7361,** 054/823-390, or 823-391. Fax 054/823-394. A/C MINIBAR TV TEL. 147 units. US$70–US$100 double; US$170 suite. AE, JCB, MC, V.

This is Hue's premier hotel, although it has close rivals. For comfort, friendliness, and location, it's quite nice. Rooms are bland chain-hotel style, smallish, clean, and comfortable, with new tile and marble bathrooms (make sure to ask for a room with recent renovations). The cheaper US$70 rooms have older carved-wood furniture. The riverview rooms are worth the extra US$10, and the pool is in a prime lounge spot by the river. The hotel also has a very nice English-speaking staff. Watch out for the hidden costs. Laundry is US$1 a piece, the exchange rate is inexplicably lower than anywhere else, and phone call costs are outrageous—even local calls are billed. Ouch! The Riverside Restaurant is Hue's most upscale, serving Vietnamese and Western dishes.

Hotel Saigon Marin. 30 Le Loi St., Hue. ☎ **054/823-526.** Fax 054/825-155. 137 units. A/C MINIBAR TV TEL. www.saigon-tourist.com/saigon_morin. E-mail: sgmorin@dng.vnn.vn. US$60–US$100 double; US$180–US$300 suite. AE, JCB, MC, V.

The Marin is a completely refurbished colonial, government-run. When you first see the outside of the Marin, with its pale pink walls and columns topped by bright purple capitals, you know you are in for something special. The whole place looks like aliens landed and gave their best shot at what a restored Southeast Asian colonial should look like. The lobby isn't that big and yet has three, count 'em, *three* chandeliers. It's hard to know what to say about the rooms. They are attractive, with reproduction French colonial furniture, nice carpet, and floral drapes, but the furniture seems to be randomly placed with no thought for style or spatial relationships. The whole effect is unsettling. Yet the whole place is certainly clean, comfortable, and deluxe, by Hue standards. Nice-sized new marble bathrooms are just that, and have hair dryers. The nice-sized pool is placed in the middle courtyard and has a outdoor cafe and well-landscaped garden to the side. The staff couldn't care less.

Huong Giang Hotel. 51 Le Loi St., Hue. ☎ **054/822-122** or 054/823-958. Fax 054/823-102 or 823-424. 150 units. A/C MINIBAR TV TEL. US$55–US$80 double; US$170 suite; US$230 royal suite. AE, JCB, MC, V.

This hotel is a veritable Asian wonderland, so enamored is it of heavy carved-wood and bamboo furnishings. Some might call it tacky, but it's great fun and well worth being your choice in Hue, as "imperial" is what the city's all about. The rooms are clean and comfortable in basic bamboo, only the bathrooms are a disappointing dormitory style, with plastic shower curtains (mine featured a Bugs Bunny motif) and no counter space. Try to get a good deal on one of the Royal Suites, with carved-wood walls, grandiose furniture with inlaid mother-of-pearl, and a massive wood room divider—sort of a mini-pagoda right in your room. The words "emperor" and "bordello" both leap to mind. The Royal Restaurant, worth a photo just for its gaudy gold-and-red-everything design alone, is for pre-arranged group dinners, where the costumed staff serves a fancy traditional dinner at a hefty price. The River Front Terrace Bar is the best place in Hue to have a drink and watch life on the river.

MODERATE

Hoa Hong Hotel II. 1 Pham Ngu Lao St., Hue. ☎ **054/824-377** or 054/826-943. Fax 054/826-949. 50 units. A/C MINIBAR TV TEL. US$30–US$60 double; US$80 suite. AE, MC, V.

Here is a nice hotel bargain in Hue. Built in 1996, the rooms are very nondescript—think navy and beige, with those polyester bedspreads again. Yet they are comfortable, with good, firm beds. The bathrooms are nice-sized, with bathtubs and hair dryers, and all is spic and span. Ask for a city view rather than a noisy street-view room. The suites have authentic Asian furniture. There are two restaurants, one of which specializes in the popular "royal dinner" theme evenings, when both staff and guests dress like emperors and empresses. The lobby has a fun little bar on one end with very expensive drinks. Tour and car rental services are available, as is round-the-clock room service. Hoa Hong II is hugely popular with tour groups, so book early.

INEXPENSIVE

Dong Loi Hotel. 11A Pham Ngu Lao St. ☎ **054/822-296** or ☎/fax 054/826-234. E-mail: interser@dng.vnn.vn. A/C TEL. US$12–US$35. No credit cards.

There are plenty of inexpensive hotels in Hue, but the Dong Loi is another particularly good bargain. Family-run, it has spotless rooms with tile floors and firm beds. The attractive bathrooms are tile, and the most expensive rooms have bathtubs. Rooms priced US$20 on up have televisions. The hotel provides tour planning and laundry services, and even has an Internet cafe. The rooms facing the back have a bonus: a free rooster wake-up call at 4am. Next door, the La Carambole restaurant, reviewed below, provides much better cuisine than your average budget hotel coffeeshop.

DINING

There are some good local dishes to sample in Hue, but relatively few spots with English menus and high-quality food. Still, the ones I found were good enough to visit more than once. Do try *bun bo Hue,* a noodle soup with pork, beef, and shredded green onions; and *banh khoi,* a thin, crispy pancake filled with ground meat and crispy vegetables.

✪ **Club Garden.** 12 Vo Thi Sau St. ☎ **054/826-327.** Main courses US$2.50–US$4; set menus US$8–US$12. No credit cards. Daily 7am–11pm. VIETNAMESE.

One of the best meals in Vietnam can be had at this unpretentious little restaurant. Seating is both outdoors and in. The menu's emphasis is on fish and crab, all prepared in the local style (grilled, in lemon leaves) and absolutely delicious. And note the prices! Their *banh khoi,* a crispy pancake stuffed with ground meat and shrimp, is the best in town. Also musts: the fried shrimp with garlic, crispy fried noodles with vegetables, and chicken cooked in lemon leaf. Dessert is fried bananas of the gods. The menu is in very good English as well as Vietnamese and French, and the family that runs the place is friendly and accommodating. Breakfast is served here as well.

Hoa Mia Restaurant. 51 Le Loi St., third floor, Huong Giang Hotel. ☎ **054/822-122.** Main courses 25,000–36,000 VND (US$1.72–US$2.48). AE, JCB, MC, V. Daily 6am–10pm. VIETNAMESE/CONTINENTAL.

A most attractive restaurant, large, open, and airy, with bamboo furniture and detailing and a great view of the Perfume River. It serves excellent local cuisine. Try *banh rom Hue,* little triangular-shaped fried rolls stuffed with ground meat, shrimp, and vegetables; crab soup with mushroom; and grilled chicken in lemon leaves. There is even wine by the glass. Their breakfast buffet is incredible, including every kind of egg and pancake, as well as Vietnamese sweets and a table full of exotic fruit. You'll have to be patient with the slow service and unseasonal Christmas Muzak, though.

La Carambole. 11A Pham Ngu Lao St. ☎ **054/822-296.** Main courses 20,000–80,000 VND (US$1.38–US$5.52); set menus US$3–US$8. V. Daily 7am–11pm. VIETNAMESE/CONTINENTAL

I came across this place on a chilly night and was warmed by the soft lighting and loud Creedence Clearwater Revival. Cheerful red tablecloths and nice wait staff made me just want to hop inside. I was excited to see "comfort food" on the menu, like chicken soup and mashed potatoes. Only the chicken soup was the Vietnamese kind and mashed potatoes were more like warm potato soup. Stick to the set menus, which offer local specialties prepared nicely. Sandwiches aren't too bad either.

Lac Thanh Restaurant. 6A Dien Tien Hoang St. ☎ **054/824674.** Main courses 7,000–40,000 VND (US$0.48–US$2.76). No credit cards. Daily 7am–10pm. VIETNAMESE.

Very good eats and a lively good time to be had here. Everybody knows it, so you'll see every under-50 wayfarer you've met during your trip here. It's basically a grubby street-side place, but one that serves very nice grilled pork wrapped in rice paper, sautéed bean sprouts, grilled crab, and spareribs, among dozens of choices. Balcony seating, too. For dessert, try the local specialty *ché nong,* a warm congee with coconut, bananas, and nuts. The glutinous texture takes some getting used to, but definitely adds entertainment value. As you approach the restaurant, you'll be mobbed by hucksters trying to take you to the knock-off next door, which is reportedly not bad either.

Riverside Restaurant. 40 Le Loi, at the Century Riverside Hotel. ☎ **054/823-390.** Main courses US$3.50–US$6. AE, JCB, MC, V. Daily all day. VIETNAMESE/CONTINENTAL.

This very nice, upscale restaurant has scenic views over the Perfume River as well as good food. The extensive menu includes dozens of varieties of noodles and fried rice, from spaghetti with cheese to Vietnamese rice noodles with seafood. Main dishes include sautéed shrimp with mushroom sauce over rice and grilled duck wrapped in lemon leaf.

ATTRACTIONS

Except for the remains of its fabulous Imperial City, Hue in itself has sadly seen the worst of the French and Vietnam wars. Most of the star attractions other than the Citadel, therefore, involve half-day or day trips outside the city.

✪ **The Citadel & Imperial City.** Admission 55,000 VND (US$3.79). Daily 7am–5:30pm.

The **Citadel** is often used as a catch-all term for Hue's Imperial City, built by emperor Gia Long beginning in 1804 for the exclusive use of the emperor and his household, much like Beijing's Forbidden City. The city actually encompasses three walled enclosures: the Exterior Exclosure or Citadel, the Yellow Enclosure or Imperial City within that, and in the very center the Forbidden Purple City where the emperor actually lived.

Beginning at the outside looking into the main entrance at the southern gate, you'll find the Flag Tower, built in 1807. It is of much significance to Vietnam's military past. In 1947 it was almost destroyed during the war against the French. Rebuilt, it was a figurehead in the American War when it was defiantly occupied by the Viet Cong for 25 days during the Tet Offensive. The palace itself was used as a field hospital for Viet Cong commandos. The tower is in three tiers, representing the natural order of earth, human beings, and heaven.

The Citadel is a square, 2-kilometer (1½-mile) wall, 7 meters (23 ft.) high and 20 meters (66 ft.) thick, with 10 gates. Ironically, it was constructed by a French military architect, though it failed to prevent the French from destroying the complex many years later. The main entrance to the Imperial City is the Ngo Mon, the southwest or "noon" gate. It encompasses an elegant pavilion known as the Belvedere of Five Phoenixes, constructed by Emperor Gia Long in 1823. It was used for important proclamations, such as announcements of the names of successful doctoral candidates (a list still hangs on the wall on the upper floor) and, most memorably, announcement of the abdication of the last emperor Bao Dai on August 13, 1945, to Ho Chi Minh.

The first structure you will approach is **Thai Hoa Palace.** Otherwise known as the Palace of Supreme Harmony, it was built in 1833. It was used as the throne room, a ceremonial hall where the emperor celebrated festivals and received courtiers; the original throne still stands. The Mandarins sat outside. In front are two mythical *ky lin* animals, which walk without their claws ever touching ground and which have piercing eyesight for watching the emperor, tracking all good and evil he does. Note the statues of the heron and turtle inside the palace's ornate lacquered interior, the heron representing nobility, and the turtle, the working person. Folklore has it that the two took turns saving each other's lives during a fire, symbolizing that the power of the emperor rests with his people, and vice versa.

The **Forbidden Purple City,** once the actual home of the emperor and his concubines, was almost completely razed in a fire in 1947. There are a few buildings left among the rubble, however. The new Royal Theater behind the square, a look-alike to the razed original, is under construction. The partially restored **Thai Binh Reading Pavilion,** to the left of it as you head north, is notable mostly for its beautifully landscaped surroundings, including a small lake with a Zen-like stone sculpture, and the ceramic and glass mosaic detailing on the roof and pillars, favored by flamboyant emperor Khai Dinh.

Turning around and facing south and the Noon Gate again, to your far right after a short walk you'll come to the splendid **Hung To Mieu** temple, built in 1804 to honor Gia Long's parents. To the left and south of it, newly restored, is **The Mieu Temple,** constructed in 1921–22 by emperor Minh Mang. Inside are funeral altars paying tribute to 10 of the last Nguyen dynasty emperors, omitting two who reigned only for days, with photos of each emperor and his empress(es) and various small offerings and knickknacks. The two empty glass containers to the side of each photo should contain bars of gold, probably an impractical idea today.

Across from The Mieu you'll see Hien Lam, or Glorious Pavilion, to the far right, with the **Nine Dynastic Urns** in front. Cast in 1835–37, each urn represents a Nguyen emperor, and is richly embellished with all the flora, fauna, and material goods Vietnam has to offer, mythical or otherwise.

✪ **Thien Mu Pagoda.** On the bank of the Perfume River. Daily 8am–5pm.

Often called the symbol of Hue, Thien Mu is one of the oldest and loveliest religious structures in Vietnam. It was constructed beginning in 1601. The Phuoc Dien Tower in front was added in 1864 by emperor Thieu Tri. Each of its seven tiers are dedicated to one of the human forms taken by Buddha, or the seven steps to enlightenment—depending upon whom you ask. There are also two buildings housing a bell reportedly weighing 2 tons, and a stele inscribed with a biography of Lord Nguyen Hoang, founder of the temple.

Once past the front gate, observe the 12 huge wooden sculptures of fearsome temple "guardians"—note the real facial hair. A complex of monastic buildings lies in the center, offering glimpses of the monks' daily routines: cooking, stacking wood, whacking weeds. Stroll all the way to the rear of the complex to look at the large graveyard at the base of the Truong Son mountains, and wander through the well-kept garden of pine trees. Try not to go between the hours of 11:30am and 2pm, when the monks are at lunch, as the rear half of the complex will be closed.

The Imperial Tombs. Admission to each 55,000 VND (US$3.79). Summer daily 6:30am–5:30pm; winter daily7am–5pm.

As befits its history as an Imperial City, Hue's environs are studded with tombs of past emperors. They are spread out over a distance, so the best way to see them is to hire a car for a half-day or take one of the many organized boat tours up the Perfume River. Altogether, there were 13 kings of the Nguyen dynasty, although only seven reigned until their death. As befits an emperor, each had tombs of stature, some as large as a small town. Most tomb complexes usually consist of a courtyard, a stele (a large stone tablet with a biography of the emperor), a temple for worship, and a pond.

Tu Duc ruled the longest of any Nguyen dynasty emperor, from 1848 to 1883. His tomb was constructed from 1864 to 1867, and has some 50 buildings. Tu Duc was a philosopher and scholar of history and literature. His reign was unfortunate: his kingdom unsuccessfully struggled against French colonialism, he fought a coup d'etat by members of his own family, and although he had 104 wives, he left no heir. The "tomb" also served as recreation grounds for the king, having been completed 16 years prior to his death. He actually engraved his own stele, in fact. The largest in Vietnam at 20 tons, it has its own pavilion in the tomb. The highlight of the grounds is the lotus-filled lake ringed by frangipani trees, with a large pavilion in the center. The main cluster of buildings includes Hoa Khiem (Harmony Modesty) Pavilion, where the king worked, which still contains items of furniture and ornaments. Minh Khiem Duong, constructed in 1866, is said to be the country's oldest surviving theater. It's great fun to poke around in the wings. There are also pieces of original furniture lying

Digging In at Vinh Moc

In the mid 1960s the Americans began bombing raids of the Vinh Linh district near the DMZ, on grounds of suspected Viet Cong complicity. The more than 600 villagers, however, refused to leave their homes and literally dug in. In fact, they dug over a mile of underground tunnels over 1965–66, and then lived in them.

The tunnels are divided into various levels, the deepest about 23 meters (76 ft.) below the surface. The complex was a fully functioning community haven, with "living rooms" for families, a conference and performance room, and an operating theater where children were delivered (you can see their pictures in the above-ground museum nearby). There are 1,728 meters (5,670 ft.) of the tunnel left today. Seven entrances point toward the sea, where, under cover of the night, the villagers would come up for air and pass munitions along to Viet Cong boats. You'll walk through about 300 meters (984 ft.) of the tunnels in a main artery that is 1.62 meters high by 1.2 meters wide (5⅓ ft. high and 4 ft. wide), going down three stages, with the clammy climate and creepy claustrophobic feeling causing perspiration to pop and hair to stand up on the back of your neck. Coming to the sea, feeling the fresh wind on your face, you'll feel relief, and also disbelief at the incredible endurance and perseverance of people who voluntarily committed themselves to enduring such conditions—who, in fact, dug themselves in.

You can see the tunnels as part of a day trip to the Demilitarized Zone (DMZ). Admission is 22,000 VND (US$1.52).

here and there, as well as a cabinet with household objects: the Queen's slippers, ornate chests, bronze and silver books. The raised box on the wall is for the actors who played emperors; the real emperor was at the platform to the left.

✪ **Khai Dinh's tomb,** completed from 1923 to 1931, is one of the world's wonders. The emperor himself wasn't particularly revered, being overly extravagant and flamboyant (reportedly he wore a belt studded with lights that he flicked on at opportune public moments). His tomb, a gaudy mix of gothic, baroque, Hindu, and Chinese Qing dynasty architecture at the top of 127 steep steps, is a reflection of the man. Inside, the two main rooms are completely covered with fabulous, intricate glass and ceramic mosaics in designs reminiscent of Tiffany and art deco. The workmanship is astounding. The outer room's ceiling was done by a fellow who used both his feet and hands to paint, in what some say was a sly mark of disrespect for the emperor. While in most tombs the location of the emperor's actual remains are a secret, Khai Minh boldly placed his under his de facto tomb itself.

Minh Mang, one of the most popular Nguyen emperors and the father of last emperor Bao Dai, built a restrained, serene, classical temple, much like Hue's Imperial City, located at the confluence of two Perfume River tributaries. Stone sculptures surround a long walkway, lined with flowers, leading up to the main buildings.

If you take the boat trip to see the tombs, note that you'll pay US$2 to US$4 for the boat ride (depending on which agent you use), *plus* 55,000 VND (US$3.79) for *each* tomb. Be prepared for when the boat pulls to shore at the first two tombs; you'll have to hire one of the motorcycle taxis at the bank to shuttle you to and from the site. You will not have enough time to walk there and back, so you're basically at their mercy. Haggle as best you can—I got one guy down to 10,000 VND (US$0.69), but they'll try to quote you something like 40,000 VND (US$2.76). But don't be too stubborn—I took the trip with others who were so insulted by the motorcycle taxis they just slumped on the bank and didn't see the tombs at all. No joke.

EXCURSION: KHE SANH & THE DMZ

Under the Geneva Accords of 1954, an agreement struck to bring peace to Indochina after its struggle with French colonists, Vietnam was divided into North and South along the Seventeenth Parallel. The two never united. During the American War, the Seventeenth Parallel, a.k.a the DMZ, or demilitarized zone between north and south, was a tense area demarcated with barbed wire and land mines in parts, bombed and defoliated into a wasteland. The area is green with growth again and completely unremarkable except for its history and the required statue at Hien Luong Bridge, which links north and south over the Ben Hai river. Nearby are strategic sites with names you may recognize: the Rockpile, Hamburger Hill, Camp Carroll, and Khe Sanh, a former U.S. marine base that was the site of some of the war's most vicious and deadly fighting. If you take a tour of the area, you see these sites as well as the Dakrong Bridge, an official entryway into the Ho Chi Minh Trail.

Warning: The route over Highway 9 to the sites are narrow, very bumpy dirt roads and wooden bridges. Rethink this trip if it's a rainy day, or if you are faint of either heart or stomach.

6 Danang & China Beach

Danang, the fourth-largest city in Vietnam, is one of the most important seaports in the central region. It played a prominent historical role in the American war, being the landing site for the first American troops officially sent to Vietnam. Even with the bustle of ships coming and going, poor Danang has to be one of the world's ugliest cities, and there isn't a major attraction save for the **Cham Museum.** It's really a must-see. Unfortunately it's been given the shaft by all the tour buses that used to make a stop here en route between Hoi An and Hue. Nowadays, if you can get them to stop for the museum, they'll only give you about 20 minutes to look.

There are a few excellent-value hotels in Danang, so an option is to actually stay in the city and take day trips to nearby Hoi An. China Beach, or My Khe, as it's known locally, is worth a stop. There's a nice light-sand coast with excellent views of the nearby Marble Mountains. The award-winning American television drama, China Beach, was based on a U.S. military recreation base a few miles north.

GETTING THERE

BY PLANE　You can fly to Danang from both Hanoi and HCMC. A taxi from the airport will cost about US$3.

BY BUS　If you're traveling on the Open Tour ticket, Danang is not a specified stop, but they'll drop you off at the Cham Museum. You'll have to call their office in either Hue or Hoi An to pick you up when you're ready to leave.

BY CAR　Danang is about 3½ hours by car from Hue, and the route covers the very scenic Hai Van Pass. Pay US$40 for the trip. From Hoi An, it's about an hour and costs US$25. This ride makes a good day trip along with the Marble Mountains.

VISITOR INFORMATION & TOURS

Vietnamtourism Danang is located at 83 Nguyen Thi Minh Khai (☎ 0511/823-660; fax 0511/821-560). They can arrange trips to the Marble Mountains and

My Son, as can nearly every hotel; except that Vietnamtourism is a lot more helpful and professional.

FAST FACTS: DANANG

Banks/Currency Exchange   Vietcombank is at 104 Le Loi St. (☎ **0511/821-955**). In a pinch you can get traveler's checks cashed at An Phu Tourist Travel, 147 Le Loi St., ☎ **0511/818-366.** Their hours of operation are better than the bank's, but their exchange rate is awful. Still, in a pinch . . .

Telephone   The city code for Danang is 511.

ACCOMMODATIONS

Bamboo Green Hotel. 158 Phan Chau Trinh St. ☎ **0511/822-996** or 0511/822-997. Fax 0511/822-998. E-mail: bamboogreen@dng.vnn.vn. 42 units. A/C MINIBAR TV TEL. US$45–US$60 double. AE, JCB, MC, V.

Operated by Vietnamtourism, this hotel opened in 1997 and is the nicest in Danang. Rooms are large, immaculate, and well-furnished in light wood (just try to overlook the hideous poly bedspreads), and the nice-sized marble bathrooms with hair dryers look brand new, as they should. Ask for a room on the top floor for a good city view. There is a big restaurant with decent Asian/Vietnamese fare and good tour services, sauna, and massage. The staff is friendly and snaps to.

Furama Resort Danang. 68 Ho Xuan Huong St., China Beach, Danang. ☎ **0511/847-333.** Fax 0511/847-220. www.interconti.com. E-mail: furamadn@hn.vnn.vn. 200 units. A/C MINIBAR TV TEL. US$140–US$200 double; US$400 suite. AE, JCB, MC, V.

The Furama is a full-service resort, about 7 miles from Danang. It's worth staying here and spending an extra day or two simply lounging around the Viet-style low-rise buildings, enjoying the beautiful beach, landscaping, and decor. Rooms are simple yet luxe: big with solid wood floors, Vietnamese-flavored furniture, and sliding doors to balconies that overlook ocean or pool. The huge modern marble bathrooms have all the amenities. There are two gorgeous swimming pools: one a minimalist still-life and the other a faux lagoon, complete with small waterfall. Prices are determined by the view, and ocean-front units are only steps from the beach. Note that most of the water sports are available only from February through September—the surf is far too rough in other months, often even for swimming. There is an hourly shuttle bus to the city. The Furama does have some kinks to work out, though: Reservations get misplaced, the staff is perhaps a bit too laid-back, and the quality of the food is uneven.

Café Indochine offers light Vietnamese and Continental meals. The Ocean Terrace serves pizza and pastas. The Hai Van Lounge and Lagoon bar serve drinks and snacks. Amenities include well-equipped health club with sauna, massage, hair salon, medical center, business center, conference and banquet rooms, 24-hour room service, baby-sitting, game room, scuba diving, snorkeling, waterskiing, surfboard rental, tennis court, driving range, karate classes, and art gallery.

Royal Hotel. 17 Quang Trung St., Danang. ☎ **0511/823-295.** Fax 0511/827-279. 28 units. A/C MINIBAR TV TEL. US$70 double; US$120 suite. Ask about seasonal discounts, which can go as high as 50%. Includes breakfast, welcome drink, and fruit basket. AE, JCB, MC, V.

Formerly the Marco Polo Hotel, this place has been a tourist standby in Danang since it was built in 1994. It's comfortable and attractive, with a floral theme rather than Asian. The small marble bathrooms are showing signs of age, but have bathtubs and hair dryers. It has three-star amenities: restaurant, tour services, business center, tennis, and nightclub. It's not as fancy, but overall it's a better bargain than the Bamboo (above).

Who Are the Cham?

There is little written history of the Cham. What we do know is mainly via Chinese written history, a few temple stelae, and the splendid religious artwork the empire created in its prime. They were a people of Indonesian descent formed in approximately the second century A.D. in Tuong Lam, along the central coast of Vietnam, while fighting to prevent Chinese domination. They declared a new land, dubbed the Lin Yi by the Chinese, that extended from Quang Binh to present-day Danang Province. The center of the civilization for most of its existence was in Indrapura, or Tra Kieu, near present-day Danang.

The Cham belonged to the Malayo-Polynesian language family, and had their own script based on Sanskrit. They lived by rice farming, fishing, and trading pepper, cinnamon bark, ivory, and wood with neighboring nations, using Hoi An as a base. Hinduism was their dominant religion, with Buddhist influences and an infusion of Islam starting in the 14th century.

In the middle of the 10th century, internal warfare, as well as battles against both the Khmer to the south and Dai Viet to the north, began to erode the Cham kingdom. By the mid-15th century, it had been almost entirely absorbed into Vietnam. By the early 1800s, there was no longer a separate Cham nation. The Cham still exist today, however, as an ethnic minority. They have their own language and customs, and their religion is still largely based on Hinduism, though a portion of them have converted to Islam. They survive through farming and the sales of handicrafts.

ATTRACTIONS

✪ **The Cham Museum.** At Tran Phu and Le Dinh Duong sts. No phone. Admission 20,000 VND (US$1.38). Daily 7am–6pm.

The Cham Museum was established in 1936 as the École Française d'Extreme Orient. It has the largest collection of Cham sculpture in the world, in works ranging from the 4th to 14th centuries, presented in a rough outdoor setting that suits the evocative, sensual sculptures well. The more than 300 pieces of sandstone artwork and temple decorations were largely influenced by Hindu and, later, Mahayana Buddhism. Among the cast of characters you'll see: symbols of Uroja, or "goddess mother," usually breasts or nipples; the linga, the phallic structure representing the god Shiva; the holy bird Garuda; the dancing girl Kinnari; the snake god Naga; and Ganesha, child of the god Shiva, with the head of an elephant. The sculptures are arranged by period, which are in turn named after the geographic regions where the sculptures were found. Note the masterpiece Tra Kieu altar of the late seventh century, with carved scenes telling the story of the Asian epic *Ramayana*. The story is of the wedding of Princess Sita. Side one tells of Prince Rama, who broke a holy vow to obtain Sita's hand. Side two tells of ambassadors sent to King Dasaratha, Prince Rama's father, to bring him the glad tidings. Side three is the actual ceremony, and side four, the celebrations after the ceremony.

Explanations are written in English and French. There is a permanent photo exhibition of Cham relics in situ at various locations throughout Vietnam that helps put everything in context.

The Marble Mountains. 7 miles south of Danang and 6 miles north of Hoi An along Hwy. 1. Admission 50,000 VND (US$3.45).

The "mountains" are actually a series of five marble and limestone formations, which the locals liken to the shape of a dragon at rest. The hills contain numerous caves, some of which have become Buddhist sanctuaries. They also served as sanctuaries for the Viet Cong during the American war. The highest mountain, Thuy Son, is climbable via steps built into the hillside. Its highlight is the Ling Ong Pagoda, a shrine within a cave. As interesting as the caves are the quarries in Non Nuoc village, at the bottom of the mountains. Fantastic animals are carved from the rock, particularly the roaring lion said to watch over the village from the peaks. Try to get a good look before you are set upon by flocks of hawkers. What's more, even if you're interested in the items they hawk—incredibly cheap mortise and pestle sets, chess sets, some of it very nice—who wants to drag *marble* all the way back home? You can easily see the mountains as part of your trip either en route to or from Hoi An.

AN EXCURSION TO MY SON

My Son, 44 miles outside of Danang, is one of the most important Cham temple sites, established in the late 4th century. The temples were constructed as a religious center for citizens of the Cham capital, Danang, from the 7th through 12th centuries. My Son may also have been used as a burial site for Cham kings after cremation. Originally, there were over 70 towers and monuments here, but bombing during the American war (the Viet Cong used My Son as a munitions warehouse) has sadly reduced many to rubble. Additionally, many of the smaller structures have been removed to the Cham museum in Danang. The complex has a very serene and spiritual setting, however, and what does remain is powerful and evocative. It's not hard to imagine what a wonder My Son must once have been.

Much of what remains today are structures built or renovated during the 10th century when the cult of Shiva, founder and protector of the kingdom, was predominant in the Cham court. Each group had at least the following structures: a **kalan,** or main tower, a gate tower in front of that with two entrances, a **mandapa** or meditation hall, and a repository building for offerings. Some have towers sheltering stelae with kingly epitaphs. A brick wall encircles the compound.

Architecturally, a temple complex shows Indian influences. Each is a microcosm of the world. The foundations are earth, the square bases are the temple itself, and the pointed roofs symbolize the heavens. The entrance of the main tower faces east, and surrounding smaller towers represent each continent. A trench, representing the oceans, surrounds each group. Vietnamese architecture is represented in decorative patterns and boat-shaped roofs.

Group A originally had 13 towers. A-1, the main tower, was a 69-foot-tall masterpiece before being destroyed in 1969. Group B shows influences from Indian and Indonesian art. Note that B-6 holds a water repository for statue-washing ceremonies. Its roof is carved with an image of the god Vishnu sitting beneath a 13-headed snake god, or **naga.** Group C generally followed an earlier architectural style called Hoa Lai, which predominated from the eighth century to the beginning of the ninth. Groups G and H were the last to be built, at around the end of the 13th century.

You can make arrangements for a half-day trip to see My Son through any tourist agent in Danang, or from Hoi An. Entrance to the site is 50,000 VND (US$3.45), and a private half-day tour with a guide is US$35 for a car, US$42 for a van. From Hoi An, the half-day seat-in-coach tour by Sinh Café costs US$2 per person.

7 Hoi An

If you go, Hoi An will be one of the highlights of your Vietnam visit. From the 16th to the 18th century, Hoi An was Vietnam's most important port and trading post, particularly in ceramics. Today, it is a quaint old town (844 structures have been designated historical landmarks) still showing the influences of the Chinese and Japanese traders who passed through and settled here. Moreover, it's small enough to cover easily on foot, wandering through the historic homes and temples on a quiet Saturday afternoon, perhaps stopping to lounge in an open-air cafe, or gaze at the endless oddities and exotic foods in the market, or take a **sampan ride** down the lazy river. In the afternoons when school is out, the streets are thronged with skipping children in spotless white shirts. While the city is eagerly courting tourism and your tourist dollars—meaning there's plenty of pesky vendors and hawkers—it's still relatively low-key and genuinely friendly.

GETTING THERE
BY PLANE OR TRAIN   Major public transport connections go through Danang. From there, you can take a car to Hoi An for US$25 through the **Vietnamtourism** office in Danang (☎ **0511/823-660**).

GETTING AROUND
Hoi An is so small you'll memorize the map in an hour or two. Most hotels and guesthouses rent out bicycles for 5,000 to 7,000 VND (US$0.34 to US$0.48) a day, as does Hoi An Tourism (see below) to explore the outer regions of the city or Cao Dai beach. **Motorbikes** are US$3 to US$5 per day and are not difficult to drive in this tiny, calm city. **Cyclos** are here and there; 10,000 VND (US$0.69) or so should get you anywhere within the city.

VISITOR INFORMATION & TOURS
The Hoi An Tourist Guiding Office, 12 Phan Chu Trinh St. (☎ **0510/862-715**), offers tours of the old town and sells the entrance ticket to the "Hoi An: World Cultural Heritage"—a one-ticket purchase offering limited admission to all of the town's museums, old houses, and Chinese assembly halls. For more information about the ticket, see "Attractions" below.

   Hoi An Tourist Service Company, inside the Hoi An Hotel, 6 Tran Hung Dao St. (☎ **0510/861-373;** fax 0510/861-636), books every type of tour of the city and surrounding areas, including China Beach and the Marble Mountains, and is a reliable operation. There are many tourist cafes, booking offices, and small hotels that can do the same job, but these specialize in backpacker minibus tours.

   The Sinh Café IV, 37 Phan Dinh Phung St. (☎ **0510/863-948**), provides bus tours and tickets onward.

Fast Facts: Hoi An

Banks/Currency Exchange   The Vietcombank branch at 4 Huong Dieu St. changes money of most major currencies and does credit card cash withdrawal transactions. Hours are Monday to Saturday 7:30am to 7pm. At no. 78 Le Loi St., 1 block up from the river, there's a money changing booth operated by Hoi An Income Bank.

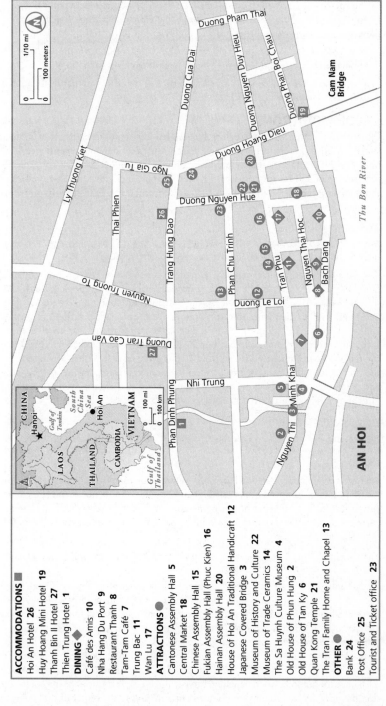

Hoi An

ACCOMMODATIONS ■
Hoi An Hotel **26**
Huy Hoang Mini Hotel **19**
Thanh Bin II Hotel **27**
Thien Trung Hotel **1**

DINING ◆
Café des Amis **10**
Nha Hang Du Port **9**
Restaurant Thanh **8**
Tam-Tam Café **7**
Trung Bac **11**
Wan Lu **17**

ATTRACTIONS ●
Cantonese Assembly Hall **5**
Central Market **18**
Chinese Assembly Hall **15**
Fukian Assembly Hall (Phuc Kien) **16**
Hainan Assembly Hall **20**
House of Hoi An Traditional Handicraft **12**
Japanese Covered Bridge **3**
Museum of History and Culture **22**
Museum of Trade Ceramics **14**
The Sa Huynh Culture Museum **4**
Old House of Phun Hung **2**
Old House of Tan Ky **6**
Quan Kong Temple **21**
The Tran Family Home and Chapel **13**

OTHER ●
Bank **24**
Post Office **25**
Tourist and Ticket office **23**

Internet/E-mail   Along Le Loi you'll find service at prices between 300 and 400 VND (a couple cents) per minute. A few places have access, but the connections are all slow, and the local ISP is down most of the time.

Post Office/Mail   The post office is at the corner of Trang Hong Dao and Huong Dieu streets and is open Monday to Saturday 6am to 9:30pm.

Telephone   The city code for Hoi An is 510. You can place international phone calls from the post office listed above.

ACCOMMODATIONS

Other than the Hoi An Hotel, below, Hoi An has a selection of budget hotels which suit its toned-down character very well. Except for a few standouts mentioned here, one is very like another, and though they are usually spotless, facilities are generally very basic, with all-in-one bathroom-shower combos. Inclusions vary; two rooms in the same hotel can have completely different amenities, so ask to see a room before booking.

MODERATE

Hoi An Hotel. 6 Tran Hung Dao St. ☎ **0510/861-373.** Fax 0510/861-636. 120 units. A/C MINIBAR TV TEL. US$26–US$60 double; US$100 suite. AE, JCB, MC, V.

The Hoi An is the top-end hotel here, and it's a good one. Don't expect anything fancy, but rooms are unusually large and impeccably clean, with tile floors and comfortable beds. Basic bathrooms are all-tile and in good condition. There are three buildings, one very new with upscale rooms: new furniture, carpeted floors. The older wing with the US$35 rooms is nearly as nice as the newer, though, so my advice is to save your money. It's tour group city but the place is big enough to handle 'em all, and the tourist services in the hotel can handle your every request. Other benefits: a very nice pool and staff, hot breakfasts, an ideal location, sauna, massage, tennis, billiards, and traditional music concerts. This is another place that charges exorbitant phone rates and cheats you on currency exchange, though.

INEXPENSIVE

Huy Hoang Mini Hotel. 73 Phan Boi Chau St. ☎ **0510/862-211.** Fax 0510/863-722. E-mail: kshuyhoang@dgn.vnn.vn. 19 units, 14 with A/C. US$10–US$25 double. No credit cards.

This is a very good bargain hotel, in a new yellow-and-white faux colonial close to the Central Market. Rooms are spotless, big, and bright, with tile floors and some older carved furniture. No phones or other amenities, and only the few US$25 rooms have bathtubs. Breakfast is served in a patio in the back with views of the river. The staff is exceedingly friendly.

Thanh Bin II Hotel. Nhi Trung St. ☎ **0510/863-715.** Fax 0510/864-192. 25 units. US$15–US$25 double. No credit cards.

The Thanh Bin II hotel is newer and nicer than its sister property, the Thanh Bin I over on Le Loi Street. The 3-story building has a very Chinese inspired lobby, with carved dark wood furnishings and cafe tables. Upstairs, the very clean and basic rooms are spacious, and just a bit loud (decor-wise, that is). The decor is a mish-mosh—somehow they've color coordinated it all. Still, I've stayed here twice and liked the place each time. There's not a musty smell to be found, bathrooms are tidy, and the staff are real friendly. If you really feel like getting wild ask for the $25 room, no. 302. This huge room sports wood paneling, carved Chinese-style furnishings (mosquito net over the bed), a nice balcony with beaded curtains, and in the center of the room—a large wooden carving of a fat, happy Buddha. I said, "Wooo! It's the Honeymoon Suite!" and all the girls in the lobby blushed and giggled.

✪ **Thien Trung Hotel.** 63 Phan Dinh Phung St. ☎ **0510/861-720** or 0510/861-769. Fax 0510/863-799. E-mail: thientrungha@dng.vnn.vn. 20 units, 15 with A/C. US$15–US$20 double. No credit cards.

This is one of the most attractive bargain places I've seen in Vietnam, which explains its popularity. The Thien Trung mini-hotel is 5 years old, and had a renovation 2 years ago. Rooms are grouped attractively around the garden, where breakfast is served. They have the de rigeur tile floors and plastic furniture, but are very bright, and the tile bathrooms are bigger and nicer than most, some with bathtubs. There is a small restaurant on the premises. Note that there are no telephones. The staff is eager and friendly.

DINING

Hoi An is a feast for the stomach as well as the eyes. Local specialties include *cao lau* (rice noodles with fresh greens, rice crackers, and croutons), white rose dumplings, shrimp in clear rice dough, and fried won ton. Seafood, particularly steamed fish, is excellent and available everywhere. Fruit shakes are another common item well worth savoring, as are the pervasive banana pancakes.

✪ **Café des Amis.** 52 Bach Dang. ☎ **0510/861-616.** Set menu 50,000 VND (US$3.45). No credit cards. Daily 6–10pm. NOUVEAU VIETNAMESE.

This unique place is going to gain a worldwide reputation soon. It serves some of the best food in Vietnam in a nothing-special setting. There is no menu, but you choose either the seafood or vegetarian course. A series of delicious dishes such as clear soup, fried won tons with shrimp, broiled fish, stuffed calamari, or scallops on the half shell is served up by very friendly chef Mr. Kim, who was once a taster in the Vietnamese army and who travels worldwide as a guest chef. Talk to him if you can; he's an interesting fellow. Asked why he doesn't choose to raise his prices to gourmet standards as well, he says, "I am a simple man. I like many friends." The specials change daily.

Nha Hang Du Port. 70 Bach Dang. No phone. Main courses 10,000–25,000 VND (US$0.69–US$1.72). No credit cards. Daily 7am–11pm. VIETNAMESE.

This place is always packed, usually by French tourists, who say they're there because they read about it in a guidebook. At the risk of jumping on the bandwagon, the food is very good. The specialty is seafood: sautéed and grilled eel, frogs, fish, and crabs. There's no ambience to speak of, however, and the riverfront setting makes you ripe prey for the seemingly countless children selling postcards and souvenirs.

Restaurant Thanh. 76 Bach Dang. ☎ **0510/861-366.** Main courses 20,000–30,000 VND (US$1.38–US$2.07). No credit cards. Daily 7am–11pm. VIETNAMESE.

There are many restaurants along the riverfront, but Thanh has a particularly poetic atmosphere, with dark wood furniture, candles, and hanging lanterns in an old Chinese house. Very romantic. A pet bird chirps along in the background. The food is simple, good, and very fresh. Their specialty is shrimp with papaya and peanuts, served with crisp rice crackers. Try also the steamed fish in banana leaf or the seafood hot pot. Strawberry or snake wine (wine with a bit of added snake blood) is available for accompaniment.

✪ **Tam-Tam Café.** 110 Nguyen Thai Hoc St. (on the second floor). ☎ **0510/862-212.** Main courses 66,000–131,000 VND (US$4.50–US$9). No credit cards. Daily 24 hrs. ITALIAN/ CONTINENTAL.

Tam-Tam is one of the coolest spots in the world, let alone Hoi An. Three French expats got together to create a bar/restaurant combo in a historic setting. The decor is very local and extremely well-done, with hanging bamboo lamps, a high wooden ceiling, and fantastic wooden figurines. The dinner menu, served in a separate restaurant room with checkered table cloths, is simple—featuring generous portions of homemade pastas, steaks, and salads—but the food is delicious. The dessert menu includes flambéed crepes, sorbet, and hot chocolate. There are two barrooms. The bigger one to the left has a pool table, book swap shelf, comfortable lounge chairs, and sofas, and is the place to hang out in Hoi An. The extensive, expensive-but-worth-it drinks menu includes creations like the Big Bamboo, a mix of rum, pineapple, orange, lemon, and ice.

Trung Bac. 87 Tran Phu. Main courses 5,000–40,000 VND (US$0.34–US$2.76). No credit cards. Daily 7am–11pm. VIETNAMESE.

Take a break while strolling along Tran Phu for this little open-air cafe. The historic building's atmosphere is nicer than those of most stalls; and the food, featuring local delights like spicy roast chicken, grilled crab, and seafood such as fried shrimp puffs on sugarcane kabobs, is also top-rate. The menu is short but has very helpful pictures. Their banana pancakes set the standard.

Wan Lu. 27 Tran Phu. ☎ **0510/861-212.** Main courses 5,000–30,000 VND (US$0.34–US$2.07). No credit cards. Daily 7am–11pm. VIETNAMESE.

The locals eat here. It's an open-air place and the atmosphere is a little rough, but portions are bigger and the food more authentic; the cau lao, for example, was properly served with a dish of hot chile sauce noticeably lacking in the tourist spots.

ATTRACTIONS

The whole town is an attraction, its narrow streets filling your eyes with the beauty of historical buildings mixed with the everyday lives of the Vietnamese who live and work here today. The oldest streets, Tran Phu and Nguyen Thai Hoc, supported Chinese immigrant merchants and their families who built traditional Chinese wooden houses, stone shophouses, and clan association houses. Many of these buildings have been restored with a tenderness that has salvaged the structure yet retained much of each building's true charm. While many today house cafes, art galleries, and silk and souvenir shops, building facades still retain their historical dignity. If you're an artist bring your sketchpad and watercolors; photographers bring plenty of film.

The Hoi An World Cultural Heritage Organization (www.hoianworldheritage.org) has the dilemma of financing the restorations and maintaining the old portions of the town. They sell a 50,000 VND (US$3.45) ticket that allows limited admission to the sights within the old town, each of which is listed below. I say limited because it's sort of a "One from column A, one from column B" sort of thing. One ticket gets you: one of the three museums, one of the three assembly halls, one of the four old houses, plus a choice of either the Japanese Bridge, the Quan Cong's Temple, or the local handicraft workshop, and finally a "wild card" that lets you see one additional place in any category that you didn't see. So, to see everything, you'll have to purchase three tickets. If you can, try to see everything. If not, I'll help you choose which things to see in the descriptions below.

Don't forget to admire the small details on the inside of each building, especially the old wooden houses that employ traditional Chinese construction methods. And don't be distracted by the tourist cafes and shops—stop and notice the trades that are worked behind some of the doors, and the locals living their everyday lives in this gorgeous setting.

THE MUSEUMS

Museum of History and Culture. 7 Nguyen Hue St. Daily 8am–7pm.

Over 2,000 years of Hoi An history are briefly covered in a circa 1653 building, with exhibits of Cham relics, trade items such as ancient ceramics, and photos of local architectural details. There are English explanations, but they are scanty. If you're seeing only one museum, make it the Museum of Trade Ceramics (below). One interesting tidbit: The name "Hoi An" literally means "water convergence" and "peace."

✪ Museum of Trade Ceramics. 80 Tran Phu St. Daily 8am–5pm.

Located in a traditional house, this museum describes the origins of Hoi An as a trade port and displays its most prominent trade item. Objects are from the 13th through 17th centuries, and include Chinese and Thai works as well. While many of the exhibits are in fragments, the real beauty of the place is that the very thorough descriptions are in English, giving you a real sense of the town's origins and history. Furthermore, the architecture and renovations of the old house are thoroughly explained, and you're free to wander through its two floors, courtyard, and anteroom. After all the scattered explanations at the other historic houses, you'll finally get a sense of what Hoi An architecture is all about.

The Sa Huynh Culture Museum. 149 Tran Phu St. Daily 8am–6pm.

After local farmers around Hoi An dug up some strange-looking pottery, archaeologists came and identified 53 sites where a pre-Cham people, called the Sa Huynh, buried their dead in ceramic jars. The two-room display here includes some of the burial jars, beaded ornaments, pottery vessels, and iron tools and weapons that have been uncovered. English descriptions are sketchy. Upstairs, the little-visited Museum of the Revolution includes such intriguing items as the umbrella "which Mr. Truong Munh Luong used for acting a fortune-teller to act revolution from 1965 to 1967." Huh? For connoisseurs only.

THE OLD HOUSES

The Old House of Phun Hung. 4 Nguyen Thi Minh Khai St. Daily 8am–5pm.

This private house, constructed in 1780, is two floors of combined architectural influences. The first floor's central roof is four-sided, showing Japanese influence, and the upstairs balcony has a Chinese rounded "turtle shell" roof with carved beam supports. The house has weathered many floods. In 1964, during a particularly bad bout, its third floor served as a refuge for other town families. The upstairs is outfitted with a trapdoor for moving furniture rapidly to safety. You may be shown around by Ms. Anh, who claims to be an eighth-generation member of the family. Tour guides at every house make such claims; however, like Quan Thang's house, the family really does seem to live here.

The Old House of Quan Thang. 77 Tran Phu St. Daily 8am–9pm.

This 300-year-old wooden house of a Fukkien-born Chinese shipmaster goes straight to the heart of Chinese culture. Inside the main room, every nook and cranny is set aside for some form of ancestral worship. Dusty photos of old family members are piled, generation upon generation, on one of the big altars. When I turned to see the other altar, in front of me was the photo of a young girl. Miss Diep Ai Hoa was the most recent member of this old bloodline to pass away, just 1 month before my visit. She was 23 years old, and her altar was lit with candles and incense, and decorated with flowers and offerings of food and favorite items. A chilly reminder that the town's tourist attractions are still vital in the lives of its residents today, as are ancient traditions.

✪ **The Tran Family Home and Chapel.** 21 Le Loi (on the corner of Le Loi and Phan Chu Trinh sts.). Daily 8am–5:30pm.

In 1802, a civil service mandarin named Tran Tu Nhuc built a family home and chapel to worship his ancestors. A favorite of Viet emperor Gia Long, he was sent to China as an ambassador, and his home reflects his high status. Elegantly designed with original Chinese antiques and royal gifts such as swords, two parts of the home are open to the public: a drawing room and an ancestral chapel. The house does a splendid job of conveying all that is exotic and interesting about these people and their period. It has even been featured as a stylish layout in a fashion magazine. The drawing room has three sections of sliding doors: the left for men, the right for women, and the center, opened only at Tet and other festivals, for dead ancestors to return home. The ancestral altar in the inner room has small boxes behind it containing relics and a biography of the deceased; their pictures hang, a little spookily, to the right of the altar. A 250-year-old book with the family history resides on a table to the right of the altar. In back of the house are a row of plants, each buried with the placenta and umbilical cord of a family child, so that the child will never forget its home. As if it could.

Old House of Tan Ky. 101 Nguyen Thai Hoc St. Daily 8am–7pm.

There have been either five or seven generations of Tans living here, depending on whom you speak with. Built over 200 years ago, the four small rooms are crammed with dark wood antiques. The room closest to the street is for greeting visiting merchants. Farther in is the living room, then the courtyard, and to the back, the bedroom. The first three are open to the public. A guide who will greet you at the door will hasten to explain how the house is a perfect melding of three architectural styles: ornate Chinese detailing on some curved roof beams, a Japanese peaked roof, and a simple Vietnamese cross-hatch roof support. The mosaic decorations on the wall and furniture are aged, intricate, and amazing. Take your time to look around.

THE ASSEMBLY HALLS

Cantonese Assembly Hall (Quang Trieu/Guangzhou Assembly Hall). 176 Tran Phu St. Daily 8am–6pm.

Built in 1885, this hall is quite ornate and colorful. All of the building materials were completed in China, brought here, then reassembled. The center garden sports a fountain with a dragon made of chipped pottery, the centerpiece. Inside, look for the statues depicting scenes from famous Cantonese operas, and in the rooms to each side, the ancestral tablets of generations past.

✪ **Fukian Assembly Hall (Phuc Kien).** 46 Tran Phu St. Daily 7am–6pm.

This is the grandest of the assembly halls, built in 1697 by Chinese merchants from Fukian Province. It is a showpiece of classical Chinese architecture, at least after you pass the first gate, which was added in 1975. It's loaded with animal themes: The fish in the mosaic fountain symbolizes scholarly achievement; the unicorn flanking the ascending stairs, wisdom; the dragon, power; the turtle, longevity; and the phoenix, nobility. The main temple is dedicated to Thien Hau, goddess of the sea, on the main altar. To the left of her is Thuan Phong Nhi, a goddess who can hear ships in a range of thousands of miles, and on the right, Thien Ly Nhan, who can see them. Go around the altar for a view of a fantastic detailed miniature boat. There are two altars to the rear of the temple, the one on the left honoring a god of prosperity and on the right, fertility. The goddess of fertility is often visited by local couples hoping for children. She is flanked by 12 fairies or midwives, one responsible for each of a baby's functions: smiling, sleeping, eating, and so forth.

OTHER SITES

✪ **Japanese Covered Bridge.** At the western end of Tran Phu St. Daily 8am–9pm.

The name of this bridge in Vietnamese, Lai Vien Kieu, means "Pagoda in Japan." No one is exactly sure who first built it in the early 1600s (it has since been renovated several times), but it is usually attributed to Hoi An's Japanese community. The dog flanking one end and the monkey at the other are considered to be sacred animals to the ancient Japanese, and my guide claimed the reasoning is that most Japanese emperors were born in either the year of the monkey or the dog by the Asian zodiac. Later I read something else that claimed maybe it meant construction began in the year of the dog and was completed in the year of the monkey. I'm sure there are many other interesting dog and monkey stories going around. Pick your favorite. The small temple inside is dedicated to Tran Vo Bac De, God of the North, beloved (or cursed) by sailors, as it is he who controls the weather.

Quan Kong Temple. 168 Tran Phu St. (on the corner of Nguyen Hue). Daily 8am–5:30pm.

This temple was built in the early 1600s to honor a famous Chin dynasty general. Highlights inside are two gargantuan 10-foot-high wooden statues flanking the main altar, one of Quan Kong's protector and one of his adopted son. They are fearsome and impressive. Reportedly the temple was a stop for merchants who came in from the nearby river to pay their respects and pray for the general's attributes of loyalty, bravery, and virtue.

Attractions Not on the World Cultural Heritage Ticket

Chinese Assembly Hall. 64 Tran Phu St. Daily 8am–5pm.

This hall was built in 1740 as a meeting place for all of the resident Chinese, regardless of their native province.

Hainan Assembly Hall. 178 Nguyen Duy Hieu St. Free admission. Daily 8am–5pm.

The Chinese merchants from Hainan Island, in the South China Sea east of Danang, built this hall. Although it is newer than most and mostly made of concrete, it is nice nevertheless.

✪ **House of Hoi An Traditional Handicraft.** 41 Le Loi St. Daily 8am–5pm.

This is basically a silk shop with an interesting gimmick you should take a look at: On the first floor you can see both a 17th-century silk loom and a working, machine-powered cotton one. On the second, you can see where silk comes from: There are trays of silkworms feeding, then a rack of worms incubating, and then a tub of hot water where the pupae's downy covering is rinsed off and then pulled, strand by strand, onto a large skein. Cool. They have the best selection of silks, both fine and raw, in many colors and weights good for clothing and for home interiors.

Central Market. At Nguyen Hue and Tran Phu sts.; bordered by the Thu Bon River to the south.

If you see one Vietnamese market, make it this one, by the river on the southeast side of the city. There are endless stalls of exotic foodstuffs and services, and a special big shed for silk tailoring at the east end (these tailors charge much less than the ones along Le Loi). Check out the ladies selling spices—curries, chile powders, cinnamon, peppercorns, especially saffron—at prices that are a steal in the West. But don't buy from the first woman you see; the stuff gets cheaper and cheaper the deeper you go into the market. Walk out to the docks to see activity there, too.

HITTING THE BEACHES

Cua Dai beach is an easy 20-minute bicycle ride from Hoi An through vistas of lagoons, rice paddies, and stilt houses. Simply follow Tran Hung Dao Street out of town for about 2 miles. It will turn into Cau Dai Street halfway to the beach. The small beach seems crowded with its orderly lines of deck chairs and endless child hawkers, but the surf and sand are good and the setting, gazing at the nearby **Cham Islands,** is spectacular. The tour companies offer boat excursions in season (Mar–Sept) to the Cham Islands, a group of seven islands about 8 miles east of Hoi An. There are also boat trips on the Thu Bon River.

SHOPPING

Once you're in Hoi An, travelers stop asking, "How many days are you staying here?" and instead ask, "How much money have you spent already?" I swear, it's a shopaholics fix. Even the most thrifty traveler manages to eke a little more out of the budget to shop.

Hoi An is a silk extravaganza. The quality and selection are the best in the country, and you'll have more peace and quiet while fitting than in Hanoi. **Silk suits** are made to order within 24 hours for about US$35; **cashmere wool** is US$45. There are countless shops, and the tailoring is all about the same quality, and fast. Overnight service is commonplace; Suits can be made in a matter of hours. A good way to choose a shop is by what you see out front—if you see a style you like it'll help with ordering. Make sure you take the time to specify your style, and be warned, if you don't clearly explain, you can get dresses and skirts back with a machine hem which is very cheap looking. Really, for tailoring I'll buy casual clothing here, but opt to buy silk in bulk to take to dressmakers back home. For the best silk selection go to no. 41 Le Loi, upstairs. Great colors and styles.

Tran Phu Street is lined with **art galleries,** and the **pottery** and **carved wood** items near the market and on Tran Phu are unique and of good quality. Along the river, lots of places sell blue and white **ceramics.** Oh, and if you're considering buying one of those lovely **Chinese lanterns,** you'll be happy to know they collapse to fit neatly in a tube for easy packing.

8 An Introduction to South Central Vietnam

South central Vietnam comprises the highlands, a land of rugged mountainous terrain mainly inhabited by members of Vietnam's ethnic minorities, and a stunning coastline bordered by small islands. Outside of two established resort destinations, **Nha Trang** and **Dalat,** the rest of the region is relatively unexplored by tourists. The area saw its share of fighting during the American war, though. Names like Buon Me Thot and Pleiku will undoubtedly ring a bell. Dalat, the top destination in the region, is popular with both Vietnamese and foreigners. It's a former French colonial outpost nestled among the hills, and still retains a serene, formal air due to the overwhelming presence of historic buildings. Nha Trang, not far from Dalat but on the coast, is also one of Vietnam's most popular destinations. The atmosphere couldn't be more different than Dalat's, however. Nha Trang is an easygoing seaside town that offers little but merrymaking, which is just as welcome in its own way.

GETTING THERE

BY PLANE   Both Nha Trang and Dalat are easily accessible by plane from both Hanoi and Saigon, plus there's a non-stop flight between the two.

BY TRAIN   Nha Trang is a stop on the north-south railway line.

BY BUS/MINIVAN   Travel between the two major cities is a 6-hour ride by bus or minivan, easily organized through a local travel agency. Both towns are included on the open ticket tours, except some open tickets will connect Ho Chi Minh City direct to Nha Trang, skipping Dalat. For details, see "Getting There" in individual town listings.

9 Nha Trang

Nha Trang at the moment is a mid-sized town of about 200,000 people, and is Vietnam's number-one resort area. While not a particularly charming town, its surf isn't bad and the beach has a breathtaking setting, with views of the more than 20 surrounding islands. There is no shortage of good places to stay and excellent fresh seafood to eat.

Unfortunately, far from becoming a gracious hideaway, Nha Trang looks like it's on the way to becoming raucous, and it might as well just go ahead. If you accept it as such, it's a fine place at which to spend 2 or 3 days frolicking in the surf, taking a snorkeling or diving cruise to the nearby islands, or enjoying the services of one of the many massage, manicure, and depilatory practitioners roaming the beach (and even the cafes). The main drag is **Tran Phu Street,** right off the ocean. It's a wide boulevard lined with palm trees off which lie most hotels and restaurants.

Culturally, there are a few things to keep you occupied: the **Pasteur Institute** is here, offering glimpses into the life and work of one of Vietnam's most famous expats; there are the interesting **Long Son Pagoda** and the well-preserved **Po Nagar Cham Temple.**

Off-season (from October through March), the surf is far too rough for swimming and sports, and you may want to rethink stopping at Nha Trang at all.

GETTING THERE

BY PLANE   Nha Trang is 1,350 kilometers (839 miles) from Hanoi and 450 kilometers (280 miles) from Saigon. Vietnam Airlines operates non-stop flights from Saigon, Hanoi, and Dalat.

BY CAR/BUS   If you choose to drive from Hoi An to Nha Trang, it's a 10-hour trip and will cost you about US$120 by car. An arduous 12-hour bus or minibus ride will cost only US$8. Nha Trang is also a stop on the Kim or Sinh Café's Open Tour, a one-way bus ticket from Hanoi to Saigon, or back the other way. They also offer overnight bus trips to Ho Chi Minh City and Hoi An, a good option if you're short on time and don't want to waste your precious daylight hours looking out the window of a tour coach.

GETTING AROUND

The main street in Nha Trang, Tran Phu, runs for about 4 kilometers (2 miles), and attractions like the Po Ngar Cham towers are yet another mile out. Biet Thu Street runs perpendicular to Tran Phu: Here's where you'll find other smaller restaurants and tour operators. Taxis are scarce, and tend to congregate around the major hotels. Renting a bike from your hotel for US$1 to US$2 a day is a very good option, as are cyclos. A cross-town trip will cost about 10,000 VND (US$0.69). In addition, motorcycle taxis can be had for 20,000 VND (US$1.38) per hour.

VISITOR INFORMATION & TOURS

You'll more than likely end up booking tickets and boat tours through your hotel in Nha Trang, or from one of the many ticketing agencies around the town and along the beach. They all sell tickets to the same boats, basically, and the prices are all the same. For bus tickets and a tour on to Dalat, contact **Sinh Café III,** 10 Biet Thu St. (☎ **058/811-981**).

Fast Facts: Nha Trang

Currency Exchange/Banks   Vietcombank's local branch is located at 17 Quang Trung St. (☎ **058/821-483**). Hours are 7:30 to 11am and 1:30 to 4pm. It offers the usual currency and traveler's check exchange and credit card cash withdrawal services. Along Biet Thu, some of the tour operators will cash traveler's checks and change money—rates are the same as at the bank (except for a small service fee) and they're open longer hours.

Internet/E-mail   Biet Thu has a cluster of Internet cafes for between 200 and 300 VND (a couple cents) per minute usage.

Post Office/Mail   The main branch is at 4 Le Loi St. (☎ **058/823-866**). Hours are 6:30am to 10pm Monday to Saturday. DHL express mail services and Internet access are available. There is another branch at 50 Le Thanh Ton.

Telephone   The city code for Nha Trang is 58.

ACCOMMODATIONS

There are many options in Nha Trang, but the scene is dominated by faceless mid-end and substandard budget choices.

EXPENSIVE

✪ **Ana Mandara Resort.** Beachside, Tran Phu Blvd. ☎ **058/829-829.** Fax 058/829-629. http://soneva-pavilion.com/ana-mandara. E-mail: resvana@dng.vnn.vn. 68 units. A/C MINIBAR TV TEL. US$152–US$196 double/villa; US$287 suite villa. AE, DC, JCB, MC, V.

It's the little things that make this resort special: the native art and handiwork in the halls and rooms, the bowl with floating flowers in the bathroom, the basin of rainwater on your private veranda for rinsing sandy feet, the burning incense in the open-air lobby. This attention to detail, as well as the secluded layout of the "Vietnamese village" units, gives the whole resort a personable, small-scale feel. Each room has a rattan rising ceiling with wood beams. Rooms are good-sized, with stylish furniture and tile floors, and the bathroom has a huge window facing a private outdoor enclosure. Very special. Thirty-six units face the beach, and others face exotic-plant landscaping (the plants are labeled, of course). The restaurant Fantastic Ana Pavilion, open 24 hours, offers a diverse international menu (see "Dining"). There's also a cocktail lounge and a pool bar. The staff is super friendly, and they mean it. The prices are reasonable as well. It's a dreamscape you will hate to leave.

MODERATE

Bao Dai Hotel (Bao Dai's Villas). Cau Da, Vinh Nguyen/Nha Trang. ☎ **058/590-147** or 058/590-148. Fax 058/590-146. E-mail: baodai@dng.vnn.vn. 40 units. A/C MINIBAR TV TEL. US$25–US$80 double. MC, V.

Next to the Ana Mandara, the Villas are the most atmospheric place to stay in Nha Trang. Built in 1923 as a seaside resort for then-emperor Bao Dai, the hotel is a cluster of plain colonial-style buildings set high on an oceanside hill. The hotel is so far out of town it's almost in another, but the peaceful atmosphere is a plus. The least expensive US$25 rooms, in two characterless new buildings, are small but nevertheless bright, spotless, and comfortable, with in-perfect-shape tile floors and bathrooms

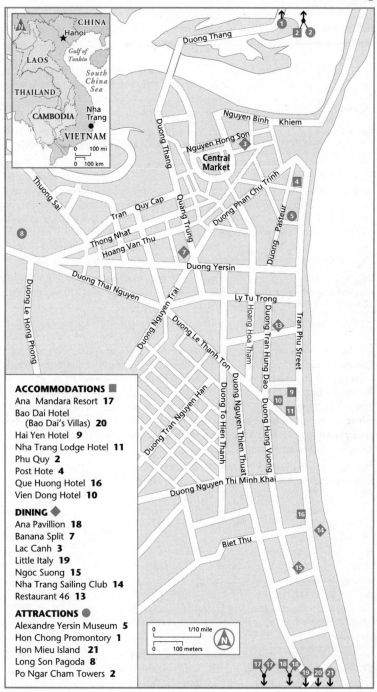

Nha Trang

CHINA
Hanoi
Gulf of Tonkin
LAOS
South China Sea
THAILAND
CAMBODIA
Nha Trang
VIETNAM

0   100 mi
0   100 km

Duong Thang
Duong Thang
Nguyen Binh   Khiem
Nguyen Hong Son
Central Market
Thuong Sai
Tran   Quy Cap
Quang Trung
Duong Phan Chu Trinh
Pasteur
Duong
Thong Nhat
Hoang Van Thu
Duong Yersin
Duong Thai Nguyen
Ly Tu Trong
Duong Le Hong Phong
Duong Nguyen Trai
Duong Le Thanh Ton
Hoang Hoa Tham
Duong Tran Hung Dao
Tran Phu Street
Duong Tran Nguyen Han
Duong To Hien Thanh
Duong Nguyen Thien Thuat
Duong Hung Vuong
Duong Nguyen Thi Minh Khai
Biet Thu

ACCOMMODATIONS ■
Ana Mandara Resort **17**
Bao Dai Hotel
   (Bao Dai's Villas) **20**
Hai Yen Hotel **9**
Nha Trang Lodge Hotel **11**
Phu Quy **2**
Post Hote **4**
Que Huong Hotel **16**
Vien Dong Hotel **10**

DINING ◆
Ana Pavillion **18**
Banana Split **7**
Lac Canh **3**
Little Italy **19**
Ngoc Suong **15**
Nha Trang Sailing Club **14**
Restaurant 46 **13**

ATTRACTIONS ●
Alexandre Yersin Museum **5**
Hon Chong Promontory **1**
Hon Mieu Island **21**
Long Son Pagoda **8**
Po Ngar Cham Towers **2**

0   1/10 mile
0   100 meters

and wood furniture. If you go for the more expensive sea-view rooms, be prepared for heavy, dark carved wood and stained carpets, though their cavernous size and shuttered windows opening onto spectacular vistas make up for a lot. The bathrooms are nothing special, but are sizable and clean, with bathtubs. The hotel also organizes scuba diving and snorkeling and boat excursions to nearby Hon Mieu Island, and there is a private cove for sunbathing. The usual transport rentals are available, including an all-day car for US$35. The staff is extremely affable. Other amenities and services include laundry, room service, and a tennis court.

Hai Yen Hotel. 40 Tran Phu St. ☎ **058/822-828** or 058/822-974. Fax 058/821-902. 110 units. A/C MINIBAR TV TEL. US$10.34–US$34.48 double; US$44.83 suite. AE, JCB, MC, V.

The Hai Yen is owned by the Thanh Hoa tourism company, the same folks who own Vien Dong, and the two are virtually indistinguishable. It's next door, and they share recreational facilities. The Hai Yen is a bit quieter, and it has outdoor hallways and an open, airier feeling. The unfortunate blue indoor-outdoor carpeting is present, however, as are the super-basic but very clean and new bathrooms. And whoops, there's that hideous plastic furniture in the deluxe rooms on up. Plastic flowers, too. The suites have even more of same, but at least there are bathtubs. The service is rather impersonal. Try to get rooms not facing noisy Tran Phu Street. There is a big indoor restaurant.

Nha Trang Lodge Hotel. 42 Tran Phu St. ☎ **058/810-500** or 058/810-900. Fax 058/ 828-800. www.nt-lodge.com. E-mail: nt-lodge@dng.vnn.vn. 124 units. A/C MINIBAR TV TEL. US$50–US$95 double; US$145 suite. AE, JCB, MC, V.

The 3-year-old lodge calls itself a "business hotel," and indeed it is a well-run and accommodating high-rise. Average-size rooms are chain-hotel style, with floral bedspreads and modern furniture, yet they are pleasing. For one, the carpet is nice and the furniture matches. The bathrooms are a nice size, with marble finishes. Everything is solid and comfortable, particularly the beds. There are in-room safes and big TVs, too. Spring for the US$95 ocean view if possible, with balcony, on an upper floor away from street noise. The big 24-hour Asian/Continental restaurant is clean and bright. There are also an efficient business center, conference rooms, disco/karaoke, barber, lounge with billiards, swimming pool, massage, tennis, room service, and travel services. The staff is well trained.

Que Huong Hotel. 60 Tran Phu Blvd. ☎ **058/825-047** or 058/827-365. Fax 058/825-344. E-mail: quehuong60@dng.vnn.vn. 45 units. A/C MINIBAR TV TEL. US$60 double; US$100 suite. MC, V.

This 1-year-old hotel is bright and bland. It is four floors of a squarish building across the street from the beach, but set back far enough from the road to be quiet. Ten minutes after leaving a room, you would be hard pressed to describe it, but the overall impression is favorable. Carpets, tasteful wood furnishings, and balconies come to mind. Beds are firm and comfortable. The bathrooms are weak—badly tiled and already showing signs of wear, though there are hair dryers. Suites have two bathrooms and are great for families. There are capable travel agents in the lobby. An Asian/ Continental restaurant feeds the hungry hordes, and to keep them amused, there are a swimming pool, tennis court, billiards, massage, sauna, and bar disco. Que Huong also offers laundry services and a barber.

Vien Dong Hotel. 1 Tran Hung Dao St. ☎ **058/821-606** or 058/821-608. Fax 058/ 821-912. 102 units. A/C MINIBAR TV TEL. US$30–US$40 double; US$70 suite. AE, JCB, MC, V.

If you're on a tour, you're probably booked here. It's big and blah and impersonal, but it's a comfortable three-star with all the amenities, and having lots of people around somehow helps. Rooms have basic blue carpet and basic yellow bedspreads and simple wood furniture, and aren't especially large. Mattresses are sturdy foam. Bathrooms are clean and tidy tile, without counters and most with simple showerhead-on-wall fixtures, although they have hair dryers. "College dorm room" comes to mind. Suites have almost unbearably ugly plastic furniture and flowers, although they also have bathtubs. There are an inviting outdoor restaurant featuring nightly music, a swimming pool, a sauna, billiards, tennis, and badminton on the premises. The lobby has a good travel services center.

INEXPENSIVE

OK Post Hotel. 2 Le Loi St. ☎ 058/821-252 or 058/821-250. Fax 058/824-205. E-mail: posthotel@dng.vnn.vn. 20 units. A/C MINIBAR TV TEL. US$17 double. MC, V.

This is a decent, unassuming budget hotel. The large rooms have old tile floors and carved wood furniture, very basic but clean. The bathrooms are large and in good condition, but only the ground floor rooms have bathtubs. The location of its attractive white colonial-style exterior is excellent; facing the ocean on a quiet stretch of Tran Phu street, it's still close to the center of town. Try for a room facing the beach. Other than Internet access, there are no services and the staff speaks little English.

Phu Quy. 54 Hung Vuong St. ☎ **058/810-609.** 12 units, 8 with A/C. US$8–US$15 double. No credit cards.

If you're looking for your basic lowest-end accommodations, you can't go wrong here. One of many narrow mini-hotels that somehow seem to stand in groups of three in Nha Trang, the Phu Quy sports small, bright, and very clean rooms with brand-new plastic furniture. The beds are comfortable and bathrooms small, with shower-in-room facilities. There are no views to speak of, but go for the top floors to escape street noise. Of course, that means climbing lots of stairs. No amenities whatsoever, but breakfasts are good and cheap at 6,000 VND (US$0.41) or so, and of course the hotel will book tickets. It is family-run, and owner Mr. Phu is as nice as they come.

DINING
EXPENSIVE

✪ **Ana Pavillion.** Tran Phu Blvd. (at the Ana Mandara Resort). ☎ **058/829-829.** Main courses 161,000–256,000 VND (US$11–US$17.50); prix fixe menus 204,000–248,000 VND (US$14–US$17). AE, JCB, MC, V. Daily 7–10pm. ASIAN/CONTINENTAL.

The Ana Pavillion serves exquisite food in an elegant ocean-front veranda, with both indoor and outdoor seating. The food is creatively prepared and beautifully presented, and portions are healthy. Try the creamed pumpkin or taro soup with shrimp, the shredded beef and avocado salad, and the Thai-style blue crabs stir-fried in curry. For dessert, there is black sticky-rice with coconut and banana fritters, and chocolate mousse served in a fresh coconut, with coconut shavings on top. Incredible. The Pavillion also offers set dinner menus for US$14 to US$17; a fabulous value.

Little Italy. Tran Phu St., Huong Duong Center (just south of the Ana Mandara resort). ☎ **058/828-964.** Main courses 40,000–60,000 VND (US$2.76–US$4.14). No credit cards. Daily 9am–10pm. CLASSIC ITALIAN.

Who knows why good Italian food is so easy to get in Vietnam? Here is yet another example. Little Italy serves up tasty pastas and salads, and the bruschetta, with good olive oil, fresh tomatoes, capers, and garlic, is to die for. The house wine, available by the glass, isn't bad, but the pizza is only so-so. Service is friendly and attentive. The casual, open-air seaside setting can also provide a good lunch experience, as guests can swim and use the restaurant's deck chairs.

MODERATE

Ngoc Suong. 16 Tran Quang Khai St. ☎ **058/827-030.** Main courses 20,000–240,000 VND (US$1.38–US$16.55). No credit cards. Daily 10am–midnight. SEAFOOD.

Nha Trang has dozens of good seafood restaurants, but this one leads the pack. In the very pleasant thatched outdoor pavilion or the vaguely nautical, softly lit interior, fresh, simply prepared seafood is served by a competent wait staff. If you like oysters, get them grilled, small but succulent. The lyrical menu includes "crabs claws enrobed in shrimp paste," "boiled pork soak in macerated mackerel" and "crab steamed in coconut milk." There are plenty of locals here adding to the congenial atmosphere.

INEXPENSIVE

Banana Split. 58 Quang Trung St. ☎ **058/829-115.** Main courses 12,000–30,000 VND (US$0.83–US$2.07) No credit cards. Daily 7am–11pm. VIETNAMESE/WESTERN.

Banana Split is the number-one roadside stall at which to meet other wanderers and have a snack, and maybe even a pedicure from the oft-visiting practitioner. It offers good pasta, spring rolls, and noodle soups, and their list of fruit shakes could well be the longest in Vietnam. The folks running the place are very friendly. Other travelers rave about the ice cream, but I still don't think it's Vietnam's strong suit. The Banana Split next door claims to be the "original," as does this one, which results in some snarling exchanges between the ladies trying to entice customers to one or the other. You probably won't notice much of a difference either way.

Lac Canh. 11 Hang Ca St. ☎ **058/821-391.** Main courses 18,000–115,000 VND (US$1.24–US$7.93). No credit cards. Daily 7am–11pm. CHINESE/VIETNAMESE.

There's nothing special about the Chinese-influenced Vietnamese cuisine served here, except for the specialty of the house: marinated prawns, fish, and fresh vegetables that you grill yourself on a rustic cast-iron flaming brazier. The place is packed with locals and tourists. Try to sit outdoors, as the atmosphere is smoky and hygiene isn't the management's top concern. Definitely the local "greasy spoon."

Nha Trang Sailing Club. 72–74 Tran Phu St. ☎ **058/826-528.** Main courses 65,000–100,000 VND (US$4.48–US$6.90). No credit cards. Daily 7am–11pm. Bar open until 2am. VIETNAMESE/CONTINENTAL.

Stop by this oceanside open-air bar/restaurant for a real Western breakfast, if nothing else. A good bet is their pancakes, uniquely not greasy and served with real butter. There are other Western standbys such as macaroni and cheese and hamburgers, tasty if not authentic, as well as the usual Nha Trang seafood selections. The setting, in a large hut, can't be beat. You can lounge on the beach and buy or swap a book from their well-stocked rack (have a chat with the rack's proprietor, who speaks excellent English and is an interesting fellow). The bar swings at night.

Restaurant 46. 6 Nguyen Chanh St. ☎ **058/816-300.** 20,000–190,000 VND (US$1.38–US$13.10). No credit cards. Daily 6am–11pm. SEAFOOD.

They've moved location from no. 46 Tran Phu, but kept the name, Restaurant 46. Still, it's very similar to many of the other name/number places in town, but this one's outstanding, as any local will tell you. Restaurant 46 serves grilled and sautéed seafood in a very unpretentious outdoor atmosphere, with plastic chairs and tablecloths under a makeshift awning. This is great place to kick back, order a cold Coke or beer, and tackle mounds of oysters, sautéed escargot, fried abalone with mushroom, or roe crabs in tamarind sauce. There is a very long, easy-to-understand English menu.

ATTRACTIONS

Po Ngar Cham Towers. 1¼ miles out of the city center at 2 Thang 4, at the end of Xom Bong Bridge. Admission 10,000 VND (US$0.69). Daily 7:30am–5pm.

This standing temple complex was built from the 8th to 13th centuries to honor goddess Yang Ino Po Ngar, mother of the kingdom. It was built over a wooden temple burned by the Javanese in 774. There were originally 10 structures; four remain. The main tower, or Po Ngar kalan, is one of the tallest Cham structures ever built. Its square tower and three-story cone roof are exemplary of Cham style. It has more remaining structural integrity than many sites, giving you a good idea of how it might have looked in all its glory. In the vestibule can be seen two pillars of carved epitaphs of Cham kings, and in the sanctuary there are two original carved doors. The statue inside is of the goddess Bharagati, a.k.a. Po Ngar, on her lotus throne. It was carved in 1050. The Po Ngar temples are still in use by local Buddhists, and the altars and smoking incense add to the intrigue of the architecture. Detracting from the whole experience are kitsch stands and endless hawkers.

Some advice: Take a taxi and perhaps see the Towers and Promontory (see below) on the same trip. A bike, cyclo, or motorbike ride along the truck-heavy road out of town is one of the most unpleasant and dangerous in all of Vietnam. If you do chance it, remember that the inner side of the street seems to be reserved for motorists going directly against the flow of traffic.

For details on Cham history, see "Who Are the Cham?," in the "Danang & China Beach" section.

Long Son Pagoda. Thai Nguyen St. Daily 8am–5pm.

The main attraction at this circa-1930s pagoda is the huge white Buddha on the hillside behind, the symbol of Nha Trang. Around the base of the Buddha are portraits of

---

Alexandre Yersin, Superman Scientist

Alexander Yersin was a French scientist and explorer born in Switzerland in 1863, a man of monumental exploits and achievements. He sailed to Indochina as an onboard doctor and ended up settling in Vietnam, where he became the country's leading expert on tropical diseases. From 1892 to 1894, he undertook surveying tasks for the French, covering land from Nha Trang to Phnom Penh. Exploring the Central Highlands in 1893 to find the best routes for roadways, Yersin came upon the Lang Bian plateau. On the journey, he survived attacks by bandits and wild elephants with no damage greater than a spear wound and a broken fibula. Upon his return, Yersin urged the French to establish a convalescence center on the cool, green hills near Lang Bian for Frenchmen adversely affected by Vietnam's moist tropical climate. Hence Dalat was founded in 1897.

From 1898 to 1902, Yersin lived in Nha Trang, founding the Pasteur Institute there. He was also inspector general at the Dalat, Saigon, and Hanoi Pasteur institutes. His most famous accomplishment, however, was isolating the bacteria that causes the plague.

Although Vietnam's major roadways do not follow the path laid out by Yersin, you will note that many streets nevertheless bear his name. He died in 1943 and is buried in Nha Trang. A museum has been established there at the site of his former offices.

monks who immolated themselves to protest against the corrupt Diem regime. After climbing the numerous flights of stairs, you'll also be rewarded with a bird's-eye view of Nha Trang.

Alexandre Yersin Museum. In the Pasteur Institute, 10 Tran Phu St. ☎ **058/822-355.** Admission 26,000 VND (US$1.79). Mon–Sat 8–11am and 2–4:30pm.

Here you can get an inkling of the work of one of Vietnam's greatest heroes, expat or not. Swiss doctor Yersin founded Dalat, isolated a plague-causing bacteria, and researched agricultural methods and meteorological forecasting, all to the great benefit of the Vietnamese. He founded the institute in 1895. On display are his desk, overflowing library, and scientific instruments.

Hon Mieu Island. The Bao Dai Hotel (☎ **058/881-049**) operates a boat trip to the island, as do the local tour operators.

The largest of the surrounding islands, Hon Mieu has a fishing village, Bai Soi, that isn't very active any longer but features many seafood restaurants. There is also an aquarium of sorts, consisting of a lake divided into three sections: one for ornamental fish, one for edible fish, and one for carnivorous varieties; there's a wharf to stand on.

SPORTS & OUTDOOR ACTIVITIES

Diving is big in Nha Trang, in season (March to September). The most professionally run operation, in terms of excellent service and safety precautions, is **Rainbow Divers.** You can find a few outlets for booking along the beach: at the **Nha Trang Sailing Club,** at the **Rainbow Bar,** and at the **Ana Mandara Resort,** or call ☎ **058/829-946.** For more information on their services and on diving in the area, check out their Web site at www.divevietnam.com. The **Nha Trang Sailing Club** (☎ **058/826-528**) also rents catamarans, jet skis, and paddleboats, and offers waterskiing and para-sailing in season.

You can also take a **boat cruise** to some of the 20 surrounding islands. The most notorious boat trip, the **"Mama Hanh-Green Hat-Don't Be Lazy-Boat Trip"** takes you out to about three different islands from 9am to 5pm. Pay US$7, which includes snorkel gear, lunch and snacks (surprisingly excellent food), and all the free local wine you can drink. Beer and sodas cost extra. I say notorious because Mama Hanh used to run a wild operation—sort of like *Animal House* on a boat, with all sorts of college fraternity-style partying. Mama Hanh has stopped accompanying the trips since September 2000. The rumor around town goes that she got busted for all the marijuana on the boat, but the truth is she just hung up her green hat and retired. She did this trip every day for 12 years. The gal must be exhausted. Now they say the trip is just not the same. She certainly was a character.

Others might enjoy the more low-key approach of competitor Mama Lanh, which is far more quiet. You can book Mama Hanh at the Nha Trang Sailing Club, Banana Split Café, or at 66 Tran Phu, ☎ **058/826-175,** and Mama Lanh's at the left-side Banana Split Café or any of the local tour operators.

NHA TRANG AFTER DARK

Nha Trang has a few lively beachfront bars where tourists congregate to swap stories. The **Nha Trang Sailing Club** at 72–74 Tran Phu St. and the **Log Bar** across from the Hai Yen Hotel have open-air bamboo hut scenes until about 1am. The rowdy bar scene is at the **Rainbow Bar** behind the Ferris wheel. Every full moon they have a bonfire party on the beach.

10 Dalat

Dalat has a unique flavor among Vietnamese towns. Founded in 1897 as a resort for French commanders weary of the Vietnamese tropics, it still has hundreds of huge colonial mansions. Some are being restored by Vietnamese nouveau riche; others are empty and decaying. Dalat's history, combined with the welcome temperate mountain climate and pastoral hillside setting, give it the feel of a European alpine resort. Which, in fact, it once was. In and around town there are also numerous pagodas to see, in serene natural settings that lend an atmosphere far different from, for example, your typical bustling Saigon temple. Dalat is also a good place in which to glimpse the influences of the Catholic Vietnamese, represented by several churches and cathedrals. Father out of town are postcard-perfect farmlands, valleys, and waterfalls. A few ethnic minorities, including the Lat and Koho, live in and around these hills, and you can visit their small villages.

Dalat is the number-one resort destination for Vietnamese couples getting married or honeymooning. If the lunar astrological signs are particularly good, it's not unusual to see 10 or so wedding parties in a single day. Many of the local scenic spots, like the Valley of Love and Lake of Sighs, pander to the giddy couples. The waterfalls are swarming with vendors, costumed "bears," and "cowboys" complete with sad-looking horses and fake pistols. A carnival air prevails. Yes, it's tacky, but isn't it interesting to see how other cultures do tacky? Plus you'll get a chance to travel, lodge, and dine with Vietnamese on a holiday, a rare opportunity.

GETTING THERE

BY PLANE   The only direct flights to Dalat are from Ho Chi Minh City (Flight time: 50 min). In Dalat, call to confirm your ticket, or direct inquiries to Vietnam Airlines at ☎ **063/822-895.** Departing, you'll pay an airport tax of 10,000 VND (US$0.69). A taxi from the airport to the city is US$3.

BY BUS/CAR   Dalat is the first stop on the "Open Tour" bus from Ho Chi Minh City, followed by Nha Trang, or vice versa. See "Getting Around," in section 2, for more information on "Open Tour" bus travel through Vietnam. If you just take a bus from Ho Chi Minh City one-way, the trip will cost US$7 (US$9 during peak season Dec–Feb). Trip time is 7 to 8 hours.

To cut travel time to about 5 to 6 hours, you can hire a private car for the trip. In Ho Chi Minh City call **Dalattourist** for booking (80 Truong Dinh St., District 1; ☎ **08/823-7176**), and the charge is US$80. If you're coming from Nha Trang, trip time is about the same, but the cost is US$70 per car. Make your booking from the Dalattourist head office in Dalat direct by calling ☎ **063/822-520.**

VISITOR INFORMATION & TOURS

The main game in town is **Dalattourist** at 02 Nguyen Thai Hoc St., on the lake at the Thanh Thuy restaurant (☎ **063/822-520;** fax 063/834-144; www.dalattourist. com; e-mail: dalatou@hcm.vnn.vn). The other popular agents have offices at Kim Café 2 c/o Dalattoserco, 9 Le Dai Hanh (☎ **063/822-479** or 063/822-366; fax 063/ 822-479); and at the Sinh Café 2, located at the Pacific Hotel, 9 Bui Thi Xuan St. (☎ **063/824-725**).

GETTING AROUND

There are no cyclos in Dalat, but walking is very pleasant in the cool air. If you have time to spend a day or afternoon walking around the town, you'll get to see all the little trippy details you miss from a van window, like the swan paddleboats on the lake, or the odd Mickey Mouse statues around the fountain at the end of the main market street. An option is to rent a car with driver (about US$25 a day with Dalattourist), rent your own motorbike for US$6, or hop on the back of somebody else's. Because the sites are often outside city limits, it makes sense to take a half- or full-day tour with Dalattourist.

Fast Facts: Dalat

Banks/Currency Exchange   Industrial & Commercial Bank, 46 Hoa Binh St. (☎ 063/822-364).

Internet/E-mail   The most accessible Internet cafe in town is on the hill that overlooks the main market street—**Viet Hung Internet Café,** 7 Nguyen Chi Thanh; ☎ **063/825-737;** e-mail: vanquan@hcm.vnn.vn. They charge VND 300 (about US$0.02) per minute.

Post Office/Mail   The main office is located at 14 Tran Phu St., across from the Novotel, and is open Monday to Saturday from 6:30am to 9:30pm.

Telephone   The area code for Dalat is 63.

ACCOMMODATIONS

With its status as a popular resort area for both foreigners and Vietnamese, Dalat offers some nice lodging choices. There are plenty of mini-hotels, but they're not of the quality you might find in Hanoi, for example. You'll note that no Dalat hotel has A/C; with the year-round temperate weather, none is needed.

VERY EXPENSIVE

✪ **Sofitel Dalat Palace.** 12 Tran Phu St. ☎ **800/221-4542** or 063/825-444. Fax 063/825-666. E-mail: sofitel@netnam2.org.vn. 43 units. MINIBAR TV TEL. US$169–US$214 double; US$319–US$414 suite. Ask about discounts and specials. AE, DC, JCB, MC, V. South side of the lake.

A palace indeed. Built in 1922 and recently renovated, this is a gorgeous historic hotel, one of only three five-star choices in Vietnam. From the huge fireplace and mosaic floor in the lobby to the hanging tapestries, 3,000-plus oil paintings, and thick swag curtains, it's a French country chateau with Southeast Asian colonial flavor. The large rooms, with glossy original wood floors, are finished with fine fabrics and throw rugs. The bathrooms feature hand-painted tiles and antique-style raised bathtubs and fixtures. Genuine antique French clocks and working reproduction telephones complete the picture, yet nothing feels overdone. Every room has a foyer and fireplace. Lakeview rooms open to a huge shared veranda with deck chairs. The high, high ceilings and huge corridors with hanging lamps contribute to the palatial feeling. Service is superb. All in all, an exquisite place that should not be missed. Le Rabelais Restaurant serves mediocre French food in an exquisite setting, but Café de La Poste is good for lunch and snacks.

EXPENSIVE

Novotel Dalat Hotel. 7 Tran Phu St. ☎ **800/221-4542** or 063/825-777. Fax 063/825-888. E-mail: novotel@netnam2.org.vn. MINIBAR TV TEL. US$119–US$139 double; US$189 suite. Discounts and specials are common. AE, DC, JCB, MC, V. Behind the Sofitel on the south side of the lake.

This is the scaled-down companion hotel to the Sofitel Palace. It was renovated in 1997 from a 1932 building that was originally the Du Parc hotel, and a lovely job was done of it. The lobby has a very interesting open-face wrought-iron lift. The smallish rooms have attractive historic touches: glossy wood floors, tasteful understated wood furniture, and molded high ceilings. The bathrooms are nice-sized and efficient, spotless, and apparently brand new. The Novotel shares amenities with the Palace (above).

MODERATE

Golf III Hotel. 4 Nguyen Thi Minh Khai St. ☎ **063/826-042** or 063/826-049. Fax 063/830-396. 78 units. MINIBAR TV TEL. US$35–US$42 double; US$50–US$70 suite. AE, JCB, MC, V. In the center of town near the main market.

The Golf is a three-star chain hotel, Vietnamese-style (Golf I and II are cheaper versions in Dalat). The big rooms have tacky purplish upholstery and Asian carved wood detailing, and are frayed just a tiny bit around the edges, though perfectly clean. It's worth springing for a deluxe US$42 double. These rooms have parquet floors rather than carpet, and bathrooms are huge and in nice shape, many with oversized sunken tubs. This is a honeymoon hotel, after all. In fact, the constant stream of Vietnamese wedding parties in and out lends a welcome festive air to the proceedings. If that's not your thing, consider staying elsewhere. Although the hotel is near the market and not far from the golf course, it is set back from the road and the rooms are relatively quiet. There are a restaurant, bar, massage, and steam bath.

INEXPENSIVE

Hang Nga Guest House. 3 Huynh Thuc Khang St. ☎ **063/822-070.** 9 units. US$29–US$60 double. AE, MC, V.

As well as being an interesting architectural experiment, Hang Nga (see "Attractions," below) is also a guesthouse. Or guest tree, you might call it—the nine small rooms are hollowed out of huge fantasy tree trunks, and each has a theme: the bear room, ant room, bamboo room, and so forth. Statues of said animals dominate the rooms, some of which have stalactites (perfect for head-bumping) and/or small fireplaces. Furniture consists of tree trunk chairs and tables and the like, and mirrors on the ceilings (I know what you're thinking). The eagle room, which Ms. Hang says represents the U.S., is the most majestic, and has a huge mosaic concrete tub, although the bear room (Russia, natch) isn't bad either, but I found the ant room the best of all. The honeymoon suite has two floors, the upper consisting solely of a bed in a nook. You can stay here for kicks, and it will be quite memorable, but don't expect it to be very comfortable. Thin foam mattresses, small rooms, and cold cement floors are the wee price you'll pay for staying in fantasyland.

✪ Hotel Dai Loi (Fortune Hotel). 3A Bui Thi Xuan. ☎ **063/837-333.** 39 units. TV TEL. US$14–US$25 double. AE, MC, V.

If you want value for money, look no further. This place opened just a couple weeks before I arrived for my research, and they've done a terrific job. Even the lowest priced rooms are terrific, with high ceilings, fresh paint, comfortable firm mattresses, marble floors, new furnishings, and nicely tiled bathrooms. Most other places in this category have musty smells and clammy feels, but not the Fortune. The place is spotless, the location near the center of town ideal, and the price is right—most doubles are in the US$14–US$15 category; the US$25 rooms have two double beds.

Ngoc Lan Hotel. 42 Nguyen Chi Thanh St., Dalat. ☎ **063/822-136** or 063/823-522. Fax 063/824-032. 33 units. MINIBAR TV TEL. US$16–US$35 double. JCB, MC, V.

This outfit is owned by Dalattourist, and is a very comfortable 10-year-old two-star alternative not far from the market. It's your classic government-run Vietnamese hotel. Rooms are huge, with hideously mismatched plastic/wood furniture and velveteen bedspreads, but are comfortable and clean, including the beds. Bathrooms are roomy as well and a tiny bit shoddy, with aged tile, but have hair dryers. The restaurant is big and dark, and resembles your local Firehouse Lodge, right down to also doubling as a dance and wedding hall. Well, you'll only be eating breakfast there, anyway. City noise permeates all the rooms, which is inevitable for such a central location. Ask for a room with a "garden view"—they're as quiet as you can get. The sweet staff speaks little English.

DINING

There is nothing outstanding about the dining scene in Dalat. Meals are simply prepared and heavily influenced by Chinese cuisine. The huge variety of local ingredients, particularly fruit and vegetables, makes for fresh-tasting food. Many small restaurants are located at Phan Dinh Phung Street. Most serve breakfast from about 7am and close around 10pm; none outside of a hotel accept credit cards. Do try the artichoke tea and strawberry jam, two local specialties.

Probably the best local spot is the clean, indoor, and relatively upscale **Ngoc Hai Restaurant,** at 6 Nguyen Thi Minh Khai St. (☎ **063/825-252**). Selections from the Western end of the spectrum include roasted chicken with potatoes, Hungarian goulash, chicken pie, and fish fritters. Tasty, inexpensive food. **Café de la Poste,** in the Palace Hotel, has good sandwiches, light meals, and desserts. It's a large, airy, upscale place, perhaps more restaurant than cafe. Selections are pricey for Dalat at 29,000 to 146,000 VND (US$2 to US$10). **Nam Do,** 6 Nguyen Thi Minh Khai St., next to Ngoc Hai Restaurant (☎ **063/824-550**), serves Chinese specialties, including hot pot. The food is non-greasy and good. There are some exotics on the menu like bear claw marinated in Chinese medicine, and grilled porcupine, but the restaurant was strangely all out of those. If there is a specialty in Dalat, vegetarian food might qualify. Try **Giac Duc** on 15 Phan Dinh Phung St. for a good US$3 meal. It's your basic concrete floor, plastic-furniture stall serving fresh vegetables, noodles, and various soups, along with imitation meat products, if you so desire. While the so-called beef ribs and prawns are interesting, stick to vegetable dishes like maize soup (which is baby corn, tofu, and mushrooms), dumplings, and "sauté miscellaneous": cabbage, tofu, and green vegetables. **Hoang Lan** at 118 Phan Dinh Phung is the backpacker favorite, with great meals with a Chinese/Vietnamese flair. Very fresh and nicely priced.

Ngyen Chi Thanh Street is lined with cafes: a noisy karaoke cafe, a chic "café des artistes," a good Internet cafe, an ice cream cafe, and a few others. If you continue up the hill, just beyond the theater, stop in at Café Tung on 6 Khu Hoa Binh. The dimly lit place is mostly filled with locals hanging out drinking tea and relaxing. The music is great, and so is the hot cocoa.

ATTRACTIONS

Much of what there is to see in Dalat hinges on the outdoors: lakes, waterfalls, and dams dominate the tourist trail. Things are spread over quite some distance, so consider a tour or renting your own car or motorbike.

Remember to avoid visiting pagodas between 11:30am and 2pm, when nuns and monks will be having their lunch. You may disturb them and also miss a valuable opportunity for a chat. It is also correct to leave a thousand VND or two in the donation box near the altar.

Dalat Market (Cho Da Lat). Central Dalat.

Huge, crowded, and stuffed with produce of all varieties, this is the top stroll-through destination in Dalat. Here's where you can see all the local specialties—and even have a try! Some of the vendors will be happy to give you a sample of some local wine or a few candied strawberries.

Xuan Huong Lake. Central Dalat.

Once a trickle originating in the Lat village, Dalat's centerpiece, Huan Huong, was created from a dam project that was finished in 1923, demolished by a storm in 1932, and reconstructed and rebuilt (with heavier stone) in 1935. You can rent windsurfing boards and swan-shaped paddleboats, although in two visits here I've yet to see anyone actually using them—I can not vouch for the cleanliness of the water.

Hang Nga Guest House and Art Gallery. 3 Huynh Thuc Khang St. ☎ **063/22-070.** Admission 5,000 VND (US$0.34). Daily 7am–7pm.

Otherwise known as the Crazy House, this is a Gaudi-meets-Sesame Street theme park designed by an eccentric Russian-trained architect. The garden features a tree-trunk couple arguing, a huge spider web, and a towering sculpted giraffe. An overhead bird-cage tunnel contraption winds throughout. Try to meet Ms. Hang Nga, of the soft voice and very heavy eye shadow, herself. The locals call her eccentric for some reason, but she's just misunderstood. You can also stay in the guesthouse, nine small rooms hollowed out of huge fantasy tree trunks (see "Accommodations").

Bao Dai's Palace. South of Xuan Huong Lake. Admission 10,000 VND (US$0.69). Daily 7am–8pm.

Completed in 1938, this monument to bad taste provided Bao Dai, Vietnam's last emperor, with a place of rest and respite with his family. Think concrete and velvet furniture. There are 26 rooms to explore, including Bao Dai's office and the bedrooms of the royal family. Deer horns from a poor animal the emperor bagged himself hang on the wall. The place has never been restored, and indeed looks veritably untouched since the emperor's ousting, which makes it all the more interesting. You can still see the grease stains on Bao Dai's hammock pillow and the ancient steam bath in which he soaked. Don't miss the etched glass map of Vietnam in the main dining room, given to Bao Dai by a group of students in 1952. The explanations are in English, and most concern Bao Dai's family. There is pathos in reading them and piecing together the mundane fate of the former royals: this prince has a "technical" job, that one is a manager for an insurance company.

Thien Vuong Pagoda. 2 miles southeast of town at the end of Khe Sanh St. Daily 9am–5pm.

Otherwise known as the "Chinese Pagoda," built as it was by the local Chinese population, this circa 1958 structure is unremarkable except for its serene setting among the hills of Dalat and the very friendly nuns who inhabit it. It does have three awe-inspiring sandalwood Buddhist statues that have been dated to the 16th century. Each is 4 meters (13 ft.) high and weighs 1½ tons. Left to right, they are Dai The Chi Bo Tat, god of power; Amithaba or Sakyamuni, Buddha; and Am Bo Tat, god of mercy.

Dalat Railway Station (Cremaillaire Railway). Near Xuan Huong Lake, off Nguyen Trai St. Admission 2,000 VND (US$0.14). Daily 8am–5pm.

Built in 1943, the Dalat station offers an atmospheric slice of Dalat's colonial history. You can see an authentic old wood-burning steamer train on the tracks to the rear, and stroll around inside looking at the iron-grilled ticket windows, empty now. Although the steamer train no longer makes tourist runs, a newer Japanese train makes a trip to Trai Mat Street and the Linh Phuoc pagoda (below). A ride costs US$5.

Linh Phuoc Pagoda. At the end of Trai Mat St. Daily 8am–5pm.

Here is another example of one of Vietnam's fantasyland glass and ceramic mosaic structures. Refurbished in 1996, this modern temple features a huge golden Buddha in the main hall, and three floors of walls and ceilings painted with fanciful murals. Go to the top floor for the eye-boggling Bodhisattva room and views of the surrounding countryside. In the garden to the right, there is a 10-foot-high dragon climbing in and out of a small lake. You can get inside of it and crawl around, too.

Su Nu Pagoda. 72 Hoang Hoa Tham St., in the Trai Ham area. Daily 9am–5pm.

Thirty nuns live at this peaceful temple. While the structure isn't very big or impressive, the Su Nu complex is small and you are free to stroll around the temple and serene gardens, usually accompanied by a nun. If you bring an interpreter, you may be invited to have a cup of tea and discuss the way of Buddha.

Datanla Waterfall. On Prenn Pass 2½ miles from Dalat. Admission 4,000 VND (US$0.28). Daily 8am–5pm.

Datanla was once a major power source for the Lat people. Today, it's a mediocre fall, pretty enough after a walk through the forest but a fully fledged tourist site. See it if you're on the way to the Truc Lam Monastery (below).

✪ Truc Lam (Bamboo Forest) Zen Monastery. On the right side of Tuyen Lam Lake, 6km (4 miles) from Dalat. Daily 7am–5pm.

Don't call this a pagoda. There's a difference, one you can feel as soon as you ascend the hill after going past the one—count 'em, one—tiny vendor. The complex was completed in 1994 with the aim of giving new life to the Truc Lam Yen Tu Zen sect, a uniquely Vietnamese form of Zen founded during the Tran dynasty (A.D.1225–1400). Adherents practice self-reliance and realization through meditation. The shrine, the main building, is notable mainly for its simple structure and peaceful air, and the quarters for nuns and monks nearby are closed to the public. However, the scenery around the monastery, with views of dam-made Tuyen Lam Lake and surrounding mountains, is breathtaking. The grounds themselves are furnished with a small man-made pond and mimosa trees. As Zen master Thich Thanh Tu said, "Life is but a dream."

Valley of Love. Phu Dong Thien Vuong St., about 2 miles north of town center. Admission 5,000 VND (US$0.34). Daily 6am–5pm.

The Valley is scenic headquarters in Dalat. You can enjoy walking amidst the rolling hills and charming lakes, all the while enjoying the antics of the Vietnamese honeymooners zipping around on motorboats and posing for pictures with local "cowboys."

Lake of Sighs (Ho Than Tho). Northeast of town, along Ho Xuan Huong Rd. Admission 5,000 VND (US$0.34). Daily 7am–5pm.

This lake has such romantic connotations for the Vietnamese, you would think it was created by a fairy godmother rather than French dam work. Legend has it that a 15-year-old girl named Thuy drowned herself after her boyfriend of the same age, Tam, fell in love with another. Her gravestone still exists on the side of the lake, marked with the incense and flowers left by other similarly heart-broken souls, even though the name on the headstone reads "Thao," not "Thuy." The place is crammed with honeymooners in paddleboats and motorboats.

Prenn Falls. At the foot of Prenn Mountain pass, 10km (6.25 miles) from Dalat. Admission 6,000 VND (US$0.41). Daily 7am–5pm.

The Prenn falls are actually quite impressive, thundering down from a great height— and you can follow a path under them, which adds some thrill factor. The Prenn experience includes cavorting costumed bears, staged photo opportunities, and vendors selling every kind of tacky knickknack available.

EXCURSION: THE LAT & CHICKEN VILLAGES

The name of Dalat is actually a colonial mispronunciation of the town's original name, Dao Lach, with *dao* meaning "water" and Lach referring to a minority tribe now known as Lat. The Lat still inhabit hills about 7½ miles outside the city, along with other minorities such as the Chil, Sré, and Koho peoples. If you go with a tour group, you'll probably see the inside of a Lat home and hear some traditional music from a small band of costumed performers. Afterwards, you'll share a communal pot of rice wine.

You can also visit the Koho. Their home is known as Chicken Village because of the 20-foot tall statue of said chicken. Why a chicken? Nobody knows. The Koho are very friendly, and you can walk around the rustic village and perhaps purchase samples of their outstanding handwoven crafts. Visiting these places independently is impossible as the government requires every visitor to be accompanied by a sanctioned guide. Dalattourist has a trip for about US$14, but you can also create your own itinerary to all the sights you can pack into 1 day for about US$20. Kim Café and Sinh Café do half-day seat-in-coach tours for about US$8, with more backpackers signing up.

SPORTS & OUTDOOR ACTIVITIES

Dalat is the perfect setting for hiking and mountain biking. Action Max (formerly Action Dalat) now books excursions through Dalattourist. Arrange trips for trekking, climbing, abseiling, mountain biking, even parachute gliding, though their office.

Golfers can try the Dalat Palace Golf Club's impressive 18-hole course. One round costs Sofitel Palace or Novotel guests US$65; all others pay US$85, plus a mandatory US$10 caddie fee. For reservations call ☎ 063/821-201.

11 Ho Chi Minh City (Saigon)

Ho Chi Minh City, or Saigon as it is once again commonly known, is a relatively young Asian city founded in the 18th century. Settled mainly by civil war refugees from north Vietnam and Chinese merchants, it quickly became a major commercial center. When the French took over a land they called Cochin China, Saigon became the capital. After the French left in 1954, Saigon remained the capital of south Vietnam until national reunification in 1975.

Saigon is still Vietnam's commercial headquarters, brash and busy, with a keen sense of its own importance. Located on the Saigon River, it's Vietnam's major port and largest city, with a population of almost five million people. True to its reputation, it is noisy, crowded, and messy. Yet Saigon is also exciting and historic, with wide downtown avenues flanked by pristine colonials. It has an attitude all its own.

Some of Saigon's tourism highlights: the **Vietnam History Museum;** the grisly **War Remnants Museum;** and **Cholon, the Chinese district,** with its pagodas and exotic stores. Dong Khoi Street—formerly fashionable Rue Catinat during the French era and Tu Do, or Freedom Street, during the American war—is still a strip of grand colonial hotels, chic shops, and cafes. The food in Saigon is some of the best Vietnam has to offer, the nightlife sparkles, and the shopping is good. The city is also a logical jumping-off point for excursions to other southerly destinations: the **Mekong Delta,** the **Cu Chi tunnels,** and **Phan Thiet beach.**

GETTING THERE

BY PLANE   Of the regional airlines, pretty much all of them fly to Vietnam including Malaysian Airlines, Thai Airways International, Silk Air/Singapore Airlines, Royal

Ho Chi Minh City (Saigon)

ACCOMMODATIONS ■
Bong Sen Hotel Annex **24**
Grand Hotel **29**
Hong Hoa Hotel **38**
Hotel Caravelle **23**
Hotel Continental **18**
Hotel Majestic **33**
Hotel Sofitel Plaza **8**
Huong Sen Hotel **26**
Kimdo Royal International Hotel **30**
Mondial Hotel **28**
New World Hotel Saigon **37**
Norfolk Hotel **21**
Omni Saigon Hotel **1**
Oscar Hotel **31**
Rex Hotel **22**
Saigon Prince Hotel **34**
Spring Hotel **17**

DINING ◆
Ancient Town **3**
BiBi **13**
Café Mogambo **14**
Camargue **15**
Cappuccino **39**
Chao Thai **12**
Lemongrass/Augustin/Globo Café **27**
Restaurant 13 **32**
Saigon Sakura **25**

ATTRACTIONS ●
Ben Thanh Market **36**
City Hall **9**
Emperor Jade Pagoda **2**
Former U.S. Embassy **9**
General Post Office (Buu Dien) **7**
Ho Chi Minh Museum **35**
Museum of the Revolution **20**
Notre Dame Cathedral **6**
Reunification Palace **5**
Saigon History Museum **10**
Saigon Opera House **16**
War Remnants Museum **4**
Zoo and Botanical Gardens **11**

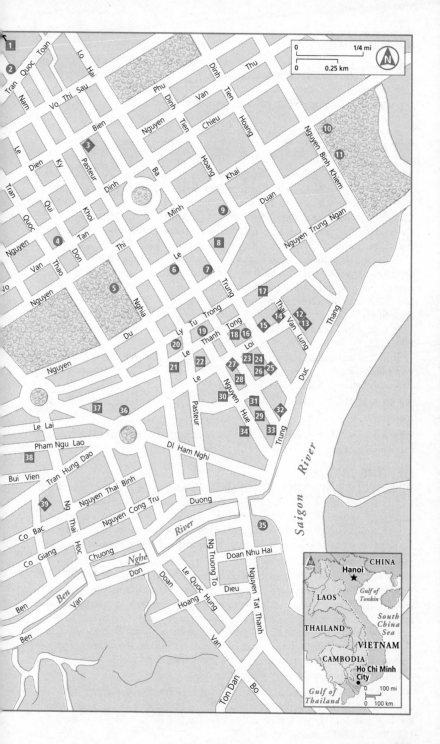

Scam Alert

If you go with a taxi driver, even a metered one, from the airport in Saigon, watch out for the hotel bait-and-switch scam. Drivers get commissions for leading tourists to one hotel or another, and it's common for them to insist that the hotel you're going to is full, or closed, or has some other problem, and to try to drop you elsewhere. Sit tight until you're at your intended destination. It may help for you to agree in writing where you're going before setting out.

Air Camboge, Lao Aviation, Garuda Indonesia, Philippine Airlines, and Cathay Pacific (from Hong Kong). My suggestion is to always check the price of the Vietnam Airlines flight first. It's usually the best fare, thanks to government controls. If you're flying to Vietnam direct from North America, look into Cathay Pacific and Eva Air for good fares and itineraries. Domestically, Saigon is linked by Vietnam Airline flights from Hanoi, Hue, Danang, Hoi An, Nha Trang, and Dalat.

At the airport in Saigon, you'll be able to change foreign currency for VND, but taxi drivers to town don't mind payment in US dollars, either. Arranging a hotel limousine to greet you will certainly make life a bit easier, but taxis are aplenty outside the arrivals hall. The trip to town is US$5, even though the cabbie will always say "Seven dollars!" Stick firmly to your offer of $5 and they always give in without too much hassle.

In town, the Vietnam Airlines office is at 116 Nguyen Hue, District 1, ☎ **08/ 829-2118,** fax 08/823-8454, to book a flight or confirm your reservation.

To get to the airport, if you can't find a taxi you can call Airport Taxi at ☎ **08/ 844-6666.** There is an international departure tax of US$12. The departure tax for domestic flights is 25,000 VND (US$1.72).

BY BUS/MINIVAN   By bus, Saigon is about 5½ hours from Dalat, the nearest major city.

BY CAR   For safety reasons alone, if you're taking wheels it is better to book a minivan with a tour or group.

GETTING AROUND
BY BICYCLE & MOTORBIKE   Saigon is blessed with the country's most chaotic traffic, so you might want to think twice before renting a motorbike or bicycle, which aren't as easily available as in other towns. You can, however, hop a motorcycle taxi— a quick trip is 5,000 VND (US$0.34), while hourly booking can be in the ballpark of US$2 per hour. OK, so it's not the safest, but it sure can save your life if you get too tired to walk!

BY CYCLO   Cyclos are available for an hourly rental of about 20,000 VND (US$1.38). But they simply are not a good option in Saigon, especially outside District 1. First, drivers have an odd habit of not speaking English (or indeed, any other language) halfway through your trip and taking you to places you never asked to see, or simply driving around in circles pretending to be confused. Second, riding in a slow, open conveyance amid thousands of motorbikes and cars is unpleasant and dangerous. Third, drive-by thefts from riders is common. And this is during daytime hours! Don't even think about it at night.

BY TAXI   Taxis are clustered around the bigger hotels and restaurants. They cost 6,000 VND (US$0.41) at flag fall and 6,000 VND or so for every kilometer after— far cheaper than in Hanoi. You can call Airport Taxi (☎ **08/844-6666**) or Saigon Taxi (☎ **08/822-6688**), among others.

BY CAR   You can simplify your sightseeing efforts if you hire a car and driver for the day from Ann's Tourist or Saigontourist (see "Visitor Information & Tours").

VISITOR INFORMATION & TOURS

Every major tourist agency has its headquarters or a branch in Saigon. They will be able to book tours and travel throughout the city and the southern region, and usually countrywide as well.

- **☉ Ann's Tourist Co.,** 58 Ton That Tung St., District 1 (☎ **08/833-2564** or 833-4356; fax 08/832-3866; www.anntours.com; e-mail: tony@anntours.com) has a great reputation that is entirely well-deserved. It's hard to imagine a friendlier, better-run travel organization. Ann's specializes in custom tours for individuals or small groups. They can be relatively expensive, but that's in comparison to the seat-in-coach cattle drive tours. These guys will help you do virtually anything you want to in Vietnam. Ask for director Tony Nong and tell him Frommer's sent you.
- **Saigontourist,** 49 Le Thanh Ton St., District 1 (☎ **08/829-8914;** fax 08/ 822-4987; e-mail: sgtvn@hcmc.netnam.vn), is a faceless, pricey, government-run group, but they'll get you where you want to go. Plus, you'll never have trouble finding them since they have outlets in practically every hotel lobby in the city.
- **Sinh Café,** 246–248 De Tham, District 1 (☎ **08/369-420** or 08/8369322; e-mail: sinhcafevietnam@hcm.vnn.vn). One of the backpacker choices for inexpensive trips and tours, on paper their tours seem exactly the same as others offered at private tour agents but with a cheaper price tag—actually, they're pretty standard tours. A good option for shoestring travelers.

Fast Facts: Ho Chi Minh City

Banks/Currency Exchange   As with elsewhere in Vietnam, you can change money in banks, hotels, and jewelry stores. The exchange rate in Saigon is better than for many smaller cities.

Major banks in Saigon: ANZ Bank, 11 Me Linh Square, District 1, ☎ **08/ 829-9319.** Citibank, 115 Nguyen Hue St., ☎ **824-2118.** HSBC, 75 Pham Hong Thai St., District 1, ☎ **08/829-2288.** Vietcombank, 29 Ben Chuong Duong, District 1, ☎ **08/829-7245.**

ATMs dispensing dollars and dong around the clock are at HSBC, ANZ Bank, and Citibank.

Embassies & Consulates   For embassies, see "Fast Facts: Hanoi," earlier in this chapter. Consulates are all in District 1, as follows: United States, 4 Le Duan St. (☎ **08/822-9433**); Canada, 235 Dong Khoi St. (☎ **08/824-5025**); Australia, 5B Ton Duc Thang St. (☎ **08/829-6035**); New Zealand, 41 Nguyen Thi Minh Khai St. (☎ **08/822-6908**); United Kingdom, 25 Le Duan St. (☎ **08/ 829-8433**).

Emergencies   For police, dial 113; fire 114; and ambulance 115. Have a translator on hand if necessary; operators don't speak English.

Internet/E-mail   Almost every upscale hotel provides Internet services in Saigon, and you can bet they charge a pretty penny. Around the city you'll find Internet service pretty easily, for an average of 200 VND (one cent) per minute. My personal favorite: thumbs up to Café Cyber Business Center for serving cocktails as well as providing full business center services! They're at 48 Dong Du

St., just off Dong Khoi in District 1, ☎ **08/823-3668;** e-mail: info@cgcybercfe. com; 300 VND per minute (US$0.02). The cheapest one I found was 150 VND—less than one cent per minute along the backpacker strip at De Tham Street, where you'll find at least a half dozen Internet cafes along 1 block.

Post Office/Mail   The main post office is located at 2 Coq Xu Paris, District 1 (☎ **08/823-2541** or 08/823-2542). It's across from the Notre Dame cathedral and is open daily from 6:30am to 10pm. There are also express mail services in the building, which is in itself a historic landmark (see "Attractions").

Safety   The biggest threat to your health in Saigon is likely to be the street traf- fic. Cross the wildly busy streets at a slow, steady pace. If you're having a really hard time getting across, find a local who is crossing and stick to his heels!

Pickpocketing is a big problem in Saigon, especially motorbike drive-bys where they slash the shoulder strap, grab the bag and drive off. Keep your bag close, and away from traffic. Hang on to your wallet, and don't wear flashy jew- elry. Be especially wary in crowded places like markets. Women alone should avoid wandering around in the evenings past 11pm or so. Contact your consulate or your hotel if you have a serious problem. If you insist on going to the local police, bring a translator. Also, the Saigon police tend to throw up their hands at "minor" infractions such as purse snatching or thievery.

Telephone   The city code for Saigon is 8. When dialing within Vietnam, the city code should be preceded by 0.

Toilets   There are no public toilets per se. Seek out hotels, restaurants, and tourist attractions.

ACCOMMODATIONS

Saigon presents the best variety of hotels in Vietnam, from deluxe business and fam- ily hotels to spotless smaller options. Most of the upper-end hotels are clustered around Nguyen Hue Street in District 1, as are the restaurants, shops, and bars.

Remember that prices listed here are guidelines only. Depending on occupancy, the season (low season in Saigon is March through October), and how long you're stay- ing, you may get up to 50% off the rack rate. Cleanliness and amenities are very easy to come by. If your room doesn't have a hair dryer or hot water, for example, you need only ask.

If you're traveling on a budget, head for De Tham, a backpacker haven loaded with guesthouses. You can get a fan-cooled room with cold water shower for as little as US$6 per night, or an air-conditioned room with hot water for around US$15. Most of these places are very basic (and a bit noisy from street traffic) but tidy, well-run, and friendly.

SAIGON'S DISTRICTS

Saigon is divided into districts, as is Hanoi, and is very easy to navigate. Find out districts (sometimes called quadrants) along with addresses, and try to group your travels accordingly. Most of the hotels, bars, shops, and restaurants are in District 1, easily covered on foot, while sightseeing attractions are spread among Districts 1, 3, and 5 (Cholon).

For this update I've noticed some hotels in Saigon have changed prices dramatically, some up, some down. In the reviews that follow, do not gauge the hotel by its price category—Saigon Prince is a four-star hotel and could never get away with charging the full rate, an eye-popping US$180 for a standard double. Likewise there's no way the well-worn and homely Kim Do Royal City Hotel can possibly compete with the Sofitel or the Omni hotel chains, but it's in the same price category. Please, when deciding on a hotel, judge the value based upon the hotel's description—when you call to make your reservations you will be quoted a "promotion rate" that more closely reflects the value of your choice.

VERY EXPENSIVE

✪ **Caravelle Hotel.** 19 Lam Son Square, District 1. ☎ **08/823-4999.** Fax 08/824-3999. www.caravellehotel.com. E-mail: hotel@caravellehotel.vnn.vn. 335 units. A/C MINIBAR TV TEL. US$130–US$190 double; from US$250 suite. AE, JCB, MC, V.

Once the rather shabby hangout of wartime journalists, the Caravelle, which had a renovation and built a new wing in 1998, is now an extremely attractive, efficient, and well-appointed hotel. It must have good feng shui, because it simply has a nice feeling to it. It certainly offers great value for the price, and attracts a goodly number of business travelers as well as tourists. The big, new rooms are well-done and well-appointed, with plush neutral furnishings and firm beds. Coffeemakers, too. Bathrooms are sizable, in marble. The executive "signature" floors have fax machines, computer hookups, VCRs, and CD players in each room. I recommend the rooftop Saigon Bar for its great view in the late afternoon and evening.

Hotel Majestic. 1 Dong Khoi St., District 1. ☎ **08/829-5514.** Fax 08/829-5510. www. majestic-saigon.com. E-mail: hotelmajestic@sgtourist.com.vn. 122 units. A/C MINIBAR TV TEL. US$150–US$215 double; from US$295 suite. AE, JCB, MC, V.

This 1925 landmark was spruced up a few years ago. On the outside, the gorgeous colonial looks a bit like a wedding cake: pink, fancy, and bright. On the inside, things have been botched up a bit. There are the original stained-glass dome and floor mosaic in the lobby, but the concrete replica of the Ben Thanh market clock and the spindly chairs in the lobby restaurant—why, why? The rooms are big; a deluxe room, for example, can be up to 42 square meters (138 sq. ft.) All feature original wood floors and light fixtures. The furniture is gaudy wooden and there are some interesting details—the TV is set into a red velveteen cabinet, for instance. Majestic suites have huge Jacuzzi bathtubs and posh gold fixtures. The pool is a bright spot, small but in an inner courtyard surrounded by palms and the hotel's picturesque shuttered innards. Try to get a quiet room facing it. The lobby lounge offers buffet meals throughout the day, a nice touch, with either a pianist or traditional music as live accompaniment. There's a restaurant, two bars, cafe, and lobby lounge. Amenities include the swimming pool, business center, conference rooms, banquet rooms, health club with sauna and massage, baby-sitting, florist, and airport transfer.

New World Hotel Saigon. 76 Le Lai St., District 1. ☎ **08/822-8888.** Fax 08/823-0710. www.newworldvietnam.com. E-mail: nwhs@hcm.vnn.vn. 542 units. A/C MINIBAR TV TEL. US$140 double; US$170 executive floor; from US$300 suite. AE, DC, JCB, MC, V.

This is a first-rate hotel, both for business people and leisure travelers. It's big, flashy, and deluxe, and has a nice bustle about it. The impeccable, plush rooms are done in a soothing array of neutrals, and the bathrooms are sharp in black and gray marble. The fat pillows are a little mushy and the beds a bit too firm, but you can't have everything. The place is loaded with amenities. The four executive floors with executive lounge have an impressive list of benefits: late check-out, all-day refreshments, free pressing, computer hookups, the whole bit, including free access to financial newswire info. If convenience is your game, it is well worth the US$30 more you'll pay over a standard double room. The staff snaps to; service is ultra-efficient. It's also one of the few places to ask straight away if you'd like a nonsmoking room.

Saigon Prince Hotel. 63 Nguyen Hue Blvd., District 1. ☎ **08/822-2999.** Fax 08/ 824-1888. 203 units. A/C MINIBAR TV TEL. US$180–US$210 double; US$350 suite. AE, DC, JCB, MC, V.

The Saigon Prince is in a good location, at the quieter end of hotel row and near several excellent restaurants. It's run by Vietnamtourism, and is a favorite of Asian businesspeople. The beige rooms are nice-sized, tasteful, and comfortable, with plush beds, carpets, and coffeemakers, and you'll be guaranteed comfort and convenience if you stay here—however, the rooms are nondescript and already showing signs of wear. The bathrooms are smart black-and-white marble. The staff is efficient but rather impersonal. Also ask about current specials like The Total Business Plan for US$90: The hotel often offers free breakfast, laundry, massage, and use of a mobile phone.

EXPENSIVE

Hotel Continental. 132–134 Dong Khoi St., District 1. ☎ **08/829-9201.** Fax 08/824-1772. 83 units. A/C MINIBAR TV TEL. US$100–US$130 double; US$160 suite. Includes breakfast, tax, and service charge.

This place is a big shame. It's not that it's so horrible, but it could be gorgeous, and it's a shambles. Built in 1890, it is the pre-eminent historic hotel in Saigon, of Somerset Maugham's *Quiet American* fame. Its last renovation was in 1980. It has a lovely colonial facade, but the lobby is overly ornate. Rooms are absolutely huge, with high ceilings. It's the red velveteen curtains and absolutely hideous bedspreads that spoil the fantasy, as do the tatty red carpets. Looks more like a cathouse. The beds are comfortable and plush, though, as are the towels. Bathrooms are big as well, clean and with bathtubs, but are plain dorm style, without counters. The standard rooms are actually the nicest. They face the rear garden instead of the noisy street, for one, and have marble floors. The restaurant is a lovely period piece, but the hotel staff is dazed and confused.

Kim Do Royal City Hotel. 133 Nguyen Hue Ave., District 1. ☎ **08/822-5914** or 08/822-5915. Fax 08/822-5913. www.kimdohotel.com. E-mail: Kimdohotel@fmail.vnn.vn. US$99–US$169 double; US$219 junior suite; US$269 executive suite. AE, DC, JCB, MC, V.

The Kimdo is the kind of place with a wooden tree trunk clock in the lobby, pink plastic hangers and polyurethane slippers in the closet, and bedspreads of some indeterminate man-made-material. It is still immensely likeable, however, thanks to its very friendly staff, good restaurant, perfect downtown location, and absolute cleanliness. It was built nearly 100 years ago, and had a renovation in 1994. The rooms have interesting Asian carved furniture, carpets, rock-hard beds (you can request a soft one), and aged bathrooms with zero counter space. There are coffeemakers, though, and everything is spotless. Rooms are big; the junior suites simply huge. On-premises dining options include the Saigon Restaurant (which serves excellent Vietnamese cuisine), two bars, and a lobby lounge. Amenities include a business center, fitness center with sauna and massage, executive floors with private elevator, airport shuttle, travel services, room service, laundry, baby-sitting, in-room safes, and medical clinic.

✪ **Norfolk Hotel.** 117 Le Thanh Ton St., District 1. ☎ **08/829-5368.** Fax 08/829-3415. E-mail: norfolk@mailser.ut-hcmc.edu.vn. 104 units. A/C MINIBAR TV TEL. US$100–US$140 double; from US$180 suite. AE, DC, JCB, MC, V.

This snappy 8-year-old Australian/Vietnamese joint venture claims to have the highest occupancy rate in town. It deserves it. Rooms are bright and good sized, furnished in slightly mismatched chain-hotel style, but everything is like new, and there are even in-room safes. The beds are soft and deluxe and the TVs large. Bathrooms are small but finished with marble. Extremely efficient and friendly, the Norfolk's staff also speaks excellent English. Its restaurant is bright and upscale, featuring extensive breakfast and lunch buffets. There are also a business center, conference room, 24-hour room service, health club with sauna, and travel services. Book early.

Omni Saigon Hotel. 251 Nguyen Van Troi St., Phu Nhuan District (District 3). ☎ **08/ 844-9222.** Fax 08/844-9198. www.marcopolohotels.com. E-mail: omnisaigonhotel@hcm. fpt.vn. 248 units. A/C MINIBAR TV TEL. US$110–US$120 double; US$150–US$160 executive floor; US$200–US$230 junior suite; from US$350 suite. AE, DC, JCB, MC, V.

Once quarters for the U.S. army (some say a base for the CIA), this hotel looks like a concrete hell from the outside. Inside is another story. The lobby, with a colonial period flavor, is gorgeous and welcoming. Rooms are perfectly comfortable, lush and well-equipped with coffeemakers and safes. The one executive floor has a small business center of its own, in-room faxes, and a particularly elegant lounge. Incredibly good beds and linens, and formal but bland decor. In addition, the Omni is renowned around town for its Sunday brunch at the Café Saigon, featuring Asian and international cuisine. Other fine choices include Lotus Court for Cantonese cuisine from Hong Kong chefs, and Nishimura, unbeatable for upscale Japanese dining. The hotel is 15 minutes from the city center in District 3, but it is also only 10 minutes from the airport, with airport transport available. The service is flawless, perhaps the best in the city.

Sofitel Plaza Saigon. 17 Le Duan Blvd., District 1. In the U.S. ☎ **800/221-4542** or 08/ 824-1555. Fax 08/824-1666. www.sofitel.com. E-mail: sofitelsgn@hcmc.netnam.vn. 292 units. A/C MINIBAR TV TEL. US$159 double; US$219 club; from US$359 business suite. AE, JCB, MC, V.

The Sofitel hotel chain is famous in Southeast Asia for finding grand old colonial dames and converting them into the most charming hotel properties. This is not one of them. Opened in 1999, it's one of the newest, and shiniest, facades on the Saigon skyline. However, what it lacks in colonial charm it more than compensates for in modern luxury, convenience, and comforts. Guest rooms are handsome, are cooling, and still have that "new car smell." You'll never be wanting for any amenity; they've thought of all your needs beforehand. The staff is some of the most helpful and professional I've seen.

MODERATE

✪ **Grand Hotel.** 8–24 Dong Khoi St., District 1. ☎ **08/823-0163.** Fax 063/823-5781. 150 units. A/C MINIBAR TV TEL. US$85–US$110 double; US$250–US$490 suite. AE, JCB, MC, V.

This is it—the Real McCoy: a 1930s colonial building, done just right. It's owned by Saigontourist—fancy that! The recently reopened, renovated Grand has a serene, tasteful atmosphere. Rooms are big, with simple dark wood furniture and huge wardrobes, and without the musty smell that plagues so many Saigon hotels. The bathrooms are small, but have big counters and hair dryers. Deluxe suites, with their own kitchen, are almost too large; there are too many chairs in the kitchen to compensate for the empty space. The amenities are all here: a big, simple outdoor pool, 24-hour room service, coffeemakers upon request, a business center, a health club with sauna and massage. The quiet atmosphere very much suggests tourist rather than business, though. Don't forget to ride in the restored iron elevator and to ogle the stunning original stained glass walls on the way up and down.

✪ **Huong Sen Hotel.** 66–70 Dong Khoi St., District 1. ☎ **08/829-9400.** Fax 08/ 829-0916. E-mail: huongsen@hcm.vnn.vn. 50 units. A/C MINIBAR TV TEL. US$52–US$95 double. AE, DC, JCB, MC, V.

This is an outstanding hotel for the price. Conveniently located on busy Dong Khoi Street, it is owned by the Vietnamese government. Rooms are big and newly renovated with simple, colorfully painted wood furniture, and floral drapes and headboards. They have nice touches like molded ceilings and marble-topped counters in the spotless bathrooms. Some have balconies. Beds are ultra-comfortable. There are a restaurant, terrace bar, sauna, massage, laundry, room service, and elevators. The staff isn't the friendliest.

Travel Tip: Minimarts & Pharmacies

There is a large store that advertises itself as "duty free," on the corners of Nguyen Hue and Le Loi streets, across from the Rex Hotel. You'll find a good selection of brand name toothpastes, face creams, sunscreens, and the like.

For 24-hour health care and pharmacy service, check International SOS, 65 Nguyen Du, District 1 (☎ **08/829-8520;** fax 08/829-8551). They're expensive but are probably your best medical choice in Saigon. They're open 24 hours and also give medical advice over the phone and have a dental clinic.

Oscar Hotel Saigon. 68A Nguyen Hue Blvd., District 1. ☎ **08/829-2959.** Fax 829-2732. E-mail: rsvn.c.century@bdvn.vnd.net. 108 units. A/C MINIBAR TV TEL. US$45–US$75 double; US$95–US$125 suite. AE, JCB, MC, V.

The Oscar, formerly the Century Hotel, has an interesting flavor. The rooms are furnished with dark furniture and, while dimly lit, are rather elegant, save for the occasional puckered carpet. Beds are the very firm brand. Baths are big, bright, and marble, very well appointed. Clientele is part business, part tourist, and the short-hall layout of the place gives rooms a secluded feel. Even though the hotel was renovated only a few years ago, it has an "older hotel" feel. It also has a business center, conference room, small cafe, lobby lounge, room service, airport transfer services, karaoke "with talented singing companions," and disco "with charming dancing partners." I know what you're thinking, but it really isn't that kind of hotel. Great location on hotel row. Its restaurant, Colours Cafe, is renowned as a good buffet and business lunch spot.

Rex Hotel. 141 Nguyen Hue Blvd., District 1. ☎ **08/829-2185** or 08/829-3115. Fax 08/829-6536. 207 units. A/C MINIBAR TV TEL. Peak season US$89–US$119 double; from US$169–US$259 suite. Off-season US$72–US$99 double; from US$135 suite. AE, JCB, MC, V.

The Rex has an unorthodox history. It used to be a French garage. It was expanded by this Vietnamese and then used by the United States Information Agency (and some say the CIA) from 1962 to 1970. Then, transformed in a massive renovation, it opened in 1990 as the hugely atmospheric government-run place it is today. The rooms are laden with bamboo detailing, on the ceilings, the mirrors, everywhere you look. The lampshades are big royal crowns, which is a hoot, and some of the suites have beaded curtains and Christmas lights over the bathroom mirrors. But the beds and pillows are incredible, firm but fat. In fact, they may claim the title of Best Beds in Vietnam. Each suite has a fax machine. The Rex is in a fabulous location downtown, across from a square that has a lively carnival atmosphere at night. It is also known for its rooftop bar with its panoramic Saigon view. There is a very nice staff to boot.

INEXPENSIVE

Bong Sen Hotel Annex. 61–63 Hai Ba Trung St., District 1. ☎ **08/823-5818.** Fax 08/823-5816. E-mail: bongsen2@hcm.vnn.vn. 57 units. A/C MINIBAR TV TEL. US$30–US$35 double; US$45 junior suite. AE, JCB, MC, V.

This small annex to the large Saigontourist-owned Bong Sen provides many of the same amenities at a much lower price. There are room service, a concierge, babysitting, and other trappings of a major hotel. The rooms are bright and attractive, with light wood furniture, new carpet, and blue tile bathrooms. Very chain-hotel floral. Rooms are on the small side, though, and the economy rooms have only one small window. The junior suite wasn't much bigger. Make sure you're getting the Annex, and not the main Bong Sen, which isn't as attractive nor as much of a value.

✪ **Hong Hoa Hotel.** 185/28 Pham Ngu Lao St., 250 De Tham St., District 1. ☎ **08/ 836-1915.** E-mail: honhoarr@hcm.vnn.vn. 7 units. A/C TEL. US$10–US$15 double. Includes tax and service charge. MC, V.

Bravo! This year-and-a-half-old mini-hotel covers all the bases for under US$15. Rooms are sizable and nicely furnished with real light wood furniture and tile floors. Only three of the rooms have bathtubs, but the rest have separate shower areas (all rooms have hot water), and all are clean, inviting, and well-designed. The mattresses are those foam pads, but they're very comfortable and the pillows carry weight. For the US$12 to US$15 rooms you can even get a TV (with satellite movies) and minibar. Downstairs is a dandy Internet center, and the room rate includes 2 hours of Internet access free every day. Stay here and you'll be satisfied at how well you've beat the system.

Mondial Hotel. 109 Dong Khoi St., District 1. ☎ **08/823-1358** or 08/829-6291. Fax 08/ 829-6273. E-mail: mondial.htl@bdvn.vnmail.vnd.net. 40 units. A/C MINIBAR TV TEL. US$30– US$45 double. AE, JCB, MC, V.

The Mondial is a very comfortable smaller-hotel option, owned by Vietnamtourism. Rooms have been recently renovated, with new carpets and new furnishings that give a freshness to the rooms—a much needed face-lift. Bathrooms, while small, are impeccable and have big marble counters. The deluxe US$45 rooms are extremely large and well laid out, and worth the extra money. There are also rooms with one twin bed available at a discount. Bonsai trees and Romanesque statuary share space in the halls, and a traditional Vietnamese song-and-dance show is presented every night at the restaurant. Travel services are available, of course.

✪ **Spring Hotel (Mua Xuan).** 44–46 Le Thanh Ton St., District 1. ☎ **08/829-7362.** Fax 08/822-1383. 45 units. A/C MINIBAR TV TEL. US$25–US$40 double; US$59 suite. Includes breakfast. AE, JCB, MC, V.

If you don't care about fancy amenities, look no further than this amazing place, with nicer rooms than many hotels twice the price. Said rooms are big and have comfy double and super-king-size beds, big TVs, and well-finished bathrooms with decorated tiles. The furniture is nice solid dark wood or light rattan, the floral motif isn't bad, and the carpeted floors are impeccably clean. Go as high up as you can to escape street noise, which is the hotel's one failing. On the other hand, it is centrally located, not far from popular Dong Khoi Street. Lowest-priced "economy" rooms have no windows. The Spring has an improbable Greco-Roman motif, with statues, colonnades, and all, but it's forgiveable, even pleasant. There are a restaurant, room service, and even a business center of sorts. The staff couldn't be nicer or more helpful.

DINING

Saigon has the largest array of restaurants in Vietnam. Virtually every cuisine is represented, all notably. Note that most restaurants close at 10:30 to 11pm. Local specialties to sample include *banh xeo*, a thin rice pancake filled with shrimp, ground pork, and bean sprouts. Try it at Banh Xia A Phu, 10 Ba Than Hai (3/2) Blvd., District 10, a very famous local restaurant with excellent fare. *Mien ga* is a delicious soup with vermicelli, chicken, mushrooms, and onions, and can be had at 140 Le Than Ton, District 1 (behind the Ben Thanh market). *Lau hai san* is a tangy seafood soup with mustard greens. It can be ordered at any seafood restaurant.

EXPENSIVE

✪ **Bi Bi.** 8A/8D Thai Van Lung, District 1. ☎ **08/829-5783.** Main courses 70,000–180,000 VND (US$4.83–US$12.41). MC, V. Daily 5–10:30pm. FRENCH/MEDITERRANEAN.

The food is the star at this small restaurant and art cafe, although the atmosphere has its charms as well. Bibi's cozy interior is fashioned with bright Mediterranean-style furnishings and impressionist paintings; the artwork collection changes periodically. A table near the front is devoted to drinking and card playing. The menu is an interesting mix: cannelloni and ratatouille, pastas and veal escalope. For dessert, there are perfectly done staples like apple crumble and cheese cake. Upstairs, there are a few sofas for drinking and lounging. The starters are almost as expensive as the main courses, and the short wine list comprises pricey selections, making this one of Saigon's more expensive choices if you don't choose the set menu. The food is well worth it.

Camargue. 16 Cao Ba Quat St., District 1. ☎ **08/824-3148.** Reservations recommended on weekend nights. Main courses 80,000–150,000 VND (US$5.52–US$10.34). AE, DC, MC, V. Daily 5:30–11pm. FRENCH/CONTINENTAL.

Camargue is two floors of enchanting surroundings in a renovated colonial. You can choose from softly lit interior or spacious outdoor terrace seating, surrounded by palm fronds. The menu changes regularly. A sampling from our visit included warm goat cheese salad, roast pork rondalet, and venison. Camargue also seems to have given tourists the nod by adding ubiquitous, lower-priced pasta dishes. The food, alas, isn't as perfect as the surroundings, presentation, and service. Excellent, but not perfect—bland salad dressing, meat a tiny bit chewy, that sort of thing. The service is first-rate, and the bar on the first floor is as fashionable as any in the country.

MODERATE

Ancient Town (Pho Xua). 211 Ter Dien Bien Phu St. (at the corner of Pasteur St.), District 3. ☎ **08/829-9625.** Main courses 50,000–70,000 VND (US$3.45–US$4.83). AE, JCB, MC, V. Daily 5:30–10:30pm. VIETNAMESE.

Ancient Town is a relatively new spot serving traditional Vietnamese fare. The setting is upscale and perfect: cane chairs, tile floors, antiques, and an elaborately carved bar. There is live traditional music nightly except for Mondays. The food is excellent. Particularly recommended are the fish soup with dill, steamed snails with ginger, baked crab, shrimp wrapped with smoked ham, and durian ice cream to finish off.

✪ **Augustin.** 10 Nguyen Thiep. ☎ **08/829-2941.** Main courses 40,000–150,000 VND (US$2.76–US$10.34). No credit cards. Daily noon–2pm and 6–11pm. FRENCH.

Tucked into a scraggly alley off Nguyen Hue Street is Augustin, a bright, lively little French restaurant, a great favorite with French expats and tourists. The food is simple yet innovative French fare: beef pot au feu, sea bass tartare with olives. Try the seafood stew, lightly seasoned with saffron and packed with fish, clams, and shrimp. The seating is quite cozy, especially as the restaurant is always full, and the Vietnamese wait staff is exceptionally friendly, speaking both French and English. The menu is bilingual, too. A large French wine list and classic dessert menu finish off a delightful meal.

Café Mogambo. 20 Bis Thi Sach St., District 1. ☎ **08/825-1311.** Main courses 55,000–185,000 VND (US$3.79–US$12.76). MC, V. Daily 7am–11pm. AMERICAN.

Run by American expat Mike and his Vietnamese wife Lani, Mogambo is the laid-back Yank hangout in Saigon. It's a small, dimly lit place with cane ceilings and walls and a few (eek) stuffed animals, as in taxidermy stuffed animals. There is a long bar with television, and a row of regulars bellied up to it. Before long, you'll be joining in the conversation and hanging out longer than you planned, too. Long, diner-style banquettes that stick to your legs are one contribution to an American experience. The other is the beef; their hamburgers and steaks are the real thing, as are the sausages and meat pies. Most entrees are 70,000 to 80,000 VND (US$4.83 to US$5.52) or so; it's the steaks that jack up the high end of the price range. Dessert is apple pie, of course, and a plain, hearty cup of coffee.

✪ **Chao Thai.** 16 Thai Van Lung, District 1. ☎ **08/824-1457.** Reservations recommended only for groups of 5 or more. Main courses 40,000–65,000 VND (US$2.76–US$4.48); set lunch menu 80,000 VND (US$5.52). AE, JCB, MC, V. Daily 10:30am–2pm and 5:30–11pm. THAI.

The food and setting are both flawless here. The restaurant is over two floors of an elegant, roomy Thai longhouse, with wide plank wood floors, black-and-white photos of Thai temples, and some small statuary. Chao Thai is famous for its fiery papaya salad, fried catfish with basil leaves, and prawn cakes with plum sauce. The flavors are subtle and not overdone; you won't leave feeling drugged on spices or too much chile. It's a popular power lunch spot, but the atmosphere is just as warm and welcoming to walk-in tourists. The service is gracious and efficient.

Globo Café. 6 Nguyen Thiep, District 1. ☎ **08/822-8855.** Main courses 60,000–85,000 VND (US$4.14–US$5.86). No credit cards. Daily 5pm–2am. CONTINENTAL.

The Globo, in an alley off hotel row, is a bar-cum-restaurant with a fun African theme: faux animal skins, drum-shaped seats at the bar. It's more subtle and sophisticated than it sounds. The dining areas are small spaces tucked at the back and on the second floor. The menu is brief but hip and excellently prepared by the resident French chef: beef filet, rib-eye steak, braised rabbit, pastas, and lasagnas. Desserts are standards like mousse, crème caramel, and lemon tart.

Lemongrass. 4 Nguyen Thiep St., District 1. ☎ **08/822-0496.** Main courses 50,000–120,000 VND (US$3.45–US$8.28). AE, MC, V. Daily 11am–2pm and 5–10pm. VIETNAMESE.

Lemongrass is renowned as one of the best Vietnamese restaurants in town. You'll rub elbows with locals, expats, and tourists alike here. The atmosphere is candlelit and intimate, very Vietnamese with cane furniture and tile floors, and yet not overly formal. The long menu emphasizes seafood and seasonal specials. Particularly outstanding are the deep-fried prawn in coconut batter and the crab sautéed in salt and pepper sauce. The portions are very healthy, Asian family-style, so go with a group if at all possible and sample as many delicacies as possible.

Saigon Sakura Restaurant. 40 Mac Thi Buoi St., District 1. ☎ **08/822-4502.** Main courses US$4–US$10. MC, V. Daily 11am–2pm and 6:30–10pm. JAPANESE.

Saigon in general is a good place to get decent Japanese food, but this place is superlative. It's not one of your fancy theme restaurants, but Sakura is packed with Japanese visitors. Need we say more? OK, we will. The sushi is fresh and bursting with flavor, the ginger is pickled just right, the tempura is delicately prepared, and the lunch special, at US$7 to US$11 for a set menu, is a great value. For that you'll get rice, beer or soft drinks, a few sushi rolls, a main course, and an array of tasty small accompaniments.

INEXPENSIVE

Cappuccino. 258 De Tham St., District 1. ☎ **08/837-1467.** Main courses 24,000–55,000 VND (US$1.66–US$3.79). No credit cards. Daily 10am–midnight. ITALIAN.

This open-air place on De Tham Street, alias Backpacker Row II, is a good place to stop for some decent pasta, pizza, or risotto. Run by an Italian expat, it has red-and-white checkered tablecloths and smells great, but don't expect miracles for these prices. Your best bet is the specialty of the house risotto dishes, which come in great portions if you're starving. However, the red house wine, although good, is served chilled, the cheese isn't mozzarella, and the fresh tomatoes aren't ripe.

✪ **Restaurant 13.** 11–17 Ngo Duc Ke, District 1. ☎ **08/829-1417.** Main courses 30,000–120,000 VND (US$2.07–US$8.28). No credit cards. Daily 6:30am–10pm. VIETNAMESE.

The atmosphere may be somewhat institutional in this eatery, but 13 serves excellent traditional Vietnamese food, and only that, in a clean spot without charging exorbitant

320 **Vietnam**

prices. The place is jolly and filled with locals, tourists, and expats. Go for the seafood, anything done in coconut broth, or the sautéed squid with citronella and red pepper. The food is carefully prepared and as carefully served. In fact, the wait staff is almost too solicitous; they'll turn the pages of your menu if you let them.

SNACKS & CAFES

While shopping on Dong Khoi, stop to savor a few moments at the Paris Deli, 31 Dong Khoi (☎ 08/829-7533), a retro spot with fantastic pastries and sandwiches. The Marine Club, 17/A4 Le Thanh Ton, District 1 (☎ 08/829-2249), which also has a hopping late-hours bar scene, is renowned around town for its brick-oven pizza.

ATTRACTIONS
ATTRACTIONS IN DISTRICT 1

Ben Thanh Market. At the intersection of Le Loi, Ham Nghi, Tran Hung Dao, and Le Lai sts., District 1.

The clock tower over the main entrance to what was formerly known as "Les Halles Centrale" is the symbol of Saigon, and the market may as well be, too. Opened first in 1914, it's crowded, a boon for pickpockets with its narrow, one-way aisles, and loaded with people clamoring to sell you cheap goods (T-shirts, aluminum wares, silk, bamboo, and lacquer) and postcards. There are so many people calling out to you, you'll feel like you're a president at a press conference. I lasted all of 10 minutes before fleeing. The wet market, with its selection of meat, fish, produce, and flowers, is easier to take.

General Post Office (Buu Dien). 2 Coq Xu Paris, District 1. Daily 6:30am–10pm.

A grand old colonial building. Check out the huge maps of Vietnam on either side of the main entrance and the huge portrait of Uncle Ho in the rear.

Saigon Opera House (Ho Chi Minh Municipal Theater). At the intersection of Le Loi and Dong Khoi sts.

This magnificent building was built at the turn of the century and renovated in the 1940s. Three stories and 1,800 seats are inside. Today, it does very little in terms of performances: opera troupes, orchestras, and ballets—nothing. But I did see a very tidy military brass band play marches on the steps outside, bright and early one Sunday morning. Everyone stopped in Lam Lon Square, their motorbikes and bicycles parked in a semicircle, and sat in silence to enjoy the treat.

Notre Dame Cathedral. Near the intersection of Dong Khoi and Nguyen Du sts., District 1.

The Neo-Romanesque cathedral was constructed between 1877 and 1883 using bricks from Marseilles and stained-glass windows from Chartres. The cathedral is closed to visitors except during Sunday services, which are in Vietnamese and English.

City Hall. Facing Nguyen Hue Blvd.

Saigon's city hall was constructed between 1902 and 1908, a fantastic ornate example of colonial architecture unfortunately not open to the public.

Former U.S. Embassy. At the corner of Le Tuan and Mac Dinh Chi sts.

There is no more embassy. A high concrete and barbed-wire wall is all that's left of the building where Americans famously fled via helicopters from the incoming Viet Cong in April 1975. It looks as though some new construction is under way, however. There is a small monument to the heroism of the Vietnamese on the sidewalk in front of the site.

✪ **Vietnam History Museum.** 2 Nguyen Binh Khiem. ☎ 08/829-8146. Admission 10,000 VND (US$0.69). Daily 8–11:30am and 1:30–4:30pm.

If there is one must-see in Saigon, this is it. The museum, in a rambling new concrete pagodalike structure, does a good job of presenting important aspects of Vietnam's southern area in particular. There is an excellent selection of Cham sculpture and the best collection of ceramics in Vietnam. Weaponry from the 14th century onward is on display, including a yard with nothing but cannons. There is a wing dedicated to ethnic minorities of the south, including photographs, costumes, and household implements. Nguyen dynasty (1700–1945) clothing and housewares are also on display. There are archaeological artifacts from prehistoric Saigon. Its 19th and early 20th century histories are shown using photos and, curiously, a female corpse unearthed as construction teams broke ground for a recent housing project. There are even some general background explanations in English, something missing from most Vietnamese museums.

Revolutionary Museum. 65 Ly Tu Trong St. ☎ **08/829-8250.** Admission 10,000 VND (US$0.69). Daily 8:30–4:30pm.

This museum, situated in a grand historical structure built in the 1880s, is one of many in Vietnam exploring a familiar theme: the struggle of the nation against the French and Americans. It is probably the best of its breed, with various photos, documents, models, and military artifacts detailing local activism as well as long military struggles. The signs are in Vietnamese only at the moment, which actually doesn't present much of a problem. There is a model of the Cu Chi tunnels, the underground network built by the North Vietnamese for weapons transport and living quarters during the American war. Outside are the typical but always interesting captured U.S. fighter planes, tanks, and artillery. Underneath the building is a series of tunnels leading to the Reunification Palace, once used by former president Ngo Dinh Diem as a hideout before his eventual capture and execution in 1962.

Zoo and Botanical Gardens. Nguyen Binh Khiem St. (next to the History Museum), District 1. No phone. Admission 8,000 VND (US$0.55). Daily sunrise–sunset.

Don't come here unless you have never, ever been to a zoo and are dying to go. The animals are in dismal conditions. The only creatures that look vaguely happy, in fact, are the monkeys, doubtless due to the constant handouts they get from the Vietnamese. As for the botanical gardens, where are they? There is some nice flora, but nothing's labeled, so it's hard to know what you're looking at. To be fair, it's probably best to go in the springtime, around Tet, to see the real flower season in the south.

Reunification Palace. 106 Nguyen Du St. Admission 15,000 VND (US$1.03). Daily 7:30–11am and 1–4pm.

Designed to be the home of former President Ngo Dinh Diem, this building is most notable for its symbolic role in the fall of Saigon in April 1975, when its gates were breached by north Vietnamese tanks and the victor's flag occupied the balcony. In the former century, the French governor general lived on the site in a building called Norodom Palace, destroyed in 1962 in an assassination attempt on Diem. The current "modern" nightmare was completed in 1966, after Diem's death. Like the Bao Dai Palace in Dalat, this is a series of rather empty rooms that are nevertheless interesting because they specialize in period kitsch and haven't been gussied up a single bit. You will tour private quarters, dining rooms, entertainment lounges, and the president's office. Most interesting is the war command room with its huge maps and old communications equipment.

OTHER DISTRICTS
✪ **Emperor Jade Pagoda (Phuoc Hai).** 73 Mai Thi Luu St., District 3. Daily 8am–5pm.

One of the most interesting pagodas in Vietnam, the Emperor Jade is filled with smoky incense and fantastic carved figurines. It was built by the Cantonese community around the turn of the century and is still buzzing with worshippers, many lounging in the front gardens. Take a moment to look at the elaborate statuary on the pagoda's roof. The dominant figure in the main hall is The Jade Emperor himself, supposedly the god of the "heavens," according to a tour guide. The emperor decides who will enter and who will be refused. He looks an awful lot like Confucius, only meaner. In an anteroom to the left you'll find Kim Hua, a goddess of fertility, and the King of Hell in another corner with his minions, who undoubtedly gets those the Jade Emperor rejects. Spooky.

⭘ **War Remnants Museum.** 28 Vo Van Tan St., District 3. ☎ **08/829-0325.** Admission 10,000 VND (US$0.69). Daily 7:30–11:30am and 1:30–5:15pm.

This museum houses a collection of machinery, weapons of all sorts, and photos documenting both the French and American wars, although the emphasis is heavily on the latter. The museum's former name was the War Crimes Museum, which should give you some tip whose side of the story is being told here. Some of the facts, including the gory photos and relics, are undeniable and gripping, however, and it's interesting to see how the Vietnamese propaganda machine works. It is at the very least a testimony to the hellishness of war. There is an entire room devoted to biological warfare, another to weaponry, and another to worldwide demonstrations for peace (and denunciations of the U.S.). The explanations, which include English translations, are amazingly thorough for a Vietnamese museum. There's a goodly collection of well-labeled bombs, planes, and tanks in the courtyard outside. Kids will love it, but you may want to think twice before taking them inside to see things like wall-size photos of the My Lai massacre and the bottled deformed fetus supposedly damaged by Agent Orange.

Giac Lam Pagoda. 118 Lac Long Quan St., District 5. Daily 8am–5pm.

Giac Lam Pagoda, built in 1744, is the oldest pagoda in Saigon. The garden in the front features the ornate tombs of venerated monks, as well as a rare bodhi tree. Next to the tree is a regular feature of Vietnamese Buddhist temples, a gleaming white statue of Quan The Am Bo Tat (Avalokitesvara, the Goddess of Mercy) standing on a lotus blossom, symbol of purity. Inside the temple is a spooky funerary chamber, with photos of monks gone by, and a central chamber chock full of statues. Take a look at the outside courtyard as well.

Ho Chi Minh Museum. 1 Nguyen Tat Thanh St., District 4. ☎ **08/825-5740.** Admission 2,000 VND (US$0.14). Tues–Sun 7:30–11:30am.

Although not as extensive as the Ho Chi Minh Museum in Hanoi, there is enough information here in pictures, writing, mementos, and other paraphernalia to give you a good idea of Ho's life and times. More accurately, the place shows you how he is regarded by the Vietnamese: as something of a god. Why else would they put the man's sandals and suit in a museum? The placard says "the khaki suit [Ho] wore from 1954–1969." It must have been very well made. Obviously, there are explanations in English. There is also an extensive section on other revolutionary heroes. However, the museum supposes that you know something about Vietnamese history, as the displays are presented without background. Walking around the rear of the museum also affords a good opportunity to gaze at the very active port on the Saigon River.

Cholon. District 5. Cholon is a sizable district bordered by Hung Vuong in the north, Nguyen Van Cu to the east, the Ben Nghe Chanel to the south, and Nguyen Thi Nho to the west.

Cholon is the Chinese district of Saigon, and probably the largest Chinatown in the world. It exists in many ways as a city quite apart from Saigon. The Chinese began to settle the area in the turn of the century, and never quite assimilated with the rest of Saigon, which causes a bit of resentment among the greater Vietnamese community. You'll sense the different environment immediately, and not only because of the Chinese-language signs.

A bustling commercial center, Cholon is a fascinating maze of temples, restaurants, jade ornaments, and medicine shops. Gone, however, are the brothels and opium dens of earlier days. You can lose yourself in the narrow streets, or hit the highlights. Here is one district, by the way, where taking a cyclo by the hour makes sense to see the sites. Start at the Binh Tay Market, on Phan Van Khoe Street, which is even more crowded than Ben Thanh and has much the same goods, but with a Chinese flavor. There's much more produce, there are medicines, spices, and cooking utensils, and plenty of hapless ducks and chickens tied in heaps. From Binh Tay, head up to Nguyen Trai, the district's main artery, to see some of the major temples on or around it. Be sure to see Quan Am, on Lao Tu Street off Luong Nhu Hoc, for its ornate exterior. Back on Nguyen Trai, Thien Hau pagoda is dedicated to the Goddess of the Sea, and was popular with seafarers making thanks for their safe trip from China to Vietnam. Finally, as you follow Nguyen Trai Street past Ly Thuong Kiet, you'll see the Cholon Mosque, the one indication of Cholon's small Muslim community.

SPORTS & OUTDOOR ACTIVITIES

There are two excellent 18-hole golf courses at the **Vietnam Golf and Country Club.** Fees are US$50 to US$80 during the week for nonmembers, depending on which course you want to play, and US$100 on Saturday and Sunday. The Clubhouse is at Long Thanh My Ward, District 9, ☎ **08/733-0126;** fax 08/733-0102.

Saigon Water Park is a newly opened facility with the usual slides and chutes. It is at **Kha Van Can,** Thu Duc District (☎ **08/897-0456**).

Tennis enthusiasts can find courts at **Lan Anh International Tennis Court,** 291 Cach Mang Than Tam, District 10 (☎ **04/862-7144**).

The pool and well-equipped gym and spa at the **Caravelle Hotel** (see "Accommodations") are available for nonguests at a day rate of 181,000 VND (US$12.41).

SHOPPING

Saigon has a good selection of silk, fashion, lacquer, embroidery, and housewares. Prices are higher than elsewhere, but the selection is more sophisticated, and Saigon's cosmopolitan atmosphere makes it somewhat easier to shop (meaning shop owners aren't immediately pushing you to buy). Stores are open 7 days a week from 8am until about 7pm. Credit cards are widely accepted, save for the markets.

Dong Khoi is Saigon's premier shopping street. Formerly Rue Catinat, it was a veritable Rue de la Paix in colonial times. The best blocks are the last two heading toward the river. Notable shops include **Heritage,** 53 Dong Khoi (☎ **08/823-5438**) for wood carvings and other ethnic arts. **Les Epices** at 25 Dong Khoi St.(☎ **08/823-6795**) also has a nice collection of lacquerware and other gift items, and **Authentique Interiors,** 38 Dong Khoi (☎ **08/822-133**), specializes in gorgeous pottery and table settings. **Viet Silk,** at 21 Dong Khoi (☎ **08/823-4860**), has a quality selection of ready-made clothing and can of course whip something up for you in a day.

Nearby Le Thanh Ton Street is another shopping avenue. Look for **Kenly Silk,** at 132 Le Thanh Ton (☎ **08/829-3847**), a brand-name supplier with the best ready-to-wear silk garments in the business. Unique, tasteful, hand-embroidered pillows, table linens and hand-woven fabrics can be found at **MC Decoration,** 92C5 Le Thanh Ton, across from the Norfolk Hotel (☎ **08/822-6003**).

Stop in at **Saigon Duty Free Shop,** at 102 Nguyen Hue (☎ **08/823-4548**) across (catty-corner) from the Rex Hotel, a full-size department store of bargains. You must have an international plane ticket and can pick up your goods at the airport upon departure.

ART GALLERIES

Galleries that are close to hotels and easy to find can be a good way to start your search for Vietnamese modern art: **Ancient Gallery** (50 Mac Thi Buoi St., District 1, near Saigon Sakura Restaurant; ☎ **08/822-7962**), **Hien Minh Gallery** (32 Dong Khoi St., District 1; ☎ **08/829-5520**), and **Particular Art Gallery** (123 Le Loi St., District 1; ☎ **08/821-3019**). If these pique your curiosity, local tourist guide Saigon Pathfinder lists about a dozen other galleries to scout out. The **Ho Chi Minh Fine Arts Museum** at 97A Pho Duc Chinh St., District 1 (☎ **08/829-4441;** Tues–Sun 9am–4:45pm; admission 10,000 VND/US$0.69) is the place to start if you're truly keen, and **Lac Hong Art Gallery,** located inside the museum (☎ **08/821-3771**) features the works of many famous Vietnamese artists.

BOOKSTORES

HCMC's official "foreign language bookstore," Xuan Thu, is at 85 Dong Khoi St. across from the Continental Hotel (☎ **08/822-4670**). There is a good selection of classics in English and French and some foreign-language newspapers. It's open daily from 7:30am to 9pm. There are also several small bookshops on De Tham Street, carrying many pirate titles and used books; some of these places do swaps.

SAIGON AFTER DARK

When Vietnam made a fresh entree on to the world scene in the mid-1990s, Ho Chi Minh City quickly became one of the hippest party towns in the east. The mood has sobered somewhat, but it's still a fun place. Everything is clustered in District 1, so move along, as the crowd does, from spot to spot.

As for cultural events, Saigon is sadly devoid of anything really terrific save a few cultural dinner and dance shows. Try to find other types of performances and you're met with blank stares.

There is lots of sex for sale, as you may have heard. Gentlemen alone are likely prey. Accepting a scooter ride from a lady, by the way, is tantamount to saying "yes" to lots more.

THE BAR SCENE

The most popular place, hands down, is **Saigon Saigon** at the top of the Caravelle Hotel at 19 Lam Son (☎ **08/823-4999**). Here you have live music and a terrific view—I heard it described as the "Hard Rock Café of Saigon." **Globo Café,** at 6 Nguyen Thiep, is a small, funky, African-themed place at which to start the evening, and has live music on Fridays. The expensive cocktails may discourage you from lingering, however. Then there's the brick-walled Irish pub **O'Briens** at 74A Hai Ba Trung (☎ **08/829-3198**).

DANCING

Apocalypse Now at 2C Thi Sach, District 1 (☎ **08/824-1463**), is a still-popular HCMC landmark, and good for a short stop on your night crawl. Try to make it toward the end of the night (or early morning), when the obvious decorations, drunk tourists, and platform-shod hookers will seem more fun than sad. Watch your belongings! Try **Zouk** for a disco right on hotel row at 119 Nguyen Hue (☎ **08/822-4378**).

MUSIC & THEATER

A few hotels stage traditional music and dance shows à la dinner theater. The **"Au Co"**
Traditional Troupe have performed abroad, but call the Skyview Restaurant at the
Mondial Hotel, their home (109 Dong Khoi St., District 1, ☎ **08/849-6291**). The
Rex Hotel (141 Nguyen Hue Blvd.; ☎ **08/829-2185**) has regular performances as
well. Call each place ahead of time to double-check the performance schedule.

12 Excursions from Ho Chi Minh City

CU CHI TUNNELS

About 65 kilometers (40 miles) northwest of Saigon lies a must-stop for most visitors.
Beginning in the late 1940s, fighters against the French army dug a network of tunnels for hiding themselves and ammo. The network was expanded during the 1960s
for the Viet Cong insurgents and then for use in the American war. By then, the tunnels reached all the way to the border of Cambodia, and were instrumental in Viet
Cong takeover of hamlets along the way. The complex was at times home to almost
10,000 Viet Cong. Entire villages basically existed underground, with meeting rooms,
kitchens, and even hospitals in the tunnels.

Today, you can crawl through a portion of the tunnels, seeing the secret trapdoors
and booby traps for intruders. Try to see the real tunnels at **Ben Dinh,** though, and
not the made-for-tourist ones at Ben Duoc. The experience is dirty and claustrophobic; at times you're crawling through the tiny, clammy openings. The usual day trip to
the tunnels includes a stop at the Cao Dai Cathedral (see below), for about US$4. Talk
to the people at either Saigontourist (49 Le Thanh Ton St., District 1; ☎ **08/**
829-8914) or Sinh Café (246–248 De Tham, District 1; ☎ **08/369-420**), who do a
daily seat-in-coach trip. You'll be charged an additional US$5 admission fee at the
entrance to the tunnels.

CAO DAI HOLY SEE (TAY NINH)

The Cao Dai religion is unique to Vietnam. It was established in 1926 by a government official named Ngo Van Chieu, who claimed spirits visited him and laid down
the tenets of a new faith. Cao Daism draws its beliefs from a variety of world religions,
including the works of great writers and philosophers (which makes sense to me). The
religion's "saints" include Jesus Christ, Victor Hugo, Joan of Arc, Confucius, and
Louis Pasteur. Its headquarters are located in a huge fantasy cathedral, constructed
between 1933 and 1955 in the town of Tay Ninh. The cathedral is painted in a mosaic
of colors with a blue sky ceiling, while followers in brightly colored caftans and white
turbans complete the rainbow spectacle. Onlookers are invited to watch the noon processional service from a balcony overhead. (See the photo section at the beginning of
this book for a photo of the Cao Dai Holy See.)

The Holy See is located at Tay Ninh, 59 miles northwest of Saigon off Highway 22.
A trip out to see the cathedral is combined with the Cu Chi Tunnels in a day trip. See
the Cu Chi Tunnel section above for tour booking information.

PHAN THIET

The target of several new resort developers, this is currently the nicest place to go if
you're looking for a **beach resort** near Saigon. It's actually a smallish fishing town on
the southeastern coast, featuring peaceful light-sand beaches and sand dunes at Mue
Ne, 12½ miles east of the town. The outstanding Nick Faldo–designed **Ocean Dunes**
Golf Course (☎ **062/821-511**) is also a big draw.

Stay at the **Coco Beach Hai Duong Resort,** Km 12.5 Ham Tien, Phan Thiet (☎ 062/847-111; fax 062/847-115; e-mail: paradise@cocobeach.net): US$60 double, US$140 suite. Or try the **Novotel Ocean Dunes Resort,** 1 Ton Duc Thang St. in the United States (☎ 800/221-4542 or 062/822-393; fax 062/825-682; www. nov-phan-thiet-vietnam.com; e-mail: novpht@hcm.vnn.vn,), next to the Ocean Dunes Golf Course: US$78 double; US$98 suite. Phan Thiet is about 3 hours east of Saigon by car on Highway 1.

✪ THE MEKONG DELTA

I can't emphasize this enough: Don't leave without seeing the Mekong Delta, at least for a day. The delta is a region of waterways formed by the Mekong, covering an area of about 60,000 kilometers (37,200 miles). Most of it is cultivated with bright green rice paddies, fruit orchards, sugarcane fields, vegetable gardens, and traditional fish farms. There are a few cities, too, but rather than any cosmopolitan area, get out to see the outlying canals by boat, a fascinating glimpse into a way of life that has survived intact for hundreds of years. As you cruise slowly along the meandering canals, you'll see locals living right beside the water, above it in stilt houses, and in some cases, in it on houseboats. Trading is conducted from boat to boat, often in canal bends teeming with boats and their wares (hung from a tall pole as a form of advertising). The people are friendly and unaffected, and the cuisine of the upper delta is delicious and leans heavily toward seafood.

Coming south from Saigon, the town you'll probably reach first is **My Tho,** but you should try to make it down at least as far as **Can Tho,** the delta's largest city. It has a bustling riverfront and waterway. About 20 miles from Can Tho is **Phung Hiep,** the biggest water market in the region. The water is literally covered by the bobbing merchants.

To cope with the necessary logistics, going with a tour agent is your best bet to the delta. All travel agents offer everything from day trips to "3 days 4 nights" tours. Our pick is **Ann's Tourist Co.,** 58 Ton That Tung St., District 1 (☎ 08/833-2564 or 08/ 833-4356; fax 08/832-3866; www.anntours.com; e-mail: tony@anntours.com), for custom-made tours with six or fewer people, at reasonable prices. The main reason to go with Ann's is the company's dedication to bringing you to places that are off the beaten path. They show you the Mekong up close and personal. For the day trip they charge about US$45 per person, for 2 days about US$85 to US$115 per person, and for 3 days about US$165 per person (prices according to two-person minimum).

Think twice about going to the delta at all during the rainy season, however. Many of the roads may be washed out or the tides too high for canal travel.

Laos 7

by Jennifer Eveland

"The Jewel of Southeast Asia." "Unforgettable." "The most perfectly preserved Southeast Asian city." Most travel literature finds it hard to describe Laos or its cities without using some kind of superlative. That is partly because the superlatives are true, and partly because Laos, landlocked and serene, is too exotic and complex to describe in a few words. Asked to do so, one can only rely on a few hard-hitting adjectives.

So what is Laos about? First, it is a nation where 60% of the people are practicing Buddhists. This fact colors every facet of life there, and is the overriding impression you'll carry away. The ornate, glittering temples on virtually every corner and the flocks of monks in colorful robes on the streets are hard to miss. So, too, is the impression that Lao people may be the friendliest on earth. Then there is the diverse population, from citified Vientiane Lao to rural hill tribes. Remains of ancient civilizations are here as well, including the odd **Plain of Jars** and **Wat Phu,** a Hindu site that may pre-date Angkor Wat. Laos also has varied enticing natural terrain to explore, from mountains in the north to jungles and tropical islands in the south.

It's a beguiling place, and one that demands you slow your pace to match its own. Strolling through a town, you may be stopped in your tracks more than once by a grand temple on the corner of a dirt road, a beautiful Lao teenager strumming her guitar, stopping to wave at you, or the toothless smile of a Lao dowager, beckoning you to come and have a peek at her new grandchild. Outside the major cities, **Vientiane** and **Luang Prabang,** travel gets tougher; but you won't hear any visitors complaining about bumpy bus rides or the lack of a four-star hotel. This is the trade-off you make for the chance to visit hill tribes living in genuinely rustic conditions, untouched by modernity.

The government says it is trying to preserve its historical and ecological treasures from massive foreign invasion, so for now the country continues to develop tourism facilities at a relatively slow pace. However, the current sketchy infrastructure is actually due more to a lack of capital than to the government's wish to protect national heritage. Laos is not only the poorest country in the region, but one of the top 10 poorest countries in the world. One gets the sense that with an injection of tourism income, things will start to happen more quickly. And if it were not for current disturbing situations within the country, this may have been Laos's path.

Since the year 2000, terrorist bombings have plagued the country. Tourist-populated areas seem to be a favorite target. Within the capital city, the morning market has been targeted, also the Wattay International Airport. In the provinces, the luxury Champasak Palace Hotel (in the town of Pakse) was hit, as was a bus heading from the capital to the southern town of Savannakhet. While these small amateur devices have not been powerful enough to cause casualties, scores have been injured. Please refer to the U.S. Department of State Travel Advisory regarding the present dangers of travel in Laos.

I've yet to find a guidebook that states clearly that Laos is under the grip of rebel insurgency by the Hmong people. A minority tribe in Laos's northern hills, they have been fighting the Lao government for over 2 decades now. Currently they occupy the areas around the Plain of Jars in Xieng Khouang, and are responsible for bandit activity along Route 7 to Xieng Khouang Province. While they have not directly claimed responsibility for the bombings, it is generally believed they are responsible.

It should also be mentioned that Lao Aviation has yet to pass any international standards for safety.

1 Getting to Know Laos

THE LAY OF THE LAND
Comprising 91,429 square miles (147,201 kilometers), roughly the size of Great Britain or the state of Utah, Laos shares borders with China and Myanmar in the north and northwest, Cambodia in the south, Thailand in the west, and Vietnam to the east. It is divided into 16 provinces. Seventy percent of its land is mountain ranges and plateaus, and with an estimated population of just over 5 million, Laos is one of the most sparsely populated countries in Asia. Natural landmarks include the Annamite mountains along the border with Vietnam, and the Mekong River, which flows from China and along Laos's border with Thailand. About 55% of the landscape is pristine tropical forest, sheltering such rare and wild animals as elephants, leopards, the Java mongoose, panthers, gibbons, and black bears.

THE REGIONS IN BRIEF
THE NORTH   Surfaced with forests and mountains, the north is populated mainly by **nomadic hill tribes,** including the Hmong (Meo), Lu, Yao, and Thai Dam. In the upper northwest, seldom explored by travelers, lie provinces Bokeo, Phangsali, and Luang Namtha, home to 39 different ethnic groups. Oudomxai Province is central north. It is a relatively unexplored area with rustic hill tribe villages and fishing towns, ideal for trekking and river tours. **Luang Prabang** Province, in the center of the region, is the major travel destination in Laos. Luang Prabang city, the first Lao capital in 1353, is a UNESCO World Heritage Site with 33 existing temples. To the southeast of Luang Prabang is Xieng Khouang, location of Laos's three highest mountains. The area is pockmarked with bomb craters, remainders of the Vietnam War. Its main attraction is the **Plain of Jars,** site of an imposing archaeological mystery, and the Hmong and Thai Dam hill tribes who live near the capital, Phonsavan. In the far northeast is Hua Phan Province.

VIENTIANE & CENTRAL LAOS   **Vientiane** is both a province and a city. It is the capital of Laos and lies along the Mekong River where it borders Thailand. A bustling town with a goodly number of historic temples for its size, it's also the most modern city in the country, with Internet cafes and high-rise hotels. Its neighboring provinces are Sayaboury to the west, and Bolkhamxay and Khammouane to the southeast.

Laos

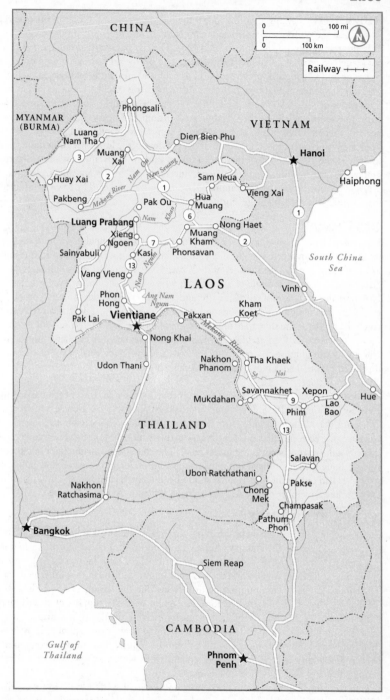

THE SOUTH   Savannakhet Province is the major commercial center in the tropical south (and the center of commerce for the country), due to its proximity to Vietnam. It is also the most populated province in Laos. The city of **Savannakhet** features classic French colonial and Chinese architecture. The **Boloven Plateau,** on the border of Saravane and Champasak provinces, is an agricultural area with teak; tea and arabica and robusta coffee plantations; fruit orchards; and cattle ranches. **Champasak,** at the confluence of the Mekong and Xe Don rivers, has been inhabited since the first century, and was once part of the Cambodian kingdom of Angkor. It is rich in culture and in ancient monuments and temples. Champasak's capital is Pakse, a former French commercial outpost. Far south of the province is the **lower Mekong delta,** also known as the "land of 4,000 islands," with its verdant landscape, flatlands, islands, and waterfalls. Sekong and Attapeu provinces are in the far southeast. They are sparsely populated, save by wild animals, and rarely see tourists. The town of Attapeu is known as "the garden village" for its tree-lined avenues.

LAOS TODAY

Landlocked Laos is one of Southeast Asia's least explored and inhabited countries, and its tourism infrastructure is still in its youthful stages. It is a fantastically unique and exotic place. Though it bears traces of its former French colonists in its buildings, language, and cuisine, it is a one-of-a-kind land where Buddhism holds sway over every facet of daily life. Colorful temples with resident monks are on nearly every corner, in towns small enough to cover on foot and to get to know locals. Travelers can relax and enjoy the sights, as the slow pace of Laos is one of its treasures, or you can enjoy more rigorous adventures such as Mekong river boating, trekking, or elephant riding. All will appreciate glimpses of rare commodities: ancient, traditional ways of life and unspoiled nature. Laos's most precious resource, however, is still its ultra-friendly and attractive citizens.

One of the last official communist governments in the world, Laos began moving to a market economy in 1986. The country's growth jumped to a 7% average through the '90s until the Asian economic crisis destroyed Thailand—Laos's main trade partner. Currently the economy depends heavily on the International Monetary Fund and other bilateral aid sources (Japan is the leader here). The country still maintains a one-party system, along with tight social and information control. It continues to follow political structures laid out by the Vietnamese, and to be influenced economically by Thailand. Laos became a member of ASEAN (Association of Southeast Asian Nations) in 1997.

A LOOK AT THE PAST

Relics suggest that humans have inhabited the area of present-day Laos since prehistoric times. However, the country's history really begins in the sixth century, when it was gradually inhabited by people from the Austro-Thai (also known as Tai) ethnic group migrating from Angkor and the area now known as Yunnan in southern China. Their loose group of communities eventually became the nation of Lang Xang, or "million elephants," under its first king Fa Ngum, with the support of the Khmer kingdom. The capital was established in Luang Prabang. In the 16th century, Vientiane grew in influence, and in 1563 King Setthathirat made it the capital of Laos. Setthathirat was a formidable man, and under him the country flourished, expanding its borders and adding several famous monuments to its landscape, including the That Luang stupa and Wat Phra Keo in Vientiane.

Unfortunately, centuries of internal strife and external warfare were to follow. In 1575, the Burmese entered Vientiane and occupied it for 7 years, while Luang Prabang remained a separate kingdom. The country was reunited under King Nokeo Koumane in 1591 and was prosperous during the 17th century, but in the early 1700s the kingdom partially acceded to Vietnamese rule. Regions opposed to the rule seceded, leaving Laos in three parts: Luang Prabang, Vientiane, and Champasak. Towards the latter end of the century, the Siamese came in and conquered all three, virtually destroying the country, especially Vientiane, when Laos vainly tried to assert its independence under King Anou in 1827.

The French arrived in 1868, hoping to add Laos to its Indochina land holdings and establish a Mekong River trade route. With Siam's acquiescence, Laos officially became a French protectorate in 1893. France ruled indirectly, using Lao royalty as a puppet regime, until the Japanese occupied Indochina briefly during World War II. After the war, Lao again became a French protectorate. This state of affairs wasn't to last long, either, as Lao nationalists, known as the Pathet Lao, allied forces with the communists struggling for independence in Vietnam. Their quest was successful; in 1954 the French granted Laos independence.

This victory wasn't absolute, however. While the communist Pathet Lao temporarily took control of the government, a right-wing coup soon followed, reducing the Pathet Lao to a guerrilla group. Despite cease-fires and international interventions, the infighting continued for years, and eventually Laos was drawn into the Vietnam War in the mid-1960s. The Viet Cong spread its activities into northeastern and southern Laos, establishing transport routes for men and weaponry. The Americans retaliated by dropping more bombs on the country than it had used in all of World War II.

Finally, a cease-fire was declared in 1973, with the Pathet Lao dominating the consensus government. Following the communist victories in Vietnam and Cambodia in 1975, the right-wing government faction succumbed for good; the remaining royals were deposed and never heard from again, and the Pathet Lao emerged victorious. The government was established under strong influence from the Vietnamese, and the first man in power was Kaysone Phomvihane, who is half-Vietnamese.

Not everyone was happy with the communist victory, however. Over the next 5 to 7 years, some 300,000 Laotians fled the country, many to the United States and Thailand. Pockets of rebel groups still remain today, particularly among the Hmong (Meo) hill tribes in the north.

THE LAO PEOPLE & CULTURE

Ethnically, Laotians fall into 68 different groups, only 47 of which are fully researched and identified. All of these fit into one of three categories. The lowlanders are **Lao Loum,** the majority group, who live along the lower Mekong and in Vientiane. The **Lao Theung,** low mountain dwellers, live on mountain slopes, and the **Lao Soung** are the hill tribes or *montagnards.* Eighty percent of the population lives in villages or small hamlets, practicing subsistence farming.

The earliest **Lao religions** were animist, and most hill tribes still practice this belief, often in combination with Buddhism. But Buddhism predominates; 60 to 80% of all Laotians are practicing Theravada Buddhists. In the morning, monks walk the streets collecting food or alms, eagerly given by the Laotians, who believe it will aid them in the next life. Laos worship regularly and can often be seen making temple visits. Most young males spend at least 3 months in a *wat,* or monastery, usually around the time of puberty or before they marry. Impressive **religious art** and **architecture** is expressed in a singular Lao style, particularly the "standing" or "praying for rain" Buddha, upright with hands pointing straight down at the earth.

Music and dance are integral to the Lao character, and you'll get a taste of it during your stay. Folk or *khaen* music is played with a reed mouth organ, often accompanied by a boxed string instrument. The *lamvong* is the national folk dance, where participants dance in concentric circles. You may also witness or take part in a *baci* ceremony, a rite used as a blessing, to perform a marriage, to say welcome or farewell, or to honor achievement. Participants sit in a circle around a bouquet of flowers, or offerings of food, and join hands, saying prayers and blessings. Strings will be tied around the celebrant's wrist, and everyone partakes of a shot or two of *lao lao,* rice wine.

Laos are friendly and easygoing, but you may find it hard to make a close friend. **Language** will usually be a barrier. There is also a sense that the Lao people are just learning how to approach their foreign visitors. Solo travelers probably have the best chance of making an entree into society. While Laos suffered brutally throughout its colonial history and most horrifically during the Vietnam War, the Lao people want to move on to peace and prosperity rather than dwell on the past. It's very unlikely that an American will be approached with recrimination. But memories are still fresh: The Lao people still deal with war fallout literally and figuratively, a result of the unexploded bombs (or UXO) that litter 50% of the country.

ETIQUETTE

The Lao are generally tolerant people, but there are a few things to keep in mind. First, upon entering a temple or wat, you must always remove your shoes. There will usually be a sign, but a good rule of thumb is to take them off before mounting the last flight of stairs. You should also take off your shoes before entering a private home, unless told otherwise.

Dress modestly. It's unusual to see bare Lao skin above the elbow or even above the mid-calf. Longer shorts and even sleeveless tops are permissible for foreigners of both sexes, but short shorts or skirts and bare bosoms and navels will cause stares and possibly offence, especially in a wat.

Men and women should avoid public displays of affection.

Women should never try to shake hands with or even hand something directly to a monk; monks are not permitted to touch women, or even to speak directly to them anywhere but inside a wat. (In a wat, they'll chat you up like mad.)

The **traditional greeting** is called the *nop* or *wai.* To perform this, place your hands together at chest level as if you are praying, but do not touch your body. Bow your head to your hands, and your upper body slightly. The nop is also used to say thank you and goodbye. Its use is fading in the big cities, but return the greeting if you're given it. In a business setting, a handshake is also appropriate.

The head is considered the most sacred part of the body, and the feet the lowliest. Therefore, do not casually touch another person's head, no matter how much you want to, and don't sit with your legs crossed or otherwise point your feet at something or someone. As in most cultures, pointing with the finger is also considered rude. If you are seated on the floor, men may sit with legs crossed, but women should tuck them to one side.

In interpersonal relations with the Lao, it helps to remember that many are strong Buddhists and take (or try to take) a gentle approach to human relationships. A person showing violence or ill temper would be regarded with surprise and disapproval. A gentle approach will take you farther here. For example, Lao are simply not that interested in haggling. One or two go-rounds are usually enough. Should you have a disagreement of any kind, keep your cool. Gentle persistence with a smile is the key.

Finally, it is considered polite to accept any food or drink offered and to at least have a taste.

LANGUAGE

The **Lao language** resembles Thai, with familiar tones and sounds found in each, yet while some vocabulary words may cross over, the two tongues—spoken and written— are quite distinct. However, many Lao understand Thai (learned from school texts and

TV), so if you've picked up some words and phrases in Thailand, they'll still be useful here. Thankfully, many people in Vientiane and Luang Prabang speak **English,** and older citizens will usually be able to speak **French. Russian** and **Chinese** are also occasionally spoken.

Like Thai, Lao has no officially recognized method of Roman alphabet transliteration. As a result, even town and street names have copious spelling irregularities, so for the vocabulary below we have chosen to list only phonetic pronunciations. Most Lao will understand you, even without tones, and will very much appreciate your efforts to speak their language.

When trying to figure out the correct pronunciation of certain names, it's helpful to remember that the original transliteration of Lao was done by Francophones, so consider the French pronunciation when faced with a new word. For example, in Vientiane (pronounced wee-en-*chan*), the wide central avenue spelled Lane Xang is pronounced *Lahn Sahng.* Also in Vientiane, Mixay sounds like *Mee-sigh.* Phonexay is *pawn-sigh.* It takes a while, but catches on.

USEFUL LAO PHRASES
Greetings

Hello	sa bai dee
Good bye	laa kawn
Thank you	khawp chai
Thank you very much	khawp chai lai lai
You're welcome/never mind	baw pen nyahng
How are you?	Sa bai dee baw?
Yes	chow/ur
No	baw/baw men
Excuse me	khaw thoot (rhymes with "put")
Where is the toilet?	soo-um yoo sai?
I don't understand.	Bo kow chai.
How much?	Tao dai?
Can you make it cheaper?	Lut dai baw?
Help!	Sue-wee dah!
Call the police!	Sue-wee un tam luat dah!
I need a/an . . .	khaw-ee tawng kahn . . .

2 Planning a Trip to Laos
VISITOR INFORMATION

The Lao Tourism Authority serves as more of an administrative arm of the government than that of an information service for visitors—as proven in their outdated collection of brochures. These color pamphlets merely provide broad brush-stroke descriptions of major attractions with absolutely no practical information. If you're still interested, you can try to obtain a few through the **National Tourism Authority of Lao P.D.R.,** 08/02 Lane Xang Ave., P.O. Box 2511, Vientiane, Lao P.D.R. (☎ **021/212-248** or 212-251; fax 021/212-769). Don't hold your breath for speedy delivery.

Lao Tourism Company (☎ **021/216-671**), the government's official travel services operation, provides limited visitor services. In addition to organizing tours in and around Vientiane city and province, they can help obtain visa extensions and offer advice on travel around the country. Write to the same address as the National Tourism Authority (above).

The official Web site for **Visit Lao Years 1999–2000, http://visit-laos.com**, is sponsored by both the Lao government and private organizations. Don't be deceived by the name; though 1999 and 2000 have passed, the information is still relevant. This user-friendly site is as detailed and as accurate as my own first-hand research. For current domestic and international news and government affairs, log on to **http://laoembassy.com**, sponsored and maintained by the Lao Embassy in Washington, DC.

ORGANIZED TOURS

In chapter 3, "Planning a Trip to Southeast Asia," we've outlined major tour operators who organize trips to Laos in addition to other Southeast Asian Destinations. Most arrange tours throughout the region, though they can plan a trip to Laos only.

It is often recommended that traveling in Laos is best done with a group. If you value independence and flexibility, you can certainly travel on your own; however, once you arrive in Laos, consider booking some arrangements through an agency— especially if your plan is to venture outside Vientiane or Luang Prabang. Getting around underdeveloped Laos can be difficult and expensive (see "Getting Around," below), and if you can hook up with a minivan or tour bus, so much the better. In addition, a tour will take care of logistics for fun things like boat cruises and raft and elephant rides. Also, it can be a pain in the neck to book hotels on your own. There will inevitably be language problems, and it will cost you a mint and take a lot of time to phone around. If you're traveling during the dry season like most people, rooms can get tight, so play it safe.

The most established and widely represented tour operators provide basic, mainstream tours to most provinces within the country for either short trips or extended visits, including in and around Vientiane, Luang Prabang, Xieng Khouang (Plain of Jars), and Champasak, plus trips to visit Laos's hill tribes. You can make arrangements with these companies from home prior to your trip, or once you've arrived in the country. Like most tour services, these companies will take the hassle out of your trip but will cost more than a do-it-yourself itinerary, the one exception being hotel rates. Prices between companies seem comparable.

- **Inter-Lao Tourism,** 07/073 Luang Prabang Rd., P.O. Box 2912, Vientiane, Lao P.D.R., ☎ **021/214-832;** fax 021/216-306; e-mail: inttour@laotel.com
- **Lane Xang Travel,** Pangkham Road, P.O. Box 4452, Vientiane, Lao P.D.R., ☎ **021/212-469;** fax 021/215-804
- **Sodetour,** Fa Ngum Street, Vientiane, Lao P.D.R., ☎ **021/216-314;** fax 021/216-313

ENTRY REQUIREMENTS

Citizens of every Western country need a valid passport and visa to visit Laos. For convenience's sake, it's best to obtain a visa prior to your trip at one of the Lao Embassy locations listed below. At an embassy, the going rate for a 15-day visa is US$35, and you'll have to wait at least 5 days for processing. Some embassies are open to granting a 30-day visa if you ask. In addition, travel agents all over Southeast Asia offer visa services—the bigger agencies are very reputable. For a fee they'll process your application and help it jump over any bureaucratic hurdles.

Laos offers three official entry sites where visas are granted upon arrival. If you're flying to Vientiane or Luang Prabang or traveling over the Friendship Bridge from Nong Khai, citizens from most Western countries can apply for a visa at the arrival checkpoint for US$30. Call your nearest Lao embassy to find out if you qualify.

Once in Laos you can extend your visa up to 30 days. To apply, head for the Immigration Office in Vientiane on Khoun Boulum Street off Lane Xang Avenue opposite

Travel Insurance

To find the **Nahiku Coffee Shop, Smoked Fish Stand,** and **Ti Gallery,** watch for mile marker 28 on the Hana Highway (no phone). Pick up locally made baked goods at the small coffee shop, then move on to the main attraction: the cast-iron smoker, which puts out smoked and grilled chicken, beef, and fresh local fish. The teriyaki-based marinade, made by the owner, adds a special touch to the fish (ono, ahi, marlin) and meats, sold for $3 a skewer.

---

the Morning Market. However, I recommend letting **Lao Tourism,** 08/02 Lane Xang Ave., adjacent to the National Tourism Authority (☎ **021/216-671**), handle it. They charge the same, US$2 for each additional day, but save you the time and hassle of dealing with civil servants yourself.

Overstaying your visa will cost you a fine of US$5 a day upon exiting the country.

LAOS EMBASSY LOCATIONS OVERSEAS

In the U.S.: Embassy of the Lao People's Democratic Republic, 2222 S St. NW, Washington, D.C., 20008 (☎ 202/332-6416; fax 202/332-4923; www.laoembassy. com); or the Lao P.D.R. Permanent Mission to the United Nations, 317 E. 51st St., New York, NY 10022 (☎ **212/832-2734;** fax 212/750-0039; www.laoembassy.com/ laomission/index.html).

In Australia: 1 Dalmain Crescent, O'Malley, Canberra, ACT 2606 (☎ **02/6286-4595;** fax 02/6290-1910).

CUSTOMS REGULATIONS

You may bring 500 cigarettes, 100 cigars, or 500g of tobacco; 1 liter of alcohol; two bottles of wine; and unlimited amounts of money, all for personal use, into Laos without taxation or penalty. Not that the Customs officials here do much, if any, searching. However, if you purchase silver or copper items during your stay, you may be required to pay duty upon exiting Laos, according to their weight. Antiques, especially Buddha images or parts thereof, are not permitted to leave the country.

MONEY

The **kip** (pronounced *keep*), the official Lao unit of currency, comes in denominations of 5,000, 2,000, 1,000, 500, 100, 50, 20, 10 and 5. Consider the exchange rate at the time of writing, US$1 = 7,600 kip—*making the largest unit of currency valued at not even one buck!* Translation: Be prepared to handle bricks of Lao cash when you exchange foreign currency.

CURRENCY EXCHANGE & RATES   At press time, the exchange rate was US$1 to 7,600 kip. I've used this rate as the standard for all currency conversions in this chapter.

Laos is very much a cash country, especially outside Vientiane. Virtually all hotel and guesthouse rates, upmarket restaurant menus, transportation charges, and expensive purchases are quoted in U.S. dollars, so it's good to be able to convert in your head quickly. For these purchases, payment is always accepted in either U.S. dollars, Thai baht, or Lao kip, so it doesn't always pay to convert all your currency into cumbersome wads of local scraps. For smaller purchases, local transportation, and pocket money, you can exchange currency at Wattay International Airport, in hotels, in banks, and on the black market, with the rate of exchange worst at hotels and best on the black market.

Traveler's checks in U.S. dollars and other major currencies are accepted in all banks in Vientiane and Luang Prabang, and some in Xieng Khouang and Pakse, but very rarely by vendors; even the American Express travel representative won't take them. In other provinces it's best to carry cash in U.S. dollars, Thai baht, or Lao kip. **Credit cards** are accepted only at major hotels or tour operators (Visa is the most widely accepted). Lao Aviation has recently begun to accept American Express, MasterCard, and Visa. You can get cash advances from your Visa card at **La Banque pour le Commerce Extérieur Lao (BCEL),** and at **Lane Xang Bank** branches in larger towns throughout the country.

LOST/STOLEN CREDIT CARDS & TRAVELER'S CHECKS   To report a lost or stolen American Express card, contact the AmEx representative in Vientiane, **Diethelm Travel,** Setthathirat Road, Namphou Square, Vientiane (☎ **021/213-833** or 215-920). If you're upcountry, you can get help from one of Diethelm's regional offices. Addresses and telephone numbers are provided in each city's corresponding section. Your card can be replaced within 3 working days.

To report a lost or stolen Visa or MasterCard you'll have to contact their customer service hot lines in Bangkok, the closest hot lines available from Laos. To report a lost or stolen credit card, you can call these service lines: **American Express** (☎ **66-2/273-0022**); **Diners Club** (☎ **66-2/238-3660**); **JCB** (Japanese Credit Bank) (☎ **66-2/631-1938**); **MasterCard** ☎ **66-2/232-2039**); and **Visa** (☎ **66-2/256-7324**).

WHEN TO GO

PEAK SEASON   High season for tourism is November through March and the month of August, when weather conditions are favorable (but accommodations run at full capacity and transportation can be overbooked).

CLIMATE   Laos's topical climate ushers in a wet monsoon season lasting from early May through October followed by a dry season from November to April. In Vientiane, average temperatures range from 71°F in January to 84°F in April. The northern regions, which include Xieng Khouang, get chilly from November to February, and can approach freezing temperatures at night in mountainous areas. Beginning in mid-February, temperatures gradually climb, and April can see temperatures over 100°F.

In order to avoid the rain and heat, the best time to visit the south is probably November through February. In the mountains of the north, May to July means still-comfortable temperatures. The monsoon season begins a bit later there as well.

PUBLIC HOLIDAYS   The major public holidays in Laos are: New Year's Day (January 1), Lunar New Year (mid-April), International Labor Day (May 1), That Luang Festival (mid-November, in Vientiane), and National Day (December 2). Businesses and government offices close for these holidays, but restaurants remain open. There are a few important festivals that you may want to catch. The **That Luang Festival** in Vientiane, during the full moon in early November, draws the faithful countrywide and from nearby Thailand. The pre-dawn gathering of thousands joins in a ceremonial offering and group prayer, and then a procession. For days afterwards, a combined trade fair and carnival offers handicrafts and flowers, games, concerts, and dance shows. Although the entire country celebrates the **Lunar New Year (Pimai Lao),** the Luang Prabang festivities include a procession, a fair, a sand-castle competition on the Mekong, a Miss New Year pageant, folk performances, and cultural shows. It's held in mid-April. Make sure you're booked and confirmed in hotels before you go. At local temples, worshippers in brightly colored silks greet the dawn on **Buddhist Lent** (Boun Khao Phansaa) by offering gifts to the monks and pouring water into the ground as a gesture of offering to their ancestors. Lent will last 3 months. The

Vientiane Boat Race Festival (Vientiane, Luang Prabang, and Savannakhet) is held the second weekend in October to mark the end of Buddhist Lent. Men and women compete in groups of 50, rowing long boats along the Mekong to the beating of drums. On **National Day,** the entire country celebrates a public holiday, while in Vientiane, you'll find parades and dancing at That Luang temple (Dec. 2).

HEALTH CONCERNS
VACCINATIONS
Laos does not require any special vaccinations to enter; however, you're recommended to have the vaccinations discussed in chapter 3 when you are going to visit Laos or any other Southeast Asian nation.

HEALTH PRECAUTIONS
In chapter 3 we discuss the major health issues that affect travelers to Southeast Asia and recommend precautions for avoiding the most common diseases.

No water in Laos is considered potable so stick with bottled water (and avoid ice), readily available from vendors all over the country. Also, Lao cuisine uses many fresh ingredients and garnishes, and condiments made from dried fish that may have been stored under unsanitary conditions. Exercise caution when eating from roadside and market stalls and smaller local restaurants.

In Laos, medical facilities are scarce and rudimentary. Emergency medical facilities exist in Vientiane, but outside the capital you'll require medical evacuation. Contact information is provided under "Fast Facts: Laos," below.

GETTING THERE
When planning travel to Laos, it's important to remember that you're not permitted to cross Laos's borders with Myanmar and Cambodia.

BY PLANE   Bangkok provides Laos's main link with global air routes; however, with regular flights from neighboring Vietnam, Cambodia, and Myanmar, it's easy to hop a direct flight from anywhere in Indochina. See each individual country chapter for carriers to the countries mentioned above.

Lao Aviation, the national carrier, coordinates international flights from its head office in Vientiane (3 Pangkham Rd., P.O. Box 4169; ☎ **021/212-051** international; www.lao-aviation.com). Lao Aviation connects Vientiane with Bangkok, Hanoi, Ho Chi Minh City, Phnom Penh, and Siem Reap. It's also possible to fly from Bangkok or Chiang Mai direct to Luang Prabang. Other convenient routes link Cambodia (Phnom Penh and Siem Reap) and Pakse in the south.

Thai Airways International, Angel Air (from Thailand), Vietnam Airlines, Royal Air Camboge, and Myanmar Airways all provide service to Laos.

If you leave Laos by air, keep 76,008 kip (US$10) tucked away safely for the **international departure tax,** paid at the airport as you pass through the immigration checkpoint.

BY TRAIN   The State Railway of Thailand's northeastern line originates at Bangkok's Hua Lampong Railway Station (☎ **02/223-7010** or 02/223-7020). Running north, it connects many major provincial capitals in Isan, Thailand's northeastern region, before terminating at Nong Khai across the Mekong from Vientiane. Once you arrive in Nong Khai, you'll need to hire a tuk-tuk from the train station to the immigration checkpoint at the Thai-Lao Friendship Bridge (about 30B or US$0.70 for the trip). The checkpoint is open daily from 8:30am to 5pm. Once across to Laos, you'll need to grab a taxi to Vientiane (which is actually not *exactly* across from Nong Khai). It should cost you about 38,004 kip (US$5).

BY BUS   From Vietnam a lot of people chose to take the bus overnight from Danang or Hué to Savannakhet. In Danang the bus leaves at 7pm every Monday, Wednesday, Thursday, and Sunday. Talk to **Vietnamtourism** (83 Nguyen Thi Minh Khai; ☎ **0511/823-660**); the cost is 190,019 kip (US$25). From Hue the bus leaves at 7pm on Tuesday and Saturday. Contact Huong Giang Tourist Company (17 Le Loi St.; ☎ **054/832-220**) for more information.

BY BOAT   Thailand and Laos maintain three official border checkpoints (not including the Friendship Bridge) along the Mekong between the two countries. The Mekong/border crossing between Thailand's Chiang Khong (near Chiang Mai) and Laos's Houeixay has proven wildly popular in the past few years with folks who want to float downriver from northern Thailand to Luang Prabang while taking in all the Mekong sights.

Visas can be secured in Chiang Mai, Chiang Rai, and Chiang Khong from travel agents and guesthouses. These are usually good for 14 days only. Once you reach Houeixay, book the passenger boat that departs every morning (arrive early!). The trip will cost 85,000 kip (US$11.18) and take about 1½ days to complete. You'll stay overnight in a local village along the way. Be prepared for all kinds of discomfort, and a chance to take home a unique traveler's yarn.

Additional crossing points along the Mekong are between Mukhdahan (Thailand) and Tha Khaek (Laos), and between Ubon Ratchathani (Thailand) and Chong Mek (Laos).

GETTING AROUND

Laos's underdeveloped infrastructure begs for endless cautions. The U.S. Department of State warns travelers against using Lao Aviation flights for unnecessary travel due to the airline's dubious history of plane maintenance. Laos has no railroads, and of the country's highway system only 40% is paved (and I use the term paved *very* loosely). Furthermore, a couple roads along the major tourism corridor are closed to foreigners as a result of "bandit activity" (read: guerilla insurgency). Travel along the Mekong is long and tiring and subject to seasonal conditions. And there is the nasty business of the aforementioned bombings in the capital and elsewhere. That said, despite these troubles, plenty of visitors continue to hop all over the country each year. If your heart is set on Laos, you will have to take your chances. However, the rewards are terrific.

Air travel presents the fastest and most convenient way to get between destinations. In fact, if you plan a trip to Xieng Khouang to see the Plain of Jars, you'll have no choice but to fly due to dangerous road conditions. Talk to Lao Aviation at their head office in Vientiane (3 Pangkham Rd.; ☎ **021/212-058;** www.lao-aviation.com) about domestic routes linking Vientiane, Luang Prabang, Xieng Khouang, Pakse, and other places around the country. Ticket prices range from about 266,027 kip (US$35) Vientiane/Xieng Khouang to 722,072 kip (US$95) Vientiane/Pakse. Lao Aviation

---

Warning: Watch Out for Unexploded Bombs

Laos is, per square inch, the most heavily bombed country in the world to date, thanks to the Vietnam War. Certain parts of the country, in the north around the Plain of Jars, and in the south around the Ho Chi Minh Trail, are laden with unexploded bombs (or unexploded ordnance—UXO), some of which are as small as a fist. There is not much of a risk to tourists, provided you avoid wandering through the unexplored jungle in risky areas and don't pick anything up. If you're traveling with children, warn them and keep an eye on them in those areas.

accepts payment in U.S. dollars, traveler's checks, Lao kip, American Express, Master-Card, and Visa. And keep in mind, for each domestic flight you take there's a **domestic departure tax** of 1,000 kip (US$0.13) payable at the airport before you board your plane.

If you have the cash to spare and don't want to waste time with Lao Aviation domestic flights, **Lao Westcoast Helicopter** (☎ **021/512-023**) will be more than happy to charter a helicopter to take you where you need to go at your convenience. You'll have to negotiate the fare for your itinerary as prices will vary on many factors.

Public buses connect Laos; however, what the Lao consider a "bus" may to the rest of the world be little more than a flatbed truck with benches. While routes from Vientiane north to Luang Prabang and south to Savannakhet are handled by private companies with relatively comfortable buses (cushioned seats and air-conditioning), other major routes sport public buses that make that old ratty grammar school bus of yours seem like limousine service. Once you get out to less populated areas, service is sketchy and really uncomfortable.

One alternative is to hire a **private vehicle,** a car with a driver (self-drive vehicles are virtually impossible to find). The most popular routes for car hire are the 8-hour trip up to Luang Prabang from Vientiane, or shorter trips throughout Vientiane Province. Also handy, car rentals provide the most convenient way around the southern parts around Pakse. Find contacts for private vehicle hires in each corresponding section to follow.

Finally, there's the magical Mekong. Sadly, Laos doesn't have any quality river transport with any sort of comfort. Backpackers are all over the **river barges** that ply between Chiang Khong in Thailand and Luang Prabang. If you're floating downriver, the trip is an interesting day and a half, full of great scenery and crazy travel companions. However, the chug upriver against the current takes about 3½ days. Trust me, you'll be homicidal after the first day. The alternative is a **speedboat** hire between the two stops, which gets you there much faster but is even more noisy and uncomfortable than the barge. It is possible to hop cargo boats between Vientiane and Luang Prabang, but they're just that . . . cargo boats.

Navigating on foot through Laos's small cities is easy. You can use **taxis** and **tuktuks** (covered carts behind motorbikes) in Vientiane, Luang Prabang, and Pakse, or rent **bicycles** and **motorbikes** in Vientiane and Luang Prabang.

TIPS ON ACCOMMODATIONS

Book your hotel early during the peak season (November through February), using travel agents and tour operators as necessary. Language difficulties can make booking outside of Vientiane almost impossible to do yourself. Don't expect discounts, either, as facilities aren't plentiful and occupancy is usually high. That said, you'll be generally happy with the standards and prices you'll encounter.

TIPS ON DINING

You'll very much enjoy the Lao cuisine, though some accuse it of being "Thai by way of China." Try it at real restaurants whenever possible, as the street stands aren't up to those in neighboring countries. You'll also find decent food of other cuisine, including French, Thai, and Italian.

TIPS ON SHOPPING

You'll undoubtedly leave with a few pieces of handwoven Lao textiles, handcrafted silver, and other lovely objects. Many things are one-of-a-kind, so if you see something you like, get it. Remember that the Lao don't particularly like bargaining, and a "no" usually means no.

Fast Facts: Laos

American Express   The country's one AmEx representative is **Diethelm Travel,** Namphou Square, Setthathirat Road, Vientiane, ☎ **021/215-920** or 213-833. *Good to know:* Diethelm will not cash American Express traveler's checks, and for lost or stolen TCs, they'll have to make all arrangements through the representative in Bangkok. On the other hand, they can handle the American Express letter holding service, and will perform emergency check cashing services.

Business Hours   With a few exceptions, hours tend to be 8:30am to noon and 1:30 to 5pm weekdays; 8am to noon Saturdays; closed Sundays. Restaurants are open from about 11am to 2pm and 6 to 10pm daily, although many are closed for lunch on Sundays.

Doctors & Dentists   Medical care in Laos is primitive by Western standards. For major problems, most foreigners choose to hop the border to Thailand for the Nong Khai Wattana General Hospital just over the Friendship Bridge. In an emergency call ☎ **66-42/465-201.** Vientiane has one International Medical Clinic, Mahosot Hospital, on Fa Ngum Road at the Mekong riverbank (☎ **021/ 214-022**). It's open 24 hours. Facilities are very basic. The doctors speak French but little English. For emergency evacuation call **Lao Westcoast Helicopter Company** in Vientiane at ☎ **021/512-023.**

Drug Laws   Opium is openly grown in northeast Laos and is easily available, as is marijuana. Neither are legal, and although you may see many travelers indulging, it is highly recommended that you don't. You may face high fines or jail if you're caught.

Electricity   Laos runs on 220-volt electrical currents. Plugs are two-pronged, with either round or flat prongs. If you're coming from the U.S. and you must bring electrical appliances, bring your own converter and adapter. Outside of Vientiane and Luang Prabang electricity is sketchy, sometimes available for a few hours a day. A surge protector is a must for laptops.

Embassies   U.S.: Thatdam Bathrolonie Road (☎ **021/212-582;** fax 021/ 212-584). **Australia:** Nehru Road, Bane Phonsay (☎ **021/413-600**). The Australian embassy also assists Canada, New Zealand, and U.K. nationals.

Emergencies   In Vientiane, for police dial ☎ **991;** fire ☎ **190;** ambulance ☎ **195.** For medical evacuation, call **Lao Westcoast Helicopter Company** at ☎ **021/512-023.**

Internet/E-mail   You can find Internet access in Vientiane, Luang Prabang, and Pakse, but not at Phonsavan. I've listed Internet cafes in each city. Prices are very cheap, and connections are generally not too slow.

Language   Lao is the major language, and many people in Vientiane and Luang Prabang speak **English.** If you've picked up Thai, feel free to use it here, as many understand it. A rare few also speak some Russian and French. See "Language," above, for more information.

Liquor Laws   There are no real liquor laws in Laos, but most bars refuse to admit patrons under the age of 18. Bars usually close around midnight.

Post Offices/Mail   A letter or postcard should take about 10 days to reach the U.S. Overseas postage runs about 800 kip (US$0.11) for 100 grams, up to 2,300 kip (US$0.30) for 500 grams. Postcards are 900 kip (US$0.12). The mail service

Telephone Dialing Info at a Glance

- **To place a call from your home country to Laos,** dial the international access code (011 in the U.S., 0011 in Australia, 0170 in New Zealand, 00 in the U.K.), plus the country code (856), plus the city or area code (21 for Vientiane, 71 for Luang Prabang) and the 6-digit phone number (for example, 011 + 856 + 21/000-000).

- **To place a call within Laos,** dial the city or area code preceded by a zero, then the 6-digit number (for example, 021/000-000). A local call costs 45 kip (US$0.01) a minute from a phone booth. You must use a phone card, which you can buy at the post office, the telephone office, and mini-marts.

- **To place a direct international call from Laos,** dial the international access code (**00**) plus the country code, the area or city code, and the number (for example, 00 + 1 + 212/000-0000).

- **International country codes** are as follows: Australia 61, Burma 95, Cambodia 855, Canada 1, Hong Kong 852, Indonesia 62, Malaysia 60, New Zealand 64, the Philippines 63, Singapore 65, U.K. 44, U.S. 1, Vietnam 84.

is reportedly unreliable, however, so if you're sending something important, use an express mail service. FedEx and DHL have offices in the major cities.

Safety   Buddhist Laos is an extremely safe country by any standard. Violent or even petty crime is not a big risk for tourists here. Quiet Vientiane isn't much of a threat, except for the traffic—there are few lights, and because traffic isn't all that heavy it moves very, very quickly. There have been rare instances of robbery or rape in remote areas. Solo travelers should take care when going too far off the beaten track, even on a day hike. Some of the country's highways, like Route 13 near Kasi and Route 7 in the northeast, are at a very high risk for rebel and bandit attacks. Check with your consulate before doing any overland travel. Of course, petty crime does exist. Watch your belongings and don't leave valuables in your hotel rooms, particularly in smaller guesthouses.

When trekking in the north or in the south around the Ho Chi Minh Trail, even in well-visited areas such as the Plain of Jars, **beware of unexploded bombs.** Don't stray into remote areas, and don't touch anything on the ground.

Telephone & Fax   The international country code for Laos is 856. Phone rates during my most recent visit: 1 minute to the U.S. 23,200 kip (US$3.05); to Canada 20,100 kip (US$2.64); to Australia 7800 kip (US$1.03); to New Zealand 15,500 kip (US$2.04); and to the U.K. 20,100 kip (US$2.64). Buy a stored-value phone card at any post office or telecom center to use at international phone booths outside. Most newer hotels have International Direct Dialing at surcharges of about 10%. Collect calls are impossible anywhere, and the long-distance companies haven't made it to Laos yet. See the "Telephone Dialing Info at a Glance" box for more information.

Local calls are 90 kip (US$0.01) per minute. Like the international phone booths, local phone booths also accept only pre-paid phone cards. Laos has no coins.

Time Zone   Laos is 7 hours ahead of Greenwich Mean Time, in the same zone as Bangkok. That makes it 12 hours ahead of the U.S. and 3 hours behind Sydney.

Tipping   Tipping has arrived in Laos, particularly in Vientiane. Feel free to tip bellhops, chauffeurs, and tour guides, and to leave 5 to 10% or round up your bill in upscale restaurants. Foreign currency, especially U.S. dollars, is appreciated.

Toilets   You'll find toilets or *hawng nam* in hotels, restaurants, tourist attractions, and even wats. Only in the very newest hotels will you find Western-style sit-down toilets, but squat-style toilets (if they have clean floors) are actually more hygienic. Bring your own paper and sanitary hand wipes. You'll notice a bowl and a pail of water nearby for flushing. Throw two to three buckets of water into the toilet.

Water   There is no potable water in Laos. Drink only boiled or bottled water, which is available on virtually every street corner. Don't take ice with your drinks, especially outside of Vientiane. You may even want to consider brushing your teeth with boiled or bottled water.

3 Vientiane

Vientiane (wee-en-*chan*) has to be one of the world's most unique capitals. Like many cities in developing countries, on arrival it's a shock. Few expect the capital of a whole country to have maybe six paved roads total. A local resident laughed at my observation, "Six? *Which six?*" It's a reminder that not only is Laos one of the poorest countries in Asia, but in the world as well.

Vientiane's small scale means you'll be constantly confronted by startling incongruities. For while it has a more than a 1,200-year history as a cosmopolitan center, today it is still a dusty town with a population of about 250,000. Many of the residents are monks in vermilion or mustard-colored robes, attending to their business at wats whose peaked roofs still dominate the local skyline. Crumbling French colonial mansions house the likes of the World Bank, International Monetary Fund, and every UN agency known to man. The airport still uses the grab-your-bag-off-the-cart method of dispensing luggage and you can ride to town in a motorized cart. At the same time, the city has Internet cafes and advertising agencies, embassies and investment advisors. It has luxury business hotels with swimming pools and gourmet restaurants with fine wines, and the streets are crowded with big, gleaming utility vehicles.

As far as tourism goes, the city was ransacked by the Vietnamese in 1828, so it lacks some of the ancient history you find in the former capital of Luang Prabang. But its temples have been beautifully reconstructed, and there are some nice colonial buildings still standing: **That Luang** is the pre-eminent temple in the country and scene of a huge festival every November; the **Patuxay victory monument** is a peculiarly Lao version of the Arc de Triomphe; the **Morning Market** has a full city block of goods to explore; and the **Mekong** glows pink at sunset. It is worth a stay of several days to take it all in and enjoy Vientiane's laid-back atmosphere while it lasts.

VISITOR INFORMATION

For the size of the country and what you'll want to do, you actually have a good choice of agents within the country. Although Laos is heavily promoting eco-tourism, there aren't many operators who will take you off the beaten track. For assistance with that, you'll have to look for agents nearer home.

- **Diethelm Travel Laos.** Namphou Square, Setthathirat Road, P.O. Box 2657, Vientiane, Lao P.D.R. (☎ **021/215-920;** fax 021/216-294). Monday to Friday 8am to noon, 1:30 to 5pm; Saturday 8am to noon. These are the most professional folks in town and they can help you arrange deluxe personalized trips or small necessities like bus tickets.

Living Without Street Addresses

You'll notice that many of the businesses in Vientiane don't seem to have street addresses. The city is so small they hardly need them. Note also that transliterations of Laos street names differ from map to map, and that "thanon" simply means street.

- **Sodetour.** 114 Quai Fa Ngum, P.O. Box 70, Vientiane, Lao P.D.R. (☎ **021/ 216-314;** fax 021/216-313). Experienced and reputable.
- **Inter-Lao Tourisme.** Setthathirat Road, P.O. Box 2912, Vientiane, Lao P.D.R. (☎ **021/214-232;** fax 021/216-306). Moderately helpful.
- **Lao Tourism.** 08/02 Lane Xang Ave., P.O. Box 2511, Vientiane, Lao P.D.R. (☎ **021/216-671;** fax 021/212-013). Government-owned, but offers some good rafting, trekking, and elephant-riding programs.

GETTING THERE

Vientiane is Laos's major international airport. For information on arriving by plane or by train, see "Getting There" in "Planning a Trip to Laos," above.

If you're arriving via Wattay International Airport in Vientiane, a taxi to town is around 30,000 kip (US$3.95) tops. Don't let the driver rip you off.

GETTING AROUND

The city lies entirely on the east side of the Mekong River (the other side is Thailand). The main streets, running parallel to each other, are Samsenthai and Setthathirat. The heart of the city is Nam Phu fountain, and many of the directions in this chapter are given in relation to it.

Central Vientiane is easily covered on foot. You can also hire a **tuk-tuk,** a covered cart behind a motorbike, or a **jumbo,** a bigger version of same. They charge about 5,000 kip to 10,000 kip (US$0.66–US$1.32) around town. You should settle the price before you ride. **Motorcycles** can be rented for 60,806 kip (US$8) or so a day— look around the Nam Phu Fountain. **Bicycles** are available at Raintrees Bookstore and guesthouses at 7,600 kip to 15,201 kip (US$1–US$2) per day. You can also rent a car with a driver for 456,046 kip (US$60) a day. Call **Asia Vehicle Rental,** 08/3 Lane Xang Ave., beside Thai Farmers Bank (☎ **021/217-493;** e-mail: avr@loxinfo.co.th).

Fast Facts: Vientiane

Banks/Currency Exchange   Banque Pour Le Commerce Extérieur Lao is on Pangkahm Street down by the river (☎ **021/213-200**). You can exchange money there in all major currencies and withdraw cash on Visa cards. You can also exchange money at Banque Setthathirat, near Wat Mixay. They are open Monday to Friday 8:30am to 3:30pm. Other banks line Lane Xang Avenue.

Internet/E-mail   PlaNet Online is at 201 Setthathirat Rd. about a block north-west of the Nam Phu Fountain (☎ **021/218-972;** e-mail: planet@laonet.net). The cost is 228 kip (US$0.03) per minute and depending on how long you're online.

Emergencies   For police dial ☎ 991; fire ☎ 190; ambulance ☎ 195. For medical evacuation, call Lao Westcoast Helicopter company at ☎ **021/512-023.**

Post Office/Mail   The General Post Office is on the corner of Thanon Khou Vieng and Lane Xang Avenue, opposite the Morning Market. Hours are

Vientiane

ACCOMMODATIONS ■
Anou Hotel **3**
Asian Pavillion Hotel **22**
Lane-Xang Hotel **18**
Lao Plaza Hotel **9**
Novotel Hotel Vientiane **1**
Royal Dokmaideng Hotel **26**
Settha Palace Hotel **8**
Tai-Pan Hotel **5**

DINING ◆
Arawan **29**
Healthy & Fresh Bakery **15**
The Hong Kong Restaurant **10**
Just For Fun Restaurant **17**
Kua Lao **21**
L'Opera **12**
La Belle Epoque **8**
Lo Stivale **14**
Nazim Restaurant **6**
Restaurant Namphou **11**

ATTRACTIONS ●
Buddha Park **31**
Morning Market **24**
Lao National Museum **6**
Phra That Luang **28**
Patuxay (Victory Monument) **27**
That Dam (Black Stupa) **23**
Wat Ho Phra Keo **19**
Wat Ong Teu **4**
Wat Si Muang **30**
Wat Si Saket **20**

OTHER ●
Diethelm Travel **13**
Immigration Office **25**
Lao Aviation **16**

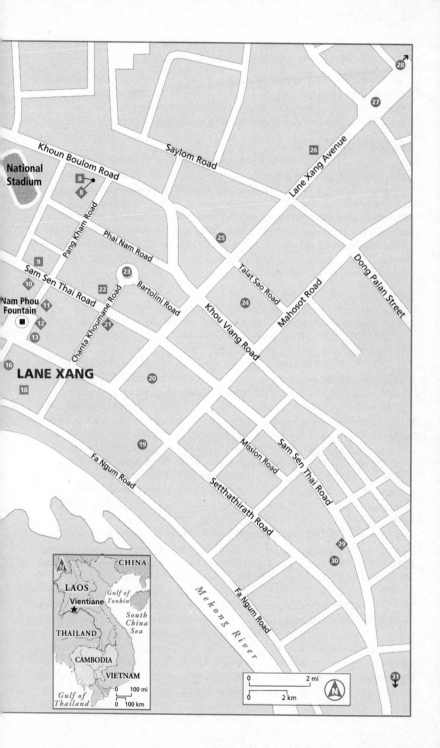

National Stadium

Khoun Boulom Road

Saylom Road

Lane Xang Avenue

8
8

26

27

28

Pang Kham Road

Phai Nam Road

25

Talat Sao Road

Mahosot Road

Dong Palan Street

9

Sam Sen Thai Road

10

23

22

Bartolini Road

Nam Phou Fountain

11

12

13

Chanta Khoumane Road

21

Khou Viang Road

24

16

LANE XANG

18

20

19

Fa Ngum Road

Mission Road

Sam Sen Thai Road

Setthathirath Road

29

30

CHINA

LAOS

Gulf of Tonkin

Vientiane

South China Sea

THAILAND

CAMBODIA

VIETNAM

Gulf of Thailand

0   100 mi
0   100 km

Mekong River

Fa Ngum Road

31

0   2 mi
0   2 km

N

Monday to Friday 8am to noon and 1 to 5pm, Saturday and Sunday 8am to noon only. EMS and FedEx services are just next door.

Telephone/Fax The central telephone office, where you can place local and International Direct Dialing (IDD) calls, is located on Setthathirat Road near Nam Phu Circle (Nam Phu Fountain), and is open from 8am to 10pm daily. You can also send faxes or telexes (does anybody send telexes anymore?).

ACCOMMODATIONS

Laos is still developing its tourism industry, so hotels are not numerous. Demand is high enough and resources scarce enough that there is little incentive for renovations and service. There simply isn't that much choice, especially in Vientiane, although there are a few nice places that get the job done. Try to book early during non-monsoon months; late November and early December are particularly busy. You can try for a discount if you come during the rainy season. Hotel prices do not include a government tax of 10%, and some tack on an additional 5 to 10% service charge. From November through February add a few dollars to the rate for peak season surcharges. All hotels provide free transport to the airport.

EXPENSIVE

Lao Plaza Hotel. 63 Samsenthai Rd., P.O. Box 6708, Vientiane. ☎ **021/218-800.** Fax 021/218-808. www.laoplazahotel.com. E-mail: lph@laoplazahotel.com. 142 units. A/C MINIBAR TV TEL. 912,091–1,064,106 kip (US$120–US$140) double; from 1,520,152 kip (US$200) suite. AE, JCB, MC, V.

This 1997 hotel and business center is bland but plush and comfortable, with international-standard accommodations and amenities. It's a good choice for business travelers, who comprise 90% of the hotel population. Sizable rooms are either beige or blue, with solid wood furniture in perfect condition, thick rugs, firm beds, small marble bathrooms, robes, and hair dryers. You can even get a computer and Internet hookup in your room. Nonsmoking rooms are available on two floors. The pool is big and inviting. Lao Plaza's staff is professional enough, but not especially friendly or helpful. Guests have to pay 60,806 kip (US$8) to use the gym, and the hotel charges 11,401 kip (US$1.50) for a 3-minute local phone call (I can't imagine what the international charges are like). Amenities include a business center with Internet access, conference rooms, banquet facilities, sauna, Jacuzzi, massage, nightclub, beer garden, bookstore, and exceptional gift shops. The May Yuan restaurant has admirable Chinese food. The Plaza also has a cafe with buffet meals, and a deli/bakery.

Novotel Hotel Vientiane. Unit 9, Samsenthai Rd., P.O. Box 585, Vientiane. ☎ **800/221-4542** or 021/213-570. Fax 021/213-572. E-mail: novotlao@loxinfo.co.th. 220 units. 532,053–1,368,137 kip (US$70–US$180) double; from 2,432,243 kip (US$320) suite. AE, MC, V.

This is a lovely hotel; the lobby, with an art-deco theme and domed ceiling painted with blue skies and white clouds, is a place in which you might enjoy lingering. The renovated top-floor rooms have subdued, elegant dark carpets and wood furniture, and marble bathrooms with nice big counters. The older "standard" rooms are less luxe, with cane furniture, pastel colors, and tile bathrooms. Deluxe rooms include free laundry, local calls, and complimentary drinks. All rooms are spotless, with hair dryers and coffeemakers. The amiable French chef runs a fantastic restaurant, with indoor and outdoor-by-the-pool seating. His weekend brunch buffet is not to be missed; and though the daily breakfast buffet may be expensive at 60,806 kip (US$8), it's well worth it if you're hungry. The incredibly helpful staff will learn your name quickly. Facilities and services include a business center with Internet access, executive lounge, swimming pool, health club with sauna and massage, 24-hour room service, free transportation to the town center, good gift shop, bookstore, and disco.

MODERATE

Royal Dokmaideng Hotel. Lane Xang Ave., P.O. Box 3925, Vientiane ☎ **021/214-455.** Fax 021/214-454. 40 units. A/C MINIBAR TV TEL. 212,821–304,030 kip (US$28–US$40) double; 456,046 kip (US$60) suite. AE, MC, V.

A very good value can be found in this clean, friendly, 5-year-old hotel, which has reduced its rates by 50% to boost occupancy. The big rooms have attractive carpet and nice wood furnishings, with comfortable beds and plump pillows. There are nice-sized marble bathrooms, although I can't praise the moldy shower curtains or the sporadic lack of hot water. There are hair dryers, and you can get hot water thermoses upon request. The suites are huge and excellent for families. The Chinese restaurant is bright and inviting, and so is the pool. There is even a gym with a Jacuzzi and massage services for 34,203 kip (US$4.50) an hour!. The hotel is a favorite with Chinese tour groups, which means ask for a nonsmoking room when you book, and book early to get one. Also, don't go for the standard rooms, which aren't that much cheaper at 212,821 kip (US$28) and aren't nearly as nice.

✪ **Settha Palace Hotel.** 6 Pang Kham St., P.O. Box 1618. ☎ **021/217-581.** Fax 021/ 217-583. E-mail: settha@laonet.net. 48 units. A/C MINIBAR TV TEL. 418,042–570,057 kip (US$55–US$75) double; from 1,337,734 kip (US$176) suite. AE, MC, V.

Look no further; this turn-of-the-century French colonial mansion has been lovingly restored, offering the most charming address in Vientiane hands down. Opened in August 1999, this intimate hotel has small but cozy rooms with antique detail and modern conveniences. I loved the high ceilings, wood floors, dark wood reproduction furnishings (including four-poster beds), and dramatic black and white tiled bathrooms. And you don't need to leave the modern world behind; you've got full amenities in the bathroom and satellite TV. Hotel facilities include an outdoor swimming pool with Jacuzzi and a business center. Settha Palace also houses the finest dining venue in the capital. La Belle Epoque serves French and Continental cuisine that's not too bad in a setting that can't be beat. The staff here is unbeatable—they win first prize for friendly and efficient service. In any other city a hotel of this caliber would cost four times as much, at least.

Tai-Pan Hotel. 22/3 Francois Ngin Rd., Ban Mixay, Muong Chanthabury, Vientiane. ☎ **021/216-907.** Fax 021/216-223. E-mail: taipan@lox2.loxinfo.co.th. 44 units. A/C MINIBAR TV TEL. 425,643–456,046 kip (US$56–US$60) double; 539,654 kip (US$71) junior suite; from 615,662 kip (US$81) suite. AE, MC, V.

This very attractive, 7-year-old midsize hotel is located in a good location downtown by the Mekong. The large rooms, all spotless, bright, and cheerful, have shiny parquet floors, painted wood furniture, and floral bedspreads. The sizable bathrooms are done in white, clean tile, and have bathtubs. Ask for a third-floor room with a balcony and river view. Nice, friendly staff. There are a business center, conference rooms, health club with sauna, complimentary airport transfer, fruit basket, and International Direct Dialing (IDD). There's also a Western/Lao restaurant. Nonsmoking rooms are available.

INEXPENSIVE

✪ **Anou Hotel.** 01–03 Heng Boun St., Vientiane. ☎ **021/213-630.** Fax 021/213-632. E-mail: anouhotel@microtec.com.la. 40 units. A/C MINIBAR TV TEL. 152,015 kip (US$20) double; 228,023 kip (US$30) suite. AE, MC, V.

Here's a bargain for you. The Anou has clean, bright, good-sized rooms, some with clean beige carpet and others with hardwood floors. The beds are spotless and comfortable, and the bathrooms are among the cleanest in Laos, with tile floors and walls and nice marble counters. Some of the bathrooms are shower-in-room, without bathtubs, so let the hotel know if that matters to you. The suites are simply huge and all have wood floors, but there are only three of them. The downstairs restaurant is very inviting, and the hotel has a nice location in downtown Chinatown, surrounded by shops and restaurants.

Asian Pavilion Hotel. 379 Samsenthai Rd., Vientiane. ☎ **021/213-430** or 213-431. Fax 021/213-432. 45 units. A/C MINIBAR TV TEL. 190,019 kip (US$25) double; 266,027 kip (US$35) suite. AE, JCB, MC, V.

Five years ago this place might have done just fine, but now it can rate only as a bargain hotel. The rooms, while clean, are a decorator's nightmare and have ugly red carpet and slightly scuffed furniture. The beds are perfectly comfortable and spotless. The bathrooms are showing signs of age, but they do have bathtubs. English speakers are a minimum among the staff, and there are some listless-looking locals continually hanging out in the lobby watching football. The downtown location is convenient but can be noisy. There is a nice-looking restaurant and travel service on the premises. No elevators.

Lane-Xang Hotel. Fa Ngum Rd., P.O. Box 280, Vientiane. ☎ **021/214-102.** Fax 021/214-108. 109 units. A/C MINIBAR TV TEL. 190,019 kip (US$25) double; 342,034–418,042 kip (US$45–US$55) suite. AE, V.

This 40-year-old hotel, once the prize of Vientiane, is a low-end hotel today. There are tons of amenities, including two restaurants, a bar, a swimming pool, a gym with sauna and massage, elevators, and tennis courts. The rooms are nice-sized and comfortable, with clean beds and wood floors, but they are old. That means decrepit closets and peeling wallpaper. The showers have that all-too-common mold problem, too. Ask for a room with a river view. Here "single" means one bed, not one person. Do not consider a suite, whatever you do: the plastic furniture and puckered carpets are just horrendous, and the bathrooms very run down.

DINING

French is very big in the Lao capital, and good restaurants of this ilk (along with a few serving Italian) actually outnumber those serving native Lao fare. It may sound like a pity, but the food is generally so good and so reasonably priced that you probably won't complain. There's usually a decent French wine list, or you can try *lao lao* (rice wine served warm, with or without herbs), snake blood, tree bark, or elephant innards. A few other local specialties to watch out for are *khao poun,* rice vermicelli with vegetables, meat or chiles in coconut milk; *laap,* minced meat, chicken or fish tossed with fresh mint leaves; or a tasty Lao-style pâté. Try sticky rice, eaten with the hands, as an accompaniment.

EXPENSIVE

✪ **La Belle Epoque.** Settha Palace Hotel. 6 Pang Kham St., P.O. Box 1618. ☎ **021/217-581.** Main courses 53,205–98,810 kip (US$7–US$13). AE, MC, V. Open daily 6am–10:30pm. FRENCH/CONTINENTAL

This restaurant is at the top of dining experiences in Vientiane—the place for a power lunch or to entertain friends. Inside the Settha Palace Hotel, a newly renovated colonial mansion, you can't beat the atmosphere—colonial elegance mixed with Vientiane's laid-back feel. The service is just the same—efficient and quick but with a friendliness that's sincere. The menu covers a wide range of French and Continental specialties with meat, game, and seafood prepared quite nicely. My rack of lamb was terrific, and cost 98,810 kip (that's US$13)—I felt like a criminal. Tell me where you can find this type of cuisine, service, and ambience for these prices anywhere else in the world. Certainly not back at home—take advantage while you can. Bon appetit.

The Hong Kong Restaurant. 80/4 Samsenthai Rd., across from the Lao Hotel Plaza. ☎ **021/213-241.** Main courses 38,003–102,610 kip (US$5–US$13.50). No credit cards. Daily 11:30am–2pm and 6–10pm. CANTONESE/SICHUAN.

The Hong Kong (run by a bunch of folks from Beijing) is a favorite among Laos's Chinese community. The decor is standard Chinese restaurant—indoors and clean. The very fresh vegetable and soup dishes are a little under-spiced, even for Cantonese food, but the seafood specialties are good. The garlic shrimp is a must, as is the stir-fried crab with ginger. The food is surprisingly pricey, but that's probably unavoidable given the scarcity of some of the ingredients. The English menu has helpful pictures.

L'Opera. On the Fountain Circle. ☎ **021/215-099.** Main courses 34,203–64,606 kip (US$4.50–US$8.50). AE, V. Daily 11:30am–2pm, 6–10pm. ITALIAN.

Real Italian. Even if you've got good Italian at home, come here for the toothsome homemade egg noodle pasta, nice Italian wine list, and fantastic authentic desserts and espresso. There is a large selection of pizzas—pizza Lao is a surprisingly good combination of tomatoes, cheese, chiles, Lao sausage, and pineapple. The ambience is very good—a rather formal Italy-meets-Lao—with linen tablecloths, brick walls, and cane furniture. Very popular with expats.

Restaurant Namphou. On the Fountain Circle. ☎ **021/216-248.** Main courses 34,203–87,409 kip (US$4.50–US$11.50). AE, V. Daily 11am–3pm and 6:30–11:30pm. ASIAN/CONTINENTAL.

The ambience couldn't be better than it is here in this intimate dining room: semi-casual native Lao yet formal enough for a business lunch. The menu is rather eclectic, a seeming combination of Thai, Lao, French, and Continental. Specialties of the house are filet mignon, a hamburger with bleu cheese, and stewed deer in wine sauce. The management is extremely friendly and the service and food are both excellent.

MODERATE

✪ **Kua Lao.** 111 Samsenthai Rd. (at the intersection of Chanta Khoumane). ☎ **021/214813.** Main courses 9,805–12,769 kip (US$1.29–US$1.68); 76,008 kip (US$10) set menu. Daily 11am–2pm and 5–11:30pm. LAO.

Kua Lao is the premier Lao restaurant in the country, serving traditional Lao cuisine in a traditional setting. It's situated in a restored colonial, with a series of dining rooms. The extensive menu goes on for pages, but thankfully has English descriptions and pictures to help out. Order one of the many specialties cooked in clay hot pots. The US$10 (76,008 kip) set menu has numerous courses and is a very good idea for sampling varied delicacies, especially if you're dining with fewer than four people. There is an entire page of vegetarian entrees, and another entire page of something you don't see often: traditional Lao desserts. There is also a French wine list, and music accompanies dinner. Everything is fantastic.

✪ **Le Silapa.** 17/1 Sihom Rd., Ban Haysok. ☎ **021/219-689.** Main courses 22,422–119,712 kip (US$2.95–US$15.75). MC, V. Open Mon–Sat 11:30am–2pm; 6–10pm. FRENCH/CONTINENTAL

New on the local scene, this cozy little bistro was recommended to me by Vientiane's foreign residents, all of whom had nothing but praise for the food and the atmosphere here. I had lunch and (blame it on the wine list) promptly lost my notes, so have nothing concrete to report. I ate fish. Very delicious fish. And the decor? Very nice. Did I mention the wine list? Just go. It's a small intimate, friendly place. They had to beg me to leave.

Lo Stivale. 44/2 Thanon Setthathirat, opposite Wat Ong Teu. ☎ **021/215-561.** Main courses 30,403–60,806 kip (US$4–US$8). AE, V. Daily 11am–10pm. ITALIAN.

In a pseudo-Italian, candlelit environment, Lo Stivale features the usual pastas and meat entrees. The real highlight, though, is the pizza. Reputed to be the best in town, it certainly is delicious. The pies are big, with an ultra-thin, crackerlike crust and generous fresh toppings.

INEXPENSIVE

Arawan. 478 Samsenthai Rd., about 2 blocks past Wat Simuang. ☎ **021/215-373.** Main courses 8,969–30,023 kip (US$1.18–US$3.95). No credit cards. Daily 11am–2pm and 5–10pm. RUSTIC FRENCH.

For inexpensive grilled or one-pot meals, try Arawan. The menu features all manner of meats: chicken, pork, steak (imported from New Zealand), chacroute. The food is fresh, simply prepared, and very good. Most entrees are served with salad and French fries. There are other French specialties to be had as well such as coq au vin and ragoût de mouton. Arawan has no ambience to speak of, but the place is clean and inviting, and has an amiable French proprietor, who will be eager to chat with you—that is, if you speak some French. The menu has English translations. Most main courses go up to only about 15,000 kip; it's the steaks that cost the big bucks.

Just For Fun Restaurant. 57/2 Phangkhoum Rd., opposite Lao Aviation. ☎ **021/213-642.** Main courses 10,641–13,681 kip (US$1.40–US$1.80). No credit cards. Daily 9am–9pm. VEGETARIAN/THAI/LAO/INTERNATIONAL.

This seems like the place to kick back and relax. Here you can learn and read about many of the non-governmental organizations that operate in Laos and the Mekong region—and possibly run into the people who work for them. Specialties here are one-plate dishes with rice, noodles, soups, and salads. The Thai items are quite tasty and you can substitute tofu for meat in any dish. J.F.F. also sells some local handicrafts.

Nazim Restaurant. Fa Ngoum Rd. ☎ **021/223-480.** Main courses 7,981–19,002 kip (US$1.05–US$2.50). No credit cards. Daily 11am–11pm. INDIAN.

The choice here is wide open. You get northern and southern Indian cuisine—from tandoor to thosai. Biriyani dishes make for great one-plate meals. Plus they've got Indian-inspired Malay dishes like roti canai and mee or nasi goreng. Unbelievable, the extent of their cooking talents—but everything comes out great. And cheap—it's a backpacker favorite, so pull up a chair, order another beer, and meet some new friends.

SNACKS & CAFES

Stop at the **Healthy & Fresh Bakery** at 44/4 Ban Xieng Yeun, Setthathirat Road (two doors down from Le Santal). It's everything it says it is, and great-tasting as well. It also serves quiche and salads along with breads and sweets, and fantastic coffee. **The Scandinavian Bakery,** off Nam Phu Fountain Circle, has specialties from that region (and daily bread specials) and is always packed with travelers. A spot to stop and sample Lao food very inexpensively (as well as take in the scenery) is the **Dong Phalan night market** on Talat Nong Duoang Road, not far from the Novotel. You can graze on such Lao snacks as kabobs and spring rolls and stuff yourself for less than 10,033 kip (US$1.32) at the **Lao Hotel Plaza Beer Garden** at 63 Samsenthai Rd. There is also a string of small open-air eateries facing the Mekong River on Fa Ngum Road, between Pangkham and Nokeo Khumman streets. **PVO,** an open-air stall next to the Lao Paris Hotel on Samsenthai Road, serves outstanding Vietnamese *pho* (noodle soup) and spring rolls for 3,500 kip (US$0.46).

ATTRACTIONS

While Vientiane doesn't have the sheer number of wats enjoyed by Luang Prabang, they still dominate the list of must-sees here. Most sights are still within the city limits, which means you'll be able to cover them on foot, getting to know the city intimately as you go.

✪ **Phra That Luang.** At the end of That Luang Rd. Admission 1,000 kip (US$0.13). Daily 8am–noon and 1–4pm.

This is the pre-eminent temple in Lao, actually a 148-foot-tall stupa. It is not the original; the first, built in 1566 by King Setthathirat over the ruins of a 12th-century Khmer temple, was destroyed when the Siamese sacked Vientiane in 1828. It was rebuilt by the French in 1900, but the Lao people criticized it as not being true to the original. It was torn down in 1930 and remodeled to become the temple you see today. As you approach, the statue in front depicts Setthathirat. After you enter the first courtyard, look to the left to see a sacred bodhi tree, the same variety as that under which Buddha sat to achieve enlightenment. It has a tall, slim trunk, and the shape of its foliage is almost perfectly round. According to the Laotians, bodhi trees only appear in sacred places. You'll never see one, for example, in someone's backyard. The stupa is built in stages. On the second level there are 30 small stupas, representing the 30 Buddhist perfections, or stages to enlightenment. That Luang is the site of one of Lao's most important temple festivals, which takes place in early November.

Morning Market (Talaat Sao). On Talat Sao Rd., off Lane Xang Ave. Daily 7am–5pm.

You could poke around peacefully for hours in this huge market, with its three buildings full of produce, electronics, and handicrafts of all types. Best of all, the atmosphere is very low-key. No one will follow you, shriek at you, or hassle you to buy. It's an excellent source of gifts and souvenirs.

Wat Ho Phra Keo. On Thanon Setthathirat, opposite Wat Sisaket. Admission 1,000 kip (US$0.13). Daily 8am–noon and 1–4pm.

Also built by King Setthathirat in 1566, Phra Keo was constructed to house an emerald Buddha the king took from Thailand (which the Thais took back in 1779). Today there are no monks in residence, and the wat is actually a museum of religious art, including a Khmer stone Buddha and a wooden copy of the famous Luang Prabang Buddha. In the garden, there's a transplanted jar from the Plain of Jars (see section 5, below).

Lao National Museum. Samsenthai Rd., near the Lao Plaza Hotel. Admission 3,000 kip (US$0.39). Daily 8am–noon and 1–4pm.

Housed in an interesting old colonial that was once used for government offices, the Museum of the Revolution has photos, artifacts, and re-creations of the Lao struggle for independence against the French and Americans. The exhibits (firearms, chairs used by national heroes, and the like) are rather scanty, barely scratching the surface of such a complicated subject, but most are in English at least. Archaeological finds and maps presented on the first floor (probably because there is no other museum to house them at present) help make a visit here worthwhile. Actually, one of the most interesting exhibits is in the last room before you exit, sort of a Laos trade and commodities exhibit of produce, handiwork, and manufactured goods. Though dated, it will give you some idea of Laos's geography and commerce.

Patuxay (Victory Monument). At the end of Lane Xang Ave. Admission 1,000 kip (US$0.13). Daily 8am–4pm.

This monument was completed in 1968 and dedicated to those who fought in the war of independence against the French. Ironically, the monument is an arch modeled on the Parisian Arc de Triomphe. Its detailing is typically Lao, however, with many *kinnari* figures—half woman, half bird. It's an imposing sight, and you can climb up for a good city view.

Wat Si Saket. At the corner of Setthathirat and Lane Xang avenues. Admission 1,000 kip (US$0.13). Daily 8am–noon and 1–4pm.

Wat Si Saket, completed in 1818, is the only temple in Vientiane to survive the pillaging of the city by the Siamese in 1828, perhaps because the temple is built in traditional Thai style. It is renowned for the more than 10,000 Buddha images in the outer courtyard, of all shapes and sizes, in every possible nook and cranny. Look for Buddha characteristics that are unique to Laos: the standing or "praying for rain" Buddha; or the pose with arms up and palms facing forward, the "stop fighting" or calling for peace Buddha. The pose where Buddha points the right hand downward signifies a rejection of evil, and a calling to mother earth for wisdom and assistance. Lao Buddhas also have exaggerated nipples and square noses, to emphasize that Buddha is no longer human. The sim features a Khmer-style Buddha seated on a coiled cobra for protection.

Wat Ong Teu. Intersection of Setthathirat and Chou Anou roads. Daily 8am–5pm.

Wat Ong Teu is in a particularly auspicious location, surrounded by four temples: Wat Inpeng to the north, Wat Mixay to the south, Wat Haysok to the east, and Wat Chan to the west. Its name comes from its most famous inhabitant, a huge *(ongteu)* bronze Buddha. The temple, famous for its beautifully carved wooden facade, was built in the early 16th century, and rebuilt in the 19th and 20th centuries. It also serves as a national center for Buddhist studies.

That Dam (the Black Stupa). At the intersection of Thanons Chanta Khumman and Bartholomie.

This ancient stupa was probably constructed in the 15th century or even earlier, though it has never been dated. It is rumored to be the resting place of a mighty *naga*, or seven-headed dragon, that protected the local residents during the Thai invasion in the early 1800s.

Wat Si Muang. East on Samsenthai, near where it joins Setthathirat. Daily 8am–5pm.

Wat Si Muang, another 1566 Setthathirat creation, houses the foundation pillar of the city. According to legend, a pregnant woman named Nang Si, inspired by the gods to sacrifice herself, jumped into the pit right before the stone was lowered. She has now become a sort of patron saint for the city. The temple is very popular as a result, and is the site of a colorful procession 2 days before the That Luang festival every November.

Buddha Park. About 24km (15 miles) southeast of town. Admission 500 kip (US$0.07), plus an additional 500 kip for jumbo parking and 500 kip to use a camera. Daily 7:30am–5:30pm.

Buddha Park is more like a fanciful sculpture garden, full of Hindu and Buddhist statues created in the 1950s by a shamanist priest named Luang Pu. They are captivating, whether they are snarling, reposing, or saving maidens in distress (or carrying them to their doom, it's hard to tell). The huge reclining Buddha is outstanding; you can climb on its arm for a photo. There is also a big concrete dome to climb, itself filled with sculptures. The half-hour jumbo ride to get here, should you choose that route, is very dusty, but fulfilling: you get a clear view of Thailand across the Mekong.

SPORTS & OUTDOOR ACTIVITIES

While you may not usually think of joining in on local sports activities on your vacation, the laid-back local Hash House Harriers seems to invite socializing in addition to a weekly run. It certainly attracts interesting people, full of great stories. The

Vientiane HHH have a **family run** every Monday evening at 5:30pm. Information on venues can be found at the Phimphone Mini-market on the corner of Khumman and Samsenthai streets. Vientiane is small and clean enough to make this a fun experience, and a chance to meet expats. (Drinking follows.) Every Saturday at the field near the U.S. Ambassador's residence there is **softball** starting at 3:30pm. For information, call ☎ **021/413-273** (days).

SHOPPING

Laos is famous for its handwoven silk textiles. You can buy them in fabric or in ready-made wall hangings, accessories, and clothing. Silver is everywhere, in jewelry and ornamental objects. The main shopping streets are **Samsenthai** and **Setthathirat**, around the Nam Phu fountain area. Be sure to visit **Satri Lao Silk,** at 79/4 Setthathirat, for fabrics, clothing, and housewares; and **Carol Cassidy** off Setthathirat on Nokeo Khumman (☎ **021/212-123**), who designs her own fabrics using traditional Lao motifs as a base. **Ikho 2,** Phangkhoum Road next to Just For Fun Restaurant, is also a good gift shop. I liked the unusual furniture and artworks displayed at T'shop Lai Gallery (Vat Inpeng Street, ☎ **021/223-178**). Very unique, but a bit more pricey than other places; however, they take Visa. They'll ship your purchases home, too. Good for gifts, check out the cut-work household linens: bedspreads, kitchen textiles, place settings, plus baby items in great colors and quality at Camacrafts, on Neokeokumon (☎ **021/416-597**). For a broad selection of silver and gold jewelry, check the shop on the corner of Samsenthai and Pangkham roads. You can also find native handicrafts: silver, textiles, and carved wood housewares, in the **Talaat Sao morning market** on Lane Xang Avenue.

VIENTIANE AFTER DARK

There are a few places around town to meet and greet other English-speakers. The **Fountain Grill,** surrounding Nam Phu fountain, is the hot spot for expats and travelers. There is also a wine bar, **Le Cave de Chateaux,** on Fountain Circle. The **Lao Plaza Hotel** has a nightclub/disco and popular beer garden, and the **Novotel** has a happening disco. Be careful if you're strolling about after dark, though, as Vientiane has a goodly number of open sewers.

EXCURSIONS FROM VIENTIANE

Vang Vieng. 4 hours north of Vientiane by bus.

Surrounded by mountains, limestone caves, and karst formations (underground caves and caverns formed by the movement of water), Vang Vieng is an appealing village in majestic surroundings. Travelers come here for the hiking and spelunking in the numerous surrounding caves. You may want to stay a night or two, especially to break up a long overland trip to Luang Prabang. The best place in town is the **Hotel Nam Xong** (☎ **021/213-506**), with clean, tile-floor, air-conditioned rooms and a magnificent view of a private lake. Double rooms are around 190,019 kip (US$25), including breakfast. Inquire at any travel agency for bus tickets to Vang Vieng. Diethelm Travel (see "Planning a Trip to Laos," above) offers rafting/trekking/caving tours on the Nam Xong River, which passes through the town.

Lao Pako. About 39km (24 miles) north of Vientiane on the Nam Ngum River.

Here's your chance to visit a Lao "resort," developed with ecotourism in mind. Lodging is in traditional slant-roofed longhouses, which cost from 45,000 kip (US$5.92) for a double room to 65,000 (US$8.55) for your own private bungalow. There isn't much to do except relax, trek, visit villages, and take a few rafting trips, but the experience will doubtless prove interesting. To get there, you can take a local bus for an hour or rent a vehicle. To inquire, call the resort's Vientiane office at ☎ **021/222-925** or fax 021/212-981.

4 Luang Prabang

There's something magical about Luang Prabang. Maybe it's the way the early morning sunlight catches the saffron of the monks' robes as they make their way through the streets seeking their morning meal in return for blessings. Or the way the ancient temples come alive, their striking architectural presence reverberating with the sounds of chants. Could be the sights of the back streets where the everyday life of the Lao people who live here, working trades in the alleys and along the river, become so accessible to an outsider. Or maybe it's the feeling you get at the end of a busy day when you saunter drowsily home, a lazy afternoon sun casting long shadows off the lovely French country houses on all sides of your view. Down by the banks of the river, ladies gather to chat in the shade of huge leafy trees, while you find a comfortable cafe to rest your tired dogs and toast the sunset over the Mekong with a cool cocktail. This small town has magic— so many come and get lost in its charm. Allow yourself at least 3 days to sink into the city's languid rhythms, but beware, you may end up staying longer than you planned.

Literally meaning "great holy image," Luang Prabang has been named one of UNESCO's World Heritage Sites for its aged religious and colonial structures. The first capital of Laos, it has remained relatively untouched by war or even by the ravages of time. Thirty-three temples and wats stand in the small, gracefully laid-out town on the banks of the Mekong and Nam Khan rivers, each temple more beautiful than the next.

VISITOR INFORMATION & TOURS

A few companies in town provide tour services.

- **Diethelm Travel,** Sakarinh Road, near the Villa Santi (☎ **071/212-277;** fax 071/212-032). Monday to Saturday 8am to noon; 2 to 5pm. Diethelm arranges city tours and excursions to out-of-town sights.
- **Sodetour,** 105/6 Souvannabalang Rd. near the boat docks on the river (☎ **071/ 212-092**). Monday to Friday 8am to noon and 1:30 to 4pm, Saturday 8am to noon. Very professional outfit.

GETTING THERE

BY PLANE　Lao Aviation has three daily flights from Vientiane to Luang Prabang for 418,042 kip (US$55) one-way, and also connects Luang Prabang to Xieng Khouang daily for 266,027 kip (US$35). The Luang Prabang airport also handles international flights from Chiang Mai and Bangkok in Thailand. This airport allows you to get a visa on arrival. Outside the airport, if you haven't arranged pickup via your hotel, try to hop a jumbo with other travelers—the more passengers, the better the rate. For flight information call the Lao Aviation office in Luang Prabang at ☎ **071/ 212-172.**

BY BUS/MINIVAN　The overland route to Luang Prabang from Vientiane takes about 11 hours by public bus, depending on how many times it breaks down. However, the jaw-dropping scenery, past the mountains and limestone formations at Vang Vieng and several Hmong hill villages along the way, is well worth making the trip by land at least once. The bus costs 30,000 kip (US$3.95). It departs from the Morning Market several times a day (☎ **021/216-507**).

Luang Prabang

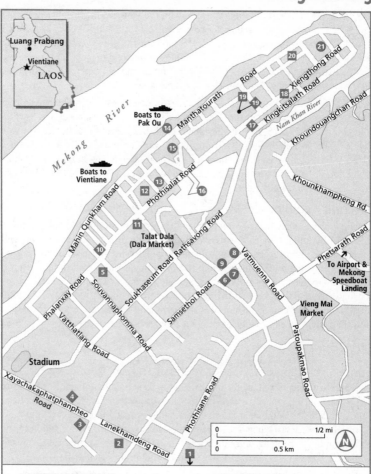

ACCOMMODATIONS ◼
L'hotel Souvannaphoum **5**
Le Calao **21**
Manoluk Hotel **2**
New Luang Prabang Hotel **12**
Pan Sea Hotel **1**
Phousi Hotel **11**
Say Nam Khan Guest House **18**
Villa Santi **19**

DINING ◆
Café des Arts **17**
Indochina Spirit **10**
Malee Lao Food **3**
Restaurat Locaux **17**
Sinxay Restaurant at the Villa Sinxay **4**
Villa Santi **19**
Visoun Restaurant **6**

ATTRACTIONS ●
Mount Phu Si (Phousi) **16**
Royal Palace Museum **15**
That Makmo **8**
Wat Mai **13**
Wat Wisunalat/Visounarath **9**
Wat Xieng Thong **21**

OTHER ●
Boat Pier (to Pak Ou Caves) **14**
Immigration Office **7**

BY JEEP OR TRUCK   Taking the mountain route by jeep or truck (it's not very safe to go by car) takes 7 hours and will cost about 1,748,175 kip (US$230) for the trip plus 456,046 kip (US$60) per day PLUS extra for the driver's meals and accommodations. If it seems steep, blame all the non-governmental organizations operating in Laos for driving up the prices—they all get reimbursed from expense accounts (in case you were wondering where your charity money ends up).

BY BOAT   It is possible to travel by boat from Vientiane to Luang Prabang, depending on the season, which in turn affects the depth of the river. Speedboats leave from the port (☎ 021/215-924) if they get enough passengers to make the trip worthwhile. The 8-hour trip is uncomfortable and noisy, and costs 160,000 kip (US$21.05). Don't even think about the slowboat—the 5 day/4 nights trip will drive you insane what with sleeping on a mat and so forth. It costs 89,000 kip (US$11.71) and also departs from the port.

GETTING AROUND

Luang Prabang is easy to cover on foot, and if you get tired, tuk-tuks and jumbos cost about 1,000 kip (US$0.13) a trip. For sights outside the city, jumbos usually gather along Xieng Thong Road across from the popular cafes and restaurants; prices are negotiable. At the time of my research the government was not allowing foreign visitors access to motorcycles and bicycles. No one knew why. I found a place next to the Luang Prabang Bakery that rented me a bike on the sly for 10,000 kip (US$1.32) per day. Note: The Western spelling of many street and wat names is very inconsistent, and the same road can change names as it progresses through the city.

Fast Facts: Luang Prabang

Banks/Currency Exchange   The Lane Xang Bank is at Phothisarat Road, next to the New Luang Prabang Hotel. Hours: Monday to Saturday 8:30am to 3:30am. Closed Sundays and holidays. You can exchange cash and traveler's checks in most major currencies to kip and withdraw cash using a Visa card. There's another Lane Xang money changing office on Xieng Thong Road next to the Luang Prabang Bakery. You can also change money at hotels and on the black market.

Emergencies   For police, dial ☎ 071/212-453; for a medical emergency call ☎ 071/252-049.

Post Office/Mail   The post office is on the corner of Phothisarat and Kitsalat roads, across from Luang Prabang Travel and Tourism. Hours are Monday to Friday 8am to noon and 1 to 5pm, Saturday 8am to noon.

Internet—Look for PlaNet Online on Phothisarat Rd. (the main restaurant drag), on the corner of Ban Wat Sene (☎ 071/252-291). They have another branch at the other end of Phothisarat, 3 blocks past the Palace Museum.

Telephone   The city code for Luang Prabang is 71. Dial a "0" first inside Laos. The telephone center in town, as it were, consists of two booths around the corner from the post office on Thanon Kitsalat. You can buy local and international phone cards in an office across the street.

ACCOMMODATIONS

There are numerous places to stay in the city, most loaded with atmosphere. Don't expect any real bargains, as demand is high in the dry season from November through February. During this time, book early and expect prices listed below to carry a peak season surcharge. Service is, shall I say, relaxed, as befits Luang Prabang, and moldy

Travel Warning: Bandits on Highway 13

Bandits and rebels occasionally attack public and tour buses on Highway 13 from Vientiane, just past Luang Prabang. There have been no attacks involving tourists in the past few years, but attacks involving Lao nationals still occasionally occur. Security has improved—there are army stations in the risky areas—but check with your embassy before you go.

bathrooms seem to be a common problem. Amenities like hair dryers, coffeemakers, and working televisions are rare.

EXPENSIVE

Pan Sea Hotel. Phou Vao St., P.O. Box 50, Luang Prabang. ☎ **071/212-194.** Fax 071/212-534. www.pansea.com. 59 units. A/C MINIBAR TV TEL. 380,038 kip (US$50) double; 866,487–1,033,703 kip (US$114–US$136) suite. Additional charges apply during peak season Nov–Feb. AE, MC, V.

This is touted as the "best hotel in Luang Prabang," doubtless because it offers the most amenities and is nearly always full with French tour groups. It does have a small swimming pool, but it's rather far outside the town center. Transportation to town is available upon request; or rather when the driver is available. Rooms are smallish, with parquet floors and balconies that take advantage of the hotel's location on a quiet hilltop. The beds are comfortable and the wood furniture modern and attractive. There are marble bathrooms with bathtubs, but they could use some strong detergent around the grouting and they are not air-conditioned (they're doored-off from the bedrooms, which do have A/C). The staff is very young and friendly, but could use a bit of training. There's a good indoor Lao/French restaurant.

MODERATE

L'hotel Souvannaphoum. Phothisarath Rd., Namphou Square, P.O. Box 741, Luang Prabang. ☎ **071/212-200.** Fax 071/212-577. 25 units. A/C. 395,240 kip (US$52) double; 570,057 kip (US$75) suite. AE, V.

The Souvannaphoum was formerly the villa of Prince Souvannaphouma, which accounts for the beautiful, quiet setting, lobby, restaurant, and bar here. Most of the hotel is open-air and decorated with a colonial Southeast Asian country house theme. The rooms are surprisingly basic but clean and comfortable, with nice wooden floors and marble bathrooms. The decor and amenities stop there, though. The two suites (the former royal bedrooms) are the exception, and are absolutely huge and well-decorated. You'll feel royal if you spring for one of them. Otherwise, at least ask for a room with a balcony. The staff is friendly and tries to be helpful, when you can find them. Telephone and laundry services are available, as is assistance with travel services when the Inter-Lao Tourism desk is manned, which unfortunately isn't often. The open-air restaurant is very good.

Le Calao. Thanon Khaem Khong (on the Mekong River, close to Wat Xieng Thuong), Luang Prabang. ☎ **071/212-100.** 5 units. A/C. 380,038 kip (US$50) double. V.

A newly restored 1904 villa on the banks of the Mekong, Le Calao has arched balconies, wood floors, and an outdoor dining pavilion. Its location, size, and decor are unique and picturesque. The rooms are a nice size and very comfortable, with wood furniture and tile floors, and have been well-designed to further the colonial feel of the place. The beds are firm and comfortable. Bathrooms have wood cabinetry but are otherwise rather spartan, with no bathtubs. There seems to be a staff of one. Given these factors and the lack of other amenities, the price seems expensive, even with the view. Still, it has ambience.

Manoluk Hotel. 121/3 Phou Vao St., Luang Prabang. ☎ **071/212-250** or 071/212-509. Fax 071/212-508. 30 units. A/C MINIBAR TV TEL. 266,027 kip (US$35) double; 532,053 kip (US$70) suite. AE, V.

An interesting choice, the Manoluk. The rooms are large and have polished wood floors and ceilings, burl tables and chairs, and amazingly comfortable beds. The bathrooms are similarly large, finished with tile, and clean for Luang Prabang. (They even have hair dryers.) The huge restaurant and second-floor lounge, complete with wooden deer heads, give the place the feel of a lodge. (A good feeling, it should be stressed.) The staff seems to be nonexistent, save for a person or two at the front desk watching the lobby television. Somehow, that seems to suit the laid-back, private feel of the place. There are motorcycles and bicycles for rent.

✪ Phousi Hotel. Setthathirat Rd., Luang Prabang. ☎ **071/212192.** Fax 071/212719. 43 units. A/C MINIBAR TV TEL. 212,821–243,224 kip (US$28–US$32) double; 342,034 kip (US$45) family rooms. MC, V.

For all-round comfort and convenience, this is probably your best bet in Luang Prabang. The rooms are neat and clean, with nice teak furniture and floral fabrics, and spotless big tiled bathrooms. The more expensive doubles have wood floors. The hotel is situated in a prime downtown spot, across from the Market. At night it glitters with strings of lights (a very nice, rather than tacky, effect in magical Luang Prabang), and traditional musicians serenade. The staff is accommodating and efficient. Try to book early, as it's a tour group favorite.

✪ Villa Santi. P.O. Box 681, Sakkarine St., Luang Prabang. ☎ **071/212-267.** Fax 071/252-158. 25 units. 418,042 kip (US$55 double); 494,049 kip (US$65) suite. AE, MC, V.

Formerly the residence of Lao princess Manili, this low-key villa reopened in 1992. The setting is quiet, with the rooms surrounding an inner garden. Rooms have parquet floors and teak furniture, and the tile bathrooms look brand new. Everything is spotless. A new wing was built 4 years ago, not quite as atmospheric as the old. Only four rooms have king-sized beds, so be sure to specify when you book if that's what you want. The overall charm and the convenient downtown location make this one of the top choices in Luang Prabang. There are restaurants in both the old and new wings; the one in the old wing has a slightly better atmosphere (see "Dining," below).

INEXPENSIVE

New Luang Prabang Hotel. Sisavangvong Rd., Luang Prabang. ☎ **071/212-264.** Fax 071/212-804. 15 units. A/C MINIBAR TEL. 228,023 kip (US$30) double. No credit cards.

The New Luang Prabang is a minihotel. The rooms are much nicer than the faded-carpet hallways; they're clean, with nice parquet floors. Beds come in sets of two twins only, but they are comfortable and clean. Bathrooms have no separate showers or tubs; it's the all-in-one variety. The hotel is smack in the middle of the downtown area; there is no better location. The staff is very nice, but don't expect the service or facilities of a real hotel. No elevators.

Say Nam Khan Guest House. Ban Wat Sene (off Kingkitsalath Rd.), Luang Prabang. ☎ 071/212-976. Fax 071/213-009. 14 units. A/C. 114,011–190,019 kip (US$15–US$25) double. No credit cards.

This little place in a renovated colonial building on the banks of the Nam Kham River is just plain charming. The smallish rooms have comfortable beds and wood furniture. The bathrooms are clean, tile with shower-in-room. Some of the rooms have ugly red carpet, others a teak floor. Located within walking distance of the main restaurant row.

DINING

Pull up a chair. There is a great variety of inexpensive restaurants in Luang Prabang, all exemplary of the town's friendly atmosphere. What we've called "restaurant row" is easily found along the end of Phothisarat Street as it turns into Xieng Thong. It's also about the only place in town alive past 9pm–before it quickly dies at 11pm.

Café des Arts. Xieng Thong Rd. (on "restaurant row"). No telephone. Main courses 3,800–12,500 kip (US$0.50–US$1.64). No credit cards. Daily 7am–11pm. FRENCH/CONTINENTAL.

The specialty here is "make your own salad" with six ingredients picked from a long list. Your trusty reviewer can vouch for the cleanliness of the fresh greens. Pasta, hamburgers, crepes, filet de boeuf, and tartines round out the very appetizing menu. Breakfast is omelets galore. Open-air like all the others on restaurant row, Café des Arts has a better atmosphere than most, with real tables and chairs with linen tablecloths, and black-and-white prints on the walls.

✪ Indochina Spirit. Ban Vat That 52, opposite the fountain across from L'hotel Souvannaphoum. ☎ **071/252-372.** Main courses 7,000–20,000 kip (US$0.92–US$2.63). Daily 8am–11pm. LAO/THAI.

This restaurant may be new, but the house it is located in dates back 70 years. This gorgeous traditional Lao home has been put to lovely use. Indochina Spirit has done a great job in the simple local décor inside, and charming garden dining outside. The menu features some traditional Luang Prabang dishes, and lots of Thai selections.

Malee Lao Food. Near the intersection of Phu Wao and Samsenthai. Main courses 3,500–15,000 kip (US$0.46–US$1.97). Daily 10am–10pm. LAO.

Malee Lao dishes up inexpensive and delicious local cuisine in a large, casual, open-air setting crammed with backpackers. Curries predominate; try the chicken curry soup, which is actually big pieces of chicken and potato in sauce. It's best eaten sopped up by hand with sticky rice. The *oolam* is a Luang Prabang specialty: eggplant, meat, and mixed vegetable soup flavored with a singular bitter root. The cute kids of the household are constantly playing and running around, which adds to the very friendly atmosphere. Always crowded at dinner.

Restaurat Locaux. 23/6 Phothisarat Rd. Main courses 3,000–8,000 kip (US$0.39–US$1.05). No credit cards. Daily 7am–11pm. LAO.

Locaux is a very casual open-air stall that serves all manner of Lao specialties. Everything is tasty, particularly the green spring rolls made with fresh vegetables. You may need to work up your nerve to order "fried Hairdo vet flour," "banana flabbier," "fried chicken + girdle + coconuts," and especially "fried sewer & sauce," but the food is much better than the English here. In a pinch, check out your neighbor's plate and ask for what he's having.

Sinxay Restaurant at the Villa Sinxay. Phu Vao Rd. ☎ **071/212-587.** Main courses 8,000–18,000 kip (US$1.05–US$2.37). No credit cards. Daily 7am–10pm. LAO/FRENCH.

Sinxay serves local specialties in a well-designed, open-air villa. It has long had a reputation of serving some of the best Lao food in town. The cuisine is creative and excellent, especially for the price. Fried chicken in bamboo, stewed aulam boar (with a bitter herb unique to Luang Prabang), and laap with fish all easily passed muster. But the place is known for one special local dish, orlam beef, which is flavored with dill. Very nice.

✪ Villa Santi. Sakkarine St., Luang Prabang (in the Villa Santi Hotel). ☎ **071/212-267.** Main courses 15,202–45,605 kip (US$2–US$6). V. Daily 7am–10pm. LAO/CONTINENTAL.

Villa Santi provides exquisite food on the upper floor of a restored colonial villa. The food is local and traditional Lao, along with some creative Asian-influenced Continental: I have to recommend the *khao pounh nam pik*—a Luang Prabang specialty. Villa Santi makes this noodle soup with a luxuriously creamy coconut curry broth and packs it with chunks of fresh fish on the top. It's a dream! Also try *mok pa* (steamed fish cooked in banana leaves), and pork brochettes with lemongrass. The most exotic item on the menu is probably the wild boar pepper steak. It's more tender than you might think, and worth every penny of the 45,605 kip (US$6) it costs. The desserts are scrumptious: bananas flambéed in Cointreau, fruit salad in rum. There are more casual offerings for lunch, including hamburgers. The restaurant has indoor and outdoor balcony seating. Most evenings there is traditional music and dancing in the courtyard below, and the restaurant is casual enough to allow you to stroll to the window for a look. Dining will be a memorable experience.

Visoun Restaurant. Visounnalat (also spelled Wisunalat) Rd., next to the immigration office. ☎ **071/212-268.** Main courses 8,000–18,000 kip (US$1.05–US$2.37). No credit cards. Daily 7am–9pm. CHINESE.

This low-scale open-air restaurant has a very casual environment, but it serves tasty Chinese food. The menu is a bit hard to decipher, getting no more specific than "fried chicken" or "pork with long beans," but the food is fresh and good. Visoun has a very large vegetarian selection as well.

ATTRACTIONS

Royal Palace Museum. Phothisarat Rd. Admission 10,000 kip (US$1.32). Mon–Sat 8–11am and 1:30–4pm. (Warning: at 11am they will kick you out, and you'll have to pay *again* if you come back after lunch.)

The palace, built for King Sisavang Vong from 1904 to 1909, was the royal residence until the Pathet Lao seized control of the country in 1975. The last Lao king, Sisavang Vattana, and his family were exiled to a remote region in the northern part of the country and never heard from again. Rumor has it that they perished in a prison camp, though the government has never said so. The palace remains now as a repository of treasures, rather scanty but still interesting. You can begin your tour by walking the length of the long porch; the gated, open room to your right has one of the museum's top attractions, an 83-centimeter-high golden standing Buddha that was a gift to King Fa Ngum from a Khmer king. It's the namesake of Luang Prabang, "holy image." This is only a copy, however; the real thing is in a vault of the State Bank. To your right on the inside, note the fantastic murals on the wall of the receiving room, painted in 1930. Each panel is shown to best effect as the sun hits it at different times of the day. The main throne room features lavish colored glass murals and, in a cabinet near the door, the coronation robes of the last prince. Throughout the palace are numerous *ding sun* drums, huge priceless bronze floor ornaments, some of them 1,000 years old.

Outside the palace, a large Soviet-made statue of Sisavang Vong, the first king under the Lao constitution, waves to your left. The temple on the right as you face the palace, Phra Bang, has doors created by Thid Tud, considered Laos's greatest sculptor. The temple is reportedly being renovated to house the golden standing Pra Bang Buddha.

Wat Mai. Phothisarat Rd., near the Lane Xang Bank.

Wat Mai is considered one of the jewels of Luang Prabang. Its golden bas-relief facade tells the story of Phravet, one of the last avatars, or reincarnations, of the Buddha. It held the Pra Bang Buddha from 1894 until 1947. Stop by here at 5:30pm for the evening prayers, when the monks chant in harmony.

Mount Phu Si (Phousi). Admission 8,000 kip (US$1.05).

Rising from the center of town, Phu Si has temples scattered on all sides of its slopes, and a panoramic view of the entire town from its top. **That Chomsi Stupa,** built in 1804, is its crowning glory. Taking the path to the northeast, you will pass **Wat Tham Phousi,** which has a large-bellied Buddha, Kaccayana. **Wat Phra Bat Nua,** farther down, has a yard-long footprint of the Buddha. Be prepared for the 355 steps to get there. Try to make the hike, which will take about 2 hours with sightseeing, in the early morning or late afternoon to escape the sun's burning rays.

Wat Xieng Thong. At the end of Thanon Xieng Thong. Admission 5,000 kip (US$0.66). Daily 8am–6pm.

Xieng Thong is considered the premier wat of Luang Prabang. Built in 1560 by King Say Setthathirat, it is situated at the tip of a peninsula jutting out into the Mekong. Xieng Thong survived numerous invading armies intact, making its facade one of the oldest in the city. One of the outstanding characteristics of the complex is the several glass mosaics. Note the "tree of life" on the side of the sim. Facing the courtyard from the sim's steps, the building on the right contains the funeral chariot of King Sisavang Vong with its seven-headed *naga* (snake) decor. The chariot was carved by venerated Lao sculptor Thid Tun. There are also some artifacts inside, including ancient marionettes. Facing the sim, the building on the left, dubbed the "red chapel," has a rare statue of a reclining Buddha that dates back to the temple's construction. Its exterior is adorned with a mosaic depicting a popular folk tale.

Wat Wisunalat/Visounarath. At the end of Thanon Wisunalat. Admission 5,000 kip (US$0.66). Daily 8am–5pm.

Wisunalat is known for its absolutely huge golden Buddha in the sim, the largest in town at easily 6.1 meters (20 ft.) tall. The wat was constructed in 1512 and held the famous Pra Bang Buddha from 1513 to 1894. On the grounds facing the sim is the famous **That Makmo,** or watermelon stupa, a survivor since 1504. Wat Aham is a few steps away from the Wisunalat sim.

SHOPPING

Luang Prabang features a fantastic array of the handwoven textiles for which Laos is well known, so stock up here. In the parking lot across the street from Luang Prabang Travel, a group of Hmong women sell embroidered items, also good buys. You can buy 100% gold jewelry at good prices in and around the Morning Market, although the workmanship is crude. There are a few shops with excellent handicrafts on Phothisarat Road across from Wat Hosian.

EXCURSIONS FROM LUANG PRABANG

Pak Ou (Tam Ting) Caves. On the banks of the Mekong, 35km (22 miles) from Luang Prabang. Admission to both caves: 8,000 kip (US$1.05).

The Pak Ou caves are two crannies in the side of a mountain stuffed with thousands of old Buddha images. The site has long been sacred for the Lao, even prior to Buddhism, when they worshiped spirits. The lower cave has over 4,000 images, ranging from 3 inches to 9 feet tall, stuck in nooks and crannies. The upper cave is actually even more interesting. Its Buddha images are placed far back into the cliff, so you'll need to bring a flashlight. The real highlight of a trip to the caves, though, is the breathtaking view of the mountains during the 2-hour boat ride. The trip will usually include a stop at Ban Xang Hai, a village specializing in production of Lao whiskey.

Many tour agencies charge exorbitant prices for half-day tours, as much as 152,015 kip (US$20) if you go alone. But you can simply stroll along yourself by the boat wharf, across from the Palace Museum on the river, and hire your own vessel. Expect to pay about 76,008 kip (US$10) for a boat of 3. Many will try to charge around 114,001 kip to 152,015 kip (US$15 or US$20); bargain like a maniac.

Kuang Si Falls. 36km (20 miles) south of town.

The Kuang Si falls are a spectacular sight: a huge, tiered waterfall with pristine pools below. Viewing them is a good excuse to get out of town for a bit and see the surrounding countryside, but expect the falls to be crowded with tourists and Laotians. You'll probably need to take a tuk-tuk or jumbo to go there independently, which means a 2-hour ride along bumpy, dusty roads. Negotiate with the drivers along Phothisarat Rd.; fares will be around 76,008 kip (US$10) for a group of four. You can also hire a boat (at the docks opposite the Palace Museum) to take you down the Mekong (about 100,000 kip or US$13.16; 1 hour down, 2 hours back), then jump to a jumbo for a brief overland trip to the falls. *Note:* During the dry season, from November to May, don't waste your time as the falls are only a trickle.

Tad Se Falls. 21km (13 miles) southeast of the city.

Tad Se falls are a 35-minute drive east of town by tuk-tuk or motorbike. While the falls are on a much smaller scale than Kuang Si, you do have a good chance of a private viewing, as most tourists haven't discovered them yet. Like Kuang Si, they are many small tiered formations rather than one huge stream. Drivers charge about 50,000 kip (US$6.58) for up to three or four passengers. Note: As with the Kuang Si Falls, during the dry season, from November to May, don't waste your time as the falls are only a trickle.

Ban Phanom Weaving Village. About 4km (2½ miles) outside of town on Patoupakmao, past Wat Phonphao.

The Lu clan of Ban Phanom came originally from Xixuangbana in southern China, and have been weavers for hundreds of years. The village is an interesting bike ride or stop on the way back from one of the waterfalls, but don't expect rustic authenticity. Yes, there is an entire shed devoted to handweaving here, and some chickens on the loose, but the whole village has the feel of a special show for tourists. Nonetheless, it has one of the best and cheapest selections of handwoven fabric in the whole country. If you hop in a tuk-tuk, you can combine this trip with the Wat Phon Phao (see below) for about 30,000 kip (US$3.95) for up to four people (about 3 hours total).

Wat Phon Phao (Peacefulness Temple). About 5km (3 miles) out of town, on the way to Ban Phanom. Mon–Fri 8–10am and 2–4pm.

Also known as the Golden Stupa, this temple has five floors of interesting murals depicting Buddhist tales and other temples and wats in Luang Prabang. The view of the town at the tiny upper room is worth the tuk-tuk ride from the center of town. See Ban Phanom listing above for trip details.

Across the Mekong River. Charter your own boat for about 2,000 kip (US$0.26) at the boat docks opposite the Royal Palace Museum.

Charter your own boat and go across to the relatively uninhabited side of the Mekong, right before it meets up with the Nam Khan. Taking a path to the east, you'll pass through a village that isn't posing for tourists. **Wat Them Xieng Mien,** which you'll come to next, has some Buddhist caves to wander through. Bring your own flashlight and inquire at the wat to enter. **Wat Chom Piet** is an abandoned wat reportedly built in the 16th century. Ask the gatekeeper there to open the doors for you. Finally, **Wat Long Khoun,** in a serene setting on the riverbank, once served as a religious retreat for Laos's royals.

5 Xieng Khouang & the Plain of Jars

Xieng Khouang, whose top attraction is the Plain of Jars, is relatively well developed for tourism compared to other provinces in the north—"relatively" being the operative word here. Its capital city, Phonsavan, has one of those "This is the far edge of the earth" feeling, even though it's slowly growing. Electricity is only available between 6pm and 11pm, so bring a torch (or at least a lighter). The Jars are the big ticket item here, but I assure you, the views of the surrounding countryside almost steal the show. Many people skip this part of the country altogether, but I'll tell ya, it's my favorite part of the country for the chance to learn about the mysterious Jars, and also about the rebel activities that take place in the hills around the area, and the de-mining projects going on here and in other parts of the country. You may also want to see one of the nearby hill tribe villages.

GETTING THERE

Lao Aviation flies from Vientiane to Phonsavan every day except Saturday for 281,228 kip (US$37) one-way, or you can fly from Luang Prabang four times a week for 266,027 kip (US$35). Once you arrive in Phonsavan it is mandatory for you to register with the authorities. And make sure you reconfirm your flight out of there *every day until you leave* to guarantee a seat back. Either your hotel or tour agent will greet you, or you can hitch a ride to town with one of the touts waiting to book you into his guesthouse.

Traveling by road from Vientiane is impossible due to bandit activities on the highways. Overland from Luang Prabang involves several grueling days on public buses, trucks—anything going in your direction. It's not recommended.

GETTING AROUND

Once you get to Phonsavan, your best bet is to hook up with a local tour company to get to the Plain of Jars and surrounding villages.

ACCOMMODATIONS & DINING

For years the best spot in town has been the **Auberge de la Plaine des Jarres** cabin-style bungalows with fireplaces nestled in a pine forest above the town (☎ and fax **061/312-044;** e-mail: plainjar@samart.co.th). Rates are 342,034 kip to 380,038 kip (US$45 to US$50) for a double room. These days they're a bit musty. Tour operators are now turning to the new **Phou Chanh Resort** (☎ **061/312-264**), where rates are 266,027 kip to 304,030 kip (US$35 to US$40) for a double room. Each pine cabin houses two double rooms and a family room with a fireplace, so it's the perfect place if you're traveling in a group of four. Unfortunately, both of these places are cut off from the main town.

The town itself has a bizarre assortment of hotels, all of which are either government owned proletariat-styled bunkers, and guesthouses, some of which are friendly and welcoming. I highly recommend **Maly Guesthouse,** operated by **Sousath Travel.** The owner, Mr. Sousath, is a local legend, full of information about the Plain of Jars

Travel Warning: Beware of Unexploded Ordnance

Xieng Khouang Province is one of the most heavily bombed areas on earth. UXO, or unexploded ordnance, is numerous, particularly in the form of small cluster bombs, blue or gray metal balls about the size of a fist. Don't stray into uninhabited unexplored areas, and don't touch anything on the ground.

and the rest of the region. Rooms range from 60,806 kip to 418,042 kip (US$8 to US$55), depending on amenities.

If you don't care to dine at your hotel, venture into town, where you'll find noodle and snack shops on the main street.

ATTRACTIONS

✪ The **Plain of Jars** is both a stunning sight and an archaeological mystery. Hundreds of jars of varying sizes, the largest a bit over 2.7 meters (9 ft.) high, cover a plateau stretching across 24 kilometers (15 miles). There are believed to be about 13 different sites.

The origin of the jars is unknown. Nobody knows who made them, where the people responsible came from or what ever happened to them. According to local folklore, an ancient king stored wine in the jars that was then drunk in celebration of a war victory. Dead war heroes are said to have been buried in the empty jars.

The jars have been dated to about 2,000 years, and the most popular theory today is that the jars were indeed used as funerary urns. Bones, ashes, bronze ornaments, and iron tools have been recovered on the site; however, nothing has ever been found *inside* a jar. In the 1990s archeological groups from Australia were permitted to study the sites, but a full-scale investigation has not been permitted by the Lao government. However, some believe the mystery is close to being solved.

The standard tour takes you to three sites (some claim to take you to four as a marketing gimmick). As far as tours go, you get what you pay for. The big travel agencies all handle Plain of Jars tours, but aren't really worth the steep price. One exception is **Sousath Travel** (at the **Maly Guesthouse,** P.O. Box 649, ☎ **061/312-031;** fax 061/312-395). See "Accommodations & Dining," above. For 380,038 kip (US$50), you get a Jeep with an English-speaking guide with all kinds of fascinating information about the jars, the history, the region, and anything else that comes to mind. If you pay 190,019 kip (US$25) with one of the independent operators in town, you'll get a guy in a truck who speaks enough English to tell you the jars were used for whiskey. If you pay 10,000 kip (US$1.32), you'll take a tuk-tuk to Site 1 where you'll be told the jars were used to make sticky rice.

Warning: According to the Mines Advisory Group operating in the area, not one jar site has ever been officially declared mine-free. Now there's an attraction you don't get at Disneyland. Stick to the well-beaten paths.

6 Pakse & Champasak Province

The town called Champasak was once a capital of the pre-Angkorian kingdom of Champasak, and the site of the ancient temple Wat Phu, second only to Cambodia's Angkor Wat in historical importance in the region. Today, the town of Champasak is visited via Pakse, southern Laos's largest city. (Keep in mind the relevance of "largest city" when we're talking about Laos.) Pakse is also the starting point for a few attractions in the southern provinces, including the Bolaven Plateau and the islands of the Mekong.

VISITOR INFORMATION

For visitor information, contact **Diethelm Travel** off 13 Road, 1 block past the Sodetour office (☎ **021/212-596**).

FAST FACTS: XIENG KHOUANG & THE PLAIN OF JARS

Banks **BCEC Bank** is along the riverbank in the town, while Lane Xang and Lao May Bank have outlets on No. 13 Road.

Internet   On No. 13 Road across from Lao May Bank look for **T&K.** Service is not always available.

GETTING THERE

BY PLANE   Lao Aviation flies each morning from Vientiane to Pakse at a cost of 722,072 kip (US$95) one-way. The airport in Pakse is on the opposite side of the river from the main town. Flag down a passing tuk-tuk, and expect to pay 2,000 kip (US$0.26) for a shared ride, or 5,000 kip (US$0.66) if you're alone. The Lao Aviation office is along the river past the BCEC bank; ☎ **031/212-252.**

BY BUS   If you dare to take this route, don't say I didn't warn you. You can take a private bus from Vientiane to Savannakhet for 8 hours of relative comfort, then transfer to a public bus for the rest of the trip—10 to 12 hours in a nasty bus with broken seats. The forest is your only rest stop.

ACCOMMODATIONS & DINING

There are four main hotels in town. The **Sala Champa Hotel** is an old French villa offering doubles for 304,030 kip or US$40 (No. 14 Road, Pakse District, P.O. Box 504; ☎ **031/212-273**). The **Champasak Palace Hotel,** a grand old place, was formerly the palace of Prince Bounome (No. 13 Road, Pakse District, P.O. Box 718; ☎ **031/212-263;** fax 031/212-781); they charge anywhere between 136,814 kip and 266,027 kip (US$18 to US$35) for a double, including breakfast. Another nice colonial is the **Hotel Residence du Champa** (No. 13 Road, Pakse District, P.O. Box 504; ☎ **031/212-120;** fax 031/212-765); it's 334,433 kip (US$44) for a double, including breakfast. Finally, there's the **Souksamlane Hotel** (No. 14 Road, Pakse District; ☎ **031/212-002**), a bit lower on the scale but still clean and with air-conditioning, which charges as low as 152,015 kip (US$20) for a double.

The Champasak Palace Hotel serves some of the best food in town, mainly Chinese fare. Otherwise, you can check out the few restaurants around the Pakse Hotel, near the central market.

ATTRACTIONS

Pakse, the capital of the province, was a turn-of-the-century French administrative post. It's noted for its handwoven silks and cotton, which you'll find (along with much more) at the lively outdoor market. Textiles here are incredibly inexpensive. You'll be too shocked at the low prices to even bargain. To find the market, walk along the river by the boat landing.

The most interesting sights are out of town. For no-muss-no-fuss, Diethelm Travel does a good job planning trips for you and making all arrangements, and it will be even better if you can arrange it all in Vientiane prior to your arrival. Yes, it is possible to do these trips yourself, but a lot of your success depends on weather conditions and bargaining skills—a trip to the Mekong islands can take a couple days just to get there if you dare attempt some of the "budget travel" methods you may hear about.

✪ **Wat Phu.** Almost 14km (9 miles) southwest of Champasak; 45km (28 miles) from Pakse. Admission 2,000 kip (US$0.26). Daily 8am–4:30pm.

This ancient temple, which dates back from the 6th to the 11th centuries, could be one of the highlights of your visit to Laos. Some say the temple's grand layout inspired Cambodia's Angkor Wat.

Wat Phu was built as a Hindu homage to the god Shiva, on a site that may have been previously used for animist worship. The complex is located on a plateau 1,207 kilometers (750 miles) above sea level. It is built symmetrically, with a broad causeway as the central axis. The structure immediately behind the large reservoir is recent, constructed by Lao royalty for officiating ceremonies and water games. The causeway behind this passes two pond basins, one on either side, and two worship pavilions, one for each gender. Behind these, along the steps to the next level, are, to the right, the former site of the galleries, and, to the left, the Nandi pavilion, a dedication to the bull, Shiva's traditional mount.

On the upper level is the main sanctuary, with some non-historic Buddhist statues. Originally a linga, a Shiva phallus, stood here, bathed in water from the spring behind the complex. The sanctuary was reportedly a site of human sacrifices from the pre–Wat Phu temple era. Today, during a ceremony taking place on the fourth day of the waxing moon in the sixth lunar month, a bull is ritually slaughtered by members of a nearby Mon-Khmer (an ethnic group closely related to the Khmer) tribe in honor of the founding father of Wat Phu. What you will probably see, however, is a view of the temple's surroundings, including the spring, which is considered sacred, and Lao travelers dipping themselves into the water to receive its blessings. Contact Diethelm Travel (see information above) to make the trip by car (trip cost: 228,023 kip or US$30) or, if the weather permits, by boat up the Mekong (190,019 kip or US$25).

Bolaven Plateau and Tad Lo Resort. Bolavan is northeast of Champasak Province; Tad Lo is 100km (62 miles) northeast of Pakse.

Bordering Champasak and Savarane provinces, the Bolaven Plateau is the site of teak, rubber, tea, and coffee plantations; cattle ranges; and rustic villages. It is home to various Mon-Khmer ethnic groups (including the Laven, for which the area is named) living in thatch huts and keeping traditions thousands of years old. You'll be able to visit their villages (some are close to the Tad Lo resort) and waterfalls of the nearby Set River, and observe local agricultural practices.

An excellent place to stay is the **Tad Lo Lodge,** an eco-tourism resort where you can live in simple bungalows and ride elephants. Diethelm Travel charges 76,008 kip (US$10) per day during the busy season for this trip, and can book you at the Tad Lo Lodge for between 114,011 kip (US$15) and 228,023 kip (US$30) per night for a double.

Don Khong Island. 5 hours by boat from Pakse.

Don Khong is the largest of the spectacular lower Mekong islands, not far from the border with Cambodia. **Ban Khone Nua** is a small village on the island with old colonial buildings and the remains of a French railway. Sights in the area include two impressive **waterfalls,** Li Phi and Khon Phapheng. Phapheng is the biggest waterfall in Southeast Asia. By boat, you can also travel to the area known as Si Pan Don, or the Four Thousand Islands. There is one island in particular where you may be able to catch sight of the rare Irrawaddy freshwater dolphins if you're traveling January through March.

You can also overnight on the island. The best choice is **Sala Donekhong,** with basic lodgings in a teak house at 3 Kanghong St. at 266,027 kip (US$35) per night for a double.

Diethelm Travel handles the trip this way; you'll take a boat one-way (their boat is much nicer than the local boats on the river—with a toilet even!), for 684,068 kip (US$90) per person.

Singapore 8

by Jennifer Eveland

Singapore thrives on a history that has absorbed a multitude of foreign elements over almost 2 centuries, melding them into a unique modern national identity. Beginning with the landing of Sir Stamford Raffles in 1819, add to the mix the original Malay inhabitants, immigrating waves of Chinese traders and workers, Indian businessmen and laborers, Arab merchants, British colonials, European adventure-seekers, and an assortment of Southeast Asian settlers—this tiny island rose from the ingenuity of those who worked and lived together here. Today, all recognize each group's importance to the heritage of the land, each adding unique contributions to a culture and identity we know as Singaporean.

With all its shopping malls, fast-food outlets, imported fashion, and steel skyscrapers, Singapore could look like any other contemporary city you've ever visited—but to peel through the layers is to understand that life here is far more complex. While the outer layers are startlingly Western, just underneath lies a curious area where East blends with West in language, cuisine, attitude, and style. At the core, you'll find a sensibility rooted in the cultural heritage of values, religion, superstition, and memory. In Singapore, nothing is ever as it appears to be.

For me this is where the fascination begins. I detect so many things familiar in this city, only to discover how these imported ideas have been altered to fit the local identity. Like the Singaporean shop house—a jumble of colonial architectural mandates, European tastes, Chinese superstitions, and Malay finery. Or Singlish, the unofficial local tongue, combining English language with Chinese grammar, common Malay phrases, and Hokkien slang to form a *patois* unique to this part of the world. This transformation of cultures has been going on for almost 2 centuries. So, in a sense, Singapore is no different today than it was 100 years ago. And in this I find my "authentic" travel experience.

1 Getting to Know Singapore

THE LAY OF THE LAND

The country is made up of one main island, Singapore, and around 60 smaller ones, some of which—like Sentosa, Pulau Ubin, Kusu, and St. John's Island—are popular retreats. The main island is shaped like a flat, horizontal diamond, measuring in at just over 42 kilometers (25 miles) from east to west and almost 23 kilometers (14 miles) north

Singapore

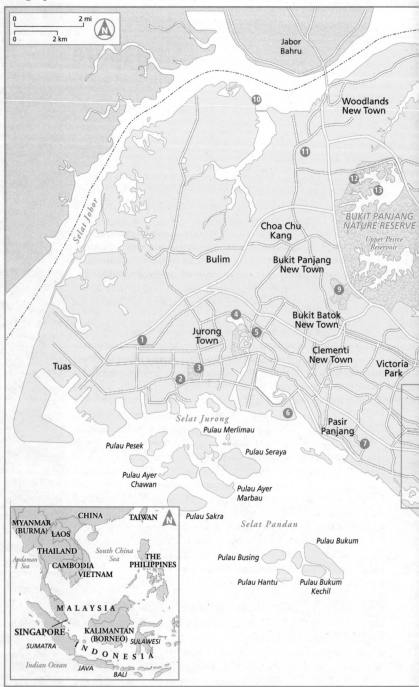

0 2 mi
0 2 km

Jabor
Bahru

Woodlands
New Town

BUKIT PANJANG
NATURE RESERVE

Upper Peirce
Reservoir

Choa Chu
Kang

Bulim

Bukit Panjang
New Town

Bukit Batok
New Town

Jurong
Town

Clementi
New Town

Victoria
Park

Tuas

Selat Jurong

Pulau Merlimau

Pasir
Panjang

Pulau Pesek

Pulau Seraya

Pulau Ayer
Chawan

Pulau Ayer
Marbau

Pulau Sakra

Selat Pandan

Pulau Bukum

Pulau Busing

THE
PHILIPPINES

Pulau Hantu

Pulau Bukum
Kechil

CHINA

MYANMAR
(BURMA)   LAOS

TAIWAN

THAILAND
CAMBODIA
VIETNAM

South China
Sea

Andaman
Sea

MALAYSIA

SINGAPORE

KALIMANTAN
(BORNEO)   SULAWESI

SUMATRA

INDONESIA

Indian Ocean   JAVA

BALI

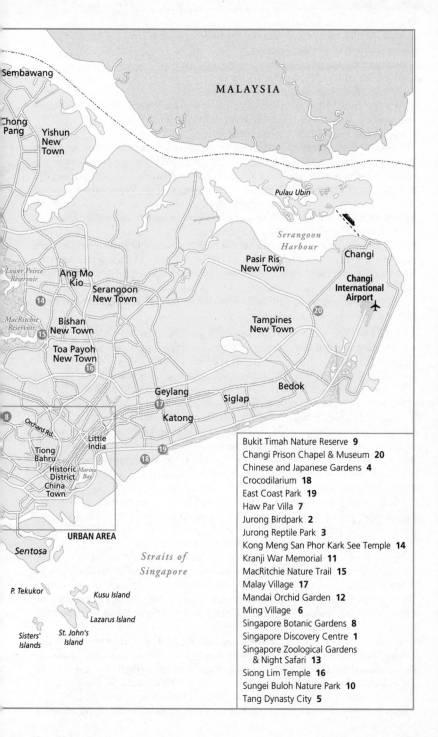

Sembawang

MALAYSIA

Chong
Pang

Yishun
New
Town

Pulau Ubin

Serangoon
Harbour

Pasir Ris
New Town

Changi

Changi
International
Airport

Lower Peirce
Reservoir

Ang Mo
Kio

Serangoon
New Town

⑭

MacRitchie
Reservoir

Bishan
New Town

⑮

Tampines
New Town

⑳

Toa Payoh
New Town

⑯

Geylang

Bedok

⑧

Orchard Rd.

⑰

Siglap

Katong

Little
India

Tiong
Bahru

⑱ ⑲

Historic
District
China
Town

Marina
Bay

URBAN AREA

Sentosa

Straits of
Singapore

P. Tekukor

Kusu Island

Lazarus Island

Sisters'
Islands

St. John's
Island

to south. With a total land area of only 584.8 square kilometers (351 sq. miles), Singapore is almost shockingly tiny.

Singapore's geographical position, sitting approximately 137 kilometers (82 miles) north of the equator, means that its climate offers uniform temperatures, plentiful rainfall, and high, high humidity.

As a city-state, Singapore is basically a city that *is* the country. That doesn't necessarily mean that the entire country is urban, but that the whole of the country and the city is "Singapore," without provincial divisions.

Singapore does, however, have an urban center and smaller suburban neighborhoods: The urban area centers around the Singapore River at the southern point of the island, and within it are neighborhood divisions: the **Historic District** (also referred to as the city center or cultural district), **Chinatown, Tanjong Pagar** (which is oftentimes lumped together with Chinatown due to its close proximity), the **Orchard Road area, Little India,** and **Kampong Glam** (also referred to as the Arab District).

Just beyond the urban area lie suburban neighborhoods. Some older suburbs, like **Katong** and **Geylang,** date from the turn of the 20th century. Others are new, and are therefore referred to as "HDB New Towns." (HDB stands for "Housing Development Board," the government agency responsible for public housing.) HDB New Towns such as **Ang Mo Kio** or **Toa Payoh** are clusters of public housing units, each with their own network of supporting businesses: provision shops, restaurants, health-care facilities, and sometimes shopping malls.

THE CITY   The urban center of Singapore spans quite far from edge to edge, so walking from one end to the other—say, from Tanjong Pagar to Kampong Glam—might be a bit much. However, once you become handy with local maps, you'll be constantly surprised at how close the individual districts are to one another.

The main focal point of the city is the **Singapore River,** which on a map is located at the southern point of the island, flowing west to east into the Marina. It's here that Sir Stamford Raffles, a British administrator, landed and built his settlement for the East India Trading Company. As trade prospered, the banks of the river were expanded to handle commerce, behind which neighborhoods and administrative offices took root. In 1822, Raffles developed a Town Plan, which allocated neighborhoods to each of the races who'd come in droves to find work and begin new lives. The lines drawn then still remain today, shaping the major ethnic enclaves within the city limits.

On the south bank of the river, go-downs (warehouses) were built along the waterside, behind which offices and residences sprang up for the Chinese community of merchants and "coolie" laborers who worked the river and sea trade. Raffles named this section **Chinatown,** a name that stands today.

Neighboring Chinatown to the southwest is **Tanjong Pagar,** a small district where wealthy Chinese and Eurasians built plantations and manors. With the development of the steamship, Keppel Harbour, a deep natural harbor just off the shore of Tanjong Pagar, was built up to receive the larger vessels. Tanjong Pagar quickly developed into a commercial and residential area filled with workers who flocked there to support the industry.

In these early days, both Chinatown and Tanjong Pagar were amazing sites of city activity. Row houses lined the streets, with shops on the bottom floors and homes on the second and third floors. Chinese coolie laborers commonly lived 16 to a room, and the area flourished with gambling casinos, clubs, and opium dens for them to spend their spare time and money. Indians also thronged to the area to work on the docks, a small reminder that although races had their own areas, they were never exclusive communities.

As recently as the 1970s, a walk down the streets in this area was an adventure: The shops housed Chinese craftsmen and artists; on the streets, hawkers peddled food and other merchandise. Calligrapher scribes set up shop on sidewalks to write letters for a fee. Housewives would bustle, running their daily errands; children would dash out of every corner; and bamboo poles hung laundry from upper stories. Today, however, both of these districts are sleepy by comparison. Modern HDB apartment buildings have siphoned residents off to the suburbs, and though the Urban Redevelopment Authority has renovated many of the old shop houses in an attempt to preserve history, they're now tenanted by law offices and architectural, public relations, and advertising firms. About the only time you'll see this place hustle anymore is during weekday lunchtime, when all the professionals dash out for a bite.

The **north bank** was originally reserved for colonial administrative buildings, and is today commonly referred to as the **Historic District.** The center point was The Padang, the field on which the Europeans would play sports and hold outdoor ceremonies. Around the field, the Parliament Building, Supreme Court, City Hall, and other municipal buildings sprang up in grand style, and behind these buildings, Government Hill—the present-day **Fort Canning Park**—was the home of the governors. The Esplanade along the waterfront was a center for European social activities and music gatherings, when colonists would don their finest Western styles and walk the park under parasols or cruise in horse-drawn carriages. These days, the Historic District is still the center of most of the government's operations, and close by high-rise hotels and shopping malls have been built. The area on the bank of the river is celebrated as Raffles's landing site.

To the northwest of the Historic District, in the areas along **Orchard Road and Tanglin,** a residential area was created for Europeans and Eurasians. Homes and plantations were eventually replaced by apartment buildings and shops, and in the early 1970s, luxury hotels ushered tourism into the area in full force. In the 1980s, huge shopping malls sprang up along the sides of Orchard Road, turning the landscape into the shopping hub it continues to be. The Tanglin area is home to most of the foreign embassies in Singapore.

The original landscape of **Little India** made it a natural location for an Indian settlement, as the Indians were the original cattle hands and traders in Singapore; the area's natural grasses and springs provided their cattle with food and water, while bamboo groves supplied necessary lumber for their pens. Later, with the establishment of a jail nearby, Indian convict laborers, and the Indian workers who supplied services to them, came to the area for work and ended up staying. Today, while fewer Indians actually reside in this district, Little India is still the heartbeat of Indian culture in Singapore; shops here sell the clothing, cultural, and religious items, and imported goods from "back home" that keep the Indian community linked to their cultural heritage. Although the Indian community in Singapore is a minority in its numbers, you wouldn't think so on Sundays, when all the workers have their day off and come to the streets here to socialize and relax.

Like Little India, the area around **Bugis Street** is adjacent to the Historic District. This neighborhood was originally allocated for the Bugis settlers who came from the island of Celebes, part of Indonesia. The Bugis were welcomed in Singapore, and because they originated from a society based on seafaring and trading, they became master shipbuilders. Today, regrettably, nothing remains of Bugis culture outside of the national museums. In fact, for most locals, Bugis Street is better remembered as a 1970s den of iniquity where transvestites, transsexuals, and other sex performers would stage seedy Bangkok-style shows and beauty contests. The government "cleaned up" Bugis Street in the 1980s, so that all that remains is a huge shopping mall and a sanitized night market.

Kampong Glam, the neighborhood beyond Bugis Street, was given to Sultan Hussein and his family as part of his agreement to turn control of Singapore over to Raffles. Here he built his *istana* (palace) and the Sultan Mosque, and the area subsequently filled with Malay and Arab Muslims who imparted a distinct Islamic flavor to the neighborhood. The presence of the Sultan Mosque assures that area remains a focal point of Singapore Muslim society, but the istana has fallen into disrepair and serves as a sad reminder of the economic condition into which Singapore's Malay community has fallen. **Arab Street** is perhaps the most popular area attraction for tourists and locals, who come to find deals on textiles and regional crafts.

Two areas of the city center are relatively new, having been built atop huge parcels of reclaimed land. Where the eastern edges of Chinatown and Tanjong Pagar once touched the water's edge, land reclamation created the present-day downtown business district, which is named after its central thoroughfare, **Shenton Way.** This Wall Street–like district is home to the magnificent skyscrapers that grace Singapore's skyline and to the banks and businesses that have made the place an international financial capital. During weekday business hours (9am to 5pm), Shenton Way is packed with scurrying businesspeople. After hours and on weekends, it's nothing more than a quiet forest of concrete, metal, and glass.

The other reclaimed area is **Marina Bay,** on the other side of the river, just east of the Historic District. **Suntec City,** Southeast Asia's largest convention and exhibition center, is located here, and has become the linchpin of a thriving hotel, shopping mall, and amusement zone.

OUTSIDE THE URBAN AREA   The heart of the city centers around the Singapore River, but outside the city proper are suburban neighborhoods and rural areas. In the immediate outskirts of the main urban area are the older suburban neighborhoods, such as **Katong, Geyland,** and **Holland Villiage.** Beyond these are the newer suburbs, called **HDB New Towns.** The HDB , or Housing Development Board, is responsible for creating large towns, such as **Ang Mo Kio** and **Toa Payoh,** each have their own network of supporting businesses: restaurants, schools, shops, health-care facilities, and sometimes department stores.

2 Planning a Trip to Singapore

VISITOR INFORMATION

The long arm of the **Singapore Tourism Board (STB)** reaches many overseas audiences through its branch offices, which will gladly provide brochures and booklets to help you plan your trip, and through their Web site, at **www.newasia-singapore.com.** The STB also has Web sites with special tips directed specifically for American and Canadian travelers. If you're traveling from the States, look up **www.singapore-usa.com**; from Canada, try **www.singapore-ca.com.**

IN THE UNITED STATES

- **New York:** 590 Fifth Ave., 12th Floor, New York, NY 10036 (☎ **212/302-4861;** fax 212/302-4801)
- **Chicago:** Two Prudential Plaza, 180 North Stetson Ave., Suite 2615, Chicago, IL 60601 (☎ **312/938-1888;** fax 312/938-0086)
- **Los Angeles:** 8484 Wilshire Blvd., Suite 510, Beverly Hills, CA 90211 (☎ **323/852-1901;** fax 323/852-0129)

IN CANADA

- **Toronto:** The Standard Life Centre, 121 King St. West, Suite 1000, Toronto, Ontario, Canada M5H 3T9 (☎ **416/363-88 98;** fax 416/363-5752)

IN THE UNITED KINGDOM

- **London:** 1st Floor, Carrington House, 126–130 Regent St., London W1R 5FE, United Kingdom (☎ **207/4370033;** fax 207/7342191)

IN AUSTRALIA & NEW ZEALAND

- **Sydney:** Level 11, AWA Building, 47 York St., Sydney NSW 2000, Australia (☎ **2/9290-2888;** fax 2/9290-2555)

IN SINGAPORE

- **Tourism Court:** 1 Orchard Spring Lane, across the street from Traders Hotel (☎ **65/736-6622;** fax 65/736-9423. Their toll-free Touristline in Singapore is ☎ **1800/736-2000.**)

ENTRY REQUIREMENTS

To enter Singapore, you must have a valid passport. Visitors from the United States, Canada, Australia, New Zealand, and the United Kingdom are not required to obtain a visa prior to their arrival. A **Social Visit Pass** (with combined social and business status) good for up to 30 days will be awarded upon entry for travelers arriving by plane, or for 14 days if your trip is by ship or overland from Malaysia. Good news for U.S. passport holders: In fall 1999 the United States allowed Singaporeans to travel socially in the United States without a visa, so Singapore has reciprocated by allowing Americans a 3-month social/business-class Social Visit Pass upon entry. Be advised, this and all other types of passes are at the discretion of the Immigration officer, who may not award you the full amount of time. Singapore is trying to cut down on foreigners living here without proper documentation—many make illegal "Visa Runs" to Malaysia to allow them to stay longer in Singapore. However, if this is your first trip to Singapore, you should have no problems.

The **Singapore Immigration & Registration (SIR) Department** operates a 24-hour automated inquiry system for questions about visa requirements at ☎ **65/391-6100,** but if you need to speak to a representative, call between the hours of 8am and 5pm Monday through Friday, or 8am and 1pm on Saturday. The Singapore Immigration & Registration office is located at 10 Kallang Rd., SIR Building (above the Lavender MRT station). Business hours are Monday through Friday 8am to 5pm and Saturdays 8am to 1pm. For immigration information on the net, visit the Ministry of Home Affairs Web site at www.mha.gov.sg.

CUSTOMS REGULATIONS

The following items are not allowed through customs unless you have authorization or an import permit: animals; birds and their by-products; plants; endangered species or items made from these species; arms and explosives; bulletproof clothing; toy guns of any type; weapons, including decorative swords and knives; cigarette lighters in the shape of pistols; toy coins; pornographic prerecorded videotapes and cassettes, books, or magazines; controlled substances; poisons; materials that may be considered treasonable (plutonium, military maps—that kind of thing). For all pharmaceutical drugs, especially sleeping pills, depressants, or stimulants, you must provide a prescription from your physician authorizing personal use for your well-being. There's no restriction

Urban Singapore Neighborhoods

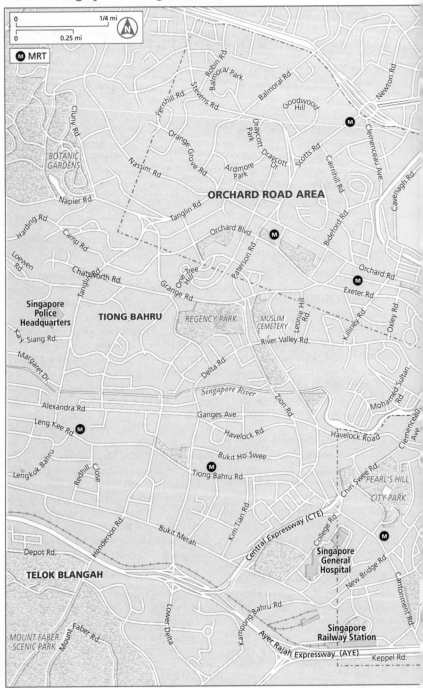

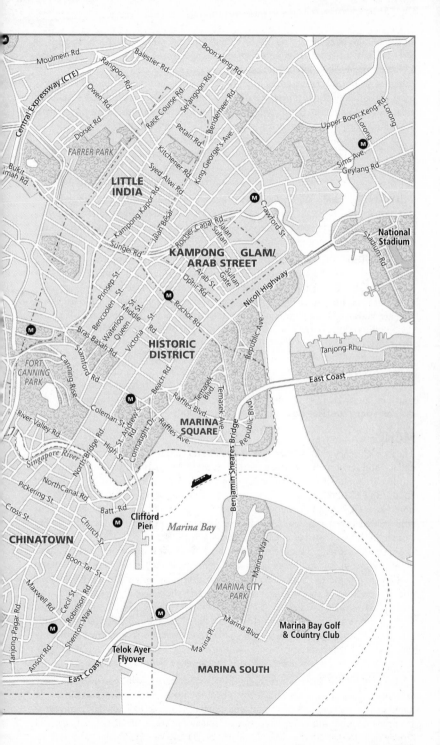

on the amount of currency you can bring into Singapore. For those above 18 years of age who have arrived from countries other than Malaysia and have spent more than 48 hours outside Singapore, allowable duty-free concessions are 1 liter of spirits; 1 liter of wine; and 1 liter of either port, sherry, or beer, all of which must be intended for personal consumption only. There are no duty-free concessions on cigarettes or other tobacco items. If you exceed the duty-free limitations, you can bring your excess items in upon payment of goods and services tax (GST) and customs duty.

All inquiries can be directed to the **Customs Office** at Changi International Airport (☎ **65/542-7058**) or to the automated customs hot line at ☎ **65/355-2000** (Monday to Friday 8am to 5pm, Saturday 8am to noon). A detailed rundown can be found on the Net at the Ministry of Home Affairs home page **www.mha.gov.sg**.

DEPARTURE TAX When you leave Singapore you'll be required to pay a **departure tax** of S$15 (US$9). Nowadays, this tax is usually added onto your airfare. Ask your airline if this is the case. If not, coupons for the amount can be purchased at most hotels, travel agencies, and airline offices.

THE TOURIST REFUND SCHEME Singapore has a great incentive for travelers to drop big bucks: the Tourist Refund Scheme. If you purchase goods at a value of S$300 (US$179.65) or more at a shop that displays the Tax Free Shopping sign, customs will reimburse the 3% GST (goods and services tax) you paid for the purchase. You are allowed to pool receipts from different retailers for purchases of S$100 (US$59.90) or more. Here's how it works: When you purchase the item(s), apply with the retailer for a Tax Free Shopping Check. When you're leaving Singapore, present your Shopping Checks and the items purchased at the Tax Refund Counters located in the Departure Hall at Changi Airport's terminals 1 or 2. Within 12 weeks, you'll receive a check for the GST refund—or, if you used a credit card for the purchase, your bill can be credited (a surcharge may be levied). For more information, contact the **Singapore Tourism Board** at ☎ **800/736-2000**.

MONEY
The local currency unit is the **Singapore dollar.** It's commonly referred to as the "Sing dollar," and retail prices are often marked as S$ (a designation I've used throughout this book). Notes are issued in denominations of S$1, S$2, S$5, S$10, S$50, S$100, S$500, and S$1,000. Notes vary in size and color from denomination to denomination. Coins are issued in denominations of S1¢, S5¢, S10¢, S20¢, S50¢, and the fat, gold-colored S$1. Singapore has an interchangeability agreement with Brunei, so the Brunei dollar is accepted as equal to the Singapore dollar.

Singapore's currency weathered the Southeast Asian economic crisis in 1997 rather successfully, so if you were hoping for a more favorable exchange rate, you're looking in the wrong place; the Sing dollar has decreased in value only slightly from precrisis rates. At the time of this writing, exchange rates on the Singapore dollar were as follows: US$1 = S$1.67, Can$1 = S$1.14, £1 = S$2.70, A$1 = S$1.07, NZ$1 = S85¢. These are the exchange rates used throughout this chapter, but before you begin budgeting your trip, I suggest you obtain the latest conversions so you don't suffer any shocks at the last minute.

For up-to-date money conversion, visit the currency chart at www.cnn.

CURRENCY EXCHANGE While hotels and banks will perform currency exchanges, you'll get a better rate at any one of the many money changers that can be found in all the shopping malls and major shopping districts (look for the certificate of government authorization). Many shops are also authorized to change money, and will display signs to that effect. Money changers usually give you the official going rate for the day, and sometimes the difference in rate between hotels and money changers can be as much as US8¢ to the dollar. Lastly, while some hotels and shops may accept your foreign currency as payment, they will always calculate the exchange rate in their favor.

AUTOMATED-TELLER MACHINES   Singapore has thousands of conveniently located 24-hour automated-teller machines (ATMs). Whether you're in your hotel, a shopping mall, or a suburban neighborhood, I'd be surprised if you're more than 1 or 2 blocks from an ATM—ask your concierge or any passerby and they can direct you. With debit cards on the MasterCard/Cirrus or Visa/PLUS systems, you can withdraw Singapore currency from any of these machines, and your bank will deduct the amount from your account at that day's official exchange rate. This is a very good way to access cash for the most favorable currency rate, but make sure you check with your bank before you leave home, to find out what your daily withdrawal limits are. It's also a good idea to keep track of ATM charges—while Singapore banks do not charge for the service, your home financial institution can levy a fee of up to US$1.50 per transaction for this convenience.

TRAVELER'S CHECKS   The two most easily recognizable traveler's checks in Singapore are issued from American Express and Thomas Cook. They can be cashed at banks and hotels, but money changers will cash them at the day's official exchange rate (as opposed to charging a fee or giving their own rate). Upon occasion they may try to charge a fee, but if you indicate you'll take your business elsewhere they may change their minds. To cash a traveler's check you will need to show your passport. Occasionally, an international driver's license or your driver's license from home will suffice.

CREDIT CARDS   American Express (AE) is accepted widely, as are Diners Club (DC), MasterCard (MC), Japan Credit Bureau (JCB), and Visa (V), though you'll find that some budget hotels, smaller shops, and restaurants will accept no credit cards at all. Purchases made with credit cards will appear on your bill at the exchange rate on the day your charge is posted, *not* what the rate was on the day the purchase was made. It's also worth noting that if your signature is slightly different on the slip than it is on your card, shop owners will make you redo the slip. They're real sticklers for signature details, so don't leave out a middle initial or forget to cross a T.

American Express is a recommended asset for all who venture overseas. Their Charge Card Guarantee Service allows you to cash personal checks up to US$1,000 every 21 calendar days while you travel. (Note that if the checks are not honored by your financial institution, American Express will charge it to your bill and will freeze your account until the entire amount is recovered.) For more information, check the American Express Web site at **www.americanexpress.com**. In Singapore, the American Express office's 24-hour membership services hot line is ☎ **1800/732-2244.** The 24-hour traveler's check refund hot line is ☎ **1800/738-3383; MasterCard** has toll-free access to report lost or stolen cards. In Singapore dial ☎ **1800/110-0113** to reach MasterCard's Global Service Emergency Assistance for International Travelers; for **Visa's** Emergency Assistance number call their local toll-free hot line at ☎ **1800/580-7500.** For both MasterCard and Visa, there are other services available, but it depends on the type of card you hold and the institution that issued it. Contact your issuing institution before your trip to find out what travel benefits you're eligible to receive.

WHEN TO GO

The busy season is from January to June. In the late summer months, business travel dies down, and in fall, even tourism drops off somewhat, making the season ripe for budget-minded visitors. These may be the best times to get a deal. Probably the worst time to negotiate will be between Christmas and the Chinese New Year.

CLIMATE At approximately 137 kilometers (82 miles) north of the equator, with exposure to the sea on three sides, it's a sure bet that Singapore will be hot and humid year-round. Temperatures remain uniform, with a daily average of 80.6°F (26.7°C), afternoon temperatures reaching as high as 87.44°F (30.8°C), and an average sunrise temperature as low as 75.03°F (23.9°C). Relative humidity often exceeds 90% at night and in the early morning. Even on a "dry" afternoon, don't expect it to drop much below 60%. (The daily average is 84.4% relative humidity.) Rain falls year-round, much of it coming down in sudden downpours that end abruptly and are followed immediately by the sun.

The Northeast Monsoon occurs between December and March, when temperatures are slightly cooler, relatively speaking, than other times of the year. The heaviest rainfall occurs between November and January, with daily showers that sometimes last for long periods of time; at other times, it comes down in short heavy gusts and goes quickly away. Wind speeds are rarely anything more than light. The Southwest Monsoon falls between June and September. Temperatures are higher and, interestingly, it's during this time of year that Singapore gets the *least* rain (with the very least reported in July).

In between monsoons, thunderstorms are frequent. Also interesting, the number of daylight hours and number of nighttime hours remains almost constant year-round. February is the sunniest month, while December is generally more overcast.

PUBLIC HOLIDAYS & EVENTS There are 11 official public holidays: New Year's Day, Chinese New Year or Lunar New Year (2 days), Hari Raya Puasa, Good Friday, Hari Raya Haji, Labour Day, Vesak Day, National Day, Deepavali, and Christmas Day. On these days, expect government offices, banks, and some shops to be closed.

Holidays and festivals are well publicized by the **Singapore Tourism Board** (STB), which loves to introduce the world to the joys of all Singapore's cultures. A call or visit to an STB office either before your trip or once you arrive will let you know the what, where, and when of all that's happening during your stay. See the listing of STB offices in the United States, Canada, the United Kingdom, and Australia under "Visitor Information," earlier in this chapter. Its Web site at **www.newasia-singapore.com** also has information about upcoming holidays and festivals.

HEALTH CONCERNS

Generally speaking, you'll have no problem with the food in Singapore, other than the possible digestive problems you may experience simply because you're not used to the ingredients. All fruits and vegetables should be thoroughly washed to rinse away any bacteria. Chinese restaurants in Singapore still use monosodium glutamate (MSG), the flavor enhancer that was blamed for everything from fluid retention to migraine headaches, and has been squeezed out of most Chinese restaurant cuisine in the West. The MSG connection has just started to catch on here, but not in full force. Many restaurants can now prepare dishes without MSG upon request, but smaller places will probably think you're insane for asking.

Singapore doesn't require that you have any **vaccinations** to enter the country, but strongly recommends immunization against diphtheria, tetanus, hepatitis A and B, and typhoid. If you're particularly worried, follow their advice; if you're the intrepid type, ignore it. While there's no risk of contracting malaria (the country's been declared malaria-free for decades by the World Health Organization), there is a similar deadly virus, **dengue fever** (also just called dengue), that's carried by mosquitoes and has no immunization. Symptoms of dengue fever include sudden fever and tiny red spotty rashes on the body. If you suspect you've contracted dengue, seek medical attention immediately (see the listing of hospitals under "Fast Facts," later in this chapter). If left untreated, this disease can cause internal hemorrhaging and even death. Your best protection is to wear insect repellent, especially if you're heading out to the zoo, bird park, or any of the gardens or nature preserves.

For further health and insurance information, see chapter 3.

GETTING THERE
By Plane

If you're hunting for the best airfare, there are a few things you can do. First, plan your trip for the low-volume season, which runs from September 1 to November 30. Between January 1 and May 31, you'll pay the highest fares. Plan your travel on weekdays only, and, if you can, plan to stay for at least a full week. Book your reservations in advance—waiting until the last minute can mean you'll pay sky-high rates. Also, if you have access to the Internet, there are a number of great sites that'll search out super fares for you. See chapter 3 for more information.

FROM THE UNITED STATES   Singapore Airlines (☎ 800/742-3333 in the U.S.; 65/223-6030 in Singapore; www.singaporeair.com) has a daily flight from New York, two daily flights from Los Angeles, two daily flights from San Francisco (only one on Sunday), and a flight four times weekly from Newark, New Jersey. Flights originating from the East Coast travel over Europe, stopping in either Frankfurt or Amsterdam. Flights from the West Coast stop over in either Tokyo or Hong Kong. United Airlines (☎ 800/241-6522; 65/873-3533 in Singapore; www.ual.com) has daily flights connecting pretty much every major city in the United States with Singapore via the Pacific route. Expect a stopover in Tokyo en route. Northwest Airlines (☎ 800/447-4747; 65/336-3371 in Singapore; www.nwa.com) links all major U.S. airports with daily direct flights to Singapore from the following ports of exit: New York, Detroit, Minneapolis, Los Angeles, Seattle, and San Francisco, with direct flights from Las Vegas on Mondays and Thursdays only. All flights have one short stopover in Tokyo.

FROM CANADA   Singapore Airlines (☎ 604/681-7488; 65/223-6030 in Singapore; www.singaporeair.com) has flights from Vancouver three times a week, with a stopover in Seoul.

FROM THE UNITED KINGDOM   Singapore Airlines (☎ 181/747-0007 in London; 161-832-3346 in Manchester; 65/223-6030 in Singapore; www.singaporeair.com) has three daily flights departing from London's Heathrow Airport with a daily connection from Manchester. Depending on the day of departure, these flights stop over in either Amsterdam, Zurich, or Bombay. **British Airways** (☎ 0345/222111 local call from anywhere within the U.K.; 65/839-7788 in Singapore; www.british-airways.com) has daily nonstop flights from London. **Qantas Airways Ltd.** (☎ 0345/747767; 65/839-7788 in Singapore; www.qantas.com) has daily nonstop flights on weekdays and flights twice daily on weekends from London.

FROM AUSTRALIA   Singapore Airlines (☎ 65/223-6030 in Singapore; www.singaporeair.com) has twice-daily flights from Melbourne (☎ 3/9254-0300) and Sydney (☎ 2/9350-0100); three dailies from Perth (☎ 8/9265-0500); a daily from Brisbane (☎ 7/3259-0717); flights from Adelaide (☎ 8/8203-0800) four times a week; and from Cairns (☎ 70/317-538) three times a week. **Qantas Airways Ltd.** (☎ 2/131313 toll free; 65/839-7788 in Singapore; www.qantas.com) links all major airports in Australia with daily direct flights to Singapore from Sydney and Melbourne. **British Airways** (☎ 8/9425-7711 in Perth; 7/3223-3133 in Brisbane; 65/839-7788 in Singapore; www.british-airways.com) has daily flights from Perth and Brisbane.

British Airways and Qantas work in partnership to provide routing from Australia, so be sure to consult Qantas for connecting flights form your city.

FROM NEW ZEALAND   Singapore Airlines (☎ 3032129 in Auckland; 3668003 in Christchurch; www.singaporeair.com) has daily flights from Auckland and Christchurch. Air New Zealand (☎ 0800/737000; www.airnewzealand.co.nz) has daily flights from Christchurch and a daily flight from Auckland in partnership with Singapore Airlines (so you can still use or accumulate frequent-flyer miles for this trip).

Getting Into Town from the Airport

Most visitors to Singapore will land at **Changi International Airport,** which is located toward the far eastern corner of the island. Compared to so many other international airports, Changi is a dream come true, providing clean and very efficient space and facilities. Expect to find in-transit accommodations, restaurants, duty-free shops, money changers, ATMs, car-rental desks, accommodation assistance, and tourist information all marked with clear signs. As you arrive, keep your eyes peeled for the many Singapore Tourism Board brochures that are so handily displayed throughout the terminal.

The city is easily accessible by public transportation. A **taxi** trip to the city center will cost around S$22 to S$25 (US$13.15 to US$14.95) and takes around 20 minutes. You'll traverse the wide Airport Boulevard to the Pan-Island Expressway (PIE) or the East Coast Parkway (ECP), past public housing estates and other residential neighborhoods in the eastern part of the island, over causeways, and into the city center.

CityCab offers an **airport shuttle,** a six-seater maxicab that traverses between the airport and the major hotel areas. It covers most hotels, and is very flexible about drop-offs and pickups within the central areas, including MRT (subway) stations. Bookings are made at the airport shuttle counter in the arrival terminal or by calling ☎ 65/553-3880. Pay S$7 (US$4.20) for adults and S$5 (US$3) for children directly to the driver.

A couple of **buses** run from the airport into the city as well. SBS bus no. 16 will take you on a route to Orchard Road and Raffles City (in the Historic District). SBS bus no. 36 runs a direct route to and from the airport and Orchard Road. Both bus stops are located in the basement of the arrival terminal. A trip to town will be about S$1.30 (US$0.78).

For **arrival and departure information,** you can call Changi International Airport toll-free at ☎ 1800/542-4422.

BY TRAIN

The Keretapi Tanah Melayu Berhad railroad company runs express and local trains from **Malaysia to Singapore** four times daily. In Kuala Lumpur, contact KTMB at ☎ 03/274-7434, or see their Web site at www.ktmb.com.my. The fare from KL is RM60 (US$15.80), RM26 (US$6.85), and RM14.80 (US$3.90) for 1st, 2nd, and 3rd class travel, respectively. All trains let you off at the Singapore Railway Station (☎ 65/222-5165) on Keppel Road in Tanjong Pagar, not far from the city center. Money-changing services are available in the station. A taxi into town is not expensive from here.

The *Eastern & Oriental Express,* sister to the Venice Simplon-Orient-Express, runs once a week between Singapore and Bangkok in exquisite luxury, with occasional departures between Bangkok and Chiang Mai. For international reservations from the U.S. and Canada call ☎ 800/524-2420, from Australia ☎ 3/9699-9766, from New Zealand ☎ 9/379-3708, and from the U.K. ☎ 171/805-5100. From Singapore contact E&O in Singapore at (☎ 65/392-3500).

BY BUS

Buses to Singapore from almost all cities in Malaysia will let you off at either the Ban Sen Terminal at the corner of Queen Street and Arab Street in Kampong Glam or at the crossroads of Lavender Street and Kallang Bahru. From Kuala Lumpur buses leave from the **Kuala Lumpur Railway Station** (Plusliner/NiCE, ☎ **04227-2760,** costs around RM55/US$14.45). Buses from Johor Bharu depart from **Larkin Bus Terminal** (Singapore-Johor Ekspress, ☎ **07/223-2276,** RM2.40/US$0.63).

BY FERRY

From the **Johor Ferry Terminal** (☎ **07/251-7404**) in Tanjung Belungkor on the East coast of Malaysia you can catch a FerryLink ferry four times daily and be in Singapore in 45 minutes. One-way fare for adults is MR15 (US$3.95). The ferry lets you off at Changi Ferry Terminal (no phone) on the east coast of Singapore. Taxis do not ply this route, so call a CityCab at ☎ 65/552-2222 to come fetch you. *Also note:* Changi Ferry Terminal does not have money-changing services. **FerryLink's Singapore** contact numbers are ☎ **65/545-3600;** fax 65/545-5040.

From **Tioman Island** you can catch an Auto Batam Ferries and Tours ferry to Singapore at the Berjaya Jetty every day at 2:30pm. Please note this service does not operate from mid-October to early March due to the monsoon season. The ferries let you off at Singapore's Tanah Merah Ferry Terminal, in the eastern part of the island. The terminal has money-changing facilities and a taxi queue outside. Auto Batam's contact in Singapore is ☎ 65/271-4866.

Tanah Merah Ferry Terminal is also home to companies that serve nearby Batam, a popular day trip, and Bintan, an Indonesian island resort area.

GETTING AROUND

The many inexpensive mass transit options make getting around Singapore pretty easy. Of course, **taxis** always simplify the ground transportation dilemma. They're also very affordable, and, by and large, drivers are helpful and honest if not downright personable. The **Mass Rapid Transit (MRT)** subway service has four lines that run over two main routes (roughly east-west and north-south) and are very easy to figure out. **Buses** present more of a challenge because there are so many routes snaking all over the island, but they're a great way to see the country while getting where you want to go. In the bus section, below, I've thrown in some tips that will hopefully demystify the bus experience for you.

Of course, if you're just strolling around the urban limits, many of the sights within the various neighborhoods are within walking distance, and indeed, some of the neighborhoods are only short walks from each other—getting from Chinatown to the Historic District only requires crossing over the Singapore River, and from Little India to Kampong Glam is not far at all. However, I advise against trying to get from, say, Chinatown (in the west) to Kampong Glam (in the east). The distance can be somewhat prohibitive, especially in the heat.

BY PUBLIC TRANSPORTATION Stored-fare **TransitLink fare cards** can be used on both the subway and the buses, and can be purchased at TransitLink offices in the MRT stations. These save you the bother of trying to dig up exact change for bus meters; plus, if you transfer from a bus to the MRT, or between buses, you'll save S$0.25. The card does carry a S$2 (US$1.20) deposit—for a S$12 (US$7.20) initial investment, you'll get S$10 (US$6) worth of travel credit. At the end of your stay, you can cash in your card for the remaining value, and still get one extra trip for about S$0.10.

BY MASS RAPID TRANSIT (MRT)   The MRT is Singapore's subway system. It's cool, clean, safe, and reliable, providing service from the far west reaches of the island to the far east parts on the east-west line and running in a loop around the north part of the island on the north-south line. The lines are color coded to make it easy to find the train you're looking for (see the MRT Transit map in this chapter for specifics). The two lines intersect at the Raffles Place Interchange in Chinatown/Shenton Way, at City Hall in the Historic District, and in the western part of the island at the Jurong East Interchange. (By the way, don't let the "East" fool you—Jurong East is actually in the western part of the island.) MRT operating hours vary between lines and stops, with the earliest train beginning service daily at 5:15am and the last train ending at 12:47am.

Fares range from S$0.60 to S$1.50 (US$0.36 to US$0.90), depending on which stations you travel between. System charts are prominently displayed in all MRT stations to help you find your appropriate fare, which you pay with a TransitLink fare card. Single-fare cards can be purchased at vending machines at MRT stations. See above for information on stored-fare cards. (One caution: A fare card can not be used by two people for the same trip; each must have his own.)

TransitLink also has a Special Edition Tourist Souvenir Ticket, which is good for MRT use only. For S$7 (US$4.20) you can buy a fare card with S$6 (US$3.60) stored value, which you can take home as a souvenir after your trip. It saves you a dollar off the standard deposit, but no refunds can be made on leftover value.

For more information, call TransitLink TeleInfo at ☎ **1800/779-9366** (daily 24 hours).

BY BUS   Singapore's bus system comprises an extensive web of routes that reach virtually everywhere on the island. It can be intimidating for newcomers, but once you get your feet wet, you'll feel right at home. There are two main bus services, **SBS (Singapore Bus Service)** and **TIBS (Trans-Island Bus Service).** Most buses are clean, but not all are air-conditioned.

Start off first by purchasing the latest edition of the **TransitLink Guide** for about S$1.40 (US$0.84) at the TransitLink office in any MRT station, at a bus interchange, or at selected bookstores around the city. This tiny book is a very handy guide that details each route and stop, indicating connections with MRT stations and fares for each trip. Next to the guide, the best thing to do is simply ask people for help. At any crowded bus stop there will always be somebody who speaks English and is willing to help out a lost stranger. You can also ask the bus driver where you need to go, and he'll tell you the fare, how to get there, and even when to get off.

All buses have a couple of fare machines close to the driver. Feed the machine your TransitLink card then push the button with the corresponding fare (it's pretty much an honor system to make sure you pay the correct rate). You'll get a receipt back with your fare stamped on it. Sometimes the authorities come around and check to see that people are paying the correct fare, and if you've made a mistake, this is a good time to play up the ignorant tourist routine—otherwise you could be charged the highest fare as punishment. The best thing to do? Ask the driver to tell you the correct fare for where you want to go. It'll be anywhere between S$0.55 and S$1.50 (US$0.33 and US$0.90). If you're paying cash, be sure to have exact change; place the coins in the box by the driver and announce your fare to him. He'll issue a ticket, which will pop out of a slot on one of the TransitLink machines.

The **Tourist Day Ticket** is a great deal for travelers. The 1-day pass costs S$10 (US$6), good for 12 rides on either SBS or TIBS buses or the MRT. Using one of these will save you having to worry about calculating the correct fare or coming up

MRT Transit System

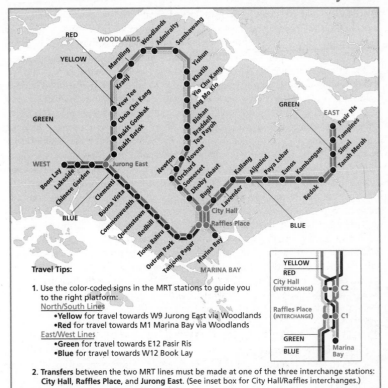

Travel Tips:

1. Use the color-coded signs in the MRT stations to guide you to the right platform:
   <u>North/South Lines</u>
   - **Yellow** for travel towards W9 Jurong East via Woodlands
   - **Red** for travel towards M1 Marina Bay via Woodlands
   <u>East/West Lines</u>
   - **Green** for travel towards E12 Pasir Ris
   - **Blue** for travel towards W12 Book Lay

2. **Transfers** between the two MRT lines must be made at one of the three interchange stations: **City Hall**, **Raffles Place**, and **Jurong East**. (See inset box for City Hall/Raffles interchanges.)

with exact change. You can pick one up at any TransitLink office and at hotels, money changers, provisioner shops, or travel agents. Unfortunately, there's no handy sign identifying which shops sell them, so you'll have to ask around.

For more information, contact either of the two operating bus lines during standard business hours: **Singapore Bus Service** (SBS) (☎ **1800/287-2727**) or the **Trans-Island Bus Service** (TIBS) (☎ **1800/482-5433**).

BY TROLLEY You have a couple of trolley options, both services offered for the convenience of travelers, making stops at most major tourist destinations. The **Singapore Trolley** shuttles down Orchard Road, through the Historic District and the Singapore River, and down to Marina Square. For S$14.90 (US$8.90) adults and S$9.90 (US$5.95) children, you can enjoy unlimited rides during your stay (this price also includes a free riverboat tour). Buy your tickets either from your hotel's front desk or directly from the driver. Call Singapore Explorer at ☎ **65/339-6833.**

Singapore Airlines hosts the SIA Hop-on bus. Plying between Bugis Junction, Suntec City, the Historic District, the Singapore River, Chinatown, and the Singapore Botanic Gardens, the Hop-on comes every 30 minutes between the hours of 8:30am and 7pm. Unlimited rides for 1 day cost S$5 (US$3) adults and S$3 (US$1.80) children. Buy your tickets from your hotel's front desk, from a Singapore Airlines office, or from the bus drivers. If you've traveled to Singapore via Singapore Airlines, you're entitled to free passage aboard the Hop-on. Just show your ticket to the driver. For more information call **Singapore Airlines** at ☎ **65/223-6030.**

BY TAXI Taxis are a very convenient and affordable way to get around Singapore, and there's every chance you'll get a good conversation with the driver into the bargain. Despite this, I advise against relying completely on taxicabs, since Singapore's excellent public transportation system will take you practically anywhere you need to go for a fraction of the price. Even in the middle of nowhere there's always a bus route to take you to familiar territory—just remember to keep your TransitLink Guide (see above) handy, so you'll know where the bus you're about to hop is headed.

In town, all of the shopping malls, hotels, and major buildings have taxi queues, which you're expected to use. During lunch hours and the evening rush, the queues can be very long; though by and large taxis are convenient, don't count on finding one fast during the evening rush hours between 5pm and 7pm. Especially if it's raining, you'll be waiting for an hour, easy. Everybody wants a cab at this time, and for some strange reason this is the time the cabbies choose to change shifts. Brilliant. During this time, I recommend you call to book a taxi pickup. You pay a little extra, but believe me, some days it can really be worth it.

Most destinations in the main parts of the island can be reached fairly inexpensively, while trips to the outlying attractions can cost between S$10 and S$15 (US$6 and US$9) one-way. If you're at an attraction or restaurant outside of the central part of the city where it is more difficult to hail a cab on the street, you can ask the cashier or service counter attendant to call a taxi for you. The extra charge for pickup is between S$2.80 and S$3.20 (US$1.70 and US$1.90) depending on the cab company (Comfort is the cheapest). Call these main cab companies for bookings: **CityCab** (cash payment ☎ **65/552-2222;** credit card payment ☎ **65/553-8888**), **Comfort** (☎ **65/ 552-1111**), and **TIBS** (☎ **65/481-1211**).

All taxis charge the metered fare, which is S$2.40 (US$1.45) for the first kilometer and S$0.10 for each additional 225 to 240 meters or 30 seconds of waiting. Extra fares are levied on top of the metered fare depending on where you're going and when you go. At times, figuring your fare seems more like a riddle. Here's a summary:

Trips during peak hours: Between the hours of 7:30am and 9:30am Monday to Friday, 4:30pm to 7pm Monday to Friday, and 11:30am to 2pm on Saturdays, trips will carry an additional S$1 (US$0.60) peak-period surcharge. But if you're traveling outside the Central Business District (CBD), you won't need to pay this surcharge during the morning rush. (To accurately outline the boundaries of the CBD, I'd need to fill a couple encyclopedic volumes, so for this purpose, let's just say it's basically Orchard Road, the Historic District, Chinatown, and Shenton Way—basically.)

Additional charges rack up each time you travel through an Electronic Road Pricing (ERP) scheme underpass. On the Central Expressway (CTE), Pan-Island Expressway (PIE), and selected thoroughfares in the CBD, charges from S$0.30 to S$1.70 (US$0.18 to US$1) are calculated by an electronic box on the driver's dashboard. The driver will add this amount to your fare.

And for special torture, here's some **more charges:** From midnight to 6am, add 50% to your fare. From 6pm on the eve of a public holiday to midnight the following day, you pay an additional S$1. From Changi or Seletar Airports add S$3 (US$1.80). And for credit card payments add 10%.

BY CAR Singapore's public transportation systems are so extensive, efficient, and inexpensive that you shouldn't need a car to enjoy your stay. In fact, I don't advise it. It is expensive due to government taxation of motor vehicles, you have to drive on the left side of the road, all foreign drivers need a valid international driver's license, and you have to deal with confusing parking regulations. If you insist, however, **Avis** (☎ **65/542-8855**) and **Hertz** (☎ **65/737-1668**) have offices at Changi Airport. Both also offer hourly rentals of chauffeur-driven vehicles.

Fast Facts: Singapore

American Express   The American Express office is located at no. 01–04/05 Winslan House, Killiney Road (a short walk from Orchard Road). The direct line for travel services is ☎ **65/235-5788.** The 24-hour membership services hot line is ☎ **1800/732-2244.** The 24-hour traveler's check refund hot line is ☎ **1800/738-3383.** See the "Money" section earlier in this chapter for more details on member privileges.

Baby-Sitters   Most hotels will arrange for a reliable baby-sitter with at least 24 hours' advance notice.

Business Hours   **Shopping centers** are open Monday through Saturday from 10am to 8pm, and stay open until 10pm on some public holidays. **Banks** are open from 9:30am to 3pm Monday through Friday, and from 9am to 11am on Saturdays. **Restaurants** open at lunchtime from around 11am to 2:30pm, and for dinner they reopen at around 6pm and take last order sometime around 10pm. **Nightclubs** stay open until midnight on weekdays and until 2am on Fridays and Saturdays. **Government offices** are open from 9am to 5pm Monday through Friday and from 9am to 3pm on Saturdays. **Post offices** conduct business from 8:30am to 5pm on weekdays and from 8:30am to 1pm on Saturdays.

Cameras & Film   There are many camera equipment shops in the malls on **Orchard Road,** and some will take repairs. Avoid the shops in Far East Plaza and Lucky Plaza, as these are not as reputable. Film is readily available everywhere at prices comparable to those in the West. Many of the major shopping centers have fast and inexpensive film-developing services, and developing quality is generally excellent.

Climate   See "When to Go," earlier in this chapter.

Credit Cards   To report lost or stolen credit cards, the number to call for **American Express** is ☎ **1800/732-2244.** For **MasterCard,** the toll-free Emergency Assistance hot line is ☎ **1800/110-0113.** For **Visa,** call toll-free ☎ **1800/110-0344.** If your **Diners Club** card is lost or stolen, call locally ☎ **65/292-7055.**

Crime   Because of harsh laws, strict enforcement, and traditional cultural beliefs, there is not a lot of crime in Singapore. Murder and rape are almost nonexistent. A few pickpockets do creep around tourist-populated areas, though, so take care. All hotels have either a safe deposit box in the rooms or a safe behind the front desk. The only other thieves you need to be aware of are shop owners who may overcharge you for purchases, all in the sport of savvy salesmanship.

   Also, you probably don't want to become a criminal yourself. Violations that bring on large fines include littering, jaywalking, smoking in prohibited areas, and failing to obey taxi queues (meaning that if there's a taxi queue nearby, it's against the law to hail a cab out of the queue).

   The number to call for a **police emergency** is ☎ **999.**

Currency   See "Money," earlier in this chapter.

Customs   See "Customs Regulations," earlier in this chapter.

Dentists   Dental care in Singapore is excellent, and most procedures will cost less than they would at home. Some hospitals offer emergency dental care at affordable rates, should you need dental care during your trip.

Doctors   Most hotels have in-house doctors on call 24 hours a day. A visit to a private physician can cost anywhere from S$25 to S$100 (US$15 to US$60). In the event of a medical emergency call ☎ **995** for an ambulance.

Driving Rules   See "Getting Around," earlier in this chapter.

Drug Laws   If you are caught in possession of morphine quantities exceeding 30 grams, heroin exceeding 15 grams, cocaine 30 grams, marijuana 500 grams, hashish 200 grams, or opium 1.2 grams, the Singapore government will consider you to be a drug trafficker and you will receive the death penalty—no questions asked. See the "Customs Regulations" section earlier in this chapter for more details.

Electricity   Standard electrical current is 220 volts AC (50 cycles). Consult your concierge to see if your hotel has converters and plug adapters in-house for you to use. If you are using sensitive equipment, do not trust the cheap voltage transformers. Nowadays, a lot of electrical equipment—including portable radios and laptop computers—comes with built-in converters, so you can follow the manufacturer's directions for changing them over. FYI, videocassettes taped on different voltage currents are recorded on machines with different record and playback cycles. Prerecorded videotapes are not interchangeable between currents unless you have special equipment that can play either kind.

Embassies   Foreign missions in Singapore are as follows: **United States,** 30 Hill St. (☎) **65/338-0251**); **Canada,** 80 Anson Rd., 14/15–00 IBM Towers (☎ **65/225-6363**); **Australia,** 25 Napier Rd. (☎ **65/737-9311**); **New Zealand,** 13 Nassim Rd. (☎ **65/235-9966**); **United Kingdom,** Taglin Rd. (☎ **65/473-9333**).

Emergencies   For police dial ☎ **999.** For medical or fire emergencies call ☎ **995.**

Hairdressers/Barbers   Most major hotels have unisex salons, and you can find them in many shopping malls as well. For the gentleman who wants a really special shave 'n' a haircut, you can always try the back alley behind the Allsagoff School off Sultan Road in Kampong Glam. They don't make places like these anymore.

Hitchhiking   Definitely not recommended in Singapore. Heaven knows what punishment you'll invite.

Holidays   See "Public Holidays & Events," under "When to Go," earlier in this chapter.

Hospitals   If you need to seek emergency medical attention, go to either of the following centrally located private hospitals: **Mount Elizabeth Hospital Ltd.,** 3 Mount Elizabeth Rd., near Orchard Road (☎ **65/737-2666**), or **Singapore General Hospital,** Outram Road, in Chinatown (☎ **65/222-3322**). Medical care in Singapore is of superior quality. In fact, throngs of ASEAN (Association of Southeast Asian Nations) neighbors make annual trips to Singapore for their physical examinations and other medical treatments. You can be assured of excellent care, should you need it.

Internet   Internet cafes are becoming common throughout the city, with usage costs between S$4 and S$5 (US$2.40–US$3) per hour (keep in mind, if you use the Internet in your hotel's business center, you'll pay a much higher price). Almost every shopping mall has one, especially along Orchard Road, and there are cybercafes in both terminals at Changi Airport. In town, along Orchard

Road, try **Cyber Arena Internet Point II,** Cuppage Terrace, 39 Orchard Rd. (☎ **65/738-1540**), or **E-Net Cyberspace,** 1 Scotts Rd., Shaw Centre no. 05–10 (☎ **65/835-2338**). In the Historic District, there are a few in Stamford House, just across from City Hall MRT Station. Check out **Chills Café,** no. 01–01 Stamford House, 39 Stamford Rd. (☎ **65/883-1016**).

Language   The official languages are Malay, Chinese (Mandarin), Tamil, and English. Malay is the national language while English is the language for government operations, law, and major financial transactions. Most Singaporeans are at least bilingual, with many speaking one or more dialects of Chinese, English, and some Malay.

Laundry   Almost all Singaporeans have washing machines in their homes, so the concept of self-service laundry is not terribly common here. There are some laundries listed in the Singapore Yellow Pages directory, but most of them are out in the Housing Board developments, so it may be a trek. A few hotels offer self-service launderettes, and most of them have a laundry service, but you'll pay inflated prices for clean clothes.

Liquor Laws   The legal age for alcohol purchase and consumption is 18 years. Some of the smaller clubs rarely check identification, but the larger ones will, and sometimes require patrons to be 21 years to enter, just to weed out younger crowds. Public drunk-and-disorderly behavior is against the law, and may snag you for up to S$1,000 in fines for the first offense, or even imprisonment—which is unlikely, but still a great way to ruin a vacation. There are strict drinking and driving laws, and roadblocks are set up on weekends to catch party people on their way home to the housing developments.

Mail   Most hotels have mail services at the front counter. **Singapore Post** has centrally located offices at no. 04–15 Ngee Ann City/Takashimaya Shopping Centre (☎ **65/738-6899**); Tang's department store at 320 Orchard Rd. no. 03–00 (☎ **65/738-5899**); Chinatown Point, 133 New Bridge Rd. no. 02–42/43/44 (☎ **65/538-7899**); Change Alley, 16 Collyer Quay no. 02–02 Hitachi Tower (☎ **65/538-6899**); and 231 Bain St. no. 01–03 Bras Basah Complex (☎ **65/339-8899**). Plus there are five branches at Changi International Airport. For all general inquiries, dial ☎ **65/1605** for the Singapore Post hot line.

The going rate for international airmail letters to North America and Europe is S$1 (US$0.06) for 20 grams plus S$0.35 (US$0.21) for each additional 10 grams. For international airmail service to Australia and New Zealand, the rate is S$0.70 (US$0.42) for 20 grams plus S$0.30 (US$0.18) for each additional 10 grams. Postcards and aerograms to all destinations are S$0.50 (US$0.30).

Your hotel will accept mail sent for you at its address. For other mail services, refer to the section on American Express under "Money," earlier in this chapter—American Express has a special mail delivery and holding deal for card members.

Maps   The *Singapore Street Directory,* a book detailing every section of the island, is carried by most taxi drivers, and can be very helpful if you're trying to get someplace and he either doesn't know where it is or can't understand you. The street listing in the front will direct you to the corresponding map. A good cabbie can take it from there. Other good maps of the major city areas can be found in free STB publications, while there are also a few commercially produced maps sold in all major bookstores here.

Newspapers & Magazines   Local English newspapers available are the *International Herald Tribune, The Business Times, The Straits Times,* and *USA Today International.* Following an article criticizing the Singapore government, the *Asian Wall Street Journal* was banned from wide distribution in Singapore. Most of the major hotels are allowed to carry it, though, so ask around and you can find one. *The New Paper* is an "alternative publication" that may be a useful source for finding out what's happening around town. Major hotels, bookstores, and magazine shops sell a wide variety of international magazines.

Pets   Singapore has strict quarantine regulations, and I'll be shocked if you can find a hotel that will take pets. Keep poochie at home.

Pharmacies/Chemists   Guardian Pharmacies fills prescriptions with name brand drugs (from a licensed physician within Singapore), and carries a large selection of toiletry items. Convenient locations include no. B1–05 Centrepoint Shopping Centre (☎ **65/737-4835**); Changi International Airport Terminal 2 (☎ **65/545-4233**); no. 02–139 Marina Square (☎ **65/333-9565**); and no. B1–04 Raffles Place MRT Station (☎ **65/535-2762**).

Police   Given the strict law enforcement reputation in Singapore, you can bet the officers here don't have the greatest senses of humor. If you find yourself being questioned about anything, big or small, be dead serious and most respectful. For emergencies, call ☎ **999.** If you need to call the police headquarters, dial ☎ **65/235-9111.**

   If you are arrested, you have the right to legal council, but only when the police decide you can exercise that right. You get no call unless they give you permission. Bottom line: Don't get arrested.

Radio/TV   There are five channels in Singapore, four of which are mostly English-language programming. These days, more shows are being produced locally, but there's still a heavy rotation of the latest hits from the United States, the United Kingdom, and Australia. The larger hotels all have HBO and some have CNN, as well as other satellite programming.

   There are five FM radio stations, which broadcast in all of the national languages.

Rest Rooms/Toilets   Rest rooms are easy to find in Singapore and most of the time they are clean. Note that the authorities levy fines for not flushing, though I've never seen anyone actually come in and check. The more modern facilities will have toilet bowls, but you won't get out of Singapore alive without encountering a "squatty potty"—a small porcelain bowl in the floor over which you are expected to hover. Be prepared. If you head out to beach areas or to surrounding islands, bring spare tissue. Every once in a blue moon, I've encountered some old lady who stands outside the door and charges you a dime to use the toilet, but it's rare.

Safety   Singapore is a pretty safe place by any standards. There's very little violent crime, even late at night. If you stay out, there's very little worry about making it home safe. If your children are missing, they probably aren't kidnapped, but are being consoled by a friendly passerby while they search for you. This may sound naive, but the Chinese are culturally a very family oriented people, and most would never dream of harming a child.

   In recent years, some pickpocketing has been reported. Hotel safe deposit boxes are the best way to secure valuables, and traveler's checks solve theft problems in a jiff.

Smoking   It's against the law to smoke in public buses, elevators, theaters, cinemas, air-conditioned restaurants, shopping centers, government offices, and taxi queues.

Taxes   Many hotels and restaurants will advertise rates followed by "+++." The first + is the goods and services tax (GST), which is levied at 3% of the purchase. The second + is 1% cess (a 1% tax levied by the STB on all tourism-related activities). The third is a 10% gratuity. See the "Customs Regulations" section earlier in this chapter for information on the GST Tourist Refund Scheme, which lets you recover the GST for purchases of goods over S$300 (US$179.65) in value.

Taxis   See "Getting Around," earlier in this chapter.

Telegrams & Wiring Money   See "Money," earlier in this chapter for information on wiring money. To send a telegram, consult your hotel. Many of them offer this service for a fee.

Telephones & Faxes   Almost all hotels will send faxes locally and internationally for you and add the charge to your bill. **Public phones** are abundant and can be operated by coins or by phone cards, which can be purchased in increments of S$2, S$5, and S$10 (US$1.20, US$3, and US$6) values at post offices, provisioners shops, and some money changers. The charge for a local call is S$0.10 for 3 minutes. A tone will interrupt your call when your time is up to remind you to add another coin. Calls to numbers beginning with 1800 are toll free within Singapore.

International Direct Dialing (IDD) is the long-distance service used by most hotels, businesses, and private residences in Singapore, with direct dialing to 218 countries. Depending on where you are calling, there is rarely a delay or echo on the line, and reception is incredibly clear.

Telephone Dialing Info at a Glance

- **To place a call from your home country to Singapore:** Dial the international access code (011 in the U.S., 0011 in Australia, or 00 in the U.K., Ireland, and New Zealand), plus the country code (**65**), plus the seven-digit phone number (for example, 011-65/000-0000). Note that many hotels have toll-free numbers for calling from all these countries; where this is the case, I've listed them in the individual hotel reviews.

- **To call Malaysia from Singapore:** Via an operator, dial **109**. To call direct, dial the access code for the trunk line that links the two countries (007) plus Malaysia's country code (60) plus the city code and the number (for example, 005-60/000-0000).

- **To place a direct international call from Singapore:** Dial the international access code (001), the country code (U.S. and Canada 1, Australia 61, Republic of Ireland 353, New Zealand 64, U.K. 44), the area or city code, and the number.

- To reach the international operator: Dial 104.

- **To place a call within Singapore:** Dial the seven-digit number. The "65" prefix need not be used. Toll-free numbers in Singapore use the standard "1-800" prefix.

  Other useful numbers are for the **time** (☎ 1711), and for the **weather** (☎ 65/542-7788). For **telephone directory assistance,** dial **100**.

Before you leave your home country, contact your long-distance provider to see if they offer a **long-distance calling card,** which will allow you to access their international operators and have your calls charged to your home phone bill at their rates. Singapore has some of the lowest international call rates in the world, but unfortunately, hotels charge a whopping surcharge for these calls.

Time　Singapore Standard Time is 8 hours ahead of Greenwich mean time (GMT). International time differences will change during daylight saving or summer time. Basic time differences are: New York –13, Los Angeles –16, Montreal –13, Vancouver –16, London –8, Brisbane +3, Darwin +1, Melbourne +2, Sydney +3, and Auckland +4. For the current time within Singapore, call ☎ **1711.**

Tipping　Tipping is discouraged at hotels, bars, and in taxis. Basically, the deal here is not to tip. A gratuity is automatically added into guest checks, and there's no need to slip anyone an extra buck for carrying bags or such. It's not expected.

Tourist Offices　See "Visitor Information," earlier in this chapter.

Water　Tap water in Singapore passes World Health Organization standards and is potable.

Yellow Pages　The Singapore Yellow Pages is the place to start for any need that may come up. They are standard in most hotel rooms. They're rarely found at public phones, but shopkeepers may let you take a peek at theirs if you ask nicely.

3 Accommodations

Budget accommodations are not a high priority in Singapore. Between the business community's demand for luxury on the one hand and the inflated Singaporean real estate market on the other, room prices tend to be high. What this means for leisure travelers is that you may end up paying for a business center you'll never use or a 24-hour stress-reliever masseuse you'll never call—and all this without the benefit of a corporate discount rate. Don't fret, though: there's a range of accommodations out there—you just have to know where to find 'em.

In considering where you'll stay, think about what you'll be doing in Singapore—that way, you can choose a hotel that's close to the particular action that suits you. (On the other hand, since Singapore is a small place and public transportation is excellent, nothing's really ever too far away.)

Orchard Road has the largest cluster of hotels in the city, and is right in the heart of Singaporean shopping mania—the malls and wide sidewalks where locals and tourists stroll to see and be seen. The **Historic District** has hotels that are near museums and sights, while those in **Marina Bay** center more around the business professionals who come to Singapore for Suntec City, the giant convention and exhibition center located there. **Chinatown** and **Tanjong Pagar** have some lovely boutique hotels in quaint back streets, and **Shenton Way** has a couple of high-rise places for the convenience of people doing business in the downtown business district. Many hotels have free morning and evening shuttle buses to Orchard Road, Suntec City, and Shenton Way. I've also listed two hotels on **Sentosa,** an island to the south that's a popular day or weekend trip for many Singaporeans. (It's connected to Singapore by a causeway.)

Rates for double rooms range from as low as S$80 (US$47.90) at the Strand on Bencoolen (a famous backpacker's strip) to as high as S$650 (US$389.20) a night at the exclusive Raffles Hotel. Average rooms are usually in the S$200 to S$300 (US$119.75 to US$179.65) range, but keep in mind that **although all prices listed in this chapter are the going rates, they rarely represent what you'll actually pay.**

In fact, you should *never* have to pay the advertised rate in a Singapore hotel, as many offer promotional rates. When you call for your reservation, always ask what special deals they are running and how you can get the lowest price for your room. Many times hotels that have just completed renovations offer discounts, and most have special weekend or long-term stay programs. Also be sure to inquire about free add-ons. Complimentary breakfast and other services can have added value that make a difference in the end.

For the purposes of this guide, I've divided hotels into the categories **very expensive,** S$400 (US$239.50) and up; **expensive,** S$300 to S$400 (US$179.65 to US$239.50); **moderate,** S$200 to S$300 (US$119.75 to US$179.65); and **inexpensive,** under S$200 (US$119.75).

TAXES & SERVICE CHARGES   All rates listed are in Singapore dollars, with U.S. dollar equivalents provided as well (remember to check the exchange rate when you're planning, though, since it may fluctuate). Most rates do not include the so-called "+++" taxes and charges: the 10% service charge, 3% goods and services tax (GST), and 1% cess (a 1% tax levied by the STB on all tourism-related activities). Keep these in mind when figuring your budget. Some budget hotels will quote discount rates inclusive of all taxes.

THE BUSY SEASON   The busy season is from January to around June. In the late summer months, business travel dies down and hotels try to make up for drooping occupancy rates by going after the leisure market. In fall, even tourism drops off somewhat, making the season ripe for budget-minded visitors. These may be the best times to get a deal. Probably the worst time to negotiate will be between Christmas and the Chinese New Year, when folks travel on vacation and to see their families.

MAKING RESERVATIONS ON THE GROUND   If you are not able to make a reservation before your trip, there is a **reservation service** available at Changi International Airport. The Singapore Hotel Association operates desks in both Terminals 1 and 2, with reservation services based upon room availability for many hotels. Discounts for these arrangements are sometimes as high as 30%. The desks are open daily from 7:30am to 11:30pm.

THE HISTORIC DISTRICT
VERY EXPENSIVE

✪ **Raffles Hotel.** 1 Beach Rd., Singapore 189673. ☎ **800/525-4800** in the U.S. and Canada, 008/251-958 in Australia, 0800/441098 in New Zealand, 0800/964470 in the U.K., or 65/337-1886. Fax 65/339-7650. www.raffles.com. E-mail: raffles@pacific.net.sg. 104 suites. A/C MINIBAR TV TEL. S$650–S$6,000 (US$389.20–US$3,592.80) suite. AE, DC, JCB, MC, V. Near City Hall MRT.

Raffles Hotel has been legendary since its establishment in 1887. Named after Singapore's first British colonial administrator, Sir Stamford Raffles, it was founded by the Armenian Sarkies brothers. Originally, it was a bungalow, but by the 1920s and 1930s it had expanded to become a mecca for celebrities like Charlie Chaplin and Douglas Fairbanks, for writers like Somerset Maugham and Noël Coward, and for various and sundry kings, sultans, and politicians. Always at the center of Singapore's colonial high life, it's hosted balls, tea dances, and jazz functions, and during World War II was the last rallying point for the British in the face of Japanese occupation and the first place for refugee prisoners of war released from concentration camps. In 1987, the Raffles Hotel was declared a landmark and restored to its early 20th-century splendor, with grand arches, 14-foot molded ceilings with spinning fans, tiled teak and marble floors, Oriental carpets, and period furnishings. Outside, the facade of the main building was

Urban Singapore Accommodations & Dining

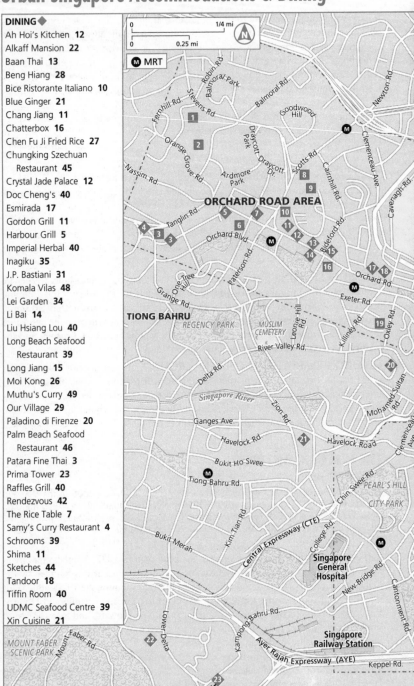

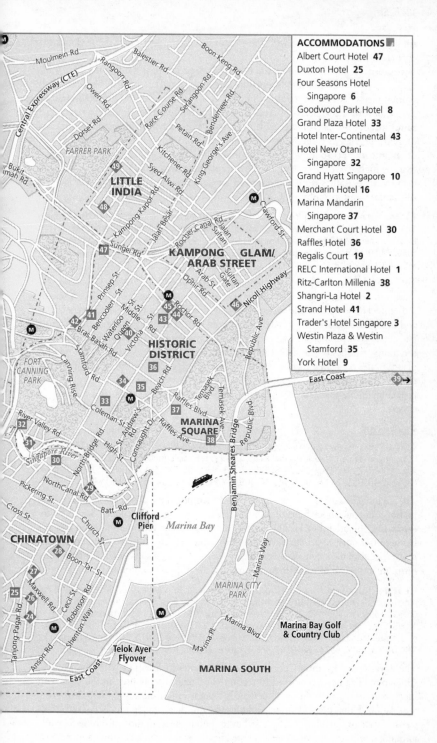

similarly restored, complete with the elegant cast-iron portico and the verandas that encircle the upper stories.

Because it is a national landmark, thousands of people pass through the open lobby each day, so in addition there's a private inner lobby marked off for "residents" only. Nothing feels better than walking along the dark teak floors of the verandahs, past little rattan-furnished relaxation areas overlooking the green tropical courtyards. Each suite entrance is like a private apartment door: Enter past the living and dining area dressed in Oriental carpets and reproduction furniture, then pass through louvered doors into the bedroom with its four-poster bed and beautiful armoire, ceiling fan twirling high above. Now imagine you're a colonial traveler, fresh in town from a long ocean voyage. Raffles is the only hotel in Singapore where you can still fully play out this fantasy, and it can be a lot of fun.

✪ **The Ritz-Carlton, Millenia Singapore.** 7 Raffles Ave., Singapore 039799. ☎ **800/ 241-3333** in the U.S. and Canada, or 65/337-8888. Fax 65/338-0001. www.ritzcarlton.com. E-mail: reservation@ritz-carlton.com.sg. 608 units. A/C MINIBAR TV TEL. S$430–S$475 (US$257.50–US$284.45) double; S$550–S$5,000 (US$329.35–US$2,994) suite. AE, DC, JCB, MC, V. 10-min. walk to City Hall MRT.

Touted as the ultimate in Singapore luxury hotels, The Ritz-Carlton, Millenia, is just that, but you have to love ultramodern design. The space-age lobby is like a science museum: The sculptures and artworks displayed throughout this place are very daring and innovative. Luckily for residents, the guest rooms display a great deal of warmth and coziness in comparison. All rooms have spectacular views of either Kallang Bay or the more majestic Marina Bay. Even the bathrooms have views, as the huge tubs are placed under octagonal picture windows so you can gaze as you bathe. Oh, the decadence! Guest rooms here are about 25% larger than most five-star rooms elsewhere, providing ample space for lovely seating areas, big two-poster beds, and full walk-in closets.

EXPENSIVE

Grand Plaza Parkroyal. 10 Coleman St., Singapore 179809. ☎ **800/44-UTELL** in the U.S. and Canada, or 65/336-3456. Fax 65/339-9311. E-mail: gph01@pacific.net.sg. 338 units. A/C MINIBAR TV TEL. S$300–S$320 (US$179.65–US$191.60) double; S$500–S$1,200 (US$299.40–US$718.55) suite. AE, DC, JCB, MC, V. 5-min. walk to City Hall MRT.

The Grand Plaza was built on top of (and incorporating) 2 blocks of prewar shop houses, and you can see hints of shop house detail throughout the lobby, which is otherwise like any other hotel's. The old alleyway that ran between the shop house blocks has been transformed into a courtyard where dinner is served alfresco. Guest rooms are of average size, have considerable closet space, and sport sharp Italian contemporary furniture in natural tones, with homey touches like snuggly comforters on all the beds.

✪ **Hotel Inter-Continental Singapore.** 80 Middle Rd., Singapore 188966 (near Bugis Junction). ☎ **800/327-0200** in the U.S. and Canada, 008/221-335 in Australia (Sydney 02/9232-1199), 800/442-215 in New Zealand, 0345/581-444 in the U.K. (London 181/847-2277), or 65/338-7600. Fax 65/338-7366. www.interconti.com. E-mail: singapore@interconti.com. 406 units. A/C MINIBAR TV TEL. S$410 (US$245.51) double; S$580–S$3,800 (US$347.30–US$2,275.45) suite. AE, DC, JCB, MC, V. Bugis MRT.

The government let Inter-Continental build a hotel in this spot with one ironclad stipulation: The hotel chain had to retain the original shop houses on the block and incorporate them into the hotel design. No preservation, no hotel. Reinforcing the foundation, Hotel Inter-Continental built up from there, giving touches of old architectural style to the lobby, lounge, and other public areas on the bottom floors while imbuing it with the feel of a modern hotel. Features like beamed ceilings and wooden staircases are warmly accentuated with Chinese and European antique reproductions, Oriental carpets, and local artworks. The second and third floors have "Shop House Rooms" styled with such Peranakan trappings as carved hardwood furnishings and floral linens, and with homey touches like potted plants and carpets over wooden floors. These rooms are very unique, presenting a surprising element of local flair that you don't often find in large chain hotels. Guest rooms on higher levels are large, with formal European styling and large luxurious bathrooms.

✪ **Marina Mandarin Singapore.** 6 Raffles Blvd., Marina Square, Singapore 039594. ☎ **65/338-3388.** Fax 65/339-4977. www.marina-mandarin.com.sg. E-mail: mmsrevn@pacific.net.sg. 575 units. S$340–S$420 (US$203.60–US$251.50) double; S$460 (US$275.45) executive club; S$600–S$3,000 (US$359.30–US$1,796.40) suite. AE, DC, JCB, MC, V. 10-min. walk to City Hall MRT.

There are a few hotels in the Marina Bay area built around the atrium concept, and of them, this one is the loveliest. The atrium lobby opens up to ceiling skylights 21 stories above, guest corridor balconies fringed with vines line the sides, and in the center hangs a glistening metal mobile sculpture in red and gold. One of the most surprising details is the melodic chirping of caged songbirds, which fills the open space every morning. In the evening, live classical music from the lobby bar drifts upwards. The guest rooms are equally impressive: large and cool, with two desk spaces and balconies standard for each room. Try to get the Marina view for that famous Shenton Way skyline towering above the bay. All bathrooms have double sinks, a separate shower and tub, and a bidet.

MODERATE

Hotel New Otani Singapore. 177A River Valley Rd., Singapore 179031. ☎ **800/421-8795** in the U.S. and Canada, 800/273-2294 in California, or 65/338-3333. Fax 65/339-2854. www.newotani.co.jp. E-mail: newotani@singnet.com.sg. 408 units. A/C MINIBAR TV TEL. S$300–S$320 (US$179.65–US$191.60) double; S$600–S$700 (US$359.30–US$419.15) suite. AE, DC, JCB, MC, V. Far from MRT stations.

The Hotel New Otani sits along the Singapore River just next to Clarke Quay (a popular spot for nightlife, dining, and shopping) and a stroll away from the Historic District. At night, you have access to nearby Boat Quay bars and restaurants to one side and to the unique clubs of Mohamed Sultan Road on the other. The hotel was renovated in 1993, and recent additions (to all rooms) include multimedia PCs with Microsoft Office and tourist information. Internet access and computer games are also available for an extra charge. All rooms have small balconies with good views of the river, the financial district, Fort Canning Park, and Chinatown, and the standard rooms have large luxurious bathrooms like those you typically see in more deluxe accommodations. Facilities include a large outdoor pool and a fitness center with aerobics, Jacuzzi, sauna, facials, and massage (you can even get a massage poolside). The hotel runs daily shuttle service to Orchard Road, Shenton Way, and Marina Square.

✪ **The Westin Stamford & Westin Plaza.** 2 Stamford Rd., Singapore 178882. ☎ **800/WESTIN-1** in the U.S. and Canada, or 65/338-8585. Fax 65/338-2862. www.westinsingapore.com. E-mail: westin1@singnet.com.sg. 2,046 units. A/C MINIBAR TV TEL. Westin Stamford: S$340–S$360 (US$203.60–US$215.55) double; S$380 (US$227.55) executive club; S$450–S$1,700 (US$269.45–US$1,017.95) suite. Westin Plaza: S$360–S$380 (US$215.55–US$227.55) double; S$400 (US$239.50) executive club. AE, DC, JCB, MC, V. City Centre MRT.

The combined Westin Stamford and Westin Plaza hotels, an impressive complex comprising 2,046 combined guest rooms, the Raffles City Convention Centre, plus 12 food and beverage outlets, sits directly atop the Raffles City Shopping Complex and City Hall MRT station just in the center of town. Both hotels opened in 1986, with special acclaim for The Westin Stamford as the Guinness Book of World Records' tallest hotel in the world. Its 70 floors measure in at 226.13 meters (735 ft.) and offer some pretty spectacular views. Funny thing: The rooms in The Westin Stamford are less expensive than those in The Westin Plaza. Go for the views, and save money!

Guest rooms are slightly larger than average and feature balconies; the rooms' light pastel decor gives a feeling of freshness. If you plan to conduct business in Singapore, The Westin offers guest offices for S$390 (US$234). Ask about their weekend promotional rates.

INEXPENSIVE

✪ Albert Court Hotel. 180 Albert St., Singapore 189971. ☎ **65/339-3939.** Fax 65/339-3252. www.fareast.com.sg/hotels. E-mail: sales.mktg@albertcourt.com.sg. 136 units. A/C MINIBAR TV TEL. S$120 (US$71.85) double. AE, DC, JCB, MC, V. 5-min. walk to Bugis MRT.

The Albert Court was first conceived as part of the Urban Renewal Authority's master plan to revitalize this block, which involved the restoration of two rows of prewar shop houses. The eight-story boutique hotel that emerged has all the Western comforts but has retained the charm of its shop house roots. Decorators placed local Peranakan touches everywhere, from the carved teak panels in traditional floral design to the antique china cups used for tea service in the rooms. (Guaranteed: The sight of these cups brings misty-eyed nostalgia to the hearts of Singaporeans.) Guest room details like the teak molding, floral batik bedspreads, bathroom tiles in bright Peranakan colors, and old-time brass electrical switches give this place true local charm and distinction. Room service is available from 7am to 11pm.

✪ Strand Hotel. 25 Bencoolen St., Singapore 189619. ☎ **65/338-1866.** Fax 65/338-1330. 130 units. A/C TV TEL. S$65 (US$38.90) double; S$80 (US$47.90) triple; S$100 (US$59.90) 4-person sharing. AE, DC, MC, V. 10-min. walk to City Hall MRT.

The Strand is by far the best of the backpacker places in Singapore. The lobby is far nicer than you'd expect, and your S$65 a night gets you a clean and neat room. Although there are some hints that you really are staying in a budget hotel—older decor and uncoordinated furniture sets, for instance—the place provides some little niceties, like hotel stationery. The no-frills bathrooms are clean and adequate. There are no coffee- and tea-making facilities, but there is 24-hour room service and a cafe on the premises. Free parking is available.

CHINATOWN

✪ Duxton Hotel. 83 Duxton Rd., Singapore 089540. ☎ **800/552-6844** in the U.S. and Canada, 800/251-664 in Australia, 800/446-110 in New Zealand, or 65/227-7678. Fax 65/227-1232. http://duxtonhotels.com.sg. E-mail: duxton@singnet.com.sg. 50 units. A/C MINIBAR TV TEL. S$180 (US$107.80) double; S$240 (US$143.70) suite. Rates include full English breakfast. AE, DC, JCB, MC, V. 5-min. walk to Tanjong Pagar MRT.

The Duxton was one of the first accommodations in Singapore to experiment with the boutique hotel concept, transforming its shop house structure into a small hotel and doing it with an elegance that's earned great international acclaim. From the outside, the place has old-world charm equal to any lamplit European cobblestone street, but step inside and there are very few details to remind you that you are in a quaint old shop house—or in the historic Chinese district, for that matter. It's a sophisticated and romantic little place, done entirely in turn-of-the-century styling that includes reproduction Chippendale furniture, hand-painted wall papers, and pen-and-ink Audubon-style drawings. Each room is different (to fit the structure of the building), but even with the limited spaces they have to work with, they've succeeded in creating rooms that feel airy and open. Garden suites feature a lovely little courtyard.

Merchant Court Hotel. 20 Merchant Rd., Singapore 058281. ☎ **800/637-7200** in the U.S. and Canada, 800/655-147 in Australia, 800/442-519 in New Zealand, 800/252-840 in the U.K., or 65/337-2288. Fax 65/334-0606. www.raffles.com/ril. 476 units. A/C MINIBAR TV TEL. S$305–S$335 (US$182.65–US$200.60) double; S$810–S$1,500 (US$485.05–US$898.20) suite. AE, DC, JCB, MC, V. 10-min. walk to Raffles Place MRT.

Merchant Court's convenient location and facilities make it very popular with leisure travelers. Situated on the Singapore River, the hotel has easy access not only to Chinatown and the Historic District, but also to Clarke Quay and Boat Quay, with their multitude of dining and nightlife options. While this new hotel's guest rooms aren't the biggest in the city, I never felt claustrophobic due to the large windows, fresh decor, and cooling atmosphere. Try to get a room with a view of the river or landscaped pool area.

ORCHARD ROAD AREA
VERY EXPENSIVE

✪ **Four Seasons Hotel Singapore.** 190 Orchard Blvd., Singapore 248646. ☎ **800/332-3442** in the U.S., 800/268-6282 in Canada, or 65/734-1110. Fax 65/733-0682. www.fourseasons.com. E-mail: fssrez@magix.com.sg. 254 units. A/C MINIBAR TV TEL. S$475–S$500 (US$284.45–US$299.40) double; S$530 (US$317.35) executive club; S$620–S$4,500 (US$371.25–US$2,694.60) suite. AE, DC, JCB, MC, V. 5-min. walk to Orchard MRT.

A lot of upmarket hotels will try to convince you that staying with them is like visiting a wealthy friend. Four Seasons actually delivers. The guest rooms are very spacious and inviting, and even the standard rooms have creature comforts you'd expect from a suite, such as complimentary fruit, terry bathrobes and slippers, CD and video disc players, and an extensive complimentary video disc and CD library that the concierge is just waiting to deliver selections from to your room. Each room has two-line speakerphones with voice mail and an additional data port. The Italian marble bathrooms have double vanities, deep tubs, bidets, and surround speakers from the TV and stereo. Did I mention remote-control drapes? Everything here is comfort and elegance done to perfection (in fact, the beds here are *so* comfortable that they've sold almost 100 in the gift shop—no kidding!). In the waiting area off the lobby you can sink into soft sofas and appreciate the antiques and artwork selected from the owner's private collection. Consider a standard room here before a suite in a less expensive hotel. You won't regret it.

✪ **Goodwood Park Hotel.** 22 Scotts Rd., Singapore 228221. ☎ **800/772-3890** in the U.S., 800/665-5919 in Canada, 800/89-95-20 in the U.K., or 65/737-7411. Fax 65/732-8558. 235 units. A/C MINIBAR TV TEL. S$425–S$465 (US$254.50–US$278.45) double; S$615–S$650 (US$368.25–US$389.20) poolside suite; S$888–S$3,000 (US$531.75–US$1,796.40) suite. AE, DC, JCB, MC, V. 5-min. walk to Orchard MRT.

The Goodwood Park Hotel, a national landmark built in 1900, resembles a castle along the Rhine—having served originally as the Teutonia Club, a social club for the German community. During World War II, high-ranking Japanese military used it as a residence, and 3 years later it served as a British war crimes court before being converted into a hotel. Since then the hotel has expanded from 60 rooms to 235, and has hosted a long list of international celebrities and dignitaries.

For the money, there are more luxurious facilities, but while most hotels have bigger and better business and fitness centers (Goodwood has *the* smallest fitness center), only the Raffles Hotel can rival Goodwood Park's historic significance. The poolside suites off the Mayfair Pool are fabulous in slate tiles and polished wood, offering direct access to the small Mayfair Pool with its lush Balinese-style landscaping. There are also suites off the main pool, which is much larger but offers little privacy from the lobby and surrounding restaurants. The original building has large and airy guest rooms, but beware of the showers, which have handheld showerheads that clip to the wall, making it difficult to aim and impossible to keep the water from splashing out all over the bathroom floor. The extremely attentive staff always serves with a smile.

○ Grand Hyatt Singapore. 10–12 Scotts Rd., Singapore 228211. ☎ **800/228-9000** in the U.S., or 65/738-1234. Fax 65/732-1696. www.hyatt.com. 693 units. S$340–S$450 (US$203.60–US$269.45) double; S$490–S$3,800 (US$293.40–US$2,275.45) suite. AE, DC, JCB, MC, V. Near Orchard MRT.

Rumor has it that, despite its fantastic location, this hotel was doing pretty poorly until they had a feng shui master come in and evaluate it for redecorating. According to the Chinese monk, because the lobby entrance was a wall of flat glass doors that ran parallel to the long reception desk in front, all the hotel's money was flowing from the desk right out the doors and into the street. To correct the problem, the doors are now set at right angles to each other, a fountain was built in the rear, and the reception was moved around a corner to the right of the lobby. Since then, the hotel has enjoyed some of the highest occupancy rates in town. Feng shui or not, the new decor is modern, sleek, and sophisticated, an elegant combination of polished black marble and deep wood. Quiet corridors with great artwork lead to bright guest rooms distinguished by small glass-enclosed alcoves looking over the hotel gardens. Bathrooms are large, with lots of marble counter space.

EXPENSIVE

Mandarin Singapore. 333 Orchard Rd., Singapore 238867. ☎ **800/380-9957** in the U.S. and Canada, or 65/737-4411. Fax 65/235-6688. www.meritus-hotels.com. E-mail: rmresvn@ singnet.com.sg. 1,235 units. A/C MINIBAR TV TEL S$400 (US$239.50) double; S$450 (US$269.45) club; S$580–S$2,800 (US$347.30–US$1,676.65) suite. AE, DC, JCB, MC, V. Near Orchard MRT.

Smack in the center of Orchard Road is the Mandarin Hotel, a two-tower complex with Singapore's most famous revolving restaurant topping it off like a little hat. The 39-story Main Tower opened in 1973, and with the opening of the South Wing 10 years later the number of rooms expanded to 1,200. Massive renovations of both wings and most of the facilities were completed in 1995. True to its name, the hotel is decorated in Chinese style, from the huge lobby mural of the "87 Taoist Immortals" to the black-and-red Ming-design carpet murals and black lacquer-style guest room entrances. The South Wing is predominantly for leisure travelers, who have access to the tower from the side of the hotel off Orchard Road. The guest rooms here are slightly smaller and furnished with Chinese-style dark wood modular units. The guest rooms in the Main Tower are brighter and larger.

○ Shangri-La Hotel. Orange Grove Rd., Singapore 258350. ☎ **800/942-5050** in the U.S. and Canada, 800/222448 in Australia, 0800/442179 in New Zealand, or 65/737-3644. Fax 65/733-3257. www.shangri-la.com. 760 units. A/C MINIBAR TV TEL. S$405 (US$242.50) Tower double; S$490 (US$293.40) Garden double; S$440 (US$263.45) horizon club; S$550 (US$329.35) Valley double; S$1,000–S$3,200 (US$598.80–US$1,916.15) suite. AE, DC, JCB, MC, V. 10-min. walk to Orchard MRT.

It may not be as centrally located as other hotels in the area, but the Shangri-La is a lovely place, with strolling gardens, a putting course, and an outdoor pool paradise that are great diversions from the hustle and bustle all around. Maybe that's why visiting VIPs like George Bush, Benazir Bhutto, and Nelson Mandela have all stayed here.

The hotel has three wings: The Tower Wing is the oldest, housing the lobby and most of the guest rooms, which were recently renovated. The Garden Wing's bougainvillea-laden balconies, half of which overlook the tropical atrium with its cascading waterfall and exotic plants, drip with tropical magic—these rooms feel the most like resort rooms. The exclusive Valley Wing has a private entrance and very spacious rooms, linked to the main tower by a sky bridge that looks out over the hotel's 6 hectares (15 acres) of landscaped lawns, fruit trees, and flowers.

○ **Traders Hotel Singapore.** 1A Cuscaden Rd., Singapore 249716. ☎ **800/942-5050** in the U.S. and Canada, 800/222448 in Australia, 0800/442179 in New Zealand, or 65/738-2222. Fax 65/831-4314. www.shangri-la.com. 543 units. A/C TV TEL. S$275–S$320 (US$164.65–US$191.60) double; S$355 (US$212.55) club; S$490–S$1,000 (US$293.40–US$598.80) studio apt and suite. AE, DC, JCB, MC, V. 10-min. walk to Orchard MRT.

A fantastic bargain for leisure travelers in Singapore, Traders advertises itself as a "value-for-money" hotel. A spin-off of Shangri-La (see above), this hotel anticipates the special needs of travelers and tries on all levels to accommodate them. Rooms have an empty fridge that can be stocked from the supermarket next door (show your room card key at nearby Tanglin Mall for discounts from many of the shops); there are spanking clean self-service launderette facilities with ironing boards on six floors; and there are vending machines and ice machines. They even provide a hospitality lounge for guests to use after check-out, with seating areas, work spaces with data ports, card phones, safe-deposit boxes, vending machines, and a shower.

Guest rooms are smaller than average, but feature child-size sofa beds and large drawers for storage. The large, landscaped pool area has a great poolside alfresco cafe, Ah Hoi's Kitchen, serving up tasty Chinese dishes at reasonable prices. Hotel facilities include a data port in each room and a fitness center with outdoor Jacuzzi, sauna, steam, massage, and facial services. Services include voice mail and free shuttle service to Orchard Road, Shangri-La Hotel, Shangri-La Rasa Sentosa Resort, Suntec City, and Shenton Way business district. Be sure to ask about promotion rates when you book your room. If you're planning to stay longer than 2 weeks, they have a long-stay program that offers discount meals, laundry and business center services, and half-price launderette tokens.

York Hotel Singapore. 21 Mount Elizabeth, Singapore 228516. ☎ **800/223-5652** in the U.S. and Canada, 800/553-549 in Australia, 800/447-555 in New Zealand, 800/89-88-52 in the U.K., or 65/737-0511. Fax 65/732-1217. www.yorkhotel.com.sg. E-mail: enquiry@yorkhotel.com.sg. 406 units. A/C MINIBAR TV TEL. S$265–S$285 (US$158.70–US$170.65) double; S$260 (US$155.70) cabana; S$400 (US$239.50) split-level cabana; S$430–S$910 (US$257.50–US$544.90) suite. AE, DC, JCB, MC, V. 10-min. walk to Orchard MRT.

This small tourist-class hotel can boast some of the most consistently professional and courteous staff I've encountered. A short walk from Orchard, York is convenient though far enough removed to provide a relaxing atmosphere. A recent renovation has redressed previously flavorless rooms in a sharp contemporary style in light woods, natural tones, and simple lines. Combined with an already spacious room, the result is an airy, cooling effect. Bathrooms throughout are downright huge. Cabana rooms look out to a pool and sundeck decorated with giant palms. Despite surrounding buildings, it doesn't feel claustrophobic, as do some of the more centrally situated hotels. There's a Jacuzzi, but the business center is tiny and there's no fitness center at all. Guests in single-occupancy rooms are often upgraded to doubles.

INEXPENSIVE

Regalis Court. 64 Lloyd Rd., Singapore 239113. ☎ **65/734-7117.** Fax 65/736-1651. 43 units. A/C TV TEL. S$145–S$165 (US$86.85–US$98.80) double. Rates include continental breakfast. AE, DC, JCB, MC, V. 10-min. walk from Somerset MRT.

For a bit of local charm at an affordable price, Regalis Court is a favorite. Centrally located just 10 minutes' walk form Orchard Road, this old charming bungalow has been restored beautifully and outfitted with Peranakan-inspired touches. Everything here will make you feel as if you're staying in a quaint guest house rather than a hotel, from the open-air lobby (under the porte cochere) and corridors to the guest rooms, which have comforting touches like teakwood furnishings, textile wall hangings, Oriental throws over wooden floors, and bamboo chick blinds to keep out the sun. Although guest rooms are slightly smaller than conventional rooms, they are still quite comfortable. Facilities are few. They also offer laundry services, a steam room, and car hire.

✪ **RELC International Hotel.** 30 Orange Grove Rd., Singapore 258352. ☎ **65/ 737-9044.** Fax 65/733-9976. www.hotel-web.com. E-mail: relcih@singnet.com.sg. 128 units. A/C TV TEL. S$110 (US$65.85) double; S$165 (US$98.80) suite. Rates include American breakfast for 2. DC, JCB, MC, V. 10-min. walk to Orchard MRT.

For real value, my money is on RELC. Sure the location is terrific (only a 10-minute walk to Orchard Road), but the added value is in the quality of the facility. I found the service and convenience here superior to some hotels in the higher priced categories. RELC has four types of rooms—superior twin, executive twin, Hollywood queen, and alcove suite—but no matter what the size, none of the rooms ever feel cluttered, close, or cramped. All rooms have balconies, TVs with two movie channels, and a fridge with free juice boxes and snacks. Bathrooms are large, with full-length tubs and hair dryers standard. If you're interested in the higher-priced rooms, I'd choose the Hollywood queen over the alcove suite—its decor is better and it can sleep a family very comfortably. The "superior" rooms don't have coffee- and tea-making facilities. A self-service launderette is available.

4 Dining

Dining out in Singapore is the central focus of family quality time, the best excuse for getting together with friends, and the proper way to close that business deal. That's why you find such a huge selection of local, regional, and international cuisine here, served in settings that range from bustling hawker centers to grand and glamorous palaces of gastronomy. But to simply say "If You Like Food You'll Love Singapore!" doesn't do justice to the modern concept of eating in this place. The various ethnic restaurants, with their traditional decor and serving styles, hold their own special sense of theater for foreigners, but Singaporeans don't stop there, dreaming up new concepts in cuisine and ambience to add fresh dimensions to the fine art of dining. For a twist, new variations on traditions pop up, like the French-service Chinese cuisine at Chang Jiang or the East-meets-West New Asia cuisine dished up at Doc Cheng's. Theme restaurants turn regular meals into attractions. Take, for example, Imperial Herbal's intriguing predinner medical examination or House of Mao's Cultural Revolution menu.

Many of Singapore's best restaurants are in its hotels, whether they're run by the hotel itself or operated by outfits just renting the space. Hotels generally offer a wide variety of cuisine, and coffee shops almost always have Western selections. Shopping malls have everything from food courts with local fast food to mid-priced and upmarket establishments. Western fast-food outlets are always easy to find—McDonald's burgers, Dunkin' Donuts, or Starbucks coffee—but if you want something a little more local, you'll find coffee shops (called *kopitiam*) and small home-cookin' mom-and-pop joints down every back street. Then there are hawker centers, where, under one roof, the meal choices go on and on.

CHINESE CUISINE The large Chinese population in Singapore makes this obviously the most common type of food you'll find, and by right, any good description of

Singaporean food should begin with the most prevalent Chinese regional styles. Many Chinese restaurants in the West are lumped into one category—Chinese—with only mild acknowledgment of Cantonese, Szechuan and dim sum. But China's a big place, and its size is reflected in its many different tastes, ingredients, and preparation styles.

MALAY CUISINE   Malay cuisine combines Indonesian and Thai flavors, blending ginger, turmeric, chiles, lemongrass, and dried shrimp paste to make unique curries. Heavy on coconut milk and peanuts, Malay food can at times be on the sweet side. The most popular Malay curries are **rendang,** a dry, dark, and heavy coconut-based curry served over meat; **sambal,** a red and spicy chile sauce; and **sambal belacan,** a condiment of fresh chiles, dried shrimp paste, and lime juice.

PERANAKAN CUISINE   Peranakan cuisine came out of the Straits-born Chinese community and combines such mainland Chinese ingredients as noodles and oyster sauces with local Malay flavors of coconut milk and peanuts.

INDIAN CUISINE   Southern Indian food is a superhot blend of spices in a coconut milk base. Rice is the staple, along with thin breads such as *prata* and *dosai,* which are good for curling into shovels to scoop up drippy curries. Vegetarian dishes are abundant, a result of Hindu-mandated vegetarianism, and use lots of chickpeas and lentils in curry and chile gravies. **Vindaloo,** meat or poultry in a tangy and spicy sauce, is also well known.

   Banana leaf restaurants, surely the most interesting way to experience southern Indian food in Singapore, serve up meals on banana leaves cut like place mats. It's very informal. Spoons and forks are provided, but if you want to act local and use your hands, remember to use your right hand only, and don't forget to wash up before and after at the tap. **Northern Indian food** combines yogurts and creams with a milder, more delicate blend of herbs and chiles than is found in its southern neighbor. It's served most often with breads like fluffy *nans* and flat *chapatis.* Marinated meats like chicken or fish, cooked in the tandoor clay oven, is always the highlight of a northern Indian meal. Northern Indian restaurants are more upmarket and expensive than the southern ones, but while they offer more of the comforts associated with dining out, the southern banana leaf experience is more of an adventure.

   One tip for eating very spicy foods is to mix a larger proportion of rice to gravy. Don't drink in between bites, but eat through the burn. Your brow may sweat but your mouth will build a tolerance as you eat, and the flavors will come through more fully.

SEAFOOD   One cannot describe Singaporean food without mentioning the abundance of fresh seafood. But most important is the uniquely Singaporean chile crab, chopped and smothered in a thick tangy chile sauce. Restaurants hold competitions to judge who has the best. Pepper crabs and black pepper crayfish are also a thrill. Instead of chile sauce, these shellfish are served in a thick black-pepper-and-soy sauce.

FRUITS   A walk through a wet market at any time of year will show you just what wonders the tropics can produce. Varieties of banana, fresh coconut, papaya, mango, and pineapple are just a few of the fresh and juicy fruits available year-round; in addition, Southeast Asia has an amazing selection of exotic and almost unimaginable fruits. From the light and juicy **star fruit** to the red and hairy **rambutan,** they are all worthy of a try, either whole or juiced.

   Dare it if you will, the fruit to sample—the veritable king of fruits—is the **durian,** a large, green, spiky fruit that, when cut open, smells worse than old tennis shoes. The "best" ones are in season every June, when Singaporeans go wild over them. In case you're curious, the fruit has a creamy texture and tastes lightly sweet and deeply musky.

TIPS ON DINING

Of course, in any foreign land, the exotic cuisine isn't the only thing that keeps you guessing. Lucky for you, the following tips will make dining no problem.

- Most restaurants are open for lunch as early as 11am, but close around 2:30 or 3pm to give them a chance to set up for dinner, which begins around 6pm. Where closing times are listed, that is the time when the last order is taken.
- **Don't tip.** Restaurants always add a gratuity to the bill, and to give extra cash can be embarrassing for the wait staff.
- Some restaurants, especially the more fashionable or upscale ones, may require that **reservations** be made up to a couple days in advance. Reservations are always recommended for Saturday and Sunday lunch and dinner, as eating is a favorite national pastime and a lot of families take meals out for weekend quality time.
- Because Singapore is so hot, "dress casual" (meaning a shirt and slacks for men and a dress or skirt/slacks and top for women) is always a safe bet in moderate to expensive restaurants. For the very expensive restaurants, formal is required. For the cheap places, come as you are, as long as you're decent.

ORDERING WINE WITH DINNER   Singaporeans have become more wine savvy in recent years, and have begun importing estate-bottled wines from California, Australia, New Zealand, France, and Germany. However, these bottles are heavily taxed. A bottle of wine with dinner starts at around S$50 and a single glass runs between S$10 and S$25 (US$6 and US$15), depending on the wine and the restaurant. Chinese restaurants usually don't charge corkage fees for bringing your own.

LUNCH & DINNER COSTS   **Lunch** at a hawker center can be as cheap as S$3.50 (US$2.10), truly a bargain. Many places have set-price buffet lunches, but these can be as high as S$45 (US$26.95). Indian restaurants are great deals for inexpensive buffet lunches, which can be found as reasonably as S$10 (US$6) per person for all you can eat. For **dinner** You can expect to pay as much as S$145 (US$86.85) per person at a **very expensive** restaurant. At an **expensive** restaurant, expect dinner to run between S$50 and S$80 (US$29.95 and US$47.90) per person. At a **moderate** restaurant, dinner for one can be as low as S$25 (US$14.95) and as high as S$50 (US$29.95). Some dinners can be under S$5 (US$3) at hawker stalls, and up to around S$15 (US$9) for one if you eat at local restaurants. Fortunately, Singapore is not only a haven for cultural gastric diversity, but it's also possible to eat exotic foods here to your heart's content, all while maintaining a shoestring budget.

Note: See map "Singapore Accommodations & Dining," above.

THE HISTORIC DISTRICT
VERY EXPENSIVE

Inagiku. The Westin Plaza Level 3, 2 Stamford Rd. ☎ **65/431-6156.** Reservations recommended. Set lunch S$30–S$50 (US$17.95–US$29.95), set dinner S$60–S$180 (US$35.95–US$107.80). AE, DC, JCB, MC, V. Daily noon–2:30pm and 6:30–10:30pm. JAPANESE.

Inagiku serves excellent Japanese food that gets top marks for ingredients, preparation, and presentation. House favorites include sashimi, tempura, and teppanyaki—with separate dining areas for tempura and a sushi bar. The tokusen sashimi morikimi is masterful in its presentation: An assortment of raw fish—including salmon, prawns, and clams—is laid out in an ice-filled shell inside of which nestles the skeleton of a whole fish. It's odd and delightful at the same time. I recommend the tempura moriawase, a combination of seafood and vegetables that's very lightly deep fried. Also highly recommended are the teppanyaki prawns. In addition to sake, they also have a good selection of wines.

✪ **Raffles Grill.** Raffles Hotel, 1 Beach Rd. ☎ **65/331-1611.** Reservations recommended. Main courses S$42–S$52 (US$25.15–US$31.15); set dinner S$120 and S$130 (US$71.85 and US$77.85) per person. AE, DC, MC, V. Mon–Fri noon–2:30pm and 7–10pm; Sat–Sun 7–10pm. FRENCH.

Dining in the grande dame of Singapore achieves a level of sophistication unmatched by any other five-star restaurant. The architectural charm and historic significance of the old hotel will transform dinner into a cultural event, but don't just come here for the ambience; the food is outstanding as well. Three set dinners allow you to select from the à la carte menu dishes like roasted veal tenderloin or roasted rack of suckling pig, the latter a highly recommended choice for its juicy meat under crispy mouth-watering skin. The 400-label wine list (going back to 1890 vintages) could be a history lesson, and if you'd like you can request the cellar master to select a wine to match each course. The fabulously attentive service from the wait staff will make you feel like you own the place. Formal dress is required.

EXPENSIVE

✪ **Compass Rose.** The Westin Stamford, 2 Stamford Rd., Level 70. ☎ **65/338-8585.** Reservations recommended. Buffet lunch Mon–Sat S$36 (US$21.55), Sun and public holidays S$41.90 (US$25.10); dinner entrees S$40.50–S$45 (US$24.25–US$26.95). AE, DC, JCB, MC, V. Daily noon–2:30pm and 6:30–10:30pm. CONTINENTAL.

What a view! From the top of the Westin Stamford, the tallest hotel in the world, you can see out past the marina to Malaysia and Indonesia—and the restaurant's three-tier design means every table has a view. It's decorated with contemporary-styled Roman arches, pediments, and columns, and when the sun sets, the whole place turns the many colors of the sky. Lunch is an extensive display of seafood served in a host of international recipes, with chefs searing scallops to order. Don't even talk about the dessert buffet—it's so tantalizing you'll think the altitude has gotten to your head. Dinner is à la carte, with dishes inspired by lighter tastes and low-fat recipes. Try the peppered lobster tail and sea scallops with hot garlic sauce. The Dutch veal tenderloin and grilled goose liver is served with a pumpkin rosette, carrot, and tarragon cream sauce. For dessert, order the sample plate.

J.P. Bastiani. 3A River Valley Rd., Clarke Quay Merchant's Court no. 01–12. ☎ **65/433-0156.** Reservations recommended for lunch, required for dinner. Main courses S$29–S$42 (US$17.35–US$25.15). AE, DC, MC, V. Mon–Fri 11:30am–2:30pm and 6:30–10:30pm; Sat–Sun 6:30–11pm. MEDITERRANEAN.

The real-life J. P. Bastiani owned a pineapple cannery at Clarke Quay; today, he lends his name to this cozy Mediterranean place, with its walled courtyard patio in the back for cocktails, a wine cellar with a huge international collection on the first floor, and a gorgeous dining room upstairs that's just dripping with romance. Their seafood dishes are the best, with a choice of a delicious coriander-crusted salmon with ginger and onion confit, or the pan-roasted sea bass, which is stuffed with leeks and potato. You can also try one of their excellent meat entrees such as rack of lamb or filet mignon. The dishes are rich and servings are quite large, so make a mental note in advance to save room for their fantastic tiramisu.

✪ **Lei Garden.** 30 Victoria St., CHIJMES no. 01–24. ☎ **65/339-3822.** Reservations required. Small dishes S$18–S$58 (US$10.80–US$34.75). AE, DC, JCB, MC, V. Daily 11:30am–2:30pm and 6–10:30pm. CANTONESE.

Lei Garden, with three locations in Singapore, six in Hong Kong and Kowloon, and two in Guangzhou, lives up to a great reputation for the highest quality Cantonese cuisine in one of the most elegant settings. Actually, of the three local branches, this one is special for the unique ambience of CHIJMES just outside its towering picture windows. Highly recommended dishes are the "Buddha jumps over the wall," a very popular Chinese soup made from abalone, fish maw (stomach), shark's fin, and Chinese ham. It's generally served on special occasions. To make the beggar's chicken, they take a whole stuffed chicken and wrap and bake it in a lotus leaf covered in yam, which makes the chicken moist with a delicate flavor you'll never forget. For either of these dishes, you must place your order at least 24 hours in advance when you make your dinner reservation. Also try the barbecued Peking duck, which is exquisite. A small selection of French and Chinese wines are available.

✪ **Paladino di Firenze.** 7 Mohamed Sultan Rd. (off River Valley Rd.). ☎ **65/738-0917.** Reservations required for dinner. Main courses S$38–S$48 (US$22.75–US$28.75). AE, DC, JCB, MC, V. Daily noon–2:30pm and 7–10:30pm. NORTHERN ITALIAN.

This has to be one of the most romantic and cozy restaurants in Singapore. There's not a lot of space in its old restored shop house setting, but they don't overcrowd the tables, separating little areas with plantings and crazy little metal trees. Whitewashed exposed-brick walls and Oriental carpets on the floor create a homey feeling, while copper- and gold-colored tablecloths add shimmer in the candlelight. The northern Italian cuisine here is excellent. The Crespelle alla Paladino are Tuscan-inspired home-made crepes filled with beef, fresh mushrooms, and Parmesan, but the osso bucco, braised veal shanks, is the most highly recommended dish here. They have a large selection of wines to choose from. Make your reservations early because this place is small and very popular. After dinner, stroll the trendy clubs along Mohamed Sultan Road.

Tiffin Room. Raffles Hotel, 1 Beach Rd. ☎ **65/337-1886.** Reservations recommended. All meals served buffet style. Breakfast S$30 (US$17.95); lunch S$35 (US$20.95); high tea S$26.50 (US$15.85); dinner S$45 (US$26.95). AE, DC, JCB, MC, V. Daily 7:30–10am, noon–2pm, 3:30–5pm (high tea), and 7–10pm. SOUTHERN INDIAN/TIFFIN CURRY.

Tiffin curry came from India and is named after the three-tiered containers that Indian workers would use to carry their lunch. The tiffin box idea was stolen by the British colonists, who changed around the recipes a bit so they weren't as spicy. The cuisine that evolved is pretty much what you'll find served at Raffles's Tiffin Room, where a buffet spread lets you select from a variety of curries, chutneys, rice, and Indian breads. The restaurant is just inside the lobby entrance of Raffles Hotel and carries the trademark Raffles elegance throughout its decor.

MODERATE

Chungking Szechuan Restaurant. 200 Victoria St., no. 02–53/54 Parco Bugis Junction. ☎ **65/337-9915.** Reservations recommended. Small dishes S$8–S$48 (US$4.80–US$28.75). AE, DC, JCB, MC, V. Mon–Fri 11:15am–2:30pm and 6:15–10:30pm. SZECHUAN/\ CANTONESE.

In a large, well-lit space, Chungking doesn't have a hint of Chinese kitsch typical to other restaurants of this category, but rather chooses a more contemporary understated decor. Located on the second floor of Parco Bugis Junction shopping mall, its large windows open up the room and provide views of the streets below, which are flanked with shop houses. The menu features dishes that blend two styles: Cantonese and spicy Szechuan. The Szechuan smoked duck is a favorite, either a half or full bird, smoked with Chinese tea leaves and herbs in a sweet black sauce. For a lighter dish, try the steamed filet of codfish deep fried in a soybean crust topped with a light soy sauce. Deep-fried live prawns with special peppercorn Szechuan sauce leave a tingle in the mouth, but never fear, the staff is very flexible about spice. Chungking also serves the standard dim sum lunch. The owner is a wine connoisseur, and has stocked some lovely wines, but they'll never charge corkage if you bring your own.

✪ **Doc Cheng's.** Raffles Hotel Arcade no. 02–20, Level 2. ☎ **65/331-1761.** Reservations recommended. Main courses S$21.50–S$31.50 (US$12.85–US$18.85). AE, DC, MC, V. Mon–Fri noon–2pm and 7–10pm; Sat–Sun 7–10pm. FUSION.

They call themselves "The Restaurant for Restorative Foods," but you won't find any ancient Chinese secrets here. Doc Cheng, the hero of the joint, was part man and part mythological colonial figure. Educated in Western medicine in England, he was a sought-after physician who became a local celebrity and notorious drunk. His concept of restorative foods is therefore rather skewed, but the restaurant banks on the decadence of the attraction and serves up "transethnic" dishes smothered in tongue-in-cheek humor. Guest chefs make the menu ever changing—the latest and greatest, an unbelievably scrumptious tamarind charcoal beef short ribs dish on portobello mushrooms. Equally well prepared (though lighter) is the charcoal-fried shutome swordfish on risotto. The house wine is a Riesling (sweet wines are more popular with Singaporeans) from Raffles's own vineyard. Three separate dining areas allow you to dine under the verandah, on the patio, or in cozy booths inside.

✪ **Imperial Herbal.** Metropole Hotel, 3rd Floor, 41 Seah St. (near Raffles Hotel). ☎ **65/337-0491.** Reservations recommended for lunch, required for dinner. Small dishes S$14–S$24 (US$8.40–US$14.35). AE, DC, JCB, MC, V. Daily 11:30am–2:30pm and 6:30–10:30pm. HERBAL.

People come again and again for the healing powers of the food served here, enriched with herbs and other secret ingredients prescribed by a resident Chinese herbalist. Upon entering, go to the right, where you'll find the herb counter. The herbalist, who is also trained in Western medicine, will ask for the symptoms of what ails you and take your pulse. While you sit and order, he'll prepare a packet of ingredients and ship them off to the kitchen, where they'll be added to the food in preparation. Surprisingly, dishes turn out tasty, without the anticipated medicinal aftertaste. If all this isn't wild enough for you, order the scorpion.

The herbalist is in-house every day but Sunday. It's always good to call ahead, though, as he's the main attraction. When you leave, present him with a small *ang pau*—a gift of cash in a red envelope—maybe S$5 or S$7 (US$3 or US$4.20). Red envelopes are available in any card or gift shop.

Liu Hsiang Lou. Allson Hotel, 101 Victoria St. ☎ **65/336-0811.** Reservations recommended. Small dishes S$12–S$44 (US$7.20–US$26.35). AE, DC, JCB, MC, V. Daily 11:30am–2:30pm and 6:30–10:30pm. SZECHUAN.

As you enter there's a veritable zoo of tanks filled with lobsters, long-neck clams, and frogs—you can buddy up to your dinner while you wait for your table. In addition to seafood, Liu Hsiang Lou also specializes in amazingly tender venison, which can be prepared sautéed with black pepper, dried red chile, garlic, or chives. Camphor- and tea-smoked duck is a fragrant and delicious Szechuan specialty, and they prepare it marinated in authentic style and bring it out in thin slices for you to wrap in pancakes with plum sauce. *Soon hock* is fish steamed with a tasty mix of tofu, mushrooms, vegetables, and chile. The most popular dishes are the sautéed diced chicken with dried red chile and the sour and spicy soup with shredded meat and fish maw (stomach). In addition, they have lunch hour dim sum. Carved rosewood chairs and landscape paintings make for a warm atmosphere.

Shrooms. CHIJMES, 30 Victoria St. ☎ **65/336-2268.** Reservations recommended. Main courses S$31–S$36.50 (US$18.55–US$21.85). AE, DC, JCB, MC, V. Daily 11:30am–2:30pm and 6:30–10:30pm. FUSION.

In one of the most exquisite locations in the city—atop the CHIJMES complex—Shrooms occupies a glorious hall in elegant sparse-contempo style; however, the atmosphere is wonderfully casual. With a mixture of Indian, Chinese, and Western selections, there'll be something for everyone on this menu, but I highly recommend the tandoori selections (both breads and meats), which are just perfect. Shrooms also operates a cafe downstairs, with lighter choices (the tandoori sandwich is weird and amazing at the same time). After dinner, the place turns into a nightclub, so stick around.

INEXPENSIVE

Bukhara. 3C River Valley Rd., no. 01–44 Clarke Quay. ☎ **65/338-1411.** Reservations recommended. Lunch buffet S$13.60 (US$8.15); dinner buffet S$19.90 (US$11.90). AE, DC, JCB, MC, V. Daily noon–2:30pm and 6:30–10:30pm. NORTHERN INDIAN.

I like to recommend Bukhara for the buffet, which is a great way to savor many treats without going over the top with the expense. Tandoori lamb kabobs, fish, prawns, chicken, and more will make meat lovers' eyes pop—the food just keeps coming. Plus, tandoori veggies like cauliflower and stuffed potatoes and peppers are also quite good. The decor is a little bit India-kitsch, with carved stonelike accents and beat-up wooden chairs. The buffet also includes breads and dal. You can also order from an à la carte menu of standard northern Indian fare. If you're in Clarke Quay, this is the best choice in this price range.

✪ **Nonya and Baba.** 262 River Valley Rd. (close to the Imperial Hotel). ☎ **65/734-1386.** Reservations recommended. Small dishes S$6–S$8 (US$3.60–US$4.80). AE, DC, JCB, MC, V. Daily 11am–2:30pm and 6–9:45pm. PERANAKAN.

Like a little Peranakan coffee shop, Nonya and Baba serves a menu of traditional standards from time-honored recipes. It's frequented by locals, many of whom come to eat Straits-Chinese comfort food like Mom used to make. The menu has about 16 dishes, with photos and very detailed descriptions of the preparations and ingredients of each, and the staff is willing and able to help you decide. *Sambal udang,* a dry sambal over prawns and tomatoes, seems to be the favorite for Westerners. The same goes for the *satay ayam* (chicken satay). *Otak otak,* fish cake with chile and shrimp paste wrapped in banana leaf and grilled, makes a great snack. However, a most special dish is the *ayam buah keluak,* whose preparation time includes 3 days to soak-crack the hard Indonesian nuts to get to the black paste inside, which is then mixed with shrimp and pork, restuffed, then fried. The ambience here is very local, with coffee shop–style marble-top tables and chairs à la Peranakan. The walls are decorated with framed *kebayas* (formal Nonya embroidered blouses), some batiks, and photos of the house specialties.

✪ **Our Village.** 46 Boat Quay (take elevator to 5th floor). ☎ **65/538-3058.** Reservations recommended on weekends. Main courses S$9–S$20 (US$5.40–US$12). AE, MC, V. Mon–Fri 11:30am–1:30pm and 6–10:30pm; Sat–Sun 6–10:30pm. NORTHERN INDIAN.

With its antique white walls stuccoed in delicate and exotic patterns and glistening with tiny silver mirrors, you'll feel like you're in an Indian fairyland here. Even the ceiling twinkles with silver stars, and hanging lanterns provide a subtle glow for the heavenly atmosphere—it's a perfect setting for a delicate dinner. Everything here is handmade from hand-selected imported ingredients, some of them coming from secret sources. In fact, the staff is so protective of its recipes, you'd almost think their secret ingredient was opium—and you'll be floating so high after tasting the food that it might as well be. There are vegetarian selections as well as meats (no beef or pork) prepared in luscious gravies or in the tandoor oven. The dishes are light and healthy, with all natural ingredients and not too much salt.

Rendezvous. no. 02–02 Hotel Rendezvous, 9 Bras Basah Rd. ☎ **65/339-7508.** Meat dishes sold per piece S$3–S$5 (US$1.80–US$3). AE, DC, MC, V. Daily 11am–9pm. Closed on public holidays. INDO-MALAY.

I was sad when, after a few months away from Singapore, I couldn't find Rendezvous at its previous location in Raffles City Shopping Center, only to learn it had shifted to a nicer space at the new (coincidentally named?) Rendezvous Hotel. Line up to select from a large number Malay dishes, cafeteria style, like sambal squid in a spicy sauce of chile and shrimp paste, and beef rendang, in a dark spicy curry gravy. The wait staff will bring your order to your table. The coffee shop setting is as far from glamorous as the last Rendezvous, but on the wall black-and-white photos trace the restaurant's history back to its opening in the early '50s. It's a great place to experiment with a new cuisine.

Sketches. 200 Victoria St., no. 01–85/86/87 Parco Bugis Junction. ☎ **65/339-8386.** S$10.50 (US$6.30) hungry; S$14.50 (US$8.70) starving. AE, DC, JCB, MC, V. Daily 11am–10pm. ITALIAN.

Pasta is always an easy and agreeable choice, and sometimes when you're traveling, familiar tastes can be welcome from time to time. Not only is this place fast, inexpensive, and good, it's also pretty unique. The concept is "Design-a-Pasta," where they give you a menu on which is a series of boxes you check off: one set for pasta type; one set for sauce type; another for add-ins like meats, mushrooms, and garlic; and boxes for chile, Parmesan, and pine nuts. The kitchen is in the center of the restaurant, with bar seating all around. This is the best place to be if you want to watch those cooks hustle through menu card after menu card—it's a great show. You can also sit at one of the tables in the restaurant or out on the patio inside the shopping mall, but then you'd miss the fun of eating here.

CHINATOWN
VERY EXPENSIVE
✪ **L'Aigle d'Or.** 83 Duxton Rd., Duxton Hotel. ☎ **65/227-7678.** Reservations recommended. Main courses S$75–S$96 (US$44.90–US$57.50); set lunch S$36 (US$21.60). AE, DC, MC, V. Daily noon–2pm and 7–10pm. FRENCH.

L'Aigle d'Or's reputation in Singapore is second to none, and after you dine here, you'll understand why. The French menu is perfection, the setting is classic, and the staff is extremely attentive and charming. Like many of the other European restaurants in Singapore, their menu changes regularly with the seasons, so you may find different dishes than on your last visit. This time around the menu featured a gorgeous veal rib, panfried and tender. For something different, try the panfried foie gras and rhubarb ravioli, a current house specialty and unbelievably tasty in a tangy raspberry sauce. As you would expect, the wine list is top of the line, the cheese selection is excellent, and the desserts are unmentionable. If you're looking for someplace truly special, you can't do better.

MODERATE
✪ **House of Mao.** 51 Telok Ayer St., no. 03–02 China Square Food Centre. ☎ **65/533-0660.** Reservations recommended. Main courses S$8–S$34 (US$4.80–US$20.35). AE, DC, JCB, MC, V. Daily 11:30am–2:30pm and 6:30–10pm. HUNAN.

Only in Singapore will you find a Cultural Revolution theme restaurant. Start with the Gang of Four cocktail before ordering your Long March chicken—you think I'm kidding. Actually, for a campy place, the food is great: Hunan style, which means plenty of chile. The viceroy chicken was supposed to be real spicy, but I found it quite nice and tangy. Venison is also featured on the menu, as well as a nice assortment of vegetable and (very flavorful) tofu dishes. Vegetarians beware: All these dishes are prepared with some sort of shredded meats. I laughed out loud at the hilarious menu, the Red Guard staff uniforms, and the memorabilia. Maybe Mao really will live to be a thousand years after all.

INEXPENSIVE

Beng Hiang. 112–116 Amoy St. ☎ **65/221-6695.** Reservations recommended on weekends. Small dishes S$8–S$20 (US$4.80–US$12). AE, MC, V. Daily 11:30am–2:30pm and 6–9:30pm. HOKKIEN.

This modest little place is perhaps the best way to find Hokkien food. Situated in a shop house on Amoy Street in the heart of Hokkien Chinatown, you can have a taste of a cuisine rarely found in restaurants. The spiced sausage and fried prawn balls are served dry to be dipped in sweet black soy sauce. Fish maw thick soup is similar to a shark's fin soup, and has egg, mushrooms, crabmeat, carrots, and shredded bamboo. Hokkien-style noodles with pork and prawn is the most popular dish. Calligraphy and Chinese landscape paintings make the low-key decor pretty.

Blue Ginger. 97 Tanjong Pagar Rd. ☎ **65/222-3928.** Reservations required for lunch, recommended for dinner. Main courses S$6.50–S$22.80 (US$3.90–US$13.65). AE, MC, V. Daily 11:30am–2:30pm and 6–10pm. PERANAKAN.

The standard belief is that Malay and Peranakan cooking is reserved for home-cooked meals, and therefore restaurants are not as plentiful—and where they do exist, are very informal. Not so at Blue Ginger, where traditional and modern mix beautifully in a style so fitting for Singapore. Snuggled in a shop house, the decor combines clean and neat lines of contemporary styling with paintings by local artists and touches of Peranakan flair like carved wooden screens. The cuisine is Peranakan from traditional recipes, making for some very authentic food—definitely something you can't get back home. A good appetizer is the *ngo heong:* fried rolls of pork and prawn that are deliciously flavored with spices but not at all hot. A wonderful entree is the *ayam panggang* "Blue Ginger," really tender grilled boneless thigh and drumstick with a mild coconut-milk sauce. One of the most popular dishes is the *ayam buah keluak,* a traditional chicken dish made with a hard black Indonesian nut with sweet meat inside. The favorite dessert here is durian *chendol,* red beans and pandan jelly in coconut milk with durian puree. Served with shaved ice on top, it smells strong.

Chen Fu Ji Fried Rice. 7 Erskine Rd. ☎ **65/323-0260.** Reservations not accepted. S$10–S$20 (US$6–US$12). No credit cards. Daily noon–2:30pm and 6–9:45pm. SINGA-POREAN CUISINE/FRIED RICE.

With bright green walls glaring under fluorescent lighting, the fast-food ambience is nothing to write home about, but once you try the fried rice here, you'll never be able to eat it anywhere else again, ever. These people take loving care of each fluffy grain, frying the egg evenly throughout. The other ingredients are added abundantly, and there's no hint of oil. On the top is a crown of shredded crabmeat. If you've never been an aficionado, you'll be one now. Other dishes are served here to accompany, and their soups are also very good.

Moi Kong. 22 Murray St. (between Maxwell House and Fairfield Methodist Church). ☎ 65/221-7758. Reservations recommended on weekends. Small dishes S$4–S$30 (US$2.40–US$17.95). AE, MC, V. Daily 11:30am–2:30pm and 5:30–10pm. HAKKA.

Located down a back alley called Murray Food Court, Moi Kong is a restaurant that looks more like somebody's kitchen, from the plastic tablecloths and dishes to tea served in simple glasses. The staff is very helpful about offering suggestions from the Hakka menu, dishes that are heavier on tofu and flavored more with homemade Chinese wine. Try house specialties like red wine prawn or salted chicken baked and served plain. The deep-fried bean curd stuffed with minced pork and fish is a traditional standard and can be served either dry or braised with black bean sauce. If you don't believe the food here is top rate, just ask Jackie Chan, whose happy photos are on the wall by the cash register!

LITTLE INDIA

✪ **Komala Vilas.** 76/78 Serangoon Rd. ☎ 65/293-6980. Reservations not accepted. Dosai S$2 (US$1.20); lunch for 2 S$8 (US$4.80). No credit cards. Daily 11:30am–3pm and 6:30–10:30pm. SOUTHERN INDIAN.

Komala Vilas is famous with Singaporeans of every race. Don't expect the height of ambience—it's pure fast food—but to sit here during a packed and noisy lunch hour is to see all walks of life come through the doors. They serve vegetarian dishes southern-Indian style, so there's nothing fancy about the food; it's just plain good. Order the dosai, a huge, thin pancake used to scoop up luscious and hearty gravies and curries. Even for carnivores, it's very satisfying. What's more, it's cheap: two samosas, dosai, and an assortment of stew-style gravies (dal) for two is only S$8 (US$4.80) with tea. For a quick fast-food meal, this place is second to none.

Muthu's Curry Restaurant. 76/78 Race Course Rd. ☎ 65/293-2389 or 65/293-7029. Reservations not accepted. Main course S$3.50–S$6.50 (US$2.10–US$3.90); fish head curry from S$16 (US$9.55). AE, DC, JCB, MC, V. Daily 10am–10pm. SOUTHERN INDIAN.

We're not talking the height of dining elegance here. It's more like somebody's kitchen where the chairs don't match, but you know there's got to be a reason this place is packed at mealtimes with a crowd of folks from construction workers to businesspeople. The list of specialties is long and includes crab masala, chicken biryani, and mutton curry, and fish cutlet and fried chicken sold by the piece. Of course you can get the local favorite, fish head curry (this is a great place to try it). The fish head floats in a huge portion of curry soup, its eye staring and teeth grinning. The cheek meat is the best part of the fish, but to be real polite, let your friend eat the eye. Go toward the end of mealtime, so you don't get lost in the rush and can find staff with more time to help you out.

ORCHARD ROAD AREA
EXPENSIVE

Bice Ristorante Italiano. Goodwood Park Hotel, 22 Scotts Rd. ☎ 65/735-3711. Main courses S$24–S$45 (US$14.35–US$26.95). AE, DC, MC, V. Daily noon–3:30pm and 6–10:30pm. Closed Christmas, New Year's, and Chinese New Year. ITALIAN.

Beatrice—or "Mama Bice" as she's known in Italy—opened her first restaurant in Milano 2 years ago, and has since opened two others, one in New York and one in Singapore. There's plenty of space, carved out into dining areas by plantings and unique displays of wooden shipping crates. Their chef hails from Milan and serves Mama Bice's family recipes of flavors inspired by her northern Italian ancestry. The lamb is tender and fresh and the pasta a perfect al dente. Because of the space, the wait for a table is short, but the bar as you walk in is a nice place to have a glass of wine before your meal. Bice has the largest selection of Italian wines in the city.

Chang Jiang. Goodwood Park Hotel, 22 Scotts Rd. ☎ **65/730-1752.** Reservations recommended. Small dishes S$15–S$58 (US$9–US$34.75). AE, DC, JCB, MC, V. Daily noon–2:30pm and 7–10:30pm. SHANGHAINESE.

The small and elegant Chang Jiang is a unique blend of Chinese food and European style. A fine setting, which mixes refined Continental ambience with Chinese accents, has a view of the courtyard and pool of the historic Goodwood Park Hotel through its large draped picture windows. The food is Chinese, but the service is French Gueridon style, in which dishes are presented to diners and taken to a side table to be portioned into individual servings. Some dishes are prepared while you watch, especially coffee, which is a veritable chemistry showcase. A couple of the more sumptuous dishes are the tangy and crunchy crisp eel wuxi and the sweet batter-dipped prawns with sesame seed and salad sauce. If you order the Beijing duck, after the traditional pancake dish they serve the shredded meat in a delicious sauce with green bean noodles.

✪ Esmirada. 180 Orchard Rd., no. 01–01 Peranakan Place ☎ **65/735-3476.** Reservations recommended for dinner. Main courses S$24–S$42 (US$14.35–US$25.15). AE, DC, MC, V. Daily noon–midnight. MEDITERRANEAN.

Ask any expatriate about restaurants and you'll hear about Esmirada. This place revels in the joys of good food and drink, bringing laughter and fun to the traditional act of breaking bread with friends and family. Evening meals can get loud and lively, so don't be surprised if the whole place gets up and dances on the tables. (And don't be surprised if your waiter joins in!) The menu is easy: There's one dish each from Italy, Spain, Greece, France, Yugoslavia, Portugal, and Morocco, and they never change. Huge portions are served family style, from big bowls of salad to shish kabob skewers hanging from a rack, all placed in the center of the table so everyone can dig in. Don't even bother with paella anywhere else—this is the best. The place is small, so make your reservations early. Stucco walls, wrought-iron details, and terra-cotta floors are mixed with wooden Indonesian tables and chairs with kilim cushions in an East-meets-West style that works very nicely.

Gordon Grill. Goodwood Park Hotel, 22 Scotts Rd. ☎ **65/730-1744.** Reservations recommended. Main courses S$32–S$50 (US$19.15–US$29.95) and up. AE, DC, JCB, MC, V. Daily noon–2.30pm and 7–11:30pm. ENGLISH/SCOTTISH.

Bringing meat and potatoes to the high life, Gordon Grill wheels out a carving cart full of the most tender prime rib and sirloin you could imagine, cut to your desired thickness. The menu of traditional English and Scottish fare includes house specialties like the panfried goose liver with apple and port wine sauce appetizer and the house recipe for (perfect) lobster bisque. Featured entrees are the mixed seafood grill of lobster, garoupa (grouper), scallops, and prawns in a lemon butter sauce and roast duck breast glazed with honey and black pepper. The traditional English sherry trifle is the dessert to order here, but if you want a little taste of everything, the dessert variation lets you have small portions of each dessert, with fresh fruit. The dining room, which is small and warmly set with dark tartan carpeting and portraits of stately Scotsmen, feels more comfortable than claustrophobic, and light piano music drifts in from the lounge next door. Dress formal.

✪ Harbour Grill. Hilton International Singapore, 581 Orchard Rd. ☎ **65/730-3393.** Reservations recommended. Main courses S$34–S$36 (US$20.35–US$21.55); 2 courses S$55 (US$32.95), 3 courses S$75 (US$44.90), 4 courses S$90 (US$53.90) per person. AE, DC, MC, V. Daily noon–2:30pm and 7–10:30pm. CONTINENTAL.

Grilled seafood and U.S. prime rib are perfectly prepared and served with attentive style in this award-winning restaurant. The Continental cuisine is lighter than most, with recipes that focus on the natural freshness of their ingredients rather than on creams and fat. Caesar salad is made at your table so you can request your preferred blend of ingredients, and the oyster bar serves fresh oysters from around the world. For the main course, the prime rib is the best and most requested entree, but the rack of lamb is another option worth considering—it melts in your mouth. Guest chefs from international culinary capitals are flown in for monthly specials. The place is small and cozy, with exposed brick and a finishing kitchen in the dining room. Windows have been replaced with murals of the Singapore harbor in the 1850s, but in the evenings it is still airy and fresh-feeling.

✪ **Li Bai.** Sheraton Towers, 39 Scotts Rd. ☎ **65/839-5623.** Reservations required. Main courses S$18–S$48 (US$10.80–US$28.75) and up. AE, DC, MC, V. Daily noon–2:30pm and 6:30–10:30pm. CANTONESE.

Chinese restaurants are typically unimaginative in the decor department—slapping up a landscape brush painting or two here and there is sometimes about as far as they go. Not at Li Bai, though, which is very sleekly decorated in contemporary black and red lacquer, with huge vases of soft pussy willows dotted about. Creative chefs and guest chefs turn out a constantly evolving menu, refining specialties, and jade and silver chopsticks and white bone china add opulent touches to their flawless meals. Make sure you ask for their most recent creations—they're guaranteed to please. Or try the farm chicken smoked with jasmine tea, a succulent dish. The crab fried rice is fabulous, with generous chunks of fresh meat, and the beef in mushroom and garlic brown sauce is some of the most tender meat you'll ever feast upon. The wine list is international, with many vintages to choose from.

✪ **Shima.** Goodwood Park Hotel, 22 Scotts Rd. ☎ **65/734-6281.** Reservations recommended. Dinner sets S$39–S$100 (US$23.35–US$59.90) and up per person. AE, DC, JCB, MC, V. Daily noon–2:30pm and 6:30–10:30pm. JAPANESE.

Downstairs is the tiny sushi and sashimi bar in clean and simple sushi-bar style. Upstairs is the main restaurant, a sprawling space divided up into specialty groupings of tables depending on your desired meal, from the teppanyaki grill to the yakinuku barbecue at the table. Its dark and cozy clubhouse feel brightens with area lighting for each table, creating interesting visuals as you walk in. The menu is complete, from Japanese steamboat buffet to the best Kobe beef in Singapore. For the most sumptuous feast with theater, go for the grill, prepared table-side with all the chopping, slicing, dicing, and cleaver-juggling you could want. Special sets are featured, and the lunch menu is discounted quite a bit. Specify what you intend to eat when you make your reservations.

MODERATE

✪ **Ah Hoi's Kitchen.** Traders Hotel, 1A Cuscaden Rd., 4th level. ☎ **65/831-4373.** Reservations recommended. Main courses S$8–S$26.50 (US$4.80–$15.85). AE, DC, JCB, MC, V. Daily 11:30am–2:30pm and 6:30–10:30pm. SINGAPOREAN.

I like Ah Hoi's for its casual charm and its selection of authentic local cuisine. The menu is extensive, specializing in local favorites like fried black pepper *kuay teow* (noodles), *sambal kang kong* (vegetable), and fabulous grilled seafood. The alfresco poolside pavilion location gives it a real "vacation in the tropics" sort of relaxed feel—think of a hawker center without the dingy florescent bulbs, greasy tables, and sludgy floor. Also good here is the chile crab—if you can't make it out to the seafood places on the east coast of the island it's the best alternative for tasting this local treat. Make sure you order the fresh lime juice. It's very cooling.

Baan Thai. 381 Orchard Rd., no. 04–23 Ngee Ann City. ☎ **65/735-5562.** Reservations recommended. Main courses S$9–S$35 (US$5.40–US$20.95). AE, DC, JCB, MC, V. Daily 11am–2:30pm and 6:30–10:30pm. THAI.

Spotless and well lit, Baan Thai is fitted out with an exotic decor, from the giant Thai Buddha that greets you in the reception area to dining nooks sectioned off with carved wooden screens. Every detail is beautifully integrated, from hanging oil lamps to antique artworks and curio items down to the celadon green plates. A fiery dish to try is the *pla khao lard plik,* charcoal-grilled garoupa (grouper) topped with chile. The *phad Thai* is fried rice noodles with prawn and chicken in a tamarind, chile, and peanut sauce. Thai green curry gravy combines lemongrass, lemon leaf, garlic, and green chile in a base of coconut and is served over your choice of chicken, pork, or beef. It's nice and spicy, but the cook will adjust the spice to taste upon request. Or you can go for the green curry, a traditional Thai favorite, and very good here.

Crystal Jade Palace. 391 Orchard Rd., no. 04–19 Ngee Ann City. ☎ **65/735-2388.** Reservations required. Small dishes S$12–S$38 (US$7.20–US$22.75); set lunch for 2 from S$50 (US$29.95). AE, DC, JCB, MC, V. Daily 11:30am–2:30pm and 6:30–10:30pm. CANTONESE.

Although Crystal Jade Palace is an upmarket choice, it's a fantastic way to try Chinese food as it was intended. From the aquariums of soon-to-be-seafood-delights at the entrance you can survey the rows of big round tables (and some small ones, too) packed with happy diners, feasting away. The food here is authentic Cantonese, prepared by Hong Kong master chefs. Dim sum, fresh seafood, and barbecue dishes accompany exotic shark's fin and baby abalone. Scallop dishes are very popular and can be prepared either sautéed with cashews, chile, and soy; panfried with chiles, white pepper, and salt; or sautéed with green vegetables. The tender panfried cod in light honey sauce proves worthy of its reputation as a time-honored favorite. For a unique soup, try the double-boiled winter melon with mixed meats, mushroom, crab, and dried scallop served in the halved melon shell. You can order Chinese or French wines to accompany your meal.

Long Jiang. Crown Prince Hotel, 270 Orchard Rd. ☎ **65/734-9056.** Reservations required Sat–Sun, and public holidays. Buffet lunch S$28 (US$16.75); buffet dinner S$32 (US$19.15). AE, DC, JCB, MC, V. Daily buffet lunch 11:45am–2:30pm, buffet dinner 7–10:30pm. SZECHUAN.

Long Jiang is the best way for beginners to experiment with Chinese Szechuan cuisine. Lunch and dinner are served all-you-can-eat buffet style, but rather than trek up to a lukewarm spread with plate in hand, you can eyeball a menu complete with photos of each dish. The portions are small, and you can order as many as you like, which means you can try different tastes without committing to only one or two dishes you're not sure about. They also have an à la carte menu with specialties like crispy chicken with hot sesame sauce, fried string beans with minced meat, and sautéed prawn with dried chile (which is only moderately spicy). The atmosphere is rather plain, with some Chinese touches.

Patara Fine Thai. no. 03–14 Tanglin Mall, 163 Tanglin Rd. ☎ **65/737-0818.** Reservations recommended for lunch, required for dinner. Main courses S$17–S$30 (US$10.20–US$17.95). AE, DC, MC, V. Daily noon–2:30pm and 6–10:30pm. THAI.

Patara may say fine dining in its name, but the food here is home cooking: not too haute, not too traditional. Seafood and vegetable are big here. Deep-fried garoupa (grouper) is served in a sweet sauce with chile that can be added sparingly upon request. Curries are popular, too. The roast duck curry in red curry paste with tomatoes, rambutans, and pineapple is juicy and hot. For something really different,

Patara's own invention, the Thai taco isn't exactly traditional, but is good, filled with chicken, shrimp, and sprouts. Their green curry, one of my favorites, is perhaps the best in town. Their Thai-style iced tea (which isn't on the menu, so you'll have to ask for it) is fragrant and flowery. A small selection of wines is also available.

Tandoor. Holiday Inn Parkview, 11 Cavenagh Rd. ☎ **65/730-0153.** Reservations recommended. Main courses S$11–S$40 (US$6.60–US$23.95). AE, DC, MC, V. Daily noon–2:30pm and 7–10:30pm. NORTHERN INDIAN.

Live music takes center stage in this small restaurant, adorned with carpets, artwork, and wood floors and furnishings. Entrees prepared in their tandoor oven come out flavorful and not as salty as most tandoori dishes. The tandoori lobster is rich, but the chef's specialty is crab *lababdar:* crabmeat, onions, and tomato sautéed in a coconut gravy. Fresh cottage cheese is made in-house for fresh and light *saag panir,* a favorite here. Chefs keep a close eye on the spices to ensure the spice enhances the flavor rather than drowning it out—more times than not, customers ask them to add *more* spices. A final course of creamy masala tea perks you up and aids digestion. If you're curious, the tandoor oven is behind a glass wall in the back, so you can watch them prepare your food.

INEXPENSIVE

✪ **Chatterbox.** Mandarin Hotel, 333 Orchard Rd. ☎ **65/737-4411.** Reservations recommended for lunch and dinner. Main courses S$15–S$39 (US$9–US$23.35). AE, DC, JCB, MC, V. Daily 24 hours. SINGAPOREAN/WESTERN.

If you'd like to try the local favorites but don't want to deal with street food, then Chatterbox is the place for you. Their Hainanese chicken rice is highly acclaimed, and other dishes—like nasi lemak, laksa, and carrot cake—are as close to the street as you can get. For a quick and tasty snack, order *tahu goreng,* deep-fried tofu in peanut chile sauce. This is also a good place to experiment with some of those really weird local drinks. *Chin chow* is the dark brown grass jelly drink; *cendol* is green jelly, red beans, palm sugar, and coconut milk; and *bandung* is the pink rose syrup milk with jelly. For dessert, order the ever-favorite sago pudding, made from the hearts of the sago palm. This informal and lively coffee shop dishes out room service for the Mandarin Hotel and is open 24 hours a day.

✪ **The Rice Table.** International Building, 360 Orchard Rd., no. 02–09. ☎ **65/835-3783.** Lunch buffet S$12.80 (US$7.65); dinner buffet S$18.50 (US$11.10). AE, DC, MC, V. Tues–Sun noon–2:30pm and 6–9:30pm. INDONESIAN.

Indonesian Dutch rijsttafel, a service of many small Indonesian dishes (up to almost 20) with rice, is imitated buffet style at the Rice Table, so if the rijsttafel at Alkaff Mansion (see above) tickles your fancy but you don't want to drop the kind of money they charge, you can try something similar here. Stuff yourself on favorite Indo-Malay wonders like beef rendang, chicken satay, otak otak, and sotong assam (squid) for a very reasonable price. Their recipes are nice and tasty. Expect to pay extra for your drinks and desserts.

RESTAURANTS A LITTLE FARTHER OUT

There are some other really fantastic dining finds if you're willing to hop in a cab for 10 or 15 minutes. These places are worth the trip—for a chance to dine along the water at UDMC or amid lush terrace gardens at Alkaff Mansion, or to just go for superior seafood at Long Beach Seafood Restaurant. And don't worry about finding your way back: Most places always have cabs milling about. If not, restaurant staff will always help you call a taxi.

EXPENSIVE

Alkaff Mansion. 10 Telok Blangah Green (off Henderson Rd.), Telok Blangah Hill Park. ☎ **65/278-6979.** Reservations recommended. Set rijstaffel menu S$60 (US$35.95) per person; buffet S$35 (US$20.95) per person. AE, DC, JCB, MC, V. Daily 7pm–midnight. INDONESIAN.

Alkaff Mansion was built by the wealthy Arab Alkaff family not as a home, but as a place to throw elaborate parties, and true to its mission, Alkaff Mansion is tops for elegant ambience. The mansion allows for indoor and outdoor patio dining at small tables glistening with starched white linens and small candles. The forest outside is a stunning backdrop. The dinner cuisine here is rijsttafel—home-style Indonesian fare that was influenced by Dutch tastes and is served in set menus that rotate weekly. A typical set dinner might include *gado gado* (a cold salad with sweet peanut sauce) and a soup. To announce the main course, a gong is sounded and ladies dressed in traditional kebaya sarongs carry out the dishes on platters. Main courses include the *siakap masak asam turnis* (fish in a tangy sauce); the *udang kara kuning*, which is a great choice for lobster; and the crayfish in chile sauce. In rijstaffel tradition, the dinner is served with rice, which is accompanied by an array of condiments like varieties of sambal and achar. Downstairs, Alkaff serves a huge buffet with nightly changing themes. I strongly recommend this place for a truly unique and memorable dining experience.

MODERATE

Long Beach Seafood Restaurant. 1018 East Coast Pkwy. ☎ **65/445-8833.** Reservations recommended. Seafood is sold by weight according to seasonal prices. Most dishes S$9–S$16 (US$5.40–US$9.60). AE, DC, JCB, MC, V. Daily 5pm–1:15am. SEAFOOD.

They really pack 'em in at this place. Tables are crammed together in what resembles a big indoor pavilion, complete with festive lights and the sounds of mighty feasting. This is one of the best places for fresh seafood of all kinds: fishes like garoupa (grouper), sea bass, marble goby, and kingfish, and other creatures of the sea from prawns to crayfish. The chile crab here is good, but the house specialty is really the pepper crab, chopped and deliciously smothered in a thick concoction of black pepper and soy. Huge chunks of crayfish are also tasty in the black pepper sauce, and can be served in variations like barbecue, sambal, steamed with garlic, or in a bean sauce. Don't forget to order buns so you can sop up the sauce. You can also get vegetable, chicken, beef, or venison dishes to complement, or choose from their menu selection of local favorites.

Palm Beach Seafood Restaurant. 5 Stadium Walk, no. 03–04 Leisure Park. ☎ **65/344-3088.** Reservations strongly recommended for weekends. Seafood is sold by the gram according to seasonal prices. Most small dishes S$12–S$28 (US$7.20–US$16.75). AE, MC, V. Daily noon–2:30pm and 6–11:30pm. SEAFOOD.

When eating scrumptious local seafood you usually find yourself in some casual open-air setting or extremely underdressed dining hall, so don't let the upscale setting at Palm Beach fool you: The food is as great as any dingy seaside joint, and very reasonably priced. Australian lobster graces the finest dish here—cooked in a clay pot with coconut milk and chile sauce. Their chile crab is also great, but to me seems a bit "local" for such a swank place. Besides, it's very messy. A gift shop outside lets you bring home jars of hot pot sauce, achar (sweet sauce), chile sauce, and sambal.

Prima Tower. 201 Keppel Rd. ☎ **65/272-8822.** Reservations required. Small dishes S$14–S$50 (US$8.40–US$29.95) and up. AE, DC, MC, V. Daily 11am–2:30pm and 6:30–10:30pm. Closed Chinese New Year. BEIJING.

One of the main attractions here is the fact that the restaurant revolves, giving you an ever-changing view of the city from your table. The other main attraction is the food, which is Beijing-style Chinese. Naturally, the best dish is the Peking duck, which has been a house specialty since this restaurant opened 20 years ago. All of the noodles for the noodle dishes are prepared in-house using traditional recipes and techniques, so the word of the day is *fresh*. Try them with minced pork and chopped cucumber in a sweet sauce. The restaurant manager comes to each table to present the daily specials. It's a good time to chat him up for the best dishes and ask questions about the menu.

Xin Cuisine. Concorde Hotel, 317 Outram Rd., Level 4. ☎ **65/732-3337.** Reservations recommended. Small dishes S$10–S$30 (US$6–US$17.95). AE, DC, JCB, MC, V. Daily noon–2.30pm and 6:30–10:30pm. HERBAL/CANTONESE.

A recent trend is to bring back the Chinese tradition of preparing foods that have special qualities for beauty, health, and vitality, balancing the body's yin and yang and restoring energy. Xin (new) cuisine transforms these concepts into light and flavorful creations, listed in a menu that's literally a book. The chef is famous for East-meets-West creations, but be assured, the cuisine is mostly Chinese. The concentrated seafood soup with chicken and spinach is a light and delicious broth that's neither too thick nor thin and has chunks of meat and shredded spinach. Stewed Mongolian rack of lamb is obviously not Cantonese, but is as tender as butter and served in a sweet brown sauce with buns to soak up the gravy. The steamed eggplant with toasted sesame seed is fantastic, with warm tender slices served in soy sauce. For the more adventurous, they serve up a mean hasma scrambled egg whites. Hasma is frog glands, which are believed to improve the complexion. The dish is a little alarming to some, but served with a hint of ginger and scooped onto walnut melba toast, it's actually quite nice.

INEXPENSIVE

✪ **Samy's Curry Restaurant.** Block 25 Dempsey Rd. ☎ **65/472-2080.** Reservations not accepted. Sold by the scoop or piece, S$0.80–S$3 (US$0.50–US$1.80). V. Daily 11am–3pm and 6–10pm. No alcohol served. SOUTHERN INDIAN.

There are many places in Singapore to get good southern Indian banana leaf, but none quite so unique as Samy's out at Dempsey Road. Part of the Singapore Civil Service Clubhouse, at lunchtime nonmembers must pay S$0.50 to get in the door. Not that there's much of a door, because Samy's is situated in a huge, high-ceilinged, open-air hall, with shutters thrown back and fans whirring above. Wash your hands at the back and have a seat and soon someone will slap a banana leaf place mat in front of you. A blob of white rice will be placed in the center, and then buckets of vegetables, chicken, mutton, fish, prawn, and you name it will be brought out, swimming in the richest and spiciest curries to ever pass your lips. Take a peek in each bucket, shake your head yes when you see one your like, and a scoop will be dumped on your banana leaf. Eat with your right hand or with a fork and spoon. When you're done, wipe the sweat from your brow, fold the banana leaf away from you, and place your tableware on top.

Samy's serves no alcohol, but the fresh lime juice is nice and cooling.

✪ **UDMC Seafood Centre.** Block 1202 East Coast Pkwy. Seafood dishes are charged by weight, with dishes from around S$12 (US$7.20). AE, DC, MC, V. Daily 5pm–midnight. SEAFOOD.

Eight seafood restaurants are lined side by side in 2 blocks, their fronts open to the view of the sea outside. UDMC is a fantastic way to eat seafood Singapore style, in the open air, in restaurants that are more like grand stalls than anything else. Eat the famous local chile crab and pepper crab here, along with all sorts of squid, fish, and scallop dishes. Noodle dishes are also available, as are vegetable dishes and other meats. But the seafood is the thing to come for. Of the eight restaurants, there's no saying which is the best, as everyone seems to have their own opinions about this one or that one (personally, I like Jumbo at the far eastern end of the row). Some restaurants accept Japan Credit Bank. Have a nice stroll along the walkway and gaze out to the water while you decide which one to go for.

HAWKER CENTERS

Hawker centers—large groupings of informal open-air food stalls—were Singapore's answer to fast and cheap food in the days before McDonald's came along, and are still the best way to sample every kind of Singaporean cuisine. They can be intimidating for newcomers, especially during the busy lunch or dinner rush, when they turn into fast-paced carnivals, so if it's your first time, try this: First, walk around to every stall to see what they have to offer. The stalls will have large signs displaying principal menu items, and you should feel free to ask questions, too, before placing your order. Special stalls have drinks only. The fresh lime goes with any dish, but to be truly local, grab a giant bottle of Tiger beer.

Next, find a table. Some stalls have their own tables for you to use; otherwise, sit anywhere you can and when you order let the hawker know where you are (tables usually have numbers to simplify). If it's crowded and you find a couple of free seats at an already occupied table, politely ask if they are taken, and if the answer is no, have a seat—it's perfectly customary. Your food will be brought to you, and you are expected to pay upon delivery. When you're finished, don't clear your own plates, and don't stack them. Some stalls may observe strict religious customs that require different plates for different foods, and getting other scraps on their plates may be offensive.

For the record, all hawkers are licensed by the government, which inspects them and enforces health standards.

The most notorious hawker center in Singapore is **Newton.** Located at Newton Circus, the intersection of Scotts Road, Newton Road, and Bukit Timah/Dunearn Road, this place is notorious, as opposed to famous, for being an overcommercialized tourist spectacle where busloads of foreigners come and gawk at the Singaporean fast-food experience. All in all, if you want to check it out, it is a good initiation before moving on to the real places. **Lau Pa Set Festival Village** (Telok Ayer Market) is located in Chinatown at the corner of Raffles Way and Boon Tat Street, and sometimes gets touristy, too, but for the record, both Newton and Lau Pa Set are open 24 hours.

In the Historic District there are a few. Try the one on Hill Street next to the Central Fire Station or the one on Stamford Road between the National Museum and Armenian Street intersection. You'll also find a couple on Victoria Street on either side of Allson Hotel, and another at Bugis night market.

In Little India, Zhujiao Centre is a nice-size hawker center. **On Orchard Road,** try Cuppage Terrace, just beyond the Centrepoint Shopping Centre.

One place that's been near and dear to Singaporeans for years (though now they've mostly been chased away by overcommercialization) is the ✪ **Satay Club.** It used to be down at the Esplanade, but constant building and land reclamation efforts moved it around a bunch of times, and so they eventually moved it to Clarke Quay off River Valley Road. Yes, it is very touristy now, but still worth a visit. Satay, by the way, is perhaps the most popular Malay dish of all time. The small kabobs of meat are skewered onto the stiff veins of palm leaves and barbecued over a hibachi. Order them by the stick. They come with cucumbers and onion on the side, and a bowl of peanut chile sauce to dunk it all in. Find yourself a table, get some beer, order yourself up a whole plate, and you'll be happy as a clam, whether you look like a tourist or not.

5 Attractions

A note: Many of the sights to see in Singapore are not of the "pay your fee and see the show" variety, but rather historic buildings, monuments, and places of religious worship. The city's historic buildings, such as City Hall or Parliament House, must be appreciated from the outside, their significance lying in their unique architecture and historical context combined with the sensual effect of the surrounding city. Monuments and statues tell the stories of events and heroes important to Singapore both in the past and present. The places of worship listed in this section are open to the public and free of entrance charge. Expect temples to be open from sunup to sundown. Visiting hours are not specific to the hour, but, unless it's a holiday (when hours may be extended), you can expect these places to be open during daylight hours.

THE HISTORIC DISTRICT

Fort Canning Park. Major entrances are from the Hill St. Food Centre, Percival Rd. (Drama Centre), Fort Canning Aquarium, National Library Carpark, and Canning Walk (behind Park Mall). Free admission. Dhoby Gaut or City Hall MRT.

When Stamford Raffles first navigated the Singapore River, he was already envisioning a port settlement, and had designs to build his own home atop the hill that is today this park. His home, a simple wooden structure (at the site of the present-day lookout point), later became a residence for Singapore's Residents and Governors. In 1860, the house was torn down to make way for **Fort Canning,** which was built to quell British fears of invasion but instead quickly became the laughingstock of the island. In 1907 the fort was demolished to make way for a reservoir. Today, the only reminders of the old fort are some of the walls and the Fort Gate, a deep stone structure. Behind its huge wooden door you'll find a narrow staircase that leads to the roof of the structure.

Fort Canning was also the site of a **European cemetery.** To make improvements in the park, the graves were exhumed and the stones placed within the walls surrounding the outdoor performance field that slopes from the Music and Drama Society building. A large Gothic monument was erected in memory of James Napier Brooke, infant son of William Napier, Singapore's first Law Agent, and his wife, Maria Frances, the widow of prolific architect George Coleman. Although no records exist, Coleman probably designed the cupolas as well as two small monuments over unknown graves. The Music and Drama Society building itself was built in 1938. Close by, in the wall, are the tombstones of Coleman and of Jose D'Almeida, a wealthy Portuguese merchant.

Singapore Philatelic Museum. 23B Coleman St. ☎ **65/337-3888.** Admission S$2 (US$1.20) adults, S$1 (US$0.60) children and seniors. Tues–Sun 9am–4:30pm. Take the MRT to City Hall and walk toward Coleman St.

This building, constructed in 1895 to house the Methodist Book Room, recently underwent a S$7 million restoration and reopened as the Philatelic Museum in 1995. Exhibits include a fine collection of old stamps issued to commemorate historically important events, first-day covers, antique printing plates, postal service memorabilia, and private collections. Visitors can trace the development of a stamp from idea to the finished sheet, and you can even design your own. Free guided tours are available upon request.

✪ **Armenian Church.** 60 Hill St., across from the Grand Plaza Hotel.

The first permanent Christian church in Singapore, it was funded primarily by the Armenian community, which was at one time quite powerful. Today, few Singaporeans

Urban Singapore Attractions

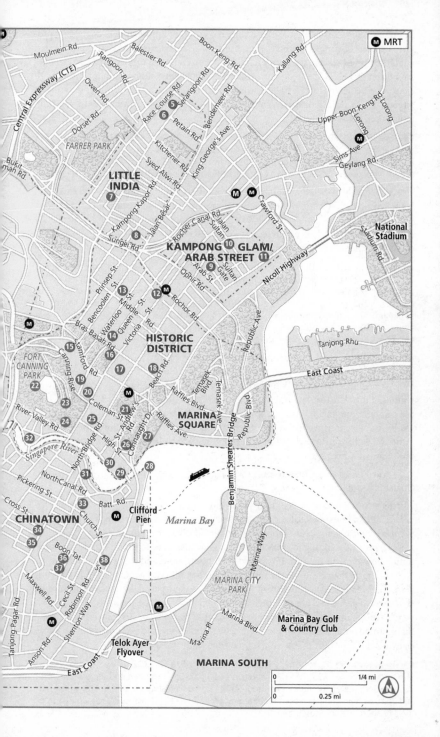

Moulmein Rd.

Rangoon Rd.

Balestier Rd.

Boon Keng Rd.

Kallang Rd.

Owen Rd.

Central Expressway (CTE)

Dorset Rd.

Race Course Rd.

Serangoon Rd.

Bendemeer Rd.

⑤

Petain Rd.

Upper Boon Keng Rd. Lorong

FARRER PARK

Kitchener Rd.

King George's Ave.

Sims Ave.

Geylang Rd.

Bukit mah Rd.

LITTLE INDIA

Syed Alwi Rd.

⑦

Kampong Kapor Rd.

Jalan Besar

Rochor Canal Rd.

Crawford St.

Ⓜ Ⓜ

National Stadium

Stadium Rd.

Sungei Rd.

⑧

KAMPONG ⑩ GLAM/ ARAB STREET ⑪

Prinsen St.

⑨

Arab St.

Sultan Gate

Ophir Rd.

Nicoll Highway

⑬

Bencoolen St.

Middle St.

Ⓜ ⑫

Rochor Rd.

Republic Ave.

Tanjong Rhu

Bras Basah Rd.

Waterloo St.

Queen St.

Victoria St.

HISTORIC DISTRICT

East Coast

Ⓜ

Stamford Rd.

⑭

⑯

Beach Rd.

Temasek Blvd.

FORT CANNING PARK

Canning Rise

⑰

⑱

Raffles Blvd.

Temasek Ave.

Republic Blvd.

㉒

⑲

⑳

Coleman St.

Ⓜ

Raffles Ave.

MARINA SQUARE

㉓

㉑

St. Andrew's

Benjamin Sheares Bridge

River Valley Rd.

㉔

㉕

High St.

Connaught Dr.

㉖ ㉗

North Bridge Rd.

㉜

Singapore River

㉚

㉙

㉘

Marina Bay

NorthCanal Rd.

㉛

Marina Way

Pickering St.

㉝

Batt. Rd.

Clifford Pier

Cross St.

CHINATOWN

Church St.

Ⓜ

MARINA CITY PARK

㉞

㉟

Boon Tat

㊱ ㊲

㊳

St.

Maxwell Rd.

Cecil St.

Robinson Way

Ⓜ

Marina Blvd.

Marina Bay Golf & Country Club

Tanjong Pagar Rd.

Anson Rd.

Shenton Way

Telok Ayer Flyover

Marina Pl.

MARINA SOUTH

East Coast

| 0 | | 1/4 mi |
| 0 | 0.25 mi | |

N

can trace their heritage back to this influential group of immigrants. Designed by prolific architect George Coleman, the church was consecrated in 1836 and the last appointed priest serving the parish retired in 1936. Although regular Armenian services are no longer held, other religious organizations make use of the church from time to time. The cemetery in the back of the church is the burial site of many prominent Armenians, including Ashgen Agnes Joachim, discoverer of the Vanda Miss Joachim, Singapore's national flower.

✪ **Asian Civilisations Museum.** 39 Armenian St. ☎ **65/332-3015.** Admission S$3 (US$1.80) adults, S$1.50 (US$0.90) children and seniors. Tues–Sun 9am–5:30pm (extended hours Wed until 9pm). Free guided tours in English Tues–Fri 11am, 2pm, and 3:30pm, with an extra tour on weekends at 2:45pm. City Hall MRT, and follow Stamford Rd. to Armenian St.

The old Tao Nan School, which dates from 1910, was completely renovated and reopened in 1997 to house the Asian Civilisations Museum. Beautiful and clear displays display fine collections of jade, calligraphy, ceramics, furniture, and artworks, all offering visitors the chance to trace the archipelago's rich Chinese heritage. Changing exhibits in the temporary galleries represent the other Asian civilizations.

✪ **Singapore History Museum.** Stamford Rd., across the street from Bras Basah Park. ☎ **65/375-2510.** www.museum.org.sg/nhb.html. Admission S$3 (US$1.80) adults, S$1.50 (US$0.90) children and seniors. Museum admission plus 3-D movie ticket: adults S$4 (US$2.40), children and seniors S$2 (US$1.20). Tues–Sun 9am–5:30pm (extended hours Wed until 9am). Free guided tours in English Tues–Fri 11am and 2pm, with an extra tour on weekends at 3:30pm. "The Singapore Story—Overcoming the Odds: A 3-D Experience" show times Tues–Sun every hour 10:30am–3:30pm.

Originally called Raffles Museum, the museum was opened in 1887, in a handsome example of neo-Palladian architecture designed by colonial architect Henry McCallum. It was the first of its kind in Southeast Asia, housing a superb collection of regional natural history specimens and ethnographic displays. In both 1907 and 1916, the museum outgrew its space and was enlarged. Renamed the National Museum in 1969, its collections went through a transformation, focusing on Singapore's history rather than that of the archipelago. Several years later, it became known as the Singapore History Museum.

Kuan Yin Thong Hood Cho Temple. Waterloo St., about 1½ blocks from Bras Basah Rd. Open to the public during the day.

There's a steady stream of people at Kuan Yin Temple on auspicious days of the Chinese calendar, as many locals believe that wishes made here come true. The procedure is simple: Wear shoes easily slipped off before entering the temple. Light several joss sticks. Pray to the local god, pray to the sky god, then turn to the side and pray some more. Now pick up the container filled with inscriptions and shake it until one stick falls out. After that, head for the interpretation box office to get a piece of paper with verses in Mandarin and English to look up what your particular inscription means. (For a small fee, there are interpreters outside.) Now for the payback: If your wish comes true, be prepared to return to the temple and offer fruits and flowers to say thanks (oranges, pears, and apples are a thoughtful choice and jasmine petals are especially nice). (You want that wish to come true, don't you?)

✪ **Singapore Art Museum.** 71 Bras Basah Rd. ☎ **65/332-3222.** www.museum.org.sg/ nhb.html. Admission S$3 (US$1.80) adults, S$1.50 (US$0.90) children and seniors. Tues–Sun 9am–5:30pm (extended hours Wed until 9pm). Free guided tours in English Tues–Fri 11am and 2pm, with additional weekend tour at 3:30pm. City Hall MRT, across Bras Basah Park from the Singapore History Museum.

The Singapore Art Museum (SAM) officially opened in 1996 to house an impressive collection of over 3,000 pieces of art and sculpture, most of it by Singaporean and Malay artists. A large collection of Southeast Asian pieces rotates regularly, as well as visiting international exhibits. Once a Catholic boys' school established in 1852, SAM has retained some visible reminders of its former occupants: Above the front door of the main building you can still see inscribed "St. Joseph's Institution," and a bronze-toned, cast-iron statue of St. John Baptist de la Salle with two children stands in its original place.

Cathedral of the Good Shepherd. 4 Queen St., at the corner of Queen St. and Bras Basah Rd. Open to the public during the day.

This cathedral was Singapore's first permanent Catholic church. Built in the 1840s, it brought together many elements of a fractured parish—Portuguese, French, and Spanish—to worship under one roof. Designed in a Latin cross pattern, much of its architecture is reminiscent of St. Martin-In-The-Fields and St. Paul's in Covent Garden.

✪ CHIJMES (Convent of the Holy Infant Jesus). 30 Victoria St. Free admission. 1-hour historical tour in English Mon–Fri 11am and 3pm, Sat 11am, S\$5 (US\$3) per person.

CHIJMES (pronounced "Chimes) is a bustling enclave of retail shops, restaurants, and nightspots. It's difficult to imagine this was once a convent which, at its founding in 1854, consisted of a lone, simply constructed bungalow. After decades of buildings and add-ons, this collection of unique yet perfectly-blended structures was enclosed within walls, forming peaceful courtyards and open spaces encompassing an entire city block. In late 1983, the convent relocated to the suburbs, and some of the block was leveled to make way for the MRT Headquarters. Thankfully, most of the block survived and the Singapore government, in planning the renovation of this desirable piece of real estate, wisely kept the integrity of the architecture. For an evening out, the atmosphere at CHIJMES is exquisitely romantic. At the same time, you can enjoy a special decadence when you party in one of the popular bars here.

✪ Raffles Hotel. 1 Beach Rd. ☎ **65/337-1886.**

Built in 1887 to accommodate the increasing upper-class trade, Raffles Hotel was originally only a couple of bungalows with 10 rooms, but, oh, the view of the sea was perfection. The owners, Armenian brothers named Sarkies, already had a couple of prosperous hotels in Southeast Asia (the Eastern & Oriental in Penang and The Strand in Rangoon) and were well versed in the business. It wasn't long before they added a pair of wings and completed the main building—and reading rooms, verandahs, dining rooms, a grand lobby, the Bar and Billiard Room, a ballroom, and a string of shops. By 1899, electricity was turning the cooling fans and providing the pleasing glow of comfort.

As it made its madcap dash through the twenties, the hotel was the place to see and be seen. Vacancies were unheard of. Hungry Singaporeans and guests from other hotels, eager for a glimpse of the fabulous dining room, were turned away for lack of reservations. The crowded ballroom was jumping every night of the week. It was during this time that Raffles's guest book included famous authors like Somerset Maugham, Rudyard Kipling, Joseph Conrad and Noël Coward. These were indeed the glory years, but the lovely glimmer from the chandeliers soon faded with the stark arrival of the Great Depression. Raffles managed to limp through that dark time—and, darker still, through the Japanese occupation—and later pull back from the brink of bankruptcy to undergo modernization in the fifties. But fresher, brighter, more opulent hotels were taking root on Orchard Road, pushing the "grand old lady" to the back seat.

The hotel was in limbo for a period of time due to legal matters, and in 1961 it passed through several financial institutions to land on the doorstep of the Development Bank of Singapore (DBS). It was probably this journey that saved the Raffles from a haphazard renovation nightmare. Instead, history-minded renovators selected 1915 as a benchmark and, with a few changes here and there, faithfully restored the hotel to that era's magnificence and splendor. Today, the hotel's restaurants and nightlife draw thousands of visitors daily to its open lobby, its theater playhouse, the Raffles Hotel Museum, and 65 exclusive boutiques. Its 15 restaurants and bars—especially the Tiffin Room, Raffles Grill, and Doc Cheng's—are a wonder, as is its famous Bar and Billiards Room and Long Bar.

Bugis Street / Bugis Junction. Bugis MRT stop, across from Parco Bugis Junction shopping mall.

If you happened to visit Singapore in the seventies, and remember Bugis as a haven for transvestites and sex shows, you're in for a big surprise. Bugis Street ain't what it used to be. In place of the decadence is a giant shopping mall, Parco Bugis Junction. A little of the past still lingers at the **Boom Boom Room** (no. 02–04 New Bugis Village, 3 New Bridge Rd.; ☎ **65/339-8187**), where nightly shows feature the most beautiful transvestites belting out hits by Barbra Streisand and Judy Garland. There's also a night market with a few bargains on cheap chic, curio items, accessories, and video discs.

The area around Bugis Street has a more benign history. The Bugis, fierce and respected warriors, were some of the first people to settle in Singapore in its early years. Raffles took note of their boatbuilding skills and, as part of his master town plan, included Bugis Town to attract more of them to the island.

✪ St. Andrew's Cathedral. Coleman St., between North Bridge Rd. and St. Andrew's Rd., across from the Padang. Open during daylight hours.

Designed by George Coleman and erected on a site selected by Sir Stamford Raffles himself, St. Andrew's was the colonial's Anglican Church. Completed toward the end of the 1830s, its tower and spire were added several years later to accord the edifice more stature. By 1852, because of massive damage sustained from lightning strikes, the cathedral was deemed unsafe and was torn down. The cathedral that now stands on the site was completed in 1860. Of English Gothic Revival design, the cathedral is one of the few standing churches of this style in the region.

City Hall (Municipal Building). St. Andrew's Rd., across from the Padang. Entrance to the visitor's gallery is permitted, but all other areas are off limits.

During the Japanese occupation, City Hall was a major headquarters, and it was here in 1945 that Admiral Lord Louis Mountbatten accepted the Japanese surrender. In 1951, the Royal Proclamation from King George VI was read here declaring that Singapore would henceforth be known as a city. Fourteen years later, Prime Minister Lee Kuan Yew announced to its citizens that Singapore would henceforth be called an independent republic.

City Hall, along with the Supreme Court, was judiciously sited to take full advantage of the prime location. Magnificent Corinthian columns march across the front of the symmetrically designed building, while inside, two courtyards lend an ambience of informality to otherwise officious surroundings. For all its magnificence and historical fame, however, its architect, F. D. Meadows, relied too heavily on European influence. The many windows afford no protection from the sun, and the entrance leaves pedestrians unsheltered from the elements. In defining the very nobility of the Singapore government, it appears the Singaporean climate wasn't taken into consideration.

Supreme Court. St. Andrew's Rd., across from the Padang. Closed to visitors, but worth seeing from the outside.

The Supreme Court stands on the site of the old Hotel de L'Europe, a rival of the Raffles Hotel until it went bankrupt in the 1930s. The court's structure, a classical style favored for official buildings the world over, was completed in 1939. With its spare adornment and architectural simplicity, the edifice has a no-nonsense, utilitarian attitude, and the sculptures across the front, executed by the Italian sculptor Cavaliere Rodolpho Nolli, echo what transpires within. *Justice* is the most breathtaking, standing 2.7 meters (9 ft.) high and weighing almost 4 tons. Kneeling on either side of her are representations of *Supplication* and *Thankfulness.* To the far left are *Deceit* and *Violence.* To the far right, a bull represents *Prosperity* and two children hold wheat, to depict *Abundance.*

Two and a half million bricks were used in building this structure, but take a moment to note the stonework: It's fake! Really a gypsum type of plaster, it was applied by Chinese plasterers who'd fled from Shanghai during the Sino-Japanese conflict, and molded to give the appearance of granite.

While taking in the exterior, look up at the dome, which is a copy of the dome of St. Paul's Cathedral in London. The dome covers the courtyard, which is surrounded by the four major portions of the Supreme Court building.

The Padang. St. Andrew's Rd. and Connaught Dr.

This large field—officially called Padang Besar but known as the Padang—has witnessed its share of historical events. It is bordered on one end by the Singapore Recreation Club and on the other end by the Singapore Cricket Club, and flanked by City Hall. The Padang is mainly used for public and sporting events—pleasant activities—but in the 1940s it felt more forlorn footsteps when the invading Japanese forced the entire European community onto the field. There they waited while the occupation officers dickered over a suitable location for the "conquered." Presently, they ordered all British, Australian, and Allied troops as well as European prisoners on the 22-kilometer march to Changi.

An interesting side note: Frank Ward, designer of the Supreme Court, had big plans for the Padang and surrounding buildings. He would have demolished the Cricket Club, Parliament House, and the Victoria Hall & Theatre to erect an enormous government block if World War II hadn't arrived, ruining his chances.

Parliament House. 1 High St., at the south end of the Padang, next to the Supreme Court. Closed to the general public, but worth seeing from the outside.

Parliament House, built in 1826, is probably Singapore's oldest surviving structure, even though it has been renovated so many times it no longer looks the way it was originally constructed. The original house was designed by architect George D. Coleman, who had helped Raffles with his Town Plan of 1822. Coleman's design was in the English neo-Palladian style. Simple and well suited to the tropics, this style was popular at the time with Calcutta merchants. Major alterations have left very little behind of Coleman's design, however, replacing it with an eclectic French classical style, but some of his work survives. Today, the building has been transformed once again, into part of a larger S$80 million Parliament Complex.

The bronze elephant in front of Parliament House was a gift to Singapore in 1872 from His Majesty Somdeth Phra Paraminda Maha Chulalongkorn (Rama V), Supreme King of Siam, as a token of gratitude following his stay in the previous year.

Victoria Theatre and Concert Hall. 9 Empress Place, at the southern end of the Padang. ☎ 65/339-6120.

Designed by colonial engineer John Bennett in a Victorian Revival style that was fashionable in Britain at the time, the theater portion was built in 1862 as the Town Hall. Victoria Memorial Hall was built in 1905 as a memorial to Queen Victoria, retaining the same style of the old building. The clock tower was added a year later. In 1909, with its name changed to Victoria Theatre, the hall opened with an amateur production of the *Pirates of Penzance.* Another notable performance occurred when Noël Coward passed through Singapore and stepped in at the last moment to help out a traveling English theatrical company that had lost a leading man. The building looks much the same as it did then, though of course the interiors have been modernized. It was completely renovated in 1979, conserving all the original details, and was renamed Victoria Concert Hall. It has since housed the Singapore Symphony Orchestra and various performance companies.

Statue of Raffles. Victoria Theatre and Concert Hall.

This sculpture of Sir Stamford Raffles was erected on the Padang in 1887 and moved to its present position after getting in the way of one too many cricket matches. During the Japanese occupation, the statue was placed in the Singapore History Museum (then the Raffles Museum), and was replaced here in 1945. The local joke is that Raffles's arm is outstretched to the Bank of China building, and his pockets are empty. (Translation: In terms of wealth in Singapore, it's Chinese one, Brits nil.)

Empress Place Building. 1 Empress Place, at the southern end of the Padang next to the Parliament Building.

Standing as a symbol of British colonial authority as travelers entered the Singapore River, Empress Place Building housed almost the entire government bureaucracy around the year 1905, and was a government office until the 1980s, housing the Registry of Births and Deaths and the Citizenship Registry. Every Singaporean at some point passed through its doors. In the late 1980s, the government offices moved out and the building was restored as an historical cultural exhibition venue.

The oldest portion is the part nearest Parliament House; it was designed by colonial engineer J. F. A. McNair and built by convict labor between June 1864 and December 1867. Four major additions and other renovations have been faithful to his original design. Inside, there are many surviving details, including plaster moldings, cornices, and architraves. It is currently being renovated as the second phase of the Asian Civilisations Museum.

Raffles Landing Site. North Boat Quay.

The polymarble statue at this site was unveiled in 1972. It was made from plaster casts of the original 1887 figure located in front of the Victoria Theatre and Concert Hall (see above), and stands on what is believed to be the site where Sir Stamford Raffles landed on January 29, 1819.

ALONG THE RIVER

The Singapore River had always been the heart of life in Singapore even before Raffles landed, but for many years during the 20th century life here was dead—quite literally. Rapid urban development that began in the 1950s turned the river into a giant sewer, killing all plant and animal life in it. In the mid-1980s, though, the government began a large and surprisingly successful cleanup project, and shortly thereafter, the buildings at Boat Quay and Clarke Quay were restored. Now the areas on both banks of the river offer entertainment, food, and pubs day and night.

Boat Quay. Located on the south bank of the Singapore River between Cavenagh Bridge and Elgin Bridge.

Known as "the belly of the carp" by the local Chinese because of its shape, this area was once notorious for its opium dens and coolie shops. Nowadays, thriving restaurants boast every cuisine imaginable and the rocking nightlife offers up a variety of sounds—jazz, rock, blues, Indian, and Caribe—that are lively enough to get any couch potato tapping his feet.

Clarke Quay. River Valley Rd. west of Coleman Bridge.

The largest of the waterfront developments, Clarke Quay was named for the second governor of Singapore, Sir Andrew Clarke. In the 1880s, a pineapple cannery, iron foundry, and numerous warehouses made this area bustle. Today, with 60 restored warehouses hosting restaurants and a shopping section known as Clarke Quay Factory Stores, the Quay still hops. **River House,** formerly the home of a *towkay* (company president), occupies the oldest building. The **Bar Gelateria Bellavista** ice cream parlor (River Valley Road at Coleman Bridge) was once the ice house. On Thursdays and Fridays from 6:30 to 8:15pm, enthusiasts can catch a **Chinese opera performance** and makeup demonstration—it's a treat to watch. Get up early on Sunday, forgo the comics section and take in the **flea market,** which opens at 9am and lasts all day. You'll find lots of bargains on unusual finds.

Merlion Park. South bank, at the mouth of the Singapore River, near the Anderson Bridge. Free admission. Daily 7am–10pm.

The Merlion is Singapore's half-lion, half-fish national symbol, the lion representing Singapore's roots as the "Lion City" and the fish representing the nation's close ties to the sea. Bet you think a magical and awe-inspiring beast like this has been around in tales for hundreds of years, right? No such luck. Rather, he was the creation of some scheming mind at the Singapore Tourism Board in the early 1970s. Talk about the collision of ancient culture and the modern world. Despite the Merlion's commercial beginnings, he's been adopted as the national symbol and spouts continuously every day at the mouth of the Singapore River from 10am to noon. Aside from the beastie himself, there's nothing to do in the park, and in fact, the best Merlion viewing can actually be done from Esplanade Park (see below).

Esplanade Park. Connaught Dr., on the marina, running from the mouth of the Singapore River along the Padang to Raffles Ave. Open daily until midnight.

Esplanade Park and Queen Elizabeth Walk, two of the most famous parks in Singapore, were established in 1943 on land reclaimed from the sea. Several memorials are located here. The first is a fountain built in 1857 to honor **Tan Kim Seng,** who gave a great sum of money toward the building of a waterworks. Another monument, **the Cenotaph,** commemorates the 124 Singaporeans who died in World War I; it was dedicated by the Prince of Wales. On the reverse side, the names of those who died in World War II have been inscribed. The third prominent memorial is dedicated to **Major General Lim Bo Seng,** a member of the Singaporean underground resistance in World War II who was captured and killed by the Japanese. His memorial was unveiled in 1954 on the 10th anniversary of his death. These days, the park is a little bit of a mess due to the nearby construction of Singapore's new Theatres on the Bay, modeled after the Sydney Opera House.

Chettiar's Hindu Temple (aka the Tank Road Temple). 15 Tank Rd., close to the intersection of Clemenceau Ave. and River Valley Rd.

One of the richest and grandest of its kind in Southeast Asia, the Tank Road Temple is most famous for a **thoonganai maadam,** a statue of an elephant's backside in a seated position. It's said that there are only four others of the kind, located in four temples in India. The original temple was completed in 1860, restored in 1962, and practically rebuilt in 1984.

Used daily for worship, the temple is also the culmination point of Thaipusam, a celebration of thanks, and the Festival of Navarathiri.

CHINATOWN/TANJONG PAGAR

Wak Hai Cheng Bio Temple. 30–B Phillip St., at the corner of Phillip St. and Church St.

Like most of Singapore's Chinese temples, Wak Hai Cheng Bio had its start as a simple wood-and-thatch shrine where sailors, when they got off their ships, would go to express their gratitude for sailing safely to their destination. Before the major land reclamation projects shifted the shoreline outward, the temple was close to the water's edge, and so it was named "Temple of the Calm Sea Built by the Guangzhou People." It's a Teochew temple, located in a part of Chinatown populated mostly by the Teochews. The temple itself is quite a visual treat, with ceramic figurines and pagodas adorning the roof, and every nook and cranny of the structure adorned with tiny three-dimensional reliefs that depict scenes from Chinese operas. The spiral joss hanging in the courtyard adds an additional picturesque effect.

Nagore Durgha Shrine. 140 Telok Ayer St., at the corner of Telok Ayer St. and Boon Tat St. ☎ 65/324-0021.

Although this is a Muslim place of worship, it is not a mosque, but a shrine, built to commemorate a visit to the island by a Muslim holy man of the Chulia people (Muslim merchants and money-lenders from India's Coromandel Coast), who was traveling around Southeast Asia spreading the word of Indian Islam. The most interesting visual feature is its facade: Two arched windows flank an arched doorway, with columns in between. Above these is a "miniature palace"—a massive replica of the facade of a palace, with tiny cutout windows and a small arched doorway in the middle. The cutouts in white plaster make it look like lace. From the corners of the facade, two 14-level minarets rise, with three little domed cutouts on each level and onion domes on top. Inside, the prayer halls and two shrines are painted and decorated in shockingly tacky colors.

✪ **Thian Hock Keng Temple.** 158 Telok Ayer St., ½ block beyond Nagore Durgha Shrine.

Thian Hock Keng, the "Temple of Heavenly Bliss," is one of the oldest Chinese temples in Singapore. Before land reclamation, when the shoreline came right up to Telok Ayer Road, the first Chinese sailors landed here and immediately built a shrine, a small wood-and-thatch structure, to pray to the goddess Ma Po Cho for allowing their voyage to be safely completed. For each subsequent boatload of Chinese sailors, the shrine was always the first stop upon landing. Ma Po Cho, the Mother of the Heavenly Sages, was the patron goddess of sailors, and every Chinese junk of the day had an altar dedicated to her. The temple that stands today was built in 1841 over the shrine with funds from the Hokkien community. All of the building materials were imported from China, except for the gates, which came from Glasgow, Scotland, and the tiles on the facade, which are from Holland.

Al-Abrar Mosque. 192 Telok Ayer St., near the corner of Telok Ayer St. and Amoy St., near Thian Hock Keng Temple.

This mosque was originally erected as a thatched building in 1827 and was also called Masjid Chulia and Kuchu Palli, which in Tamil means "hut mosque." The building that stands today was built in the 1850s, and even though it faces Mecca, the complex conforms with the grid of the neighborhood's city streets. In the late 1980s, the mosque underwent major renovations which enlarged the mihrab and stripped away some of the ornamental qualities of the columns in the building. The one-story prayer hall was extended upward into a two-story gallery. Little touches like the timber window panels and fanlight windows have been carried over into the new renovations.

Lau Pa Sat Festival Pavilion. 18 Raffles Quay, located in the entire block flanked by Robinson Rd., Cross St., Shenton Way, and Boon Tat St.

Though it used to be well beloved, the locals think this place has become an atrocity. Once the happy little hawker center known as Telok Ayer Market, it began life as a wet market, selling fruits, vegetables, and other foodstuffs. Now it's part hawker center, part Western fast-food outlets, and all tourist. Lau Pa Sat is one of the few hawker centers that's open 24 hours, in case you need a coffee or snack before retiring.

✪ **Sri Mariamman Hindu Temple.** 244 South Bridge Rd., at the corner of South Bridge Rd. and Pagoda St.

As the oldest Hindu temple in Singapore, Sri Mariamman has been the central point of Hindu tradition and culture. In its early years, the temple housed new immigrants while they established themselves and also served as social center for the community. Today, the main celebration here is the Thimithi Festival in October or November. The shrine is dedicated to the goddess Sri Mariamman, who is known for curing disease, but as is the case at all other Hindu temples, the entire pantheon of Hindu gods are present to be worshipped as well.

✪ **Jamae Mosque.** 18 South Bridge Rd., at the corner of South Bridge Rd. and Mosque St.

Jamae Mosque was built by the Chulias, Tamil Muslims who were some of the earlier immigrants to Singapore, and who had a very influential hold over Indian Muslim life centered in the Chinatown area. It was the Chulias who built not only this mosque, but Masjid Al-Abrar and the Nagore Durgha Shrine as well. Jamae Mosque dates from 1827, but wasn't completed until the early 1830s. The mosque stands today almost exactly as it did then.

LITTLE INDIA

Abdul Gafoor Mosque. 41 Dunlop St., between Perak Rd. and Jalan Besar.

Abdul Gafoor Mosque is actually a mosque complex consisting of the original mosque, a row of shop houses facing Dunlop Street, a prayer hall, and another row of houses ornamented with crescent moons and stars, facing the mosque. The original mosque was called Masjid Al-Abrar, and is commemorated on a granite plaque above what could have been either the entrance gate or the mosque itself. It still stands, and even though it is badly dilapidated, retains some of its original beauty. One beautiful detail is the sunburst above the main entrance, its rays decorated with Arabic calligraphy.

✪ **Sri Veerama Kaliamman Temple.** On Serangoon Rd. at Veerasamy Rd. Daily 8am–noon and 5:30–8:30pm.

This Hindu temple is used primarily for the worship of Shiva's wife Kali, who destroys ignorance, maintains world order, and blesses those who strive for knowledge of God. The box on the walkway to the front entrance is for smashing coconuts, a symbolic smashing of the ego, asking God to show "the humble way." The coconuts have two small "eyes" at one end so they can "see" the personal obstacles to humility they are being asked to smash. Inside the temple in the main hall are three altars, the center one for Kali (depicted with 16 arms and wearing a necklace of human skulls) and two altars on either side for her two sons—Ganesh, the elephant god, and Murugan, the four-headed child god. To the right is an altar with nine statues representing the nine planets. Circle the altar and pray to your planet for help with a specific trouble.

Sri Perumal Temple. 397 Serangoon Rd., ½ block past Perumal Rd. Best times to visit are daily 7–11am or 5–7:30pm.

Sri Perumal Temple is devoted to the worship of Vishnu. As part of the Hindu trinity, Vishnu is the sustainer balancing out Brahma the creator and Shiva the destroyer. When the world is out of whack, he rushes to its aid, reincarnating himself to show mankind that there are always new directions for development.

The temple was built in 1855, and was most recently renovated in 1992. During Thaipusam, the main festival celebrated here, male devotees who have made vows over the year carry *kavadi*—huge steel racks decorated with flowers and fruits and held onto their bodies by skewers and hooks—to show their thanks and devotion, while women carry milk pots in a parade from Sri Perumal Temple to Chettiar's Temple on Tank Road.

✪ **Sakya Muni Buddha Gaya (or the Temple of a Thousand Lights).** On Race Course Rd., 1 block past Perumal Rd. Daily 7:30am–4:45pm.

Thai elements influence this temple, from the chedi (stupa) roofline to the huge Thai-style Buddha image inside. Often this temple is brushed off as strange and tacky, but there are all sorts of surprises inside, making the place a veritable Buddha theme park. On the right side of the altar, statues of baby boddhisattvas receive toys and sweets from worshippers. Around the base of the altar, murals depict scenes from the life of Prince Siddhartha (Buddha) as he searches for enlightenment. Follow them around to the back of the hall and you'll find a small doorway to a chamber under the altar. Another Buddha image reclines inside, this one shown at the end of his life, beneath the Yellow Seraka tree. On the left side of the main part of the hall is a replica of a footprint left by the Buddha in Ceylon. Next to that is a wheel of fortune. For 50¢ you get one spin.

ARAB STREET/KAMPONG GLAM

✪ **Sultan Mosque.** 3 Muscat St. Daily 9am–1pm and 2–4pm. No visiting is allowed during mass congregation Fri 11:30am–2:30pm.

Though there are more than 80 mosques on the island of Singapore, Sultan Mosque is the real center of the Muslim community. The mosque that stands today is the second Sultan Mosque to be built on this site. The first was built in 1826, partially funded by the East India Company as part of their agreement to leave Kampong Glam to Sultan Hussein and his family in return for sovereign rights to Singapore. The present mosque was built in 1928 and was funded by donations from the Muslim community. The Saracenic flavor of the onion domes, topped with crescent moons and stars, are complemented by Mogul cupolas. Funny thing, though: The mosque was designed by an Irish guy named Denis Santry, who was working for the architectural firm Swan and McLaren.

Sultan Mosque, like all the others, does not permit shorts, miniskirts, low necklines, or other revealing clothing to be worn inside. However, they do realize that non-Muslim travelers like to be comfortable as they tour around, and provide cloaks free of charge. They hang just to the right as you walk up the stairs.

✪ **Istana Kampong Glam.** Located at the end of Sultan Gate, 1 block past the intersection of Sultan Gate, Bagdad St., and Pahang St. This is a private residence, therefore no entry is permitted.

The Istana Kampong Glam hardly seems a fitting palace for Singapore's former royal family, but there's a fascinating and controversial story behind its current state of sad disrepair. In 1819, Sultan Hussein signed the original treaty that permitted the British East India Trading Company to set up operations in Singapore. Then, in 1824, he signed a new treaty in which he gave up his sovereign rights to the country in return for Kampong Glam (which became his personal residence) and an annual stipend for himself and his descendants. Shortly after his death some 11 years later, his son, Sultan Ali, built the palace. The family fortunes began to dwindle over the years that followed, and a decades-long dispute arose between Ali's descendants over ownership rights to the estate. In the late 1890s, they went to court, where it was decided that no one had the rights as the successor to the sultanate, and the land was reverted to the state, though the family was allowed to remain in the house. Trouble is, since the place had become state owned, the family lost the authority to improve the buildings of the compound, which is why they've fallen into the dilapidated condition you see today.

✪ **Hajjah Fatimah Mosque.** 4001 Beach Rd., past Jalan Sultan.

Hajjah Fatimah was a wealthy businesswoman from Malacca and something of a local socialite. She had originally built a home on this site, but after it had been robbed a couple of times and later set fire to, she decided to build a mosque here and moved to another home. Inside the high walls of the compound are the prayer hall, an ablution area, gardens and mausoleums, and a few other buildings. You can walk around the main prayer halls to the garden cemeteries, where flat square headstones mark the graves of women and round ones mark the graves of men. Hajjah Fatimah is buried in a private room to the side the main prayer hall, along with her daughter and son-in-law.

ORCHARD ROAD AREA
The Istana and Sri Temasek. Orchard Rd., between Claymore Rd. and Scotts Rd.

This building serves as the official residence of the President of the Republic of Singapore. Used mainly for state and ceremonial occasions, the grounds are open to every citizen on selected public holidays, though they're not generally open for visits. The house's domain includes several other houses of senior colonial civil servants

✪ **Peranakan Place.** Located at the intersection of Emerald Hill and Orchard Rd.

The houses along Emerald Hill have all been renovated and the street has been closed to vehicular traffic. As you pass Emerald Hill though, don't just blow it off as a tourist trap. Walk through the cafe area and out the back. All of the terrace houses have been redone, and magnificently. The facades have been freshly painted and the tiles polished, and the dark wood details add a contrast that is truly elegant. When these places were renovated, they could be purchased for a song, but as Singaporeans began grasping at their heritage in recent years, their value shot up, and now these homes fetch huge sums.

WESTERN SINGAPORE ATTRACTIONS
The attractions grouped in this section are on the west side of Singapore, beginning from the Singapore Botanic Gardens at the edge of the urban area all the way out to the Singapore Discovery Centre past Jurong. Remember, if you're traveling around this area, that transportation can be problematic, as the MRT system rarely goes direct to any of these places, taxis can be hard to find, and bus routes get more complex. Keep the telephone number for taxi booking handy. Sometimes ticket sales people at each attraction can help and make the call for you.

Bukit Timah Nature Reserve. 177 Hindhede Dr. ☎ **1800/468-5736.** Free admission. Daily 7am–7pm. MRT to Newton, then TIBS bus no. 171 or SBS bus no. 182 to park entrance.

Bukit Timah Nature Reserve is pure primary rain forest. Believed to be as old as 1 million years, it's the only place on the island with vegetation that exists exactly as it was before the British settled here. The park is more than 81 hectares (202 acres) of soaring canopy teeming with mammals and birds and a lush undergrowth with more bugs, butterflies, and reptiles than you can shake a vine at. Here you can see more than 700 plant species, many of which are exotic ferns, plus mammals like long-tailed macaques, squirrels, and lemurs. There's a visitor center and four well-marked paths, one of which leads to Singapore's highest point. At 163 meters (535 ft.) above sea level, don't expect a nosebleed, but some of the scenic views of the island are really nice. Along another walkway is Singapore's oldest tree, estimated to be 400 years old. Also at Bukit Timah is Hindhede Quarry, which filled up with water at some point, so you can take a dip and cool off during your hike.

✪ **Jurong BirdPark.** 2 Jurong Hill. ☎ **65/265-0022.** Admission S$10.30 (US$6.15) adults, S$4.10 (US$2.45) children under 12, S$7.21 (US$4.30) seniors. Panorail: adults S$2.50 (US$1.50), children under 12 S$1 (US$0.60). Mon–Fri 9am–6pm; Sat–Sun and public holidays 8am–6pm. MRT to Boon Lay Station, transfer to SBS no. 194 or 251.

Jurong BirdPark, with a collection of 8,000 birds from more than 600 species, showcases Southeast Asian breeds plus other colorful tropical beauties, some of which are endangered. The more than 20 hectares (49½ acres) can be easily walked or, for a couple dollars extra, you can ride the panorail for a bird's-eye view (so to speak) of the grounds. I enjoy the Waterfall Aviary, the world's largest walk-in aviary. It's an up-close-and-personal experience with African and South American birds, plus a pretty walk over pathways and babbling brooks through landscaped tropical forest. This is where you'll also see the world's tallest man-made waterfall, but the true feat of engineering here is the panorail station, built inside the aviary. Another smaller walk-in aviary is for Southeast Asian endangered bird species; at noon every day this aviary experiences a man-made thunderstorm. The daily guided tours and regularly scheduled feeding times are enlightening. Other bird exhibits are the flamingo pools, the World of Darkness (featuring nocturnal birds), and the penguin parade, a favorite for Singaporeans, who adore all things arctic.

Two shows feature birds of prey either acting out their natural instincts or performing falconry tricks. The **Fuji World of Hawks** is at 10am and the **King of the Skies** is at 4pm. The **All-Star Birdshow** takes place at 11am and 3pm, with trained parrots that race bikes and birds that perform all sorts of silliness, including staged birdie misbehaviors. Try to come between 9am and 11am for breakfast among hanging cages of chirping birds at the **Songbird Terrace.**

Jurong Reptile Park. 241 Jalan Ahmad Ibrahim. ☎ **65/261-8866.** Admission S$7 (US$4) adults, S$3.50 (US$2.10) children under 12 and seniors. Daily 9am–6pm. MRT to Boon Lay Station, transfer to SBS no. 194 or 251.

The newly renovated Jurong Reptile Park (fixed up just in time, as the older facility was smelling up the entire neighborhood) houses more than 50 species of reptiles from the region and around the world. Feedings are fun, as are the reptile shows (at 11:45am and 2pm daily). Snakes are happy to wrap themselves around your neck for a souvenir photo (10:30am and 5pm daily). In itself, it's no reason to trek out to Jurong, but makes a convenient add-on to a visit to the Jurong BirdPark.

Haw Par Villa Tiger Balm Gardens. 262 Pasir Panjang Rd. ☎ **65/774-0300.** Admission S$5 (US$3) adults, S$2.50 (US$1.50) children. Daily 9am–5pm. MRT to Buona Vista and transfer to bus no. 200.

In 1935, brothers Haw Boon Haw and Haw Boon Par—creators of Tiger Balm, the camphor and menthol rub that comes in those cool little pots—took their fortune and opened Tiger Balm Gardens as a venue for teaching traditional Chinese values. They made more than 1,000 statues and life-size dioramas depicting Chinese legends and historic tales and illustrating morality and Confucian beliefs. Many of these were grue-some and bloody and some of them were really entertaining.

But Tiger Balm Gardens suffered a horrible fate. In 1985, it was converted into an amusement park and reopened as Haw Par Villa. Most of the statues and scenes were taken away and replaced with rides. Well, business did not exactly boom. In fact, the park has been losing money fast. But recently, in an attempt to regain some of the original Tiger Balm Garden edge, they replaced many of the old statues, some of which are a great backdrop for really kitschy vacation photos. Last year they also low-ered the admission price from S$16 for adults to the more affordable S$5 they charge today. Catch the two theme rides: the Tales of China Boat Ride and the Wrath of the Water Gods Flume.

Tang Dynasty City. 2 Yuan Ching Rd. ☎ **65/261-1116.** Admission S$15.45 (US$9.25) adults, S$10.30 (US$6.15) children to 12. Daily 10am–4pm. MRT to Lakeside, then transfer to SBS no. 154 or 240.

This theme park re-creates Xian, the Chinese capital city during the Tang Dynasty (A.D. 618–907), the "Golden Age" of Chinese history for great achievements in the sciences, architecture, religion, and the arts, and for trade along the silk road. To build the reproduction city, around 80 workers who specialized in period buildings were brought in from China, as were all the green bricks and slates, roof tiles, 50,000 kilos of white jade, and almost S$5 million worth of antiques. As you make your way through the narrow streets you can check out the shops showcasing artisans who carve chops (the stone stamps carved with Chinese characters that artists use to sign paint-ings and calligraphy) and eggshells (real eggshells, carved with intricate and delicate lace designs), and perform the tea ceremony. In some buildings you can walk upstairs, especially at the three-story "pleasure home." The Buddhist temple that was built for the city has come into use as an actual temple for visitors to the park.

The wax museum has more than 100 historical Chinese figures including Confu-cius and Genghis Khan. And if you think wax museums are creepy, you have to see the animated figures of Sun Yat-sen and Mao Zedong shouting propaganda. There are 2,000 reproduction terra-cotta warriors in an underground tomb display, plus Ghost Mansion, featuring Japanese-engineered illusions.

✪ **Chinese and Japanese Gardens.** 1 Chinese Garden Rd. ☎ **65/264-3455.** Admission S$4.50 (US$2.70) adults, S$2 (US$1.20) children. Daily 9am–6pm. MRT to Chinese Garden or bus nos. 335, 180, and 154.

Situated on two islands in Jurong lake, the gardens are reached by an overpass and joined by the Bridge of Double Beauty. The **Chinese Garden** dedicates most of its area to "northern style" landscape architecture. The style of imperial gardens, the northern style integrates brightly colored buildings with the surroundings to com-pensate for northern China's absence of rich plant growth and natural scenery. The Stoneboat is a replica of the stone boat at the Summer Palace in Beijing; inside the Pure Air of the Universe building are courtyards and a pond; and there is a seven-story pagoda, the odd number of floors symbolizing continuity. Around the gardens, spe-cial attention has been paid to the placement of rock formations to resemble true nature, and also to the qualities of the rocks themselves, which can represent the forces of yin and yang, male and female, passivity or activity, and so on.

I like the Garden of Beauty, in Suzhou style, representing the southern style of land-scape architecture. Southern gardens were built predominantly by scholars, poets, and men of wealth. Sometimes called Black-and-White gardens, these smaller gardens had more fine detail, featuring subdued colors as the plants and elements of the rich natural landscape gave them plenty to work with. Inside the Suzhou garden are 2,000 pots of *penjiang* (bonsai) and displays of small rocks.

While the Chinese garden is more visually stimulating, the **Japanese garden** is intended to evoke feeling. Marble-chip paths lead the way so that as you walk you can hear your own footsteps and meditate on the sound. They also serve to slow the journey for better gazing upon the scenery. The Keisein, or "Dry Garden," uses white pebbles to create images of streams. Ten stone lanterns, a small traditional house, and a rest house are nestled among two ponds with smaller islands joined by bridges.

There are toilets situated at stops along the way, as well as benches to have a rest or to just take in the sights. Paddleboats can be rented for S$5 (US$3) per hour just outside the main entrance.

✪ **Singapore Botanic Gardens.** Main entrance at corner of Cluny Rd. and Holland Rd. ☎ **1800/471-7300** toll free in Singapore. Free admission. Daily 4am–11:30pm (closing at midnight on weekends). The National Orchid Garden: adults S$2 (US$1.20), children under 12 and seniors S$1 (US$0.60). Daily 8:30am–7pm. MRT to Orchard. Take SBS no. 7, 105, 106, 123, or 174 from Orchard Blvd.

In 1822 Singapore's first botanic garden was started at Fort Canning by Sir Stamford Raffles. After it lost funding, the present Botanic Garden came into being in 1859 thanks to the efforts of a horticulture society; it was later turned over to the government for upkeep. More than just a garden, this space occupied an important place in the region's economic development when "Mad" Henry Ridley, one of the garden's directors, imported Brazilian rubber tree seedlings from Great Britain. He devised improved latex-trapping methods and led the campaign to convince reluctant coffee growers to switch plantation crops. The garden also pioneered orchid hybridization, breeding a number of internationally acclaimed varieties.

Carved out within the tropical setting lies a rose garden, a sundial garden with pruned hedges, a banana plantation, a spice garden, and sculptures by international artists dotted around the area. As you wander, look for the cannonball tree (named for its cannonball-shaped fruit), para rubber trees, teak trees, bamboos, and a huge array of palms, including the sealing wax palm—distinguished by its bright scarlet stalks—and the rumbia palm, which bears the pearl sago. The fruit of the silk-cotton tree is a pod filled with silky stuffing that was once used for stuffing pillows. Flowers like bougainvilleas and heliconias add beautiful color.

The **National Orchid Garden** is 3 hectares (7.4 acres) of gorgeous orchids growing along landscaped walks. The English Garden features hybrids developed here and named after famous visitors to the garden—there's the Margaret Thatcher, the Benazir Bhutto, the Vaclav Havel, and more. The gift shops sell live hydroponic orchids in test tubes for unique souvenirs.

The gardens have three lakes. Symphony Lake surrounds an island band shell for "Concert in the Park" performances by the local symphony and international entertainers like Chris de Burg. Call visitor services at ☎ **65/471-7361** for performance schedules.

Singapore Science Centre. 15 Science Centre Rd., off Jurong Town Hall Rd. ☎ **65/ 560-3316.** www.sci-ctr.edu.sg/. Admission S$3 (US$1.80) adults, S$1.50 (US$0.90) children under 16, S$2.50 (US$1.50) seniors. Tues–Sun and public holidays 10am–6pm. Take the West Coast Attractions bus (see above) or MRT to Jurong East then SBS no. 66 or 335.

Featuring hands-on exhibits in true science-center spirit. You can play in the Atrium, Physical Sciences Gallery, Life Sciences Gallery, and Hall of Science. Unfortunately, many of the exhibits are worn and tired from overuse and abuse. The Technology Gallery is one of the more interesting exhibits if you can wrestle the kids away from the machines, and the aromatics display, with blindfolded "guess the herb or spice" corner, is so popular they're thinking of upgrading it from temporary status. Singapore Airlines has redone the new "On Wings We Fly" Aviation Gallery. Also notable are the section on the cleaning of the Singapore River and showcased educational projects from university students. The Omni Theatre planetarium has a projection booth encased in glass so you can check out how it works.

✪ **Singapore Discovery Centre.** 510 Upper Jurong Rd. ☎ **65/792-6188.** www.asian connect.com/sdc. Admission S$9 (US$5.40) adults, S$5 (US$3) children under 12; simulator ride S$4 (US$2.40); Shooting Gallery S$3 (US$1.80). Tues–Fri 9am–7pm; Sat–Sun and public holidays 9am–8pm. MRT to Boon Lay; transfer to SBS no. 192 or 193.

The original plan was to build a military history museum here, but then planners began to wonder if maybe the concept wouldn't bring people running. What they came up with instead is a fascinating display of the latest military technology with hands-on exhibits that cannot be resisted—one of 19 interactive information kiosks, for instance, lets you design tanks and ships. Airborne Rangers, a virtual reality experience, lets you parachute from a plane and manipulate your landing to safety. In the motion simulator, feel your seat move in tandem with the fighter pilot on the screen. The Shooting Gallery is a computer-simulated combat firing range using real but decommissioned M16 rifles. Other attractions are an exhibit of 14 significant events in Singapore history, including the fall of Singapore, self-government, racial riots, and housing block development. And then there's Tintoy Theatre, where the robot Tintoy conducts an entertaining lecture on warfare! Tintoy fights a war, seeking the help of Sun Tzu and other ancient military tacticians. IMAX features roll at the five-story iWERKS Theatre regularly. When you get hungry, there's a fast-food court.

You can also have a 30-minute bus tour of the neighboring Singapore Air Force Training Institute free with SDC admission. Inquire about tour times at the front counter.

Ming Village. 32 Pandan Rd. ☎ **65/265-7711.** Free admission and free guided tour. Daily 9am–6pm. MRT to Clementi, then SBS no. 78. Ming Village offers a free Singapore Trolley shuttle from Paragon by Sogo on Orchard Rd. and from the Raffles Hotel bus stop at 9:20am and 9:30am respectively, and also at 10:30am and 10:40am respectively.

Tour a pottery factory that employs traditional pottery-making techniques from the Ming and Qing dynasties and watch the process from mold making, hand throwing, and hand painting to glazing each piece. After the tour, shop from their large selection of beautiful antique reproduction dishes, vases, urns, and more. Certificates of authenticity are provided, which describe the history of each piece. They are happy to arrange overseas shipping for your treasures, or if you want to carry it home, they'll wrap it very securely.

CENTRAL & NORTHERN SINGAPORE ATTRACTIONS

The northern part of Singapore contains most of the island's nature reserves and parks. Here's where you'll find the Singapore Zoological Gardens, in addition to some sights with historical and religious significance. Despite the presence of the **MRT** in the area, there is not any simple way to get from attraction to attraction with ease. Bus transfers to and from MRT stops is the way to go—or you could stick to taxi cabs.

Kranji War Memorial. Woodlands Rd., located in the very northern part of the island. MRT to Bugis. From Rochore Rd., take SBS no. 170.

Kranji Cemetery commemorates the men and women who fought and died in World War II. Prisoners of war in a camp nearby began a burial ground here, and after the war it was enlarged to provide space for all the casualties. The Kranji War Cemetery is the site of 4,000 graves of servicemen, while the Singapore State Cemetery memorializes the names of over 20,000 who died and have no known graves. Stones are laid geometrically on a slope with a view of the Strait of Johor. The memorial itself is designed to represent the three arms of the services.

⊙ **Siong Lim Temple.** 184–E Jalan Toa Payoh. Located in Toa Payoh New Town. Take MRT to Toa Payoh, then take a taxi.

This temple, in English "the Twin Groves of the Lotus Mountain Temple," has a great story behind its founding. One night in 1898, Hokkien businessman Low Kim Pong and his son had the same dream—of a golden light shining from the West. The following day, the two went to the western shore and waited until, moments before sundown, a ship appeared carrying a group of Hokkien Buddhist monks and nuns on their way to China after a pilgrimage to India. Low Kim Pong vowed to build a monastery if they would stay in Singapore. They did.

Laid out according to feng shui principles, the buildings include the Dharma Hall, a main prayer hall, and drum and bell towers. They are arranged in *cong lin* style, a rare type of monastery design with a universal layout so that no matter how vast the grounds are, any monk can find his way around. The entrance hall has granite wall panels carved with scenes from Chinese history. The main prayer hall has fantastic details in the ceiling, wood panels, and other wood carvings. In the back is a shrine to Kuan Yin, Goddess of Mercy.

Originally built amid farmland, the temple became surrounded by suburban highrise apartments in the 1950s and 1960s, with the Toa Payoh Housing Development Board New Town project and the Pan-Island Expressway creeping close by.

⊙ **Kong Meng San Phor Kark See Temple.** Bright Hill Dr. Located in the center of the island to the east of Bukit Panjang Nature Preserve. Bright Hill Dr. is off Ang Mo Kio Ave. Take MRT to Bishan, then take a taxi.

The largest and most modern religious complex on the island, this place, called Phor Kark See for short, is comprised of prayer and meditation halls, a hospice, gardens, and a vegetarian restaurant. The largest building is the Chinese-style Hall of Great Compassion. There is also the octagonal Hall of Great Virtue and a towering pagoda. For S$0.50 you can buy flower petals to place in a dish at the Buddha's feet. Compared to other temples on the island, Phor Kark See seems shiny—having only been built in 1981. As a result, the religious images inside carry a strange, almost artificial, cartoon air about them.

If you're curious, find the crematorium in the back of the complex. Arrive on Sundays after 1pm and wait for the funeral processions to arrive. Chairs line the side and back of the hall, and attendees do not mind if you sit quietly and observe, as long as you are respectful. The scene is not for the faint of heart, but makes for a touching moment of cultural difference and human similarity.

Sun Yat Sen Villa. 12 Tai Gin Rd., near Toa Payoh New Town. No phone. Free admission. Mon–Fri 9am–5pm; Sat–Sun and public holidays 9am–4pm. Take the MRT to Toa Payoh, then take a taxi.

Dr. Sun Yat-sen visited Singapore eight times to raise funds for his revolution in China, and made Singapore his headquarters for gaining the support of overseas Chinese in Southeast Asia. A wealthy Chinese merchant built the villa around 1880 for his mistress, and a later owner permitted Dr. Sun Yat-sen to use it. The house reflects the classic bungalow style, which is becoming endangered in modern Singapore. Its typical bungalow features include a projecting carport with a sitting room overhead, verandas with striped blinds, second-story cast-iron railings, and first-story masonry balustrades. A covered walkway leads to kitchen and servants' quarters in the back.

Inside, the life of Dr. Sen is traced in photos and watercolors, from his birth in southern China through his creation of a revolutionary organization. Restorations are planned to convert it into the Sun Yat Sen Nanyang Memorial Hall.

Sasanaransi Buddhist Temple. 14 Tai Gin Rd., located next to the Sun Yat Sen Villa near Toa Payoh New Town. Daily 6:30am–9pm. Chanting: Sun 9:30am, Wed 8pm, and Sat 7:30pm. Take MRT to Toa Payoh, then take a taxi.

Known simply as the Burmese Buddhist Temple, this was founded by a Burmese expatriate to serve the overseas Burmese Buddhist community. His partner, an herbal doctor also from Burma, traveled home to buy a 10-ton block of marble from which was carved the 11-foot-tall Buddha image that sits in the main hall, surrounded by an aura of brightly colored lights. The original temple was off Serangoon Road in Little India, and was moved here in 1991 at the request of the Housing Development Board. On the third story is a standing Buddha image in gold, and murals of events in the Buddha's life.

Mandai Orchid Gardens. Mandai Lake Rd., on the route to the Singapore Zoological Gardens. ☎ **65/269-1036.** Admission S$2 (US$1.20) adults, S$0.50 (US$0.30) children under 12. Daily 8:30am–5:30pm. MRT to Ang Mo Kio and SBS no. 138.

Owned and operated by Singapore Orchids Pte Ltd to breed and cultivate hybrids for international export, the gardens double as an STB tourist attraction. Arranged in English garden style, orchid varieties are separated in beds that are surrounded by grassy lawn. Tree-growing varieties prefer the shade of the covered canopy. On display is Singapore's national flower, the Vanda Miss Joaquim, a natural hybrid in shades of light purple. Behind the gift shop is the Water Garden, where a stroll will reveal many houseplants common to the West, as you would find them in the wild.

✪ Singapore Zoological Gardens. 80 Mandai Lake Rd., at the western edge of the Bukit Panjang Nature Reserve, on the Seletar Reservoir. ☎ **65/269-3411.** www.asianconnect.com/zoo. Admission S$10.30 (US$6.15) adults, S$4.60 (US$2.75) children under 12. Discounts for seniors. Daily 8:30am–6pm. MRT to Ang Mo Kio and take SBS no. 138.

They call themselves the Open Zoo because, rather than coop the animals in jailed enclosures, they let them roam freely in landscaped areas. Beasts of the world are kept where they are supposed to be using psychological restraints and physical barriers that are disguised behind waterfalls, vegetation, and moats. Some animals are grouped with other species to show them coexisting as they would in nature. For instance, the white rhinoceros is neighborly with the wildebeest and ostrich—not that wildebeests and ostriches make the best company, but certainly contempt is better than boredom. Guinea and pea fowl, Emperor tamarins, and other creatures are free roaming and not shy; however, if you spot a water monitor or long-tailed macaque, know that they're not zoo residents—just locals looking for a free meal.

Major zoo features are the Primate Kingdom, Wild Africa, the Reptile Garden, the children's petting zoo, and underwater views of polar bears, sea lions, and penguins. Daily shows include primate and reptile shows at 10:30am and 2:30pm, and elephant and sea lion shows at 11:30am and 3:30pm. You can take your photograph with an orangutan, chimpanzee, or snake, and there are elephant and camel rides, too.

The literature they provide includes half-day and full-day agendas to help you see the most while you're there. The best time to arrive, however, is at 9am, to have breakfast with an orangutan, which feasts on fruits, putting on a hilarious and very memorable show. If you miss that, you can also have tea with it at 4pm. Another good time to go is just after a rain, when the animals cool off and get frisky.

✪ Night Safari. Singapore Zoological Gardens, 80 Mandai Lake Rd., at the western edge of the Bukit Panjang Nature Reserve, on the Seletar Reservoir. ☎ **65/269-3411.** www.asianconnect.com/zoo/. Admission S$15.45 (US$9.25) adults, S$10.30 (US$6.15) children under 12. Daily 7:30pm–midnight. Ticket sales close at 11pm. Entrance Plaza, restaurant, and fast-food outlet open from 6:30pm. MRT to Ang Mo Kio and take SBS no. 138.

Singapore takes advantage of its unchanging tropical climate and static ratio of daylight to night to bring you the world's first open-concept zoo for nocturnal animals. Here, as in the zoological gardens, animals live in landscaped areas, their barriers virtually unseen by visitors. These areas are dimly lit to create a moonlit effect, and a guided tram leads you through "regions" designed to resemble the Himalayan foothills, the jungles of Africa, and, naturally, Southeast Asia. Some of the free-range prairie animals come very close to the tram. The 45-minute ride covers almost 3½ kilometers (2 miles), and has regular stops to get off and have a rest or stroll along trails for closer views of smaller creatures.

Staff, placed at regular intervals along the trails, help you find your way, though it's almost impossible to get lost along the trails; however, it is nighttime, you are in the forest, and it can be spooky. The guides are there more or less to add peace of mind (and all speak English). Flash photography is strictly prohibited, and be sure to bring plenty of insect repellent. A weirder tip: Check out the bathrooms. They're all open-air, Bali style.

Sungei Buloh Nature Park. 301 Neo Tiew Crescent. ☎ **65/794-1401.** Admission S$1 (US$0.60) adults, S$0.50 (US$0.30) children and seniors. Mon–Fri 7:30am–7pm; Sat–Sun and public holidays 7am–7pm. Audiovisual show Mon–Sat 9am, 11am, 1pm, 3pm and 5pm; hourly Sun and public holidays. MRT to Kranji, bus no. 925 to Kranji Reservoir Dam. Cross causeway to park entrance.

Located to the very north of the island and devoted to the wetland habitat and mangrove forests that are so common to the region, 87-hectare (218-acre) Sungei Buloh is out of the way, and not the easiest place to get to, but it's a beautiful park, with constructed paths and boardwalks taking you through tangles of mangroves, soupy marshes, grassy spots, and coconut groves. Of the flora and fauna, the most spectacular sights here are the birds, of which there are somewhere between 140 and 170 species in residence or just passing through for the winter. Of the migratory birds, some have traveled from as far as Siberia to escape the cold months from September to March. Bird observatories are set up at different spots along the paths. Also, even though you're in the middle of nowhere, Sungei Buloh has a visitor center, a cafeteria, and souvenirs.

MacRitchie Nature Trail. Central Catchment Nature Reserve. No phone. Free admission. From Orchard Rd. take bus no. 132 from the Orchard Parade Hotel. From Raffles City take bus no. 130. Get off at the bus stop near Little Sisters of the Poor. Next to Little Sisters of the Poor, follow the paved walkway, which turns into the trail.

Of all the nature reserves in Singapore, the Central Catchment Nature Reserve is the largest at 2,000 hectares (5,000 acres). Located in the center of the island, it's home to four of Singapore's reservoirs: MacRitchie, Seletar, Pierce, and Upper Pierce. The rain forest here is secondary forest, but the animals don't care; they're just as happy with the place. There's one path for walking and jogging (no bicycles allowed) that stretches 3 kilometers (1.8 miles) from its start in the southeast corner of the reserve, turning to the edge of MacRitchie Reservoir then letting you out at the Singapore Island Country Club.

EASTERN SINGAPORE ATTRACTIONS

The East Coast leads from the edge of Singapore's urban area to the tip of the eastern part, at Changi Point. Eastern Singapore is home to the Changi International Airport, nearby Changi Prison, and the long stretch of East Coast Park along the shoreline. The

MRT heads east in this region, but swerves northward at the end of the line. A popular **bus line** for east coast attractions not reached by MRT is the SBS no. 2, which takes you to Changi Prison, Changi Point, Malay Village, and East Coast Park (a short walk from Joo Chiat Centre).

✪ **Malay Village.** 39 Geylang Serai, in the suburb of Geylang, an easy walk from the MRT station. ☎ **65/748-4700** or 65/740-8860. Free admission to village. Kampong Days and Cultural Museum: adults S$5 (US$3), children S$3 (US$1.80). Mon–Fri 10am–9pm; Sat–Sun and public holidays 10am–10pm. MRT to Paya Lebar.

In 1985, Malay Village opened in Geylang as a theme village to showcase Malay culture. The Cultural Museum is a collection of artifacts from Malay culture, including household items, musical instruments, and a replica of a wedding dais and traditional beaded ceremonial bed. Kampung Days lets you to walk through a kampung house (or Malay village house) as it would have looked in the 1950s and 1960s. The 25-minute **Lagenda Fantasy show** is more for kids, using multi-image projection, Surround Sound, and lights to tell tales from the *Arabian Nights* and the legend of Sang Nila Utama, the founder of Temasek (Singapore). The village has souvenir shops mixed with places that sell everything from antique knives to caged birds.

Two in-house groups perform **traditional Malaysian and Indonesian dances** in the late afternoons and evenings. Call during the day on Saturday to find out if they'll be performing the **Kuda Kepang** in the evening. If you're lucky enough to catch it, it's a long performance but worth the wait because at the end the dancers are put in a trance and walk on glass, eat glass, and rip coconuts to shreds with their teeth. Arrive early because the place gets packed with locals.

✪ **Changi Prison Chapel and Museum.** 169 Sims Ave., off Upper Changi Rd., in the same general area as the airport. ☎ **65/543-0893.** Free admission. Mon–Sat 10am–5pm. Closed Sun and public holidays. Changi Prison Chapel Sun Service (all are welcome) 5:30–6:30pm. MRT to Tanah Merah station, then transfer to SBS no. 2.

Upon successful occupation of Singapore, the Japanese marched all British, Australian, and allied European prisoners to Changi by foot, where they lived in a prison camp for 3 years, suffering overcrowding, disease, and malnutrition. Prisoners were cut off from the outside world except to leave the camp for labor duties. The hospital conditions were terrible; some prisoners suffered public beatings, and many died. In an effort to keep hope alive, they built a small chapel from wood and attap. Years later, at the request of former POWs and their families and friends, the government built this replica.

The museum displays sketches by W. R. M. Haxworth and secret photos taken by George Aspinall—both men POWs who were imprisoned here. Displayed with descriptions, the pictures, along with writings and other objects from the camp, bring this period to life, depicting the day-to-day horror with a touch of high morale.

The Singapore Crocodilarium. 730 East Coast Pkwy., running along East Coast Park. ☎ **65/447-3722.** Admission S$2 (US$1.20) adults, S$1 (US$0.60) children under 12. Daily 9am–5pm. MRT to Paya Lebar or Eunos and take a taxi.

Head to the Crocodilarium if you're interested in seeing alligators from India and four types of crocodiles—from Singapore, Africa, Louisiana, and Caiman (South Africa). Of the total 1,800 crocodiles that reside here, 500 are on display. The Singapore crocodile, one of the largest, reaches a maximum size of 5.5 meters (6 yd.) and can weigh up to 500 kilograms (1,100 lb.). They're pretty fierce because they have bigger heads, which means bigger mouths. However, midsize ones are the most dangerous to people because they have better mobility on land. Every so often the place picks up when a couple of them have a brutish fight. On a sweeter note, the Crocodilarium has approximately 400 births per year. Some young ones are on display—and they're very cute—but the Crocodilarium won't let you see the newborn babies because they're delicate and spook easily. While many are intended for the booming pelt industry, some are just for show. A huge gift shop peddles crocodile products, which are made both in-house and imported from outside designers. Here you can also find ostrich hide, stingray skin, and antelope pelt goods. The best way to get back to town is to ask the front counter to call you a cab.

Republic of Singapore Air Force Museum. Blk. 78 Cranwell Rd. off Loyang Ave. Changi Camp. Free admission. Tues–Sun 10am–4:30pm. SBS no. 2 or 9.

Established in 1988, this museum tracks the evolution of the Republic of Singapore Air Force with exhibits of historical artifacts and records and displays of aircraft, missiles, and dioramas with audiovisual effects.

East Coast Park. East Coast Pkwy. No phone. Free admission. MRT to Bedok, bus no. 31, or on Sun and public holidays bus no. 401.

East Coast Park is a narrow strip of reclaimed land, only 8.5 kilometers long, tucked in between the shoreline and East Coast Parkway, and serves as a hangout for Singaporean families on the weekends. Moms and dads barbecue under the trees while the kids swim at the beach, which is nothing more than a narrow lump of grainy sand sloping into yellow-green water that has more seaweed than a sushi bar. Paths for bicycling, in-line skating, walking, or jogging run the length of the park, and are crowded on weekends and public and school holidays. On Sundays, you'll find kite flyers in the open grassy parts.

Because East Coast Park is so long, getting to the place you'd like to hang out can be a bit confusing. Many of the locators I've included sound funny (for example, Carpark C), but are recognizable landmarks for taxi drivers. Sailing, windsurfing, and other sea sports happen at the far end of the park, at the Lagoon, which is closer to Changi Airport than it is to the city. Taxi drivers are all familiar with the Lagoon as a landmark. Unfortunately, public transportation to the park is tough—you should bring a good map, and expect to do a little walking from any major thoroughfare.

East Coast Park is home to a few other interesting places. **UDMC Seafood Centre** is located not far from the lagoon, and **Big Splash**—Singapore's first water park with water slides, wave pools, and river rides—is not too far away, at 902 East Coast Pkwy. (☎ 65/345-6762).

SENTOSA ISLAND

In the 1880s, Sentosa, then known as Pulau Blakang Mati, was a hub of British military activity, with hilltop forts built to protect the harbor from sea invasion from all sides. Today, it has become a weekend getaway spot and Singapore's answer to Disneyland all rolled into one. You'll find a lot of people recommending Sentosa as a must-see on your vacation, and while many travelers do visit the island for some part of their trip, it might not be the best way to spend your time if you're only in town for a few days. Basically, for those who like to do hard-core cultural and historical-immersion vacations, Sentosa will seem too contrived and cartoonish—just check out the Images of Singapore exhibit and go home. But for those who just want a good time, it delivers.

If you tried to see everything on the island, you'd need at least 3 days, but a day is just enough to see and do the best. If you want to get out of the city, the beaches are cooling and well stocked with activities, and resorts like the Beaufort are tranquil and romantic. If you're into the museum scene, there are some very well-presented historical exhibits and nature showcases. If you want to keep the kids happy, there's a water park, theme parks, and amusement rides. For your sense of adventure, you can never go wrong with Underwater World. Free with your Sentosa admission are the Fountain Gardens and Musical Fountain, the Enchanted Garden of Tembusu, the Dragon Trail Nature Walk, and the beaches.

If you're spending the day, there are numerous restaurants and a couple of food courts. For overnights, the Shangri-La's Rasa Sentosa Resort and the Beaufort Sentosa, Singapore, are popular hotel options. For general **Sentosa inquiries,** call ☎ **65/ 275-0388.**

GETTING THERE

Private cars are not allowed entry to the island except between the hours of 6:30pm and 3am, but there are more than a few other ways to get to Sentosa. The cable car and ferry fares are exclusive of Sentosa admission charges, which you are required to pay upon arrival; bus fares include your admission charge. **Island admission** is S$5 (US$3) for adults and S$3 (US$1.80) for children. Admission in the evenings (after 6:30pm) is S$3 (US$1.80) for adults and S$1.80 (US$1.10) for children. Tickets can be purchased at the following booths: Mount Faber Cable Car Station, World Trade Centre Ferry Departure Hall, Cable Car Towers (next to the World Trade Centre), Cable Car Plaza (on Sentosa), Sentosa Information Booth 4 (at the start of the causeway, opposite Kentucky Fried Chicken), and Sentosa Information Booth 3 (at the end of the causeway bridge, upon entering Sentosa). Many attractions require purchase of additional tickets, which you can get at the entrance of each.

BY CABLE CAR   Cable cars depart from the top of Mount Faber and from the World Trade Centre daily from 8:30am to 9pm at a cost of S$6.90 (US$4.15) for adults and S$3.90 (US$2.35) for children. The ticket is good for a round-trip, and you can decide where you choose to depart and arrive (at either Mt. Faber or the World Trade Centre every 5 or 10 minutes on the Singapore side) for one price. Plan at least one trip on the cable car because the view of Singapore, Sentosa, and especially the container port is really fantastic from up there. The round-trip cable car ticket is also good for a return on the ferry, in case you've had enough view. Be warned: If you return to Singapore at the Mt. Faber stop, you'll have to walk down the mountain to find a cab or bus.

BY FERRY   The ferry departs from the World Trade Centre on weekdays from 9:30am to 9pm at 20-minute intervals, and on weekends and public holidays from 8:30am to 9pm at 15-minute intervals. The round-trip fare for both adults and children is S$2.30 (US$1.40), and one way is S$1.30 (US$0.78).

BY BUS   **Sentosa Bus Service Leisure Pte Ltd** operates bus service to and from Sentosa. Service A operates between 7:15am and 11:30pm daily from the World Trade Centre (WTC) Bus Terminal. Services C and M run from the Tiong Bahru MRT Station between 7:20am and 11:30pm daily. Service E stops along Orchard Road at Lucky Plaza, the Mandarin Hotel, Peranakan Place, Le Meridien Hotel, Plaza Singapura, and then Bencoolen Street, POSB Headquarters, Raffles City and Pan Pacific Hotel, and operates from 10am to 10:45pm daily. Fares run from S$6 to S$7 (US$3.60 to US$4.20) for adults and S$4 to S$5 (US$2.40 to US$3) for children, depending on which bus you catch from where. Fares are paid to the driver as you board and the Sentosa admission fee is included in your fare. The last bus out of Sentosa is at 11:30pm.

BY TAXI   Taxis are only allowed to drop off and pick up passengers at the Beaufort Sentosa, Singapore; Shangri-La's Rasa Sentosa Resort; and NTUC Sentosa Beach Resort. The taxi fare from 6am to 6:30pm is S$3 (US$1.80) per person; however, after 6:30pm you must pay a flat fare of S$12 (US$7.20) per car. After 9pm the price drops to S$6 (US$3.60).

Getting Around

Once on Sentosa, a free monorail operates from 9am to 10pm daily at 10-minute intervals to shuttle you around to the various areas. If you're staying at one of the island's major hotels, you can take advantage of their free shuttle services to get into Singapore's urban area.

Seeing the Sights

The attractions that you get free with your Sentosa admission are the **Fountain Gardens** and **Musical Fountain,** the **Enchanted Garden of Tembusu,** the **Dragon Trail Nature Walk,** and the **beaches.**

The **Fountain Gardens,** just behind the Ferry Terminal, are geometric European-style gardens with groomed pathways and shady arbors. In the center is an amphitheater of sorts, the focus of which is a fountain—actually three fountains—that creates water effects with patterns of sprays and varying heights. During regular shows throughout the day, the fountains burst to the sounds of everything from marches to Elton John. At night, they turn on the lights for color effects.

The **Flower Terrace** starts behind the Ferry Terminal through the Fountain Garden and creeps up the side of the hill beyond. The slope has a steep grade, but pathways meander to offer some relief from the climb. Still, in the heat, you won't be taking this one fast.

The **Enchanted Garden of Tembusu,** in a corner of the Fountain Garden, is a shady grove of Tembusu trees and MacArthur palms. In the evenings, the garden is lit with tiny lights for a touch of romance.

The **Dragon Trail Nature Walk** takes advantage of the island's natural forest for a 1½-kilometer (1-mile) stroll through secondary rain forest. In addition to the variety of dragon sculptures, there are also local squirrels, monkeys, lizards, and wild white cockatoos to try to spot.

Sentosa has three beaches, **Siloso Beach** on the western end and **Central Beach** and **Tanjong Beach** on the eastern end, each dressed in tall coconut palms and flowering trees. At ✪ Central Beach, deck chairs, beach umbrellas, and a variety of **water-sports equipment** like pedal boats, aqua bikes, fun bugs, canoes, surfboards, and banana boats are available for hire at nominal charges. **Bicycles** are also available for hire at the bicycle kiosk at Siloso Beach. Shower and changing facilities, food kiosks, and snack bars are at rest stations. Siloso Beach is open at night for barbecue picnics, and has a really nice view of the tiny lights of ships anchored in the port. About once a month, rumors spread throughout the island about a **full-moon party** on Siloso that lasts until the sun comes up. They're never publicized, but are anticipated by the many folks looking for an alternative to the bar scene at night. Ask around at the bars, and they'll let you know if there's something going on.

For beach activities like volleyball, check out the offerings at the Shangri-La's Rasa Sentosa Resort. Hotel guests get first dibs, but many activities and equipment are available to the public at reasonable charges.

Unless noted, all of the following Sentosa attractions have admission charges separate from the Sentosa charge, and operating hours that differ from place to place.

Asian Village. ☎ 65/275-0338. Free admission. Daily 10am–9pm. Adventure Asia daily 10am–7pm. Monorail stop 1.

They set up this festival village around a tiny lake, with three zones representing the architectural moods of East, South, and Southeast Asia. Only there's no people! The original concept included bustling shops, street performers, traditional dance numbers,

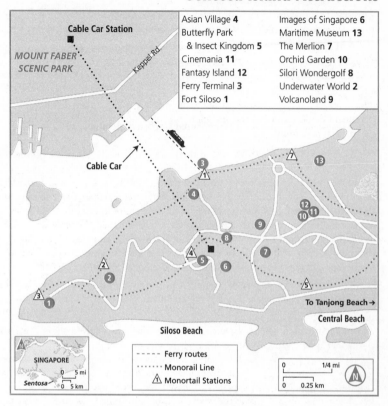

Asian Village **4**	Images of Singapore **6**
Butterfly Park	Maritime Museum **13**
& Insect Kingdom **5**	The Merlion **7**
Cinemania **11**	Orchid Garden **10**
Fantasy Island **12**	Silori Wondergolf **8**
Ferry Terminal **3**	Underwater World **2**
Fort Siloso **1**	Volcanoland **9**

Cable Car Station

MOUNT FABER
SCENIC PARK

Keppel Rd.

Cable Car

To Tanjong Beach →

Central Beach

Siloso Beach

SINGAPORE

Sentosa

- - - - Ferry routes
· · · · · · Monorail Line
⚠ Monortail Stations

0   1/4 mi

0   0.25 km

and regular shows in their auditorium, but not enough visitors came to the attraction, so most of the shops are empty and the dancers were laid off. You can paddleboat around the lake for S$5 (US$3) per half hour.

In the back of the village find **Adventure Asia,** with 10 rides tucked inside a shady grove. Ten bucks (US$6) gets you unlimited rides—not a bad deal.

Maritime Museum. ☎ **65/270-8855.** Free admission. Daily 10am–7pm. Closest to monorail stop 7, then walk along Gateway Ave.

Nautical paraphernalia buffs rejoice: Here's a showcase devoted to Singapore's ever-important connection to the sea. From ship models to artifacts, sea charts, and photos, the museum tells the story of 14 centuries of maritime life.

✪ **Fantasy Island.** ☎ **65/275-1088.** Admission S$16 (US$9.60) adults, S$10 (US$6) children 3–12. Daily 10am–7pm. Monorail stop 7.

If you have a few hours and a swimsuit, this place is a great time. Try out all kinds of water slides, water tunnels, surf rides, rapids, and a simulated lazy river running around the whole park. For the little ones, there are tree houses with water toys, special slides, and a kiddie pool. Changing rooms are available, there's a food outlet, and a first-aid team is on duty.

Cinemania. ☎ **65/373-0159.** Admission S$10 (US$6) adults, S$6 (US$3.60) children. Daily 11am–8pm. Monorail stop 7.

At this 3-D audiovisual ride with motion simulator, they rotate three films at a time from a library of 25 titles like *Cosmic Pinball, Desert Duel,* and *Runaway Train.* Call ahead for titles and show times.

Sentosa Orchid Gardens. ☎ 65/278-1940. Adults S$3.30 (US$2), children S$2 (US$1.20). Daily 9am–6:30pm. Monorail stop 1; the Orchid Garden is to the east of the Fountain Gardens.

This place is more geared toward the theme-party scene, so you're better off at the National Orchid Garden at the Singapore Botanic Gardens or at Mandai Orchids to see the best collections.

The Merlion. ☎ 65/275-0388. Admission S$3 (US$1.80) adults, S$2 (US$1.20) children. Daily 9am–10pm. Monorail stop 1 and 4.

Imagine, if you will, 12 towering stories of that half-lion, half-fish creature, the Merlion. That's a lot of mythical beast. Admission buys you an elevator ride to the ninth floor, where you can peer out the mouth, and to the top of its head for a 360° view of Singapore, Sentosa, and even Indonesia. Be at the Fountain Gardens at 7:30pm, 8:30pm, and 9:30pm nightly for the "Rise of the Merlion" show, where they light up the thing with 16,000 fiber-optic lights and shoot red lasers out its eyes. Poor Merlion. Hope this never happens to the national symbol of *your* home country.

VolcanoLand. ☎ 65/275-1828. Admission S$12 (US$7.20) adults, S$6 (US$3.60) children. Daily 10am–7pm. Monorail stop 1 or 4.

It's hard to say whether VolcanoLand is amusing or whether it's touristy and weird. The main attraction here is the ancient Central American "active volcano," a walk-through exhibit that takes you on a journey to the center of the Earth with a mythological explorer and his Jules Verne–style robot buddy. Inside the "volcano" there's a multimedia show about the mysteries of life and the universe and a simulated volcano eruption. Besides its being completely contrived, the special-effects creations are by far less cheesy than most. Outside the volcano in the rest of the small park are the not-very-politically-correct "Live Tribal Performances," like the Mayan Parade costume and dance ceremonies and the "Volcano Ritual Performance" to celebrate having survived the volcano's "eruption."

✪ Images of Singapore. ☎ 65/275-0388. Admission S$5 (US$3) adults, S$3 (US$1.80) children. Daily 9am–9pm. Monorail stop 4.

Images of Singapore is without a doubt one of the main reasons to come to Sentosa. There are three parts to this museum/exhibit: the Pioneers of Singapore and the Surrender Chambers—which date back as far as I can remember—and Festivals of Singapore, a recent addition. Pioneers of Singapore is an exhibit of beautifully constructed life-size dioramas that place figures like Sultan Hussein, Sir Stamford Raffles, Tan Tock Seng, and Naraina Pillai, to name just a few pioneers. The **Festivals of Singapore,** is another life-size diorama exhibit depicting a few of the major festivals and traditions of the Chinese, Malay, Indian, and Peranakan cultures in Singapore. Try to catch the video presentation at the end—a tribute to Singapore's strides in "cultural integration" told in true "It's a small world after all" style.

Butterfly Park and Insect Kingdom Museum of Singapore. ☎ 65/275-0013. Admission S$6 (US$3.60) adults, S$3 (US$1.80) children. Daily 9am–6:30pm. Monorail stop 4.

This walk-in enclosure provides an up-close view of some 60 live species of native butterflies, from cocoon to adult. At the Insect Kingdom, the exhibits are mostly dead, but extensive, with its collection carrying more than 2,500 bugs. Live ones to see include scorpions, tarantulas, and the very weird dead leaf mantis.

✪ **Underwater World.** ☎ **65/275-0030.** Admission S$13 (US$7.80) adults, S$7 (US$4.20) children. Daily 9am–9pm. Monorail stop 2.

Underwater World is without a doubt one of the most visited attractions on Sentosa. Everybody comes for the tunnel: 83 meters of transparent acrylic tube through which you glide on a conveyor belt, gaping at sharks, stingrays, eels, and other creatures of the sea drifting by, above and on both sides. Among many activities to choose from is an **underwater walk** or **swim with the sharks.** For an additional fee you get 30 minutes underwater attached to a hose for fresh air while you walk through schools and play with the fish. Or the same amount buys you 90 minutes of scuba diving in the shark tank. For both you must be over 18 years of age, and of course for the latter you must be able to prove scuba certification.

✪ **Fort Siloso.** ☎ **65/275-0388.** Admission S$3 (US$1.80) adults, S$2 (US$1.20) children. Daily 9am–7pm. Monorail stop 3.

Fort Siloso guarded Keppel Harbour from invasion in the 1880s. It's one of three forts built on Sentosa, and it later became a military camp in World War II. The buildings have been decorated to resemble a barracks, kitchen, laundry, and military offices as they looked back in those days. In places, you can explore the underground tunnels and ammunition holds, but they're not as extensive as you would hope they'd be.

6 Sports & Recreation

BEACHES   Besides the beach at East Coast Park (see "Eastern Singapore Attractions," above) and those on Sentosa Island (see above) you can try the smaller beach at Changi Village, called Changi Point. From the shore, you have a panoramic view of Malaysia, Indonesia, and several smaller islands that belong to Singapore. The beach is calm, and frequented mostly by locals who set up camps and barbecues to hang out all day. There's kayak rentals along the beach, and in Changi Village you'll find, in addition to a huge hawker center, quite a few international restaurants and pubs to hang out in and have a fresh seafood lunch when you get hungry. To get there take SBS bus no. 2 from either the Tanah Merah or Bedok MRT stations.

On Kusu and St. John's Islands there are quiet swimming lagoons, a couple of which have quite nice views of the city. Some people head out to Sisters Island for swimming, but the trip is a bit expensive for just a dip.

BICYCLE RENTALS   Bicycles are not for rent within the city limits, and traffic does not really allow for cycling on city streets, so sightseeing by bicycle is not recommended for city touring. Bicycles can be rented at **East Coast Park** from Ling Choo Hong (☎ **65/449-7305**), near the hawker center at Carpark E; SDK Recreation (☎ **65/445-2969**), near McDonald's at Carpark C; or Wimbledon Cafeteria & Bicycle Rental (☎ **65/444-3928**), near the windsurfing rental places at the lagoon. All of these are open 7 days from about 9am to 8 or 9pm. Rentals are all in the neighborhood of S$4 to S$8 (US$2.40 to US$4.80) per hour, depending on the type and quality bike you're looking for. Identification may be requested. On **Sentosa Island** try SDK Recreation (☎ **65/272-8738**), located at Siloso Beach off Siloso Road, a short walk from Underwater World. It's open 7 days from around 10am to 6:30 or 7pm. Rental for a standard bicycle is S$4 (US$2.40) per hour. A mountain bike goes for S$8 (US$4.80) per hour. Identification is required. In **Pulau Ubin,** there are a number of places to rent bikes right where you get off the ferry. The shops are generally open between 8am and 6pm and will charge between S$5 (US$3) and S$8 (US$4.80) per hour, depending on which bike you choose. Most rental agents will have a map of the island for you—take it. Even though it doesn't look too impressive, it'll be a great help.

GOLF Golf is a very popular sport in Singapore. There are quite a few clubs, and though some of them are exclusively for members only, many places are open for limited play by nonmembers. All will require you bring a par certificate. Most hotel concierges will be glad to make arrangements for you, and this may be the best way to go.

Best bets are the **Changi Golf Club,** 20 Netheravon Rd. (tel] **65/545-5133**); **Jurong Country Club,** 9 Science Centre Rd. (☎ **65/560-5655**); **Seletar Base Golf Course,** 244 Oxford St., 3 Park Lane. (☎ **65/481-4745**); and **Sentosa Golf Club,** 27 Bukit Manis Rd., Sentosa Island (☎ **65/275-0022**).

SCUBA DIVING If you're heading for one of the beach areas on Sentosa, or out at East Coast Park or Changi Point, you can rent canoes with paddles and life jackets for about S$6 to S$10 per hour (US$3.60 to US$6) for a one-person model or S$8 to S$12 per hour (US$4.80 to US$7.20) for a two-person canoe, depending on the make and quality of the canoe and gear. These outfits are small operators on the beach; look for their stacks of canoes on display. Basically, they only have phone contact if the guy on duty that day brought his own personal hand phone. For the best experience, I recommend canoeing out at Changi Point, where your rental person must point out to you the international boundaries between Singaporean, Malaysian, and Indonesian waters, and which islands you're permitted to land on.

TENNIS Quite a few hotels in the city provide tennis courts for guests, many floodlit for night play (which allows you to avoid the midday heat), and even a few that can arrange lessons, so be sure to check out listings for hotel facilities above. You'll have to travel about 15 minutes by taxi from the city center to reach the **Singapore Tennis Centre** on East Coast Parkway near the East Coast Park (☎ **65/442-5966**). Their courts are open to the public for day and evening play. Weekdays offer discount rates of S$8.50 (US$5.10) per hour, while weekday evening peak hours (between 6 and 9pm) jump to S$12.50 (US$7.50). Weekends and public holidays expect to pay S$12.50 (US$7.50) per hour also. If you need to stay closer to town, you can play at the **Tanglin Sports Centre** on Minden Road (☎ **65/473-7236**). Court costs are S$3.50 (US$2.10) per hour on weekdays, with charges upped to S$9.50 (US$5.70) on weekday nights from 6 to 10pm, on weekends and all public holidays.

WATERSKIING The Kallang River, located to the east of the city, has hosted quite a few international waterskiing tournaments. If this is your sport, contact the **Cowabunga Ski Centre,** the authority in Singapore. Located at Kallang Riverside Park, 10 Stadium Lane (☎ **65/344-8813**), they'll arrange lessons for adults and children and waterskiing by the hour. Beginner courses will set you back S$140 (US$84) for five half-hour lessons, while more experienced skiers can hire a boat plus equipment for S$80 (US$48) on weekdays and S$100 (US$60) on weekends. They're open on weekdays from noon to 7pm and weekends from 9am to 7pm. Call in advance for a reservation.

WINDSURFING & SAILING You'll find both windsurf boards and sailboats for rent at the lagoon in **East Coast Park,** which is where these activities primarily take place. The largest and most reputable firm to approach has to be the **Europa Sailing Club** at 1212 East Coast Parkway (☎ **65/449-5118**). For S$20/hour (US$12) you can rent a small sailboat, while windsurf boards go for about the same. Expect to leave around S$30 (US$18) deposit. While Europa does offer courses, instruction is really not recommended for short-term visitors since classes usually occur over extended periods of time on a set schedule.

7 Shopping

In Singapore, shopping is a sport—from the practiced glide through haute couture boutiques to skillful back-alley bargaining to win the best prices on Asian treasures. The shopping here is always exciting, with something to satiate every pro shopper's appetite. See the "Customs Regulations" section earlier in this chapter for information on the GST Tourist Refund Scheme, which lets you recover the GST for purchases of goods over S$300 (US$179.65) in value.

HOURS   Shopping malls are generally open from 10am to 8pm Monday through Saturday, with some stores keeping shorter Sunday hours. The malls sometimes remain open until 10pm on holidays. Smaller shops are open from around 10am to 5pm Monday through Saturday, but are almost always closed on Sundays. Hours will vary from shop to shop. Arab Street is closed on Sundays.

PRICES   Almost all of the stores in shopping malls have fixed prices. Sometimes these stores will have seasonal sales, especially in July, when they have the month-long **Great Singapore Sale,** during which prices are marked down, sometimes up to 50% or 75%. In the smaller shops and at street vendors, prices are never marked, and people will quote you higher prices than the going rate, in anticipation of the bargaining ritual. These are the places to find good prices, if you negotiate well.

DUTY-FREE ITEMS   Changi International Airport has a large duty-free shop that carries cigarettes, liquor, wine, perfumes, cosmetics, watches, jewelry, and other designer accessories. There's also a chain of duty-free stores in Singapore called DFS. Their main branch is at Millennia Walk, next to the Pan Pacific Hotel down by Marina Square (Millennia Walk, ☎ 65/332-2118). The store is huge and impressive, but unfortunately, the only truly duty-free items are liquor and cigarettes, which you can arrange to pick up at the airport before you depart—everything else carries the standard 3% GST. Feel free to apply for the Tourist Refund Scheme here, though.

ORCHARD ROAD AREA   The malls on Orchard Road are a tourist attraction in their own right, with smaller boutiques and specialty shops intermingled with huge department stores. **Takashimaya** and **Isetan** have been imported from Japan. **Lane Crawford** comes out of the West, as does **Kmart. John Little Pte. Ltd.** is one of the oldest department stores in Singapore, followed by **Robinson's. Tang's** is historic, having grown from a cart-full of merchandise nurtured by the business savvy of local entrepreneur C. K. Tang. Boutiques range from the younger styles of **Stussy** and **Guess?** to the sophisticated fashions of **Chanel** and **Salvatore Ferragamo.** You'll also find antiques, Oriental carpets, art galleries and curio shops, Tower Records and HMV music stores, Kinokuniya and Borders bookstores, video arcades, and scores of restaurants, local food courts, fast-food joints, and coffeehouses—even a few discos, which open in the evenings. It's hard to say when Orchard Road is not crowded, but it's definitely a mob scene on weekends, when folks have the free time to come and hang around, looking for fun.

Some of the larger and more exciting malls to check out are **Centrepoint,** 176 Orchard Rd.; **Ngee Ann City/Takashimaya Shopping Centre,** 391 Orchard Rd.; **Specialists' Shopping Center,** 277 Orchard Rd; and **Wisma Atria,** 435 Orchard Rd. The **Hilton Shopping Gallery,** 581 Orchard Rd., deals only in exclusive top-designer boutiques.

At **Far East Plaza,** 14 Scotts Rd, and **Lucky Plaza,** 304 Orchard Rd., there are some bargains to be had on electronics, camera equipment, and luggage, among other things, but be wary of rip-off deals. **Eyeglasses** are a surprising bargain in Singapore.

A reputable outlet is Capitol Optical at no. 03–132, Far East Plaza (☎ **65/ 736-0365**). If you're in the mood for **jewels,** the most trusted dealer in Singapore is **Larry Jewelry (S) Pte. Ltd.,** Orchard Towers, Level 1, 400 Orchard (☎ **65/ 732-3222**), but be prepared to drop a dime. **Royal Selangor,** the famous Malaysian pewter manufacturer since 1885, has eight outlets in Singapore. The Orchard branch is at no. 02–40 Paragon by Sogo, 290 Orchard Rd. The **Tanglin Shopping Centre** (Tanglin Rd., at the northern end of Orchard) is a treasure trove of antiques dealers and carpet shops. For the best selection of carpets visit **Hassan's Carpets,** no. 03–01/06 Tanglin Shopping Center (☎ **65/737-5626**).

THE HISTORIC DISTRICT   While the Historic District doesn't have as many malls as the Orchard Road area, it still has some good shopping. **Raffles City Shopping Centre** can be overwhelming in its size, but convenient because it sits right atop the City Hall MRT stop. Men's and women's fashions, books, cosmetics, and accessories are sold in shops here, along with gifts. One of my favorite places to go, however, is the very upmarket **Raffles Hotel Shopping Arcade,** 328 North Bridge Rd. These shops are mostly haute couture; however, there is the Raffles Hotel gift shop for interesting souvenirs. For golfers, there's a Jack Nicklaus signature store.

CHINATOWN   In Chinatown, I've stumbled on some of my most precious treasures. My all-time favorite gift idea? Spend an afternoon learning the traditional Chinese tea ceremony at either **The Tea Village,** 45A–51A Pagoda St. (☎ **65/ 221-7825**), or **The Tea Chapter,** 9A Neil Rd. (☎ **65/226-1175**), then head down to **D'Art Station,** 65 Pagoda St. (☎ **65/225-8307**), to pick up a good quality tea set and accessories. After a stop at **Kwong Chen Beverage Trading,** 16 Smith St. (☎ **65/ 223-6927**), for some Chinese teas in handsome tins, you'll be ready to give a fabulous gift—not just a tea set, but your own cultural performance as well, as you teach your friends a new art. While the teas are really inexpensive, they're packed in lovely tins— great to buy lots to bring back as smaller gifts.

Another neat place, **Gary Lee,** 20 Smith St. (☎ **65/221-8129**), carries a fantastic selection of linens imported from China. These hand-embroidered gems include bedding, dining linens, tea towels and handkerchiefs, and other decorative items for the home. They're priced right, and won't break on the trip back home. For something a little more unusual, check out **Chinatown Joss Stick & Ceremonial Trading,** 54 Smith St. (☎ **65/227-6821**), or **Siong Moh Paper Products,** 39 Mosque St. (☎ **65/ 224-3125**), both of which carry a full line of ceremonial items. Pick up some joss sticks (temple incense) or joss paper (books of thin sheets of paper, stamped in reds and yellows with bits of gold and silver leaf). Definitely a conversation piece, as is the Hell Money, stacks of "money" that believers burn at the temple for their ancestors to use in the afterlife. Perfect for that friend who has everything? Also, if you duck over to **Sago Lane** while you're in the neighborhood, there are a few souvenir shops that sell Chinese kites and Cantonese Opera masks—cool for kids.

For one-stop souvenir shopping, you can tick off half your shopping list at Chinatown Point, a.k.a. the **Singapore Handicraft Center,** 133 New Bridge Rd. The best gifts there include hand-carved chops, or Chinese seals. **Chinatown Seal Carving Souvenir,** no. 03–72 (☎ **65/534-0761**), has an absolutely enormous selection of carved stone, wood, bone, glass, and ivory chops ready to be carved to your specifications. Simple designs are really quite affordable, while some of the more elaborate chops and carvings fetch a handsome sum. At **Inherited Arts & Crafts,** no. 03–69 (☎ **65/534-1197**), you can commission a personalized Chinese scroll painting or calligraphy piece. The handiwork work is quite beautiful. Amid the many jade and gold shops at Chinatown Point, **La Belle Collection,** no. 04–53 (☎ **534-0231**), stands out for its jewelry crafted from orchids. The coating lets the flowers' natural colors show, while delicate gold touches add a little extra sparkle.

For Chinese goods, however, nothing beats **Yue Hwa,** 70 Eu Tong Sen St. (☎ **65/ 538-4222**). This five-story Chinese Emporium is an attraction in its own right. Their superb inventory includes all manner of silk wear (robes, underwear, blouses), embroidery and house linens, bolt silks, tailoring services (for perfect mandarin dresses!), cloisonne jewelry and gifts, lacquerware, pottery, musical instruments, traditional Chinese clothing for men and women (from scholars' robes to coolie duds!), jade and gold, cashmere, traditional items, art supplies, herbs, home furnishings—I could go on and on. Plan to send some time here.

ARAB STREET   shop for handicrafts from Malaysia and Indonesia. I go for sarongs at **Hadjee Textiles,** 75 Arab St. (☎ **65/298-1943**), for their stacks of folded sarongs in beautiful colors and traditional patterns. They're perfect for traveling, as they're lightweight but can serve you well as a dressy skirt, bedsheet, beach blanket, window shade, bath towel, or whatever you need—when I'm on the road I can't live without mine. Buy a few here and the prices really drop. If you're in the market for a more masculine sarong, **Goodwill Trading,** 56 Arab St. (☎ **298-3205**), specializes in pulicat, or the plaid sarongs worn by Malay men. For modern styles of batik, check out **Basharahil Brothers,** 99–101 Arab St. (☎ **65/296-0432**), for their very interesting designs, but don't forget to see their collection of fine silk batiks in the back. For batik household linens, you can't beat **Maruti Textiles,** 93 Arab St. (☎ **65/392-0253**), where you'll find high-quality place mats and napkins, tablecloths, pillow covers, and quilts. The buyer for this shop has a good eye for style.

I've also found a few shops on Arab Street that carry handicrafts from other countries in Southeast Asia. **Memoirs,** 18 Baghdad St. (☎ **65/294-5900**), sells mostly Indonesian crafts, from carved and hand-painted decorative items to scored leather shadow puppets and unusual teak gifts. **Ahn Yeu Em De Paris,** 15 Baghdad St. (☎ **65/292-1523**), carries boxes of velvet hand-beaded evening shoes, made in Vietnam. So inexpensive! For antiques and curios, try **Gim Joo Trading,** 16 Baghdad St. (☎ **65/293-5638**), a jumble of the unusual, some of it old. A departure from the more packed and dusty places here, **Suraya Betawj,** 67 Arab St. (☎ **65/398-1607**), carries gorgeous Indonesian and Malaysian crafted housewares in contemporary design—the type you normally find for huge prices in shopping catalogues back home.

Other unique treasures include the large assortment of fragrance oils at **Aljunied Brothers,** 91 Arab St. (☎ **65/291-8368**). Muslims are forbidden from consuming alcohol in any form (a proscription that includes the wearing of alcohol-based perfumes as well), so these oil-based perfumes re-create designer scents plus other floral and wood creations. Check out their delicate cut-glass bottles and atomizers as well. Finally, for the crafter in your life, **Kin Lee & Co.,** 109 Arab St. (☎ **65/291-1411**), carries a complete line of patterns and accessories to make local Peranakan beaded slippers. In vivid colors and floral designs, these traditional slippers were always made by hand, to be attached later to a wooden sole. The finished versions are exquisite, plus they're fun to make.

LITTLE INDIA   The best shopping is on Serangoon Road, where Singapore's Indian community shops for Indian imports and cultural items. Little India offers all sorts of small finds, especially throughout Little India Arcade (48 Serangoon Rd.) and just across the street on Campbell Lane at **Kuna's,** no. 3 Campbell Lane (☎ **65/ 294-2700**). Here you can buy inexpensive Indian costume jewelry like bangles, earrings, and necklaces in exotic designs, and a wide assortment of decorative dots (called *pottu* in Tamil) to grace your forehead. Indian handicrafts include brass work, wood carvings, dyed tapestries, woven cotton household linens, small curio items, very inexpensive incense, colorful pictures of Hindu gods, and other ceremonial items. Look here also for Indian cooking pots and household items. If after you pick up these items you care to try your hand at making your own curry, head for **Mannan Impex,** 118 Serangoon (☎ **65/299-8424**), to peruse all the necessary spices.

OUTDOOR MARKETS   A few outdoor markets still exist in Singapore, though it ain't like the old days. At the Bugis MRT station, across from Parco Bugis Junction, a well-established **night market** (which is also open during the day) delivers overpriced cheap chic, some curio items, accessories, and video compact discs (VCDs) to tourists. In **Chinatown,** on the corner of South Bridge Road and Cross Street, look for the old guys who come out with blankets full of odd merchandise—old watches, coins, jewelry, Mao paraphernalia, Peranakan pottery, and local artifacts from decades past. There's not many of these guys there, but for impromptu markets, I thought their merchandise was far more imaginative than at Bugis. If you're really desperate for a **flea market,** you can always head for the field between Little India and Arab Street (just behind the Johor bus terminal), where you'll find about five times more vendors than at Chinatown, but be warned: The goods are weird. Old nasty shoes, Barry Gibb records, broken radios—the same crap you'd see at garage sales back home, only local style. It could be interesting culturally. If you're in the mood.

8 Singapore After Dark

What do you want to do tonight? Do you want to go out for a cultural experience and find a traditional dance or music performance or a Chinese opera, or do you want to put on your finery and rub elbows with society at the symphony? If it's live performance you're looking for, you have your choice not only of the local dance and theater troupes but of the many West End and Broadway shows that come through on international tours. Or you may want to try a local performance—smaller theater groups have lately been hitting nerves and funny bones through stage portrayals of life in the Garden City. Singapore has been transforming itself into a center for the arts in this part of the world, and is beginning to achieve the level of sophistication you'd come to expect from a Western city. If partying it up is more your speed, there's all kinds of nighttime revelry going on. Society may seem puritanical during the daylight hours, but once the night comes, the clubs get crazy.

INFORMATION   Major cultural festivals are highly publicized by the Singapore Tourism Board (STB), so one stop by their office will probably provide enough info to fill your evening agenda for your whole trip. Another source is the *Straits Times,* which lists events around town, as well as the *New Paper,* which also lists musical events like local bands and international rock and pop tours. Both of these papers also provide cinema listings and theater reviews.

TICKETS   Two ticket agents, TicketCharge and Sistic, handle bookings for almost all theater performances, concert dates, and special events. You can find out about schedules before your visit through their Web sites: www.ticketcharge.net and www.sistic.com.sg. When in Singapore, stop by one of their centrally located outlets to pick up a schedule, or call them for more information. Call **TicketCharge** at ☎ **65/296-2929** or head for Centrepoint, Forum–The Shopping Mall, Funan–The IT Mall, Marina Square Shopping Centre, Tanglin Mall, or the Substation. For **Sistic** bookings call ☎ **65/348-5555,** or see them at the Victoria Concert Hall Box Office, Bugis Junction, Raffles Shopping Centre, Scotts, Specialists' Shopping Center, Suntec

Mall, Takashimaya Shopping Centre, or Wisma Atria. The STB also carries information about current and coming events.

HOURS   Theater and dance performances can begin anywhere between 7:30 and 9pm. Be sure to call for the exact time. Many bars open in the late afternoon, a few as early as lunchtime. Disco and entertainment clubs usually open around 6pm, but generally don't get lively until 10 or 11pm. Closing time for bars and clubs is at 1 or 2am on weekdays, 3am on weekends.

DRINK PRICES   Because of the government's added tariff, alcoholic beverage prices are high everywhere, whether in a hotel bar or a neighborhood pub. "House pour" drinks (generics) are between S$10 and S$13 (US$6 and US$7.80). A glass of house wine will cost between S$10 and S$15 (US$6 and US$9), depending if it's a red or a white. Local draft beer (Tiger), brewed in Singapore, is on average S$10 (US$6). Almost every bar and club has a happy hour before 7:30pm and discounts can be up to 50% off for house pours and drafts. Most of the disco and entertainment clubs charge steep covers, but they will usually include one drink. Hooray for ladies' nights—at least 1 night during the week—when those of the feminine persuasion get in for free.

DRESS CODE   Many clubs will require smart casual attire. Feel free to be trendy, but stay away from shorts, T-shirts, sneakers, and torn jeans. Be forewarned that you may be turned away if not properly dressed. Many locals dress up for their night on the town, either in elegant garb or trend-setting threads, although a certain amount of respectability is always expected.

SAFETY   You'll be fairly safe out during the wee hours in most parts of the city, and even a single woman alone has little to worry about. Occasionally, groups of young men may cat call, but by and large those groups are not hanging out in the more cosmopolitan areas. On the weekends, police set up barricades around the city to pick up drunk drivers, so if you rent a car, be careful about your alcohol intake, or appoint a designated driver. Otherwise, you can get home safely in a taxi, which fortunately isn't too hard to find even late at night, with one exception: When Boat Quay clubs close, there's usually a mob of revelers scrambling for cabs. (Note that after midnight, a 50% surcharge is added to the fare, so make sure you don't drink away your ride home!)

THEATER, DANCE & MUSICAL PERFORMANCE

Singapore is not a cultural backwater. Professional and amateur theater companies, dance troupes, opera companies, and musical groups offer a wide variety of not only Asian performances, but Western as well. Broadway road shows don't stop in San Francisco, where the road ends, but continue on to include Singapore in their itineraries. Major musical performers from opera to rock stars have been equally as successful. The Merce Cunningham Dance Company and the Bolshoi Ballet have both graced the boards, and the New York Philharmonic, under the baton of maestro Zubin Mehta, thrilled Singaporeans and visitors alike.

The **Singapore Symphony Orchestra,** 11 Empress Place, 2nd Storey, Victoria Hall (☎ **65/338-1230;** www.sso.org.sg), performs every weekend at the Victoria Concert Hall, with regular special guest appearances by international celebrities. Concerts begin at 8:15pm on Fridays and Saturdays, and tickets range from S$8 to S$50 (US$4.80 to US$29.95). Sistic handles bookings for SSO performances, so call their hot line at ☎ 65/348-5555, or visit their main office at the Victoria Concert Hall Box Office or one of their other locations listed above in this chapter.

Singapore also hosts the Malaysian Philharmonic Orchestra, plus events such as the International Piano Festival.

The **Singapore Lyric Opera,** Stamford Arts Centre, 155 Waterloo St. no. 03–06 (☎ 65/336-1929), also appears at the Victoria Concert Hall regularly. Call them for upcoming schedules, or call Sistic at the Victoria Concert Hall Box Office (☎ 65/348-5555).

The **Singapore Chinese Orchestra,** the only professional Chinese orchestra in Singapore, has won several awards for its classic Chinese interpretations. Ticket prices vary from S$8 to S$20 (US$4.80 to US$12). Contact them c/o People's Association, Block B, Room 5, No. 9 Stadium Link (☎ 65/440-3839; www.sco-music.org.sg). Ticket sales are handled by Sistic.

BARS & CLUBS

Singaporeans love to go out at night, whether it's to lounge around in a cozy wine bar or to jump around on a dance floor until 3 in the morning. And this city has become pretty eclectic in its entertainment choices, so you'll find everything from live jazz to Elvis, from garage rock to techno, world beat, or just plain rock. The truth is, the nightlife is happening. Local celebrities and the young, wealthy, and beautiful are the heroes of the scene, and their quest for the "coolest" spot keeps the club scene on its toes. The listings here are keyed in to help you find the latest or most interesting place. *A tip:* At press time, the most happening bars and clubs were anything on Mohamed Sultan Road and the new Chinese-chic Lan Kwai Fong. Start from there.

I recommend **Bojangles** (174 Killiney Rd., ☎ 65/734-5446) because it's got a great location, but manages to stay off tourist agendas. The happy hour specials are some of the best in Singapore. **Brewerkz** (no. 01–05 Riverside Point, 30 Merchant Rd. ☎ 65/438-7438), with outside seating along the river and an airy contemporary style inside—like a giant IKEA room built around brewing kettles and copper pipes—brews the best house beer in Singapore. In the basement of the Grand Hyatt Regency, **Brix** (10–12 Scotts Rd., ☎ 65/738-1234) is a nice place for those who prefer a more discriminating kind of fun. The Music Bar features live jazz and R&B, while the Wine & Whiskey Bar serves up a fine selection of wines, scotch, and cognacs.

Elvis' Place (no. B1–13 The Concourse Shopping Mall, 298 Beach Rd. ☎ 65/299-8403) is home to the delightful world of Elvis Wee, Singapore's resident Elvis Presley tribute artist and local celebrity. He hangs out at the bar and loves to talk about Elvis, life, and the world, and is very gracious when you ask for a photo or autograph. As for the bar, it's no bigger than a postage stamp, but on Friday and Saturday nights the place rocks. **The Fat Frog** (45 Armenian St. (behind the Substation) ☎ 65/338-6201) is more a cafe than a bar, and draws folks who prefer conversation without intrusive music.

Of all the choices along Boat Quay, **Harry's Quayside Bar,** (28 Boat Quay. ☎ 65/538-3029) the official after-work drink stop for finance professionals from nearby Shenton Way, is the most classy, and even though it's also the most popular, you can usually get a seat. **Hu'u Bar** at Singapore Art Museum, 71 Bras Basah Rd. ☎ 65/338-6828. the best part of the place is the music, a smooth mix of acid jazz that's both sophisticated and funky. If you're looking for a real bar-type bar, JJ Mahoney comes pretty close (58 Duxton Rd. ☎ 65/225-6225)—and they also have Karoke.

The Long Bar at Raffles Hotel (1 Beach Rd. ☎ 65/337-1886) is a nice little gem of a bar, even if it is touristy and expensive. **Muddy Murphys** (no. B1–01/01–06 Orchard Hotel Shopping Arcade, 442 Orchard Rd. ☎ 65/735-0400) is one of a few Irish bars in Singapore. Irish music rounds out the ambience created by the mostly Irish imported trappings around the place.

The Next Page (17 Mohamed Sultan Rd. ☎ 65/235-6967) is a stand out for ambience, which is a freaky Chinese dream in an old Singaporean shop house. The crowd is mainly young professionals who by late night have been known to dance on the bar (and not only on weekends). The back has a bit more space for seating, darts, and a pool table.

Down Peranakan Place there are a few bars, one of which is **No. 5** (5 Emerald Hill ☎ 65/732-0818). No. 5 is a cool, dark place just dripping with Southeast Asian ambience, from its old shop house exterior to its partially crumbling interior walls hung with rich wood carvings.

If you want to catch some jazz head to **Sax** (23 Cuppage Terrace, ☎ 65/ 835-3090), a not-so-highbrow jazz evening, try Saxophone, a hole-in-the-wall place with great live jazz and blues every day except Monday from about 9:45pm till around 12:30am. **Somerset's Bar** at The Westin Stamford and Westin Plaza Hotels (2 Stamford Rd. ☎ 65/431-5332) serves quite a lot of patrons, mostly jazz lovers who come for the best live jazz in the city.

There are a few stand outs in the disco catergory, one which is **Buzz** (88 Circular Rd. ☎ 65/536-9557). Buzz isn't as glitzy and high profile as some of the other dance clubs in Singapore, but everyone who goes out at night knows about it. Its many regulars come back again and again to dance to eighties music, which sometimes includes a tune or two you'd never thought you'd hear again. A great choice if you just want to party without all the aftertaste. The popular **Lan Kwai Fong** (50 Eu Tong Sen St. ☎ 65/534-3233) occupies a traditional medical hall in Chinatown. The restored building and its contents are so completely authentic that you'd think it was a stop on the Chinatown walking tour—don't forget to find the wine bar at the top floor.

Zouk/Phuture/Velvet Underground (Jiak Kim St. ☎ 65/738-2988) is Singapore's first innovative danceteria, comprised of three warehouses joined together. They play the best in modern music, so even if you're not much of a groover you can still have fun watching the party from the many levels that tower above the dance floor. If you need a bit more intimacy in your nightlife, Velvet Underground, within the Zouk complex, drips in red velvet and soft lighting—a good complement to the more soulful sounds spinning here. The newer addition to Zouk, Phuture, draws a younger, more hip-hop-loving crowd than VU. Including the wine bar outside, Zouk is basically your one-stop shopping for a party, and in Singapore, this place is legendary. (Payment of the highest cover charge among the three clubs in the complex allows admission to the other clubs as well.)

GAY & LESBIAN NIGHTSPOTS

It seems a few of Singapore's more better known gay and lesbian spots have closed down in the past couple of years, but new places are popping up regularly. The Web has listings at www2.best.com/~utopia/tipsing.htm, but I've found some of these to be outdated. For the latest info, I'd recommend one of the chat rooms recommended at the address above, and talk to the experts. Recent word has it that Velvet Underground, part of the **Zouk** complex (see above), welcomes a mixed clientele of gays, lesbians, and straight folks. In addition to the places I've listed below, there are a couple of gay bars that have asked to remain unlisted in this book, so ask around for a better sense of the scene in Singapore.

Inner Circle (78 Tanjong Pagar Rd.; ☎ 65/222-8462) is a pretty small and dark place, with a tiny bar, a large karaoke screen, and not much more to write home about. Most of the clientele are Singaporeans, but the staff is very friendly and open, and assure me that Westerners, although not frequent guests, are very welcome and will definitely have a good time. **Babylon** (52 Tanjong Pagar Rd.; ☎ 65/227-7466) is a small, gay karaoke club. The crowd at this bar is younger and might not be as open as at Inner Circle, but try it out anyway.

9

Malaysia

by Jennifer Eveland

Compared with spicy Thailand to the north and cosmopolitan Singapore to the south, Malaysia is a relative secret to many from the West, and most travelers to Southeast Asia skip over it, opting for more heavily traversed routes.

Boy, are they missing out. Those who venture here wander through streets awash with international influences from colonial times and trek through mysterious rain forests and caves, often without another tourist in sight. They relax peacefully under palms on lazy white beaches that fade into blue, blue waters. They spy the bright colors of batik sarongs hanging to dry in the breeze. They hear the melodic drone of the Muslim call to prayer seeping from exotic mosques. They taste culinary masterpieces served in modest local shops—from Malay with its deep mellow spices to succulent seafood punctuated by brilliant chile sauces. In Malaysia I'm always thrilled to witness life without the distracting glare of the tourism industry, and I leave impressed by how accessible Malaysia is to outsiders while remaining true to its heritage.

Malaysia just doesn't get the tourism press it deserves, but it's not because foreign travelers aren't welcome. True, the Malaysian Tourism Board has almost no international advertising campaign—and you'll be hard-pressed to get any useful information out of them—but everyone from government officials in Kuala Lumpur to boat hands in Penang seems delighted to see the smiling face of a traveler who has discovered just how beautiful their country is.

This chapter covers the major destinations of peninsular Malaysia. We begin with the country's capital, **Kuala Lumpur,** then tour the peninsula's west coast—the cities of **Johor Bahru, Malacca** (Melaka), the hill resorts at **Cameron** and **Genting Highlands,** plus islands like the popular **Penang** and the luxurious **Langkawi.** Next we take you up the east coast of the peninsula, through resort areas such as **Desaru, Kuantan, Cherating,** and the small and charming **Tioman Island,** all the way north to the culturally stimulating cities of **Kuala Terengganu** and **Kota Bharu.** My coverage will also include **Taman Negara,** peninsular Malaysia's largest national forest. Finally, we cross the South China Sea to the island of Borneo, where the Malaysian states of **Sarawak** and **Sabah** feature Malaysia's most impressive forests as well as unique and diverse cultures.

Malaysia is easily accessible to the rest of the world through its international airport in Kuala Lumpur. Or if you want to hop from another country in the region, daily flights to Malaysia's many smaller airports give you access to all parts of the country, and you can also travel by car, bus, or train from Singapore or Thailand.

1 Getting to Know Malaysia

THE LAY OF THE LAND

Malaysia's territory covers peninsular Malaysia—bordering Thailand in the north just across from Singapore in the south—and two states on the island of Borneo, Sabah and Sarawak, approximately 240 kilometers (150 miles) east across the South China Sea. All 13 of its states total 336,700 square kilometers (202,020 sq. miles) of land. Of this area, **Peninsular Malaysia** makes up about 465,000 square kilometers (134,680 sq. miles) and contains 11 of Malaysia's 13 states: Kedah, Perlis, Penang, and Perak are in the northwest; Kelantan and Terengganu are in the northeast; Selangor, Negeri Sembilan, and Melaka are about midway down the peninsula on the western side; Pahang, along the east coast, sprawls inward to cover most of the central area (which is mostly forest preserve); and Johor covers the entire southern tip from east to west, with two vehicular causeways linking it to Singapore, just over the Strait of Johor. Kuala Lumpur, the nation's capital, appears on a map to be located in the center of the state of Selangor, but it is actually a federal district similar to Washington, D.C., in the United States.

On **Borneo,** Sarawak and Sabah share the landmass with Indonesia's Kalimantan. Also sharing the island, in a tiny nook on the Sarawak coast, is the tiny oil-rich Sultanate of Brunei Darussalam.

Back on the peninsula, the major cities can be found closer to the coastline, many having built on old trade or mining settlements, usually near one of Malaysia's many rivers.

Tropical evergreen forests, estimated to be some of the oldest in the world, cover more than 70% of Malaysia. The country's diverse terrain allows for a range of forest types, such as montane forests, sparsely wooded tangles at higher elevations; lowland forests, the dense tropical jungle type; mangrove forests along the waters' edge; and peat swamp forest along the waterways. On the peninsula, three national forests—Taman Negara (or "National Forest") and Kenong Rimba Park, both inland, and Endau Rompin National Park, located toward the southern end of the peninsula—welcome visitors regularly, for quiet nature walks to observe wildlife or hearty adventures like white-water rafting, mountain climbing, caving, and jungle trekking. Similarly, the many national forests of Sabah and Sarawak provide a multitude of memorable experiences, which can include brushes with the indigenous peoples of the forests.

Surrounded by the South China Sea on the east coast and the Strait of Malacca on the west, the waters off the peninsula vary in terms of sea life (and beach life). The waters off the east coast house a living coral reef, good waters, and gorgeous tropical beaches, while more southerly parts host beach resort areas. By way of contrast, the surf

Abbreviating Malaysia

The first tip here is that people are always abbreviating Kuala Lumpur to KL. Okay, that's pretty obvious. But these people will abbreviate everything else they can get away with. So, Johor Bahru becomes JB, Kota Bharu KB, Kota Kinabalu, KK—you get the picture. Malaysia itself is often shortened to M'sia. To make it easier for you, the only shortened version I've used in this book is KL.

Peninsular Malaysia

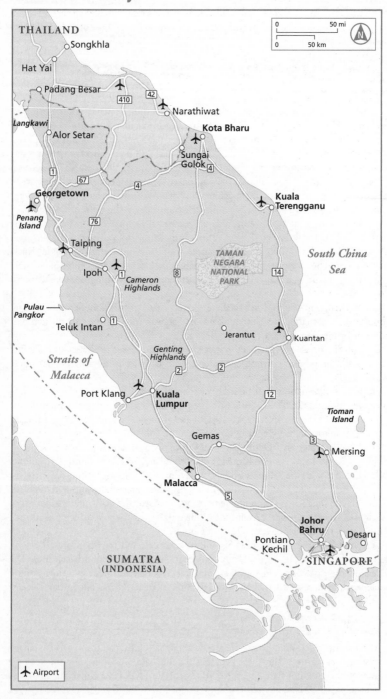

in southern portions of the Strait of Malacca is choppy and cloudy from shipping traffic—hardly ideal for diving or for the perfect Bali Hai vacation. But once you get as far north as Penang, the waters become beautiful again. Meanwhile, the sea coast of Sabah and Sarawak count numerous resort areas that are ideal for beach vacationing and scuba diving. In fact, one of the world's top 10 dive sites is located at Sipadan in Sabah.

MALAYSIA'S PEOPLE, ETIQUETTE & CUSTOMS

The mix of cultural influences in Malaysia is the result of centuries of immigration and trade with the outside world, particularly with Arab nations, China, and India. Early groups of incoming foreigners brought wealth from around the world, plus their own unique cultural heritages and religions. Further, once imported, each culture remained largely intact; that is, none have truly been homogenized. Traditional temples and churches exist side by side with mosques.

Likewise, **traditional art forms** of various cultures are still practiced in Malaysia, most notably in the areas of dance and performance art. Chinese opera, Indian dance, and Malay martial arts are all very popular cultural activities. Silat, originating from a martial arts form (and still practiced as such by many), is a dance performed by men and women. Religious and cultural festivals are open for everyone to appreciate and enjoy. Unique arts and traditions of indigenous people distinguish Sabah and Sarawak from the rest of the country.

Traditional **Malaysian music** is very similar to Indonesian music. Heavy on rhythms, its constant drum beats underneath the light repetitive melodies of the stringed gamelan (no relation at all to the Indonesian metallophone gamelan, with its gongs and xylophones), will entrance you with its simple beauty.

Questions of etiquette in Malaysia are very similar to those in Singapore, so please see chapter 8 for more information.

2 Planning a Trip to Malaysia

VISITOR INFORMATION

The **Malaysia Tourism Board (MTB)** can provide some information by way of pamphlets and advice before your trip, but keep in mind they are not yet as sophisticated as other tourist boards around the world. Much of the information they provide is vague, broad-stroke descriptions with few concrete details that are useful for the traveler. Overseas offices are located as follows.

IN THE UNITED STATES

- **New York:** 595 Madison Ave., Suite 1800, New York, NY 10022 (☎ **212/ 754-1113;** fax 212/754-1116)
- **Los Angeles:** 818 W. 7th St., Suite 804, Los Angeles, CA 90017 (☎ **213/ 689-9702;** fax 213/689-1530)

IN CANADA

- **Vancouver:** 830 Burrard St., Vancouver, B.C., Canada V6Z 2K4 (☎ **604/ 689-8899;** fax 604/689-8804)

IN AUSTRALIA

- **Sydney:** 65 York St., Sydney, NSW 2000, Australia (☎ **02/9299-4441;** fax 02/ 9262-2026)
- **Perth:** 56 William St., Perth, WA 6000, Australia (☎ **08/9481-0400;** fax 08/ 9321-1421)

IN THE UNITED KINGDOM

- **London:** 57 Trafalgar Square, London, WC2N 5DU, UK (☎ **071/930-7932;** fax 071/930-9015)
- **In Malaysia:** 17th Floor, Menara Dato' Onn, Putra World Trade Centre, 45 Jalan Tun Ismail, 50480 Kuala Lumpur (☎ **03/293-5188;** fax 03/293-5884).

For MTB offices in other cities, refer to individual city listings. The official Web site of the Malaysia Tourism Board is http://tourism.gov.my.

ENTRY REQUIREMENTS

To enter the country you must have a valid passport. Citizens of the United States do not need visas for tourism and business visits, and upon entry are granted a Social/Business Visit Pass good for up to 3 months. Citizens of Canada, Australia, New Zealand, and the United Kingdom can also enter the country without a visa, and will be granted up to 30 days pass upon entry. For other countries, please consult the nearest Malaysian consulate before your trip for visa regulations. Also note: Travelers holding Israeli passports are not permitted to travel within Malaysia (likewise, Malaysians are forbidden from traveling to Israel).

While in Malaysia, should you need to contact an official representative from your home country, the following contact information in Kuala Lumpur can help: **United States Embassy** ☎ 03/2168-5000; **Canadian High Commission** ☎ 03/243-9499;

Australian High Commission ☎ 03/240-6642; **New Zealand High Commission** ☎ 03/201-0846; and **British High Commission** ☎ 03/248-2122.

If you are arriving from an area in which yellow fever has been reported, you will be required to show proof of yellow fever vaccination. Contact your nearest MTB office to research the specific areas that fall into this category.

CUSTOMS REGULATIONS

With regard to currency, you can bring into the country as many foreign currency notes or traveler's checks as you please, but you are not allowed to leave the country with more foreign currency or traveler's checks than you had when you arrived. Due to controls on currency speculation in recent years, the government is keeping an eye on every ringgit. Regarding Malaysian currency, you are not permitted to carry in or take out more than RM1,000 per person. Upon entry, you'll be asked to complete a form issued by the Central Bank of Malaysia (Bank Negara Malaysia) stating the value of all currencies carried. This form is to be held with your passport until, on departure, you'll be asked to re-tally your cash on hand and submit the form to customs personnel.

Social visitors can enter Malaysia with 1 liter of hard alcohol and one carton of cigarettes without paying duty—anything over that amount is subject to local taxes. Prohibited items include firearms and ammunition, daggers and knives, and pornographic materials. Be advised that Malaysia enforces a very strict drug abuse policy that includes the death sentence for convicted drug traffickers.

MONEY

Malaysia's currency is the **Malaysian ringgit.** It's also commonly referred to as the Malaysian dollar, but prices are marked as RM (a designation I've used throughout this book). Notes are issued in denominations of RM2, RM5, RM10, RM20, RM50, RM100, RM500, and RM1000. One ringgit is equal to 100 sen. Coins come in denominations of 1, 5, 10, 20, and 50 sen, and there's also a 1-ringgit coin.

Following the dramatic decline in the value of its currency during the Southeast Asian economic crisis, the Malaysian government has sought to stabilize the ringgit to ward off currency speculation by pegging the ringgit at an artificial exchange rate. At the time of writing, exchange rates were RM3.79 to US$1.

CURRENCY EXCHANGE   Currency can be changed at banks and hotels, but you'll get a more favorable rate if you go to one of the money changers that seem to be everywhere; in shopping centers, in little lanes, and in small stores—just look for signs. They're often men in tiny booths with a lit display on the wall behind them showing the exchange rate. All major currencies are generally accepted, and there is never a problem with the U.S. dollar.

For up-to-date money conversion, visit CNN's Web site at www.cnn.com/travel/currency, or the currency chart at www.xe.net/ict.

AUTOMATED-TELLER MACHINES   Kuala Lumpur, Penang, and Johor Bahru have quite a few automated teller machines (ATMs) scattered around, but they're few and far between in the smaller towns. In addition, some ATMs do not accept credit cards or debit cards from your home bank. I have found that debit cards on the MasterCard/Cirrus or Visa/PLUS networks are almost always accepted at **Maybank,** with at least one location in every major town. Cash is dispensed in ringgit deducted from your account at the day's rate.

TRAVELER'S CHECKS   Generally, travelers to Malaysia will never go wrong with American Express and Thomas Cook traveler's checks, which can be cashed at banks, hotels, and licensed money changers. Unfortunately, they are often not accepted at smaller shops. Even in some big restaurants and department stores, many cashiers don't know how to process these checks, which might lead to a long and frustrating wait.

CREDIT CARDS   Credit cards are widely accepted at hotels and restaurants, and at many shops as well. Most popular are American Express, MasterCard, and Visa. Some banks may also be willing to advance cash against your credit card, but you have to ask around because this facility is not available everywhere.

In Malaysia, to report a **lost or stolen card,** call American Express via the nearest **American Express** representative office (see individual city listings), or the head office in Kuala Lumpur (☎ **603/213-0000**); for **MasterCard** Emergency Assistance for International Visitors call ☎ **1-800/88-4594,** and for **Visa** Emergency Assistance call ☎ **1-800/80-1066.** Both numbers are toll-free from anywhere in the country.

WHEN TO GO

There are two **peak seasons** in Malaysia, one in winter and another in summer. The peak winter tourist season falls roughly from the beginning of December to the end of January, covering the major winter holidays—Christmas, New Year's Day, Chinese New Year, and Hari Raya. These dates can change according to the full moon, which dictates the exact dates of the Chinese New Year and Hari Raya holidays. Note that due to the monsoon at this time (November through March), the east coast of peninsular Malaysia is rainy and the waters are rough. Resort areas, especially Tioman, are deserted and oftentimes closed. Tourist traffic slows down from February through the end of May, then picks up again in June. The peak summer season falls in the months of June, July, and August, and can last into mid-September. After September it's quiet again until December. Both seasons experience approximately equal tourist traffic, but in summer months that traffic may ebb and flow.

CLIMATE   Climate considerations will play a role in your plans. If you plan to visit any of the east coast resort areas, the low season is between November and March, when the monsoon tides make the water too choppy for water sports and beach activities. On the west coast, the rainy season is from April through May, and again from October through November.

The temperature is basically static year-round. Daily averages are between 67°F and 90°F (21°C and 32°C). Temperatures in the hill resorts get a little cooler, averaging 67°F (21°C) during the day and 50°F (10°C) at night.

CLOTHING CONSIDERATIONS   You will want to pack light, loose-fitting clothes, sticking mostly to natural fibers. Women have additional clothing requirements, as it can sometimes be uncomfortable walking through Muslim streets wearing short shorts or a sleeveless top—in many areas people *will* stare. The traditional dress for Good Muslim Women in Malaysia is that which covers the body, including the legs, arms, and head. And while many Malay women choose to continue this tradition (and with color and pizzazz, I might add), those who do not are still perfectly acceptable within Malaysia's contemporary society. As a female traveler I pack slacks and jeans, long skirts and dresses (below the knee is fine), and loose-fitting, short-sleeved cotton tops. In modern cities such as Kuala Lumpur, Johor Bahru, Malacca, Penang, and Kuching, I don't feel conspicuous in modest walking shorts, and at beach resorts I'm the first to throw on my bikini and head for the water. I always bring one light-weight long-sleeved blouse and a scarf large enough to cover my head—visits to mosques require it. If you get worried about what's appropriate, the best thing to do is to look around you and follow suit.

A tip for both male and female travelers is to wear shoes that are easily removed. Local custom asks that you remove your shoes before entering any home or place of worship.

PUBLIC HOLIDAYS & EVENTS   During Malaysia's official public holidays, expect government offices to be closed, as well as some shops and restaurants, depending on the ethnicity of the shop owner or restaurant owner. **Hari Raya Puasa** and **Chinese New Year** fall close to the same dates, during which time you can expect many shop and restaurant closings. However, during these holidays, look out for special sales and celebrations. Also count on public parks, shopping malls, and beaches to be more crowded during public holidays, as locals will be taking advantage of their time off.

Official public holidays fall as follows: Hari Raya Aidil Fitri (December or January), New Year's Day (January 1), Chinese New Year (January or February), Hari-Raya Aidil-Adha (March or April), Wesak Day (May), Prophet Mohammed's Birthday (June 26), National Day (August 31), and Christmas (December 25). Where general dates are given above, expect these holidays to shift from year to year depending on the lunar calendar. The MTB can help you with exact dates as you plan your trip. In addition, each state has a public holiday to celebrate the birthday of the state Sultan.

HEALTH & INSURANCE

The **tap water** in Kuala Lumpur is supposedly potable, but I don't recommend drinking it—in fact, I don't recommend drinking tap water anywhere in Malaysia. Bottled water is inexpensive enough and readily available at convenience stores and food stalls. **Food** prepared in hawker centers is generally safe—I have yet to experience trouble and I'll eat almost anywhere. If you buy fresh fruit, wash it well with bottled water and carefully peel the skin off before eating it.

Malaria has not been a major threat in most parts of Malaysia, even Malaysian Borneo. **Dengue fever,** on the other hand, which is also carried by mosquitoes, remains a constant threat in most areas, especially rural parts. Dengue, if left untreated, can cause fatal internal hemorrhaging, so if you come down with a sudden fever or skin rash, consult a physician immediately. There are no prophylactic treatments for dengue; the best protection is to wear plenty of insect repellent. Choose a product that contains DEET or is specifically formulated to be effective in the tropics.

For further health and insurance information, see chapter 3.

GETTING THERE
BY PLANE

Malaysia has five international airports—at Kuala Lumpur, Penang, Langkawi, Kota Kinabalu and Kuching—and 14 domestic airports at locations that include Johor Bahru, Kota Bharu, Kuantan, and Kuala Terengganu. Specific airport information is listed with coverage of each city.

A passenger service charge, or **airport departure tax,** is levied on all flights. A tax of RM5 (US$1.30) for domestic flights and RM40 (US$10.50) for international flights is usually included when you pay for your ticket.

Few Western carriers fly directly to Malaysia. If Malaysian Airlines does not have suitable routes directly from your home country, you'll have to contact another airline to work out a route that connects to one of Malaysia Airline's routes.

FROM THE UNITED STATES   Malaysia Airlines (☎ 800/552-9264) flies at least once daily from Los Angeles to Kuala Lumpur, and three times a week from New York.

FROM CANADA   North American carriers will have to connect with a Malaysian Airlines flight, either in East Asia or in Europe.

FROM THE UNITED KINGDOM Malaysia Airlines (☎ **0171/341-2020**) has two daily nonstop flights from London Heathrow airport, operating domestic connections from Glasgow, Edinburgh, Teesside, Leeds Bradford, and Manchester. **British Airways** (☎ **0345/222111,** a local call from anywhere within the U.K.) departs London for KL daily, except on Mondays and Fridays.

FROM AUSTRALIA Malaysia Airlines (☎ **02/132627**) flies directly to Kuala Lumpur from Perth, Adelaide, Brisbane, Darwin, Sydney, and Melbourne, and flies connecting routes via one of these airports from Cairns, Coolangatta, Canberra, and Hobart. **Qantas Airlines** (☎ **02/131211**) provides service from Sydney to KL on Tuesday, Friday, and Saturday.

FROM NEW ZEALAND Malaysia Airlines (☎ **09/373-2741** or 0800/657-472) flies a direct route from Auckland with connecting service from Wellington, Christchurch, Dunedin, and Palmeston.

BY TRAIN

FROM SINGAPORE The Keretapi Tanah Melayu Berhad (KTM), Malaysia's rail system, runs express and local trains that connect the cities along the west coast of Malaysia with Singapore to the south and Thailand to the north. Trains depart three times daily from the **Singapore Railway Station** (☎ **65/222-5165**), on Keppel Road in Tanjong Pagar, not far from the city center. About five daily trains to Johor Bahru cost S$4.20 (US$2.50) for first-class passage, S$1.90 (US$1.15) for second class, and S$1.10 (US$.65) for third class for the half-hour journey. **Johor Bahru's train station** is very centrally located at Jalan Campbell (☎ **07/223-4727**), and taxis are easy to find. Trains to Kuala Lumpur depart five times daily for fares from S$60 (US$36) for first class, S$26 (US$15.60) for second class, and S$14.80 (US$8.90) for third. The trip takes around 6 hours. The Kuala Lumpur Central Railway Station is on Jalan Hishamuddin (☎ **03/273-8000**), also centrally located, with a taxi line. For Butterworth (Penang), the fare is S$118.50 (US$71.10) first class, S$51.40 (US$30.85) second class, and S$29.20 (US$17.50) third class. You will have to change trains in Kuala Lumpur. Please refer to the section on Penang for specific coverage about "getting there" options.

FROM THAILAND KTM's international service departs from the **Hua Lamphong Railway Station** (☎ **662/223-7010** or 662/223-7020) in Bangkok, with operations to Hua Hin, Surat Thani, Nakhon Si Thammarat, and Hat Yai in Thailand's southern peninsula. The final stop in Malaysia is at Butterworth (Penang), so passage to KL will require you to catch a connecting train onward. The daily service departs at 3:15pm and takes approximately 22 hours from Bangkok to Butterworth. There is no first- or third-class service on this train, only air-conditioned second class; upper berth goes for 940B (US$25.40), and lower is 1,010B (US$27.30).

For a fascinating journey from Thailand, you can catch the **Eastern & Orient Express (E&O),** which operates a route between Bangkok, Kuala Lumpur, and Singapore. Traveling in the luxurious style for which the Orient Express is renowned, you'll finish the entire journey in about 42 hours. Compartments are classed as Sleeper (approximately US$1,248 per person double occupancy), State (US$1,758 per person double occupancy), and Presidential (US$3,270 per person double occupancy). All fares include meals on the train. Overseas reservations for the E&O Express can be made through a travel agent or, from the United States and Canada, call ☎ **800/524-2420,** from Australia ☎ **3/9699-9766,** from New Zealand ☎ **9/379-3708,** and from the United Kingdom ☎ **171/805-5100.** From Singapore, Malaysia, and Thailand contact the E&O office in Singapore at ☎ **65/392-3500.**

BY BUS

From Singapore, there are many bus routes to Malaysia. The easiest depart from the Johor-Singapore bus terminal at the corner of Queen Street and Arab Street. Buses to Kuala Lumpur leave three times daily and cost S$25 (US$6.60). Contact **The Singapore-KL bus service** at ☎ **65/292-8254.** They drop you at a field outside the city—thank goodness there's a regular shuttle to Puduraya Bus Terminal in central Kuala Lumpur for only RM1, but be prepared to line up (and try to have an RM1 coin handy). Buses to Johor Bahru and Malacca can also be picked up at this terminal, leaving at regular intervals throughout the day. Call ☎ **65/292-8149** for buses to Johor Bahru (S$2.10/US$0.55) and ☎ **65/293-5915** for buses to Malacca (S$11/US$2.90). If you wish to travel by bus to a smaller destination, the best way is to hop a bus to Johor Bahru and then transfer to a bus to your final stop.

From Thailand, you can grab a bus in either Bangkok or Hat Yai (in the Southern part of the country) heading for Malaysia. I don't recommend the bus trip from Bangkok. It's just far too long a journey to be confined to a bus. You're better off taking the train. From Hat Yai, many buses leave regularly for northern Malaysian destinations, particularly Butterworth (Penang).

BY TAXI (FROM SINGAPORE)

From the Johor-Singapore bus terminal at Queen and Arab streets, the **Singapore Johor Taxi Operators Association** (☎ **65/296-7054**) can drive you to Johor Bahru for S$28 (US$16.80) if you get to the terminal yourself, or S$40 (US$24) if you ask them to pick you up at your hotel.

BY FERRY

Ferries are really only convenient for travel to Desaru and Tioman Island in Malaysia. For specific information, please refer to each section in this chapter.

BY CAR

For convenience, driving to Malaysia from Singapore can't be beat. You can go where you want to go, when you want to go, and without the hassle of public transportation—but it is quite expensive. Cars can be rented in Singapore (see chapter 8 for details), then driven to and even dropped off in Malaysia. A slightly cheaper option is taking the ferry from Singapore to Johor and renting there.

GETTING AROUND

The modernization of Malaysia has made travel here—whether it's by plane, train, bus, taxi, or self-driven car—easier and more convenient than ever. Malaysia Airlines has service to every major destination within the peninsula and East Malaysia. Buses have a massive web of routes between every city and town. Train service up the western coast and out to the east provides even more options. And a unique travel offering—the **outstation taxi**—is available to and from every city on the peninsula. All the options make it convenient enough for you to plan to hop from city to city and not waste too much precious vacation time.

By and large, all the modes of transportation between cities are reasonably comfortable. Air travel can be the most costly of the alternatives, followed by outstation taxis, then buses and trains.

BY PLANE

Malaysia Airlines links from its hub in Kuala Lumpur (☎ **03/746-3000**) to the cities of Johor Bahru (☎ **607/334-1001**), Kota Bharu (☎ **609/744-7000**), Kota Kinabalu

(☎ **6088/213-555**), Kuala Terengganu (☎ **609/622-1415**), Kuantan (☎ **609/515-7055**), Kuching (☎ **6082/246-622**), Langkawi (☎ **604/966-6622**), Penang (☎ **604/262-0011**), and other smaller cities not covered in this volume. These listed phone numbers are for Malaysia Airlines reservations offices in each city. Individual airport information is provided in sections for each city that follows. One-way domestic fares can average RM75 (US$19.75) to RM200 (US$52.65).

BY TRAIN

The Keretapi Tanah Melayu Berhad (KTM) provides train service throughout peninsular Malaysia. Trains run from north to south between the Thai border and Singapore, with stops between including Butterworth (Penang), Kuala Lumpur, and Johor Bahru. There is a second line that branches off this line at Gemas, midway between Johor Bahru and KL, and heads northeast to Tempas near Kota Bharu. Fares range from RM55.50 (US$14.60) for first class between Johor Bahru and KL, to RM114 (US$30) for first class passage between Johor Bahru and Butterworth. Train station information is provided for each city in individual city headings within this chapter.

KTM has a **good deal for students.** For US$38, the ISSA Explorer Pass will get you anywhere in Malaysia for a week (US$50 for 2 weeks, US$60 for 3 weeks). The deal applies only to students under 30 who carry an ISIC International Student Identity Card, Go Card, or Youth Hostel Card. It's good for travel on second class only. Call Kuala Lumpur (☎ **03/442-4722** or fax 03/443-3707) for more information. You can also obtain a similar deal for rail travel in neighboring Thailand as well.

BY BUS

Malaysia's intercity coach system is extensive, reliable, and inexpensive. Buses depart several times daily for many destinations on the peninsula, and fares are charged according to the distance you travel. Air-conditioned express bus service (called Executive Coach service or Business Class) will cost you more, but since the fares are so inexpensive, it's well worth your while to spend the couple of extra dollars for the comfort. For an idea of price, it costs about RM16.30 (US$4.35) for service from KL to Johor Bahru, and RM18 (US$4.75) from KL to Penang. While there are more than a few independent bus companies around, I've stuck to only the two major route providers, **Transnasional** and **Park May** (which operate the NiCE and Plusliner buses). I've found these companies to be more reliable and comfortable than the others. For each city covered, I've listed bus terminal locations, but scheduling information must be obtained from the bus company itself.

BY TAXI

You can take special hired cars, called **outstation taxis,** between every city and state on the peninsula. Rates depend on the distance you plan to travel. They are fixed, and stated at the beginning of the trip, but many times can be bargained down. In Kuala Lumpur, go to the second level of the Puduraya Bus Terminal to find cabs that will take you outside the city, or call the Kuala Lumpur Outstation Taxi Service Station, 123 Jalan Sultan, Kuala Lumpur (☎ **03/238-3525**). A taxi from KL to Malacca will cost you approximately RM120 (US$31.60), KL to Cameron Highlands RM180 (US$47.40), KL to Butterworth or Johor Bahru RM220 (US$57.90). Outstation taxi stand locations are included under each individual city heading.

Also, within each of the smaller cities, feel free to negotiate with unmetered taxis for hourly, half-day, or daily rates. It's an excellent way to get around for sightseeing and shopping without transportation hassles. Hourly rates are anywhere from RM15 (US$3.95) to RM25 (US$6.60).

BY CAR

As recently as the 1970s, there was trouble with roadside crime—bandits stopping cars and holding up the travelers inside. Fortunately for drivers in Malaysia, this is a thing of the past. In the mid 1990s, Malaysia opened the North-South Highway, running from Bukit Kayu Hitam in the north on the Thai border to Johor Bahru at the southern tip of the peninsula. The highway (and the lack of bandits) has made travel along the west coast of Malaysia easy. There are rest areas with toilets, food outlets, and emergency telephones at intervals along the way. There is also a toll that varies depending on the distance you're traveling.

Driving along the east coast of Malaysia is actually much more pleasant than driving along the west coast. The highway is narrower and older, but it takes you through oil palm and rubber plantations, and the essence of kampung Malaysia permeates throughout. As you near villages you'll often have to slow down and swerve past cows and goats, which are really quite oblivious to oncoming traffic. You have to get very close to honk at them before they move.

The speed limit on highways is 110 kilometers per hour. On the minor highways the limit ranges from 70 to 90 kilometers per hour. Do not speed, as there are traffic police strategically situated around certain bends.

Distances between major towns are: From KL to Johor Bahru, 368 kilometers (221 miles); from KL to Malacca, 144 kilometers (86 miles); from KL to Kuantan, 259 kilometers (155 miles); from KL to Butterworth, 369 kilometers (221 miles); from Johor Bahru to Malacca, 224 kilometers (134 miles); from Johor Bahru to Kuantan, 325 kilometers (195 miles); from Johor Bahru to Mersing, 134 kilometers (80 miles); from Johor Bahru to Butterworth, 737 kilometers (442 miles).

To rent a car in Malaysia, you must produce a driver's license from your home country that shows you have been driving at least 2 years. There are desks for major car-rental services at the international airports in Kuala Lumpur and Penang, and additional outlets throughout the country (see individual city sections for this information).

Hitchhiking is not common among locals and I don't really think it's advisable for you either. The buses between cities are very affordable, so it's a much better idea to opt for those instead.

TIPS ON ACCOMMODATIONS

Peak months of the year for hotels in western peninsular Malaysia are December through February and July through September. For the east coast the busy times are July through September. You will need to make reservations well in advance to secure your room during these months.

TAXES & SERVICE CHARGES All the nonbudget hotels charge 10% service charge and 5% government tax. As such, there is no need to tip. But bellhops still tend to be tipped at least RM2 per bag and car jockeys or valets should be tipped at least RM4 or more.

TIPS ON DINING

Malaysian food seems to get its origins from India's rich curries influenced by Thailand's herbs and spices. You'll find delicious blends of coconut milk and curry, shrimp paste and chiles, accented by exotic flavors of galangal (similar to turmeric), lime, and lemongrass. Sometimes pungent, a few of the dishes have a deep flavor from fermented shrimp paste that is an acquired taste for Western palates. By and large, Malaysian food is delicious, but in multicultural Malaysia, so is the Chinese food, the Peranakan food, the Indian food—the list goes on. The Chinese brought their own flavors from their points of origin in the regions of Southern China. Teochew, Cantonese, and Szechuan are all styles of Chinese cuisine you'll find throughout the country. Peranakan food is unique to Malacca, Penang, and Singapore. The Peranakans or "Straits Chinese" combined local ingredients with some traditional Chinese dishes to create an entirely new culinary form. And Indian food, both Northern and Southern, can be found in most every city, particularly in the western part of the peninsula. And, of course you'll find gorgeous fresh seafood almost everywhere.

I strongly recommend eating in a hawker stall when you can, especially in Penang, which is famous for its local cuisine.

Also, many Malaysians eat with their hands off banana leaves when they are having *nasi padang* or *nasi kandar* (rice with mixed dishes). This is absolutely acceptable. If you choose to follow suit, wash your hands first and try to use your right hand, as the left is considered unclean (traditionally, it's the hand used to wash after a visit to the toilet). While almost all of the food you encounter in a hawker center will be safe for eating, it is advisable to go for freshly cooked hot or soupy dishes. Don't risk the pre-cooked items.

Also, avoid having ice in your drink in the smaller towns, as it may come from a dubious water supply. If you ask for water, either make sure it's boiled or buy mineral water.

TAXES & SERVICE CHARGES   A 10% service charge and 5% government tax are levied in proper restaurants, but hawkers charge a flat price.

TIPS ON SHOPPING

Shopping is a huge attraction for tourists in Malaysia. In addition to modern fashions and electronics, there are great local handicrafts. In each city section, I've listed some great places to go for local shopping.

For **handicrafts,** prices can vary. There are many handicraft centers, such as Karyaneka, with outlets in cities all over the country, where goods can be priced a bit higher but where you are assured of good quality. Alternatively, you could hunt out bargains in markets and at roadside stores in little towns, which can be much more fun.

Batik is one of the most popular arts in Malaysia, and the fabric can be purchased just about anywhere in the country. Batik can be fashioned into outfits and scarves or purchased as sarongs. Another beautiful Malaysian textile craft is songket weaving. These beautiful cloths are woven with metallic threads. Sometimes songket cloth is patterned into modern clothing, but usually it is sold as sarongs.

Traditional wood carvings have become popular collectors' items. Carvings by *orang asli* groups in peninsular Malaysia and by the indigenous tribes of Sabah and Sarawak have traditional uses in households or are employed for ceremonial purposes to cast off evil spirits and cure illness. They have become much sought after by tourists.

Malaysia's **pewter products** are famous. Selangor Pewter is the brand that seems to have the most outlets and representation. You can get anything from a picture frame to dinner sets.

Silver designs are very refined, and jewelry and fine home items are still made by local artisans, especially in the northern parts of the peninsula. In addition, craft items such as *wayang kulit* (shadow puppets) and *wau* (colorful Malay kites) make great gifts and souvenirs.

SUGGESTED ITINERARIES

Planning a trip to Malaysia requires a few considerations. It's important to consider the time required for traveling around the country. The trip overland from Singapore to Penang, for instance, takes up a whole day. Similarly, flying from, say, Langkawi Island to Kota Kinabalu can also take up a whole day. If your time is limited, your best bet is to narrow down your destinations within Malaysia depending on the activities that are important to you.

While Kuala Lumpur presents the most obvious choice of destinations, if you have only 3 days I'd recommend **Malacca** for its cultural charm, **Penang** for its British colonial history and good food, **Langkawi** for its luxurious beach resorts, or **Tioman Island** for laid-back beach bumming. Each is easily accessible by air, bus, or ferry from Singapore, and your travel time will be minimal. If you have a week, you can add **Kuala Lumpur** to your itinerary, or maybe a 3-day trip to **Taman Negara,** peninsular Malaysia's most exciting national park.

The most ideal itinerary would be 10 days to 2 weeks. If you're free, I'd recommend traveling north from Singapore, stopping in Malacca, Kuala Lumpur, Penang, and Langkawi. A nice trip up the east coast of the peninsula would also require at least 10 days to visit Tioman Island, Kuantan, Kuala Terengganu, and Kota Bahru.

Planning trips to **Sabah and Sarawak** usually require more time because most of the more fascinating activities here involve wildlife tours, outdoor adventure, and visits to indigenous villages, all of which require travel to the interior—quite a time-consuming proposition, but well worth the investment. Try to budget at least 10 days to enjoy any of these activities.

Fast Facts: Malaysia

American Express   See individual city sections for offices.

Business Hours   Banks are open from 10am to 3pm Monday through Friday and 9:30 to 11:30am on Saturday. **Government offices** are open from 8am to 12:45pm and 2 to 4:15pm Monday through Friday and from 8am to 12:45pm on Saturday. **Smaller shops** like provision stores may open as early as 6 or 6:30am and close as late as 9pm, especially those near the wet markets. Many such stores are closed on Saturday evenings and Sunday afternoons and are busiest before lunch. Other shops are open 9:30am to 7pm. **Department stores and shops in malls** tend to open later, about 10:30am or 11am till 8:30pm or 9pm throughout the week. Bars, except for those in Penang and the seedier bars in Johor Bahru, must close at 1am. Note that in Kuala Terengganu and Kota Bharu the weekday runs from Saturday to Wednesday. Above hours generally apply to that part of the country too.

Dentists & Doctors   Consultation and treatment fees vary greatly depending on whether the practitioner you have visited operates from a private or public clinic. Your best bet is at a private medical center if your ailment appears serious. These are often expensive but, being virtual minihospitals, they have the latest equipment. If you just have a flu, it's quite safe to go to a normal MD—most doctors have been trained overseas, and will display diplomas on their walls. The fee at a private center ranges from RM20 to RM45 (US$5.25 to US$11.85). Call ☎ **999** for emergencies.

Drug Laws   As in Singapore, the death sentence is mandatory for drug trafficking (defined as being in possession of more than 15 grams of heroin or morphine, 200 grams of marijuana or hashish, or 40 grams of cocaine). For lesser quantities you'll be thrown in jail for a very long time and flogged with a cane.

Electricity The voltage used in Malaysia is 220-240 volts AC (50 cycles). The three-point square plugs are used, so buy an adapter if you plan to bring any appliances. Also, many larger hotels can provide adapters upon request.

Internet/E-mail Service is available to almost all of the nation, and I have found Internet cafes in the most surprisingly remote places. While the major international hotels will have access for their guests in the business center, charges can be very steep. Still, most locally operated hotels do not offer this service for their guests. For each city I have listed at least one alternative, usually for a very inexpensive hourly cost of RM5 to RM10 (US$1.30 to US$2.65).

Language The national language is Bahasa Malaysia, although English is widely spoken. Chinese dialects and Tamil are also spoken.

Liquor Laws Liquor is sold in pubs and supermarkets in all big cities, or in provision stores. You'll hardly find any sold at Tioman though, so bring your own if you're headed there and wish to imbibe. A recent ruling requires pubs and other nightspots to officially close by 1am.

Newspapers & Magazines English-language papers the *New Straits Times, The Star, The Sun,* and *The Edge* can be bought in hotel lobbies and magazine stands. Of the local KL magazines, *Day & Night* has great listings and local "what's happening" information for travelers.

Postal Services Post office locations in each city covered are provided in each section. Overseas airmail postage rates are as follows: RM0.50 (US$0.13) for postcards and RM1.50 (US$0.39) for a 100-gram letter.

Safety/Crime While you'll find occasional news reports about robberies in the countryside, there's not a whole lot of crime going on, especially crime that would impact your trip. There's very little crime against tourists like pickpocketing and purse slashing. Still, hotels without in-room safes will keep valuables in the hotel safe for you. Be careful when traveling on overnight trains and buses where there are great opportunities for theft (many times by fellow tourists, believe it or not). Keep your valuables close to you as you sleep.

Taxes Hotels add a 5% government tax to all hotel rates, plus an additional 10% service charge. Larger restaurants also figure the same 5% tax into your bill, plus a 10% service charge, whereas small coffee shops and hawker stalls don't charge anything above the cost of the meal. While most tourist goods (such as crafts, camera equipment, sports equipment, and cosmetics, and select small electronic items) are tax-free, a small, scaled tax is issued on various other goods such as clothing, shoes, and accessories that you'd buy in the larger shopping malls and department stores.

Telephones & Faxes Most hotels have **international direct dialing** service and will charge extra for calls made using the service. **Local calls** can be made from public phones using coins or phone cards. Half the public phones (the coin ones) don't seem to work in Malaysia, though they'll happily eat your money. Among those that do work, one point of confusion stems from the fact that some phones take only 20 sen or 50 sen coins while others take 10 sen coins. Those that take the larger coins usually have an option for follow-on calls. If you've only spoken a short time and need to make another call, don't hang up after the first call; instead, just press the follow-on button and you can make another local call; otherwise you lose your credit.

Phone cards can be purchased at convenience stores for stored value amounts. While these cards are much more handy than coins, there are three companies

Telephone Dialing Info at a Glance

- **To place a call from your home country to Malaysia:** Dial the international access code (011 in the U.S., 0011 in Australia, or 00 in the U.K., Ireland, and New Zealand), plus the country code (60), plus the Malaysia area code (Cameron Highlands 5, Desaru 7, Genting Highlands 9, Johor Bahru 7, Kuala Lumpur 3, Kuala Terengganu 9, Kota Bharu 9, Kota Kinabalu 88, Kuantan 9, Kuching 82, Langkawi 4, Malacca 6, Mersing 7, Penang 4, Tioman 9), followed by the six-, seven-, or eight-digit phone number (for example, from the U.S. to Kuala Lumpur, you'd dial 011-60-3/000-0000).

- **To place a direct international call from Malaysia:** Dial the international access code (00), plus the country code of the place you are dialing (U.S. and Canada 1, Australia 61, Republic of Ireland 353, New Zealand 64, U.K. 44), plus the area/city code and the residential number.

- **To reach the international operator:** Dial 108.

- **To place a call within Malaysia:** You must use area codes if calling between states. Note that for calls within the country, area codes are preceded by a zero (Cameron Highlands 05, Desaru 07, Genting Highlands 09, Johor Bahru 07, Kuala Lumpur 03, Kuala Terengganu 09, Kota Bharu 09, Kota Kinabalu 088, Kuantan 09, Kuching 082, Langkawi 04, Malacca 06, Mersing 07, Penang 04, Tioman 09).

providing coin phone service in Malaysia, and each of them only accepts their own phone cards. Telekom, represented by blue phone boxes, is the most reliable one I've found, and locations are more abundant than the two others.

International calls can be made from phones that use cards, or from a Telekom office.

Television   Guests in larger hotels will sometimes get satellite channels such as HBO, Star TV, or CNN. Another in-house movie alternative, Vision Four, pre-programs videos throughout the day. Local TV stations TV2, TV5, and TV7 show English-language comedies, movies, and documentaries.

Time   Malaysia is 8 hours ahead of Greenwich mean time, 16 hours ahead of U.S. Pacific standard time, 13 hours ahead of eastern standard time, and 2 hours behind Sydney. There is no daylight saving time.

Tipping   People don't tip, except to bellhops and car jockeys. For these, an amount not less than RM4 is okay.

Toilets   To find a public toilet, ask for the *tandas*. In Malay, *lelaki* is male and *perempuan* is female. Be prepared for pay toilets. Coin collectors sit outside almost every public facility, taking RM20 per person, RM30 if you want paper. Once inside, you'll find it obvious that the money doesn't go for cleaning crews.

Water   Water in Kuala Lumpur is supposed to be potable, but most locals boil the water before drinking it—and if that's not a tip-off, I don't know what is. I advise against drinking the tap water anywhere in Malaysia. Hotels will supply bottled water in your room. If they charge you for it, expect inflated prices. A 1.5-liter bottle goes for RM7 in a hotel minibar, but RM2 at 7-Eleven.

3 Kuala Lumpur

The most popular destinations in Malaysia dot the west coast of the peninsula where the main rail line passes through, connecting Singapore with Kuala Lumpur and on to Bangkok.

The convenience of train travel isn't the only draw of this part of the country; it also holds some of Malaysia's most significant historical towns. As you travel north from Singapore, **Johor Bahru** makes for a great day trip for those with only a short time to experience Malaysia. Three hours north of Johor Bahru, the sleepy town of **Malacca** reveals the evidence of hundreds of years of Western conquest and rule. Three hours north of Malacca, and you're in **Kuala Lumpur,** the cosmopolitan capital of the country, full of shopping, culture, history, and nightlife. Close by, **Genting Highlands** draws tourists from all over the region for the casino excitement, while the more relaxed **Cameron Highlands** offers a cool and charming respite from Southeast Asia's blaring heat. Still farther north, **Penang,** possibly Malaysia's most popular destination, retains all the charm of an old-time Southeast Asian waterfront town, full of romance (and great food!), with the added advantage of beach resorts nearby. Still farther north, just before you reach the Thai border, **Langkawi** proves that there are still a few tropical paradise islands left on the planet that are not swarming with tourists.

Kuala Lumpur (or KL as it is commonly known) is more often than not a traveler's point of entry to Malaysia. As the capital it is the most modern and developed city in the country, with contemporary high-rises and world-class hotels, glitzy shopping malls and international cuisine.

The city began sometime around 1857 as a small mining town at the spot where the Gombak and Klang rivers meet, at the spot where the Masjid Jame sits in the center of the city. Fueled by tin mining in the nearby Klang river valley, the town grew under the business interests of three officials: a local Malay raja Abdullah, a British resident, and a Chinese headman (Kapitan China). The industry and village attracted Chinese laborers, Malays from nearby villages, and Indian immigrants who followed the British, and as the town grew, colonial buildings that housed local administrative offices were erected around Merdeka Square, close to Masjid Jame and bounded by Jalan Sultan Hishamuddin and Jalan Kuching. The town, and later the city, spread outward from this center.

Life in KL had many difficult starts and stops then—tin was subject to price fluctuations, the Chinese were involved in clan "wars," but worst of all, malaria was killing thousands. Still, in the late 1800s KL overcame its hurdles to become the capital of the State of Selangor, and later the capital of the Federated Malay States (Perak, Selangor, Negeri Sembilan, and Pahang) and got its big break as the hub of the Malayan network of rail lines. Its development continued to accelerate, save for during the Japanese occupation (1942–45), and in 1957, with newly won independence from Britain, Malaysia declared Kuala Lumpur its national capital.

Today the original city center at **Merdeka Square** is the core of KL's history. Buildings like the Sultan Abdul Samad Building, the Royal Selangor Club, and the Kuala Lumpur Railway Station are gorgeous examples of British style peppered with Moorish flavor. South of this area is KL's **Chinatown.** Along Jalan Petaling and surrounding areas are markets, shops, food stalls, and the bustling life of the Chinese community. There's also a **Little India** in KL, around the area occupied by Masjid Jame, where you'll find flower stalls, Indian Muslim and Malay costumes, and traditional items. Across the river you'll find **Lake Gardens,** a large sanctuary that houses Kuala Lumpur's bird park, butterfly park, and other attractions and gardens. Modern

Kuala Lumpur

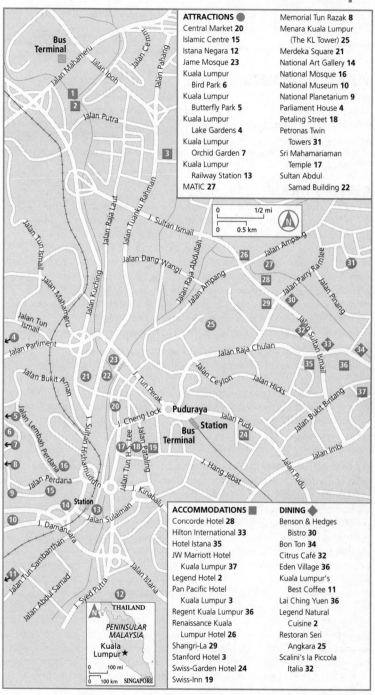

ATTRACTIONS ●
Central Market **20**
Islamic Centre **15**
Istana Negara **12**
Jame Mosque **23**
Kuala Lumpur
    Bird Park **6**
Kuala Lumpur
    Butterfly Park **5**
Kuala Lumpur
    Lake Gardens **4**
Kuala Lumpur
    Orchid Garden **7**
Kuala Lumpur
    Railway Station **13**
MATIC **27**

Memorial Tun Razak **8**
Menara Kuala Lumpur
    (The KL Tower) **25**
Merdeka Square **21**
National Art Gallery **14**
National Mosque **16**
National Museum **10**
National Planetarium **9**
Parliament House **4**
Petaling Street **18**
Petronas Twin
    Towers **31**
Sri Mahamariaman
    Temple **17**
Sultan Abdul
    Samad Building **22**

ACCOMMODATIONS ■
Concorde Hotel **28**
Hilton International **33**
Hotel Istana **35**
JW Marriott Hotel
    Kuala Lumpur **37**
Legend Hotel **2**
Pan Pacific Hotel
    Kuala Lumpur **3**
Regent Kuala Lumpur **36**
Renaissance Kuala
    Lumpur Hotel **26**
Shangri-La **29**
Stanford Hotel **3**
Swiss-Garden Hotel **24**
Swiss-Inn **19**

DINING ◆
Benson & Hedges
    Bistro **30**
Bon Ton **34**
Citrus Café **32**
Eden Village **36**
Kuala Lumpur's
    Best Coffee **11**
Lai Ching Yuen **36**
Legend Natural
    Cuisine **2**
Restoran Seri
    Angkara **25**
Scalini's la Piccola
    Italia **32**

Kuala Lumpur is rooted in the city's **"Golden Triangle,"** bounded by Jalan Ampang, Jalan Tun Razak, and Jalan Imbi. This section is home to most of KL's hotels, office complexes, shopping malls, and sights like the KL Tower and the Petronas Twin Towers, the tallest buildings in the world.

VISITOR INFORMATION

In Kuala Lumpur, the Malaysia Tourism Board has several offices. The largest is at the MATIC, the Malaysia Tourist Information Complex (see "Attractions," below), located on 109 Jalan Ampang (☎ **03/254-3929**); another is located at the Kuala Lumpur Railway Station, Jalan Sultan Hishamuddin (☎ **03/274-6063**); and another is at the Putra World Trade Centre, Level 2, Menara Dato 'Onn, 45 Jalan Tun Ismail (☎ **03/441-1295**).

GETTING THERE

BY PLANE   The new Kuala Lumpur International Airport (KLIA) (☎ **03/ 8776-0259**) opened in June 1998. Although its first 2 or 3 months had quite a few operational problems (such as misdirected baggage and confusing sign boards), the government has worked hard to fix the problems and the airport runs smoothly today. Located in Sepang, 53 kilometers (32 miles) outside the city, KLIA is a huge complex with business centers, dining facilities, a fitness center, medical services, shopping, post offices, and an airport hotel operated by Pan Pacific (☎ **03/8787-3333**). While there are money changers, they are few and far between, so hop on the first line you see, and don't assume there's another one just around the corner.

From KLIA, domestic flights can be taken to almost every major city in the country.

Getting into Town from the Airport   There's an **express bus service** that operates until midnight daily that takes you as far as the Tun Razak Hockey Stadium. The Luxury Coach (RM25/US$6.60) departs every 15 minutes, and the Semi Luxury (RM18/US$4.75) every half hour. City **taxis** are not permitted to pick up fares from the airport, but from the stadium you can take a taxi to the city. **Airport Limousines** (☎ **03/8787-3678**) operates round the clock. Coupons must be purchased at the arrival concourse for Premier Service (Mercedes, RM91.70/US$24.15) or Budget Service (Malaysian-built Proton, RM66.70/US$17.55).

BY BUS   There's more than one bus terminal in Kuala Lumpur, and it can be somewhat confusing. The main bus terminal, **Puduraya Bus Terminal,** is on Jalan Pudu right in the center of town—literally. Buses heading in and out of the station block traffic along already congested city streets, spewing noxious gasses. The terminal itself is hot, filthy, and noisy; the heavy metal boom box wars between the provision shops is amusing for about 30 seconds. This terminal handles bus routes to all over the country, but more specifically to areas on the west coast from north to south. Buses to Penang or Malacca will leave from here. I think Puduraya is a mess to be avoided at all costs. It is a well-kept secret that many business-class and executive coaches to Penang, Johor Bahru, and Singapore depart peacefully from the **KL Railway Station,** which is a far saner alternative.

The other main terminals are the **Putra Bus Terminal** on Jalan Tun Ismail just across from the Putra World Trade Centre, and the **Pekililing terminal** on Jalan Ipoh, also not far from Putra WTC. Both terminals deal primarily with buses to east coast cities such as Kota Bharu, Kuala Terengganu, and Kuantan.

The bus terminals have no telephone numbers in their own right. Inquiries must be made directly to individual bus companies.

BY TAXI   The outstation taxi stand in Kuala Lumpur is located at **Puduraya Bus Terminal** on Jalan Pudu. Call ☎ **03/238-3525** for booking to any city on the peninsula. Fares will run you about RM180 (US$47.35) to Cameron Highlands, RM120 (US$31.60) to Malacca, RM220 (US$57.90) to Johor Bahru, and RM220 (US$57.90) to Penang and to Kuantan. These taxis can pick you up at your hotel for an additional RM10 (US$2.65) upon request.

GETTING AROUND

Kuala Lumpur is a prime example of a city that was not planned, per se, from a master graph of streets. Rather, because of its beginnings as an outpost, it grew as it needed to, expanding outward and swallowing up suburbs. The result is a tangled web of streets too narrow to support the traffic of a capital city. Cars and buses weave through one-way lanes, with countless motorbikes sneaking in and out, sometimes in the opposite direction of traffic or up on the sidewalks. Expect traffic jams in the morning rush between 6 and 9am, and again between 4 and 7pm. At other times, taxis are a convenient way of getting around, as the LRT (commuter railway) doesn't hit areas most frequented by tourists, and buses are hot and crowded with some very confusing routes. Walking can also be frustrating. Many sidewalks are in poor condition, with buckled tiles and gaping gutters. The heat can be prohibitive as well. However, areas within the colonial heart of the city, Chinatown, Little India, and some areas in the Golden Triangle are within walking distance of each other.

BY TAXI   Taxis around town can be waved down by the side of the road, or can be caught at taxi stands outside shopping complexes or hotels. The metered fare is RM2 (US$0.55) for the first kilometer and an additional 10 sen for each 200 meters after that. Between midnight and 6am you'll be charged an extra 50% of the total fare. If you call ahead for a cab, there's an extra charge of RM1 (US$0.25). Government regulations have made it compulsory for cabbies to charge the metered fare, but some still try to fix a price, which is invariably higher than what the metered fare would be.

   To request a cab pickup, call **KL Hotline Cab** at (☎ **03/255-3399**).

BY BUS   There are regular city buses and minibuses to take you around the city. The fare is 20 sen for the first kilometer and 5 sen for each additional kilometer. Know, however, that the buses in Kuala Lumpur are not dependable. You can wait at a stop for a long time only to find when the bus arrives that it's hot and packed so full that passengers seem to be hanging out every window. It's not the most relaxing way to get around.

BY RAIL   The **LRT,** or Light Rail Transit, has opened its first phase in Kuala Lumpur. It covers a 12-kilometer (7.4-mile) circuit, with 13 stops between Jalan Sultan Ismail and Jalan Ampang. The cost is 75 sen between stations, the longest ride costing RM2.95 (US$0.78). Tickets are purchased at LRT stations. Stored-value cards can be purchased in increments of RM20 and RM50 (US$5.25 and US$13.15). The system operates from 6am to midnight daily, with trains coming around every 5 to 10 minutes.

ON FOOT   The heat and humidity can make walking between attractions pretty uncomfortable. However, sometimes the traffic is so unbearable that you'll get where you're going much faster by strapping on your tennis shoes and hiking it.

Fast Facts: Kuala Lumpur

American Express   The main office for American Express is located in KL at The Weld 18th floor, Jalan Raja Chulan (☎ **03/2163-5000**).

Banks/Currency Exchange   You'll also find headquarters for all Malaysian and many international **banks,** most of which have outlets along Jalan Sultan Ismail plus ATMs at countless locations throughout the city. Look for **money changers** in just about every shopping mall; they're a better bargain than banks or hotel cashiers.

Emergencies   If you have a **medical emergency,** the number to dial is ☎ **999.** This is the same number for **police and fire emergencies** as well.

Internet/E-mail   Internet and e-mail service in KL will run about RM6 per hour for usage. I like **MasterWorld SurfNet Café,** 23 Jalan Petaling, M floor (technically it's on Jalan Cheng Lock around the corner; ☎ **03/201-0133**), which charges RM6 (US$1.58) per hour. For convenience, you can also try the **Travelers Network Station Cyber Café** on the second floor at the KL train station (☎ **03/2272-2237**), with rates of RM6 (US$1.60) per hour. If you're near the KL City Centre, try **Café Caravali,** Lot 346, 3rd floor next to the cinema (☎ **03/382-9033**). It's a bit more expensive (RM10/US$2.65 per hour), but is a nice setting.

Post Office   KL's General Post Office, on Jalan Sultan Hishamuddin (☎ 03/2274-1122) can be pretty overwhelming. If you can, try to use your hotel's mail service for a much easier time.

For more Fast Facts about Malaysia, see "Planning a Trip to Malaysia" on p. 456.

ACCOMMODATIONS

There are dozens of hotels in Kuala Lumpur, most of them within city limits; an especially large number of them are in the Golden Triangle area. Other hotels listed in this section are located in the Chinatown area, within walking distance of plenty of shopping attractions and nightlife.

VERY EXPENSIVE

✪ **The Regent Kuala Lumpur.** 160 Jalan Bukit Bintang, 55100 Kuala Lumpur. ☎ **800/545-4000** in the U.S. and Canada, 800/022-800 from Australia; 0800/440-800 from New Zealand; 0800/282-245 in the U.K., or 03/241-8000. Fax 03/242-1441. 468 units. A/C MINIBAR TV TEL. RM575 (US$151.30) double; RM748–RM2,070 (US$196.85–US$544.75) suite. AE, DC, JCB, MC, V.

Of the five-star properties in Kuala Lumpur, nobody delivers first-class accommodations with the finesse of The Regent. The lobby and guest rooms are contemporary and elegant, without a single sacrifice to comfort. Touches like soft armchairs and cozy comforters in each room will make you want to check in and never leave, and the large marble bathrooms will make you feel like a million bucks even on a bad hair day. The outdoor pool is a palm-lined free-form escape, and the fitness center is state-of-the-art, with sauna, steam, spa, and Jacuzzi.

Renaissance Kuala Lumpur Hotel. Corner of Jalan Sultan Ismail and Jalan Ampang, 50450 Kuala Lumpur. ☎ **800/HOTELS-1** in the U.S. and Canada, 800/222431 in Australia (Sydney 02/251-8484), 0800/441111 in New Zealand, 0800/181738 in the U.K., 800/7272 toll free in Malaysia, or 03/262-2233. Fax 03/263-1122. 400 units. A/C MINIBAR TV TEL. RM535 (US$140.80) double; RM755 (US$198.70) executive double; from RM955 (US$251.30) suite. AE, DC, JCB, MC, V.

The Renaissance is definitely geared to satisfy the needs of very discriminating travelers, and has become a very elegant address in KL. The lobby is a huge oval colonnade with a domed ceiling and massive marble columns rising from the sides of a geometric starburst on the floor. You could be walking into a futuristic version of Washington, D.C.'s Capitol Building. The guest rooms have an equally "official" feel to them—very bold and impressive, and completely European in style. In fact, you'll never know you're in Malaysia. Facilities include a very large free-form outdoor pool with beautiful landscaped terraces. The fitness center is one of the largest I've seen— and one of the most active, attracting private members from outside the hotel. It also has Jacuzzi and sauna. Other facilities include two outdoor tennis courts, a launderette, and a shopping arcade.

EXPENSIVE

Hotel Istana. 73 Jalan Raja Chulan, 50200 Kuala Lumpur. ☎ **03/241-9988.** Fax 03/ 244-0111. 593 units. A/C MINIBAR TV TEL. RM495–RM530 (US$130.25–US$139.45) double; RM625 (US$164.45) executive club; RM1,095 (US$288.15) suite. AE, DC, JCB, MC, V.

Fashioned after a Malay palace, Hotel Istana is rich with Moorish architectural elements, and songket weaving patterns are featured in decor elements throughout. The guest rooms have Malaysian touches like handwoven carpets and upholstery in local fabric designs, capturing the exotic flavor of the culture without sacrificing modern comfort and convenience. Located on Jalan Raja Chulan, Istana is in a favorable Golden Triangle location, within walking distance of shopping and some of the sights in that area. Ask about big rate discounts in the summer months.

JW Marriott Hotel Kuala Lumpur. 183 Jalan Bukit Bintang, 55100 Kuala Lumpur. ☎ **800/228-9290** in the U.S. and Canada, 800/251259 in Australia (Sydney 02/299-1614), 0800/221222 in the U.K., or 03/925-9000. Fax 03/925-7000. 552 units. A/C MINIBAR TV TEL. RM500 (US$131.60) double; RM600 (US$157.90) executive double; RM1,000 (US$263.15) suite. AE, DC, JCB, MC, V.

Opened in July 1997, the Marriott is one of the newer hotels in town. The smallish lobby area still allows for a very dramatic entrance, complete with wrought-iron filigree and marble. The modern guest rooms have a sleek, European flavor, decorated in deep greens and reds with plush carpeting, large desks, and a leather executive chair for great work space. The staff is very motivated and enthusiastic. Another great plus: The hotel is next door to some of the most upmarket and trendy shopping complexes in the city.

✪ **Kuala Lumpur Hilton International.** Jalan Sultan Ismail, 50250 Kuala Lumpur. ☎ **800/445-8667** in the U.S. Fax 03/244-2157. www.hilton.com. 577 units. A/C MINIBAR TV TEL. RM483 (US$127.10) double; RM860–RM5,080 (US$226.30–US$1,336.85) suite. AE, DC, JCB, MC, V.

The Hilton opened in 1973, making it the first world-class hotel in Kuala Lumpur. Situated on Jalan Sultan Ismail, it's in the middle of the business and shopping heart of the city. The hotel is set back from the road, stately and quiet, giving guests a bit of peace and quiet. The guest rooms are very spacious, with separate dressing areas, a sitting area, and nice desk space. City view rooms deliver fantastically on what they promise.

The Pan Pacific Hotel Kuala Lumpur. Jalan Putra, P.O. Box 11468, 50746 Kuala Lumpur. ☎ **800/327-8585** in the U.S. and Canada, 800/625959 in Australia (Sydney 02/923-37888), or 03/442-5555. Fax 03/441-7236. 565 units. A/C MINIBAR TV TEL. RM520–RM650 (US$136.85–US$171.05) double; from RM960 (US$252.65) suite. AE, DC, JCB, MC, V.

One thing you'll love about staying at the Pan Pacific is the view from the glass elevator as you drift up to your floor. The atrium lobby inside is bright and airy and filled with the scent of jasmine, and the hotel staff handles the demands of its international clientele with courtesy and professionalism. The rooms are spacious and stately. Sunken windows with lattice work frame each view.

✪ **The Shangri-La Hotel Kuala Lumpur.** 11 Jalan Sultan Ismail, 50250 Kuala Lumpur.
☎ **800/942-5050** in the U.S. and Canada, 800/222448 in Australia, 0800/442179 in New
Zealand, or 03/232-2388. Fax 03/202-1245. 681 units. A/C MINIBAR TV TEL. RM420–RM505
(US$110.55–US$132.90) double; RM575 (US$151.30) executive club room; RM1,300
(US$342.10) suite. AE, DC, JCB, MC, V.

I don't know how they do it, but Shangri-La can always take what could easily be a
dull building in a busy city and turn it into a resort-style garden oasis. Their property
in KL is no different. With attention paid to landscaping and greenery, the hotel is
one of the more attractive places to stay in town. The guest rooms are large with cooling colors and nice views of the city.

MODERATE

✪ **Concorde Hotel Kuala Lumpur.** 2 Jalan Sultan Ismail, 50250 Kuala Lumpur. ☎ **03/
244-2200.** Fax 03/244-1628. 610 units. A/C MINIBAR TV TEL. RM320 (US$84.20) double;
RM530–RM1,880 (US$139.45–US$494.75) suite. AE, DC, JCB, MC, V.

Jalan Sultan Ismail is the address for the big names in hotels, like Shangri-La and
Hilton, but tucked alongside the giants is the Concorde, a very reasonably priced
choice. What's best about staying here is that you don't sacrifice amenities and services
for the lower cost. Although rooms are not as large as those in the major hotels, they're
well outfitted in an up-to-date style that can compete with the best of them. Choose
the Concorde if you'd like location and comfort for less. It also has a small outdoor
pool facing a fitness center. A well-equipped business center adds additional value.

The Legend Hotel. Putra Place, 100 Jalan Putra, 50350 Kuala Lumpur. ☎ **800/637-7200**
in the U.S., 1800/655147 in Australia, 0800/25-28-40 in the U.K., or 03/442-9888. Fax 03/
443-0700. 400 units. A/C MINIBAR TV TEL. RM380–RM530 (US$100–US$139.45) double;
RM630 (US$165.80) legend crest; RM830 (US$218.40) executive suite. AE, DC, JCB, MC, V.

Lovely marble in earthy tones creates a luxurious atmosphere in the Legend's public
space, which is enhanced with Chinese touches such as carved wood furniture and
terra-cotta warrior statues—and since the lobby is located nine stories above street
level, there's not the usual commotion in it. Guest rooms are spacious, and all overlook the city, but ask to face the Twin Towers for the best view. Also, the less expensive rooms seem to have the nicest decor, with soft tones and modern touches. The
Crest rooms are rather strange—mine had a bright pink frilly bedcover. Facilities
include an outdoor pool, fitness center with Jacuzzi and sauna, squash courts, a launderette, and a shopping arcade.

✪ **Swiss-Garden Hotel.** 117 Jalan Pudu, 55100 Kuala Lumpur. ☎ **03/241-3333.** Fax 03/
241-5555. www.sgihotels.com.my. 326 units. A/C MINIBAR TV TEL. RM320–RM390
(US$84.20–US$102.65) double; RM430–RM600 (US$113.15–US$157.90) suite. AE, DC, JCB,
MC, V.

For mid-range prices, Swiss-Garden offers reliable comfort, a good location, and
affordability that attracts many leisure travelers to its doors. It also knows how to make
you feel right at home, with a friendly staff (the concierge is on the ball) and a hotel
lobby bar that actually gets patronized (by travelers having cool cocktails at the end of
a busy day of sightseeing). The guest rooms are simply furnished, but are neat and
comfortable. Swiss-Garden is just walking distance from KL's lively Chinatown district, and close to the Puduraya bus station. Facilities include an outdoor pool and a
fitness center.

INEXPENSIVE

Stanford Hotel. 449 Jalan Tuanku Abdul Rahman, 50100 Kuala Lumpur. ☎ **03/291-9833.**
Fax 03/291-3103. 168 units. A/C TV TEL. RM166–RM235 (US$43.70–US$61.85) double.
AE, MC, V.

The Stanford Hotel is a good alternative for the budget-conscious traveler. The lobby feels like a mini-version of a more upmarket hotel, and with new carpeting in the corridors and guest rooms, fresh paint, and refurbished furnishings and bathrooms, the place provides accommodations that are good value for your money. And some of the rooms even have lovely views of the Petronas Twin Towers. Discounted rates as low as RM100 can be had if you ask about promotions. Facilities are thin, with only a small business center and a coffeehouse serving up decent local dishes.

✪ **Swiss-Inn.** 62 Jalan Sultan, 50000 Kuala Lumpur. ☎ **03/232-3333.** Fax 03/201-6699. www.sgihotels.com.my. 110 units. A/C TV TEL. RM150–RM184 (US$39.45–$48.40) double. AE, DC, JCB, MC, V.

You can't beat the Swiss-Inn for comfortable and modern accommodations in Kuala Lumpur. Tucked away in the heart of Chinatown, just beyond this hotel's small lobby is the action of the street markets and hawkers. The place is small, and offers almost no facilities, but the compact rooms are clean and adequate. Best yet, discounts here can bring the rates down under RM100 (beware, lower category rooms have no windows). Make sure you reserve your room early, because this place runs at high occupancy year-round. The hotel offers in-house movies and has a 24-hour sidewalk coffee house. Guests have access to the Swiss-Garden Hotel's fitness center.

DINING

Kuala Lumpur is very cosmopolitan. Here you'll find not only delicious and exotic cuisine, but some pretty trendy settings.

Benson & Hedges Bistro. Ground floor, Life Centre, Jalan Sultan Ismail. ☎ **03/2164-4426.** Reservations not accepted. Main courses RM13.50–RM35 (US$3.55–US$9.20). AE, DC, MC, V. Daily 7–10am and 11am–3pm; Sun–Thurs 6pm–midnight, Fri–Sat 6pm–2am. TEX-MEX/AMERICAN.

The latest in trendy hangouts, this bistro is part coffee bar and part restaurant, decorated in contemporary style, with mood lighting glistening off bronze coffee bean dispensers. While it's not a place for a special night out, it is an excellent choice for a quick and easy bite in a fun and laid-back atmosphere. Staff is dressed in black, with casual and hip attitudes. Good entrees are the chicken piccata, roast duck lasagna, or blackened rack of lamb. Reservations are not accepted, and on the weekends the wait can be long, partly because no one will ever rush you to get you out. In short, be there early.

✪ **Bon Ton.** No.7 Jalan Kia Peng. ☎ **03/241-3611.** Reservations recommended. Main courses RM20–RM55 (US$5.25–US$14.45); set meals RM40–RM101 (US$10.55–US$26.60). AE, DC, MC, V. Mon–Fri noon–2:30pm; daily 6–10:30pm. ASIAN MIX.

Let me tell you about my favorite restaurant in Kuala Lumpur. First, Bon Ton has an incredible atmosphere. In a 1930s bungalow that was once a school, the place winds through room after room, its walls painted in bright hues and furnished with an assortment of mix-and-matched teak tables, chairs, and antiques. Second, the menu is fabulous. While à la carte is available, Bon Ton puts together theme set meals. You have 12 to chose from, including Nonya, Malacca Portuguese, Traditional Malay, even vegetarian. They're all brilliant.

Citrus Café. 19 Jalan Sultan Ismail. ☎ **03/242-5188.** Main courses RM24–RM46 (US$6.30–US$12.10). AE, DC, JCB, MC, V. Daily noon–2:30pm and 6–10:30pm. ASIAN MIX.

This place has become very popular with the yuppie international set—locals, expatriates, and tourists alike. The theme is Asia, contemporary style, and is reflected in the decor, music, and cuisine, which ranges from Malay to Thai to Japanese, with some Western elements thrown in too. The dining room, sushi bar, and terrace cafe are sparse and minimal. Dishes like the rotisserie chicken and the special sushi rolls are served in portions to share at your table.

○ Eden Village. 260 Jalan Raja Chulan. ☎ **03/241-4027.** Reservations recommended. Main courses RM18–RM100 (US$4.75–US$26.30) and up. AE, MC, V. Sun 7pm–midnight, Mon–Sat noon–3pm and 7pm–midnight. SEAFOOD.

Uniquely designed inside and out to resemble a Malay house, Eden Village has great local atmosphere. Waitresses are clad in traditional *sarong kebaya,* and serve up popular dishes like braised shark's fin in a clay pot with crabmeat and roe, and the Kingdom of the Sea (a half lobster baked with prawns, crab, and cuttlefish). The terrace seating is the best in the house.

○ Lai Ching Yuen. The Regent Kuala Lumpur, 160 Jalan Bukit Bintang. ☎ **03/249-4250.** Reservations recommended. Main courses RM26–RM58 (US$6.85–US$15.25). AE, DC, JCB, MC, V. Daily noon–2:30pm and 6:30–10:30pm. CANTONESE.

In the Regent's signature elegant style, dining is truly fine at Lai Ching Yuen. With delicacies like shark's fin, bird's nest, abalone, and barbecue specialties, the menu is extensive. A lunchtime dim sum and set lunch menu are also excellent. Each dish is presented as a piece of art. The restaurant is large and sectioned with etched glass panels. Gorgeous accents are added with modern Chinese art and silver and jade table settings.

Legend Natural Cuisine. The Legend Hotel and Apartments, 100 Jalan Putra. ☎ **03/442-9888.** Reservations recommended for lunch and dinner; required for high tea. Main courses RM38–RM55 (US$10–US$14.45). AE, DC, JCB, MC, V. Daily 6:30am–1am. INTERNATIONAL.

Legend Natural Cuisine's menu is selected by dieticians, its dishes incorporating organically grown produce and calorie-conscious recipes with a mind toward health awareness. Off the Legend Hotel's lobby, the restaurant is spacious and cozy, and the food is so good you'll never know it's healthy. It's easy to forget about dieting when you're traveling, but Legend's Natural Cuisine makes it incredibly easy to stick to one. Try the rack of lamb, and the forest mushroom soup is an unbelievably good appetizer.

Restoran Seri Angkasa. Jalan Punchak, off Jalan P. Ramlee. ☎ **03/208-5055.** Reservations recommended. Lunch buffet RM55 (US$14.45); dinner buffet RM75 (US$19.75). AE, DC, MC, V. Daily noon–2:30pm, 3:30pm–5:30pm, and 6:30–11pm. MALAYSIAN.

At the top of the Menara KL (KL Tower) is Restoran Seri Angkasa, a revolving restaurant with the best view in the city. Better still, it's a great way to try all the Malay-, Chinese-, and Indian-inspired local dishes at a convenient buffet, with a chance to taste just about everything you have room for—like nasi goring, clay-pot noodles, or beef rendang.

○ Scalini's la Piccola Italia. 19 Jalan Sultan Ismail. ☎ **03/245-3211.** Reservations recommended. Main courses RM26–RM58 (US$6.85–US$15.25). AE, DC, MC, V. Sun–Thurs noon–2:30pm and 6–10:30pm, Fri noon–2:30pm and 6–11pm, Sat 6–11pm. ITALIAN.

Four chefs from Italy create the dishes that make Scalini's a favorite among KL locals and expatriates. From a very extensive menu you can select pasta, fish, and meat, as well as a large selection of pizzas. The specials are superb and change all the time. Some of the best dishes are salmon with creamed asparagus sauce and ravioli with goat cheese and zucchini. Scalini's has a large wine selection (that is actually part of the romantic decor) with labels from California, Australia, New Zealand, France, and, of course, Italy.

ATTRACTIONS

Most of Kuala Lumpur's historic sights are located in the area around Merdeka Square/Jalan Hishamuddin area, while many of the gardens, parks, and museums are out at Lake Gardens. Taxi fare between the two areas will run you about RM5.

✪ Central Market. Jalan Benteng. ☎ **03/2274-6542.** Daily 10am–10pm. Shops until 8pm.

The original Central Market, built in 1936, used to be a wet market, but the place is now a cultural center (air-conditioned!) for local artists and craftspeople selling antiques, crafts, and curios. It is a fantastic place for buying Malaysian crafts and souvenirs, with two floors of shops to chose from. The Central Market also stages evening performances (at 8:15pm) of Malay martial arts, Indian classical dance, or Chinese orchestra. Call the number above for performance information.

Islamic Centre. Jalan Perdana. ☎ **03/2274-9333.** Sat–Thurs 7:30am–4:45pm; Fri 7:30am–12:15pm and 2:30–4:45pm.

The seat of Islamic learning in Kuala Lumpur, the center has displays of Islamic texts, artifacts, porcelain, and weaponry.

Istana Negara. Jalan Negara. No phone.

Closed to the public, this is the official residence of the king. You can peek through the gates at the istana (palace) and its lovely grounds.

✪ Jame Mosque (Masjid Jame). Jalan Tun Terak. No phone.

The first settlers landed in Kuala Lumpur at the spot where the Gombak and Klang rivers meet, and in 1909 a mosque was built here. Styled after an Indian Muslim design, it is one of the oldest mosques in the city.

Kuala Lumpur Bird Park. Jalan Perdana. ☎ **03/274-2042.** RM3 (US$0.79) adults, RM1 (US$0.26) children. Daily 9am–5pm.

Nestled in beautifully landscaped gardens, the bird park has over 2,000 birds within its 3.2 hectares (8 acres).

Kuala Lumpur Butterfly Park. Jalan Cenderasari. ☎ **03/293-4799.** RM4 (US$1.05) adults, RM2 (US$0.53) children. Daily 9am–6pm.

Over 6,000 butterflies belonging to 120 species make their home in this park, which has been landscaped with more than 15,000 plants to simulate the butterflies' natural rain forest environment. There are also other small animals and an insect museum.

Kuala Lumpur Lake Gardens (Taman Tasik Perdana). Enter via Jalan Parliament. Free admission. Daily 9am–6pm. No phone.

Built around an artificial lake, the 91.6-hectare (229-acre) park has plenty of space for jogging and rowing, and has a playground for the kids. It's the most popular park in Kuala Lumpur.

Kuala Lumpur Orchid Garden. Jalan Perdana. ☎ **03/293-0191.** RM1 (US$0.26) adults, RM0.50 (US$0.13) children. Daily 9am–6pm.

This garden has a collection of over 800 orchid species from Malaysia, and also contains thousands of international varieties.

Kuala Lumpur Railway Station. Jalan Sultan Hishamuddin. ☎ **03/274-9422.** Daily 7:30am–10:30pm.

Built in 1910, the KL Railway Station is a beautiful example of Moorish architecture.

MATIC (Malaysia Tourist Information Complex). Jalan Ampang. ☎ **03/2164-3929.** Daily 9am–6pm.

At MATIC you'll find an exhibit hall, tourist information services for Kuala Lumpur and Malaysia, and other travel-planning services. On Tuesdays, Thursdays, Saturdays, and Sundays, there are cultural shows at 2pm. Shows are RM2 (US$0.53) for adults, RM1 (US$0.26) for children.

Memorial Tun Razak. Jalan Perdana. ☎ **03/291-2111.** Free admission. Tues–Thurs and Sat–Sun 9am–6pm, Fri 9am–noon and 3–6pm.

Tun Razak was Malaysia's second prime minister, and this museum is filled with his personal and official memorabilia.

✪ **Menara Kuala Lumpur (The KL Tower).** Bukit Nanas. ☎ **03/208-5448.** RM8 (US$2.10) adults, RM3 (US$0.79) children. Daily 10am–10pm.

Standing 421 meters (1,389 ft.) tall, this concrete structure is the third tallest tower in the world, and the views from the top reach to the far corners of the city and beyond. At the top, the glass windows are fashioned after the Shah Mosque in Isfahan, Iran.

Merdeka Square. Jalan Raja.

Surrounded by colonial architecture with an exotic local flair, the square is a large field that was once the site of British social and sporting events. These days, Malaysia holds its spectacular Independence Day celebrations on the field, which is home to the world's tallest flagpole, standing at 100 meters (330 ft.).

National Art Gallery. Jalan Sultan Hishamuddin (across from the KL Railway Station). ☎ **03/4025-4990.** Free admission. Sat–Thurs 10am–6pm, Fri 10am–noon and 3–6pm.

The building that now houses the National Art Gallery was built as the Majestic Hotel in 1932 and has been restored to display contemporary works by Malaysian artists. There are international exhibits as well.

National Mosque (Masjid Negara). Jalan Sultan Hishamuddin (near the KL Railway Station). No phone.

Built in a modern design, the most distinguishing features of the mosque are its 73-meter (243-ft.) minaret and the umbrella-shaped roof, which is said to symbolize a newly independent Malaysia's aspirations for the future. Could be true, as the place was built in 1965, the year Singapore split from Malaysia.

✪ **National Museum (Muzim Negara).** Jalan Damansara. ☎ **03/282-6255.** Admission RM1 (US$0.26) adults, free children under 10. Sat–Thurs 9am–6pm, Fri 9am–noon and 3–6pm.

Located at Lake Gardens, the museum has more than 1,000 items of historic, cultural, and traditional significance, including art, weapons, musical instruments, and costumes.

National Planetarium. Lake Gardens. ☎ **03/2273-5484.** Admission to exhibition hall RM1 (US$0.26), children under 10 free; extra charges for screenings. Sat–Thurs 10am–7pm, Fri 10am–noon and 2:30–7pm.

The National Planetarium has a Space Hall with touch-screen interactive computers and hands-on experiments, a Viewing Gallery with binoculars for a panoramic view of the city, and an Ancient Observatory Park with models of Chinese and Indian astronomy systems. The Space Theatre has two different outer space shows.

Parliament House. Jalan Parliament. No phone. Parliament sessions are not open to the public.

In the Lake Gardens area, the Parliament House is a modern building housing the country's administrative offices, which were once in the Sultan Abdul Samad Building at Merdeka Square.

○ **Petaling Street.**

This is the center of KL's Chinatown district. By day, stroll past hawker stalls, dim sum shops, wet markets, and all sorts of shops, from pawn shops to coffin makers. At night, a crazy bazaar (which is terribly crowded) pops up—look for designer knockoffs, fake watches, and pirate VCDs (Video CD) here.

Petronas Twin Towers. Kuala Lumpur City Centre. No phone.

After 5 years of planning and building, Petronas Twin Towers has been completed. Standing at a whopping 451.9 meters (1,482 ft.) above street level, the towers are the tallest buildings in the world. From the outside, the structures are designed with the kind of geometric patterns common to Islamic architecture, and on levels 41 and 42 the two towers are linked by a bridge. Opened just after the regional economic crisis, the 88 floors of each tower are half empty—not because tourists aren't allowed in to look around, but because they can't rent the space.

Sri Mahamariaman Temple. Jalan Bandar. No phone.

With a recent face-lift (Hindu temples must renovate every 12 years), this bright temple livens the gray street scene around. It's a beautiful temple tucked away in a narrow street in KL's Chinatown area, which was built by Thambusamy Pillai, a pillar of old KL's Indian community.

Sultan Abdul Samad Building. Jalan Raja. No phone.

In 1897 this exotic building was designed by Regent Alfred John Bidwell, a colonial architect responsible for many of the buildings in Singapore. He chose a style called "Muhammadan" or "Neo-saracenic," which combines Indian Muslim architecture with Gothic and other Western elements. Built to house government administrative offices, today it is the home of Malaysia's Supreme and High Courts.

GOLF

People from all over Asia flock to Malaysia for its golf courses, many of which are excellent standard courses designed by pros. For a good time, call **Bangi Golf Resort,** No. 1 Persiaran Bandar, Bandar Baru Bangi, 43650 Selangor (☎ **03/825-3728;** fax 03/825-3726); it has 18 holes, par 72, designed by Ronald Fream, with greens fees of RM100 (US$26.30) weekdays, RM170 (US$44.75) weekends and holidays. **The Mines Resort & Golf Club,** 10 1/5 mile, Jalan Sungei Besi, 43300 Seri Kembangan, Selangor (☎ **03/943-2288**), features 18 holes, par 71, designed by Robert Trent Jones Jr., with greens fees of RM280 (US$73.70) weekdays, RM350 (US$92.10) weekend and holidays. **Suajana Golf & Country Club,** km. 3, Jalan Lapangan Terbang Sultan Abdul Aziz Shah, 46783 Subang Selangor (☎ **03/746-1466;** fax 03/746-7818), has two 18-hole courses, each par 72, deigned by Robert Trent Jones Jr., with greens fees of RM170 (US$44.75) weekdays, RM290 (US$76.30) weekends and holidays.

SHOPPING

Kuala Lumpur is a truly great place to shop. In recent years, mall after mall has risen from city lots, filled with hundreds of retail outlets selling everything from haute couture to cheap chic clothing, electronic goods, jewelry, and arts and crafts. The major **shopping malls** are located in the area around Jalan Bukit Bintang and Jalan Sultan

Ismail. There are also a few malls along Jalan Ampang. **Suria KLCC,** located just beneath the Petronas Twin Towers, has to be KL's best and brightest mall, and its largest. If you purchase electronics, make sure you get an international warranty.

Still the best place for Malaysian handicrafts, the huge **Central Market** on Jalan Benteng (☎ 03/2274-6542) keeps any shopper saturated for hours. There you'll find a jumble of local artists and craftspeople selling their wares in the heart of town. It's also a good place to find Malaysian handicrafts from other regions of the country. One specific shop I like to recommend for Malaysian handicrafts is **Karyaneka,** Lot B, Kompleks Budaya Kraf (☎ 03/264-4344), with a warehouse selection of assorted goods from around the country, all of it fine quality.

Another favorite shopping haunt in KL is **Chinatown,** along Petaling Street. Day and night, it's a great place to wander and bargain for knockoff designer clothing and accessories, sunglasses, T-shirts, souvenirs, fake watches, and pirated videos.

Pasar malam (night markets) are very popular evening activities in KL. Whole blocks are taken up with these brightly lit and bustling markets packed with stalls selling everything you can dream of. They are likely to pop up anywhere in the city. Two good bets for catching one: Go to Jalan Haji Taib after dark until 10pm. On Saturday nights, head for Jalan Tuanku Abdul Rahman.

NIGHTLIFE

There's nightlife to spare in KL, from fashionable lounges to sprawling discos to pubs perfect for lounging. Basically, you can expect to pay about RM11 to RM20 (US$2.90 to US$5.25) for a pint of beer, depending on what and where you order. While quite a few pubs are open for lunch, most clubs won't open until about 6pm or 7pm. These places must all close by 1am, so don't plan on staying out too late. Nearly all have a happy hour, usually between 5 and 7pm, when drink discounts apply to draft beers and "house-pour" (lower shelf) mixed drinks. Generally, you're expected to wear dress casual clothing for these places, but avoid old jeans, tennis shoes, and very revealing outfits.

While there are some very good places in Kuala Lumpur, the true nightlife spot is in a place called ✪ **Bangsar,** just outside the city limits. It's 2 or 3 blocks of bars, cafes, and restaurants that cater to a variety of tastes (in fact, so many expatriates hang out there, they call it Kweiloh Lumpur, "Foreigner Lumpur" in Mandarin). Every taxi driver knows where it is. Get in and ask to go to Jalan Telawi Tiga in Bangsar (fare should be no more than RM5 or RM6), and once there it's very easy to catch a cab back to town. Begin at **The Roof** (☎ 03/282-7168), a three-story open-air cafe/bar that looks like a crazy Louisiana cathouse (you really can't miss it). From there you can try **Echo** (☎ 03/248-3022) for some funky dance music; **Grappa** (☎ 03/287-0080), a sophisticated wine bar; or **Finnegan's** (☎ 03/284-0187), a very rowdy Irish bar. And that's only the beginning.

Back in Kuala Lumpur, there are some very good bars and pubs that I'd recommend. **Bier Keller,** on the ground floor, Menara Haw Par, Jalan Sultan Ismail (☎ 03/201-3313), serves German beers in tankards and traditional German cuisine such as sauerkraut and beer bread. **Delaney's,** ground floor, Park Royal Hotel, Jalan Sultan Ismail (☎ 03/241-5195), has a good selection of draft beers.

For a little live music with your drinks, the **Hard Rock Café,** Wisma Concorde, Jalan Sultan Ismail next to Concorde Hotel (☎ 03/244-4152), hosts the best of the regional bands, which play nightly for a crowd of locals, tourists, and expatriates who take their parties very seriously.

While many of the larger dance clubs in the city cater to young clientele, a good choice for a more upscale dance party is **Modesto's,** Rohas Berkasa, Jalan P. Ramlee (☎ **03/381-1998**).

4 Johor Bahru

Johor Bahru, the capital of the state of Johor, is at the southern tip of the Malaysian peninsula, where Malaysia's north-south highway comes to its southern terminus. Since it's just over the causeway from Singapore, a very short jump by car, bus, or train, it's a popular point of entry to Malaysia. Johor Bahru, or "JB," is not the most fascinating destination in Malaysia, but for a quick day visit from Singapore or as a stopover en route to other Malaysian destinations, it offers some good shopping, sightseeing, and dining.

VISITOR INFORMATION

The Malaysia Tourism Board office in Johor Bahru is at **The Johor Tourist Information Centre (JOTIC),** centrally located on Jalan Ayer Molek, on the second floor (☎ **07/224-2000**). Information is available not only for Johor Bahru, but for the state of Johor as well.

GETTING THERE

BY CAR   If you arrive by car via the causeway you will clear the immigration checkpoint (☎ **07/223-5007**) upon entering the Malaysia side.

BY BUS   Buses to and from other parts of Malaysia are based at the Larkin Bus Terminal off Jalan Garuda in the northern part of the city. Taxis are available at the terminal to take you to the city. The easiest way to catch a bus from KL is at the KL Railway Station. **Plusliner** (☎ **03/227-2760**) runs service 10 times daily for RM16.30 (US$4.30). The trip takes just under 6 hours. Most all other cities in Malaysia have service to Johor Bahru. Consult each city section for bus terminal information. From Singapore, the **Singapore-Johor Express** (☎ **65/292-8149**) operates every 10 minutes between 6:30am and midnight from the Ban Sen Terminal at Queen Street near Arab Street, Singapore. The cost for the half-hour trip is S$2.10 (US$1.25).

If you're looking to depart Johor Bahru via bus, contact one of the following companies at Larkin for route information: **Transnasional** (☎ **07/224-5182**) or **Plusliner/NiCE** (☎ **07/222-3317**).

BY TRAIN   The **Keretapi Tanah Melayu Berhad** (KTM) trains arrive and depart from the Johor Bahru Railway Station at Jalan Tun Abdul Razak, opposite Merlin Tower (☎ **07/223-4727**). Catch trains from KL's railway station (☎ **03/274-7434**) four times daily for a cost between RM13.70 and RM55.50 (US$3.60 and US$14.60), depending on the class you travel. From the **Singapore Railway Station** (☎ **65/222-5165**), on Keppel Road in Tanjong Pagar, the short trip is between S$1.10 and S$4.20 (US$0.66 and US$2.50).

BY PLANE   The **Sultan Ismail Airport,** 30 to 40 minutes outside the city (☎ **07/599-4737**), has regular flights to and from major cities in Malaysia and also from Singapore. The airport tax is RM20 (US$5.25) for international flights and RM5 (US$1.30) for domestic, but this is usually reflected in the price of the ticket. For reservations on **Malaysian Airlines** flights call ☎ **07/334-1001** in Johor Bahru. A taxi from the airport to the city center will run you RM20 to RM25 (US$5.25 to US$6.60) per person. There's also a **Hertz** counter, but to make your reservation you must call their downtown office at ☎ **07/223-7520.** A RM4 (US$1.05) coach service runs between the airport and the JOTIC tourist information center in town. If you use this service for departures, make sure you catch the coach at least 2 hours before departure time. Call ☎ **07/221-7481** for more information.

BY TAXI   Outstation taxis can bring you to Johor Bahru from any major city on the peninsula. From KL's Puduraya Bus Terminal (☎ **03/238-3525** Outstation Taxi) the cost is about RM220 (US$57.90). For taxi stands in other cities please refer to each city's section. For taxi hiring from Johor Bahru call ☎ **07/223-4494.** The outstation taxi stand is located at Larkin Bus Terminal, but for an extra RM10 (US$2.65) they'll pick you up at your hotel.

GETTING AROUND
As in Kuala Lumpur, taxis charge a metered fare, RM2.05 (US$0.54) for the first kilometer and an additional 10 sen for each 200 meters after that. Between midnight and 6am you'll be charged an extra 50% of the total fare. For taxi pickup there's an extra RM1 charge. Call **Citycab** at ☎ **07/354-0007.**

Fast Facts: Johor Bahru

American Express   The American Express office is located at Mansfield Travel, ground floor, New Orchid Plaza, Jalan Wong Ah Fook (☎ **07/224-9511**).

Banks/Currency Exchange   Major banks are located in the city center, and **money changers** at shopping malls and at JOTIC.

Internet/E-mail   For **Internet** connection, I recommend the conveniently located **Weblinks Connexions** in the JOTIC center on Jalan Ayer Molek, L1-2 (☎ **07/225-1287**). They charge RM2.50 (US$0.66) per hour.

Post Office   The main **post office** is on Jalan Dato Onn (☎ **07/223-2555**), just around the corner from JOTIC.

For more Fast Facts about Malaysia, see "Planning a Trip to Malaysia" on p. 456.

ACCOMMODATIONS
Several international chains have accommodations in JB. Most are intended for the business set, but holiday travelers will find the accommodations very comfortable.

The Holiday Inn Crowne Plaza. Jalan Dato Sulaiman, Century Garden, 80990 Johor Bahru, Johor. ☎ **800/465-4329** in the U.S. and Canada, 800/221066 in Australia, 0800/442222 in New Zealand, 0800/987121 in the U.K., or 07/332-3800. Fax 07/331-8884. 350 units. A/C MINIBAR TV TEL. RM370 (US$97.35) double; RM550 (US$144.75) suite. AE, DC, JCB, MC, V.

While this hotel is not walking distance from the city center, it was the first five-star business-class hotel in Johor Bahru, and is larger than the other hotels in the city. It's comfortable and not overly formal, with furniture in traditional fabrics, wood paneling details, and marble floors in the lobby. VCRs are available upon request, with RM15 (US$3.90) video rentals. Services include airport shuttle and valet service. Facilities include a business center, a mid-size outdoor pool, one squash court, and a fitness center with sauna, steam bath, and massage; there is also a shopping complex attached. Recent deals offered by the hotel include a 50% discount off the suite rate.

✪ **The Hyatt Regency.** Jalan Sungai Chat, P.O. Box 222, 80720 Johor Bahru, Johor. ☎ **800/233-1234** or 07/222-1234. Fax 07/223-2718. 400 units. A/C MINIBAR TV TEL. RM420–RM480 (US$110.55–US$126.30) double; RM500–RM600 (US$131.60–US$157.90) executive floor; from RM800 (US$210.55) suite. AE, DC, JCB, MC, V.

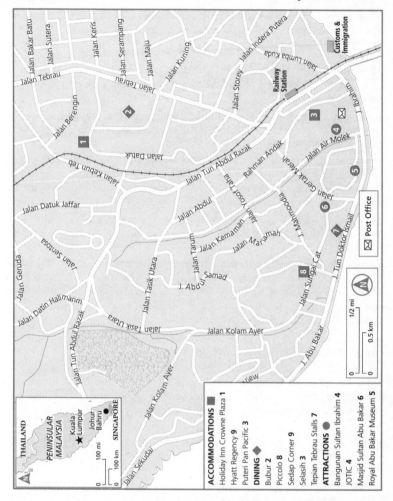

ACCOMMODATIONS ■
Holiday Inn Crowne Plaza **1**
Hyatt Regency **9**
Puteri Pan Pacific **3**
DINING ◆
Bubur **2**
Piccolo **8**
Sedap Corner **9**
Selasih **3**
Tepian Tebrau Stalls **7**
ATTRACTIONS ●
Bangunan Sultan Ibrahim **4**
JOTIC **4**
Masjid Sultan Abu Bakar **6**
Royal Abu Bakar Museum **5**

⌖ Customs & Immigration

■ Post Office

The Hyatt is near the City Square but likes to fancy itself as a city resort, focusing on landscaped gardens and greenery around the premises—the private lagoon-style pool, with gardens seen from the glass windows of the main lobby, is surely spectacular. The deluxe rooms are located better than the others, with views of Singapore and fabulous sunsets. Facilities include a business center, two tennis courts, and a fitness center with sauna, Jacuzzi, and massage. Discount packages are available.

The Puteri Pan Pacific. "The Kotaraya," P.O. Box 293, 80730 Johor Bahru, Johor. ☎ **07/ 223-3333,** or 800/8533 toll-free in Malaysia. Fax 07/223-6622. 460 units. A/C MINIBAR TV TEL. RM330–RM400 (US$86.85–US$105.25) double; RM450–RM2,000 (US$118.40– US$526.30) suite. AE, DC, JCB, MC, V.

The good news about the Puteri is it's located in the heart of the city, near attractions and shopping. The bad news is it is a very busy hotel and human traffic makes it noisy and somewhat on the run-down side. Nevertheless, little traditional touches to the decor make the Pan Pacific unique. Be sure to ask about special discounts, which can bring the price down by as much as half! Facilities include an outdoor pool, tennis and squash courts, fitness center, saunas, steam room, and business center.

DINING

The majority of fine dining in Johor Bahru is in the hotels. Outside the hotels you can sample some great local cuisine, both Malay and Chinese, and wonderful seafood from the city's hawker stalls.

Bubur. 191 Jalan Harimau, Century Garden. ☎ **07/335-5891.** Reservations held for a half hour only. Main courses RM7–RM12 (US$1.85–US$3.15). AE, MC, V. Daily 11am–5am except 4 days into the Chinese New Year. TAIWAN CHINESE.

For fast, inexpensive eats you can even order for take-out, try this place. It's a family restaurant, so it can get pretty lively. The staff is quick and attentive without being imposing. Best dishes are the traditional braised pork in soy sauce and the grilled butterfish in black bean sauce.

✪ **Piccolo.** Hyatt Regency, Jalan Sungai Chat. ☎ **07/222-1234.** Main courses RM20–RM58 (US$5.25–US$15.25). AE, DC, JCB, MC, V. Daily 11:30am–2:30pm and 6:30–10:30pm. ITALIAN.

Perhaps the most popular restaurant for the expatriate community in Johor Bahru, Piccolo's lush lagoon-style poolside ambience has a very tropical and relaxed feel. Under the timber awning, the high ceiling and bamboo blinds make for romantic terrace dining. The antipasto is wonderful, as are dishes like chicken with shrimp and spinach. The grilled seafood is outstanding.

Sedap Corner. 11 Jalan Abdul Samad. ☎ **07/224-6566.** Reservations recommended. Main courses RM4.50–RM24 (US$1.20–US$6.30), though most dishes no more than RM6 (US$1.60). No credit cards. Daily 9am–9:45pm. THAI/CHINESE/MALAY.

Sedap Corner is very popular with the locals. It's dressed down in metal chairs and Formica-top tables, with a coffee shop feel. Local dishes like sambal sabah, otak-otak, and fish head curry are house specials, and you don't have to worry about them being too spicy.

✪ **Selasih.** The Puteri Pan Pacific, "The Kotaraya." ☎ **07/223-3333,** ext. 3151. Reservations recommended. Buffet lunch RM28 (US$7.35); buffet dinner RM40 (US$10.55). AE, DC, JCB, MC, V. Daily 11:30am–2:30pm; Fri–Sat 6:30pm–10:30pm. MALAY.

For a broad-range sampling of Malaysian cuisine, try Selasih, which has a daily buffet spread of more than 70 items featuring regional dishes from all over the country. Each night, the dinner buffet is accompanied by traditional Malay music and dance performances. Children and seniors receive a 50% discount.

ATTRACTIONS

The sights in Johor Bahru are few, but there are some interesting museums and a beautiful istana and mosque. It's a fabulous place to stay for a day, especially if it's a day trip from Singapore, but to stay longer may be stretching the point.

Bangunan Sultan Ibrahim (State Secretariat Building). Jalan Abdul Ibrahim. No phone.

The saracenic flavor of this building makes it feel older than it truly is. Built in 1940, today it houses the State Secretariat.

Masjid Sultan Abu Bakar. Jalan Masjid. No phone.

This mosque was commissioned by Sultan Ibrahim in 1890 after the death of his father, Sultan Abu Bakar. It took 8 years and RM400,000 to build, and is one of the most beautiful mosques in Malaysia—at least from the outside. The inside? I can't tell

Hawker Centers

The ✪ **Tepian Tebrau Stalls** in Jalan Skudai (along the seafront) and the stalls near the **Central Market** offer cheap local eats in hawker-center style. The dish that puts Johor Bahru on the map, *ikan bakar* (barbecued fish with chiles), is out of this world at the Tepian Tebrau stalls.

---

you. I showed up in "good Muslim woman" clothing, took off my shoes, and crept up to the outer area (where I know women are allowed), and a Haji flew out of an office and shooed me off in a flurry. He asked if I was Muslim, I said no, and he said I wasn't allowed in. When I reported this to the tourism office at JOTIC, they thought I was nuts, and said anyone with proper attire could enter the appropriate sections. Let me know if you get in.

✪ **Royal Abu Bakar Museum.** Grand Palace, Johor. Jalan Tun Dr Ismail. ☎ **07/223-0555.** RM26.60 (US$7) adults, RM11.40 (US$3) children under 12. Sat–Thurs 9am–5pm.

Also called the Istana Besar, this gorgeous royal palace was built by Sultan Abu Bakar in 1866. Today it houses the royal collection of international treasures, costumes, historical documents, fine art from the family collection, and relics of the Sultanate.

SPORTS & THE OUTDOORS

In addition to its cities and towns, Johor also has some beautiful nature to take in, which is doubly good if you have only a short time to see Malaysia and can't afford to travel north to some of the larger national parks.

Johor Endau Rompin National Park is about 488 square kilometers (293 sq. miles) of lowland forest. There's jungle trekking through 26 kilometers (16 miles) of trails and over rivers to see diverse tropical plant species, colorful birds, and wild animals. Unfortunately, you'll have to be a camper to really enjoy the park, as this is the only accommodation you'll get. Still, for those who love the great outdoors, first contact the National Parks (Johor) Corporation, JKR 475, Bukit Timbalan, Johor Bahru (☎ **07/223-7471**), for entry permission. You'll have to take an outstation taxi from Johor Bahru (cost: RM60/US$15.80); for booking, call ☎ **07/223-4494** to Kluang. The taxi driver will drop you at the shuttle to the park entrance. Take this shuttle (which you'll prearrange through the National Parks Board) to the park entrance at Kahang. The 3-hour trip costs RM350 (US$92.10) for two people, then you'll have to pay the RM20 (US$5.25) per-person entrance fee to the park. They can rent you all the gear you'll need, but you must bring your own food, and remember to boil your drinking water at least 10 minutes to get it into a potable condition.

The **Waterfalls at Lombong,** near Kota Tinggi, measuring about 34 meters (112 ft.) high, are about 56 kilometers (34 miles) northeast of Johor Bahru. You can cool off in the pools below the falls and enjoy the area's chalets, camping facilities, restaurant, and food stalls. An outstation taxi will also take you to the falls, which are a little off the track on your way east to Desaru. The cost would also be around RM60 (US$15.80).

GOLF

Johor is a favorite destination for **golf** enthusiasts. The Royal Johor Country Club and Pulai Springs Country Club are just outside Johor Bahru and offer a range of country club facilities, while other courses require a bit more traveling time, but offer resort-style accommodations. *One note of caution:* If you play in Johor, especially at the Royal Johor Country Club, don't wear yellow. It is the official color of the sultan, and is worn only by him when he visits the courses.

The most famous course has to be the **Royal Johor Country Club,** 3211, Jalan Larkin, 80200 Johor Bahru, Johor (☎ **07/223-3322;** fax 07/224-0729). This 18-hole, par-72 course provides the favored game of the Sultan of Johor, so they don't accept walk-ins. You must contact the club manager beforehand to obtain admission. Once you've received his okay, expect to pay RM105 (US$27.65) for weekday play and RM210 (US$55.25) for weekends. Other courses to try include **Palm Resort Golf & Country Club,** Jalan Persiaran Golf, off Jalan Jumbo, 81250 Senai, Johor (☎ **07/599-6222;** fax 07/599-6001), with two 18-hole courses, par 72 and 74, and greens fees RM150 (US$39.45) weekdays, RM250 to RM325 (US$65.80 to US$85.55) weekends; **Pulai Springs Country Club,** km 20 Jalan Pontian Lama, 81110 Pulai, Johor (☎ **07/521-2121;** fax 07/521-1818), with two 18-hole courses (both par 72) and greens fees of RM80 to RM100 (US$21.05 to US$26.30) weekdays, RM180 to RM200 (US$47.35 to US$52.65) weekends; or the **Ponderosa Golf & Country Club,** 10-C Jalan Bumi Hijau 3, Taman Molek, 81100 Johor Bahru, Johor (☎ **07/354-9999;** fax 07/355-7400), with 18 holes, par 72, and greens fees of RM80 (US$21.05) weekdays, RM150 (US$39.45) weekends.

SHOPPING

The **Johor Craftown Handicraft Centre,** 36 Jalan Skudai, off Jalan Abu Bakar (☎ **07/236-7346**), has, in addition to a collection of local crafts, demonstration performances of handicrafts techniques. **JOTIC,** 2 Jalan Ayer Molek (☎ **07/224-2000**), is a shopping mall with tourist information, cultural performances, exhibits, demonstrations of crafts, and restaurants.

5 Malacca

While the destinations on the east coast are ideal for resort-style beach getaways, the cities on the west coast are perfect for vacations filled with culture and history, and Malacca is one of the best places to start. The attraction here is the city's cultural heritage, around which a substantial tourism industry has grown. If you're visiting, a little knowledge of this history will help you understand and appreciate all there is to see.

Malacca was founded around 1400 by Parameswara, called **Iskander Shah** in the Malay Annals. After he was chased from Palembang in southern Sumatra by invading Javanese, he set up a kingdom in Singapore (Temasek), and after being overthrown by invaders there, he ran up the west coast of the Malay peninsula to Malacca, where he settled and established a port city. The site was an ideal mid-point in the east-west trade route and was in a favorable spot to take advantage of the two monsoons that dominated shipping routes. Malacca soon drew the attention of the Chinese, and the city maintained very close relations with the mainland as a trading partner and a political ally. The Javanese were also eager to trade in Malacca, as were Muslim merchants. After Parameswara's death in 1414, his son, Mahkota Iskander Shah, converted to Islam and became the first sultan of Malacca. The word of Islam quickly spread throughout the local population.

During the 15th century, Malacca was ruled by a succession of wise sultans who expanded the wealth and stability of the economy, built up the administration's coffers, extended the sultanate to the far reaches of the Malay peninsula, Singapore, and parts of northern Sumatra, and thwarted repeated attacks by the Siamese. The success of the empire was drawing international attention.

The Portuguese were one of the powers eyeing the port and formulating plans to dominate the east-west trade route, establish the naval supremacy of Portugal, and

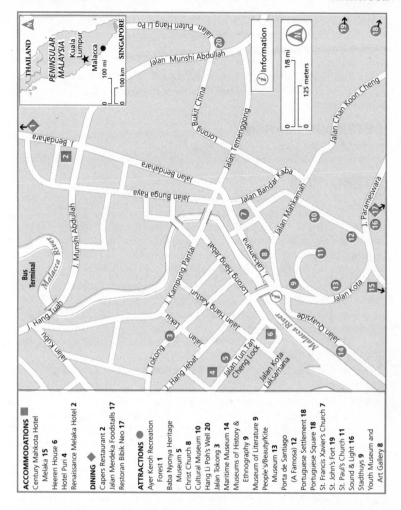

THAILAND

PENINSULAR MALAYSIA

Kuala Lumpur

Malacca

SINGAPORE

100 mi

100 km

Jalan Puteri Hang Li Po

Jalan Munshi Abdullah

i Information

N

1/8 mi

125 meters

Jalan Chan Koon Cheng

J. Bendahara

Jalan Bendahara

Bukit China

Lorong

Jalan Temenggong

Jalan Bunga Raya

Jalan Bandar Kaba

J. Munshi Abdullah

Malacca River

Bus Terminal

Jalan Mahkamah

Jalan Parameswara

J. Laksamana

J. Kampung Pantai

Lorong Hang Jebat

Jalan Hang Kasturi

Jalan Kota

Malacca River

Jalan Quayside

Jalan Kota Laksamana

Jalan Tun Tan Cheng Lock

Cheng Lock

Lekiu

J. Tokong

J. Hang Jebat

J. Hang Tuah

Jalan Kubu

ACCOMMODATIONS
Century Mahkota Hotel Melaka **15**
Heeren House **6**
Hotel Puri **4**
Renaissance Melaka Hotel **2**

DINING
Capers Restaurant **2**
Jalan Merdeka Foodstalls **17**
Restoran Bibik Neo **17**

ATTRACTIONS
Ayer Keroh Recreation Forest **1**
Baba Nyonya Heritage Museum **5**
Christ Church **8**
Cultural Museum **10**
Hang Li Poh's Well **20**
Jalan Tokong **3**
Maritime Museum **14**
Museums of History & Ethnography **9**
Museum of Literature **9**
People's/Beauty/Kite Museum **13**
Porta de Santiago (A Famosa) **12**
Portuguese Settlement **18**
Portuguese Square **18**
St. Francis Xavier's Church **7**
St. John's Fort **19**
St. Paul's Church **11**
Sound & Light **16**
Stadthuys **9**
Youth Museum and Art Gallery **8**

promote Christianity in the region. They struck in 1511 and conquered Malacca in a battle that lasted only a month. It is believed the local Malaccans had become accustomed to the comforts of affluence and turned soft and vulnerable. After the defeat, the sultanate fled to Johor, where it reestablished the seat of Malay power. Malacca would never again be ruled by a sultan. The Portuguese looted the city and sent its riches off to Lisbon.

The Portuguese were also the first of a chain of ruling foreign powers who would struggle in vain to retain the early economic success of the city. The foreign conquerors had a major strike against them: Their Christianity alienated the locals and repelled Muslim traders. The city quickly became nothing more than a sleepy outpost.

In 1641, the Dutch, with the help of Johor, conquered Malacca and controlled the city until 1795. Again, the Dutch were unsuccessful in rebuilding the glory of past prosperity in Malacca, and the city continued to sleep.

In 1795, the Dutch traded Malacca to the British in return for Bencoolen in Sumatra, being far more concerned with their Indonesian interests anyway. Malacca became a permanent British settlement in 1811, but by this time it had become so poor and alienated that it was impossible to bring it back to life.

The final blow came in 1941, when the city fell under Japanese occupation for 4 years. It wasn't until 1957 that Malacca, along with the rest of Malaysia, gained full independence.

VISITOR INFORMATION

Surprisingly, there is no Malaysia Tourism Board office in Malacca, but there is a locally operated **Malacca Tourism Centre** in the Town Square (☎ **06/283-6538**).

GETTING THERE

While there is an airport in Malacca, it's not open for any flights due to lack of demand. And while Malacca doesn't have a proper train station, the KTM stops at Tampin (☎ **06/441-1034**), 38 kilometers (23.75 miles) north of the city. It's not the most convenient way in and out of Malacca, but if you decide to stop en route between Kuala Lumpur and Johor Bahru, you can easily catch a waiting taxi to your hotel in town for between RM35 and RM40 (US$9.20 and US$10.55).

BY BUS   From Singapore, contact **Malacca-Singapore Express** at ☎ **65/293-5915.** Buses depart seven times daily for the 4½-hour trip (S$11/US$6.60). From Johor Bahru's Larkin Bus Terminal, **Jebat Ekspress** (☎ **07/223-3712**) has five daily buses at a cost of RM9 (US$2.35). From KL's Puduraya Bus Terminal on Jalan Pudu, **Transnasional** (☎ **03/230-5044**) has hourly buses between 8am and 10pm for RM6.80 (US$1.80).

The bus station in Malacca is at Jalan Kilang, within the city. Taxis are easy to find from here.

BY TAXI   Outstation taxis can bring you here from any major city, including Johor Bahru (about RM120/US$31.60) and Kuala Lumpur (RM120/US$31.60). Taxi reservation numbers are listed in each city's section. The outstation taxi stand in Malacca is at the bus terminal on Jalan Kilang. There's no number for reservations.

GETTING AROUND

Most of the historic sights around the town square are well within walking distance. For other trips **taxis** are the most convenient way around, but are at times difficult to find. They're also not as clearly marked as in KL or Johor Bahru. They are also not metered, so be prepared to bargain. Basically, no matter what you do, you'll always be charged a higher rate than a local. Tourists are almost always quoted at RM10 (US$2.65) for local trips. Malaysians pay RM5 (US$1.30). You should try to bargain for a price somewhere in between. Trips to Ayer Keroh will cost about RM20 (US$5.25).

Trishaws (bicycle rickshaws) are all over the historic areas of town, and in Malacca they're renowned for being very, very garishly decorated (which adds to the fun!). Negotiate for hourly rates of about RM15 (US$3.95).

Fast Facts: Malacca

Banks/Currency Exchange   Major banks are located in the historic center of town, with a couple along Jalan Putra.

Internet/E-mail   The most centrally located **Internet** connection is E-netlink Cyber Café, 54 Jalan Parameswara (☎ **06/292-1969**), for RM3 (US$0.79) per hour.

Post Office   The most convenient **post office** location is on Jalan Laksamana (☎ **06/284-8440**).

For more Fast Facts about Malaysia, see "Planning a Trip to Malaysia" on p. 456.

ACCOMMODATIONS

Malacca is not very large, and most of the places to stay are well within walking distance of attractions, shopping, and restaurants.

Century Mahkota Hotel Melaka. Jalan Merdeka, 75000 Malacca. ☎ **800/536-7361** in the U.S., or 06/281-2828. Fax 06/281-2323. 617 units. A/C MINIBAR TV TEL. RM350 (US$92.10) double; RM350–RM650 (US$92.10–US$171.05) 1–3-bedroom apt. AE, DC, JCB, MC, V.

Located along the waterfront, the hotel is walking distance from sightseeing, historical areas, shopping, and commercial centers. It's a suite hotel and while it's not luxurious, its rooms are more like holiday apartments, making it a good choice for families. The views are of either the pools, the shopping mall across the street, or the muddy reclaimed seafront. Facilities include two outdoor pools, a fitness center with sauna and massage, tennis and squash courts, a children's playground, a game room, minigolf and access to nearby golf, and a business center. It's across the street from the largest shopping mall in Malacca.

✪ **Heeren House.** 1 Jalan Tun Tan Cheng Lock, 75200 Malacca. ☎ **06/281-4241.** Fax 06/281-4239. 7 units. A/C TV TEL. Sun–Thurs RM129–RM139 (US$33.95–US$36.60) double; RM239 (US$62.90) family suite. No credit cards.

This is the place to stay in Malacca for a taste of the local culture. Started by a local family, the guest house is a renovated 100-year-old building furnished in traditional Peranakan and colonial style and located right in the heart of historical European Malacca. All the bedrooms have views of the Malacca River, and outside the front door of the hotel is a winding stretch of old buildings housing antiques shops. Just walk out and wander. The rooms on the higher floors are somewhat larger. Laundry service is available, and there's a cafe and gift shop on the premises.

Hotel Puri. 118 Jalan Tun Tan Cheng Lock, 75200 Malacca. ☎ **06/282-5588.** Fax 06/281-5588. 50 units. A/C TV TEL. RM150 (US$39.45) double; RM245 (US$64.45) suite. Rates include breakfast. AE, MC, V.

In the olden days, Jalan Tun Tan Cheng Lock was known as "Millionaire Row" for all the wealthy families that lived here. This old "mansion" has been converted into a guest house, its tiled parlor has become a lobby, and the courtyard is where breakfast is served each morning. While Hotel Puri isn't big on space, it is big on value (discount rates can be pretty low). Rooms are very clean, and while not overly stylish, are comfortable enough for any weary traveler. Friendly and responsive staff add to the appeal.

✪ **Renaissance Melaka Hotel.** Jalan Bendahara, 75100 Malacca. ☎ **06/284-8888** in Malaysia or 800/601-1882 in Singapore. Fax 06/284-9269. 316 units. A/C MINIBAR TV TEL. RM437 (US$115) double; RM495–RM4,025 (US$130.25–US$1,059.20) suite. AE, JCB, MC, V.

Renaissance is one of the more posh hotels in Malacca, and, according to business travelers, is the most reliable place for quality accommodations—but aside from the pieces of Peranakan porcelain and art in the public areas, you could almost believe you weren't in Malacca at all. The hotel is, however, situated in a good location, though you'll still need a taxi to most of the sights. Renovations were completed 2 years ago to upgrade the guest rooms, which are fairly large and filled with Western comforts. Don't expect much from the views, as the hotel is in a more business-minded part of the city. No historical landmarks to gaze upon here. Facilities include an outdoor pool; fitness center with massage, sauna, and steam; two indoor squash courts; a tour operator desk; and a beauty salon. Golf is located nearby.

DINING

In Malacca you'll find the typical mix of authentic Malay and Chinese food, and as the city was the major settling place for the Peranakans in Malaysia, their unique style of food is featured in many of the local restaurants.

A good recommendation for a quick bite at lunch or dinner if you're strolling in the historical area is the long string of **open-air food stalls** along Jalan Merdeka, just between Mahkota Plaza Shopping and Warrior Square. **Mama Fatso's** is especially good for Chinese style seafood and Malay sambal curry. A good meal will run you about RM35 to RM40 (US$9.20 to US$10.55) per person. And believe me, it's a good meal.

✪ **Capers Restaurant.** Renaissance Melaka Hotel, Jalan Bendahara. ☎ **06/284-8888.** Reservations recommended. Main courses RM20–RM48 (US$5.25–US$12.65). AE, DC, MC, V. Mon–Sat 6:30–10:30pm. CONTINENTAL.

This is the only fine-dining establishment in Malacca at the moment, which means it is quite formal and pricey. Warm lighting and crystal and silver flatware are only a few of the many details that add to the elegant and romantic atmosphere. The signature dishes, like grilled tenderloin, come from the charcoal grill. The panfried sea bass is served quite artfully in a ginger and dill sauce over bok choy and potatoes. Their wine list is large and international (including Portuguese selections, in keeping with the Malacca theme).

Portuguese Settlement. Jalan d'Albuquerque off Jalan Ujon Pasir. No phone. Main courses RM15–RM20 (US$3.95–US$5.25) per person. No credit cards. Open nightly from 6pm. PORTUGUESE MALACCA

For a taste of Portuguese Malacca head down to the Portuguese Settlement, where open-air food stalls by the water sell an assortment of dishes inspired by these former colonial rulers, including many fresh seafood offerings. Saturday nights are best when, at 8pm, there's a cultural show with music and dancing.

✪ **Restoran Bibik Neo.** No. 6, ground floor, Jalan Merdeka, Taman Melaka Raya. ☎ **06/281-7054.** Reservations recommended. Main courses RM5–RM15 (US$1.30–US$3.95). AE, DC, MC, V. Daily 11am–3pm and 6–10pm. PERANAKAN.

For a taste of the local cuisine, the traditional Nyonya food here is delicious and very reasonably priced. And while the restaurant isn't exactly tops in terms of decor, be assured that the food here is excellent and authentic. Ikan assam with eggplant is a mild fish curry that's very rich and tasty, but I always go for the otak-otak (pounded fish and spices baked in a banana leaf).

ATTRACTIONS

To really understand what you're seeing in Malacca you have to understand a bit about the history, so be sure to read the introduction at the beginning of this section. Most of the really great historical places are on either side of the Malacca River. Start at Stadthuys (the old town hall) and you'll see most of Malacca pretty quickly.

MUSEUMS

✪ **Baba Nyonya Heritage Museum.** 48/50 Jalan Tun Tan Cheng Lock. ☎ **06/283-1273.** Admission RM8 (US$2.10) adults, RM 4 (US$1.05) children. Daily 10am–12:30pm and 2–4:30pm.

Called Millionaire's Row, Jalan Tun Ten Cheng Lock is lined with row houses that were built by the Dutch and later bought by wealthy Peranakans; the architectural style reflects their East-meets-West lifestyle. The Baba Nyonya Heritage Museum sits at nos. 48 and 50 as a museum of Peranakan heritage. The entrance fee includes a guided tour.

✪ **The Cultural Museum.** Kota Rd., next to Porta de Santiago. ☎ **06/282-6526.** Admission RM1.50 (US$0.39) adults, RM0.50 (US$0.13) children. Sat–Thurs 9am–6pm, Fri 9am–12:45pm and 2:45–6pm.

A replica of the former palace of Sultan Mansur Syah (1456–77), this museum was rebuilt according to historical descriptions to house a fine collection of cultural artifacts such as clothing, weaponry, and royal items.

The Maritime Museum and the Royal Malaysian Navy Museum. Quayside Rd. ☎ **06/282-6526.** Admission RM2.50 (US$0.66) adults, RM0.50 (US$0.13) children. Sat–Thurs 9am–6pm, Fri 9am–12:45pm and 2:45–6pm.

These two museums are located across the street from one another but share admission fees. The Maritime Museum is in a restored 16th-century Portuguese ship, with exhibits dedicated to Malacca's history with the sea. The Navy Museum is a modern display of Malaysia's less-pleasant relationship with the sea.

✪ **The Museums of History & Ethnography and The Museum of Literature.** Stadthuys. Located at the circle intersection of Jalan Quayside, Jalan Laksamana, and Jalan Chan Koon Cheng. ☎ **06/282-6526.** Admission RM2.50 (US$0.66) adults, RM0.50 (US$0.13) children. Sat–Thurs 9am–6pm, Fri 9am–12:45pm and 2:45–6pm.

The Stadthuys Town Hall was built by the Dutch in 1650, and it's now home to the Malacca Ethnographical and Historical Museum, which displays customs and traditions of all the peoples of Malacca, and takes you through the rich history of this city. Behind Stadthuys, the Museum of Literature includes old historical accounts and local legends. Admission price is for both exhibits.

The Peoples Museum, The Museum of Beauty, The Kite Museum, and the Governor of Melaka's Gallery. Kota Rd. ☎ **06/282-6526.** Admission RM2.50 (US$0.66) adults, RM0.50 (US$0.13) children. Sat–Thurs 9am–6pm, Fri 9am–12:45pm and 2:45–6pm.

This strange collection of displays is housed under one roof. The Peoples Museum is the story of development in Malacca. The Museum of Beauty is a look at cultural differences of beauty throughout time and around the world. The Kite Museum features the traditions of making and flying *wau* (kites) in Malaysia, and the governor's personal collection is on exhibit at the Governor's Gallery.

The Youth Museums and Art Gallery. Laksamana Rd. ☎ **06/282-6526.** Admission RM1 adults (US$0.26), RM0.50 (US$0.13) children. Sat–Thurs 9am–6pm, Fri 9am–12:45pm and 2:45–6pm.

In the old General Post office are these displays dedicated to Malaysia's youth organizations and to the nation's finest artists. An unusual combination.

HISTORICAL SITES

Christ Church. Located on Jalan Laksamana. No phone.

The Dutch built this place in 1753 as a Dutch Reform Church, and its architectural details include such wonders as ceiling beams cut from a single tree and a Last Supper glazed tile motif above the altar. It was later consecrated as an Anglican church, and mass is still performed today in English, Chinese, and Tamil.

Hang Li Poh's Well. Located off Jalan Laksamana Cheng Ho (Jalan Panjang). No phone.

Also called "Sultan's Well," Hang Li Poh's Well was built in 1495 to commemorate the marriage of Chinese Princess Hang Li Poh to Sultan Mansor Shah. It is now a wishing well, and folks say that if you toss a coin in, you'll someday return to Malacca.

✪ **Jalan Tokong.**

Not far from Jalan Tun Tan Cheng Lock is Jalan Tokong, called the "Street of Harmony" by the locals because it has three coexisting places of worship: the Kampong Kling Mosque, the Cheng Hoon Teng Temple, and the Sri Poyyatha Vinayar Moorthi Temple.

✪ **Porta de Santiago (A Famosa).** Located on Jalan Kota, at the intersection of Jalan Parameswara. No phone.

Once the site of a Portuguese fortress called A Famosa, all that remains today of the fortress is the entrance gate, which was saved from demolition by Sir Stamford Raffles. When the British East India Company demolished the place, Raffles realized the arch's historical value and saved it. The fort was built in 1512, but the inscription above the arch, "Anno 1607," marks the date when the Dutch overthrew the Portuguese.

Portuguese Settlement and Portuguese Square. Located down Jalan d'Albuquerque off Jalan Ujon Pasir in the southern part of the city.

The Portuguese Settlement is an enclave once designated for Portuguese settlers after they conquered Malacca in 1511. Some elements of their presence remain in the Lisbon-style architecture. Later, in 1920, the area was a Eurasian neighborhood. In the center of the settlement, Portuguese Square is a modern attraction with Portuguese restaurants, handicrafts, souvenirs, and cultural shows. It was built in 1985 in an architectural style to reflect the surrounding flavor of Portugal.

St. John's Fort. Located off Lorong Bukit Senjuang. No phone.

The fort, built by the Dutch in the late 18th century, sits on top of St. John's Hill. Funny how the cannons point inland, huh? At the time, threats to the city came from land. It was named after a Portuguese church to St. John the Baptist, which originally occupied the site.

St. Paul's Church. Located behind Porta de Santiago. No phone.

The church was built by the Portuguese in 1521, but when the Dutch came in, they made it part of A Famosa, converting the altar into a cannon mount. The open tomb inside was once the resting place of St. Francis Xavier, a missionary who spread Catholicism throughout Southeast Asia, and whose remains were later moved to Goa.

St. Francis Xavier's Church. Located on Jalan Laksamana. No phone.

This church was built in 1849 and dedicated to St. Francis Xavier, a Jesuit who brought Catholicism to Malacca and other parts of Southeast Asia.

Sound & Light. Warrior Square, Jalan Kota. ☎ **06/282-6526.** Admission RM5 (US$1.30) adults, RM2 (US$0.53) children. Shows nightly at 9:30pm.

The Museums Department has developed a sound-and-light show at the Warrior Square, the large field in the historical center of the city, which narrates the story of Malacca's early history, lighting up the historical buildings in the area for added punch. This is a good activity when you first arrive to help you get your historical bearings.

OTHER ATTRACTIONS

Outside of Malacca is the 202 hectares (500 acres) of forest that make up **Ayer Keroh Recreational Forest,** where many attractions have been built. A taxi from Malacca will run you about RM20 (US$5.25). See the **Reptile Park** (☎ 06/231-9136), admission RM4 (US$1.05) adult, RM2 (US$0.53) child, open daily 9am to 6pm; the **Butterfly & Reptile Sanctuary** (☎ 06/232-0033), admission RM5 (US$1.30) adult, RM3 (US$0.79) child, open daily 8:30am to 5:30pm; **The Malacca Zoo** (☎ 06/232-4053), admission RM3 (US$0.79) adult, RM1 (US$0.26) child, open daily 9am to 6pm; and the **Taman Mini Malaysia/Mini ASEAN** (☎ 06/231-6087), admission RM5 (US$1.30) adult, RM2 (US$0.53) child, open 9am to 5pm daily.

SHOPPING

Antiques hunting has been a major draw to Malacca for decades. Distinct Peranakan and teak furniture, porcelain, and household items fetch quite a price these days, due to a steady increase in demand for these rare treasures. The area down and around **Jalan Tun Tan Cheng Lok** sports many little antiques shops that are filled with as many gorgeous items as any local museum. Whether you're buying or just looking, it's a fun way to spend an afternoon.

Modern shopping malls are sprouting up in Malacca, the biggest being the **Mahkota Parade** on Jalan Merdeka, just south of the field (Warrior Square) in the historic district. Two hundred retail stores sell everything from books to clothing.

For crafts, start at **Karyaneka** (☎ 06/284-3270) on Jalan Laksamana close to the Town Square. If you travel down Laksamana you'll find all sorts of small crafts and souvenir shops.

There's also a daily **flea market** on the north end of the field (Warrior Square) just in the historic district. Try your bargaining skills here for batiks, baskets, regional crafts, and souvenirs.

6 Genting Highlands

Genting Highlands, the "City of Entertainment," serves as Malaysia's answer to Las Vegas, complete with bright lights (that can be seen from Kuala Lumpur) and gambling. And while most people come here to gamble, there's a wide range of other activities, although most of them seem to serve the purpose of entertaining the kids while you bet their college funds at the roulette wheel. Still, nestled in the cool mountains above the capital city, it's a hop from town and a fun diversion from all that *culture!*

VISITOR INFORMATION

The Genting Highlands Resort is owned and operated by Resorts World Berhad, who'll be glad to provide you with any further information. For hotel reservations call ☎ 03/262-3555 or fax 03/261-6611. You can also visit their central office at Wisma Genting on Jalan Sultan Ismail in KL.

GETTING THERE

For buses from Kuala Lumpur, call Genting Highlands Transport, operating buses every half hour from 6:30am to 9pm daily from the Pekeliling Bus Terminal on Jalan Ipoh. The cost for one-way is RM2.60 (US$0.68) and the trip takes 1 hour. The bus lets you off at the foot of the hill, where you take the cable car to the top for RM3 (US$0.79). For bus information, call ☎ 03/441-0173.

You can also get there by hiring an outstation taxi. The cost is RM40 (US$10.55) and can be arranged by calling the Puduraya outstation taxi stand at ☎ 03/238-3525.

ACCOMMODATIONS

There are four hotels of varying prices within the resort. Rates vary depending on whether it's the low season, shoulder season, peak season, or super peak. The calendar changes each year, but basically weekends are peak, as well as the last week in November through the end of December. Super peak times are around Christmas, the calendar New Year, and Chinese New Year, with a few other days dotted over the summer. With the above exceptions, weekdays are generally low season.

Genting Hotel. Genting Highlands 69000, Pahang Darul Makmur. ☎ **03/211-1118.** Fax 03/211-1888. 700 units. A/C MINIBAR TV TEL. Low season RM190 (US$50) double; shoulder RM230 (US$60.55) double; peak RM280 (US$73.70) double; super peak RM350 (US$92.10) double. AE, MC, V.

Genting Hotel is a newer property in the resort complex, and is linked directly to the casino. Promotional rates can be as low as RM97 for low period weekdays.

Highlands Hotel. Genting Highlands 69000, Pahang Darul Makmur. ☎ **03/211-1118.** Fax 03/211-1888. 875 units. A/C MINIBAR TV TEL. Low season RM210 (US$55.25)double; shoulder RM250 (US$65.80) double; peak RM300 (US$78.95) double; super peak RM370 (US$97.35) double. AE, MC, V.

Highlands Hotel's main attraction is its direct link to the casino. You'll pay the highest rate here, as promotional rates in this hotel are very rare.

Resort Hotel. Genting Highlands 69000, Pahang Darul Makmur. ☎ **03/211-1118.** Fax 03/211-1888. 800 units. A/C MINIBAR TV TEL. Low season RM160 (US$42.10) double; shoulder RM190 (US$50) double; peak RM230 (US$60.55) double; super peak RM 290 (US$76.30) double. AE, MC, V.

Resort Hotel is comparable to the Theme Park Hotel below, but it's a little newer and the double occupancy rooms all have two double beds and standing showers only.

Theme Park Hotel. Genting Highlands 69000, Pahang Darul Makmur. ☎ **03/211-1118.** Fax 03/211-1888. 440 units. A/C MINIBAR TV TEL. Low season RM120 (US$31.60) double; shoulder RM 160 (US$42.10) double; peak RM200 (US$52.65) double; super peak RM220 (US$57.90) double. AE, MC, V.

The Theme Park Hotel is a little less expensive than the others, primarily because it's a little older and you must walk outside to reach the casino. Promotional rates during the week can be as low as RM62 for up to three people in one room.

DINING & ENTERTAINMENT

Genting doesn't stop at the casinos when it comes to nightlife. International entertainers perform pop concerts, and the theaters put on everything from lion dance competitions to Wild West shows to magic extravaganzas. The **Genting International Showroom,** on the second floor of the Genting Hotel, hosts a show package, with theater-seating tickets starting from RM40 (US$10.55) and cocktail seats starting at RM50 (US$13.15), drinks not included. For dining, the most highly recommended place is **The Peak Restaurant & Lounge,** Genting's fine dining restaurant on the 17th floor of the Genting Hotel. Ask about special one-price combination dinner and show tickets.

ATTRACTIONS

Gambling, gambling, and more gambling. The **resort casino** is open 24 hours. Entry is a refundable deposit of RM200 (US$52.65) whether you're a guest at the resort or just visiting for the day. By the way, you must be at least 21 years old to enter the casino. Inside it's a gambler's paradise, with all the games you'd care to wager a bet on, including blackjack, roulette, and baccarat.

For outdoor excitement, the resort has an **outdoor pond** with boats and a **horse ranch** with riding for all levels of experience. For somewhat less excitement (but better photo ops) the **cable car ride** down the mountain from the resort offers aerial views of the Malaysian jungle. A one-way fare is RM3 (US$0.79) for adults and children; Sunday to Thursday 8am to 7:30pm and Friday and Saturday 8am to 8:30pm. Additional facilities include a bowling alley and an indoor heated pool. The **Awana Golf and Country Club** (☎ 03/211-3025; fax 03/211-3535) is the premier golf course in Genting.

For children, there's the huge **Genting Theme Park** (☎ 03/211-1118; ext. 58240), covering 100,000 square feet and mostly filled with rides, plus many Western fast-food eating outlets, games, and other attractions. The Outdoor Theme Park has four roller coasters, flume rides, and a balloon ride, while the Indoor Theme Park has a Space Odyssey roller coaster and a motion simulator. Don't miss the Disco Bumper Cars! Admission to both parks is free, but to ride the rides you'll have to buy a 1-day unlimited ride pass, which will set you back RM30 (US$7.90) for adults and RM18 (US$4.75) for children. The Outdoor Theme Park is open Monday to Friday 10am to 6:45pm, Saturday and Sunday 8am to 7:45pm; Indoor Theme Park daily 9am to 2am.

7 Cameron Highlands

Although Cameron Highlands is in Pahang, it is most often accessed via Kuala Lumpur. Located in the hills, Cameron Highlands has a cool climate, which makes it the perfect place for luxury resorts tailored to weekend getaways by Malaysians, Singaporeans, and international travelers.

Ringlet is the first town you see as you travel up the highlands. It is the main agricultural center. Travel farther up the elevation to **Tanah Rata,** the major tourism town in the Highlands, where you'll find chalets, cottages, and bungalows. The town basically consists of shops along one side of the main street (Jalan Sultan Ahmad Shah) and food stalls and the bus terminal on the other. **Brinchang,** at 1,524 meters (5,029 ft.) above sea level, is the highest town, surrounding a market square where there are shops, Tudor inns, rose gardens, and a Buddhist temple.

Temperatures in the Cameron Highlands average 70°F (21°C) during the day and 50°F (10°C) at night. There are paths for lovely treks though the countryside and to peaks of surrounding mountains. Two waterfalls, the Robinson Falls and Parit Falls, have pools at their feet where you can have a swim.

VISITOR INFORMATION

There are no visitor information services here. They've been closed for a very long time, and have no immediate plans for reopening.

GETTING THERE

Kurnia Bistari Express Bus (☎ 05/491-2978) operates between Kuala Lumpur and Tanah Rata four times daily for RM10.10 (US$2.65) one-way. They don't accept bookings in Kuala Lumpur, asking you to just show up at Puduraya bus terminal to buy your ticket and board the next bus. Kurnia Bistari also provides service to and from Penang two times daily for RM14.10 (US$3.70). The bus terminal is in the center of town along the main drag. Just next to it is the taxi stand. It's a two-horse town; you can't miss either of them. **Outstation taxis** from KL will cost RM180 (US$47.35) for the trip. Call ☎ 03/238-3525 for booking. For trips from Cameron Highlands call ☎ 05/491-2355. Taxis are cheaper on the way back because they don't have to climb the mountains.

GETTING AROUND

Walking in each town is a snap because the places are so small, but the towns are far apart, so a walk between them could take up much time. There are local buses that ply at odd times between them for around RM3 (US$0.79), or you could pick up one of the ancient, unmarked taxis and cruise between towns for RM4 (US$1.05).

Fast Facts: Cameron Highlands

Banks/Currency Exchange You'll find **banks** with ATMs and money-changing services along the main road in Tanah Rata.

Post Office The local **post office** is also in Tanah Rata (☎ **05/491-1051**).

For more Fast Facts about Malaysia, see "Planning a Trip to Malaysia" on p. 456.

ACCOMMODATIONS

✪ **The Cool Point Hotel.** 891 Persiaran Dayang Endah, 39000 Tanah Rata, Cameron Highlands, Pahang Darul Makmur. ☎ **05/491-4914.** Fax 05/491-4070. 47 units. A/C TV TEL. Off-season RM90–RM140 (US$23.70–US$36.85) double; peak season RM125–RM180 (US$32.90–US$47.35) double. MC, V.

Cool Point has an outstanding location, a 2-minute walk to Tanah Rata. While the modern building has some Tudor-like styling on the outside, the rooms inside are pretty standard, but the place is very clean. Make sure you book your room early. This place is always a sellout. Cool Point also has a restaurant serving local and Western dishes.

✪ **The Smokehouse Hotel.** Tanah Rata, Cameron Highlands, Pahang Darul Makmur. ☎ **05/491-1215.** Fax 05/491-1214. 13 units. TEL. RM440–RM680 (US$115.80–US$178.95) suite. AE, DC, MC, V.

Situated between Tanah Rata and Brinchang is a gorgeous Tudor mansion with lush gardens outside and a stunning old world ambience inside. Built in 1937 as a country house in the heyday of colonial British getaways, the conversion into a hotel has kept the place happily in the 1930s. Guest suites have four-poster beds and antique furnishings, and are stocked with plush amenities. The hotel encourages guests to play golf at the neighboring course, sit for afternoon tea with strawberry confections, or trek along nearby paths (for which they'll provide a picnic basket). It's all a bizarre escape from Malaysia, but an extremely charming one.

DINING

For fine dining in a restaurant, the continental cuisine at **The Smokehouse Hotel** (☎ **05/491-1215**) is really your only option. And although it's pricey, it's top rate. As for a more local experience, there's an alfresco **food court** along the Main Street in Tanah Rata that serves excellent Indo-Malay and western dishes for breakfast, lunch, and dinner at unbeatable prices. Also along Main Street are **cafes** that are good for dinner but seem even more popular for a cold afternoon beer.

ATTRACTIONS

Most of the sights can be seen in a day, but it's difficult to plan your time well. In Cameron Highlands I recommend trying one of the sightseeing outfits in either Brinchang or Tanah Rata, as getting around on your own can be quite difficult. **C. S. Travel & Tours,** 47 Main Rd., Tanah Rata (☎ **05/491-1200;** fax 05/491-2390), is a highly reputable agency that will plan half-day tours for RM15 (US$3.95) or full days starting from RM80 (US$21.05). On your average tour you'll see the Boh tea plantation and factory, flower nurseries, rose gardens, strawberry farms, butterfly farms, and the Sam Poh Buddhist Temple. You're required to pay admission to each attraction yourself. They also provide **trekking and overnight camping tours** in the surrounding hills with local trail guides. Treks are RM30 (US$7.90), camping RM150 (US$39.45) for 2 days/1 night. Bookings are requested at least 1 day in advance. Also, pretty much every hotel can arrange these services for you.

GOLF

If you want to hit around some balls, **Padang Golf,** Main Road between Tanah Rata and Brinchang (☎ 05/491-1126), has 18 holes at par 71, with greens fees around RM42 (US$11.05) on weekdays and RM63 (US$16.60) on weekends. They also provide club rentals, caddies, shoes, and carts.

8 Penang

Penang is unique in Malaysia because, for all intents and purposes, Penang has it all. Tioman Island (see p. 515 below) may have beaches and nature, but it has no shopping or historical sights to speak of. And while Malacca has historical sights and museums, it hasn't a good beach for miles. Similarly, while KL has shopping, nightlife, and attractions, it also has no beach resorts. Penang has all of it: beaches, history, diverse culture, shopping, food—you name it, it has it. If you only have a short time to visit Malaysia but want to take in as wide an experience as you can, Penang is your place.

Since Malaysia's independence in 1957, Penang has had relatively good financial success. Today the state of Penang is made up of the island and a small strip of land on the Malaysian mainland. Georgetown is the seat of government for the state. Penang Island is 285 square kilometers (171 sq. miles) and has a population of a little more than one million. Surprisingly, the population is mostly Chinese (59%), followed by Malays (32%) and Indians (7%).

VISITOR INFORMATION

The main **Malaysia Tourism Board (MTB)** office is located at No. 10 Jalan Tun Syed Sheh Barakbah (☎ 04/261-9067), just across from the clock tower by Fort Cornwallis. There's another information center at **Penang International Airport** (☎ 04/ 643-0501) and a branch on the third level at **KOMTAR** (Kompleks Tun Abdul Razak) on Jalan Penang (☎ 04/261-4461).

GETTING THERE

BY PLANE   **Penang International Airport** (☎ 04/643-0811) has direct flights from Singapore about seven times daily (Singapore Airlines toll-free in Singapore ☎ 1-800/223-8888; Malaysia Airlines ☎ 65/336-6777). From KL, Malaysia Airlines has two flights daily (☎ 03/746-3000). The airport is 20 kilometers (12 miles) from the city. To get into town, you must purchase fixed-rate coupons for taxis (RM23/US$6.05 to Georgetown; RM35/US$9.20 to Batu Feringgi). There's also the **Penang Yellow Bus Company** bus no. 83, which will take you to Weld Quay in Georgetown.

There are also car rentals at the airport. Talk to **Hertz** (☎ 04/643-0208) or **Budget** (☎ 04/643-6025).

BY TRAIN   By rail, the trip from KL to Butterworth takes 6 hours and costs RM58.50 (US$15.40) first-class passage, RM25.40 (US$6.70) for second class, and

RM14.40 (US$3.80) for third class. Three trains leave daily. Call the **KL Railway Station** (☎ **03/274-7434**) for schedule information.

The train will let you off at the **Butterworth Railway Station** (☎ **04/334-7962**), on Jalan Bagan Dalam (near the ferry terminal) in Butterworth, on the Malaysian mainland. From there, you can take a taxi to the island or head for the ferry close by.

BY BUS   Many buses will bring you only to Butterworth, so if you want the trip to take you all the way onto the island, make sure you buy a ticket that specifically says Penang. These buses will let you out at **KOMTAR** on Jalan Gladstone across from the Shangri-La Hotel. If you're dropped in Butterworth at the bus terminal on Jalan Bagan Dalam (next to the ferry terminal), you'll need to grab a taxi or take the ferry to the island.

In KL, **Plusliner/NiCE** (☎ **03/272-2760**) departs from the KL Train Station regularly. The NiCE Executive Express coaches leave four times daily, costing RM45 (US$11.85), while the Plusliner standard coaches head for Butterworth three times daily (RM16.50/US$4.35) and Penang island eight times daily (RM18/US$4.75). The trip takes about 4½ hours.

For buses back to KL call the **S. E. Bus Line** (☎ **04/262-8723**) at the main bus terminal in the basement at KOMTAR.

BY FERRY   The ferry to Penang is nestled between the Butterworth Railway Station and the Butterworth bus terminal. It operates 24 hours a day and takes 20 minutes from pier to pier. From 6am to midnight ferries leave every 10 minutes. From midnight to 1:20am boats run every half hour and from 1:20 to 6am they run hourly. Purchase your passage by dropping 60 sen (US$0.16) exact change in the turnstile (there's a change booth if you don't have it). Fare is paid only on the trip to Penang. The return is free. The ferry lets you off at **Pengalan Raja Tun Udah,** Weld Quay (☎ **04/210-2363**).

The ferry will also take cars for a fee of RM7 (US$1.85), which includes passenger fees.

BY TAXI   The outstation taxi stand is in Butterworth (☎ **04/323-2045**). Fares to Butterworth from KL will be about RM240 (US$63.15).

BY CAR   If you're driving you can cross over the 13½-kilometer (8-mile) Penang Bridge, the longest bridge in Southeast Asia. All cars are charged RM7 (US$1.85) for the trip to Penang. It's free on the return.

GETTING AROUND

BY TAXI   Taxis are abundant, but be warned they do not use meters, so you must agree on the price before you ride. Most trips within the city are between RM3 and RM6. If you're staying out at the Batu Feringgi beach resort area, expect taxis to town to run RM20 (US$5.25); RM30 (US$7.90) at night. The ride is about 15 or 20 minutes, but can take 30 during rush hour.

BY BUS   Buses also run all over the island, and are well used by tourists, who don't want to spring RM20 every time they want to go to the beach. The most popular route is the **Hin Bus Co. (Blue Bus) no. 93,** which operates every 10 minutes between Pengkalan Weld (Weld Quay) in Georgetown and the beach resorts at Batu Feringgi. It makes stops at KOMTAR Shopping Plaza and also at the ferry terminal. Fare is RM1 (US$0.25). Give your money to the nice ticket person on board.

CAR RENTAL   Hertz has an office in Georgetown at 38 Farquhar St. (☎ **04/263-5914**).

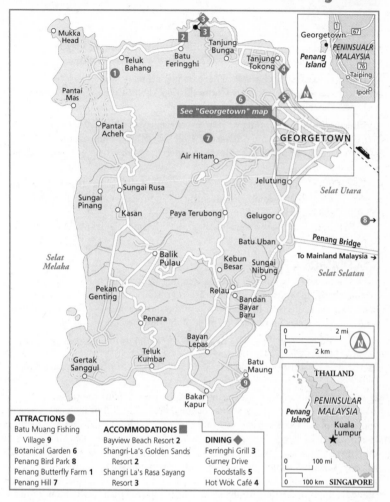

Penang Island

See "Georgetown" map

ATTRACTIONS ●
Batu Muang Fishing
 Village **9**
Botanical Garden **6**
Penang Bird Park **8**
Penang Butterfly Farm **1**
Penang Hill **7**

ACCOMMODATIONS ■
Bayview Beach Resort **2**
Shangri-La's Golden Sands
 Resort **2**
Shangri La's Rasa Sayang
 Resort **3**

DINING ◆
Ferringhi Grill **3**
Gurney Drive
 Foodstalls **5**
Hot Wok Café **4**

BY BICYCLE & MOTORCYCLE   Along Batu Feringgi there are bicycles and motorcycles available for rent.

BY TRISHAW   In Georgetown it's possible to find some trishaw action for about RM15 (US$3.95) an hour. It's fun and I recommend it for traveling between sights, at least for an hour or two.

ON FOOT   I think everyone should walk at least part of the time to see the sights of Georgetown, because in between each landmark and exhibit there's so much more to see. A taxi, even a trishaw, will whisk you right by back alleys where elderly hair-cutters set up alfresco shops, bicycle repairmen sit fixing tubes in front of their stores, and Chinese grannies fan themselves in the shade. The streets of Georgetown are stimulating, with the sights of old trades still being plied on these living streets, the noise of everyday life, and the exotic smells of an old Southeast Asian port. Give yourself at least a day here.

Fast Facts: Penang

American Express   AmEx has an office in Georgetown at Mayflower Acme Tours, Tan Chong Building, 274 Victoria St. (☎ **04/262-6196**).

Banks/Currency Exchange   The banking center of Georgetown is in the downtown area (close to Fort Cornwallis) on Leboh Pantai, Leboh Union and Leboh Downing.

Internet/E-mail   For Internet service in town, try **sTc Net Café**, 221 Chulia St. (☎ **04/264-3378**), which charges RM6 (US$1.60) per hour. Out on Batu Feringgi head for **Cyber By the Beach,** Golden Sands Resort (☎ **04/881-2096**), with fees of RM5 (US$1.30) per hour.

Post Office   The main post office in Georgetown is on Leboh Downing (☎ **04/261-9222**). Another convenient location is out on Jalan Batu Feringgi (☎ **04/881-2555**).

For more Fast Facts about Malaysia, see "Planning a Trip to Malaysia" on p. 456.

ACCOMMODATIONS

While Georgetown has many hotels right in the city for convenient sightseeing, many visitors choose to stay at one of the beach resorts 30 minutes away at Batu Feringgi. Trips back and forth can be a bother (regardless of the resorts' free shuttle services), but if you're not staying in a resort, most of the finer beaches are off limits.

The Bayview Beach Resort. Batu Feringgi Beach, 11100 Penang. ☎ **04/881-2123.** Fax 04/881-2140. 366 units. A/C MINIBAR TV TEL. RM402.50 (US$105.90) hill-view double; RM483 (US$127.10) sea-view double; RM655.50 (US$172.50) hill-view suite; RM862.50 (US$226.95) sea-view suite. AE, DC, JCB, MC, V.

Located right on Batu Feringgi Beach, the Bayview is a relaxing resort with all the conveniences you look for in a large international hotel. The feel of the place is spacious and airy, an ambience carried over into the rooms—the standard double room, for instance, is quite large. Rooms facing the road have views of the neighboring condominium complex, and can be noisy. Get the sea view so you can take advantage of your balcony. Facilities include an outdoor pool, squash and tennis courts, billiards, table tennis, and a fitness center with Jacuzzi, sauna, and steam. Cycling, parasailing, waterskiing, sailing, windsurfing, canoeing, and boat trips to beachside barbecues and fishing spots are all available. Recent discount packages offer 50% discounts off all categories of rooms.

Cathay Hotel. No. 15 Leith St., Georgetown 10200, Penang. ☎ **04/262-6271.** Fax 04/263-9300. 37 units. TV. RM59.80 (US$15.75) double without A/C, RM69 (US$18.15) double with A/C. No credit cards.

The Cathay is highly recommended for its location and price. Within walking distance of the city attractions, it's definitely a budget place, but it has a charming faded elegance. Housed in a traditional Chinese prewar mansion, nice touches include high ceilings, mosaic tile and wood floors, and whitewashed walls. The decor features Chinese lanterns and ceiling fans. You won't find a budget hotel with more style and respectability. The only real faults are the small, old bathrooms and the lack of room service or laundry services.

✪ **The City Bayview Hotel, Penang.** 25–A Farquhar St., Georgetown 10200 Penang. ☎ **04/263-3161.** Fax 04/263-4124. 176 units. A/C MINIBAR TV TEL. RM300–RM350 (US$78.95–US$92.10) double. AE, DC, MC, V.

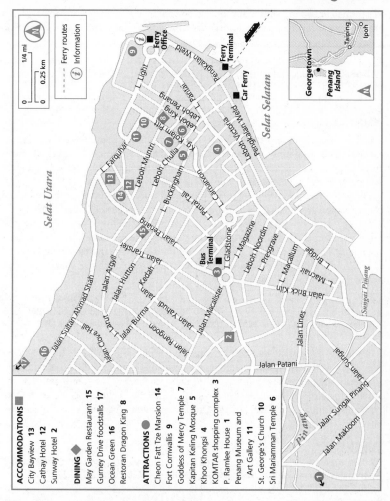

Situated on Farquhar Street, City Bayview has a convenient location for visitors who want to take in the historic and cultural sights of Georgetown. A new wing opened last year featuring large guest rooms that have style and amenities that bring the hotel up to date (before this it hadn't seen renovation since 1975!). Newly renovated suites in the old wing have been completely updated with new furnishings and amenities.

Shangri-La's Golden Sands Resort. Batu Feringgi Beach, 11100 Penang. ☎ **800/ 942-5050** in the U.S. and Canada, 800/222448 in Australia, 0800/442179 in New Zealand, or 04/881-1911. Fax 04/881-1880. www.shangri-la.com. 395 units. A/C MINIBAR TV TEL. RM430–RM610 (US$113.15–US$160.55) double; RM1,250 (US$328.95) suite. AE, DC, JCB, MC, V.

Rasa Sayang's little sister property is located just next door. A newer resort, it is priced lower than the Rasa Sayang, so it attracts more families. The beach, pool area, and public spaces fill up fast in the morning, and folks are occupied all day with beach sports like parasailing and jet skiing, and pool games. For the younger set, a kids' club keeps small ones busy while mom and dad do "boring stuff." Rooms are large with full amenities, and the higher priced categories have views of the pool and sea. Better still, guests here can use the facilities at Rasa Sayang.

✪ **Shangri-La's Rasa Sayang Resort.** Batu Feringgi Beach, 11100 Penang. ☎ **800/ 942-5050** in the U.S. and Canada, 800/222448 in Australia, 0800/442179 in New Zealand, or 04/881-1811. Fax 04/881-1984. www.shangri-la.com. 515 units. A/C MINIBAR TV TEL. RM580–RM680 (US$152.65–US$178.95) double; RM780 (US$205.25) deluxe sea-facing double; RM740 (US$194.75) deluxe garden/patio room; from RM1,000 (US$263.15) suite. AE, DC, JCB, MC, V.

Of all the beachfront resorts on Penang, Rasa Sayang is the finest. It has been here the longest, celebrating its 25-year anniversary in 1998, so it had the first pick of beachfront property and plenty of space to create lush gardens and pool areas. Get a room looking over the pool area, and your private balcony will face the picturesque palm-lined beach. The free-form pool is sprawled amid tropical landscaping and cafes, and the rest of the grounds have strolling gardens that are romantically illuminated in the evenings. The hotel is both elegant and relaxed, with Malay-style decor in the public areas and rooms. You'll also appreciate the good seafood restaurants nearby. Facilities include an outdoor pool, fitness center, small putting green, and table tennis. Guests have access to nearby tennis courts, sailing, boating, and waterskiing. Make sure to ask about the incredible bargain packages.

Sunway Hotel. 33 New Lane, Georgetown 10400 Penang. ☎ **04/229-9988.** Fax 04/228-8899. 262 units. A/C MINIBAR TV TEL. RM330 (US$86.85) double; RM600 (US$157.90) suite. Ask about discounts as low as 165RM (US$43.40) for a double, including American breakfast. AE, DC, MC, V.

The Sunway is centrally located in Georgetown, near the KOMTAR shopping complex and the Penang Museum. Built in 1994, the hotel is warm and elegant, with marble details and a new and modern feel to the open spaces. The rooms are fresh and spacious, and rooms on all sides have views of the city. Facilities include an outdoor pool and a fitness center with Jacuzzi. The hotel can arrange tennis, squash, and sauna at nearby facilities.

DINING

✪ **Feringgi Grill.** Shangri-La's Rasa Sayang Resort, Batu Feringgi Beach. ☎ **04/881-1811.** Reservations recommended. Main courses RM49.50–RM68 (US$13.05–US$17.90). Daily 7–10:30pm. CONTINENTAL.

The Feringgi Grill is comparable to any five-star hotel grill anywhere. From the dreamy lobster bisque to the carving cart of perfectly grilled top-quality meats flown in from all over the world, you'll be living the good life with each bite. A good wine selection will help revive you when you think you've died and gone to heaven. And don't even mention the desserts—the whole cart is a sore temptation sent straight from hell. Feringgi is perfect for a romantic dinner, or a change from all that char koay teow you've been eating in town.

✪ **Hot Wok Café.** 125–D Desa Tanjung, Jalan Tanjung. ☎ **04/899-0858.** Reservations recommended for weekends. Main courses RM9–RM15 (US$2.35–US$3.95). AE, DC, MC, V. Daily 11am–3pm and 6–11pm. PERANAKAN.

This place is the number-one recommended Peranakan restaurant in the city, and small wonder: The food is great and the atmosphere is fabulous. Filled with local treasures such as wooden lattice work, wooden lanterns, carved Peranakan cabinets, tapestries, and carved wood panels, the decor will make you want to just sit back, relax, and take in sights you'd only ever see in a Peranakan home. Their curry capitan, a famous local dish, is curry chicken stuffed with potatoes, with a thick delicious coconut-based gravy. The house specialty is a mean *perut ikan* (fish intestine with roe and vegetable).

✪ **May Garden Restaurant.** 70 Jalan Penang. ☎ **04/261-6806.** Reservations recommended. Main courses start at RM8 (US$2.10); seafood priced by weight in kilograms. AE, DC, MC, V. Daily noon–3pm and 6–10:30pm. CANTONESE.

This is a top Cantonese restaurant in Georgetown, and while it's noisy and not too big on ambience, it has excellent food. But how many Chinese do *you* know who go to places for ambience? It's the food that counts! Outstanding dishes include the tofu and broccoli topped with sea snail slices or the fresh steamed live prawns. They also have suckling pig and Peking duck. Don't agree to all the daily specials or you'll be paying a fortune.

✪ **Ocean Green.** 48F Jalan Sultan Ahmad Shah. ☎ **04/226-2681.** Reservations recommended. Main courses from RM12 (US$3.15); seafood priced according to market value. Daily 9am–11pm. AE, MC, V. SEAFOOD.

I can't rave enough about Ocean Green. If the beautiful sea view and ocean breezes don't make you weep with joy, the food certainly will. A long list of fresh seafood is prepared steamed or fried, with your choice of chile, black bean, sweet and sour, or curry sauces. On the advice of a local food expert, I tried the lobster thermidor, expensive but divine, and the chicken wings stuffed with minced chicken, prawns, and gravy.

Restoran Dragon King. 99 Leboh Bishop. ☎ **04/261-8035.** Main courses RM8–RM20 (US$2.10–US$5.25). No credit cards. Daily 11am–3pm and 6–10pm. PERANAKAN.

Penang is famous around the world for delicious local Peranakan dishes, and Dragon King is a good place to sample the local cuisine at its finest. It was opened 20 years ago by a group of local teachers who wanted to revive the traditional dishes cooked by their mothers. In terms of decor, the place is nothing to shout about—just a coffee shop with tile floors and folding chairs—but all the curries are hand blended to perfection. Their curry capitan will make you weep with joy, it's so rich. But come early for the otak-otak, or it might sell out. While Dragon King is hopping at lunchtime, dinner is quiet.

FOOD STALL DINING

No section on Penang dining would be complete without full coverage of the local food stall scene, which is famous. Penang hawkers can make any dish you've had in Malaysia, Singapore, or even southern Thailand better. I had slimy char koay teow in Singapore and swore off the stuff forever. After being forced to try it in Penang (where the fried flat noodles and seafood are a specialty dish), I was completely addicted. Penang may be attractive for many things—history, culture, nature—but it is loved for its food.

Gurney Drive Foodstalls, toward the water just down from the intersection with Jalan Kelawai, is the biggest and most popular hawker center. It has all kinds of food, including local dishes with every influence: Chinese, Malay, Indian. In addition to the above-mentioned char koay teow, there's *char bee hoon* (a fried thin rice noodle), *laksa* (fish soup with noodles), *murtabak* (a sort of curry mutton burrito), *oh chien* (oyster omelette with chile dip), and *rojak* (a spicy fruit and seafood salad). After you've eaten your way through Gurney Drive, you can try the stalls on **Jalan Burmah** near the Lai Lai Supermarket.

ATTRACTIONS
IN GEORGETOWN

✪ **Cheong Fatt Tze Mansion.** Lebuhraya Leith. No phone. Admission RM12 (US$3.15) adults and children. Open for guided tours only Thurs–Fri at 9am.

Cheong Fatt Tze (1840–1917), once dubbed "China's Rockefeller" by *The New York Times,* built a vast commercial empire in Southeast Asia, first in Indonesia, then in Singapore. He came to Penang in 1890 and continued his success, giving some of his spoils to build schools throughout the region. His mansion, where he lived with his eight wives, was built between 1896 and 1904. Inside are lavish adornments—stained glass, crown moldings, gilded wood-carved doors, ceramic ornaments, and seven staircases.

✪ **Fort Cornwallis.** Lebuhraya Light. No phone. Admission RM1 (US$0.26) adults, RM0.50 (US$0.13) children. Daily 8am–7pm.

Fort Cornwallis is built on the site where Capt. Francis Light, founder of Penang, first landed in 1786. The fort was first built in 1793, but this site was an unlikely spot to defend the city from invasion. In 1810 it was rebuilt in an attempt to make up for initial strategic planning errors. In the shape of a star, the only actual buildings still standing are the outer walls, a gunpowder magazine, and a small Christian chapel. The magazine houses an exhibit of old photos and historical accounts of the old fort.

Goddess of Mercy Temple. Leboh Pitt. No phone.

Dedicated jointly to Kuan Yin, the goddess of mercy, and Ma Po Cho, the patron saint of sea travelers, this is the oldest Chinese temple in Penang. On the 19th of each second, sixth, and ninth month of the lunar calendar, Kuan Yin is celebrated with Chinese operas and puppet shows.

Kapitan Keling Mosque. Jalan Masjid Kapitan Keling (Leboh Pitt). No phone.

Captain Light donated a large parcel of land on this spot for the settlement's sizable Indian Muslim community to build a mosque and graveyard. The leader of the community, known as Kapitan Keling (or Kling, which ironically was once a racial slur against Indians in the region), built a brick mosque here. Later, in 1801, he imported builders and materials from India for a new, brilliant mosque. Expansions in the 1900s topped the mosque with stunning domes and turrets, adding extensions and new roofs.

✪ **Khoo Khongsi.** Lebuhraya Cannon. ☎ **604/261-4609.** Free admission. Daily 9am–5pm.

The Chinese who migrated to Southeast Asia created clan associations in their new homes. Based on common heritage, these social groups formed the core of Chinese life in the new homelands. The Khoo clan, who immigrated from Hokkien province in China, acquired this spot in 1851 and set to work building row houses, administrative buildings, and a clan temple around a large square. The temple here now was actually built in 1906 after a fire destroyed its predecessor. It was believed the original was too ornate, provoking the wrath of the gods. One look at the current temple, a Chinese baroque masterpiece, and you'll wonder how that could possibly be. Come here in August for Chinese operas.

P. Ramlee House. Jalan P. Ramlee. No phone. Free admission. Daily 9am–5pm.

This is the house where legendary Malaysian actor, director, singer, composer, and prominent figurehead of the Malaysian film industry P. Ramlee (1928–73) was born and raised. A gallery of photos from his life and personal memorabilia offer a glimpse of local culture even those who've never heard of him can appreciate.

✪ **Penang Museum and Art Gallery.** Lebuhraya Farquahar. ☎ **04/261-3144.** Free admission. Open Sat–Thurs 9am–5pm.

The historical society has put together this marvelous collection of ethnological and historical findings from Penang, tracing the port's history and diverse cultures through time. It's filled with paintings, photos, costumes, and antiques among much more, all presented with fascinating facts and trivia. Upstairs is an art gallery. Originally the Penang Free School, the building was built in two phases, the first half in 1896 and the second in 1906. Only half of the building remains; the other was bombed to the ground in World War II. It's a favorite stop on a sightseeing itinerary because it's *air-conditioned!*

St. George's Church. Farquhar St. No phone.

Built by Rev. R. S. Hutchins (who was also responsible for the Free School next door, home of the Penang Museum) and Capt. Robert N. Smith, whose paintings hang in the museum, this church was completed in 1818. While the outside is almost as it was then, the contents were completely looted during World War II. All that remains are the font and the bishop's chair.

Sri Mariamman Temple. Lebuhraya Queen. No phone.

This Hindu temple was built in 1833 by a Chettiar, a group of Southern Indian Muslims, and received a major face-lift in 1978 with the help of Madras sculptors. The Hindu Navarithri festival is held here, whereby devotees parade Sri Mariamman, a Hindu goddess worshipped for her powers to cure disease, through the streets in a night procession. It is also the starting point of the Thaipusam Festival, which leads to a temple on Jalan Waterfall.

OUTSIDE GEORGETOWN

Batu Muang Fishing Village. Southeast tip of Penang. No central phone.

If it's a local fishing village you'd like to see, here's a good one. This village is special for its shrine to Admiral Cheng Ho, the early Chinese sea adventurer.

✪ **Botanical Garden.** About a 5- or 10-min. drive west of Georgetown. ☎ **604/228-6248.** Free admission. Daily 5am–8pm.

Covering 30 hectares (70 acres) of landscaped grounds, this botanic garden was established by the British in 1884, with grounds that are perfect for a shady walk and a ton of fun if you love monkeys. They're crawling all over the place and will think nothing of stepping forward for a peanut (which you can buy beneath the "do not feed the monkeys" sign). Also in the gardens are a jogging track and kiddie park.

Penang Bird Park. Jalan Teluk, Seberang Jaya. ☎ **04/399-1899.** Admission RM10 (US$2.65) adults, RM5 (US$1.30) children. Daily 9am–7pm.

The Bird Park is not on Penang Island, but on the mainland part of Penang state. The 2-hectare (5-acre) park is home to some 200 bird species from Malaysia and around the world.

Penang Butterfly Farm. Jalan Teluk Bahang. ☎ **04/881-1253.** Admission RM5 (US$1.30) adults, RM2 (US$0.53) children over 5; free children under 5. Mon–Fri 9am–5pm, Sat–Sun 9am–6pm.

The Penang Butterfly Farm, located toward the northwest corner of the island, is the largest in the world. On its 0.8-hectare (2-acre) landscaped grounds there are more than 4,000 flying butterflies from 120 species. At 10am and 3pm there are informative butterfly shows. Don't forget the insect exhibit—there are about 2,000 or so bugs.

✪ **Penang Hill.** A 20–30-min. drive southwest from Georgetown. The funicular station is on Jalan Stesen Keretapi Bukit.

Covered with jungle growth and 20 nature trails, the hill is great for trekking. Or you can go to Ayer Hitam, a town in the central part of Penang, and take the **Keretapi Bukit Bendera** funicular railway to the top. It sends trains up and down the hill every half hour from 6:30am to 10:30pm weekdays and until midnight on weekends, and costs RM4 (US$1.05) for adults and RM2 (US$0.53) for children. If you prefer to make the trek on foot, go to the "Moon Gate" at the entrance to the Botanical Gardens for a 5.5-kilometer (9-mile), 3-hour hike to the summit.

SHOPPING

The first place anyone here will recommend you to go for shopping is **KOMTAR.** Short for "Kompleks Tun Abdul Razak," it is the largest shopping complex in Penang, a full 65 stories of clothing shops, restaurants, and a couple of large department stores. There's a **duty-free shop** on the 57th floor. On the third floor is a **tourist information center.**

Good shopping finds in Penang are batik, pewter products, locally produced curios, paintings, antiques, pottery, and jewelry. If you care to walk around in search of finds, there are a few streets in Georgetown that are the hub of shopping activity. In the city center, the area around Jalan Penang, Lebuhraya Campbell, Lebuhraya Kapitan Keling, Lebuhraya Chulia, and Lebuhraya Pantai is near the Sri Mariamman Temple, the Penang Museum, the Kapitan Keling Mosque, and other sites of historic interest. Here you'll find everything from local crafts to souvenirs and fashion, and maybe even a bargain or two. Most of these shops are open from 10am to 10pm daily.

Out at Batu Feringgi, the main road turns into a fun **night bazaar** every evening just at dark. During the day, there are also some good shops for batik and souvenirs.

NIGHTLIFE

Clubs in Penang stay open a little later than in the rest of Malaysia, and some even stay open until 3am on the weekends.

If you're looking for a bar that's a little out of the ordinary, visit **20 Leith Street,** 11–A Lebuh Leith (☎ **04/261-6301**). Located in an old 1930s house, the place has seating areas fitted with traditional antique furniture in each room of the house. Possibly the most notorious bar in Penang is the **Hong Kong Bar,** 371 Lebuh Chulia (☎ **04/261-9796**), which opened in 1920 and was a regular hangout for military personnel based in Butterworth. It has an extraordinary archive of photos of the servicemen who have patronized the place throughout the years, plus a collection of medals, plaques, and buoys from ships.

For dancing, the resorts in Batu Feringgi have the better discos. **Borsalino,** Penang Park Royal, 1 Batu Ferringhi Beach (☎ **04/881-1133,** ext. 8844), is popular, with upbeat dance music and slick disco decor. Much of the clientele seems to remember when disco meant doing the hustle. **Zulu's Seaside Paradise,** Paradise Tanjung Bungah (☎ **04/890-8808**), is a world-beat dance club, spinning African, reggae, and other danceable international music.

Hard Life Café, 363 Lebuh Chulia (☎ **04/262-1740**), is an interesting alternative hangout. Decorated with Rastafarian paraphernalia, the place fills up with backpackers, who sometimes aren't as laid back as Mr. Marley would hope they'd be. Still, it's fun to check out the books where guests comment on their favorite (or least favorite) travel haunts in Southeast Asia.

9 Langkawi

Where the beautiful Andaman Sea meets the Strait of Malacca, Langkawi Island positions itself as one of the best emerging island paradise destinations in the region. Since 1990, the Malaysian Tourism Board has dedicated itself to promoting the island and developing it as an ideal travel spot. Now, after a decade of work, the island has proven itself as one of this country's holiday gems.

Its biggest competition comes from Phuket, Thailand's beach-lover fantasy to the north. But, day for day and dollar for dollar, I'd take Langkawi over Phuket hands down. Why? Well, despite being pumped up by government money and promotional campaigns, Langkawi remains relatively unheard of on the travel scene. So, while you get the same balmy weather, gorgeous beaches, fun water sports, and great seafood, you also avoid the horrible effects of tourism gone awry—inflated prices, annoying touts, and overcrowding. Besides, I've stayed in almost every luxury property on Phuket, and can testify that Langkawi's finest resorts can compete with pride.

This small island also claims a Hollywood credit, starring in the 1999 film *Anna and the King*. Langkawi played the part of Thailand to Jodie Foster's Anna Leonowens and Chow Yun Fat's King Mongkut (Rama IV). The Thais wouldn't allow the filmmakers to shoot on location in their kingdom (and rightly so, as King Mongkut, their revered Father of Modern Thailand, has been continuously portrayed in the West as a stubborn, immature fop who got all his great ideas from a common English tutor—indeed, historians agree that according to many well-documented sources, Anna Leonowens's famous account of her time at the Royal Palace had more basis in her imagination than in reality), so Hollywood turned to neighboring Malaysia for location filming. The palatial Thai-style buildings constructed for the set have never been torn down, and you can still hear all kinds of local gossip about the film's stars.

Technically, Langkawi is a cluster of islands, the largest of which serves as the main focal point. Ask how many islands actually make up Langkawi and you'll hear either 104 or 99. The official MTB response? "Both are correct. It depends on the tide!" On Langkawi Island itself, the main town, **Kuah,** provides the island's administrative needs, while on the western and northern shores, the beaches have been developed with resorts. The west-coast beaches of **Pantai Cenang** and **Pantai Tengah** are the most developed; however, the concept of development here should be taken in relative terms. To the north, **Datai Bay** and **Tanjung Rhu** host the island's two finest, and most secluded, resorts.

One final note: Malaysia has declared Langkawi a duty-free zone, so take a peek at some of the shopping in town, and enjoy RM4 (US$1.05) beers!

VISITOR INFORMATION

The MTB office is unfortunately situated in Kuah town on Jalan Persiaran Putra, so most travelers miss it completely, instead heading straight for the beach areas. If you'd like to pick up some of their information, ask your taxi driver to stop on the way to your resort. For specific queries, you can also call them at ☎ **04/966-7789.** If you're arriving by plane, there's another MTB office at the airport (☎ **04/955-7155**).

GETTING THERE

BY PLANE   Malaysia Airways makes Langkawi very convenient from either mainland Malaysia or Singapore. From KL, two daily flights depart for Langkawi's International Airport (☎ **04/955-1322**). Call Malaysia Airline's ticketing office in KL

(☎ **03/746-300**) or their reservations line on Langkawi (☎ **04/966-6622**). From Singapore, Malaysian Airlines flies direct daily, but has numerous other flights with stops in either KL or Penang. For Singapore reservations call ☎ **65/336-6777.**

The best thing to do is prearrange a **shuttle pickup** from your resort; otherwise you can just grab a taxi out in front of the airport. To Pantai Cenang or Pantai Tengah, the fare should be about RM25 (US$6.60), while to the farther resorts at Tanjung Rhu and Datai Bay it will be as high as RM40 (US$10.55). To call for a pickup from the airport dial ☎ **04/955-1800.**

BY TRAIN Taking the train can be a bit of a hassle, because the nearest stop (in Alor Setar) is quite far from the jetty to the island, requiring a cab transfer. Still, if you prefer rail, hop on the overnight train from KL (the only train), which will put you in to Alor Setar at around 6am. Just outside the train station you can find the taxi stand, with cabs to take you to the Kuala Kedah jetty for RM10 (US$2.65). Call the KL Railway Station at ☎ **03/274-7434** or the Alor Setar Railway Station at ☎ **04/ 731-4045** for further details.

BY BUS To be honest, I don't really recommend using this route. If you're coming from KL, the bus ride is long and uncomfortable, catching the taxi transfer to the jetty can be problematic, and by the time you reach the island you'll need a vacation from your vacation. Fly or use the train. If you're coming from Penang, the direct ferry is wonderfully convenient.

BY FERRY From the jetty at Kuala Kedah, there are about five companies that provide ferry service to the island (trip time: about 1 hour and 45 minutes; cost: RM15/US$3.95). Contact LADA Holdings at ☎ **04/762-3823** in Kuala Kedah or ☎ **04/966-8823** in Langkawi; Langkawi Ferry Services at ☎ **04/762-4524** in Kuala Kedah or ☎ **04/966-9439;** or Nautica Ferries at ☎ **04/762-1201** in Kuala Kedah or ☎ **04/966-7868** in Langkawi. Ferries let you off at the main ferry terminal in Kuah, where you can hop a taxi to your resort for between RM30 and RM40 (US$7.90 and US$10.55).

If you're coming from Penang, the ferry is the way to go. **Bahagia Express** has a morning and afternoon speedboat from Weld Quay in Georgetown for RM35 (US$9.20). Call them in Penang at ☎ **04/263-1943** or visit their office across from the clock tower, just next to the main tourism board office. If you're heading from Langkawi to Penang, you can call Bahagia in Langkawi at ☎ **04/966-5784.**

GETTING AROUND

BY TAXI Taxis generally hang around the airport, the main jetty, the taxi stand in Kuah, and some major hotels. From anywhere in between, your best bet is to call the taxi stand for a pickup (☎ **04/966-5249**). Keep in mind, if you're going as far as one side of the island to the other, your fare can go as high as RM40 (US$10.55).

CAR & MOTORCYCLE RENTAL At the airport and from agents in the complex behind the main jetty, car rentals can be arranged starting at RM60 (US$15.80) per day. This is for the standard, no-frills model—actually, mine was more reminiscent of some of the junkers I drove throughout college, but it still got me around. Insurance policies are lax, as are rental regulations. My rental guys seemed more concerned with my passport documents than with my driver's license. If you're out on the beach at Cenang or Tengah, a few places rent Jeeps and motorcycles from RM80 (US$21.05) per day and RM30 (US$7.90) per day, respectively. Pick a good helmet.

BY FOOT The main beaches at Cenang and Tengah can be walked quite nicely; however, don't expect to be able to walk around to other parts of the island.

Langkawi

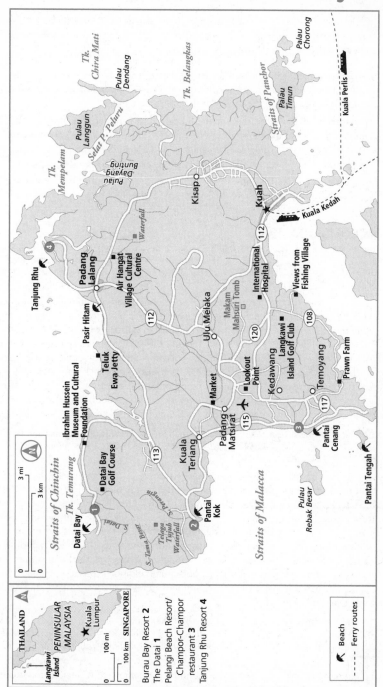

Straits of Chinchin

Straits of Malacca

Straits of Panchor

Kuala Perlis

Palau Chorong

Palau Timun

Pulau Dendang

Pulau Langgun

Pulau Dayang Bunting

Kisap

Kuah

Kuala Kedah

Tk. Chira Mati

Tk. Belangkas

Tk. Mempelam

Tk. Peluru
Salat P. Peluru

Tanjung Rhu

Padang Lalang

Pasir Hitam

Air Hangat Village Cultural Centre

Waterfall

Ulu Melaka

Makam Mahsuri Tomb

International Hospital

Views from Fishing Village

Langkawi Island Golf Club

Teluk Ewa Jetty

Ibrahim Hussein Museum and Cultural Foundation

Datai Bay Golf Course

Kedawang

Temoyang

Prawn Farm

Lookout Point

Market

Padang Matsirat

Kuala Teriang

Pantai Cenang

Pantai Tengah

Datai Bay

Pantai Kok

Teluga Tujuh Waterfall

S. Tanak Besar

S. Datai

S. Penuragun

Pulau Rebak Besar

112

112

120

108

117

113

115

Tk. Temurang

3 mi

3 km

THAILAND

PENINSULAR MALAYSIA

Langkawi Island

Kuala Lumpur

SINGAPORE

100 mi

100 km

Burau Bay Resort **2**
The Datai **1**
Pelangi Beach Resort/
Champor-Champor restaurant **3**
Tanjung Rhu Resort **4**

Beach

Ferry routes

Fast Facts: Langkawi

Banks/Currency Exchange   The only major bank branches seem sadly located far from the beach areas, in Kuah town, mostly around the blocks across the street from the Night Hawker Center (off Jalan Persiaran Putra). Money changers keep long hours out at Pantai Cenang and Pantai Tengah, but for other resorts you'll have to change your money at the resort itself.

Internet/E-mail   Along the Pantai Cenang and Pantai Tengah main road, you'll find at least a half dozen small Internet places. The Shop, a small convenience store along the strip, provides service for RM6 (US$1.60) per hour.

Post Office   The main **post office** is in Kuah at the LADA Kompleks on Jalan Persiaran Putra (☎ **04/966-7271**). Otherwise, use your resort's mail services.

For more Fast Facts about Malaysia, see "Planning a Trip to Malaysia" on p. 456.

ACCOMMODATIONS

Burau Bay Resort. Teluk Burau, 07000 Langkawi, Kedah. ☎ **04/959-1061.** Fax 04/959-1172. 150 units. A/C MINIBAR TV TEL. RM250 (US$65.80) garden-view chalet; RM280 (US$73.70) sea-view chalet; RM370 (US$97.35) family chalet; RM735 (US$193.40) royal chalet. AE, DC, JCB, MC, V.

Pelangi's little-sister property, Burau offers beachside resort accommodations for less money than its upscale sibling. Not nearly as ritzy, this place feels more like summer camp than a resort. All guest rooms are contained in cabanas, with simple decor that's a bit on the older side. For the price, though, they offer value for money. The only restaurant serves local cuisine and Western selections alfresco. All rooms have in-house movies. Burau also organizes golf, massage, Jeep treks, jungle treks, mountain biking, tennis, canoeing, catamaran sailing, jet skiing, scuba diving, snorkeling, fishing, waterskiing, windsurfing, and yachting. Facilities include an outdoor pool, daily shuttle to town, overnight room service, games pavilion, and provision shop.

✪ **The Datai.** Jalan Teluk Datai, Langkawi, Kedah. ☎ **04/959-2500.** A/C MINIBAR TV TEL. US$279 double; US$320–US$470 villa; US$470–US$1,380 suite. Prices jump about 50% Dec–Jan. AE, DC, MC, V.

Aesthetically speaking, this is one of my favorite resorts in Southeast Asia, coming damn close to heaven. It is simply elegant and elegantly simple. I love how the resort blends with its natural jungle surroundings. There's literally nothing to distract you from the beauty of this place. The rooms delight, with lovely daybeds looking out to your private balcony. Minimalist in design, the decor's color schemes stick close to natural, with rosewood tones, deep local tapestries, and regal celadon upholstery. Designer body-care products make an evening in the oversized bathrooms pure joy. Villas carry through the same theme, but ensure additional privacy. My one complaint? The beach is inferior to others on the island—the narrow strip of sand flanks a bay that's full of rocks.

✪ **Pelangi Beach Resort.** Pantai Cenang, 07000 Langkawi, Kedah, Malaysia. ☎ **04/955-1001.** Fax 04/955-1122. 350 units. A/C MINIBAR TV TEL. RM513–RM563 (US$135–US$148.15) double; RM820–RM1,520 (US$215.80–US$400) suite. AE, DC, JCB, MC, V.

For those who prefer a more active vacation, I recommend Pelangi. A top-quality resort, this place stands out from neighboring five-star resorts for its sheer fun. A long list of organized sports and leisure pastimes make it especially attractive for families, but surprisingly, I never found children to be a distraction here. Pelangi's 51 ethnic wooden chalets are huge inside, and are divided into either one, two, or four guest rooms. You'll be welcomed by vaulted ceilings, modern bathrooms, and large living spaces. But it's the little things you'll love—I didn't want to get out of bed and leave my squishy down pillows and snuggly bedding! In addition, Pelangi's location, near the central beach strip for island life, means you're not cloistered away from the rest of civilization.

✪ **Tanjung Rhu Resort.** Tanjung Rhu, Mukim Ayer Hangat, Langkawi, Kedah. 138 units. A/C MINIBAR TV TEL. US$205–US$440 double. AE, DC, JCB, MC, V.

Everyone on the island will agree that the beach at Tanjung Rhu—a wide crescent wrapped around a perfect bay—wins first prize, no contest. It's spectacular. This resort claims 1,100 acres, monopolizing the scene for extra privacy, but it has its pros and cons. The pros? Guest rooms are enormous and decorated with a sensitivity to the environment, from natural materials to organic recycled-paper wrapped toiletries. The cons? Make sure you don't book your vacation during a Malaysian or Singaporean school vacation, since the place draws families like flies, and believe me the kids will buzz all over the place. Still, during between-holiday downtime, I love this resort's friendly and casual atmosphere—and, of course, the beach.

DINING

If you're out at one of the more secluded resorts, chances are you'll stay there for most of your meals. However, if you're at Pantai Cenang or Pantai Tengah, I strongly recommend taking a stroll down to **Champor-Champor** just across the road in the Pelangi Resort (☎ **04/955-1449**). If you're in Kuah town looking for something good to eat, the best local dining experience can be found at the evening **hawker stalls** just along the waterfront near the taxi stand. A long row of hawkers cook up every kind of local favorite, including seafood dishes. You can't get any cheaper or more laid-back. After dinner, from here it's easy to flag down a taxi back to your resort.

Finally, I'm not one to bash places, but I got suckered by a glossy brochure for **Barn Thai**—a Thai restaurant on the eastern side of the island built deep inside a thick mangrove forest. Sound interesting? The food was terrible and overpriced while the atmosphere was destroyed by busloads of tourists. Stay away.

ATTRACTIONS

Most visitors will come for the **beaches.** All resorts are pretty much self-contained units, planning numerous water-sports activities, trekking adventures, sports, and tours to local attractions.

For a fun day trip I recommend taking one of the local boat trips to some of Langkawi's other islands. Most diving trips take you out to **Payar Marine Park** for two dives per day. Off Payar Island, a floating platform drifts above a stunning coral reef, where dive operators and snorkel gear rentals are available (there's also a glass-bottom boat if you don't want to get wet). Day trips to other **surrounding islands** such as Pualu Singa Besar, Pulau Langgun, Pulau Rebak, or Pulau Beras Basah give you a day of peaceful sun-soaking and swimming. The full day trip to Payar Island floating reef platform costs RM170 (US$44.75), but dives and rental of snorkel gear cost extra. If you want to hop around to nice secluded island beaches, the half-day **island hopping tour** costs RM45 (US$11.85). The half-day **round-island tour** also stops at a few attractions, including the Batik Art Village (RM30/US$7.90). In Langkawi call Asian Overland at ☎ **04/955-2002,** or talk to your hotel tour desk operator.

Perhaps one of the loveliest additions to Langkawi's attractions is the **Ibrahim Hussein Museum and Cultural Foundation,** Pasir Tengkorak, Jalan Datai (☎ 04/959-4669). The artistic devotion of the foundation's namesake fueled the creation of this enchanting modern space designed to showcase Malaysia's contribution to the international fine arts scene. If you can pull yourself from the beach for any one activity in Langkawi, this is the one I recommend. Mr. Hussein has created a museum worthy of international attention. Truly a gem. It's open daily from 10am to 5pm; adults RM7 (US$1.85), children free.

SHOPPING

Langkawi's designated Duty Free Port status makes shopping here quite fun and very popular. In Kuah town, the Sime Darby Duty Free Shop, **Langkawi Duty Free,** 64 Persiaran Putra, Pekan Kuah (☎ 04/966-6052), carries the largest selection of apparel, chocolates, cigarettes, footwear, liquor, and perfumes. You can also check out the duty-free wares at the **Kuah Jetty Point,** Lot 2.0 and 2.15 Jetty Kuah (☎ 04/966-8771). They also stage a free cultural dance show every day except Thursday and Friday at noon and again at 4pm. Another fun shopping experience, the **Craft Cultural Complex,** situated on the northern side of the island (☎ 04/959-1913), has the best handicrafts shopping on the island.

10 Desaru

Desaru is an odd place. If it weren't for the resorts here, it probably wouldn't be a place at all. A large arch appears over the road as you approach, welcoming you to the resort town, while just outside there's not much to speak of. Situated along 17 kilometers (10 miles) of sandy beach on the South China Sea, this collection of six resorts and campgrounds has become a very popular vacation spot. Its claim to fame? It's close to Singapore, which means the great majority (up to 90%) of folks who come are Singaporeans or expatriates on weekend getaways for beaches and golf. Desaru gets jam packed on these days, and is not very conducive to relaxation. With this in mind, plan on a trip to Desaru from Monday through Thursday (and not during a public holiday). Still, in all Desaru has a far way to go before it's overdeveloped.

Once in Desaru, you'll probably be staying within your resort most of the time. All have pools and beachfronts with varieties of water sports. The staff at the front desks can arrange golf for you at the local course.

GETTING THERE

You can reach Desaru over well-laid roads by **car** from Johor Bahru, or **outstation taxis** from Johor can deliver you to Desaru for about RM100 (US$26.30). For booking call ☎ 07/223-4494. The number to call for outstation taxis from Desaru is ☎ 07/823-6916. They can take you to Kota Tinggi (see Johor's "Sports & the Outdoors," p. 485) for RM50 (US$13.15) or to Mersing for RM130 (US$34.20).

From the Changi Ferry Terminal on the east coast of Singapore, **FerryLink** (☎ 65/545-3600) departs daily at 8:15am, 11:15am, 2:15pm, and 5:15pm. The trip is S$19 (US$11.40) one-way and S$26 (US$15.55) round-trip. Children cost S$11.50 (US$6.90) and S$16 (US$9.60) respectively. The trip is a slow and peaceful 45 minutes to the jetty at Tanjong Belungkor (☎ 07/251-7404). From here you can prearrange shuttle service with your resort, or you can go it alone with one of the outstation taxis that wait outside the jetty building (RM40/US$10.55 with air-conditioning, RM25/US$6.60 without). The ride takes a half hour.

GETTING AROUND

The resorts at Desaru are self-contained, with restaurants and activities, including golf, water sports and nature treks. Should you require other services, the front desk of any resort can help you out.

ACCOMMODATIONS

✪ **Desaru Golden Beach Hotel.** P.O. Box 50, Tanjung Penawar, 81907 Kota Tinggi, Johor. ☎ **07/822-1101.** Fax 07/822-1480. Singapore reservations ☎ 65/235-5476. 57 units, 115 villas. A/C MINIBAR TV TEL. Weekdays RM170 (US$44.75) double; RM190 (US$50) villa. Weekends RM240 (US$63.15) double; RM260 (US$68.40) villa. AE, DC, JCB, MC, V.

Desaru Golden Beach Resort is casual and comfortable, with a tropical open-air lobby with a high timbered ceiling to allow for cool breezes. The standard rooms face the parking area and garden, while the superior rooms face the sea, and are assigned on a first-come, first-served basis. The villas are like small apartments, and their balconies have plenty of space for sitting with a cool drink. And while their privacy is nice, one feature I don't like is that the villas have carpeting, which makes the rooms feel warm. The double rooms off the lobby feel cooler and fresher with clean tiled floors. Dining options are a seafood restaurant and another offering local dishes. Facilities include a large outdoor lagoon pool, access to the fitness center at Desaru Perdana Beach Resort, a Jacuzzi, two outdoor tennis courts, water sports equipment, and bicycle rental.

The main attraction here besides the beach is **golfing,** which the resort is happy to arrange for you. See below for course details.

Desaru Perdana Beach Resort. P.O. Box 29, Bandar Penawar, 81900 Kota Tinggi, Johor. ☎ **07/822-2222,** or Singapore reservations 65/223-2157 (for reservations from Singapore, rates are quoted in S$). Fax 07/822-2223.. 229 units. Weekdays RM330 (US$86.85) garden-view double; RM340 (US$89.45) sea-view double; RM500 (US$131.60) suite. Weekends RM350 (US$92.10) garden-view double; RM360 (US$94.75) sea-view double; RM600 (US$157.90) suite. AE, DC, MC, V.

An upmarket resort, this property attracts a more varied group of international guests (especially Japanese). It's newer than the others, so the architectural styling has a more modern distinction. The Bali-style open-air lobby features a paneled ceiling and high wooden beams. Guest rooms are also very up-to-date, with new furnishings in Western styles and all the amenities. Perdana, unlike the older Golden Beach, fills huge blocks of buildings, which on the outside look like condominiums, while Golden Beach is smaller and a little more spread out.

Perdana has three restaurants, Japanese, Chinese and Continental, and a bar with live entertainment nightly. Facilities include a large outdoor pool, small fitness center, Jacuzzi, sauna, tennis courts, water-sports equipment, and souvenir shop.

DESARU OUTDOORS

It goes without saying that many visitors come for the **golf.** Guests at any of the resorts can arrange golf through their resort's front desk. The **Desaru Golf & Country Club,** P.O. Box 57, Tanjung Penawar, 81907 Kota Tinggi, Johor (☎ **07/822-2333;** fax 07/822-1855), has 45 holes and an 18-hole Robert Trent Jones Jr. course. Greens fees for 18 holes on weekends and public holidays are RM150 (US$39.45) and RM90 (US$23.70) Monday through Friday. Club rentals, shoes, carts, and buggies are available for rent, and caddy fees run about RM30 (US$7.90). Be sure to confirm your reservation 2 weeks beforehand.

Beach activities include parasailing and windsurfing (with instruction), canoeing, jet skiing, waterskiing, fishing (including night fishing), snorkeling, and speedboat rides. The resorts can also arrange hikes in the nearby jungle, horseback riding, go-carts, tennis, volleyball, and other activities.

11 Mersing

Mersing is not so much a destination in itself but more a jump-off point for ferries to the islands on the East Coast of Malaysia, such as Tioman. Nobody really stays in Mersing unless he's missed the boat—literally. There are a couple of good seafood restaurants in town, but otherwise it's just a small, relaxed fishing town.

GETTING THERE

The main focal point of the town is the **R&R Plaza,** by the main jetty to Tioman. Here you'll find the bus terminal just behind the food stalls (which are great to graze at as you wait for a ferry or bus). In front of these are the offices where you book the ferry or speedboats to Tioman. Outside of R&R are taxis—some local, some outstation, none metered. Local trips are about RM5 (US$1.30). You can also hire outstation taxis to other cities from R&R Plaza. Expect to pay RM140 (US$36.85) to Kuantan, and RM120 (US$31.60) to Johor Bahru.

SPM Ekspress operates daily **bus** service from KL's Puduraya Bus Terminal to Mersing (☎ **03/202-5255** in KL). From Johor Bahru take Johora Express from the Larkin Terminal (☎ **07/224-8280**). They have a daily bus costing RM7 (US$1.85) for the trip. For outgoing bus information from Mersing, call **Johora Express** at (☎ **07/ 799-5227**).

ACCOMMODATIONS

While Mersing has no world-class accommodations or resorts, you will find basic accommodations suitable for those just passin' through.

Mersing Inn. 38 Jalan Ismail, next to the Parkson supermarket, 86800, Mersing, Johor. ☎ **07/799-2288.** Fax 07/799-1919. 40 units. RM65 (US$17.10) double. MC.

The rooms here are small but clean, but some do not have air-conditioning, so be sure to specify. Others don't have televisions or telephones. There are private bathrooms for each room, however.

✪ **Timotel.** 839 Jalan Endau, 86800, Mersing, Johor. ☎ **07/799-5888.** Fax 07/799-5333. 50 units. A/C MINIBAR TV TEL. RM98–RM126 (US$25.80–US$33.15) double; RM189–RM210 (US$49.75–US$55.25) suite. AE, MC.

This hotel, one of the newest and most pleasant in Mersing, has clean and neat rooms and modern conveniences like room service and laundry services. The hotel provides free transfers to and from the jetty. There's a fitness center, and bicycle rental can be arranged.

DINING

Just as with the hotels in Mersing, none of the restaurants are particularly "fine." There is, however, some pretty good seafood to be eaten here, if you don't mind a really low-key and colloquial dining experience. Neither of the places below has a phone, and if they did they probably wouldn't use them for silly things like taking reservations. Just head on down and find a table.

Ee lo Restoran. Jalan Abu Bakar, next to the roundabout beside the newspaper shop. No phone. Main courses RM5–RM10 (US$1.30–US$2.65). No credit cards. Daily 9am–10pm.

Here is the best place to eat while waiting for your boat. About a 5-minute walk from R&R Plaza, this coffee shop has menu items like mee hoon and kuay teow, Hainan chicken rice, and all sorts of seafood and vegetable dishes. The steamed prawns are succulent, and Ee lo serves an unusual dish—stir-fried vegetables in milk—which is quite tasty.

Mersing Seafood Restaurant. Jalan Ismail, next to the Shell station. No phone. Noodle dishes RM3 (US$0.79) and up; other dishes RM10 (US$2.65) and up. MC. Daily 12:30pm–midnight. CHINESE/SEAFOOD.

You won't need a reservation here, even though it gets crowded on weekends. The service is lousy and the place is a little grubby, but the food is so good nobody seems to care. It's also air-conditioned. Prices will range according to season. Some great dishes to try are the deep-fried squid stuffed with salted egg yolk, the bamboo or asparagus clams fried in chile sauce, or the sautéed garlic prawns.

12 Tioman Island

Tioman Island is by far the most popular destination on Malaysia's east coast. Although it's in the state of Pahang, Tioman's mainland gateway, Mersing, is in Johor. The island is only 39 kilometers (23.4 miles) long and 12 kilometers (7.2 miles) wide, with sandy beaches, clear water with sea life and coral reefs, and jungle mountain-trekking trails with streams and waterfalls. So idyllic is the setting that Tioman was the location for the 1950s Hollywood film *South Pacific.*

Despite heavy tourist traffic, Tioman has retained much of its tropical island charm, perhaps by virtue of the fact that few large hotels have been built on it. However, some parts are becoming very commercial, particularly **Kampung Tekek,** which is where you arrive at either the main jetty or the airport. A paved stretch of road runs up the west coast, between Tekek and Berjaya Tioman Beach Resort (the only true resort on the island), and this area is more built up than the rest of the island. *Built up* is really a relative term; trust me, it's a one-horse town. If you trek overland from Tekek to the east coast, you'll find beaches that are more peaceful and serene.

There is a small local population on the island living in the kampungs (villages), but at almost any given time there are fewer locals than tourists, most of whom come from Singapore and other parts of Malaysia. Most are there for the scuba and beaches, but from November through February you won't find many tourists. Monsoon tides make Tioman inaccessible by ferry, and not the most perfect vacation in the tropics.

Activity is spread throughout the kampungs along the shores of the island. Each of these places has some sort of accommodation facilities, most of them very basic chalets, with some access to canteens or restaurants. The lay of the land looks like this: On the west side of the island are most of the kampungs. **Tekek** is about midway from north to south. It's the only kampung with a paved road, which is only a few kilometers long. North of Tekek is **Kampung Air Batang** (also called ABC), and north of that is **Salang.** Both of these kampungs have paved walking paths connecting them with Tekek and with each other. The path from ABC to Tekek is lighted at night. A hike between kampungs takes about 30 to 40 minutes.

South of Tekek is the **Berjaya Tioman Resort,** and south of that is **Kampung Paya** and **Kampung Genting.** Neither Paya nor Genting is accessible via walking path. I haven't covered either of them in this section because, frankly, I don't recommend you stay there. The main snorkel, dive, and fishing operators, as well as the better places to eat, are in other kampungs, and while Paya and Genting are secluded, their beaches are not particularly good. So while most of the touting in Mersing is for accommodations in Paya and Genting, beware. I've seen plenty of travelers take up these offers, only to change kampungs within a day or two.

If you really want seclusion, head for **Juara,** the only kampung on the eastern side of the island. The beach is also the island's finest, but be prepared for provision of only the most minimal of human necessities. Juara is connected with Tekek by a hiking trail over the hills in the center of the island, and while the locals can make the trip in just over an hour, most of us will need two. If you're making the hike, be sure to leave no later than 4pm to allow time to make it before dark.

GETTING THERE

Flights to Tioman originate from Kuala Lumpur, operated by a private airline, **Berjaya Air,** coordinated by the folks at the Best Western Berjaya Tioman Beach Resort on Tioman. However, you need not stay at the resort to book passage on these flights. When considering travel to Tioman, keep in mind the monsoon. Berjaya Air does operate a daily flight during low season, but many times flights are cancelled due to inclement weather conditions. During the lovely months of March through October, Berjaya flies twice daily. Call their KL office for reservations at ☎ **03/746-8228.** Their office in Tioman is at the Berjaya Resort (☎ **09/419-1000**). The airport in Tioman is in Kampung Tekek, just across from the main jetty. If you're staying at Berjaya Tioman, a shuttle will fetch you; however, if you plan to stay elsewhere, you're on your own. See "Getting Around," below.

Aside from air travel, your other option is to travel by one of the 10 **speedboats** that depart from Mersing each day. Book passage on one of them from the many booking agents huddled around the dock near Mersing's R&R Plaza. They're basically all the same, each reserving trips on the same boats. Boats leave Mersing Jetty at intervals that depend on the tide. The trip takes around 1½ hours and can cost between RM20 and RM25 (US$5.25 and US$6.60), depending on the power of the boat you hire. The last boat leaves for Tioman between 5 and 6pm every evening. If you miss this boat, you're stuck in Mersing for the night. If you're not sure when you want to leave Tioman, you can purchase a one-way trip, then when you're ready to return, just show up at the jetty in Tekek before 8am. You can buy a ticket then and catch the morning boat back.

From Singapore, **Auto Batam Ferries & Tours** (☎ **65/524-7105**) operates a daily ferry at 8:30am from the Tanah Merah Ferry Terminal for S$148 to S$168 (US$88.60 to US$100.60) adults and S$58 to S$93 (US$34.75 to US$55.70) for children. The ferry takes 4 hours to reach the Berjaya resort, which is also where you catch the ferry back to Singapore at 2:30pm each day.

GETTING AROUND

Aside from walking the trails between kampungs (see introduction), the most popular mode of transport is **water taxi.** Each village has a jetty; you can either pay your fare at tour offices located near the foot of the pier, or pay the captain directly. The taxis stop operating past nightfall, so make sure you get home before 6 or 7pm. A few sample fares: from Tekek to ABC is RM12 (US$3.15) per person, to Salang RM20 (US$5.25), to Juara RM60 (US$15.80). Also, these guys don't like to shuttle around only one person, so if there's only one of you, be prepared to pay double.

Tioman Travel Tips
_____

If you have not already acquired a good **mosquito repellent,** do so before heading to Tioman. You'll need something with DEET. Tioman mosquitoes are hungry. If you plan to stay in one of the smaller chalet places, you might want to invest in a mosquito net. Also, bring a **flashlight** to help you get around after sunset.

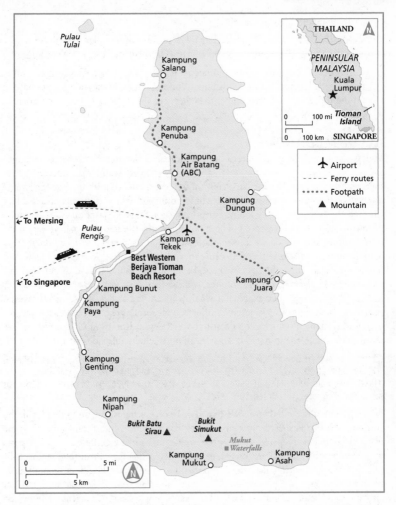

Note that water taxis usually don't hang around Juara. If you're looking to get back to civilization by boat, you either have to get lucky with a supplies-delivery boat or wait for a taxi to make a drop-off (which can be days). Otherwise, there's a daily **sea bus** at 3pm that can take you to the other kampungs.

In Tekek, where paved roads allow, many locals have motorbikes, and some will scoot you someplace for anywhere between RM5 and RM10 (US$1.30 and US$2.65).

Fast Facts: Tioman Island

Banks/Currency Exchange   You'll find money changers who accept traveler's checks in Tekek at the airport, by the jetty, and at Berjaya Tioman Resort. Other places will take traveler's checks, and some of the smaller accommodations now accept them as payment. The best idea for a better rate is to cash them at a bank on the mainland before you go.

Internet/E-mail   Internet access is in Tekek or from the couple of small shops in Salang. Rates run between RM5 and RM10 (US$1.30 and US$2.65) per hour.

Telephones   There are public phones at Tekek, ABC, and Salang, which you can use with Telekom phone cards bought on the island. Most guest houses have nothing more than cellular phones that they will allow guests to use—at a price.

For more Fast Facts about Malaysia, see "Planning a Trip to Malaysia" on p. 456.

ACCOMMODATIONS

Unless you stay at the Best Western Berjaya Tioman Beach Resort, expect to be roughing it. For some travelers, the Berjaya Tioman, with its wonderful modern conveniences, is what it takes to make a tropical island experience relaxing. Your shower is always warm, you can order food to your room, and you can arrange any activity through the concierge in the lobby. For others, though, real relaxation comes from an escape from modern distractions. The small **chalets in the kampungs** have very minimal facilities and few or no conveniences such as hot showers and telephones. Why would you want to stay in them? Because they're simple, quiet, close to the beach, and less touristy than the resort. You will also have to trek around to find dining options, as few of these places have canteens. Yes, you sacrifice a lot, but the peaceful nature of the island is a more idyllic experience when you stay at a chalet. Be warned, however, that touts at the jetty in Mersing will offer you all sorts of really, really cheap accommodations, many of which are so rustic they're beyond Robinson Crusoe. Those I've listed under "The Kampungs," below, are all on the habitable side of rustic.

⦿ **Best Western Berjaya Tioman Beach Resort.** Tioman Island, Pahang Darul Makmur. ☎ **09/419-1000.** Fax 09/419-1718. 380 units. A/C MINIBAR TV TEL. Mar–Oct RM260 (US$68.40) double; RM360 (US$94.75) chalet; RM430–RM975 (US$113.15–US$256.60) suite. Nov–Feb rates discounted 50%. AE, DC, MC, V.

Berjaya Tioman is the only true Western-style resort on the island, and provides all the conveniences you'd expect from a chain hotel. For modern comforts and golf, this is the place to be, but be prepared to be in the middle of Tourist Central. A range of sports opportunities and facilities are offered, including scuba diving, windsurfing, sailing, fishing, snorkeling, canoeing, glass-bottom boat rides, horseback riding, four tennis courts, swimming pools, spa pool, water slide, children's playground, 18-hole international championship standard golf course with pro shop, jungle treks, slot machines and video games, billiards, and boat trips to nearby islands. Four restaurants provide perhaps the best dining on the island, including a nightly beachside seafood buffet. Services include complimentary airport transfers, foreign currency exchange, and laundry services. Berjaya carries a full line of water-sports equipment for guests, a PADI dive operator on the premises, plus a nine-hole golf course (which is really not too spectacular).

DINING

You won't find fantastic food on the island. Most cuisine consists of simple sandwiches and local food, unless you dine at Berjaya Resort, where the choices are much more extensive. There are inexpensive provision shops here and there. Beer is available in Tekek and Salang, and at Nazri's Place, a restaurant in the very southern part of ABC.

THE KAMPUNGS
KAMPUNG ABC

This village lines a long rocky beach that is not the best for swimming in spots, but ABC is very laid-back and comfortable in other ways. Chalets line the pathway along the beach, where you'll find small shady picnic areas and hammocks to swing in. While ABC is well populated by travelers, the people here tend to be more relaxed.

The nicest place to stay is **Air Batang Beach Cabanas,** Kampung Air Batang, 86800 Mersing (no phone). Creeping up the side of the hill, these chalets, many with views of the sea, are the largest and newest in the kampung. Rates go from RM120 (US$31.60) for units with air-conditioning and RM70 (US$18.40) for those without. All cabins have private toilets with cold shower. Cash is accepted, but not credit cards or traveler's checks.

Really the only place to eat here is **Nazri's place** in the south end of the beach, which serves breakfast, lunch, and fish or chicken barbecue dinner daily.

B&J Diving Centre (☎ 09/419-1218) has a branch along the path. They charge RM150 (US$39.45) for two dives in 1 day, usually to nearby Chebeh and Sapoy Islands. They also have PADI courses and accept MasterCard and Visa. Daily snorkeling rentals are RM20 (US$5.25).

✪ KAMPUNG JUARA

Juara is where to go if you really want to get away from it all. A gorgeous cove of crystal blue waters and wide clean sand make for the best beach on the island. Come here expecting to rough it, though. Most of the chalets here are terrible, some only slightly more accommodating than dog houses. There are no phones, only one TV, one place to eat (**The Happy Café,** which has the one TV and a few small convenience store items), and no air-conditioning anywhere. But I still found a quite decent place to stay. On the north end of the beach is **Juara Bay Village Resort,** with 20 rooms that go for RM30 (US$7.90) for hill views and RM40 (US$10.55) for sea views. Credit cards aren't accepted here. Each room has a fan and private bathroom, and they're all good-sized and clean. Communications services to this side of the island have yet to be developed, making reservations impossible, so you'll just have to show up and try your luck. If no rooms are available (hardly likely), there are other choices around.

KAMPUNG SALANG

This kampung is a happening spot. Snuggled in a big cove of lovely beach and blue water, the village has relatively more conveniences for visitors, such as a choice of eating places serving continental and local seafood dishes for a song, a few bars, money changers, convenience stores, and places to make international calls. It is not a metropolis by any standard, though, and accommodations remain basic.

A good place to stay is **Salang Indah Resorts,** Kampung Salang, Tioman (☎ 09/419-5015; fax 09/419-5024). Choices of rooms vary from fan-cooled hillside chalets at RM25 (US$6.55), to air-conditioned hillside chalets at RM90 (US$23.70) and sea-view chalets for between RM130 (US$34.20) and RM150 (US$39.45). Air-conditioned chalets also feature hot-water showers.

Both **B&J** (☎ 09/419-5555) and **Dive Asia** (☎ 09/419-5017) have offices in Salang. See above locations for prices and services.

KAMPUNG TEKEK

Kampung Tekek is the center of life on Tioman, which means it's the busiest spot, and while there are small accommodations here—as well as some convenience stores (open from 7am to 11pm), souvenir shops, and restaurants—you're better off in one of the other kampungs. The best dining is to the side of the main jetty, where you'll find open-air seafood stalls selling soups, noodle dishes, and seafood and vegetable dishes, at very inexpensive prices.

Just beyond the stalls is the office for **Dive Asia** (☎ 09/419-1337). Daily dives usually hit two or three spots: Chebeh Island, Malang rocks, and Labas Island. With equipment rentals an excursion costs about RM150 (US$39.45). Night dives to Pirate Reef run about RM80 (US$21.05). You can also enroll for a PADI open-water course starting at RM745 (US$196.05). Dive Asia accepts MasterCard and Visa. Mask and snorkel equipment rentals go for RM20 (US$5.25) per day. There is also a Dive Asia branch at Salang. For bookings feel free to e-mail them at diveasia@tm.net.my.

TIOMAN OUTDOORS

After you're waterlogged, you can trek the trail from Tekek to Juara, and some of the paths along the west coast. The hike across the island will take around 2 hours. Bring water and mosquito repellent, and don't try it unless you are reasonably fit.

At the southern part of the island are Bukit Batu Sirau and Bukit Simukut, **"The Famous Twin Peaks,"** and closer to the water near Kampung Mukut are the **Mukut Waterfalls.** There are two smallish pools for taking a dip. Some regular trails exist, but it's inadvisable to venture too far from them because the forest gets dense and it can be tough to find your way back. Negotiate with water taxis to bring you down and pick you up.

13 Kuantan

Kuantan is the capital of Pahang Darul Makmur, the largest state in Malaysia, covering about 35,960 square kilometers (22,475 sq. miles). Travelers come to Pahang for the beautiful beaches, which stretch all the way up the east coast, and for inland jungle forests that promise adventures in trekking, climbing, and river rafting. Much of **Taman Negara,** Malaysia's national forest preserve, is in this state, although most people access the forest via Kuala Lumpur. Kuantan, although it's the capital, doesn't have the feel of a big city. If you're staying at the beach at **Telok Chempedak,** 5 kilometers (3.1 miles) north of Kuantan, the atmosphere is even more relaxed.

VISITOR INFORMATION

There is a **Tourist Information Centre** (☎ 09/517-1624) located on Jalan Penjara in the center of town. Staff here are exceptionally helpful and good at answering specific inquiries.

GETTING THERE

BY AIR   Malaysia Airlines has a daily flight from KL. For reservations call (☎ 03/746-3000). Flights arrive at the Sultan Ahmad Shah Airport (☎ 09/538-1291). Just outside the airport is a taxi stand where you can get a cab to Kuantan for RM25 (US$6.60) or to Cherating for RM60 (US$15.80).

BY BUS   Bus routes service Kuantan from all parts of the peninsula. If you're coming from KL, **Plusliner** (☎ 03/442-1256) departs from the Putra Bus Terminal, opposite from the Putra World Trade Centre. Seven daily buses make the trip for RM11.70 (US$3.10). From Mersing, **Transnasional/Naelia** (☎ 07/799-3155) has two daily coaches to Kuantan for RM10.40 (US$2.75). The bus terminal in Kuantan is in **Kompleks Makmur.** Taxis at the stand just outside the terminal can take you to town for RM10 (US$2.65).

For buses from Kuantan to other destinations call **Plusliner** at ☎ 09/515-0991 or **Transnasional** at ☎ 09/515-6740.

BY TAXI   Outstation taxis from KL (☎ 03/238-3525) will cost RM220 (US$57.90). From Johor Bahru the fare will be about RM150 (US$39.45), and from Mersing RM100 (US$26.30). For outstation taxi booking from Kuantan call ☎ 09/513-6950. The stand is at the bus terminal.

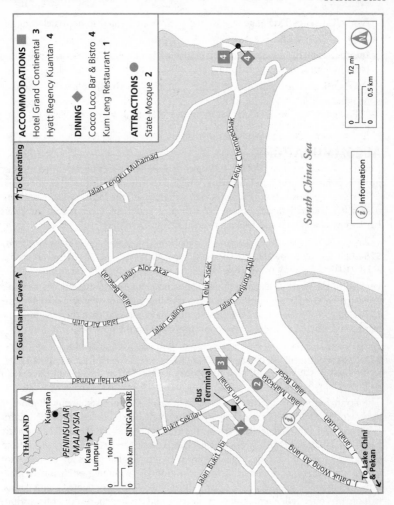

ACCOMMODATIONS ■
Hotel Grand Continental **3**
Hyatt Regency Kuantan **4**

DINING ◆
Cocco Loco Bar & Bistro **4**
Kum Leng Restaurant **1**

ATTRACTIONS ●
State Mosque **2**

South China Sea

ⓘ Information

To Cherating ↑

To Gua Charah Caves ↑

Jalan Tengku Muhamad

Jalan Alor Akar

Jalan Beserah

Jalan Air Putih

Jalan Galing

J. Teluk Chempedak

J. Teluk Sisek

J. Teluk Cempedak

Jalan Tanjung Api

Jalan Haji Ahmad

THAILAND
Kuantan
PENINSULAR
MALAYSIA
Kuala
Lumpur ★
SINGAPORE
100 mi
100 km

Bus Terminal ■

J. Tun Ismail

Jalan Mahkota

Jalan Besar

J. Bukit Sekilau

J. Bukit Ubi

J. Datuk Wong Ah Jang

J. Tanah Putih

To Lake Chini & Pekan ↓

GETTING AROUND

The areas in the town's center are nice for walking. Otherwise stick with **taxis,** which can be waved down on any street. If you need to arrange for a pickup, call the taxi stand at the bus terminal at ☎ **09/513-4478.** There's also a stand behind the Tourist Information Centre where you'll be sure to find a cab in a pinch. Taxis here are not metered, so you must negotiate the fare before you set out. This is a good deal when you want to hire someone for a few hours to take you around the city. Rates are from RM15 (US$3.95) per hour. Use taxis to travel to areas of interest outside the city that are covered later in this section.

Fast Facts: Kuantan

American Express   The American Express office is at Mayflower Acme Tours, Ground floor, Sultan Ahmad Shah Airport (☎ **09/538-3490**).

Banks/Currency Exchange   Most major banks are located appropriately along Jalan Bank, near the State Mosque.

Internet/E-mail   Internet service is available from a couple of cafes at the Kompleks Makmur; check the shopping mall adjacent to the bus terminal.

Post Office   The central post office (☎ **09/552-1078**) is near the State Mosque on Jln. Haji Abdul Aziz.

For more Fast Facts about Malaysia, see "Planning a Trip to Malaysia" on p. 456.

ACCOMMODATIONS

Kuantan is not a very large place, and most of those who vacation here prefer to stay just a little farther north, in **Cherating,** which is more established as a resort destination. If staying in Kuantan is important to you, though, the Hotel Grand Continental is a fine, centrally located place. Near the beach at Telok Chempedak, the Hyatt Regency is as romantic and relaxing as any place at Cherating.

Hotel Grand Continental. Jalan Gambut, 25000 Kuantan, Pahang Darul Makmur. ☎ **09/ 515-8888.** Fax 09/515-9999. 202 units. A/C MINIBAR TV TEL. RM222 (US$58.40) double; RM360 (US$94.75) suite. AE, DC, JCB, MC, V.

Located in the heart of Kuantan, this hotel is near the central mosque. It's a simple three-star hotel, with new and adequate facilities that are somewhat reminiscent of the 1970s. The front view of the bridge and river is more pleasant than the view from the rear rooms. There's a fitness center, pool, and shops on the premises.

✪ **Hyatt Regency Kuantan.** Telok Chempedak, 25050 Kuantan, Pahang. ☎ **800/ 233-1234** from the U.S., or 09/566-1234. Fax 09/567-7577. 336 units. A/C MINIBAR TV TEL. RM391–RM450 (US$102.90–US$118.40) double; RM841–RM956 (US$221.30–US$251.60) suite. AE, DC, JCB, MC, V.

The Hyatt Regency is located on the beach at Telok Chempedak, about 10 minutes outside of Kuantan proper. The long stretch of sandy beach bordering it is perfect for relaxation and fun, and in the evening the crashing waves are the perfect romantic backdrop. Hyatt has built a five-star resort here, and it is five-star in every sense, from outstanding facilities to large, well-appointed rooms. Higher prices are of course for rooms with sea views. Facilities include two outdoor swimming pools (one a more active family frolic spot, while the other is quiet and calm), three lighted tennis courts, two squash courts, table tennis, darts, volleyball, and a water-sports center with windsurfing, sailing, waterskiing, and jet skis. The hotel is near locations for golf, jogging, and jungle hikes.

Hyatt has **the best bar in Kuantan,** oftentimes with a live band nightly. They also offer a few dining choices, including a great coffee shop for local and Western fare, plus the Cocco Loco Bistro & Bar, a good choice for Italian.

DINING

You can find both seafood and local food in Kuantan, but like the other smaller destinations in Malaysia, you'll be hard-pressed to find fine dining outside of the larger hotels. The best evening activities are centered around the beach area at Telok Chempedak.

Cocco Loco Bistro & Bar. Hyatt Regency Kuantan, Telok Chempedak. ☎ **09/566-1234,** ext. 7700. Reservations recommended. Main courses RM20–RM48 (US$5.25–US$12.65). AE, DC, JCB, MC, V. Daily noon–2:30pm and 6–10:30pm. ITALIAN.

For a little fine dining in Kuantan, your best bet is at the Hyatt's Italian restaurant, Cocco Loco. Local seafood like sea bass and prawns is transformed into beautiful entrees, with light sauces and the freshest ingredients. They have a good wine list with many international labels. If you arrive early, you can still see the ocean from huge glass windows. However, even after dark, Cocco Loco has a beautiful atmosphere enhanced by romantic lights, terra-cotta floors, and bright table linens.

Kum Leng Restoran. E-897/899/901 Jalan Bukit Ubi, Kuantan. ☎ **09/513-4446.** Seafood priced according to seasonal availability; other dishes can be as low as RM5 (US$1.30) for fried tofu or as high as RM100 (US$26.30) for shark's fin. No credit cards. Daily 11:30am–2:30pm and 5:30–10:30pm. CANTONESE.

Kum Leng is one of the top restaurants in Kuantan. A bit cramped, it's always doing a good business but there's rarely a wait. Try the fried chicken with dry chile topped with onions and cashew nuts, or the fried chile prawns with shells. They're very fresh and not too spicy.

ATTRACTIONS

Kuantan can really be seen in a day. While there are a few fun crafts shops, the place is not exactly a hotbed of culture. The main attraction in town is the huge **State Mosque,** which is quite beautiful inside and out, with a distinct dome, minarets, and stained glass. Late afternoon is the best time to see it, when the light really shines through the glass.

SHOPPING

You can have a nice walk down **Jalan Besar,** sampling local delicacies sold on the street and shopping in the smaller craft and souvenir shops. Visit **HM Batik & Handicraft,** 45 N–1, Bangunan LKNP, Jalan Besar (☎ **09/552-8477**), and **Kedai Mat Jais B. Talib,** 45N–8, Bangunan LKNP, Jalan Besar (☎ **09/555-2860**), for good selections of batiks and crafts. **Batik RM** has a showroom on Jalan Besar (2–C Medan Pelancung, ☎ **09/514-2008**), but the showroom out on Jalan Tanah Puteh (☎ **09/513-9631**) is much more fun. Tours around the back allow you to watch the waxing and dyeing processes. Their showroom has some great batik fashions—more stylish than so much of the batik clothing that you find in the markets.

ATTRACTIONS OUTSIDE KUANTAN

Pahang is home to peninsular Malaysia's most stunning forests. With Kuantan as your starting point, it's an easy jump out to these spots for a day or half-day trip.

Gua Charah caves are about 25 kilometers (15.6 miles) outside of Kuantan. Also called Pancing caves (they're located at a town called Pancing), one of the caves in the network is a temple, home to a huge reclining Buddha. It is said that the monk caretaker, who has grown very old, is having difficulty finding another monk who will take over his duties at the caves. An outstation taxi can take you there for RM80 (US$21.05).

Also fun is **Lake Chini,** 12 freshwater lakes that have local legends that rival Loch Ness. They say that there once was an ancient Khmer city at the site of the lakes, but it is now buried deep under the water, protected by monsters. Some have tried to find both city and monsters, but have come up with nothing. Boats are there to take you across the lake to an *orang asli* (indigenous peoples) kampung to see the native way of life. Lake Chini is 60 kilometers (38 miles) southwest of Kuantan, and an outstation taxi can bring you for RM80 (US$21.05).

Just south of Kuantan is **Pekan,** which for history and culture buffs is far more interesting then Kuantan. Pekan is called "the Royal City" because it is where the Sultan of Pahang resides in a beautiful Malay-style istana. The **State Museum** on Jalan Sultan Ahmad has displays depicting the history of Pahang and its royal family, as well as sunken treasures from old Chinese junks. Outstation taxis to Pekan are RM20 (US$5.25).

GOLF

The **Royal Pahang Golf Club** is near Kuantan's beach resort area on Jalan Teluk Chempedak (☎ 09/567-5811; fax 09/567-1170). Your hotel will be happy to make all necessary reservations for you.

14 Cherating

Because Kuantan is such a small town, some travelers coming through these parts choose to stay 47 kilometers (28 miles) north in ✪ Cherating. This area supports a few international-class resorts along the beautiful beachfront of the South China Sea. Funny thing: Compared to Kuantan, the town of Cherating has even fewer things to do, and guests tend not to stray too far from their resort. Self-contained units, they each offer a few dining choices, arrange all the water-sports facilities and outdoor activities you have time for, and can even provide transport to and from Kuantan if you need to see a little "big city life." Windsurfers take note: Cherating is world famous for excellent conditions, and the home of a few international competitions and exhibitions. Resorts can also arrange trips through the mangroves up the Cherating River in a hired bumboat, and trips to crafts shops and cultural shows. A little more than 11 kilometers (6.8 miles) north of Cherating is Chendor Beach, one of the peninsula's special beaches where giant leatherback turtles lay their eggs from May to October.

ACCOMMODATIONS

Club Med. Correspondence through KL office only via Vacances, Suite 1.1, 1st Floor Bangunan MAS, Jalan Sultan Ismail, 50250 Kuala Lumpur. ☎ **03/261-4599.** Fax 03/261-7229. www.clubmed.com. E-mail: cmkul@po.jaring.my. 315 units. A/C MINIBAR TEL. Weekdays (Sun–Fri) RM300 (US$78.95) per adult, RM30–RM180 (US$7.90–US$47.35) per child; weekends (Sat) RM350 (US$92.10) per adult, RM35–RM210 (US$9.20–US$55.25) per child. Peak season (Christmas, New Year's, and Chinese New Year) RM420 (US$110.55) per adult, RM42–RM252 (US$11.05–US$66.30) per child. AE, DC, MC, V.

The world-renowned Club Med occupies a lovely stretch of beachfront property along the coastline here. On 200 private acres, you can expect this resort chain to take complete care of all your holiday needs. This compound of Malay-style wooden houses contains very contemporary but natural furnishings, with nice little balconies for each. Everything is absolutely spotless. A note: If you're new to Club Med, they'll require a membership fee of RM80 for adults only, added on to your booking (Club Med really is a club, you see). They'll also be happy to arrange all your transportation from KL for an additional cost.

For fun, try their outdoor swimming pool, sailing activities, windsurfing, kayaking, tennis (six lighted courts), squash, badminton, cricket, archery, volleyball, wall-scaling, and a circus school with flying trapeze! They also coordinate jungle walks and batik lessons. Almost all above activities are included in your daily rate. At extra cost, there's also a nearby golf course. A daily international buffet features Malay, Indian, Korean, Japanese, and Chinese cuisine, while the Pantai features grilled seafood and meats and Vesuvio opens in the evenings for Italian fare. After that, head for the nightclub and bar.

Holiday Villa Cherating. Lot 1303, Mukin Sungai Karang, 26080 Kuantan, Pahang Darul Makmur. ☎ **09/581-9500.** Fax 09/581-9178. 150 units. A/C MINIBAR TV TEL. RM110–RM190 (US$28.95–US$50) double; RM230–RM295 (US$60.55–US$77.65) suite. AE, DC, JCB, MC, V.

What a resort! This 4-hectare (10-acre) coastline property has three different wings to choose from: The Capital Wing houses modern amenities similar to any international-class hotel, while the Village Wing and the Palace Wing have chalets, longhouses, and istanas. The 13 Village Wing chalets are each decorated in the style of one of the thirteen Malay states, and its kampung feel makes it perfect for unwinding. The chalets in both wings range from simple two-bedroom accommodations to a Sarawak longhouse with 10 guest rooms and private balconies to a replica of the Istana Lama Sri Menanti in Negeri Sembilan.

Facilities include two outdoor pools, two outdoor spa pools, a children's wading pool, a game room, three outdoor tennis courts, two indoor badminton courts, a fitness center, sauna, massage, a beauty parlor, and a water sports center (with windsurfing, beach surfing, catamaran, sailing, parasailing, scuba diving, jet scooters, canoeing, and boating). Also available are sightseeing tours, island excursions, fishing, and golfing.

15 Taman Negara National Park

Malaysia's most famous national park, Taman Negara, covers 434,300 hectares (1,085,750 acres) of primary rain forest estimated to be as old as 130 million years, and encompasses within its borders Gunung Tahan, peninsular Malaysia's highest peak at 2,187 meters (2,392 ft.) above sea level.

Prepare to see lush vegetation and rare orchids, some 250 bird species, and maybe, if you're lucky, some barking deer, tapir, elephants, tigers, leopards, and rhinos. As for primates, there are long-tailed macaques, leaf monkeys, gibbons, and more. Malaysia has taken the preservation of this forest seriously since the early part of the century, so Taman Negara showcases efforts to keep this land in as pristine a state as possible while still allowing humans to appreciate the splendor.

There are outdoor activities for any level of adventurer. Short jungle walks to observe nature are lovely, but then so are the hard-core 9-day treks or climbs up Gunung Tahan. There are also overnight trips to night hides where you can observe animals up close. The **jungle canopy walk** is the longest in the world, and at 25 meters (83 ft.) above ground, the view is spectacular. There are also rivers for rafting and swimming, fishing spots, and a couple of caves.

VISITOR INFORMATION

Call the Kuala Tahan Office, Taman Negara Resort, Kuala Tahan, Jerantut, 27000 Pahang (☎ **609/263-500;** fax 609/261-5000).

GETTING THERE

The entrance to the park is at **Kuala Tembeling,** which can be reached in 3 hours by road from Kuala Lumpur. By far the easiest way to visit the national park is through a **travel operator,** who will arrange your transport to the park, accommodation, meals, and activities. Taman Negara Resort (see below) is the largest operator, with a few others providing excellent packages as well.

Outstation taxis from Puduraya Bus Terminal (☎ 03/238-3525) will cost about RM150 (US$39.45) to the park entrance. From there you must venture upstream 2 hours by boat to the Taman Negara Resort (below). The **KTM,** Malaysia's rail system, also travels to this area. Get off at the Tembeling station to catch the boat into the park, or at Jerantut if you need a place to stay overnight (there isn't really any place to stay at Tembeling). From KL (☎ 03/274-7434) there's a special evening train running to Jerantut at 8:20pm. From Johor Bahru, stop at Tembeling. Call KTM at

(☎ **07/223-3040**) for inquiries about their morning train. Budget your fare at RM38 (US$10) for second-class passage.

ACCOMMODATIONS

Nusa Camp. Bookings through Kuala Lumpur Office: Malaysia Tourist Information Centre (MATIC), 109 Jalan Ampang. ☎ **03/2162-7682.** Fax 03/2162-7682. Accommodations range from Malay houses at RM100 (US$26.30) per night to A-frame chalets at RM55 (US$14.45) or 4-person hostel for RM15 (US$3.95). You can also rent a tent for RM15 (US$3.95). Meals cost RM11–RM20 (US$2.90–US$5.25), and the boat ride goes for RM38 (US$10), return.

Nusa Camp will send you to the park, put you up in their own kampung house, chalet, or hostel accommodations, and guide your activities for you. See range for accommodations and meals above. Once there, they have numerous guided trips out into the wilds: a night safari (2 hours; RM35/US$9.20 per person); or night walk (1 hr.; RM20/US$5.25); a trip to see an orang asli village (4 hrs.; RM45/US$11.85); tubing down rapids (2 hrs.; RM30/US$7.90); overnight hikes (RM90/US$23.70); overnight river fishing trips (RM150/US$39.45); a trip to the canopy walkway (4 hrs.; RM80/US$39.45); or an overnight trip to explore caves (RM220/US$57.90).

Taman Negara Resort. Kuala Tahan Office, Taman Negara Resort, Kuala Tahan, Jerantut, 27000 Pahang. ☎ **09/266-3500.** Fax 09/266-1500. (Or contact Kuala Lumpur Sales Office, Lot G.01A, Ground Floor, Kompleks Antarabangsa, Jalan Sultan Ismail, 50250 Kuala Lumpur; ☎ 03/245-5585; fax 03/245-5430.) Accommodations come in many styles: a bungalow suite for families (RM600/US$157.90); chalet (RM216/US$56.85) and chalet suite (RM300/US$78.95), both good for couples; standard guest house rooms in a motel-style longhouse (RM165/US$43.40); and dormitory hostels for budget travelers (RM40.25/US$10.60). All prices above are per night. The Explorer Package runs RM482 (US$126.85) per person for 3 days and 2 nights, or RM775 (US$203.95) per person for 4 days and 3 nights.

Taman Negara Resort, well established in the business of hosting visitors to the park, organizes trips for 3 days and 2 nights or for 4 days and 3 nights, as well as an à la carte deal where you pay for lodging (see above) and activities separately. Explorer visitors check into the chalets, which are air-conditioned with attached bathroom, and enjoy a full itinerary of activities included in the package price. À la carte activities include a 3-hour jungle trek (RM20/US$5.25 per person), a 1½-hour night jungle walk (RM13/US$3.40), the half-day Lata Berkoh river trip with swimming (RM45/US$11.84 per person), a 2-hour cave exploration (RM35/US$9.20), and a trip down the rapids in a rubber raft (RM25/US$6.60). Shuttle transfers from KL (4 hours) are an extra RM50 (US$13.15) per person, and the boat trip to the resort is either RM38 (US$10) for the 3-hour traditional wooden boat or RM60 (US$15.80) for the 1-hour speedboat.

16 Kuala Terengganu

The capital of the state of Terengganu, Kuala Terengganu has far more exciting activities to offer a visitor than its southern capital neighbor, Kuantan. And yet, many travelers to Malaysia often skip this part of the country for the more beaten paths. So why should you consider coming here? **Malaysian crafts.** Kuala Terengganu has the best cottage industries for Malaysian crafts—better than anywhere else on the peninsula. Terengganu artisans specialize in everything from boat building to kite making, and it is here that you can see it all happen.

Kuala Terengganu is small and easy to navigate, clustered around a port at the mouth of the Terengganu River. Many livelihoods revolve around the sea, so most of the activity, even today, focuses on the areas closest to the jetties. Life here is slow

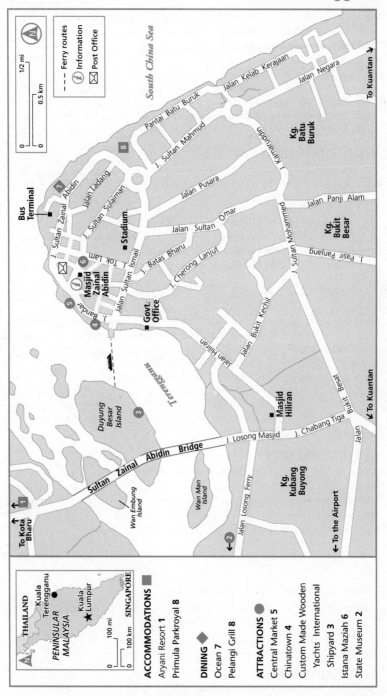

South China Sea

- - - Ferry routes
ⓘ Information
⊠ Post Office

1/2 mi
0.5 km
0
0

To Kuantan →

Jalan Kelab Kerajaan
Jalan Negara

Pantai Batu Buruk
Jalan Kamaruddin

Kg. Batu Buruk

Jalan Ladang
Jalan Sultan Mahmud

Jalan Pusara
Jalan Panji Alam

Bus Terminal
J. Sultan Zainal Abidin
Jalan Sulaman

Stadium

Jalan Sultan Omar

Kg. Bukit Besar
J. Pasir Panjang

J. Tok Lam
Jalan Sultan Ismail
Jalan Batas Bharu
J. Cherong Lanjut
Jalan Sultan Mohammed

ⓘ
⊠
Masjid Zainal Abidin

Jalan Bukit Kechil

Govt. Office
J. Bandar

Jalan Hiliran

Terengganu

Masjid Hiliran

Bukit Besat

To Kuantan →

Duyung Besar Island

Sultan Zainal Abidin Bridge
J. Losong Masjid
J. Chabang Tiga

Wan Embung Island
Wan Man Island

Kg. Kubang Buyong

Jalan Losong Ferry

→ To the Airport

← To Kota Bharu

THAILAND

Kuala Terengganu

Kuala Lumpur
★

PENINSULAR MALAYSIA

SINGAPORE

100 mi
100 km
0
0

ACCOMMODATIONS ■
Aryani Resort **1**
Primula Parkroyal **8**

DINING ◆
Ocean **7**
Pelangi Grill **8**

ATTRACTIONS ●
Central Market **5**
Chinatown **4**
Custom Made Wooden
Yachts International
Shipyard **3**
Istana Maziah **6**
State Museum **2**

paced and comfortable, and very Muslim, owing to its proximity to orthodox Muslim Kelantan in the north. It is a sedate town, so don't come here for the nightlife. As opposed to its west coast contemporaries, this city is mostly Malay (about 90%), so it's here that you see Malay culture in a more pure form, with fewer outside influences.

The local business week is from Saturday to Wednesday, so be prepared for that when you plan your time here. Also important to know: Terengganu is a dry state. Alcoholic beverages cannot be purchased in stores, and there is only one bar in town, at the Primula Parkroyal Resort (listed below). Chinese restaurants are also permitted to sell beer to diners.

VISITOR INFORMATION

The Tourism Information Centre is on Jalan Sultan Zainal Abidin just next to the post office and across from the central market. The number there is (☎ **09/622-1553**).

GETTING THERE

Malaysia Airlines has two daily flights from KL to Kuala Terengganu's Sultan Mahmud Airport. The reservations number in KL is ☎ **03/746-3000.** For local airport information call ☎ **09/666-4204.** For Malaysian Airlines bookings from Kuala Terengganu call ☎ **09/622-1415.** From the airport, a taxi to town is about RM15 (US$395).

The **MPKT Bus Terminal** is located on Jalan Sultan Zainal Abidin next to the water. Plusliner (☎ **03/443-4285**) has two daily buses from KL, departing from the Putra Bus Terminal opposite the Putra World Trade Centre. The trip time is 8 hours, with tickets priced at RM21.60 (US$5.70). From Kuantan you can also catch the Plusliner bus heading from KL to Kuala Terengganu via Kuantan. For buses out of Kuala Terengganu call Plusliner at (☎ **09/622-7067**).

Outstation taxis from Kuantan will cost RM90 (US$23.70). Call ☎ **09/513-6950** for booking. From Kota Bharu taxis will be around RM80 (US$21.05) (RM56/US$14.75 without air-conditioning). The number for the taxi stand there is ☎ **09/748-1386.** Outstation taxi bookings from Kuala Terengganu can be arranged by calling ☎ **09/622-1581.**

GETTING AROUND

While you can stroll around the downtown areas with ease, getting to many of the bigger attractions will require a **taxi.** To call and arrange for a car, dial ☎ **09/622-1581,** or arrange through your hotel concierge. It's a good idea to hire these guys for a half or whole day, so you can go around to places and not worry how you'll get back. Rates will be around RM15 (US$3.95) per hour.

Fast Facts: Kuala Terengganu

Banks   Most **banks** are on Jalan Sultan Ismail.

Post Office   The main **post office** is on Jalan Sultan Zainal Abidin (☎ **09/622-7555**), next to the Tourist Information Centre.

For more Fast Facts about Malaysia, see "Planning a Trip to Malaysia" on p. 456.

ACCOMMODATIONS

✪ **The Aryani Resort.** Jalan Rhu Tapai–Merang, 21010 Setiu, Terengganu, Malaysia. ☎ **09/624-1111** or 09/624-4489. Fax 09/624-8007. 20 units. MINIBAR TV TEL. RM560–RM656 (US$147.35–US$172.65) double; RM808 (US$212.65) modern suite; RM1,055 (US$277.65) heritage suite. AE, DC, JCB, MC, V.

Two and a half years ago, Raja Dato' Bahrin Shah Raja Ahmad (a most royal name) opened his dream resort. An internationally celebrated architect, he'd previously designed the State Museum and wished to translate the beautiful lines of Terengganu style into a special resort. The resulting Aryani is stunning—organic, stimulating, unique and, best of all, peaceful. In a rural 9-acre spot by the sea, the rooms are private bungalows situated like a village. Inside, each is masterfully decorated to suit both traditional style and modern comfort. The Heritage Suite wins the prize: a 100-year-old timber palace, restored and rebuilt on the site, it's appointed with fine antiques. The design of the outdoor pool is practically an optical illusion, and the spa (for massage and beauty treatments) is in its own Malay house. The resort's rural location has both a plus and a minus: On the plus side it's secluded; on the minus it's 45 minutes from Kuala Terengganu. The resort can also arrange boat trips, tours to town, and golfing.

✪ **Primula Parkroyal Kuala Terengganu.** Jalan Persinggahan, P.O. Box 43, 20904, Kuala Terengganu, Terengganu Darul Iman, Malaysia. ☎ **800/835-7742** from the U.S. and Canada; 800/363-300 from Australia (Sydney 02/9935-8313); 0800/801-111 from New Zealand; 09/622-2100 or 09/623-3722. Fax 09/623-3360. 249 units. A/C MINIBAR TV TEL. RM320 (US$84.20) double; RM400 (US$105.25) suite. AE, DC, MC, V.

A top pick for accommodations in Kuala Terengganu is the Parkroyal. The first resort to open in this area, it commands the best section of beach the city has to offer and still is very close to the downtown area. It has full resort facilities, which include three excellent restaurants and the only bar in the city (perhaps even in the state). Make sure you get a room facing the sea—the view is dreamy. Other facilities include an outdoor pool, grassy lawns, water-sports facilities, a lobby shop, and a kid's club.

DINING

Ocean. Lot 2679 Jalan Sultan Janah Apitin (by the waterfront). ☎ **09/623-9154.** Reservations not accepted. Main courses RM10–RM25 (US$2.65–US$6.60); seafood sold according to market prices. MC, V. Daily noon–2:30pm and 5:30pm–midnight. CHINESE/SEAFOOD.

One of the most celebrated seafood restaurants in town, Ocean prepares tender prawns, light butterfish, and juicy crab in local and Chinese recipes that are very good. Don't count on much from the alfresco decor. To be honest, the place looks more or less like a warehouse, but the views of the sea help. So does the beer, which Ocean is permitted to serve.

Pelangi Grill. Primula Parkroyal, Jalan Persinggahan. ☎ **09/622-2100.** Main courses RM10–RM24 (US$2.65–US$6.30). AE, DC, JCB, MC, V. Daily noon–11pm. LOCAL/CONTINENTAL.

In an open-air lanai facing the sea and the resort's gardens, this delightful multilevel outdoor cafe is good for either family meals or romantic dinners. The main level is set for standard menu items, which includes the house specialties, sizzling dishes of prawn or beef, plus pizzas and a great assortment of local and Western entrees. The lower patio is set for steamboat, a fondue-style dinner where you place chunks of fish and meats into boiling broth at your table. A small assortment of international wines is available.

ATTRACTIONS

✪ **Central Market.** Jalan Sultan Zainal Abidin.

Open daily from very early until about 7pm, the central market is a huge maze of shops selling every craft made in the region. There's basket weaving for everything from place mats to beach mats. Batik comes in sarongs (with some very unique patterns), ready-made clothing, and household linens. Songket, beautiful fabric woven with gold and silver threads, is sold by the piece or sarong. Brass-ware pots, candlesticks, and curios are piled high and glistening. Every handicraft item you can think of is here, waiting for you to bargain and bring it home. And when you're done, venture to the back of the market and check out the produce, dried goods, and seafood in the wet market.

Chinatown. Jalan Bandar.

While Terengganu has only a small Chinese population, its Chinatown is still quite interesting. This street of shop houses close to the water is still alive, only today many of the shops are art galleries and boutiques, showcasing only the finest regional arts. Also along Jalan Bandar you can find travel agents for trips to nearby islands.

✪ **Custom Made Wooden Yachts International Shipyard.** 3592 Duyong Besar. ☎ **09/623-2072.**

Abdullah bin Muda's family has been building ships by hand for generations. Now Mr. Abdullah is an old-timer, but he gets around, balancing on the planks that surround the dry-docked hulls of his latest masterpieces. He makes fishing boats in Western and Asian styles, as well as luxury yachts—all handmade, all from wood. While Mr. Abdullah doesn't speak any English, he'll let you explore the boats on your own, and even tell you how much money he's getting for them. You'll weep when you hear how inexpensive his fine work is.

Istana Maziah. Jalan Masji. No phone.

Probably one of the least ornate istanas in Malaysia, this lovely yellow and white royal palace, built in 1897, is today mainly used for state and royal ceremonies. It is not open to the public. Tucked away down the narrow winding street is its neighbor, the Masjid (mosque) Abidin.

✪ **State Museum.** Bukit Losong. ☎ **09/622-1444.** Admission RM5 (US$1.30) adults, RM2 (US$0.53) children. Sat–Thurs 9am–5pm.

The buildings that house the museum's collection were built specifically for this purpose. Designed by a member of the Terengganu royal family, an internationally renowned architect who also built the nearby Aryani resort, it reflects the stunning Terengganu architectural style. Atop stilts (16 of them, the traditional number) with high sloping roofs, the three main buildings are connected by elevated walkways. Inside are fine collections that illustrate the history and cultural traditions of the state.

TERENGGANU'S HANDICRAFTS

Chendering, an industrial town about 40 minutes' drive south of Kuala Terengganu, is where you'll find major handicraft production—factories and showrooms of batiks and other lovely items. All these places are located along one stretch of highway, but all are too far apart to walk to. Plan to hire a taxi by the hour to shuttle you between them; they're about a 5-minute hop between each if you're driving. Also, while you're in the area, stop by the **Masjid Tengku Tengah Zahara,** which is only 5 kilometers outside of the town. The mosque is more commonly referred to as the Floating Mosque, as it is built in a lake and appears to be floating on the top.

Noor Arfa. Lot 1048 K Kawasan Perindustrian Chendering. ☎ **09/617-5700.** Sat–Thurs 8am–5pm.

Noor Arfa is Malaysia's largest producer of hand-painted batik. This former cottage-industry business now employs 200 workers to create ready-to-wear fashions that are esteemed as designer labels throughout the country. There's also a shop in town at Aked Mara, A3 Jalan Sultan Zainal Abidin (☎ **09/623-5173**).

Suteramas. Zkawasan Perindustrian Chendering. ☎ **09/617-1355.** Free admission. Sat–Wed 9am–5pm.

Suteramas specializes in batik painting on fine quality silks. At this, their factory showroom, you can buy their latest creations or just watch them being made. Not only do they dye the cloth, they make it from their own worm stock.

✪ **Terengganu Craft Cultural Centre.** Lot 2195 Kawasan Perindustrian Chendering. ☎ **09/617-1033.** Sat–Wed 8am–5pm, Thurs 8am–12:45pm.

Operated by the Malaysian Handicraft Development Corporation, The Craft Cultural Center, also called Budaya Craft, not only sells handicrafts, but also has blocks of warehouses where artisans create the work. See batik painting, brass casting, basket weaving, and wood carving as well as other local crafts in progress.

TERANGGANU'S OUTDOORS

If you are in Terengganu between May and August, you've arrived just in time to see the **baby leatherback turtles.** For hundreds of years, possibly more, giant leatherback turtles have come to the shore here by the thousands. The females crawl to the beaches where they dig holes in which to lay their eggs. Sixty days later, the small turtles hatch and scurry for the water. In recent decades the turtles have had trouble carrying out their ritual, with development and poaching putting severe hardships on the population. Of the babies that are hatched, many never make it to the deep sea. At the Department of Fisheries of the State of Terengganu (Taman Perikanan Chendering; ☎ **09/917-3353**) there is a sanctuary that collects the eggs from the beaches, incubates them in hatcheries, then sets the babies free. They welcome visitors to their exhibits about turtles and the sanctuary's activities, and to midnight watches to see mothers lay eggs and babies hatch. These activities are free of charge.

The first marine park in Malaysia, the **Terengganu Marine Park,** is situated around the nine islands of the Redang archipelago, 45 kilometers (28 miles) northeast of Kuala Terengganu and 27 kilometers (17 miles) out to sea. Sporting the best coral reefs and dive conditions off peninsular Malaysia, the park attracts divers with its many excellent sites. The largest of the islands is Pulau Redang (Redang Island), where most people stay in resorts on overnight diving excursions. Begin with an hour's drive to the northern jetty town of Merang (not to be confused with Marang, which is in the south), followed by an overwater trip to any one of the islands for scuba, snorkeling, and swimming.

Coral Redang Island Resort is one of the best in Redang, with 40 detached and semidetached bungalows and standard rooms on idyllic gardens next to the beach. They specialize in Eco Diving, with everything from beginner PADI courses to boat dives and night dives, with equipment rental as well. The resort also has snorkeling gear. Contact Coral Redang at 137A, 1st Floor, Jalan Sultan Zainal Abidin, Kuala Terenganu (☎ **09/623-6200;** fax 09/623-6300).

17 Kota Bharu

In the northeast corner of peninsular Malaysia, bordering Thailand, is the state of **Kelantan.** Few tourists head this far north up the east coast, but it's a fascinating journey for those interested in seeing Malaysia as it might have been without so many foreign influences. Kelantan owes its character to the mountain range that runs north to south through the interior, slicing the peninsula in half. The state is populated mostly by Malays and Bumiputeras, with only tiny factions of Chinese and Indian residents and almost no traces of British colonialism. Not surprisingly, Kelantan is the heart of traditional Islam in modern Malaysia. While the government in KL constructs social policies based upon a more open and tolerant Islam, religious and government leaders in Kelantan can be counted on to put forth a strong Muslim ideal where they feel they may have influence. Indeed, the state has one of only two ministers that are not members of Dr. Mahathir's leading UMNO party.

Kota Bharu, the state capital, is the heart of the region. The area is rich in Malay cultural heritage, as evidenced in the continuing interest in arts like *silat* (Malay martial arts), *wayang kulit* (puppetry), *gasing* (top-spinning), and *wau* (kite flying). For the record, you won't find too much traditional music or dance, as women are forbidden from entertaining in public. Also beware that the state has strict laws controlling the sale of alcoholic beverages, which cannot be purchased in stores, hotels, or most restaurants. You will not find a single bar. Chinese restaurants, however, are permitted to sell beer to their patrons, but will probably not allow you to take any away.

VISITOR INFORMATION
You'll find the Kelantan Tourist Information Centre at Jalan Sultan Ibrahim (☎ 09/748-5534).

GETTING THERE
BY AIR   From KL, Malaysia Airlines (☎ 03/746-3000) flies twice daily. You'll land at Kota Bharu's Sultan Ismail Petra Airport (☎ 09/773-7000), about 20 minutes outside the city. A taxi to town shouldn't be any more than RM25 (US$6.60). The Malaysia Airlines office in town is at Ground Floor, Kompleks Yakin, Jalan Gajah Mati (☎ 09/744-7000).

BY TRAIN   The KTM runs a line through the center of the peninsula all the way to the Thai border. The Wakaf Bharu station is closest to the city, and taxis are available, or you can take local bus nos. 19 or 27. For train information in KL call ☎ 03/274-7424.

BY BUS   Kota Bharu's bus terminal is at Jalan Padang Garong off Jalan Doktor. Buses bring you here from all corners of the peninsula. From KL call Transnasional at Puduraya Bus Terminal (☎ 03/230-3300). They've got two dailies at a cost of RM22 (US$5.80). From Kuala Terengganu's bus terminal, Transnasional (☎ 09/623-8384) has six buses daily for RM7.50 (US$2). To find out about buses out of Kota Bharu, call ☎ 09/747-4330. The taxi stand is just across the street, and you may be hounded by all sorts of gypsy cabs, people with cars who are not proper taxi drivers but who will take you places to make some extra cash. They're basically honest.

BY TAXI   The local taxi stand across from the bus terminal also acts as the outstation taxi stand. To reserve a car the number is ☎ 09/748-1386. Taxis from Kuala Terengganu run about RM80 (US$21.05).

GETTING AROUND
One thing I like about Kota Bharu is how most of the major museums are located in one central area, so walking to them is very easy. For the beach and cottage industry areas you'll need to hire a **taxi.** The main taxi stand is at Jalan Padang Garong; call ☎ 09/748-1386 for booking. Daily and half-day rates can be negotiated for about RM15 (US$3.95) per hour. Trips around town will be between RM5 and RM10 (US$1.30 and US$2.65).

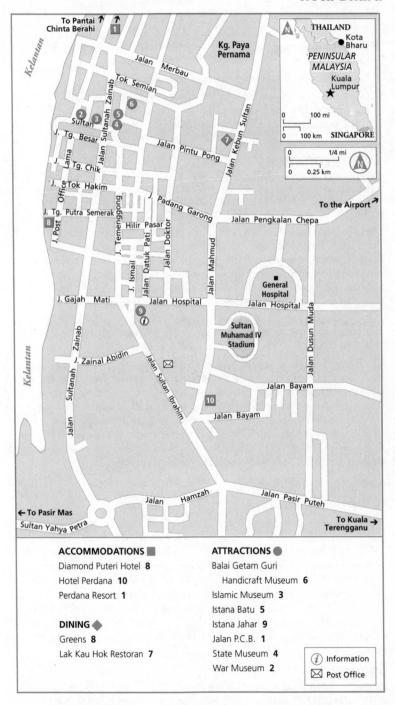

Kota Bharu

THAILAND

Kota Bharu

PENINSULAR MALAYSIA

Kuala Lumpur

SINGAPORE

0 100 mi
0 100 km

0 1/4 mi
0 0.25 km

Kelantan

To Pantai Chinta Berahi

Kg. Paya Pernama

Jalan Merbau

Tok Semian

Sultan

J. Tg. Besar

J. Lama

J. Tg. Chik

J. Tok Hakim

J. Office

J. Tg. Putra Semerak

J. Post

Jalan Sultanah Zainab

Jalan Pintu Pong

Jalan Kebun Sultan

J. Padang Garong

Jalan Pengkalan Chepa

To the Airport

Hilir Pasar

J. Temenggong

Jalan Datuk Pati

Jalan Doktor

Jalan Mahmud

J. Ismail

J. Gajah Mati

Jalan Hospital

General Hospital

Jalan Hospital

Sultan Muhamad IV Stadium

Jalan Dusun Muda

J. Zainab

J. Zainal Abidin

Jalan Sultan Ibrahim

Sultanah

Jalan

Jalan Bayam

Jalan Bayam

To Pasir Mas

Jalan Hamzah

Jalan Pasir Puteh

Sultan Yahya Petra

To Kuala Terengganu

ACCOMMODATIONS

Diamond Puteri Hotel **8**
Hotel Perdana **10**
Perdana Resort **1**

DINING

Greens **8**
Lak Kau Hok Restoran **7**

ATTRACTIONS

Balai Getam Guri
   Handicraft Museum **6**
Islamic Museum **3**
Istana Batu **5**
Istana Jahar **9**
Jalan P.C.B. **1**
State Museum **4**
War Museum **2**

(i) Information
✉ Post Office

Fast Facts: Kota Bharu

Banks/Currency Exchange   Find these at Jalan Pitum Pong and Jalan Kebun Sultan.

Post Office   The main post office is at Jalan Sultan Ismail (☎ **09/748-4033**).

Internet/E-mail   Look for Internet service at Perdana Cyber Café just inside Perdana Superbowl next to (naturally) the Hotel Perdana.

For more Fast Facts about Malaysia, see "Planning a Trip to Malaysia" on p. 456.

ACCOMMODATIONS

✪ **Diamond Puteri Hotel.** Jalan Post Office Lama, 1500 Kota Bharu, Kelantan. ☎ **09/743-9988,** or Kuala Lumpur sales office 03/413-0448. Fax 09/743-8388. 311 units. A/C MINIBAR TV TEL. RM220–RM255 (US$57.90–US$67.10) double; RM320 (US$84.20) suite. AE, DC, MC, V.

Does Diamond Puteri lead Kota Bharu into the 21st century, or at least bring it up to the 20th? Either way, it's the city's first shiny new five-star hotel, opened just in time for the economic crisis and still struggling to come into its own, but still full of all the modern conveniences. Guest rooms are welcoming and bright. The location by the Kelantan River doesn't offer the fabulous view you'd hope for, which makes the outdoor pool area not as inviting. They also have a fitness center with a sauna.

Hotel Perdana. Jalan Mahmood, P.O. Box 222, 15720 Kota Bharu, Kelantan. ☎ **09/748-5000.** Fax 09/744-7621. 178 units. A/C MINIBAR TV TEL. RM125–RM140 (US$32.90–US$36.85) double; RM600 (US$157.90) suite.

The premier business-class hotel in Kota Bharu for years, Perdana was unrivaled until the Diamond Puteri opened in 1998. Perdana won't seem as fancy anymore, but it's still a good choice for affordable and comfortable accommodations in the city. The small guest rooms need a little refurbishing, but are spick-and-span. Besides, the rates are good for the quality of the facility. Unusual for a hotel, Perdana boasts a bowling alley (!) and more conventional hotel facilities such as an outdoor swimming pool, a fitness center (which is not exactly state-of-the-art), sauna, and steam bath. Sports activities like tennis and squash also make the hotel attractive.

Perdana Resort. Jalan Kuala Pa'Amat, Pantai Cahaya Bulan, P.O. Box 121, 15710 Kota Bharu, Kelantan, Malaysia. ☎ **09/774-4000.** Fax 09/774-4980. 117 units. A/C MINIBAR TV TEL. RM170–RM210 (US$44.75–US$55.25) chalet. AE, DC, MC, V.

For a little beach fun in Kota Bharu, head for Perdana Resort, just about the only beach resort in the area, and perhaps the only beach where you can wear a Western-style bathing suit and not feel out of place. The individual chalets make for great privacy, each with its own porch outside and bathroom inside. They're also spacious, so if you want to put in an extra bed or two for an additional RM30, you'll still have ample room to get around. Perdana will arrange whatever beach activity you desire, from paddle boats to canoeing, beach volleyball, and fishing trips. They also have outdoor tennis, bicycle rentals, horseback riding, kite flying, and a host of other amusements to keep you busy. When you can't take anymore, collapse in the giant free-form pool.

DINING

Greens. Diamond Puteri Hotel, Jalan Post Office Lama. ☎ **09/743-9988.** Main courses RM10–RM38 (US$2.65–US$10). AE, DC, MC, V. Daily 7am–midnight. WESTERN/LOCAL.

Done up in a simple cafe style, Greens has yet to grow into its surroundings in the new Diamond Puteri Hotel. Serving as the coffee shop for the hotel, it is open from early in the morning till late at night and features a wide range of dishes. Choose from familiar Western favorites or try their specialty local Kelantanese selections (which are the best dishes), such as *ayam perchik* (chicken in a coconut and fish stock gravy), a favorite in these parts.

Lak Kau Hok Restoran. 2959 Jalan Kebun Sultan. ☎ **09/748-3762.** RM8–RM25 (US$2.10–US$6.60). No credit cards. Daily 11am–2:30pm and 6–10pm. CHINESE/SEAFOOD.

Kota Bharu isn't all that boring a town at night. Head down to Chinatown's Jalan Kebun Sultan where the streets get lively. Walk past glowing restaurants, hawker stalls, and friends out for a chat and a stroll, and when you reach the little house that is Lak Kau Hok, head inside. The smells of garlic and chiles will seduce you from the moment you enter, and after specialties like steamed garlic prawns and steamed fish Teochew style (with vegetables and mushrooms sautéed in a rich gravy), you'll be very happy you came. Did I mention they serve beer?

ATTRACTIONS

✪ **Padang Merdeka museums.** At the end of Jalan Hilir Kota. ☎ **09/744-4666.** Sat–Thurs 8:30am–4:45pm.

Centered around the Padang Merdeka are five of the most significant sights in Kota Bharu, run by the Kelantan State Museum Corporation. At the **Istana Jahar** (adults RM3/US$0.79, children RM1.50/US$0.39), Kelantan traditional costumes, antiques, and musical instruments are displayed in context of their usage in royal ceremonies. **Istana Batu** (adults RM2/US$0.53, children RM1/US$0.26) takes you through a photographic journey of Kelantan's royal family, and offers a peek at their lifestyle through the past 200 years. The **Balai Getam Guri** handicraft museum (adults RM1/US$0.26, children RM.50/US$0.13) showcases the finest in Kelantanese textiles, basketry, embroidery, batik printing, and silversmithing. You'll also be able to buy crafts in the shops within the compound. The **Islamic Museum (Muzium Islam)** (adults RM1/US$0.26, children RM0.50/US$0.13) teaches everything you might want to know about Islam in this state, with a focus on Islamic arts and Kelantan's role in spreading Islam in the region. Finally there is the **War Museum (Bank Kerapu)** (adults RM2/US$0.53, children RM1/US$0.26), which tells the story of Kelantan during World War II in a 1912 bank building that survived the invasion.

✪ **State Museum (Muzium Negeri).** Jalan Hospital. ☎ **09/744-4666.** RM2 (US$0.53) adults, RM1 (US$0.26) children. Sat–Thurs 8:30am–4:45pm.

It's been a long time since this old building served as the colonial land office, but in 1990 major renovations gave it a new life. It now houses the Kelantan Art Gallery, including ceramics, traditional musical instruments, and cultural pastimes exhibits.

SHOPPING

For great local handicrafts shopping, visitors to Kelantan need go no further than **Jalan P.C.B.,** the road that leads to P.C.B. beach from Kota Bharu's Chinatown area. Hire a taxi and stop at every roadside factory, showroom, shop, and crafts house (the place crawls with them!) and you'll satisfy every shopping itch that needs scratching. Some wonderful places to try are **Wisma Songket Kampung Penambang,** Jalan P.C.B. (☎ 09/744-7757), for songket cloth and clothing, and to see the ladies weaving the fine cloth. The local kite man, **Haji Wan Hussen bin Haji Ibrahim,** makes and sells kites out of his home at 328–A Kampong Redong Tikat, Jalan P.C.B. (☎ **09/744-0462**), and will invite you in for a look. He'll pack them sturdily so you can airmail them home. Also, **Pantas Songket & Batik Manufacturer,** Kampung Penambang, Jalan P.C.B. (☎ **09/744-1616**), has a nice selection of batik clothing and sarongs, plus some pieces of songket cloth.

In town, if you'd like to buy some silver, good (and inexpensive) filigree jewelry collections and silver housewares are to be had at **Mohamed Salleh & Sons,** 1260B Jalan Sultanah Zainab (☎ **09/748-3401**), and **K. B. Permai,** 5406–C Jalan Sultanah Zainab (☎ **09/748-5661**).

In the small but lively Chinatown area look for **A. Zahari Antik,** 3953–B Jalan Kebin Sultan (☎ **09/744-3548**), where you can shop for old treasures like keris (Malay daggers with wavy blades, of which this place has a great selection) as well as pottery, carvings, and brass.

Finally, for a little local shopping experience, check out the giant **Pasar Besar wet market** on Jalan Parit Dalam. Behind the produce and fish stands are shops for cheap bargains.

18 East Malaysia: Borneo

Borneo for the past 2 centuries has been the epitome of adventure travel. While bustling ports like Penang, Malacca, and Singapore attracted early travelers with dollars in their eyes, Borneo attracted those with adventure in their hearts. Today, the island still draws visitors who seek new and unusual experiences, and few leave disappointed. Rivers meander through dense tropical rain forests, beaches stretch for miles, and caves snake out longer than any in the world. All sorts of creatures you'd never imagine live in the rain forest: deer the size of house cats, owls only 6 inches tall, the odd probiscus monkey, and the orangutan, whose only other natural home is Sumatra. It's also home to the largest flower in the world, the Rafflesia, spanning up to a meter (about 3 ft.) wide. Small wonder this place has special interest for scientists and researchers the world around.

The people of Borneo can be credited for most of the alluring tales of early travels. The exotically adorned tribes of warring headhunters and pirates of yesteryear, some of whom still live lifestyles little changed (though both headhunting and piracy are now illegal), today share their mysterious cultures and colorful traditions openly with outsiders.

Add to all of this the fabulous tale of the White Raja of Sarawak, Sir James Brooke, whose family ruled the state for just over 100 years, and you have a land filled with allure, mystery, and romance unlike any other.

Malaysia, Brunei Darussalam, and Indonesia have divided the island of Borneo. Indonesia claims Kalimantan to the south and east, and the Malaysian states of **Sarawak** and Sabah lie to the north and northwest. The small sultanate of Brunei is nestled between the two Malaysian states on the western coastline.

SARAWAK

Tropical rain forest accounts for more than 70% of Sarawak's total land mass, providing homes for not only exotic species of plants and animals, but for the different ethnic groups who are indigenous to the area. With more than 10 national parks and four wildlife preserves, Malaysia shows its commitment to conserving the delicate balance of life here, while allowing small gateways for travelers to appreciate Sarawak's natural wonders. A network of rivers connects the inland areas to the rest of the world, and a boat trip to visit tribal communities and trek into caves and jungles can prove to be the most memorable attraction going.

Every visitor to Sarawak starts out from **Kuching,** the capital city. With a population of some 400,000 people, it's small but oddly cosmopolitan. In addition to local tribes that gave up forest living, the city has large populations of Malays, Chinese, Indians, and Europeans, most of whom migrated in the last 2 centuries. The city sits at the mouth of the Kuching River, which will be your main artery for trips inland. Before you head off for the river, though, check out the many delights of this mysterious colonial kingdom.

KUCHING

The perfect introduction to Sarawak begins in its capital. Kuching's museums, cultural exhibits, and historical attractions will help you form an overview of the history, people, and natural wonders of the state. In Kuching your introduction to Sarawak will be comfortable and fun; culture by day and good food and fun by night. Kuching, meaning "cat" in Malay, also has a wonderful sense of humor, featuring monuments and exhibits to its feline mascot on almost every corner.

Visitor Information

The Sarawak Tourism Board's **Visitor Information Centre** has literature and staff that can answer any question about activities in the state and city. This is actually the best place to start planning any trips to Sarawak's wonderful national parks, as the main office for the parks board operates from here. Really, they're just incredibly informed and are so welcoming, feel free to take advantage. You'll find them at the Padang Merdeka next to the Sarawak Museum (☎ **082/423-600**).

Getting There

Almost all travelers to Sarawak enter via Kuching International Airport, just outside the city. Malaysia Airlines (☎ **03/746-3000** in KL) flies here about 10 times daily from KL. In addition, there are nonstop flights from the Malaysian cities of Johor Bahru and Kota Kinabalu. Malaysia Airlines also connects Kuching with direct flights from Singapore, Bandar Seri Bagawan in Brunei, Hong Kong, and Manila. The number for Malaysia Airlines in Kuching is ☎ **082/246-622.** For airport information call ☎ **082/454-255.**

Taxis from the airport use coupons that you purchase outside the arrival hall. Priced according to zones, most trips to the central parts of town will be RM16 (US$4.20).

Getting Around

Centered around a padang, or large ceremonial field, Kuching resembles many other Malaysian cities. Buildings of beautiful colonial style rise on the edges of the field; many of these today house Sarawak's museums. The main sights, as well as the Chinatown area and the riverfront, are easily accessible by foot. Taxis are also available, and do not use meters; most rides around town are quoted at RM6 (US$1.60). Taxis can be waved down from the side of the road, or if you're in the Chinatown area the main taxi stand is near Gambier Road near the end of the India Street Pedestrian Mall. For a taxi call ☎ **082/348-898.**

Fast Facts: Sarawak

American Express The American Express office is located at Cph Travel Agencies, 70 Padungan Rd. (☎ **082/242-289**).

Banks/Currency Exchange Major banks have branches on Tunku Abdul Rahman Road near Holiday Inn Kuching, or in the downtown area around Khoo Hun Yeang Road.

Internet/E-mail For a good Internet cafe try Cyber City, No. 46 Ground Floor Block D (☎ **082/428-318**), just behind Riverside Complex Shopping Mall, charging RM6 per hour (US$1.60).

Post Office The central post office is on Jalan Tun Abang Haji Openg (☎ **082/245-952**).

For more Fast Facts about Malaysia, see "Planning a Trip to Malaysia" on p. 456.

Accommodations

Holiday Inn Kuching. P.O. Box 2362, Jalan Tunku Abdul Rahman, 93100 Kuching, Sarawak, Malaysia. ☎ **082/423-111.** Fax 082/426-169. 305 units. A/C MINIBAR TV TEL. RM288–RM345 (US$76–US$91) double; RM575 (US$152) and up suite. AE, DC, JCB, MC, V.

Holiday Inn offers Western-style accommodations at a moderate price, and you'll appreciate its location in an excellent part of town. It sits along the bank of the Kuching River, so to get to the main riverside area you need only stroll 10 minutes past some of the city's unique historical and cultural sights, shopping, and good places to dine. Catering to a diverse group of leisure travelers and businesspeople, the hotel has spacious, modern, and comfortable rooms, and while there are few bells and whistles, you won't want for convenience. The outdoor swimming pool and excellent fitness center facility will help you unwind, and the small shopping arcade has one of the best collections of books on Sarawak that can be found in the city.

Kuching

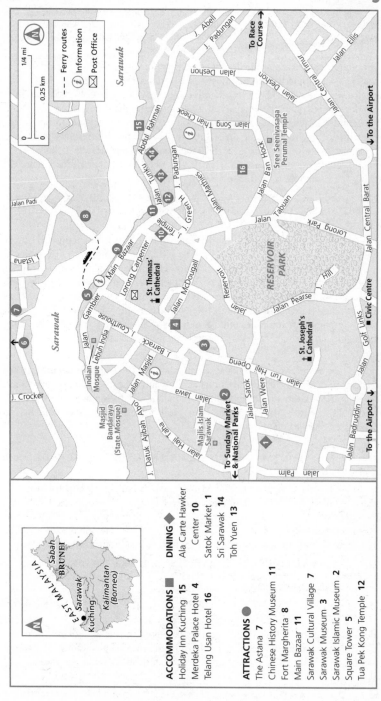

ACCOMMODATIONS ■
Holiday Inn Kuching **15**
Merdeka Palace Hotel **4**
Telang Usan Hotel **16**

ATTRACTIONS ●
The Astana **7**
Chinese History Museum **11**
Fort Margherita **8**
Main Bazaar **11**
Sarawak Cultural Village **7**
Sarawak Museum **3**
Sarawak Islamic Museum **2**
Square Tower **5**
Tua Pek Kong Temple **12**

DINING ◆
Ala Carte Hawker
  Center **10**
Satok Market **1**
Sri Sarawak **14**
Toh Yuen **13**

⭘ **Merdeka Palace Hotel.** Jalan Tun Abang Haji Openg, 93000 Kuching, Sarawak, Malaysia. ☎ **082/258-000.** Fax 082/425-400. 214 units. A/C MINIBAR TV TEL. RM210–RM385 (US$55.25–US$101.30) double; RM646–RM790 (US$170–US$207.90) suite. AE, DC, JCB, MC, V.

Towering over the Padang Merdeka in the center of town is the Merdeka Palace, practically a landmark in its own right (as soon as you see the easily distinguishable tower, you'll always know where you are). This is one of the most fashionable addresses in the city, for guests as well as banquets and functions. From the large marble lobby to the mezzanine shopping arcade stuffed with designer tenants, its reputation for elegance is justified. Large rooms come dressed in European-inspired furnishings and fabrics. Try to get a view of the padang, as the less expensive rooms face the parking lot. The rooftop outdoor swimming pool is small, but the fully equipped fitness center has sauna and steam rooms, plus massage.

⭘ **Telang Usan Hotel.** Ban Hock Road, P.O. Box 1579, 93732 Kuching, Sarawak, Malaysia. ☎ **082/415-588.** Fax 082/245-316. 66 units. A/C TV TEL. RM140–RM200 (US$36.85–US$52.65) double. AE, DC, JCB, MC, V.

While in Kuching I like to stay at the Telang Usan Hotel. It's not as flashy as the higher priced places, but it's a fantastic bargain for a good room. Most guests here are leisure travelers, and in fact, many are repeat visitors. The small public areas sport murals in local Iban style, revealing the origin of the hotel's owner and operator. While rooms are small and decor is not completely up-to-date, they're spotless. Some rooms have only standing showers, so be sure to specify when making your reservation if a long bath is important to you. The coffee shop serves local and Western food from 7am to midnight, and the higher category rooms have minibars.

Dining

In addition to the two conventional restaurants listed below, Kuching's **hawker center** food stalls offer a culinary adventure at affordable prices. A good centrally located center is at **Ala Carte** on Lebuh Temple. It's indoor and air-conditioned. Also try the food stalls at **Satok Market** out at Jalan Satok for excellent Malay, Chinese, and Sarawakian cuisine.

⭘ **Sri Sarawak.** Crowne Plaza Riverside Kuching, Jalan Tunku Abdul Rahman. ☎ **082/247-777.** Main courses RM8–RM22 (US$2.10–US$5.80). AE, DC, JCB, MC, V. Daily noon–2:30pm and 6–10:30pm. MALAY.

Sri Sarawak is the only place to find Malay food in a fine-dining establishment. The restaurant occupies the 18th floor of the Crowne Plaza hotel, with views all around to the city below. The friendly and helpful staff is more than happy to help you navigate the menu, which includes Sarawak specialties such as *umai*, raw fish that's "cooked" in lime juice with onion, ginger, and chile. I'm addicted and want everyone to try it!

Toh Yuen. Kuching Hilton, Jalan Tunku Abdul Rahman. ☎ **082/248-200.** Reservations recommended on weekends. RM14–RM48 (US$3.70–US$12.65). AE, DC, JCB, MC, V. Daily 11:30am–2:30pm and 6:30–10:30pm. CHINESE.

One of the premier Chinese restaurants in Kuching, Toh Yueh serves excellently prepared dishes that are as pleasing to the eye as they are to the palate. Chef's specialties like butter prawns melt in your mouth, as do any of the many bean curd selections and crunchy vegetable dishes. Beware, portions are huge! Call ahead for special promotions for weekend lunch and dinner, which can be surprisingly low priced.

Attractions

⭘ **The Astana and Fort Margherita.** Across the Sarawak River from town. Museum: no phone. Fort: ☎ **082/244-232.** Free admission. Tues–Sun 9am–5pm.

At the waterfront by the Square Tower you'll find water taxis to take you across the river to see these two reminders of the White Rajas of Sarawak. The Astana, built in 1870 by Raja Charles Brooke, the second raja of Sarawak, is now the official residence of the governor. It is not open to the public, but visitors may still walk in the gardens. The best view of the Astana, however is from the water.

Raja Charles Brooke's wife, Ranee Margaret, gave her name to Fort Margherita, which was erected in 1870 to protect the city of Kuching. Inside the great castlelike building is a police museum, the most interesting sights of which are the depictions of criminal punishment.

Chinese History Museum. Corner of Main Bazaar and Jalan Tunku Abdul Rahman. No phone. Free admission. Daily 9am–5pm.

Built in 1912, this old Chinese Chamber of Commerce Building is the perfect venue for a museum that traces the history of Chinese communities in Sarawak. Though small, it's centrally located and a convenient stop while you're in the area.

Main Bazaar. Along the river.

Main Bazaar, the major thoroughfare along the river, is home to Kuching's antiques and handicraft shops. If you're walking along the river, a little time in these shops is like a walk through a traditional handicrafts art gallery. You'll also find souvenir shops and some nice T-shirt silk-screeners.

✪ **Sarawak Cultural Village.** Kampung Budaya Sarawak, Pantai Damai, Santubong. ☎ **082/846-411.** RM45 (US$11.85) adults, RM22.50 (US$5.90) children. Daily 9am–5pm.

What appears to be a contrived theme park turns out to be a really fun place to learn about Sarawak's indigenous people. Built around a lagoon, the park re-creates the various styles of longhouse dwellings of each of the major tribes. Inside each house are representative members of each tribe displaying cultural artifacts and performing music, teaching dart blowing, and showing off carving talents. Give yourself plenty of time to stick around and talk with the people, who are recruited from villages inland and love to tell stories about their homes and traditions. Performers dance and display costumes at 11:30am and 4:30 daily. A shuttle bus leaves at regular intervals from the Holiday Inn Kuching on Jalan Abell.

Sarawak Islamic Museum. Jalan P. Ramlee. ☎ **082/244-232.** Free admission. Sat–Thurs 9am–5pm; Fri 9am–12:45pm and 3–5pm.

A splendid array of Muslim artifacts at this quiet and serene museum depicts the history of Islam and its spread to Southeast Asia. Local customs and history are also highlighted. While women are not required to cover their heads, respectable attire that covers the legs and arms is requested.

✪ **Sarawak Museum.** Jalan Tun Haji Openg. ☎ **082/244-232.** Free admission. Sat–Thurs 9am–5pm; Fri 9am–12:45pm and 3–5pm.

Two branches, one old and one new, display exhibits of the natural history, indigenous peoples, and culture of Sarawak, plus the state's colonial and modern history. The two branches are connected by an overhead walkway above Jalan Tun Haji Openg. The wildlife exhibit is a bit musty, but the arts and artifacts in the other sections are well tended. A tiny aquarium sits neglected behind the old branch, but the gardens here are lovely.

Square Tower. Jalan Gambier near the riverfront. ☎ **082/426-093.**

The tower, built in 1879, served as a prison camp, but today the waterfront real estate is better served by a tourist information center. The Square Tower is also a prime starting place for a stroll along the riverside, and is where you'll also find out about cultural performances and exhibitions held at the waterfront; or call the number above for performance schedules.

Tua Pek Kong Temple. Junction of Jalan Tunku Abdul Rahman and Jalan Padungan. No phone.

At a main crossroads near the river stands the oldest Chinese temple in Sarawak. While officially it is dated at 1876, most locals acknowledge the true date of its beginnings as 1843. It's still lively in form and spirit, with colorful dragons tumbling along the walls and incense filling the air.

Touring Local Culture

When you come to Sarawak everyone will tell you that you must take a trip to witness **life in a longhouse.** It is perhaps one of the most unique experiences you'll have, and is a lot easier to arrange than it sounds. Many good tour operators in Kuching take visitors out to longhouse communities, where guests are invited to stay for 1 or more nights. You'll eat local food, experience daily culture, and view traditional pastimes and ceremonies. On longer tours you may stop at more than one village to get a cross-cultural comparison of two or more different tribes. Good tour operators to speak to about arranging a trip are **Borneo Adventure,** 55 Main Bazaar (☎ **082/245-175;** fax 082/422-626), and **Telang Usan Travel & Tours,** Ban Hock Road (☎ **082/236-945;** fax 082/236-589). These agencies can also arrange trips into Sarawak's national parks.

TOURING SARAWAK'S NATIONAL PARKS

Before planning any trip into the national parks, travelers must contact the **National Parks Booking Office** at the Visitors Information Centre next to the Sarawak Museum (☎ **082/248-088;** fax 082/256-301). You will need to acquire permission to enter any park, and be advised on park safety and regulations. I recommend you visit the office itself. Situated inside the Tourism Board office, the staff here knows about every trip activity and can advise on accommodations options and all forms of transportation to and from the parks, and can even book your trip for you. They'll also screen tourism videos of the parks for you in their conference room, to help you decide which parks are best for your interests.

Bako National Park, established in 1957, is Sarawak's oldest National Park. An area of 2,728 hectares (6,820 acres) combines mangrove forest, lowland jungle, and high plains covered in scrub. Throughout the park you'll see the pitcher plant and other strange carnivorous plants, plus long-tailed macaques, monitor lizards, bearded pigs, and the unique probiscus monkey. Because the park is only 37 kilometers (22 miles) from Kuching, trips here are extremely convenient.

A new project, the **Matang Wildlife Centre,** about an hour outside of Kuching, gives endangered wildlife a home, provides researchers with insights into wildlife conservation, and educates visitors about the animals and their habitat. For day trips, no parks department permission is required.

Gunung Gading National Park, about a 2-hour drive west of Kuching, sprawls 4,106 hectares (10,265 acres) over rugged mountains to beautiful beach spots along the coast. Day-trippers and overnighters come to get a glimpse of the Rafflesia, the largest flower in the world. The flowers are short-lived and temperamental, but the national parks office will let you know if there are any in bloom.

Gunung Mulu National Park provides an amazing adventure with its astounding underground network of caves. The park claims the world's largest cave passage (Deer Cave), the world's largest natural chamber (Sarawak Chamber), and Southeast Asia's longest cave (Clearwater Cave). No fewer than 18 caves offer explorers trips of varying degrees of difficulty, from simple treks with minimal gear to technically difficult caves that require specialized equipment and skills. Aboveground is 544 square kilometers (326 sq. miles) of primary rain forest, peat swamps, and mountainous forests teeming with mammals, birds, and unusual insects. Located in the north of Sarawak, Mulu is very close to the Brunei border.

Niah National Park, while interesting to nature buffs, is more fascinating for those interested in archaeology. From 1954 to 1967 explorers excavated a prehistoric site inside Niah's extensive cave network. The site dates as far back as 40,000 years, and is believed to have been continuously occupied until some 2,000 years ago. The **Niah Great Cave,** which contains the site, revealed sharp stone implements, pottery vessels, and animal and botanical remains. Near the mouth of the cave is a burial ground dating from Paleolithic times. The **Painted Cave,** also within Niah's cave network, is a magnificent gallery of mystical cave paintings and coffins that were buried here between A.D. 1 and A.D. 780. While a visit to the park requires parks department permission, further information on the excavation sites can be obtained from the Sarawak Museum (☎ **082/244-232;** fax 082/246-680).

10 Bali & Lombok

by Lynn A. Levine with Mary Herczog

I arrived at the airport in Bali, armed with vague visions of a tropical paradise. At the airport I met a couple who, after only 1 week of a planned 3-week honeymoon, were disgusted enough to flee from the island. Hmmm. After my visit I thought, "Did we really visit the same place, or were they simply unrealistic in their idea of an earthly paradise?" Bali is every bit what you'd imagine: a treasure of sensual pleasures for the eyes, ears, and taste buds. The geology alone makes a stopover here more than worth the trouble, studded as it is with volcanic peaks, bubbling springs, tropical exoticism, and stunning beaches. Even the nonbeliever will appreciate why the earliest inhabitants found sacredness at almost every turn, erecting stunning works of craftsmanship and architecture just as eye-popping as the marketing videos depict them. Daily ceremonies abound—tooth fillings, weddings, and cremations—drawing elaborately dressed women with ornate fruit offerings balanced on their heads, and men unselfconsciously adorned with colorful sarongs and traditional headdresses. The soothing music of the *gamelan* and the calming resonance of bamboo wind chimes are an unobtrusive fixture in the background, and the pungent fruits of the Spice Islands lend a pleasingly complex and aggressive flavor to the local cuisine. But Bali would be just another tropical paradise without the Balinese, a culture so rich, layered, and completely unique to this extraordinary place, that expats who have lived here 20 years say with a sigh, "The longer I stay, the less I understand it."

The main religion on the island, Agama Hindu Dharma, with all the pomp and ceremony that goes along with it, is the central force in the life of the Balinese: a distinct blend of Hindu, Buddhist, Javanese, and ancient indigenous beliefs. Beauty and harmony, essentials of the belief system, are played out in an almost improbable artistry in everything the Balinese lay their hands on, and with such an abundance of raw materials, why not? Fresh flowers are strewn everywhere and replaced daily. Complicated centerpieces of woven bamboo and elephant grass are the hotel staff's way of welcoming you to their home. You'll see beauty in every corner of their world: in intricate woodcarved archways, elaborately gilded doorways, batik textiles, and not least of all on the faces of the natives. If Bali didn't actually materialize into this world as the "Island of the Gods," the island must now be at the top of the gods' lists of prime real estate. Not far behind the deities is a stampede of cultural voyeurs, but rather than resent the attention, the locals look upon these intruders with something akin to amused patience, as we fumble unknowingly into the courtyards of private homes, lured by the spectacle of bright ribbons and abundant pyramids of the finest fruits. Let's not forget either that the quality of life on Bali is uplifted well above that of other islands in Southeast Asia, so it would be difficult for the Balinese to ignore the advantages of commerce.

So what scared away the honeymooners? Whatever heights of perfection you will reach by immersing yourself in the warmth, spirituality, and color of this island, there's no mistaking its third world roots. Since anyone arriving on the island is wealthy enough to afford the plane ticket, we are seen by many as little more than wallets with legs. Savvy locals understand the strength of the dollar and will squeeze you often. There's nothing more sobering than being coerced into a donation for a temple that an impending ceremony prevented you from entering or, upon making a donation, hearing the phrase, "Oh, so little?" Admittedly, the surface "noise" can be quite maddening, but once accustomed to it, either by sequester or by resignation, the magnificence of the island, the dignity of the people, and the bounty of Mother Nature will undoubtedly shine brighter.

BALI TODAY

As with any undiscovered paradise that isn't so undiscovered any more, Bali buffs mourn the loss of the island's innocence. But Bali has always been a magnet for tourists and expats, and if its economy is now almost solely based on tourism (and rice), well, at least they have one.

But to say that it's changed is only telling part of the truth. Sure, 25 years ago there were virtually no hotels on Kuta Beach. Twenty-five years ago, there was no electricity in Ubud, and now there's a cybercafe on every corner. Peddlers ("touts") and hustlers—usually opportunists imported from Java—have grown in numbers and aggressiveness, determined to take advantage of the walking wallets that are American, European, and Australian visitors. And yet, the essential Bali has not changed. The Balinese ritualized way of life remains precisely as it always has been.

BALI & THE INDONESIAN CRISIS

The riots and protests that erupted in Indonesia in 1998 were the result of 3 decades of military rule and struggles to bring the world's fourth most populous country into the modern global economy. Chafing under the virtual dictatorship of President Suharto, the Indonesians finally revolted, with demonstrations turning into riots that made headlines around the world. In June of 1999, Indonesians witnessed their first free parliamentary election since 1955, ousting Suharto, and electing Abdurrahman Wahid, a highly respected Sufi cleric and able politician, as president. But riots, bombings, and protests continue to plague the country, specifically in Aceh, East Timor, and Irian Jaya, where separatist movements have little support both locally and internationally. (As of this writing, Abdurrahman Wahid stands accused of presidential misconduct in connection with a corruption scandal, the outcome of which is yet to be seen.)

With its tourist-based economy and Hindu religion, Bali has remained largely unaffected by the tumultuous and unpredictable economic and social problems recently wracking the rest of the country. Indeed, during the riots, the U.S. State Department told all tourists to come home immediately. Those on Bali, by and large, looked around, saw everything was normal, and stayed put, leaving me to suspect that the State Department warning was nothing more than economic leverage during a particularly politicized time aimed at withholding tourist dollars. However, some tourists

Bali

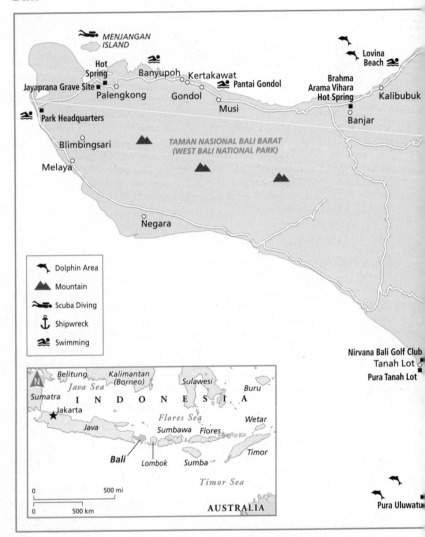

have stayed away out of fear, while others simply have found it harder to get there, thanks to decreased flights (particularly when the state airline, Garuda, ceased being able to offer international flights).

At press time, matters were still too unpredictable and unstable to offer any strong opinions about Indonesia's—or Bali's—future. I can say that at the moment Bali remains a safe, peaceful place to visit, despite any other Indonesian troubles.

LEARNING MORE ABOUT BALI

To learn more about Bali, we cannot recommend Fred Eisenman's two-volume *Bali: Sekala & Niskala* (Periplus Editions) highly enough. It can be obtained in the U.S. or throughout Bali, particularly in Ubud. Eisenman spends part of the year in Jimbaran,

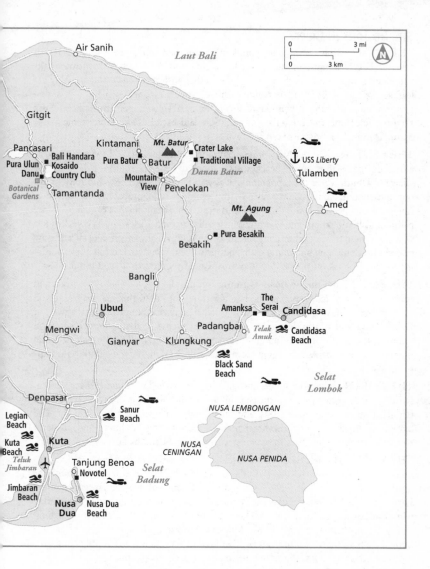

and his writing about all aspects of Balinese culture—society, religion, tradition, art, and so on—is lovingly detailed, and most readable and accessible.

1 Getting to Know Bali

THE LAY OF THE LAND

Bali may be a small island, but it doesn't lack topographic variety. How accommodating of it to have something for every taste. The island is divided in half, east/west, by a volcanic mountain chain, and scored length-wise by deep river gorges. (Thanks to these, most traffic on the island has to be north-south, though a few major bridges have helped.) You can find photo-ready terraced colonial rice paddies, white sand beaches with clear blue aqua water, mountain lakes, forests, and more.

THE REGIONS IN BRIEF

THE SOUTH   This is the most populous part of the island and the most visited by tourists, largely because of the beautiful beaches and coral reefs that surround the peninsula at the bottom of the island. It is also the most commercial and arguably the least scenic part of the island, flat and beachlike. **Kuta** is a highly trafficked tourist destination, most desirable if you like to surf or enjoy a Tijuana-type atmosphere. **Nusa Dua** is a resort manufactured for tourists, more laid-back but also more sterile, while **Sanur** is roughly a cross between the two.

THE CENTER   Between the commercialization and build-up and the more sparse, flat landscape adjacent to the beaches, it's a shock to leave the south for the engaging village of **Ubud,** where the topography gives way to verdant greenery and hilly (if not outright mountainous) countryside. In my opinion—and probably only the most single-minded beach fan will disagree—this is the most beautiful area of Bali, with rice paddies, lush vegetation, and charming little villages. Nonetheless, in its own low-key way, the center is every bit as commercial as the south; many of the communities are geared toward nothing but selling crafts to tourists, and Ubud itself is full of touts seeking to make a buck off the hordes of visitors. But given the setting, you mind it less.

THE EAST   From the landmark **Gunung Agung,** the volcano that is the heart and center of Bali and its people, to the beaches along the coast, this may be the region that offers the most appealing diversity. You'll find terrific snorkeling and diving at **Candi Dasa** and nearby locations, without the intense level of commercialization found in the South. Inland, mountain lovers and climbers will find much to please them in the Gunung Agung region (complete with Besakih, the most important temple in Bali).

THE NORTH   Here the mountains and beaches virtually collide (expect a steep, twisting, turning ride to get to the coastline), and the climate is dry. Volcanic mountain lakes provide marvelous vistas, and surprisingly chilly temperatures at night. The black sand beaches of **Lovina** attract many visitors fleeing the hustle and bustle of Kuta, but the place manages to remain relatively relaxed and mellow.

THE WEST   This is a relatively undeveloped part of Bali, with a mountainous terrain mostly given over to the **Bali Barat National Park.** The few attractions for tourists in the area include the famous temple of **Tanah Lot,** the big **Sangeh Monkey Forest,** and the fabulous coral reef at **Pemutan** (usually done as a day diving or snorkel trip from Lovina or Candi Dasa). A Javanese influence can be felt here in everything from religion (with a stronger Muslim presence) to food. Though its charms are less immediate than those of other parts of Bali (and its few main roads fiercely crowded), the West does offer a less tourist-intensive experience of the island.

A LOOK AT THE PAST

In just the last half century, Bali has been surrounded by remarkable change and turmoil—the birth of an independent Indonesia and its attempts to modernize, a bloody coup that brought about strong-arm military rule and, in the late '90s, violent protests, religious conflicts, and economic upheavals bringing a tentative return to democracy. Yet somehow, little of that seems to have touched Bali directly. The island goes on at its own pace.

The first indication that Bali is charmed as well as charming may have come at the time of the very first contact from the West, when, in 1588, a Portuguese ship seeking spice trade hit a reef and sank. Survivors who reached the shore were treated well but forbidden to leave. Nine years later, when three Dutch sailors landed to scout the island, only one returned—the other two were so charmed by the island that they stayed.

Perhaps the island itself exerts some power over visitors. As distinct as Balinese life is, its people and culture originated elsewhere. Evidence of settlement goes back to the Neolithic period of around 3000 B.C. Chinese-rooted culture made its way to the island around 800 B.C. By about A.D. 900, Buddhist and Hindu peoples had migrated from India and Southeast Asia, and for several hundred years, rule of Bali alternated between home and conquerors from Java. In 1343 the Hindu **Majapahit kingdom of East Java** imposed its religious and social structure on the island, but that kingdom's reach soon began to erode in the face of a growth of the Islamic religion, and in 1515 the core of the Majapahit hierarchy fled to Bali, cementing the island's Javanese-originated culture. Somehow Bali remained Hindu as Islam swept to domination of all the surrounding islands. It experienced a flowering of art and culture still called the Golden Age, which gradually faded as the royal family fell into decline and regional ruling factions fragmented Balinese life.

The first real Western presence was established in 1601 when a Dutch contingent came to set up formal relations, and a trade agreement was established. Various other attempts to expand relations were largely rebuffed—even as the Dutch East India Company expanded throughout the area—save for the shipping of Balinese slaves to Dutch and French merchants. In the era of Napoleon, Holland's East Indian holdings passed first to the French, then to the British, who returned them to the Dutch in the peace agreement following Napoleon's Waterloo defeat in 1815.

The modern era of internationalism was initiated in the 1830s by Danish trader Mads Lange, who operated directly with the rajas and bypassed the Dutch completely. That didn't sit well with the Dutch, and after several years of tension and shows of force on both sides, the Balinese formally recognized Dutch sovereignty. For several decades Dutch rule remained uneasy but strong—especially in the north, where its trade administration was based. Cultural tension was manifested most dramatically in resistance to the Dutch edict ending the practice of suttee, the ritual practice in which widows would throw themselves on their late husbands' funeral pyres.

Perhaps the most dramatic and tragic event in Balinese history came in 1906 when, under a Dutch blockade at Badung precipitated by the looting of a wrecked Chinese trading vessel, natives found themselves in a desperate situation. With Dutch troops landing at Sanur and moving in through Denpasar, the Balinese lost any hope and, to the horror of the Dutch, marched directly into open fire in a mass suicide. A similar scene was repeated in 1908, and Dutch control of Bali was total by 1909.

Over the next couple of decades, a steady stream of European settlers and visitors came—doctors and teachers at first, followed by the first tourists, artists, and cultural explorers. By the 1930s, Bali's reputation as a magical paradise was spreading rapidly, and such figures as anthropologist Margaret Mead, artist Walter Spies, and Canadian composer Colin McPhee became the island's most prominent proselytizers.

World War II saw an exodus of foreigners with the arrival of Japanese troops. For Indonesians, it was a time of both strain under the brief Japanese occupation and revelation in light of the damage done to Dutch control. Shortly after the end of the war in 1945, Nationalist Party founder **Sukarno,** a thorn in the side of the Dutch since the '20s, announced a declaration of Indonesian independence and was named president. The Dutch fought the movement, but withdrew under international pressure in 1949, allowing the creation of the Republic of Indonesia. Inevitably, perhaps, economic and social uncertainties undermined the democracy, and after just 10 years, parliament was dissolved and a new "guided democracy" was installed.

Bali was hit very hard by the economic problems, and maintained at best an uneasy relation with Jakarta, which wasn't helped by its Hindu status in the Islamic nation. Sukarno's reign ended in 1965 when army major-general **Suharto** seized control in the wake of a supposed—and highly suspect—failed Communist coup. Bloody conflicts continued for several years and as many as 100,000 Balinese were killed, some as suspected Communists, others because of their Chinese heritage.

When Suharto officially became Indonesia's second president in 1968, the military gained a far-reaching influence over national affairs. During the next 3 decades, until the major economic crisis of 1997, Indonesia enjoyed a period of prosperity, in spite of allegations against Suharto that accuse him of having embezzled $570 million of state funds during his time in office. Chafing under the virtual dictatorship of President Suharto, the Indonesians finally revolted, with demonstrations turning into riots that made headlines around the world. In June of 1999, Indonesians witnessed their first free parliamentary election since 1955, ousting Suharto and electing Abdurrahman Wahid, a highly respected Sufi cleric and adept politician, as president. But riots, bombings, and protests continue to plague the country, specifically in Aceh, East Timor, and Irian Jaya, where separatist movements have little support both locally and internationally.

Increased governmental attention to tourism in Bali in the '60s and '70s helped increase its special position in Indonesia, and has given it something of a protected status (after all, Bali's a tax cash cow). A steadily increasing influx of Australian surfers drawn by the waves at Kuta and spiritual seekers attracted to Ubud made tourism in Bali one of the few sources of stability in the Indonesian economy, and stimulated the eventual and continuing development of the island as an upscale resort destination.

CEREMONY & CELEBRATION: BALI'S PEOPLE & CULTURE
RELIGION

The Balinese are a deeply spiritual people and their religion is seamlessly incorporated into every facet of their day-to-day existence. Over 90% of the population is **Hindu,** with the minority made up of Muslims, Buddhists, and Christians. Balinese Hinduism is related to, but different from, Hinduism as practiced in India. Indeed, Balinese Hinduism has incorporated elements of Buddhism. There are no formal prayers, and the complexities of the Hindu teachings are usually left to the priests. Instead, the Balinese focus on pleasing God through aesthetic rituals and ceremonies.

There is one Supreme Being in Bali Hinduism. Since there can be no physical representation of this Being, it is symbolized in temples and shrines by an empty throne. The Supreme God has other godly manifestations, though, which is why Hinduism is erroneously seen as polytheistic. The three main forms are Brahma the Creator, Shiva the Destroyer, and Vishnu the Preserver. Their symbolic colors—red, white, and black, respectively—turn up over and over again in celebrations.

Balinese Hindus believe in dharma and adharma, order and disorder, and the need for balance between them. There can be no good without evil. Disease is as much a part of life as health; it's when disease takes over that disorder reigns. To achieve harmony, the forces of good must be saluted with offerings, while the forces of bad must be appeased.

The classic notions of karma, reincarnation, and enlightenment are also found here. One's behavior contributes to one's karma: Accumulate enough cosmic brownie points, and you will achieve enlightenment and be liberated from the cycle of life, death, rebirth. Another important concept is that of animism, or the belief that all things have a spirit and are alive. The stone statues that represent gods are not gods themselves, but they do have a spirit and are considered alive, as are all trees, plants, water—you name it. You will see daily offerings made to the river, to the stone gods by your hotel or at a bridge, or in someone's car. This belief makes Bali seem totally alive. Contrast it with Lombok, which like the rest of Indonesia is predominantly Muslim, and you'll see how less vital it seems.

Add to this Bali's complex system of rituals, which govern every facet of life from birth to death. There is always some kind of ceremony, great and small, going on somewhere. Every morning, the Balinese place little offerings, delicate boxes made of leaves containing bits of rice, small flowers, and incense, in various places, to thank the gods and make the day go well. You will see these all over the streets, where they get stepped on or eaten by dogs—because once anything has been offered to the gods, its worth is spent and it is discarded. The amount of effort that goes into these elaborate but ultimately disposable offerings is astonishing.

Beyond these small daily offerings there are the ceremonies. Temple anniversary celebrations, tooth filings, cremations—every day, all over Bali, something is happening. The Tourism Board puts out a pamphlet listing the biggest ceremonies, but family events happen constantly. Particularly in a place like Ubud, something will be going on just about every day you are there. See that parade of gorgeously dressed Balinese, with towering offerings of fruit and flowers meticulously arranged in complex patterns balanced precariously on their heads, marching along to rhythmic music? They are on their way to a ceremony of some sort. Follow them. Really—it's okay, even expected. As long as you are respectful, the locals enjoy it when tourists come to watch. What does respectful mean? Well, first of all, it means proper dress. You need not be as glammed up as the Balinese, who will be bedecked in elaborate sarong outfits of the most fantastic cloth (the makeup of the outfits changes depending on what is being celebrated), but you must be wearing a sarong and sash yourself, and your arms should be covered to at least the elbow.

TEMPLES

Every village must have at least one temple, but one temple is really three: the *pura puseh,* the main central temple, dedicated to Vishnu; the *pura desa,* the everyday temple dedicated to Brahma; and the *pura dalem,* the temple of the dead, dedicated to Shiva. Add to these the small temples or shrines found in nearly every home, hotel, and restaurant, and all the little shrines along the road and riversides, and you have an idea of why this is called the "Island of the Gods." There are over 20,000, in fact.

Consequently, temples lose their ability to thrill rather early on, particularly since, to Western eyes, they aren't all that magnificent. These aren't the glittering piles of sequins you find in Thailand, but rather open-air constructions of brick and stone (and not even that many statues). One looks pretty much exactly like the next, with subtle differences of course, until you get to the north, where temples are festooned in elaborate, fanciful carvings.

Once inside a temple, you need not stick to the back wall, though you might prefer to start out that way. More often than not, the locals will pull you to the front so you can see what's going on, and even encourage you to take pictures. (But don't do so unless given permission.) If you are lucky, you might be asked to partake of some Balinese coffee or even a meal. Ask someone to explain what you're seeing—don't be shy. If they don't want to talk, or can't speak English, they may well find someone who can. Often it's a ceremony honoring an anniversary of the temple you are in (held at 6- and 12-month marks).

CELEBRATIONS

The big three events in Bali are tooth filings, weddings, and cremations. **Tooth filing** is a rite of maturation, wherein the sharp front teeth, especially the canines, are filed down smooth (the idea being to differentiate humans from the animals.) This can happen at any age, even after death, but is most often done to adolescents, who by that age have already been through the nearly dozen rituals that marked their first few days on the planet. Believe it or not, it's quite fun to watch the participants grimace through this rite of passage, then smile in a mirror afterward, admiring their new set of adult choppers. (The Balinese will be grinning like crazy.) **Weddings** are self explanatory but colorful events. But it's at cremations where the Balinese pull out all the stops.

Cremation is the only way a soul can be freed of its earthly self and travel to its next incarnation (or to enlightenment). Death is a joyous occasion in Bali, full of floats and fanfare that can resemble a Mardi Gras parade. Complicated towers (the higher the caste, the higher the tower—limited only by power lines) hold the body, carried aloft by cheering men, who turn the tower in circles to send the spirit to heaven, then take it to the burning ground. There the body is placed in receptacles resembling fabulous creatures (winged lions, bulls and so forth, again determined by caste), and set on fire. Sometimes the body won't burn quickly enough, and it is poked at, often mocked, to help free the spirit from its now-useless fleshy vessel and send it on its way. This is an extraordinarily beautiful and moving rite and marvelous to witness, even for Western-ers whose view of death is so different from that of the Balinese. Cremations are expen-sive and so not as common as other ceremonies; sometimes, bodies have to be buried until such time (from a few months to many years) the family can afford the proper send-off. To share costs, they are also often group affairs. There are tours that take tourists to a cremation, which might be worth going on if it's your only shot at seeing one, but they can be somewhat embellished for the visitors.

Feel free to ask around about upcoming celebrations, but be sure to get confirma-tion from more than one person. If you are staying at a losmen, let your hosts know you would like to go to temple with them. Be aware, though, that Bali operates on "rubber time," which means a cremation scheduled for noon will happen promptly at 5pm. But hanging out has its own rewards. That's when you might get invited to din-ner, or if nothing else, you get to listen to some music and observe real life in action. Compared to Western church-going, celebrations in Bali are very casual: women gos-sip, children play, and dogs wander temple grounds freely, snacking on offerings. A priest chants, people pray and then get up, and others take their places. The Balinese videotape and shoot photos. (You should not, unless someone tells you it's okay, but they probably will.) Again, they are generally most welcoming, provided you act with dignity and respect. Imagine being this receptive to a total stranger at a family funeral, and you have an idea of what kind of people the Balinese are.

MUSIC & DANCE

Bali is "where musical sounds are as [much a] part of the atmosphere as the palm trees, the spicy smells and the charmingly beautiful people. The music is fantastically rich—melodically, rhythmically, texturally (such orchestration!) and above all formally."

So wrote British composer Benjamin Britten to a friend while visiting Bali in Janu-ary 1956. It was the sounds of the **gamelan**—the bright-sounding metal percussion ensembles that accompany just about every celebration and ceremony here—that turned Britten's head. And he was hardly the first major Western music figure to be infected. Claude Debussy was transfixed by gamelan music at a Java pavilion of the 1898 Paris Exposition—which is evident in such impressionist orchestral lynchpins as "La Mer." Canadian Colin McPhee lived outside of Ubud in the '30s, an experience recounted in his book *A House in Bali*. Lou Harrison has written for American varia-tions of gamelan ensembles, and anyone hearing the music of Steve Reich or Philip Glass has, essentially, already had the gamelan experience.

But you don't have to be a trained musician to be transformed by the magic of Balinese music. It's everywhere, pouring from tapes played in shops and restaurants (though today you're just as likely to hear Bob Marley or Tracy Chapman in the bigger communities), accompanying both staged dance performances and temple festivals, weddings and tooth filings. The upscale hotels generally have two or three players chiming musical greetings to arrivals in the lobby.

The word *gong* is of Indonesian origin. Know that, and you've got a head start in understanding the archipelago's music—especially the vibrant Balinese brand. The gentler style featuring light sounds of metallophones and flute that you'll certainly hear played on tapes or CDs in many restaurants, shops, and hotels is likely from Java or Sudan. It was from the courtly music of Java that Balinese gamelan evolved, the style and its tools brought to the island by fleeing Hindu royalty in the 16th century. That style remained until 1915, when in the north of Bali a movement bloomed for a distinctive sound called **kebyar,** which means lightning flash. Indeed, that's a terrific description of the style, notable for its sudden bursts of sound emerging from more tranquil lines.

And still today in the daily life of Bali, and even in many presentations made just for tourists, the local music of the gamelan and such vocal relatives as the **kecak (monkey chant)** is an essential feature. Every banjar has a gamelan (or at least, in poorer areas, access to one), with musicians (not true professionals, but your workaday crew of drivers, farmers, shopkeepers, artisans, and the like).

Make no mistake: This is not folk music. It's highly structured, highly disciplined classical music, even more so (in the conventional Western sense) than Indian classical music. Though the music is not written, it is also not improvised, per se. That would be virtually impossible given the precision and intricacy of the musical mosaics produced, requiring years of study and practice.

As for dance, the most common in public performance are the **legong** and **barong dances,** intricate ballets presenting, as much Balinese art does, scenes from the epic *Mahabarata* or *Ramayana.* The latter, in particular, is highly entertaining, involving an evil witch, magic dragon, and men in a trance jabbing daggers at their own chests (how real the trance is probably depends on the setting). Many major hotels offer dance performances, and in Ubud at the central Palace and other locations there's one pretty much every night. Information can be had at the tourist center, but ask around and you might find a real (nontourist) performance taking place at an accessible village. Numerous tapes and CDs of these are available, some with the chanted/sung narration that accompanies performances, some just the music.

Ditto for the music of the wayang kulit—the **shadow puppet plays,** in which intricately cut leather figures are used to project images against a screen, again depicting a tale from one of the Hindu epics, all manipulated masterfully by a puppeteer who also does all the voices (often injecting news, gossip, topical humor and even crude jokes) to the accompaniment of a small gamelan ensemble.

The other major example of "traditional" music is the **kecak,** a very dramatic and visual a cappella piece featuring as many as 100 men depicting a saga of a monkey king and his warriors, featuring bursts of simian-styled chanting that gives the style its onomatopoeic name. Intriguingly, though, the kecak and to some extent the other generally seen performances are actually the invention of Westerners. In Balinese culture, where there's no distinction between sacred and secular, there is no real tradition of performance for performance's sake rather than for real ceremony. But in the '30s, artist Walter Spies, living in Bali, was asked to arrange some dance performances for a visiting filmmaker, and that was accomplished by using excerpts and pastiches of the true things. As tourism grew, the demand for such things grew as well, and today they are ubiquitous.

Gamelan isn't the only music you'll hear in Bali. An enticing brand of Indonesian pop, called **dangdut,** is a blend of Indian film music and Arabic pop. Sinewy and sexy, it has been used as a vehicle for topics that had generally been taboo.

ARTS & CRAFTS

A tourist in Bali will see everything from profusely carved and decorated temples bedecked in shimmering fabrics, to winsome cat-shaped doorstops in faux-Appalachian folk style, to a perfect art-nouveau sideboard being carved under a bamboo rain cover. The volume and diversity of production on the island is stunning.

It is impossible to speak of Balinese art without speaking of Balinese culture as well. The rituals and celebrations that are a daily part of the Bali-Hindu religion and culture create a constant demand for traditional artwork. Even in the International Airport, Ngurah Rai, every doorway is decorated with the grotesque floral gargoyle called Karang Bhoma. Its purpose is not merely decorative, but to protect against evil influences. (Curious that it repeatedly appears over the doors tourists pass through as they enter Bali.) The novelty of baroque wedding cake decorative demons, dragons, and indecipherable deities will wear off even before you reach your hotel.

One reason there is so much art is that there are so many artists. The Balinese culture does not marginalize artistic activity the way Western cultures have. In fact, the rituals of Bali demand a level of aesthetic perfection that requires the average person to be able to recognize, if not create, beauty. The Balinese hold that their gods will only accept offerings that are aesthetically pleasing, from stone carvings to body posture (considered an offering like any other). A second reason for the preponderance of traditional art is that much of it is disposable. Elaborately decorated and carved coffins are cremated along with the deceased. And many other rituals render the objects used in them unusable a second time.

Climate plays a role in the arts as well. The humidity makes works of art decay rapidly, so that they require frequent replacement. This is particularly true of the very perishable palm ornaments and rice-paste sculptures, ikat weavings and carved masks used in sacred performances, but it is also true even of the stone and bricks of the temples themselves. The blue-gray tufa stone, called "paras" by the Balinese, absorbs water like a sponge and sprouts moss and fungi within a single rainy season. A 10-year-old shrine can look older than Angkor Wat, or the Pyramids.

For the collector interested in coming home with something representative of Bali, it is worth a brief enumeration of traditional art forms.

Traditional sculpture consists of **stone and wood carving** representing a variety of Balinese gods and guardians. Some of the wood carvings are used as temporary bodies for the gods to inhabit during rituals, others designate rank and are placed in the rafters of thatched living quarters. The area uphill of Ubud around Tegalalang, Pakadui, and Pujung specializes in wood carving. You can travel through entire villages inhabited by hundreds of half-finished eagle-faced Garudas. Of course, the next village might be full of slightly distorted Donald Ducks.

Stone statues, often frightening to look at, flank the gateways of palaces and temples, guarding against demonic forces. Stone is carved in Batubalan, Blabatuh, and Batuan, downhill from Ubud on the road to Sanur. Most are too large and heavy to transport, but small "replicas" of traditional forms are also produced. If you buy one, wrap it well, as Balinese stone is very brittle. A few statues are carved in hardened concrete, and some black lava stone sculptures are imported from Java, but being made of harder stone, these have far less detail.

Masks are another traditional sculptural form. They depict a wide range of characters used in both sacred and secular performances. Masks of the grotesque bug-eyed demoness Rangda are often seen hanging in garlands outside souvenir shops, seemingly bereft of any menace in their mass-produced multiplicity. But beware: The Balinese hold that even a tourist mask may become inhabited if it possesses the proper qualities.

The features of heroes, heroines, villains, monsters, and clowns are fixed by ancient canons that allow for only limited interpretation. What that means is that they all tend to look alike. When looking at a cluster of 50 or so identical masks of Rama, hero of the Hindu *Ramayana* epic, it is difficult to visualize how his green serenity might look twelve thousand miles away on your wall. But sure enough, removed from the company of his legion of cloned companions, Rama is magnificent. Look for eyes that focus on a spot somewhere to the front of the mask. Turn it with your hand and watch the eyes to see if they convey a sense of seeing. Don't bother searching for antiques; they are well-faked and rare to boot—and probably haunted.

For those with an interest in two-dimensional art, there are the ancient stylized **paintings** of deities and the delicately carved "lontar" palm frond books, both still produced on the island. The center of this archaic painting style is now in the eastern territories of Bali near Klungklung. Perhaps the best example is seen in the painted ceiling of the Kerta Gosa in the town of Klungklung itself. Works of art in this Kamasan style are harder to find than the paintings, which have become one of the chief "modern" art forms of Bali.

Based in the Gianyar district in central Bali are several "schools" of wood carving and painting originating in a fortunate blend of Balinese and Western traditions. In the 1920s and '30s, and again in the late '50s and '60s, Balinese artists collaborated with foreign artists to create new styles that diverged from the traditional forms. Some of the foreign artists were expatriates who came to live on Bali for many years. **Walter Spies,** a German, and **Rudolf Bonnet,** a Dutchman, influenced Balinese art and artists in the pre–World War II years. Spies, patronized by the aristocratic Sukowati family, built a house on the site of the current Tjampuhan Hotel in Ubud that became a kind of expat mecca in Bali. He has achieved mythic status as the prime mover of the modern Balinese art movement, helping create the now-famous kecak dance, the Pita Maha art society, and the Bali Museum in Denpasar. He is credited with inspiring a Balinese traditional painter, Anak Agung Gede Soberat, to work with scenes from daily life instead of mythology, thus initiating a new style of painting, and with guiding the development of the elongated sculptural style now so ubiquitous on Bali. His own paintings, at once meticulous and moody, are a fusion of cultural forms.

Despite the fertile contribution Spies and his followers brought to Bali, their fame unjustly overshadows the sources of their inspiration. **I Gusti Nyoman Lempad** was already a master carver when, at Spies' suggestion, he turned to ink drawing and produced a half century of masterpieces. **Ida Bagus Njana**'s various carving styles, from abstractly modified human forms to simple female studies, became style setters for the island. There are of course others by the score to be discovered by anyone with the determination to look.

Getting Married in Bali

Tourists have come to love getting married on Bali (though the Balinese turn their noses up at it). If you want to get married legally on the island (as opposed to a simple vow renewal), you need to do some planning in advance. Contact **Bali Weddings International:** Jalan Padanggalak no. 4, Sanur (☎ **361-287516;** fax 361-286262; www.baliweddingsint.com/; e-mail: info@baliweddingsint.com).

Nowadays, the variety of painting styles available is as diverse as the artists producing them, and the profusion of choices can be hypnotic. Be patient, and be aesthetically demanding. You will find your masterpiece if you search. And remember, it's better to possess a small masterpiece than a large mediocrity.

LANGUAGE

English is widely spoken throughout Bali, particularly in the major tourist areas. While not everyone is fluent, most of the people you will be dealing with will speak enough English that you can communicate with them. Many of the employees in the better hotels speak other languages as well.

The Balinese speak both Indonesian and Balinese—the former when out in public, the latter at home. Aside from the tendency towards seemingly jaw breaking polysyllabic phrases, Indonesian is not that hard to learn—pronunciation is pretty straightforward and spelling is mostly phonetic. Balinese is much more complicated, not least because there are actually three levels of it—high, middle, and low—used depending on the class and authority of the person to whom you are speaking. Don't even try to learn it, but do worry about Indonesian—not because you need it, but because embarrassingly few tourists bother to even learn to say "Hello" or "Thank you" in their host country's language. People will be delighted that you took the time to learn how to exchange pleasantries. Besides, I've often noticed that *"Tidak, terima kasih"* works better to get rid of a persistent tout than "No, thank you."

Often, you will be asked "Where are you going?" This is actually a routine, polite question that may not require an answer, but often it's a way of then asking if you need transport. If you don't, just say "Jalan jalan," which means "Just walking." And if they are truly insistent, to the point of huge annoyance, you can resort to "Pergi!" ("Go away!").

2 Planning a Trip to Bali

VISITOR INFORMATION

Recently, the few Indonesian/Bali tourism offices outside of the country have been either shut down or incorporated into their nearest embassy/consulate. No matter; the information they gave was sketchy in terms of usefulness at best. There are other better sources for getting what you need to know. The thick, multilingual *Visitor's Guide to Bali,* is a nice introduction to the island, full of information, annual events, and even a mini–phone directory. Visit the Web site at **www.asiapages.com.sg** to find out how to obtain a copy.

The best Web site for information on accommodations, sightseeing, events, and just about everything else you can imagine is **Bali Paradise Online at www.bali-paradise. com**. It gives the impression that it is run by the government, but it is not. Another, though less complete, Web site is **Bali Online (www.indo.com)**, which offers a less expansive range of the same information. The self-proclaimed "Bali Information Mega Site," **www.onbali.com**, is another great source for planning your trip. For information on the art scene in Bali, log onto **www.baliecho.com**, the electronic arm of Bali's tourism, art, and culture magazine.

IN BALI   There are six **Information Centers** operated by the Department of Tourism where booklets and brochures are available free of charge (when actually available, that is). They are at **Ngurah Rai International Airport** (☎ **361-751011**); in **Ubud** at the crossroad of Monkey Forest Road and Jalan Raya Ubud (the main road; no phone); in **Kuta** at Jalan Benasari 36B, Legian (☎ **361-754090**); in

Denpasar at Jalan Parman Niti Mandala (☎ 362-222387); and in **Singaraja** at Jalan Veteran 23 (☎ 361-225141).

Better still is the efficient **Badung Government Tourist Office** in Kuta (Jalan Raya Kuta no.2, ☎ 361-756176), serving mostly the island's southern regencies, but often stocked with useful general information on the island, including a calendar of events. **Baliplus** informational pamphlets are available at over 70 hotels and 140 tourist locations on the island, or you can call or e-mail for your free copy (☎ 361-758671; e-mail: Baliplus@denpasar.wasantara.net.id).

ENTRY REQUIREMENTS

Visitors from the U.S., Australia, most of Europe, New Zealand, and Canada do not need visas. They will be given a stamp that allows them to stay for 60 days, provided they are entering the country through an officially designated gateway: Ngurah Rai Airport or the seaports of Padang Bai and Benoa. If you want to stay longer than 60 days, you must get a tourist or business visa *before* coming to Indonesia. Tourist visas are valid only for 4 weeks and can not be extended, while business visas can be extended for 6 months at Indonesian immigration offices.

CUSTOMS REGULATIONS

Customs allows you to bring in, duty-free, 200 cigarettes or 50 cigars and 2 pounds of tobacco; cameras and film; 2 liters of alcohol; and perfume clearly intended for personal use. Forbidden are guns, weapons, narcotics, pornography (leave it at home if you're unsure how it's defined), and printed matter with Chinese characters. Plants and fresh fruit may also be confiscated.

MONEY

The currency of Indonesia is the **rupiah,** from the Sanskrit word for wrought silver, *rupya.* Coins are available in denominations of Rp25, 50, 100, and even occasionally 5 and 10. Notes are Rp100, 500, 1000, 5000, 10,000, 20,000, 50,000 and 100,000.

The following bills are no longer in circulation: the 1992 pink Rp10,000, 1992 greenish 20,000 bill, or blue Rp50,000 with ex-president Suharto's picture.

CURRENCY EXCHANGE & RATES   With the economic problems Indonesia is currently facing, Bali has become a bargain for tourists. In less than 2 years, the **rupiah** went from about 1,000 to the dollar to 10,000 and more. During recent trips, the exchange rate fluctuated wildly hour by hour. It is hard to say at press time precisely what things should cost—even the prices listed (collected at a rate of 9,000 rupiahs to the dollar) could be entirely different by the time you arrive. But no matter what the exchange rate, Bali is still going to be an inexpensive destination once you get there, particularly when it comes to food, souvenirs, and sightseeing.

Most major hotels offer **exchange services,** but their rates are almost always pitiful to the point of extortion.

Mom and Pop "authorized money exchange" places are thick as flies along the streets, each with rates more attractive than the next. **AVOID THESE,** unless you're researching a paper on scams and outright thievery. Some of their tricks include the bait and switch of decimal points on the calculator, broken or rigged calculators, or the less benign reneging on whether commission is included or not. The most abhorrent maneuver is palming a handful of bills off the counter when you're not looking (*never* close a deal until that counted wad of bills is in your hand). My advice is to search out one of the countless state-sponsored locations of **Wartel Telecommunications Service.** The rates here may appear lower, but if you factor in the money you saved by not being robbed, plus the avoidance of a potentially vacation-ruining headache, you come out ahead.

ATMs are becoming more common—there is at least one in most major tourist areas—and often give you a much better exchange rate. The same is true for **credit cards,** but their use is still mostly limited to the major hotels, restaurants, and shops.

WHEN TO GO

PEAK SEASON   The high tourist season is July and August, along with the weeks surrounding Christmas and New Year's, when prices are higher and tourist traffic considerably increased. Try to avoid these times, as well as February and March (given the increased heat and humidity).

CLIMATE   Bali is just below the equator, so the weather is more or less constant year-round (always some variation of hot and humid). A day is nearly always 12 hours long—from 6am to 6pm. The rainy season lasts from October to April, with nearly daily monsoons. Rain usually comes in short, violent bursts that often stop within an hour (though at night it can last a few hours). The humidity is at its crushing worst during this period (there are times when you think you're breathing water) and the hottest months are February, March, and April. Temperatures are mostly in the 80s all year long. Sweaters are only necessary if you are staying up by the volcanoes or mountains, where it can get nippy at night.

PUBLIC HOLIDAYS   Public holidays are New Year's Day (January 1), Idul Fitri (celebration of the end of Ramadan; late February), Nyepi (a major purification ritual and a time when Balinese are supposed to sit at home, silent; late March), Good Friday and Easter Sunday (late March/early April), Muslim New Year (mid-May), Indonesia Independence Day (August 17), Ascension Day of Mohammed (early December), and Christmas (December 25).

HEALTH CONCERNS

No inoculations are required, but it's always a good idea to get shots for hepatitis A, tetanus, polio, and typhoid (ideally, you've already had some of these). You might consult with your doctor or the CDC Web site if anything further is currently suggested. **Malaria** is only a concern if you plan to be out in remote villages near rice paddies after dark and not a concern in the tourist areas of Bali (indeed, the CDC has declared it malaria-free). The anxious can take malaria pills (you must start this regimen at least 2 to 3 weeks prior to entering an infected area), but be aware that the prevention is sometimes almost as bad as the disease. You probably should not pet strange dogs—there are many stray dogs in Bali, and nearly all of them have some kind of mange, or possibly rabies.

You absolutely cannot drink the water on Bali, but bottled water is cheap and readily available. Just about every hotel will supply you with a couple bottles or a jug of boiled water—remember to use it when brushing your teeth as well (although I didn't, and I'm still alive to tell the tale). Restaurants in tourist areas are used to supplying safe water, complete with ice made from boiled water, but if you want to be extra safe, ask for no ice, and *air minum* (drinking water). Salads, too, are generally safe in tourist areas. As always, you can help avoid "Bali belly" (the Indonesian version of Montezuma's Revenge) by sticking to foods that have been peeled or well cooked.

Travel Tip

When you leave Bali, there will be an **airport departure tax.** Ask your hotel for the current rate (at the time of this writing Rp50,000/US$5.55).

Travel Tip

Patria Travel at 621 Second Ave., 2nd floor, New York, NY 10016 (☎ **212-779-8628;** www.patriatravel.com; e-mail: sales@patriatravel.com), specializes in tailor-made packages for independent travelers to Indonesia; count on them for discounted fares with many of the major carriers flying into Bali.

When in doubt, you can also get meat-free dishes.
   When Bali belly does sneak up on you, here's a few tips:

- Be sure to replenish the **liquids** in your system, as dehydration is going to be your most serious threat.
- Stock up on the local equivalent of Gatorade (an electrolyte replacement drink) called **Pocari Sweat,** packaged in soft-drink cans.
- Go to the nearest chemist and pick up some **charcoal pills** and a few doses of gastrolyte.
- When you feel like your stomach is ready to handle something slightly more substantial, seek out a few containers of **Yakult,** a very sweet milk-based drink a step below yogurt (or pick up some yogurt).
- Then go to sleep and wait it out.

WHAT TO PACK

Given the heat and humidity, loose cotton clothing is essential in Bali. Though the Balinese do dress up, informality among foreigners has come to be expected. (See "Cultural Dos & Don'ts," above, about modesty in dress.) I suggest packing a minimal amount of clothing and buying more climate-appropriate wear once you get to Bali. You might also consider giving away all your clothes at the end of your stay, as Western clothes, even underwear, are luxury items for the Balinese. It's a nice thing to do and you'll have more room in your luggage for souvenirs.

GETTING THERE
BY PLANE

FROM THE U.S. & CANADA   As of press time, **China Air** (☎ 800/227-5118 in the U.S.) and **Eva Air** (☎ **800/695-1188**), with **Garuda Indonesia,** both through Taipei; **Singapore Air** (☎ **800/742-3333**) through Singapore; and **Nippon** (☎ **800/235-9262**) through Osaka fly to Bali from the U.S. with no obligatory overnight stay. Flights with overnight stays are available on **Continental** (☎ **800/231-0856**) and **Cathay Pacific** (☎ **800/233-2742**).

FROM THE U.K.   Bali is served from Europe by **Cathay Pacific** via Hong Kong; tickets can be purchased from British Air (☎ **0345/222111**), **Singapore Air** (☎ **7470007**), and **Air France** (☎ **0181/742-6600**).

FROM AUSTRALIA & NEW ZEALAND   Flights from Australia and New Zealand can be booked through **Qantas** (☎ **131211;** www.qantas.com.au).

Getting to Your Destination from the Airport

Ngurah Rai, Bali's airport, is considered to be in Denpasar, but it's really 13 kilometers (8 miles) southwest. Given that, and how close you are to your real tourist destinations, there is probably no reason to ever go to Denpasar proper. Though it's not an unpleasant big city, it holds no real attractions for tourists. Instead, change a small amount of money from one of the exchange windows at the airport (check them all out—often the ones farthest down the row have the best rates), and exit the terminal.

There is no public transportation at the airport; no buses, no bemos, no horse-carts. Instead, tourists have two choices: either grab any one of an unlimited selection of unscrupulous cab drivers, or have your hotel send a car. I recommend the latter; not only are the rates comparable to the official rates at the airport, but you will avoid any bad first impressions caused by seemingly harmless taxi scams. Don't believe me? OK, head outside and look for the **official taxi window** counter near Customs. There are set rates to just about every major tourist area. You pay at this window and they will get your car for you. Do *not* use anyone who comes up directly to you offering to give you a ride; they will charge considerably higher rates.

GETTING AROUND

BY CAR   You can rent cars in Bali, but it's not recommended. Roads are not clearly marked—if marked at all—and even with a good map, there's a good chance you will get lost in the middle of nowhere. The Balinese are also wild drivers. Given how cheap and easy it is to get a tourist shuttle to most of the areas you want to go to, or to hire someone to drive you, it's best to avoid the headache. If you do decide to drive, just remember five things: (1) you will need an International Driver's License or a locally issued Tourist Driving License; (2) traffic is on the left hand side; (3) a honk from behind you means someone wants to pass, so move over; (4) the Balinese *always* have the right-of-way. Once they have gone by, then it's your turn; (5) any damage caused to life, limb, personal property, or family poultry will be on *your* bill.

BY MOTORBIKE   Motorbikes are even more dangerous than cars. You will see your share of bloody crashes (and how close do you think medical care is?). If you do decide to take the risk (and admittedly, it's a nice way to see the island), save them for remote areas where the traffic isn't so bad, and please be careful. The same driving license requirements for cars apply to motorbikes and scooters.

BY PUBLIC TRANSPORTATION   Blue and brown vans called *bemos* operate as buses in Bali. They work pretty well, in a sort of mysterious way. They have regular routes, but these aren't really written down. Just ask someone where the regular pickup is, and which bemo to take to get you where you want to go. Prices are also similarly secretive, and bemo drivers have no qualms about charging tourists lots more than locals. Ask one of the latter how much the ride really should cost. All things considered, bemos are better for short hops (around town, for example) than long distances, which may require many changes of vehicle.

It's tiresome, negotiating for every last kilometer, isn't it? Metered taxis do exist; they're blue or yellow and run mostly in Kuta and Sanur, though they can be hired to take you to nearby resorts like Nusa Dua. Make sure they put their meter on, though.

BY PRIVATE TRANSPORTATION   There are two solid options for traveling around Bali, and both work quite well. Regular **tourist shuttles** run between all the major locales. These are reliable and cheap, though air-conditioned vehicles charge more. You can book them through a tourist office or your hotel, or just find one on your own—many stores will have signs advertising shuttle service. **Perama,** considered the most reliable operator, has offices in most tourist centers. The main office is in Kuta (☎ **361-751551**).

BY BOAT   There are several companies offering sometimes overlapping and competing service by sea to the nearby islands of Nusa Penida and Nusa Lembongan, and to Lombok. **Bounty Cruises** (☎ **361-7333333** or 361-726666) has daily hydrofoil service leaving at 9am from Bali's Benoa Harbor to Nusa Lembongan (30 min.; US$25), that continues on to Lombok's Sengiggi Beach (add 2½ hrs.; US$35) before

Obtaining a Tourist Driver's License

A Tourist Driver's License can be obtained at the **Foreign License Service** (☎ 361-243-939) at Jalan Agung Tresna no. 14 in Renon. Head to the service window for foreigners in the Pelayanan Samsat building, BPKB Section. To apply, you'll need photocopies of the photo and I.D. pages of your passport and the visa page if applicable, plus Rp75,000 (US$8.30) in cash. The office is open Monday to Thursday and Saturday 8:30am to 2:30pm; and Fridays from 8:30am to 1pm. (If you're caught driving without a license, I'm told that Rp5,000/US$0.55 is a satisfactory bribe.)

arriving at Gili Meno (add 30 min.; US$40), one of the three islands in the small island group offshore of Lombok. **Bali Hai Cruises** (☎ 361-720331) has day trips to Lembongan Island, and some to Lombok. Sail Sensations (☎ 361-725864) has day sailing and starlight dining. For a luxury alternative, **Wakalouka** (☎ 361-484085), run by the same people who bring you the Waka group of boutique hotels, will transport you in style to their exclusive property on Nusa Lembongan. Most of these offer a **dinner sunset cruise** or **day trips** that make great outings, with activities that include ocean rafting, diving, snorkeling, banana boat rides, and just plain lazing.

WHEN YES MEANS YES . . . AND NO

It seems simple enough—you ask a transport guide if he can take you from point A to point B, and he says yes. You negotiate the price and 10 minutes later, after some uncertain turns and squinty looks, he pulls up in front of point Q. You realize that he had no idea where you wanted to go and was only guessing the whole way.

Welcome to one of the peculiarities of Balinese culture that, if you don't learn to navigate around it, could drive you nuts. The transport guide in question wasn't trying to scam you when he said he knew where you wanted to go. He simply didn't want to disappoint you with a negative answer. Balinese will do anything to avoid disappointing someone, even if it means not exactly telling the truth, and there seems to be no sense that taking someone on a wild goose chase will be a greater disappointment.

So what to do about it? First, don't take a condescending attitude. It's merely a cultural difference. But make sure that a driver (or shopkeeper, or whomever you've asked something) really understands and really means yes. Have a map or written directions to show, or at least ask the question several different ways until you're confident that you're going to get what you've asked for. Then sit back and enjoy the ride.

The other option is hiring a **transport guide.** You won't have any trouble finding one (avoiding them is the problem). In Ubud and other tourist spots, men cluster the streets, endlessly shouting, "Transport? Transport? Yes? Tomorrow? Yes?" Short or long distances, hire by the day, the hour, or the week—just figure out exactly where you want to go, and what you think you would want to pay. (You may base an appropriate cost on what a taxi or shuttle would charge.) You have to bargain—you will know when they've gone as low as they can or want to, because they will probably refuse to drive you. If the one you've picked isn't going low enough, try somebody else. Be sure to write down your exact destination to avoid any possible misunderstanding. Also make it clear that you do not want to go to any crafts place—generally, the guy will take you to someone who jacks up their prices to pay for his cut.

TOUR GUIDES   Hiring a private tour guide can be more expensive than just using a transport guide off the street, but then again, you will get what you pay for. Trained professionals are rare in Bali—many a so-called "tour guide" doesn't have as good a

---

A Note on Addresses & Phone Numbers

Street addresses in Bali can be somewhat sketchy, I've made every attempt to provide precise addresses here, but in smaller towns the address of a hotel or restaurant may simply be "on the main street." Don't worry: These places will be impossible to miss. As for phone numbers, if no phone number is listed for an establishment, chances are there's no phone.

---

command of English as you would like, nor as studied a sense of history. (Balinese don't always know much about their past.) So someone who can really illuminate matters for you, plus, ideally, tell you about their own experiences within the culture, is worth paying for. It doesn't matter where the office is located—they can pick you up and take you anywhere, using your own itinerary or one they create for you. Expect to pay not only for the guide, but for the car, driver, and gas as well, all of which can run just over US$100 total for a day.

ACCOMMODATIONS

The range of hotel options in Bali is truly mind-boggling: from a US$5-a-night (or less) bungalow with breakfast in the morning, to a US$900-a-night villa with your own retinue of servants. In the middle are an ever-increasing number of native bungalows that can only be described as sublime. At high-end or luxury properties, often all you gain is increased and better frills, from A/C (a standard upgrade in more "modest" properties), to an in-room VCD player. Think about that when booking a hotel. And don't stay every night in a Western chain. Sure, they offer applicable familiar comforts, and considerable consistency, but then why didn't you book a trip to Hawaii instead? Don't overlook **losmen/homestay locations,** where you often end up rubbing elbows with the proprietor's family (and dogs, chickens, and so on). Expect fans instead of A/C, and no hot water (hard to get used to, but sometimes worth the experience). The good news is that many losmen have converted their squat toilets into the Western kind with a seat. In exchange, you'll get a bargain place to stay, often with a complete breakfast that leaves you full all afternoon, and a chance to observe some real Balinese life.

Try a variety of hotels of varying quality and price, and instead of mourning lost creature comforts, consider what you gain in terms of local interaction and adventure. You will come home with a greater appreciation of the Balinese, and much better stories. Another option is to stay in a village—not just one on the fringes of, say, Ubud, but way off the beaten path. You can check with locals for suggestions, look for possibilities in the budget section of the **BaliOnline** service (**www.indo.com**), or call Guna at Santa Bali Travel (see "Tour Guides" under "When Yes Means Yes . . . and No," above) and ask him about the very comfortable homestay recently erected in his village.

Prices tend to fluctuate with the popularity of a region. Some of the most expensive choices are found on the ocean, and in ever-delightful, and thus ever-popular, Ubud. Moving off the main street, or out of the main action, you may find that prices drop astonishingly. One of the highest quality hotels on the island is located on Amed, a largely undeveloped fishing village 2 hours (part of it on a bumpy, unpaved dirt road) from Candi Dasa, the nearest built-up community. The hotel costs a fraction of what a luxury hotel would elsewhere. But even on the outskirts of Ubud are some excellent options for ridiculously low prices. The remoteness, though, does make some guests feel too isolated—especially if you don't have a car.

A NOTE ON PRICES   Here's a big hint about how to further conquer high prices: The published rates are just that—the published rates. More than one hotel, after giving us their official rates, then said, "Now here's what we *really* charge," whereupon the price sometimes dropped by as much as half. The so-called "discounts" offered on the Internet on hotel Web sites are actually closer to the real price range. The brave of heart might want to only reserve their first night, and then just try and see what they can find once they get there. I noted many potential guests just showing up at some of the fanciest and most expensive hotels and demanding to know how the hotel would make it worth their while to stay. This won't always pan out—in high season, forget about it—but if you are looking for bargains—and possibly luxury as well— making reservations in advance is not always the best for your budget. Besides, there are more losmen/homestays than you can count in Bali, and someone, somewhere, will have a room, for probably a heck of a lot cheaper than you think.

A final word about the rates: almost all the hotels charge what they call **plus plus**— a 21% government tax and service charge on top of the quoted rates. They also charge from US$15 to more than US$50 extra per room during high season (the 2 or 3 weeks around Christmas and New Year's, and July and August). Many places automatically include breakfast, but if you book through a travel agent (who might well get you a bargain price), they often negotiate meal plans into the room rate, which may or may not be to your advantage given how cheap restaurants outside the hotel will usually be.

RESTAURANTS & DINING

One of your most difficult tasks in Bali will be sampling some good old home cooking. Nobody seems to want to serve true Balinese or Indonesian food, possibly dissuaded by the fear that the real thing is just too spicy and exotic for non-locals. The choices are these: succumb to the coaxings of sidewalk staff at these "authentic" warungs (serving French fries!) chanting "yes, yes" to entice you in for a meal, risk 3 days in bed with a fever by sampling some roadside grub, or surrender to the call of high quality international and (dare I say it) fusion menus sprouting up all over the island.

Best of all, as long as you stay away from the largely pricey hotel restaurants, food in Bali is quite cheap, and local fare is always less expensive than European dishes. **Vegetarians** will also be quite happy, as many places have a veggie-only menu. And while the names of dishes will be the same from place to place, you might be surprised at how different the interpretations are.

Caution should always be exercised about food consumption, but greater care is taken in all the tourist areas; I ate uncooked green salads everywhere listed here and never experienced a problem. At all times, and particularly in tourist areas where most of the dining options run towards the aforementioned expensive hotel restaurants, or generic tourist-geared restaurants, I encourage you to try real **warungs.** Warung is actually the word for restaurant, and many places are called this, but authentic ones, mostly frequented by locals, are sort of little cafes—slightly grimy stores with just three or so seats for dining. Don't be put off by appearances; I've had some of my best meals in Bali at places like these, for literally pennies. If food prep concerns are an issue, order items fried (so to ensure thorough cooking) and without meat. Our standby is *nasi goreng* (fried rice), without meat, which is always prepared slightly differently, and always delicious.

Indonesian dishes you are most likely to encounter: *nasi goreng* (fried rice, usually topped with an egg); *mie goreng* (fried noodles); *nasi campur* (can be a plate of boiled rice with sides of meat and veggies, but often a sampler plate of different tastes offered by the restaurant, ranging from fish wrapped in banana leaves to deep-fried corn fritters); *ayam goreng* (fried chicken, often tough, scrawny birds); *gado gado* (salad with peanut sauce, served hot or cold); *satay* (small chunks of meat on skewers served with peanut sauce—more innovatively, the meat has been minced and spiced. Padang food (sold in little cafes called *rumah makan* Padang) is spicy tidbits (fried fish or chicken, various veggie dishes) piled up in dishes—you pick what you want or let them choose. They fill a plate for you and charge you by the amount; it's usually quite cheap.

Specifically Balinese food is harder to come by, mostly because the Balinese don't eat in warungs much, but rather at home, or at festivals. But the dishes are spectacular, particularly ***babi guleng,*** generally a feast of roasted suckling pig turned into several rich dishes, and ***betutu bebek,*** or smoked duck. Both need to be ordered a day in advance.

SHOPPING

The selection, presentation, and sheer amount of arts and crafts available for purchase in Bali (see "Arts & Crafts," in section 1), is mind-boggling, especially when you realize you *have to have it all.* There's something for all budgets, from trinkets that cost pennies to paintings and furniture that can cost many thousands of dollars. Between fabrics, clothing, wood and stone carvings, paintings, and doodads of varying quality, it's a shopper's paradise. The important thing to remember is that everything runs the gamut; clothing can be high designer quality, or it can fall apart after you've worn it only twice; wood can be carved to order or mass-produced. Don't buy the first frame you see; you are likely to see thousands more.

Shopping in Bali is something like a mental contact sport. Only a few places have fixed prices; everywhere else, bargaining is the name of the game. It's simple, really. Whoever has the most stamina wins. It works like this: the seller offers the first price, which to a well-heeled rube sounds pretty good. In fact, it's often 10 times what the item is really worth. So the savvy then offer an amount substantially lower, whereupon the seller gasps, smiles, and shakes his head with dismay, but comes down a notch as a favor to you. The haggling continues, and sometimes you'll get fed up and leave, but they'll drag you back, offering to "make morning price just for you, for good luck." And so it goes until, ideally, you both reach a mutually satisfactory price (or not; there are plenty more of that next door). These people are very good at what they do, and most of us are not, so the fainthearted give up early on and pay more than they need to.

Here are some tips to remember:

1. If you start by countering with an amount that is half their original price, they've already won. Don't worry that your offer seems outrageously low; their price is outrageously high to begin with, and the melodramatic reaction is all part of the act.
2. Take your time to shop around, for a few days even, before you begin to actually shell out money, so that you know what's out there. Start with an easy item—a

---

Shopping Tip

Many of the big names in **sporting goods** crank out merchandise manufactured in Indonesia, translating to lower prices if you know where to look. There's a Nike shop in Kuta Square (see "Shopping" under "Kuta"), and Athletes Foot locations on Jalan Melasti in Legian and in the Galleria shopping center (see "Shopping" under "Nusa Dua"). As mentioned above, the real name of the buying game in Bali, in terms of quality for value, is to commission something. This can be anything from a wood carving to a garment. The latter doesn't take as long, but in either case you must bring plenty of drawings or photos so that the creator will have a good blueprint to go by.

sarong for temple wear, for example. (As of this writing, sarongs were about Rp20,000 to Rp30,000, depending on the quality of the cloth.) Attempting to buy a sarong from a couple different sellers demonstrates that there is indeed ultimately a bottom line (at least, for tourists; Balinese will always pay less, and that's as it should be).

3. Head for the hills (or do your shopping out of the main areas). Remember, sparse tourists translates into better bargains.

4. Don't hesitate to walk away if negotiations aren't going your way. Not only will there always be someone else to buy from, but this can sometimes be an effective bargaining tool. Suddenly, the price may drop dramatically. Or if you return the next day, they may be even more inclined to work with you. But remember, once you've agreed on a price, that means you've bought it. Reneging at that point is considered very rude.

5. Above all, relax. Someone will always have the item you wanted for less than you paid, or your friend will have gotten a better deal elsewhere. Often tourists get so caught up in negotiations, determined to get a bargain, that they fail to realize they are literally dickering over dimes. Remember, you can't get that item at home, and even if you can, how much more would you have to pay for it? (As an example, those flying wood creatures that are all over Ubud for about Rp40,000 will, in a certain New Orleans import shop, set you back US$40 to US$70.)

Fast Facts: Bali

American Express   There is a branch c/o Pacto Travel Agency in the Bali Beach Hotel in Sanur (☎ **361-288449**); and in Panin Bank at Jalan Legian 80X, Kuta (☎ **361-751-058**).

Business Hours   Most places keep "daylight hours," which on the equator pretty much means 6am to 6pm. (Or a little later.)

Doctors & Dentists   Ask your hotel for a referral—many have a doctor on call. In Kuta, try the **Bali International Medical Centre** (Jalan Bypass Ngurah Rai no. 100X, ☎ **361-761263**). It's open daily from 8am to midnight and sometimes will send someone to your hotel. There is a general hospital in Denpasar, but for any serious problems, go home as soon as possible for treatment. For dentists, ask your hotel for a referral.

Drug Laws   Though you may be offered hash and marijuana at every turn, Indonesia officially takes drug offenses very seriously, and you run the risk of getting busted readily (because, as a tourist, they rather assume you are using drugs) and languishing in jail for 9 or more years.

Electricity   Currents may be either 110 volts, 50 AC; or 220 to 240 volts, 50 AC.

Embassies/Consulates   United States: Jalan Hayam Wuruk no. 188, Denpasar (☎ **361-233605**). **Australia (Canada, New Zealand,** and **Great Britain** also have their representatives here): Jalan Prof. Moch, Yamin 51, Denpasar (☎ **361-235092**). Or, in Jakarta: **Canada:** Wisma Metropolitan I, 5th floor, Jalan Jen. Sudirman, Kav. 29, Jakarta (☎ **021-510709**). **Great Britain:** Jalan Thamrin 75, Jakarta (☎ **021-330904**).

Emergencies   The number for the police is 110, ambulance 118, fire 113.

Telephone Dialing Info at a Glance

- **To place a call from your home country to Bali,** dial the international access code (011 in the U.S., 0011 in Australia, 0170 in New Zealand, 00 in the U.K.), plus Indonesia's country code (62), plus the area code (361 for Kuta, Jimbaran, Nusa Dua, Sanur, and Ubud; 362 for Lovina; 363 for Candi Dasa; 370 for Lombok), followed by the 6-digit phone number (for example, from the U.S. to Lovina, you'd dial 011 + 62 + 362 + 000000).
- **To place a call within Indonesia,** you must use area codes if calling between states. Note that for calls within the country, area codes are all preceded by a zero (i.e., Lovina 0362, Candi Dasa 0363, Lombok 0370, etc.).
- **To place a direct international call from Indonesia,** dial the international access code (001), plus the country code of the place you are dialing, plus the area code, plus the residential number of the other party.
- To reach the international operator, dial 102.
- **International country codes** are as follows: Australia 61, Burma 95, Cambodia 855, Canada 1, Hong Kong 852, Laos 856, Malaysia 60, New Zealand 64, the Philippines 63, Singapore 65, Thailand 66, U.K. 44, U.S. 1, Vietnam 84.

Hospitals   There is a main hospital in Denpasar, but for any serious ailment, get back to your own country as soon as you can; or evacuate to Hong Kong, Singapore, KL, or Bangkok.

Internet/E-mail   Internet cafes are springing up all over Bali (and, realizing that the majority of travelers use Hotmail, have a direct link to same), but the connections can still be painfully slow, particularly early to mid-evening when everyone in Indonesia (so it seems) is checking their e-mail. Since the cafes charge by the minute, you can rack up quite a bill just trying to read your mail. Go at off hours and if the connection seems slow, sign off and come back again some other time. Many hotels also will let you use their Internet connection to read e-mail.

Language   The Balinese speak both Indonesian and Balinese—the former when out in public, the latter at home. English is widely spoken throughout Bali, particularly in the major tourist areas. While not everyone is fluent, most of the people you will be dealing with will speak enough English that you can communicate with them. (For more information, see "Language," earlier in this chapter.)

Liquor Laws   You won't find liquor in any Muslim restaurant, but you will find it otherwise readily available throughout Bali, particularly the potent rice spirit *arak* and, of course, Bali Hai beer.

Police   The phone number for the police is **110.**

Post Office/Mail   Your hotel can send mail for you, or you can go to the post office in Denpasar (Jalan Raya Puputan Renon, ☎ **361-223568**). Other branches are in Kuta, Ubud, and Sanur. For big items, there are packing and shipping services in all major tourist areas. Cost is determined either by size or weight.

Safety/Crime   Bali is by and large a safe place to be, even after dark. Violent crime is rare. However, pickpockets are not, so you should exercise considerable caution by using a money belt, particularly in crowded tourist areas, and be careful not to flash large wads of cash (it's rude, besides). If you find yourself in need of assistance, contact the **Guardian Angels Tourist Police** (there are 265 of these angels dressed in blue) at ☎ **361-763753** 24 hours a day.

Many hotels offer safety deposit boxes, and it would be best to keep extra cash and other valuables in them. If nothing else, make sure your suitcase has a good lock on it. Even the best hotel can't always guarantee security for valuables left lying in plain sight.

Taxes   Most hotels and restaurants add a "plus plus" to the bill—a 10% and 11% combination of sales tax and service charge, for a total of 21%.

Telephones   As many hotels charge a great deal even for using your calling card, you are better off using **Wartel's** privately owned public phones. There's one in every tourist center, though some work better than others. Some also have Internet services.

Time   Bali is Greenwich Mean Time plus 8 hours, except during daylight saving time, which they do not observe. That's 13 hours ahead of Eastern standard time in the U.S., and 16 hours ahead of Pacific standard time.

Tipping   Tipping is not required, and not even encouraged. Most restaurants include a "service charge" in the "plus plus" added to the bill. If you feel you must tip when dining, just leave a very small amount. More often than not, the recipient will be surprised.

Toilets   Western style toilets with seats are becoming more common than the Asian squat variety, though cheap losmen/homestays and some less touristy public places still have the latter. Always carry some toilet paper with you or you may have to use your hand (the left one only, please) and the dip bucket available.

Water   Avoid tap water in Bali unless properly boiled. Bottled water is available everywhere, and restaurants in tourist areas seem to use it as a matter of course, but you should always ask to be sure.

3 Kuta

Intrepid travelers arriving at Denpasar's Ngurah Rai Airport information booth looking for directions are systematically shooed off to Kuta. (After all, isn't everyone going there?) If you're young, brave, and a die-hard "yahoo" (Australian for face-painter), then maybe you'll understand why the little seaside town of Kuta burgeoned into an indistinguishable string of seaside municipalities that host one massive and rowdy party. Australian rugby players love it. But hearty middle-aged English couples murmur words like "trash" and "worthless" when describing their experience in Kuta.

You're probably thinking "Can it be as bad as all that?" Well, it's not for nothing that the hotels are consistently full. As a rule, I myself try never to stay within a 1 kilometer radius of a McDonald's, Wendy's or Dunkin Donuts. But some people enjoy being in the thick of the action. It's a quick 10 minutes from the airport, especially convenient for Australians in for a quickie weekend in the tropics. Some even maintain a loyal following of beach locals for things like toenail painting, massages, and gifts, resulting in other potential scavengers keeping a respectable distance. But still, Kuta is made up of narrow streets and alleys, with pedestrians crammed between honking, muffler-less cars and motorbikes and some of the most aggressive touts on the island.

The best compromise of all, short of staying elsewhere on the island, is to follow the flow of tourism out of the eye of the hurricane. The beaches just north of Kuta Beach are actually quite nice, namely, the quieter shores of Legian and the downright upscale sands of Seminyak. Some of the best dining on the island is located here as well.

GETTING THERE

Kuta is virtually right next to the airport, so many, if not most, hotels offer free airport pick-up. There are also **taxis** galore, but be sure to take the official ones to get the set rates, usually one-tenth of what unofficial drivers will charge. As you exit the terminal, turn to your left and look for the window where you give your destination, pay your fare, and are assigned a cab.

GETTING AROUND

Kuta is a big rectangle. The two main north-south streets are Jalan Pantai Kuta, running next to the ocean, and Jalan Legian. They are connected by Jalan Melasti at the top and bisected, sometimes in a crooked, meandering way, by Jalan Benesari, Poppies Gang I and II, and a few small alleys. You can easily **walk** all this, or take the reasonably priced blue and yellow **metered taxis** (but not the unofficial ones offered by touts). Kuta gradually becomes Legian and then Seminyak to the north—as you walk up Jalan Legian, you won't even notice where one ends and the other begins. The further up the beach you go, the more likely you are to encounter dogs and children frolicking on the sand. Currents are equally strong up here with no reefs to protect swimmers from the wrath of the Indian Ocean.

Fast Facts: Kuta

Banks/Currency Exchange   There is an ATM in the Kuta Square shopping mall (about halfway down on the left). Wartel outlets are found all around the main streets.

Internet/E-mail   Internet cafes almost outnumber transport guides in Kuta. Most charge by the minute, so negotiate before logging on if your Internet cafe posts hourly rates. On the northern fringes of Legian and Seminyak, head over to **Bali Cyber Cafe & Restaurant** (Jalan Pura Bagus Taruna no. 4, at Kuta Palace Road, Legian; ☎ **361-761326**), which charges Rp24,000 per hour; **Legian Cyber C@fe** (Jalan Sahadewa no. 21, Legian; ☎ **361-752-138**), open 9am to 10pm, which charges Rp30,000 per hour; or the air-conditioned **Goa 2001 cyber cafe** (Jalan Raya Seminyak, Seminyak; ☎ **361-731178**), open 9am to 2am for Rp16,000 per hour.

Post Office/Mail   There is a main post office, but it's not conveniently located. There are also some postal agents, and your hotel can send mail for you.

Telephones   The area code in Kuta is 361.

ACCOMMODATIONS

Kuta Beach, while still a booming resort, is now just a caricature of what it used to be. Amidst the frat-boy bustle, we've managed to find a handful of standouts, but discovered that those in-the-know are seeking refuge in the beaches just to the north, in **Legian** and **Seminyak.** We've found a few gems here too, but even here, if aggressive-to-the-point-of-hostile touts are not your idea of a relaxing day at the beach, I suggest you base yourself elsewhere.

KUTA BEACH

Bounty Hotel. Poppies Gang II, Jalan Segara Batu Bolong no. 18, Kuta, Bali. ☎ **361-753030.** Fax 361-752121. 166 units. A/C MINIBAR TV TEL. US$93 double; US$103 deluxe. AE, DC, MV, V. Free parking.

The biggest thing going on at Poppies Gang II, the Bounty is clearly a party-down hotel, but at least one that feels like it is in Bali. The rooms are decidedly Western-style (with familiar comforts like hair dryers), though they do have wood floors and are decorated with Balinese fabric. Standard rooms are slightly smaller than deluxe, with the wash basin in the room. Be careful—seemingly complimentary snacks left out for you are really from the minibar. The complex, arranged around an attractive pool, features stone carvings and red tile ornamentation. The hotel (always a good place to grab a cab) is positioned equal walking distance between the beach and the shopping on Legian, and the same people own the **Bounty Bar & Restaurant** over there, which is one of the area's most happening late-night spots. That fact and the fliers advertising various party spots gives you an idea of the clientele.

✪ Hard Rock Hotel. Jalan Pantai, Banjar Pande Mas, Kuta, Bali. ☎ **361-761869.** Fax 361-761868. E-mail: bookings@hrbc-bali.co.id. 418 units. A/C MINIBAR TV TEL. US$170–US$180 double; US$350–US$550 suite. AE, DC, JCB, MC, V. Free parking.

On principle, I despise the Hard Rock Cafe's cultural imperialism and wouldn't eat at one on a bet. And so, fully prepared to extend that attitude to this hotel, instead I was utterly disarmed by its fanciful, whimsical design that while entirely un-Balinese is so delightful I forgot to care. Quickly move past the lobby (where the staff speaks excellent English), with its usual dubious memorabilia (once-used guitars, gold records), and head down brightly colored corridors labeled after different musical genres (psychedelic, blues, alternative). The color scheme extends into rooms that can best be called *cabana moderne.* They are light and airy, with a photo of an artist from the corridor genre, while unbleached cottons with the Hard Rock logo cover the bed. The bathrooms are done in playful geometrics—be sure to steal that cotton laundry bag. The fun continues with the pool—the largest in Bali, a sprawling monster with slides and its own beach (nonguests can use it for a fee, and rooms in the "deluxe block" have their own private pool. There's an outdoor living room, an MTV-style sitting area, an in-house radio station, and a recording studio where you can play out your own musician fantasies. Sure, rock blares 24/7 in the lobby, which has a popular bar, and in other public areas, but the fabulous kids' playroom—"Little Rock"—and that pool make it a great option for boomer families. This is not the place to stay if you want to experience even a modicum of Balinese culture, but it still is a model of modern hotel design.

Hotel Restu Bali. Jalan Raya Legian no. 113, Kuta, Bali. ☎ **361-751251.** Fax 361-751252. E-mail: restubali@denpasar.wasantara.net.id. 41 units. A/C TV TEL. US$35–US$55 double. Rates include breakfast. AE, JCB, MC, V. Free parking.

Technically, this is in Legian, but it's on Kuta's main shopping drag of Jalan Raya, which means you often end up wandering by here. It's about a 10-minute walk to the beach, but right in the middle of nighttime action. The deceptively simple small property is actually a long, narrow rabbit's warren of different tropical nooks and crannies. For all the hustle and bustle outside, it's unbelievably serene. Standard rooms have wicker furniture and stark but good bathrooms. The Puri Deluxe are bungalow style, with thatched roofs and woven mats covering the walls and private patios. Bathrooms are the same, but the sink is in the room. Two very nice swimming pools spill into gurgling fountain pools—some of which are right outside a handful of rooms, creating a noise that some might find soothing but others distracting.

Natour Kuta. Jalan Pantai Kuta no. 1, Kuta, Bali. ☎ **361-751361.** Fax 361-751362 or 361/ 753958. E-mail: nkbh@denpasar.wasantara.net.id. 137 units. A/C MINIBAR TV TEL. US$100–US$130 double; US$175–US$350 suites. AE, DC, JCB, MC, V. Free parking.

This is the only hotel in Kuta that is right on the beach—and at a spot on the beach that while still not good for swimming is better for dipping up to your knees. If your other passion is shopping, being right next to Kuta Square makes this the most per-fectly situated hotel for you. Pleasant also is the butterfly-shaped pool on the way to the beach, which provides a nice spot for viewing the sunset. All this means you won't be spending too much time in the unimaginatively decorated long and narrow rooms—though try to get a third floor standard, which has an ocean view. Skip the more costly bungalows in back, which provide little more than some faux privacy or romance (even the bathrooms are the same size as standard). The beach access and pool may make this a good choice for families. For dining, there's a steak and seafood restaurant, coffee shop, and two bars, plus frequent buffet dinner shows.

✪ Poppies II Cottages. Poppies Lane I, Kuta, Bali. ☎ **361-751059.** Fax 361-752364. E-mail: info@bali.poppies.net. 21 units (4 additional units at the older Poppies II). A/C MINI-BAR TEL. US$85 double. AE, DC, MC, V. Free parking.

This is by far the best mid-range hotel in Kuta, with its individual and atmospheric thatched cottages set among gorgeous gardens abloom with a riot of bougainvillea. The small swimming pool, designed to look like a natural pond, complete with rock formations, is perhaps the prettiest in town, and is surrounded by many nooks for lounging. It's hard to leave such a spot for the madness of Kuta. The rooms, truth be told, aren't that special (despite a recent upgrade), but the open-air bathrooms are in marble, complete with a small sunken tub. An interesting touch is the Internet Cot-tage, where homesick guests can have their own e-mail address and Web page while in residence.

The original Poppies Cottages, a bit of a distance away, are less of a bargain, as the bungalows there badly need a face-lift (particularly the large but deeply drab bath-rooms). They only look shabbier compared with similar places around town that give you more amenities (like A/C, telephone, and an on-site pool) for around the same price. You can use the fabulous pool at the other Poppies, but it's a long, hot walk away.

LEGIAN

Padma Hotel. Jalan Padma no. 1, Legian, Bali. ☎ **361-752111.** Fax 361-752140. 403 units. A/C MINIBAR TV TEL. US$260 double; US$325–US$1,750 suite. AE, DC, JCB, MC, V. Free parking.

This sprawling complex way up the beach in Legian has plenty of activities that make it attractive for families. Others may find it a bit out of the way from the heart of Kuta action (though there are shops and touts aplenty just outside the gate). Rooms have slightly better than average Bali furniture. Standard rooms, in a four-story high-rise, have a balcony, but only deluxe rooms have good views. Family rooms open onto a patio and the garden, but all rooms have the same size bathroom. The pool is large and angular. There is a grassy place before you get to the actual beach that is kept tout-free for better beach enjoyment (which is still good only for surfing, not swimming). The many local culturally geared activities (egg painting, instrument demonstration) are admirable, but all that non–air-conditioned space means a long hot walk to any part of the complex. Padma is home to seven restaurants and three bars.

Puri Tantra Bungalows. Jalan Padma Utara 50X, Legian, Bali. ☎ and fax **361-753195.** 6 units, all with bathroom. US$40 bungalow. No credit cards.

Kuta

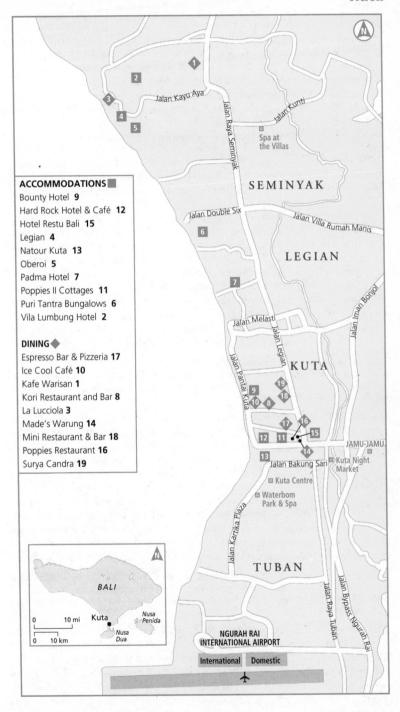

ACCOMMODATIONS ■
Bounty Hotel **9**
Hard Rock Hotel & Café **12**
Hotel Restu Bali **15**
Legian **4**
Natour Kuta **13**
Oberoi **5**
Padma Hotel **7**
Poppies II Cottages **11**
Puri Tantra Bungalows **6**
Vila Lumbung Hotel **2**

DINING ◆
Espresso Bar & Pizzeria **17**
Ice Cool Café **10**
Kafe Warisan **1**
Kori Restaurant and Bar **8**
La Lucciola **3**
Made's Warung **14**
Mini Restaurant & Bar **18**
Poppies Restaurant **16**
Surya Candra **19**

Tucked unobtrusively behind a mahogany door in a garden off the beach at Legian, this is one of the area's more intimate and peaceful choices. The six individual bungalows line a garden path that makes its way through the Yudana family's backyard, and if your luck holds out, you may find yourself romping with their big and fluffy dogs. The cottages consist of the main room and a dressing room alcove; outdoor bathrooms have sunken tubs and an interesting striated shell tiling pattern. Traditional narrow gilded Balinese portals open onto a terrace or patio, some with bamboo furniture, or you can grab one of the garden lounges and relax on the lawn. During the off or slow season, you may have to go hunting for the owners, but it's worth the effort.

SEMINYAK

✪ Legian. Jalan Laksmana, Seminyak, Kuta, Bali 80361. ☎ **361-730622.** Fax 361-730623. 70 units, all with bathroom. AC MINIBAR TV TEL. US$305–US$710 suite. AE, DC, JCB, MC, V. Free parking.

Only 3 years old, the Legian had tough competition when it staked a beachfront spot next to the Oberoi. The cement structure topped by a tile roof reminiscent of a pagoda may stray a bit into the bland, but with the lawns and pool facing the beach, it's easy to see how the planners justified sinking all of their investment into the rooms. This is Indonesian high style imported from Jakarta—it's actually amazing what wonderful things they can do with inlaid shell, coconut wood, and bamboo fibers. All rooms come with a terrace that faces the sea, complete with an outdoor day bed that's almost too pretty to muss up. Actually, all rooms are suites; guests, dubious as to how much space they really need, frequently ask for something smaller. Bikes are free to guests, solving the transportation problem for those with relatively strong thighs.

Oberoi. Jalan Laksmana, Seminyak, Kuta, Bali 80361. ☎ **361-730361.** Fax 361-730791. www.oberoihotels.com. E-mail: obrblres@indosat.net.id. 75 units, all with bathroom. AC MINIBAR TV TEL. US$240–US$700 garden view cottage or villa; US$290–US$800 ocean view. AE, DC, JCB, MC, V. Free parking.

The first hotel in Seminyak and one of the Leading Hotels of the World, the Oberoi has attracted the likes of Henry Kissinger, Julia Roberts, and the British musician Donovan. The property is composed of individual *lanais*—native (and politically incorrect) bungalows of coral stone with wood beams and thatch roofs. Rooms are visually bland, but the amenities are first class all the way: futon beds, glass and marble in the outdoor baths, sunken tubs, and goodies like slippers, robes, and flip-flops for the beach. Nine villas have their own private pool, along with a VCD player (we peasants in the standard units only get a VCR). Already several years old, however, the beachfront grounds and poolside area are looking a little weatherworn. There's a mini outdoor amphitheater for the schedule of traditional dances (Tuesdays, Thursdays, and Saturdays). And guests can take advantage of on-site motorbike rental for US$6!

Vila Lumbung Hotel. Jalan Raya Petitenget no. 100X, Kuta, Bali. ☎ **361-482220.** Fax 361-489970. www.HotelLumbung.com. E-mail: info@HotelLumbung.com. 20 units. A/C MINIBAR TV TEL. US$150–US$200 bungalow; US$405 deluxe villa. Rates include breakfast and taxes. MC, V.

Exotic luxury is difficult to resist, especially when it lies in such close proximity to some of the best meals in Kuta (i.e., Kafe Warisan, La Lucciola). Vila Lumbung is laid out amidst landscaped tropical gardens, with two and three-story grass-roof villas designed in the manner of the Balinese "lumbung"—a building traditionally used for storing rice. (Think upscale Oriental barn.) Two-story bungalows consist of upstairs and downstairs units, offering a choice of either a private terrace or balcony. I prefer the upstairs units because of the presence of architectural elements like the narrow "dome" which, here, has been transformed into a bright and cozy lounging "bale." Furniture is of coconut wood and teak (although I would have preferred monotone natural fibers for the sofa and bedspreads), and the cool tile terrazzo floors are refreshing on your feet. The only potential drawback of the property is that it lies on the opposite side of the road from the sea, but the bi-level pool—with a waterfall, cave, and bubble pool— is a lovely respite from the rough sea and aggressive touts.

DINING

The variety in Kuta is stunning, thanks to all the homesick tourists who can't do without their German, Italian, and American favorite. Unfortunately, this translates into a stunning variety of bad and mediocre food, but there *are* a couple of standouts, listed below. Besides these, if you absolutely must, there is the **Hard Rock Cafe,** which offers probably the best burger on the island (but I don't want to hear about it), and the two hotel restaurants directly across from the beach, which offer safe and solid, if unexciting, tourist specialties and fresh fish.

KUTA BEACH

Espresso Bar & Pizzeria. Jalan Legian 83, Kuta. ☎ **361-752576.** Reservations not accepted. Main courses Rp4,900–Rp17,500. Daily 10am–1am. PIZZA, MEXICAN.

Pizza is the true international food, and it's interesting to see a local country's spin on this reliable item. Here, it's thin crust, light on the sauce, heavy on the cheese, with a variety of toppings (chicken, shrimp, veggies and . . . squid). Best of all, it's from a wood-fired brick oven! This spaghetti-Western themed place is just one of many restaurants serving pizza in Kuta, but one of the few that specialize in it. That, and the oven, does mean that you pay twice what you would in a warung. It also serves burgers, Mexican fare, and pasta. I say stick with the pizza; an individual 10-inch with various toppings runs about Rp16,000. Toss in a fancy ice cream dessert, banana fritters, espresso (including Italy's fab Illy coffee) or "Happy Soda" (cream and hyper-sweet syrup) and you've got a nice cheap snack or light meal, Western style.

Ice Cool Cafe. Poppies Gang II (opposite the Bounty Hotel), Kuta. Rp6,500 (scoops), Rp10,000 (shakes). Daily 8am–11pm. ICE CREAM.

This slightly larger than a sidewalk stand ice cream parlor claims to have the best ice cream in Bali—that may well be true. Certainly, places that offer scoops rather than premade bars are rare, and the selection of flavors here is fairly wide. Try a "thick shake" (as everywhere in Bali, if you get a regular shake, the consistency is like water) of fruit juice or a smoothie.

✪ Kori Restaurant and Bar. Poppies Gang II, Kuta. ☎ **361-758605.** Lunch main courses Rp12,000–Rp32,500; dinner main courses Rp29,500–Rp118,500. AE, DC, JCB, MC, V. Daily 11:30am–11pm. EUROPEAN/STEAKHOUSE.

Valet parking in the narrow and chaotic Poppies Gang II? For a meal prepared by no less than a former member of the Four Season's stable of chefs, nothing but the finest. You can choose to sit in the dining room, or on one of the more romantic cushioned bamboo platforms that bridge the narrow garden oasis. In deference to the heat, the lunch menu is somewhat light, featuring *malai köftes* (spicy vegetarian fritters in a curry sauce), the mouth-burning Bali chile burger (if you dare), or Bangers (veal sausages) for the carnivore. The dinner menu has all the bells and whistles with steakhouse-type entrees: try the mixed grill of U.S. beef loin, spare ribs, pork cutlet and Nuerberger sausages, or order up the Singapore chile crab, savory and spicy fresh black Bali crabs served with a big 'ole bib. Topping the high end of the menu is the giant seafood grill, cooked and served on a hot lava stone. To finish off, there's a respectable stock of brandy and cognac.

Made's Warung. Br. Pando Mas, Kuta. ☎ **316-755297.** Reservations not accepted. Main courses Rp12,000–Rp26,000. AE, MC, V (on orders of Rp80,000 or more). Daily 8am–12am. INDONESIAN.

This is a Kuta tradition that may serve what you think will be your best meal, until you eat much better Indonesian food elsewhere on the island. Still, this is a reliable, bustling, confusing open-air warung on a noisy street, whose popularity means possibly sharing a table. Gado gado, satay (especially pork), and curries are all recommended, and you can get plenty of food (for a slightly light meal) for about US$2. Fun surprises on the menu include bagel and smoked marlin, tofu burgers, Caesar salad, and vegemite for an Aussie breakfast. They also have a large beverage selection, from iced coffee drinks to considerably potent booze (the menu warns you).

Mini Restaurant & Bar. Legian St., Kuta. ☎ **361-751651.** Reservations not accepted. Main courses Rp16,000–Rp22,000 (seafood by weight and somewhat higher). AE, MC, V. Daily 10am–noon. SEAFOOD.

One of two restaurants right next to each other that serve fresh fish out of a tank, this is the larger of the two—a cavernous, thatched-roof place. You choose your fish and preparation (steamed, barbecued, or fried). They—and I—recommend it fried, though the prices go up considerably. But a whole snapper runs about US$6 and easily serves two. Shellfish—enormous prawns and lobster—really hit the ceiling price-wise. Or go ahead and order the frog legs. Fish comes with choice of sauce: butter garlic (not that great, but the marinated onions are), sweet and sour, and soya. The menu offers many, many cocktails and some appealing frothy drinks. They do *babi guleng* combinations (with advance order), and also offer local, Chinese, and European dishes.

Poppies Restaurant. Poppies Cottages, Poppies Lane I, Kuta. ☎ **361-751059.** Reservations recommended. Men must wear shirts. Main courses Rp19,500–Rp37,000. AE, MC, V. Daily 8am–11pm. INDONESIAN/EUROPEAN.

Poppies is a veritable tradition thanks to its 25 years of serving Indonesian and not-so-Indonesian specialties. Some think it's severely overrated, but if you need Italian or French-style pork, beef, or chicken, you will be happy here, but you will pay extra for it. It's certainly the prettiest restaurant in town, with a garden setting, a mass of crawling vines overhead keeping the hot sun at bay, and babbling pools and waterfalls. Indonesian dishes include an outstanding *ikan pepes*—mashed fish cooked in a banana leaf (sort of a fish tamale) with nicely hot spices and served with an even spicier collection of vegetables they called "pickles." The *mie goreng,* loaded with shrimp and vegetables, is also good. Service is slow, but this is a good place to dawdle.

Surya Candra. Jalan Legian 83, Kuta. ☎ **361-752576.** Main courses Rp13,000–Rp23,000. DC, MC, V. Daily noon–midnight. SEAFOOD.

Exactly the same idea as the Mini Restaurant right next door—pick your fish victim out of the tank, tell them how you want it, sit, and eat. Those looking for more intimacy might prefer it here, since it is somewhat smaller than the inappropriately named Mini. Otherwise, why not have a progressive fish dinner and compare the two?

SEMINYAK

✪ **Kafe Warisan.** Jalan Kerobokan, (Kerobokan) Seminyak. ☎ **361-731-175.** Reservations required. Main courses Rp77,000–Rp99,000. AE, MC, V. Mon–Sat 11am–4pm and 7–11pm. FRENCH.

Kafe Warisan is no secret: an unscientific poll of the best restaurants on the island inevitably put this address at the top of the list. The gracious setting—in an open courtyard under the protection of frangipani trees and overlooking rice paddies—is just a prelude to the sophistication of the menu, and the personalized place card is a nice touch too. Now for the hard part: selection by elimination. With so many mouth-watering options to choose from, it's obvious that you'll be eating here more than once. Here's a tip: the house favorite appetizer is the plate of escargots, here stuffed into roasted mushrooms and topped with a pesto butter. For main dishes, Kafe Warisan serves the best steaks on the island, the finest cuts of meat imported from Australia (they know their audience). With any luck, you'll land here on a day when the venison tenderloin graces the special menu. There's a wide selection of non–red meat dishes, including a grilled Tasmanian salmon, a seafood fricassee, and a grilled rosemary chicken breast. There's also an extensive wine list that will set you back Rp145,000 to Rp1,300,000 (US$16 to US$144 for the 1984 Margaux), plus a choice of California wines by the glass (skip the reds, unless you like yours chilled). Stop by the boutique on your way to finger through a collection of beaded dresses, silk sarongs, jewelry, antique batik, and other collectibles.

Ku Dé Ta. Jalan Oberoi 9, Seminyak. ☎ **361-736969.** Main courses Rp30,000–Rp40,000 (US$3.33–US$4.44). AE, MC, V. Daily 7am–midnight (food service). BISTRO.

Ku Dé Ta is yet another "Europe meets Asia," Kuta area's newest (as of this writing) international bistro aimed at an upscale clientele. Romantic lighting and elegant min-imalist decor blur the lines between indoor and outdoor dining; daytime the ambience is dominated by the restaurant's proximity to the beach. Add both an elegant bar and lounge area and a cigar lounge—complete with putting green—to the equation, and you've got an all-purpose evening out. Happily, what comes out of the kitchen makes you want to stay: try the signature dish of slow-roasted, Asian-sauced duck with a star anise and pear essence or the chile and sea-salted squid, with a mango and green papaya marmalade. The cigar lounge is open from 6pm until late.

✪ **La Lucciola.** Oberoi Rd., Kayu Aya Beach, Legian. ☎ **361-730838.** Breakfast Rp12,500–Rp28,000; main courses Rp23,000–Rp96,000. AE, MC, V. Daily 8am–midnight. ITALIAN.

If there's a see-and-be-seen spot among the Kuta crowd, it's the brand-new La Lucci-ola. Even breakfast draws the beautiful people, and why not, with its prime beachfront location on this deserted stretch of Legian. With morning eye-poppers like ricotta hot cakes, smoked salmon scrambled eggs on toasted focaccia, and a mythical plate of hash browns, it's no wonder. You'll find yourself equally bewitched by the dinner menu, with choice offerings like lemongrass bok choy risotto with sesame ginger poached snapper, chicken and soba noodle salad with a soy sesame dressing, or a delectable loin of pork, chargrilled with apples and served with a pumpkin puree and onion relish. Even writing this is torture. End with a bracing espresso and the white chocolate pra-line pannacotta, and you won't even mind that you were strong-armed into giving a donation to the adjacent temple in order to enter the parking lot.

OUTDOOR ACTIVITIES & WATER SPORTS

Obviously, **surfing** is number one in Kuta, as enthusiasts from all over are drawn to its stupendous breakers. You can't swing a dead cat here without hitting a surfer. Blame Bob Koke, who claims to have first brought the sport to Bali from Hawaii.

The best surfing is between March and July, though it's still good as late as Octo-ber. Tubes Bar (see "Kuta After Dark," below) will have a list of tide charts and other important information, though the plethora of surf shops should be able to help you as well. You can also take lessons from the **Cheyne Horan School of Surf** (☎ 361-756735). The breaks along the beach all have their good points, (beginners should stick to the surf off Kuta and Legian beach, where they'll find safety in the sandy beaches), but the legendary surf is at the low reef breaks and "barrels" of **Kuta Reef** (out from the southern end of the beach). You either have to paddle to get there (it takes about half an hour) or pay an outrigger at Jimbaran to take you.

Unfortunately, the same surf makes recreational **swimming** virtually impossible. The waves crash sharply in, and before them, the water barely covers the ankles. Even past the breakers, the current can be too strong. Pay close attention to swimming warnings and restrictions and be very careful if you do swim. Tanning and splashing to cool off are about all that's left to do. Few hotels in Kuta are right on the beach, and two beach chairs and umbrellas rent for Rp35,000 a day.

Other water sports are similarly disappointing—there is no good snorkeling or diving—any dive shop will send you to Sanur, Nusa Dua, or Candi Dasa. For better ocean swimming, and for parasailing, head to Jimbaran Bay, which is only a few kilometers away.

Another option is **Waterbom Park & Spa,** Jalan Kartika Plaza, Tuban, Kuta (☎ 361-755676), just south of Kuta. A water park with slides, a lazy river, and spa facilities, it makes for an ideal family outing. Should your hotel not have a pool, you can pay for a day pass to the monster one at the **Hard Rock Hotel.** The biggest in Bali, it also has several large water slides, plus a faux beach.

SHOPPING

With the touts constantly in your face, shopping in Kuta will seem mandatory. Certainly, you won't lack for quantity—but quality will have to wait until Ubud. Hucksters will constantly wave knockoff brand-name colognes, cheap hats, and dubious wristwatches at you. The streets (particularly Poppies Gang II) are lined with stalls offering tie-dyed sarongs, sarong skirts (with actual ties), shorts, and swimsuits. **Sarongs** are cheaper and nicer elsewhere, but then again, too nice in many cases to use as a swimsuit cover-up, so if that's what you're looking for, here is the place to buy. In any event, given the hard sell, this might be the place to hone your bargaining skills—being cheated by a savvy Kuta salesperson is probably an essential Bali shopping rite of passage. There are regular fixed-price stores, but nothing you can't live without.

Kuta Square is the place to go if you miss Western-style shopping—i.e., fixed prices and mall goods. On the first street right past the Natour Hotel is a shopping mall that could be called Brand Name Row, with Nike, Polo, and Armani stores, plus fast food places like McDonald's, KFC, and Round Table. There is also a CyberCafe here, and an ATM halfway down on the left. Check out **Dive Indonesia** at the entrance to Matahari for any diving gear you failed to bring along.

The **ABC Bookstore,** Jalan Pantai Kuta no. 41E (☎ 361-752745), offers used books with quite a few English-language selections—mostly of the beach blanket variety undoubtedly left behind by tourists. A treasure does sneak in occasionally, however. Buy a book, bring it back when you are done, and get half price back. They're open from 10am to 9pm.

KUTA AFTER DARK

Except for the early morning hours, when the transplanted partiers are sleeping off last night's binge, Kuta IS party central. There's so much going on here, and so comparatively little elsewhere, you have to wonder if it all didn't just migrate over. Kuta nightlife doesn't even really kick in until after 11pm, and then it goes nearly until dawn—every night. In theory, each place has an individual atmosphere and attracts its own clientele, but unless you are a connoisseur, one nightclub or bar looks pretty much like the next. You can either find your own to call home or switch around, sampling everything Kuta has to offer.

Women should be aware of the Bali rent boys. These are young men who want nothing more than to attach themselves to a Western girlfriend, for a few days or a lifetime (who cares, as long as she pays the bills?). They aren't threatening, and can be quite handsome and attentive. Just know what you are getting into.

Kuta really rages (the verb of the moment) in December and January, when the spring break/frat party mentality that is always prevalent hits a fever pitch. If you aren't there then, you can always join the nonlegendary, twice weekly (Tuesday and Saturday) Peanuts Pub Crawl, which picks up at several hotels and takes you to a few different nightspots, including both Peanuts I and II (both on Jalan Legian). By the time they return you to your hotel the next morning, don't expect to remember much of what you did the night before.

Or you could skip all that and do what the locals do: hang out by the food stalls on the beach on Friday and Saturday nights until midnight.

CLUBS

Of course, there are many more than those listed here, but these are some of the most high-profile clubs in town.

Bounty Ship I. Jalan Legian. ☎ **361-752529.** No cover Sun–Fri (1 drink minimum), Rp10,000 Sat. Daily 10pm–3am.

Here's where the tourists go to get ship-faced—it's built to look like a galleon, with a restaurant on the "deck" and a dance club below in the "hull," housing a bar and dance floor, with live bands some nights and deejays others. If it sounds cheesy, well, it is. But the club gets lively, with a young crowd. And on Tuesdays you can walk the plank. They've got a mini-bungee set-up from a board overhanging the dance floor.

Hard Rock Cafe. Jalan Raya Kuta. ☎ **361-755661.** Occasional cover.

The most upscale place in town, and popular with locals as well as yuppie tourists, the Hard Rock Cafe has earned its place as the premiere locale for live music in Kuta. Live bands play nightly starting around 11pm until at least 1am, but action can go on until dawn.

Peanuts II. Jalan Legian or Jalan Melasti (2 entrances). No phone. Occasional cover.

Not the hottest game in town, except by reputation, but surrounded by other bars to get you oiled up before you head in. Either come especially for the rowdy pub crawl, or on other days come to avoid it. There's live music nightly and a disco out the back for all-nighters.

BARS

Again, there are too many bars to mention, so we've selected the most popular, less adolescent types. You might also check out the bar in the lobby of the **Hard Rock Hotel** (☎ **361-755661**), which is a classy, lively place that often has live music as well.

Goa 2001. Jalan Seminyak 1. ☎ **361-730592.** No cover. Daily 7pm–2am.

This is one of the island's oldest hangouts and a Kuta mainstay (they just change the year). The music is smooth Latino in a Balinese environment—great for people-watching and relaxing—adult style.

Hulu Café. Jalan Menu, Legian. No phone. Cover Rp10,000 (US$1.11). Tues–Sun 4pm–2am.

It's shoulder to shoulder on Wednesday, Friday, and Sunday nights at this gay bar, for arguably the best drag show in Indonesia (yes, there are others), featuring some of Bali's best talent. Shows begin around 10:30pm, and Saturday nights are reserved for the "Search for a Tragedy" amateur night. Let's see how these guys look *out* of sarongs!

Kori Restaurant and Bar. Poppies Gang II. ☎ **361-758605.** No cover.

The valet parking should give you an idea of what to expect: relaxed, cozy, pricey. Kori also has a cozy cigar salon with pool table, or you can show off your newly acquired tan draped at the bar—imported wine in hand.

The Living Room. Jalan Petitenget, Seminyak. ☎ **0818-358223.** Daily 7pm–midnight.

This newly opened restaurant didn't cut the mustard among my discerning crowd, but while it's too soon to render a definitive verdict on the validity of the menu, we've decided to wait it out on the open-air terrace with one of the over 100 international wines clogging up the wine cellar.

Q Bar and Café. Jalan Dyana Pura, Abimayu Arcade, Seminyak. ☎ **361-730927.** No cover. Daily 5pm–2am.

The "strip's" newest addition adds some class to a rowdy party that's already gotten out of hand. OK, so it's considered a gay bar, but thanks to the (gay) owner, you can count on a stylish and quirky place to relax. There's a restaurant serving light foods, theme parties, fashion shows, and guest DJs. And cocktails are jumbo.

DAY TRIPS FROM KUTA

The following destinations are easy day trips from either Kuta or Ubud. (Tanah Lot is somewhat closer to Kuta.) Tour companies often combine them as a package, or you can go through your hotel or your own transport guide.

Tanah Lot. 15km (9.3 miles) west of Denpasar. Admission Rp3,000. Open during daylight hours.

Though it's not particularly near anything else, and not all that remarkable architecturally, Tanah Lot is a popular tourist destination, so expect possibly the biggest crowds you will encounter at a temple. Its popularity is due partly to its ease as a day trip from Kuta, but also because of the undeniably spectacular setting, high on craggy bluffs overlooking the Java Sea. This is a truly magnificent example of how well temples in Bali are wedded to their locations, be they lakeside, mountainside, or seaside.

Tanah Lot is said to have been founded by a Brahmin priest in the 16th century. A rivalry with the local, established priest nearly led to his expulsion; instead, he meditated so hard he pushed Tanah Lot "out to sea," where it rests on an inlet that actually becomes an island at high tide. (The walk from the car park is not as long nor as steep as at many other sights, and there are no stairs.) Non-Hindus can't actually enter the temple, but have access to other parts of the complex, strung out across the rocks, and many of these afford a good view. The photo ops provided here are superb, though shutterbugs tend to spoil the meditative qualities of the place. Try to come close to sunset, when Tanah Lot is truly glorious. Skip the touristy snake cave; instead, if the tides allow, wade out to the part of the temple complex that's at your back when you reach the snake cave. It's beautiful and a much better use of time.

Sangeh Monkey Forest. 31km (19 miles) north of Denpasar. Admission Rp3,000. Open during daylight hours.

The Sangeh Monkey Forest is much bigger than the somewhat more high-profile Monkey Forest in Ubud, with majestic trees and even more monkeys. So if you are simian fan, you should go (Sangeh is often combined with trips to Tanah Lot.) A personal "guide" will take you through the forest. It's an enjoyable walk, full of atmosphere thanks to the monkeys and the 17th-century temple they seem to guard. At the end, the guide will attempt to take you to his or her stall. The monkeys are even more wild and fearless than the ones in Ubud, which means fabulous close-ups for photos,

Tee Off Over Tanah Lot

The **Nirwana Bali Golf Club** (Jalan Raya Tanah Lot, Tabanan; ☎ **361-815970;** fax 361-815962; www.nirwanabaligolf.com; e-mail: reservation@ nirwanabaligolf.com) is a sublime experience for golf junkies. The golf course sits on a 101-hectare (250-acre) tract of land only 30 minutes north of the airport, that includes an 18-hole, par-72 championship course designed by Greg Norman, the five-star **Le Meridien Spa and Resort** (www.lemeridien-bali.com/), plus a development of residential villas. It's exclusively private, yet encourages visitors and tourists to use the facilities. At these Westernized prices, it's no wonder.

Nirwana's course incorporates rice paddies and creeks into greens that rise high above the Indian Ocean. Three challenging holes run along the cliff's edge with sweeping views of the sea, but it's the signature seventh hole that draws sighs of wonderment: a line drive into dramatic views of the sacred temple of Tanah Lot, perched on a rocky islet. Nirwana employs a Course Marshall, whose sole duty is to cruise the greens and monitor the speed of the game. Carts are required and are included in the green fee, along with an enchanting and well-trained caddy from the all-female caddy team.

Green fees are available for 9 or 18 holes, and differ for outside visitors and those staying at Le Meridien. Guests of the hotel pay US$72 for a full round (nine holes US$52), while day-trippers pay a whopping US$125/US$70.

In addition to their regular rates, Le Meridien offers a "Simply Golf" package, along with special rates for "the Weekender," "Family Retreat," and "Spa and Lifestyle."

---

but it also means you must be careful not to bring any foodstuffs (they *will* find it on you, and none-too-gently) or any valuables, as they are larcenous beasts. You can also see huge fruit bats flying overhead like vultures. At the end, there is a stand where you can hold a tamed bat to admire its wingspan—touristy, of course (the point being to buy a photo), but it's a thrill to examine one of these up close.

4 Jimbaran

Jimbaran is easily overlooked, because it's so small and because flashy Kuta is right next door. Pity, because this is the nicest beach in South Bali, with some of the purest sand and clearest water around, protected enough so that the water is usually calm, and perfect for swimming. Jimbaran was abruptly elevated to new heights of resort distinction when the Four Seasons' goose laid a golden egg here. But despite increasing development (and indeed, if you squint and cut out the hotels at the top and bottom of the bay's curve), everything looks much like it did 20 or more years ago. A fishing village still exists here, and locals took advantage of the new local business and set up rows of shacks on the beach where cheap fish is grilled to order all day long.

You'll probably get the most memorable seafood feast of your stay in here. Jimbaran is utterly romantic in the flickering candlelight and simply fabulous nightly sunsets.

Removed from the pulse of the island, most people say that the Four Seasons is the only reason to come, but I disagree. Access to the rest of the island is definitely limited, but for a taste of what an undiscovered Bali may have been like, Jimbaran is worth an overnight stay, or at the very least an afternoon with a wonderful meal.

GETTING THERE

Jimbaran is on the road to Nusa Dua, so bemos go there frequently from Kuta and the airport. You'll have to walk in from the main road, though, as the beach area is hidden down several access lanes. Cabs are also easy to grab at either location.

GETTING AROUND

As Jimbaran really is just a few hotels, there are few other facilities. Consult your hotel for currency exchange, Internet access, postal service, and telephone service.

ACCOMMODATIONS

✪ **Four Seasons at Jimbaran Bay.** Jimbaran 80361, Bali. ☎ **361-701010.** Fax 361-701020. www.fourseasons.com. 147 units. A/C MINIBAR TV TEL. US$550 1-bedroom villa; US$750 and up 2-bedroom and Royal Villa. AE, DC, MC, V. Free parking.

This hotel is what comes to mind when you imagine a luxury resort, and yet it's so organic to its setting and so in harmony with its culture that you don't miss out (much) by staying here.

The Four Seasons' exquisitely landscaped grounds drape along a hillside that leads down to the bay. The layout is meant to suggest a series of Balinese villages, with each set of accommodations like a traditional, multistructure Bali home, within its own walled compound. A typical thatched villa consists of a good-sized bedroom; generous dressing room; and large marbled bathroom with oversized tub, many thick towels and fancy amenities, his and her sinks, and both an indoor and outdoor garden shower (water comes out a bamboo pipe). There is an open-air sitting room decorated better than most of our living rooms at home, a little shrine, and best of all, your own private plunge pool. All this with a view of the blue sea. Posh? You bet. Each set of villas has its own staff ready to serve you or drive you around the expansive grounds in golf carts. The horizon pool matches the ocean it seems to blend into, and there are other small dipping and soaking pools. Staff waits to hand you towels, ice water, and icy sprays to keep the heat at bay. A library has quite a good collection of books and videos—each villa comes with a VCR. You can walk or be driven in a golf cart down to the beach, passing bales (open-air pavilions) and viewing spots down the way, to the luxe beach club, featuring all the same amenities as the pool. Who can begrudge the honeymooners who hole up here for days, rarely venturing to the outside world?

As usual, the Four Season leaves little for guests to desire: 24-hour room service, CD players, VCRs, hair dryers, safes, turndown, laundry and dry cleaning, newspapers, library and lounge with books and videos, airport transfers, free transfer to Four Seasons Sayan (including packing on request), full service spa, tennis courts, fitness center, art gallery, boutique, meeting facilities, tour desk, three restaurants, two bars, dance programs, and gallery.

Pansea Puri Bali. Jalan Uluwatu, Jimbarann, Bali 80361. ☎ **361-701605.** Fax 361-701320. www.pansea.com. E-mail: panseabl@indosat.net.id. 41 cottages. AC MINIBAR TV TEL. US$190–US$290 cottage. AE, DC, JCB, MC, V.

The pioneer resort on Jimbaran's beach, the Pansea has watched its clientele wither away over the years, most recently due to defections to the Four Seasons at the far end of the bay. But you don't have to pay top dollar to enjoy Jimbaran, and you don't have to go all the way to Lombok to experience authentic local beach color. Renovated in 1996, the Pansea features self-contained garden cottages set back from the beach and arranged around lily ponds, coconut trees, and Balinese statues. All cottages have indoor and outdoor terraces (with outdoor deck shower) with sun umbrellas, secluded behind checkered bamboo fences. Rooms are well presented in carved teak, with a fruit bowl to greet you upon check-in. Mosquito netting is always a nice touch, as is a naturalist decor of linen under thatched roofs, while bathrooms pass muster with goodies like a separate water closet, hair dryer, and batik robes to slip on after you step out of the sunken tub.

DINING

Jimbaran, with its row of ✪ **fish shacks** on the beach, offers one of the best basic meals you'll eat in Bali. Simply choose your weapon: live lobster at Rp200,000 per kilo (½ kilo should do a person OK, unless you're my gluttonous brother); crab or prawns, the most costly; or a huge fish stored in one of the Styrofoam coolers to round out a less expensive feast. A snapper big enough for two and served with an array of dipping sauces, rice, tomato cucumber salad and spinach cooked in sweet chile, topped off with fruit, ran me an easy Rp30,000 (around US$3), and that was with iced tea.

It's smoky (so you may want to take the wind direction into account when choosing your stall) and hot during the day, and there will be a war between you and a swarm of hungry flies. Still, this was the best eating experience I had in Bali.

There are two main clusters of stalls. The more romantic is the beach-side row of candle-lit tables just north of the Pan Sea Bungalows, though I hear the more honest scales are located over in the shadow of the Four Seasons Hotel. Whichever spot you pick, you're ensured a stunning sunset. (Tip: two full ½ liter bottles of water should weigh about 1.2 kilos; don't feel shy about checking the scales before you buy.) If you want something a little more conventional, try the Four Season's **PJ's** (located between the fish shacks and the hotel), which serves pizza, seafood, and Mexican specialties.

5 Nusa Dua

In the 1970s, a French firm, commissioned by the Indonesian government, came up with the idea for a self-contained resort complex to "minimize the impact of tourism on the Balinese culture." They chose this 300-hectare tract of undeveloped land, devoid of any infrastructure, and basically transformed it into a theme park. Eighteen years after the groundbreaking of the first five-star property (the Nusa Dua Beach Hotel, in 1983), Nusa Dua is home to a daunting lineup of five-star all-inclusive properties, secluded in a manicured and sterile atmosphere that any all-American gated subdivision would be proud of. Granted, the beaches are clean, the beaches are blissfully tout-free, but the only local culture you'll be exposed to is the nightly folklore show. Still, it's suitable for families and business conventions. No risk of impacting local culture here.

Exiting the gated area to the north of the local Club Med, the smooth and freshly paved roadway gives way to a refreshingly chaotic series of bumpy twists and turns past an alarming number of mediocre all-inclusives. But finally, the thatched pavilions of the Novotel appear, within easy walking distance of a pleasantly sparse number of warungs, dive shops, and souvenir stands, lending credibility to the idea of an all-in-one vacation.

GETTING THERE

Couldn't be easier. Most hotels in Nusa Dua offer airport pickup, but you can find shuttles and/or cheap taxis at the airport and in Kuta. (Be sure to take only the official blue and yellow metered taxis in Kuta.) Bemos from Denpasar go to Nusa Dua by way of Kuta and Jimbaran.

GETTING AROUND

These big spreads make it so comfortable you don't want or even have to leave the grounds—but even the most starry-eyed honeymooner might want a break from expensive hotel meals. There isn't much to see other than the Galleria shopping mall (as if!) and the village of Bulau, located on the other side of the massive gates that mark the entrance to the resort. Still, Bulau and the fishing village of Benoa at the north end of the peninsula are worth spending time in to get some Bali flavor. Getting around **on foot** can be a hot and dusty proposition on the main road, which runs parallel to the beach on the other side of the hotels. Walk along the beach instead (there's a paved walkway part of the way). **Don't take cabs,** which can take forever to get to your hotel, or your hotel's own transport, which, unless it's free, can cost 10 times as much as a cab. Better choices are the **local shuttle**—Rp2,000 per person (every 40 minutes) or the free **Galleria shuttle** (every 15 minutes); or just grab a **transport guide** off the street.

Fast Facts: Nusa Dua

Everything you could possibly need is in the hotels.

Banks/Currency Exchange   Consult your hotel for currency exchange.

Internet/E-mail   There is a Wartel with Internet service in Bualu.

Post Office/Mail   There is a postal agent at the Galleria shopping center.

Telephone   The area code in Nusa Dua is 361.

ACCOMMODATIONS
VERY EXPENSIVE

Nusa Dua Beach Hotel and Spa. P.O. Box 1028, Denpasar, Bali. ☎ **361-771219**/771210. Fax 361-772617. www.nusaduahotel.com. E-mail: sales@nusaduahotel.com. 380 units. A/C MINIBAR TV TEL. US$150–US$230 double; US$300–US$2,800 suite. AE, DC, JCB, MC, V. Free parking.

There are some things this hotel does very well, and it has a lot more local style than some of the other resorts, designed as it was based on palaces of an earlier era. However, the bulk of the regular rooms—called Superior—are smaller and more ordinary (despite some Balinese art on the walls) than the price should warrant. The Deluxe and Palace rooms are bigger (although the Deluxe rooms still have no counter space by the sink), with Balinese fabric on the beds and, for the Palace rooms, CD and video players, wood carvings, Jacuzzi tubs, and free breakfast and afternoon tea. There are two swimming pools, a good-sized geometric one and a lagoon version right on the beach. The best amenity, though, is the exquisite spa. You can get a massage in the bright, open-air, thatched pavilion, then crash on a Bali-style bed set in a fountain of water. It's deeply romantic and relaxing. There is even a lap pool, should you have the strength. The gym, too, is well-equipped with all the right machines and free weights, nicely air-conditioned, with plenty of icy towels and fruit.

Sheraton Laguna Nusa Dua. P.O. Box 77, Nusa Dua Beach 80363, Bali. ☎ **800/ 325-3535** or 361-771327. Fax 361-771326. www.sheraton.com. 276 units. A/C MINIBAR TV TEL. US$245–US$400 double; US$490–US$1,200 suite. AE, DC, MC, V.

There is something to be said for being able to step directly from your hotel room into the swimming pool—in this case, a serpentine monster complete with several sandy beaches, that winds its seemingly endless way through the property.

Nusa Dua

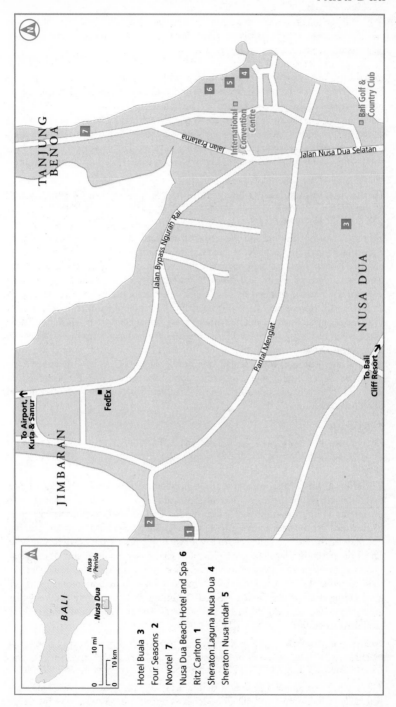

Hotel Buala **3**

Four Seasons **2**

Novotel **7**

Nusa Dua Beach Hotel and Spa **6**

Ritz Carlton **1**

Sheraton Laguna Nusa Dua **4**

Sheraton Nusa Indah **5**

This is the Sheraton's trump card in the area, and thanks to the design of the pool and gardens, even at full capacity, you don't feel like a number. It's as good as it sounds. The rooms are lavish but a bit flower-fussy, with a brash and brassy, vaguely tropical decor, but the huge wood and marble bathrooms make up for it. Additional luxury touches include in-room check-in (complete with fruity drinks and snacks), 24-hour butler service (no need for a coffeemaker), and your own personalized stationery and business cards to use while in residence. The housekeepers don't use trolleys, so quiet rules the day. The extensive grounds are so big, though, that a walk to the ocean is an endeavor. The additional swimming pools are something of a letdown—only 58 of the rooms have swim-up access and none have ocean views. The pampering is all well and good—OK, *really* good—especially that relaxation candle fired up by the turndown service.

✪ **Sheraton Nusa Indah.** P.O. Box 36, Nusa Dua Beach 80363, Bali. ☎ **800/325-3535** or 361-771906. Fax 361-771908. www.sheraton.com. 358 units. A/C MINIBAR TV TEL. US$195–US$240 double. AE, DC, MC, V. Free parking.

Short on character, but long on Western creature comforts, the Nusa Indah makes for a most satisfying resort experience. The size is daunting—beginning with the airplane hangar–sized lobby (air-conditioned, which is rare in Bali), big enough to accommodate the conference groups that make up the majority of its clientele. The thatched pavilion bar warmed at night by candlelight helps bring it down to size, as does the attentive staff. Rooms have dark wood paneling and smooth parquet floors, with colorful local fabric on beds (which also have heavy down comforters—lush, but hardly necessary in this heat). Large marble bathrooms have a separate area for the toilet, and a sit-down shower or sunken tub. Standard rooms have a divider between the sitting area and the bedroom, while deluxe rooms are entirely open. Views are either of the garden or the pool; some rooms on higher floors have ocean views. Between the giant pool and the beach are open-air pavilions (*bales*) laid with cushions—perfect for serious all-day relaxing.

EXPENSIVE

Hotel Bualu. P.O. Box 6, Nusa Dua, Bali. ☎ **361-771310** or 361-771311. Fax 361-771313. 50 units. A/C MINIBAR TV TEL. US$95 double; US$120 suite. AE, DC, JCB, MC, V. Free parking.

The Hotel Bualu is what passes for a budget hotel in Nusa Dua. It was actually the first hotel to open in the resort (30 years ago), and if it's hard to live in the shadow of the mighty Hilton across the way, the marvelous, friendly staff more than make up for it. You don't get the bells and whistles of the big resorts here, but then again, you may not want them, and you don't have to pay for them. They have their own private beach across the street, but feel free to use the beach chairs (and pools) of any of the bigger resorts as well. The rooms were some of my favorites: fairly standard rectangles with terra cotta tile floors, carved wood trim, batik bedspreads on comfortable beds, and glass sliding doors to the garden veranda. Additions such as a lovely children's playground, carriage rides around town, and pony rides on the beach make this good for families on a budget.

✪ **Novotel.** Jalan Pratama Tanjung Benoa, P.O. Box 39, Nusa Dua 80361, Bali. ☎ **361-772239.** Fax 361-772237. www.novotelbali.com. E-mail: info@novotelbali.com. 192 units. A/C MINIBAR TV TEL. US$130–US$150 double; US$250 beach cabana. AE, DC, JCB, MC, V.

This is what a Bali hotel beach resort should be; it's the only hotel in Nusa Dua where you really feel like you're in Bali. Considerable creative thought went into the design, with sandstone, soft adobe patinas, thatched roofs, and carvings that form a unique space quite different from a generic tropical resort. It's gorgeous and very special. It's also way up at the northern end of the peninsula, removed from the rest of the tourist area—which could be an asset or a drawback. It does mean that right outside the grounds is the quite authentic fishing village of Benoa—a good trade-off, I think. The resort is on both sides of the main street—the more expensive ocean side has easier beach access, but the "garden" side is quieter, although often reserved by groups. Up here, the ocean is much deeper and better for swimming. Rooms are big, bright, and airy, decorated in coconut wood and a minimalist Asian style that other hotels are beginning to copy. Better still, for the price, are the "Beach Cabanas," even bigger suites in semi-private bungalows (two per pavilion) complete with outdoor stone tubs—most of them honeymoon-worthy. The three swimming pools all have their own flair (including one with stone ledges for lounging on while stone heads spit cooling water on you), though none are very big. Tons of activities (including aerobics, soccer, Balinese dance lessons, cooking classes, pool games, a kids' club with many goodies, and free tennis during the day) will keep you from feeling bored, but there is also a free shuttle down into Nusa Dua should you feel the need. But given that this is the best of both worlds—a terrific resort and real Bali right outside—it's hard to see that you would.

DINING

If you've got the budget for it, you can eat very well in Nusa Dua. The problem is that most of the restaurants are in the hotels, and are priced accordingly—sky high in some cases, even by Western standards. And you are kind of trapped, particularly if the lazy days make you unwilling to stir very far. Options, should you be able to mobilize, include walking into town to find a warung, or better still, getting a ride up to Benoa, the fishing village on the north end of peninsula and eating at a warung there, where prices will be cheap and the fish fresh. Another solution is the supermarket in the Galleria, which offers cheap snacks and drinks, plus cereal and washed fruit, which could provide a budget alternative to pricey hotel breakfasts.

The Italian Restaurant at Amanusa. Nusa Dua (past the Bali Golf and Country Club). ☎ **361-772333**. Appetizers Rp 120,000–Rp180,000; main courses Rp180,000–Rp210,000. AE, DC, JCB, MC, V. Daily 6:30–11pm (last order at 10pm). ITALIAN.

OK, so I had to correct the spelling of some of the menu items. While surprising considering the cachet of the resort, what was not surprising was the superiority of the meal. The venue is expectantly exquisite, under lofty ceilings and overlooking the pool and Colonnade. The outside courtyard sits in an amphitheater where dinner is often garnished with traditional Balinese performances. The Sydney-trained chef, Sean Flakelar, oversees a parade of Italian recipes executed to perfection, like the *carpaccio di tonno alla Genovese* (raw tuna with olive oil and lemon), *agnolotti di cape sante* (half moon ravioli with shellfish sauce) and *tonno ai ferri* (grilled tuna served with eggplant caviar). Top the meal off with a cool version of the *cassata Neapolitana* or skip directly to the selection of ports, cognacs, and liqueurs, and you may be feeling a bit godfather-like yourself.

✪ **Kolak Restaurant.** Hotel Bualu. ☎ **361-771310** or 361-771311. Reservations recommended. Main courses Rp16,000–Rp38,000. AE, DC, JCB, MC, V. Daily 10am–11pm. INDONESIAN.

This is one hotel restaurant that is quite reasonable, and quite tasty. Located in the Hotel Bualu, the oldest hotel in Nusa Dua, Kolak offers authentic (in an upper middle–class way) Indonesian food, in little pavilions containing just four tables each, set around the swimming pool. Try the Rijstaffel, a sort of Indonesian sampler platter

(Rp45,000 per person, with a two-person minimum). On a recent visit, it featured *tahu telor* (Indonesian omelet), *empel pedas* (fried beef in spicy sauce), *pepes ikan* (fish in banana leaves), *sate, dere udang* (shrimp curry), *gado gado*, and a lot more. (No, I couldn't finish it all.) Most of it was spicy and all of it flavorful, except for the watered-down shrimp curry. Bigger appetites could try the Seafood Parade (Rp150,000), a platter of grilled whole fish, prawns, squid, lobster with veggies, fried rice, and mixed salad—two people could easily share without going hungry. They also offer an American breakfast for under US$4—considerably cheaper than at the other hotels.

Matsuri Japanese. Galleria, Nusa Dua. ☎ **361-772267.** Reservations recommended. Set meals Rp100,000–Rp160,000. AE, DC, JCB, MC, V. Daily 11am–11pm. JAPANESE.

Not the cheapest choice among the many cafes and such in the Galleria, but better than average Japanese food nonetheless. The set meals are quite large (the entree comes with appetizer, veggies, rice, miso soup, steamed egg with shrimp and chicken, pickles, and dessert) and two people could easily make a meal out of one, particularly if you throw in some sushi. (A 12-piece tuna roll, featuring butter-soft fish in larger portions than in the U.S., was US$3.) Try the ginger fried pork, thin strips of meat that look suspiciously like bacon (but taste nothing like it). It was delicious.

Raja's Table. Nusa Dua Beach Hotel. ☎ **361-771-210,** ext. 626. Reservations required. Set meals from Rp105,000 for 1 course to Rp230,000 for 5 courses; lobster surcharge Rp60,000. AE, DC, JCB, MC, V. Daily noon–10:30pm. ASIAN.

Who can resist the combination of exotic and elegant entrees based on specialties of the Asia-Pacific region? Not me, as I struggled between the sautéed ginger pepper lobster and the crispy prawns in Vietnamese mint with spicy ginger and a tropical fruit salsa. Gourmet Asian it is. The Korean *bolgogi* (for two) is a sesame seed marinated feast of beef cooked at the table and served with kimchee and other spicy side dishes. Lunch is slightly less tremendous given the heat, with main courses at Rp55,000 to Rp95,000, and the bonus is the panoramic view of the beachfront and swimming pool.

TOURS

To find a travel agent or guide, try either the busy **Tunas Indonesia Tours & Travel** at Jalan D. Tamblingan 107 (☎ **361-288056**); or **Santa Bali Tours and Travel** at the Grand Bali Hotel (☎ **361-287628**).

OUTDOOR ACTIVITIES & WATER SPORTS

The surf and swim situation here is the opposite of Kuta's. The surf is a considerable distance offshore, making swimming in the clear blue-green water most pleasant. At high tide, that is; it's not very deep to begin with, and at low tide the water can recede so much you can practically walk out to where the surf ought to be. Except in the wet season, when the outer reef (opposite the public beach past the Hilton) turns into a popular surf break. This makes for interesting shell-gathering, at least. Jet skiing and windsurfing are also popular, but dive excursions, all arranged by the hotels, will probably take you to areas closer to Sanur, or to Amed and Tambulen in the northeast.

Golf enthusiasts will be thrilled with the 18-hole championship course at the **Bali Golf and Country Club** (☎ **361-771791**). Covering 3 acres in the loveliest of settings across the street from the Galleria and the Hyatt, it looks like golf nirvana to these eyes. You'll pay for it though: greens fees are US$125.

SHOPPING

You can get all the same goods as in Kuta (endless sarongs and the like) in the village of **Bualu.** Not far past the gates dividing the resort from the village are several collections of outdoor stalls, with somewhat less persistent salespeople than in Kuta, and cheaper goods.

Meanwhile, the **Galleria** (suspiciously like an American outdoor outlet mall) gives you both Western-style shopping and the ability to buy local crafts without hassle and bargaining. Merchandise is geared (and priced) towards a more upscale clientele and if you've got the cash, there's actually some quality items to be had. Check out the silk and gold weaves of **Gallery Samarcanda,** where luxury items are tagged with three-digit (and up) numbers in U.S. dollars. There is a Keris Department Store that carries foreign name brands like Esprit, Versace, and Benetton, and an American Express office. Attached to Keris is a fully stocked **handicrafts center,** with souvenir items of better quality than that you find along the beaches (but not as luxurious as in the hotel boutiques), with (fairly high) fixed prices to boot. Granted, you could probably bargain for a better price elsewhere, but the convenience and selection is appealing. There's also a supermarket that stocks dry goods and many snack-worthy items.

NUSA DUA AFTER DARK

All of the hotels offer some kind of music at night—and frequent Balinese dance and music programs, though these usually come as part of a costly buffet dinner package. (These are usually beach or pool-side and open-air, and you can get a partially obstructed but free show if you lurk around the edges.) Candle-lit lounge-hopping should keep you busy for a few nights, but if you're looking for seriously rowdy nightlife, this might be a good time to check out Kuta.

6 Sanur

Sanur is probably the perfect compromise between hectic, maddening Kuta and sterile Nusa Dua. It's not terribly threatening to the first-time Bali visitor, who may still be looking for more for beach fun than anything else, but real life is still plenty in evidence here. It's also a manageable size, with Kuta-type shops, of slightly better quality and slightly less aggressive hustle, on the main streets. The beach is very nice, with better swimming than in Kuta and a paved walkway for promenading (though somewhat aggressive touts show up here, as do beggars, which is unusual for Bali).

GETTING THERE

Many hotels offer airport pickup, and there are regular shuttles from Kuta and all other major tourist areas, as well as fixed-price cab rides from the airport. Bemos go from Denpasar's Tegal Station.

GETTING AROUND

More than likely, your feet will handle most of your in-Sanur travel, either on the main roads or along the mostly paved beach walkway. **Bemos** do run up and down the main streets, and there are also metered blue taxis.

Fast Facts: Sanur

Banks/Currency Exchange   There is an American Express office in the Grand Bali Beach Hotel and two Wartel locations on the strip.

Internet/E-mail   Internet access with or without air-con; take your pick along the main drag. Santai Homestay on Jalan D. Tamblingan offers Internet access, in addition to accommodations and a bookstore.

Telephone   The area code in Sanur is 361.

ACCOMMODATIONS

With the exception of the losmen, all of the following are beachfront locations, generally set back quite a distance from the street (sometimes involving a spooky walk down a darkish lane at night).

VERY EXPENSIVE

Bali Hyatt. Jalan Danau Tamblingan, Sanur, P.O. Box 392, Bali. ☎ **361-281234.** Fax 361-287693. www.hyatt.com. E-mail: bhyatt@dps.mega.net.id. 400 units. A/C MINIBAR TV TEL. US$200–US$285 double; US$600 and up suite. AE, DC, JCB, MC, V. Free parking.

A massive property a short walk from the center of Sanur, this property would make any Wall Street executive very happy. The buildings date back to 1973 and show their age, as does, to a lesser extent, the inside decor. Bits of local crafts show up in the bedrooms, but the marble bathrooms, with pretty fixtures, are much more interesting. Better are the more expensive Regency Club rooms, with Bali tile and wood, terraces with fans, complimentary breakfast, all-day coffee, evening cocktails, and newspapers. Even if it's not as innovative or fanciful as some newer offerings by other chains, the name brand is secure, and it might work well for families thanks to all the modern activities. The quite extensive though perhaps over-manicured grounds could be fun to get lost in, with two pools, including a large one with waterfalls, bridges, temples, and other bits of interest. They have security on their beach, and a shuttle that goes to their property in Nusa Dua every 2 hours. A fancy new spa offers body treatments and massage.

For dining, Cupak Bistro and Wantilan Cafe offer different levels of Indonesian and Western cuisine; you can have Italian at Pizza Ria, Chinese at Telega Naga, and grilled specialties at Omang-Omang. There are three bars, including a piano bar and an espresso stop with live entertainment.

✪ **Tandjung Sari.** Jalan Danau Tamblingan no. 41, Sanur, Denpasar 80228, Bali. ☎ **361-288441.** Fax 361-287930. www.baliparadise.com/tandjungsairhotel. E-mail: tansri@dps.mega.net.id. 26 units. A/C MINIBAR TEL. US$160–US$275 double. Free parking.

Essentially the first boutique hotel in Bali, the Tandjung Sari opened in 1962 and was rewarded by a mention from Anaïs Nin in her diaries (as if there was anything she didn't write about in her diaries). Almost 40 years later, the Tandjung Sari remains the sensuous delight it was as the pioneer hotel on Sanur Beach. The hotel is a rabbit's warren of secret nooks and crannies, with stone statues, ponds, flowers, and surprises at every turn. All units are constructed the traditional Balinese way, most with their own private gardens and bales (outdoor pavilions for relaxing). The bathrooms are just dandy, some with outdoor garden showers (check out the fossilized leaf prints), and huge sunken tubs indoors big enough for two. The rectangular swimming pool is pretty, but sandwiched uncomfortably between a cushy open-air library and the very fine restaurant, so swimmers feel a bit exposed. Basically, you just need to show up with a swimsuit and toothbrush, because the management has thought of everything else: a change of sarongs for daytime, creamy soft nightshirts for bedtime, straw hats, and hefty beach towels. See the review of the excellent Tandjung Sari restaurant below.

MODERATE

✪ **Hotel La Taverna.** P.O. Box 3040, Denpasar 80228, Bali. ☎ **361-288497.** Fax 361-287126. www.asiatravel.com/La Taverna. E-mail: lataverna@dps.mega.net.id. 34 units. A/C MINIBAR TEL. US$110–US$135 double; US$180–US$240 suite. AE, DC, JCB, MC, V. Free parking.

Although it's a bit of faded grandeur, there's no bland European hotel room decor or apartment complex landscaping here. Rooms have been 75% renovated and are full of

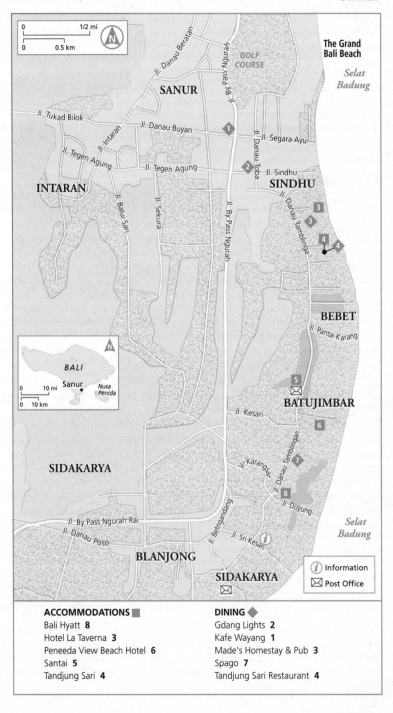

The Grand
Bali Beach

*Selat
Badung*

GOLF
COURSE

Jl. Danau Beratan

SANUR

Jl. Tukad Bilok

Jl. Intaran

Jl. Danau Buyan

Jl. By Pass Ngurah

Jl. Segara Ayu

Jl. Danau Toba

Jl. Sindhu

SINDHU

Jl. Tegen Agung

Jl. Tegen Agung

INTARAN

Jl. Balui Sari

Jl. Sekura

Jl. By Pass Ngurah

Jl. Danau Tamblinga

BEBET

Jl. Pantai Karang

BALI

Sanur

Nusa
Penida

0   10 mi
0   10 km

BATUJIMBAR

Jl. Kesari

Jl. Danau Tamblingan

SIDAKARYA

Jl. Karangsari

Spago

Jl. Duyung

Jl. By Pass Ngurah Rai

Jl. Danau Poso

Jl. Betngandang

Jl. Sri Kesari

*Selat
Badung*

BLANJONG

SIDAKARYA

i Information

Post Office

ACCOMMODATIONS ■
Bali Hyatt **8**
Hotel La Taverna **3**
Peneeda View Beach Hotel **6**
Santai **5**
Tandjung Sari **4**

DINING ◆
Gdang Lights **2**
Kafe Wayang **1**
Made's Homestay & Pub **3**
Spago **7**
Tandjung Sari Restaurant **4**

exquisite details: carved wood antique furnishings, batik or ikat fabric on windows and beds, traditional carved wood Bali doors leading to bathrooms (but the tall should be warned—these doors are very small), separate sunken dressing areas, sunken tubs, and so on. The rooms are small though (size increases with price), and in some cases a bit cramped. Claustrophobics in particular might want to request the ones with thatched roofs, which have higher ceilings. The pretty, quiet, foliage-filled grounds are complete with stone statues and a babbling brook and fountain. The pool is next to, but not right on, the beach. Not a luxury resort, but with style like this, it's no wonder the American ambassador to Indonesia stays here (in Room 31) when he's in town. The Beach Restaurant offers fresh seafood and Italian favorites, aided by their own brick-oven pizza. Movies are shown in the lobby every night.

INEXPENSIVE

Peneeda View Beach Hotel. Jalan Danu Tamblingan no. 89, Sanur, Bali. ☎ **361-288425.** Fax 361-286224. 44 units. A/C MINIBAR TEL. US$45–US$60 double or suite. AE, MC, V. Free parking.

This hotel has enough Bali/Asian flavor to distinguish it from other sadly ubiquitous generic hotels. It is a bit worn around the edge and lacking in certain amenities, but the staff is so friendly, and the handcarved screen in the lobby is *sooo* irresistible. Rooms are all in cottages—two rooms with connecting doors, with basic tile floors. Bali antiques and carvings help make them a little less spare than losmen. The two pools are apartment-building style, set amidst adequate gardens, and there is a private beach. Special touches include free afternoon coffee and tea poolside or in the lobby, free snorkeling once a week, four free mountain bikes (first come, first served), evening laser disc movies and live music, and an on-site bakery. Dine all day with an ocean view at the Nusa Lemobongan Beachside Restaurant, or have lunch at the Peneeda Poolside bar. Occasionally, they offer cultural dance evenings.

Santai. Jalan Danua Tamblingan 148, Sanur, Bali. ☎ **361-281684** or 361-281685. Fax 361-287314. www.webcom.com/pplh. E-mail: pplhbali@denpasar.wasantara.net.id. 16 units. A/C TV TEL. Rp150,000 (US$16) double. Rates include breakfast. MC, V. Free parking.

This is a great budget option if only for the socially conscious, '60s collective attitude that fuels it. Appealing alone is the assemblage of visitors camped out in the cozy open-air reading room. It's operated by a nongovernmental organization that seeks to promote awareness and responsibility for Indonesia's environment. Homestay-style rooms are simple without being dreary, well maintained in a two-story building around a small pool, with low-end baths. Other services include a health food restaurant, a combination Internet cafe and bookstore/library, a gift shop, a swimming pool, and conference room and business facilities.

LOSMEN

Made's Home Stay. Jalan Danua Tamblingan 74 (across the street from La Taverna), Sanur, Bali. ☎ **361-288152.** Fax 361-288152. www.madeshomestay.com. E-mail: mades@madeshomestay. com. 15 units. Rp150,000 double with fan; Rp200,000 double with A/C. Rates include breakfast. No credit cards.

A little pricey for something that bills itself as a "homestay," but it's very clean, all rooms have tubs, and there is a small pool. That, the attached pub, and the air conditioning may make the rate increase worth it. Carved wooden doors bright with red and gilt paint lead to rooms that make cute attempts at frilly bedclothes and the like—totally out of place, but charming.

DINING

Several new establishments have begun to fill the void of dining in Sanur, which, up to recently, was confined to the hotels or tourist-oriented *warungs*—where french fries were a staple side dish. (Such places are marked by their use of bamboo furniture and checked tablecloths, and of course, by the french fries—I'd avoid these.) There are a few decent options near the tourist path, and these are listed below.

Gadang Lights Cafe. Jalan Tandakan 5, Sanur. ☎ **361-282424.** Main courses Rp14,000–Rp25,000. No credit cards. Daily 10am–11pm. INDONESIAN/BALINESE/ASIAN.

A quick look at the menu and many veteran travelers might pass this place by. It's not that the food's half bad, but it is heavy on non-Balinese selections. But I'm a sucker for garden lanterns and ambience, so I gave this one a try.

After 5 minutes at Gadang Lights, it's easy to see why customers keep coming back time and time again. The owner, Nyoman Sudika, who built the pavilion and decorative garden from the ground up, treats this as a labor of love. Try the *jukut asam,* a spiced fish-based broth of coconut milk with corn and spinach that makes up for the short list of local specialties. There's also a large selection of Chinese, Thai, and Italian dishes.

Spago. Jalan Danau Tamblingan 79, Sanur. ☎ **361-288335.** Tapas Rp9,500–Rp18,500; main courses Rp17,500–Rp52,500. MC, V. Daily 11am–11pm. INDONESIAN/INTERNATIONAL

No relation to the power-making icon in L.A., Spago is Sanur's newest addition, opened in fall 2000 by an Austrian expat. While the menu bears no resemblance to anything Balinese, you're guaranteed a delicious and creative meal, from the tapas (shrimp fritters, stuffed vine leaves) to the southern tastes (empanadillas—spicy lamb ragout in a puff pastry shell). You may find the food a bit heavy for lunch in the tropics, though, so I'd save this one for the evening.

✪ **Tandjung Sari Restaurant.** Jalan Danau Tamblingan no. 41 (in Tandjung Sari Hotel), Bali. ☎ **361-288441.** Reservations recommended. Main courses Rp22,000–Rp98,500. AE, MC, V. Daily 7pm–1am. INDONESIAN/BALINESE.

Generally, prominent hotel restaurants can be relied on for adequate food catering to the tastes of timid tourists and for higher-than-average prices. The excellent restaurant at the Tandjung Sari is an exception. It's open air, not too big, and you dine by the shimmering pool with the nearby waves crashing in your ears. The small menu doesn't look like much, but the portions are good-sized and quite tasty. I love the pork sate, which arrives on a small grill—simple, but perfectly cooked and with a lovely flavor—and the *bebek betutu,* a spicy duck, Bali-style, which should make your mouth very happy.

Warung Choice Bakery. Jalan D Tamblingan, Sanur. Main courses Rp6,500–Rp19,000. No credit cards. Daily 7am–10pm. BALINESE.

An example of the many rather ordinary warungs, though this one does have a bakery some have found worthy of note. The food sounded fine on the menu—Thai shrimp pumpkin in coconut and fresh basil cooked in coconut cream sauce, Angsohi fish with sweet and sour sauce, sautéed shrimp and veggies. It wasn't bad, just bland. Better was the fresh honeydew juice. If you haven't had good Bali food, you'd probably find it delicious, and so in that sense, this might not be a bad place to start.

OUTDOOR ACTIVITIES & WATER SPORTS

Water sports are big in Sanur and most of the island's dive shops are based here. That's curious, as the local diving and snorkeling isn't all that good—experienced divers will probably end up taking day trips with dive masters to Nusa Lembongan or Nusa Penida. Snorkeling is either at a reef about a kilometer out to sea from the Bali Hyatt (you can wade out there at low tide), or a little farther offshore. But currents can often be strong, making the experience unpleasant and reducing visibility. Not that it matters, as neither the coral nor the fish are that extraordinary. Sanur is a decent place to dive for inexperienced divers or those looking to brush up on their skills, but soon you will probably want to try other options. Glass-bottom boat rides are also popular, as is a certain amount of sailing. Most hotels will hook you up with dive masters, or you can go directly to the operators (as some hotels do). You can feel comfortable in the hands of **Crystal Divers** (Sanur ☎ **361-286737;** www.crystal-divers.com), **Sanur Dive College** (Sanur ☎ **361-284025;** www.sanurdivecollege.com), and **Archipelago Dive Sarana** (Kuta Paradiso Hotel ☎ **361-287666;** Taman Sari Bungalows ☎ **362-93264;** www.archipelago.com), all of whom give good advice and can be relied on for sound instruction.

Ocean swimming is a mixed bag; the water can be slightly rough at high tide, and too salty and shallow at low. Still, waves are usually nonexistent right at shore, so dipping at any time is possible. Surfing happens off shore, with inconsistent reefs 1 to 3 kilometers (0.62 to 1.24 miles) out in front of the Bali Hyatt and the Grand Bali Hotel. **Waterskis** and **jetskis** are also for hire along Sanur Beach.

Golfers may enjoy the easy nine-hole course at the **Grand Bali Beach Hotel** (☎ **361-288511,** ext. 1388).

SHOPPING

There are plenty of opportunities for bargaining here, with wares that land squarely between what's found in Kuta and the somewhat better merchandise of Ubud. You'll find shops along the Jalan Danau Tamblingan, and a market with many stalls just off the northern end of the beach (on the left after the giant lobster). The level of hucksterism can be just as annoying as in Kuta—be prepared to be virtually physically pulled into a stall—but there are somewhat fewer sellers and so the pressure feels slightly less intense. **Alas Arum Agung Supermarket** on Jalan Danau Tamblingan (slightly south of Spago) is a one-stop shop for groceries and other goodies you'd like to take home, plus there's a fairly large selection of fixed-price souvenirs. You might also check out the beautiful ikat and handwoven fabrics and made-to-order garments at **Nogo,** Jalan Danau Tamblingan 208 (☎ **361-28832**).

SANUR AFTER DARK

If your interpretation of nightlife is serious partying, drinking, and late hours, you are better off heading over to Kuta for the evening. Otherwise, the local hotels have bars, some of which can be interesting scenes, particularly the beachfront one at the **Tandjung Sari.** They also have regular Balinese entertainment, generally packaged as a show and dinner buffet, but the quality of these is better in Ubud, or even Kuta. **La Taverna Bar** also has a beachfront spot, and a live quartet playing songs from the '70s, '80s and '90s every Wednesday and Saturday night. If you can tear yourself away for the seafront romance, there's the **Lazer Sports Bar,** located on the main drag (across from the Tandjung Sari), where nightly matches are listed outside for the benefit of all who walk by. They also provide free transport from within Sanur. If you've already begun checking out real-estate in the area, you can get a feel for the expat scene at **Kafé Wayang** (corner of Jalan Bypass Ngurah Rai and Jalan Hang Tuah), an Asian-style tapas bar with live music every Friday night.

7 Ubud

Arriving at Bali's Ngurah Rai International Airport, I overheard a lone backpacker ask the people manning the tourist kiosk for information on where to go. "Kuta is where all the people go," was the indifferent reply, one that forced me to unceremoniously butt in with my two cents. "You may want to consider Ubud."

The sun-and-fun atmosphere of Kuta is fine for the Australian and New Zealand market, who invest only 3 hours and bargain basement prices on airline shuttles to the island. But for the rest of us who live around the corner from the St. Barts, Hawaii, or St. Remo, a simple beach bum holiday isn't going to justify flying halfway around the world. And so it shouldn't. There's no mistaking Ubud for a rural or pastoral village, but if your aim is to expose—no, immerse—yourself in the Balinese culture, there's no reason to go anywhere else. About the only thing it doesn't have is a beach, but again, you can easily day-trip to Nusa Dua, Sanur, Candi Dasa, or Jimbaran for that. But I guarantee that once you arrive, you'll kick yourself for having "wasted" your time elsewhere, and that you'll never want to leave.

Ubud feeds the pulse of the island. It is the richest region in Bali for art production, which is possibly why so many expat artists have made their homes here. Its arteries have long ago extended beyond the boundaries of the small art community it was 75 years ago, but this commercial boom has only helped to create a surreal atmosphere of refinement and artistry. The confines of the town are just unable to contain the explosion of high quality galleries, shops, and the newest trend: spas.

Meanwhile, the locals' commitment to spiritual life continues, and there always seems to be some ceremony or other going on. Ubud is also the closest thing going to a central Bali location; just about everything you might want to see is an easy day (or even half-day) trip from here, which makes it a good jumping-off point. It's also got a disarming collection of some of the finest hotels in Asia, as well as some of the best and most lush scenery of any significant center on the island: phosphorescent rice paddies, virgin jungle, gorges, ravines, and river valleys. Any side street will lead you into a parallel universe of rural fantasy, a dramatic transformation from the glossy commercialism of Ubud's main thoroughfares. It's no wonder many non-Balinese have come here for a visit and never left.

GETTING THERE

Many hotels in the area offer hotel pickup, and taxis will come here from the airport, about an hour away. Bemos drop you in the center of town, while the tourist shuttles have their own stops, usually on one of the two main drags.

GETTING AROUND

The sound that will be ringing in your ears and haunting your dreams for many days to come is, "Transport? Transport? Yes? Transport? Tomorrow? Yes?" This is the unending mantra of hopeful young men with **minivans,** ready to be hired by the trip, the hour, the day, or even the week. You don't really need them within the town. Ubud is small enough that **walking** is the preferred method of transportation, though admittedly there can be a fair amount of ground to cover. What's more, they'll overcharge you horribly for short distances. Use them only to get to sights outside of town. Hotels away from the main action generally provide regular **shuttles** into town. If you are staying at a losmen or other low-budget hotel without a shuttle, you can always grab a **bemo** (making sure not to get ripped off there either), or perhaps **rent a motorbike**

Ubud

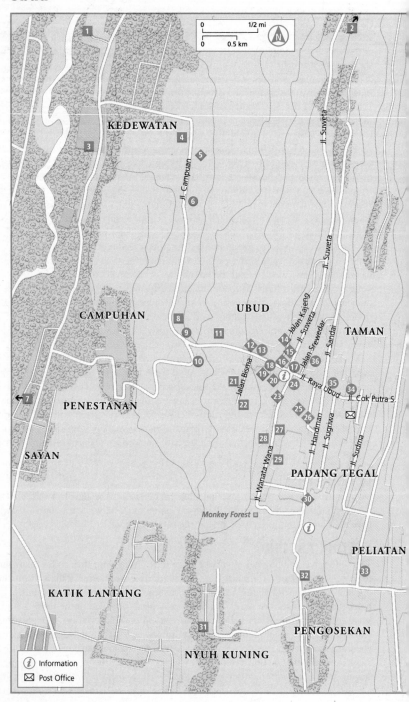

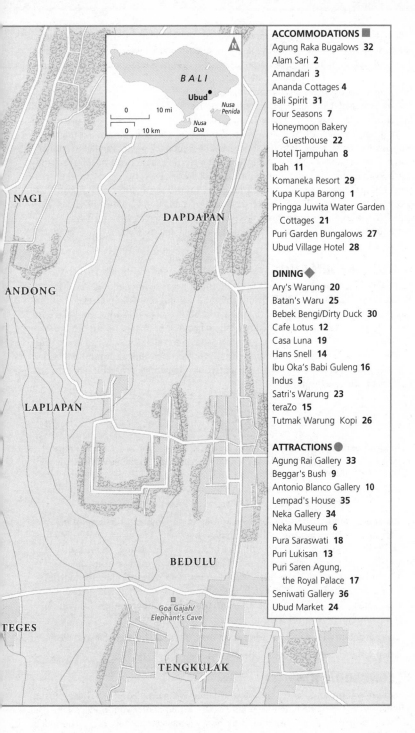

ACCOMMODATIONS ■
Agung Raka Bugalows **32**
Alam Sari **2**
Amandari **3**
Ananda Cottages **4**
Bali Spirit **31**
Four Seasons **7**
Honeymoon Bakery
  Guesthouse **22**
Hotel Tjampuhan **8**
Ibah **11**
Komaneka Resort **29**
Kupa Kupa Barong **1**
Pringga Juwita Water Garden
  Cottages **21**
Puri Garden Bungalows **27**
Ubud Village Hotel **28**

DINING ◆
Ary's Warung **20**
Batan's Waru **25**
Bebek Bengi/Dirty Duck **30**
Cafe Lotus **12**
Casa Luna **19**
Hans Snell **14**
Ibu Oka's Babi Guleng **16**
Indus **5**
Satri's Warung **23**
teraZo **15**
Tutmak Warung Kopi **26**

ATTRACTIONS ●
Agung Rai Gallery **33**
Beggar's Bush **9**
Antonio Blanco Gallery **10**
Lempad's House **35**
Neka Gallery **34**
Neka Museum **6**
Pura Saraswati **18**
Puri Lukisan **13**
Puri Saren Agung,
  the Royal Palace **17**
Seniwati Gallery **36**
Ubud Market **24**

BALI
Ubud
Nusa Penida
Nusa Dua
0   10 mi
0   10 km

NAGI

DAPDAPAN

ANDONG

LAPLAPAN

BEDULU

Goa Gajah/
Elephant's Cave

TEGES

TENGKULAK

(about US$5 per day) if you're an experienced enough rider. I found getting around (even to points beyond Ubud) by bicycle one of the more pleasant ways of spending a day. **Bicycles** are for hire at two or three street-side locations along Monkey Forest Road (near the Ulun Ubud Hotel) for about Rp20,000 per day for two bikes (although negotiations started much higher).

The layout of Ubud is slightly more complicated than the more or less one-road beach communities you may have encountered prior to coming here. The main street is the Jalan Raya, which runs east-west. Perpendicular to it is Monkey Forest Road, which runs north-south and does indeed end in a monkey forest. Parallel to Monkey Forest Road, to the east, is Jalan Hanoman. Intersecting these two roads, by the land-mark football field, is Jalan Dewi Shinta. As Jalan Raya goes west, it crosses the Cam-puhan gorge, takes a hard right, and becomes a north-south street called Jalan Raya Campuhan (this area is no longer technically Ubud, but Campuhan). It all runs together—indeed, the boundaries of several nearby villages, including Sayan, where the Four Seasons is located, meld into those of Ubud, and you won't even notice you've left town.

VISITOR INFORMATION

Jalan Raya Ubud, on the south side of the street, near the intersection with Monkey Forest Road (☎ **361-973285**), is not the most helpful tourism office ever, but cer-tainly friendly and a good place to go for touristy facts, such as times and places of dance programs (ask them for a copy of the schedule), or to sign up for other events such as packages to see cremations, shuttles, and so forth. They'll also book day trips around the island for you—assuming they've got the one you want running that day. Tourist agencies exist all over town, each offering competitive prices for day trips and shuttles to other tourist areas.

Fast Facts: Ubud

Banks/Currency Exchange   There is an ATM next door to Casa Luna restau-rant on Jalan Raya, as well as several on the Main Road on the way to Laplapan. Money changers are everywhere, and exchange rates seem to get better the far-ther away you get from the main intersection. US$100 gets a better rate than US$50, and traveler's checks seem to get better rates than bank notes.

Internet/E-mail   Internet cafes have sprung up in Ubud, and it's impossible to take more than two steps without tripping over one. The Roda Internet Cafe (Jalan Bisma) bills itself as the "Internet in a rice paddy." Closer to the center of town is the Jineng Business Center (Jalan Hanoman, across from the Dirty Duck), open 8am to 10pm daily, with the most computers and fastest modems. Or try a true cafe, Bali 3000 Internet Café and Art Gallery, on Jalan Raya, past the market, away from the center of town. It has five computers that always seem to be full, but at least you can sip something while you wait.

Post Office/Mail   The post office is on the main road, but very far to the east.

Telephone   The area code in Ubud is 361.

ACCOMMODATIONS

The sheer volume and variety of hotels in Ubud is amazing. And as Ubud gains in popularity, the big-name hotels keep moving in. But no matter your budget, here you really do find everything, from sublime honeymoon compounds to the humblest *alang alang* (thatch roof) cottage. If you had the opportunity to inspect them all, you'd definitely run up against the dilemma that I did of selecting just a choice few. No matter where you choose to stay, you'll groan over the one you didn't stay in. They're all just that wonderful. Here we've listed an assortment, both in central Ubud and some a ways away. In most cases, the latter are either a calorie burning but doable walk, or the hotels have reliable shuttles into town. And what you lose in immediate access you make up for in drop-dead gorgeous scenery. If you're game, you can book your first few nights and look around for something else (or something cheaper) once you've arrived. Regardless of how many nights you reserve, there's little chance you'll get stuck without a place to rest your head—if nothing else, there are countless losmen in Ubud and the surrounding villages.

VERY EXPENSIVE

✪ **Amandari.** Kedewatan, Ubud, Bali. ☎ **361-975333.** Fax 361-975335. E-mail: amandari@indosat.net. 29 units. A/C MINIBAR TEL. US$520–US$950 double; US$1,255–US$2,400 1-, 2-, and 3-bedroom villas. AE, DC, JCB, MC, V. Free parking.

If you have ample disposable income, this exquisite hotel is an excellent place to part with it. It's also the place to rub elbows with the rich and famous for whom nothing but the Amandari, and its pampering, will do. (Mick Jagger and Jerry Hall got married here.) Laid out like the world's fanciest Balinese village, the rooms are all huge thatched stone cottage suites, full of delicate Balinese luxuries, each enclosed in its own walled compound. Some are two-story and have their own private pool. Bathrooms are similarly generously sized, with many fluffy towels, a large shower inside and a tub outdoors. And the service—well, let's say you get what you pay for. It's all set on an eye-popping gorge, though the view is not as spectacular as the one over at the Kupu Kupu Barong hotel. However, its famous emerald green horizon pool (the water spills over the far edge), which mimics the exact color of the gorge, is marvelously engineered to blend seamlessly with the green beyond—it's the best pool in Ubud. And they even love children! Other amenities are hair dryers, CD player, cordless telephones, turndown, tennis court, gym, beauty salon, laundry, tour desk, 24-hour room service, newspapers, massage, complimentary baby-sitting, courtesy car, water sports, trekking, excellent library, and shops. The one terrific restaurant has a bar and serves local and European favorites. There is a free shuttle to Ubud (the hotel is about a 15-minute drive away), but it's hard to imagine wanting to leave very often. If you can't afford to stay here, don't feel bad—neither can I. But let's meet up for lunch at the restaurant and admire that pool, okay?

✪ **Four Seasons Resort at Sayan.** Sayan, Ubud, Gianyar Bali 80571. ☎ **361-977577.** Fax 361-977588. www.fourseasons.com. 46 units. A/C MINIBAR TV TEL. US$375–US$425 suite; US$52–US$2,400 villa. AE, DC, MC, V.

This recently opened Four Seasons is an architectural wonder, a masterpiece of planning that takes full advantage of its extraordinary setting right on the River Ayung. It's incredibly posh, of course, though not intimidatingly so, unless a fashion photo shoot on the lobby's open-air edge makes you want to crawl into a hole. To enter, you cross a long bridge leading into a pond that appears to rest in a bowl formed by its green surroundings, thus evoking the volcanic crater lakes found elsewhere on the island. You then descend a staircase and learn that, improbably, this pond rests on top of the lobby and the rest of the hotel. From here on out, the design is ultra-modern, yet not at the expense of Balinese style. Rooms are either in two-story suites (bedroom below the sitting area), deluxe suites that are somehow even fancier, and high-end villas with private plunge pools. All the interiors are done in gleaming woods and natural fabrics and are full of precious local art and artifacts. Expect luxurious bathrooms (two to every suite/villa) with huge tubs, showers and dressing areas, and more thick towels than a linen shop. Every room has views of the deep green gorge and/or the river, with in-room sound systems to help you set the mood. The bi-level horizon pool (not as big as you might expect) follows the serpentine shape of the river, which you can also walk down to and dangle your feet in (it's a bit too rough to swim in). Pampering, of course, is at a maximum, and includes "seamless" transfer between here and the resort at Jimbaran Bay; they take care of everything, including, if you wish, your packing.

There is a regular shuttle to Ubud, which is only about 10 minutes away, but as of this writing the last shuttle is at 3pm (this may change), which sort of strands you at the hotel, where the food is excellent, but expensive. (If you are actually on a budget—which is hard to believe if you are staying here—or just want to have some local Sayan flavor, turn left immediately outside the hotel gates and walk down the street about 5 minutes to Cafe Sayan, at the Tamen Bebek homestay. It's a solidly good cafe where I had some terrific nasi goreng and mie goreng.) The hotel has regular weekly free entertainment, featuring local musicians and dancers—these serve as superior samplers of Balinese dance. I should note that the building of this hotel caused some controversy, as it took over a sacred bathing place for the local people. On the other hand, it also employs many people from the village of Sayan who would have had to move elsewhere for employment.

Ibah. Campuhan, Ubud, P.O. Box 193, Bali. ☎ **361-974466.** Fax 361-974467. www. ibahbali.com. E-mail: sales@ibah.com. 11 units. A/C TV TEL. US$225–US$285 double; US$400 and US$470 villa. AE, DC, JCB, MC, V. Free parking.

A fairly new resort on the tail edges of the main Ubud action, this is probably the most romantic hotel you'll find this close to town. It's a special combination of Indonesian style and Western comforts. The very big rooms have spare, clean lines that employ lots of wood and natural fabrics, including a four-poster canopy bed hung with mosquito netting. Good-sized bathrooms have either outdoor or wood floor showers. All rooms have spacious verandas or patios—you pay extra for a view of thatched roofs, trees and hills, but it might be worth it. One deluxe room has a tricky spiral staircase, while the Rose suite has a glimpse into the neighboring Gardenia suite bathroom (shouldn't reveal anything too intimate, but still). The grounds make good use of the hilly land, with all kinds of secret nooks and crannies, including a roughly heart-shaped swimming pool with two alcoves built into the walls next to it for cozy poolside tête à têtes. (The drawback is all the steep, potentially slippery stairs.) Spa and massage are in a lush wood and muslin-draped room, and there is a particularly sexy indoor Jacuzzi that turns the sacred into the profane by evoking a temple bath.

✪ Kupu Kupu Barong. Kedewatan, Ubud, Bali. ☎ **361-975478.** Fax 361-975079. www. bali-paradise.com. E-mail: kkbarong@indosat.net.id. 19 units. A/C MINIBAR TEL. US$335–US$405 double; US$699 suite. AE, DC, MC, V. Free parking.

The major selling point of this luxury boutique hotel of bungalows is the view—so breathtaking it's hard to tear yourself away. The hotel is set on a deep green gorge with a river rushing far below, palm trees rising above rice fields—with a million-dollar view like that, expensive rooms almost seem like a bargain. (Truth be told, some rooms have better views than others, but even the least impressive are extraordinary.) Deluxe bungalows are arranged in a straight line (bed, tub, sitting area), while everything in two-story luxury bungalows directly faces the windows, the better to take advantage of the main attraction. Wherever you end up will be comfortable and spacious, and you'll find yourself doing everything without looking down, so riveted will you be by the windows. The decor is plain—after all, what could compete?—but aesthetically pleasing. Bathrooms are in pieces—tub here, sink there, closet way over there—and this gives even more room, but not much counter space. The two small pools are refreshing, but oddly they're the only areas that don't overlook the view, but this may change, as the hotel is scheduled to expand to 30 units, including new suites with private plunge pools. The long distance into town is minimized by free, reliable shuttle service every hour until 11pm. Guests with disabilities should request rooms near the entrance to avoid the many stairs. There's a highly praised restaurant, and one bar.

EXPENSIVE

Bali Spirit Hotel and Spa. P.O. Box 189, Nyuh Kuning Village, Ubud 80571, Bali. ☎ 361-974013. Fax 361-974012. www.bali-paradise.com/balispirit. E-mail: balispirit@bali-paradise.com. 19 units. A/C TEL. US$95–US$135 double; US$145 villa. Rates include breakfast. AE, MC, V. Free parking.

Located considerably south of the main section of Ubud in the village of Nyuh Kuning, this is a relatively reasonable alternative to the really high-end luxury hotels like the Amandari and Kupu Kupu Barong, largely thanks to a stunning hillside setting overlooking a river gorge. The rooms are not as luxurious, but you wouldn't know that unless you compared them in person. As it is, they are eye-poppers: comfortable, well-appointed, and bigger than average, some with thatched roofs and Bali fabrics. The pool is a decent size, and there are traditional Balinese bathing pools in the holy river. There's also a fine spa with a full range of services. That and the free chauffeured car to take you wherever you want to go "at a moment's notice" makes this a plenty pampering experience.

✪ **Komaneka Resort.** Monkey Forest Rd. ☎ **361-976090.** Fax 361-977140. www.komaneka.com. E-mail: Komaneka@indosat.net.id. 17 units. A/C MINIBAR TEL. US$135–US$190 double; US$210–US$230 garden and pool villa. AE, DC, JCB, MC, V. Free parking.

This new property is right on Monkey Forest Road, clean, modern, but still locally stylish, and the only one at this level in central Ubud. It's also the only property where you can opt for the (newly constructed) villa with private pool this close to the action. It's meant to be a modern luxury hotel, Bali style, but unlike other attempts, it doesn't come off looking like a suburban condo. Occupying a long, narrow space (flat and with downstairs rooms, which might make this a better choice for guests with disabilities), ending in a rectangular pool, guests are well away from street noise, with views of gardens and rice paddies. The rooms are outfitted in lots of natural woods and fabrics, and the beds are hung with cheesecloth-like netting suspended from the thatched ceiling. Deluxe rooms have deconstructed bathrooms that, while lacking in any real walls, are still arranged for privacy. Suites are bigger and have cushioned window seats, with well-stocked bathrooms featuring big marble baths and showers with wood floors.

MODERATE

Agung Raka Bungalows. Pengosekan Village (2km south of Ubud center). ☎ **361-975757.** Fax 361-975546. 22 bungalows, all with bathroom. TEL. US$67 standard villa; US$73–US$137 bungalow; US$175–US$200 Kingdom or Honeymoon suite. MC, V.

Whether you're looking for higher- or lower-end accommodations, you certainly won't have to sacrifice Balinese style here. You'll be waving to straw-hatted women whacking rice stalks on the grounds, as the bungalows are arranged around a series of working rice paddies. The property lies on the fringes of Ubud, and thanks to the thriving village art community, you'll hardly know you've left. Lower end bungalows are basic two-story wood and bamboo constructions with rudimentary outdoor bathrooms at the back and a staircase up to a cozy bedroom. Superior bungalows are a drastic step up—single occupancy A-frames with teak and *bedeg* (woven bamboo) accents and TV.

The bath "rooms" here are large modern courtyard facilities that include both a tile bathtub and a stone floor shower. The suites are to die for: a dizzying spectacle of stone and marble, big enough for four but romantic enough for two—there's even an actual throne in one suite's bathroom garden: a toilet set in solitude under its own canopied hut. How's that for easy living?

✪ **Alam Sari.** Keliki, Tromoi Pos 03, Kantor Pos Tegallalang, Gianyar 80561, Bali (9km/5.5 miles north of Ubud). ☎ and fax **361-240308.** www.alamsari.com. E-mail: info@alamsari. com. 10 units. A/C MINIBAR TEL. US$80 double; US$90 suite; US$150 family unit. AE, DC, JCB, MC, V. Free parking.

This is the very model of what a modern Bali hotel should be; its combination of comfort, social responsibility, setting, and price set a standard I sincerely hope other hotels will follow. Everything the Alam Sari does is with thought towards local economy, ecology, and culture. So all room furnishings, from wood furniture to brightly dyed fabrics, are entirely Indonesian made. (Try to get the room with the marvelous antique wood canopy bed.) They use solar heating and recycled paper, and waste disposal is done with a minimum of environmental impact. The only music you hear is live. They employ a large number of villagers from neighboring Keliki (known for its miniature painting), sell local wares in the hotel shop, and encourage guests to go into the village to view life there—a terrific change from the usual resort ivory tower. Not only are the rooms quite pretty, but there is a gorge view, complete with looming volcano, nearly as good as the one found at Kupu Kupu Barong, at a fraction of the price. (Admittedly, this one has a road cutting through it, and traffic noise intrudes.) The seclusion and opportunity for interaction with village life makes up for the 20-plus minute drive into Ubud. This remoteness does mean relying on the hotel for all services—they charge for transport to and from Ubud, but are fast and reliable. Cost-conscious guests might want to fill their room fridge with snacks and breakfast items. There's an excellent Balinese-style restaurant (strictly no MSG!) and bar, which features live (and unamplified) Bali music at night.

✪ **Ananda Cottages.** Campuhan, Ubud. ☎ **361/975-376.** Fax 361/975-375. http:// members.xoom.com/ananda-bali/. E-mail: anandaubud@denpasar.wasantara.net.id. 54 units, all with bathroom. MINIBAR TEL. US$40–US$50 double without A/C; US$60–US$70 double with A/C. AE, MC, V.

Ever so slightly north of Ubud proper, Ananda Cottages is far enough from the town center to discourage tourist hoards, yet atmospheric enough for the Balinese experience you were hoping for. The cottages and rooms are arranged around working rice terraces; in order to get to your room, you'll have to follow the paths and terrace retaining walls which, at night, are lit with mini coal-fed torch-like flames (if it's your first time, you'll probably get lost, but there's always somebody around to steer you in the right direction). The cottages, bi-level structures of brick with bamboo pavilion roofs, contain individual units, classified as either upstairs or downstairs. About half the rooms of these bi-level structures are air-conditioned, but the best rooms, both with or without a/c, are undoubtedly downstairs. These have scrumptious Balinese outdoor baths, and outdoor patio living rooms off the front. Upstairs rooms are nice, with modern baths and small verandas, but the true Balinese experience is downstairs. There is a small swimming pool at the extreme back of the property on a raised rice terrace. There's also a restaurant, and an outdoor area for communal TV watching.

Hotel Tjampuhan. Jalan Raya Campuhan. P.O. Box 198, Ubud 80571, Bali. ☎ **361-975368.** Fax 361-975137. www.indo.com/hotels/tjampuhan. E-mail: tjampuhan@indo.net.id. 64 units. US$70 double with fan; US$115 double with A/C; US$175 Walter Spies' (2-bedroom) house. Rates include breakfast and shuttle to Ubud center. AE, MC, V.

From its somewhat innocuous position on the road into Ubud, Hotel Tjampuhan astonishes the unexpected visitor with a lush and tropical sanctuary terraced down a ravine above the sacred Tjampuhan River and the 900-year-old Gunung Lebah Temple. The hotel was built in 1928 for guests of the prince of Ubud, and was chosen by the Western artists Walter Spies and Rudolf Bonnet as headquarters for their art association, Pita Maha. All units enjoy natural Balinese thatched roofs, and modern bathrooms with either step up or sunken tubs, but admittedly, and in spite of coconut wood features and bamboo mats, they could easily reflect a bit more native style. Fan-cooled rooms, called "Agung Rooms," are slightly smaller than "Raja Rooms," and you'll forfeit the view here as well. Splurge for a Raja Room (or even Spies' own villa), which gives the impression of being somewhat more gracious thanks to a fairly large veranda overlooking the gorge. But the real draw at the Tjampuhan are the grounds, which are full of stonework, plants, moss and—alas—steps, all leading down to the river. There are two very pretty pondlike pools, and one additional one with cold spring water, perfect for hot days.

Pringga Juwita Water Garden Cottages. Jalan Bisma, Ubud 80571, Bali. ☎ and fax **361-975734.** E-mail: pringga@dps.mega.net.id. 17 units. US$65–US$80 double. JCB, MC, V. Free parking.

This is a popular small hotel heavy on the atmosphere thanks to the streams, lily ponds, and bubbling fountains that make the grounds more water than earth. Add plenty of stonework dripping with moss and you've got one lush place. Some people have complained about a smell of mold, while others find it perfection. (They spray for mosquitoes, by the way.) Deluxe rooms are two stories; downstairs is a totally open-air lounging area and open-air marble bathroom; up some treacherous stairs is the bedroom, simple but for mahogany flooring and carved archways. It's all terribly characteristic, but not for anyone with disabilities.

Ubud Village Hotel. Jalan Monkey Forest, Ubud, Bali. ☎ **361-975571** or 361-974701. Fax 361-975069. 28 units. A/C MINIBAR TV TEL. US$60–US$90 double. Rates include breakfast. MC, V. Free parking.

Ubud Village Hotel makes the best of its Monkey Forest Road location; actual room decor is beige and generic, but units make up for the bland interior deficiency with garden porches and courtyards that become blissfully private behind a set of double garden doors. When not lounging outside; your sarong carelessly agape, most likely you'll be pampering yourself in the open-air stone and coral bathroom, steeped in the oversized polished tile in-ground bath, complete with a pair of steps down from your slippers. If you turn the volume up loud enough, you can watch TV from the tub through the picture window that separates bathroom from bedroom. There's also a shower and a drying rack. There's a refreshing pool, and the hotel engages a masseuse, for a relaxing outdoor rubdown (or in your room, if you prefer) in your own poolside platform bed.

Services include a bar, a restaurant, and airport transfers.

INEXPENSIVE

Puri Garden Bungalows. Monkey Forest Rd. ☎ **361-975395.** Fax 361-976188. 8 units. US$25 double. Rates include breakfast. MC, V.

A bit more upscale than your average losmen, so it's a good budget alternative. Rooms and baths (all clean and big enough not to be claustrophobic) are larger than in an average losmen. Rooms have bamboo on the walls and rushes on the floor, while bathrooms are nicely tiled. There's no A/C, only fans, but there is hot water. Second-story rooms have bathrooms down a steep flight of stairs, making middle-of-the-night calls of nature precarious. It's all arranged around a nice Buddha-adorned garden with fish ponds.

LOSMEN

In addition to the ones below, there are literally dozens of losmen to chose from in Ubud. Just walk down Monkey Forest Road or the Jalan Hanoman, or better still, turn down any little alley or side street that cuts across them. The **Ubud Sari Health Resort** (Jalan Kajeng 35; ☎ 361-974393; see "Pamper Yourself," below) has a couple of rooms that, while not the best accommodations offered, even by losmen status, do come with free use of sauna and other spa facilities and invitations for the morning yoga class.

Feel free to poke around until you find one that suits you—often there will be four or five within a few feet of each other. When inquiring about the price, it's a good idea to feign misunderstanding and ask for written confirmation, because it's not unheard of that the rates mysteriously increase upon check-out.

Esty's House. Jalan Dewi Sita, Maruti Lane, Ubud. ☎ **361-977679.** 6 units. Rp35,000 double (cold water and fan only). Rates include breakfast. No credit cards.

A recently opened homestay, built specifically as such. It's very clean and comfortable, though the rooms are basic. Each room has an agreeable tiled patio sitting area in front. The owners, a congenial young couple, have a laundry (and gift shop) on the premises, which is awfully handy for grubby travelers.

✪ **Honeymoon Bakery Guesthouse.** Jalan Raya, Ubud, Bali. ☎ **361-973283.** Fax 361-973282. www.bali-paradise.com/casaluna. E-mail: casaluna@bali-paradise.com. 6 units. Rp150,000–Rp200,000 double. Rates include breakfast.

A step up from the typical losmen (with hot and cold water and prices to match), but I think it's worth it. You are literally staying in the backyard (which, despite the mailing address, is actually on a dirt road, Jalan Bisma) of the people who bring you Casa Luna, Indus, and the Honeymoon Bakery, so boy do you get a good breakfast! (Frothy fruity drinks; thick, creamy homemade yogurt and fresh fruit; your choice of other goodies including thin green banana pancakes with coconut and cane syrup—I didn't need lunch.) Rooms are big enough (two to a bungalow), with small but lovely carved wooden canopy beds with mosquito netting, set in a charming garden overrun with plants, birds, pets, children, and treasures. This is also where they hold their cooking classes, which is mighty handy. The staff is far more attentive than any found at a luxury hotel—they can really spoil you.

Kajeng Homestay. Jalan Kajeng 29, Ubud, Bali. ☎ **361-975018.** 12 units. Rp45,000–Rp75,000 double. Rates include breakfast. No credit cards.

Just up from the main Ubud road, this losmen doesn't look like much upon entering, but it's surprisingly pretty in the back, with a big lily pond and quite a good view of the valley. Rooms are clean, with tile, and porches. There's hot water only in the most expensive rooms, but all rooms have fans.

Rice Paddy Bungalows. Off Monkey Forest Rd. (at end of tiny alley about halfway down, just after Puri Garden Hotel). 6 units. Rp40,000–Rp60,000 double. Rates include breakfast.

A nice garden complex whose rooms have high ceilings, tiled floors, basic baths with Western toilets, and hand-held showers. Half the rooms are upstairs. Only two have hot water and another two have ceiling fans.

DINING

The tourist explosion in Ubud has done wonders for the state of dining affairs here, where (aside from a few stellar standouts near Kuta), you'll be hard put avoiding some of the finest meals you will enjoy on the island. The only complaint might be the general absence of typically local dishes, mitigated by the innovative synthesis of Asian flavors with Western tastes. You'll be pleasantly surprised at how well you can eat on sums of money that at home would barely cover the aperitif, but there are ways of emptying your wallet. While we don't usually encourage the insular hotel dining, you'll be guaranteed a first class dining experience at **the Ayung Terrace at the Four Seasons, The Terrace Restaurant at Amandari,** the **Kupu-Kupu Barong** or the **Ibah** (all mentioned in "Accommodations," above). To justify those Western prices, each of these restaurants occupy panoramic patios with spectacular views of the Ayung River Valley. Unless noted, reservations are not required at the restaurants below.

Ary's Warung. Main St. Main courses Rp25,500–Rp58,100 (duck, lamb, and salmon much higher—up to Rp120,000); set menu Rp145,000. No credit cards. Daily 7:30am–1am. MODERN INDONESIAN.

Ary's gourmet European and Indonesian specialties have many fans, but I love their honey ginger lime drink (with or without alcohol), which has helped us get through many a hot Bali day. (Consider also trying the honey mango mint, or banana lemon honey.) Ary's is particularly nice at night, when it's lit by candles and you can sit up on the second floor and watch the action in the busy street below, or bats catching bugs at the streetlights next to you. For appetizers, try the gazpacho, a generous bowl full of icy fresh flavor—perfect for a hot day—or the grilled goat cheese salad. Chicken crepes are surprisingly un-mushy (crepes are tricky, but they do them right), stuffed with chicken, tomatoes, and leeks sautéed in garlic and white wine, with a creamy spinach sauce. Rendang Pedang is a West Sumatran beef dish simmered in coconut with local herbs—it's got a kick that sneaks up on you.

✪ Batan's Waru. Jalan Dewi Sita, Ubud. ☎ **361-977528.** Main courses Rp15,500–Rp34,500. MC, V. Daily 8am–12am. INDONESIAN/EUROPEAN.

This is everyone's new favorite Ubud dining spot, tucked away on the pleasant cross street just before the football field. It's particularly moody at night when they light up the street entrance with candles. Here you'll find a full menu with a number of traditional dishes beyond the usual suspects, and plenty of vegetarian options. For an appetizer, try *urap pakis*—wild fern tips with roasted coconut and spices; or the *lempur ayam*—chicken dumplings simmered in a banana leaf. "Uncle Karaman's Humus" is spicy and comes with grilled pepper flat bread and tomato mint relish, and everything is served with a dish of spicy hot condiments. Finish off with a perfect cup of decaf Illy-brand espresso, and you've topped off a happy meal. They also do smoked duck and a babi guleng feast, with a day's advance order.

Bebek Bengil/Dirty Duck. Padang Tegel (at the end of the street as it hooks into Monkey Forest Rd.), Ubud, Bali. ☎ **361-975489.** Main courses Rp12,500–Rp28,500. MC, V. Daily 11am–11pm. INDONESIAN/EUROPEAN.

Yes, they serve duck here—the famous house specialty, crispy duck stewed in Indonesian spices, then deep fried. One serving is half a duck, ready to be torn to bits with your fingers. Fans of this Ubud institution (i.e., David Bowie), love that the duck here is not greasy, but I've heard complaints that the meat is a bit dry (though the skin is delightfully fatty). Other poultry includes stuffed chicken (with shiitake, sprouts, and spinach). The menu also includes salads and well-stuffed, crunchy sandwiches. Grilled tuna salad with lemon cumin vinaigrette is a light and healthy option, and not overly dressed. There are veggie options, including a mushroom cashew pate appetizer.

Cafe Lotus. Ubud Main Rd. ☎ **361-975-660.** Appetizers Rp11,500–Rp20,000; main courses Rp22,500–Rp40,000. No credit cards. Daily 9am–10pm. MODERN INDONESIAN/INTERNATIONAL.

The food here isn't half bad, but the real reason to come to Cafe Lotus is for the chance to dine in the shadow of the Pura Saraswati. This is Ubud's architectural treat, although you can sit at a table the way your mother intended, the bamboo platform seating above the lily pads is infinitely more exotic, and the breeze is nice too. It seems as if the menu is meant to tease, taking traditionally Western items like fettuccine and turning them into fiery dishes of hot chiles, black olives, and hearts of palm. The Balinese Sate Lilit, a mixed fish kabob with a hint of coconut, is served on skewers and presented on a plate the size of a boat. Not bad for the view.

Casa Luna. Main St. ☎ **361-973282.** Main courses Rp9,000–Rp33,000. No credit cards. Daily 8am–1am. ECLECTIC.

This innovative restaurant wouldn't be out of place in San Francisco—in fact, I know some dedicated Northern California foodies who dream of Casa Luna's chicken satay. One of the widest menus in Ubud, it has dazzling versions of local cuisine and nouvelle food from pumpkin ravioli to Mediterranean tofu. It's all imaginative, fresh, and beautifully prepared. The big, healthy salads make Californians happy, as does the long list of frothy juice blends like pineapple, carrot and honey or turmeric, lemon and honey. Or try an avocado shake. But despite their skill with Western dishes, you should really see how they are bringing Indonesian food into the modern era. Try the nasi campur or the ikan Bali and see how these traditional dishes fly. Save room for dessert; the Casa Luna bakery made Ubud history a long time ago with its recipes for decadent brownies with ice cream and the Black Mischief cake. Since you won't be able to try everything, I bet you will end up eating here more than once.

Hans Snell's. Jalan Kajeng. ☎ **361-975699.** Main courses Rp9,000–Rp23,000. MC, V. Daily 9:30am–10pm. INDONESIAN.

An enjoyable walk up a cobblestone street and then a turn to the left (follow the signs) into a nice garden setting brings you to Hans Snell's. I know people who say they've eaten the best meal of their lives here, but I found the menu hit or miss. A decided hit was the *opor ayam,* a lightly smoked chicken simmered in coconut milk and spices that elicited cries of "Outstanding!" Skip, however, the really ordinary lemon chicken. Nothing is too spicy, but they will turn up the heat on request. Beware of waiters who might take advantage of slow nights and try to sell you crafts from their village (so they say).

Ibu Oka's Babi Guleng. Jalan Suweta (across from the Palace, right before the Bambu restaurant). No credit cards. Open daily, no regular hours. BALINESE.

If you want to sample *babi guleng,* roast suckling pig, without the caloric commitment of the full feast, come here. The recipe is a family secret, roasted with a special blend of spices and chile. Slightly better than a shack, right across from the Palace, this is one of those roadside eateries you've been spying suspiciously—but longingly. You sit at low tables and get a paper plate full of spicy roast pig and crunchy pig parts, even spicier vegetables, and rice.

Think of it as fast food, Bali style. Rp18,000 got us two orders of pig, two waters, and immense satisfaction. Pig may not be served on temple days.

Indus. Jalan Raya Sargingan, Campuhan, Ubud. ☎ **361-977684.** Dress "neat casual." Main courses Rp17,000–Rp34,000. No credit cards. Daily 7:30am–11pm. ECLECTIC.

A recent offering from the Casa Luna people, this eclectic restaurant is easily the "must do" place in town. Don't let that scare you away, but do admire the graceful pillars, the use of marble, the lovely pale carved wood furniture, and the setting overlooking the Tjampuhan ridge. The view alone (not to mention the constant breeze wafting through) makes it worth the trip, but guests of the chic resorts up this way will be grateful for something this good so close by. Try such intriguing offerings as beetroot and feta empanadas, grilled calamari tostada, or some of the wraps and sandwiches—and don't overlook the fresh tuna and prawn crepes with lime leaves, coriander, and wasabi. Homemade ice creams include ginger, palm sugar, and black rice flavors, or opt for the dreamy chocolate mocha tart. Abstainers get to choose from the usual Casa Luna offerings of healthy "smoothie" type juices.

✪ **Satri's Warung.** Monkey Forest Rd. (east side, 1-min. walk from Main Rd.—look for second yellow beer sign). ☎ **361-973279.** Main courses Rp4,500–Rp9,500; banana chicken for 2 Rp50,000. Daily 8am–11pm. INDONESIAN/BALINESE.

When I want to torture myself, I think, "I could be eating banana chicken at Satri's right now." Hidden in a dirt-floored courtyard, off a twisting corridor, it's one of the finest warungs in all of Bali. The very friendly Satri serves her exceptionally good Indonesian food in generous portions—I know some vegetarians who ate here every single night for a month—but the reason to come, and dream about it afterward, is the banana chicken. Order it a day in advance, then feast on a whole chicken, marinated and glazed in a luscious sauce, succulent and falling off the bone, artfully arranged and served with heaping plates of equally delicious salad and cooked vegetables, and a large bowl of rice. Smoked duck is a similarly rapturous experience and must also be ordered a day in advance. (Top it off with fresh-squeezed lemonade.) Don't miss this restaurant, even if you don't have time for the chicken or duck. (But you'll make the time.)

teraZo. Jalan Suweta, Ubud. ☎ **361-978-941.** Main courses Rp17,000–Rp34,000. Daily 8am–11pm. AE, MC, V. MEDITERRANEAN.

This new offshoot of the popular Batan Waru (also reviewed in this section), has quickly become Ubud's restaurant of the moment. The spacious interior is simple yet welcoming, terraced behind a garden and decorative fountains. Considering the reach of the menu, the food is surprisingly good. The cool gazpacho made of ripe tomatoes is a welcome starter in the tropical heat, although I'm glad I didn't pass up the spring rolls—deep fried shrimp and noodles wrapped in rice paper and served with a delicate mint sauce. The eight-layer pie is an irresistible challenge to the heat, but a worthy pastry crust filled with smoked blue marlin, spinach, ricotta, and mushrooms. Purists may want to stick to the Asian-influenced dishes like the *nasi kuning*—yellow coconut rice with raisins, cashews, and strips of egg; or the *kue tiaun*—stir-fried rice noodles, chicken, and local greens. There's also a tempting breakfast menu: Start your day out right with the ricotta blintzes with a hint of cardamom and topped with a raspberry coulis.

✪ **Tutmak Warung Kopi.** Jalan Dewi Sita. ☎ **361-975754.** Main courses Rp10,000–Rp30,000. No credit cards. Daily 9am–11pm. INDONESIAN/EUROPEAN.

Though it bills itself as a warung, this would be called a cafe anywhere else, complete with nouvelle cuisine and modern art on the walls. "Warung Kopi" actually means coffeehouse, boasting the best coffee in Bali (it's darn good), and making this place a breakfast staple. Lunch and dinner menus de-emphasize local cuisine (though I do like their nasi campur) in favor of rich pastas, chicken Dijonaisse, grilled sausages, and "organic salads." I love the spicy chicken sandwich, on fat baguette bread, with a fresh salad on the side—not in the least Balinese, but a fine change of pace. Parents will be pleased with the kids' menu (this is about the only place that has one) including half sandwiches and similarly pint-sized portions. Kids—and parents—can then fill up on fancy desserts from lime and mango mousse to Orange Dream cake (the owner used to be a pastry chef).

ATTRACTIONS

Pura Saraswati. Jalan Raya Ubud, Ubud. Daily during daylight hours.

The royal family commissioned this temple and water garden, dedicated to the Hindu goddess of art and learning, at the end of the 19th century. The main shrine is covered in fine carvings, and the bale houses giant *barong* masks. The restaurant Cafe Lotus is situated at the front, on the main street, so that diners can look out over the lovely grounds.

Puri Saren Agung, the Royal Palace. Jalan Raya, Ubud. Daily during daylight hours.

From the late 19th century to the mid-1940s, this was the seat for the local ruler. It's a series of elegant and well-preserved pavilions, many of them decorated incongruously with colonial-era European furniture. Visitors are welcome to stroll around, though there are no signs indicating what you are looking at, so it palls quickly. Every night, dance performances are held in the courtyard, and it is by far the best and most dramatic setting for these in Ubud. Part of the complex functions as a hotel, which for atmosphere and central location can't be beat, but I found the staff, though not unfriendly, decidedly distracted and unhelpful. (Still, if the thought of palace romance thrills you, call ☎ **361-975057,** or fax 361-975137.)

MUSEUMS

Blame German artist Walter Spies, who arrived here in 1928, for Ubud's long relationship with artists. Well, with Western artists, since the Balinese are plenty artistic on their own, hence the many galleries in town. Unfortunately, tourists spend much of their time shopping for identical, often shoddy crafts, and ignore some of the extraordinary art on display in the local museums. There are two highly recommended museums in the vicinity; take the time to check one or both out. If nothing else, it's a crash course in Balinese art appreciation and will help you enormously should you decide to upgrade from tacky souvenirs to more expensive purchases in the local galleries (see "Art Galleries," below).

Antonio Blanco's House and Art Gallery. Jalan Campuhan, Ubud (just past the bridge). ☎ **361-975502.** Admission Rp5,000. Daily during daylight hours.

Antonio Blanco is a nutty guy, a Catalan expat artist who really loves topless Bali girls (including his wife, who is featured in many of his paintings) and himself, not necessarily in that order. He's often around and will strike up a conversation on a dime. Decide for yourself whether his unabashed paintings are art, but don't miss his inspired multi-media pieces.

✪ **Neka Museum.** Jalan Raya Campuhan (about 10 min. north of central Ubud, near Ananda Cottages), Ubud. ☎ **361-975074** or 361-975034. Admission Rp10,000. Daily 9am–5pm.

This is the place to be introduced to Balinese art, and it's a lot more accessible than you might think. The museum was founded in 1982 by Suteja Neka, a former schoolteacher and art patron. It's housed in several pavilions, the order and contents of which keep changing (signs and a guard will tell you where to go). The art comes with well-written, highly informative English-language labels, so there is no need to buy an expensive guide. Things to look for: In the second room of the first pavilion, which shows the four major schools of Balinese painting, I love the striking black and white "Pandawas in Disguise" and the acid flashback "Demonic Sacrifice." The Ubud-style paintings reflect various aspects of village life, and depict some scenes that—provided you've been getting out enough—should be very familiar to you. The artist Sonit seems to be a Balinese Gauguin, with his use of bold splashy colors. The two paintings collectively called "Mutual Attraction" (housed in the last pavilion) were put next to each other only after it was noticed that the man in one seemed to be admiring or leering after the woman in the other. Finally, in the photography archive, don't miss the black and white photos from the 1930s and '40s by Robert Koke, author of *Our Hotel in Bali,* and notice how very little has changed for the Balinese people in the last 5 or 6 decades. It's too bad more of this art isn't available in reproduction, but the Neka Museum does have a good book available to fill a bit of that void. Do look at the view of the Campuhan Gorge from the Smit Pavilion. It explains why so many artists, Western and Balinese, have been inspired here, and may well inspire you to take up painting yourself.

✪ **Puri Lukisan.** Jalan Raya Ubud, Ubud. ☎ **361-975136.** Admission Rp8,000. Daily 8am–4pm.

A major renovation has turned a formerly dilapidated display into something nearly on a par with the Neka Museum. Some feel it even exceeds its more prominent counterpart, thanks in part to the Puri Lukisan's gorgeous garden setting, complete with lily ponds, rice paddies, and maybe even a water buffalo. It was founded in 1956 by a prince of Ubud and a Dutch artist to help preserve the history and heritage of the changing Bali arts, particularly as they become ever-more corrupted by the ravenous tourist industry. There is an invaluable cross-section of styles to be seen here, paintings and sculptures that show the evolution of Balinese art, and a changing exhibit by young local artists.

✪ **Seniwati Gallery of Art by Women.** Jalan Sriwedari 2B, Banjar Taman, Ubud. ☎ **361-975485.** Free admission. Daily 10am–5pm.

Like most museums, the Neka and the Puri Lukisan have a small ratio of female artists to male. This museum/gallery was founded to display often-overlooked art by women, and as a place for those who sometimes find themselves without a voice to express themselves. Both local and expat artists on are display, and some of the work is deeply powerful and moving. Besides fine art, the museum also includes pottery/ceramics, wood carving, and textiles. (I only wish there were more active displays of women creating these crafts—it would make a purchase more meaningful.) The permanent collection, special events showcase, gallery where art can be purchased, and various workshops help promote local female art and provide a place for an exchange of ideas, techniques, and information. They have a shop on Jalan Raya that sells high-quality crafts entirely made by village women.

OUTDOOR ACTIVITIES & WATER SPORTS

Monkey Forest. Monkey Forest Rd. Rp3,000. Daily during daylight hours.

Yes, there is a monkey forest at the southern end of Monkey Forest Road. Towering trees cluster around to make a home for a troop of bad-tempered but endlessly photogenic primates, who swing from branches, cannonball into pools of water, engage in seemingly anthropomorphic activity, and generally delight photo-snapping visitors. Signs warn you not to feed them, while locals cluster beneath the signs selling you bananas and nuts for precisely that purpose. Do so if you must, but do not tease the critters, who are grumpy enough as it is—just hand them the food. Make sure you have no other food on you, as they will smell it. They also are known to snatch at dangling or glittering objects, or dig their teeth into an offensive rubber soled sandal. There is a temple for the dead within the forest, and the track also leads to Nyuhkuning, a wood-carving village.

BIRD WATCHING

Noted British naturalist and ornithologist Victor Mason leads bird-watching tours Tuesday, Friday, Saturday, and Sunday beginning at 9:30am from Victor's pub, the Beggar's Bush (at the Tjampuhan Bridge). It costs US$33, which includes water and lunch at Beggar's Bush after. Not too strenuous, it's suitable for all mobile ages, and Mason says you should see about 30 of the 100 or so varieties of birds in the area. (Birders I know point out that birds are most active and visible during the early morning and tend to be gone by 9:30am, so they doubt how many you might see. It's a nice walk anyway.) Bring binoculars if you can, though they should have a spare pair. Call **Bali Bird Walks** at ☎ **361-975009** for more details.

You can also go to the village of **Petulu,** northeast of Ubud, where every evening around 6pm countless white herons arrive to roost overnight in the trees. Local legend has it they are the reincarnated souls of the dead. To get there, take Tegalalang-Pujung road north from the T junction at the eastern edge of Ubud, go about 1½ kilometers, turn left at the fork, then go another 1½ kilometers.

ELEPHANT RIDING

It may be called **Elephant Safari,** but the experience at ✪ **Elephant Safari Park,** Jalan Bypass Ngurah Rai, Pesanggaran (☎ **361-721480;** fax 361-721481), is less safari and more elephant ride—but when was the last time you took one of those? The elephants, native to Sumatra, are beautifully cared for—indeed, elephant experts say these are the best-tended and most content they've ever seen. They live in a park that seems to be a model for ecologically and culturally minded attractions. The owners have worked carefully with locals from Taro Village, previously one of Bali's most remote and untouched villages, to make sure they have improved conditions, not destroyed local culture. (This means trying to find ways of reducing the sacred white cow population without killing them. Note their graves as you take your ride.) After learning some elephant facts (biology, care and feeding, threats, preservation), you can feed a pachyderm (they like sugar cane and yams). Then you are loaded two by two onto your beast (the *mahout,* or guide, sits on its neck), and off you go for a somewhat jostling, swaying trip through the nearby jungle. (It's not all that jungle-y, but who cares? You're riding an elephant.) Be sure to ask questions; guides are all knowledgeable about local flora, customs, and elephants.

But only after the ride is over does the real fun begin: the optional elephant bath. This entails mounting an elephant bareback, arms about a guide's waist, and riding along as the animal slowly walks into a deep pool of (clean) river water. At the handler's command, the elephant rears up and plunges in to its knees, submerging you up to your chin. Shampoo is optional.

This may well have been the most fun I had in Bali. Bring your swimsuit (or not—I went in my clothes), hold on tight because you could fall off from laughing too hard, make sure someone other than a family member is taking your picture because they will surely screw it up as they laugh too hard, but don't miss this part of the excursion. Don't forget the words *"Gajah bagus"* (excellent elephant), and give that elephant a yam.

Safaris are US$39 to US$56 for adults, US$29 to US$38 for children. Family packages are available. The park is open daily, and reservations are recommended.

RAFTING & TREKKING

Just west of Ubud is the Ayung River, where everyone comes for white-water rafting and kayaking. The rapids probably aren't that impressive for experienced rafters (the wet season promises more challenging rapids), but the scenery along the way is, with rice paddies, deep gorges, and photo-op waterfalls. The following two companies book 2-hour trips that include all equipment, hotel pickup, and lunch. Your hotel can also make the reservations.

Bali Adventure Tours. Jalan Bypass Ngurah Rai, Pesanggaran. ☎ **361-721480.** Fax 361-721481. www.baliadventuretours.com.

Packages may include the elephant safari described above, or other treks (jungle, nature reserves, rice paddies). The same people also book mountain cycling. White-water rafting (including transfers, instruction, equipment, and hot showers after-wards) is US$59 for adults, US$40 for children. Kayaking is US$58 per adult (no children).

✪ **Sobek.** Jalan Tirta Ening 9, Bypass Ngurah Rai, Sanur. ☎ **361-287059.** Fax 361-289448.

This adventure outlet earns raves from customers for its professionalism and eye for details and comfort. Rafting (including transfers, lunch, changing facilities, and equipment) is US$68 for adults, US$45 for children under 12. They also offer kayak-ing, cycling, and trekking, plus package combos of everything.

WALKING

By far, one of the most delightful activities in Ubud is walking. And I don't mean just past all those shops. Ubud is surrounded by fascinating villages, scenic rice paddies, gorges, and rivers, and there are roads and paths that lead to all of them. You can just wander, but I strongly urge you to buy a copy of the **Ubud Surroundings map,** avail-able in bookstores, grocery stores, and newsstands throughout town (particularly on the Jalan Raya). It shows all the roads and trails and gives suggestions on where to go and what to see. Try walking to the village of **Penestanan,** just west of the Campuhan Bridge. Ascend the stairs directly opposite the Hotel Tjampuhan (on Jalan Raya Cam-puhan) and follow the path over the river and through the woods (really), turning left at the crossroads with Penestanan's main street. This will eventually bring you back down a steep road that ends about where Jalan Raya Campuhan turns into Jalan Raya Ubud.

You can also try the most popular walk in Ubud (and certainly my favorite), the **Campuhan Ridge walk.** Follow the Jalan Raya downhill as it curves. Right before the bridge, past the Ibah on the right-hand side, there is a path that heads down from the road. When it forks, don't go towards the river, but scramble briefly uphill to the right, then follow the path. It will take you through a temple, then up a hill to follow along the gorge. It's a breathtaking vista of green rice paddies, sheer cliffs, and trees, and you may well have it to yourself, aside from a friendly local or two. The friend who first told me about this walk (saying it's his favorite in the world) suggested that you start at around 6am, walk for about an hour, then turn around and come back just in time for breakfast—well before the morning heat sets in. You can also keep going; the path leads through two tiny settlements. After the temple of the second one, the road forks. If you go left it leads you back down to the Campuhan road, about 1 kilometer (0.62 miles) above the Neka Museum (from there I suggest you catch a bemo or other transport, as the walk back to Ubud is a bit dicey with all the cars). If you go right you'll eventually arrive at the village of Keliki. From there, it's about a 2-hour walk to Ubud, though you can always go to the Hotel Alam Sari just outside Keliki for a meal and a ride back to town.

Or just grab any likely looking path or road and see where it goes. You won't have quite the sense of discovery and wonderment visitors did when Ubud and the sur-rounding villages were less built up, but the beauty remains undiminished.

SHOPPING

Adding to its other delights, Ubud is Shopping Central. With a range from the tackiest, cheapest, mass-produced (yet lovely still) souvenirs to say-goodbye-to-the-college-fund priced art, you are likely to find something here to commemorate your trip. Do like friends of mine did and entirely decorate your house with Ubud crafts, carvings, and fabric. Or do like I do and get all your Christmas shopping done on a budget.

The amount of goods available can be overwhelming, particularly since many carry nearly identical items. Before buying anything, you might want to check out the **Ubud Market,** at the southeast corner of Monkey Forest Road and Jalan Raya Ubud (open during daylight hours). It's a real market, great noisy fun, with dozens of stalls selling goods intended for locals (check these out for bargains), produce, livestock, and the like, among the tourist kitsch. This is a good place to pick up a sarong and sash, if you haven't yet, or to start working on a more climate-appropriate wardrobe. It also functions somewhat as a wholesale market—many of the stores buy their goods here. Bargaining can be a bit tougher here, owing to some really hard-nosed (but often quite charming) lady proprietors. You might well get better prices elsewhere, but at least you can get an idea of what to pay. If you arrive first thing in the morning you can try some of the snacks the ladies bring to sell.

For more shopping, just walk down **Monkey Forest Road, Jalan Raya Ubud,** and **Jalan Hanoman.** Shop after shop is filled with gorgeous sarongs, wood carvings, mobiles, various flying creatures, jewelry, incense, pottery, gaily colored–shirts, and so on. It's nearly all geared towards tourists, and you'll have to sort out the treasures from the dreck. In between are some shops with more legitimate merchandise, a few of which are noted below. All should be fixed price. Higher quality items—and higher prices—are found on Jalan Raya Ubud west of Monkey Forest Road.

Several nearby crafts villages seem to be entirely devoted to some kind of commercial production. **Mas,** on the bemo route to Ubud from the south, is the most prominent wood-carving village, but there is also **Tegalalang** to the north. **Batubulan,** to the south, specializes in stone carving, while **Celuk** is where you find silver jewelry. **Batuan** and **Keliki** are major art centers, with their own distinctive styles. The sheer amount of apparently identical goods for sale in these places can be bewildering, but if you have the patience you can find (or commission) treasures. All are accessible by bemo, though it can be a wearying trip involving several changes. Unfortunately, your other choice is a transport guide, who will certainly get a cut of the then probably inflated price of whatever you buy (here's where I'd opt for a scooter or car, but *be careful*).

ART GALLERIES

There are art galleries galore in Ubud; the following are just the most highly regarded or highest profile. Go take a look at what's on display at the Neka or the Puri Lukisan (see "Museums," above) to familiarize yourself with the different styles of art (and get an idea of what is good quality) before leaping into a purchase. Also consider patronizing the **Seniwati Gallery of Art by Women** (see "Museums," above), Jalan Sriwedari 2B.

Agung Rai Fine Art Gallery (☎ 361-974228; Jalan Peliatan, Peliatan; open daily except holidays 8am to 6pm), is a highly regarded source for artwork for all budgets. Agung Rai founded the museum in 1996 with art collected since he was a kid; it's now a collection of a huge number of Balinese paintings. The exterior of the gallery honors Balinese beauty too, poised on the edge of a rice field with views of the Gunung Agung in the distance, a dubious but delicious spot for a hip espresso bar. **Hans Snell's Gallery,** Jalan Kajeng, Ubud (☎ 361-975699; open daily 8am to 8pm), is owned by Dutch expat Snel, who moved to Bali and married his teenage model. Snel has worked

You'll be bargaining with more leverage if your adversaries don't know you're from the mighty U.S. of A. This is your chance to take advantage of any bilingual skills you may have acquired along the way, and remember, it's a second language for the shopkeeper too. Also, avoid falling for the innocent question, "Where are you staying?" as prices rise accordingly for those holing up at the Four Seasons. Eye up the homestays on your way to the market and adopt one for the duration of your market tour.

in a variety of styles, most recently abstract compositions. The former home of Ubud's most significant artist, I Gusti Nyoman Lempad, **Lempad's House,** Jalan Raya (open daily 8am to 6pm), is unfortunately less a museum of his work (most of which is at the Neka Museum) than a gallery showcasing a group of painters calling themselves "Puri Lempad." Owned by the founder of the Neka Museum, **Neka Gallery,** Jalan Raya (☎ 361-975639; open daily 8am to 7pm), is more than reliable for good quality art in all price ranges. It includes artists from all over Indonesia.

BOOKS

Cintra Bookshop, Dewi Sita Street (☎ 361-973295), has used books well organized by language and some by category—even alphabetized! Opposite the post office, the ✪ **Ganesha Bookstore,** Jalan Raya (☎ 361-976339), is an oasis for serious readers. Ganesha is delightfully low on Danielle Steel and high on a wide assortment of both new and used novels, classics, and nonfiction in several languages, with a fine selection of Bali-related items. They also carry a small but strong selection of CDs and tapes, along with good Balinese crafts, especially musical instruments. Owner Ketut Yuliarsa keeps his own instruments in a loft upstairs, where he gives hands-on classes every Tuesday evening—a great way to learn a little about the local music, whether you're an experienced pro or a tin ear.

HOUSEHOLD ITEMS

Owned by the Casa Luna folks, and located on the corner of Jalan Raya and Jalan Bisma in Campuhan, **Casa Luna Homewares** has everything you need to decorate your house in Bali style, including gorgeous pillows, wall hangings, bed coverings, and kitchen ware.

JEWELRY

Treasures, the boutique inside Ary's Warung (☎ 361-976697) on Jalan Raya Ubud, specializes in jewelry created by the best area designers, using precious metals and stones.

TEXTILES

Monkey Forest Road seems to be a hotbed for quality in the textile department, excluding galleries. The best of locally made ikats, songkets, and endeks can be found at **Wardanis** on Monkey Forest Road. **Jani's Place** (☎ 361-975358), also on Monkey Forest Road, has textiles from all over Indonesia, including ikat weaves in cotton and silk.

CLASSES

There are various ever-changing classes in art and dance instruction throughout Ubud—keep your eyes peeled for bulletin boards and other signs advertising them.

Yoga is offered at the **Ubud Sari Health Spa** (see "Pamper Yourself," below). See above for information about the **Ganesha Bookstore**'s music classes.

⊙ **Casa Luna Cooking School.** Jalan Raya. ☎ **361-973282.** http://bali-paradise.com/ casaluna. Classes Mon 10am–2pm, Tues (market tour) 8am–noon, Wed 10am–2pm. Rp100,000 per person. Book in advance.

Janet de Neefe runs this cooking school in the backyard of her lovely home, where she'll teach you how to cook just like she does—or close enough to impress your friends. Learn to make that fabulous spiced fish in banana leaves you passed up at Indus restaurant, or the green pancakes she serves for breakfast at her homestay. On Tuesdays, you go to the Ubud market, buy what's there, and spontaneously turn it into something delicious. Best of all, there's a feast at the end!

Meditation Shop. Monkey Forest Rd. ☎ **361-976206.**

Your New Age center, offering silent meditation hours and instruction in meditation (an interesting concept), along with metaphysical literature.

UBUD AFTER DARK

Fed by the demand of an ever-expanding tourist base, Ubud's nightlife scene is slowly transforming from nil to relatively sedate, and that's fine with many of us. Many of the restaurants, at least, are now staying open after 9pm, and some show laser disc **movies** nightly. One of the more popular venues is the **Jazz Cafe,** Jalan Sukma 2 (4 streets east of Monkey Forest Rd., just off the main road; ☎ **361-976594;** open 7:30 to 10:30pm), one of the few true nightspots in town. Live performances of surprisingly good jazz bands—including one that combines modern jazz with gamelan (Tuesdays only)—are scheduled Tuesday through Saturday; make a reservation if you want a table for lunch or dinner. **Sai Sai** on Monkey Forest Road (☎ **361-976698;** open 7:30 to 11pm) gets pretty busy on Saturday nights, but remains romantically quiet and congenial during the "down" times. Gamelan music is featured on Tuesday nights. Down the street is the **Funkey Monkey** (☎ **361-903729;** open noon to 1am), a cocktail bar for the cooler crowd, where a live DJ spins the latest dance music (closed Mondays). Personally, we think you should live it up a little and spring for a choice wine savored in the shrine to style that is the **Four Seasons** (☎ **361-977577**).

PERFORMANCES

There are usually several dance, music, and shadow puppet performances to choose from every night in Ubud, both at the **Palace** (the recommended location) and other nearby stages (when needed, transportation is included). Barong, legong, kecak, gamelan, abbreviated dance performances of the *Mahabarata* and *Ramayana*—it's all there for you to sample in various forms. If you have time for only one, a barong performance at the Ubud Palace would be your best bet. Barong is highly visual, employing both acting and dance. It's both comedic and dramatic, and comes close to what Westerners would consider a traditional narrative, which also makes it suitable for children. Seeing a performance of anything at the palace, where the stage is in the dramatic courtyard, is a treat in and of itself.

It's easy to learn what's on the performance agenda; boys will come up to you in the street every day trying to sell tickets for that evening's program. Or you can plan ahead by getting a schedule at the tourist office on Jalan Raya. You can purchase tickets at the venue in question, or indeed from the street boys. Check prices in advance, just in case. As of this writing, tickets were about Rp20,000.

8 Sights & Destinations near Ubud

The following are sights that are either quite close to Ubud or can easily be done in a half-day trip, even in combination with other spots. (Though if you want to really linger, this will take up an entire day.) Some are quite popular on the tourist track and thus often incredibly crowded. If you go earlier in the day, both the crowds and the heat will be more bearable, but you'll find that the hours near closing are just as pleasant, since many of the touts may have already closed up shop and gone home. Don't just settle for the hot spots—many of the locations neglected by tourists make for far better viewing anyway.

All sacred locations will insist on a sarong and sash. Most will provide them for free, or for a small fee (less than Rp1,000), but you will look more stylish—not to mention polite—if you come with your own. There will be locals offering to be your guide at every site. You don't really need them, and their information may be highly suspect—but then again, they could be entertaining. Be sure, however, to negotiate a firm price ahead of time, and be prepared for them to insist at the end that that price was quite a bit higher than actually agreed upon.

There are **organized tours** that go to many, but not all, of these sights—check with the various tourist agencies in town to see if one or two fit the bill. Or you can grab one of those pesky **transport guides** and tell them for once that yes, you really do want transport. Believe it or not, they are reliable, being desperate for business, and if you negotiate a time and place they will show up. Have your itinerary clearly written down—nothing I have listed here is unusual, and any guide who acts even vaguely puzzled should not be hired. Decide in advance how much you want to spend for a day or half-day's worth of someone's time and gas. You will have to negotiate (chances are they will start quite high), and be sure to make it clear that you do not want to go to any shops (assuming you don't) and won't pay the full price if somehow you do accidentally end up at one. You might also ask your guide to tell you exactly where you are when he lets you off at a site, since there often aren't clear signs ("Hmm, is this Titra Empul or Yeh Pulu?"). And don't forget to tip at the end of the day (10% or so should be fine).

BESAKIH
About 20km (12 miles) N of Klungklung

This is the so-called "Mother Temple"—the center of Bali Hinduism and the most important temple in Bali. Set on the slopes of the volcanic Gunung Agung, the highest mountain in Bali, with a grand and marvelous view, it is one of the top tourist sights on the island. Admission is Rp3,000; the temple is open daily during daylight hours.

However, I have to warn you: if you are expecting to see the St. Peter's Basilica of Bali, forget it. Culturally, Besakih is monumentally significant, being the holiest temple in Bali, but architecturally, it's more like a big village church (to continue with the analogy from another religion and culture). Further, Besakih is not just one temple, but a series of temples in a compound. And non-Hindus are not allowed inside the walls of any of the temples. So the best a camera-toting tourist can hope for is a glimpse over a wall, or through an open door. There are no signs, markers, maps, or information brochures anywhere (it is a working religious compound and not a museum or other tourist-oriented construction) and so even when you do see something, it's unlikely you will know what you are looking at. The touts are so insistent that it's almost worth paying one of them; even if their information is dubious, at least it's something. The view is wonderful when it isn't raining or threatening to rain, and clouds aren't entirely obscuring it. Add to this a very long, steepish walk up from the car park, and this becomes a less-than-rewarding experience.

Besakih is the oldest and largest of Bali's roughly 20,000 temples. It may date back as far as the 8th or 10th centuries, but the first hard records of it come from the 14th and 15th centuries. There are 22 temples spread over about 3 kilometers (2 miles) in the complex, which was destroyed by an earthquake in 1917, and heavily damaged again in the 1963 eruption. It has since been well restored. The three main temples venerate the Hindu holy trinity. The **Pura Penataran Agung** (originally a funeral temple for the Gelgel kings dynasty and the island's central temple) is more or less in the center; it's the largest and is dedicated to Shiva. **Pura Batu Medog,** diagonal from Penataran Agung's upper left corner, is dedicated to Vishnu. **Pura Kiduling Kreteg,** off from the right upper Penataran Agung corner, is dedicated to Brahma. The notable feature of Penataran Agung is its giant stairway, lined by seven levels of carved figures, with characters on the right from the *Ramayana* and the ones on the left from the *Mahabarata*.

To best enjoy Besakih, try to arrive early in the morning, ahead of the busloads of tourists. Or come during the Bhata Turun Kabeh, a month-long festival celebrating the time the gods descend from the heavens to hang out in Besakih. It usually falls during March or April; check the calendar of festivals issued annually by the Bali government tourist office.

In passing, the little warungs among the shops lining the car park at the base of the hill are quite cheap and tasty.

GUNUNG AGUNG

At 3,014 meters (9,888 ft.), the tallest mountain in Bali, Gunung Agung is utterly sacred to the Balinese, who like to sleep with their heads facing it. The mountain is believed to have been created by the gods, and is the center of the world. It can be seen from most points (provided clouds aren't in the way) in east Bali.

Gunung Agung is the center of one of the greatest modern-day Bali disasters. In 1963, as plans were being made for the once-a-century ceremony Eka Dasa Rudra, the great ritual held to purify the entire island and to ensure good luck (which hadn't been held in several centuries, so no one thought it would matter that it was not the correct year for it), the long-dormant volcano began to rumble. The ceremony went ahead on March 8, even as ash rained down on the probably glum participants. The volcano erupted on March 17, pouring lava down and spewing poisonous gas. As many as 2,000 people were killed, and another 100,000 lost their homes. East Bali was a near total wreck and it took many years to rebuild, with scars still visible. As for the ceremony, it was held again in 1979—the year it should have been held in the first place—and this time went off without a hitch.

You can climb the now-quiet Gunung Agung, but it is a serious trek that absolutely calls for a guide (the trails are not well marked) and proper supplies. Most hotels can arrange for it, but figure you will have to start climbing in the middle of the night or very early in the morning to make the top by sunrise.

OTHER SIGHTS NEAR UBUD

For sights nearer to "home," consider hiring a bicycle for amblings into neighboring villages; I found the physical effort of pedaling all day long an ample tradeoff for the countless "hellos" offered by smiling natives unaccustomed to seeing many outsiders rolling through their midst. Of course, they don't smile less when you're on a scooter, though the engine does drown out the laughter and the moment passes much more quickly.

Goa Gajah/Elephant Cave. About halfway between Ubud and Mas, approximately 2km (1.2 miles) to the east. Admission Rp3,100. Daily during daylight hours.

The mouth of this man-made cave doesn't quite look like an elephant, which makes the legend that that is how it got its name suspect. In any case, Goa Gajah was built in the 11th century, probably as a type of monk's cell. Inside the small, dark, and clammy cave are statues of Ganesha to the left (most definitely an elephant) and three phallic emblems of Siwa to the right. Outside to the left of the cave is a worn statue of a woman with children; she's both a Balinese folk heroine and a Buddhist goddess, so Goa Gajah seems to have been both Hindu and Buddhist. There is also a large rectangular bathing area, and just beyond it, steps leading to a pretty ravine, where there are some statues of Buddha.

✪ **Yeh Pulu.** 1km (0.62 mile) south of signs just east of Goa Gajah. Admission Rp3,000. Daily during daylight hours.

This is one of our favorite Bali sights, a row of bas-relief carvings in a rock face. It's pretty, simple, intriguing, and for some reason largely unvisited by tourists. You can actually walk to Yeh Pulu from Goa Gajah, but it's through some rice paddies, and you do need one of those guides to help you find it. If you arrive by car, after paying your fee you will have a medium-length walk through a rice field, past a bathing place on the left (don't turn in there or you may startle some naked bathers). The carvings date back at least 400 years, and while no one is exactly sure what the five panels depict, they do seem to tell the story of a hunt. Note the religious and cultural details on the figures, culminating with a statue of Ganesha. A slightly nutty older woman may bless you with holy water and ask for a donation. Go ahead and give it to her; we could all use an extra blessing.

Pura Panti Pasek Gelgel/Pura Gunung Kawi. Sebatu. About 9km (5.6 miles) northeast of Ubud. Admission Rp3,000. Daily during daylight hours.

On the grounds of these two pretty temples in the village of Sebatu you find lovely little bathing pools of holy water, fed by mountain springs. The place was undergoing renovation recently, even though it was already fairly well maintained. A priest occasionally offers guests (of which there aren't many non-Balinese) treats like rice balls with a cane syrup center. Take one and then have a dip in the pool, making sure you go to the appropriate gender section. (For the main Gunung Kawi, see below.)

✪ **Gunung Kawi.** 12km (7.4 miles) northeast of Ubud. Admission Rp3,000. Daily during daylight hours.

Hands down my favorite Bali sight, and inexplicably neglected by tourists. If I do my job right, that's going to change, but it will still be worth a look. Here you find the so-called "royal tombs" or *chandi.* Actually, no one knows what they really are—no ashes or bones were found inside, so they were probably memorials or cenotaphs, and the best guess is they were built to honor 11th-century King Udayana and his consorts and concubines. They are rare stone monuments, set deep in niches, all carved directly out of the mountain face (rather like Mount Rushmore). No identifying marks, aside from some cryptic faded writing, were found on them. To reach them, you walk down a steep flight of 300 steps (and yes, you'll have to walk back up), which brings you to a small gorge. Go to the left, and view the first set of tombs, which honor the King's minor wives. The second set, for the King and his favorite wives, are arguably even better. They're across the river, all the way through the temple complex; turn left and walk through the complex until you actually exit it, down some steps towards the river (note the cavelike monks' cells carved out of the mountain along the way). The monolithic tombs stand silent and enigmatic, mysterious and awesome, in a lovely setting

Pamper Yourself

The spa phenomenon is more pronounced in Ubud than anywhere else on the island, where massages in all price ranges are available in equally jaw-dropping settings. It would be impossible to list them all, but in addition to the ones listed below, other notables include the sunken carved stone grotto pools in the **Tjampuhan Spa** (Hotel Tjampuhan, Jalan Raya Campuhan; ☎ 361-975368); and the **Natura** in Laplapan (3km northeast of Ubud; ☎ 361-978666), whose private treatment rooms overlook the Petanu River Valley, surrounded by a tropical rain forest.

Employing the Ayurvedic traditions (the Hindu holistic "science of life") and accenting earthly elements, **the Four Seasons Spa at Sayan** (☎ 361-701010) uses locally grown spices, natural clays, herbs, and flowers to create a menu of exclusive therapies. Given the stress of this journalist's job, the *Chakra Dhara* was just what the witch doctor ordered: using herbal oil on key energy points, all of my toxic blockages were cleared and my *chakra* flow was restored.

More affordable but no less transcendent is the **Ubud Sari Health Resort,** Jalan Kajeng 35 (☎ 361-974393), where in addition to spa and beauty salon services in a lush and tranquil garden setting, they offer all sorts of healing treatments (chiropractic, high colonics, aromatherapy). There's also an on-site healer who claims to be able to diagnose problems through psychic powers. Prices are from US$9 for a ½ hour massage to US$47 for a firming and reducing full body wrap.

of green gorge and rushing river; you could probably spend hours just staring at them. A tenth tomb, possibly of an advisor, is back across the river, to your left through marshy rice paddies as you head towards the exit.

Titra Empul. About 500m north of Gunung Kawi turnoff. Admission Rp3,000. Daily during daylight hours.

The holy water of Titra Empul is considered the most sacred on Bali, and it is part of a ritual following recovery from a serious illness to come bathe here. The waters burble up in a clear cool blue from a black silt–bottomed rectangular pool; legend has it that a warrior pierced a stone here and let loose the healing liquid, which saved his poisoned army. There are separate bathing places for different body parts and different kinds of people, and along with the Balinese who come here there are usually hordes of jabbering tourists brought in by the busload. (Come in the early morning to miss the bulk of them.) Take a healing dip if you like, and notice the modern building on the clifftop to your right; it was used by Indonesian President Suharto or the Balinese governor, who liked to pick out the best looking of the naked local gals and summon them up for closer encounters.

9 Candi Dasa

Candi Dasa hasn't gotten raves from the press, especially given the sorry non-state of the area's "beaches." Thanks to enthusiastic but overly rapid development, Candi Dasa's coral reefs were largely destroyed, leaving the beaches so exposed that the sand eroded away, replaced by nasty, foot-cutting coral. The engineering of man-made sea walls has already begun to show patches of accumulated sand, but in the meantime, we'll just have to content ourselves with sandless rocky access to the area's azure waters.

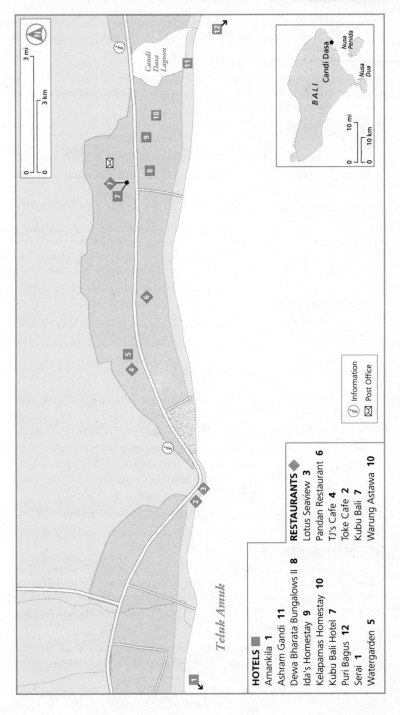

Candi Dasa

Teluk Amuk

Candi Dasa Lagoon

HOTELS
Amankila **1**
Ashram Gandi **11**
Dewa Bharata Bungalows II **8**
Ida's Homestay **9**
Kelapamas Homestay **10**
Kubu Bali Hotel **7**
Puri Bagus **12**
Serai **1**
Watergarden **5**

RESTAURANTS ◆
Lotus Seaview **3**
Pandan Restaurant **6**
TJ's Cafe **4**
Toke Cafe **2**
Kubu Bali **7**
Warung Astawa **10**

i Information
⊠ Post Office

B A L I
Candi Dasa
Nusa Penida
Nusa Dua

10 mi
10 km

3 mi
3 km

Another option nearby is the village of **Padangbai,** in the westernmost part of the bay, where you'll experience something closer to village life and gain easy access to the best snorkeling in the area, but lose some of the tourist infrastructure. But the main reason to camp out in Candi Dasa is to take advantage of the peace, relaxation, and historical riches of the eastern corner of the island (See "Sights & Destinations Near Candi Dasa," below). You can also find some of the island's finest accommodations here (Amankila) and some respectable runners-up.

GETTING THERE

There are shuttles from all major tourist areas to Candi Dasa, and most of the hotels offer airport pickup for a fee. The most comfortable option, however, is to negotiate "transport" with a local in his private car or jeep (if you don't like his vehicle, ask somebody else).

GETTING AROUND

There isn't much to the town of Candi Dasa itself—just one road, parallel to the beach—so your feet will do you just fine. Hotels just outside the center (or farther in the case of the Amankila and the Serai) generally offer regular **shuttles** into town, or, if you prefer, **motorbike** rental. **Bemos** also travel frequently up and down the main strip.

TOUR OPERATORS

There are a number of tour offices on Candi Dasa's main street, including the reliable **Perama.**

Fast Facts: Candi Dasa

Banks/Currency Exchange   Money changers are all up and down the main street, offering competitive prices.

Car/Motorbike Rental   Safari on the main street (☎ **363-41707**) is a reliable and friendly tourist point, with a selection of cars, jeeps, and motorbikes.

Internet   Safari on the main street (☎ **363-41707**) has Internet service, as does Tarunga Beach Bungalows, also on the main street.

Post Office/Mail   Asri Shop on the main street offers postal services.

Telephone   Go to the Kubu Bali Hotel, on the main street. Candi Dasa's area code is 363.

ACCOMMODATIONS

There are not quite as many accommodation choices in Candi Dasa as one might think, but between the high end, ultra-luxurious Amankila and the several basic losmen, there is enough of a range to satisfy everyone. If you choose to stay in Padangbai, losmen are the only option. They're easy to find, and pretty much all the same.

VERY EXPENSIVE

✪ **Amankila.** Manggis. ☎ **361-771267** (reservations), or 363-41333. Fax 361-771266 (reservations), or 363-41555. 35 units. A/C MINIBAR TEL. US$550–US$750 double; US$1,700 2-bedroom suite. AE, DC, JCB, MC, V. Free parking.

This is the seaside cousin of the Ubud gorge–based Amandari, with another breathtaking view (this one of the ocean) and prices to match. And the fact that they brought along pillows for you for the ride back in their SUV is always a good sign. The hotel is located on a bluff somewhat outside of Candi Dasa, but a full guest book (in low season) and the conversion of several rooms to those with private pools shows that this clientele couldn't care less how far from town they were. Enjoy ruling over a large bungalow with a sleeping room dominated by a solid wood four-poster canopy bed, an enormous dressing area/bathroom, and cushioned windows. (Prices are higher for ocean views and private pools.) An elegant, well-stocked library puts the pitiful shelves of weather-beaten volumes other hotels call their library to shame. The Amankila has the only beach in Candi Dasa with sand—and a breathtaking bi-level pool, whose water matches the color of the ocean it seems to spill into. One restaurant serves breakfast and lunch; another serves dinner. There's also a bar.

EXPENSIVE

✪ **Puri Bagus.** P.O. Box 129, Candi Dasa, Karangasem 80801, Bali. ☎ **363-41131.** Fax 363-41290. www.balimart.com/bagushotels.htm. E-mail: pdcandi@denpasar.wasantara.net.id. 15 units. A/C MINIBAR TEL. US$115–US$135 double; US$350 villa. AE, DC, MC, V. Free parking.

A lengthy but doable walk from the center of town, this is a compromise between the high-priced Amankila or Serai and the lesser hotels in Candi Dasa. Pretty and romantic, it's the best of its class. The grounds zigzag around the land jutting into the ocean, which laps right up to the edge, with steps down to the beach. Good-sized bungalows are airy and light thanks to many big windows, and Balinese music plays in them to greet you. Each has a small but clean and pretty sitting area, an open-air bath with hand-held showers (these are just a little frayed around the edges—probably weather-worn). The U-shaped swimming pool has a very deep section for scuba practice and a large shallow area for kids. There's an expensive but tasty restaurant with a fine ocean view, and two bars. Dance programs and movies are offered at night, plus a full range of daily free activities.

Serai. Buitan, Manggis, Karangasem, Bali 80871. ☎ **363-41011.** Fax 363-41015. www. ghmhotels.com. E-mail: seraimanggis@ghmhotels.com. 58 units. A/C MINIBAR TV TEL. US$130–US$185 double; US$260–US$285 suite. AE, DC, JCB, MC, V. Free parking.

From the outside, this comfortable, newish place may look more like a boxy concrete singles apartment complex, but beyond the facade is a vision worthy of a magazine cover. In spite of the starkness, the staff is unpretentious and disarmingly friendly. Rooms are stylish, luxurious, and easy on the eye, and there are some nice touches like afternoon tea and treats on your patio (or balcony, if you're upstairs). The vast lawn, in the midst of which is a bigger than average pool surrounded by teak lounges, leads to a large pebble beach. You'll need to take advantage of the house transportation if you want to get into town, but this won't seem like such a hardship when you consider that "town" is going to offer a different type of travel experience than the one you're looking for by staying here. A particularly interesting bonus is the cooking school.

MODERATE

✪ **Watergarden.** Main St., Candi Dasa. ☎ **363-41540.** Fax 363-41164. www. watergardenhotel.com. E-mail: info@watergardenhotel.com. 14 units. TEL. US$70–US$80 double; US$160 2-bedroom suite. AE, MC, V. Free parking.

One of the better-looking properties in Candi Dasa, the Watergarden ends up with many repeat guests. The simple thatched individual bungalows are unimaginatively decorated, but plenty comfortable (though only some have A/C). Each has a wide veranda overlooking one of the many lily ponds (occupied by some rather aggressive koi) that bisect the grounds and give the hotel its name. The lack of directional signs (at this writing) makes finding your bungalow among the twisting paths and bridges an adventure. (Be ready for lost guests to bumble into your space, or at least look in your windows.) The most private rooms are 11 and 12, at the back, but they're also the farthest walk. Only deluxe rooms have A/C. For dining, see the review of TJ's and bar below.

INEXPENSIVE

Ashram Gandhi Candi Dasa. Main St., Candi Dasa. ☎ and fax **361-225145** (reservations), or 363-41108. 14 units. US$20–US$35 double. Only married couples can share rooms. Includes 3 vegetarian meals a day. 3-night minimum stay.

Yes, this is a real ashram, and they are serious about it. It's a truly unique experience to stay here, with a number of pros and cons. The pros: It's an ashram (recently featured in a travel article in the *New York Times*), and you are welcome to join in all daily activities including prayer routines, yoga, meditation, English classes, and cleaning (the place has to stay clean somehow), though it's not required. The vegetarian (naturally) meals are by all accounts quite good, and you can't beat the peaceful vibe. On the other hand, this is a commune—30 people live here full-time, and there is a kindergarten school on the grounds. Amenities are minimal—cold water and fan only (though it's not uncomfortable at all)—and they do prohibit smoking, alcohol, non-married couples sharing rooms, and nudity on their beach. However, it's a nice location, wrapping around the lagoon, with grazing cows and a well-stocked reading room (many books on religion). The outside walls of the buildings feature quotes from Gandhi ("Learn to be your own judge and you will be happy"). Guides are available for touring and day trips.

Dewa Bharata Bungalows. Main St., Candi Dasa. ☎ **363-41090.** Fax 363-41091. 24 units. US$20–US$23 double with fan; US$25–US$35 double with A/C. Rates include breakfast. Free parking.

A good budget choice if you're looking for something a step above a losmen. It's essentially the same idea in terms of rooms and furnishings, but with a slight upgrade in each. Bathrooms are clean, with showers only. Outside, the tiled pavilions have lots of Bali frills and are set amidst a manicured garden. There is a small pool (which you don't get at a losmen) that overlooks the beach and is particularly nice for a budget place.

✪ **Kubu Bali.** Main St., Candi Dasa. ☎ **363-41532** or 363-41256. Fax 363-41531. 20 units. A/C TEL. US$55 double; US$65 suite. JCB, MC, V. Free parking.

A great value for the price, the Kubu Bali is an extremely comfortable and well thought-out hotel. It's tucked away off the main street amidst a ravine of rice terraces, perched on endlessly scenic levels of cobblestone gardens, statues, benches, aviaries, and pavilions terraced up the hillside.

The handsomely decorated individual bungalows are bright and airy, with simple touches and comfortable amenities. The bathrooms present the perfect compromise of modern tile (and porcelain) grafted onto a stone shower open to the sky. Each cottage has a porch and lounging couches, as well as its own sundeck. At the uppermost reaches of the hill, the grounds are crowned by an extremely pretty pool with views of the ocean and islands. There's room service (food until 10pm, drinks 24 hours), and an excellent restaurant (see below).

LOSMEN

✪ **Ida's Homestay.** Main St., Candi Dasa. ☎ and fax **363-41096.** 6 units. Rp60,000–Rp90,000 double. Rates include breakfast.

They've done a lot with a little in this popular homestay. Comfortable cottages on idyllic seaside grounds feature cold water and fan only. If that scares you off, I assure you that after a look, you'll be sorely tempted. That is, if you don't mind sharing the lawns with a few grazing bovines and crowing chickens. Opt for the two-story cottage with an upstairs double bed and nice sitting area.

Kelapamas Homestay. Main St., Candi Dasa. P.O. Box 103, Amlapura 80801, Bali. ☎ and fax **363-41947.** 24 units. Rp60,000–Rp200,000 double (with A/C and bathtub). Rates include breakfast.

Thatched and bamboo cottages of varying sturdiness and comfort are arranged around well-maintained, grassy grounds. Expat artists on a small trust fund make this their home away from home. Prices go up with A/C and proximity to the ocean, but the ones directly facing the beach (which has a sheltered place for swimming) are probably worth the price increase. Unlike other homestays, they offer such amenities as a small restaurant, massage (Rp30,000 per hour), motorbike rental, and tour and snorkeling arrangements.

DINING

Kubu Bali. Kubu Bali Hotel. Reservations not required. Main courses Rp12,500–Rp35,000 (prawns higher). MC, V. Daily 9am–10pm. INDONESIAN/SEAFOOD.

This is possibly the nicest looking restaurant in town, with pavilions bedecked with elaborate chandeliers, arranged among ponds, and set with large marble tables. The big open kitchen (which helps ease fears about food sanitation) is at the entrance. It churns out a large menu, heavy on fish prepared all ways. You are better off having dessert at TJ's, however.

Lotus Seaview. Candi Dasa Beach. ☎ **363-41257.** Main courses Rp13,000–Rp33,000. AE, MC, V. Daily 8am–10pm. INDONESIAN/SEAFOOD.

Located at the nominal entrance to Candi Dasa, but a small walk from the center of things (take advantage of their free shuttle service), this branch of the Lotus restaurants offers slightly more interesting variations on the local fare—in other words, everything isn't deep fried. Choices include pastas, dishes "for meat lovers," or satay grilled on your table. The ocean setting, under Balinese pavilions, is utterly swell. Try the grilled fish satay, or the *udang goreng,* sautéed shrimp with garlic, tomatoes, onions, and Balinese veggies. Or drop in after snorkeling for pineapple, banana, and papaya mixed fruit—it's nearly as sweet as an ice cream shake. Whatever you do, don't miss the *very* dense chocolate mousse—a barely whipped pure chocolate concoction. Happy hours include a coffee and dessert special, and they serve high tea.

Pandan Restaurant. Candi Dasa Beach. ☎ 363-41541. Main courses Rp10,000–Rp50,000. No credit cards. Daily 8am–12am. SEAFOOD.

This place is right on the beach, with sand underfoot and the sound of waves crashing in your ears. Don't be deceived by the overwhelming number of "fried" options on the menu; unless it says battered and fried, what they really mean is *stir-fried.* Grilled fresh fish, which is more expensive, comes with a garlic sauce. Usually "fresh fish" means tuna, but they do sometimes have snapper (coated in some mild chiles), which must be purchased whole but can easily feed two or more people.

TJ's. In the Watergarden Hotel, Main St., Candi Dasa. ☎ **363-41540.** Main courses Rp10,000–Rp30,000. AE, MC, V. Daily 8am–midnight. INDONESIAN.

Considered the best restaurant in Candi Dasa, with prices to match. Still, the presentation is quite nice; note that satay comes on little grills with actual glowing embers. The bar is one of the few nighttime hangouts in town, even if the atmosphere is a little less Bali and a little more Tahiti/tropical island.

You could just come for dessert; try the moist Chocolate Ecstasy Cake, with little bits of orange peel—more interesting than the Wicked Chocolate Cake.

Warung Astawa. Main St., Candi Dasa. ☎ **363-41363.** Main courses Rp6,000–Rp16,000. Daily 8am–11pm. INDONESIAN/CHINESE.

It's hard to find good breakfast places around Candi Dasa—probably because most people eat at their hotels—and many places wait until evening to bring out their dinner and buffet specials. But this little warung has won raves for its morning meal: pancakes, fruit salad, and tomato and cheese omelets all get a thumbs up. At night you can taste their spring rolls and shrimp cocktails while watching Balinese dancers.

OUTDOOR ACTIVITIES & WATER SPORTS

Water sports are the main reason for coming to Candi Dasa, with extremely healthy reefs and an array of marine life.

You can snorkel at two spots: The Blue Lagoon, at the western end of the bay, or by Padangbai (about 40 minutes by outrigger boat), which has otherworldly coral worthy of National Geographic. Due to strong currents, area diving is mainly drift diving, making these waters appropriate for more advanced divers. The rough waters around Gili Mimpang, the small island directly off the coast, may be better for divers than snorkelers, as are the small nearby islands of Gili Tepekong and Gili Biaha. Other good spots for diving are Padangbai; Amed, a bit north of Candi Dasa (which also has perhaps the best snorkeling on Bali); or Tulamben, considered one of the finest diving spots on the island. The sunken wreck of the USS *Liberty* has been offshore at Tulamben since World War II.

Snorkeling and diving trips can be arranged through your hotel, with one of several operators along the main road (a couple are listed below), or with someone you just meet on the beach (this could be the cheapest, but he may not have the right equipment.) For snorkeling, I booked through my hotel, which just used a local fisherman, but he was excellent—good equipment, plenty of safety precautions, and a strong knowledge of the area.

As for swimming, the water between the "beach" and the seawalls is shallow, but good for a dip; beyond the walls it can be too rough.

DIVE SHOPS

The following shops can arrange diving trips around Candi Dasa or anywhere else in Bali, and most dive trips include equipment rental and lunch.

Divelite. Main St. (beach side), Candi Dasa. ☎ **363-41669.**

This new diving facility seems superior to the other well-established operations, and certainly more confidence-inspiring than the street shacks. The manager is very friendly and helpful. They offer a full range of diving trips, from snorkeling to extensive excursions and diving instruction; they have low-season prices; and they host a party at the shop every day after the dive.

Maoka Dive Center. Main St., Candi Dasa. ☎ **363-41463.**

Offers a full range of diving options, from introductory dives and dive courses to trips out, which call for a minimum of two people. A 4-day program of instruction is US$265 per person.

SHOPPING

Shopping isn't much to write home about in Candi Dasa, but the absence of hard-selling touts can come as a relief. The **Asri Shop** (☎ **363-41098**), opposite the beach on the main street, is one exception, offering a cross-section of decent goods at fixed prices. There are a couple of bookstores in the area as well, including the **Candi Bookstore** on the main street, but most of what they offer is sun-faded used volumes.

CANDI DASA AFTER DARK

Candi Dasa is pretty low-key at night, probably because most people come for the water sports and need to get to bed early for the best snorkeling and diving in the morning. The main beach road, opposite from the ocean, has several little bars and restaurants, most of which offer laser disc movies as entertainment at night. A few offer a bit more, and are listed below. Nightly dance programs are offered at the **Warung Candi Agung,** Main Street (☎ 363-41157)—the price includes a buffet dinner and transport from your hotel. Tuesday through Friday at 9pm, the **Pandan Harum Stage** on Main Street offers Barong and Legong dance. Or you could just hang out with the adventurer types at **TJ's** bar, in the Watergarden Hotel.

Legenda. Main St., Candi Dasa. No phone.

Legenda calls itself a rock cafe, but it's really a reggae place, so either Bob Marley or live bands wail most evenings. It gets busier later in the evening.

Koeno Cafe. Main St., Candi Dasa.

The newest addition to Candi Dasa, Koeno Cafe takes thirsts to new levels of backwater urban chic. Pillows are strewn along the streetside banquettes, but you may want to belly up to the bar and hang out with the exuberantly friendly staff. For now, the menu is exclusively in bottles and thick fruit shakes, but Koeno's employees assured me that a menu of grills was slated to arrive in the near future.

10   Sights & Destinations near Candi Dasa

TO THE NORTH

Amed. 2 hrs. north of Candi Dasa.

The fishing village of Amed is an increasingly popular tourist destination, despite its relative inaccessibility—it's about 2 hours north of Candi Dasa, the last bit along a harsh dirt road. The snorkeling here is possibly the best in Bali. You can come here as a day trip from Candi Dasa (all the diving places offer trips), or even Ubud (it's easy to arrange land transport), but you might want to spend the night. Lodging options are limited to either losmen or the very posh **Hotel Indra Udhyana,** just outside of town. The latter offers luxurious bungalows (around US$160 for a double) with balconies or verandas, air-conditioning, TV, and telephones. I've heard even Princess Diana was a guest here. The hotel is at Amed Beach, Bunutan, P.O. Box 119, Jalan Katrangan no. 22, Karangasem 80852, Bali. The phone number is ☎ 361-241107; fax 361-234903; www.indo.com/hotels/indra-udhyana; e-mail: hiuamed@ indosat. net.id.

Tenganan. 8km (5 miles) north of Candi Dasa.

An original Bali Aga village, Tenganan is lauded as a well-preserved slice of Bali village life, with everything here much as it has been for centuries. In reality, once tourists started to come and villagers figured out what a cash cow they had on their hands, the place became uncomfortably like a theme park—call it Bali Land. Sure, cottages line the quaint, car-less cobblestone streets, and traditions are still adhered to with a strictness found nowhere else on the island. And yes, this is the only place in Indonesia where they still make double ikat cloth. But you have to pay an enforced "donation" to enter, and it doesn't help that you are treated like a giant walking wallet, as stall after stall tries to attract you to identical wares. And how can the uninformed know if they are buying genuine, good quality ikat cloth anyway?

Tirtha Gangga Royal Bathing Pools. 20km (12.4 miles) north of Candi Dasa. Admission Rp3,000. Daily during daylight hours.

This Water Palace was built in 1947 by the last raja of the region, and was obviously sited with views of Gunung Agung and the Lombok Strait in mind. It was partly demolished by both earthquake and volcanic eruption, which means that much of what you see is a modern restoration of something that wasn't that old to begin with. Still, the restoration was a good one, and if you like water as much as the raja did, you will enjoy the many fountains, water-spitting stone figures, and pools of this serene, parklike place. Be sure to bring your bathing suit; you can swim here for a small fee. At least one of the pools is well-maintained and on a hot day, you will regret not taking advantage of its cool waters. There is also a homestay on the premises.

BETWEEN CANDI DASA & UBUD

Goa Lowah/Bat Cave. 10km (6.2 miles) east of Klungkung. Admission Rp3,000. Daily during daylight hours.

A pretty little temple, a big snake, and bats—lots of bats. Some complain about the smell and mess (bats are an untidy bunch of flying rodents), but others (myself among them) find the scene too surreal and fascinating to care. It's like something right out of *The Jungle Book,* with the large python coiled around that ancient-appearing throne, just waiting for his next, easy meal, and countless squeaking bats hanging from the ceiling. The cave is said to be the mouth of a tunnel that reaches all the way to Gunung Agung and Besakih. Watch out for touts at the entrance offering you "free" necklaces; they will demand money for them when you leave.

Klungkung. 26km (16 miles) southeast of Ubud.

More or less on the road to Candi Dasa from Ubud, Klungkung was the seat of the local raja until the last one died in 1965. It's a rather interesting, almost colonial-looking town, worth poking around a bit. Note the shops more or less across and catty corner from the parking lot across from the palace, where you can you can get gorgeous, elaborate, real temple wear—as opposed to what you would normally buy in tourist areas.

Taman Gili. In Klungkung. Admission Rp3,000. Daily during daylight hours.

The Taman Gili gardens contain the only remnants of the Semara Pura Royal Palace, and are referred to as the palace by guides. Very little remains of the palace, which was mostly destroyed by fighting in 1908, but two main buildings are set in the relaxing gardens. The **Kerta Gosa** is an open-air pavilion, once the Hall of Justice, notable for its famous painted ceiling, a nine-level mural showing scenes and characters featured in wayang puppet theater. The murals have been restored many times, and nothing remains of the original. Still, they are interesting and virtually unique. The paintings show all sorts of punishments in store for the wicked, and probably made the accused brought here for trial tremble. The **Bale Kambung,** a floating pavilion entirely surrounded by a moat, was reserved for tooth-filing ceremonies. Its ceiling, also gaily and elaborately painted, illustrates Balinese astronomy and folk tales. There is a museum on the property that lacks any explanatory aids, but within its virtual junk shop hodgepodge display are some fascinating items, including relics and photos of the royal family. Don't overlook (as if you could) that photo-op brick and stone gateway to the right of the Bale Kambung.

BETWEEN CANDI DASA & LOVINA

Gunung Batur and Lake Batur. 62km (38.4 miles) north of Ubud.

Gunung Batur is the most sacred mountain in Bali after Gunung Agung. It's a beautiful sight thanks to the volcanic lake near its peak (the biggest in Bali), and the smoke that still pours from it. You can see lava tracks streaking down its side and villages built on or near them—an act of great faith, considering that its last eruption was in 1926 (surely it must be feeling due again?). You can hike Batur more easily than Agung, even without a guide, though having one can be handy.

The best place to view Lake Batur and the volcano is from **Penelokan,** a village on the lake crater rim, whose name means "Place to Look." It's a heck of a view, provided the weather cooperates (clouds are not conducive to vistas). You can improve your odds by arriving early in the morning.

That this is a scenic tourist spot has not been lost on the locals, and some of the most aggressive touts on the island will be here waiting for you. The word "no" is like a dog whistle; they can't hear it. Their phenomenally irritating and incredible persistence, and the small fee you have to pay even to enter Penelokan (around Rp3,000 per person) may make this a hassle you might want to avoid—if you thought you could avoid touts *anywhere on the island.* Then again, it's a beautiful volcanic crater—sure you want to miss it? (There is actually an alternative; see Pura Ulun Danu Batur review, below.)

Pura Ulun Danu Batur. 4km (2.48 miles) north of Penelokan.

This is the second most important temple in Bali after Besakih, and in my opinion, far more striking. As a bonus, it rests on the lip of the lake crater, so you have a peaceful way to get much of that fabulous view without the touts, who aren't permitted inside. (Though not only do you have to run a gauntlet of them to enter, lately they've set up camp between the temple and the rim and do try to call to you and get your attention.)

There are quite a few shrines within the temple complex (300 are ultimately planned), which is dedicated to the goddess of the crater lake, but the one that stands out is the 11-roofed meru (a pagoda-style shrine) in the inner courtyard.

Lake Bratan and Pura Ulun Danu Bratan. 48km (30 miles) north of Denpasar. Admission Rp3,000. Daily during daylight hours.

This is a beautiful lake set in a long-defunct volcanic crater whose serenity seems impossible to shatter—that is, unless you are here during tourist season, when the water is full of buzzing boats and the like. It's directly on the way to Lovina, and so worth stopping to look at, certainly for the temple, Pura Ulun Danu Batur. Dedicated to the water goddess, and an important directional temple, it's the one that shows up in all the guidebook photographs, with its meru set beautifully against a backdrop of water, almost appearing to float there. Truth be told, it photographs somewhat better than it looks in person, so photo op buffs will be the happiest for coming here. But anyone will be pleased with the pretty manicured grounds, not quite so cluttered with tourists as you might think, with a multi-level shrine to Buddha.

11 Lovina

Somewhat removed from the pulse of the island, Lovina attracts those looking to truly "get away from it all." Its real draw though, are the dolphins that frolic off shore every morning, making the swimming and snorkeling here even more wondrous than if you were just communing with the other pretty marine life. It's also the logical jumping-off point for diving trips along the northern part of the island, including the magical Menjangan island, part of the Bali Barat National Park. There'll be a price to pay beyond the monetary one, though. It's a hike over dizzy mountain roads. This inaccessibility keeps tourism down to a pitch low enough to cause a disturbing level of aggressiveness in the locals, whose relentless hovering prevents you from a truly relaxing day on the area's black sand beaches. Don't expect a tourist infrastructure equal to that of the southern part of the island; we're basically talking about a sparse stretch of six small villages that blend together in a row along the ocean (Pemaron, Tukadmungga, Anturan, Kalibukbuk, Kaliasem, and Temukus; Kalibukbuk is where the main action is). But since you will be doubtless staying feet from the ocean, viewing the gorgeous sunset just means stepping right outside your room.

GETTING AROUND

The main road (that's what it's called) runs parallel to the coast, with two tiny (and easily missed) side streets coming off it, in Kalibukbuk, to the ocean. **Jalan Bina Ria** is the western street and **Ketapang** is the eastern one. Most losmen and restaurants are found on these streets and alleys coming off them, with a few more less interesting ones along the main road. If you are staying right here, walking is not a problem (though as mentioned, walking along the beach can be a hassle), and motorbikes can be rented. Many of the hotels farther out have **shuttles** to this main area, but it's easy to grab any **bemo** that zips up and down along the main road. Just be sure you know where you want to be let off—they often don't speak much English.

Fast Facts: Lovina

Banks/Currency Exchange Money changers are along the main road (as are some banks), and the Jalan Bina Ria.

Internet/E-mail Spice Cyber (☎ 362-41509), located in Spice Dive, a dive shop on Jalan Bina Ria, offers e-mail and fax service from 10am to 9pm daily for Rp30,000 per hour.

Post Office/Mail There is no post office proper, but there are agents on the main road (or just hand your envelopes to your hotel to mail for you).

Telephone Find one on the main road west of Jalan Bina Ria. The area code for Lovina is 362.

ACCOMMODATIONS

With two exceptions, the level of accommodations in Lovina are basic; for the most part, the luxury hotels have not yet invaded here. All properties are on the beach unless otherwise noted, though none have truly private beaches—leaving the hotel grounds for the sand means being suddenly surrounded by a swarm of touts who don't care that you've already booked a dolphin watching or snorkeling trip. (For some reason, these folks largely disappear near sunset, so a walk to and from town then is most enjoyable.)

VERY EXPENSIVE

✪ **Damai Lovina Hotel.** Jalan Damai, Kayuputih Lovina, Singaraja, Bali. ☎ **45-331-48034** reservations from North America and Europe, or 362-41008. Fax 362-41009. www.damai. com. 8 units. A/C MINIBAR TEL. US$160–US$185 double. Rates include breakfast. MC, V. Free parking.

The motto of this hotel is "hard to find, hard to leave," and I can solemnly assure you that this is correct. Located way up the hill overlooking Lovina, what you lose in beach access, you gain in some of the finest accommodations in Bali. It's a nearly perfect little jewel of a place, the brainchild of a Danish expat. Rooms are all villas, and they are all utterly beautiful, with gorgeous teak furniture, Balinese fabric on the furnishings, many windows, and a four-poster canopy bed draped with cheese cloth. More carved wood leads to the dressing areas and bathrooms, which have green stone outdoor showers, wood sinks and vanities, and amenities in glass bottles. Deluxe villas have a bigger bath and an outdoor Jacuzzi spa tub, and a sitting area with a low-set table with a sunken area for your feet. Some rooms have an ocean view. The grounds overlook a panorama of green hills and gorge and blue ocean—a spectacular view no matter where you look—with a small, lovely pool that seems to spill into the surroundings. For those worried about being so far (15 to 20 minutes) from the ocean, there's a free shuttle to the beach all day long. It's virtually the comfort and style of an Amandari at a fraction of the cost. See the review below of the terrific Damai Restaurant, but note it's very expensive at night unless you have meals built into your room rates, so plan to go into Lovina for dinner most evenings (or stock your fridge with snacks). Guests are also invited to partake in Damai's 1- or 2-day cooking courses, which include instruction on Balinese basics, a morning market tour, and a tour of the hotel's organic farm.

EXPENSIVE

Mas Lovina Cottages. Jalan Raya Lovina, Kalibukbuk, Bali. ☎ **362-41237.** Fax 362-41236. E-mail: maslovina@bali-paradise.com. 20 units. A/C MINIBAR TV. US$80 double; US$150 2-bedroom family cottage. AE, JCB, MC, V.

These "cottages" are actually two-story cabinlike structures, with two bedrooms that share a living room and kitchen area. The space is wonderful, and the bathrooms are big, with tubs, and nicely tiled, but the furniture is shabby and uncomfortable. It's nothing a good face-lift wouldn't fix, but at these prices it's probably not worth it except for families. Each half of the cottage (bedroom plus living room or kitchen, a rarity in Bali) can be rented separately, or you can take the entire structure. The pool is by far the largest in Lovina, and it's virtually right on the beach (though touts tend to hang over the walls, trying to get your attention). The same company owns the **Hotel Bali Danau Buyan,** at nearby Lake Buyan (Jalan Raya Bedugul, Pancasari, ☎ 362-21351), and it's basically the same layout and rates, but the location on a mountain overlooking the lake provides a different, rather peaceful experience you might want to look into for a night.

✪ **Puri Bagus Lovina.** P.O. Box 225, Lovina, Singaraja, Bali. ☎ **362-21430.** Fax 362-22627. www. puri-bagus.com/index_lovina.htm. E-mail: pblovina@denpasar.wasantara.net.id. 40 units. A/C MINIBAR TV TEL. US$125–US$150 double; US$350 suite. AE, DC, JCB, MC, V. Free parking.

If you want luxury (or close to it) accommodations, without the isolation and lack of beach access that comes with the Damai, here is your other option. This is a splendid place (better than their property in Candi Dasa), decidedly high-end (but more afford-able than comparable Bali beach resorts), and imaginative without being funky like most Lovina hotels. Rooms, all in villas, are simple but elegant and comfortable, dec-orated with bits of Bali fabric and paintings. Prices vary according to the view (rice paddy, garden, or ocean), but they all have high thatched ceilings with glass at the top to keep the air in and the bugs out. Large bathrooms come with both indoor and out-door showers, and there are big verandas, some of which look right out to the sea. Suites will get you a private pool, CD player, and a basic tub, and some have kitchens. The landscaped grounds go right to the seawall (there is no beach but there are steps into the water), with several small cushioned *bales* overlooking the blue Java sea. A pretty blue amorphous pool also peers out at the ocean (sometimes you share the water with the hotel's four ducks). Facilities and services include water sports, bicycles, sight-seeing excursions, free shuttle to Lovina, 24-hour room service, car rental, sundries shop, boutique, laundry, safety deposit boxes, and massage. For dining, there's a small seafood restaurant with outdoor kitchen, and a second restaurant that serves Balinese items. There is a poolside bar. Occasional evening entertainment is offered.

MODERATE

Hotel Aneka Lovina. Jalan Rayan Lovina, Singaraja, Bali. ☎ **362-41121** or 362-41122. Fax 362-41827. www.aneka-hotels.com/anekalovina.htm. 59 units. A/C MINIBAR TV TEL. US$50–US$70 double. AE, MC, V. Free parking.

This is a typical mid-range Lovina Beach accommodation—not bad at all, just not all that memorable. Rooms here are in thatched cottages set in pretty Bali garden grounds (complete with a dolphin fountain). Standard rooms are boring, with tiny basic bath-rooms, but second-story rooms offer nice views of green and thatch. Deluxe rooms are bigger, with carved wooden doors that lead to slightly less disappointing interiors—bamboo furniture, and bigger bathrooms, some with tubs. For size and less oppressive decor, these are a better deal. The small pool has a swim-up bar, and the waterfall-flanked stage offers occasional nighttime entertainment. There's one seafood restaurant and one offering the usual assortment of Indonesian and European fare. A pool bar and bars inside both restaurants occasionally provide nighttime entertainment.

INEXPENSIVE

Aditya Beach Bungalows. P.O. Box 134, Singaraja 81101, Bali. ☎ **362-41059.** Fax 362-41342. www.indo.com/hotels/aditya/. 42 units. US$25–US$45 double. Rates include breakfast. AE, MC, V. Free parking.

This big property looks impressive from a distance (you can see it when out on the water snorkeling or dolphin watching), but it's really just an adequate budget choice. High-end rooms are big, clean, thatched and oceanfront, with slightly shabby furniture and slightly smelly bathrooms (sinks are actually in the rooms). They do have air-conditioning and televisions. Oddly, the cheaper standard rooms in a two-story concrete block are somewhat nicer, with Bali fabric and less grim bathrooms. Skip the low-end, fan-only US$25 standard, which is very old. The swimming pool is nothing special, despite some spitting fountains. There's a restaurant that serves Indonesian, European, and Chinese food. The bar serves "many kind drinks with qualified bartender."

✪ **Rambutan Beach Cottages.** P.O. Box 195, Singaraja, Bali. ☎ **362-41388.** Fax 362-41057. www.indo.com/hotels/rambutan/. E-mail: Rambutan@indo.com. 33 units. US$15–US$55 double; US$85–US$180 villa. Discounts for Internet bookings. Rates include taxes and breakfast. JCB, MC, V. Free parking.

By far the best budget option in Lovina. All rooms are in two-story red and white bungalows that are set among the prettiest tropical garden around. Budget rooms (US$15) are better than others in this price range, but better still are standards and superiors, with hot water and TVs (and A/C in superiors) and plenty of very nice Indonesian carved wood furniture and Bali fabrics. The rooms are big and bright, with funky-tiled, slightly shabby bathrooms. The three villas get you the luxury of the southern part of the island at half price. These are furnished with classic teak furniture, A/C, TV, VCD, and minibar, and you even get your own private garden and gazebo. The pool looks like a small blue pond. There is a small children's area and a slightly run-down badminton court. The staff is friendly (and can arrange water sports and tours) and speaks decent English, and it's just a short walk to the beach.

LOSMEN

Angsoka. Jalan Bina Ria, Lovina Beach, Bali. ☎ **362-41841.** Fax 362-41023. 38 units. Rp50,000–Rp150,000 double. Rates include breakfast. No credit cards.

A friendly place, with very clean and comfortable losmen-style rooms. As the price goes up, so does the amount of space and the quality of the bathrooms, and you gain fans, showers, tubs and, finally, A/C. At these prices, spring for the latter. Some rooms are in small bungalows (which curiously have inferior bathrooms), and some come with high bamboo ceilings. There are a small pool and a tiny temple on the grounds.

Astina Seaside Cottages. P.O. Box 141, Singaraja, Bali. Lovina Beach (500m from main road), Kalibukbuk. ☎ **362-41187.** 16 units. Rp50,000–Rp80,000 double. Rates include breakfast. No credit cards.

A friendly losmen with all rooms in cottages or bungalows. The more you pay, the more you get: private baths, ceiling fans, even a welcome drink and fruit basket! The paint is chipped, but they do have carved wood beds. Cold water only.

Bayu Kartika Beach Bungalows. Jalan Ketapang, Kalibukbuk, Lovina Beach. ☎ **362-41055.** Fax 362-41219. 24 units. Rp105,000–Rp255,000 double. Rates include taxes and breakfast. No credit cards.

This is a very popular place—travelers you would expect to find at higher-end locations proclaimed great satisfaction with these accommodations. Rooms are all duplex bungalows (some with garden baths), sprawled out in a large garden setting with ponds, a fountain, and a swimming pool. As room prices go higher, you gain A/C and hot water. The location, adjacent to the beach, can't be beat. Phones and TV may also be added to some rooms. There's a small restaurant and bar overlooking the beach.

DINING

With perhaps one exception, dining in Lovina is a pretty dull proposition. Most of the options, outside of hotels, are on the main street or on Jalan Bina Ria, which runs perpendicular from it to the beach. Wander the latter and pick a restaurant at random—it will be okay, but probably nothing special. (They do often offer dance programs and competing buffets spilling over with food.)

Arya's @ Planet Lovina. On the main road. ☎ **362-41797.** Main courses Rp6,500–Rp18,500. No credit cards. Daily 8:30am–11pm. INDONESIAN.

The former Arya's, whose new name now spoofs Planet Hollywood, used to serve the best desserts in Lovina. Alas, these (including apple crumble, brownies, and "Fruity Planet Surprise") have gone downhill, and the rest of the menu features merely adequate food (admittedly, in a pleasant enough atmosphere). It does have lots of cocktails, dessert coffee, and dubiously "healthy" drinks (orange, spinach, and ginger with milk, egg and honey—all in one glass).

✪ **Damai Restaurant.** Jalan Damai (in Hotel Damai), Kayuputih, Lovina. ☎ **362-41008.** Reservations recommended. Lunch main courses Rp62,000–Rp88,000; dinner set menu Rp396,000. AE, MC, V. Daily 11am–3pm and 7–10pm. NOUVELLE INDONESIAN.

Apparently, the proprietor of the Damai is a foodie, having imported his own gourmet chef, Per Thoestesen, whose claim to greatness extends from the kitchens of the French legend Paul Bocuse to guest appearances on Danish television. If you aren't staying here, do make the trip up the mountain. Skip the expensive (outrageously so by Bali standards) set dinner menu (you can't see the marvelous ocean/mountain view at night anyway), and come up for lunch. You will pay more than you would for an average Bali meal, but the same perfect, world-class meal back in the U.S. would cost at least four times as much. The menu is limited (perhaps only four entree choices, and two appetizers), but more than sufficient, given its emphasis on freshness—the hotel's organic farm provides 80% of the kitchen's fresh produce. Melt-in-the-mouth panfried fish was topped with a heavenly creamy dill sauce. Fried chicken is really also panfried, served with a spicy ginger sauce. Chicken sate was more Chinese in flavor than Balinese. The presentation was modern, simple, and elegant, with small portions, but the contents were rich, so the amounts proved just right. And if you really wish to spend more money, the many expensive bottles of wine can bring your bill up to staggering heights.

Surya Restaurant & Bar. Main St., Kalibukbuk. Main courses Rp6,500–Rp18,000. No credit cards. Daily 8am–10pm. INDONESIAN/SEAFOOD.

Surya is a popular and reliable local restaurant, well situated on the main drag, that serves everything a hungry traveler could want—brunch, seafood, local specialties, pizza, and a happy hour with a range of booze and mixed drinks.

Warung Kopi Bali. Jalan Binara, Singaraja. ☎ **362-41361.** Main courses Rp6,500–Rp20,900. No credit cards. Daily 8am–11pm. INDONESIAN/SEAFOOD.

Probably a bit better than the other tourist-oriented restaurants along the Jalan Bina Ria. They serve garlicky seafood kabobs, the notable flavors of *pepes isi laut* (marinated shrimp, tuna, and veggies made with Balinese sauce all grilled together in a banana leaf), and the big, good value seafood basket that combines more garlicky tuna, sweet-and-sour shrimp, deep-fried squid, fries, and rather nice vegetables. As at other places, you get a free shot and some tepid garlic bread at happy hour.

Warung Made Cafe. Jalan Main St. (right next to Aditya Hotel). ☎ **362-41239.** Main courses Rp6,500–Rp16,500. No credit cards. Daily 8am–11pm. Indonesian.

A bit noisy because it's on the busy main street, but a nice menu of Bali, veggie (including several good salads), and seafood items. It's also an "ice cream parlor" as envisioned by Jimmy Buffet, offering concoctions with various flavors, sauces, and whipped cream. In addition to the usual suspects, try a papaya or avocado shake or a "Lovina Sunset" sundae. Don't ask what they all contain—the friendly staff speaks minimal English and can't really tell you. Continue to cool yourself down with their many sweet and lethal tropical cocktails (fruit juice and Bali brews figure heavily). A bulletin board has much info of interest to a traveler, and at night there is live music or "bring your own tape or CD."

OUTDOOR ACTIVITIES & WATER SPORTS

The crystal-clear water, which is often as calm as glass, makes for some very fine **swimming**—though the dark sand can cloud the first several feet or even yards. But persist; not too far out you can actually **snorkel** without a guide, as coral begins rather close to shore. There aren't that many fish this close, but look for the cobalt blue starfish. There's better snorkeling on the reefs a few hundred yards away, but you'll need a guide with a boat. These reefs have been badly damaged over the years, but there are still a great variety of psychedelic fish, sometimes in impressive numbers. Be sure your guide brings some bread so you can feed the fish; being at the center of a cloud of tropical fish, all nibbling at your fingers, is a thrill. The reefs aren't significant enough for experienced divers, most of whom go to the premiere dive site in Bali, **Menjangan Island** (see "Sights near Lovina," below) to the west, or **Amed** and **Tulamben** to the east. Trips can be booked through dive shops in town. Snorkeling can be booked by just about any hotel or losmen, but frankly, many of the lesser-end hotels just flag someone down on the beach. You could do that on your own and get the same person for less money. The disadvantage is that these guys may not have very good, or enough, equipment; a dive shop should be able to guarantee better standards.

Finally, there is **dolphin watching,** for which Lovina is famous and for which I have mixed feelings. At about 5:30am every morning, dozens of boats go out full of tourists, to sit offshore and wait for the morning dolphin-feeding migration. This can involve a pretty long wait, which most of the time is rewarded by at least a few, and perhaps dozens of leaping dolphins. The way the boats chase the creatures so that their customers can get a good look is uncomfortably reminiscent of the touts on the beach chasing down hapless tourists. It's hard to say how the dolphins feel—they come back every morning, after all—but still. That said, I can also say that the moment your boat is surrounded by leaping, laughing Flippers may well be one of your grandest in Bali. Dolphin watching can be arranged by any hotel, or you can go flag down the same guy on the beach who took you snorkeling.

DIVE SHOPS

Spice Dive, Jalan Rina Bia (☎ **362-41509;** www.damai.com/spicedive/), is a five-star PADI dive center, offering a full range of diving facilities and excursions, as well as Internet service. **Baruna,** Main Road, Kalibukbuk (☎ **362-23775**), offers snorkeling and dolphin watching.

SIGHTS NEAR LOVINA

All of these require transport, either your own (motorbike or car) or something you've arranged with a transport guide. Most hotels will also book day excursions.

Gitgit Waterfall. 11km (6.8 miles) south of Singaraja. Admission Rp3,000. Daily during daylight hours.

If you take the mountain roads through Bedugal and past Lakes Bratan, Buyan, and Tambingan, you will pass by Gitgit waterfall on your way to Lovina. Park on one side of the street (whatever you do, don't eat at the restaurant there with its ghastly buffet), cross the road, pay the entrance fee, and make your lengthy way down a twisty concrete path and stairs. Once past the many stalls, you'll come across a small temple and a thrilling 45-meter (148-ft.) freefalling waterfall. Cool off in the pool at its base, and admire the considerable jungle foliage before making the hot climb back up.

Brahma Vihara Asrama Buddhist Monastery. 10km (6.2 miles) southwest of Lovina.

Built in 1970, this is the only Buddhist monastery in Bali. It attracts regular pilgrims (including, once, the Dalai Lama). It was severely damaged in the 1976 earthquake, but has been completely restored. It's brightly colored, with a fine gold Buddha statue, but truth be told, Zen students will find it of the most interest, while everyone else will only note how different the architecture is from Hindu temples.

Air Panas Hot Springs. 6km (3.7 miles) east of Lovina, or 1km from the monastery—turn left at the crossroads as you go downhill, then left at the next major crossroads, and from there follow the signs. Admission Rp3,000. Daily 8am–6pm.

These are some of the nicest and best-maintained hot springs on the island and generally not very crowded. Be sure to cover yourself with a sarong when not bathing, conveniently available at the above-average aggressive touts before the entrance.

✪ **Pura Bejai.** About 8km (5 miles) east of Singaraja, 200m (656 ft.) up a small road to the north.

This small temple barely rates a mention in most guidebooks, but it's one of my all-time favorites, because of its unusual look. Festooned with a riot of carvings— demons, gods, monsters, animals, you name it—it gives you a good idea of how different the temples of the north are from the cookie-cutter ones of the south.

Pura Dalem Jagaraga. Main road above, 400m (1,312 ft.) past the turning for Pura Bejai, 4km (2.48 miles) down.

About 1 kilometer to the north of the town of Jagaraga (where the Balinese fought a great battle against the Dutch in 1848) is a temple covered in editorializing comic strip–type panel carvings that show how simple village pursuits like kite flying and fishing were corrupted by the arrival of the Dutch. The favorite photo-op is on the right hand side: two Dutch men driving a Model T, being held up by a Balinese Clyde Barker.

✪ **Pura Meduwe Karang at Kubutambahan.** 12km (7.4 miles) east of Singarajah.

More extraordinary and unusual carvings characterize one of the largest temples in the north: figures from the *Ramayana,* soft porn, monkeys, village life, and most famously, a shorts-wearing bicyclist about to turn a dog-chased rat into roadkill. Folklore has it this is Dutch artist WOJ Nieuwenkamp.

✪ **Air Saneh.** 6km (3.7 miles) from Kubutambahan. Admission Rp3,000. Daily 7am–7pm.

This is a freezing-cold—oh, isn't that nice?—freshwater springs in a rock-lined natural swimming pool, set in pleasing gardens that overlook the sea. It's just enough off the beaten path so that it's often uncrowded (with the possible exception of school holidays and package tour days; weekdays seem best)—a delicious little secret I am blowing here. Don't be shy; bring your bathing suit and jump in. There are clean changing rooms.

Menjangan Island. 1½ miles off the northwest coast.

Part of the Bali Barat National Park, and itself declared a national marine reserve, Menjangan Island is graced with the most beautiful coral reef in all of Bali. And since it's anything but convenient to get to—it's over an hour by boat from Lovina and much longer through the park road—it's remained blissfully underappreciated. Expect glassy waters alive with bannerfish, sunfish, hawksbill turtles, gorgons, clownfish, and further down, reef sharks, all of which will find you a most interesting intruder.

A recent addition to this quiet island is the Waka Shorea, one of several luxury resorts in the Waka stable and the only resort permitted in all of the national park. They met the challenge admirably, with an eco-conscious property of thatched chalets and villas designed to exist in harmony with the landscape. The bush hogs seem to approve, wandering undeterred into your front yard. For information on the resort, contact the Waka Shorea at ☎ **361-484085;** fax 361-484767; www.wakaexperience. com; e-mail: sales@wakaexperience.com (US$157 bungalow; US$218 villa).

Several dive shops in Lovina offer dive-boat trips to Menjangan Island; day trips with Spice Dive (☎ **362-41509**) cost US$50. You can also hole at the boutique Mimpi Resort Menjangana, opposite the island, on the mainland and on the fringes of the park (☎ **82-8362729;** fax 82-8362728; www.mimpi.com). It's got a PADI dive center, spa facilities, and a thermal spring on the grounds (US$90–US$325 rooms and villas).

12 Lombok

People talk about Lombok being what Bali was more than 20 years ago, but Lombok is more than just an escape from tourist buildup that sees more annual visitors on the island than Balinese. It's a flight *to* the rugged landscapes of an as yet unspoiled slice of rural Indonesia. Geographically, the two islands are separated by the Wallace Line, a deep trench that marks the meeting point of the Asian and Australian tectonic plates. In fact, the more easterly you travel on the island of Lombok, the drier and scrubbier the brush becomes, and the more likely you are to encounter bird species endemic to Australia. No elephants or rhinos here.

Lombok is significantly drier than Bali, especially in the south, where millions of years of volcanic runoff have mellowed into a vast expanse of gently rolling hills that fans out from the island's lone looming volcano, **Gunung Rinjani.** Arriving perpendicular to the southern coastline, these hills culminate in spectacular, rocky shores and half-moon bays with brilliant white sands. It's less fertile than Bali and has thus been a poorer relation since long before Westerners sailed these waters.

But it's not only geology that sets Lombok apart from its more illustrious neighbor. The people of Lombok are predominantly Islamic rather than Hindu (although most of the people in tourism are Hindu), though as in Bali, ancient animist beliefs still color the practice of religion, influenced by indigenous elements left over from the ancient Sasak people. Except for a rare staging of the **Gendang war dance,** these elements are not as evident as in Bali—no endless parade of temple processions or sidewalks strewn with offerings, no ever-present ceremony and music. As such, potential developers talk about the island's culture as being "unsuitable" for tourist consumption because officials haven't yet figured out a way to package it for a tourist audience.

Beach Etiquette

Part of the reason to visit Lombok is the clear aqua water and the fine white sand of the beaches, many of which you can have all to yourself. But please note that while these bits of paradise tend to make you dress—or rather, undress—like Adam and Eve before the fall, remember that this is a Moslem island, and you should cover up once you are off the sand—and maybe even on it. Even if some locals are used to nearly naked tourists, that doesn't mean it's the polite thing to do. I'm not suggesting entire *djellabahs* or the like (locals don't even wear them), nor does this apply to when you are on your hotel grounds. Just demonstrate a little local courtesy and keep your top on while sunbathing, and cover up that cute bikini when you leave the beach.

Most likely these developers either misunderstand or underestimate their potential audience. Those who venture to Lombok are looking for something slightly more rugged and a little less manufactured, and the island is still in a position to oblige. Visitors are primarily drawn by the unspoiled beaches and the **snorkeling and diving** off the shores of Lombok and the nearby **Gili Islands.** The truly intrepid challenge the peak of **Mt. Rinjani.** But admittedly, few know about the stunning day treks around the volcano, or are aware of the other natural and cultural attractions Lombok has to offer: the **monkey forest** at Pusuk; the **waterfalls** of Senaru and Mayung Putik; and the northern village of **Bayan,** home to the oldest mosque on the island, and the first place in Islam to celebrate Mohammad's birthday. The parade of daily life is no less fascinating, with carts drawn by small ponies (the most common mode of transportation on the island) or communal trucks loaded with perhaps 20 people going to or from town and market. **Hindu temples and water gardens** offer quite pleasant sightseeing prospects, while the food (the name Lombok means chile pepper, so Sasak cooking has a kick) is every bit as rewarding as Balinese warung fare. **Crafts** are also a big attraction and the island's inhabitants are known for an their artistry in everything from decorative items (the gecko is big over here); pottery (OK, not very practical); baskets; wonderfully utilitarian platters, bowls and jars made of bamboo, wood, reeds, shells and ceramics; and woven textiles: colorfully intricate ikat throws and brilliant songket sarongs woven with threads of gold. A visit to the many villages specializing in these crafts will be a highlight of your trip, and many producers are eager to show visitors how their wares are made.

There is one drawback, however, evident the moment you land on solid ground. The locals are desperate—potential guides, masseuses, porters, drivers, boatmen, watch salesmen, earring vendors, and toenail-painters swarm like flies, and it almost never lets up. It's enough to make you fearful of leaving your hotel. The solution is a painless and inexpensive one: buy a ring (about $2); wallow in a massage (US$1.50); give your shoulder a break (US$0.10); and have a beachfront pedicure ($1)—all for less than you'll spend at the airport newsstand. The transformation will be sudden; with the pressures of a sale out of the way, the locals relax and display an uncanny level of kindness, warmth, and good nature.

GETTING THERE

There are three ways to get to Lombok—by ferry, by hydrofoil, and by plane. If time is an issue, the latter is not necessarily your best choice. Although it's actually cheaper than the hydrofoil, the risk of getting stuck at the airport may not outweigh that ferry

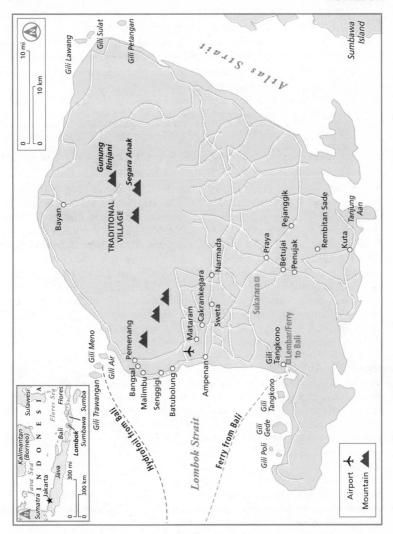

ride. If pressed for time, you can risk a day trip by plane or grab a package day tour designed around a typical tourist agenda (a little shopping, a little beachgoing), available by hydrofoil. But if your goal is island exploration, particularly searching out those private white-sand beaches, 1 day is not enough.

Any travel office on Bali can book your Lombok trip (try the always reliable **Parama**). They can arrange bus transfer packages too, so inquire about this if your hotel does not offer shuttle service at the harbor (most do at the airport).

BY FERRY The ferry (☎ **361-721212**) leaves Padang Bai (just south of Candi Dasa) twice a day, arriving about 4 hours (Rp15,000/US$1.66) later at Lempar.

BY HYDROFOIL Bounty Cruises is your best bet, making the trip daily from Benoa Harbor (just north of Nusa Dua, ☎ **361-7333333**), Bali at 9am and stopping, literally, on Senggigi Beach and the Gili Islands (2½ hr.; US$35). The Mabua Express

Travel Tip

Getting on and off transportation means you will be swarmed by locals insisting on carrying your bags. Some have the audacity to withhold your luggage unless you agree to pay them sometimes unreasonable sums. If at all possible, carry a bag with a shoulder strap, or be unfaltering in your refusal.

If that doesn't work, agree on a price before moving on (Rp1,000 or Rp2,000 per bag should be fine, unless you want to give more).

(☎ **361-721212**) departs from Benoa and arrives in Lempar about 2 hours later (US$25 to US$30). Always check to confirm departure times!

BY PLANE   Merpati (☎ **361-263918** or 361-751374; www.merpati.co.id) and **Garuda National** (☎ **361-227825,** 361-772231, or 361-751179; www.garuda-indonesia.com/) fly several times daily to Lombok's **Selaparang Airport** (20 min.; approximately US$30) from Bali and Jakarta respectively. (Other airlines flying into Lombok include the new **Air Mark** and the frequently insolvent **Bouraq.**) **Silkair** (☎ **370-628254;** fax 370-628292), the regional wing of Singapore Airlines (www.silkair.net/), flies from Singapore daily. If you're planning on a quick hop over from Bali, note that frequent delays can turn a 20-minute flight into an infuriating several-hour ordeal, stranding you at the airport—this makes a relaxing 2½-hour boat ride seem all the more attractive, doesn't it? Flights are also sometimes consolidated and/or canceled, so if you are making a day trip, you should double-check that your flight back is still running.

GETTING AROUND

You have two choices of public transportation: **bemos** and **horse-drawn carts.** Given those options, even though traffic is nearly as chaotic as on Bali (and those horse-drawn carts just add to the mayhem), you might be better off **renting a car,** especially if you want to go exploring by yourself instead of on a hotel's planned day-tour. Your hotel can set you up with a rental, or you can get one at the airport when you arrive. **Motorbikes** are an attractive option, particularly for searching out private beaches, but if you don't already know how to ride one, this is not the place to learn. A simple—though admittedly more costly—option is to have your hotel arrange for a car and driver for you.

For excursions to the Gili Islands, you have two reliable options: either hop on one of the transport hydrofoils (Bounty Cruises stops at Senggigi Beach on its way to and from the Gili Islands) or head up to one of the seafront villages to the north and hire a local boatman (try Malimbu, Bangsal, or Pemenang villages). The going rate for a round-trip outrigger to Gili Meno is about Rp100,000 (US$11).

A public ferry leaves from Bangsal Harbor, but because the schedule is so unreliable, there have been stories of tourists getting stranded out at the islands and then paying exorbitant sums just to get back to Lombok. It's also possible that these stories are spread to benefit the local boatmen.

Fast Facts: Lombok

Banks/Currency Exchange   There are two new ATM locations in Senggigi: Bank BDI (next to Silk Air and the Pacific Supermarket) and Bank BCA (near the turnoff to the Senggigi Beach Hotel). Don't rely entirely on these, however. Money changers abound in the main tourist areas, and there are banks in Mataram.

Health/Safety   Lombok is still considered a high-risk area for rabies. If you're headed off to feed the monkeys, leave the food at home, wear long pants and closed shoes, and don't provoke them. If bitten, you'll need to begin the series of painful rabies shots *immediately* (and don't let anyone tell you otherwise).

Internet/E-mail   From no telephones to back-to-back Internet cafes. Lombok, or more accurately, Senggigi Beach, has come a long way. There are several clustered along the southern end of Jalan Raya Senggigi (near Bayan Restaurant). Rates are Rp200 per minute and Rp12,000 per hour.

Post Office/Mail   There are post offices in Mataram and one in the center of Senggigi, but your hotel can also mail for you.

Telephones   There are several telephones in the center of Senggigi.

AMPENAN–MATARAM–CAKRANEGARA–SWETA

Together, these four towns, a few kilometers south of the airport, make up one sprawling mass that actually is far less oppressive and suffocating than you would expect from an Indonesian city. True tourist sights are few, but poking around here, especially around the local market (described as "shocking" by foreigners), can be surprisingly interesting, and this is probably the only place you're guaranteed a true Sasak meal (read: fire hot. Really.). It's also a good place to pick up cheap spices, especially vanilla. Still, nearly all tourists quickly move on to more beach-appropriate locales, like Senggigi and Kuta.

SENGGIGI

Senggigi, 12 kilometers (7.4 miles) north of Mataram, is the main beach resort for Lombok where most tourists end up. The beaches aren't as outstanding as those found farther south, but it's really not a fair comparison, as those in the south are *really* outstanding. But since Senggigi is the only place on the island to have a tourist infrastructure, and because it enjoys a good proximity to various Lombok sights, it's probably the best place for the causal visitor, particularly one planning only a short trip to Lombok.

Water sports can be arranged by your hotel, or you can call **Dream Divers** (☎ **370-693738**) to arrange scuba diving, lessons, snorkeling trips, and windsurfing. There are dives right in front of the Senggigi Beach Hotel, but most dive trips take you to the Gili Islands. For shopping and other basic needs, the **Senggigi Square,** right across the street from the Sheraton, is a brightly colored, rather abstract mall (of original and whimsical enough architecture that it did not offend our sensibilities) that contains boutiques, gift shops, money changers, and a travel agent.

ACCOMMODATIONS

Lombok has already come a long way since the days when shacks on the beach were your only overnight options. Five-star luxury properties have already begun to sprout up along the western coastline above Senggigi (the Oberoi, for one; ☎ **370-638444;** fax 370-632496; www.oberoihotels.com), attracting a more exclusive clientele to the island. Thankfully, those of us in the middle range still have more than an ample selection of places to stay, from simple yet comfortable, to simply divine.

✪ **Alang Alang.** Jalan Raya Mangsit, Senggigi, Lombok. ☎ **370-693518.** Fax 370-693194. www.alang-alang-villas.com. E-mail: hotel@alang-alang-villas.com. 19 units. A/C MINIBAR TEL. US$80 deluxe bungalow; US$450 2-bedroom villa (capacity 6). MC, V.

A few miles up the road from Senggigi Beach makes a world of difference. The Alang Alang, meaning "thatched roof" in Indonesian, is that perfectly characteristic property you hoped to find at the end of your travels. Granted, it's characteristic of Bali, and you *are* on Lombok, but let's not get picky. It's small scale, affordable, beachfront, and far enough away from any real center of things to discourage touts. All but three of the bungalow units have "au naturel" outdoor baths and showers, while inside are simple yet boutique rooms featuring carved platform beds, embroidered mosquito netting, and soaps wrapped in dried coconut leaves. Get a bunch of friends together and rent out the villa, a veritable Raja's palace compound with its own private beachfront swimming pool, kitchen, dining area, and two sensual outdoor baths, both with the john out under the stars. There's also a romantic oceanfront restaurant.

Pool Villa Club at the Senggigi Beach Hotel. Jl. Pantai Senggigi, Mataram 83010, Lombok. ☎ **370-693210.** Fax 370-693200. www.aerowisata.co.id/poolvillaclub.html. E-mail: villas@indo.net.id. 16 villas. A/C MINIBAR TV TEL. US$380 villa. Rates include breakfast. AE, DC, JCB, MC, V.

Billed as a "hotel within a hotel," the Pool Villa Club adds a level of exclusivity to Senggigi Beach aimed at one-upping the nearby Sheraton. Do they succeed? At this level of self-indulgence, they sure do, but I'd say that for any property that provides in-room espresso machines. Villas are all duplexes, with separate living room, dining room, and upstairs bedroom with balcony. A rear terrace, furnished with teak lounges, gives direct access to the lagoon pool that snakes through the property, but also provides the option of lounging in your own private sunken sandstone Jacuzzi. The swimming pool is even equipped with a special time release chlorination system that keeps the pool open day and night. As for the style, I'd gladly transport the whole lot back home, including the all-natural doo-dads crafted of from banana tree fibers to the personalize amenities supplied by Bvlgari. Bathrooms are equally over the top, separated from the bedroom by lovely sliding doors and outfitted with an enormous marble sunken bath, a separate W.C., and a handy dressing room/luggage storage area. Honeymooners have already begun to flock to this slice of romance, so let's just hope that those lower level sofabeds that encourage families remain vacant for the time being.

Senggigi Beach Hotel. Jalan Pantai Senggigi, Senggigi, P.O. Box 1001, Mataram 83010, Lombok. ☎ **370-693210/19.** Fax 370-693200. www.aerowisata.com/seng.html. E-mail: hsa@mataram.wasantara.net.id. 149 units. A/C MINIBAR TV TEL. US$130 double; US$160–US$250 bungalow. AE, DC, JCB, MC, V.

Located down an unprepossessing dirt lane, these equally unassuming accommodations get the job done in a comfortable but standard beach motel kind of way. Bungalows are slightly nicer, with somewhat bigger baths and bamboo walls, and half of them have outdoor showers. (Guests here are also welcomed with a cake with their name on it.) Each bungalow houses two rooms and some have connecting doors, so this might be a good option for families. Kids might also like running around the quite large grounds. The pool is disappointingly unimaginative, but its slightly inland location provides welcome relief from the beach touts. There is a spa on-site, three restaurants (frequent evening theme dinners), and three bars.

Sheraton Senggigi. Jalan Raya Senggigi km 8, Senggigi, P.O. Box 1154, Mataram 83015, Lombok. ☎ **800-325-3535** or 370-693333. Fax 370-693140. www.sheraton.com. E-mail: sheraton@indo.net.id. 156 units. A/C MINIBAR TV TEL. US$170–US$190 double (deluxe rm); US$400–US$500 suite; US$1,100 beachfront villa. AE, DC, JCB, MC, V.

This is not as lavish a property compared to the Bali-based Sheratons, but everything is plenty comfortable. The highly efficient, helpful staff speaks excellent English; the newly redone lobby is tropical elegant; and the ocean-side garden lines the seaside setting with a profusion of lush plants. But though bright and cheerful, the rooms are in a rather uninspiring Western style. There's lots of tropical colors and wood and nice-sized bathrooms, and all rooms technically have an ocean view, although the rampant foliage can obscure it. The fine free-form pool with a water slide right through a giant's head is a step in the right direction. Thanks to a full-time security guard, the beach is clear of vendors, but you may want to hang around the grounds instead for a shot at petting the resort's pet deer grazing about the compound (no more venison for me). A recently completed beachfront spa pavilion ensures a stylish level of pampering, so you should absolutely ask your travel agent or the hotel's booking office about their fine vacation getaway packages. There are three quite good restaurants (see review below of Kebun Anggrek) and two bars, one with a lovely view of the sunset. Every night they have a theme dinner.

DINING

Restaurants in Senggigi are generally of fairly good quality, though few are all that special. The following are all in the same area on Jalan Raya, roughly in the center of Senggigi action, which makes it easy to start looking for nightlife after dinner. Consider also asking your hotel to help you find a genuine Sasak warung, so you can try some of their spicy, original dishes (I especially like the way they do fish). **Taman Senggigi** (Jalan Raya Senggigi; ☎ 370-693842; main courses Rp25,000 to Rp50,000; MC, V; daily from 7am to 11pm) serves Indonesian and international dishes in a lush garden. ✪ **Gili Masak** (Jalan Raya Senggigi; ☎ 370-693105; main courses Rp25,000 to Rp40,000; MC, V; open daily 8am to 11pm) has a creative menu rich in spices that turns locally grown produce into scrumptious representations of Indonesian fare, all prepared with purified water. **Circus** (Jalan Raya Senggigi; ☎ 370-693820; main courses Rp17,000 to Rp37,000; no credit cards; daily 8am to 11pm) may not be the most alluring setup in town, but you're guaranteed a fix of authentic Italian pasta (and Indonesian selections), prepared under the watchful eye of Roberto, a resident Italian, who believes there's no excuse for bad food. Or stick to the familiar atmosphere of one of the hotel restaurants. Particularly good are the ✪ **Alang Alang** (☎ 370-693518; main courses Rp22,000 to Rp40,000; MC, V; open daily 8am to 11pm; see "Accommodations," above), probably the most romantic restaurant on the island and one that predates the bungalows; Sheraton's **Kebun Anggrek** (☎ 370-693333), which serves international cuisine daily from 5am to 11pm (main courses are Rp55,000 to Rp120,000); or the romantic Beach Comber at the Pool Villa Club (☎ 370- 693210), a seafood- and French-style brasserie with main courses from Rp32,500 to Rp80,000; open daily to nonguests 6 to 10pm.

ATTRACTIONS

Batu Bolong Temple. 1km (0.62 miles) south of Senggigi (near the Jayakarta Hotel). Daily during daylight hours.

There isn't much in the way of sights in Senggigi, but this temple, perched on a rocky ledge, should help fill that void. It's not so much historical as it is pretty, offering good views and photo ops. But that's enough, particularly if you find yourself going through temple withdrawal after Bali's profusion of them. Admire the hole in the rock where virgins were once sacrificed in the good old days—or at least, in someone's vivid imagination.

Puri Mayura Water Palace. Jalan Selaparang, Cakranegara. Admission Rp1,500. Daily during daylight hours.

Much as I hate to keep comparing poor Lombok unfavorably to Bali, this 18th-century water palace isn't nearly the dazzler that Tirtha Gangga is. It's more like the palace at Klungklung, with a floating bale (all that's left of the original structure, destroyed in 1894 by the Dutch) set in the middle of a good-sized artificial lake. Water pours from spouts, and it's pretty and peaceful, particularly in the bustling city, but it's no more than a nice rest stop.

GILI ISLANDS

Just to the northwest of Lombok are three small islands that offer some of the best snorkeling and diving in this area. Many tourists take day diving trips from as far away as Bali to enjoy them, but once out here, you'll kick yourself for not staying at least 1 night. Unfortunately, the golden goose is slowly being strangled, as constant mooring, shell removal, and other commercial activities linked to the tourist trade are starting to destroy the reefs. The range of fish is impressive, however, though currents can be rough and visibility not what it should be. Snorkelers will be happy with spots right off the beaches at the north of **Gili Trawangan** and **Gili Meno,** and should probably skip going out into deeper water with the divers. **Gili Air** is the most accessible island, close to shore, while Gili Meno has better fish and brilliant blue coral, and is recommended for beginners. Gili Trawangan is the farthest away, but rewards you with the most reliably good diving. Dive shops in Senggigi and the local hotels will arrange trips out to the islands. **Dream Divers** (☎ 370-693738; www.dreamdivers.com) is one of the biggest and supposedly best organized outfitters, but shop around, and check out **Blue Marlin** and **Indonesian Divers** too.

The islands do offer the most basic of overnight accommodations (mostly losmen), but remember that there's no fresh water out here, either to drink (bring your own bottles) or to shower. The biggest and most popular among the expat crowd is the ✪ **Villa Ombak** on Gili Trawangan (☎ 370-642336; fax 370-642337; www. hotelombak.com; e-mail: info@hotelombak.com), an irresistibly natural oasis draped in bougainvillea, of traditional Sasak duplex cottages (no fresh water; showers are cold sea water; US$68 to US$85). The saltwater pool and body treatment center were inaugurated in November 2000 (pool use for nonguests is Rp25,000 per day).

KUTA

Not to be confused with the Bali Kuta—this Kuta has absolutely nothing in common with the one over in Bali. Except maybe the surfing. Actually, Kuta, Lombok, located 30 kilometers (18.6 miles) south of Mataram, is little more than a wide spot in the road running parallel to a sweeping bay. Across the road are some of the finest virgin white-sand beaches on the whole island, backed by an open plain of flatlands and low-lying reeds. Thanks to the 3-foot barrel waves, Kuta's recently been discovered by a small circuit of die-hard divers, and by the looks of the Wartel location going up (at the junction near the Matahari Inn), somebody is betting on Kuta as the island's next tourist center. For now, it's still blissfully silent.

Kuta is currently home to only three hotels: the Novotel, the Matahari, and an unmentionable surfer dive. That may change, and not necessarily for the better, if the developers have their way and turn this into Lombok's Nusa Dua, so go now. It's easy to find your own private beach—just get a ride from the Novotel, or take your own car or motorbike and head down the road a ways. There are plenty of beaches to go around, all with clear, aqua-blue waters and a sense, however false, that you are the first person to set foot on them. You aren't—so be careful with your belongings while swimming. Some of these beaches have self-appointed locals who will guard your possessions or rent you shade from the sun. It's petty larceny, but you might as well pay them to avoid an argument.

ACCOMMODATIONS

Matahari Inn. Kuta Beach, Lombok. ☎ **370-655000.** Fax 370-654832. www. lombokonline.com/matahari. E-mail: matahari@mataram.wasantara.net.id. 6 villas. A/C MINI-BAR TV. Rp250,000 (US$27) double. Rates include taxes and breakfast. No credit cards.

For a less overwhelming resort feel (as well as price tag), the Matahari is an excellent alternative to the Novotel. In fact, many of their guests take one look at the Matahari villas and transfer over here for the duration of their stay. (The Matahari has lower-end facilities, but since the villas are so accessible, I found them unworthy.) The six villas are thatched Sasak-style bungalows, all arranged around a small swimming pool in a garden behind the hotel's other motel-style facilities. They are surprisingly plush, decorated with furnishings of inlaid wood or carved and gilded pieces Balinese style. The bathroom is also unexpected: comfortable and modern facilities (including a bathtub) in an outdoor garden. The Matahari staff is gracious and helpful, and is available to arrange excursions, and activities like beach sports and horseback riding.

✪ **Novotel Lombok.** Mandalika Resort Pantai Putri Nyale, Pujut Lombok Tengah, Nusa Tenggara Barat. ☎ **370-653333.** Fax 370-653555. www.novotel-lombok.com. E-mail: hotel@lnovotel-lombok.com. 108 units. A/C MINIBAR TV TEL. US$130–US$150 double (deluxe rm); US$250 bungalow or villa. AE, DC, JCB, MC, V.

They say you either love or hate *The Flintstones* feel you get from the Novotel, but I loved it and wouldn't hesitate to make it a destination all its own. It is off the beaten track; however, there is nothing—and I mean nothing—near here. (The hotel does offers excursions, and the guides/drivers for these can be exceptionally good.) The standard rooms, in sandstone blocks, are arranged around bungalows constructed to look like the distinctive Sasak villages you pass on the way to Kuta (see above). The bungalows offer more space, and have their own swimming pool. Otherwise, all rooms are essentially the same, with all-natural fabrics and woods dotting the rafters, and extra touches like telephones of coconut fiber and interior gecko accents. The staff is superb, all genuinely friendly, and most speak excellent English. The property is big and confusing enough to require a map at first, but blundering around will ultimately take you to an elevated pool not unlike a Mayan pyramid, plus a series of fountains you can splash in. And all of it overlooks the purest white beach and clear water with nothing to spoil the view but the hills and sky. And all this within steps of all sorts of cushy comforts, from towels to icy bottles of water—just the right way to effect a romantic, luxurious getaway. A disadvantage of staying here is that until refrigeration migrates to this side of the island (I got food poisoning out here), you're confined to dining at the superb, but expensive offerings at the hotel's restaurants (try to get a meal plan when booking).

DINING

Sadly, the lack of tourist turnover translates into food of dubious freshness. Having traced an extended and extremely unpleasant bout of food poisoning to one of the more reassuring roadside options, I'd hesitate to send you anywhere where a refrigerator isn't immediately handy. Maybe you'll have better luck than I did; good bets are the Matahari Inn and the Kuta Indah Hotel and Restaurant, but I'd stick to the Novotel.

TANJUNG SEGER, TANJUNG AAN & TANJUNG PEDAU BEACHES

These three beaches are among the most superb in this part of Lombok—though if it's not high season, other tourists in the area may confine themselves to the comfortable Novotel beach. All are located within 5 kilometers (3 miles) of the Novotel—you can ask there or at any shack along the road how to find them. If you're planning to rent a surfboard from one of the local boys along the road, verify the condition of the board (some have been repaired repeatedly), and that in the event of problems, you won't be held liable.

RAMBITAN & SADE

You can't miss the traditional Sasak villages of Rambitan and Sade 8 kilometers (5 miles) and 6 kilometers (3.7 miles) north of Kuta, respectively. Not only do you have to drive through them to get to Kuta, but their distinctive thatched huts, with unusual, almost whimsical peaked roofs, almost look like a community for elves—that is, if elves used dung in their building construction. This is the look, rightly or wrongly, that the Novotel is trying to copy with its own upscale hotel villas, but this has been the real thing for centuries. Both are set up to receive visitors (and their donations), making the whole thing smack of disheartening commercialism. Regardless, since the nightly cost of those Novotel villas is probably more than one of these inhabitant's annual income, it would be gracious to help support the inspiration and the real people who live there.

GUNUNG RINJANI

The massive bulk of Indonesia's second highest mountain, a volcano, spreads across 65 kilometers (40 miles) of the north part of Lombok. Way up near the top—but actually still another day's climb from the peak—is the awe-inspiring crater lake **Segera Anak.** You can't see it unless you're at the top, but only the hardiest should attempt such a superhuman climb—not to mention the cold night such an ascent forces you to spend near the summit. If "because it's there" is your motto, by all means try it, but you must have a guide and proper trek arranged for you (hotels in Senggigi and Kuta can do this). Once at the top, if the weather gods are kind, you'll be able to wave at Bali's Gunung Agung volcano.

Be aware of the current dangers however: Incidents of attacks on the rim and along the trails by (potentially violent) bandits have been reported, even against groups with police escort (suspicion has it that a local contingent of the expeditions are in cahoots with the bandits, and that the booty is divided). I suggest you put this trek off until better economic times come to Lombok.

CRAFTS VILLAGES

About 22 kilometers (13.6 miles) south of Sweta you'll find a group of villages, centered around Praya, that specialize in different types of crafts. There are other crafts villages on Lombok, but this particular center is right on the route to Kuta from the airport and Senggigi, and has become a regular stop on the tourist circuit. It's your call whether you actually want to stop here (though some guides either make it mandatory, or at least smooth-talk you into it). While it is educational to learn about the various crafts—the intricacies of ikat songket weaving, for example, are astonishing and the skills demonstrated by its makers humbling—the hard sell that can come at the end, when you are virtually turned upside down to shake the money out of your pockets, can be off-putting to say the least. If you're a serious buyer though, it's a great way to practice your bargaining skills, and the reward will be some fine trophies for your home. You'll find ikat weaving in **Sukarara** and **Pejanggik,** rattan baskets in **Baleke,** wood carving in **Sukaraja** and **Senanti,** and pottery in **Penujak.** This last village is part of the 10-year-old Lombok Craft Project, which seeks to raise the standard of living among the potter families, who have been practicing their craft since the 16th century. You've seen this stuff for sale in Bali and didn't know it (Lombok pottery is quite distinctive)—come buy it from the source and support a good cause.

TAMAN NARMADA

This sprawling complex of terraces and lakes 10 kilometers (6 miles) east of Carkrane-gara seems to go on forever. It was built by an aging raja in the late 1700s, who sup-posedly modeled it on the lake at Gunung Rinjani; it does kind of look like it, if you squint. Like many sights on Lombok, it's not all that remarkable if you just breeze in for a quick look (though there is a rather sweet little temple to poke around in). Bet-ter you should bring your swimsuit and spend part of a day here—its parks make for pleasurable ambles and the water is fine for dipping, and more, as evidenced by the shrieking, naked local boys who splash around and cannonball off pedestals. It's open during daylight hours, and admission is Rp1,000.

Geography, climate, and culture. Who would have imagined that this seemingly benign combination of forces could align to produce traditions and practices consid-ered by the West to be so utterly self-indulgent? Eastern cultures believe in the main-tenance of life forces through muscular manipulation and relaxation, along with the use of *jamu*—traditional medicine practiced through the use of natural means. Toss into the recipe an abundance of indigenous tropical botanicals along with centuries of home-grown medicinal brews, and you've got a spa experience Westerners are eager to empty their wallets on. Of course, it's only natural that the Balinese have developed it into an art form.

There's definitely something irresistible about spending "coffee money" (excuse any perceived financial arrogance) on an otherwise unattainable disposable luxury, but remember, in Bali, it's just as easy to spend $200 on a back rub as $2. At the low end (and I'm not talking about those beachfront rubdowns), quality is sort of a crap shoot. Because you're never guaranteed consistency in staff, you'll never know until your hour is up whether you're in for a not-unpleasant surface rubbing or a celestially satisfying (and borderline painful) deep tissue massage. But when it comes to self-indulgence, who wants mediocrity? With Bali's spa industry growing at exponential rates, it's dif-ficult to sort out all of the options, and next to impossible not to sample at least one product every day, especially since each spa offers settings more sensual, serene, lush, and lavish than the next. In all cases, appointments are usually necessary.

As the dominant "chain" spa on the island, **The Mandara Spa** will keep cropping up as the operator of a number of in-house hotel spas, but don't let the idea of a fran-chise discourage you from the treatments they offer. Extra special locations are the Chedi in Ubud (their first), where the ultimate indulgence is an oversized flower-filled bathtub that sits dramatically in a serene lotus pond; the private Spa Villa at the Ibah in Ubud, where warm timbers and folds of cascading fabric create an opulent and meditative mood; and the Mandara Spa at The Legian in Seminyak, which combines exotic Indonesian body elixirs in an environment of understated elegance with sensory bliss. (Rates vary according to locations.)

In the southern part of the island, The **Spa Villa at the Sheraton Laguna** is the spa's crowning feature. Imagine a palace bathroom of marble, stone, and hand-carved wood, with an intimate dining nook for a post-workout appetite. The villa also fea-tures a mosaic tiled Jacuzzi, a waterfall shower, facilities for dual massage, and an enor-mous and plush bed for relaxation (or whatever). A 3-hour treatment, which typically includes a half-hour body scrub, a 1-hour body massage, a collagen treatment, an herbal bath, and use of the standard spa facilities (gym, sauna, cold plunge pool) costs US$200 per person.

Winning extra points for ambience is the **Jamu-Jamu Spa in The Villas** (Jalan Kunti 118X, Seminyak; call ☎ 361-730840 for reservation and pickup; there's a second location at the DFS—located above the DFS Galleria on Jalan Bypass Nygurah Rai, 2 kilometers from the international airport), set in a Moorish-style palatial environment of grace and tranquility. The secrets of "jamu," referring to the traditional use of herbs for health and well-being, have been handed down from mother to daughter for centuries. Jamu-Jamu furthers the tradition, with all natural, organically grown (whenever possible), and hand-cultivated products. Treatments are aimed at achieving both inner and outer beauty; you can take advantage of a 3-day total rejuvenation retreat, or pop in on your last day for a 15-minute pre-flight "booster."

A name in Indonesia that is synonymous with expertise in "jamu" is **Martha Tilaar,** founder and president of the country's foremost cosmetic company and namesake of her own successful chain of spas, totaling eight throughout Indonesia. Martha Tilaar spas (in Bali, ☎ **361-777662,** Jalan Bypass Ngurah Rai, Taman Mumbul, open 10am to 10pm) feature the Dewi Sri line of aromatic spa products, blended according to once-secret recipes used by the princesses occupying the royal palace in Yogyakarta. Traditional body treatments range in price from US$50 and up, and include therapies like the *Lulur Malih Warni* (an exfoliating process that cleanses and softens skin) and the *Ken Dedes* (a series of treatments including a masque, massage, herbal bath, and eyebrow-raising "body smoke" best described as a smoke douche).

The Philippines

11

by Lynn A. Levine

The Philippines has a marketing problem. Lacking the mystery of Malaysia or Indonesia, less prominent than her turbulent neighbors Vietnam, Laos, and Cambodia, and seemingly not as magical as Thailand, the Philippines have a difficult time convincing travelers why they should actually go there. Encounters with Westerners within Philippine borders overwhelmingly revealed that their presence was due exclusively to business, or to a connection with an embassy, or on behalf of a mission, or simply by accident.

The biggest obstacle in traveling around the Philippines is an appalling lack of an infrastructure. Roads are either pockmarked, washed away, or nonexistent, making a 100-kilometer excursion close to a 3-hour ordeal—that's without traffic. Internal airlines and charters may get you quickly from point "A" to point "B," but when the real attractions are at point "C," you'll still have to factor in a half or whole day of often unpleasant road travel.

Another major deterrent to traveling in the Philippines is the widespread disregard for natural resources. Besides the problem of deforestation, fishermen routinely drop dynamite or inject cyanide into coral reefs hoping to optimize the catch and minimize the effort (dynamite renders enough whole corpses to make it worthwhile, and low levels of cyanide simply stun the fish). Meanwhile, fishermen are ignorant (or apathetic) of the impact they are having on the environment and on future food sources. Almost as disastrous is that without the reefs, scuba diving—a significant percentage of the tourism industry in the Philippines—will go elsewhere. Several private and foreign organizations have become active in educating and activating the local population towards healthy practices (in some cases the results are already evident, as in El Nido), and one would hope that these efforts reap noticeable rewards.

So why go? War buffs and veterans like the Philippines for historical reasons. Honeymooners can find considerable romance in a select number of all-inclusive native-style luxury resorts, but frankly, not many will appreciate the degradation on the way to the front gate. Another unqualified justification for going is that it's scandalously inexpensive. And certain remote areas of the country are some of the most lovely I've ever.

So it seems that the Philippines is a destination for the hearty category of **adventure traveler.** Less concerned with hot running water and the inconveniences of the road (and plenty of time on your hands), an intrepid soul will find wonder in the scenic hiking trails, underground caves, crisp watering holes, and unspoiled native villages. Once beyond the anarchy and filth of the nearest town, the Philippines becomes a rural vision of simplicity, of high spirits and of warmth. Occupying over 7,100 islands (and that's only at low tide), the unspoiled natural resources of the hinterland provide an endless sea of choices for sun, fun, and adventure, with a rare number of tribespeople hidden in the mountains—far beyond the prying eye of the tourist.

Unfortunately, these are not the experiences you will find by following a guidebook. In the sections to follow, I have tried to include a handful of select destinations considered to be the "anchors" of tourism in the Philippines. You will no doubt want to go beyond these suggested locations to experience the geography, topography, and traditions of the land—if you don't mind a few hardships along the way.

1 Getting to Know the Philippines

THE LAY OF THE LAND

The Philippines are southeast of Hong Kong and northeast of Indonesia, bordered on the west by the South China Sea and on the east by the Pacific Ocean. Borneo is only 24 kilometers (15 miles) from the country's southernmost point.

THE ISLANDS IN BRIEF

The 7,107 islands and islets that make up the Philippine archipelago form a landmass about the same size as Italy. Its sprawling shape, with a coastline that extends more than 17,742 kilometers (11,000 miles), makes it seem much larger than it really is.

The country is divided into three main island groups: **Luzon, the Visayas,** and **Mindanao.** The northern island of Luzon (home to Manila), together with the islands of Mindoro and Palawan, is the largest of the three groups. The Visayan Islands from the central region include Cebu, Bohol, Negros, Panay (with Boracay), Samar, and Leyte. Mindanao is the second largest island in the south and it contains the island chains of Camiguin, Basilan, and the infamous Sulu islands—we don't recommend you visit these areas as they are extremely unstable.

The diversity of the islands and the varying experiences that each offers are only limited by your tolerance for lack of amenities. Are you a one-stop resort hound who likes all the creature comforts of island living at your fingertips? Try the resorts of **Boracay** or **Cebu's Mactan Island.** Both offer blindingly white-sand beaches, teeth-numbing cool fruit shakes to sip while you soak, and a funky, leisurely mood that will have even the most wound-up executives building sandcastles. Or are you a Teva-toting hiker whose idea of a vacation involves unpredictable, adrenaline-raising treks or diving hundreds of miles from shore? Consider **Palawan,** the "last frontier" of the Philippines. Palawan's exclusive resorts provide the best of both worlds for the traveler who likes a bit of pampering with his or her adventure. The islands of **Bohol** and **Mindoro** have excellent diving for both pros and novices. On Mindoro, the party vibe and friendly nature of Puerto Galera attract expatriates from Manila and locals alike. Bohol has an authentic mix of village life and pristine beaches, especially on Panglao island.And finally, Luzon, the biggest island of the archipelago, is home to the cosmopolitan capital, Manila, and the small towns of the province along the Central Cordillera Mountains. In this mountainous region you'll find the Ifugao tribespeople and their miraculously cultivated Banaue rice terraces; the caving opportunities and burial caves of Sagada; and farther north, the Spanish-influenced historic town of Vigan, where horse-drawn carriages can trot you through the cobblestone streets.

The Philippines

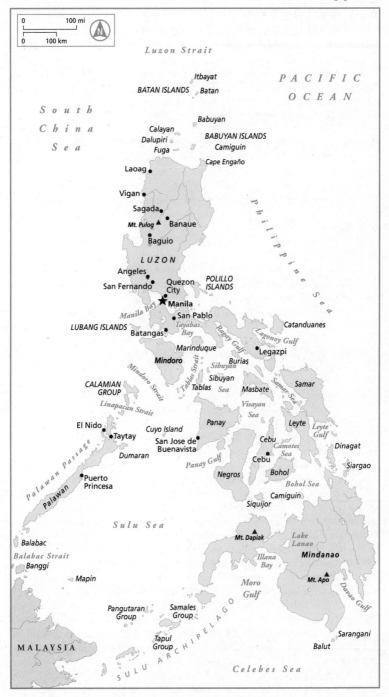

A LOOK AT THE PAST

The first inhabitants of the Philippines arrived as early as 300,000 years ago, probably migrating over a land bridge from the Asian mainland. The Negrito, a tribe located near Mt. Pinatubo, arrived 25,000 years ago, but were driven back by several waves of immigrants from modern-day Indonesia and Malaysia. In 1380, the Arab-taught Makdum arrived in the Sulu archipelago and established what became a powerful Islamic sphere of influence over the next hundred years.

When **Ferdinand Magellan** arrived in 1521 he claimed the archipelago for Spain, but 20 days later he was killed by the Cebuan chieftain, Lapu-Lapu. Another determined conquistador, Ruy Lopez de Villalobos, followed in 1543 and named the territory Filipinas, after the king of Spain. In 1565 the Spanish began to permanently occupy the territory, and by 1571 the entire country—except for the strictly Islamic Sulu archipelago—was under Spanish control.

The Spanish hold was challenged by outside forces, especially by the Dutch and the British. But it was the Filipinos themselves who ultimately started an independence movement.

After almost 400 years of colonial domination, the Philippines sided with the Americans to expel the Spanish, only to submit once again to the indignity of occupation, this time at the hands of the Americans, who purchased the islands from Spain for US$20 million. That same year, the Philippines had had enough, and embarked on a campaign to oust the Americans, a conflict that would last the next 3 years.

Before recognizing the Filipinos' desire for independence and ultimately letting go, the Americans introduced their system of schooling, government, democratic ideals, and improved sanitation. In 1935, Manuel L. Quezon was sworn in as the first president of the Philippine Commonwealth. But in 1942, Japan invaded the country, brutally interrupting the process of transition from colony to independent nation. Filipino and American troops, under the direction of **General Douglas MacArthur,** resisted Japan's advance until MacArthur was ordered by President Roosevelt to retreat. "I shall return," was MacArthur's famous promise, and after years of oppression, rebellion, and disarray under Japanese rule, MacArthur did return and seized control once again, in 1944. The Philippines achieved full independence again in 1946, and Manuel Roxas was sworn in as president of the Philippine Republic.

Ferdinand Marcos was elected president in 1965, and hopes ran high that he would be able to control the political and economic deterioration that had gripped the country since the end of the war. Instead, in 1972 he declared martial law, "to handle the economic crisis and the peace-and-order situation." He continued to rule virtually as a dictator until 1986, when communist and Muslim guerrillas attacked his regime, and he was accused of ballot-rigging and fraud. A snap election saw the opposition parties rally around **Corazon Aquino,** widow of a prominent opposition figure whose 1983 assassination had sparked massive anti-government protests. Cory Aquino initiated a program of nonviolent civil unrest that resulted in Marcos and his beauty-queen wife, Imelda, fleeing the country to Hawaii, where Marcos died in 1989.

Aquino re-established the democratic institutions of the country, but failed to tackle economic problems or win over the military or the powerful Filipino elite. U.S. influence in the country diminished following the 1991 Mt. Pinatubo eruption, which destroyed the United States Air Base, and after the Philippine Senate refused to ratify the lease on the Subic Bay Naval Station. Aquino survived seven coup attempts in 6 years and was succeeded by her defense minister, **Fidel Ramos,** in 1992. Finally, progress was starting to be seen and felt by the Filipino people and the international community. Ramos succeeded in revitalizing the economy, attracting foreign investment and defusing long-running tensions with the Muslim National Liberation Front.

In 1998 he was replaced by the Philippines' answer to Ronald Reagan, former actor Joseph Estrada.

THE PHILIPPINES TODAY

The Philippines is still recovering from the political upheaval that resulted in the resignation of President Joseph Estrada at the end of 2000. Elected by the largest number of votes in any democratic election ever held in the Philippines, former film star Joseph Estrada is accused of having accepted (even solicited) payoffs associated with illegal gambling dealings totaling US$11 million, a figure that takes on new character in relation to the average person's day wage of $5. The presidential post was assumed by his vice president, Gloria Macapagal-Arroyo, who has, to date, garnered the support of the country, on a platform of combatting flagrant corruption, cronyism, and immorality in government.

Another sticking point for the body politic of the country has been a violent civil war, centered in the southern island province of Mindanao. Hardly a recent phenomenon, the Moro movement on Mindanao, active since 1521, resisted Spanish and then American colonial rule, and conflict continued after Philippine independence. Muslim resentment in the region flared as a result of large-scale migrations of Christians from other Filipino regions, which reduced the Muslims to a minority on the island. The most recent example of this was the kidnapping of 20 guests at the Dos Palmsa resort in Palawan   at the hands of the Abu Sayyaf. Discrimination, land-occupation, and the destruction caused by Christian vigilantes fueled the movement's desire for a separate Islamic state. Abject poverty fuels the fire, especially when tourists are seen as endless fonts of cash.

The 1996 peace agreement between the Philippine government and the Moro National Liberation Front (MNLF), which supposedly marked an end to the MNLF's 26-year military struggle for autonomy, served to cover up rather than address the basic problems of economic, social, and religious disaffection felt by the Muslim south. The breakaway faction from the MNLF, the militant Moro Islamic Liberation Front (MILF), disagreed with the deal and waged a guerrilla war against government troops for independence on the island. Kidnapping incidents and the peace and order in this area were making headlines throughout the international community, and their secessionist program of political and military pressure on the government remains a key threat to stability in the Philippines. A toppling government doesn't help.

CUISINE

Although Filipino food is a fusion of foreign and indigenous influences, historians speculate that 80% of Filipino dishes derive from the Spanish kitchen. As in any cuisine based on a poor economy, there is no limitation on what is eaten at what time of day. Rice is the main staple and is the centerpiece of every meal, including breakfast (hotels accommodate American sensibilities by offering eggs and toast). Expect to see items like *bangus* (milkfish), *kare-kare* (oxtail), and tons of *lechon kawali* (whole roasted pig). Chinese influences are seen in the noodle dishes like *bihon, miki, sotanghon, mami, lomi,* and *miswa* and often go by the collective name of *pancit.* Shops that specialize in noodles are appropriately named *panciterias.* The egg roll makes the transition in *lumpia,* stuffed with delicacies like *ubod* (heart of palm) or other local vegetables.

The name of the dish often suggests how it is prepared. *Prito* means fried, *ihaw* or *inihaw* means grilled or broiled. *Adobo* is anything prepared with vinegar and garlic, offering a flavor not unlike American southern barbecue. *Paksiw* means to stew in sour fruit or vinegar; *ginataan* refers to anything cooked in coconut milk. *Sinigang* is usually a fish based sour soup, but it's not uncommon to see this on a menu as a chicken or beef *sinigang.*

The **seafood** is so much fresher (not to mention cheaper) than at most places that even people who don't like fish may be converted. The most plentiful types are *lapu-lapu* (grouper), *bangus* (milkfish), blue marlin, and *tanguigue,* all excellent either simply grilled or stewed in soy and ginger.

When traveling around, do venture into the local specialties (balut, a fertilized egg embryo eaten semi-raw, is a delicacy; you'll see locals sucking back eggs on street corners—a custom I never considered for myself). El Nido, meaning "the nest" in Spanish, is named for the birds nests perched high on the area's cliffs; the mucus used to hold the nest together is a rare treat in China. In the province of Laguna, be sure to try the *kesong puti,* a white cheese made of caribao milk. Los Baños is synonymous with *buko pie,* a semi-sweet, semi-creamy pie make of coconut meat. At hundreds of roadside stands throughout the archipelago, you can certainly pick up a gummy rice treat made with brown sugar and wrapped in a banana leaf—the name changes from locality to locality.

The **fruits** are amazing: Treat yourself to the familiar mangoes, papaya, avocado, and guava, and to lesser-known fruits like lanzones (beige clusters of fruit) and the smelly durian. Many of these are transformed into refreshing tropical shakes or as simple ades. **Calamansi** is limeade that short on sugar and can leave your lips puckered for hours. For hard drinkers, **Tanduay Rum** is unbelievably cheap and popular here. San Miguel is the country's best known brand of beer.

RELIGION

The Spanish missionaries came, they saw, and they surely conquered, converting over 90% of the population to Christianity, of whom 80% are **Roman Catholic** and 6% are **Protestant.** About 4% of Filipinos belong to the **Philippine Independent Church,** also known as the Aglipay, an early 20th-century sect that is closely related to the Anglican and Episcopalian churches. In the south, on the island of Mindanao and along the Sulu archipelago, the Spanish were not so successful in anchoring Christian ideals. About 5% of Filipinos, concentrated mostly in these areas, are **Muslim.**

ETIQUETTE

Seldom will you find a people who so enjoy the company of their Western visitors. Their curious nature often results in personal questions about your age, your family, your children (or lack thereof—a sad state of affairs as far as they are concerned). More often than not guests in Filipino homes are offered the best seat at the dining table and almost always served the host's finest dish. Perhaps due to their long association with Spain, Filipinos are emotional and passionate about life, food, and fiestas in a way that seems more Latin than Asian.

The Filipino attitude of *bahala na* (come what may) is a source of strength, but it often results in complacency. Just remember that you are in their country, where time is not of the essence, and relax. Filipino pride demands that once a confrontation begins, there is no backing down, so try to avoid talking politics, religion, or corruption and avoid taking on an aggressive stance in situations where life doesn't go your way—it will get you nowhere but angry. Filipinos are aware of the problems in their country but are not prepared to listen to foreign visitors pointing those problems out and voicing criticism. They love talking about their families though!

Here's a quick checklist to help you navigate through the culture:

- A deadpan raising of the eyebrows means "yes." But remember that Filipinos hate to say no, so keep your antenna up for any hesitation—a surefire signal to ignore anything that comes after it.
- The gesture we recognize as "go away" or "goodbye" (a wave with palms down) signifies "come here."

- One hisses and makes a kissing-type noise to get attention.
- Pursed lips point in a particular direction.
- It is customary to leave some food on the plate to show you've had enough.
- Don't be punctual for social meetings. Arrive at least 30 minutes late if you want to be really polite.
- It is customary to take off your shoes before entering a home.
- For women travelers, be prepared to answer the question, "Do you have a companion?" or "Where is your companion?"
- For business travelers, punctuality is expected.
- And be sure not to leave home without your business cards, as Filipinos like to know who they are dealing with.

LANGUAGE

Although there are nearly 2,000 regional languages scattered throughout the Philippines archipelago, 90% of the populace speaks one of eight major languages (Tagalog, Cebuano, Hiligaynon/Ilonggo, Waray, Bicol, Ilocano, Kapampangan, Pangasinan) or one of their subgroups. Don't get alarmed; a century of American occupation (both by the military and by retirees) ensures the widespread use of English. In fact, all governmental and official matters are conducted, by law, in English. In the interest of nationalism, there is a push to make **Tagalog** the official national language, and already you can hear the stuttered cadence of an English fallen into disuse.

English will get you by everywhere, but there are definitely some quirks that we'd like to point out. For one, Filipinos answer positively to a negative question. If you ask a taxi driver, "You don't know where you're going?" the reply will be "Yes," which actually means "No." In fact, Filipinos hate to say no, or "I don't know," preferring to beat around the bush, indulge in euphemisms, or flat out lie. This can be frustrating when you want a straight answer or prompt service, and at the very least, completely confusing. Make a point of avoiding negative questions and above all, be patient. Carrying over the idea that Filipinos hate to say no or to disappoint you by telling you something they think you don't want to hear, if you sense any hesitation toward a question, it's basically safe to say that you can disregard everything that follows.

USEFUL PHILIPPINE PHRASES

Most Filipinos speak at least three languages: Tagalog (the national language) and their own regional dialect are usually supplemented by American English and sometimes Spanish.

Although you will, in most cases, not need to use any Tagalog, the Filipinos get a real kick out of any attempt, botched or not. In Tagalog, *p* and *f* are often interchangeably pronounced and used. The written *p* can be pronounced as an *f.* You'll notice this even carries over into English (*Filipinas* pronounced *Pilipinas* and *food* pronounced *pood.*) Double vowels are pronounced separately, for example Ta-al Volcano. *I* is pronounced *ee.* The nasal combination *ng* is pronounced "nang" and *mga* is pronounced "manga." Using *po* (masculine) or *ho* (feminine) signifies respect and should be used whenever talking with an older person. Basically the words are pronounced phonetically—how it looks is usually how it's pronounced.

English	Tagalog	Pronounced
Welcome	Mabuhay	Mah-*boo*-ha-ee
Good morning	Magandang umaga	Mah-gahn-*dahng* oo-*mah*-gah
Good night	Magandang gabi	Mah-gahn-*dahng ga-bi*
I'm fine	Mabuti	Ma-boot-ee
How are you?	Kumusta ka	Kuh-moos-tah ka

English	Tagalog	Pronounced
Please	Paki	*Pah*-kee
Thank you	Salamat	Sah-*lah*-maht
You're welcome	Walang anuman	Wahl-*ahng* ah-noo-*mahn*
What time is it?	Anong oras na ba?	Ah-nong *oh*-rahs nah bah
What is your name?	Anong pangalan mo?	Pahng-*ahl*-ahn
Where is the . . .	Nasaan ang . . .	Nah-sah-*ahn* ahng . . .
Toilet?		CR comfort room?
Bus/jeepney?	Bus/djipney sa?	
Do you have A/C?	Mayroon bang air-condition?	May-oh-*oon* bahng air-condition?
The bill, please	Akina ang kuwenta ko	AH-keenah *kwehn*-tuh koh
How much is this?	Magkano ito?	ee-*toh*
Yes/No	Oo/Hindi	*Oh-oh*/Hihn-*dee*

2 Planning a Trip to the Philippines

VISITOR INFORMATION

With some of the most diverse marine life in Southeast Asia and a cache of world-class dive spots, the underwater aficionado may want to do a bit of advance planning. In the case of diving the Tubbataha Reef or other sites requiring a live-aboard, this is essential. **Dive Buddies** (☎ 02/899-0838; fax 02/899-7393; e-mail: divephil@ mnl.sequel.net) and **Whitetip Divers** (☎ 02/521-0433; fax 02/522-1165), both located in Manila, are two travel agencies specializing in diving the Philippines. For live-aboards, there's the **MY Island Explorer** operated by Cruise & Island Adventure, 714 Jose Abad Santos Ave, San Juan, Metro Manila (☎ 02/726-0115; fax 02/724-7601; www.scubaworld.com.ph); the **MY Jinn Sulu,** Queen Anne Palawan Inc., c/o the Trattoria Terrace in Puerto Princesa (☎ 48/212-751l; fax 48/212-894); **MY Thor Viking,** c/o Swagman Travel (☎ 45/322-5133; fax 45/322-9467; e-mail: bookings@swaggy.com); and **MY Nautikia,** PCP Holiday Cruises Inc., Herald Suites Building, 2168 P. Tamo Ave., Makati (☎ 02/759-6270; fax 02/759-6282; e-mail: nautika@mnl.sequel.net).

Adventure trips by sea kayak are another popular but under-organized activity. Thanks to **Mountain Travel Sobek** (☎ 888/687-6235 or 510/527-8100; London: 1494/448-901; www.mtsobek.com) the islets, mangroves, and lagoons of the archipelago, particularly of northern Palawan, are gaining in adventure mystique. **Tribal Adventure Tours** (☎ 2/823-2725; fax 2/823-2988; www.sequel.net/~tribal; e-mail: tribal@mnl.sequel.net) is one of the more respected locally run outfitters. Both arrange kayaking "safaris," in the spectacularly untouched marine wilderness around Palawan.

The long arm of the Philippine Department of Tourism (DOT) reaches many potential overseas visitors through its branch offices, which will gladly provide brochures and booklets to help you plan your trip (including those under the financial auspices of the DOT itself—a dubious relationship at best). Below is a listing of several DOT offices in the English-speaking world. You can also check out their Web site at **www.tourism.gov.ph** or the one connected with the Philippine Convention and Visitors Corporation at **www.dotpcvc.gov.ph**.

IN THE UNITED STATES

- **New York:** Philippine Center, 556 5th Ave., New York, NY 10036 (☎ 212/575-7915; fax 212/302-6759; www.pcgny.com/).

- **Los Angeles:** 3660 Wilshire Blvd., Ste. 285, Los Angeles, CA 90010 (☎ **213/ 487-4527;** fax 213/386-4063; www.philconsul-la.org/).
- **San Francisco:** 447 Sutter St., no. 507, San Francisco, CA 94108 (☎ **415/ 956-4060;** fax 415/956-2093; e-mail: pdotsf@aol.com).

IN CANADA

- **Toronto:** Philippine Consulate General, 151 Bloor St. West, Suite 365, Toronto, Ontario, Canada M5S 1S4 (☎ **416/922-7181;** fax 416/922-2638; www.philcongen-toronto.com/).

IN AUSTRALIA

- **Sydney:** Wynyard House, Suite 703, Level 7, 301 George St., Sydney 2000 (☎ **612/9299-6815** or 9299-6506; fax 612/9299-6817; e-mail: ptsydney@ozemail.com.au).

IN THE UNITED KINGDOM

- **London:** 146 Cromwell Rd., London SW74EF (☎ **207/835-1100;** fax 207/ 835-1926; e-mail: tourism@pdot.co.uk).

WEB SITES

- **www.dotpcvc.gov.ph** is a one-stop shopping site operated by the Department of Tourism and the Philippines Convention and Visitors Corporation.
- **www.philippine.org** is a great site for information on the Philippines' various provinces, and interesting links.
- **www.asiatravel.com** is a valuable resource with information on hotels throughout Asia, particularly resorts that offer promo rates.
- **www.sino.net/asean/philippn.html,** titled "Tourist Information," gives all the expected facts on visas, customs, weather, accommodations, and more.

ENTRY REQUIREMENTS

Visas are not required for visits up to 21 days, provided that you have a valid passport and a return ticket. If you wish to stay longer than 21 days, you'll need to apply for a "visa waver," good for a total of 59 days. It's best to handle this prior to your departure, as immigration lines are long, government workers are slow, and you'll be vulnerable to corrupt government workers imposing compulsory "express lane" fees (they're not) or just plain illegal fees.

The truly fearless (or those of you who accidentally overstayed your 21-day welcome) can brave the system by presenting yourselves at one of the Immigration offices in Manila, Angeles, Cebu City, and San Fernando. Bring extra passport photos if you will be applying for a visa. If you plan an even longer stay, direct your visa inquiries to the Philippine embassy or consulate in your home country. For anyone interested in retiring in the Philippines, there is a **Philippine Retirement Authority,** 15th floor, Antel 2000, Corporate Center, 121 Valero St., Salcedo Village, Makati, Manila (☎ 2/751-9300 to 9303; www.force2020.com/).

Actual fees for this visa waver include an application fee (P1,000), visa waver fee (P500), and a legal research fee (P20). The *non-compulsory* express lane fee can be yours for only P500. (At the time of this writing, the total P2,020 equaled about US$40.)

PHILIPPINE EMBASSY LOCATION

- **In the United States:** 1600 Massachusetts Ave. NW, Washington, D.C. 20036 (☎ **202/467-9300;** www.embassyonline.com); also, Philippine Consulate, 56 5th Ave., 3rd floor, New York, NY 10036 (☎ **212/575-7915**).

- **In Canada:** 130 Albert St., Ottawa, Ontario K104G5 (☎ **613/233-1121;** www.philembassyca.org).
- **In Australia:** 1 Moonah Place, Yarralumla, ACT 2600 Canberra (☎ **06/ 273-2535;** www.philembassy.au.com/).
- **In New Zealand:** 50 Hobson St., Thurndon, Wellington (☎ **04/472-9921**).
- **In the United Kingdom:** 9A Palace Green London W8 4QE (☎ **207/ 937-1600;** fax 207/937-2925; www.Philemb.Demon.Co.Uk/).

CUSTOMS REGULATIONS

Any amount over US$3,000 brought into the country must be declared. You are allowed to bring in 400 cigarettes or two tins of tobacco, and two bottles of alcoholic beverages not to exceed 1 liter each. When you leave the Philippines you have to pay a departure tax of P500 (US$10; either currency accepted). If you are returning to the U.S., you may take back US$400 worth of goods purchased in the Philippines. Duty-free items include 200 cigarettes or 100 cigars (no Cuban cigars), a liter of alcohol, and most handicraft goods. Shells, coral, animals, or produce are not allowed.

MONEY

The Philippine currency is the **peso.** It's divided into 100 centavos. Coins come in denominations of 1, 5, 10, and 25 centavos and 1 and 5 pesos. Banknotes are in denominations of 5, 10, 20, 50, 100, 500, and 1,000 pesos.

CURRENCY EXCHANGE & RATES   As I was finishing my research, efforts at impeaching President Estrada had just begun, causing the peso to fall to an historic 50 pesos to the U.S. dollar. To obtain the latest conversions, go to CNN's Web site at **www.cnn.com/travel/currency**. In Manila, currency can be changed at banks (Monday through Friday from 9am to 3pm) and hotels, but for a more favorable rate (other than through your ATM card) try one of the money changers scattered throughout all major city centers and at the airport. If you're near a Shoe Mart, change your money at their currency exchange desk, as they have the best rates.

All major currencies are accepted, but you will have better luck with U.S. dollars. In the smaller towns you'll have to keep your eyes peeled for a "money changer," because it will be more difficult to find a bank or hotel to exchange money, especially at rates you can live with. If you're headed out along the roads less traveled, you'll need to carry a wad of cash with you, as there are no banks (indeed, there is no money). Be sure to load up on small bills like 10, 20, 50 and 100 peso notes, because rarely will anyone change for large ones. The wad will weigh down your pocket but ultimately save you time and patience.

It seems the farther you get from Manila (or other larger cities) the lower the exchange rate you receive. One way around this is to pay for as much as you can with a credit card—the exchange rate is calculated based on your home country's exchange rate, not the local rate.

Several hundred bank branches throughout the country are equipped with **automated-teller machines.** Cirrus ATMs are more plentiful than PLUS and can be found at Citibank and Philippine National Bank branches throughout the country. **Unionbank,** located in most of the big cities (Manila, Cebu, Davao), is affiliated with PLUS. ATM locator services are available through MasterCard/Cirrus and Visa/PLUS. Simply dial the operator, request an international collect call, and dial: **MasterCard/Cirrus** (☎ 314/275-6690) or **Visa/PLUS** (☎ 410/581-7931).

Most major **credit cards** (MasterCard, Visa, American Express, Diners Club, Japan Credit Bank) are widely accepted. Cash withdrawals can be made at any Equitable Bank branch with your Visa or MasterCard. You can get cash or traveler's checks with your American Express card at the **American Express** Bank in Manila, 6750 Ayala Ave., Makati (☎ 2/818-6731).

LOST/STOLEN CREDIT CARDS & TRAVELER'S CHECKS   MasterCard has a toll-free Global Service Emergency Assistance for International Visitors hot line at ☎ 800/110-0113; the international collect call number is ☎ 314/275-6690; **Visa**'s toll-free hot line is ☎ 800/345-1345, or call collect at ☎ 410/581-7931. The number to call for **American Express** is ☎ 800/732-2244. The 24-hour traveler's check refund line for **American Express** is ☎ 800/738-3383; for **Thomas Cook,** it's ☎ 800/223-7373.

CARRYING MONEY   As with any foreign country, the most sensible way to carry money, checks, tickets, and documents is in money belts or secret pockets. In other words, don't be flashy with your valuables, and try not to advertise what's in your wallet by what you wear on your back.

WHEN TO GO

High season lasts from March through May, a scorching hot and dry season and ideal for a traveler planning to spend time at the beach (prices will be higher for accommodations and transportation during this time). Harvest festivals like Flores de Mayo also take place during these hot summer months.

Actually, the most pleasant time to visit the Philippines is during the warm, sunny days and balmy nights that last from November to February. The heat and humidity relent somewhat, leaving dryer air and refreshing breezes (except along the Pacific coast, which can be wet at this time) and temperatures that range from 20°C to 28°C (68°F to 82°F). The southwest monsoon brings on the rains from June to October, with July and August being the wettest months. If you're planning to head to the mountain provinces for hiking or caving, try to avoid the rains, because not only will roads be muddy (sometimes impassable) and flights unpredictable, the trails will be slippery and dangerous. It's important to remain flexible during the rainy season, as typhoons are unpredictable. At the mere threat of a typhoon, all means of transportation will halt, leaving you stranded for days on end.

PUBLIC HOLIDAYS   Businesses, banks, and government are closed on New Year's Day (Jan. 1), Good Friday (the Friday before Easter), Araw ng Kagitingan (Apr. 19), Labor Day (May 1), Independence Day (June 12), National Hero's Day (Aug. 30), Bonifacio Day (Nov. 30), Christmas Day (Dec. 25), and Rizal Day (Dec. 31). All Saints Day (Nov. 1) and Christmas Eve (Dec. 24) are not official holidays, but are usually treated as such.

Christmas is celebrated as early as September (during any month that ends in "ber") throughout the country, but the major festivals such as Ati-Atihan, Sinulog, and Dinagyang take place in January. This makes late December to January a crowded time to visit, and getting around can be quite a push-and-shove experience.

HEALTH CONCERNS

The two biggest threats to your health in the Philippines are the heat and mosquitoes. Heat and humidity can hit you hard if you're not used to them, and can result in prickly heat, **heat exhaustion, heat stroke, dehydration,** and fungal **infections.** Drink lots of (purified or bottled) fluids, especially water. And obviously, take it easy with the sun. Mosquitoes are at their most bothersome after the sun sets, so plan your outdoor time and bring lots of repellent. **Malaria,** carried by the nocturnal anopheles mosquito, is only a consideration if you're headed to rural areas (confirmed in remote areas of Luzon, Basilan, Mindoro Palawan, Mindanao, and the Sulu Archipelago) and in the provinces of Bohol, Catanduanes, Cebu, and Leyte. If you think you will be in an infected area, be sure to begin a regimen of tablet *suppressants* (there is no preventative) *before you go.* If backpacking or camping out is on your itinerary, or if your adventure includes overnights in rooms where the windows will be opened, we strongly suggest bringing a hanging mosquito net or bivy sack, which pops up like a tent over any bed. Both are portable and durable and can be found at most outdoor supply stores or army/navy stores. (**Dengue fever** is also rare but present and transmitted via the early morning mosquito.)

Even more unpleasant but easily avoided are the fresh water parasites that cause **schistosomiasis.** While abundant in the Philippines, they are easily avoided, as most of the fresh water is murky and absolutely unappealing. Stick to salt water and the hotel pool and you should be fine.

Take care with even seemingly minor scratches, because the humidity and heat encourage bacterial infections, easily preventable with the application of antibacterial cream.

If you do become seriously ill, your hotel should be able to recommend a good place to go for treatment, or contact your embassy. Public facilities are below par here, so ask about the nearest private hospital, and be prepared to pay the bill in full.

DIETARY PRECAUTIONS

They say the water is potable in Manila, but I recommend the very affordable bottled water, or purified water (that includes the ice) just in case. Purification tablets are also available in local drug stores. As with visiting any foreign country, there is always the inevitable bowel adjustment to new food, water, climate, and stress. Anti-diarrhea medicine may help, and oral rehydration salts may help severe cases of dehydration brought on by diarrhea or intense heat.

VACCINATIONS

Unless you have been to cholera or yellow-fever regions, no vaccinations are required. Tetanus shots are recommended for divers and snorkelers.

GETTING THERE
BY PLANE

Air travel is the only sure bet to get to the Philippines. There are no regular passenger ships to the country. A few cruise ships stop here, but not long enough to allow passengers much time to explore the country.

Manila's **Ninoy Aquino International Airport** is the main port of entry, followed by Cebu's **Mactan International Airport** (flights from Hong Kong, Singapore, Malaysia, and Japan).

FROM THE U.S. & CANADA   Flying in from the U.S. or Canada will take you, including stopovers, about 24 hours from the East Coast, 14 to 18 hours from the West Coast (Philippine Airlines makes the trip from San Francisco and Los Angeles in an easy 11½ hours). You will lose at least 12 hours going, but when you return to the U.S. you will arrive before you left, thanks to that mysterious International Date Line. **Philippine Airlines (PAL)** (☎ **800/435-9725**) makes the crossing in an unprecedented 11½ hours from the West Coast. A partnership with a stellar **National Airlines** (☎ **888/757-5387;** www.nationalairlines.com) will connect you from points east, but you'll have to gear up for a short stopover at the slot machines in their hub in Vegas.

Other airlines with service to Manila include: **Cathay Pacific** (☎ 800/233-2742); **Continental** (☎ 800/231-0856); **Japan Airlines** (☎ 800/525-3663); **Korean**

> ## Travel Tip: Insurance for Active Pursuits
>
> If your itinerary includes diving, caving, kayaking, or other adrenaline-pumping activities, keep in mind that some policies won't cover them. Before setting off on your adventure, verify what kind of coverage you have under your current insurance policy. (See chapter 3 for more information on travel insurance.)

(☎ 671/649-3301); **Northwest** (☎ 800/225-2525); and **United** (☎ 800/241-6522). PAL has **Canadian offices** in Vancouver and Toronto, and Cathay Pacific offers regular flights between Vancouver and Manila, with a stopover in Hong Kong.

An increasingly popular way of traveling to Eastern destinations like Manila and Hong Kong is with courier airlines like DHL, Federal Express, Skypack, and TNT Courier. Your assignment as an air courier is easy. You'll travel coach class on regularly scheduled airlines accompanying air freight checked as passenger baggage. All you have to do is carry the freight documents and hand them over to the courier company representative at your destination. A Web site to check out with valuable information on courier flights is www.aircourier.org/.

FROM THE U.K.   **British Airways** is at ☎ **0845/773-3377**; www.british-airways. com. London is probably the bucket shop capital of the world, so for those who are not familiar with them, these are travel agencies that offer discounted tickets released by airlines eager to fill seats, even if it means at a reduced profit. Magazines that feature ads for bucket shop deals in the U.K. are *Time Out, City Limits, LAM, Trailfinder, Australasian Express,* and specialized magazines like *The Geographical Magazine, Traveler, Wanderlust,* and *Business Traveler.*

FROM AUSTRALIA   **PAL** (☎ **612/9079-2020**) offers direct service to Manila from Sidney. **Qantas Airlines** (☎ **131313;** www.qantas.com) flies from Melbourne, Adelaide, Brisbane, and Sydney. **Air Niugini** (☎ **612/92901544**) flies to Manila with a stopover in Port Moresby. **STA** (☎ **02/92121255** in Sydney) is one of the best discount agencies, with offices in Sydney, Perth, Melbourne, Adelaide, Canberra, Brisbane, and Hobart.

FROM NEW ZEALAND   **Thai Airways International** (☎ **65/224-2011**) offers the cheapest flights, via Bangkok. Because there are no direct flights from New Zealand to Manila, there are few bargains. Small student discounts may be available through **New Zealand Student Travel Services** (☎ **64/95256901**).

REGIONAL CONNECTIONS   **PAL** (☎ **800/435-9725; www.philippineair. com**) connects numerous Asian cities with their main hub in Manila, and their secondary hub in Cebu. Service includes flights to/from Xiamen, China; Hong Kong, Singapore, Seoul, Tokyo, Osaka, Kuala Lumpur, Riyadh, Cairo, Abu Dhabi, and Dubai. This list is not exhaustive, so check to see if your desired departure city is served as well.

Several regional airlines fly into Subic Bay International Airport (☎ **47/252-9360** to 66), located about 4 hours north of Manila by bus. Air Asia (☎ **47/252-1888**) has flights from Kuala Lumpur, Kuching, Penang, and Malaysia; Dragon Air (☎ **47/252-3836;** www.dragonair.com) has flights from Hong Kong; China Southern Airlines (☎ **47/252-3836;** www.cs-air.com) has flights from Shenzen, Shanghai, and Canton; and Far Eastern Transport (tel] **47/252-9491;** www.fat.com.tw) flies from Kaoshiung and Taipei. Contact the **SBMA Tourism Department** (☎ **47/252-4242**) for further information on these flights.

GETTING AROUND
BY PLANE

For the most part the domestic airlines run on a pretty reliable schedule. However, during peak seasons and holidays, many flights will be booked up, and during bad weather, services will obviously be delayed or cancelled. **PAL** (☎ 2/855-8888) has the greatest number of flights to the largest number of destinations, with **Air Philippines** (☎ 2/843-7001) running a close second, but many of these flights are suspended during low season. Call ahead for information.

PAL is currently marketing its Jetsetter Pass, a 12-coupon booklet that costs P24,000 to P30,000, depending on whether the bulk of your travel will be between Manila and the Visayas or Manila and the southern provinces. Fares are inclusive of Aviation Security Fee & Terminal Fee (except for Manila and Cebu). The coupons are valid for 1 year from the date of purchase and can only be obtained from within the Philippines. **Air Philippines** is also considering a similar bargain fare, so be sure to inquire.

Other domestic air services covering regularly scheduled routes are operated **Asian Spirit** (☎ 2/840-3811; www.asianspirit.com), with flights to Baguio, Tagbilaran, and Caticlan; **Cebu Pacific** (☎ 2/636-4938; www.cebupacificair.com), with flights to Cebu, Davao, Dumaguete, and Kalibo; **Pacific Air** (☎ 2/832-2731-32, 891-6252) to Caticlan, Iloilo, and Busuango; **A. Soriano Aviation** (☎ 2/831-5380; www.boracayair.com) to El Nido, Boracay, and Caticlan; and **SEAir** (☎ 2/891-8701; www.flyseair.com) with flights to Busuanga, Cebu, Caticlan, El Nido, and Puerto Princesa.

You will also be required to pay a "terminal fee" at the airports; it's P500 (US$10) for international flights and P100 (US$2) for domestic flights.

BY TAXI

In Manila, Cebu, and other major cities, taxis are everywhere, pretty reliable and very affordable. They are usually easy to flag down and most have air-conditioning. The question to ask before you take off is whether the meter works. Many drivers will have you believe their meters don't work and charge you much more than the trip should cost. They'll also try to charge more because of traffic. There's *always* traffic, so let them know you're not a sucker. The meter starts at P20 (US$0.40) and increases at a very slow pace. In traffic the meter barely moves, so do tip the driver for his time and patience. Taxis that wait outside major hotels will charge you more than regular taxis; you may want to just stroll to the street and hail down a metered taxi.

BY BUS

Buses are usually a great way to see the country, but after endless hours of identical roadside shacks, you'll just want it all to be over. Most routes are around 10 hours, with some longer routes running on overnight schedules. You will be able to tell which buses are reputable by scanning them at the stations; avoid the ones with lopsided axles that are dirty with rust and dents. **Victory Liner** (☎ 2/361-1506) is one of the most dependable, comfortable, and safe companies. Other companies with service out of Manila are **Baliwag Transit** (points north, including Pampanga), ☎ 2/912-3343; **Dangwa** (points north including Baguio and Banaue); and **BLTB** (Batangas, Legazpi, Tagaytay and other points south of Manila).

Generally, buses are cheap, efficient, and fairly reliable, unless unpaved roads have been washed out or mud slides have occurred in the northern provinces. Seat reservations are not necessary. Tickets are purchased at designated counters in the terminal, or you can simply pay the conductor while en route. Non-air-conditioned buses tend also to be gritty and unroadworthy, so be sure to ask about air-conditioning when you call to verify times and schedules. Express buses (usually the air-conditioned ones) have fewer stops, and you can expect a pretty bad B movie or Chuckie horror flick—although with any luck, you'll get a pirated new release. Street vendors will board the buses at several stops offering everything from Celine Dion cassettes to chewy pig skin, so while this food is OK to eat, you may want to pack a sandwich or carry a bag of Chips Ahoy. There are also meal stops at local restaurants, but there's no guarantee that the food will be fresh, hot, or edible, and the toilets are undeniably the worst I've ever seen. It's also not uncommon for tires to blow more than once over the course of a trip, but don't worry—the driver and his minions will have it changed before you know what happened.

BY TRICYCLE

You will quickly get used to the sound and smell of the motorized and pedal tricycles (pedicabs) that jam the dusty or muddy streets in the provinces and small towns. They carry two to three passengers in their sidecars, and one on the pillion behind the driver (although I've seen one of these babies hauling up to eight). You'll be surprised at the way these things can climb. Expect to pay anywhere from P5 to P20 (US$0.10 to US$0.40) per person for "a special ride," meaning you will not be sharing the ride with any other passengers. In an attempt to rake as much as 500% over the actual cost of the ride, drivers will rarely quote you the correct local rate, so it is best to ask an unconcerned local before boarding and then simply hand over the money at the end. The exhaust can be choking, so I advise bringing a bandanna to help filter out the fumes.

BY TRAIN OR LIGHT RAIL TRANSIT

Nobody takes the train. It's that simple. The Philippine National Railway (PNR) is old, slow, rickety, unreliable, and seedy. In Manila, however, the Light Rail Transit (LRT) and the brand new Metrostar Express (MRT) provide the most painless, carbon monoxide–free, traffic-less way to cross the city. (See "Getting Around," in the Manila section below.)

BY BOAT

Ships, ferries, launches, pumpboats, and *bancas* (motorized outriggers) are the main means of inter-island transport. Manila is the jump-off point to major provinces and cities; Cebu is the secondary link between the Visayas and Mindanao. Fares vary according to level of comfort, service, and regularity. Accommodations range from luxury cabin suites with private facilities to tarpaulin deck cots with disgusting toilets and saltwater bucket baths. (Bring plenty of snack foods and toilet paper for these rides.) An air-conditioned cabin for four costs between P500 and P1,200 (US$12.50 to US$30) per person, including meals, depending on the destination. Once again, the harbor in Manila is quite rowdy with activity and people. Be prepared to be hassled, coerced, and watched, and hold onto your bags.

You can book tickets through any travel agent or purchase them at the pier at the shipping lines' harbor offices. Two main lines include **Asuncion Shipping Lines,** Pier 2, North Harbor (☎ 2/204024), and **WG&A,** Pier 14 (☎ 2/894-3211 or 2/245-4061 through 2/245-4080; e-mail: reservations@wgasuperferry.com), one of the nicest and most reliable ferries, with service to Cebu, Negros, Palawan, Panay, and Mindanao. Tickets for all shipping lines can be obtained on the day of departure at the pier, but it is best to book at least 2 days in advance, especially during the peak months of December and January. Schedules are published in national dailies such as the *Philippine Daily Inquirer,* the *Business Daily,* and the *Manila Bulletin.* Motor launches service longer routes between smaller ports. Schedules are subject to delays, as the captain will wait for the boat to fill up before departing.

Ferry boats service medium to large outlying islands. These are small vessels where passengers sit on deck chairs for periods of travel lasting from about 30 minutes to 2 hours. Cebu has regular ferry boat departures for shorter routes such as Bohol, Dumaguete, and Dapitan, as well as longer routes for Surigao, Cabayan de Oro, and Zamboanga on Mindanao.

Note that there are numerous **ferry accidents** every year in the Philippines, and having taken several, few of which would be called seaworthy back home, I can see why. The tragic incident in September 1998 killed about 400 people, and caused legislatures to call for stricter regulations. Use your best judgment. If you feel uncomfortable boarding a ferry that looks leaky, lopsided, and top-heavy, look for an alternative. And always locate the life vests as soon as you board.

Pumpboats and **bancas** are motorized and nonmotorized outrigger boats that either ply short island crossings or run along the coast from port to port.

The latest addition to the sea-lanes are high-speed **catamarans** and **hydrofoils**—fast, comfortable, and clean. Cebu is the main port for these vessels, with routes to Visayan ports and to Northern Mindanao. Passage usually costs from P40 to P1,000 (US$0.80 to US$20). Food and drinks can usually be purchased at an on-board snack bar.

BY CAR

The traffic in Manila is the worst I have ever seen, and sitting idle amidst all of those beggars and cheap toy vendors is not my idea of a vacation. If you must, though, the familiar rental car agencies are here, where you can either rent a car to drive yourself (you must have an international driver's license or a valid license from your home

---

Inter-Island Travel Tips

- Airlines often change their flight schedules during peak months. Reconfirm your flights at least 2 days before the date of departure. Call your travel agent, the airline itself, or the concierge in your hotel for assistance.

- Domestic airlines require passengers to check in at least 45 minutes before departure time. Otherwise, they will release your seat in favor of wait-listed passengers. The airports are crowded and hectic during peak seasons, so come even earlier to cut down on stress and hassle.

- Airlines impose a "no-show" fee for reservations that have not been cancelled. If you have to cancel your flight, do so at least 2 days in advance.

- If you have to board a boat from the North Harbor in Manila, don't wear expensive jewelry, be extra careful with your belongings, and guard your bag with your life (hold it in front of you).

- You will be hassled to death at ports and piers; the swarms of people selling their services is unrelenting, and they don't take no for an answer. Wait for crowds to thin out at the pier before disembarking from the boat, so the hawkers will have already found their victims.

- Porters working the terminals are legitimate freelancers; don't forget to tip them for agressively "volunteering" to carry your bags, Most are very helpful, going so far as to expedite your check-ins and transfers. (All that for P10 to P20 or about US$0.25.)

country) or hire the services of a driver. Hiring a driver is the best way to go, a cheap luxury used by most expats and many Filipinos. Hired drivers know the roads and understand their rules (or lack thereof). They can negotiate with traffic police and can be a valuable source of information. In Manila call: **Avis** (☎ 2/734-5851); **Budget** (☎ 2/818-7363); **Dollar** (☎ 2/844-3120); or **Nissan Rent-A-Car** (desk at the airport; ☎ 2/816-1808), and they'll direct you to the closest location. Rental cars are also available in Baguio and other points on Luzon, Cebu, and Bohol.

TIPS ON ACCOMMODATIONS

As with most of the Southeast Asian countries in this book, the currency crisis throughout the region and the shortage of tourists has left many hotel rooms vacant. While bargaining hasn't yet entered the Filipino psyche, always ask for seasonal discounts, especially if you're traveling during the low season. If you plan on staying at the same place for a few days you should definitely ask for a reduced rate, because some of the smaller resorts and beach bungalows will come down as much as 40% off the rack rate if bookings are slim. In this section, prices are quoted in U.S. dollars only whenever the hotel rates are routinely provided in that currency, otherwise, rates are quoted in both dollars and pesos (at the exchange rate in force at the time of this writing: P50 to US$1).

TIPS ON DINING

Festering poverty, apathy, and the absence of public works have resulted in the need for vigilance whenever food is involved. The lack of funds for maintenance have blurred the lines between the "in" and "out" pipes, and the lack of hot water prevents any reasonable attempt at hygiene. Absolutely don't drink the water, not even from a fresh water source as there's always a vagrant caribao on higher ground. That is, unless you find a summer of recovery from dengue fever or typhoid an appealing prospect.

That's not to say that you'll drop 30 pounds during your stay in the Philippines. The food here is actually quite delicious, taking on the flavors and styles of the various cultures that migrated or dominated the archipelago. While exploring the familiar Italian or French cuisines, do venture toward the local delicacies like lapu-lapu fish, or, for the more adventurous (don't count me among them), balut—an egg embryo eaten semi-raw. But don't be scared away from all local dishes, which rely heavily on vinegar and calamansi juice (local lime) for flavoring.

In extreme situations, you'll be faced with a local *turo-turo* (roadside pots where you point at what you want; even many Filipinos avoid these) or starvation. Not all street stalls are to be avoided—stick to the ones where the food is hot (this is essential; lukewarm or cold food has had a chance to ferment). Ask for a glass of hot water to dip your utensils; the locals do.

And the question you've all been asking yourselves? Do they really eat dog? Sure, primarily in the northern provinces of Northern Luzon, but it's not as widely eaten as assumed, and it's not disguised as any other meat. It's just considered another food source, particularly when there's nothing else around. In some households, dog meat (*aso*) is a delicacy, and obtained at a premium. Filipinos recognize that we Westerners find the practice shocking, and try to convince us that consumption is either in decline, or no longer practiced.

Fast Facts: The Philippines

American Express   In Manila, the American Express office is located in the Ace Building, corner of Rada and de la Rosa streets, Legazpi Village, Makati, Manila. It's open from 8:30am to 5pm weekdays, 8:30am to noon Saturdays. The direct line for travel services is ☎ **2/814-4770** to **73**. In Cebu, the office is in the PCI Bank Bldg., by the U.S. Consulate, Gorordo Avenue, 2nd floor (☎ **32/ 232-2970**). It's open weekdays from 8:30am to 4pm, 8:30am to 11am Saturday. American Express's 24-hour traveler's check refund hot line is ☎ **800/ 738-3383.**

Thomas Cook has an office at Skyland Plaza Building, in Manila (☎ **2/ 816-3701**); and on the ground floor of Metro Bank Plaza, Osmena Boulevard, in Cebu (☎ **32/219-229**).

Bookstores   In Manila, the **National Book Center** in Robinson's Mall, Ermita, has a current selection of best-selling books, magazines, and Filipino literature. They also have a wide selection of travel guides (should you happen to lose this one). There are branches in Cebu City also.

Business Hours   Private and government offices are usually open from 8am or 9am to 5pm, Monday through Friday (some private offices open on Saturday mornings too). Most shopping centers, stores, and supermarkets open at 10am and close at 7pm (malls may stay open until 8 or 8pm); during December, stores stay open until 10pm. Banks are open Monday through Friday from 9am to 3pm.

Cameras & Film   There are many camera equipment shops in Manila. **One-Stop Photo Center** at SM Megamall (☎ **2/633-5041**) is in a convenient location, with another branch in the Shangri-la Plaza in Makati (☎ **2/632-1543**). Film is readily available everywhere at prices comparable to those in the West. Most malls have fast, inexpensive, and good-quality film developing. There are also photo labs for the photo enthusiast who wants more specialized developing; **New City Studio Photography** is one such lab, located at Robinson's Galleria, Ortigas Avenue (☎ **2/636-4891**).

Doctors & Dentists   Most of the top hotels have a doctor on the premises available 24 hours a day. Otherwise, if you need emergency medical treatment, go to **Makati Medical Center** (☎ **2/815-9911**). (It's good enough for the president.) Treatment is inexpensive in the Philippines, and most medicines are available in cities, but usually under local brand names.

We wouldn't recommend dental care outside of Manila. If you do need it, try to get a recommendation from your hotel concierge, or one of the private hospitals in the city. Most procedures will cost less here than they would at home.

Drug Laws   Penalties are extremely strict for possession, use, or trafficking of illegal drugs in the Philippines. Convicted offenders can expect jail sentences, fines, or even the death penalty. This applies to possession of over 750g of marijuana, 50g of hashish, 200g of shabu (a methamphetamine, a.k.a speed), or 40g of heroin, cocaine, opium, or morphine.

Earthquakes   The Philippines is rocked by tremors and earthquakes quite often enough that you don't even feel them. If you think its going to be a big one, seek cover under tables, beds, or door frames to protect yourself from falling debris; or head to solid open ground.

Electricity   The country's electric power is set at 220–240 volts AC; however, some hotels come equipped with outlets for 110–120 volts too (some of these are limited to low powered devices like razors; others support appliances like hair dryers). Outlets are often identified for appropriate voltage, but if you are not sure, ask first before using it. Housekeeping at most big hotels can provide things like converters and plug adapters and electric razors for you to use, and many better hotels provide hair dryers as a rule.

Power failures, called "brownouts," are very common in the Philippines, even in Manila. Pack a flashlight and maybe a candle or two (the Museum Store sells artsy "credit card lights" for US$6.95). In the countryside or coastal towns, electricity is run off generators that usually have curfews of 10pm or 12am.

Embassies   The **U.S. Embassy** is located at 1201 Roxas Blvd., Manila (☎ **2/ 523-1001;** fax 2/522-4361; http://usembassy.state.gov/manila/). The **Canadian Embassy** is at Allied Bank Center, Ayala Avenue, Makati, Manila (☎ **2/ 810-8861**). The **Australian Embassy** is at Salustiana Ty Tower, 2nd floor, 104 Paseo de Roxas, Makati, Manila (☎ **2/817-7911** or 2/750-2840). The **New Zealand Embassy** is at Gammon Center Building, Alfaro St. Salcedo Village, Makati, Manila (☎ **2/818-0916**). The **Embassy of the U.K.** is at LV Locsin Building, Ayala Avenue, Makati, Manila (☎ **2/810-8861**).

Emergencies   For police, dial **166.** For medical or fire emergencies, dial **7575.**

Doctors/Hospitals   In Manila, most hotels either have an in-house doctor available or can suggest a reputable doctor for whatever you may need. Makati Medical Center (☎ **2/815-9911**) is the best around. A few others are: Saint Lukes Medical Center (☎ **2/722-0901**); Cardinal Santos Medical Center (☎ **2/721-3361**); and Medical City General Hospital (☎ **2/631-8626**).

Internet/E-mail   Internet cafes can be found throughout the Philippines, even in some pretty remote places. Wherever there are phone lines, you can bet someone is connected. Most of the bigger hotels in Manila and Cebu offer Internet access in their business centers, and some even have individual hookup in the rooms. A sure bet is the mall, where there's bound to be a few.

Language   Tagalog is the most widely spoken of the native languages, but English is widely spoken.

Liquor Laws   The legal age for alcohol purchase and consumption is 18 years, although IDs are rarely checked. Bars and clubs don't stick to any official closing time, but it's generally 2 to 4am. (Most bar owners will stay open until the last customer leaves.) Don't worry about finishing that beer before you venture to the bar next door; it's common practice to BYOB to most places.

Post Offices/Mail   Most tourist hotels offer postal services at the front counter. Post offices are open Monday to Friday from 8am to 5pm. Airmail letters to North America and Europe cost P11 (US$0.22), and to Australia and New Zealand, P10 (US$0.20). Postcards cost P8 (US$0.16), regardless of the destination, but you'll be better off slipping these into an envelope, because postcard delivery, and mail in general, is slow. Courier companies in Manila include **DHL** (☎ **2/895-0511**); **Federal Express** (☎ **2/833-3604**); and **UPS** (☎ **2/ 832-1516**).

Police   The emergency services are pretty reliable in Manila. On remote islands such as Palawan, however, expect the grocer clerk to wear many hats (police chief, fire chief, judge, and doctor). These fellas may not be the most reliable or helpful of civil servants. For police emergencies, dial **166.**

Safety/Crime   As in any country, theft, extortion, and assaults on tourists can probably be avoided with a little common sense and foresight. Almost everyone has caught wind of the kidnappings (mostly of Chinese and Japanese businessmen) that occur here, which the country is seriously cracking down on. Obviously, if you are flaunting cash, wearing expensive jewelry, or leaving your room unlocked, you are asking for trouble. It is best to keep valuables and excess cash in your hotel's safe-deposit box until you need them. When walking around, keep your money, passports, and camera hidden. Consider wearing a money belt, or a small purse with the straps hidden under a shirt and tucked into your pants. Also, shoes tend to disappear on ferries, so if you kick your shoes off, keep a watchful eye on them.

Manila isn't the safest place at night, so take a taxi if you have to go out. Rural towns tend to be poorly lit, so unless you have your flashlight, you will probably want to be inside anyway. Single women tend to be targets for all sorts of creative victimizations: girls having been robbed by taxi drivers after having succumbed to sleeping gas sprayed by the driver. Men are not exempt; it's practically impossible to advance 5 feet without an invitation to a nearby girlie bar. Be forewarned that the girls will swoop down en masse, and that even if you don't order a thing, your total bill will be very high. Let's just hope you can pay up.

We strongly advise staying away from portions of **Mindanao,** particularly the southern islands of **Basilan, Sulu, Tawi-Tawi,** and **Jolo,** which are inhabited by rebels and pirates. The Philippine government and the Moro National Liberation Front (MNLF) signed a peace agreement in 1996 supposedly ending the MNLF's 24-year military struggle for autonomy in Mindanao. However, peace remains elusive following the rise of the militant Moro Islamic Liberation Front (MILF), which opposes the agreement. Best just to stay away.

The U.S state department erges visitors to the Philippines to exercise extreme caution. There have been incidents of the kidnapping of tourists, sporadic bus hijackings, and bombings.

Taxes   Visitors tend to get slammed at top hotels and resorts when it comes to taxes (most hotels set their own tax on food, lodging, and excursions); however, the official taxes are: hotel 0.75%; restaurants 10%; and sales or VAT (Value Added Tax) 1%. Purchases usually indicate if VAT is included in the price.

Telephone & Faxes   Phone service is good in the Philippines, and reception is incredibly clear. Phone booths come in two varieties: coin-operated and Fonkard Plus, for calls using prepaid cards, which are available at most major hotels and post offices. The cost for a local 3-minute call is around 2 pesos. Dial ☎ **114** for directory assistance.

Hotels charge a ridiculous rate for international calls, and there's usually a 10% surcharge. If you don't have a calling card already, I suggest you get one; the rates will be much cheaper. Almost all hotels will send local or international faxes and will add the charge to your bill.

Time   Philippine Standard Time is 8 hours ahead of Greenwich Mean Time (GMT). International time differences will change during daylight saving, or summer time. Time differences during standard time are: U.S. East Coast: −13, U.S. West Coast: −16, London: −8, Darwin: +1, Melbourne: +2, Brisbane and Sydney: +3.

Tipping   Tipping in restaurants and hotels is optional but always appreciated. Generally a 5 to 10% tip is sufficient. At finer restaurants, the service charge is usually included in the bill.

Toilets   Bathrooms are called "comfort rooms," or the "CR," but sadly, more often than not, they're not. Some are downright alive and crawling while others are clean and comfortable. If you're taking a bus into Northern Luzon or into rural areas, be prepared for anything, and **never ever** step outside without toilet paper. In the countryside, plumbing hasn't made its debut yet, so you will be introduced to the "hand operated flush"—a plastic ladle or bucket is provided in a nearby barrel of standing water; simply dump some down the toilet. You will

---

Telephone Dialing Info at a Glance

• **To place a call from your home country to the Philippines,** dial the international access code (011 in the U.S., 0011 in Australia, 0170 in New Zealand, or 00 in the U.K.), the country code (**63**), the city or area code (see below), and then the seven-digit phone number.

• **To place a call within the Philippines,** use the area code of the city you are trying to call, then simply dial the seven-digit number. In some cases, you will find only five-digit numbers. These old numbers still work but will soon be replaced. Some area codes are: Manila 2, Cebu 32, Bohol 38, Baguio 74, Batangas 43, Puerto Princesa 48, Boracay 36, and Puerto Galera 912.

• **To place a direct international call from the Philippines,** dial the international country code (for the U.S. and Canada 01, for Australia 61, for New Zealand 64, and for the U.K. 44), then the area or city code, then the number (for example, 01 + 212/999-9999).

---

also notice that most toilets, except for in the nice hotels, lack toilet seats. It's likely that the seats are expensive and sold separately, but we were told that women here actually stand up on the seat instead of sitting. Never ever flush paper (definitely no sanitary napkins or tampons—if you can find any)!

Water   Poverty and corruption have resulted in a deterioration of an already dubious infrastructure, a situation that has resulted in rusted and broken-down pipes and a blurring of the lines between the "in" and "out" pipes. Unless you're hoping to contract tuberculosis, confine your water consumption to *sealed* bottled water.

3 Manila

Well, at least they're trying. Rising from the wasteland of uncollected garbage and the oppressive stench of urban blight are the bursts of governmental initiatives aimed at reclaiming not only a city, but a culture. The Metropolitan Museum features a surprising collection of thoughtful and vibrant art by local and international artists, the Orchidarium creates an oasis of calm within a madhouse of congestion, the new MRT raises hopes over the possibility of relieving overworked roadways, and hundreds of lighted orbs optimistically illuminate an otherwise seedy and avoidable corner of Rizal Park.

As a stopover for leaps into the cultural and natural attractions of the Philippines, Manila is a necessary evil. But after weeks of hiking mountains devoid of hot water or of days stranded (by the weather) on a forsaken shore, Manila begins to look good. So while you're here, it's worth a day or two to open yourself up to the historic context of the Filipino people, to find out where they come from, and to get some insights into where they are headed.

GETTING THERE

See "Getting There" above, since you'll almost certainly be arriving by air from abroad.

You'll be swarmed at the arrivals gate by representatives touting "official rates." There are no official rates. Just what the **airport taxis** (private companies that serve the airport) charge. Theoretically rates are fixed (even adjacent stands charge different amounts), but if you show a modicum of interest or hesitation as you walk away, I guarantee that someone will blurt out a lower rate. You could also try picking up a metered

Manila

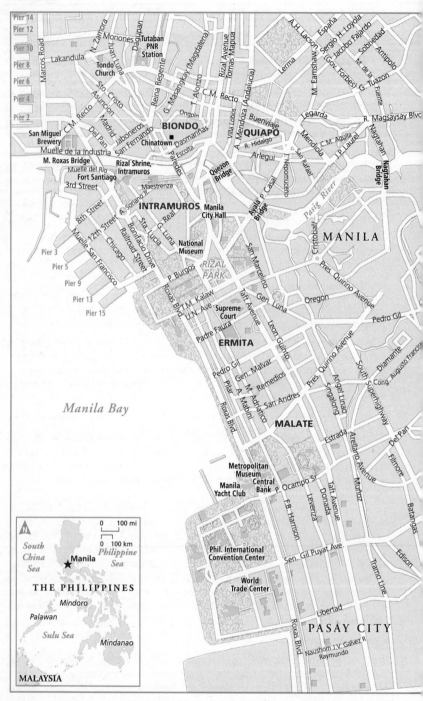

Pier 14
Pier 12
Pier 10
Pier 8
Pier 6
Pier 4
Pier 2

Marcos Road
Lakandula
N. Zamora
Moriones
Juan Luna
Dagupan
Tutaban PNR Station

Tondo Church
Sto Cristo
Asuncion
Madrid
Jaboneros
San Fernando
Reina Regente
G. Masangkay (Magdalena)
T. Alonzo
Ongpin
C.M. Recto
Rizal Avenue
Tomas Mapua

A.H. Lacson
Sergio H. Loyola
España
(Gov. Forbes)
M. Earnshaw
Lerma
Antipolo
M. de la Fuente
G. Tuazon
Sobriedad
Jacobo Fajardo

San Miguel Brewery
C.M. Recto
Del Pan
Muelle de la Industria
M. Roxas Bridge
Muelle del Rio
Fort Santiago
3rd Street

BIONDO
Chinatown
Dasmariñas
Escolta
Paredes
Villa Lobos
A. Mendoza (Andalucia)
Buenviaje
R. Hidalgo
QUIAPO
Legarda
Mendiola
C.M. Aguila
J.P. Laurel
San Rafael
Arlegui
J. Nepomuceno
R. Magsaysay Blvd

Rizal Shrine, Intramuros
Quezon Bridge
Maestrenza
Ayala Bridge
P. Casal

Nagtahan Bridge

Pasig River

8th Street
12th Street
Chicago
Muelle San Francisco
Pier 3
Pier 5
Pier 9
Pier 13
Pier 15

A. Soriano Jr.
Sta. Lucia
Bonifacio Drive
Railroad Street
G. Luna
INTRAMUROS
Manila City Hall
National Museum
P. Burgos
Roxas Blvd
RIZAL PARK
T.M. Kalaw
U.N. Ave.
Supreme Court
Padre Faura

San Marcelino
Taft Avenue
Gen. Luna
Leon Guinto
Oregon
Pres. Quirino Avenue
MANILA
Cristobal
Pedro Gil

ERMITA
Pedro Gil
Pilar
M. Adriatico
A. Mabini
Gen. Malvar
M. Remedios
San Andres
Pres. Quirino Avenue
Estrada
Singalong
Angel Linao
Arellano Avenue
Muñoz
South Superhighway
Cong. Augusto Francisco
Diamante
Del Pan
Filmore
Batangas

Manila Bay

Roxas Blvd
MALATE
Metropolitan Museum
Manila Yacht Club
Central Bank
P. Ocampo Sr.
F.B. Harrison
Leveriza
Donada
Taft Avenue

Phil. International Convention Center

World Trade Center

Sen. Gil Puyat Ave.
Tramo Line
Edison

Libertad
PASAY CITY
Roxas Blvd
Naushom J.V. Galvez R.
Raymundo

Inset map

N

0   100 mi
0   100 km

South China Sea
Manila
Philippine Sea

THE PHILIPPINES
Mindoro
Palawan
Sulu Sea
Mindanao

MALAYSIA

666

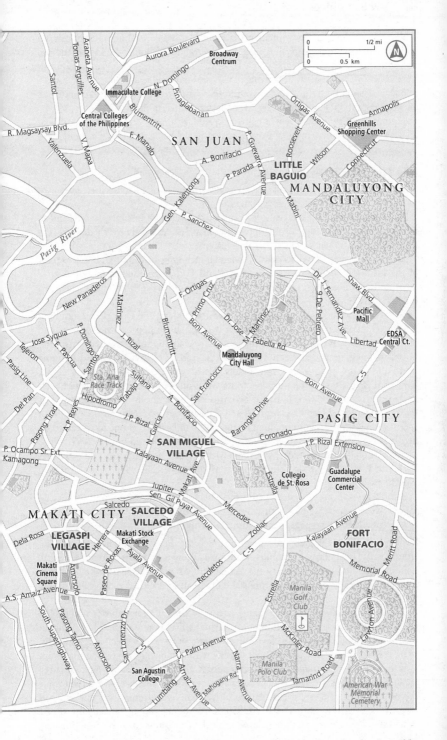

cab at the departures gate (dropping off fares on their way out), but not even this is a guarantee of a hassle-free arrival. A metered ride from the airport to Makati should run no more than P100 (US$2) and about P150 (US$3) for downtown Manila. Remember that you will most likely be arriving in the wee hours and feeling like an overcooked noodle; do yourself a favor and pay your hotel to pick you up. Hotel pickup rates are between P450 (US$8.50) and P900 (US$18) depending on the hotel.

If you're one of the lucky few to nab a metered taxi, that 1) turns on the meter, and 2) takes the most direct route, the fare to downtown Manila should run around P100 (US$2).

GETTING AROUND

Manila is a sprawling metropolis that's actually a number of separate cities, each with its own mayor and municipal government.

Most newcomers find the city's disorganized, seemingly unplanned layout hard to navigate. But in the middle of this apparently shapeless sprawl are clearly defined centers, each with its own unique illogical character.

South of the river, the oldest part of Manila, including **Intramuros,** is where most of the historical and cultural interest lies. **Rizal Park,** stretching from Taft Avenue down to Roxas Boulevard on the bay, lies just south of here in what might be termed the main city center.

South of Rizal Park is the tourist belt of **Ermita, Malate,** and **Pasay City,** with their hotels, restaurants, trendy cafes, handicraft shops, bookshops, airline offices, and travel agencies. **Remedios Circle** is the bohemian section of Malate where artists and musicians hang, sleep, and strum. Linking all these areas is **Roxas Boulevard,** running north and south along Manila Bay. Before World War II this was the most elegant boulevard in the city, with stuccoed white mansions and walled villas whose well-groomed gardens and lawns lined the beachfront. Now it's home to five-star bay-view hotels, the **Cultural Center Complex,** and the **Metropolitan Museum.**

Just to the east is the cosmopolitan financial hub of **Makati.** Home to Gucci stores, high-rise condominium complexes, office tower blocks, and top hotels, this is where the rich, the famous, the expat, and the powerful reside and relax. In nearby **Forbes Park** you'll find the Manila Polo Club and Manila Golf Club, along with a thriving nightlife scene.

Although you'll probably take taxis everywhere, it's always a good idea to have an idea of where you are, so pick yourself up a good map of Manila. **"EZ" Maps** are sold at most hotels and newspaper stands throughout the city.

BY TAXI   This is the preferred way of getting around town, but don't expect to get around very fast. During rush hours it can take as long as 2 hours to travel a painful 4 kilometers. This is partly due to the lack of traffic signals and signs, which has cars creeping across gridlocked intersections and doing all sorts of illegal things, including driving against oncoming traffic.

Taxis are everywhere, are cheap, pretty safe (see "Safety/Crime," above), and easy to identify, as most have a light indicator on top and writing on the side. They're thankfully also air-conditioned! Hotel taxis usually have a fixed rate for specific destinations, so unless you prefer the reassurance of dealing with a known quantity, you may want to walk down the street and hail one for yourself. Before you take off, make sure the meter is working, as drivers will convince you that it's broken only to charge you triple the usual fare. In the rare event that the driver refuses to comply, get out and hail another cab. Meters start at P20 (US$0.50) and inch up by increments of P1 (US$0.03). You can spend an hour driving all the way across town and still only pay about P100 (US$2). Make sure to carry small bills, because drivers often don't have any change (or so they say). You should leave a tip of 5 to 10%.

BY RENTAL CAR   See "Getting Around," earlier in this chapter.

BY BUS & JEEPNEY   Both types of vehicles pulse through most of Manila's major thoroughfares. Few of the city buses and none of the jeepneys are air-conditioned, and they're all pretty run-down. To boot, the locals will eye you up and down like you're crazy, but everybody has to ride a jeepney at least once. Buses display their final destination on the front; jeepney routes are fixed and written on the side. But unless you like suffocating heat and exhaust, just take a taxi.

BY PEDICAB, TRICYCLE, OR CALESA   Looking more like cartoon props, these throwbacks to a less gentler time are indispensable modes of transportation to the locals. None are allowed on major roads, so unless you're headed deep into the back streets, it's unlikely you'll need to use any of these in Manila. The pedicab is a pedal bike attached to a sidecar; a tricycle is a motorized version of the same thing. Both charge a minimum of P3 up to P10, but you may have a hard time convincing the driver to accept this from you, as foreigners are usually charged more.

BY LIGHT RAIL TRANSIT (LRT) & METROSTAR EXPRESS (MRT)   The LRT elevated railway system speeds through stations from Caloocan in the north to Baclaran in the south, while the brand new *air-conditioned* MRT hugs the city's eastern perimeter from Taft Avenue (just north of the airport) through Ortigas and Quezon City (a Phase 2 extension west to Monumento is planned for the future). Buy a token for a flat rate of P11.50 (US$0.23) at staffed booths. The LRT and MRT are open from 5:30am to 9:30pm. Try to avoid carrying bulky loads while riding these trains, as they is often full.

BY HORSE-DRAWN CARRIAGE   *Calesas,* as they are known, operate in Manila's Chinatown, Rizal Park, and Intramuros, and along Roxas Boulevard. The two-person horse-drawn calesa is more or less a tourist attraction, with fares beginning at P20 depending on the distance. As always, negotiate the fare before boarding one.

ON FOOT   You can do it, but Manila is not really a pleasant walking town. There's nothing very pretty to look at, the sidewalks are for either nonexistent or unable to accommodate the flow of people, and the exhaust fumes are overwhelming (expect a layer of grit to form on your skin within seconds).

VISITOR INFORMATION

The **Department of Tourism** (DOT) has several regional offices. Stop by the tourist information desk when you arrive at the airport in Manila or Cebu City. The main branch of the DOT at Rizal Park has maps, brochures, and nifty computer printouts for all the provinces with run-downs on accommodations, transportation, and attractions. Call ☎ **2/523-8411** or stop by between 8am and 5pm weekdays. There is also a **tourist assistance hot line** available 24 hours Monday through Saturday, ☎ **2/524-1660.**

Fast Facts: Manila

Banks/Currency Exchange   Currency can be changed at banks (Monday through Friday from 9am to 3pm) and hotels, but for a more favorable rate try one of the money changers scattered throughout the city centers and at the airport. All major currencies are accepted, but you will have more luck with U.S. dollars.

Laundry   All hotels offer laundry service, generally at prices inflated above their cost. Since these prices are still relatively cheap, it's probably easier to entrust your soiled clothing to housekeeping, but the truly independent minded traveler may want to spread the wealth around by patronizing one of the many laundries dotting downtown Manila. In Makati, you can call **Lavandera Co** (☎ **2/ 893-3412**) for free pickup and delivery between 6am and 10pm daily. Lavandera guarantees same-day service at no extra charge, for the easy price of P50 (US$1) per kilo (minimum 3 kilos, but who cares?).

Pharmacy   Most hotels stock the basics, like shampoo, toothpaste, aspirin, hairspray, and feminine products (sorry, no tampons!), in their gift shop. Otherwise, try **La Botica Inc.,** located in SM Megamall, ☎ **2/634-2222; Emilene's Pharmacy Inc.,** at East Service Rd., ☎ **2/842-3186;** or one of the **Mercury Drug Corp** outlets around the city (the main store is in the Mercury Drug Corp Bldg, Quezon City, ☎ **2/911-5071**).

Post Office   Most hotels offer mail service. Rizal Park Post Office, located by the park, near the Manila Hotel in Ermita, is not too busy. They are open Monday to Friday, 8am to 5pm, and Saturday until noon. If you are in Makati, a more convenient location is the Makati Central Post Office at Gil Puyat Avenue, Makati. The hours are the same.

Telephone   See "Fast Facts," earlier in this chapter. For calls within Manila no prefix is necessary. From a hotel you usually have to dial 9 for an outside line. Directory assistance is 114.

Transit Information   If you have any questions on routes and prices you can call the 24-hour tourist hot line at ☎ **2/524-1660.**

ACCOMMODATIONS

In a city where venturing outside is tantamount to stepping into a slum, it's no small relief to put a crisp, shiny lobby between you and the front door. Fortunately, hotels in Manila merit their star-studded status, in reliable luxury chains like the Shangri-La, the Inter-Continental, and the Peninsula. The influence of these five-star properties have elevated the standards of hotels in the metro Manila area, where for once, you can actually take for granted the availability of 24-hour hot water and a top sheet.

When choosing a neighborhood, Ermita and Malate are closest to the tourist areas and less congested with people and traffic than Makati. Nightlife is abundant here, and the city's countercultural and artistic community tends to congregate in this area. If business is your priority, Makati, Manila's business and financial district, is where you need to be. Stores, dining, and hotels are all top-notch in this area, but rush hours can be a nightmare.

Hotel rates are listed in pesos along with the current equivalent in U.S. dollars; in the case where the hotel rates are provided in U.S. dollars, only this rate is provided.

ERMITA/MALATE
Very Expensive

✪ **Manila Hotel.** One Rizal Park, 1099 Manila. ☎ **800/9-MNL-HTL** or 2/527-0011. Fax 2/527-0022 to 24. www.manila-hotel.com.ph. E-mail: resvn@manila-hotel.com.ph. 500 units. A/C MINIBAR TV TEL. P12,500–P15,000 (US$250–US$300) double; P16,250–P125,000 (US$325–US$2,500) suite. AE, DC, JCB, MC, V.

Without a doubt Manila's most famous hotel, the Manila hotel has stood as witness to the lives, loves, triumphs, and heartbreaks of a city for 7 decades. It's certainly the most representative of Filipino culture, in spite of the unfortunate laminated poster and ruby

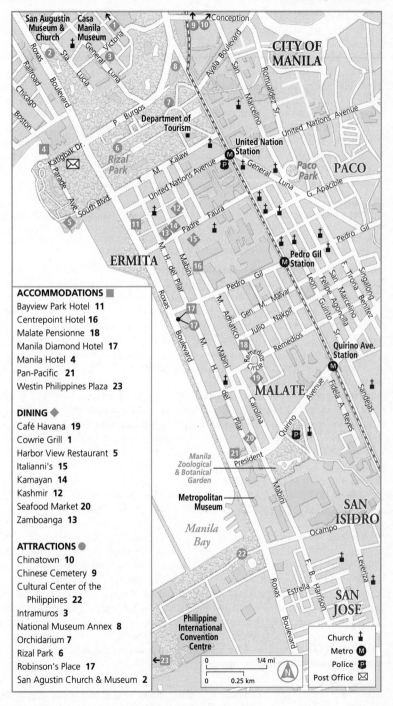

San Augustin Casa
Museum & Manila
Church Museum

Victoria

San Augustin Museum & Church

Roxas
Sta. Lucia
General Luna

Railroad
Boulevard

Chicago

Boston

Katigbak Dr.

Parade

South Blvd.

Ave.

P. Burgos

Department of
Tourism

Rizal
Park

T. M. Kalaw

United Nations Avenue

ERMITA

Roxas

M. H. del Pilar

Mabini

Padre Faura

Conception

CITY OF
MANILA

Ayala Boulevard

San Marcelino

Romualdez Sr.

United Nations Avenue

Department of
Tourism

United Nation
Station

Paco
Park

PACO

General
Luna

G. Apacible

Pedro Gil

Pedro Gil
Station

Leon
Felipe Agoncilla
San Marcelino
Guinto
F. Tirona Benitez
Singalong

ACCOMMODATIONS ■
Bayview Park Hotel **11**
Centrepoint Hotel **16**
Malate Pensionne **18**
Manila Diamond Hotel **17**
Manila Hotel **4**
Pan-Pacific **21**
Westin Philippines Plaza **23**

DINING ◆
Café Havana **19**
Cowrie Grill **1**
Harbor View Restaurant **5**
Italianni's **15**
Kamayan **14**
Kashmir **12**
Seafood Market **20**
Zamboanga **13**

ATTRACTIONS ●
Chinatown **10**
Chinese Cemetery **9**
Cultural Center of the
Philippines **22**
Intramuros **3**
National Museum Annex **8**
Orchidarium **7**
Rizal Park **6**
Robinson's Place **17**
San Agustin Church & Museum **2**

Pedro Gil

M. Adriatico

Gen. M. Malvar

Julio Nakpil

Remedios

Quirino Ave.
Station

Remedios
Circle

MALATE

Carolina

M. H. del Pilar

Mabini

Fidela A. Reyes

Quirino Avenue

Sandejas

Manila
Zoological
& Botanical
Garden

Metropolitan
Museum

Manila
Bay

Ocampo

SAN
ISIDRO

Quirino

President

F. B. Harrison

Roxas

Estrella

SAN
JOSE

Leveriza

Mabini

Philippine
International
Convention
Centre

0   1/4 mi
0   0.25 km

Church ✝
Metro Ⓜ
Police Ⓟ
Post Office ✉

red accents recently added by the hotel's new (Chinese) management. Since its opening in 1912, the hotel, nestled between the walled city of Intramuros and the famed Manila Bay, has hosted everyone from Ernest Hemingway to John F. Kennedy, with Michael Jackson and the Beatles in between. WW II buffs can even take advantage of the General MacArthur suite, a re-creation of the room he occupied for 6 years, although priority for this museum-like room goes to diplomats and presidents. Rooms exude a turn-of-the-century charm, with four-poster beds, old world fabrics and textures, and ceiling fans. Rooms in the 18-story wing, added in 1970, are less expensive—and less charming—than rooms in the original building. All the first-class amenities you would expect are here, but the height of luxury is in the Penthouse and Presidential suites, with their live-in butlers, indoor swimming pools, and helipads. While poking around the lobby, ask the concierge for a look at the Archive Room, a cluttered historical of the hotel's 88 years. Dining options include Japanese and Italian.

Expensive

✪ The Pan Pacific. M. Adriatico and Gen. Malvar St., Malate, Manila. ☎ **800/327-8585** in North America or 2/536-0788 in Manila. Fax 2/526-6503. www.panpac.com. E-mail: rsvn-manila@panpac.com.ph. 240 units. A/C MINIBAR TV TEL. P9,500–P11,500 (US$190–US$230) double; P12,500–P625,000 (US$250–US$1,250) suite. AE, DC, JCB, MC, V.

As the only true luxury hotel in the Malate/Ermita area, the Pan Pacific isn't in direct competition with its closest rivals, the Peninsula and the Shangri-La over in Makati. And just when a seasoned traveler thinks there's nothing left to impress, the Pan Pacific exceeds your expectations by installing televisions above the lip of the bathtub—with remote. Its actual claim to fame, however, is as the first butler hotel in Manila, a reputation they maintain in grand style. Double doors herald expansive mirrors reflecting Italian marble and sandblasted glass in the bathrooms, which also come with a separate shower stall. Countertop goodies are impressive too: bath salts and a loofah sponge just about outdo every other place I've been in that department, and they even throw in a traveling toothbrush set along with the usual five-star amenities. The elegant down duvet comforter and sea of pillows are a nice touch, as is the in-room iron and ironing board. Spacious and technologically advanced, every room has dual phone lines (IDD/NDD Internet ready), personal computers on granite desks, fax/printers, and your very own drip coffeemaker.

Moderate

✪ Bayview Park Hotel. 1118 Roxas Blvd., Ermita, Manila (corner of United Nations Ave.). ☎ **2/526-1555.** Fax 2/522-3040. E-mail: bookings@bayview.com.ph. 285 units. A/C MINI-BAR TV TEL. P5,750–P6,500 (US$115–US$130) double; P7,000–P9,250 (US$140–US$185) suite. AE, DC, MC, V.

Quality and value are why the Bayview is popular, and a complete overhaul in 1996 ensures that this combination is achieved without compromising luxury. Its location across from the U.S. embassy is prime, overlooking the bay and within easy walking distance of attractions, but you don't pay sky-high prices for it. They offer a range of corporate, bay-view, and executive suites; you'll enjoy the best views from the junior suite's corner room. All standard and superior rooms are equipped with gadgets like individual bed-side panel control, coffeemakers, and deposit boxes, and many rooms are interconnected for a large family or business gathering. The tranquil rooftop garden and pool rival anything you'd see at the Peninsula, and the modest but effective fitness center offers massage services.

Inexpensive

Malate Pensionne. 1771 M Adriatico St., Malate, Manila. ☎ **2/596-672.** Fax 2/597-119. 45 units, 48 dorm beds. P1,050–P1,500 (US$21–US$30) room with A/C and private

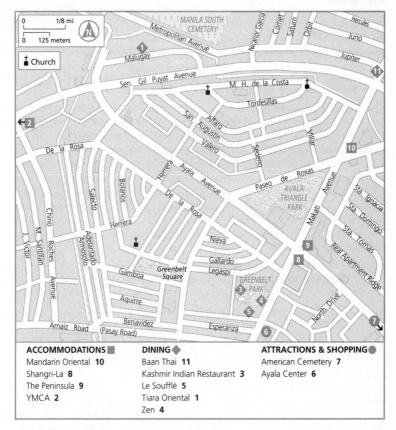

ACCOMMODATIONS ■
Mandarin Oriental **10**
Shangri-La **8**
The Peninsula **9**
YMCA **2**

DINING ◆
Baan Thai **11**
Kashmir Indian Restaurant **3**
Le Soufflé **5**
Tiara Oriental **1**
Zen **4**

ATTRACTIONS & SHOPPING ●
American Cemetery **7**
Ayala Center **6**

bathroom; P850 (US$9) room with fan and private bathroom; P550–P800 (US$11–US$8) room with fan and common bathroom; P275 (US$5.50) per person in dorm with fan. AE.

The cozy atmosphere and budget prices make this the most popular pension in Metro Manila. The rooms are clean, the sheets smell good, the water is hot, and the staff is super helpful and knowledgeable. The antiques in each room add a charming, warm touch. You'll even find a business center with e-mail. The restaurant and cafe are fine if you don't feel like wandering out at night, and they've even got vegetarian options.

MAKATI
Very Expensive
Mandarin Oriental. Paseo de Roxas and Makati Ave., Makati, Manila. ☎ **2/750-8888.** Fax 2/817-2472. www.mandarin-oriental.com. E-mail: reservations-momnl@momnl.com. 464 units. A/C MINIBAR TV TEL. P14,500–P22,00 (US$290–US$440) double; P24,500–P43,500 (US$490–US$870) suite. AE, DC, JCB, MC, V.

In a sea of five-star luxury hotels, service separates this hotel from its competitors, attracting its loyal business clientele for its high quality personalized attention. Employees warmly welcome you and shoo you along the red carpet that leads to the elevators and up to your room. The rooms are soothing, in muted, relaxing tones, with a huge desk that makes it easy to spread out your laptop and files. Bathrooms are sleek, in all marble and porcelain. All suites come with fax machines, which in standard rooms are available on request. For dining, there's a dizzying array of cross-cultural options to please every palate.

The Peninsula. 1226 Makati City, Manila (corner of Ayala and Makati Ave.). ☎ **2/810-3456.** Fax 2/815-4825. www.peninsula.com. E-mail: tpm@peninsula.com. 500 units. A/C MINIBAR TV TEL. P14,750–P17750 (US$295–US$355) double; P21,500–P135,00 (US$430–US$2,700) suite. AE, DC, JCB, MC, V.

The Peninsula is one of the classiest, most elegant hotels in Manila. It certainly has the best lobby, with enormous tapestries and bright natural light filtering through gracefully arched glass windows. A grand curving staircase takes you up past the piano accompaniment to the lobby lounge and the popular Conservatory Bar and Grill. Rooms are airy and come equipped with fax machines and a handsome wooden entertainment center with a large TV. The comfortable bathrooms have separate shower, tub, and toilet areas. For dining, you'll feel important at such high-society palate pleasers as Old Manila featuring excellent selections from various Asian cuisines (☎ **2/812-3456;** main courses P450 to P745 or US$9 to 14.90); and The Lobby, for 24-hour food and live music, a hot spot for politicians and the social elite. There's also an Italian restaurant, a bar, and an à la carte buffet.

Shangri-La Hotel. P.O. Box 4191, MCPO 1281, Makati, Manila (corner of Ayala and Makati aves). ☎ **800/942-5050** in the U.S. and Canada; 800/222-448 in Australia; 0800/442-5050 in New Zealand, 44 181/747-8485 in the U.K.; 2/813-8888. Fax 2/813-5499. www.ShangriLa.com. 703 units. A/C MINIBAR TV TEL. P15,000 (US$300) deluxe room; 15,750P–P19,500 (US$315–US$390) executive room; P19,500–P24,750 (US$390–US$495) horizon room; P67,750–P145,000 (US$1,355–US$2,900) presidential suite. AE, DC, MC, V.

Keep your tie buttoned for this very professional resort catering to the international business executive. The design is as varied as the diverse corporate moguls who stay here. Compared to the more pure-bred designs of other top hotels in the area, it's a decorative mutt—*Gone With the Wind* meets Malaysia. And for some reason they think it's a good idea to flip pancakes in the lobby. But in terms of service the Shangri-La is second to none, and carries with it the reputation of a premier Asian hotel chain. The Makati location is perfect for exclusive shopping and business dealings. The rooms are exceptionally spacious and appointed with coffeemaker, a convenient push-button control panel by the bed, and a separate shower stall in the marble bathroom. The suites are huge and luxurious, radiating a timeless ambience and making you feel like royalty.

Moderate

Tiara Oriental. 7248 Malugay St., Makati City (near Makati Medical Center). ☎ **2/729-7888.** Fax 2/729-4916. www.Tiara.com.ph. E-mail: Sales@Tiara.com.ph. 114 units, all with bathroom. A/C MINIBAR TV TEL. P4,750–P5,000 (US$95–US$100) double; P6,000–P1000 (US$120–US$220) suite. AE, DC, JCB, MC, V.

This moderately priced hotel is perfect for businesspeople who want a four-star boutique environment without all the fuss of mass-produced luxury. The Tiara Oriental glitters behind a crisp marble lobby and gold accents in the rooms, which are elegantly simple. The hotel's smaller size doesn't require you to compromise on the necessary amenities; there's a business center with secretarial services and Internet access, and other services such as messengers, freight and travel arrangements, and any place that offers the possibility of renting alright by me. And it's the only gig in town with in-room instructions on what to do during an earthquake (this is good). The hotel provides shuttle service to the Makati Shopping Center, so you're not entirely reliant on the basic hotel cafe for all your meals (which incidentally served me only those breakfast Danishes I had picked out of the basket the prior morning).

Inexpensive

City Garden. Makati corner of Kalayaan Ave., Makati City. ☎ **2/899-1111.** Fax 2/899-1415. www.citygardenhotels.com. E-mail: garden@iconn.com.ph. 160 units, all with bathroom. A/C MINIBAR TV TEL. P1,500–P1,900 (US$30–US$38) double; P2,100–P2,300 (US$42–US$46) suite. Children under 12 stay free without extra bed. Promo rates for long stays. AE, DC, JCB, MC, V.

This stylish newcomer is a breath of fresh air in the middle of a traditionally stuffy neighborhood of business class elitism. Rooms may be considered a bit on the small side, but space concerns are balanced by the pristine parquet floors, orthopedic mattresses, and pleasing design of the room. Even the television is sleek and streamlined, and the management expects to have installed Internet access into the viewing system by the publication of this book. The panoramas are even good, especially from the rooftop recreation area, which includes an outdoor swimming pool, modern fitness center, spa, sauna, and restaurant. There's also a business center, a travel agency, non-smoking rooms, and a helipad for those wishing to beat the city traffic.

YMCA. 7 Sacred Heart Plaza St. (off Dao St.), San Antonio Village, Makati (near Makati Central Post Office). ☎ **2/899-6101.** Fax 2/899-6097. 30 units. A/C TV TEL. P1,130–P1,265 (US$22.60–US$25.30) double; P2,213–P2,582 (US$44.26–US$51.64) suite for 3–6 persons. AE, DC, MC, V.

Unexpectedly tucked into the residential back streets of Makati, the YMCA is pretty much what you would expect, with rooms in need of a paint job and the familiar odor of a dorm room. The Spanish-influenced building, a cement pillared construction with a triangular pediment and wrought iron posts, makes it a bit less institutional, and it *is* a great place to meet other travelers. They also offer cheap, dormitory-style accommodations, although it can be quite noisy and hard to sleep. Facilities include a pool, small gym, and tennis and basketball courts. There's also a decent restaurant serving local and continental dishes.

ALONG ROXAS BOULEVARD

Expensive

Manila Diamond Hotel. Roxas Blvd. at the corner of Dr. J Quintos St., Manila. ☎ **2/526-2211.** Fax 2/526-2255. www.diamondhotel.com. E-mail: Diamond@cnl.net. 500 units. A/C MINIBAR TV TEL. P12,000–P13,000 (US$240–US$260) superior single or double; P13,000–P20,000 US$260–US$400) deluxe single or double; P15,000–P100,000 (US$300–US$2,000) executive floor suite. AE, DC, JCB, MC, V.

A 15-minute walk to Rizal Park, the Diamond Hotel straddles the best of Manila between the tourist district and the business center. As a reliable Japanese-owned chain hotel, it's popular with business executives and, obviously, visiting Japanese. The lavish combination of black granite, marble, and opulent gold leaf creates an elegant early 1900s art deco/postmodern design throughout the lobby and the rooms, which come equipped with fluffy down beds and both 110 and 220 voltage. Wide bay windows in all the rooms afford at least partially magnificent views of Manila Bay and the illuminated skyline, a perfect ambience for reading your complimentary copy of *TIME*. Rooms are also equipped for fax and computer hookup.

PASAY (NEAR THE AIRPORT)

Very Expensive

Westin Philippines Plaza. Cultural Center Complex, Roxas Blvd., Pasay City. ☎ **800/625-5144** in the U.S.; 800/1651-0701 or 2/551-5555 in Manila. Fax 2/551-5610. 670 units. A/C MINIBAR TV TEL. P15,000–P17,500 (US$300–US$350) double; P22,750–P156,400 (US$455–US$3,128) suite. Weekly promotional rates. AE, DC, JCB, MC, V.

The fabled sunsets of Manila are the backdrop to this resortlike hotel complex on the bay, which caters mostly to international business travelers who want to take advantage of its convenient location and vacation-like atmosphere. Taking up some of the primest real estate on the water's edge of the CCP complex, the Westin is close enough to the hustle and bustle of downtown, but not so near to the airport that you're stranded.

The hotel has a huge pool that curves around water slides and a poolside bar that hosts cultural performances and barbecues. Golfers can also hone up on their accuracy at the on-premise putting green. The best views are from the "pool-view" rooms that overlook the bay, and rooms and bathrooms are spacious and first-class. Service is excellent. There are several top quality restaurants, a great bakery, a disco, and a bar with Guinness on tap.

DINING

If you crave it, Manila's got it, whether you are looking for gourmet dining or a quick-and-cheap but tasty meal. There's plenty of that familiar, salty, greasy, American fast food to choose from here, an unfortunate legacy of the country's later colonial years. If you can pry yourself away from T.G.I. Friday's, the Hard Rock Cafe, the Fashion Cafe, Chilis, Benihana, McDonald's, Wendy's, Dominos, Pizza Hut, Shakey's, Kentucky Fried Chicken, Kenny Roger's Roasters, and Texas Chicken, there's plenty of worthy menus around town. Below we've listed the most popular, but these are by no means the only places with good food and atmosphere. No fuss meals (they also deliver!) can be had at the **Aristcrat** chain, considered a pioneer in BBQ chicken since 1936, and every bit as finger-lickin' good as they say (what's more, they don't use MSG). If dietary hygiene is not a concern, you can venture over to the fairly reliable **turo-turos** near the Lyceum of the Philippines in Intramuros (along Muralla) or choose your fish and method of cooking over at the **Seaside Market** near the Baclaran flea market. In Makati, restaurants are grouped along Pasay Road, Makati Avenue, and Jupiter Street, with the bigger selections (sorry folks) found inside the more environmentally appealing malls.

Mixed up in the cauldron of modern cultures—from the Dutch, to the Spanish, to the Chinese and Japanese—and buried under the surface of the ubiquitous American fast food and mall experience—is a uniquely Filipino character.

ERMITA/MALATE

Café Havana. 1903 M. Adriatico (at Remedios St.), Malate. ☎ 2/521-8097. Main courses P220–P445 (US$4.40–US$8.90). AE, DC, MC, V. Daily 11am–2am. CUBAN.

It's easy to spot this muy popular corner hacienda, with its windows that surround the entire facade. The airy inside is just as festive, with hardwood floors, pastel paintings, and interesting Cuban knickknacks decorating the bar and restaurant. At lunchtime, the scene turns corporate with the suit-and-tie type taking advantage of the lunch special. They have great pork sandwiches and tasty Cuban kabobs. Most entrees come with an accompaniment of Spanish rice and an array of dipping sauces, including hot spicy chiles.

Dinnertime finds an eclectic mix of people, and after dinner the bar gets pretty packed. Impromptu dancing is not uncommon at any hour, and even the waiters seem to always be moving their hips and clapping. It's kind of hard to keep still with the sensual beat of Latino music blasting from the speakers.

Harbor View Restaurant. On Manila Bay, South Gate A, South Blvd., Rizal Park, Ermita. ☎ 2/524-1532. Main courses P80–P330 (US$1.60–US$6.60). AE, DC, JCB, MC, V. Daily 11am–midnight. FILIPINO/SEAFOOD.

This restaurant jutting out over the harbor is considered one of the most romantic spots in Manila. The white plastic tables create an unpretentious crab house atmosphere, where you can watch the boats passing by. When the mercury drops, the breeze is relaxing, and you can dance to the tunes of Frank Sinatra and the other swingers playing over the sound system. The menu ranges from your basic cheeseburger to the more exotic *sugpo sa Taba ng Talangka* (prawns in crab fat), with or without a sprinkling of chicharon (crispy fried pork skin) with more basic options like tuna, shrimp, and mussels. The mango salad is refreshing, with chopped green mangos, onion, and tomato seasoned with *baboong* sauce. The menu also features an ample variety of frozen drinks, making this a perfect stop for an after-dinner drink as well.

✪ **Kamayan.** 523 Padre Faura cor. M. Adriatico, Ermita, Manila. ☎ **2/528-1723.** (A second location is at 47 Pasay Rd., Makati; ☎ **2/845-3604.**) Main courses P130–P654 (US$2.60–US$13.08). Shellfish priced per 100 grams. AE, DC, MC, V. Daily 11am–11pm. FILIPINO.

According to folklore, eating with one's bare hands used to be seen as the ultimate pleasure, a way of celebrating the plentiful feast. Well, it's certainly a messy hoot, as even the saucy shellfish entrees are tackled with your hands.

The squeamish get silverware, and everyone gets an unlimited supply of wet-wipes. It's a rather touristy venue, but according to locals it's a must-stop for great-tasting Filipino food, and the atmosphere is better than that of nearby Zamboanga, with its roving serenading band. If you're feeling adventurous, order the *nilalang bulalo* (cow foot soup) or the enormous sweet and sour prawns. Portions are huge, service is almost overly attentive, and the atmosphere is fun and lively.

✪ **Kashmir.** Padre Faura, Ermita. ☎ **2/524-6851.** (A second location is in the Festejo Building, 816 Pasay Rd., Makati; ☎ 2/844-4924.) Main courses P250–P600 (US$6.25–US$15). AE, DC, JCB, MC, V. Daily 11am–11pm. INDIAN/MALAYSIAN.

With a variety of sauces ranging from tomato cream and butter, to coconut milk with spices, to spicy tandoori, it's no wonder Kashmir's cuisine ranks among the top five in the city with locals and expats alike. It's also one of the very few places you can get a fix of yogurt, prepared here in several cool and creamy lassi flavors. The space is small, dimly lit, and quiet; the food is anything but. There are plenty of vegetable main courses and rice specialties to choose from, including the house pride chicken tandoori. A sure palate pleaser is the Kesu Pullao, a subtle, saffron-seasoned rice dish, and in all cases, you'll be offered the option of mild or spicy (not for the wimpy). Most main courses come with an assortment of mango chutney, mint sauce, and a spicy crushed pickles-and-ginger dip. Those wary of spicy food might try the T-bone steaks and lamb chops in a milder mushroom sauce.

Seafood Market. Ambassador Hotel, Mabini St., Malate. ☎ **2/524-7756.** Entree with soup and salad P400–P800 (US$8–US$16). AE, DC, MC, V. SEAFOOD.

There is a method to this seafood madness. First, grab a cart or basket and pick out a fresh lobster, crab, lapu-lapu (a delicious local white fish related to the grouper), or one of the many other mouthwatering creatures on offer. Put it in a plastic bag, but wrap it tightly, as they get jumpy when they're out of the water. Then select how you want your fish prepared from a long list of options. Try the delicious *sinigang ni hipon,* which is a sour-ish tamarind-based soup with prawns and local vegetables, the classic sweet and sour lapu-lapu or simply grilled fish.

Zamboanga. 1619 Macario Adriatico St., Ermita, Manila. ☎ **2/525-7638** or 2/521-9836. Reservations recommended during peak season. Main courses P80–P400 (US$1.60–US$8). AE, DC, MC, V. Daily 9am–11pm. FILIPINO/SEAFOOD.

The gifts of the sea are truly appreciated here, their flavor brought out with delicious Filipino sauces and spices. The menu will need interpretation, which only goes to show how authentic the dishes are here. The wait staff is very friendly and will gladly stand over you for as long as it takes until you are clear about what's what. The local specialty *adobo* is good, as is Fisherman's Delight, a delectable assortment of fresh oysters, crabs, shellfish, and crustaceans, steamed and delicately spiced. If seafood is not your thing, there are plenty of noodle, rice, and vegetarian dishes. All main courses come in a native basket lined with banana leaves. One word of caution: If you order the pig, you get the whole pig—head and all! The attraction here is the traditional cultural show, the only one connected to a restaurant.

MAKATI

Cabalen. Glorietta Park, Ayala Center Mall, Makati. ☎ **2/893-5915** (also inside Robinsons Place, Malate). All you can eat buffet P220 (US$4.40). AE, DC, JCB, MC, V. Daily 11am–10pm.

A casual and amiable restaurant of *molave* wood tables and chairs and folk songs playing in the background, Cabalen serves up traditional Filipino entrees heavy on influences from the Campanga region of central Luzon. Myself a boycotter of buffet meals in general, here, the buffet is the best way to go, offering a thorough sampling of exotic selections. Typical dishes include *bopiz* (kidney), *gatang kohol* (snails in coconut milk*)*, *ensalata ampalaya* (a bitter vegetable with garlic and ginger), and *laing* (a root vegetable in coconut milk. There's also an abundant choice of pork, beef, and fish stews, as well as Chinese influenced fried *lumpia, pinakbet* (noodles), and *adobos* (traditional barbeque). Finish off with some local ice cream or one of the rice-based puddings (yam, corn, or plain milk), or go for broke with the fried banana.

Le Souffle. 2nd Floor, Josephine Building, Makati Ave. at West Dr., Ayala Center, Makati. ☎ **2/812-3287.** Main courses P395–P750 (US$7.90–US$15). AE, DC, MC, V. Daily 11am–3pm and 6–11pm (the bar stays open until 1am). FRENCH/MEDITERRANEAN.

"If the ingredients are here, we will do our best!" is the chef's motto, who defends the brevity of Souffle's written menu by ensuring the quality of the kitchen's output—limited only by the ingredients currently on hand. Some of the chef's best dishes have been unique requests from guests, including the decadent panfried goose liver. The menu offers such unique dishes as rack of lamb, confit de canard, and grilled lapu-lapu in a warm tarragon/tomato vinaigrette served with crispy vegetable julienne topped with sour cream and paprika. In support of diners eating as they please, there is no distinction between appetizers and main courses, a policy that creates just the right mix of sophistication and casualness. There's also an excellent wine bar.

L'eau Vive in Asia. 1499 Paz M. Guazon Ave. (formerly Otis), Paco, Manila. ☎ **2/563-8558** or 2/563-8559. Reservations recommended. Main courses P250–P600 (US$5–US$12). AE, DC, MC, V. Daily 11am–3pm and 7–11pm. FRENCH.

This missionary settlement run by Carmelite nuns serves up authentic French cuisine, including frog legs in garlic butter and rabbit in white wine cream sauce. Not only is the food delicious, but it's beautifully arranged with complementary colors and textures. The lapu-lapu à la bouillabaisse is excellent, filled with shrimp and tomato in a delicate white wine cream sauce, and served with fettuccine noodles. The service is cordial and attentive (they are nuns, after all), and because the place is somewhat off the beaten track, in a rather run-down area, it's quiet and sometimes a little empty. To warm your heart and spirit, catch the 9:30pm prayer, when local street children kneel down in front of the garden courtyard and the statue of Mary and sing along to "Ave Maria."

ATTRACTIONS

Rather than giving an exhaustive list of sights to see in Manila, below are a few of the more interesting things to see in the city. There are plenty of guided city tours available through most hotels; however, most of the sights below are easy to reach, and taxi drivers will be familiar with all of them.

ERMITA/MALATE

Intramuros. North of Rizal Park. Admission P50 (US$1). Daily 8am–6pm.

When Spanish colonizers had Cebu under their belt, and when they recognized the strategic advantages of Manila Bay, the Spaniards transferred the capital to Manila. That same year, in 1571, they started the construction of a walled city, a fortified seat for the Spanish Empire in the East. Named for the land "within the walls," the historic area of Manila called Intramuros is the most popular sightseeing destination and a respite from this cramped, crowded, and chaotic city. The 4.5-kilometer-long outer wall encloses an area of 64 hectares (158 acres), so you may want to take advantage of the tour of Intramuros by horse-and-buggy for P600 (US$12; the short version around the plaza in front of Fort Santiago, just after the ticket window, is only P40 (US$0.80). If you just like to poke around the garrison and chapel at your own pace, you can follow in the final footsteps of José Rizal, or simply relax on the overgrown ramparts formerly used as defense. Sights within the walls of Intramuros include Fort Santiago, San Agustin Church (both listed below), and the Plaza San Luiz Complex (listed under Casa Manila, below, and which includes an arcade of souvenir boutiques, an outdoor cafe, and a restaurant).

Fort Santiago. Northwest corner of Intramuros. No phone. Entrance included with admission to Intramuros. Daily 8am–6pm.

Fort Santiago was begun in 1571 and was completed 150 years later with the use of Filipino forced labor. The fortress was used as Spain's main military defense position in the islands, as well as a prison for Filipinos during both the Spanish and Japanese occupations.

Beyond the training oval, now a peaceful garden, is the Rizal Shrine (Tuesday through Sunday 8am to noon and 1 to 5pm; donations welcome), a collection of Rizal memorabilia housed in the prison where, in 1896, the national hero spent the final 2 months of his life. The exhibit includes relics of the man, his various books and manuscripts, various paraphernalia acquired on his trips abroad, and the actual vertebra where the executioner's bullet lodged (he was shot in the back).

San Agustin Church and Museum. Real and General Luna sts. (within the walls of Intramuros). Admission P45 (US$0.90). Daily 9am–noon and 1–5pm.

San Agustin is the oldest church in the Philippines, and the oldest structure to survive the destructive bombing of WWII.

The Monastery, originally used as the living quarters, housed a classroom, refectory, vestry, sacristy, library, and infirmary of the Augustinians. The baroque church was restored and turned into a museum in 1973, and houses the Ayala Chapel along the left nave, maintained by the auspicious Ayalas themselves in the manner of a Middle-Age aristocracy, and the tomb of Miguel Lopez de Lagazpi (left of the altar), who founded the city of Manila in 1572. In the monastery, arranged around a pretty cloister, is a showcasing of Filipino, Spanish, Chinese, and Mexican art, a collection of religious sculpture and objects, and an interesting collection of photos of 19th-century Manila.

✪ **Casa Manila.** Real & General Luna sts. (right across from San Agustin Church). ☎ **2/ 496-793** or 2/483-275. Admission P40 (US$0.80). Tues–Sun 9am–6pm.

Lodged within the Plaza San Luiz Complex, a reconstruction of nine traditional Spanish colonial houses, Casa Manila embodies 19th-century design, with original adobe stones, European furnishings and decor, and Philippine weavings. The house reveals a bit of 19th century culture, swathed in mirrors and elaborate carvings that denoted a family's wealth. The layout provides a window into 19th century Manila as well, with a ground floor anteroom for unwanted guests, tax collectors, and amorous callers; the first level bachelor's bedroom (removed for discreet comings and goings); an impressive array of kitchen utensils; and a "dual latrine."

Rizal Park. Roxas Blvd. and Untied Nations Ave. (just outside the walls of Intramuros).

Rizal Park honors the nationalist hero who was executed here at dawn by the Spanish on December 30, 1898. Stroll around to see his bronze statue and the Japanese gardens, and stop in the Department of Tourism along the park, on TM Kalaw St. You might even catch a free Sunday concert or get a delicious mango shake at the nearby Manila Hotel.

The National Museum Annex. Padres Burgos St. (a short walk from Rizal Park). ☎ **2/ 494-450.** Admission P100 (US$2). Mon–Sat 8:30am–noon and 1–5pm.

The Philippine National Museum opened this annex in 1999 to provide a unified space for exhibitions on Filipino culture and heritage. The best stuff is found on the third floor, from prehistoric findings from Palawan to a comprehensive and instructive ethnological display. You'll see a fossilized skullcap of Tabon Man, and an extensive exhibition of tribal artifacts and representations indicative of life throughout the ancient archipelago.

Check out the museum's Maritime Heritage Gallery located on the second floor, featuring seven native boats that have been carbon-dated to between 890 and 710 B.C. Of special interest are the recovered items from the *San Diego*, a Dutch ship sunk in 1600. Tough times were these, where Ming Dynasty china served as ordinary tableware (intact and on display here).

Coconut Palace. CCP/Cultural Center of the Philippines (orange buses and jeepneys circle the complex continually). ☎ **2/832-0223.** Admission P100 (US$2); includes 30-minute guided visit. Tues–Sun 9am–4:30pm. Closed holidays. If the entrance gate is closed, ring for admission.

Built for the Pope in anticipation of his visit to Manila in 1978, this stately palace is constructed almost entirely from organic materials. Ultimately, the Pope declined the offer to stay here, stating that the palace was much too opulent for his use. Instead, I suspect that political correctness compelled him to hole up at the home of the local ecclesiastic leaders, given that close to an entire forest must have been chopped down to build the thing. You see, 90% of the building is made of coconut lumber, frond fibers, and other indigenous materials. It is rather beautiful, though, and like the controversy over wearing fur, the thing *is* already dead. So I felt justified in oohing and ahhing over this collection of hexagonal shapes repeated in the building's wings and flooring. Images of coconut shells and banana fronds appear in the chandeliers, and a oyster farm of capiz shells filter in natural light. Mostly used for wedding receptions, maybe they'll take my idea for a garden cafe seriously, because the lush garden grounds and unrivaled view of Manila Bay are currently enjoyed by just a handful of staff members.

It's clear that they're on the right track. The ✪ **Orchidarium** (entrance near Teodoro E. Valencia Circle; ☎ **2/527-6376**) is open Tuesday through Sunday 9am to 5pm. Admission is P100 adults; P60 students/seniors; it includes entrance to the Butterfly Pavilion and a starter kit for growing orchids, planting a tree, or caring for butterflies. The city gatekeeper to 50 of the 180 genera of indigenous orchids, opened on October 28, 2000. The Orchidarium is one large planned nature trail, sophisticated enough to appeal to tree huggers, with areas entitled Fern Gully, Dendro Hill, Brome

Beds, Heli Pad, and Scented Green. The gardens are targeted at a younger audience, however, to instill a level of natural appreciation in a highly impressionable audience. Attractions feature a **Butterfly Pavilion** of about 1,500 butterflies (they're deaf, so the highway traffic on the other side of the wall has no effect); a **Rain Forest** which has three waterfalls and jug-shaped carnivorous pitcher plants; and a **House of Reptiles** (called by staff members the House of Representatives). Optional hands-on activities include a rock climbing wall (P50/US$1), and a fishing pond (P25/US$0.50), set among sensitively sculpted sections like the Rocky Trail, the Water Experience, the Orchid Gallery, the Trellis of Waves, and the Philippine Species Island. An exhibition area and curio shop occupy the center island, where a fine dining restaurant recently opened.

OUTSIDE THE CITY CENTER

Chinatown. Quintin Paredes and Ongpin sts. Binondo.

Located in the old districts of San Nicolas and Binondo, you'll know you've entered Chinatown when you pass through the three Chinese-Philippine friendship arches called the Arch of Goodwill. Not for the faint of heart, Chinatown is as authentically unkempt as they come, split down the middle by the main artery of Ongpin Street. Gold jewelry, Chinese ceramics, porcelains, and fresh or preserved fruits and meats vie for your time, but most people just come for a traditional Chinese herbal remedy in some of the oldest apothecaries in the city. Here you can pick up an emulsion for strong bones and teeth or "essence of chicken," said to restore mental alertness and physical energy (sounds like mom's chicken soup) or a more basic ginseng. The charming Carvajal Street briefly runs parallel to Ongpin near the Binondo Church, a narrow lane barely wide enough for the bales of cogon grass and produce stalls that force patrons to walk single file. Grab a *hopia,* an interesting dumpling-like pastry, from any of the bakeries, or flag down a *calesa,* the horse-drawn carriages that frequent Chinatown.

The Chinese Cemetery. North of Santa Cruz, along Aurora Ave. and Jose Abad Santos St.

This cemetery is more like a well-kept suburb. In fact, the dead are better off than the living inhabitants of the squatter towns surrounding it. Some house-size tombs are complete with mailboxes, air-conditioning, and even fax machines to make the afterlife as comfortable and convenient as life on earth was. Guides are recommended, as they have some fascinating tales to tell about the area, and it's easy to lose yourself in the many alleys that branch through the cemetery.

The American Cemetery. Fort Bonifacio in Makati; 2km from where Ayala Ave. meets Edsa (Epifanio de los Santos Ave.). Free admission. Daily 6:30am–5pm. Arrival best by taxi.

War buffs and veterans will probably be drawn to the American Cemetery, the largest American burial ground outside the U.S. Laid out on 52 hectares (128 acres) of land donated to the U.S. by the Philippines in 1964, the cemetery is the final resting place

---

Where to Tee off on Luzon

If you are interested in getting in a few rounds of golf, Manila and the surrounding area have plenty of courses to choose from. Some are for members only, but the following are open to tourists: **Aguinaldo Golf Club,** Quezon City (☎ 2/911-8142); **Fort Bonifacio Golf Club,** Fort Bonifacio, Makati (☎ 2/812-7521); **Philippine Navy Gold Club,** BNS Fort Bonifacio, Makati (☎ 2/819-2780); **Calatagan Golf Club,** Calatagan, Batangas (☎ 42/818-6961).

for the 17,000 soldiers who died in the Philippines and surrounding Pacific during World War II. Tiled mosaic mural maps clearly illustrate the historic battles inside the stark circular memorial, so you don't have to be a World War II history buff to appreciate the significance of the site.

SHOPPING
SHOPPING CENTERS

Once I returned from the Philippines, all of this local merchandise with "Made in the Philippines" started jumping out at me: handicrafts, novelty items, and high-priced designer wear that cost pennies to produce. Subtract customs taxes, middlemen's fees, and hundreds of percentage markup and you can only imagine how much fun you'll have in the malls of Manila and Cebu. Obviously, items with labels like Swatch, Nautica, Calvin Klein, and Ralph Lauren price their merchandise based on the current value of the U.S. dollar, so there'll be no bargains there. But you can find relatively high quality locally made goods for a fraction of what you'd pay back home (I hit pay dirt at a little store in Robinson's Mall called Oxygen).

Ermita/Malate
Robinson's Place. Along M. Adriatico St. in Ermita, next to Manila Midtown Hotel.

For unique antiques, knickknacks, jewelry, coins, and woodwork, go to **Yamasawa** on the third floor. **Hanuman Music and Crafts** offers a selection of hand drums with Philippine tribal designs and traditional rattan weaving. They also carry hand-sculpted pottery and bowls, incense, and New Age books and music.

Harrison Plaza. Between A. Mabini and M. Adriatico sts. in Malate.

This plaza has two major department stores under its roof: **Shoemart** (SM) and the upscale **Rustan's** (operated by Marks and Spencer). On the first floor is an antique shop called **Kabul.** On the second floor, **Fo Kuang Yuen** sells Chinese decorative objects, statues, and small samples of jewelry made of jade and other semi-precious stones. Check out the bargain stalls on the ground floor's center atrium for gift items.

Makati
Ayala Commercial Center. Between Edsa, Ayala Ave., Makati Ave., and Pasay Rd.

This is a vast, sprawling complex, so use the convenient map displays or the user-friendly Automated Shoppers Guides (ASGs) located at the ends of hallways. **Island Spice** and **Pidro** offer tropical clothing, light cotton shirts, T-shirts, shorts, and sarongs. **The Museum Shop** and **Things** sell art reproductions, statues, and a few native souvenirs.

For Filipino antiques go to **Goldcrest Square;** even if you don't intend to buy anything, it's still a great place to see how Spanish, Chinese, Japanese, and American influences have blended with tribal Filipino culture. At **Tesoro's** you'll find wearable native dresses as well as woven and embroidered items like place mats and tablecloths made from indigenous materials.

You can find very convincing knockoffs of names like Ferragamo, Gucci, and Bulova at **Goldcrest,** the freshly opened indoor version of a flea market. Makati's residents and commuters find that these stalls, which carry knockoffs of the latest fashions, toys, and gadgets, are more convenient than their inspiration, Greenhills.

SM Megamall. Along Edsa Ave., near the Hotel Inter-Continental.

This is said to be the largest mall in the country, with six floors of shops and 12 cinemas. Stores like **Old Manila** and **Memory Lane** display Philippine-made furnishings, small antiques, and old books and jewelry. **Tahanan** is a good place to find modern basketwork. And have I mentioned shoes? Check out the ever-popular **Shoemart** department store. If the heat gets to you, there's an ice-skating rink.

Shangri-La Plaza. Right beside SM Megamall, bordered by Edsa Ave. and Shaw Blvd.

This exclusive mall is home to Rustan's Department Store and a range of high-end boutiques and stores. The main attraction here is an eight-story atrium with live trees and a musical fountain.

OPEN MARKETS

No trip to Manila is complete without venturing to the open markets where local artists, weavers, sculptors, and the like spread their livelihood out for all to see. You will need some bargaining expertise to get through the experience; if you don't have it, you're a sitting duck.

Central Market, in Santa Cruz by Quezon Avenue, is a good place to go for fabrics and clothes. It's a fairly large sprawl and it's open every day, weather permitting. **Baclaran,** just off Roxas Boulevard on the way in from (or to) the airport (if you're not taking a taxi: from Ermita take a jeepney headed for Baclaran and take it to the end, or hop on the LRT to the last station; from Makati take a bus marked "Baclaran" or "NAIA"/Nino Aquino Int'l Airport), is a low quality local clothing and handicrafts market. If you're looking for straw, rattan, or carved wood handicrafts in an authentic (read: filthy) environment, venture into the neighborhood market of Quiapo. A bracing foray into the wet market is definitely a shocking eye-opener; guaranteed to turn even the most seasoned traveler into a vegetarian.

MANILA AFTER DARK

At first glance, it may appear that karaoke rules the Filipino night, but you'll be surprised at the variety of nightlife the city has to offer. The sterile atmosphere of the city's countless malls is eminently appealing to locals, who flock to this artificial refuge from the grubby outside world.

It's not uncommon to overlap a shopping expedition with dinner, and dinner with a movie. The malls also maintain a concentration of theme pubs like the Hard Rock Cafe, TGI Fridays, Streetlife, and The Brewery, where the lines are consistently long. The Malate/Ermita area has a bohemian, laid-back atmosphere, while Makati hosts more of a jet-setting scene. For reasons of convenience, we're leaving out the up-and-coming scene in Quezon City, which is too far away for the casual visitor.

While waiting for the sun to set and the bars to open, why not hop on the **Manila Bay Sunset Cruise** (consult your hotel concierges for info) leaving nightly at 5pm from the Harbor View Pier (near the Manila Hotel, off South Drive). The cruise costs P40/US$0.80.

Café Adriatico. 1900 M. Adriatico St., Malate, Manila (at Remedios Circle). ☎ **2/ 521-6682.** Sun–Thurs 11am–midnight; Fri–Sat until 2am.

Very popular for dinnertime romantic interludes or a simple after hours cup of coffee, Café Adriatico's adult atmosphere is a perfect place to see how middle class Manila lives. Its location on Remedios circle even makes a (short) nighttime walk possible. The menu certainly covers its bases, with Filipino selections, Continental cuisine, and recipes from around the Southeast Asian region, rounded off by the cabaret tunes played by the resident British pianist.

Café Provençale. Unit 5 & 6 Puerta de Isabel 11 (along Muralla St.) at Magallanes Dr., Intramuros. ☎ **2/527-4251.** Mon–Sat 11am–11pm; later hours on weekend evenings.

Taking up two stone vaulted spaces of the old city walls in what may have been a hospital or even a morgue, Café Provençale offers some adult nightlife in a historic setting. One vault has been renovated into a sleek and modern billiard room and bar, an urban reconstruction of chrome and stainless steel that serves as both a meeting place and after-dinner destination for the restaurant in the adjacent vault. The Swiss born son of two Brits (married to a Filipina) makes his debut as restaurateur and head chef after an auspicious period of employment in the kitchens of the Manila Hotel, so you're guaranteed a superior Mediterranean meal next door for less than you'd pay a parking attendant at home.

Giraffe. 6750 Ayala Ave., facing the Glorietta Circle, Makati. No cover.

In direct competition with Venezia (see below), Giraffe attracts the cocktail crowd of Manila's younger power people. Called "gay-raf" in certain circles, it's also a magnet for Manila's gay crowd. Grab a seat at the trendy, circular bar, or take the spiral stairs to the balcony area above. The left side of the bar is where most gay patrons hang out. This place gets pretty packed and, as at Venezia, dress code is enforced.

Heckle & Jeckle Café & Bar. Ground floor, Villa Bldg., Jupiter St., corner of Makati Ave., Makati. ☎ **2/890-6904.** Daily 11am–4am.

Named after the two cartoon magpies, people come to this bar to play a game of pool or to listen to the live band every Thursday to Saturday. Come between 8 and 10pm to avail yourself of the P175 (US$3.50) drink-till-you-drop special. They also make a mean pizza, and cocktail lovers should try the *Heckle Special.*

Prince of Wales Pub. Basement, New Plaza Building, near the Greenbelt Center, Makati. ☎ **2/815-4274.**

This British-style pub is the friendliest in town and very popular among expatriates and tourists. If you're homesick, this might be the place to come. Perhaps have a dart game or two, or just head for the bar and start chatting. Aside from the usual British pub grub, P.O.W. serves Middle Eastern specialties like hummus, and the popular *mishman,* a spicy dish of shrimp, chicken, or beef on a bed of water cabbage and chile peppers. It goes great with a beer. Lunchtime here is more businesslike, but the atmosphere is still relaxed. Honorable mention goes to **Blarney Stone,** the only bar in town that has Guinness on tap. It's on the Upper Basement floor, Glass Tower Building, Palanca Jr. St., Legazpi Village, Makati (☎ **2/818-6541**).

Republic of Malate. 1769 Mabini St., Malate. ☎ **2/303-3529.** Cover P250 (US$5) includes 1 standard drink.

Pop diva Kuh Ledesma owns this eminently of-the-moment night club, and her pop status ensures standing room only. Latin Nights at the Republic is a favorite, featuring an up and coming band accompanied by a local vocalist every Thursday.

Timbuktu/Java Hut. 618 Nakpil St., Malate. ☎ **2/303-7103** and 2/303-3763. Mon–Thurs 7pm–2am; Fri–Sat until late.

The juxtaposition of a hip restaurant over an upscale coffee bar is somewhat accidental but makes choosing a suitable environment for your mood that much easier. The Java Hut offers Filipino food in a laid-back and beachy locale of throw pillows and batik lanterns. If you've been scared off by that balut (the duck embryo you see locals scarfing up on street corners), you may be brave enough to have a go at it soaked in a thick camouflaging gravy spiced with chile and garlic, with a stiff local beer to toss back to lessen the trauma. Downstairs, Timbuktu challenges all of the city's Starbucks (there are 23 outlets in the city) with their coffee originals like the JFK (cocoa and milk sprinkled with Oreos) or the Portofino (Kahlua, cream, nutmeg, and cherry). What's more, both venues accept orders from the other.

✪ **Venezia Bar and Restaurant.** Ground Floor, Glorietta II, Ayala Center, Makati. ☎ **2/845-1732.**

This is the posh place where Manila's jet set and local expats come to see and be seen. The huge L-shaped, fully stocked bar is set in a Venetian-style, almost gothic decor. If the plushy art-nouveau bar chairs don't do it for you, have a seat at one of the tables. Dance to the funky beats, then kick up your feet and smoke a cigar while soaking in the trendiness all around you. Stylish clothes and shoes are required, and men must wear shirts with collars.

4 Excursions from Manila

The provincial roads leading south out of Metro Manila lumber painfully away from the seething city towards greener pastures. For the most part neglected by the local administrators, provincial communities stretch out in an endless parade of corrugated roadside shacks, emaciated dogs, and rusty steel rooftops. Obviously, the further away you get from the city, the more pastoral the land becomes, making the provinces within reasonable driving distance a playground for the well-to-do city dwellers.

There are a number of day or overnight trips (depending on your tolerance for traffic) you can take from Manila. (See the section on Northern Luzon for information on the Mount Pinatubo trek, also within easy reach of the city.) Most of these destinations are within 3 hours or less of the city; depending on your travel style, you can either go it alone or book an inexpensive tour through your hotel or a travel agency in Manila. Try **Baron Travel** (☎ 2/817-4926), with offices in major hotels such as the **Holiday Inn** and the Pan Pacific, and others scattered throughout the city.

CORREGIDOR

Of vital strategic importance in World War II was the tadpole-shaped island of Corregidor, standing guard at the entrance to the Bay of Manila 26 miles west of the capital and just offshore of the Bataan Peninsula to the north. From 1902 to 1922, Corregidor island was fortified by the American military as part of the "Harbor Defenses of Manila and Subic Bay," but construction was halted with the Washington Disarmament Treaty of 1922, which bound the U.S. to cease improvements on existing fortifications in colonies west of the International Dateline. Under a guise of "public works," two more projects were completed in top secret: the bomb-proof Malinta Tunnel and the Navy Radio Intercept Tunnel, whose purpose was to obtain and decode radio messages coming from Japan.

The island is administered by the Corregidor Visitor's Information Center, which offers a walk-in loop tour by way of bus or jeepney. This option isn't so convenient, though, as the public ferry to the island leaves from Bataan. Student packages and promotions are available from Manila; for information, contact the **Corregidor Foundation** (☎ 525-3420; fax 523-5605; www.tourism.gov.ph; e-mail: cfi-dot@compass.com.ph) or the Corregidor Visitor's Information Center in the CCP Bay Cruise Terminal A (☎ 2/834-5048).

Sun Cruises, Inc. operates package tours from Manila, leaving Monday through Friday from the CCP Bay Cruise Terminal A on Roxas Boulevard at 8am (boarding is at 7:30; Saturday and Sunday additional tour leaves at 10am). For information contact Sun Cruises at ☎ **2/524-0333;** fax 2/521-5850. For reservations, call ☎ **2/831-8140;** fax 2/834-1523; e-mail: suncruises@magsaysay.com.ph.

TAGAYTAY RIDGE TOUR/TAAL VOLCANO TREK

About a 1½-hour drive south of Manila lies the city of Tagaytay, a narrow municipality stretched along part of the perimeter of the ridge high above the calm waters of Lake Taal and its picturesque occupant, Taal Volcano. At 686 meters (2,250 ft.) above sea level, the city enjoys panoramic views of the volcano as well as the lush green mountain ranges at your back (the best views of the lake are obscured by facilities lining the ridge, but fortunately, a few of these are notable places for slaking hunger and thirst or resting weary feet after a day's expedition at the volcano). The city's altitude also promises a slightly less insufferable heat than its neighbors at lower heights, as well as an abundant variety of crops like pineapples, papaya, ginger, and camote (sweet potato) suited to milder climes.

Lake Taal's origins were as a low-lying valley, until geology resculpted and inundated its contents. A history of deadly eruptions resulted in a fate not unlike that of the city of Pompeii, Italy; in fact, recent findings claim that Lake Taal conceals a buried city beneath its waters.

The volcano juts out of the center of the lake on its own island amid landscapes of ash and cinder, and despite being one of the country's smallest volcanoes, it has been the site of many of its most powerful eruptions. Scientists monitor the island closely for signs of impending activity, so you can safely hike or ride a pony to the island's many natural wonders, including the irresistible (but challenging to get to) Crater Lake, with its famous "island in a lake on an island in a lake on an island." After trekking up the slope of the volcano, you can swim in the warm waters and wonder at the smoke coming up from cracks in the earth.

Hotels and travel agencies run regular half-day and full-day trekking **excursions** to the Taal Volcano depending on whether or not you want to get down and dirty. The half-day trip will get you a taste of the area for about P1,300 per person (minimum two passengers; P1,800 with lunch); the full-day trekking tour includes a canoe ride, lunch, round-trip transfers, and guide for P3,000 per person (minimum 2 passengers; P5,000 per person). You can also do the trek on horseback.

The City of Tagaytay operates a friendly **Tourism and Cultural Development Office** inside the City Hall (from 11th Airborne monument, take a jeepney headed to the right) if you're interested in the historical and economic aspects of the city (☎ **46/ 860-0697;** e-mail:fnt@mozcom.com).

PAGSANJAN FALLS TOUR

The Pagsanjan Gorge is one of nature's wonders turned tourist attraction. The famed falls, a thundering sheet of falling water, is actually called Magdapio Falls, and is the pinnacle of an amusement ride that is commonly known as "shooting the rapids." (My personal experience was more like a trickle. . . .) There's no denying the scenic value of the ride as you travel upstream, then back down along the Pagsanjan River, at the base of 400-foot-high cliffs that are home to a lush forest wilderness. In fact, if Pagsanjan gives you a sense of déjà vu, it's probably because you have seen it in such movies as *Apocalypse Now* or *Born on the 4th of July.*

All of the resorts fronting the Pagsanjan River offer the **river excursion to the waterfalls** (whose actual name is the Magdapio Falls). Prices are the same no matter where you go, at P580 (around US$12) per person (note: based on two or three per boat; if you're traveling alone, you'll either have to pay double or negotiate a better rate, if it's a slow day).

The "ride" consists of a native canoe (yours) being propelled (and frequently lifted over boulders) upstream by two highly expert and sufficiently bored boatmen. About 7 kilometers and 2 hours later, you arrive at the falls, where a crudely-made raft will take you the few meters through the pounding falls for a brief look at Devil's Cave and back (P50/US$1 extra).

You can also book the Pagsanjan excursion as a day tour from Manila through your hotel or any travel agency in Manila. A typical day tour will include lunch, the canoe ride, and round-trip transportation for about P2,500 (US$50).

Be sure to take along a waterproof bag for cameras and film. Also, wear clothing that will wring out and dry overnight; in this high humidity, jeans shorts can take up to 3 days to dry.

SUBIC BAY FREEPORT ZONE

Throughout the past few centuries, Spanish, Japanese, and American troops have all recognized the strategic importance of Subic Bay in the push towards the dominance of Manila. Today, it's a matter of economics; the former American naval base established here in 1901 and abandoned in 1992 has been developed, uplifted, and given the special designation as a "Freeport," a governmental arm designed as a self-sustaining industrial, commercial, financial, and investment zone.

The Freeport covers an area of 18,000 hectares, (44,460 acres), 6,000 of which have been developed for industrial purposes. The remaining 12,000 hectares are protected, and represent one of the last preserved forests in central Luzon. Only the native Aita people, veritable hermits of the forest, are exempt from the prohibition against hunting or logging.

The zone is enclosed by a security gate, a seeming slap in the face to the characteristically disorderly town of Olongapo outside the entrance gates. But this somewhat artificial and secure zone elicits a sigh of relief for its pristine bay and scenic Zambales Mountains, where families of monkeys scurrying alongside the road are a common sight. Thanks to over a century of military activity, the area waters provide an arena for world class diving.

Fixed on achieving international competitiveness, the powers behind Subic Bay are at full throttle, implementing industrial and environmentally viable projects with increased tourism as the prize. From the pristine and gloriously undeveloped shores of Subic Bay, to internationally competitive facilities, the Subic Bay Freeport is an ideal one-stop destination offering truly unspoiled beaches, living forests, wildlife attractions, water sports, horseback riding, *and* duty-free shopping. The Subic Bay Metropolitan Authority maintains a very active **Tourism Department** at Building 662, Second Floor, Barryman Street (near the Legenda Hotel). For general information or details on any of the activities listed below, call ☎ **47/252-4242** or fax 47/252-4561, or check out their Web site at **www.sbma.com**.

✪ MOUNT PINATUBO

After 600 years of silence, on June 15, 1991, Mt. Pinatubo blew its top, blasting 20,000 tons of sulfur dioxide 25 miles high and forming a cloud that encircled the globe within 21 days. It's no doubt that the world experienced some of its most glorious sunsets during those 3 weeks, but that was a heavy price, counted in the loss of around 42,000 homes, over 100,000 acres of cropland, and the lives of 900. At least this time the locals had some warning. The last time the volcano erupted, area residents weren't so lucky.

Ten years later, some of the farmers have returned, eking a living out of rice fields covered in hardened lava by carving bonsai trays, bowls, lanterns, and other household objects, as well as other souvenirs for the weekend trekker. And always in the shadow of this 1,759-meter (5,770-ft.) high menace.

That destruction can be so overpoweringly stunning is an intriguing cosmic strategy, resulting in a stream of naturalists and eco-tourists willing to put their bodies through some intense physical stress for the pleasure of a few moments of awe. Treks to the crater can be completed in one or two overnights; you can decide whether those nights will be spent between sheets or in a sleeping bag. The hike up to the crater, not including transport to the village "base camp," will take 3 to 6 hours, depending on which village you choose to set out from; prices run from around US$100 to US$150 per person. A good portion of the hike is on sandy ash, which will require more effort, but the reward for your troubles will be a hard-to-beat swim in the stunning crater lake. There's no protection up here, so watch out for sunburn, pack enough water (included in most tours), and wear a hat with a brim.

Swagman Travel (☎ 2/524-5816 in Manila or 45/322-5133 in Angeles City) arranges two night treks camping overnight in the lahar (lava) fields, but tours can be arranged through any travel agency. For the more comfort-minded, **Baron Travel** (☎ 2/817-4926) runs weekend packages with overnights at the Holiday Inn in Clark.

5 Northern Luzon

More than anywhere else in the Philippines, the provinces of Northern Luzon have managed to retain their purely indigenous and uncolonized traditions. In many of these areas you can still see Ibaloi, Kankana-ey, Ifugao, Bontoc, Kalinga, Gaddang, and a few other tribes, generically (and somewhat derogatorily) known as Igorots. The most unaffected by Western culture live reclusive lives beyond the prying eye of the tourist, living and cultivating as they have for centuries. The longevity of these tribes is due to the mighty Cordillero Mountains, which run the length of Northern Luzon and create a topography that was less than welcoming to invading Spaniards.

Not much has changed over the centuries, as the only access into the region is limited by a single, rough and rocky, and often unsurfaced road that is all but impassable under the best of conditions. The hardship of the arrival has managed to keep tourism and development in check, so that time stands still in villages around Banaue, where livelihood continues to depend on a staggering landscape of rice terraces rivaling any of the seven wonders of the ancient world. In remote villages, tribes live off the lands, have tribal meetings of elders, and continue the practice of exhuming the corpses of dead relatives and storing the remains in blankets in a corner of their hut.

In Sagada, the Earth reveals her hidden treasures in underground caves, where the "hanging coffins" still represent an ancient, if not endangered, burial site. But most impressive of all is the general absence of intrusive electrical wires, and the ability to gain insight into the simplicity of life without modern encumbrances.

GETTING INTO THE REGION

Manila is the jumping-off point for all points north. You can definitely capture the flavor of this region from the seat of a bus, but when traveling into the Cordilleras, you may want to seriously think through how much road travel you can endure. Some of the roads heading north through the mountains are more of an adventure than the destination itself, but a 10-hour odyssey of being jostled around like Mexican jumping bean might be too much for even the most intrepid traveler. When mapping out your route, consider how much travel time you can or are willing to endure, and make sure you stay long enough to make it worth the trouble. Also remember that the rainy season and typhoons can seriously impede ground travel.

BY BUS   Several companies run regular bus service into Northern Luzon: **Dangwa Tranco** (☎ 2/731-2859) and **Victory Liner** (☎ 2/361-1506) both have air-conditioned buses that make several daily trips. From Manila, gauge about 9 hours. The terminals of the individual bus companies are scattered throughout Manila, so

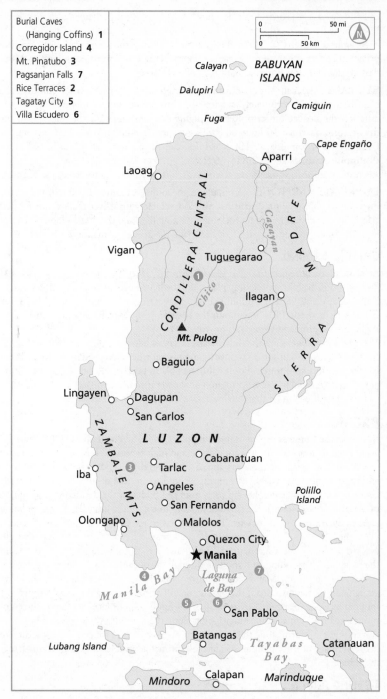

Burial Caves
  (Hanging Coffins) **1**
Corregidor Island **4**
Mt. Pinatubo **3**
Pagsanjan Falls **7**
Rice Terraces **2**
Tagatay City **5**
Villa Escudero **6**

0   50 mi
0   50 km

Calayan   BABUYAN
              ISLANDS

Dalupiri

Camiguin

Fuga

Cape Engaño

Aparri

Laoag

C
O
R
D
I
L
L
E
R
A

C
E
N
T
R
A
L

Cagayan

Vigan

Tuguegarao

1

Chico

2

Ilagan

▲
Mt. Pulog

S
I
E
R
R
A

M
A
D
R
E

Baguio

Lingayen

Dagupan

San Carlos

L U Z O N

Z
A
M
B
A
L
E

M
T
S
.

3

Cabanatuan

Tarlac

Iba

Angeles

San Fernando

*Polillo
Island*

Olongapo

Malolos

Quezon City

★ **Manila**

4

Manila Bay

*Laguna
de Bay*

7

5

6

San Pablo

Batangas

*Tayabas
Bay*

Catanauan

Lubang Island

Mindoro

Calapan

Marinduque

call first, or ask a taxi driver if he knows how to reach a particular terminal. Most likely, he will.

Swagman Travel (☎ 2/523-8541; e-mail: fly-bus@mozcom.com) also organizes private coach service from the Swagman Hotel Narra Hotel in Angeles daily on Monday, Wednesday, and Friday at 8am for P600 (US$12).

BY PLANE Loakan Airport outside of Baguio offers the only option for air travel into the region. Unfortunately, service is erratic; at the time of this writing, all was quiet on the Loakan air strip. Regular flights usually resume for the duration of the dry season and cut a 10-hour odyssey down to 50 minutes from Manila (roughly P1,200/US$24 round-trip). For schedules, call **Asian Spirit** at ☎ 2/840-3811 or **Philippine Airlines** at ☎ 2/816-6691.

From the airport, you can take a rental car, bus, or jeepney to wherever you're going.

BY PRIVATE CAR/TOUR A popular compromise is to hire a car and driver for the duration of your stay up north. An off-road vehicle with driver costs about P5,000 (US$100) per day and includes fuel, tolls, parking fees, and the driver's food and lodging. Any travel agency or hotel desk can make the arrangements for you.

GETTING AROUND

Avis on Harrison Road (☎ 74/442-4018), and **Hertz** on Session Road (☎ 74/442-3045) in Baguio are the only places in Northern Luzon where you can rent a car. Rates are available with or without a driver. Expect to pay around P14,000 for a 4-day rental with drive and P8,000 without, but because of the appalling nature of the roads, I wouldn't recommend trying this on your own.

Buses and jeepneys are the only means of travel between towns and villages up in the Cordilleras (and in some cases, you can only get where you're going on foot). Buses ply the long-distance routes, but it's also possible to hop on and off one of these if it's going your way when you want to go. For shorter distances, you can take a tricycle.

In Sagada and Bontoc there are no taxis, only jeepneys and tricycles.

BAGUIO

Known as the "summer capital of the Philippines," at 1, 524 meters (5,000 ft.) above sea level, Baguio's fortune is in its cool climate and high elevation. The American military was the first to recognize the area's appeal, setting aside a 535-acre military reservation amidst the pine trees in 1903 as a retreat for soldiers in need of some R&R. Today the city is a busy urban center, having risen from the rubble of the devastating earthquake of 1991. A popular retreat for city-folk looking to escape the heat, Baguio's population soars in the summer months, when the Manila-based judicial system transfers the courts up to the highlands. To accommodate the flow, Baguio has developed into a fairly well-evolved provincial outpost, offering leisure activities to the office-worn like boat rides in the park, horseback riding, and strolling through the unexpectedly hygienic city market.

But beyond a mini Manila, the most remarkable thing about Baguio is the drive along winding Kennon Road, the 33-kilometer (21-mile) scenic route up through the mountains along treacherous cliffs and past the famous "lion's face" landmark—a sculpture carved into a huge stone outcropping along the roadside. Waterfalls and hot mineral springs gush forth along the journey, so you may want to gauge some extra time to take advantage of these natural wonders, oftentimes accessible via death-defying hanging bridges.

GETTING AROUND

For information on getting to Baguio City, see "Getting Into the Region," above. Except for the immediate downtown area, Baguio City is too big to stroll around.

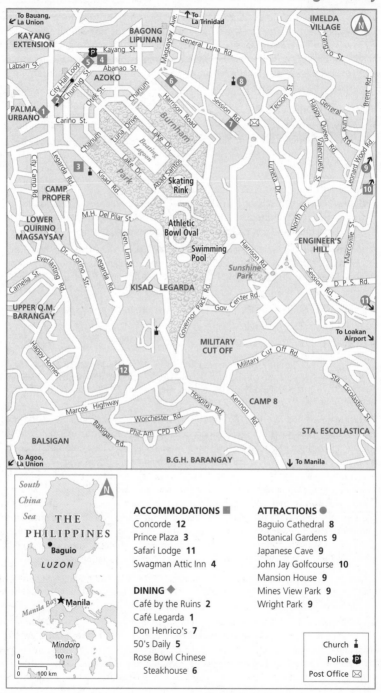

Baguio City

To Bauang, La Union ←
KAYANG EXTENSION
BAGONG LIPUNAN
To La Trinidad ↑
IMELDA VILLAGE

Labsan St.
Kayang St.
KAYANG EXTENSION
Magsaysay Ave.
General Luna Rd.
Yang-co St.
Brent Rd.

City Hall Loop
Chuntug St.
Abanao St.
AZOKO
Chanum
Harrison Road
Session Rd.
Tecson St.
Happy Queen Rd.
General Luna Rd.
Leonard Wood Rd.

PALMA URBANO
Cariño St.
Otek St.
Luna Drive
Lake Dr.
Burnham
Boating Lagoon
Session Rd.
Valenzuela St.

City Camp Rd.
Legarda Rd.
Chanum
Lake Dr.
Park
Abad Santos
Skating Rink
Luneta Dr.
North Dr.

CAMP PROPER
Kisad Rd.
M.H. Del Pilar St.
Athletic Bowl Oval
ENGINEER'S HILL
Marcoville St.

LOWER QUIRINO MAGSAYSAY
Dr. Cariño Str.
Gen. Lim St.
Swimming Pool
Harrison Rd.
Session Rd. 2
D.P.S. Rd.

Everlasting St.
Legarda Rd.
KISAD LEGARDA
Sunshine Park
To Loakan Airport ↘

Camelia St.
UPPER Q.M. BARANGAY
Governor Pack Rd.
Gov. Center Rd.
MILITARY CUT OFF

Happy Homes
Military Cut Off Rd.
Sta. Escolastica St.

Marcos Highway
Worchester Rd.
Hospital Rd.
Kennon Rd.
CAMP 8
STA. ESCOLASTICA

BALSIGAN
Balsigan Rd.
Phil-Am CPD Rd.

To Agoo, La Union ←
B.G.H. BARANGAY
To Manila ↓

South China Sea
THE PHILIPPINES
LUZON
Baguio
Manila Bay
Manila
Mindoro
0   100 mi
0   100 km

ACCOMMODATIONS ■
Concorde 12
Prince Plaza 3
Safari Lodge 11
Swagman Attic Inn 4

DINING ◆
Café by the Ruins 2
Café Legarda 1
Don Henrico's 7
50's Daily 5
Rose Bowl Chinese
   Steakhouse 6

ATTRACTIONS ●
Baguio Cathedral 8
Botanical Gardens 9
Japanese Cave 9
John Jay Golfcourse 10
Mansion House 9
Mines View Park 9
Wright Park 9

Church ✝
Police P
Post Office ✉

Jeepneys and taxis are available to take you to your hotel, or to provide transport in and around Baguio City. Taxi drivers will swarm you at the bus and air terminals, so it's not a surprise to learn that many also lend their services as tour guides. Locals on hotel-commissions will also descend upon you even before your feet hit the ground, so if you arrive without a hotel reservation, you can tempt fate or, if you're arriving at the airport, you can consult the people over at the tourism information counter.

VISITOR INFORMATION

The **Department of Tourism** is on Governor Pack Road (☎ 74/442-6708; fax 74/442-8848). It's open daily from 8am to noon and 1 to 5pm.

Fast Facts: Baguio

Banks/Currency Exchange   In addition to the numerous ATM machines around town, the Philippine National Bank on Session Road has money withdrawal machines and can exchange traveler's checks and currency.

Internet/E-mail   CyberSpace (☎ 74/443-8730), at the Mt. Crest Hotel on Legarda Road, offers e-mail and Internet access. You can also log on at Future Place Internet Café (☎ 074/304-2586) on Governor Pack Road at the Victoria Liner and Auto Bus depot.

Post Office/Mail   The local post office is located on Upper Session Road.

Telephone   The area code is 74.

ACCOMMODATIONS

Concorde Hotel. Europa Center, Legarda Rd., Baguio. ☎ 74/443-2039 to 58. Fax 74/443-2060. www2.mozcom.com/-concorde. E-mail: concorde@mozcom.com. 139 units. TV TEL. P1,782–P2,970 (US$39.60–US$66) double; P4,026–P4,488 (US$89.46–US$99.73) suite. AE, DC, MC, V.

By far the best hotel in town, the Concorde's appeal is mostly in its unique and rustic architecture. This hotel has great atmosphere, with exposed brick, natural light that trickles in through the high atrium, and curved stairways that combine to form a peaceful and cozy feel. The patio furniture is made out of logs and sticks—a nice touch that complements the all-natural ambience the hotel has succeeded in achieving. The rooms, while neat and clean, are pretty basic, with wide-planked hardwood floors, spare furnishings, and small windows set above eye level, so if possible, you may want to opt for the deluxe suite for a bit more comfort. For those of you who hit the pillow early, be forewarned: the hotel has a disco that's open from 10pm to 3am, but you can always work off any accumulated steam in the hotel's fitness center. There's also a 24-hour cafe, as well as both Chinese and Japanese restaurants.

Prince Plaza Hotel. No. 17 Legarda Rd., Baguio. ☎ 74/442-5082. Fax 74/442-5093. 48 units. TV. P1,500–P1,700 (US$33.33–US$37.77) double; P3,000 (US$66.66) deluxe suite; P3,500 (US$77.77) apt. AE, MC, V.

The lobby of this hotel near Burnham Park feels almost sanitary, decorated in shiny, almost lacquered grays and whites, with Mexican tile windows. The rooms are fairly large and neat, with excellent views of the highlands. All come with two double beds, large TVs, carpeting, and plenty of closet space. Bathrooms have hot and cold showers with a pull-out showerhead. The Shabu Shabu Restaurant dishes up good local cuisine, and there is a coffee shop. The deluxe rooms are the best value, with balcony, living area, minibar, and separate standup shower and bathtub. There is a loud discotheque in the hotel that stays open until 11pm, so if you are an early sleeper it may drive you crazy.

Safari Lodge. 191 Leonard Wood Rd. ☎ **74/442-2419.** Fax 74/444-2994. 14 rms, all with bathroom. P1,000–P1,500 (US$20–US$30) double; P2,000–P3,000 (US$40–US$60) family room. No credit cards.

When you're up in the mountains, this is exactly the kind of place you're hoping to find. The Safari Lodge was a private home converted into a lodge, but the hunting retreat ambience remains in the collection of boar, tiger, caribao, elephant, and even hyena heads adorning the main hall. Rooms are spacious and woodsy and furnished with gloriously clean and modern tile bathrooms. Family rooms and duplexes accommodate from five to seven people, so they're great for big families.

Swagman Attic Inn. 90 Abanao St. ☎ **74/442-5139.** Fax 74/442-9859. For Manila reservations to any Swagman's Inn, 2/523-8541. 20 units. TV TEL. P750 (US$18.75) single; P1,200 (US$30) double. MC, V. Near open-air markets.

This Australian-run place, popular with backpackers, offers decent accommodations for low-end prices. The Swagman name seems to be everywhere in the Philippines, with their travel agencies and inns scattered throughout most tourist destinations. This particular inn was a shell of its former self the day I arrived; current renovations are enlarging and upgrading accommodations in anticipation of a major influx of Australians by early 2001. Swagman offers travel agency and money-changing services, and there's a laundry facility (Spin City) right next door.

DINING

Café by the Ruins. No. 25 Chuntug St., in front of City Hall. ☎ **74/442-4010.** Main courses P48–P158 (US$1–US$3). DC, MC, V. Daily 7am–10pm. BAKED GOODS/FILIPINO.

Exotic, tropical, and relaxed are the words that describe this interesting place, a pseudo outdoor cafe sheltered in the remains of a bombed-out building. The nominal ruins are what's left of the governor's home and garden that was partially destroyed by U.S. forces during World War I. You can see the remains of them among the arches and the adjoining vine-covered gazebo. A huge bamboo-thatched roof and rice-papered lanterns create a subtle twilit effect, but aside from the atmosphere, the food here is delicious, ranging from regional Cordilleran to European; try the chicken Palawan stewed in coconut milk and basil. Check out the fresh bread counter, if the aroma doesn't stop you in your tracks.

Café Legarda. Legarda Rd. at Urbano St., Baguio. ☎ **74/443-9421.** Main courses P164–P544 (US$3.65–US$12). MC, V. Daily 6am–midnight. CONTINENTAL/SEAFOOD.

One of the better run restaurants in town if not the least characteristic is Café Legarda, a favorite among locals for the selection of steaks and seafood at reasonable prices. The menu also offers fresh pastas, soups, and breads, and seafood main courses including prawns stuffed with crabmeat and an especially good charbroiled blue marlin. They cook with a lot of butter, so the cholesterol conscious should ask them to go easy.

Don Henrico's. Session Rd., Baguio. ☎ **74/442-8802.** Pizzas P140–P420 (US$2.80–US$8.40). DC, MC, V. Daily 10am–12am. ITALIAN.

This brightly lit pizza joint is a happening place that serves pizza, pasta, and more. You'll be overwhelmed by the variety of pizzas to choose from: taco, pesto chicken, Viking with anchovy, caper mushroom, and tomato, and of course Chicago deep-dish and New York–style pizza. And you've got the option of choosing a small, medium, or large pie, depending on the size of your appetite. There's also a double stuffed version, for gluttons or the really hungry. If that's not enough to choose from, you can create your own. The dessert menu is just as overwhelming, from tiramisu, to blueberry cheesecake, to the choco mango—double dark chocolate cake stuffed with mango and clouds of whipped cream filling. Take-out and delivery are available for a 10% charge.

Rose Bowl Chinese Steakhouse. 21 Harrison Rd. ☎ **074/442-4213.** Main courses P129–P899 (US$2.50–US$18). Courses feed 4 to 6 people. AE, DC, JCB, MC, V. Daily 6am–11pm. CHINESE/AMERICAN.

This popular reincarnation of the oldest restaurant in Baguio is still one of the more popular restaurants in town, founded by the current owner's grandfather. Its casual atmosphere and family-sized portions are just two things that have attracted patrons for years, not to mention the optimum quality of the ingredients (no MSG, except for some residual in the oyster sauce). The huge menu offers the popular chop suey, chow mein, noodle dishes, seafood, and, for the less adventurous, good ol' American style steaks and burgers. The crabmeat rice is an interesting combination, or try the Fisherman's Pearls—meatballs with quail eggs and tofu in a sweet and sour sauce.

50's Daily. 88 Abanao St., Baguio. ☎ **74/442-4839.** All main courses around P55 (US$1.10). No credit cards. Daily 8am–4am.

Advancing the atmosphere of Baguio as a former American base, 50's Daily combines almost as many themes as Disney. It's a diner, a nighttime hangout, a coffee shop, and a roller rink all rolled into one—or does the wait staff wear skates for speedy service? You can order a UFO sandwich, served in a native "flying saucer" filled with your choice of *adobo*, or stick with the old BLT reliable. There are local foods on the menu as well, including *bangus* (milk fish) and *congee* (Chinese porridge).

ATTRACTIONS

There are several points of interest in Baguio: **Baguio Cathedral,** at the highest end of Session Road, Baguio's main street; **Mansion House,** the summer home of Philippine presidents until World War II, when it was destroyed, then rebuilt; and **Wright Park,** near Mansion House, a great place to walk or rent ponies.

The **Botanical Gardens** displays the rich flora of the Cordilleras and a collection of Igorot folk art and architecture. Ifugao in their traditional garb stand at the entrance in the hopes that you'll pay them a few pesos for a picture. It's not *National Geographic*-worthy, but it will look good in your photo album. You can also hunt for treasure in the **Japanese Cave,** said to contain a stash hidden by General Yamashita during the war.

John Jay, the former U.S. military camp, is now a **golf** course with steep **hiking** trails. The lodging office has trail maps. **Mines View Park** should be the cap of your long day of touring, with incredible views on a clear day. Most hotels offer tour guides.

SHOPPING

For traditional Igorot weavings visit **Easter Weaving Room, Inc.** on Easter Road (☎ 74/442-4972), where downstairs you can watch the weavers manipulating the wooden machines to create all sorts of geometric patterns. **Ibay's Silver Shop,** on Governor Pack Road (☎ 74/442-7082; in the Lions Building), sells interesting charms, bracelets, and anything else made of silver, though prices are not as cheap as you would expect. In the back room you can see them melting down junk scrap silver and pouring it into bar molds. Finally, everyone's favorite spot in Baguio is the **city market,** on Magsaysay Avenue, where you'll find anything and everything traditional, hand-made, or edible. Be sure to hold on to your valuables while working your way through the market.

✪ SAGADA

No place could be more enchanting than this small village tucked away among green mountains and rice terraces—most people who come here find that it's one of the highlights of their trip. The mountain air is fresh and cool (pollution is still minimal), the people are friendly and laid-back, and the hiking opportunities are fantastic. Nature is alive and well here, and ancestral land is protected by the elders.

The area has found its way onto the backpacker's itinerary for the underground honeycomb of caves that lies beneath the town and the hanging coffins. It is a traditional Ifugao practice to hang the wooden coffins of the dead in caves and along the tall limestone cliffs; these **hanging coffins** are a must-see for the benefit of your friends back home (see "Hiking & Caving," below).

GETTING THERE

You have the choice of arriving via Banaue or Baguio City, depending on where you're coming from. For the **Manila-Banaue-Bontoc-Sagada** route (13 to 14 hours), a **Dangwa Tranco bus** leaves the Cubao terminal once a day at 7am for the 9-hour trip to Banaue. A daily jeepney leaves Banaue at 7:30am for the 2- to 3-hour ride to Bontoc. In Bontoc, jeepneys leave from outside Nellie's Eatery on Bontoc's main street several times a day for the 2-hour ride up to Sagada.

For the **Manila-Baguio-Sagada** route (12 to 13 hours): There are many bus companies that travel the popular direct route (6 hours) to Baguio, but **Victory Liner** leaves hourly and is air-conditioned and comfortable. From Baguio, several early morning **Lizardo** buses (☎ 74/422-1060) depart from the Dangwa Terminal starting at 6:30am. The trip to Sagada takes you along the scenic Halsema Highway, also known as the Mountain Trail. The trip takes about 7 or 9 hours with stops for snacks and lunch.

VISITOR INFORMATION

For maps and detailed information on the caves and trails, go to the very small **tourism window** in the Municipal Hall Building, which also houses the Sagada Environmental Guides Association (SEGA) Information Center. You can hire a guide here with a lamp for cave exploration.

ACCOMMODATIONS

Neither phones nor hot water heaters have found it here yet, and in many homes, salt is a luxurious commodity. Few inns have running water, and what they lack in amenities is made up for in charm. It's exactly this natural, untouched spirit that visitors find so endearing. Family-owned guesthouses are the main source of accommodation, although a big hotel was recently built and you can actually get hot water. Mattresses are little more than varying thicknesses of foam, and you will have to get used to waking up with the roosters.

Masferre Café and Inn. Past the Municipal Hall on the left. No phone. 7 units. P100 (US$2) per person. No credit cards.

Popular with the backpacking crowd, this place is very cozy and clean. Windows (in the rooms that have them) swing out like those in a country cottage. Rooms have two single beds, and there are two common baths in the inn. The proprietress is the widow of Eduardo Masferre, who spent his life documenting the mountain life of the Ifugao tribespeople. His beautiful black and white photographs are displayed in the dining area.

Olahbinan Resthouse. Next to the Prime Hotel, down the stairs on your left. 11 units. P80–P150 (US$1.60–US$3) double. No credit cards.

One of the larger guesthouses, Olahbinan has 11 comfortable and clean rooms, a restaurant with a fireplace, and an upstairs balcony with excellent views. They also have running hot water.

Sagada Guest House. Up from the central bus stop. No phone. 15 units. P70–P200 (US$1.40–US$4) double. No credit cards.

Owned by the ex-mayor, Sagada Guest House will provide essential accommodations and a great meal in its cafe.

Sagada Prime Hotel. A 5-minute walk past the Municipal Hall on your left. 43 units. P600 (US$12) double with common bathroom; P1,000 (US$20) double with private bathroom. No credit cards.

This is Sagada's first official hotel, opened in March 1997. It offers spacious rooms and a large restaurant serving meals and drinks at reasonable prices. Always negotiate room rates during the low season.

St. Joseph's Rest House. Up the hill to the right as you come into town. No phone. 29 units. P60 (US$1.20) per person for dorm room; P100 (US$2) per person for double. No credit cards.

Originally a convent, this cozy cottage was converted into Sagada's first guesthouse by St. Mary's Mission in the 1970s. It's now managed by the Episcopal Diocese of the northern Philippines. The grounds are the most beautiful in town, with all sorts of manicured flowers and bushes in front and back. Rooms are small and quaint, with hot water showers. Noisier, dorm-style rooms are also available. Amenities include a large restaurant, a gift shop selling local crafts, and secured garage parking for anyone who may have rented a car for the journey here.

DINING

In addition to the guesthouses, there are several cafes in town, offering a variety of choices at any time of the day or early evening. (Most close at 9pm.) It's customary in Sagada to reserve meals in advance. This may seem like an inconvenience, but realize that you are getting a home-cooked meal, and whatever you request has to be slaughtered. (Many turn vegetarian at the prospect.) Next door to the Municipal Hall is **Shamrock Café,** providing breakfast, lunch, dinner, snacks, and nighttime guitar playing. Lots of tourists come here, so it's a good place to share information with other travelers. **The Log Cabin,** down the hill from Shamrock, will give you delicious European-style food, including lasagna and omelets. They have an excellent music selection. **Alfredo's Cabin** is a cozy melange of tribal statues and motifs where you can eat fettuccine Alfredo, potatoes au gratin, or curried rice, all best enjoyed by the romance of the fireplace.

Masferre Inn and Country Café both have excellent local dishes as well as hamburgers, pancakes, and other European/American dishes.

HIKING & CAVING

The hiking around Sagada is stunning, challenging, and often grimy. You can get a guide to take you along a short 2-hour tour, or go the distance for the 6-hour haul. Wear biker shorts or grungy clothing that you don't mind getting dirty. You can wear hiking boots, but waterproof sandals are better, as you will be walking in water.

Sumaging (Big Cave) is the one most popular attraction with tourists. It's a 40-minute walk from Sagada on the Suyo Road, which winds its way through the simple villages and above beautiful rice terraces and rivers. Exploring the cave takes about 3 hours, looking at Mother Nature's unusual limestone sculptures, creatively named the pig pen, giant's foot, pregnant woman, and Romeo and Juliet. The first part of the climb is slippery, partly due to the moisture on the limestone, but also from the gooey bat droppings from overhead. (Bring wet wipes!) The second part of the exploration is done barefoot, mostly over sandpaper-like calcium formations. Thankfully you'll be getting wet—a perfect opportunity to wash the dung off your clothes. Toward the end you reach "the tunnel," an appropriately named claustrophobically narrow space, navigated using a rope and all the upper body strength you can muster. The claustrophobic should simply take a deep breath; you'll be out of the tunnel and into a huge domed space in under 2 minutes. It's great, adventurous fun, and perfectly appropriate for those of us who are less than in tip-top shape.

Lumiang is a 30-minute walk from Sagada on the way to the Big Cave, down a path to your left. This burial cave, where many old and a few newer coffins are stacked, is well worth a visit. You can see the coffins right at the entrance of the cave, without going inside. The bodies are still intact and old, and since the thin wooden covers to the coffins are not bolted on, you can see the bones still peacefully tucked in the fetal position. Do not remove anything from these sacred areas. A local elder told me about a tourist who took a bone or two and the next day fell and broke his leg. Believe what you will, respect the dead, and don't tempt fate.

Loko-ong (Crystal Cave) has been closed for quite some time now thanks to tourists from hell who raped it of its stalactites and stalagmites. It may re-open, so it's worth a check to find out when you arrive. This cave is definitely for the more adventurous, requiring more physical exertion, some rope climbing, and swimming.

The paths that lead to **Echo Valley** are overgrown, and you may find yourself wandering around in circles for hours. That's OK though, considering how beautiful the area surrounding the valley is and assuming you brought along enough water. The path leads through an old cemetery and past some hanging coffins and small burial caves along the way. You'll even see "death chairs," once used to prop up the body during mourning periods. Echo Valley has beautiful views of limestone cliffs, some with coffins hanging.

Set amidst rice terraces and only 25 minutes from town, **Bokong Waterfall** is a popular spot for both locals and visitors. The falls are small but spill into a deep pool—an ideal spot for a picnic or quick dip. Just past Sagada Weaving, take the cement steps to the left. Follow the path down to the river, cross over, and head upstream. **Bomod-ok** is a bigger waterfall, but farther away. To get there, you'll have to walk along the Banga-an Road for about an hour, then go down the cement steps just past the Banga-an Elementary School. Another hour's walk will take you down the path through the village of **Fidelisan** and some rice terraces to the waterfall.

Mt. Ampacao is the highest peak in Sagada, at 1,889 meters (6,198 ft.). You will need a lot of endurance for the 2-hour hike to the top. You can pick wild blueberries on the slopes, and from September to December it's on the flight path of migratory birds.

Mt. Polis, if not exceedingly beautiful, is a test of endurance. On its old Spanish trail are waterfalls, forests, villages, and great vistas. Start early in the morning with a water bottle and packed lunch for the 8-hour round-trip.

BANAUE

Up in the mountains, far from civilization, is the Philippines that we've all imagined. While modernity infiltrates the lives of the mountain people, it's still the land that dictates the way they live. The name for the people who live in this region, Ifugao, comes from *ipugo,* meaning eaters of rice, a staple food said to have been a gift from the gods. The rice terraces were built as a tribute to the heavens in thanks for the sustaining food. Sheltered by the rugged mountains during the days of Spanish colonialism, the Ifugaos managed to maintain their culture as farmers and miners, with well-developed customs of their own.

Travel Tip

You can change your dollars or traveler's checks over at RSR General Merchandise in the Trade Center (the commercial area) for better rates than at the Banaue Hotel.

GETTING THERE

BY BUS **Dangwa Tranco** has early morning daily buses leaving from Manila to Banaue. The trip takes about 10 hours. Some try to break up the trip by spending some time along the way in Baguio, but the ride from Baguio to Banaue can hit the 9 hour mark, canceling out in my mind any justification for doing so. If you're thinking of a combo trip anyway, **Autobus Transport** (☎ **74/36873** or 74/32227) runs a night bus from Baguio to Banaue that'll get you in at 4:30am, in addition to the regular daily bus services.

If you're planning a triangular tour of the region beginning in Baguio (7 hours from Manila), you can either head directly to Sagada (7 hours from Baguio) or to Banaue (9 hours from Baguio). Between Banaue and Sagada, you must change jeepneys in Bontoc; all told it's about 3½ to 4 hours (and possibly 5) between the two. If you're thinking that that's a lot of traveling, it is, so plan on enough time on the ground to make it worth your trouble.

ACCOMMODATIONS & DINING

While home-made guest houses abound, the **Banaue Hotel and Youth Hostel** (Just outside town, on the main road (ask the bus driver to leave you off at the entrance); ☎ **73/386-4087** (Manila reservations ☎ 2/524-2809 or 2/523-5949). Fax 73/386-4048 or 2/521-2532. E-mail: sales@philtourism.com.) is Banaue's only true hotel, and a welcome relief after the tortuous journey into the mountains. The Banaue Hotel is owned and operated by the Philippine Dept. of Tourism, which manages to maintain a level of quality and cleanliness superior to its other properties. During the low season, this place can feel like something out of *The Shining;* don't be surprised if you are the only one staying here.

If you plan on staying a few days in Banaue, you will obviously want some variety in your meals. The Banaue Restaurant serves a good and hearty breakfast and dinner. Besides the Banaue Restaurant, local guesthouses have good fare for cheap prices. **Halfway Lodge,** on the road to Mayoyao; **Sanafe Lodge,** beside the bus stop and across from the market; **Café Jam,** just down the street near the Town Hall; and **Stairway Lodge,** near Halfway Lodge, all offer excellent local dishes.

HIKES AROUND BANAUE

The rice paddies and retaining walls around Banaue are a hiker's dream. Trails skirt treacherous drop-offs of rice paddy retaining walls, or follow dirt paths pounded by children making their way to the nearest village schoolroom. Hikes lasting from a few minutes to all day are all right outside your doorstep. The Department of Tourism can provide **maps** of the area including hiking trails. Don't leave home without water, and take special care in the rainy season, as trails become dangerously slippery.

The ✪ **Village of Batad** is the most popular trek and will take you the whole day. Plan two, because you won't want to leave. Native village customs have ceded to Levis, Coca-Cola and corrugated rooftops, but the essential simplicity of life without running water or electricity remains. Bathing is accomplished with a ladle and fresh mountain water, and sections of guide books (like this one) are completed by candlelight.

The journey to Batad is in two steps: you have to get transport for the 12-kilometer (7-mile) ride (by tricycle about 45 minutes) to the start of the trail. From there it's a two-hour hike, half of which is uphill and fairly strenuous; the second half is more or less downhill. (Make sure you arrange for your transport to be waiting for you at the drop-off junction for your ride back to town. If you decide to "wing it," remember that jeepneys are heading into town in the early morning.)

Once arrived, there's nothing to do but relax, have a drink, and set out for some more hikes along narrow paths and dangerous retaining walls that any Western mother would blanch at. Don't be put off by the children offering to be your guide or asking for pens—tourists who've come before have made the mistake of handing out stuff—an act of kindness that encourages negative behavior. If you want to bring something useful to the village, bring candles, salt, and matches, and hand them over to the innkeeper.

The **Village of Bang-an** is an alternative for those who aren't up for the strenuous hike to Batad. It's only 2 kilometers in from the junction leading to Batad. Just before sunset, you can see rainbows against the setting sun at the horizon.

Tam–an village is perfect for a late-night walk, just before sunset. Simply walk down the 240 steps from behind the Banaue Hotel pool. It's supposedly a traditional Ifugao village, but you will find more corrugated metal roofs than thatched huts (the *nipa* needs to be replaced every 2 years or so, making the metal more economical). Plenty of pigs, chickens, monkeys, and children, though. Villagers will take a break from beating rice stalks to ask you if you'd like to see their ancestral bones, dragged out from the honored corner of the hut wrapped in a burlap sack. Interesting custom, that will cost you as much as P150 (US$3). They're more than happy to strike up a conversation though, and point you graciously on your merry way.

Guihob Natural Pool is a 4-kilometer (2½-mile) ride or a 45-minute hike along the road from the town center to this streaming oasis of fresh spring water. Pick up some sandwiches and bring your bathing suit for a numbing swim and gear yourself up for the inevitable reappearance of sweatballs on the return hike. You can also stop here on your way back from Batad, since it's on the way.

6 Mindoro

Puerto Galera is actually a series of towns and beaches strung out on and around a protuberant land mass unmistakably shaped like the tail of a large whale. Its charm is largely due to the land formations that create a natural harbor spotted with a number of protective islets. The natural shelter afforded by the combination of completely enclosed bays and the mountain ranges behind was recognized in 1572, when the "Port of Galleons" was founded as a Spanish provincial capitol and a valuable refuge for trade ships making the journey in and out of the Spice Islands (Indonesia). Maybe they were enchanted by the magical streaks of lightning that light up the skies regularly at sundown.

Puerto Galera was declared a preserved area under a 1973 UNESCO program, a move that enticed the more intrepid traveler to see what the fuss was all about. Ironically, it was the arrival of tourism that turned the tide of local fortunes; local fishermen now earn miraculous sums as *banqueros* (boat taxi drivers), making even the most lucrative dynamite fishing intake look like peanuts.

Puerto Galera's protected status, the self-policing policy of local tour operators, and the availability of alternate income for former fishermen, have allowed for a resurgence in marine life. Puerto Galera's reefs are flourishing, and in turn its corals support over 2,500 species of marine life, possibly the most diverse marine ecosystem in the Philippines.

Besides diving and beachcombing, the untouched island of Mindoro has some challenging and rewarding hikes. Among the most popular trails are the ones that takes you up into a native village, or under a thundering waterfall.

GETTING THERE

BY PLANE   There are no commercial flights to Puerto Galera. But if you really want to make a holiday out of it, you can hire a private helicopter for US$1,000 or a seaplane for US$350. Call ☎ **973/497-503** for more information.

BY BUS & FERRY   The trip is in two legs: by road from Manila to Batangas (2 hours), then across to Mindoro Island by boat or ferry (another 2 hours). A daily combo trip operated jointly by the Si-Kat Ferries and the **Centrepoint Hotel** (Mabini St., Ermita, Manila; ☎ **2/521-2751**) starts in the early morning in front of the hotel. The air-conditioned bus takes you to Batangas City Pier just in time to catch the last (usually around midday) *Si-Kat II* ferry to Puerto Galera for the price of (US$7). Tickets can be purchased at the hotel.

Taxis in Manila will also take you to Batangas for about P1,000 (US$25), or you can catch a JAM, Tritran, or BLTB bus (around P101/US$2, with a/c) to the pier. One reliable ferry option is **DSL Fastcraft M/V** *Blue Eagle,* which leaves daily at 7am and 1:30pm (P120/US$2.40 for 60 minutes). The return ferry leaves PG at 11:30am and 3:30pm; there's an additional 10:15am run on Fridays and Saturdays from Batangas Pier that leaves PG at 9am.

Viva Shipping Lines (☎ **43/723-6072**) is the massive local car ferry (2 hours; P88 (US$1.76), which leaves Batangas several times a day. Be aware that these ferries dock over at Balatero Pier, so avoid arriving after dark, as there will be zero transport options once you arrive. To counter the inevitability of last minute changes in ferry schedules, be sure to call the Tourist Information office at the pier ahead of time at ☎ **43/723-9963.**

Note: Use your judgment before boarding a ferry. Many of these outriggers look as if they're on their last bamboo leg, and in some cases all it will take is one rough bit of surf to topple the thing. If it's floating crooked and dressed in rust, don't get on (the boatmen should really encourage the fatter people to sit on the lower deck, because these things seem frightfully top-heavy!). If you arrive at the pier after the last ferry, usually after 5pm, you can hire a private *banca* to take you across to Mindoro for about P2,000 (US$50). You will be besieged by people offering their bancas who will insist that there are no more ferries, but don't take anybody's word for it. Seek out someone official or go to the terminal and ask to be sure.

GETTING AROUND

Most visitors who visit Puerto Galera town don't stay for long, not because the town lacks in fishing town appeal, but because the beaches, resorts, and bars are located elsewhere. Better hotels will have a boat waiting for you at the dock, but if you're traveling spontaneously, you can get to the neighboring beaches by jeepney, tricycle, or *banca.* If you want to get a feel for Puerto Galera town, you can spend the night in one of the several (practically identical) crash pads for about P500 (US$10) a night, of which the Puerto Galera Resort Hotel is the best (Conception Street, right up from the wharf; ☎ **43/442-0160;** booking: Ermita, Manila; ☎ 2/525-4641; fax 2/ 522-2968).

Most of the popular beaches, and subsequently the most developed, dot the northern tip of the whale's fin. Except for Coco Beach, which is accessible along the beach only at low tide, it's possible to walk along the beach or over the rocks between Big Laguna, Small Laguna, and Sabang.

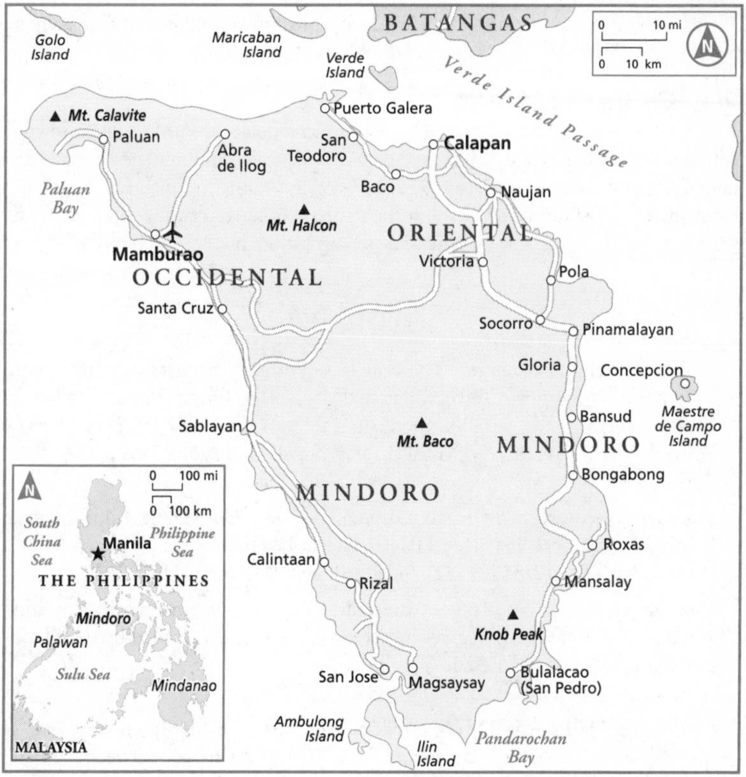

A succession of potholes called the road runs the length of the fin from Sabang, past Encenada Beach, through Puerto Galera town and on to Balatero (where all ferry traffic will eventually be transferred), San Isidro (White Beach), Aninuan Beach, and Talipanan Beach. All of these points are accessible (and more expensive) if reached by sea.

BY JEEPNEY The trip from Puerto Galera to Sabang Beach takes 20 minutes, for P10 (US$0.20). From Sabang you can walk to Big La Laguna or Small La Laguna Beach, but you'll want to travel light, as the beaches are not right next door. Jeepneys to neighboring Talipanan take 35 minutes, for P20 (US$0.40); to Aninuan, it's 20 minutes for P15 (US$0.30); and to White Beach, it's 10 minutes, for P10 (US$0.20).

BY TRICYCLE I'm not sure how they pedal the mostly uphill, pot-holed route, but they do. A "regular" trip costs the locals P5 to P10 (US$0.10 to US$0.20) to Sabang Beach, but the drivers will find a way to get you to pay at least P50 (US$1). Obviously, prices for a special trip (when you're the only one they take) will have to be negotiated.

BY BANCA OR PUMPBOAT This is the best way to see the lay of the islands. The local *banqueros* banded together to form a cooperative, which has resulted in prices higher than what you'd expect to pay in the Philippines (and double what they were last year), but it's well worth it. Each beach has a queue of boats for hire at fixed prices. Prices for rides to the various islands from the pier at Puerto Galera are: San Antonio, 10 minutes, P120 (US$2.40); Coco Beach, 15 minutes, P150 (US$3); Big La Laguna, 18 minutes, P180 (US$3.60); Small La Laguna, 20 minutes, P200 (US$4); Sabang,

23 minutes, P230 (US$4.60); White Beach, 40 minutes, P450 (US$9); Talipanan, 60 minutes, P500 (US$10). Fares are doubled after dark.

VISITOR INFORMATION

There is a Tourist Information Center right on the docks of Puerto Galera town, but you may want to make any travel arrangements, ask questions, and get maps at **Swagman Travel** on Sabang Beach, ☎ **912/347-6993,** or at their Small La Laguna Beach location, ☎ **912/306-6585.** Also, most resorts will have accurate, up-to-date information on what to see and do here and packages available.

Fast Facts: Mindoro

Banks/Currency Exchange There are lots of money changers along the pier in Puerto Galera. Swagman Travel will exchange cash and traveler's checks and make card advances. They have locations in Puerto Galera (☎ **912/319-9587**), Sabang Beach (☎ **912/347-6993**), and Small La Laguna Beach (☎ **912/306-6585**).

Doctors/Hospitals Provincial Hospital (☎ **43/288-4186**); Palm Medical Clinic (☎ **912/352-9519**); and Puerto Galera Lying in Clinic for pharmacy and lab services (☎ **912/352-9531**) are all in Puerto Galera.

Emergencies Dial ☎ 166 for the police. For serious emergencies requiring evacuation to a hospital, free helicopter air-lift service is provided by the Philippine Army Search and Rescue Squad. Contact any of the resorts and they will radio for you, or call ☎ **912/305-0652.**

Internet/E-Mail Asia Divers provides e-mail service (no Internet access) at both locations, on Sabang Beach and Small La Laguna Beach, between 8am and 5pm. The Atlantis Resort Hotel (see below) also offers e-mail access.

Police The Puerto Galera Police Station is at the intersection above the docks in Puerto Galera (☎ **973/800-168**).

Post Office/Mail The easiest place to drop off mail is at Swagman's Travel on Sabang Beach or at La Laguna Beach Club on Big La Laguna Beach (☎ **973/855-545**). There is a post office near the church next to the basketball court.

Telephone International and long-distance calls can be made at Swagman's Travel in Sabang Beach or at any of the bigger resorts like La Laguna Beach Club. Phone service in Puerto Galera is on cellular phones, which are not always reliable.

ACCOMMODATIONS

Puerto Galera—or "PG," as expatriates and locals affectionately call their playground—plays host to incredible opportunities for diving and snorkeling, lounging at the beach, and rowdy nightlife, making it a popular destination for world-weary divers, as well as escapees from Manila.

PUERTO GALERA

✪ Coco Beach Resort. Puerto Galera, Mindoro. ☎ **917/377-2115** or 917/890-1426. Booking: Roxas Blvd., Manila, ☎ 2/521-5260 or call the resort directly: ☎ 2/521-5260. Fax 2/526-6903. www.cocobeach.com. E-mail: info@info.com. 80 units. P2,250 (US$45) per person double; P3,250–P4,250 (US$65–US$85) per person suite. Includes round-trip transfers from Manila, buffet breakfasts, tax,and service. Rates are considerably lower for successive nights. 25% Christmas supplement. Minimum stays for Easter Week and Chinese New Year. AE, DC, MC, V.

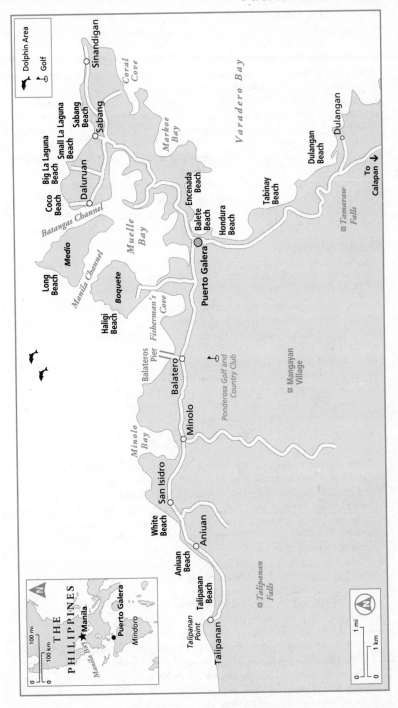

Rarely would you equate the absence of hot water and air-conditioning and the need for mosquito netting with "high end," but on the semi-virgin shores of Coco Beach's own private island, it's actually so. This resort doesn't have much in the way of comfortable amenities—it lacks hot water, A/C, and TV—but the bamboo four-poster bed with draped netting, the tribal artifacts, and the hammocks swinging from the bungalow terrace make up the difference. Bathrooms are large, covered with white tiles and plants, and some have walls built out of pieced-together coral. The setting is idyllic: bamboo and rattan huts stacked up the hillside above the resort's very own stretch of white sand. The resort complex is a gardener's dreamscape filled with lilacs, orchids, azaleas, and other exotic flowers, which combined with the bungalows, create a treehouse atmosphere offering peace and privacy at an unbeatable price. If the term "ecotourism" is used loosely around here to drum up business, they actually practice what they preach, basing the system on a sort of communal one, where employees are treated like family, and guests in turn are treated as if they were guests in someone's private home. There's a large lagoon-shaped pool and kiddie extension with water slide, along with a tennis court, a golf course overlooking the harbor, and a shopping arcade.

SABANG BEACH

Atlantis Resort Hotel. Sabang Beach, Puerto Galera, Mindoro. ☎ **973/497-503** or 912/308-0672. www.atlantishotel.com. E-mail: georg@atlantishotel.com. 29 units. A/C MINI-BAR TV. P2,750 (US$55) double; P3,250–P5,250 (US$65–US$105) suite. AE, DC, MC, V.

If you're not the type to consider hot water an optional amenity, this is said to be the best and most comfortable hotel in Puerto Galera. The contemporary Spanish-Mediterranean decor, with its terra-cotta tile and white stucco walls, make the place feel like a cross between a Greek isle and an underwater amusement park. White bridges lead to separate castles peeking through the palm trees. They even have a "Flintstones House" for families with children. Each room looks sculpted, with curved stucco shelving units and beds that are supposed to impart the idea of a coral reef. The

---

The *Coco Explorer*

Aware that the Philippines' top destinations are relative neighbors, the owners of Coco Beach have taken the guesswork (and unpleasantness) out of land transport and bundled the best of the islands into one week-long seafaring fest aboard the *Coco Explorer.* The ship houses 20 small inside cabins and 36 outside cabins, each with wash basins. (Shower and toilet facilities are shared but separate for men and women.) It's not a luxury liner, but it's much better than a live-aboard, and the cruising makes it all worth it.

The 7-day itinerary includes Boracay; the Palawan's northern group of islands including Coron Bay, Dicalubuan, Malcapuya, Sangat Island and Black Island; and Apa Reef and Pandan Island on western Mindoro. Prices for 7 days range from P24,500 to P29,500 (US$490 to US$590), including (optional) all meals. The hop-on/hop-off rate between any two ports (2 days and 1 night) is US$78 to US$88. (Credit cards are accepted for on-board incidentals only.)

You can also hop on and off according to your own schedule; any 2 days and 1 night (from one port to another) costs P3,900 to P4,440 (US$78 to US$88).

For information and bookings contact *Coco Explorer*'s **Manila office** in Legaspi Towers 300, Roxas Blvd. (☎ **2/526-4594;** fax 2/526-6903; www.cocoexplorer. com) or book through any travel agent.

secluded suites have private terraces, and rooms are airy, quiet, and clean. The tiled bathrooms are spacious, with pedestal sinks and separate shower rooms. Atlantis is in the heart of town, so if nightlife is your priority, you're where it all happens. Otherwise, there's only few shops and a dirt walkway to separate you from the nighttime revelries. There are a pool, billiards, five-star dive shop, e-mail and faxing, laundry, baby-sitting, beauty parlor, small fitness room, and massage.

Big Apple Dive Resort. Sabang Beach, Puerto Galera, Mindoro. ☎ **912/308-1120.** E-mail: Big-apple@qinet.net. A/C TV. 21 units. P1,000 (US$20) double. AE, DC, MC, V.

Located on the beach, close to the restaurants, this beachfront crash pad is a popular place for European divers. Its advantage over the other budget dive resorts (besides the hot water) is its billiard room and the nice swimming pool. Only two rooms actually front the beach—the rest are set back along an alleyway perpendicular to the beach. Standard rooms just have a fan, while deluxe rooms offer air-conditioning, a double bed, and television, and some have kitchenettes.

SMALL LA LAGUNA

El Galleon. Small La Laguna, Puerto Galera, Mindoro. ☎ **973/782-094.** Fax 973/865-252. E-mail: allan@asiadivers.com. A/C. 25 units. P2,050 (US$41) standard; P2500–P3000 (US$50–US$60) deluxe. AE, DC, MC, V.

At El Galleon, built high along a cliff on the beach, you'll get excellent seaside breezes and views, but you'll have to endure many zigzagging steps to get up to your room. At least the rooms are equipped with intercoms, so you can make requests or have laundry and food delivered to you without having to make the long trip down. The setting is exotic and tropical, and you can enjoy it all from your own private verandah. Rooms are cozy, with the bed set on a step-up platform and bay windows all around. Built-in window seats and handmade tapestries create a rustic atmosphere. Some mattresses are springy and lumpy, while others are just right, so do the test before you choose your room. The triangular-shaped pool featuring a huge palm tree is right next to the pavilion restaurant that dishes up excellent international cuisine. It's popular with divers, as its famous owner, Allan Nash, also owns Asia Divers and the Point Shooter Bar.

☼ Portofino Resort. Small La Laguna Beach, Puerto Galera, Mindoro. ☎ **973/776-704.** www.portofino.com.ph. E-mail: Resort@portofino.com.ph. 25 units. A/C TV TEL. P2,000–P3,000 (US$40–60) deluxe studio; P3,500–P6,750 (US$70–US$135) suite. AE, DC, MC, V.

You'll feel like you are staying in a private hacienda along the Spanish Mediterranean at Portofino (which incidentally, is in Italy), whose accommodations include studios and one- and two-bedroom suites. Every unit is outfitted slightly differently, with fully equipped kitchens (microwave, toaster oven, coffeemaker, blender, dishes, mugs), tiled bathrooms, contemporary rattan beds, handmade batik prints, and stained glass windows in the foyer. Room no. 31 even has a Jacuzzi. And yes, Portofino has hot water. You'll have incredible views of the beach and Verde Island across the bay. And if a view just doesn't do it for you, the beach is only a stone's throw away past the stone pool and waterfall. The clientele tends to include Filipino executives, embassy employees, and European families.

IN THE HILLS

☼ Tanawin Lodge. Palangan, Puerto Galera. Booking office: in Manila ☎ **2/551-7307.** Fax 43/442-0112. 6 units, all with bathroom. P5,700–P7,000 (US$114–US$140) double. Rates include round-trip transfers from Manila, buffet breakfasts, and fruit basket. Rates are considerably lower for successive nights. 20% off packaged rates June–Oct. No credit cards.

Ten minutes by tricycle above Puerto Galera town is Tanawin Lodge, a rustic paradise offering infinite intimacy and seclusion. Landscaped into a terraced slope up in the mountains, Tanawin Lodge offers often blustery breezes and views of the bays peeking through the lush and swaying palm fronds. The three standard rooms occupy the small circular tower attached to the dining area, and enjoy the shared rail balcony. But a stay at the Tanawin would be disappointing if you didn't snag one of the freestanding cottages—rustically refined thatched huts enhanced by modern amenities. The best cottage is the "Snail's House" suite, a delicious chalet/hut big enough for four, with its own private verandah overlooking the bay, an oversized marble bathroom, and a barrel-shaped tile kitchen. The lodge's swimming pool sits atop a small rise with views, and a 15-minute walk down a path on the side of the hill will take you down to a secluded cove.

DINING

You can tell that tourism is booming by the new constructions underway by locals hoping to get in on the gold rush. Many new restaurants are popping up at the far end of Sabang Beach, offering authentic *ihaw-ihaw* (mixed grills) and other local food. Another consequence of the prosperity in PG is that general quality is getting better. But don't expect any enclosed or fine-dining establishments, just open-air restaurants under traditional thatched roofs.

SABANG BEACH

Le Bistrot Brasserie and Pizzeria. Sabang Beach. Main courses P220–P340 (US$4.40–US$6.80). No credit cards. Daily noon–midnight; until 3am on weekends. FRENCH.

Le Bistrot was opened by a Swiss ex-patriot couple in 1984, and since then, the two have never turned back, having been honored by the local government with Filipino citizens for their good works. The food here is delicious, whether you order one of the bistrot's signature pizzas or go for the gusto. Try the chicken à la Maltaise and you will get two large boneless chicken breasts sautéed in olive oil and marinated in kalamansi (a limelike fruit grown locally), chile, and honey. Most main courses come with ratatouille—zucchini, tomatoes, and red and green peppers mixed together in a spicy tomato sauce—excellent for dipping in their crispy French bread. Lamb lovers will appreciate the pungent leg of lamb with mashed potatoes, although the beef fondue is awfully tempting. The restaurant has remained humble with darts and billiards hall, and there have been tournaments held every Saturday since 1984. There's a well stocked bar, graced with a selection of French, Californian, and Australian wines.

Relax Thai Restaurant. Sabang Beach, Puerto Galera, Mindoro. Main courses P120–P250 (US$2.40–US$5). No credit cards. Daily 7–11pm. THAI.

Marietta, the gracious and cordial cook and part owner of Relax Thai, cooks the most authentic Thai red, yellow, and green curry; all the herbs are cut fresh from her backyard garden. The other dishes don't taste very Thai, but they're still good. It's a nice, relaxing option if you're tired of classic Filipino cuisine. It's also renowned for having the cleanest bathroom in town. Check it out for yourself.

Ristorante de Franco. Atlantis Resort, Sabang Beach. Main courses P250–P450 (US$5–US$9). AE, DC, MC, V. Daily 7am–11pm. SOUTHERN ITALIAN.

Franco is his name and Italian is his game. Atlantis resort's restaurant serves classic Italian cuisine, some of the best food on the beach. Appetizers include bruschetta or oven-baked eggplant with cheese. Choose from seafood specialties, homemade pastas with a variety of sauces, meat dishes, and homemade pizzas. The beef gives new meaning to "tender" loin—it's like butter. Called the "wool shed" by its Aussie visitors, the space is as rustic as a hangar, yet relaxing and quiet. They have a large drink menu including French and Italian wine and sangria. And for dessert, if you have room, try the crepes, zabaglione, or banana split. Franco will prepare any special requests not on the menu, with a money-back guarantee if you are less than satisfied. Mangia!

Sunshine Coast Bar and Restaurant. Sabang Beach, next to South Sea Divers. Main courses P80–P180 (US$1.60–US$3.60). No credit cards. Daily 6:30am–11pm. INTERNATIONAL.

This place is very popular with the locals for its varied offerings and cheap prices. Most tourists come for either the English, Japanese, Filipino, or American breakfast. Or, depending on what kind of evening you've had, try the frequently ordered "feeling shitty breakfast": coffee, Coke, and two cigarettes. What it lacks in atmosphere it makes up for with good humor.

Tamarind Restaurant and Music Pub. Sabang Beach. Main courses P120–P300 (US$2.40–US$6). MC, V. Daily 7am–midnight. FILIPINO.

Tamarind juice, tamarind fish, tamarind coffee, tamarind chicken—this place lives up to its name. The wooden menu and authentic bamboo furnishings set this local place apart from the rest. Sit inside the jungle of hanging, standing, and potted plants, or enjoy the ocean breezes on the beachfront terrace. (This is not recommended during high tide though.) The food is typical Filipino–nothing extraordinary, although the tamarind fish special is good, seasoned with paprika, tomato, tamarind juice, and shrimp. And it's the only place in Puerto Galera where I saw crab and lobster on the menu, but you have to give advance notice so they can fish it out for you. And if you feel like a cup of joe, they have more than enough choices for any caffeine connoisseur.

SMALL LA LAGUNA BEACH

El Galleon Beach Resort Restaurant. Small La Laguna Beach. Main courses P40–P300 (US$0.80–US$6). AE, MC, V accepted for amounts over P1,000 (US$20). Daily 6am–midnight. INTERNATIONAL.

The witty humor and honesty of the menu is typical of its Australian owner. This is a hub for divers, who chat away on their cell phones. The menu is broad, with slices of pizza, peel 'n' eat shrimp, cheese fondue, Filipino dishes, soups, even peanut butter-and-jelly sandwiches. With 3 days' notice you can have a goat. A must-try is the spicy tomato-based fish soup, loaded with lapu-lapu, parsley, and thyme.

Full Moon Restaurant. Small La Laguna Beach. ☎ **973/751-968.** Main courses P120–P280 (US$2.40–US$5.60). No credit cards. Daily 6:30am–midnight. FILIPINO.

This no-frills beachfront diner is another favorite of PG regulars. A small chalk board lists the daily menu: potato patties, lamb shepherd's pie, and lasagna, but they'll make you a special plate of local food on request. There's a large assortment of seafood, beef steaks, and ice cold beer. Try their homemade rye bread and the vegemite spread, which Aussies claim is to them what spinach is to Popeye. Monday nights, feast on a barbecue roast while watching a video.

Portofino Resort. Small La Laguna Beach. ☎ **973/776-704.** Main courses P180–P320 (US$3.60–US$6.40). MC, V (additional 8% fee when using credit cards). Daily 6am–midnight. STEAKS/MEXICAN.

The recently completed restaurant and bar will make you feel like you've been transported to a cliff-side villa on the Mediterranean. It's worth getting a cheap drink here simply to be able to use the pool that overlooks the beach. The food is well worth a visit too. Sit next to the lopo birds if the chatter doesn't annoy you and enjoy main courses like beef tenderloin or rib-eye steak, charcoal broiled to your liking and served with steamed vegetables, rice, or stuffed baked potatoes. They have a selection of sandwiches and Mexican-style platters, and ask about their daily specials. Portofino's claim to fame is their ice cream: Black Forest, rocky road, strawberry, and chunky mascapuno (nuts) are just a few you can choose from to make magnolia double Dutch sundaes, banana splits, or milk shakes.

BIG LA LAGUNA BEACH

La Laguna Beach Club. Big La Laguna Beach. ☎ **973/855-545.** Main courses P200–P450 (US$4–US$9). AE, DC, MC, V. Daily 6:30am–10pm. INTERNATIONAL.

For good eats and good reading at the same time, check out La Laguna's nine-page menu; it's a literary masterpiece. The main characters are the delicious seafood selections, like prawns with ginger, onion, chile, garlic, and rice. Follow along as the plot changes to spaghetti and pizza, then comes the gut-busting meat chapter. Feel free to request anything that's not on the menu. Service is prompt and the atmosphere is peaceful, especially by the pool. A warning to those who fear felines: They will beg and mew until some soft-hearted visitor drops a morsel, but they will scatter like flies as soon as you pick up a stone. Prices are a bit higher here than at other places.

DIVING

Most of the more than 30 dive sites around Puerto Galera are within 10 minutes of the three main beaches. Dive sites begin at a depth of 5 meters or less and increase in difficulty to deep sea dives and high powered drift dives. Deep trenches and vibrantly colorful reefs characterize Puerto Galera's waters, with dives sporting names like "the canyons," "the fishbowl," and "the washing machine." There are also numerous wrecks, a shark cave, and a true wall with a drop-off of more than 50 meters. The number of dive shops around Puerto Galera is overwhelming, as are the options for diving and certification. All have up-to-date equipment and are PADI recognized. In **Small La Laguna Beach** there are **Action Divers,** ☎ 973/751-968; and **Asia Divers,** ☎ 973/782-094. In **Sabang Beach** there's the **Atlantic Dive Resort,** ☎ 912/308-0672; the **Big Apple Dive Resort,** ☎ 912/308-1120; **Capt'n Greggs Resort,** ☎ 912/306-5267; **Cocktail Divers,** ☎ 912/306-5828; **Octopus Divers,** ☎ 912/313-4486; and **South Sea Divers,** ☎ 912/332-4286. And in **Big La Laguna,** there's the **La Laguna Dive Center,** ☎ 912/306-5622. All of these places pretty much offer the same prices and go to the same sights. Asia Divers, a national chain, is probably the best known, but Sky Tellman, owner of South Sea Divers, has the longest tenure in Puerto Galera.

MINDORO AFTER DARK

Sabang Beach is pretty much where the action is. Unfortunately, the arrival of party-seeking diver dudes has had its negative effects, which can be observed in the nights at Sabang Beach, which is more commonly known by the locals as "hooker central." The seedy side of Sabang doesn't diminish its appeal for cruising up and down the strip, which has the potential to get really rowdy at night. If you're a little dubious about which bar to go into, check out **Eddie's Place** (☎ 0912/305-8591 and ask for Eddie Garcia), a great new beachfront bar and billiards hall, which was recently reincarnated from Dico's Stop. You can sit under the *ugon* grass umbrellas and enjoy the sea breeze any time of the day or night—it's open 24 hours a day.

7 Cebu/Mactan Island

In the 1970s, Cebu was promoted as the "Pearl of the Orient," a move that attracted unsuspecting sun-seekers unaware that they were traveling to the Philippines. In truth, except for a few unexceptional points of interest, Cebu City has little to offer, so the fact that there's any tourism at all is a result of Mactan Island's high end resorts, the nearby golf courses, and direct flights from Tokyo. On Cebu's resort-lined Mactan Island, Japanese comprise 50% of annual tourist arrivals. So, Cebu's advantage is this airport, which now receives direct flights daily from Kalibo (Boracay), Manila, and Tokyo. Unfortunately, the influx of Japanese has elevated prices at resorts on Mactan Island (conveniently connected to Cebu City by two bridges), creating a package environment less appealing to a more earthy explorer.

CEBU CITY/MACTAN ISLAND
GETTING THERE
BY PLANE   The new **Mactan International Airport** is the nicest and cleanest in the country. **Philippine Airlines** (☎ 2/816-6691) has three daily flights and **Air Philippines** (☎ 2/843-7770) has five daily flights. **Cebu Pacific** (☎ 2/636-4938) offers seven daily flights from Manila and from Kalibo (Boracay), lasting just over an hour. **SEAir** (☎ 32/341-3021) runs a charter flight between Caticlan (Boracay) to Cebu as well. A one-way ticket will cost you under P2,000 (US$40), depending on the availability of promotional rates. It's twice as much for a round-trip. It is also possible to arrange your international ticket direct to Cebu. Check with your travel agent or with Philippines Airlines, which offers a program called "Cebu Express." Airport tax for international passengers in Cebu is P400 (US$8). The departure tax for flights out of Mactan International Airport are P400 (US$8) for international flights and P50 (US$1) for domestic.

BY BOAT   **WG&A SuperFerry** (☎ 2/245-4061) makes daily trips to Cebu from Manila costing about P1,265 to P6,600 (US$25 to US$132). Count on 21 to 22 hours.

VISITOR INFORMATION
The **Department of Tourism** office is located at GMC Plaza Building, Cebu City, ☎ 32/254-2811. There is also a **tourist information counter** at Mactan International Airport, ☎ 32/340-2486 or locally, 32/340-2450. In case you are in need of any special services, the **U.S. Consulate** is in the PCIB Building, 3rd floor, Gorordo Avenue, ☎ 32/231-1261. **The Honorary Consul of the U.K.** is in the Villa Terrace Homes, Greenhills Road Casuntingan, Mandaue City, ☎ 32/346-0269. **Canada's Honorary Consul** is at 45-L Andres Abellana St., Cebu City, ☎ 32/254-4749. (There are no consulates for Australia or New Zealand in Cebu.)

Fast Facts: Cebu City/Mactan Island

Banks/Currency Exchange   The Philippine National Bank on Osmena Boulevard, ☎ 32/253-1663; Standard Chartered Bank on Burgos Street, across from City Hall, ☎ 32/709-85; and Citibank, Osmena Boulevard, ☎ 32/255-9333, all can change traveler's checks and foreign currency. Most big resorts and hotels also have currency exchange, although at a less favorable rate. Banking hours are Monday to Friday 9am to 3pm. ATMs are open 24 hours. You'll find an American Express Office on the 2nd floor of the PCI Bank Building, on Gorordo Avenue (☎ 32/232-2970). It's open weekdays from 8:30am to 4pm and on Saturday from 8:30am to 11am. Thomas Cook (☎ 32/219-229) has an office at the ground floor of Metro Bank Plaza, Osmena Boulevard. It's open weekdays from 8:30am to 4pm and 8:30am to 11am on Saturday.

Doctors/Hospitals   Cebu Doctor's Hospital, Osmena Boulevard, near the Provincial Capitol Building (☎ 32/253-7511), is a reputable place to deal with any emergencies that may arise. They also have one of three decompression chambers in the country (of the other two, one is barely held together with spit and glue and the other is privately owned).

Emergencies   Dial ☎ **166** for the police. Cebu also has an emergency tourist assistance hot line to help you with any situations involving crime, theft, or illness. It's ☎ **32/254-4023.**

Internet/E-Mail   Better bring your own hookup to Cebu. Resorts on Mactan Island can provide e-mail service, but you won't be able to surf the Web.

Police   Cebu City Police Station (☎ **32/253-5636**) is on Jose L. Briones Street; or Lapu-Lapu City Police (☎ **32/340-0250**) is by the public market off S. Osmena Street on Mactan Island.

Post Office/Mail   The main post office in Cebu City is located in the Quezon Building, near Plaza Independencia (☎ **32/346-1851**). On Mactan Island there is a post office by the Lapu-Lapu City Hall off A.C. Cortes Avenue. Most resorts on the island will post letters or postcards for you, which is much easier.

Telephone   You'll notice both five- and seven-digit numbers here. The five-digit numbers are part of the old system and will soon be completely replaced. Hotels are equipped with IDD (International Direct Dial) and NDD (National Direct Dial). Cebu's area code is 32. There are international phone boxes sprinkled throughout the city, or calls can be made at the Philippine Long Distance Telephone Company (PLDT) on Osmena Boulevard, ☎ **32/253-1961.**

ACCOMMODATIONS

It's a dubious honor that Cebu City has earned itself a description as "the Manila of the South." As a sprawling hub for business and manufacturing, there is a demand for five star luxury properties geared to businessmen and their laptops. **The Cebu Plaza** (Nivel Hills, Lahug, ☎ **32/231-1231;** fax 32/231-2071. Manila reservations: ☎ 2/634-7505;. fax 2/634-7509; E-mail: Cphres@cebu.webling.com) and the **Cebu City Marriott** (Cebu Business Park, Cebu City, ☎ **800/888-2233** or 32/232-6100; fax 32/232-6101; E-mail: Ccmhotel@mozcom.com) offer eminently respectable digs for fly-by-nighters, but anybody looking to enjoy their time in this neck of the woods stays on Mactan Island, preferably with views of the Bohol Strait.

On Mactan Island you have many choices. Among the pricier resorts is pricier side **Plantation Bay** (Marigondon, ☎ **32/340-5900;** fax 32/340-5988; www.plantationbay.com; E-mail: rsvns@plantationbay.com.) offers a slice of turn-of-the-century romance and Southern comfort. It has been admitted as a member of the Small Luxury Hotels of the World Association. But all honors aside, it truly is a quaint village that succeeds in balancing colonial plantation simplicity with beach resort luxury. **The Shangri-La's Mactan Island Resort** (☎ **32/231-0288;** fax 32/231-1688; www.shangri-la.com; E-mail reservations: srsvn@mac-shangri-la.com) remains the only international deluxe resort hotel in the country. Rooms resemble those you can find in any major city in the world, with modern amenities and private balconies.

The **Cebu White Sands Beach Resort** (☎ **32/340-5960;** fax 32/340-5969. www.gsilink.com/user/wsands; E-mail: whitesands@cbu.skyinet.net.) is a fine boutique resort that retains a turn-of-the-century ambience, with an antique collection the owners proudly display throughout the lobby and the rooms.

You'll find cheaper prices and lot of promo rates at **Costabella Tropical Beach Hotel** (☎ **32/253-0828;** Reservations: Cebu City, ☎ 32/231-4244, 2787, or 3273; fax 32/253-0563). This Mediterranean-style villa is a bit understated in comparison to the other resorts nearby, but the main reason for choosing this resort is for the

DINING ◆
Cowrie Cove **9**
The Garden Patio **10**
Magellan's Landing Euro Pub
  and Restaurant **11**
No Problem Restaurant **12**

ACCOMMODATIONS ■
Cebu Marine **13**
Cebu White Sands Beach Resort **4**
Club KonTiki **3**
Costabella Tropical Beach Hotel **6**
Delta Philippine Dream **1**
Maribago Bluewater Beach Resort **5**
Plantation Bay **2**
Shangri-La **8**
Tambuli Beach Villa & Club **7**

beach, which is larger than others. **The Maribago Bluewater Beach Resort** (☎ **32/ 492-0100** or 32/232-5411; fax 32/492-0128. Reservations: Makati, Manila, ☎ 2/ 817-5751. Fax 2/845-0680; www.bluewateresort.com; E-mail: bluwater@mozcom. com), also offers lower rate and is authentic Philippines, down to the bamboo hangers, fuzzy slippers, umbrellas, and custom paintings done by a worker at the resort. The **Tambuli Beach Villa and Club** (☎ **32/232-4811** to 4819; Reservations: Cebu City, 32/254-0640; fax 32/53097; www.tambuli.com; E-mail: Tambuli@mozcom. com.) is comprised of two neighboring facilities. Together, the resort boasts the longest stretch of beach of any resort on this part of the island

DINING

Because of the distances that will require hotel transportation (tricycles tend to disappear after dark), much of your dining will probably be in your hotel. If you've got any ambition, you can head over to the fisherman's wharf or go hotel-hopping. Besides two standouts at the **Shangri-La**—Cowrie Cove and The Garden Patio—, try one of the several options at **Plantation Bay** (☎ 32/844-5024): **Fiji Restaurant** is a casual waterfront pavilion. The smart **Kilimanjaro Kafé** sits in the middle of the expanse of water, and has an international menu. Both are surrounded by netting, providing protection from annoying mosquitoes and hungry flies. Otherwise, Plantation Bay hosts a jazz bonfire dinner Wednesday to Saturday called **"Rhythm By the Bay."** If you decide to head to Fisherman's Wharf try the **No Problem Restaurant** (near the Magellan Marker ☎ 32/495-8101).

8 Bohol

Bohol Island, southeast of Cebu in the center of the Philippine archipelago, may not have as much to offer as some of the other island destinations, but the island's attractions are quite unique and varied. Most people head right to the Chocolate Hills, a surreal landscape of thousands of hills, but there's much more to Bohol than these. There are numerous caves, some with fantastic swimming holes, natural parks, centuries-old churches, hanging bridges, waterfalls, and beautiful beaches. Bohol is also a diver's playground—its diverse marine life and coral reefs are rated among the best in the world.

The people are some of the friendliest in the Philippines, giving you a true sense of village life.

GETTING THERE

BY PLANE   Philippine Airlines (☎ **2/816-6691**) and **Asian Spirit** (☎ **2/840-3811**) run the 2-hour daily flight from Manila to Tagbilaran, Bohol's capital, for about P2,300 (US$46) one-way. Tricycles to the city center at Agora Market should cost P5 (US$0.10) per person. Three people can fit if one doesn't mind straddling the bike. Tricycles to Alona Beach on Panglao Island should cost P150 to P200 (US$3 to US$4) total for the ride. Otherwise, you can flag an air-conditioned taxi for about P300 (US$6) to Panglao Island. Taxis are generally not metered; you'll have to negotiate with the driver.

Another option is to fly into Cebu City (see "Getting There," above), and take a taxi to the pier (Pier 4, North Reclamation Area) for the 90-minute ferry to Bohol. **Supercat** (☎ **32/232-4511**) leaves two to four times daily according to an ever changing schedule (always call ahead) for P320 (US$6.40 plus P20 terminal fee); **OceanJet** has departures from Pier 1 at 5:30am, 9:30am, and 5:30pm daily (confirm these times too!), for the same price. You can take a tricycle into town from the pier for about P5 per person, or even to Panglao Island, for about P100 (US$2), although it will take about an hour to get there. Taxis are quicker and will cost about P200 (US$4).

BY BOAT   WG&A Superferry, Pier 4 North Harbor, Manila (☎ **2/894-3211** or 2/893-2211), makes the 31 hour voyage to Bohol Fridays and Sundays for P600 (US$12). You can get private cabins for a bit more, but the air-conditioning usually doesn't work, and cabins can be a bit stale-smelling and unpleasant. Bunks occupy the higher decks and come with padding if you wish.

GETTING AROUND

BY BUS   You probably won't want to get around by bus, unless you're into the idea of getting stuffed in next to somebody's sack of belongings in a hot bus along sweltering and dusty roads. Nevertheless, linking the main outlying towns to Tagbilaran are the St. Jude Bus Lines at the bus terminal on East Butalid Street. They cost about P50 (US$1) for a 2-hour trip.

BY RENTAL CAR   Bohol Travel and Tours on Carlos P. Garcia Avenue in Tagbilaran (☎ **38/411-3840** or 38/411-2984) can arrange a rental car and driver for you, for around P1,500 to P2,000 (US$30 to US$40) a day. Your hotel can also arrange this, but a better resort will charge you heavily for the service.

BY MOTORBIKE   This is the best way to get around and see the island. An all-day rental will run you P600 (US$12) and can be arranged at **Bohol Travel and Tours** on

Cebu & Bohol

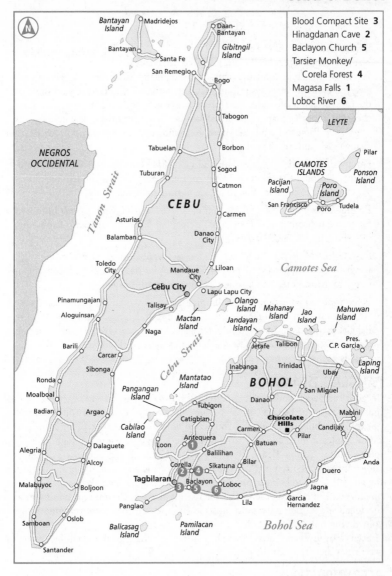

Blood Compact Site **3**
Hinagdanan Cave **2**
Baclayon Church **5**
Tarsier Monkey/
   Corela Forest **4**
Magasa Falls **1**
Loboc River **6**

Carlos P. Garcia Avenue in Tagbilaran (☎ **38/411-3840** or 38/411-2984). On Alona Beach, try **Sunshine Travel and Tours.** Ask for Jessie.

VISITOR INFORMATION

There is no tourism office in Tagbilaran, but **Bohol Travel and Tours** (☎ **38/411-3840**) or **Sunshine Travel and Tours** (no phone) can arrange island tours and handle ticket bookings and confirmations, visa information, and accommodations.

Fast Facts: Bohol

Banks/Currency Exchange In Tagbilaran, Allied Bank and Philippine National Bank on Carlos P. Garcia Avenue will change cash and traveler's checks. Several of the banks along the main road (Tagbilaran Road) have ATMs and can give you cash on your MasterCard, but unfortunately, you can't rely on these, as they are often out of service. You'll have better luck changing money or traveler's checks at a money changer in the market area (ask your driver; he'll know where to go). On Panglao Island, the Alona Kew and Aquatica resorts on Alona Beach change cash and traveler's checks.

Doctors/Hospitals Ramiro Hospital (☎ 38/411-3515) and Tabilaran Community Hospital (☎ 38/411-3324) are small facilities, but the serious injuries get carried onto the ferry bound for Cebu on a stretcher.

Emergencies Dial ☎ 166 for police, ☎ 161 for fire, and ☎ 32/340-5643 for rescue helicopter. A decompression chamber is located at Camp Lapu-Lapu in Cebu City, ☎ 32/310-709.

Post Office/Mail In Tagbilaran it's on JS Torralba Street, near the town hall. Panglao town also has a small post office, but it's far and thoroughly inconvenient to get to. Most hotels can post letters and post cards for you.

Telephone Tagbilaran: The Philippine Long Distance Telephone Company (PLDT) on Noli Me Tangere Street offers fax and long distance service. On Panglao Island there are only cell phones and hotel lines. Overseas and local calls can be placed at the Alona Kew Resort and most of the dive shops. The area code is 38.

PANGLAO ISLAND

Because Panglao Island boasts superb dive sites and white sandy beaches that rival the white sands of Boracay, it has become the obvious choice for travelers looking to explore Bohol and its waters. You really won't find tourist facilities elsewhere in Bohol, unless you're looking to stay in the smoggy eyesore of Tagbilaran. The serene, sleepy **Alona Beach** is where the die-hard diving action is, usually the choice for visitors interested in little more than basic accommodations. Thankfully, the beach has yet to be overrun with tourists and shooter bars, leaving a deliciously unadorned and relaxed beach atmosphere. But however charming it is to swim with the locals' dogs, there are more upscale facilities nearby, without compromising your diving holiday.

See "Getting There," above for information on getting to the island by taxi or tricycle from the airport or the pier.

ACCOMMODATIONS

Along Alona Beach are numerous native-style resorts that all offer comfortable, convenient cottages, and most have restaurants. Don't expect hot water or air-conditioning, though. **Pyramid Resort, Alonaville Beach Resort,** and **Aquatica Resort** all charge about P500 to P700 (US$10 to US$14) for a cottage, and provide mosquito nets. **Bohol Divers Lodge** offers a variety of rooms, some air-conditioned (P2,200/US$44), and some simply standard with common bath (P480/US$9.60). It's a good place to meet other divers. The charming **Alona Tropical** (P800 to P1,800, or US$16 to US$36) offers perfect location and accommodations, with and without A/C, for a budget price. It's situated at the far north end of the beach, where it's quiet and less crowded. And the food here is the best on the beach.

Alona Kew White Beach Resort. ☎ **912/516-2904.** Booking: Tagbilaran City, Bohol, ☎ 38/411-2615, 411-4686. Fax 38/411-2471. E-mail: Alonakew@mozcom.com. 35 units. A/C. P850 (US$17) standard double with fan; P1,000 (US$20) deluxe cottage with fan; P1,900 (US$38) A/C superior; P2,200 (US$44) A/C suite. AE, DC, JCB, MC, V.

Among the native-style cottages that populate the beach, the ones at Alona Kew are the nicest. It's as central as you can get, and is the only resort that actually has beach furniture for your use. The cottages are serviceable, with mother-of-pearl lamps, warm subdued lighting, tile floors, and a vanity table with large mirror. There is a large wardrobe, mattresses are firm and thick (not the foam kind), and sheets are high quality. Rooms 8, 10, 12, and 14 are beachfront, giving you the best views and easy access to the white sand.

Elsewhere on & around Panglao Island

Ananyana Beach Resort. Doljo Beach. Panglao Island. Bohol. ☎ and fax **38/502-8101.** www.ananyana.com. E-mail: info@ananyana.com. 10 units, all with bathroom. A/C MINIBAR. P3,000 (US$60) suite; P6,000 (US$120) family suite. Add 8% for payment by credit card. AE, JCB, MC, V.

Newly opened as of Christmas 2000, the Ananyana promises good things, thanks to the skilled management of Patrick and Emma, partners and entrepreneurs associated with Savedra over in Alona Beach. The resort combines local materials with Balinese sensibilities, which translates into extensive landscaping for optimum privacy, blissful therapeutic massages, and yoga instruction. There's even a Japanese tatami relaxation area. All rooms were designed as suites with ocean views, outdoor spaces (the upstairs rooms have balconies), and an attention to detail. The family suites—good for four— even have a Balinese style semi open bath with garden. A well-staffed activity center and dive shop (affiliated with Savedra; see "Scuba Diving" under "Moalboal" above) ensure you can't miss the natural wonders of the area. The resort provides transfers from both Mactan Airport in Cebu (US$35 per person) and from Tagbilaran (US$15 per person).

Balicasag Dive Resort. Balicasag Island, Panglao, Bohol. ☎ **912/516-2675.** Booking: Makati, Manila, ☎ **2/812-1984.** Fax 2/812-1164. 20 units. P1,400 (US$28) double. AE, DC, JCB, MC, V.

Balicasag is home to some of the best reefs in Bohol, and it attracts serious divers, mostly on day trips. Once the day's balance of boats clear out, there's nothing but natural bliss. It's especially popular with the Japanese. The cottages are comfortable but basic: little more than a place to rest your head. There is no hot water or air-conditioning, just a fan. The grounds are beautiful and quiet, thanks to its solitary location. They have a restaurant, billiard table, volleyball, and, of course, excellent diving facilities.

Bohol Beach Club. Panglao Island. ☎ **38/411-5222** to 5224. Fax 38/411-5226. Booking: UN Ave., Ermita, Manila, ☎ **2/522-2302** or 2/522-2303. Fax 2/522-2304. 65 units. A/C MINIBAR TV TEL. P2,750 (US$55) double. AE, DC, JCB, MC, V.

Once the best resort on Bohol, this popular beach complex is the perfect getaway for families. From the main pavilion, you walk through a path lined with palm trees and spotlights to the bungalows. All the traditional-style rooms are covered with *cogon* grass, giving them that deserted isle appearance. The tile floors inside are perfect for sweeping away sand, and the mattresses are thick and comfortable. The marble bathroom has hot and cold water, with excellent water pressure, and there is plenty of closet space. All bungalows are along the private beach, so you walk out your front door and your feet touch the sand. The strategically placed hammocks hanging between palm trees are the only thing between you and the perfect water—watch out for sea urchins though. Enjoy a massage, swim, or the Jacuzzi after playing tennis or eating from their buffet or Peammila ("good taste") Bar.

✪ **Panglao Island Nature Resort.** Bingag, Dauis, Bohol. ☎ **38/411-2599.** Fax 38/411-5866. www.panglaoisland.com. E-mail: metroctr@mozcom.com. 39 units, all with bathroom. A/C MINIBAR TV TEL. P6,250 (US$125) room in quaduplex; P7,500 (US$150) duplex; P10,000 (US$200) bungalow. AE, DC, JCB, MC, V.

Designed by the same eminent architect who built the revered Amanpulo, Panglao Island Nature Resort has been designed with an eye to luxury and impossible detail, from the woven basket servers for bath towels and amenities, to the in-room mosquito zapper, to the water spigot outside your cottage door to wash away the day's sand. The cottages are arranged on a cliff, solidly constructed and true to a modern Filipino sensibility. Windows line all or a portion of every wall, providing almost wraparound views of the sea or the tamed jungle, including floor to ceiling picture windows in the shower stall. Late sleepers or those taking advantage of some private time have the option of lowering the tasselled bamboo shades, but a sunrise over the coral waters of the Bohol Strait as seen through your sliding glass doors is hard to resist. Verandahs are great for lounging or watching the sunset after a dip in your own private (cold water) Jacuzzi, and each unit comes equipped with a drying rack and umbrellas for excessive rain or shine. Room furnishings represent the finest of what Filipino craftspeople have to offer, with rattan headboards, the odd coconut tree trunk popping out of the walls, and a fabulous comfy chair of tightly woven twine and muslin. Panglao offers a selection of day tours, compensating for the main drawback to staying on this side of the island, which is the lack of transportation, so you're not entirely reliant on the hotel van. Luckily, the restaurant is outstanding (see "Dining," below). Also, peak swimming hours occur at low tide, effectively limiting you to a swim in the panoramic waterfall lagoon pool instead, or better yet, in the eerily silent underwater cave pool.

DINING

Alona Kew Restaurant. Alona Beach. ☎ **38/502-9042.** Main courses P150–P500 (US$3–US$10). AE, DC, JCB, MC, V with a minimum purchase of P500 (US$10). Daily 6am–10pm. FILIPINO/INTERNATIONAL.

More expensive than most places here, Alona Kew's open-air bamboo pavilion—decorated with conch shells galore—dishes up hearty portions of steamed crabs, sizzling *gambas* (shrimps), and other seafood. You can select your own fresh fish from the tank and they will prepare it however you wish. There are tons of sizzling platters here, from squid to tenderloin tips. They also have a variety of sauces like lemon butter, chile-tomato, Thousand Island, and their mother-in-law sauce, a spicy, sour, vinegar and soy combination.

✪ **Alona Tropical.** Alona Beach. ☎ **38/411-4517.** Main courses P90–P280 (US$1.80–US$5.60). No credit cards. Daily 5:30am–midnight. INTERNATIONAL.

On the southern part of the beach, at the end of a path that winds through rows of curvaceous palm trees along the white-sand beach, you'll find the Alona Tropical Restaurant, a native-style cabana right on the beach. The menu offers all the familiar fare, but it is by far the best on the beach. This is obvious when you see the crowd that develops after 7pm. Try the grilled chicken breast, or the pork chop with onions and a cucumber-tomato salad in a sweet vinaigrette. Down it with some wine or a fruit shake, and top it all off with a banana split.

✪ **Panglao Island Nature Resort.** Bintag, Dauis, Bohol. ☎ **38/411-2599.** Main courses P96–P144 (US$2.40–US$3.60). AE, DC, JCB, MC, V. Daily 6am–11pm. FILIPINO.

Unless they're remarkable, I generally try to avoid hotel restaurants. Because the Panglao Island Nature Resort is so removed from the main action over at Alona Beach, it was pretty much a given that I would eat there. Imagine my surprise when my selections arrived, each one fresher and more flavorful than the other. The regional specialty, prepared with a high level of expertise here, is the *kinilaw,* an entrée-sized appetizer of thick raw chunks of tanguigay in coconut milk, ginger, red onion, diced tomato, and scallions. There was hardly any room for the steamed whole lapu-lapu (grouper) when it arrived, irresistible in a crispy bacon Oriental sauce. You won't have to be a vegetarian to enjoy the *lohansay* (mixed vegetables) with tofu, or you can enjoy a large selection of carnivorous options like pork chops, spareribs, sizzling chicken, or the Filipino steak in lime, soy, and garlic. You may find yourself here two nights in a row. I did.

DIVING

Simply walk the stretch of beach and take your pick from the seven dive shops here (prices are the same, at around $17 per dive; gear and add-ons are extra). **Savedra Great White Dive Shop** is the most highly recommended, with branches on Alona Beach, at the Panglao Island Resort, and at the new Ananyana Resort. They're probably the most service oriented on the beach, plus they're friendly and fun. Their outings tend to have fewer people, making for a more intimate and fulfilling excursion. Savedra is a registered PADI center, and is the only outfitter on the beach to offer nitrox dives. They also offer action and adventure trips (river climbing, canyoning, horseback riding). **Atlantis Diver Center** (☎ **38/502-9090**) has some of the newest equipment at their branch over at the far end of the beach (in the Kalipayan Hotel).

Most dives in the area are steep wall dives. Balicasag Island, with its impressive corals, house morays, and larger fish, is one of the best dive sites in the Visayas and only 20 minutes from Alona Beach by pumpboat. One of the main attractions here is the black coral forest, where you can see batfish and other reef fish. Turtle Point is popular, named after the turtles who timidly hide in the caves 18 to 20 meters down. Pamilican Island is more popular for the several species of whales and dolphins, best seen in the early morning or late at night as they frolic offshore. Pamilican means "resting place of the mantas," so you may get a look at one of these, or some of the gorgoinians, sponges, and sea anemones in the marine sanctuary on the northwest side of the island.

HIKING

Bohol is a land of rolling hills, little of which has been explored. It's not unlikely to stumble upon a hot spring or waterfall, and spelunkers will find a wealth of challenges to explore. A guide is essential, not only to lead you to the best the island has to offer, but to keep you away from the venomous jaws of snakes. Guides are available through the **Bohol Exploration Club** in Tagbilaran (3-G. Vissara St., Tagbilaran City; ☎ **38/ 411-3119** or 38/411-4189) or through **Divine Word Outdoors Club** (Lesage Street/corner Gallares St., Tagbilaran City; ☎ **38/411-3432**, ext. 121).

SHOPPING

You can't leave Bohol without a traditional basket made from nito, bamboo, sig-id, and other vines in **Antequera,** north of Tagbilaran. Have a taxi take you there. Sunday is the perfect day to go—it's market day, so come early to get your pick of the better items. You can also find shops selling baskets in Tagbilaran, though with less variety.

In Panglao, you will no doubt see women selling shells on the beach and in small boats while you dive. These are unique-looking, deep-sea shells, and make excellent gifts. Except it's illegal to export them and they'll be confiscated at the airport.

CHOCOLATE HILLS

It turns out that this is the polite name. They're called chocolate hills because in the scorching and barren dry season, these 1,768 haycock hills resemble scoops of chocolate, or so they say. Natives of Bohol prefer the idea of a caribao with a very bad case of diarrhea. (There's another legend of a heart-broken giant having shed tears, but that one doesn't serve my purpose in this intro.)

There's a perfectly logical explanation for this surreal landscape, completed in a mere two million years. Coral deposits laid the limestone foundations of a landmass that was once submerged. Then the weather took over. When the rains came, their high acidic content dissolved the coral and shell fragments, composed of soluble calcium carbonate, eventually forming gullies that, over time, deepened and interconnected. The conical hills represent the non-eroded portion of limestone, while the ground level indicates the end of the layers of soluble limestone.

A climb up 213 steps will lead you to an observation deck where you get a 360° view of the uniform hills. It's especially magnificent at sunrise or sunset.

GETTING THERE

The best way to see Chocolate Hills and the rest of the island's sights is through an arranged 1-day tour. Bohol Travel and Tours in Tagbilaran (☎ **38/411-3840**) and Sunshine Tours and Travel on Alona Beach (no phone) can arrange an air-conditioned car for you. Expect to pay about P1,500 (US$30). Along the way you'll see Baclayon Church, the Blood Compact Site (monument to the first Spanish/Filipino treaty), Loboc River (where you can hop on a floating restaurant or catch a *banca* downriver to the nearby waterfalls), and the Tarsier monkey (a must see!). The Hills are the last stop. Otherwise, it's a long 90-minute drive (or considerably more; twice, round-trip) to see only the hills.

BY BUS   St. Jude Bus Lines go directly to the Hills. Buses leave almost hourly for Carmen from Tagbilaran's bus terminal on East Butalid Street. It's P40 (US$0.80) for the 2-hour trip. Tell the driver you want Chocolate Hills and you will be dropped off at the turnoff, where you can either walk 1 kilometer up a steep hill to the Chocolate Hills Complex, or pay P10 (US$0.20) per person for a motorbike lift.

ACCOMMODATIONS

The Chocolate Hills Complex is the only place to stay in the area. Unfortunately, it's a run-down, cobwebbed, chipped-paint, picked-foam mattress mess! You're better off doing a day tour, seeing the Hills, and returning to Tagbilaran or Panglao Island for the night. If you must stay here, do so at your own risk. Solo female travelers should be extra careful: It's never very full, doors are not very secure—and let's not even get into the peephole I discovered. The pool is the best thing going for it. The dining room is pretty good for lunch and has a terrace with great views.

ATTRACTIONS

The best way to get to these places is to hire a car. A round-trip tour will take a day and you can stop as you please at sites along the way. The bus route toward Chocolate Hills passes most of these sites, but you obviously have less control over when and where you stop.

Blood Compact Site. 10-min. ride by tricycle or taxi from Tagbilaran.

In 1565 native chieftain Datu Sikatuna forged a blood compact here with Spaniard Miguel Lopez de Legaspi to foster friendly relations between their two nations. It's considered the first treaty of friendship between the native people and the Spaniards in the Philippines. The spot is marked with a large bronze re-enactment.

Hinagdanan Cave. 6km (4 miles) from Tagbilaran (near Panglao Island Nature Resort). Admission P10 (US$0.20).

A 20-minute ride by bus or jeepney, the cave is a cathedral of underworld of stalactites and stalagmites that form sculptures in the underground pool. Take a swimsuit—you'll be sorry if you don't.

Baclayon Church. Baclayon, 7km (4 miles) from Tagbilaran City. Admission P10 (US$0.20) per person. Mon–Sat 8am–5pm, Sun 9am–5pm.

Built by the Jesuits in 1595, this is the oldest stone church in the country, and pretty well worn. The massive edifice still retains its centuries-old design. Painted murals and relics from the 16th century can be seen inside. The convent houses a museum where old urns, chalices, and other relics are preserved.

Tarsier Monkey. In the forest habitat in Corella, 10km (6 miles) northeast of Tagbilaran (but you can see them in Loay, along the road to the Chocolate Hills).

The Tarsius Syrichta is the world's smallest primate, measuring 4 to 5 inches, with a tail longer than its body. Its big brown eyes, large hairless ears, and long claws—not to mention its ability to rotate its head nearly 360° and leap like a frog—make this quite a unique animal. They are on display at the edge of the forest off the main road toward Chocolate Hills. In their open cage they are free to climb the trees or eat crickets off your arm. They're shy, but when they do, this might just be the highlight of your trip to the Philippines (I almost succumbed to a mini stuffed version). Do bring your kids to see this!

Magasa Falls. Antequera, 20km (12 miles) from Tagbilaran.

A 45-minute ride by bus or jeepney, these falls are about 25 feet tall, with verdant forest as the scenic backdrop to the placid waters.

Loboc River. In the small town of Loay. Boat rides are offered all along the river's edge.

Take a motorized pumpboat from the bamboo hanging bridge in Loay, snaking your way through the serene waters and palm-fringed banks. The hour-long ride ends at Busay Falls, where you can jump in for a swim. A small motorboat upstream costs P400 to P600 each way (US$8 to US$12; some choose to take a jeepney back, or be picked up), or P800 (US$16) round-trip to the waterfall. You can also hire a whole riverboat (generally reserved for groups) for P1,600 (US$32) plus P150 (US$3) for lunch.

Balicasag Island. 45 minutes by pumpboat from Alona Beach.

More beautiful beaches abound here, not to mention excellent scuba diving. The island is a Coast Guard reservation, and its surrounding waters are declared a fish sanctuary. It's a great day trip: Hire a boat for about P1,000 (US$20) for the day, catch some fish, and have a picnic on the island. Any of the resorts will be able to arrange boat hire.

9 Boracay

Ah, Boracay. Everything they say is true and more. Boracay hovers off the northwest corner of Aklan on Panay Island, owing its very existence to the deposits of some of the finest, most pristine sand the Sibuyan and Sulu Seas had to offer. At its longest point, Boracay stretches a mere 9 kilometers (6 miles; some reports say 7 or 8km) and is only 1 kilometer wide at its narrowest mid-section. To the west are 3 kilometers of a perfect, untainted and undeveloped expanse of sand, caressed by the impossibly transparent and shallow waters of the shoreline. The eastern end of the island acts as a barrier to the powerful winds of the Pacific, where shallow waters and relentlessly high winds form a premiere combination of conditions for windsurfing. To the north and south of the island are virgin coves protected by large coral rock slides, creating a handful of secluded and romantic spots for sunbathing. In the 1980s, the island was discovered by intrepid backpackers lured by the blinding sand and high winds, and soon after, Boracay's fate was sealed.

Boracay is blessed with an unbeatable combination of traits: a perfect beach, bargain-basement prices, and intimate beachfront bamboo huts that masquerade as "resorts." But without the beach-bum atmosphere, Boracay would be just another sunny isle. Although the native bamboo huts, under constant assault by tenacious termites, have given way to more stable structures, this has simply opened up the island's treasures to those of us accustomed to a hot shower. The unbridled success of the island—most notable in a flurry of new construction including the unfortunate appearance of "D-Mall" (a theme park style shopping center already housing an unsightly fluorescent deli and salad bar), might indicate that paradise risks getting lost in its own prosperity.

For now, the balance is perfect, the sand is still like talcum powder, the beaches are free from modern encumbrances, and shoes are still a superfluous accessory.

GETTING THERE

BY PLANE Boracay is served by two airports, **Caticlan Airport,** essentially a *nipa* hut just a stone's throw away from the boats to the island; and **Kalibo Airport,** a 2-hour bus ride east. **Asian Spirit** and **Pacific Air** have small commuter planes from Manila to Caticlan; **Air Philippines, Cebu Pacific, SEAir,** and **A. Soriano Aviation** serve Kalibo. If you're flying in from **Cebu,** both Cebu Pacific and SEAir have one flight each daily direct to Caticlan Airport. Promotional fares are frequently being offered for both airports, especially during low season; expect to pay between P1,800 and P2,500 (US$36 and US$50) each way.

From Caticlan Airport, depending on how much luggage you're carrying, simply walk over to the boat docks. A motorized tricycle will be more than available if you find that your suitcases are too heavy; but negotiate the price down considerably (P20 should do it), as the distance is eminently walkable.

The trip from Kalibo is easier than you'd think, and there are many options for transferring to the Caticlan boat docks. All of the better hotels provide free pickup at the airport, pooling their resources to have all guests ushered into a comfortable char-tered bus. For those arriving without a hotel reservation and transfer, you can either grab a spot on that chartered bus (Southwest Tours; P175/US$3.50), or hop on one of the vans providing transfer service (P100/US$2).

From Caticlan, it's a 20- to 30-minute ride on a banca; again, if you've got a reservation, you're all set, but if you're arriving independently, you'll have to hire your own. Expect to pay P60 (US$1.20) for the ride.

GETTING AROUND

ON FOOT White Beach is where all the shops, resorts, and restaurants are, and everything is within walking distance. Walking from boat station no. 1 all the way through to boat station no. 4 will take you about an hour.

BY TRICYCLE You won't have any problem finding a tricycle during the day, but at night they are hard to come by. Tricycles will normally charge P10 (US$0.25) for any point along White Beach, but as a tourist you will most likely be charged a bit more. Always agree on the price before taking off.

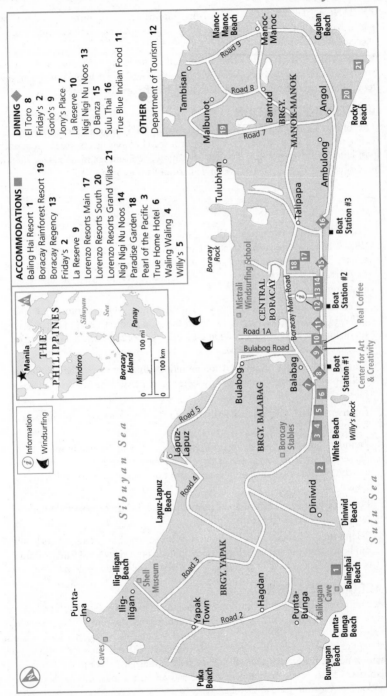

Boracay Island

ACCOMMODATIONS ■
Baling Hai Resort **1**
Boracay Rainforest Resort **19**
Boracay Regency **13**
Friday's **2**
La Reserve **9**
Lorenzo Resorts Main **17**
Lorenzo Resorts South **20**
Lorenzo Resorts Grand Villas **21**
Nigi Nigi Nu Noos **14**
Paradise Garden **18**
Pearl of the Pacific **3**
True Home Hotel **6**
Waling Waling **4**
Willy's **5**

DINING ◆
El Toro **8**
Friday's **2**
Gorio's **9**
Jony's Place **7**
La Reserve **10**
Nigi Nigi Nu Noos **13**
O Banza **15**
Sulu Thai **16**
True Blue Indian Food **11**

OTHER ●
Department of Tourism **12**

THE PHILIPPINES

★ Manila

Mindoro

Sibuyan Sea

Panay

Boracay Island

0   100 mi
0   100 km

ⓘ Information

Windsurfing

Sibuyan Sea

Sulu Sea

Punta-Ina

Caves

Ilig-Iligan Beach

Ilig-Iligan

Shell Museum

Yapak Town

Road 3

Road 2

BRGY. YAPAK

Hagdan

Punta-Bunga

Kalikugan Cave

Punta-Bunga Beach

Bunyugan Beach

Puka Beach

Balinghai Beach

Road 4

Lapuz-Lapuz Beach

Lapuz-Lapuz

Road 5

Diniwid

Diniwid Beach

BRGY. BALABAG

Boracay Stables

Bulabog

Balabag

White Beach

Willy's Rock

Bulabog Road

Road 1A

Boracay Main Road

CENTRAL BORACAY

Mistrali Windsurfing School

Boracay Rock

Tulubhan

Tambisan

Malbunot

Road 7

Road 8

Road 9

Manoc-Manoc

BRGY. MANOK-MANOK

Bantud

Talipapa

Ambulong

Angol

Rocky Beach

Cagban Beach

Manoc-Manoc Beach

Road 19

Road 20

Road 21

Real Coffee

Center for Art & Creativity

Boat Station #1

Boat Station #2

Boat Station #3

721

BY BANCA   For island hopping, diving, snorkeling, or exploring by sea, you can rent a banca almost anywhere along White Beach, or make arrangements through your resort. Rentals will cost you about P700 (US$14) for a half day.

BY BICYCLE OR MOTORBIKE   A motorbike for island exploration will cost you about P150 (US$3) an hour; bikes will cost P50 (US$1) per hour. You can arrange rentals from your resort or anywhere along White Beach.

VISITOR INFORMATION

The Tourist Center (☎ 36/288-3704 or 36/288-3705) located near boat station no. 2, is a one-stop shop where you can confirm travel arrangements, exchange money, post letters, receive packages, use their telecom services and fax machines, or shop in their shopping arcade. They are open daily from 9am to 6pm.

Fast Facts: Boracay

Banks/Currency Exchange   Allied Bank south of boat station no. 3 (☎ 36/288-3026) has a foreign exchange counter, as does the Tourist Center and most resorts. The Tourist Center will also give cash advances on credit cards for a 7.5% fee. Rates will not be very good in Boracay, so try to bring enough pesos with you.

Doctors/Hospitals   The Boracay Medical Clinic and Drugstore (☎ 36/288-3147) is along boat station no. 2, off the main road. The Metropolitan Doctor's Clinic has doctors on call 24 hours a day (☎ 36/288-6357). It's located on the Main Road near the Market.

Emergencies/Police   Call ☎ 166. For serious illness or injury, the 505 Rescue Helicopter is in full operation. Any hotel or resort will be able to contact it for you.

Internet/E-mail   Boracay has arrived onto the Internet scene. Ask me where you can go to *avoid* one.

Laundry   If you're not staying on a resort property with its own in-house laundry service, there are several places along White Beach that do laundry by weight. Try the location (no name, no phone) in front of Alice in Wonderland near boat station no. 2.

Post Office/Mail   There's a small post office in Balabag near boat station no. 2, but your best bet is the Tourist Office.

Telephone   The area code for Boracay is 36. International and national calls can be made at the Tourist Office's Telecom desk, open daily from 9am to 10pm. Many resorts also have international direct dial at the reception desk.

ACCOMMODATIONS

Accommodations on White Beach range from the rustic and basic to high-end native-style cottages or hotels with all white glove amenities. Most of the upscale resorts have staked out the wider and whiter north end of White Beach, and the further south along the beach you go, the noisier it gets (tip: the high end hotels are north of boat station no. 3). Prices vary seasonally: They peak in mid-December to the first week of January, Chinese New Year, and Easter (reservations are a must during these times), and are lowest from June to October 31.

EXPENSIVE

🔾 **Friday's Resort.** Far north end of White Beach. Bookings: 8741 Paseo De Roxas, Makati, Manila. ☎ **2/750-4488** or 2/750-8459. Fax 2/750-8457. E-mail: fridays@boracay. webquest.com. 35 units. A/C MINIBAR TV TEL. P6,000–P7,250 (US$120–US$145) deluxe; P7,250–8,500 (US$145–US$170) premier. AE, DC, JCB, MC, V.

Friday's cottages are situated on the finest part of the talcum-powder white-sand beach. Although simple and native—with walls of woven bamboo ribbons and framed mats, thatched roofs and wooden floors—it boasts air-conditioning, tiled baths, and direct-dial phones. Verandahs outside overlook the beach, face the freshwater pool, or are nestled among the tree tops. The restaurant is one of the best on Boracay. (See "Dining," below.) A plethora of leisure activities are offered, including paddleboats, windsurfing, jet skis, island tours, volleyball, and mountain biking. You are right next door to Red Coral Diving School, which is convenient for anyone considering a course. For indoor enthusiasts there are a video library and game room with billiards, darts, and table tennis.

Pearl of the Pacific Beach Resort. Balabag, White Beach. ☎ **36/288-3962.** Fax 36/ 288-3220. Bookings: Quezon City, Manila, ☎ 2/924-4480; fax 2/924-4482. 56 units. A/C MINIBAR TV TEL, except standard rms. P4,850–P7,750 (US$97–US$155) standard; P5,850– P8,750 (US$117–US$175) deluxe; P6,600– P21,000 (US$132–US$420) suite. AE, DC, JCB, MC, V.

The well-appointed rooms of this contemporary resort blend in naturally with the sprawling hills and slopes along White Beach. The design is the most original of all the resorts here; the furnishings were created by a famous Filipino designer and radiate relaxation, using neutral colors, textures, and shapes. Choose from beach-level rooms or hillside cottages, connected to the main pavilion by a funky zigzag industrial metal bridge. The cottages were recently renovated, but the suites are also very nice, with seaward views. Each suite is two levels; the beds and bathroom are on the top level, and a few steps down takes you to the living room, where two people can sleep on the sofas. The rod iron poster beds are plush and comfortable, and the bathrooms are large, with separate shower and bath, a scale, and unfinished wooden wardrobes with sliding doors. If you find yourself on the hillside and feeling a little lazy, a van can escort you down to the beach. There's fun and sports galore here, as with most resorts in the area. Just inquire at the desk. At the Princesa Rita Restaurant, you can enjoy the international cuisine and beach views in an alfresco whitewashed space with soft wood lighting and piped-in music.

🔾 **Waling Waling Beach Hotel.** Balabag, White Beach. ☎ **36/288-5555** to 5560. Fax 36/288-4555. Bookings: Manila, 2/724-2089, 727-7493. Fax 2/721-4927. 23 units. AC MINI-BAR TV TEL. P4,850–P7,150 (US$97–US$143) standard; P6,650–P9,250 (US$133–US$185) deluxe; P8,450–P11,300 (US$169–US$226) suite. AE, DC, JCB, MC, V.

What stands out about this place is that every room's private terrace looks out onto White Beach. Unlike the traditional nipa cottage style of so many other resorts here, the Mediterranean-style facade and interior will make you feel at home, with large, spacious rooms, thick mattresses, dresser drawers, and large TVs. The wooden lounge chairs and side tables are perfect for sunbathing, sipping a mango shake, or flagging down a passing masseuse. Be sure to inquire about special promo rates—excellent bargains.

Willy's Beach Resort. Balabag, White Beach. ☎ **36/288-3151** or 36/288-3395. Fax 36/288-3016. 40 units. A/C MINIBAR TV TEL. P3,700 (US$74) double; P3,900–P4,200 (US$78–US$84) suite. AE, MC, DC, V, JCB.

Right across from Boracay's most photographed landmark, Willy's Rock, is Willy's Beach Resort, an impressive Mediterranean-style villa shaded by lofty coconut and palm trees. Compared to Friday's, Pearl of the Pacific, and Waling Waling Resorts, which offer similar amenities in this neck of the beach, Willy's gives you the best value. The decor is basic, with foam mattresses. All rooms have hot showers and French doors that open onto terraces surrounding the sandy, shaded courtyard and restaurant. Breakfast is included in the price and is quite good. The palm thatched roof hangs out quite far, so if you are a natural light enthusiast, you may find the rooms a bit dark and too artificially lit. The popular beach bar offers happy hour between 5pm and 7pm. There are also room service, turndown twice daily, laundry, arranged tours, and complimentary transport to the airport.

MODERATE

✪ **Balinghai Beach Resort.** Two coves north of White Beach. ☎ **36/288-3646.** www.boracay.cc. E-mail: balinghai@boracay.cc. P3,000–P4,500 (US$60–US$90) cottage. AE, DC, JCB, MC, V.

Balinghai is hands down Boracay's winner for native authenticity, sensitivity to the environment, and perfect seclusion. Probably the most beautiful spot on the island, what used to be a sweet potato plantation now consists of five cottages secretively tucked into the cliffside, connected by steep stone trails zigzagging their way up the slope and down to the cove. The cottages are the pinnacle of romance, sporting the sublime simplicity of bamboo beams, terra-cotta tile, and local stones. The placement of the cottages optimizes the views over the Sulu Sea—even the toilet is positioned strategically to enjoy a full-on view. Rooms and verandahs are spacious, and each has its own unique flavor—a tree in the bathroom here; a circular verandah there. There's only one drawback: in the interest of absolute authenticity, there's no hot water. At Balinghai, it's actually worth it.

Boracay Regency Beach Resort. Balabag, Boracay. ☎ **36/288-6111.** Fax 36/288-6777. E-mail: regency@iloilo.net. 43 units. A/C MINIBAR TV TEL. P4,620 (US$92.40) superior; P5,280 (US$105.60) deluxe; P6,490 (US$129.80) family room; P7,920 (US$158.40) suite. Rates include breakfast for 2. AE, DC, JCB, MC, V.

A lot of individual features set this newest and most modern resort apart from similar resorts like Pearl of the Pacific, Waling Waling, and Lorenzo. It's the only place with a pool on the front beach, using fresh water from a natural underground spring on the property. This place isn't part of the Regency that we all know, though it does look and feel like a chain hotel and many of the resident expatriates consider it a place for an "older crowd." All rooms are nicely lit, furnished with dark wood and bamboo. The deluxe rooms are a bit bigger than the standard superiors, and you can soak in their bathtubs. The terraces off each room face the pool. Services include island-hopping and boat tours, ticket confirmations, laundry and pressing, safe-deposit boxes, currency exchange, and room service.

La Reserve Resort and Hotel. Akland, Boracay. ☎ **36/288-3020.** Fax 36/288-3017. E-mail: lareserv@pny-fmail@.i-next.net. 7 units. A/C MINIBAR TV. June–Nov P2,500–P5,000 (US$50–US$100) bungalow; Dec–May P4,000–P9,000 (US$80–US$180). AE, DC, MC, V.

A French-inspired retreat along white beach, La Reserve is a project of the Basque/ Bordelais owner. Some of these creatively painted bungalows are duplexes, and each of these can fit up to three people, making this an ideal place for a small family. The standout are the huge oil paintings in the bathroom—colorful motifs that will transport you into space or 10,000 leagues under the sea. The wallpaper in each room is hand-painted too. There is hot water, and the location, near boat station no. 1, is directly on the beach where all the action takes place. La Reserve is also considered to have the best restaurant on the island (see "Dining," below).

Lorenzo Resorts: Main, South and Grand Villas. Bookings: Quezon City, Manila. ☎ **2/928-0719** or 2/926-3958. Fax 62/926-1726. www.boracay-lorenzo.com. E-mail: reservations@boracay-lorenzo.com. A/C MINIBAR TV TEL. P2,000–P3,000 (US$40–US$60) main double with fan; P3,600–P5600 (US$72–US$112) main double with A/C; P5,400–P7,900 (US$108–US$158) South double. Room rates include breakfast. P2,800–P5200 (US$56–US$104) Grand Villa; P2,800–P11,000 (US$50–US$220) 1- or 2-bedroom villa. AE, DC, MC, V.

Each of the three Lorenzo properties offers guests comfortable accommodations, and no matter which one you choose, you can use any of the resorts' facilities. **Lorenzo Main** is located in the heart of White Beach and can be a bit loud. It's near the beach within a garden; the rooms, in wooden cottages with *nipa* roofing, are clean and traditionally decorated. There are two swimming pools, a game room, a disco, and a Filipino restaurant. **Lorenzo Grand Villas,** the newest of the family, is situated at the far south end of the island on a cliff that commands beautiful views of the passage between Boracay and Panay. It's bright and designed with a whimsical seaside motif that leaves you feeling peaceful and energized. The landscape is extravagant, with a pool, Asian-style ponds with fish, and the sound of chimes lingering throughout. This is the best place for families, although access to the beach involves cliff-side stairways. There are a pool and restaurant. **Lorenzo South** is probably the most convenient; it is not as loud as Lorenzo Main and not as far away as Lorenzo Villas, where transportation can be a problem. The beachfront here is secluded and the snorkeling is excellent. All rooms have a balcony facing the beach, and the suite has a Jacuzzi.

Paradise Garden Resort Hotel. Manggayad, Boracay. ☎ **36/288-3411.** Fax 36/288-3557. www.paradise-garden.com. E-mail: info@paradise-garden.com. 52 units. A/C TV MINIBAR. P4,000–P5,500 (US$80–US$110) deluxe; P5,000–P6,750 (US$100–US$135) VIP; P5,750–P32,500 (US$115–US$650) suite. AE, DC, MC, V.

Set a bit back from the beach, this hotel is set amidst a sprawl of manicured tropical gardens and natural nooks. You'll be comfortable in the spacious rooms, with hot water, air-conditioning, private terraces, and a courtyard swimming pool set in a beautiful tropical garden. The real draw of the Paradise Garden is the mansionlike extravagant two-floor royal suite, with pillars, a huge private terrace, two floors, glass paneled French doors, and unmatched personal service. They also have a golf putting green and golf cart rentals.

✪ True Home Hotel. North of Boat Station no. 1. ☎ **36/288-3784.** Fax 0917 463 0402. E-mail: truehomehotel@yahoo.com. 8 units, all with bathroom. A/C TV TEL. P3,750 (US$75) standard; P4,250 (US$85) deluxe; P4,750 (US$95) suite. Call ahead to confirm acceptance of credit cards.

From the beach, this hotel is just another innocuous and small inn. True Home would probably grab your attention if you were passing along the main road, simply because of its Spanish style carved wooden arch entrance. A shame, because this is Boracay's newest (and so far, best kept, secret). Granted, the one suite and one of the deluxe rooms are the hotel's crowning achievement: the deluxe is at ground level right on the beach, while the second floor suite enjoys a sweeping balcony—complete with pillars and a hammock—overlooking a pristine Sulu Sea. Only the rooftop restaurant has a better view. Everything is new, down to the freshly grouted modern tile bathrooms, with shiny wooden floorboards running throughout. The only caveat is the occasionally noisy bar right next door (see Blossom, under "Boracay After Dark," below), so if the music turns from soothing jazz to a test of decibels, you're well within your rights to have them tone it down.

INEXPENSIVE

Boracay Rainforest Resort. Malay, Aklan, Boracay. ☎ **36/621-1772.** 4 units. A/C MINI-BAR. P2,250 (US$45) deluxe; P3,125 (US$62.50) A/C suite. AE, DC, JCB, MC, V.

If you want to be away from the strip of resorts and have a truly personal, independent, unique vacation, this is the place—here it's just you and the rhythm of nature. Popular with stressed execs, weary urbanites, and honeymooners, the eco-conscious hideaway resort is tucked away in the middle of an ancient tropical rain forest, on a mountain overlooking a small private white-sand beach that faces the Sibuyan Sea. All cottages look like your dream childhood tree house, mounted on top of cliffs, with spectacular views from wraparound verandahs of the sea and distant islands. The rooms are well-equipped, with CD/radio, refrigerator, bathroom (no hot water), desk, queen-size bed, alarm clock, coffeemaker, and intercom to the main house where the restaurant is located. There's an outdoor bamboo bed nook, where you can snuggle up with huge oversized pillows. Transportation can be a problem, but they can provide a tricycle or their big, hummerlike vehicle. You'll have to do some daily hiking through the forest path to get to the junction for pickup.

Nigi Nigi Nu Noos. Manggayad, Boracay. Boat station no. 2. ☎ **36/288-3101.** Fax 36/288-3112. niginigi@pworld.net.ph. 21 units. A/C TEL. P1,000 (US$49–US$90) fan room cottage; P2,000 (US$62–US$112) air-conditioned cottage; P3,200 (US$62–US$112) apt. Rates reflect season. Rates include breakfast, and 7th night is free. AE, DC, MC, V.

The name is so catchy, you'll find yourself repeating it for years to come. The excellent Asian restaurant, funky art masks, and cone-shaped pagoda-style cottages will also leave an impression. It's a truly native experience, with comfortable accommodations tucked in the middle of White Beach, where you can shop and eat easily. The interiors are decorated with native materials like woven palm leafs, *cogon* grasses, cocoa bark, tropical hardwoods, and bamboo, but with the convenience of European-style bathrooms. There's also an Internet cafe (with only one computer), a souvenir shop, and a festive, popular bar.

DINING

Boracay is a culinary melting pot. Dining options are limited only by the nationalities of the island's adoptive residents and the ingredients they stuff in their luggage after a visit back home. Restaurants span the culinary globe: French, German, Swiss, Italian, Indian, Japanese, and Thai are all here side by side—and this is not the imitation stuff nor is it spoiled by mass production. Of course, fresh seafood and native cooking techniques influence the menus. You'll be forced to extend your stay on Boracay just to put a dent in your list of places to eat.

El Toro. Boat station no. 2. ☎ **36/373-6288.** Main courses P60–P395 (US$1.20–US$7.90). AE, MC, V. Daily 5:30am–11pm. SPANISH.

What a lovely place to sit. Stucco walls, stone pillars, and wood moldings around the swing windows create a breezy Mediterranean mood. The specialty of the house is the paella sangria, fresh mixed seafood combined with saffron rice and Spanish seasonings, served with sangria. The menu also has local favorites, pastas, burgers, and tacos. Feel like a whole roasted pig? Give them 24-hour notice and you're in for a gut-busting feast.

Friday's Resort. Far north end of White Beach. Main courses P120–P320 (US$2.40–US$6.40). AE, DC, JCB, MC, V. Daily 6am–midnight. INTERNATIONAL.

One of the best places on the beach for Filipino favorites and seafood, Friday's offers a casual, open-air dining experience. It's especially popular with European families. The service is excellent, and the dishes are artistically presented. You can choose continental standbys like pasta al pesto after your chef's salad, or the more adventurous Japanese sashimi or Indian tandoori. The bar concocts refreshing tropical shakes and carries an impressive wine list. In the evenings they offer "The Beach Grill," a selection of fresh seafood and meats laid out on the beach during sunset. This place is pricier than most, especially the shakes—almost double the prices found elsewhere (but we're talking dimes here, folks).

Gorio's Restaurant. Boat station no. 2, next to Aquarius Dive Shop. ☎ **36/288-3132.** Main courses P120–P170 (US$2.40–US$3.40). AE, DC, JCB, MC, V (7% surcharge added for credit cards). Daily 8am–10pm. FRENCH/ITALIAN.

You've probably noticed the women pulling and stretching noodles all day—they're preparing Gorio's fresh, homemade tagliatelle. That's the Italian part; the French contribution is the much sought-after crepes. The "Islander," made of fresh mango, banana, pineapple, vanilla ice cream, and chocolate sauce, is the winner, and the first runner-up for most people is the "Fire Ball," with mixed fresh fruits flambéed in rum. Inquire about the catch of the day and ask for unsweetened iced tea, or you're in for a cavity-inducing tea shake.

Jony's Place. Aklan, off the main road in boat station no. 1. ☎ **36/288-6119.** Main courses P120–P240 (US$2.40–US$4.80). No credit cards. Daily 7am–11pm. MEXICAN.

You won't have to run for the border here in Boracay, just to Jony's Place. The restaurant is on the non-beach side of the road, so for some, this might be a deterrent, but the food is good enough and the ambiance cozy enough to warrant a stop. Seating is outside on the sandy floor, where hanging lanterns light up the night. Choose à la carte chicken or beef tacos, enchiladas, burritos, or flautos, a fried burrito. Combo platters add spicy Mexican rice and beans. The mango daiquiri is perfect for cooling the brow and the tongue. They also deliver.

✪ **La Reserve.** Boat station no. 2. ☎ **36/288-3020.** Main courses P160–P1,600 (US$3.20–US$32 (the high end is for caviar). AE, DC, JCB, MC, V. Daily 7am–11pm. CLASSIC FRENCH.

This is fine dining with sand at your feet, palm leaves brushing against your hair, and the sea breeze at your back. Every bit of the pricey meals is worth it. You can sit in the garden or in the alfresco interior while you enjoy stuffed crab, caviar, T-bone steaks, or tanguegue fish with mango sauce. The dishes, though truly rich, are all prepared and presented in a light nouvelle cuisine style that goes easy on the stomach. And no meal is complete without a good glass of wine; the owner prides himself on his collection of 5,000 bottles. Prices range from US$15 a bottle to—gulp—US$1,320! Desserts tend to be rich, gooey, and caloric. After all this gastronomic love-making, light up one of their Havana cigars.

Nigi Nigi Nu Noos. Boat station no. 2. ☎ **36/288-3101.** Main courses P80–P200 (US$1.60–US$4). Cash only. 2-for-1 happy hour 5–7pm (local beers and mixed drinks). Daily 7am–midnight. THAI/CHINESE.

There's that name again. The mellow exotic birds, giant carved masks, and sea breezes make you feel like you're on the island of Dr. Moreau. The place is always packed with a cool crowd eating in the open-air restaurant, drinking at the beach-side bar, or melting to jazz in the jazz and blues area. Ginger is favored in the cooking, and they offer the most eclectic mix of meat preparations I've seen on the island: beef with ginger, Burmese chicken with coconut milk, and honey lemon glazed chicken. Stay and daydream or play a game of backgammon after your meal.

Sulu Thai. Boat Station no. 3. ☎ **36/288-3400.** Main courses P80–P190 (US$1.60–US$3.80). Cash only. Daily 7am–10pm. THAI.

This is a great place for people-watching on the "beach expressway." It's nothing much to look at (hardly the height of elegant dining) but they serve great Thai food. The menu is heavy with crab, fish, meat, rice, egg, soup, and noodle dishes. The sautéed mixed seafood with basil leaves is cooked perfectly, with snappy shrimp, chewy squid, and succulent crab. Word on the beach is that this is better than Siam Thai Restaurant farther up the beach.

✪ **O Banza.** Next to Swagman's Travel; near Lorenzo Main (boat station no. 2), Boracay. ☎ **36/288-5167.** Main courses P220–P600 (US$4.40–US$12). PORTUGUESE.

Wow. This rather unremarkable grouping of outdoor tables right along the beachfront bath that runs along White Beach serves some of the best food I've eaten *anywhere*. It's no wonder: with the flavors of the homeland (the olive oil, chorizo, wine, and olives are hand-carried from Portugal) and the business savvy of an ex-attorney turned beach bum, you can expect a grossly oversized and truly wonderful Mediterranean meal. Drown yourself in the *arroz de mariscos,* a transcendent cross between a risotto and a paella abundant in (cooked) marine life. The *pataniscas de bacalhau* (cod dumplings with rice) is a house specialty, but you'll need to order this in advance to allow for preparation. The menu also offers meat kabobs, steak, innovative salads like octopus or chickpea, and a luscious green (tastier and juicier) lobster. In the summer, O Banza hosts a nightly seafood barbecue on the beach, a food fest that attracts groups of Boracay's permanent expats and lots of lucky accidental arrivals.

True Blue Indian Food. Malay, in boat station no. 2 on the main walkway. ☎ **36/288-3142.** Main courses P105–P295 (US$2–US$5.90). Cash only. Daily 9am–noon and 6–11:30pm. NORTHERN INDIAN.

Bring the candles and incense and sharpen your yoga skills for this excellent Indian restaurant. You'll be taking your shoes off and sitting on oversized floor pillows on the top floor wooden terrace, where rice paper lamps cast distorted shadows and create a subdued atmosphere. The menu is equally satisfying, with spicy chicken, meat, and vegetarian dishes; tandoori; masala; and the usual unleavened bread dishes like chapati. Funky, spiritual world music plays in the background.

SPORTS & OUTDOOR ACTIVITIES
HITTING THE BEACHES

Now for the reason you came here. The beaches are fabulous, and not just **White Beach,** the island's life blood. White Beach is where all the action is, including massage vendors who comb the beach and shallow waters. The north end of White Beach is very scenic and less congested.

The beaches above the boulders to the north of White Beach offer some of the more secluded and scenic spots. Try **Diniwid Beach,** at the far north end of White Beach, or the rocky inlet of **Baling Hai Beach,** a bit further up. The best "compromise" will be to simply hire a sailing catamaran and go on a circular tour of the island, stopping at whim.

SCUBA DIVING

The clear sea off Boracay—you can see 30 kilometers (100 ft.) or more through the water—offers a variety of sites, including walls, bat caves, coral formations, and tidal surges. The sealife is abundant, including sharks, barracuda, tuna, sturgeon, pennant coral fish, sweetlips, jacks, large eagle rays, sea snakes, barrel sponges, lapu-lapu, and lionfish. Most sites are only a few minutes offshore, so you can go for a dive in the morning and be eating lunch by noon. The diving may not be the best in the Philippines— the coral isn't as abundant or beautiful as at Palawan or Bohol— but the variety of sites will appeal to all types of divers.

There are about 20 scuba schools on this small island, so you can imagine the competition. All offer the same prices, around US$18 if you've got your own equipment; US$25 without, and about US$40 for an introductory dive. Prices for an open water course are US$275 to US$300. **Calypso Diving** (☎ 36/288-3206) is the island's only PADI five-star IDC center. **Red Coral Diving School** (☎ 36/288-3486), near Friday's Resort, comes highly recommended, as Miguel (or "Mike") is a member of the Philippine Coast Guard and president of the Boracay Scuba Divers Association. Other shops that come highly recommended are the newer **FishEye Divers** (☎ 36/288-6090)**, Victory Divers** (☎ 36/288-3209), **Lapu-Lapu** (☎ 36/288-3302), and **Aquarius Scuba Diving** (☎ 36/288-3332).

WINDSURFING

Several factors contribute to the superiority of Boracay as a windsurfing wonderland. First, the *amihan,* or strong Pacific winds, howl straight into the island's east end, right into the welcoming arms of Bulabog Beach. Blocking the swells about 500 meters offshore is a protective coral reef, resulting in a bay of flat, clear water under steady and heavy winds. The conditions are optimum for the Funboard Cup, a challenge against mother nature that attracts the best and brightest athletes in this corner of the world. Beginners are better off over at White Beach, where the winds are somewhat tamer, and the waters just as calm. **Mistrali Windsurfing School** on Bulabog Beach (☎ 36/288-3876; open November to April) is the main outfitter for windsurfing and instruction. Rates are about P600 (US$12) per hour.

SNORKELING

Snorkeling is good at Lapuz-Lapuz, Ilig-Iligan, Crocodile Island, and Yapak. If you didn't bring gear, you can rent it from any dive shop, or at your resort.

Tribal Adventure Tours, located at Sandcastles Resort on boat station no. 1 (☎ 36/288-3207; fax 36/288-3449), offer eco-friendly, tailor-made kayaking, trekking, mountain biking, and caving tours in and around Boracay. They don't stick to any set itinerary, and will be happy to create a package for you combining any or all of these activities.

TENNIS & GOLF

Tirol and Tirol Resort (☎ 36/238-3165), next to the tourist office, will rent out rackets and balls for about P150 (US$3.75) for an hour's play. **Fairways and Blue-water Resort Golf and Country Club** (☎ 36/288-3191), north of White Beach, has an 18-hole par 72 Graham Marsh–designed golf course. It's normally for members only, but occasionally it's open to nonmembers—check with your resort to find out. A tricycle can take you there.

SHOPPING

If the many vendors that wander the beaches don't have what you want, check out the selection of souvenirs, carvings, T-shirts, and sarongs at the **Talipapa Flea Market** at the southern end of boat station 2. Another excellent shop along the main strip (next to Bom Boms) near boat station 2 is the **Center for Art, Creativity and Consciousness,** a shop stocked with unique, locally made artwork, including jewelry, woven items, and a large collection of drums.

BORACAY AFTER DARK

As if the party waits for the bars and discos to open. Even if life on Boracay is one significantly mellowed Spring Break, starlight illuminates a completely different side to the island. The night takes over all along White Beach. The current "in" discos are **Beachcomber** (boat station no. 1), **Bazzura** (boat station no. 2), or **Sulo Bar** (boat station no. 3). **Moondogs** (boat station no. 1) offers a commemorative T-shirt to anyone still standing after 15 shots, and your name gets added to a plaque. **Titay Main Garden Theater Restaurant and Bar** (boat station no. 3) hosts performances of ethnic dance and music. You'll need to take a tricycle to get here. For a more relaxed and less adolescent night out, **Bom Bom** is the newest arrival on the boat station no. 2 scene, it's got the most interesting music, and deliciously unfussy hammocks and bamboo swings scattered on the sand beneath coconut trees. **Summer Place** is a cozy restaurant of bamboo beds and armchairs doubling as a billiard hall with a similar gimmick to that at Moondog—only here the goal is a measly six shots. Down at the south end near boat station no. 3 is the **Jazzed Up Café** (☎ 36/288-5170), a relative newcomer where you can listen to live jazz and Latin music. Near boat station no. 1 (next to True Home) is **Blossom,** an intimate outdoor bar with stools right above the high tide line. The torchlight and two lone tables make for a very romantic evening, particularly when the music selection steers towards the soothing (it doesn't always, but the bartender is very amenable to requests).

10 Palawan

Palawan has been described by naturalists as "the Last Frontier," a title that attempts to convey the virgin and untamed nature of the island. While the rest of the Philippines is largely uncharted frontier as well, Palawan is noteworthy because of its geology and climate, a combination that sustains a level of biological diversity not seen elsewhere in the archipelago. Palawan is home to many species of wildlife not found anywhere else, including several (aggressive) species of monkeys, bear cats, civets, mouse deer, the scaly ant-eater, and the swift, a species of bird whose nests are a culinary delicacy. Nevertheless, environmentalists and local resorts must maintain a constant vigilance in protecting the environment, a necessary act of self-preservation in the face of abominable fishing and logging practices. In addition to the numerous first-class resorts in El Nido, Amanpulo, and offshore Puerto Princesa, there's a wealth provided by Mother Nature certainly worth a bit of effort to experience, like the unique geology of the Underground River, the pre-historic Tabon Man from the southern Tabon caves, the cliffs of Bacuit Bay, the otherworldly beauty of the waters around Coron Island, and the Tubbataha Reef. Don't forget your mosquito repellent, and this is a good time to think about a malaria prophylactic.

GETTING THERE

BY PLANE   You will need to assess where you will be spending the majority of your time before booking a flight to Palawan. If you're headed to **Puerto Princesa, Air Philippines** (☎ 2/843-7770) and **Philippine Airlines** (☎ 2/816-6691) have daily flights; a round-trip fare will cost you about P4,000 (US$80). **SEAir** (☎ 2/891-8708) flies to Puerto on Fridays and Sundays only; fares are about the same.

For entry into northern **Palawan,** the private charter **A. Soriano** (☎ 2/804-0408) has regular service (from twice daily to twice weekly, depending on the season) from Manila to their private airstrip in **El Nido** for P4,600 (US$92) one-way. Passengers on these flights are usually headed to the El Nido Resorts (there's a partnership between the airline and resort), so if you're not reserved at either Miniloc Island or

Palawan Island

South

China

Sea

Mindoro Strait

Busuanga Island
Busuanga
Coron
Coron Island
CALAMANIAN GROUP
Culion
Culion Island

Linapacan Strait
Linapacan

El Nido Marine Reserve
El Nido

Taytay Bay
Taytay
Dumaran

San Vincente
Roxas

St. Paul Subterranean National Park (Underground River)
Sabang

Honda Bay ▣ Islands in Honda Bay
Puerto Princesa
Irawan Crocodile Farm
Iwahig Prison Farm
area of inset

Aborlan

Palawan Passage

Narra

Sulu Sea

Quezon
Taban Caves

Rizal

Brooke's Point

Batarasa

Balabac

Balabac Strait

Puerto Princesa

National Hwy.
National Hwy.
National Hwy.

Malvar St.

National Hwy.

Fundador Rd.
AIRPORT

J. Rizal Ave.
J. Rizal Ave.

Money Changer

A. Abeug Sr.Rd.

ACCOMMODATIONS ■
Asturias Hotel **2**
Casalinda **7**
Hotel Fleurie **4**
Legend Hotel **3**
Trattoria Inn **5**

DINING ◆
Badjao Seafront Restaurant **8**
Ka Lui **6**
Marina de Bay **1**
Swiss Bistro **5**

Lagen Island, you could possibly get bumped. **SEAir** (☎ **2/891-8708**) also services El Nido for about P3,900 (US$78).

Asian Spirit (☎ **2/840-3811** to 2/840-3814) and **SEAir** (☎ **2/891-8708**) fly the Manila–**Coron** route daily (into Busuanga, in northern Palawan) in a small prop plane, both for about P2,000 (US$40) one-way.

Thank God for **SEAir,** which offers the **only connecting flights** between Puerto Princesa and El Nido, and between Puerto and Busuanga, saving you a lengthy and unnecessarily complicated return through Manila or, worse, a torturous jeepney ride. Flights are Fridays and Saturdays only; it's P1,500 from Puerto to El Nido and P2,000 to Busuanga. (See also "Getting There," under El Nido and Coron, below.)

BY BOAT   WG&A SuperFerry, Pier 4, North Harbor, Manila (☎ 2/894-3211), makes two trips a week to **Puerto Princesa** from Manila during peak season; the trip takes about 24 hours. This is the most reliable, clean, and comfortable sea travel in the country; accommodations range from economy class to your own private cabin with air-conditioning for P1,195 to P4,200 with meals (US$24 to US$84; prices available without meals as well). There are other ferries likened to traveling in a timber box, but you get what you pay for.

PUERTO PRINCESA

Puerto Princesa has been successful in hitching itself to Palawan's bandwagon as the "last frontier," but beyond serving as a convenient gateway to the mid and southern sections of the island (appropriate for the more hard-core adventure traveler), Puerto can best be described as just another Filipino backwater with nice accommodations and mediocre sights at best. It's better than most towns (relatively speaking), but unless you relish unromantic walks inhaling tricycle soot or spending the better part of your day driving on rocky paths, you'll want to spend as little time here as possible. The nearby (2-3 hours by private car) St. Paul Subterranean River National Park and Underground River is a fascinating natural resource worth the trouble, but best enjoyed as an overnight rather than one of the lengthy and exhausting drive-by day excursions offered by local tour operators (be prepared for minimal facilities).

VISITOR INFORMATION

The **City Tourism Office,** to the right as you exit the airport in **Puerto Princesa** (☎ 48/433-2983), can offer you information, mostly on Puerto Princesa. There is also a **tourist information counter** at the arrival terminal in the airport. It's open daily until planes leave. For more island-wide information, check the **Provisional Tourist Office** (☎ 48/433-2968) on the ground floor of the Capitol building complex on Rizal Avenue.

Fast Facts: Puerto Princesa

Banks/Currency Exchange   All banks in Palawan will ask to see your passport and a copy of purchase receipts for traveler's checks. You'll have an easier time at one of the many money changers located along Rizal Avenue in Puerto Princesa. And their rates are decent too. Philippine National Bank on the corner of Rizal Avenue and Valencia Street, Puerto Princesa (☎ 48/433-2321), is open Monday to Friday 9am to 3pm. There are no ATMs in Palawan.

Doctors/Hospitals   The private Adventist Hospital (☎ 48/433-2156) is located on San Pedro Street in Puerto Princesa.

Emergencies   The emergency police assistance number is ☎ **166.**

Internet/E-mail   George & Bob's Internet Café and game shop (☎ **48/434-5005**) on Rizal Avenue (past the Trattoria Inn) offers Internet access in a pleasantly clean, air-conditioned environment.

Police   Puerto Princesa's Police Station (☎ **48/433-2818** or 48/433-2101) is on Peneyra Road. Outside of Puerto Princesa, you can get assistance from the local Municipal Hall. Just ask someone where it is.

Post Office   Most towns have post offices, but mail will arrive faster if you send it from Puerto Princesa or Manila.

Safety   Because of reports of unwarranted harassment (and the kidnapping of tourists) by the local Muslims, take extreme precaution. Women traveling alone should be especially careful in southern Palawan. Malaria is also more of a risk in the south (but don't let your guard down in the north).

Telephone   The area code for Puerto Princesa is 48. You can make international and local calls from most hotels in Puerto Princesa, and at Piltel on Roxas Street or RCPI on Rizal Avenue, both phone service providers. Other parts of Palawan either don't have phone service or are serviced by cellular phones. If you need to make a call in these areas, check with a local dive shop.

ACCOMMODATIONS
Moderate to Expensive

Asturias Hotel. South National Hwy., Tiniguiban Heights. Puerto Princesa. ☎ **48/434-3851.** Fax 48/434-3750. www.angelfire.com/rnb/asturiashotel/. E-mail: asturias@pal-onl.com. 60 units, all with bathroom. A/C MINIBAR TV TEL. P2,000–P4,250 (US$40–US$85) double. AE, MC, V.

With so many other great options in town, the Asturias has one ace in the hole: the "showcase" garden pool, sunken into the central landscaped garden. The hotel is built in a Spanish Mediterranean style, and all guest rooms open onto the garden, keeping you in touch with the outdoors. Rooms are very simply furnished in white textures and wrought iron furniture, and a very few out-of-place modern architectural touches. The room phones have fast Internet lines, though, and the standard doubles are fairly large (the deluxe is cavernous). And if you're staying elsewhere, a day pass for use of the pool costs only P100.

✪ Dos Palmas Resort. Arreceffi Island, Honda Bay, Puerto Princesa. ☎ **48/434-3118.** Fax 48/434-3119. www.dospalmas.com.ph. E-mail: 2palmas@mozcom.com. 50 units, all with bathroom. A/C. P14,000 (US$280) 2 nights double in garden cottage; P18,000 (US$360) 2 nights double in duplex bay cottage. Rates include 10% service charge, 6 meals, use of resort facilities (excluding marine sports equipment), transfers to and from airport. Promotional packages available. JCB, MC, V.

Despite the success of Dos Palmas and its commitment towards environmental responsibility, this resort has been overlooked by the higher Filipino powers because they think the owner—a 24-year old who took over the family business after his father's death—is too rich. Not a good reason to discount Dos Palmas, an island hideaway that reeks of native style luxury and holiday self-indulgence. The 10 bay suites are the crowned jewel of the property, freestanding whitewashed cottages at the end of a long pier, topped by the architectural equivalent of a field hat. The island sits at the far end of Honda Bay surrounded by a "an integrated marine ecosystem" of thick mangrove forests, Seagram beds, and coral reefs, so that the main highlight of staying here is to take advantage of the marine activities. When not peering under the surface of the water or tooling through the mangrove forest, you can always paddle out on your kayak to the end of the nearby sandbar for a nap.

Hotel Fleuris. Lacao St., Puerto Princesa. ☎ 48/434-4338. www.fleuris.cjb.net. E-mail: hfleruis@mozcom.com. 47 units, all with bathroom. A/C MINIBAR TV TEL. P2,200 (US$44) deluxe; P3,000 (US$60) suite. AE, JCB, MC, V.

Rooms are crisp and clean in this newest elegant boutique hotel in Puerto Princesa. Pillows are soft, mattresses are firm, and it was the first hotel I'd stayed in without any leaky plumbing. The staff is also some of the most sincerely friendly you'll encounter in the archipelago.

✪ **Legend Hotel.** Malvar St., Puerto Princesa. ☎ 48/433-9076. Fax 48/433-9076. E-mail: legendpp@mozcom.com. 100 units, all with bathroom. A/C MINIBAR TV TEL. P2,678–P3,652 (US$54–US$73) double; P4,626–P5,844 (US$92–US$117). suite. Rates include tax. AE, DC, JCB, MC, V.

Only a year old, this is the new best hotel in Puerto Princesa. From the looks of the business center, function rooms, and fitness center, it's geared to a more business minded traveler, but who wouldn't appreciate elegant guest rooms, tasteful locally made furniture, and plush bathrobes? At the time of this writing, the Legend was putting the final touches on a swimming pool, just about blowing the competition out the water. Expect impeccable services, free transfers to and from the airport, and rates up to 40% below those stated above.

Inexpensive

✪ **Casalinda Tourist Inn and Restaurant.** Trinidad Rd., Rizal Ave., Puerto Princesa. ☎ 48/433-2606. Fax 48/433-2309. E-mail: casalind@mozcom.com. 12 units. TEL. P750 (US$15) double with A/C; 450 ($9) double with fan. No credit cards.

Owned by an American and his Filipina wife, Casalinda is the best place in town if you're looking for native authenticity. The peace and quiet of its off-road location helps create a relaxed, island mood, as does the tropical courtyard lined with palm and banana trees, where you can grab a lawn chair and just hang out. Like Casalinda's native neighbors, rooms are constructed of bamboo, rattan, and suwali walls, and provide little more than the basic 5-inch foam mattress and air-conditioning in eight of the units. The trade-off here is the lack of hot water, but if you can handle it for a day or two, the ambience and price can't be beat.

Trattoria Inn and Swiss Bistro. 353 Rizal Ave., Puerto Princesa (right on the main road). ☎ 48/433-2719 or 48/433-4985. Fax 48/433-8171. www.palawan.net/trattori/ palawan.html. E-mail: www.queenannedivers.com/trathome/index.html. 17 units. A/C TV TEL. P270–P350 (US$5.40–US$7) double with common bathroom; P490–P580 (US$9.80–US$11.60) double with air and semi-private bathroom; P750 (US$15) double with air and private bathroom. AE, DC, MC, V.

Imagine Gilligan's hut with e-mail. Remarkably, this native-style inn continues to be popular with the backpacker crowed, unaware (or unconcerned) that there's a better alternative just across the street. But the crowds keep on coming, in no small part to the knowledgeable on-site travel agency and popular bistro out back. The *sawali* thatched huts have seen better days, and the bathrooms are for the shoe-string budget conscious only.

DINING

Badjao Seafront Restaurant. Abueg Rd., Puerto Princesa. ☎ 48/433-3501. Main courses P65–P350 (US$1.30–US$7); set menu P220 (US$4.40). JCB, MC, V. Daily 8am–11pm. FILIPINO/SEAFOOD.

The clientele of this restaurant is decidedly upscale, even if the food is only satisfactory. But the romance of dining in an open pavilion on stilts over the mangroves and shallow tide is irresistible, especially under the overwhelming glow of a full moon. Stick with the reliable lapu-lapu, steamed or with butter and parsley, and definitely order a plate of the local seaweed, a house specialty. Be sure to arrange for a ride back to your hotel, or else you'll be stuck out here until sunrise.

✪ **Restaurant of the Ecological Cultural Development Center.** Vietnamese Village (13km north of Puerto Princesa). No phone. Main courses P38–P125 (US$0.76–US$2.50). Daily 8am–10pm. No credit cards. VIETNAMESE.

My one meal at this restaurant made me sad for not having covered the Vietnamese portion of this book. I could have been eating like this daily. The restaurant is run by a holistic-minded import who wholeheartedly supports the mind-body connection. The menu reflects this ideology, with locally grown organic ingredients, lots of vegetables, and a complete ban on soft drinks! Even the tofu is homemade. Don't miss the pork pie, a deceptively delicate mousse of ground steamed pork and spices, or the shrimp, mango and mint salad. Dishes are healthy, well prepared, and irresistible to your palate. The ECDC also has seriously budget accommodations, and Che Nhat Giao, the manager, will organize local tours.

✪ **Ka Lui.** Rizal Ave., Puerto Princesa. ☎ **48/433-2580.** Main courses P250–P320 (US$5–US$6.40). MC, V. Mon–Sat 11am–2pm and 6–11pm. FILIPINO.

Ka Lui is the handiwork of Louie Oliva, a local character whose friendly attitudes transfer over to the name (Ka Lui means Pal Louis). The native *nipa* and bamboo structure provides the most thoroughly Filipino atmosphere you'll find on the island (next to eating in a bare hut); guests are even required to remove their shoes before entering. Decorative pillows and tribal wall hangings, all crafted locally, add to the quirk and cozy feel of the place. The menu is heavy on fish and vegetables, but most regulars stop in several times a week for the four-course set meal, which comes with tuna steak, lobster, vegetables, soup, and fruit (P275/US$5.50).

Marina de Bay. Purok Sandiwa, Barangay Tiniguiban. Puerto Princesa. ☎ **433-5163.** Reservations suggested. Main courses P200–P395 (US$5–US$8). JCB, MC, V. Daily 6am–10pm. FILIPINO/ SEAFOOD.

Little more than a covered boat dock at the end of a long pier, the only frills at this hotel "restaurant" are the lapping of the water beneath the rickety wooden slats, but if the mayor's presence is any indication, those planks will hold. It's not uncommon that items on the menu are unavailable, but for this much romance, who cares? The menu lists temptations like prawn kabob and duck in orange sauce, but you're better off just ordering the fresh catch of the day, caught in the nets right below the pier.

Trattoria Inn and Swiss Bistro. 353 Rizal Ave., Puerto Princesa. ☎ **48/433-2719** or 48/433-4985. Breakfast P140–P170 (US$2.80–US$3.40); dinner P180–P270 (US$3.60– US$5.40). AE, DC, MC, V. Daily 6am–midnight. FILIPINO/INTERNATIONAL.

This small bistro has excellent pizza and international breakfasts, and entrees like lasagna or schnitzel. And of course it's the only place around where you can get good cheese (the owner is from Switzerland). Sit inside at a cozy table, at the bar, or outside in the tropical garden. It's a popular gathering place for locals, backpackers, and expatriates in the area, and can be a valuable place to get information and advice and to share travel tales.

ATTRACTIONS

You can arrange for a tricycle to take you to most of these sights for about P200 (US$5) for a half day, or P400 (US$10) full day.

Iwahig Prison. About 25km (15½ miles) south of Puerto Princesa. 35 to 40 minutes by tricycle from Puerto Princesa.

This prison established during the American regime is a unique concept in rehabilitation. About 1,700 inmates live on the landscaped grounds (some even with their families) among orchards, coconuts, rice, and other crops. If it weren't for the tangerine-colored shirts of the workers in the fields, Iwahig would resemble a tranquil farm rather than a hard-knock prison whose convicts have committed the most serious of offenses. The prisoners have free range of the farm and are allowed to earn an income by working at some of the handicraft stores around the farm.

You can visit the farm and interact with the prisoners if you wish, but it's a long ride to do little more than see the landscape. There's also a small store filled with souvenirs crafted by the prisoners (somebody should tell them to stop carving "Palawan" on everything). When I went I had a long, interesting talk with a prisoner who, in between bumming cigarettes, kept insisting that he was charged with robbery first, then murder. I don't recommend female travelers going alone.

Crocodile Farming Institute. Halfway between Puerto Princesa and Iwahig Penal Colony. Admission P10. Mon–Fri 1:15–4:15pm, Sat 9am–noon and 1–4pm. 20–30 minutes by tricycle from Puerto Princesa.

If you're intrigued by crocodiles, you can visit a breeding farm about 30 kilometers (19 miles) away from Puerto Princesa where the prehistoric beasts are raised and observed for "conservation" purposes. When the population reaches a safety net, the alligators will be sold for meat and pocketbooks at the comely sum of P20,000 (US$400) a head. Sad, but interesting to see nonetheless. Feeding time—Monday and Thursday afternoons—is a particularly good time to go.

✪ **Tubbataha Reef.** 182km (113 miles) southeast of Puerto Princesa, in the Sulu Sea.

Without a doubt, Tubbataha Reef is the best dive site in the Philippines. The entire Tubbataha Reef was protected as a national marine park in 1988. Most divers head to the larger, isolated north reef, which plunges to a sheer vertical wall over a hundred feet deep. Shovel-nose rays, leopard sharks, giant manta rays, and reef sharks are among the full-time residents, with even larger fish occasionally turning up from the deep. It's only reached by a live-aboard boat and it's best, if not entirely necessary, to plan this trip ahead of time, as boats tend to fill up quickly, but you can also check on your arrival into Palawan to see if a spot has opened up. **ScubaWorld Dive Shop** offers 5- to 6-day outings on their live-aboard, the M/V *Explorer*, a 130-foot boat with a 24-person capacity in 12 cabins. Contact their Manila office at ☎ **2/895-3551,** 2/890-7805, or 2/890-7807; fax 2/890-8982; www.scubaworld.com.ph. March to June is the best season for general visits. March to June is good for diving, the best being April and May (diving) because this is when the winds are at their lowest. Trips average about US$150 to US$200 per person per day.

AFTER DARK

There's not much to do in Palawan after dark unless you're a karaoke fan. The appealing and modern **Karaoke Room** in the Asturias Hotel actually deviates from the norm by hosting ballroom dancing Monday to Saturday from 8pm to 2am, and for a mere P100 (US$2) you can get some much needed instruction.

ST. PAUL SUBTERRANEAN RIVER NATIONAL PARK & UNDERGROUND RIVER

This teeming Preserved Tropical Forest habitat was declared a World Heritage Site by UNESCO in 1999. Home to more than 95 species of birds and 295 different species of trees, it changes face from flat plains, to rolling hinterlands, to hills and mountain peaks, making the hike through one of the forest trails all the more irresistible. A major highlight of a visit to the park is the Underground River, an 8.2-kilometer (5-mile) subterranean artery carved through the karst limestone cliffs over the course of how long? now inhabited by thousands of (harmless) screeching bats and swiftlets.

You must secure an entry permit to enter into the park. The permit is available at the liaison officer of the **St. Paul Subterranean River National Park Office,** in the TR Santos Bldg., Junction 1, San Miguel National Highway in Puerto Princesa (☎ **48/433-2409** or 2509). Park permit: P150 (US$3) adults, P75 (US$1.50) ages 13 to 17, or P50 (US$1) ages 6 to 12. You can also purchase the permit at the park's entrance in Sabang. Additional fees: General entrance fee P30 (US$0.60); entrance to the cave P200 (US$5) adults; P100 (US$2) 17 to 20 years; P75 (US$1.50) 13 to 16 years; P50 (US$1) 6 to 12 years.

To get to the park, you'll have to find your way to Sabang. The best way to get there is with **Go Palawan,** which has an air-conditioned van that departs Puerto Princesa dailat at 7:30 am and returns at 3:30 pm. at the Trattoria Inn on Rizal Avenue, ☎ **48/433-4570** or 48/433-9344, offers the cheapest, most comfortable, and reliable means of getting to Sabang and the underground river. Otherwise, jeepneys depart daily at 7:30 am (P75/US$1.50) from the pier for intolerable 3-hour ride.

Overnight facilities on Sabang Beach are unquestionably basic and native. There are several cottages and homestays on the beach in Sabang, all charging under P400 (US$8) for the pleasure. There's the beachfront **Sabang Beach Resorts** (☎ 48/ 434-3762; fax 48/434-3762) to the right of the pier; or the A-frame native chalets at **Pat 'n Let Cottages** opposite the pier. There is also the quiet **Panaguman Beach Resort.** near the underground river (No phone, only radio transmission; Book through: Trattoria Inn, Rizal Ave., Puerto Princesa, ☎ **48/433-2719** or 48/ 433-4985. Fax 48/433-8171).

EL NIDO

This tropical cluster of limestone islets is a honeymooner's paradise. Actually, this would be considered paradise by anybody. Except for the casual and un-apprehended dynamite fisherman, what used to be a malaria infested jungle was largely left untouched until 1982, when a group of Japanese diving enthusiasts appeared on the scene and began buying up islands which, at the time, could be had for a song. The first incarnation of what is now El Nido resorts, which currently includes the resort properties of Lagen Island and Miniloc Island (the third was destroyed in a fire but can be seen on reruns of Britain's *Robinson Caruso*), was a simple diving camp, but the colorful clown fish and the over 300 species of coral were too much to resist.

Islands here no longer sell for $100, but the fact that Bacuit Bay has been declared a protected area, along with the limits set by the natural geography, have prevented the over-development that usually comes as a result of too much of a good thing. To date, the El Nido Managed Resource Protected Area sprawls over 35,283 hectares (87,149 acres) of land and 53,847 hectares (133,002 acres) of water, and at full capacity, supports slightly more than 200 people at a time (including staff and not including El Nido town). Bacuit Bay is now the home to four resorts that can accommodate most wallet sizes (Lagen, Miniloc, Dalarog, Malapacao), while the fishing village of El Nido town caters to backpackers and budget travelers in search of a basic bed and bathroom (of the many guesthouses in town, the beachfront native cottages of Lally and Abet are the best; see below).

All of the resorts and many independent outfitters in town organize excursions to the area attractions. These include but are not limited to: sunrise kayaking through the mangrove forest to watch the Eastern Reef egrets fly off to do a day's work, scuba diving or snorkeling in the coral rich coves and lagoons to diving alongside a fabulously colorful array of fish, and candle-light dinners for two on a deserted stretch of sand. Many of the islands are privately owned so that the use of a given beach can be planned and coordinated, which means that here, three's *really* a crowd.

GETTING THERE

BY PLANE   The easiest way to get to El Nido is by plane from Manila. **A. Soriano Aviation** (☎ 2/804-0760) has small twice-daily chartered flights to El Nido, at 7:30am and 3:30pm. Tickets sell for P4,600 (about US$92) each way and can be purchased only five or less days in advance (reserve ahead) at their hangar on Andrew Avenue near the airport. Air service is usually reserved for visitors staying at the resorts around El Nido, but in low season extra seats are usually available. You can check on availability of seats at **Ten Knots Office** (known as the White House) in El Nido town (no phone). SEAir flies to El Nido from Manila (P3,890/US$78) via Busuanga (P1,890/US$38 from Manila) on the way to Puerto Princesa (P1,500/US$30 from El Nido) providing the best option for travel among the highlighted destinations of Palawan.. You'll need to coordinate your plans though, as SEAir flies this route on Fridays and Sundays only.

BY BANCA   From Sabang, at the same place where you get dropped off for the Underground River, there's a small outrigger that makes the 7½-hour trip to El Nido on Thursdays and Sundays for P850 (US$17; departure 7am). It works out well if you can divide that amount between four or five people. It is a beautiful ride along the white beaches on the South China Sea, but you will be sitting up on a bench for the duration of the trip.

GETTING AROUND

The quickest and most scenic way (and in most cases, the *only* way) of getting around is by hired pumpboat, or *banca.* You'll find them along the beaches. Price varies depending on the destination and the boat operator (once again, you have to bargain). They do tend to rob you because transport is so unpredictable and hard to arrange throughout Palawan. But if you are traveling with more than one person it's less heavy on your pocket.

If you are staying at one of the resorts in El Nido, you will have access to kayaks and boats that can take you from island to island. They will also arrange for transport to and from the small **Dio Airport.** If general transportation is not included in your rates, expect to pay up to US$60 per ride. El Nido town is small, and you can get around easily by foot, although there are tricycles.

VISITOR INFORMATION

There is a **tourist office** in El Nido town (next to the post office on Calle Real Road) that can assist you with resort accommodations if you haven't already made arrangements. There are no phone lines in El Nido, only cellular phones. Bring enough pesos with you, as there is no place outside of the resorts to exchange money.

ACCOMMODATIONS

Of all the homestays and cottages in El Nido town, **Lally & Abet Cottages** (Far end of Quezon St.; ☎ 48/715-3890; fax 48/713-4019) is hands down the winner. Rooms are constructed of native *suwali* walls, and I found the rooms clean enough to go barefoot (don't underestimate this). Management arranges daily tours and cave explorations (but you can easily negotiate something on the waterfront as well).

Bacuit Bay

Prices at the following resorts are all-inclusive, covering three meals a day and all water activities except dives.

Amanpulo Resort

Throughout the archipelago, anyone in-the-know speaks of Amanpulo in hushed tones. It's the best of the best, and no less sublime than any of the other Aman Resorts around the world. A paradise retreat for the rich and famous, the sophisticated Amanpulo, meaning "peaceful island," gives its guests so much serenity and privacy that you wouldn't even know it if Robert de Niro was next door. (Rumor has it that he is a regular.) The cottages, called *casitas,* are spaciously arranged on the beach, perched on hillsides, or set between treetops. Fresh flowers are placed throughout your casita daily. The beauty of this paradise will take your breath away and it won't be easy to go back to the real world.

Flights from Manila will take you to the resort's private airstrip daily at 1:30pm. This is the only way to get here. A round-trip, on **A. Soriano Aviation Charter Flights** (☎ 2/834-0371), will cost you US$275 per adult. Be sure to call the resort for reservations and any schedule changes.

Contact the resort for more information: P.O. Box 456 Pasay Tramo Post Office, Pasay City, Manila. ☎ **2/532-4040.** Fax 2/532-4044. E-mail: manilasales@amanresorts.com.

The **Dolarog Resort** (El Nido 5313, Palawan; fax **48/433-4892**) is a secret just waiting to be discovered. If you don't want to spend hundreds at the big resorts in the area, but still crave a hut on a private secluded island with breathtaking views of the stars, sunsets, and rock formations, then Dolarog is for you. Lovers of nature need look no further than **Malapacao Island** (El Nido 5313, Palawan; fax **48/433-4892;** www.malapacao.com), the harmonious eco-conscious resort, **Malpacao Island** (situated in a cove among El Nido's Bacuit Bay Marine Sanctuary. No meat eating or smoking allowed. Integral to a stay at Malapacao are the wellness programs, which include mud baths, facials, massages, and other therapies.

You'll be pleased with **Miniloc Island Resort and Lagen Island Resort** (El Nido; ☎ **2/894-5644;** fax 2/810-3620; www.elnidoresorts.com; E-mail: elnido@mailstation. net.) that sits on its own private cove, protected at the back by a sheer limestone cliff. Miniloc attracts a mostly youthful crowd intent on a high level of activity and an even higher level of romance. Luxurious Lagen Island is the choice of a more upscale crowd, with extras like CD players, telephones, and library. Whichever island you choose, however, with all the activities at your disposal, you'll hardly be spending time in your cottage.

DINING

All resorts offer complete meal packages with your stay. However, if you venture to El Nido town, check out **Mac Mac's** on Calle Hama Road for excellent Filipino and international dishes. It's small, dark, hot, and run-down, but so is everything else in town. It's a great place to meet other travelers and talk diving. Lobsters are plentiful in the waters around El Nido, and you can get a huge one for dirt-cheap. At Mac Mac's, you can request a lobster feast in the morning, and by dinnertime Max, the proclaimed best chef in El Nido, will have it and the delicious accompaniments ready. Also try **Virgies Eatery** around the corner for excellent homestyle Filipino cuisine. (The food will be different every day.)

Outdoor Activities

DIVING & SNORKELING When you tell someone you are going diving in the Philippines, the next question is "Have you gone to El Nido?" The area is known for some of the best diving spots in the country, although many have walked away discouraged and disgusted by the scars and destruction that dynamite and cyanide fishing have caused to some of the reefs in the area. If you don't already have your certification, the El Nido Resorts (Miniloc and Lagen) and other nearby smaller resorts, like Dolarog, can arrange for instruction, dives, and snorkeling.

In El Nido town, **Mac Mac's Dive Shop** (on Calle Hama Road), operated by Max from Austria and James from the U.S., will show you great dives for a good price, and even park the boat on an island and grill fresh tuna and lapu-lapu. Be sure to let them know what kind of dive you are looking for—slow and in-depth, or quick, covering more distance and coral. Prices are P1,600 (US$32) for two dives or an intro dive, and P500 (US$10) for snorkeling, including lunch and equipment rental.

DIVING Miniloc Cove is the preferred area for divers in Bacuit Bay. More advanced divers get to experience the "tunnel dive," where the midsection opens up to a large dome where hatched fish eggs are visible.

MOUNTAIN BIKES Rentals are available at **El Nido Boutique** in town, for P30 (US$0.60) per hour or P150 (US$3) per day.

Difficult Destinations: Cambodia & Myanmar (Burma)

In preparing this guide, we were confronted with problematic political realities in Cambodia and Myanmar—realities that made us question the advisability of sending readers there. While Cambodian authorities have made direct travel to Siem Reap (with access to Angkor Wat) a welcome possibility, the rest of the country remains iffy in terms of safety. Meanwhile, the political unfairness of the government of Myanmar has influenced the international community to post sanctions against the country.

For these reasons, we present this chapter, which will introduce you to these two troubled countries, provide some background on their histories, cultures, and political situations, and suggest resources and tour operators the intrepid traveler can contact for aid in planning a trip.

1 Cambodia

Once upon a time, almost 2 millennia ago, a powerful people known as the Khmer ruled over much of present-day Southeast Asia, including parts of what is now eastern Thailand, southern Vietnam, and Laos. Theirs was a kingdom that seems to have been created in a dream, full of wondrous temples, magnificent cities rising from steamy jungles, and glorious gods.

After fighting many wars of attrition through the ages, however, the Khmer kingdom's size was chiseled away considerably. Remaining is what we know today as Cambodia, a tiny land half the size of Germany.

And the name Cambodia hardly evokes thoughts of ancient glories. To those of us born in the late 20th century, especially in the West, Cambodia suggests instead a history of oppression, civil war, genocide, drug running, and coups d'état. Constant political turbulence and the presence of gun-toting rebels, bandits, land mines, and unexploded bombs have given the country a reputation as one of the world's most dangerous places to travel, rather than a repository of man-made and natural wonders.

Yet Cambodia's beauty and history are still there to be explored. First and foremost there is **Angkor Wat,** a monumental Hindu temple breathtaking both in beauty and historical significance. It is but a part of the former lost city of Angkor, which tells the story of a civilization in its crumbling roads, buildings, and ornate bas-reliefs that decorate hundreds of feet of crumbling temple walls. There is **Phnom Penh,** the capital, tatty but charming, with crumbling French colonial architecture and a splendid palace.

Cambodia is also resplendent with natural gifts; the **Mekong River** winds its way down from Laos to almost bisect the country vertically. Its **Tonle Sap,** or Great Lake, is Southeast Asia's largest lake and is surrounded by fertile lowlands. White-sand beaches line its southwest coast.

The Cambodian people of today have their own rich culture. Eighty-five percent of the population is Khmer, with the remaining 15% Vietnamese and Chinese. Oddly, given their horrific history, Cambodians are strongly religious; 95% of the population of 11.5 million are Theravadan Buddhists, Buddhism having taken over as the country's dominant religion at the beginning of the 13th century. (A Hindu-Buddhist mix predominated previously.)

These days, it looks as if Cambodia's assets may finally be able to get their due attention. Since the formation of a new coalition government in November of 1998, relative peace has descended. Tour groups are coming back, as are independent travelers, though both usually follow a circumscribed itinerary.

While Cambodia is not yet risk-free and a trip will entail following safety precautions to the letter (see below), this land's marvels will be well worth your effort.

A TURBULENT POLITICAL PAST

Cambodia has been populated by people of the **Mon-Khmer** ethnic group, who probably migrated from the north as far back as 1,000 B.C. It was part of the kingdom of Funan, a Southeast Asian empire that also extended into Laos and Vietnam, to the sixth century, when it was briefly absorbed into a rebel nation called Chenla. It then evolved into its glorious Angkor period in the eighth century, from which sprung many of Cambodia's treasures, most notably the lost city of Angkor.

By the late 12th century, however, the Angkor kingdom began a decline, marked by internal rebellions and culminating in a loss to the Kingdom of Siam in 1431. Vietnam jousted with Siam and also had a hand in controlling the kingdom to some degree beginning in the early 17th century. The French took over completely in 1863, followed by the Japanese, then the French again. Cambodia finally regained independence in 1953 under the leadership of **Prince Norodom Sihanouk.**

Vietnamese communist outposts in the country, however, drew Cambodia into the Vietnam War. It was heavily bombed by American forces in the late 1960s. A U.S.-backed military coup followed in 1970, but in 1975 the infamous **Khmer Rouge,** led by the tyrannical **Pol Pot,** took over Cambodia, renamed it Kampuchea, and established a totalitarian regime in the name of communism. Opposition—even imaginary opposition—was brutally crushed, resulting in the death of over two million Cambodians. The civil and Vietnam wars decimated Cambodian infrastructure. It became, and still is, one of the world's poorest nations, with a mainly agrarian economy and a literacy rate of about 35%.

In response to Khmer Rouge infractions in its country, Vietnam invaded Cambodia in 1978 and occupied it with a small number of troops until 1989, installing a puppet regime led by Hun Sen as prime minister. When Vietnam departed, the United Nations stepped in and engineered a fragile coalition government between the Sihanouk and Hun Sen factions. There was never full agreement, however, and Hun Sen took over in a violent 1997 coup. The Khmer Rouge subsequently waned in power and its former leader, Pol Pot, died in 1998.

In November of 1998, a new coalition government was formed between the two leading parties leading to relative political peace. Cambodia is now leaning toward a war crimes tribunal for Khmer Rouge perpetrators, but it still has not decided how to confront its vicious and bloody past and move forward.

ATTRACTIONS

Except for hard-core independent travelers, most people come to Cambodia to see the ruins of the ancient city of **Angkor,** capital of the Khmer kingdom from 802 until 1295, and its several historical and wondrous temple complexes. A 4-day visit there will suffice (though many do it in fewer). Previously, the Cambodian government required all international visitors to enter via the international airport in **Phnom Penh** to help draw tourism to the capital city. Nowadays, due to high demand, they've allowed direct flights into **Siem Reap,** the closest city to Angkor Wat.

ANGKOR WAT

A sandstone and laterite temple complex, Angkor Wat is one of the world's marvels, the largest religious monument ever constructed. Unknown to the world until French naturalist Henri Mahout discovered it in 1861 by literally stumbling over it, the area of Angkor existed for centuries only as a myth—a wondrous city (or cities to be exact), its exact location in the Cambodian jungle unknown.

The wat is a central tower surrounded by four smaller towers, standing in a rectangle of about 850 by 1,000 meters (2,800 by 3,800 ft.) and surrounded by a moat. Built under King Suryavarman II in the 12th century, these spectral towers seem to rise from the earth's undergrowth, and are a magnificent celebration of Hinduism and of the god Vishnu. Angkor Wat is decorated by the longest bas-relief in the world, carvings depicting the customs and culture of the Khmer people, Hindu epics like the *Ramayana,* and the life of King Suryavarman. The mesmerizing figures are fashioned in a bold, curvaceous style, the figures seeming to leap off the stone wall.

There is still more in the Angkor complex, which covers 60 square miles and carries the remains of passageways, moats, temples, and palaces that represent centuries of building in the capital. **Angkor Thom,** which means "the great city" in Khmer, is famed for its fantastic 45-meter (148-ft.) central temple, **Bayon.** A Buddhist temple built under a later king, Jayavarman VII, the Bayon nevertheless follows the Hindu cosmology concept of architecture as a metaphor for the natural world. It has four huge stone faces, with one facing out, keeping watch, at each compass point. Bayon is also surrounded by two long walls with bas-relief scenes of legendary and historical events, probably painted and gilded originally. There are 51 smaller towers surrounding Bayon, each with four faces of its own.

PHNOM PENH

Phnom Penh is a town with a lengthy history, having been founded in the mid-14th century by the Khmers as a monastery and replacing Angkor Thom a century later as the country's capital. It is historically and currently a port city at the confluence of three rivers: the Mekong, Tonle Sap, and Bassac. Perhaps the city's most momentous moment was actually when it lay vacant: Following an eviction order from Pol Pot, almost all of Phnom Penh's residents moved to the countryside in 1975, to return under the authority of Vietnamese troops in 1979.

Today, Phnom Penh's 1.4 million people live in a world of semi-chaos. Prostitution, drugs, and banditry of all sorts proliferate, incongruous among the motorbikes, rickshaws, and remnants of French colonial structures. As well as soaking up the local color, as it were, you'll actually find much to see of historic interest in Phnom Penh. Its **Royal Palace** is a stone showpiece of classical Khmer architecture, decorated with bold, curvaceous motifs including the garuda, a mythic Hindu bird. The **Silver Pagoda** on the palace grounds, its floors covered with 5,000 blocks of silver weighing more than 6 tons, is another fascinating attraction. It houses a 17th-century Buddha made of Baccarat crystal, and another made almost entirely of gold and decorated with almost 10,000 diamonds.

Throughout the city you'll see the faded glory of aged **French colonial architecture.** There are also four notable wats, religious temples with resident monks.

Of more grisly interest is the **Tuol Sleng,** or Museum of Genocide, a schoolhouse-turned-prison where up to 20,000 victims of Pol Pot's excesses were tortured before being led to the Cheoung Ek, otherwise known as the killing fields, about 10 miles from Phnom Penh. There is a glass tower memorial on the spot, erected in 1988 and filled with tens of thousands of skulls arranged by age and sex.

PLANNING A TRIP TO CAMBODIA
VISITOR INFORMATION

You'll find a wealth of information (government-approved but of undetermined origin) at **www.cambodia-web.net**. A privately run information site offers excellent background information at **www.cambodia.org**. The Cambodian Embassy to the U.S. sponsors **www.embassy.org/cambodia**. Area specialist Diethelm Travel also does a good job at **www.diethelm-travel.com/cambodia/index.htm**. You can also contact **www.asiatour.com**.

WORKING WITH A TOUR OPERATOR

There are at least three good reasons to go to Cambodia on a guided tour with an experienced operator: (1) your itinerary is likely not to be adventurous; (2) without a guide, you'd miss the finer details of what you're seeing (unless you're an expert on

Cambodian history); (3) going with a group is safer. Even if you travel independently, you may want to sign up with a local tour operator (like Diethelm, below) once you're there.

Recommended tour operators:

- **Abercrombie & Kent.** 1520 Kensington Rd., Suite 212, Oakbrook, IL 60523-2141 (☎ 800/323-7308; fax 630/954-3324; www.aandktours.com)
- **Diethelm Travel.** No. 65, Street 240, P.O. Box 99, Phnom Penh, Cambodia (☎ 23/219-151; fax 23/219-150; e-mail: dtc@bigpond.com.kh; www.diethelm-travel.com). In Siem Reap: House no. 4, Road no. 6, Krum no. 1, Sangkat no. 2, Phum Taphul, Siem Reap, Cambodia (☎ 63/963-524; fax 63/963-694).

ENTRY REQUIREMENTS

All visitors are required to carry a passport and visa. A 1-month visa can be issued on arrival at the Phnom Penh or Siem Reap airports for US$20, as well as at the Poi Pet international checkpoint for travel overland between Thailand and Cambodia. Bring two passport photos for your application. If you plan to arrive by boat from Vietnam, or overland at checkpoints other than Poi Pet, you must obtain your visa prior to arrival and specify your place of entry upfront. There is no overland or water crossing between Laos and Cambodia.

CAMBODIAN EMBASSY LOCATIONS

- **In the U.S.:** 4500 16th St. NW, Washington, D.C. 20011 (☎ 202/726-7742; fax 202/726-8381; www.embassy.org/cambodia/). **In NY:** 866 UN Plaza, Suite 420, New York, NY 10017 (☎ 212/421-7626; fax 212/421-7743)
- **In Australia/New Zealand:** no. 5 Canterbury Crescent, Deakin, ACT 2600, Canberra (☎ 61-6/273-1259; fax 61-6/273-1053; www.embassyof cambodia.org.nz/)

SAFETY

It is highly recommended that you check with your home country's overseas travel departments or with the United States Department of State to be warned of travel advisories and current affairs that may affect your trip.

The days of the Khmer Rouge taking backpackers hostage have passed. Today, general lawlessness poses the biggest threat to visitors and locals alike. **Banditry** is rampant in rural areas and in Phnom Penh after dark, with tourists easy targets for mugging and purse snatching. While some travelers report seeing or hearing nothing at all untoward, others tell tales of children roaming the streets of the capital with submachine guns.

SAFETY TIPS   Now that you're properly frightened, here's the good news: The tourism route here is very well developed, and operators know exactly when and where to go. Follow their instructions. If you're going it alone, below are some straightforward safety measures recommended by the DOS that should lead to a trouble-free visit:

- Sporadic political violence is not uncommon, so avoid political gatherings or demonstrations, and avoid the vicinity of government buildings, which may betray themselves by the presence of armed guards.
- Travel only by air or hydrofoil to Siem Reap, avoiding regular boats and speed-boats, which rarely take safety precautions. Once in Siem Reap, stay in the city or near the temple complexes.
- Stay inside after dark in Phnom Penh.

- If you're traveling by road outside of urban areas, go only between the hours of 8am and 4pm.
- Land mines and unexploded ordnance can be found in rural areas in Cambodia, but especially in Battambang, Banteay Meanchey, Pursat, Siem Reap, and Kampong Thom provinces. If by some chance you find yourself in these areas, don't walk in heavily forested spots or in dry rice paddies without a local guide. Areas around small bridges on secondary roads are particularly dangerous.

DRUGS   As Cambodia is one of the world's biggest producers of cannabis—not to mention heroin, amphetamines, and other substances—petty producers abound, as do petty skirmishes. You may be tempted to buy or sample substances offered, but if caught you may face a lengthy jail sentence, which is guaranteed to be uncomfortable. Also, you'll want to be in full control of your faculties here at all times, and to avoid the unsavory characters who conduct such business.

MEDICAL SAFETY & EVACUATION INSURANCE   A word here about the Cambodian medical system, which is rudimentary at best and nonexistent at worst. Make sure that you have medical coverage for overseas travel, and that it includes emergency evacuation. For details on insurance, see chapter 3.

FOREIGN EMBASSIES IN CAMBODIA

Should you encounter problems during your visit, go to your embassy. Addresses for embassies in Phnom Penh: **U.S.,** 16, Street 228 between streets 51 and 63 (☎ **023/ 216-436;** http://usembassy.state.gov/cambodia/); **Canada,** no. 11, Senei Vanna Vaut Oum (Street 254; ☎ **023/213-470**); **Australia** (also serves New Zealanders), no. 11, Senei Vanna Vaut Oum (Street 254; ☎ **023/213-466**); and **U.K.,** no. 27–29 Botum Soriyavong (Street 75; ☎ **023/427-124**).

GETTING THERE & GETTING AROUND

Previously, international flights only arrived at Phnom Penh's Pochentong International Airport (about 15 minutes outside the city). Currently the airport is served by Dragonair, Malaysia Airlines, Silk Air (Singapore Airlines), Bangkok Airways, Lao Aviation, Vietnam Airlines, Royal Air Camboge and Royal Phnom Penh Airways—which means you can fly direct from Bangkok and U-Tapao (near Pattaya, Thailand), Hong Kong, Kuala Lumpur (Malaysia), Vientiane and Pakse (Laos), Ho Chi Minh City, and Singapore.

If you do choose to visit Phnom Penh, there are some choice hotels. My favorite is the **Hotel Le Royal** (no. 92 Rukhak Vittei Duan Penh; ☎ **023/981-888;** fax 023/ 981-168; e-mail: raffles.hlr.ghda@bigpond.com.kh,) a fabulous art-deco masterpiece dating back to 1929 that has been recently restored. Great location, too. Another famous choice is the lovely **Hotel Sofitel Cambodiana**— make sure you get a riverfront view (313 Sisowath Quay; ☎ **023/426-288;** fax 023/426-290; www. hotelcambodiana.com; e-mail: sofitel.cambodiana@bigpond.com.kh). For a great hotel bargain check out the resortlike **Juliana Hotel** (no. 16 Juliana 152 Rd., P.O. Box 2154; ☎ **023/366-070;** fax 023/880-530; e-mail: juliana@camnet.com.kh) with a great pool and facilities for leisure travelers.

To get from Phnom Penh to Siem Reap you can go the quick way, **by plane**—Siem Reap Airways, Royal Phnom Penh Airways, President Airlines, and Royal Air Camboge all fly daily. Or you can go upriver via the great Tonle Sap lake with gorgeous tropical scenery. Boat tickets for fast and slow boats can be purchased from any travel agency and tour operator in the city. Services and prices are generally the same.

Be warned! Both ways carry their own liabilities. No domestic air carrier in Cambodia has been checked against international airline safety codes. As for the boat ride, one boat sank in 1997 with no emergency equipment or safety procedures to assist passengers. In 1999, passengers aboard the fast boat faced armed robbers.

Nowadays, if you just want to see the great temples at Angkor the process is simplified with international arrivals directly to Siem Reap, the city closest to the site. Bangkok Airways flies directly from Bangkok and Phuket, and you can check flights by Silk Air, Lao Aviation, Vietnam Airlines, and Royal Camboge Airline for other routes. *Note:* the international departure tax (from both Phnom Penh or Siem Reap) is US$20; domestic is US$10 to US$4, depending on where you're flying.

In Siem Reap, the best hotel is the famous 75-year old **Grand Hotel d'Angkor** (1 Vithei Charles de Gaulle, Khum Svay Dang Kum, Siem Reap; ☎ **063/963-888;** fax 063/963-168; www.raffles.com; e-mail: ghda@bigpond.com.kh). It really completes the entire trip with a total feeling of majesty.

2 Myanmar (Burma)

Consider the travel pioneers of the 19th and early 20th century. Boarding steam ships instead of planes, these men and women pushed the limits of comfort in exchange for the romance of destinations little known to the rest of the world. They wanted to be inspired by people with ways of life untouched by the hands of modern ruin. They wanted to be charmed by mysterious customs and awed by magnificent sights. Some sought escape from civilization. Some desired thrilling adventures in dangerous lands. Others went in search of spiritual answers. Many went simply because no person—at least of their nationality—had been there before.

Nowadays such experiences are becoming increasingly difficult to find. The entire world has been mapped, and many previously unspoiled destinations now disappoint travelers who show up to find Coca-Cola billboards being erected near picturesque beaches, or local people trading colorful traditional attire for American Levi's. Mystical Asian harbors have been replaced by steel and glass cityscapes. And for the real traveler, nothing can shatter an experience like the arrival of a busload of gawking tourists.

Not so in Myanmar (formerly Burma), which seduces travelers with the promise of adventure and beauty unspoiled by the trampling hordes of Western feet. Yangon (Rangoon), the nation's capital, still resembles a postcard from the 1950s. Ancient and serene temples rise from the morning mist, uncluttered by souvenir tents and idling tour buses. Local people still stop and gaze curiously at strangers passing through. Adventure lurks in the forests and hills.

Unfortunately, the preservation of this pristine portrait has cost the Burmese people dearly. Since 1962, Myanmar has been under the strangling grip of a military junta whose "Burmese Way of Socialism" closed the country to the outside world and ground its economy to near collapse. The Burmese people struggle to survive amidst poverty, political oppression, and revolutionary violence.

So what's an interested traveler to do? On one side, the State Law and Order Restoration Council (SLORC), the ruling elite, opens its arms to foreign visitors, luring them with smiles and welcoming them to spend foreign money—money it hopes will help mask the problems of a nation it has so sadly neglected. On the other side, nongovernmental organizations that support Myanmar's pro-democracy movement are raising the call to world travelers, urging them to avoid travel to Myanmar and thus prevent the SLORC from obtaining the hard currency and global legitimacy it needs to survive.

If you yearn for an adventurous travel experience, Myanmar can satisfy your expectations. With the proper preparations, you can enjoy this hidden corner of the world with relative security, and with current and accurate information you can minimize your contributions to the damages caused by the current regime. Please travel wisely.

BURMA YESTERDAY, MYANMAR TODAY

Myanmar sits in the northwest corner of Southeast Asia, sharing borders with Thailand, Laos, China, Tibet, India, and Bangladesh. The northern regions rise and plunge with the foothills of the Himalaya mountain range. It is here that streams originate, converging in low-lying plains to form the Ayeyarwady (Irrawaddy) River. The river bisects the country before branching out into deltas, flowing southward through Myanmar's tropical southern landscape to the Andaman Sea.

The people are divided into over 67 unique ethnic groups. Descended from people who migrated in waves from central Asia, Tibet, and southern China, the many races that developed over the centuries battled each other constantly, and in some cases still do so today. The majority of the population is **Bamar,** the race of the ruling elite. Most of the other races are divisions of hill tribe peoples who share similar cultures with the people of northern Thailand and Southern China.

Theravada Buddhism is the country's ruling religion, having drifted to the country from its origins in Sri Lanka. Prior to Buddhism, the people of Burma practiced as many different forms of animism—the worship of spirit and nature gods—as there were tribes. Today, although a profound majority of the population is Buddhist, animism is still alive and well in the northern regions.

Buddhism has a far-reaching influence on the people of Myanmar. Theravada, the most orthodox of Buddhist tracts, follows strictly the teachings of the Lord Buddha. Many men and boys enter the monkhood (if only for a short time); life is conservative; and the artistic tradition of Sri Lankan Buddhism abounds, from Myanmar's many breathtaking temples to a multitude of fascinating Buddha images.

Myanmar is rich in natural resources, including rubies and other gemstones mined in the north, and teak trees, desirable for their fine hardwood lumber. Its fertile soils yield bountiful rice crops, but unfortunately, Myanmar's biggest claim to agricultural fame is the opium poppy. Hill tribe farmers in the north depend on poppies for survival, as their sale brings more money than other subsistence crops. Farmers sell the crops to manufacturers who produce and distribute the opium and heroin derivatives globally. Much of the true wealth gained by the sale is diverted to tribal rebel groups for the purchase of weapons in the fight for independence from Myanmar's ruling military junta.

HISTORY & POLITICAL TURBULENCE

Prior to the Anglo-Burmese wars, which ended in 1886, Burma had been a monarchy since the 11th century. British colonialism put the country on the world map, but failed to protect it from the invading Japanese in World War II. In 1946, following the Japanese surrender, Burma became an independent state, and a fledgling democracy began under the courageous leadership of **Aung San,** an independence hero who was able to unite Burma's many ethnic groups to form a single nation. Unfortunately, the following year, Aung San was killed in a coup. To this day, he remains a national hero, his image plastered on almost every wall in the country.

The following 15 years were wrought with domestic chaos until General Ne Win took hold of the reins. He filled government positions with high-ranking military officials, which gave rise to the all-powerful Revolutionary Council. Under a socialist decree, privatization was banished, the military ruled all affairs (including those social and economic), and the country was virtually closed to the outside world.

Since then, there have been many challenges to Ne Win's government, most of which were initiated by the country's many different ethnic minority groups. The most threatening challenge came in 1988, following a brief and rare period of relative political openness, when people began to collect and speak openly about their human rights and

Myanmar (Burma)

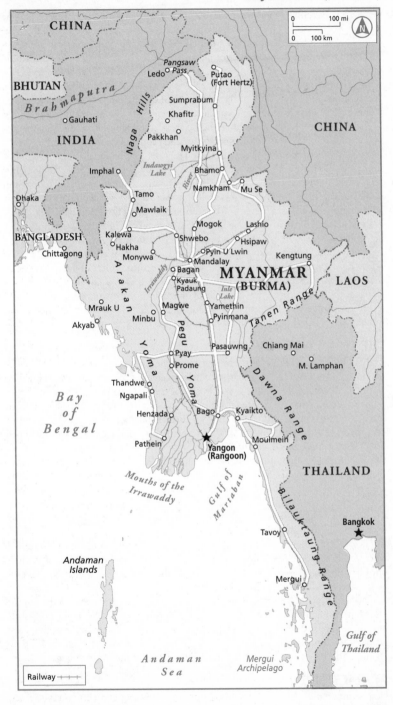

CHINA

BHUTAN

Brahmaputra

INDIA

○ Gauhati

BANGLADESH

Dhaka ○

Chittagong ○

*Bay
of
Bengal*

Ledo ○ *Pangsaw
Pass*

○ Putao
(Fort Hertz)

Sumprabum ○

Khafitr ○

Pakkhan ○

Naga Hills

Myitkyina ○

*Indawgyi
Lake*

Bhamo ○

River

Namkham ○ Mu Se ○

Imphal ○

Tamo ○

Mawlaik ○

Kalewa ○

Hakha ○

Monywa ○

Arakan

Mogok ○   Lashio ○

Shwebo ○   Hsipaw ○

○ Pyin U Lwin

○ Mandalay   Kengtung ○

Bagan ○

Kyauk ○
Padaung

Irrawaddy

Mrauk U ○

Magwe ○

*Inle
Lake*

Yamethin ○

Minbu ○

Yoma

Pyinmana ○

Akyab ○

*Pegu
Yoma*

Pasauwng ○

Chiang Mai ○

Tanen Range

Pyay ○

Prome ○

M. Lamphan ○

Thandwe ○

Ngapali ○

Henzada ○

Bago ○ Kyaikto ○

Dawna Range

Pathein ○

★ Yangon
(Rangoon)

Moulmein ○

*Mouths of the
Irrawaddy*

*Gulf of
Martaban*

THAILAND

MYANMAR
(BURMA)

LAOS

Bilauktaung Range

Tavoy ○

★ Bangkok

*Andaman
Islands*

Mergui ○

*Andaman
Sea*

*Mergui
Archipelago*

*Gulf of
Thailand*

Railway ┼┼┼┼

0 — 100 mi
0 — 100 km

democracy. In September of that year, the army retaliated with a brutal sweep, killing as many as 10,000 people. It was this massacre that drove the government to form the **State Law and Order Restoration Council (SLORC),** and inspired a young intellectual, **Aung San Suu Kyi,** daughter of independence leader Aung San, to become head of the opposition party, the pro-democracy National League for Democracy (NLD).

General elections were held in 1990, and despite the political imprisonment of Ms. Suu Kyi, the NLD won 82% of the votes. The SLORC chose to ignore the expressed wishes of the Burmese people and remained in power, imprisoning many NLD figures.

Today, Ms. Suu Kyi remains under house arrest in Myanmar's capital. She is recognized globally as the voice of democracy for the people of Burma, who suffer under strict SLORC oppression policies. In early 1999 the International Labour Organization (ILO) pointed a finger at the SLORC as a leading abuser of basic labor rights, and shortly after, a report to the United Nations Human Rights Commission (UNHCR) stated that human rights violations were on the rise, with the government intimidating citizens and preventing them from exercising fundamental rights.

In March 1999, when Aung San Suu Kyi's husband, Michael Aris, who was residing in the UK, fell critically ill with cancer, the Myanmar government refused him a visa to enter the country. Instead, the Myanmar government tried to convince Ms. Suu Kyi to leave, promising her that she'd be allowed to return. In fear of permanent exile, she remained in Myanmar, and sadly her husband passed away shortly after. The global press has accepted this as proof of the cruel manner in which the SLORC regards its people, and the people of Myanmar see the incident as yet another reason to hold Ms. Suu Kyi in the highest of esteem as the true soul of the nation.

THE SLORC & TOURISM

The SLORC opened the country to tourism in the early 1990s, and a flood of overseas hotel investors, travel agencies, and tour operators came flooding in. However, alongside reports of the country's vast wealth of cultural beauty came reports of government projects that conscripted forced labor to complete infrastructure and tourism projects. Reports in the BBC described Myanmar as "one vast labour camp," a description that *The New York Times, Daily Telegraph,* and *Financial Times* have confirmed with scenes of prisoners in chains, working under harsh and violent conditions, many times collapsing from beatings and heat exhaustion. Such labor projects increased dramatically when the SLORC declared 1996 as "Visit Myanmar Year." The BBC reported cruel labor practices during the restoration of the Royal Palace in Mandalay in preparation for 1996. A northern Burmese stated, "Ten years from now Burma won't be the same. It'll only be for the army and tourists . . . Foreigners don't know what we're going through for this tourism year."

The SLORC's hopes of attracting foreign money through tourism were crushed when Aung San Suu Kyi publicly urged tourists to refrain from visiting Myanmar until a legitimate government had been established. By the mid-90s, travel agents began to drop Myanmar packages like a bad habit.

However, over the past couple of years a new side to the argument has developed. Does boycotting tourism in Myanmar help the Burmese people? Some say no, pointing to the jobs created by the tourism industry and the access tourism gives local people to the outside world. Now, many NGOs have suggested that maybe it's time for the world to see Burma, and to expose the country to the world at large.

ATTRACTIONS

Despite international concern regarding tourism, many will chose to visit Myanmar, and understandably so. With little debate, it is a country of astounding beauty, the most famous and exquisite sight being the **Shwedagaon Pagoda** in Yangon. The construction of the pagoda remains a mystery, hidden in many local legends; however, recorded history suggests it predates the 11th century. The huge Sri Lankan–influenced, bell-shaped pagoda rises above the cityscape, a vision of glistening gold—8,688 precious solid gold plates, bejeweled in a huge fortune of diamonds, rubies, sapphires, and other gems. Inside, the stupa enshrines eight hairs from the Lord Buddha; outside, within the temple walls, is a small city of pagodas, temples, shrines, and astrological pillars.

Yangon also retains the charm of an exotic British outpost. A walk down city streets is a sensory assault of exotic city planning, with tropical colonial architecture interlaced with Burmese temples, markets, and shops.

And then there's **Bagan,** a riverside city containing over two thousand pagodas, located up the Ayeyerwady just south of Mandalay. Rivaling Cambodia's Angkor Wat, these 11th-century temples stretch as far as the eye can see, and are a stunning image of ancient Buddhist expression and a testimony to the wealth of a once mighty kingdom.

Just north of Bagan, **Mandalay** is the most visited city in Myanmar next to Yangon. The main attraction is the **Royal Palace,** a perfect square enclosed in walls over 2 kilometers in length on each side. Surrounded by a moat, the walled palace is open to the public through special guided tours that visit only the Lion's Room, where the royal throne was located, and the palace museum.

PLANNING A TRIP TO MYANMAR
VISITOR INFORMATION
While planned tours are unarguably the most convenient way to see Myanmar, non-governmental organizations are suggesting a "backpacker" route for those who are really interested in seeing "the true Burma." They urge foreign visitors to patronize family-run guest houses and restaurants, and use transportation that supports local people to ensure that your money stays out of the hands of the government and finds its way to the people who truly need it. **The Burma Project at the Open Society Institute,** 400 W. 59th St., 4th Fl., New York, NY 10019 (☎ **212/548-0632;** fax 212/548-4655; www.soros.org/burma), is a leading NGO in the struggle for democracy. Their Web site provides extensive links to facts and articles about Myanmar and its political situation.

WORKING WITH A TOUR OPERATOR
Abercrombie & Kent (1520 Kensington Rd., Suite 212, Oakbrook, IL 60523-2141; ☎ **800/323-7308;** fax 630/954-3324; www.aandktours.com.) do a fabulous job with tours in Myanmar, booking you into the best hotels and transportation options available. Another recommended agency, Diethelm Travel, is based in Southeast Asia. You can plan all or part of your trip through them. Their Yangon office is at 1 Inya Rd., Kamayut Township; ☎ **951/527-110** or 527-117; fax 951/527-135; www.diethelm-travel.com/; e-mail: leisure@diethelm.com.mm.

ENTRY REQUIREMENTS
Myanmar consulates issue visas for stays of up to 28 days. The cost is US$25, with three passport photos. An extension of up to 14 days can be granted in-country.

MYANMAR EMBASSY LOCATIONS
- **In the U.S.:** Myanmar Embassy, 2300 S St. NW, Washington, D.C. 20008 (☎ **202/332-9045**); Permanent Mission of Myanmar to the United Nations, 10 E. 77th St., New York, NY 10021 (☎ **212/535-1310**)

- **In the U.K.:** 19A Charles St., London W1X 8ER (☎ **0171/629-6966**)
- **In Australia:** 22 Arkana St., Yarralumla, Canberra A.C.T. 2600 (☎ **6102/627-33811**)
- **In Canada:** 85 Range Rd., Suite 902–903, Sandringhan, Ottawa, Ontario (☎ **613/232-6434**)
- There is no Myanmar representation in **New Zealand.**

SAFETY

It is highly recommended that you check with your home country's overseas travel departments or with the United States Department of State to be warned of travel advisories and current affairs that may affect your trip. See "Safety Tips" on p. 745, earlier in this chapter.

Medical safety & evacuation insurance is highly recommended that you obtain emergency evacuation insurance coverage for the length of your stay, in addition to your health insurance policy. A good evacuation plan will get you out of the country in situations that pose political danger, will help you secure adequate legal assistance should you be unfortunate enough to need it, and will transport you to the nearest reputable medical facility in the event of a health emergency.

FOREIGN EMBASSIES IN MYANMAR

Many countries will strongly urge that you keep in touch with your native consulate within Myanmar upon arrival and throughout your stay. In the event of an emergency, you'll be thankful that they have your travel itinerary on hand. International representatives in Myanmar are as follows: **U.S.,** 581 Merchant Rd. (☎ **951/282-055**); **U.K.,** 80 Strand Rd. (☎ **951/821-700**); **Australia,** 88 Strand Rd. (☎ **951/251-809**). There is no presence for New Zealand or Canada in Myanmar at this time.

GETTING THERE & GETTING AROUND

Travelers almost always enter Myanmar by plane. International carriers servicing Myanmar include **Myanmar Airways International** (www.maiair.com), **Thai Airways International,** and **Silk Air** (Singapore Airlines), with direct access from Bangkok, Singapore, and Hong Kong. Air Mandalay connects Thailand's Chiang Mai with Mandalay and Yangon.

Upon arrival, independent travelers will be required to cash no less than US$200 at the airport, in exchange for 200 Foreign Exchange Certificates (FEC)—1 FEC = 1 U.S. dollar. When you leave, only amounts exchanged above the original 200 can be changed back to U.S. dollars. If you've booked a tour, make sure you are issued a letter from the agency that will exempt you from the 200 FEC rule.

Once in Myanmar, the most convenient public transportation between cities is flying **Air Mandalay** (www.air-mandalay.com) or **Yangon Airways** (www.myanmars.net/ygnair), which operate between most major cities. **Myanmar Railways** will take you from Yangon to Mandalay and beyond. Buses ply between cities, as well as riverboats for stunning tours of the Ayeyerwady and its sights.

The most famous and luxurious mode of travel is to book passage aboard the **Eastern & Oriental's Road To Mandalay,** a grand river cruiser that plies between Mandalay and Bagan, with trips down to Yangon as well. Visit their Web site at www.orient-express.com or call in the **U.S.** ☎ 800/524-2420, in the **U.K.** ☎ 020/7805-5100, in **Australia** ☎ 1800/000-395, or in **New Zealand** ☎ 09/379-3708.

There are a few top quality hotels in **Yangon,** the most famous of which is **The Strand Hotel** (92 Strand Rd.; ☎ **951/243-377;** fax 951/289-880; e-mail:

reservations@strandhotel.com.mm). Built at the turn of the century, the Strand is a gorgeous monument to British colonial opulence, and the only really elegant address in the country. You'll also find excellent accommodations at **Traders Hotel Yangon** (223 Sule Pagoda Rd.; ☎ **951/242-828;** fax 951/242-800; e-mail: thyn@shangri-la.com), a business hotel with a great location operated by Shangri-La hotels. For beautiful accommodations on Inya Lake, try the **Renaissance Lake Hotel–Yangon** (37 Kabah Aye Pagoda Rd.; ☎ **951/662-866;** fax 951/665-537; e-mail: renaissanceinyalake@mptmail. net.mm).

Index

FROMMER'S® COMPLETE TRAVEL GUIDES

Alaska
Amsterdam
Argentina & Chile
Arizona
Atlanta
Australia
Austria
Bahamas
Barcelona, Madrid & Seville
Beijing
Belgium, Holland &
  Luxembourg
Bermuda
Boston
British Columbia & the
  Canadian Rockies
Budapest & the Best of Hungary
California
Canada
Cancún, Cozumel & the
  Yucatán
Cape Cod, Nantucket &
  Martha's Vineyard
Caribbean
Caribbean Cruises & Ports
  of Call
Caribbean Ports of Call
Carolinas & Georgia
Chicago
China
Colorado
Costa Rica
Denmark
Denver, Boulder & Colorado
  Springs
England
Europe

European Cruises & Ports of Call
Florida
France
Germany
Greece
Greek Islands
Hawaii
Hong Kong
Honolulu, Waikiki & Oahu
Ireland
Israel
Italy
Jamaica
Japan
Las Vegas
London
Los Angeles
Maryland & Delaware
Maui
Mexico
Montana & Wyoming
Montréal & Québec City
Munich & the Bavarian Alps
Nashville & Memphis
Nepal
New England
New Mexico
New Orleans
New York City
New Zealand
Nova Scotia, New Brunswick &
  Prince Edward Island
Oregon
Paris
Philadelphia & the Amish
  Country
Portugal

Prague & the Best of the Czech
  Republic
Provence & the Riviera
Puerto Rico
Rome
San Antonio & Austin
San Diego
San Francisco
Santa Fe, Taos & Albuquerque
Scandinavia
Scotland
Seattle & Portland
Shanghai
Singapore & Malaysia
South Africa
Southeast Asia
South Florida
South Pacific
Spain
Sweden
Switzerland
Texas
Thailand
Tokyo
Toronto
Tuscany & Umbria
USA
Utah
Vancouver & Victoria
Vermont, New Hampshire
  & Maine
Vienna & the Danube Valley
Virgin Islands
Virginia
Walt Disney World & Orlando
Washington, D.C.
Washington State

FROMMER'S® DOLLAR-A-DAY GUIDES

Australia from $50 a Day
California from $70 a Day
Caribbean from $70 a Day
England from $70 a Day
Europe from $70 a Day

Florida from $70 a Day
Hawaii from $70 a Day
Ireland from $60 a Day
Italy from $70 a Day
London from $85 a Day

New York from $80 a Day
Paris from $80 a Day
San Francisco from $60 a Day
Washington, D.C.,
  from $70 a Day

FROMMER'S® PORTABLE GUIDES

Acapulco, Ixtapa &
  Zihuatanejo
Alaska Cruises & Ports
  of Call
Amsterdam
Australia's Great Barrier Reef
Bahamas
Baja & Los Cabos
Berlin
Boston
California Wine Country
Charleston & Savannah
Chicago

Dublin
Hawaii: The Big Island
Hong Kong
Houston
Las Vegas
London
Los Angeles
Maine Coast
Maui
Miami
New Orleans
New York City
Paris

Phoenix & Scottsdale
Portland
Puerto Rico
Puerto Vallarta, Manzanillo &
  Guadalajara
San Diego
San Francisco
Seattle
Sydney
Tampa & St. Petersburg
Vancouver
Venice
Washington, D.C.

FROMMER'S® NATIONAL PARK GUIDES

Family Vacations in the
  National Parks
Grand Canyon

National Parks of the American
  West
Rocky Mountain
Yellowstone & Grand Teton

Yosemite & Sequoia/
  Kings Canyon
Zion & Bryce Canyon

FROMMER'S® MEMORABLE WALKS

Chicago
London

New York
Paris

San Francisco
Washington, D.C.

FROMMER'S® GREAT OUTDOOR GUIDES

Arizona & New Mexico
New England

Northern California
Southern California & Baja

Southern New England
Vermont & New Hampshire

FROMMER'S® BORN TO SHOP GUIDES

Born to Shop: France
Born to Shop: Hong Kong,
  Shanghai & Beijing

Born to Shop: Italy
Born to Shop: London

Born to Shop: New York
Born to Shop: Paris

FROMMER'S® IRREVERENT GUIDES

Amsterdam
Boston
Chicago
Las Vegas
London

Los Angeles
Manhattan
New Orleans
Paris
San Francisco

Seattle & Portland
Vancouver
Walt Disney World
Washington, D.C.

FROMMER'S® BEST-LOVED DRIVING TOURS

America
Britain
California
Florida

France
Germany
Ireland
Italy

New England
Scotland
Spain
Western Europe

THE UNOFFICIAL GUIDES®

Bed & Breakfasts in California
Bed & Breakfasts in
  New England
Bed & Breakfasts in the
  Northwest
Bed & Breakfasts in Southeast
Beyond Disney
Branson, Missouri
California with Kids
Chicago
Cruises
Disneyland
Florida with Kids

Golf Vacations in the
  Eastern U.S.
The Great Smoky &
  Blue Ridge Mountains
Inside Disney
Hawaii
Las Vegas
London
Mid-Atlantic with Kids
Mini Las Vegas
Mini-Mickey
New England with Kids

New Orleans
New York City
Paris
San Francisco
Skiing in the West
Southeast with Kids
Walt Disney World
Walt Disney World for
  Grown-ups
Walt Disney World for Kids
Washington, D.C.
World's Best Diving Vacations

SPECIAL-INTEREST TITLES

Frommer's Britain's Best Bed & Breakfasts and
  Country Inns
Frommer's France's Best Bed & Breakfasts and
  Country Inns
Frommer's Italy's Best Bed & Breakfasts and
  Country Inns
Frommer's Caribbean Hideaways
Frommer's Adventure Guide to Australia &
  New Zealand
Frommer's Adventure Guide to Central America
Frommer's Adventure Guide to India & Pakistan
Frommer's Adventure Guide to South America
Frommer's Adventure Guide to Southeast Asia
Frommer's Adventure Guide to Southern Africa
Frommer's Gay & Lesbian Europe
Frommer's Exploring America by RV
Hanging Out in England

Hanging Out in Europe
Hanging Out in France
Hanging Out in Ireland
Hanging Out in Italy
Hanging Out in Spain
Israel Past & Present
Frommer's The Moon
Frommer's New York City with Kids
The New York Times' Guide to Unforgettable
  Weekends
Places Rated Almanac
Retirement Places Rated
Frommer's Road Atlas Britain
Frommer's Road Atlas Europe
Frommer's Washington, D.C., with Kids
Frommer's What the Airlines Never Tell You